THEORY

AND

PRACTICE

OF

MODERN

GOVERNMENT

REVISED EDITION

BOOKS BY HERMAN FINER

Political Philosophy and Institutions

THEORY AND PRACTICE OF MODERN GOVERNMENT
(*two-volume and one-volume editions*)
MUSSOLINI'S ITALY
THE SENSE OF RESPONSIBILITY IN SOCIAL ACTION
THE ROAD TO REACTION
THE FUTURE OF GOVERNMENT

International Policy

THE UNITED NATIONS ECONOMIC AND SOCIAL COUNCIL
THE CHILEAN DEVELOPMENT CORPORATION
AMERICA'S DESTINY

Political Institutions

THE BRITISH CIVIL SERVICE
REPRESENTATIVE GOVERNMENT AND A PARLIAMENT OF INDUSTRY
FOREIGN GOVERNMENTS AT WORK

Administration

ENGLISH LOCAL GOVERNMENT
MUNICIPAL ENTERPRISE
THE TENNESSEE VALLEY AUTHORITY: LESSONS FOR INTERNATIONAL APPLICATION

THEORY

AND

PRACTICE

OF

MODERN

GOVERNMENT

REVISED EDITION

HERMAN FINER
University of Chicago

HENRY HOLT AND COMPANY
NEW YORK

To Sophie

With all the homage of Proverbs, xxxi, 10-31
"For her price is far above rubies."

Preface

THE STRONG, persisting demand by students, and general readers interested in democratic citizenship, for my *Theory and Practice of Modern Government,* whether the original two volumes or the abridged one-volume edition, has encouraged me to revise the latter.

I am immensely (though apologetically) grateful that they have not been deterred by the length of my treatise, but, rather, seem to have welcomed what I have attempted: depth with breadth; analysis with comprehension; original research, first-hand observation, and personal experience—sufficient for the student himself to acquire an independent grip of the situations discussed.

This, then, is the one-volume edition. It is now so thoroughly rewritten as to be a new work. The facts of government have been brought up to date, and the trends and ideas have been, with measure, reconsidered and refashioned, so that this work may represent the contemporary mind, hopes, and difficulties of mankind in government today. Some omissions in the one-volume edition of 1934 (for example, the American Presidency) had to be restored but were newly written. The attentive reader will see, I hope, that every opportunity has been taken, and the felt necessities met, to develop the structure where change has occurred in the provinces of action and thought. The comparison is still the governments of Britain, the United States, France, and Germany—but at the proper points the experience of nazi Germany, fascist Italy, and Soviet Russia has been adduced.

However, it would seem proper to point to a number of specific additions, though to mention them all would be to mention almost every page. A new introduction relates the character of the state, the value of political science, the problem of power, and the nature of democracy. More than earlier, the features, justification, and consequences of the democratic principle are brought out, and this is thrown into relief by the contrasting world of dictatorships. The impact of the planned economy—or democratic socialism—on electorates, parties, legislatures, executives, and civil services is traced. The classic theme of the separation of powers is rejudged. Of course, the new constitution of France, the downfall of Weimar Germany, the rise and fall of the nazi state, the peculiarities of the Soviet constitution, are analyzed in relation to their national environment and the interests they serve. The latest developments in bills of human rights are evaluated. Examination is made of the creeds and organization of political parties in democracies and dictatorships under stress of war and its aftermath. Some new things are thought on public opinion and how the various agencies of communication and education and propaganda form public policy. The busy, determined process of renewal of legislatures, cabinets, councils of ministers, and the presidency is fully displayed. Particular attention is given to legislative and popular controls over the executive branch of government, now so heavily and newly burdened with economic, social, and international responsibilities, and to the reorganization of executives, with auxiliaries for planned leadership on a broader front than ever before. The crucial problems of the civil service—to get, keep, manage, and inspire in the service of the state enough of the best minds and characters of the living generation—have been reconsidered, with novel information and perspective. And finally, we have assayed the challenge of reconciling vast multitudes of men and women with diverse values under the one peaceful dome of a common democratic habitation, and the influence of time on the political process.

Perhaps it is not amiss to say one other thing. In an age where the social sciences more than ever avow their indispensable reliance on each other for insight into the same world of social experience from different points of view, not a few scholars in sociology, anthropology, modern history, and general philosophy have found this treatise a useful companion to their own studies—even if only to define and unravel the questions they feel bound to ask of human groupings in their own particular focus of interest. Their work has certainly been indispensable to this one, as they may see.

It must be emphasized, then, that this volume is abreast of our own time. Great reforms and reconstructions have occurred in the last fifteen years, under the stress of economic disaster and total war. I have tried to make the consequences on government understandable, and this in the light of the millenial strivings of men for a state fit to live in. It should also be emphasized that this is not the two-volume edition, which is being reprinted from time to time until it also can come out in a revised form.

My small book, *The Future of Government* (London, 1946), concisely surveys political institutions and movements in the critical decade, 1932-42.

I shall be deeply gratified if this edition is of as much value to students as they have said the first was. The world certainly needs citizens who understand that the good government of oneself is the surest guarantee of durable and happy self-government in the state.

In my next work, *The Persistent Problems of Democracy,* I hope to consider not democracy's institutional involvements, but the problems of values with which it wrestles for enduring and fruitful life.

May 1, 1949   H. F.

Contents

CONTENTS

[ix]

CONTENTS

Part Four
LEGISLATURES

Part Five
CABINETS AND CHIEFS OF STATE

[x]

Tables

Illustrations

Part One

MAN'S POLITICAL URGENCIES

Justice without power is unavailing; power without justice is tyrannical. Justice without power is gainsaid, because the wicked always exist; power without justice is condemned. We must therefore combine justice and power, making what is just strong, and what is strong just.—PASCAL

On what shall man found the economy of the world which he would fain govern? If on the caprice of each man, all is confusion. If on justice, man is ignorant of it.—PASCAL

Government and the State

No human situation here and now or in the future can be identical with any situation in other times or places. What a treatise on government can teach is therefore of limited value—but it can be very far from valueless. If the situations are not identical, they are not completely different: there are recognizable similarities. We can get to know how men *are likely* to act in the social organization called "the state." We can become the prophets of the probable if not the seers of the certain. It is also not without interest to know—and not entirely impossible to know—the motives, the bodily compulsions, the spiritual insistencies that cause men to throw themselves into positions of leadership or submission. If we ask for a lesson in completely and minutely accurate prediction, we shall ask in vain, though sometimes so many similarities exist between then and now and there and here that it is a pleasant surprise to realize how much an intelligent mind can foretell, and how frequently it is possible to merit the unpopularity of those who can rightly say, "I told you so!"

Usually, however, the political scientist does not know enough about all the elements that are relevant to his own problem, and usually the material is fragmentary or unobtainable for various reasons. Furthermore, where the answer depends on a judgment of motivating forces—that is to say, in the province of what was or is in the actor's mind—the observer is seriously baffled: the actor may not merely be mistaken about his own grounds of action but he may be entirely unaware of them. The actor may be duped by his own fancy; or he may be a deliberate cheat where any of two or three or more motives may fit as an explanation satisfactory to the observer, who may yet be wrong in his choice or unable to choose with assurance. In future situations the combination of personalities and material conditions must have its own specific pattern, as also the thousand-fold various degrees and proportions of human qualities thrown against the thousand-fold diverse environment. It looks as though we might throw up our hands at the prospect of finding any value in the study of government.

We may be reassured, for we are not, of course, entirely without guidance. Intelligent thoughtfulness is obviously of central importance in weighing the similarities and differences in various situations in time and place. This intelligence—observing, comparing, making allowances for degree and circumstance, moving from the facts in the distance to those in our presence, treading tentatively through hypothesis and surmise to the point of conditional and still dismissible conviction—this intelligence is sovereign. But on what shall it feed? To talk of government alone is, in spite of the immense width of its human range, already to have narrowed the phenomena to be observed and explained. It is to focus on one marked element in history out of hundreds which might distract and confuse us. The lines are firmer because they are narrower; and being narrow they are tolerably definite. The shorter the period studied, the clearer, because the simpler, the relationships of cause and effect. The more the eye is concentrated on a single organ or process of government, the more assured the truths discoverable about it, though the less known about the things on which one has turned one's back.

PHILOSOPHY AND INSTITUTIONS

Now there are two royal paths of insight into the behavior of men and women in their social organization called "government." Along one path is pursued the exploration of the ideas, the principles, the theories of what is right and wrong, what is desirable or undesirable, as men and women have held them, sometimes in a philosophic, systematic form. The speculations begun by Plato and Aristotle are not merely whimsical amusements, ending in a chuckle or giving rise to a gasp of wonder, but serious exercises of the intellect and feeling regarding man's fate in government: they warn, they encourage, they inform. They reveal at least all the recesses of one man's mind. They display his account of how many minds and characters at a specific time struck up against the problems presented to them by the place in which they dwelt. They follow through from the urge or temptation of a purpose to the practical outcome in victory or defeat. They proclaim a highest good or supreme duty like Justice or Virtue, and then draw conclusions, from the nature of the universe and of man, on the right and logical arrangements necessary fully to subserve such ends; they explore what transformations of environment, of habits, of laws, even of man himself, are required, and how far the process can be tolerable and successful.

It will be noticed that the political theorist or philosopher does not and cannot altogether exclude a concern for institutions, however ethereal his end, however celestial his aspiration. Since political achievement is for men and through men, political achievement is through institutions, which are nothing but men acting more or less deliberately in a fairly durable concert for the attainment of a considered complex of ends. He may start as Plato did, with Justice, and arrive at the need to limit the freedom to compose poetry and songs, or to institute common ownership of almost all possessions. Or, seeking good in growth, he may, like Aristotle, find he must appease the appetite for wealth by systematic education, lest the contest for it produce destructive revolutions. Or, fearful above all of disorder and death, he may, like Hobbes, prescribe the need for armies in the hands of absolute government. Or, like a gentler man than Hobbes, like John Locke, he may proceed from the pursuit of happiness and tolerance to government by legislatures founded on popular election and the separation of powers. The political philosopher begins with an end and then finds ways and means, that is, institutions.

This present work pursues the second main track to political understanding: it examines the institutions of government as they actually work, and usually does this by showing how they evolved stage by stage. Yet it would be poor instruction if the mechanism were not related to the end for which it was established, and showed no concern for the purpose that animates and makes dynamic the whole apparatus. The philosophy is immanent in the institution of government; for government is the exercise of authority by men over men, and a philosophy guides the distribution of authority. No one can talk intelligently of the electorate without talking of Rousseau; or of the ballot without remembering John Stuart Mill; or of law courts and the Bill of Rights without Locke coming to mind; or of the nature of obedience without Aquinas's system looming in the background; or of parliamentary procedure without being prompted by Jeremy Bentham's theory of pleasure and pain; and when dictatorial political parties are under appraisal it is in the dogmatic presence of Karl Marx. But our emphasis is on institutions as they serve us today. At the minimum, the more steadily our eyes are focused on institutions, the more they are opened to the possibilities and probabilities which assist us with hints towards efficacious inventive thought, enabling us to order affairs so that the ways and means shall not get across the path of our ends and so that the ends shall be shaped according to what we have learned is not impossible.

A strong warning is necessary: the institutions of government must not be regarded as eternal and petrified. Institutions are nothing but useful or useless habits: they were acquired for a purpose, and purpose changes. The world of political reality is not the printed world of books, or of statutes, or of administrative rules and orders. The cut and dried is not political. De Tocqueville's novelty has become a commonplace: "Do not confound the institutions of government with the necessary foundations of society." The "machinery" of government consists of men, women, and children, thousands and millions of them, placed in living relationship and conducting themselves in an ordered manner: but the order is constantly changing, growing, and the purpose is changing, and with it the pattern. Government is provisional, tentative; it is a process of what has been, what is or just was, and what is about to become something else, even if only slightly different; it is in transition to the future. Ortega y Gasset, in a much misconstrued book, conveys something of my meaning:

Whether we like it or not, human life is a constant preoccupation with the future. In this actual moment we are concerned with the one that follows. Hence living is always, ceaselessly, restlessly, a *doing*. Why is it not realised that all *doing* implies bringing something future into effect? . . . Let it be clear, then, that nothing has a sense for man except in as far as it is directed towards the future.[1]

It is imperative to remember that mankind in its separate states, as in the world at large, is on its way from somewhere to another proximate destination, and then on, once again. Vista after vista of progression can be sensed. We shall soon realize that old as government is, it is in its infancy—that is the most striking impression given by contemplating it. Hence, what we here describe is transitory: a moment, if a long moment, in being and becoming. If any reader thought that the governmental arrangements we shall discuss were the final shape, the unaltering inert form, he would gravely misrepresent what the author is anxious to convey.[2]

WHY GOVERNMENT MATTERS

GOVERNMENT is man's unending adventure. It is his heaviest collective and individual burden. Yet it is his supreme hope of liberation from individual feebleness.

Government is an endless adventure because man is deficient in wisdom, virtue, strength, and material resources—deficient compared with his burgeoning capacity to imagine, to wish, to want. Every discovery or invention that carries him nearer to the fulfilment of his desires still leaves him unsatiated, for he at once spots new horizons and disparages his past imperfections.

Government, again, requires endless effort because the rich depths and complexities of human nature have not been fully fathomed, in spite of thousands of years of conscious speculation. Tomorrow always springs some unexpected variation of human circumstance and environment. No philosopher has yet succeeded in producing a completely satisfactory version of history and politics for everyone else.

The most powerful mind cannot embrace all history even if it can discover or recover the scattered, incomplete, garbled or falsified sources. The most ingenious mind cannot weave and interpret all the parts into a whole meaningful to others. The most sensitive and imaginative heart cannot give due weight to all the qualities it perceives, the weight

[1] Reprinted from *The Revolt of the Masses* by Jose Ortega y Gasset, by permission of W. W. Norton and Company, Inc. Copyright 1932 by the publishers.

[2] Cf. Karl Mannheim, *Ideology and Utopia* (London, 1939), *Diagnosis of Our Time* (London, 1943), and *Man and Society in an Age of Reconstruction* (London, 1942).

it would receive from other interpreters of mankind, of nature and events, even if the other two desiderata were fulfilled. Government, further, is endless, because the feature on which Karl Marx erroneously placed the most stress—that is, the complicated material environment—is in a continual wave of change under the gusts of the human mind, surging up from the unprompted creative unconscious.[3] Deep down in man are many insurgent, ruthless, elemental needs, below the surface of the rational and the conscious, and they will out: they give to all the institutions of government a momentum and a ferocity not explicable by the polite. These needs are the world of Schopenhauer, of Freud: of the myths of immortality, the passion for self-preservation, the thirst for ideology. Perfection of theory and perfection of practice have always just eluded the great scientists and practitioners of the art of government.

Government is an adventure, not a textbook, because its end or purpose shares the dark or bright nebulousness of man's ultimate purpose. Each philosopher adds his own end; each philosopher gives to the general term all philosophers use his particular inflection, thinking it essential. As Acton said, "Of freedom there are two hundred different definitions,"[4] and this wealth of interpretation has caused more bloodshed than anything except theology. And with every child born into the world, the total destination of mankind through government shifts, because each child possibly bears with it an amazingly new and certainly rather different idea of what constitutes felicity or truth.

Government is composed of patterns of human cooperation; the allocation and forms of authority; and procedure. That is its anatomy. Its soul lies in choosing between alternative objects of happiness

and choosing between duties and sacrifices, and effecting a proportion between them. It allows no complete rejections, but imposes a decision on a tolerable mixture of preferences, seeking and keeping power balanced against what other men and women are seeking—seeking, keeping, and changing. The institutions of government are created and amended by men to enable them the better to attain what they believe to be their happiness and to fulfil what they surmise to be their duty. We do not lose sight of the fact that the process is not altogether systematically deliberate, nor that each generation inherits much that it finds obstructive. Political institutions represent the difference between human nature in the raw and civilized man. All that separates the baby of the Stone Age from the baby born yesterday is its social heritage—government.[5] Rousseau,. however, claimed that the institutions of government were so wicked (in his time) that the Stone Age baby was the better off of the two: yet he hastened to claim that if his ideas were heeded, the golden age would arise in the future and no longer be buried in the past. As such, government is a heavy burden, for men must carry it without rest if they wish not to slither back into the ever-tempting moral slovenliness and practical defeatism of barbarity. The temptation to cease caring for government is as insidious as the temptation not to keep clean; and people think too often that they can have their cake and eat it, and even eat somebody else's. The most dangerous fallacy in government is the negligent belief that people can have what they want through government without paying the cost of production.

If a government is dictatorial, the dictatorial clique bears heavy burdens, the more so because the people do not even thank it for the things it seems to do

[3] Cf. Ernst Cassirer, *The Myth of the State* (New York, 1946), Part I, and Erich Fromm, *Man for Himself* (New York, 1947). See R. G. Collingwood, *The Idea of History* (Oxford, 1946) for what history can teach.
[4] Cf. *Essays on Freedom and Power* (Boston, 1949), p. 14.

[5] Cf. Graham Wallas, *Our Social Heritage* (London, 1925), and Robert M. McIver, *The Web of Government* (New York, 1946). Cf. also R. Lowie, *Prmitive Society* (New York, 1920) and M. J. Herskovits, *Man and His Works* (New York, 1948).

primarily for its own pleasure. If government is democratic, the burden is not abolished: it is still existent, but it is distributed. In a democracy, government is less brutal, but it exacts much more of the average man in brainwork, patience, tolerance, and sometimes asks him deliberately to decide to do violence to others, even to kill, for the public welfare. Equally exacting is the individual management of the techniques required to build and maintain a just order that embraces millions of fellow-citizens and to prevent it from being destroyed by the weight of individual and group egoism. It is not a long step from persuasion to picketing; from picketing to violent repulse of non-strikers and from that to the summons of the militia; from lockouts to machine-guns; from a general strike to mismanagement of the national economy and the violent extremism of political parties; from extreme political views to the banishment of opponents from public office and employment.

These various qualities make the study and practice of government a fascination and a duty. Government is the most massive and effective of the instruments which men have constructed to maximize their own power to be what they want to be, and this constitutes their freedom.

Everybody who knows anything knows that it is a waste of our short lives to insist on ideal perfection. Popular government, or any other for that matter, is no chronometer, with delicate apparatus of springs, wheels, balances, and escapements. It is a rough heavy bulk of machinery, that we must get to work as best we can. It goes by rude force and weight of needs, greedy interests and stubborn prejudices; it cannot be adjusted in an instant, or it may be a generation, to spin and weave new material into a well-finished cloth.[6]

GOVERNMENT IS POLITICS PLUS ADMINISTRATION

A COMPLETE act of government consists of the conversion of the desires or will of some individuals or groups into the be-

6 John Morley, *Notes on Politics and History* (New York, 1914), p. 197.

havior of others or all in the society in which they dwell. The desire or will may be related (among other ends) to morals, as in the prohibition of liquor traffic or divorce. Or it may be concerned for religion, requiring that a particular creed be taught in the public schools or be given privileges by the state. Or the prime object may be economic, for example, that monopolies be suppressed or left free or that mass unemployment be prevented. The purpose of government is to convert all such desire or will into the authorized and commanded behavior of those who live in that area of settlement we call the "state." The desire or will may emanate from one mind, or spring spontaneously from many, or be developed by a minority.

Thus, government falls roughly into two general parts, definable, if not completely severable: (1) the process of politics, and (2) the process of administration. The first comprises the origin, development, and maturing of social will, so that popular loyalties to a desire are marshalled in such a way as to establish a law or convention socially accepted or simply acquiesced in. And this involves simultaneously the stimulation of social readiness to make the direct and indirect sacrifices of time, money, economic habits and to establish the rewards and self-restraints which are necessary to support and nourish the will thus engaged. The result is a reservoir of social will and power. Administration is the use of this reservoir of social will and power by appropriate personal, mechanical, territorial, and procedural methods, in order to render specific governmental services to those entitled to them and to enforce duty where the will or ability is lacking.

As for the relative importance of the two, politics and administration, for civic welfare as for study, the first takes precedence by an incalculable distance. The machinery of administration is subordinate to the political phase of government; and it ought to be. For the political determines will and function, and these are prior to, sovereign over, and creators of, the administrative machine and procedure. First is will, then function, and then, a long distance after, administration. Administration is an applier of discretion, and the discretion is the political almost entirely unhampered in its character and free will; but administration is merely the reflection of political rule; it is a recipient of smaller amounts of discretion, and this, also, on terms of accountability to the political masters. Administration hath slain its thousands, but the political process its ten thousands. The administrator can improve the work the politician wants him to do but he cannot utterly destroy it; the man of politics can utterly destroy the administration and dictate that it shall never even come into being. A mistake of administration can do neither the good nor the harm that can be done by an act or omission or error of judgment in political decision. This gives us our sense of proportion. I have been too long concerned with my studies of administration to be suspected of disprizing administration: but to overrate its value in the entire process and apparatus of government is to make grievous mistakes in statesmanship and to distract citizens from principle by displays of gadgetry.

The relationship of the two may be suggested by the famous rhymed opinion of Alexander Pope from the *Essay on Man,* and an answer to it offered by the present author, in the same form. Thus, Pope:

> For forms of government let fools contest,
> Whate'er is best administer'd is best.

and we reply:

> But what is best must free men still decide,
> Lest leaders gull them, and officials ride.

THE DEMAND FOR RIGHTS IS THE DEMAND FOR GOVERNMENT

WHAT, then, sets government going, gives birth to its functions, and molds its organs? Every man is the abode of an interwoven complex of associative and separative tendencies, of friendly and hostile dispositions. Individual man is by himself incomplete. It is his nature to need the help of others to complete himself. He is a parasite on some, a murderer of others, to satisfy his longings, which may be noble but too powerful for self-control. Yet he also sympathizes with some of the aims of other people. Hume and Adam Smith and Edmund Burke built much of their political and economic theory on the conviction that man had a natural, indefeasible sympathy for man,[7] instinctive and general. Out of this crepitating ball of fierce energies, dynamic or static, springs forcefully a design of cooperation or domination, again in intermixed layers and seams, marvellously subtle and combined.

If man's aims were merely economic, the task of government would be very easy. That, incidentally, is why Karl Marx was able to simplify it and hand to Lenin and Stalin a misleading formula.[8] Man's mind is unbelievably rich and various, and it is because all of human nature is involved and exigent that government becomes difficult, for it is concerned with the reconciliation of diversities by persuasion, or with the settlement by force of the most complicated rights and wrongs.

The economic and social setting of modern man is amazingly complex. The state is large, comprising many millions, each of whom is a little different from the others and possessed of an exasperating stubbornness. Society is compact of a myriad involutions. Any one problem—even one as limited as whether the sale of oleomargarine should be free of restriction—is stinging in its wrapped-up obstinacies: and this is one only of thousands, many of far more moment than this. Social interdependence is exceedingly dense because the members crave a

---

[7] Cf. Basil Willey, *The Eighteenth-Century Background* (London, 1941).
[8] Stalin found that he had to learn for himself: "We have no right to expect of the classical Marxist writers, separated as they were from our day by a period of forty-five or fifty-five years, that they should have foreseen each and every zigzag of history in the future in every separate country..." Cf. *Leninism* (New York, 1942), p. 470 ff.

THE DEMAND FOR RIGHTS IS THE DEMAND FOR GOVERNMENT

high standard of living, and these, for their own purposes, belong to a plethora of occupational and social groupings each congealed by hard organization, with loyalty to insiders but some hostility to outsiders. Social interdependence rests on these groups, though not wholly. An intense conflict over what is yours and what is mine is in constant play. At the same time, an exigent demand insists on other values: the right to self-government, freedom from the encroachments of authority, freedom of speech, freedom of criticism, freedom of religious belief and practice, freedom to move or not to move about the country, freedom to invest savings wherever one will, freedom to rear a family in the ethics pleasing to the parents, freedom to have as many children as the parents please—and so on.[9]

Thus the mind of every man and woman is truly pregnant with a state. In other words, each mind is intent on supreme authority for its own values. And every such state is different. As each of us looks through the film called "state" into the recesses of his own mind, each perceives a different picture, an *order,* which in some particulars, at least, is unique for each person. To some, state means personal power; to others, money; to some, war; to others, either peace and poetic contentment or frenzy; to still others, charity or savagery. One identifies the state with the felicity of his family, another with a favorite race. Hegel saw it as the embodiment of the cunning of divine Reason; Louis XIV, as himself, grand, victorious, powerful, *le Roi Soleil.* Lenin saw the classless society; Hitler saw Germany as the noblest race with himself as servitor and master, so much better than his father, a petty customs official, loyal to a trivial part of the contemptible Austro-Hungarian state. An artist has conceived of a state in which all the citizens are tributary to the artists who govern them and reward them by producing art.[10] Acton looked on the state as either the "true demonstration of religion" or as nothing. Were we to enumerate all the different visions, we should narrate a slightly different one for every member of the human race—and that truth contains some important, far-reaching democratic consequences, which, if acknowledged, can produce peaceful government, but which, if ignored, may cause even good men to cry out for a government standing above coerced serfs.

Which of the multitude of minds and states is *right?* Each thinks he is right; but no external revelation, no technology, is available as a test to help man settle this question unqualifiedly or beyond objection by all men. Only his social devices determine the question, without settling it. The Grand Inquisitor in Dostoievsky's *Brothers Karamazov* confronted the apparition of Christ on precisely this question: whether to leave the determination of what is right to the freely questing masses and risk unrest, turbulence, riot, murder, and war; or to take choice out of the hands of the masses, stilling their unrest by bread, the circus, a myth, a hierarchy, and the infallibility of a doctrine enforced by imprisoning and torturing the disobedient.

Yet all men and women meet, and all states stand, on the same base: the demand for obedience of others to *their* special character. Each would like the world *fixed* that way, the way they think *right.* For knowingly or not, each expresses in his social energies W. H. Auden's "Canzone": [11]

> What can we know
> But panic and caprice until we know
> Our dreadful appetite demands a world
> Whose order, origin, and purpose will
> Be fluent satisfaction of our will?

How different states can be may be realized from the quickest mental comparison between the western democracies (and even among them) and fascist Italy,

---

[9] Cf. The conflict of values as portrayed in Justice Frankfurter's opinion in *Minersville School District* v. *Gobitis,* 310, U.S. 586 (1940).

[10] Clive Bell, *Civilization* (London, 1928).
[11] From *Collected Poetry* (New York, Random House, 1945), by permission of the publishers.

nazi Germany, and the Soviet Union.[12] Each represents a different conception of material and spiritual good, and each began with ideas in the minds of somebody—but not all at once, nor all under the impulse of one idea, nor irrespective of the different environments to be mastered.

Out of the contiguity of men with different impulses, and therefore different beliefs of *rights*, an order arises, precarious, contingent, on sufferance, but fairly set for some time. Some individuals and groups dominate the rest by sheer power of a physical kind, by coercion; some by persuasion; some by a mixture of these; and some by sheer energetic initiative carrying all before it over the complaisance or apathetic inertia of the rest. Some values subdue and subordinate the less potent contenders. And a state arises by this contending process of subdual and submission; as Pope says in his *Essay on Man*:

Till jarring interests of themselves create
The according music of a well-mixed state.

THE STATE

THE state that thus arises can be defined in various ways according to the point of view.[13] It may be regarded as the association in any territory that is supreme over other associations and individuals. Or, it may be envisaged as the supreme social framework. It can be defined as the supreme permeator of all with a hierarchy of values, maintainable in the end, if necessary, by force. In all these definitions, the essence of the state is in its monopoly of coercive power, declared and enforced as the only legitimate monopoly; in its very existence, which is an immanent threat; or in its active use in the naked form of force when the members of the society (who may have very wide spheres of unrestricted and unlicensed initiative) threaten the main

values and are about to disrupt the society by exercising force against each other.

This, then, is the state; and its supreme power and monopoly of coercion (which it can devolve in many ways on its own terms) is *sovereignty*.[14] The political process revolves around the acquisition of this sovereignty; the administrative, around its executive utilization. The struggle for the possession of sovereignty is also a struggle for legitimacy: men strive above all things to be *right*, to be thought *right*.[15] Whatever the form of their struggle—for acquisition of material goods, for the power to give orders to other people, for self-preservation, for a point of law or in intellectual conflict— men are desperately trying to be *right*. This, the desire to be right and to be acknowledged as right, is probably the most persistent and intense drive in all men and women, though it is disguised by the name of the things about which they claim to be right. They so strive because they crave rightness for itself: they have no rest without its assurance. They seek it, also, because without its active or passive acknowledgment, they become unsure in governmental action, fumble, act more cruelly than they perhaps wish, while the threat of disobedience or revolt pursues them down the days and nights and years.

COERCION, COMMONWEALTH, AND OBEDIENCE

GOVERNMENT may be equated with the state when we are thinking of the state in the sense just defined. Or, government may be spoken of as the more proximate agencies, like the legislature, the parties, the executive, the law courts, the police, or unemployment benefits. Or, government may mean, according to context,

[12] For a contrast cf. T. D. Weldon, *States and Morals* (New York, 1947).
[13] Cf. for various definitions, Roscoe Pound, *Outlines of Jurisprudence* (Harvard, 1943).

[14] Cf. Charles Merriam, *History of the Theory of Sovereignty since Rousseau* (New York, 1900).
[15] Cf. G. Ferrero, *The Principles of Power* (New York, 1942). And contributing to an understanding of the relationship between metaphysics, ethics, and political philosophy and practice, see K. R. Popper's brilliant and wise *The Open Society* (London, 1945).

the men who hold office at a given time. Their relationship should be clear.

Why do people obey government? Because it serves them with values, values for them; or because they are afraid of its coercion. The values are not merely material values, concrete utilities, but also spiritual satisfactions. There are rebels who reject a high standard of living because it can be bought only by a loss of spiritual freedom or by cruelty to minorities. We know from public opinion polls everywhere that some merely acquiesce out of habit—there are those everywhere who to important questions of statecraft return the answer, "Don't know!" Apathy, and interest in other aspects of living, make them subjects by nature, almost slaves by nature. Others, again, succumb to the formidable challenge of the only alternative: to establish a rival state: "What can't be cured . . . " All of us, however, for different acts of government, and at different times, obey because we fear that the force at the disposal of government, manipulated for society, would be used against us. For however well-constructed and amiable a system of government, not all the people can be pleased all the time by the laws and the administration of them. Quite large minorities may find themselves disaffected. Is the state to be disrupted, and the considerable value of order to be subverted, on each such occasion by every dissentient? We have Socrates's conscious and reasoned repudiation of this course, when the loss to him was no less than his life: he had always supported the idea of law, and, now, when it told against him, was he, by disobedience, to deny the validity of his own teaching of the value of the *idea* in the long run? For the state is an order in time: without duration, it would be altogether another thing. A point may, of course, be reached where the values of order—that is, tranquillity, regular and unviolent processes, persuasion, reasoning, debate, and the calculability of the future—may become trivial compared with the intensity of resentment at the object for which coercion may be in-

voked. This risk is always contingent in government, and the discontented will fight back, almost certainly reciting the last pages of John Locke's *Essay on Civil Government,* or the *Vindiciae contra Tyrannos* without the slightest idea that these put their justifications in neater phrases, if rather more archaically and bookishly.[16]

Did any societies ever exist without the immanence of coercion? As we push back to the state of nature or the golden age, murky or glittering in the pages of Plato, Hobbes, Locke, Rousseau, and Hume, we cannot find an actual time which will give us a certain answer to this question. As anthropology threads its way back through the centuries until the records fade into mere conjecture—except in Engels's crushing footsteps [17]—and as we introduce the results of the study of contemporary primitive societies,[18] we find that there always was and always is coercion operative in social existence. Its forms are very various, and so also are the occasions and purposes of its use. Coercion is innate in man's constitution, nature, and values. He cares so much about some things he requires for the satisfaction of his animal nature and his wonder about the value of life altogether—the nature of God, the meaning of immortality, the compulsion to feel *right*—that he is prepared to force others into the social ways of fulfilment of his needs. But it is rarely that he will use violence when he can get his own way otherwise.

Democratic government is also a user of coercion. But the legitimacy of its coercion resides in the people when acting through majority vote exercised through certain procedures. Democratic governments use coercion—armies, police

16 Cf. Charles Merriam, *Political Power* (Chicago, 1934), and Bertrand Russell, *Power* (London, 1937).
17 Cf. Frederick Engels, *The Origin of the Family, Private Property, and the State* (London, 1884).
18 Cf. W. C. McLeod, *The Origin of Government and Politics* (New York, 1924) and the works of R. H. Lowie, B. Malinowski, Robert Redfield, Ralph Linton, and Clyde Kluckhohn.

forces, prisons, fines, searches, and so on —because in spite of all the fact-finding, debate, reasoning, kindness, and a high degree of consensus, some men and women, even large proportions of the population, may be irked by measures taken by the government, even where the government is the recently elected legislature. For example, if the medical profession were converted from a free profession into a state-appointed, state-paid, state-regulated service, many medical men might very painfully feel the pressure of the coercive power of the state if they attempted disobedience or sabotage. The merit of democracy lies in its intention to get for the maximum number the maximum social benefit available through the country's resources, science, and manpower, while attempting by its methods to reduce force to a minimum. But some remnant of coercion there must be, since men have biological differences of physique, mind, and values not conciliable by persuasion.

Clearly, then, the state and government are indispensable, indeed, natural. The states of our time did, in fact, have their origin in acts of force in the service of some or other of the values held, as we have suggested above. As the grouping in a single area grew larger in population, in the complexity of occupations and ideas and values, and included more of the previously separate and different groupings, so the range of force of the triumphant government expanded and intensified. A common superior came into existence. It facilitated order, peace, and communications. In the course of time, a common morality, up to a point, was established. Oppenheimer suggests that the state was at last founded when the ruling group put to death one of its own members for committing an act of prohibited violence against one of the conquered.[19] The common superior, now permeated up to a point by the common morality, is the *constitution*—that is to say, the nexus of fundamental institu-tions prescribing the scope and rightful succession to ruling positions and the authority to use force. Or, in a phrase crude enough to miss the saving holiness, "who gets what, when and how." [20] The constitution is the autobiography of the power relationship, concrete and spiritual, in any human group, and like all autobiographies, it includes some fancies which are not lived up to, and excludes some vices which are lived only too well.

Within a nation, or any society for that matter, many groupings of human beings abound. In many respects they are like the supreme grouping, the state; but in one final quality they are not like it. Non-state social groups—like churches, business associations, labor unions, civic reform societies, professional guilds, athletic clubs, philatelic and other hobby organizations—all these, numbering thousands in modern nations, have characteristics shared by the state. For example, they have a hierarchy of authorities; they have rules of procedure; and their activities are marked by purpose, by the whole gamut of the tactics of gaining power and avoiding submission to others, and by pressures, moral and material, sometimes to the point of violence. In these things they are like the state, and their study is an indispensable accompaniment of the study of the state, because they offer additional opportunities of observation and learning, and they happen also to be part of the reason why the state is necessary.

Yet there are some very marked and decisive differences between these non-state groups and the group known as the state. *First,* in a non-state group, entrance or exit is more voluntary than in the state, where membership is involuntary and exit almost impossible unless the state grants permission. *Second,* the objects of a non-state society, with the possible exception of the churches, are very limited; they usually have a single purpose, whereas the state has always had a multiple object and today touches almost

[19] Cf. F. Oppenheimer, *The State* (New York, 1922), pp. 91-92.

[20] Cf. H. Lasswell, *Politics: Who Gets What, When and How* (New York, 1936).

every aspect of a man's life. *Third,* although the non-state groups possess some forms of pressure—for instance, refusal of membership, "blackballing," and denial of privileges, which may in some cases produce the greatest pain and economic damage (e.g. in the closed shop, refusal of communion, refusal to marry in a church, pressure against a business firm which will not come to heel)—they do not have the severity of the final coercion at the disposal of the state. *Finally,* above all, these groups, like individuals, exercise their pressures and coercion only on sufferance from the state until—because they are exacting too much from the public (as a monopoly of any kind might do) or are threatening the general welfare or security of the state (as a society of physicists or priests or political philosophers might do), or are exercising a pressure on their own members (workers not in the union, or doctors who practice group medicine, or corporations not prepared to enter buying and easing agreements that restrain trade) which is considered by society in general unduly to deprive them of life, liberty, and the pursuit of happiness—until the state limits their power so to act, on pain of fines, imprisonment, or abolition. The greater, ampler, territorially wider coercion rules the lesser ones, because the greater, ampler, territorially wider welfare embraces the lesser ones.

Within the last three centuries, the area of commonweal in the state has gradually overtaken and, in total, remarkably reduced the ancient area of coercion. Many state activities are carried out with almost universal consent, and might have full consent if some men were not too lazy to be anything but parasites on the political effort of their fellow nationals. Such governmental activities yield a utilitarian or spiritual good—for example, the regulation of transport, or the spread of free education—almost universally as the result of benefits every individual enjoys. These activities use the product of long habitual peaceful living together in one area small enough, given the means of communication, for ideas to circulate and master the individual minds and consciences.

Yet the modern state still has areas of (*a*) legitimized coercion and (*b*) coercion that is not legitimate. The latter has been inherited from primitive states of society, and the inertia of millions of men and women dispersed over wide areas has not yet overtaken the unjustified power now possessed by some which arose out of luck, force, fraud, sharper wits, or absence of scruple and enabled economic and political privileges to be established on the basis of the lack of education or good-nature of those millions. It is at that latter wrong that Marx directed the spear of his class-conscious and equalitarian principles.[21] But he exaggerated, placing all weight on the economic nature of man. Hence, he regarded the state as simply and only an instrument of the minority to suppress and exploit the propertyless majority. Hence, for Marxists, the state today is not merely the scene of commonweal and cooperation, but also the scene of combat, and of combat not merely for the values which might now be formulated if all began equal and with a clean slate, but of combat about existent hereditary coercions which conflict with contemporary conscience and therefore with will.

In the Marxian perspective, of course, the exploitative and therefore the coercive factor in the state became especially and unnaturally conspicuous and grim. Indeed, all the rest of human nature and endeavor in government, reason and love, were discarded as merely "housekeeping"! Easy for Marx, then, to argue that man's liberty and equality in the state of nature, and in the happy future, would return only when the state, identified with coercion, is overthrown, that is, when the bourgeois state crashed in ruin. No classes, no state! Abolish the former and you dissolve the latter! But, sir, how did classes start? If out of human nature, the impulses may be expected to be straining to pour out again at any time. Then,

---

21 Cf. *The Communist Manifesto* (1848) of Marx and Engels.

even on this minor ground, the state will still be needed to prevent their victorious resurgence, and so government also. For it would seem that Adam lives on after Marx and is likely to survive Stalin.[22]

SOVEREIGNTY AND RIGHTS IN DEMOCRACY

THE world has arrived at a point in time when both the commonweal and coercive factors of the state are in the hands, or about to come into the hands, of the new legitimates—the people themselves. At last, the millennial writhing of the peoples for a principle of legitimacy— that is, an ultimate moral basis for deciding the values which are to rule societies and for making those values concretely supreme, by the use of force if necessary—has gone through all the more vulnerable principles, monarchy, aristocracy, theocracy, oligarcy, ideocracy, and has arrived at the least (though still to some extent) vulnerable, *democracy*— that is, government by all, but in practice government by the majority cognizant of the respect it owes to the minority. From this generalization the U.S.S.R. and like polities are excluded, because they deny the capacity of the people to govern themselves for their own freely conceived purposes.[23]

Outside the despotisms, every man or woman is sovereign at one and the same time as he or she is a subject. From each radiate orders to others, and upon each focus commands from others, government being the medium through which are transmitted reciprocal and weighted rights and obligations. An enormous responsibility rests on each, for the rights he demands can be implemented for him in the end only by the duties his fellow men render. The richness of his happiness and fulfilment, so far as any government can facilitate this, depends on the services, that is, the subjection rendered to him by others; and they, in their turn, cannot but demand a *quid pro quo* of sovereignty over their fellows.

It is today more important than it ever was, even more important than it was when the first edition of this book appeared a few years ago, that we surrender the abstract, unreal notion, of a government and the governed in opposition to each other, as two discrete entities: one claiming duties, the other fighting for rights. The opposition may be valid for a dictatorship without popular support; and in the absolute states of the centuries before our own, it fairly well represented reality. To continue to entertain it is to make gigantic mistakes in understanding of the truth about human nature in politics and political action. It is to believe that rights originate with a government, which has an inexhaustible supply thereof; that benefits can be extracted from government by threats and laws without asking which people in the community must provide the government with its resources. It is to ignore the responsibility for government which is our burden and our privilege; it is to disregard the need for individual self-government; it is to give exigence a licensed field which is empty of the idea of mutuality. Yet some men still think this way.

The truth of this reciprocity has a sterner ring in the democratic than in the dictatorial state. It becomes more starkly evident as the whole of society, through the state, assumes more and more responsibility for social and economic regulation, becoming in some cases the employer of the labor of millions, and the manager of basic social possessions and the means of production. The older veil over economic realities—the contest between workers and capitalists—is torn away. It can no longer be used to obscure the true bases for the production of wealth: industry, discipline, punctuality, uninterrupted work, inventiveness. It can no longer be used to hide the truth about distribution of wealth: some acceptable relationship between reward and effort; the tension between the different occupa-

---

[22] Cf. Joseph A. Schumpeter, *Capitalism, Socialism, Democracy*, 2nd edition (New York, 1947), Part I.
[23] Cf. Herman Finer, *America's Destiny* (New York, 1947), Chaps. VII and IX.

tions in their respective quests for the largest possible share in the total product of industry, the need to give extra reward to those who do the most disagreeable and dangerous work. The conditions of ownership and management are rapidly changing: new incentives and an owner's sense of responsibility are called for.

The men and women in each occupation are the employers of the rest; each occupation is complementary to or in competition with other occupations. The producers of some commodities are the consumers of those produced by men and women in other industries. When government has assumed responsibility for almost all productive and distributive activities—either by nationalization or by deep regulation—it is at once the mediator among them, since they are claimants on each other, and a unifier according to a high, national hierarchy of values. But all, as the electorate, make the claims on each other through political methods, and at the same time make the national pattern. The triple responsibility is now merged in the duty of each citizen: as employer, as consumer, as statesman. And since his state is irrevocably part of the constitution of the world order, such as it is, he mingles with this trinity, his responsibility as diplomat.

To avoid disaster, and to make the utmost of ourselves in the vast areas which are the territorial foundation of each state, what an enormous amount of knowledge, sagacity, and patient judgment is needed! What a delicate balance between self-doubt and assurance, of concession and insistence! What a well-considered, rationally and sensitively elaborated apparatus! In a democracy all men and women are rulers. They have asked for it. All recent kings and queens of the past ruled under a sense of obligation, and after a proper education; the others are remembered with contempt, they were often disobeyed, some were overthrown, and a few were killed. King Demos rules on the same terms, or is killed for the same reasons. Writing in the early 16th century, an archbishop of

Turin [24] in the service of the court of France declared that three "curbs" changed tyranny to civility among monarchs and preserved them from the hatred of their subjects: religion, justice, and police. The first is commensurate with the whole Christian ethic. The second required external bodies, of a representative kind, to limit absolute power; the right of suit in civil matters against the Crown; independent judges; and the complete honoring of the laws and ordinances made by the king himself. The third required good sense; that the king take counsel before action; and that the rights of the three estates should be treated with consideration.

GEOGRAPHY AND PHYSICAL POWER

PIONEERS like Bodin and Montesquieu have accustomed us to think of government as controlled by geographical situation, climate, and race, though it must be admitted that they made some very stupid generalizations on the subject. In the course of this work we will have much occasion to observe the action and reaction of material environment and human qualities. The material environment sets the conditions within which man's ambitions and capacities may operate in government. Toynbee has made a very important feature of climate.[25] What is of more importance, since peoples move away from impossible climates or die out in them,[26] is the size and location of the country under a single government. A small area with a dense population has, other things being equal, the tremendous advantage of coherence; in swiftness of circulation of ideas, in the continuity of contact between human beings, in understanding of each other, in the likeness of their fate and interests, in the almost instinctive emergence of

---

24 Claude de Seyssel, cited in Carlyle, *Mediaeval Political Theory in the West* (London, 1936), Vol. VI, Part III, p. 220 ff.
25 Cf. *Study of History* (Oxford, 1933), Vol. I, pp. 302-15 and Vol. III, pp. 4-7.
26 Cf. F. C. Markham, *Climate and the Energy of Nations* (Oxford, 1944).

common opinion, they have immense advantages over the larger, wide-spread areas, with their population scattered thinly in small townships and in sudden vast dense clumps, with their diversities of climate, resource, and product. In the first category are countries like Britain and France, in the second countries like the United States and the U.S.S.R.[27] The former tend to develop a society with the cohesion of a family, and the similar expectations of justice and duty; the latter find it very difficult to establish articulation of social groupings and unified government.

Location exerts a profound effect on political institutions, by influencing the extent to which the community must limit the personal freedom of the individual: security and self-preservation are the factors which bear most heavily in this direction. Where nations are connected by land, especially plains, and even where rivers and mountains intervene, they come in time to fear damage or extinction or enslavement or loss of self-government. Some one, or group, or the masses of the population, decree defensive marshalling of all forces: personal conscription for the armed forces, the limitation or abolition of regional, local, or provincial autonomy, the regulation of commerce to strengthen home production of war supplies, and establishment of controls over inventors. Where the imminence of danger is less, by reason of resources and natural obstacles which still hold back the best-equipped enemy (as for Britain until the twentieth century, and for the United States till D-Day in World War II exhibited new possibilities of invasion from the sea), the liberties can be larger, as they have been, to the making of model communities. Then there is the demand which the increase of human energy makes upon the need for government. In the center of modern life stands this awful truth: that, as compared with the eighteenth century, man is now able, by the use of steam power, electric energy,

and the internal combustion engine, to do many times as much good and many times as much harm to his fellows. For whereas then the only source of energy was windpower, manpower, or horsepower, now the wind and the muscles and the stamina of horse and man are actually negligible beside man's mechanical force.

In our own day, the exploitation of a new source of energy, that of atomic fission, thrusts the problem more memorably at us. Other types of weapon, including the bacterial, rank with the atomic bomb in their danger to man. Are we to descend into a Hobbesian era, or can the genius of Thomas Paine carry the weight of uranium? A few brief observations are offered.

If political science, studying historic and contemporary man, has any axioms at all, then this is one: that any increase in the power possessed by an individual or group must, when its gravity is appreciated, be followed by an increase in social control or, in other words, the power of Government. Scattered agricultural, weak, groupings do not produce or require intense central control of power. Densely populated areas, with powerful groups jostling each other, cannot avoid it. The social control of individual power means the assumption of a controlling or counteracting power by the central authority. The history of legislation in surprisingly varied phases of social life attests this axiom.

Power means the ability to do others harm or withhold what is for their good. The power may consist in *Material* form: for example, explosives, disease germs, or swiftly-moving, and therefore lethal, mechanical vehicles. Or it may be *intellectual:* knowledge, for example, of the technique of government; or of mathematics; or of the secrets of personal relationships or activities inside one's own or foreign groups. Clever people are held in distrust. Or, thirdly, power may consist in a *spiritual* form, such as ritual, charms, incantations, doctrines about human destiny and salvation. Power to influence destiny and salvation has been claimed by various orders of priesthood, and government has

---

[27] Cf. Edward Crankshaw, *Russia and the Russians* (New York, 1947).

power is gainsaid, because the wicked always exist; power without justice is condemned. We must therefore combine justice and power, making what is just strong, and what is strong just.

Acton made his crucial test of morality even more transfixing to the man of conscience. He asserted: [36]

The greatest crime is Homicide. The accomplice is no better than the assassin; the theorist is worse. Of killing from private motives or from public, from political or religious, *eadem est ratio*. Morally, the worst is the last.

Yet there would be more murder rather than less if there were no politics, no government. Burke's injunction, which we may sum up as saying that the proper business of man is politics, would save much murder and injustice, even though it meant the steady exertion of preventive or remedial power. Burke said: [37]

It is not enough in a situation of trust in the commonwealth, that a man means well to his country; it is not enough that in his single person he never did an evil act, but always voted according to his conscience, and even harangued against every design which he apprehended to be prejudicial to the interests of his country. This innoxious and ineffectual character seems formed upon a plan of apology, and disculpation falls miserably short of the mark of public duty. That duty demands and requires that what is right should not only be made known but made prevalent; that what is evil should not only be detected, but defeated.

The implied intervention in the political process can come about by coercion or y persuasion: education would limit the rmer by making the would-be coercer alize that there are limits to the long-n value of coercion for his purposes, d that there are good reasons in moral-why coercion should be limited. Educa-would also limit coercion by indicat-how much of it there would have to unless self-government made coercion ecessary.[38]

on, *Essays on Freedom and Power*, p. 369.
ughts on *Present Discontents* (Oxford,
's Classics), Vol. II, p. 79.
Karl Mannheim, *op. cit.*; and S. Hook,

NATIONALITY

MAN is not born free, he is born national; and, being national, he is assured some freedoms he might otherwise not have had. A peculiar integrating force in modern government is that consciousness of kind that we call nationality. It is true that people appeal to others in the name of the nation—that is, the collective whole of the nation—and of patriotism for selfish purposes; yet this is evidence of a recognition of duty, courtesy, and peaceableness, in itself a spontaneous feeling of kinship, of sympathy. Nationality is a quality of a corporate personality, which the nation is, and it therefore gives unity to the state, and engenders a will above that of all its adherent individuals and groups. It is a personality in the sense that it is a complete whole, with character, outlook, energy, a history, a feeling of unity and insistence on a future, and spiritual objectives supported by energies. It is no use attempting to belittle it, as Acton did, with the adjective "criminal," or to regard it as a malady of infancy, or a silly state of mind. This is a condition of man that has taken centuries to grow; it is growth, not caprice. The corporate personality goes far in absorbing individual personalities.

Men look for Grace, and it is given to them by Place—today's local habitation of the state they live in. Most of men's elementary and ardent cravings have come to be satisfied, up to the present point of time, by and inside the corporation of men that has formed on a distinct territory in the vast wide world. A common language, a common cultural inheritance, common physical characteristics (up to a point), many years of exclusive possession of certain territories cultivated by their hands or the hands of their ancestors, make them feel at home, and they have a profound longing for home. From man's first consciousness he is played upon by the specific human and environmental influences of a Place: noises, food, light, weather, landscape, customs, occupations, songs, cattle, parents, stories, products—they grow with him and he with them: is nothing much without them. His id

Education and Modern Man (New York,

finally stepped in to subordinate such power. In whatever form power arises, the struggle arises to control it if others can be frightened, influenced, coerced, or signally rewarded by gift or immunity from harm—so long as it is recognized as a substantial influence. Consider the history of monopolies of all kinds.

In the long run, the alternatives are that the possessor of power subjects society to his own will; or that he exercises self-control, limiting or suppressing his power in a measure that is tolerated by society; or that society domesticates him and his power to its purposes and will. In bygone ages the subjection of the masses was possible. For the future it is always a menace, but becomes less and less a possibility. It must suffer defeat by the combined effect of the diffusion of knowledge, the consciousness of the collective power of the majority, and the deep-rooted faith in the right of the majority to rule. As for the exercise of self-limitation, an appropriate illustration is the possession of the world by coercion: a Genghiz Khan, an Alexander, perhaps a Napoleon, would not hesitate. But that solution to international insecurity is excluded by the democratic scruples of the Bomb-owner.

The imminence of power's effects in *time*—that is, the rapidity between its exertion and its consequences—is of the essence of the problem of control—that is, of government. The speed of its deadliness must cause a tightening of controls over the Bomb, in the sense of Justice Holmes's phrase in *Abrams* v. *United States*, that the action of government is proper where there is "a clear and imminent danger that it will bring about forthwith certain substantive evils." The emphasis is upon immediacy. The area threatened defines the size of the society urgently interested in control, and the area is defined by the range and speed of modern vehicles.

Two aspects of atomic control can be foreseen. One is the sharpening of control by each nation over its own scientists and technical workers, by means of instruments like the Official Secrets Act. It will

matter little that the nuclear expert may claim his liberty to investigate the beneficent peaceful uses of nuclear energy, for its fateful destructiveness will always be paramount in society's mind until it is conquered. There can never be a retreat to the innocent state of mind before its advent. Like all experts, the nuclear physicist will certainly and properly be brought under "civilian" control, and subordinated to a responsibility to society through government. It can be taken for granted that the impulses which mastered theocracies, plutocracies, bureaucracies, will not suffer domination by technocracies. Those who put government by priests in the second place will not let government pass to the laboratories; the repositories of test-tubes will not be allowed to house the *arcana imperii*, any more than the temples were. The greater the technologist's power for weal or woe, the more will he be controlled—and all industry ancillary to his awful magic will also be governed by society. The international implication is the certainty of national controls over industrial establishments in order to implement each government's pledge to the international organization to allow an inspectorate full access to all plants.

The implications of the coming of atomic power have yet another aspect. No firm in private industry could ever have organized the search for and succeeded in the manufacture of the Bomb. Success was achieved in a way that can be repeated for making available to mankind foods and materials for consumption which are now indicated by science as not only possible but easily possible. The world of governments will never shake off the most impressive lesson of the making of the atomic bomb:

But the greatest marvel is not the size of the enterprise, its secrecy, or its cost, but the achievement of scientific brains in putting together infinitely complex pieces of knowledge held by many men in different fields of science into a workable plan. And hardly less marvellous has been the capacity of industry to design, and of labor to operate, the machines and the methods to do things never before done so that the brain child of many minds came forth in physical shape and performed as it was supposed to do.[28]

POWER AND MORALITY

WE have already appreciated that a powerful force dwells in every man and woman, and that force is immanent and even imminent in all human affairs and comes to its consumate organization in the government of great societies. What are we to think of the use of force or power to compel other men to do our will? Our ideas can be clarified by a consideration of the disavowal of power by Acton.[29]

Power tends to corrupt and absolute power tends to corrupt absolutely. Great men are almost always bad men, even when they exercise influence not authority.

This, which is vulgarly misquoted by omission of the word "tends," is Acton's most insistent warning, while his most exacting criterion requires that the institutions of liberty must limit power.

The terms of this theory need weighing. We may omit the second part of the dictum, since if the first is right or wrong, the second part merely magnifies the rightness or wrongness; and, for the rest, it is rather in the nature of a cry of anguish.

Power corrupts. Whom does it corrupt? It must corrupt men—men in authority. But can power corrupt men of predominantly noble character? Does not power's corruptibility depend on men's natures and purposes? Can power possibly corrupt those who are originally pure in heart, really pure in heart, and not merely impure dissimulators on the road to power? If Acton utters so unproportioned a thought—and the value of history and political science lies in proportion—he is rejecting all mankind as corrupt. For all men exercise some degree of power; we have, indeed, been at pains to make clear that all of us are at some time the employers of sovereign authority! This is to speak as a monk who has fled the world,

not as a man of it. It is conceivable that Acton is right—then the conclusion would seem to be that life is not worth living in any of the forms taken by the nations and states of antiquity and modern times. Not even the holiest sect can hold up its head against Acton's doom . . . it is an escape from life and courage. It does not discriminate among men or causes or degrees of responsibility or the mixture of good and bad in every man.

Next, if power corrupts, what is corruption? Acton gives a hint:[30]

But the possession of unlimited power, which corrodes the conscience, hardens the heart, and confounds the understanding of monarchs, exercised its demoralizing influence on the illustrious democracy of Athens.

Upon this, the political scientist offers two observations. *First,* against the corruption that results from the exercise of power is to be weighed its benefits to the statesman or thinker or priest or citizen (who may be all three) who wields it. Power heightens sensitiveness; it stimulates the imagination of purposes and expedients; it generates invention; it increases compassion when it places men where they confront the sorrows which government exists to assuage and the trials that must be visited upon some in order that others may have a more abundant life; and it develops fortitude and humility. Power compels men to think, to choose, to endeavor towards the conquest of pain and the discovery of truth. Is this catalogue not at least as tenable as Acton's sweeping anathema?

It is strange, indeed, that Acton does not adduce the life of Christ or St. Paul; that he does not remember Hegel's compassion for the agony of great men; that he does not consult Marcus Aurelius; that he does not introduce in this light the mighty liberators of man (like Lincoln) whose deeds he chronicles.

The *second* observation on Acton's ban on power is the answer given him by Bishop Creighton.[31] Great men are usu-

---

[28] Official Statement on the Atomic Bomb, *New York Times,* August 7, 1945.
[29] Cf. Acton, *Essays on Freedom and Power* (Boston, 1949), p. 364.

[30] *Ibid.* p. 40.
[31] *Idem.*

ally "representative" men, that is, they are acting on behalf of others as agents or trustees. Now, most statesmen arrive at the seat of power because they have been elected, more or less directly, or have themselves, with a small group of followers, risen to authority for the fulfillment of a cause, the realization of an ideal, the battle for an order (not excluding Acton's own noble order of liberty, truth, or Christianity). The government of other men, the government of societies small or large, is dependent not only on the character of the man who governs, but also on the necessities of the human and environmental and historically determined factors in the situation. For the statesman (for ourselves) the character of other men poses the problem in power. Every man is a repository of power, expansive or statically defensive; for a man is compact of physical energy, intellect, passions, spiritual intimations, and psychological impulses and appetites; this is the alpha and omega of power in government. Power in government can only be exorcised when men dissolve; it can only be dissipated when men no longer live.

Not a single ideal to which Acton rightly attaches worth could be practically effectuated without the use of power. Furthermore, the values which men seek in establishing government, indeed in craving it—and they may be splendid, humanist values—instinct with moral splendor as Acton's were—impose the final tasks of coercion and fraud on the shoulders and the consciences of governing men. If those who govern should seek the salvation of their own souls by abjuring power, they merely shift the locus of damnation to their clients' souls, for these, then, will be compelled personally to exercise the residue of cunning and coercion for their own advantage.

Power or influence in government is the power that corrupts. And power's essence? Power is only magnification. It is a magnifier of good as well as bad, it ennobles as well as corrupts. The consequences of power are a function of the purpose and character of its agents. Gladstone, the peer of Edmund Burke, and

Acton's political idol, himself said that a minister with power could do ten times the good in office than he could out.[32] And Creighton confronted Acton with this oblique answer:[33]

I remember that in 1880 I met John Bright at dinner: he was very cross, apparently a cabinet meeting had disagreed with him. Amongst other things he said: "If the people knew what sort of men statesmen were, they would rise and hang the whole lot of them." Next day I met a young man who had been talking to Gladstone, who urged him to parliamentary life, saying: "Statesmanship is the noblest way to serve mankind."

As Acton followed actual, contemporary politics, he was constrained to admit the value of power. He commended fine causes—for example, the rights of the Irish tenant against avaricious landlords, the value of the great territorial state embracing and subduing a congeries of nationalities. But they could not triumph without the marked use of power. Indee[d] *a propos* of the former, Acton declared:

As much authority as is wanted to protec[t] few against the many, or the weak agains[t] strong, is not contrary to freedom, but th[e con]dition of freedom. The disease lies in [ ] not in the state. The other view, that t[he] dangerous enemy a nation has is its [govern]ment, is pure revolution, and was in[ ] St. Just.

As a warning, Acton's dictum [ ] But the kingdom of politics [ ] world. As a warning in polit[ics] sels us to build the machine[ry of govern]ment, write its procedures, [ ] spirit in such wise as to [ ] and balances, to promote [ ] without falling into anar[chy] and injustice, and to invi[ ] ence of mind. Acton o[ ] missed Pascal:[35]

Justice without power [ ] without justice is tyra[nny]

---

[32] Cf. p. 602 below.
[33] Acton, *op. cit.,* p. [ ]
[34] Acton, *Letters of* [Glad]stone (London, 19[ ]
[35] Blaise Pascal, *P*[ ] (New York, Mo[ ] p. 298.

[36] Act[ ]
[37] Th[e] Worl[d]
[38] Cf. [ ]

tity is made up largely of them. By the time he has reached the age of discretion and reason, when he might prefer alternatives, his senses are no longer able to conceive those alternatives without prejudice. In any case, he must continue to live and make his fortune in a place—the whole world seems hardly ready to turn nomad. Men yearn for value, not merely commodity. They want more than a stone, they need bread; they need more than bread, they need spiritual purpose and justification. They need praise: that is, they need a hierarchy of values, and an authority, something beyond them, that raises them up in their rightful place. They yearn for the divine and the holy and immortality: this collective person embraces them in its immortality.[39] The combined researches and thinking of constitutional historians, anthropologists, and psychoanalysts have demonstrated the coincidence of the locality, the home, and the divine—of Place and Grace—that is the nation. It is this local society that has in our own day amalgamated the services of religious minister, ethical leader, and spiritual healer, and combined them with the gifts of public order and increasingly of economic welfare and security. This society bestows both praise and blame, distributes honors and casts down in shame. This becomes the highest loyalty, and religion itself has been bent to serve it.

So far the world has offered the mass of common men no more vivid alternative for fervent loyalty. Though it is expressed more as a defensive and offensive force against other nations, yet its power at home does soften and inhibit the potential violence of man against man, spurs the citizen to public devotion and self-sacrifice, and clothes certain duties and rights with the quality of spontaneous naturalness. In our own day, nationality is cultivated, deliberately worshipped, for

it is seen that without it the egoisms would come nearer to breaking the society in pieces. Wherever it is not mature, there are continuing threats of breakdown of common parliamentary institutions, and always serious tensions. Government proceeds on the basis of common obligations, or relapses into logrolling. Where nationality is excessive it may be equally destructive, by subduing the life, the rights, and the scruples of the source of all life, mind, and conscience—the individual.

As we read the chapters that follow, and reflect on the conditions of leadership and of popular control of the actions of government, and consider how the entire way of life of each nation organized in its state is linked to and penetrates all others (by reason of their economic interdependence, the inseverability of their territories from each other, the rapid and passionate wildfire spread of moral feelings, the swift communications that tell all of each other's fate, charity and cruelties), as we see their resources managed by government in the interests of a few or of all, and as we observe the growing strength of each inevitably coupled with each one's fears of all—we appreciate that the constitution, the formal expression of the way of life of each nation, is, indeed, a part of the constitution of the world. One bad constitution hurts and may corrupt the rest: a good one assists to salvation.[40] The citizen is a part of the sovereign power, a diplomat in an age of open diplomacy in his own country: and as he is good and capable in his country so he works good or ill for the whole world.

THE CHARACTERISTICS OF LEADERSHIP

In all forms of government, whatever the basis of authority, we see the same qualities of leadership, though the forms and beneficiaries vary. As we progress through a review of the various organs of government, electorate, political parties, legislatures, and from time to time glimpse the executive, it is as though we were steadily ascending the steps of a pyramid up to the summit. This ascent is marked

[39] Cf. Rudolf Otto, *The Idea of the Holy* (New York, 1939); Ian Suttie, *Origins of Love and Hate* (London, 1938); Royal Institute of International Affairs, *Study of Nationality* (London, 1940); Herman Finer, *America's Destiny* (New York, 1947), Chap. 5; Hans Kohn, *Idea of Nationalism* (New York, 1945); E. H. Carr, *Nationalism and After* (London, 1946).

[40] Cf. E. S. Corwin, *The Constitution and World Organization* (Princeton, 1944).

by the brighter clarification and definition of policy, rising from the seething and multitudinously colored public opinion, upward to the ever more orderly and deliberate processes of sifting facts, formulating law, and guiding administration.

If an aphorism can be ventured, the process of government, thus viewed, shows a successive gain in Consciousness, Coherence, Constancy, and Conscientiousness—the four chief marks of statesmanship.

Consciousness means the sensing of principles and ends; the vision of the future; diagnosis of the parts in the whole design of the near or distant objective; clarity regarding the efficacy of the means to ends; equity which determines the proportionate burden each group should justly bear on the road to the goal.

Coherence signifies that all the men and the agencies serving government are brought and held together in concerted pursuit of a common end, with no gaps, no overlapping, no incongruous public declarations, no departmental or individual actions obstructive of the common end to be reached.

Constancy connotes steadiness of vision and demeanor, loyalty to purpose, attachment to rightness of policy from the beginning to the conclusion, without wavering, hesitancy, self-contradiction or caprice; it means dynamic dependability.

Conscientiousness means a sense of responsibility for achievement of consciousness, coherence and constancy in harmony with the will of the people, an ever-exacting acknowledgment of obligation. It implies responsibility for initiative.

The executive is the epitome of all these qualities found diffused in all the other organs of government. It does not displace them; it works with them. But it crystallizes the four qualities we have distinguished, qualities outstanding in the nature of government itself.

It will, therefore, never be a surprise to the political scientist, though it may be properly disturbing to all democrats, that when the society is in a crisis of self-preservation against dangers from within, and especially against dangers from without, there is a temporary vesting of additional and sometimes unlimited power in the hands of the executive. Two world wars have shown us that this is unavoidable, beneficial, and redeemable when the war is over.[41] Burke said, "A constitution without the means of change is a constitution without the means of its preservation," and we may reverse the aphorism, and say, "A constitution without the means of its preservation is a constitution that will never survive to times of peaceful change." Though we must ever be on our guard that the procedures and safeguards examined in the ensuing chapters never be subverted, we must recognize the need of exceptional measures while a crisis, in sense of "clear and present" danger, is upon us. But this is far from saying that the executive alone assumes the prerogative (that is the name for the initiative in uncharted seas of a crisis, which requires new powers or novel ways of using powers that have been unaptly distributed to the critical situation). All powers may still cooperate, but the constitutional distribution of authority will now correspond to the forces tugging at its peacetime design, and tugging it out of shape.

We have seen, then, that political institutions operate as the expression of a particular aspect of human life, and that the essential nature of this aspect is the social struggle for and the subsequent use of the supreme power within a territory. And in default of words less obscured by history, we call this supreme power the state, and its supremacy, sovereignty.

Before we embark upon the study of political institutions separately, we are faced with two problems whose discussion is a necessary prelude: first, the relationship between politics and economic institutions and processes (chapter 2), and second, the conditions of state activity (chapters 3 and 4).

41 Lindsay Rogers, *Crisis Government* (New York, 1935), and C. L. Rossiter, *Constitutional Dictatorship* (Princeton, 1948), and my review of the latter, *Columbia Law Review*, April 2, 1949.

2

Politics and Economics

INDIRECT PRODUCTION

THE economic organization of modern societies is based upon indirect production. The commodities which men and women regularly make and the services they perform are not directly for themselves; but they are at the command of others, at any rate to satisfy the demands made or likely to be made by other people.

From the standpoint of the economist, therefore, the state is an economic institution; from the standpoint of the political scientist, economic organization is a factor whose form has a necessary influence upon that of the state. That special branch of political science which is public administration is usually nothing more than economic activity conducted by public authorities. If the economic motive is strong enough, the political institution is obliged to respect its processes. That is not deplorable to the patient searcher, though it may be to the political reformer, for as Maeterlinck says: "There comes, too, a period of life when we have more joy in saying the thing that is true than in saying the thing that merely is wonderful."

Indirect production means that a great territorial gap yawns between various producers, and between producers and consumers. They do not know each other's character as in the village economy of the eighteenth century. Government is therefore required to establish standards such as weights and measures, currency, credit, conditions for "fairness" or "quality" in commerce, and the qualifications of certain professions and trades. Between mere regulation and state management lie important values of liberty and welfare, but not differences of principle.

PRODUCTION FOR FUTURE CONSUMPTION

YET modern economic organization is, in addition, marked by the fact that its methods of production are "roundabout." Commodities and services are not, as a rule, made for hand-to-mouth consumption: the planning of production for the future is necessary in every society, particularly where indirect production is so complexly organized. This is the particular and amazing difference between the nineteenth century and all others that preceded it. The production of the material welfare consumable on any one day is dependent upon concerted efforts made long before, sometimes years before, through a complicated and expensive organization of machines and men. Without preliminary calculation and organization, the goods would not be there; without the anticipated consumer, the preliminary calculation and organization would be useless.

More recently, the masses, whose authority in democratic states is final, and whose silent, stubborn wishes in dictatorial states must to a large degree be respected, have demanded social security, full employment, and a high standard of living. That is, they have a vital interest in the control over the future, and government therefore is called upon to provide the stability and foreplanning necessary to make today's productive activities intermesh with those which will come, perhaps, in distant years.

The virtue of roundabout methods of production is punctuality; all must proceed as anticipated and arranged. No single item with which men reckon may disappoint, on pain of disaster to the general plan. We have reached a stage of economic production in which the range and prediction are concerned not merely with territory but with distant time. If any one of the multitude of factors in this calculation is changed by an undue interruption of supply, grievous harm may be done to the life of many other parts of the community, which, far from being immediate parties to the dispute, are entirely innocent of it. The state, if nothing else precedes it in time and efficiency, is required to maintain the continuous fulfillment of social expectations, and, *in proportion* as these are vital to the civilization desired, obedience to the state must be unconditional. All this presses to a demand for executive stability and the diminution of political partisanship in the interests of stabilization. It calls for the prevention of industrial strife. If man as a consumer wants a high standard of living, including security, then man as a producer must not interrupt his work: continuity becomes the spirit of his laws.

DIVISION OF LABOR AND ECONOMIC GROUPS

MODERN economic organization involves political activity and institutions to respond to the effects of division of labor. To safeguard and develop their interests in the division of the product of industry, in order also to further their cultural development, men and women, engaged in similar tasks, whether in the same factory or craft or industry, form organizations. Society is divided vertically.

The community of industry bids fair to outdo in significance the community of religion or neighborhood. It helps to evolve a special allegiance to the group organization, founded on the special interests which it represents and seeks continuously to realize. It is difficult, almost impossible, for the individual member of such a group to compare the worth of his loyalty to it with his loyalty to communities and to the great community, the state, outside it, and, comparing, to rate its value lower. Such a voluntary acceptance of a secondary status comes sometimes, but not often. The respective values to be compared are so intangible and comprehensive that even a fine philosophic mind measures them with difficulty. David Hume in his *Treatise of Human Nature* observes,

Here, then, is the origin of civil government and society. Men are not able radically to cure, either in themselves or others, that narrowness of soul which makes them prefer the present to the remote.

The average man tends to modify his special occupational conceit and allegiance only when he is persuaded that the effects are, in the ultimate sum of economic good and evil, good for him, or, when not accepting the argument, he is forced into the behavior it implies. His group is unmistakably the potential subverter of the state of the day, and that state is, at a certain point, bound to "push back."

The vertical division of society has two consequences. (1) Each vocational grouping is reluctant to regard its representation in the legislature as adequately representing it. Hence the lobby and other informal or formal hearings and representative arrangements of a direct nature, such as representation on advisory boards in the government departments or, as in France and Germany in the interwar years, the existence of special occupational assemblies, or, as in Fascist Italy, the Chamber of Corporations. And (2) these organizations are the repositories of knowledge so specialized that their cooperation with representative assemblies and the civil servants is essential to sound legislation and administration.

DIVISION INTO CLASSES

Now modern industry exhibits not merely a division into separate occupations but a division between those who actually and legally control the instruments of production and those who are obliged to submit to an occupational discipline. This horizontal division of society is close to the division postulated by Karl Marx in his theory of the class struggle—proletariat and bourgeoisie.

What are the broad political implications of this feature of industrial organization? Let us first be clear about one thing. Employer and employed are equally servants of all those forces which the economist calls demand, and for which we may use the concrete term, the consumer. (The deliberately established monopolistic perversions of this principle will be considered presently.) The employer as well as the employed will receive no income unless the consumer is satisfied in the long run. Any employer, whatever his nature (kind or cruel) and whatever the method of his selection (by birth or property, or election by the workers), or whatever the nature of his industry (private entrepreneurial or nationalized), is bound to pass on to all workers the orders implied in the consumer's demand. This fundamental relationship must be respected by all political institutions; should they fail in this, they must find themselves obliged in some way to use persuasion or force to maintain their alternative.

Political tension, however, arises especially in the relationship between employer and employed from the secondary role of the employer—as the legal controller of the equipment, and, therefore, as supreme manager of the methods, processes, and conditions of work. Workers in every occupation dispute the employer's control; the workers of all occupations dispute the position of all employers, and class stands against class.

The means of production are private property, but they are instruments of production affecting national and group welfare, and nation and groups have an interest if the owner-manager should be lazy, monopolistic, or less capable than some alternative form of management. This is the view taken by left-wing politicians and labor unions and is an important basis of socialist thought. The clever, ambitious, sensitive worker cannot help harboring a sense of injustice, and we must expect to see him endeavor to remove its causes. To see this world daily slipping by and his talents unrewarded, to realize, too, that his children must possess extraordinary ability and grit to climb to the rungs where the hereditary mediocre effortlessly cling, must be for him a revolutionary incentive.

In the Soviet Union the means of production have come fully under state ownership and management [1] in order to implement equality of opportunity, the career open to the talents, and the development of invention, all of which were regarded as otherwise difficult if not impossible owing to the restrictive practices of private property. In Great Britain [2] and Western Europe, large steps have been made by the democratic processes in the same direction. In the United States, the sphere of free enterprise and ownership is still the largest in the world, but since 1932 (that is, since the Great Depression [3]) remarkable strides have been made in public regulation and socialized activity: e.g., the credit activities of the federal government, symbolized best by the Reconstruction Finance Corporation.

The close relevance of the division of labor and the formation of well-organized groups and "classes" in modern states to

[1] Cf. Alexander Baykov, *The Development of the Soviet Economic System* (New York, 1947); and Harry Schwartz, *Russia's Postwar Economy* (Syracuse, 1947); N. A. Voznesensky, *The Economy of the USSR during World War II* (Public Affairs Press, Washington, 1948); L. Gruliow, *Soviet Views on the Post-war World Economy* (Public Affairs Press, Washington, 1948).

[2] Cf. Herman Finer, "British Reconstruction and Planning," *International Labour Review* (March and April, 1948); and see other articles in the series.

[3] Merle Fainsod and Lincoln Gordon, *Government and the American Economy* (New York, 1949).

the theories of political parties is described in some detail later. Such interests and parties are not the result of personal vagaries and theoretical perversity, or of an antipatriotic, antinational plan, freely preconceived and pursued out of sheer enthusiasm for doctrine; they are the result of plainly perceptible causes, material and spiritual, directly and inseparably bound up with our present mode of economic life.

CAPITALISM, PRIVATE ENTERPRISE, AND ECONOMIC DECENTRALIZATION

AMONG the factors not yet taken into account is the actual daily management of economic resources, material and human. Modern economic organization has been peculiarly marked by its extreme and often surprising degree of decentralization —that is, omitting the example of the U.S.S.R. and allowing for great modification currently developed in other countries. The economic process has not been regulated from one center, or even from a few great centers, but almost every individual human being has been an independent center of decision, energy, and responsibility. "Economic decentralization" has been seized upon by economists anxious to emphasize the theoretical merits of the capitalistic system, while minimizing the inefficiencies of actual capitalism.[4]

The development which led to this situation is traceable to two broad classes of causes: (1) men's theories and passions concerning their worldly existence, rewards, and punishments; and (2) the theories arising from the actual experience and past failure of guild, municipal, and state control. In the first broad class of causes will be found dominant the spiritual changes which were at once the causes and effects of religious Protestantism—their victorious course beginning in the fifteenth century, and their essence being summed up in Strafford's description of the Puritans: "The very genius of

that nation of people leads them always to oppose, as well civilly as ecclesiastically, all that ever authority ordains for them." In the second class of causes, the grand factor is the influence of the physiocrats, Adam Smith, and the older economists, who expounded the lessons taught by the failures in one and a half centuries of mercantilism and its Continental types, Colbertism and cameralism.

This spiritual development and economic experience together gave birth to that extreme decentralization which until recently marked our economic organization. Individual men and women and, till late in the nineteenth century, children were neither regulated nor hindered by government in their calculation of what and how much of economic goods or services should be produced or consumed; the individual alone was responsible, and he received the reward and suffered the damage.

There is no doubt that this system, operating with minimum restraints from about 1815 to 1870, assisted an immense increase in the aggregate wealth of these countries, and that, for vastly increased populations, a greatly increased standard of living was made possible. However, a large proportion of the population in every generation since, say, 1800, has been so badly fed, housed, clothed, and educated, and so sick, that its condition has been one of permanent misery. The economic system has not prevented dark blots from staining civilization, nor has economic wellbeing gone with any regularity and certainty to those whose merits in social life were splendid but not economic.

Further, as the capitalist system developed, it was seen that its efficiency was more dependent upon large-scale regulation, that is, upon the combination of small units, than upon its old doctrine of decentralization and free competitive enterprise. By about 1845 laissez faire and its attendant social doctrines were played out; from 1880 government has with ever-accelerated speed entered as supreme regulator of the economic process, and today we are in the middle of the social battle

[4] Lionel Robbins, *Economic Basis of Class Conflict* (London, 1939); *Economic Planning and International Order* (London, 1937).

around the control of industry. The day of Samuel Smiles and John Stuart Mill's "Liberty" have gone, so far as we can now see, never to return.

THE ARRIVAL OF PLANNING

NEVERTHELESS, there has recently been a recrudescence of defenders of private enterprise, among them being Walter Lippmann (*The Good Society*) and F. A. von Hayek (*The Road to Serfdom*). Hayek challenges the compatibility of planning and democracy, stressing these arguments: (1) The best planner cannot possibly have a sufficient comprehension of the gamut of human emotions to know what is best for the public welfare. (2) Partial planning is not possible; undesired reactions may occur in areas excluded from the plan. (3) Because of conflicting interests in the legislature, and the rapidly shifting demands of an advanced technology, the administrators must arbitrarily make the rules effectuating the plan, thus violating the "rule of law." (4) Reliance will be placed on force, resulting in the most undesirable individuals holding key positions, all because the plans will not be logically defensible. The same pattern of totalitarianism following on planning, as experienced in the Germany of the 1920's and leading to the Nazi state, will be duplicated in Great Britain and the United States if they continue to encourage social engineering.[5]

Hayek, however, has overlooked several strikingly important points: (1) Total planning would be reprehensible to the people and the legislature, which always acts short of extreme ideas, whether their exponents be of the left or right. (2) As a result of several centuries of lawmaking or planning, legislative abilities have considerably increased. Consequently, planning can be delimited exclusively to the fields that the people, through their legislatures, desire. (3) When unwanted results accompany deliberately planned ends, it is always possible for society to impose decontrols. (4) The process of correcting legislative and administrative errors by repeal or amendment has never halted. (5) Careful study of the trend in administrative processes reveals the many scientific safeguards that society has developed. Practically, our alternatives are a far cry from, on the one hand, a perfect system of laissez faire, and, on the other, tyrannical public administrators who represent the logical conclusion of an invalid hypothesis based on hostility to them. We are, instead, confronted with actual industrial and commercial policies, as contrasted with present and potential government administration. (6) Lastly, it should be noted that Hayek is discussing noncomparables in predicting a Nazi-type future for Britain. The extent and type of planning to be found in any country is an outgrowth of its peculiar institutions and climate of opinion. Analysis of these theories and practices from beyond the periphery of the system is meaningless.

The trend is all against the "competition" of individuals and small firms, and all towards the creation of great trusts and combines, ordering and monopolizing the production and sale of commodities. They are economical, but they may become tyrannical, because they can not only fix prices but, avoiding competition, no longer need to improve their own efficiency. It has been calculated that about sixty per cent of prices of commodities in America are "administered" prices, or prices fixed by corporations not subject to free competition.[6] When monopolies are economical, political power is sought to help their birth; when they are tyrannical, government is called upon to offer the consumer and small producer its protection.

Political institutions have already proceeded far in their control of industry and economic distribution in all the countries we are discussing. There are variations of extent in each of them, but it is perfectly clear that the extent and forms of such control now constitute the most passion-

---

[5] For the point of time when this struggle assumed serious meaning, see Helen Lynd, *England in the Eighties* (New York, 1945).

[6] Cf. National Resources Planning Board, *Structure of the American Economy*, 1939.

ately contested question in political life. Planned economy, *Étatisme* and Syndicalism, Socialism and Guild Socialism, *Planwirtschaft* and *Gemeinwirtschaft,* Rationalization and Amalgamation, and Communism—all in their native countries and outside them—are the solutions which men, organized politically, are demanding or refusing.

It may be observed that this economic problem is both the offspring and the parent of moral "ideology." For a general attitude to the spiritual value of life regulates our economic conduct, while the economic process, according to our likes and dislikes, will be accepted, rejected, or amended according to the values, freedom, leisure, opportunity, and so on that we worship.

A special aspect of the government control of the economy is the relationship between finance and industry. The banking system is the intermediary between savers and users of capital. The banks are convenient deposit institutions and accumulate savings, and then, upon this basis, make loans for investment and business enterprise. The extent to which they risk their depositors' money has for generations been regulated by the state, since the ordinary safeguard of the withdrawal of deposits is usually ineffective once a failure has occurred. Government thus acts preventively as a support to credit, especially where investments are made abroad and alien notions of government and financial honor prevail; and this governmental control is an encouragement to saving because it assures savers that their savings will not be lost. This supply of credit for industry and commerce has become vital to the roundabout method of production, and agriculture and industries can be helped or ruined by the policy pursued by the banks. Hence the matter has become one of public economy, to be regulated by institutions with more authority to enforce such a policy than the private-profit relationship normally provides, and according to rules with an eye to the welfare of the whole body of citizens (as well as any particular bank or firm of stockbrokers or manufacturer or merchant) and with an eye also to foreign conditions and world prices.

THE NATURE OF PLANNING [7]

PLANNING has either of two general motive forces—increased production or more equitable distribution and consumption —and both require a high degree of government control of economic processes. The first motive implies the use of natural resources, labor, skill, science, and organization to the maximum degree and kind of productivity, that degree and kind being established at a central point upon the belief that an immense increase of production and a lightening of human toil can be so secured. One aspect of this order of thought is technocracy, the government of society by technical experts. The most extreme views of this kind, extreme to the point of political impossibility even perhaps in the dictatorships we already know, ignore the free expression of citizens' preferences and neglect the consequences to civic liberties and the rights of opposition. But more sensible views look to production planned for maximum consumption with an earnest and preventive eye upon the possible loss of freedom. Indeed, this is the crucial problem of modern democratic government: to discover how to plan maximum production, and distribution which will promote the maximum welfare, while pre-

---

[7] Cf. Friedrich A. Hayek and others, *Collectivist Economic Planning* (London, 1935); F. A. Hayek, *Industrialism and Economic Order* (Chicago, 1948); Rex Tugwell, *The Fourth Power, in Planning and Civic Government* (Washington, April-June, 1939); Barbara Wootton, *Lament for Economics* (New York, 1938), and *Freedom under Planning* (Chapel Hill, 1945); Friedrich Hayek, *The Road to Serfdom* (Chicago, 1945); Herman Finer, *The Road to Reaction* (Boston, 1945); John D. Millet, *Government Planning* (New York, 1948); and Rex Tugwell, review of Millett, in *Public Administration Review* (Spring, 1948). See also Oliver Franks, *Central Planning in Peace and War* (London, 1947); Lionel Robbins, *The Economic Problem in War and Peace* (London, 1947); Findlay McKenzie (ed.), *Planned Society,* (New York, 1937). See also J. M. Clark, *Alternative to Serfdom* (New York, 1948).

serving liberty of political dissent and vigorous economic experimentation.

The other motive force toward planned production begins with the idea of more equitable distribution. This means not distribution according to a man's capacity to produce (and especially not the capacity to produce in the present rather haphazard economic process) but distribution according to need. The governors of the program of production are consumption needs, not profit making which follows the indicator of effective demand. It includes also a wish for "justice" in the human relationships of production, of labor standards, workshop management, and so forth, and of a better share of the employees in the process as well as the product of industry, the process itself being a contribution to the latter. But any considerable intervention in distribution can be implemented only by control of production: that is the lesson of Soviet experience as well as the plain twice-told lesson of the war economies of all the belligerents. The movement for planning had its origins in World War I. The chief impetus came when the German generals suddenly saw that the war was not to be won quickly and that all resources, human, material and scientific, must be mobilized for a single purpose. Little as the postwar fulfillment was, relative to the promise of a better world made during World War I, something of the promise was kept. Moreover, there remained a mental and moral sense that certain social changes could no longer be denied in modern states simply on the ground that they were administratively impossible: what had been done for war could be done for welfare.

Planning had its immense difficulties even in wartime, when aggressive or defensive emotions unified mighty multitudes of men and women as to the purpose of the state.[8] For the millions of individuals were not absolutely like-minded, nor by any means identical, in their degree of sacrificial determination, or in their endurance or toleration of hard-

ships socially imposed for the purposes of victory. Therefore, the observer must ask himself questions about the effectiveness of governmental planning not merely in terms of administrative techniques and institutions, but above all in the context of the diverse and changing aims of individuals and groups. Can a plan which is far-reaching and taut be arrived at by free discussion and agreement, a plan which will not only satisfy a vast majority but continue to satisfy a majority? And is society to permit the usual free right of opposition to and criticism of that plan and its administration with the possible result of its piecemeal dismantlement or total subversion? Furthermore, there is the question whether those who plan can limit their influence to what is consciously planned only, or whether the plan will not have indirect consequences of control over the rest of individual activity. Have governments the psychological and technical ability for self-limitation in their planning activity, or must they become absolute?

Yet in various ways, unmistakably important advances were made in all countries, democratic and otherwise, along the lines indicated, as a consequence of the productive and distributive motives referred to above, and side by side with the need to take planned antidepression measures. Here and there, in the various sectors of economy, a number of public corporations arose for production purposes, while simultaneously came the establishment of more and more comprehensive social-security schemes—that is, schemes for the maintenance of the income of the unemployed and those distressed by accident, invalidism, sickness, old age, widowhood, orphanhood, etc. Along the distributive line, World War II aroused sentiments of social equity, based upon the notion of the justice of equality of sacrifice of all classes and occupations in a community at war for common survival. This culminated in such instruments as the Atlantic Charter, with the declared objective of "securing, for all, improved labor standards, economic advancement and social security," so that "all the men

---

[8] Cf. Albert Lauterbach, *Economics in Uniform* (Princeton, 1944).

in all the lands may live out their lives in freedom from fear and want." Another such pronouncement of political intention was the declaration made by President Franklin D. Roosevelt in January, 1942, of the Four Freedoms: Freedom from Fear, Freedom from Want, Freedom of Religion, and Freedom of Opinion.

As piece by piece was added, in the interwar years, to their specific organs of planning of production and social security and assistance, each nation established an agency of comprehensive planning, that is, of planmaking and of studies and investigations to that end. Later, we shall analyze the nature and effectiveness of the Economic Council in Germany, the Economic Advisory Council and royal commissions and advisory bodies in Great Britain, the *Conseil National Économique* in France; and the National Resources Planning Board in the United States. All these institutions fulfill one or both of two functions: namely, they bring together representatives of the main economic groups in the hope of securing from them both (a) intimate and expert expression of their special views and desires (essential to the education of public administrators whether as executives or as draftsmen of laws), and (b) a mutual arrangement of policy based on this expression. Or they make scientific and long-term analyses of trends requiring governmental intervention, if the government desires a particular economic or social result rather than a fortuitous result growing from the undirected operation of those trends. The Economic Advisory Council in the United Kingdom and the National Resources Planning Board in the United States were more particularly adapted to this latter objective; and of the two, the wide vision and scope of the National Resources Planning Board, its independent status as an organ of insight and foresight, and its independence of immediate politics and politicians, resulted in a considerable contribution to social prescience, if not to the adoption of executive plans.

The work of these comprehensive planning bodies achieved little, because over-

all planning, as suggested previously, is a political act on the highest level. It is a matter for the supreme executive and the legislative assembly, with the assent of the people. Any planning body of the kind mentioned, whether exclusively advisory or fitted into the governmental machinery (like the *Reichswirtschaftsrat* or the *Conseil National Économique*) cannot but be an adjunct, a subservient if useful and even indispensable organ, to the process of planning which goes on continuously in every state in the form of the more thoughtfully predictive and concerted progress of government policy.[9] It is, indeed, a mistake to place exclusive hopes in democratic countries in one single organ of planning of the character indicated. Democratic governmental systems are served, as it is, by a planning process which looks something like this:

In the center are the cabinet or the President and the legislative bodies upon whom falls the first as well as the final responsibility for results. They ultimately decide; and their decisions become not merely a plan, but a special form of plan, namely a law, which is normally followed by application in detail. Before the matter comes to the summit point of decision, however, there is a twofold process, one commencing at the cabinet or Presidential stage, while the other finds its destination there but emanates from the distance outside. In the *first* process, the cabinet or the executive or a legislative steering body develops a policy, that is, a plan—a considered pattern of desires and the will to their attainment. Through its offices it then marshals the information, the suggestions, the favorable or unfavorable reactions of, it may be, hundreds of social organizations and individuals, in order to make that plan workable, to fit it to the hard and the soft contours, and perhaps modify it when analysis proves that ambition or ideals have outstripped national capacity to fulfill them.

Simultaneously, in any highly developed society, a *second* process is going on.

9 Cf. p. 546 below.

Various societies of interested people, some occupational, some social, some religious, some anxious to give and others to receive or be protected, have their plans —that is to say, their desires that government shall make universal certain rules of civil conduct. Universities, for example, are concerned not only with teaching but with research in economic and social matters and with the possibilities laid open by natural science. Enjoying relative independence of thought, they are able to suggest long- and short-term directions and to recommend ways and means. Besides, in the last quarter of a century, there have come into existence various institutes of social research—historical, economic, statistical—for political and economic planning. Usually these are without a political party bias, though they may have very definite corporate convictions regarding the plasticity of human nature and social organization and the shape in which these ought to be molded.

In the end, however, whether or not there is a special all-comprehensive governmental organ at the top of this congerie of free planning bodies, the sifting of the plans suggested comes into the hands of the trusted professional civil servants or career public employees. These are the professional advisers of political ministers and legislators, the draftsmen of plans. In the end, to these is assigned the responsibility of converting those plans which receive the *imprimatur* of the sovereign political bodies into the behavior of the citizen. In the planning process, the chief service is rendered by these civil servants. For, though they may not create or originate the laws, they hold a strategic position for discovering and sifting and collating administrative and technical ways and means (as well as machinery) and adjusting plan to plan, not to mention facilitating the everyday execution of the result. Hence, all importance ought to be attributed to their role, no matter how well organized are the specially established private or political organs of planning. The final planners (if not the inventors or discoverers before the plans reach the stage of enactment) are the civil servants, and nothing should be allowed to obscure the view that the making of the plan and its achievements are a direct function of the quality of the civil servants. For the recognition of this proposition has a decisive bearing upon the problem of the education and recruitment of public officials. In this and other ways, the development of intervention by the state has made the problem of "bureaucracy" progressively more acute.

It may well be asked wherein planning differs from government, as traditionally practiced and taught? It does not differ in kind; and reasoning to the contrary is wrong and of ill effect. Then why use a new word? One of the reasons in the United States is to avoid use of the cursed word "socialism." But planning does add the two qualities of wider activity and more pervasive activity of government; insofar as planning is the comprehensive management of a nation's men and resources, the lateral and temporal characteristics of government are carried to lengths never before practiced in states so large. By *lateral planning* is meant that all the factors which are complementary to each other—men, resources, skills, agencies of government, environmental factors, the legal conditions, and so on—are marshaled and carried forward together, so that there is no conflict, overlapping, or underlapping, in the march of all the agents to the objective or objectives. By *temporal planning* is meant the emphasis on the foresight regarding conditions that will prevail in the future (distant, or fairly close) and the arrangement of a succession of stages in time by which each part is to be accomplished, so that all the factors are joined at the point of time set at the beginning, and no stage is so unsuccessful that the result in the far future is jeopardized. There is a heavier emphasis than in traditional government on prognosis and inventive-mindedness.

We are already becoming the beneficiaries of contemporary experience with the widest governmental planning. One of the most intelligent practitioners has thus stated his problem,[10] and it closely resembles the theory outlined above.

Planning can be divided logically into five stages:—

The first, without which none of the others can happen, is making up one's mind to plan and grasping what planning means.

The second is assembling the necessary facts and forecasts to make sure that the plan can be put on a sound practical basis.

The third stage is actually devising alternative plans and seeing what they each offer and what they each cost in terms of resources and disadvantages.

The fourth is the taking of decisions between alternative plans, including the decision what is to be planned and what is to be left unplanned.

The fifth, and by far the most extensive stage, is carrying out the plans in practice. This includes explaining them, adjusting them and devising all the necessary ways and means of ensuring that what was planned on paper does in fact happen at the right times and in the right places and in the right way.

THE TENSIONS OF ACQUISITIVE SOCIETIES

Now in all that we have so far said there is latent the likelihood and fear of social strife and misery. Why? It is because the product of industry and agriculture is in men's estimation so scarce that they strain and leap to dispute each parcel of it. Men are today ruled by the ideal of the high standard of living and are perturbed by the knowledge that even with about eight hours' steady work for five days per week, under conditions of severe industrial discipline unknown to their ancestors, the standard is difficult to attain. They are enormously greedy; they are unconscious of it; and when they meditate upon the depths of their greed they dignify it by the name of an impersonal title like the "high standard of living." Indeed, it has become the pledged objective of both the United Nations (article 56) and the International Labor Organization (Declaration of May, 1944) to achieve a high standard of living.

10 Herbert Morrison (Lord President of the Council in the Labour government), "Economic Planning," in *Public Administration* (London, Winter, 1946).

This acquisitiveness is one of the roots of our present major political problems, domestic and international. The notion is current that, above all things, the acquisition and consumption of a great amount of material wealth is man's most proper good. This ideal is not the sudden creation of any particular year or set of men, though the phrase has a history perhaps no older than a century. No deliberate weighing-up of spiritual and material values caused its establishment. In the last century and a half, western Europeans and Americans found themselves suddenly in possession of the steam capacity to acquire immense riches, to increase and multiply. They tasted of the fruit of the machine and found it good. And God came to be spelled Get.

Each generation produced its wonders, its triumphs over the earth, the seas, and the heavens, and found itself ever freer of the limitations of time and space; and the standard of living became so absorbing a religion to men, even now untouched by criticism, that those who dare to assert another standard, or come from countries where the standard of living is lower, or live and work where it is lower, are treated as damnable heretics. Protective duties are set up against countries with a lower standard. Even the Soviet state is an idolator of material wealth. Stalin has never followed Ghandi in finding a loin-cloth adequate for Russians!

The political difficulty is that this greed is for satisfactions which the common opinion of mankind calls noble, and thus produces a scramble in which all parties are right. It is true that the mere possession of riches does not necessarily result in its immoral consumption, and that for moral consumption wealth is necessary. It is even true that the more riches we have, the more may we be able to turn our attention to the pursuit of spiritual beauty and supremely virtuous activity. Yet it comes about that we can reverse Mandeville's famous saying, "Private vice; public good," and say instead, "Private good, public vice," for our very virtues are apt to embroil us in civil commotion and international war. The mother wishes to see her son do well at school and obtain a situation which shall be "nice," respectable, well-paid, and not too laborious. The father provides the necessary means to achieve such a pleasant destiny. If, however, all mothers and fathers act similarly, and if their sense of what is "respectable, well-paid, and not too much work" is of a similar quality, the result may be, indeed we have seen it to be, what all parents unite to say they condemn: war at home and abroad. Those economic and social qualities which now pass for family and national virtues inevitably affect industrial relations, and political institutions are unavoidably embroiled in them, since the supreme authority lies with them. Forsyte drives the English state, the Buddenbrooks the German, Babbit the American, and Belphégor the French.

Our preference to wash with soap made of vegetable rather than of animal fats leaves us blind to the exploitation of backward races who are employed to produce palm kernels. Labor is sweated so that the consumer may be attracted by the cry of "cheap!" For the rubber supply upon which modern transport so largely depends the cruelest atrocities were committed in Africa. For the oil which drives machinery or moves tractors in the fields of Soviet collective farms or drives our cars (Americans use eight barrels of forty-two gallons each per year), a daily war is waged between companies and nations, in which hideous strokes of force or guile determine the comparative standard of living of modern nations. For sugar the liberties of Puerto Rico and Cuba were bought and sold. We are not content with chocolate; we demand it in forms attractive to the palate and the eye. The very seasons are controlled and nature's order distorted, for we are not patient to wait until our own spring brings us young vegetables; they are ravished from sunnier climates, and even the bees are made to give up their honey by the artificial fabrication of the light and heat of summer. Every ingenuity is practiced to tear from man and nature the utmost they can give to satisfy the appetites. But Englishmen cannot ask for high dividends and high wages without rights in the Middle East and Africa; the Frenchmen cry out for the *mise en valeur* of their colonies; the Germans turned toward Russia as a field of exploitation since opportunities were denied them elsewhere; and some Americans fearfully hold their hand over their pile of dollars lest too many immigrants should knock off a few and reduce its height.

THE STATE AND POPULATION

Now, individuals, families, industries, and nations, might be as acquisitive as it is in them to be were there enough material welfare to satisfy all. For what we call "excess" is measured by the ratio between how much is demanded, the number of the applicants, and the amount available for distribution. Here's the rub. For the full strength of human passions is obliged, as the world is constituted at present, to operate through exhaustible material resources, and therefore to rage against unyielding confines.

The amount available for distribution is limited by the condition and quality of economic organization and by industrial and agricultural technique—and then the amount per head is the aggregate producible quantity divided by the number of the population.[11] At any one moment, man's ability to exploit natural resources and control the number of his kind fixes the amount of material welfare available for the satisfaction of his appetites. Man's knowledge and power over nature increase, and, therefore, the number who can live and develop their personalities as they will may increase. But the political scientist, especially when he is expected to consider the larger schemes of social amelioration, may as well abdicate at once, unless he recognizes that his answer is governed by two conditions: (1) the uncertain prospect of invention, which may

[11] Cf. Eugene Staley, *World Economic Development* (Montreal, 1944); and T. W. Schultz (ed.), *Food for the World* (Chicago, 1945).

come slowly or rapidly, but which is hardly at all amenable to direction and control; (2) increases or decreases in birth rate over a short period which it is not within political power to alter; it is very problematical whether reproduction even over a long period can be influenced by governmental plans (the inspectorate, for example, would find insuperable difficulties). It then follows that men's desires, satisfiable by economic means, may be variable within the limits set by (1) and (2), but that a limit nevertheless exists to the total amount of material welfare at any time available to realize human aspirations. This may be considered unfortunate; but it is dreadfully true.

Yet in our own time the triumphs connected with fertilizer, penicillin, electronics, the making of artificial protein foods, dietetics, and the refinement of mechanical power and of atomic energy give promise of substantial increases in per capita productivity.[12] Meanwhile the political scientist must remember that the power of the land to sustain a population establishes an ultimate, though a variable, margin to the power of political institutions; it is perhaps the most powerful of the elements which govern the extent to which the ideally good is realizable. In Britain, France, and Germany, where the population is dense in relation to resources, the problem of control of population is a continuing anxiety; in the United States and the U.S.S.R., less so.[13]

---

[12] Joseph Schumpeter, *Capitalism, Socialism, and Democracy* (New York, 1947).

[13] David Glass, *Struggle for Population* (London, 1936). In Britain, the Royal Commission on Population was appointed in March, 1944, "to examine the facts relating to the present population trends in Great Britain; to investigate the causes of these trends and consider the probable consequences; to consider what measures, if any, should be taken in the national interest to influence the future trend of population, and to make recommendations." The fifteen-member commission has received evidence at fortnightly meetings and has secured assistance from three advisory subcommittees: (1) biology and medicine, (2) economics, and (3) statistics. These scientific committees have completed several reports. Cf. W. Vogt, *Road to Survival* (New York, 1948), for policy regarding backward peoples.

PROPERTY

"PROPERTY," said Harrington, "produces Empire"; and fundamental in any economic and therefore political organization is the problem of private property. Private means exclusive, and it is clear that the power of the great association called the state must vary with the extent to which the exclusiveness of possessions is accorded by morals and law to individuals and lesser groups. Whether possessions are held to be lent for a time, or for a lifetime, or whether the power of unregulated disposition goes further, beyond the owner's lifetime, and whether the general mind of the time does or does not attach the idea of social obligation to that of property—all these things manifestly affect the nature of political institutions and the nature of the state.

Now, broadly speaking, the modern state began with the theory and the practice of the social regulation of property. According to the church, which preceded the state as the supreme community, and according to the state, which was at the outset ruled by religious traditions and even by religious ministers, a man could not do as he liked with his own. But by the middle of the eighteenth century men had escaped from the traditional morality and therefore from the state, which had sought to be its vehicle. Already in 1689 John Locke had claimed the immunity of property from arbitrary seizure by the state, that is, had claimed that property should be excluded from the sphere of the acknowledged supremacy of the state; and, before him, the Parliamentary champions against the Crown became warriors partly to safeguard their property from irregular levies by the state. Blackstone makes a profound obeisance to the English principle: "So great is the regard of the law for private property that it will not authorize the least violation of it; not even for the general good of the whole community."

The Continent was slower to extricate itself from the toils of the benevolent despots and their economists and public administrators, but when it did, in France particularly, it was with a rebellious cry, the clash of victorious arms, and a philosophy sprung from the head of the *Économistes*. The physiocrats founded their philosophy of the state upon the axiom that the absolute exclusiveness of property was the supreme condition of the greatest material welfare, and that this again resulted in the highest moral good. All the declarations of rights on the Continent and in the United States included the right to private property, and even in the German constitution of 1848 it holds a proud place.

The essence of the philosophy which supported these clauses was plain: (1) it is good that much wealth should be created; (2) the greatest amount will be created if men are certain that the reward for which they work will be exclusively theirs. We shall never be able to give a certain answer to the question: If the world between 1750 and 1850 had admitted the right of the state to regulate individual activities and the disposition of property, would there have been as much riches created with less attendant social misery? For we have no means of even guessing who would have governed, and with what competence, in the name of the state, and that is decisive of the question. We know that in the nineteenth century, Europe's population quintupled with an accompanying increase in wealth per capita, and that the Americas became populated with a very large growth of wealth. We know also that critics arose to proclaim the misery of the masses and to call attention to the advent of new industrial relations and institutions which needed social control; and that governments began, upon various principles, and under various names, to deny the exclusiveness of property, and to take away from its privateness.

Two observations may be added. *First,* when Locke stipulated that the value of the state lay in its protection of property, he also stipulated that there should be a strict limit on the amount of property which anyone could hold. *Second,* in our own day the legitimization of the kind and degree of property permissible depends upon the preparedness of the average

man to support it. Some amount of private property is essential to civil liberties; some degree of private property is essential as an incentive to production and invention. Part of the modern political struggle revolves around the determination of how much, in each case.[14] We have yet to discover the answer.

The controversies of our own day are embittered as they circle around the problem of how far the social control of property shall go.[15] Property is continually encroached upon by: (1) the right of eminent domain; (2) the police power; and (3) taxation.

(1) Eminent domain has meant the right of the state to annex private property, on payment of due compensation, for public uses, with a growing emphasis on the positive social aspect of promoting public welfare.

(2) The more significant concept of police power extends the element of compulsion in governmental acquisition of property rights to an exclusion of payment.[16] The state has "the power of promoting the public welfare by restraining and regulating the use of liberty and property." Prohibition in the United States destroyed the entire liquor industry without remuneration being made; Great Britain and Continental nations have assumed entire control of whole industries —coal and the railroads, for example— under the same power. Here is the storm center of the modern state. Whatever it does must inevitably be paid for. Most must be paid for in taxation, since per-

14 Ernest Beaglehole, *Property* (London, 1931).
15 *Principles of Political Economy*, Book II, Chap. 1, Sec. 3. Mill said: "The laws of property have never yet conformed to the principles on which the justification of private property rests. They have made property of things which never ought to be property and absolute property where only a qualified property ought to exist. They have not held the balance fairly between human beings, but have heaped impediments upon some, to give advantage to others: they have purposely fostered inequalities, and prevented all from starting fair in the race."
16 Benjamin F. Wright, *Growth of American Constitutional Law* (New York, 1942), Chap. VI.

sonal services have been discarded as un-economical and inconvenient.

(3) Every tax is a subtraction from private property; it may not be directly taken from capital, but it certainly converts the income to public use. Indeed, taxation has been called confiscation; and it is. When men fight political battles on the field of taxation they not only seek to divert public expenditure from one purpose to another more desirable one, but some of them attempt to secure that as much money as possible shall be kept in private pockets and freely disposed of by the owner, while others endeavor to draw upon private purses for public expenditure. It should be noticed also that since World War I, taxation has been established as much more consciously and considerably an instrument to regulate the volume and kind of production and employment and to combat depressions.

HE WHO HAS, GOVERNS!

FOR the time being we have said enough to indicate how and in what ways, the great society, the state, is concerned in economic institutions and motives. Engraved upon the heart of modern society, to a depth reaching to its inmost core, is the motto of a Birmingham bank: "He who has, is!" written in the vernacular and not in Latin; and those who would understand the character and functions of modern government must understand the spirit and institutions of which this motto is a symbol. For though it is not everything to modern man, it is much. "He who has, is!" That is not all. He who has, governs! Yet, who may have, may be determined by the supremacy of a just principle of government—for example, majority rule.

Even if the government were confined to these economic functions only, their persistent emergence from human weakness and collision would necessitate the establishment and operation of the state. Engels and Lenin were in gross error to believe that the "government of man" would wither away before "the administration of things."

3

State Activity: Historical Development

AMONG the manifestations of the state, its functions hold a cardinal position, and an examination of the conditions of state activity is elemental to the comprehension of the seemingly inextricable confusion of parts which constitute the state. The history of state activity falls into four periods: the first, up to the time of Adam Smith; the second, from the turn of the nineteenth century to about 1870; the third, from 1870 to the end of World War I; and the fourth, the period since that time, particularly beginning with 1929, the advent of the Great Depression.

TO 1776

ADAM SMITH's magistral work was the first systematic treatise inimical to state activity, and until his time it had seemed the right and proper policy for the state widely to regulate human activities—laissez faire, indeed, appears as a brief exception in centuries of activity by the state.

To those who erroneously believe that the modern state alone has essayed the task of positive action in a wide sphere, the town life of the fourteenth to the middle of the sixteenth century offers an emphatic contradiction. As soon as the wider territory now known as the "nation," but then known as the "realm," "commonweal," or "kingdom," attained a state of settled organization in England, France, and Prussia, and as soon as the rulers were firmly established on their thrones, what had been done in the narrow area of the town was attempted for the nation.

Soon the three great systems of state activity arose: Colbertism in France (preceded, however, by a good deal of state activity), mercantilism in England, and cameralism in Prussia and other Germanic states.[1] Trade and industry, manufactures and agriculture, prices and wages, apprenticeship and skilled craftsmanship was tightly harnessed in rules ministering to the prince's treasury, the defense, the glory, and the general welfare of the nation, as that was conceived by the prince and his counselors. The latter, as merchant adventurers, not infrequently had a personal interest in the policy they foisted on the prince. Roughly for two and a half centuries, from 1550 to 1800, the process of controlling social and economic activities was most forcible, and ever extending in its scape and detail.

Eighteenth-Century Benevolence. The age of enlightened and benevolent despotism spread everywhere. But the cameralists of Prussia supplied two things lacking elsewhere: (1) they maintained a logical and detailed program for the application of their doctrine of state activity and a tradition, developing further an already long series of treatises and teaching the old and the new to generations of

---

[1] Cf. Henri Pirenne, *Economic and Social History of Mediaeval Europe* (London, 1936); C. W. Cole, *Colbert and a Century of French Mercantilism* (New York, 1939); Eli Heckscher, *Mercantilism* (London, 1935), 2 vols

students at the universities; and (2) they also insisted, as never elsewhere, upon an administrative organization and a civil service deliberately trained in the qualifications required for their work. The Prussian people thereby enjoyed a state that was well and honestly administered (though the virtue was relative), but they were obliged to suffer restrictions which became so galling that poets and dramatists cried out against them in works which achieved the widest popularity. The full doctrine of the police state or benevolent despotism is to be found in the works of Christian Wolff. Its doctrine is also the commonly accepted code of France and England in the same century; but in England the doctrine of state activity was not extended and carried out as in France and Prussia (and Austria). While these countries had a professional civil service spread over the country and actuated by the central authority, England carried out her policy of state interference mainly with reference to foreign trade and the acquisition and development of colonies, while her domestic administration was, in its higher branches, given up to the mercies of the ignorant, slothful, and corrupt, and unpaid officers and justices of the peace of towns, counties, and parishes, and the foppish wastrels and their underlings in Westminster and Whitehall.

In view of modern controversies, it is not unimportant to note that the Russian autocracy pursued a like policy of state development of mines, forests, and frontier settlements, while toward the end of this period the framers of the American constitution were of a mercantilist frame of mind. They believed in the state fostering trade and industry.[2]

The Foundations and Price of Success. What were the spiritual foundations of these systems of state activity, and what practical effect did they have? The first question is easily answered: that is, it is easy to enumerate the influences though it is difficult to ascribe to each its proper

weight. The state was new; it had but recently emerged from the agonies of combat, and even in the eighteenth century the process of violent aggrandisement was not yet ended. In such a condition men's fears of authority, and their patriotic hopes in it, form a reservoir of energy from which self-sacrifice and obedience can be obtained, even if those sacrifices are not strictly related to the aims and ends of conquest and defense. Restrictions which would not be brooked in the ordinary state of peace and peaceful mind, when the temper would grow impatient in the normal course of industry and life, are pressed forward by the body of psychic forces to which we give the collective name patriotism, and the burden becomes a joy.

All this is bound up to some extent with the person of the king, who, everywhere the conquerer of the Pope, is said to be the Victorious, the Wise, the Peacemaker, or the Saint, *Gloriose, Serenitas, Clementia,* the Magnificent, the Great, the Just, or Very Christian, the Philosopher, and *Dei Gratia,* who certainly lives in an atmosphere, and amidst a ceremonial, in which all virtues are magnified, while vices are sedulously hidden from the contemporary populace to enrich the reading of you, the later generation.

The state entered a field in which the extent of its territory and population was a singularly important condition of success in the things men wanted—international mercantile and colonial success, and the regulation of domestic conditions to ensure this.

The sense of solidarity, we may even say the sense of state, which had enabled the municipality to frame and execute its regulations, became in the sixteenth and seventeenth centuries a national consciousness. The generation and strengthening of the national spirit in the struggles between Pope and state, the breakdown of the old settled order by the Renaissance spirit, and the awakening of enterprise and acquisitiveness by the discovery of lands and wealth in the Far East and Far West—all these gave the power of attracting and directing human

[2] Walton H. Hamilton and Douglass Adair, *The Power to Govern* (New Haven, 1937).

energies to the only unit big enough to enter into a struggle for possession, the nation, with its area and population extended as far as possible. Even now, in an age of atomic bombs, the world reckons in manpower; how much more so when the only mobile energy available was contained in the sinews of men and horses. The state of mind was one in which the desire for national power mingled with the sheer incomprehensibility of individual freedom, which might or might not have been regardful of the necessary power of the state. In England the evolution of the desire for power is marked clearly by the reign of Henry VII; of him Bacon has said that "he bowed the ancient policy of this realm from consideration of plenty to consideration of power." Now flourished the *raison d'état*.

Further, in the infancy of an organization, things are done and suffered which maturity alone can condemn and amend. What was the alternative? The very things which men feared and hated—localism, ecclesiastical strife, and oppression by tyrannical individuals and overlords. The choice among alternatives can come only when there are alternatives theoretical or actual, and at the origin of things there are, by hypothesis, none. Alternatives are the offspring of history, or, as Bacon said, "Truth is the daughter of time." The state enjoyed the benefits of an almost complete consensus. This itself was only part of a much wider state of mind, that of the Ages of Faith. The Church was still the paramount educator of youth; the English state, indeed, gave the Church of England the monopoly of it. "Man," in Kant's words, "had not yet made his exit from the state of his self-made minority." Church and princes were rarely questioned.

Two other conditions which produced state activity require emphasis: (1) the fiscal needs and policy of the government; and (2) the pressure of commercial and industrial people who pursued their own interests consciously or unconsciously under cover of claims that the nation would benefit. If the latter were powers for liberty, the liberty primarily sought was in the interests of their own acquisitions. However, the liberty gained for a few could not be restricted to their sole benefit.

Even as these conditions secured for the state that general obedience which is its very life, others were arising which eventually penetrated Leviathan and dispersed its ancient elements.

Another question has yet to be answered. Were the regulations effective? how much success did they have? what hindered that success? No answer can be given until the question is made more precise. When we ask whether they achieved their object, there is the broader object and the narrower. The broader object was said to be national strength obtained through national wealth. But this aim is constituted of a tremendous number of ingredients: the balance of trade, the increase of population, the manufacture of certain articles in sufficient quantities to ensure adequate defense in war, and so on. No exact inquiry has ever been made into the effect of mercantile regulations upon these things. We know generally that all countries prospered; but the causes of prosperity, like the growth of knowledge and the increased international division of labor, were so powerful that enrichment was possible even if the regulations were economically unsound. It is certain that all countries lost much in aggregate welfare, in order that they might be well off in some particular aspects, in the possession of certain manufactures, of colonies, and, in the case of France and England, of large and well-equipped navies. It is also certain that we cannot find any widespread challenge to the policy. Whether these values could have been obtained with less expenditure and dissatisfaction is another question, and one that has not been answered by economic historians in the kind of detail which alone would be useful to us. An incessant struggle was needed for success. There was no general spontaneous obedience to the demands of the state, and the state was compelled to explain itself and reprove its citizens or officials in preambles to statutes and in circulars, and thus secure obedience. Statute after statute complained that the previous ones had not been properly obeyed. Numerous officials were necessary, and in all countries, customs officers became the watchdogs of import and export regulations and were perhaps the best hated of all. But the inspectors of industries of various kinds were hardly less detested and deceived wherever possible. In France and Prussia, state activity at home was taken seriously and carried out by professional administrators—in Prussia by expert and specially trained men—while the central authority maintained a strict and continuous and almost vindictive superintendence over its agents. It is not amiss to observe that the Prussian public economy was much dominated by the military authorities, since the economy supplied the means for the maintenance of the standing army. The richer the economy, the bigger and better equipped the army.

In England amateurism prevailed in the local justices and the government of the towns, and the poor-law in the eighteenth century is an eloquent testimony to its insufficiency at that time and in the circumstances, and an illustration of the fact that the success of the activity of the state (like that of any individual) depends upon the ability and character of those who perform it. English commercial policy was successful through unscrupulous sacrifice of Ireland, victorious wars which brought rich colonies, and the favorable maritime situation of the country. To this success the Navigation Acts contributed. Success was bought by methods which had not taken into account an ultimate possible loss— the loss of the American colonies and all that came of that in war, commercial embargoes, and destruction of shipping. The state can often win its way, as a private individual can, if it is ready to make the future pay for the present, and nation as well as individual may accidentally stumble into such a course without deliberately intending to set present gains and losses against those of the future. If Colbert, Cromwell, Grenville, Frederick the Great, and the kings of France and their counselors could have foreseen all the consequences of their policy, they might have pursued other ends, but such knowledge is possible only when experience and science are at hand to teach, and even these have their limitations; in proportion to their magnitude, the activity of the state is seemingly successful until the day a reasoned balance is struck.

The activity of the French state was more or less successful, but at what cost? Its officials were recruited in an infamously wasteful fashion, for men like Colbert came but once in a generation. The peasantry, whose agriculture was deemed inferior to the glory of manufactures, commerce, and colonies, was so oppressed that the only possible issue was violent revolution. The crude repression, fines, imprisonments, litigation developed a mistrust and hatred of public administration (which, it seems, is hardly eradicable even now from the Frenchman, however much he may agree with state activity as a theory) and, according to some authorities, weakened all trust in self-government. But these are heavy prices, though there is no way of reckoning them in francs. Further, several generations of French men, women, and children were obliged to live under a restrictive régime which, as far as we can tell, diminished the total aggregate welfare possible in a spontaneously developing individualism. We may ask, too, would not manufactures and commerce, if left to themselves, have better satisfied the originators of restrictive schemes, if these could have observed the long-run outcome?

The Downfall of State Activity. When men had experienced these things for a couple of centuries, they began to doubt their wisdom. Opinion became rational and individualistic; where before it had been traditional and social, it now became utilitarian. The Absolute Good, whereby men judge of temporal things, changed its nature: until the middle of the eighteenth century it had been an end inseparably connected with that social grouping called the State; now the Absolute Good became charged with individual values. The Enlightenment spread: people ceased to believe, as before, in miracles, books abounded on the Order of Nature, wits like Voltaire laughed royal and religious nonsense out of men's hearts. The scientific triumphs of the seventeenth century suggested support for the individual as sovereign creator of the State. Kant crowned all by his worship of man's rational nature, and, catching fire from Rousseau, dedicated his talents to the gospel of Progress achievable in the State through man's dynamic and unfettered reason. In England Locke had created a set of doctrines which compelled men's everyday thought and behavior; the State was posterior to the welfare of the individual, and its sovereign power properly limited by the will of its individual members. Hume's skeptical mind paved the way for social teachings even more shattering to the pretensions of the State than Locke's. In brief, however much all these thinkers differed among themselves, they collectively encouraged *first,* a belief that more freedom for the individual and less State activity would be socially fruitful, and, *second,* a belief that man, guided by individual reason and untrammeled by authority, would, by the unfolding of his nature, attain a state of perfection. This second part of the general belief we know as the doctrine of Progress. These beliefs have suffered strange vicissitudes since their formulation, but they still nominally rule modern society and statecraft. We have to ask what influence they had upon the development of State activity, and the answer seems to be that at different stages and in different places they had different effects, their first general effect being to encourage practical and theoretical movements subversive of despotic though "benevolent" government. The chief systematic contributors are the physiocrats and Adam Smith.

The Physiocrats.[3] The French *Économistes,* called also the physiocrats, formed the first school of thought to break with Colbertism and mercantilism. Their system, in so far as it concerned the problem of state activity, reposed upon two pillars:

---

[3] Georges Weulersse, *Le Mouvement Physiocratique* (Paris 1910), 2 vols.

the faith that agriculture was the only true productive work, that manufactures and commerce were of little value, and that individual choice was of higher worth than state regulation. All commerce and manufactures were, to them, unproductive, and therefore all encouragements thereof were social waste, especially if they were paid for by burdens upon agriculture. Agriculture alone produced; only agricultural peoples had the most desirable qualities: they had pure morals, they increased the population, they made good soldiers. Agriculture was the occupation of the majority of the nation and provided the greater part of the royal revenues. While it thrived—and it could easily be made to thrive (recent English agricultural progress proved this)—the nation would always have a good supply of food, but without it the raw material of all industrial activities would be lacking. No other form of economic activity returned a net product over and above the labor and capital put into it.

Existing restrictions in France discouraged agriculture instead of encouraging it; for had it been free, it could have driven good economic bargains with the industrial population and so have effectively reduced the value of the privileges that manufactures obtained from the state. About the middle of the eighteenth century the best political and economic minds in France seemed all at once to be seized with a question terrible for all systems and states: "Is all this really necessary?"

The gospel was bound up with their theory of property. To them the individual right to property in its most absolute sense was indeed fundamental, for this was the motive force of economic activity. Mirabeau, the Friend of Man, identified property rights with "the necessity of opening to the activity of the individual a free career, an unlimited field." "This which is mine," he said, "is the entire universe." Nothing must force this right, and the state's only business was to see that this principle was respected. For freedom to dispose of possessions was justified by the economy of agriculture, which required the intense application of the acquisitive and preservative dispositions of man. The right of bequest encouraged men to work for ends attainable only beyond their own generation, and plans made long ahead and works erected for future benefits were the essentials of agricultural economy. The tools and capital needed would find their best use if they were left to the free disposal of those who had an immediate interest in their most gainful application. Of all forms of property, the most indispensable was property in one's own person, the freedom to work when, where, and how one liked: "La terre ne peut fructifier que sous la main des hommes libres."

Here then was logical consequence: a theory of almost complete state inactivity. Grimm fulminated against the madness of regulating everything, "la fureur de trop gouverner"; and d'Argenson had set up as the highest maxim of government, "Pas trop gouverner!" Don't govern too much!

However, it was not sufficiently convincing to say that property and liberty made for the best social good through agricultural production; it was still necessary to show how this came about. What was the motive force in individual human beings which was of such a potency and direction that it could be left to operate without state control? The answer, in brief, was this: no individual human being can seek his own good, his own personal interest, without at the same time producing the public good.

Society need not fear harm or disruption, for "every one works for others, in believing that he works for himself." This comes about because human beings realize the need for reciprocity: in order to satisfy their own appetites they are obliged to concede certain satisfactions to others. The pursuit of our own interests teaches us our rights, and, at the same time, our duties towards others.

Yet what is to prevent this individual pursuit of satisfaction from causing subversion, misery, anarchy? For not all men are good, nor is their wisdom remarkable. The physiocrats answer: the interest of

the individual, and its pursuit, must be enlightened: that is, he must be taught a philosophy of his own best interests and the natural possibilities of their satisfaction.

Government's part is to leave men alone; at the most it is to recall men to an enlightened view of their interest; and this is to be learned from the nature of things and of men. The state is properly limited to guaranteeing security, property, and liberty, and to the declaration of the principles of the social order discovered by philosophers.

The physiocrats were like all who have scrutinized the face of the heavens and discovered a God with whose promise and behavior they are intimately acquainted: admitting that He is all-powerful and all-wise, they will not let Him attend to His business alone. And, if men cannot learn His ways, they must be taught by those who pretend to know them. What, then, did the physiocrats teach as to the activity of the state? Since the laws were graven on the face of Nature, the legislator could not create laws, he could but declare them. The state should be no more than tutelary, securing property and liberty and explaining why it did so, for these explanations would bring home to citizens the *Ordre Naturelle*. "Liberty and immunity are the best administrators," and "Government has practically nothing to do except to dispense itself from doing anything." This was the logical and seriously held consequence of the physiocrats' genuine belief in their natural laws.

Though the physiocrats were lamentably in error, they had added at least two ideas of extraordinary importance to the science of state activity: (1) the idea of a natural order of social behavior which determined the proper scope and manner of governmental action. and (2) the theory that if the individual were left untrammeled, the greatest social good would result. In the first idea they themselves erred in believing that they had arrived at the complete truth, or even at the truth in the part which they had investigated. They too narrowly identified their personal beliefs with the designs of Nature. Second, their optimism was unlimited and inveterate. The most impossible explanations were invented in order not to desert the beneficent intention of Nature acting through individual self-interest. And yet the doubt remained. Indeed, this doubt was so ineradicable that the physiocrats themselves threw up the sponge and admitted that there ought to be limits to state inactivity, and that the chief limit was state education. A damnable but necessary heresy! And indeed, as the public educational activities of the great business corporations and labor unions of our own day demonstrate, a continuing, necessary heresy!

These theories did not influence French government very much. Only with the Revolution itself was there a snapping of ancient threads and a throwing off of oppressive burdens.

ADAM SMITH

In 1776, a few years after the zenith of physiocracy, appeared the work which was to exercise an influence more profound, extensive, and lasting—Adam Smith's *Wealth of Nations*. Smith thought highly of the physiocrats, though he recognized and denounced their cardinal errors. He was at one with them in their theory of human nature in society, on the existence of economic laws, and the inability of government to bring about the welfare of society better than could the untrammeled individual. He made mincemeat of the mercantile system. He showed that on its own principles it was ineffective and wasteful, and again, that those principles reduced the potential wealth of nations. Wherever the government put its finger it paid more than it obtained, and some classes lost more than any other classes gained.

Governments could not judge where human beings could best apply their work and capital. Only the individual, in his special situation, could best judge this. The argument rises to its highest burden in the famous passage upon the "invisible hand." This, and like phrases, have produced the error that Adam Smith was the creator of laissez faire. But he was in fact too clever to surrender to the utter inactivity of the state proposed by the physiocrats. He recognized that a state has other needs besides material welfare, such as defense and instruction, and that these may not be attainable in the undirected higgling of the market. He objected, quite pertinently, to the following assertion by the physiocrats: "If a nation could not prosper without the enjoyment of perfect liberty and perfect justice, there is not in the world a nation which could ever have prospered."

Adam Smith's work has had a tremendous vogue, and its native virtue was enhanced by economic and political conditions at the time of its publication. Through the channel of Göttingen University, the *Wealth of Nations* percolated into Germany; *Smithianismus* became a cult, while the book was likened to the New Testament in its social significance. In England a prime minister avowed in the House of Commons his faith in its principles. In France Jean-Baptiste Say systematized, with national clarity, the work of the master. The world believed itself given over to laissez faire.

The world need neither have rejoiced nor feared inordinately. Bad conditions themselves bring about reforms, and good conditions maintain themselves. In England some important fiscal reforms were accomplished by reason of the conditions, and by about 1846 hardly a vestige of the mercantile system was left. In Germany a small measure of local representative government was established, and the emancipation of the servile agricultural population was begun. In France, free peasant proprietorship was inaugurated and trade and industrial corporations abolished. But all these things were not merely Smithian. It has been shown, for example, for Prussia, how many other currents contributed to that strong stream which carried away the ancient controls. Stein's was an independent creative talent at least on a par with Adam Smith's.

Laissez faire was never an absolute rule of government, or even approximately absolute, or the governments would have been forced to action in at least the three directions indicated by Adam Smith. These were: (1) protecting society from violence and invasion, (2) establishing the administration of justice, and (3) providing for public works and public institutions which are profitable for society but not productive of individual profits. Between 1776 and 1876, at which later date a new impulse toward state activity successfully emerged, all governments made laws at great speed, on numerous aspects of social life, and saw to it that their rules were executed. There are few fictions so misleading as that which looks back at the early nineteenth century and says it was an "era" of laissez faire.

In France, after the abolition of state control in economic matters in the first raptures of Revolution and Restoration, dangerous and unhealthy industries were regulated, and as soon as the consequences of the Industrial Revolution, which came later in France than in England, began to loom large (that is, by about 1860), the state began to assume more and more activities in relation to them. The first great theoretical reaction against Smithian doctrines commenced in Germany. The most systematic of the Romanticists, Adam Müller, refuted the doctrine of the "invisible hand" point by point, and showed very clearly to what social evils unregulated industrial revolution tended.

There was merely a pause while civilization developed, the agricultural eighteenth century being pushed out of the way and the steam-driven nineteenth rolling in. Only the obsolete was left alone or demolished; the new and desirable was at once harnessed. In proportion as the full potency of the new energies was revealed, and as the creatures of its titanic force were molded and emplaced, promising a magnified weal or woe, men lost interest in a Natural Order which left things to run amuck, and demanded deliberate regulation. For the Natural Order had been overtaken now by a machine order. State inactivity, which the Natural Order and the *Wealth of Nations* had advocated, was carried out mainly in international trade, as far as England was concerned.

The leaders of manufacturing industries were creating fortunes, factories, and power; and as a sequel, they created schools of thought and instruments of agitation claiming freedom. In England the so-called Manchester School was established—radicals with doctrines drawn from Smith and Bentham. Smith argued free trade; Bentham argued that men best knew their own interests, and that the best government was representative government, which included all interests. The Anti-Corn Law League was its chief bloom, and anti-state interference in the regulation of working conditions another. Its influence has only of recent years been seriously counteracted. In Germany, the German Manchester School, *Manchestertum*, had no more than a very few years of authority. In France, despite brave protestations, very little was done to break down the network of defensive customs duties. In the United States, upon federation, commenced a policy of state regulation of international trade, and shortly afterwards of internal improvements— railroads, rivers, canals, roads, and posts.

Meanwhile there was a mighty fermentation in the home activities of the state, leading to a vast increase of functions between 1830 and 1870, at which date the theory of laissez faire or individualism was in a very tattered condition.

FORCES AT WORK FROM 1776 TO 1870

THE forces at work were (1) the economy of industrial environment, (2) the psychological influence of manufactures, (3) the ideas and sentiments of progress, Benthamism, and humanitarianism, and (4) democratic institutions.

The Economy of Industrial Environment. The economy of the new industries was conditioned by the nature of steam-power. The *first* result of this was congregation. It was necessary that people should be near the machines, too expensive to be installed at home. Congregation gave rise to new problems of public health administration and poor relief and the prevention and punishment of crime. In the matter of public health, the contagious nature of disease soon abolished the notion of any absolute freedom of the individual or the locality. The possibility of the rapid movement of criminals by the use of modern transport and their opportunities to hide in the byways of the large towns made it necessary to establish national regulation of training and to provide numbers of police. Furthermore, when people live in densely packed areas, social misery becomes more apparent, and becoming aware is for the more conscious of the miserable the spur to reform.

Second, the new industry and commerce required for their full extension the rapid movement of raw materials to the manufacturing centers and the rapid movement of the finished product to the consumer. Articles could be produced cheaply in proportion to the size of the market, and large-scale organization was therefore necessary. Easy movement, large capital, credit, insurance, and safeguards for a proper administration of roads were provided for, and the principles of limited liability, insurance, and banking were established.

Third, the essence of the new economy was division of labor and roundabout production. Thence the need for continuity, the political implications of which we have discussed in an earlier chapter.

Fourth, a new type of subordination came into existence with the new industry. Traditional feelings of fellowship between master and servant were now overwhelmed by the ambition to inherit the new riches promised by machines. Samuel Smiles was the great prophet of the day, and his was a gospel strangely like the dollar standards of America at the present time, themselves originating with Astor, Gould, Fiske, and Rockefeller several decades later. When both employers and employed were themselves ready to take advantage of each other—the first by the discipline of hours and wages and fines, and the second by the strike and sabotage —and were jointly ready to take advantage of the work of infants and women under conditions of revolting cruelty, common decency obliged the state to take action even against Manchester and even against the American "robber barons."

The Psychological Influence of Manufactures. The mere existence of manufactures gave men a startling sense of power. If their economic well-being was so easily obtainable by the mere institution of machines, why not their general social well-being, and their mental development? Reform of the law, which had, in 1814, been said by no less an authority than Savigny to be given to us by earlier generations and to be incapable of being remade, was now conceived of as merely one more problem in engineering.

It should be noted that this idea was already expressed by Bentham in his *Fragment on Government,* published in 1776, the same year that *Wealth of Nations* saw the light. Some contemporary writers argue (erroneously) that it is a lust for power which activates social planners, who are sometimes referred to as "social engineers." No! The impetus to economic and social planning was inherent in the new industrialism, in the discontent with its inequities, and the new sense of social power and competence suggested by machinery, scientific cause-and-effect, and invention.

The Ideas and Sentiments of Progress, Benthamism, and Humanitarianism. The effects, material and psychological, of the new system in industry did not operate merely upon a small class and very small body of political rulers. Western Europe and the United States were now committed to democratic government, and though in Germany and France its full expression was impeded for some time by conservative and royalist forces, and in England by the upper and middle classes, government now had to reckon with the wishes of the whole population. The whole virtue of democratic government lay in its promise to shorten the circuit between the impulse of popular needs and the legal and administrative response. Nor was this all:

(1) The gospel of Progress and Perfectibility had been invented on the Continent, in France and Germany.[4] Before the

----

[4] Cf. another aspect in R. H. Tawney, *Religion and the Rise of Capitalism* (London, 1929) and Max Weber, *The Protestant Ethic and the Spirit of Capitalism* (London, 1930).

end of the eighteenth century no visions of indefinite possibilities of human progress upon earth had inspired men's plans. Static or cyclical patterns limited their optimism, or else perfection was, owing to the exigencies of the censorship, conceived possible only in Utopias as far away as China or at the bottom of the Atlantic Ocean. Now, however, men said that their own country could, with a few simple legislative arrangements, become the Kingdom of Heaven. Kant saw all the generations preparing for the Perfect Generation. Godwin explained the steps to be taken, in his *Political Justice*. Malthus quarreled with his father about the possibility of reaching this happy state, and, to prove the impossibility, composed the pessimistic first *Essay on Population*. Though invented in France and Germany, the gospel had a speedier effect upon the United States and England than upon them, for these were not so acquisitive, were content with intellectual as much as material satisfactions, and were moreover, for a large part Catholic, while the other countries were Protestant, if anything. Furthermore, Germany was handicapped by its fragmentation, and in addition, neither France nor Germany had fully responsible and representative systems of parliamentary government to act as the vehicle of the new outlook.

(2) Bentham, searching for a principle of political utility which should be unflavored by the "nonsense on stilts" of Natural Rights and the Natural Order, seized on the "greatest happiness of the greatest number." This was later incorporated into the radical faith and program in all countries, and became one of those powerful ultimate dogmas which lead society very far. The dogma could, of course, have had its application in a slackening of state activity, as it did for some decades, but then the effect was the opposite because society required it.

(3) The eighteenth century had seen an extraordinary revival of humanitarian feeling and benevolence. Prison, hospital, and health reform occupied the minds of many people in England for two or three decades before the Reform Bill of 1832, and many things were accomplished.

Democratic Institutions. All these forces played upon the enfranchised classes, who, in turn, caused Parliament to undertake certain activities. The vote was to state activity what steam power was to industry: it drove the state fast and far. After 1834 Parliamentary debates, and therefore the motives of the members, became freely reported. From 1836 division lists were published by order of the House. In 1835 the first printed questions were put on the Order Paper, and year by year there was a steady increase in the number of questions asked by the government.[5] The Chartist movement demanded not only the vote and proper Parliamentary representation: men like William Lovett said: "But it is not for the mere possession of the franchise that is to benefit our country; that is only the means to a just end— the election of the best and wisest of men to solve a question which has never yet been propounded in any legislative body —namely, *how shall all the resources of our country be made to advance the intellectual and social happiness of every individual? It is not merely the removing of evils, but the establishing of remedies that can benefit the millions. . . ."* The spinners of Silesia and Lyons, and their like, were already preparing the way for radical and socialist parties in Prussia and France. In 1867 John Stuart Mill uttered his gloomy fear that the working class in a majority would certainly infringe property rights, although he had already admitted that "the laws of property . . . have not held the balance fairly between human beings, but have heaped impediments upon some, to give advantages to others: they have purposely fostered inequalities, and prevented all from starting fair in the race." By the time he came to writing his *Autobiography* he had reached

---

[5] In the United States it was not until 1873 that the *Congressional Record* was officially publishing debates and proceedings of Congress; prior to that, beginning with 1830, the *Congressional Globe* had been privately printed.

the conclusion that England required socialism.

What was the meaning of the growth of state activity? The immediate driving spirit was the unwillingness of those who achieved political sovereignty to allow the spontaneous behavior of people to have its ungoverned consequences. Human behavior was thus bent to conform with ends which individuals acting unchecked might not have pursued.

FROM THE CRISIS IN THE 1870's AND 1880's
UNTIL WORLD WAR I

STATE activity increased with the need for it, in spite of the prevailing dogma of laissez faire and self-help, and in spite of the economic theorists whose fatalistic individualism found its comprehensive expression in Mill's *Political Economy* and *Essay on Liberty*. But Mill himself was gravely worried by new longings; he could be neither entirely pessimistic nor so individualistic as his predecessors who had lived in the gloomy thirty years which began the nineteenth century.

Indeed, the full consequences of the industrial change were becoming visible and compelled the invention of institutions to cope with them. These, with the development of new doctrines and sentiments, caused the presumption in favor of laissez faire to be changed into a presumption in favor of state interference. That change came about by imperceptible but important stages in the 1870's and 1880's.

In the first place, this question had to be answered: was the state, as an arrangement producing a stable social order, to be allowed to founder from the shock of social forces making for disruption, or were these forces to be so adjusted as to allow further smooth continuance of life? All the economic interests were tugging against each other. People were becoming increasingly conscious of the cost of the new prosperity in terms of the misery of the working classes—England, again, necessarily the first.

The Social Microscope. An apparatus of exploration was invented for the social field, as mightily influential in its sphere as the invention of the microscope had been in physics and medicine. Royal commissions of inquiry, beginning with that of 1832 on the administration of towns, were every five years or so making clear the relationship between detestable social phenomena and their exact quantitative causes. What else can so assault the conscience as exact knowledge? Who can for long resist the demonstrated fact that an evil is remediable by human intervention? [6]

Thus conditions pressed, and knowledge of their effects and causes was extended. The conditions of housing, health, factories, and mines were remodeled by the state. The sectional interests which had been created by the new industry (like the railway interest and the trade unions) were incorporated into the state by measures which (1) took away from the former the power to extract to the full from other occupations what the traffic would bear, and (2) arranged for the latter the possibility of legal withdrawal of their work with the minimum danger of penalties. All these things were not accomplished without much turmoil and stress—strikes, riots, and political battles in legislatures and in the secret avenues that lead to them. Evils were not eradicated immediately knowledge was gained and conscience informed; threats and fears of violence and disorder were required to ram home the logic of social justice.

The condition of the state's continued existence is that it should every day renew itself, nourishing government with fresh powers, and expelling the remnants of that which no longer lives with wholesome vigor. Among such powers are the mind and the spirit as well as economic welfare. These were peculiarly energetic and transformative in the two decades of change. Religion had long been allied

---

[6] H. M. Clokie and J. W. Robinson, *Royal Commissions of Inquiry* (Oxford, 1937); R. Vernon and N. Mansergh, *Advisory Bodies* (Oxford, 1940); Sidney and Beatrice Webb, *Methods of Social Study* (London, 1932). It was not long before American Congressional investigating committees and committee hearings on contemplated legislation accomplished similar results.

with fatalism as to this world's goods, but now it became socially active. In England, Nonconformity was allied with Liberal politics. The Church of England gave birth to Christian Socialism. In Germany a Christian Democratic party was formed. Pope Leo XIII, in the famous encyclical of 1891, recalled Catholics to a sense of Christian social service. The fatalism of religion was challenged by the social good offered by science. Against ensconced and complacent individualism another ideal was preached—an actually living community under Christ, in which no man has a right to call anything that he has his own absolutely, but in which reside spiritual fellowship and practical cooperation. (It is relevant at this point to draw attention to the strong Christian Socialist movements in Europe after World War II, which the Vatican has had the pleasure of morally fostering as an offset to the social doctrines of the Communist party.[7] Among them are the Christian Democratic or Popular Parties of Italy, Belgium, and Germany, and the *Mouvement Républicain Populaire* of France.)

Arithmetic Becomes Argumentative. The day of absolute principles in legislative discussion had passed more surely than the day of absolute government. For statistics—the mathematical recording and analysis of social phenomena—had become a servant of government, and commodities, qualities, behavior, and nature's operations were being investigated with an arithmetic minuteness and exactitude heretofore applied only in the physical sciences. Where, before this, men had been wont to talk in terms of absolutes, while recognizing that no absolute would suffice in actual politics, a means of measurement and degree now made it easy for men to retreat from their own absolute— laissez faire, for example—and yet not fly to the opposite extreme. In France in the 1830's and 1840's the whole battle for free trade was waged around the system of customs statistics then in use, while Prussia had already for many decades con-

verted the science of statistics into an art of government. Now this habit of mind does not necessarily lead to more state activity: it may work either way and which way it works depends upon the needs of the time. In the 1870's and 1880's the statistical habit of mind finally inclined, on the balance, to overcome eternal and absolute negations of state activity, because it inculcated the view that in society we are concerned only with the more or less. Moreover, the substance of statistics showed, as we have urged already, the number of points at which social life needed social control to avoid evils and produce good.[8]

Not only did arithmetic become argumentative, but since it dealt in units of calculation—sick people, hospital beds, children attending schools, miles of public road, etc.—it became possible to establish standard reporting by local authorities to central headquarters. It became easier to get appropriate solutions of local problems made by central officials. This conduced to the efficiency of centralization: for the local and central administrators were now talking about the same thing.

The Social Conscience. All this growth in the science of statistics and in social investigation does not entirely account for the growth in state activity and the substantial reign of collectivism. We must add to other factors the growth of a social conscience. An authority upon that time describes the upper layer of society as having been overcome with "a class-consciousness of sin." Let us recall the names of

---

[7] Cf. Papal Encyclical *"Of Atheistic Communism" (Divini Redemptoris)*, March, 1937, for the general theory.

[8] In this connection, the work of the National Resources Planning Board (especially in such studies as *The Structure of American Economy, The Economics of Planning Public Works, Technological Trends and National Policy, The Problems of a Changing Population)* may be noted as sponsor of a remarkable series of analytical and prognosticatory investigations. It would seem that its findings were so incontrovertible as eventually to become compelling social policy, and therefore in 1943 a Congress without bravery abolished the Board, with directions for the disposal of its work reminiscent of the Romans who scattered salt on the ruins of Carthage so that nothing should ever grow on that site again. Cf. Chap. 26 below.

such people as Elizabeth Fry, Florence Nightingale, Octavia Hill, the Earl of Shaftesbury, Jane Addams, Sidney and Beatrice Webb,[9] each of whom changed the mind of the public to believe that the "impossible" could and ought to be done in his or her specific line of endeavor. Nor could liberalism avoid the effects of the energy released by the sense of social injustice. It was this development which caused Herbert Spencer to label Liberalism the New Toryism, and to compose his famous essays on *The Man versus the State.*

Soon this power began to be released in organized forms. After 1867, as a result of vastly different causes in different countries, almost universal suffrage was established and statesmen had to reckon with the natural desire of men to be saved from their miseries. By 1867 there was a representative if not responsible government for Germany, and by 1871 the Third Republic had been born in France. What one party promises in a democracy the other party must in the long run also promise. Mass party parliaments grew up outside Parliament, and state control over the processes of production and distribution came into the forefront of political discussions. Socialist organizations were created. At Oxford the movement in social philosophy—that of Green and Bosanquet—was in tune with the social theory of the time—indeed, led it. In France and Germany the "Socialists of the Chair" opposed reforms from above to reforms demanded by political parties.

The remaining theorists of laissez faire either were, in part, won over to the new doctrinal tendencies, or else they were successfully confuted in some famous controversies, like that between John Stuart Mill and James Fitzjames Stephen.

It is the proper end of government to reduce this wretched waste to the smallest possible amount, by taking such measures as shall cause the energies now spent by mankind in injuring one another, or in protecting themselves against injury, to be turned to the legiti-

mate employment of the human faculties, that of compelling the powers of nature to be more and more subservient to physical and moral good.

These last sentences are John Stuart Mill's and they seem to represent the position of a daring state interventionist. It would be difficult to find a match to these opinions outside the extreme socialist position even today. But this is only one of the places in which John Stuart Mill began by rehearsing the economics of 1800, only to conclude with the results of his own experience. The final words in the *Principles* were emphasized by the statement of faith in the *Autobiography.* The world was well on its way to socialism, and discussions like Mill's by stating the issues, cleared the way for it.

Mill's final statement of the case for laissez faire, that which appears in the *Essay on Liberty,* was finely confuted—and in our opinion, left quite stricken on the field of controversy—by James Fitzjames Stephen's *Liberty, Equality, and Fraternity.* The position of Stephen's book was, in regard to the main issues, also taken by Ritchie, in his little volume on *The Principles of State Interference,* an exceedingly sensible and just attack upon Herbert Spencer's *Man versus the State.* If we indicate Spencer's main thesis upon state activity, we shall hear the last and despairing trumpet call of laissez faire by a considerable mind until more recently Hayek's *Road to Serfdom* reintoned the flyblown score.

Spencer held that all legislative interference cannot help setting in motion unforeseen and unfortunate effects; that, without positive will, one legislative act inevitably and uncontrollably leads to others; that the conception is fostered that government ought to step in; that the beneficial weeding out of the weakest is impeded; that an officialdom is fostered which ever conspires to obtain more power over the people; that enslavement and despotism follow; that legislators are ignorant, especially of the "systematic study of social causation"; that the accumulation of state business results in "red

---

[9] Cf. Beatrice Webb, *Our Partnership* (New York, 1948).

tape"; that spontaneous individual activity is practically always superior to state-controlled activity.

Stephen's answer to Mill and Ritchie's answer to Spencer were much the same. They show that discussion had revealed the essential problems involved in state activity and even point to a series of maxims which would be of service to legislators. These points had become clear:

(1) The "individual" postulated by Mill and Spencer was a mere abstraction. There is no such thing, if man is to be considered as a member of society at all. This "individual" was a *wish* personal to Mill, Spencer, and others, projected into, and dominating, the whole of their discussion.

(2) The antithesis between state and individual was founded upon this false view of the "individual," and upon the fallacy that the state was a sovereign authority the power of which emanated not from the constituent individuals, but from some undiscoverable but nevertheless reprehensible source.

(3) There is not necessarily any connection between state activity and centralization; the idea that these were synonymous, so frequently introduced into controversy, was erroneous, for the possible forms of organization for state activity were many, including municipal and vocational administration.

(4) Attacks upon the incapacity of legislators and administrators, of the kind made by Spencer (more crotchety and ignorantly stubborn in this regard than Mill), were not entirely valid arguments against state activity. It is true that the success of state activity depends upon the efficiency of the instruments, and that efficacy is one element in the decision to act or not to act; but it is an argument relative to a particular set of circumstances and not an absolute argument against activity. Nevertheless, Spencer had put his finger upon an important aspect of the question. The efficiency of the instrument is indeed of critical importance. Spencer's criticism of the competence of legislators, however, invited comparison between them and the actual competence of private businessmen. Lord Pembroke in a pamphlet on *Liberty and Socialism,* published by the now long defunct Liberty and Property Defence League, made the comparison: "What," he says, "would private enterprise look like if its mistakes and failures were collected and pilloried in a similar manner?"

(5) The abstract notion of liberty itself was questioned, and it was asked, Is this more than one of many ends of which man seeks the realization? Some liberty is desirable, as well as other things, but nothing at all is attainable without a limitation of liberty. If, then, limitation is conceded, the extent of the limitation is merely a question of the more or less dependent upon the mixture of men's desires and capacities, and this varies in time and place.

(6) Stephen enunciated the questions to be asked before activity is undertaken by the state, and these were: (*a*) Is the object aimed at good (i.e., will it tend to advance the well-being of the community)? (*b*) Will the proposed means attain it? (*c*) Will they attain it at too great expense, or not (i.e., can the end be attained without doing more harm than is compensated by the benefit of its attainment)?

(7) It was further proved that the least amount of state activity possible was education: for if the masses, uneducated, were to become the legislators, all the evils prophesied by Spencer must result. But was it necessary to wait until all had been formally educated to a required standard; was not a state activity already a part of civic education, a means to reform character?

What was the net result of the development of state activity between the middle and the last quarter of the nineteenth century? The cardinal gain was the break-up of absolutes, or at least the break-up of old absolutes; for socialism, the new dispensation, was in its early days an absolute, as unmeasured as those it replaced. Further, toward the end of the century, government was actually conducting an enormous range of activities, and the immediate promise of all political parties was for more. The direction of opinion was well established: the state could effectively act, for experience had shown that it could provide the organization and the officials. Furthermore, the state ought to act; Humanity, Fraternity, Equality, and the prudent prevention of social friction and waste demanded it. From this time dates the rapid development of socialist schools of thought, and of Socialist and Labor parties in practical politics. The western world has become more and more socialistic in deed and thought. The essence of that thought is, first, that the life of the individual person shall be made to respond to a social standard established by the state, and, next, that the state shall provide for the poor a minimum of services and security, at the ultimate expense of the wealthy.

SINCE WORLD WAR I

WORLD WAR I had three effects on government: (1) it stirred social emotions; (2) it taught that if society and government deliberately planned their productive activities they could achieve remarkable results; and (3) it developed the popularization of government because the masses learned to have an additional confidence in their own ability as compared with the classes—aristocracy, or plutocracy, or politicians—who had hitherto governed.

Social Criticism, and Proposals for Governmental Action. Simultaneously, social criticism made clearer three deficiencies in society which would require to be corrected by government. These were:

(1) The rise of monopolies, which ruled production over a large field, sometimes to a 100-per cent control of certain commodities. In the United States and Great Britain an angry outcry rose against these, causing the accentuation of antitrust measures. This is still a major problem.[10] In

Germany the rise of the nation to world power, simultaneous with the industrialization of the economy, resulted in governmental favor toward monopolies, at least until the downfall of the imperial system in 1918. The question at stake everywhere is whether regulation is adequate for curbing the power of monopolies to underexploit their own productive opportunities, to continue methods less efficient than those which laws might introduce, and to buy up patents or sterilize their own inventions in order to avoid the necessity of reorganizing their plant and management, undertaking new business initiative, and working harder.[11]

It will be observed that it is entrepreneurs of this kind who lie on the path between the consumer and the technical possibilities available for increased production. They exercise a government over men.[12] The fostering of scientific advancement and technological development has become a major concern of all modern governments, not least the dictatorial ones, and substantial financial assistance (accompanied by general programs of research) is rendered by governments for these purposes.

The protection of invention by patent law has also required to be seriously reviewed, for the idea that anyone who receives a protection for an invention then has so high a degree of property in it that he need not use the invention or can sell it to a suppressor has become abhorrent to a society in quest of more wealth and less toil.[13]

(2) The movements for intervention of governments to secure equality became highly marked. This development was partly the result of the equalitarian no-

---

[10] Cf. A. E. Burns, *The Decline of Competition* (New York, 1936); Joan Robinson, *The Economics of Imperfect Competition* (Cambridge, 1933); J. M. Keynes, *General Theory of Employment, Interest, and Money* (London, 1935); and Alvin Hansen, *Fiscal Policy and Business Cycles* (New York, 1941) and *Economic Policy and Full Employment* (New York, 1947).

[11] Cf. House of Commons *Debates*, April 22, 1948, on Royal Commissions Bill to inquire into monopolies.
[12] Cf. Robert Brady, *Business as a System of Power* (New York, 1943).
[13] Cf. Vannevar Bush, *Science, the Endless Frontier* (Washington, 1945); Hearings on the Kilgore Bill on National Science Foundation (1946: S.R. 146, 79th Cong.); Walton H. Hamilton, *Anti-Trust in Action* (Washington: Temporary National Economic Committee, 1940).

tions developed during World War I, and partly the result of the practical policy and governmental activity of the Soviet Union, where the interested world was observing the idea of equality (that is, educational opportunity unobstructed by family and business privilege) and the reduction of inequalities that stem from inheritance and the power of property owners to direct the work of the propertyless. These movements were combined with the view that in many respects the system of private enterprise (that is, the relationship between the free producer and his customer) could not adequately deliver the goods—for example, in housing, health, diet, education. Hence the impetus in all nations to supply these through public authorities at less than cost or altogether without charge.

(3) The grave inequalities of property and income were revealed more clearly by statistical analysis and presentation. For example, in President Roosevelt's message of April 29, 1938, incorporating the recommendations of the Temporary National Economic Committee, he cited these facts: For the year 1935 to 1936, 47 per cent of American family units had incomes of less than $1000, and less than 1½ per cent at the top received the same total income as the 47 per cent at the bottom. Of the corporations reporting income for 1935, 0.1 per cent earned 50 per cent of the net income, and 4 per cent earned 84 of the net profits; 0.1 per cent of the corporations reporting assets owned 52 per cent of the total assets. The gist of the matter was put by the President in his second inaugural address: "I see one third of a nation ill-housed, ill-clad, ill-fed."

The remedies for these evils—if they are to preserve the incentive of men and women to produce, while safeguarding their political and civil liberties—are highly complicated. They require, within a gradually and democratically developed system of governmental activity, the carefully organized techniques of popular acceptance, popular control, parliamentary surveillance, and administrative arrange-ments of personnel, departments, and territorial decentralization.

With the increasing severity of depressions, the government's role in attempting to prevent these downswings in the business cycle is assuming supreme importance. In the United States the Council of Economic Advisers, established by the Employment Act of 1946, is symptomatic of this development. Its function is to advise the President and Congress on the state of the economy, recommending anti-depression measures.[14]

The type of governmental action that can be pursued includes all facets of economic life, specifically:

(1) Fiscal and tax policy. During a depression, governmental outlays will exceed its receipts. Large-scale expenditures —a planned series of public works, for example—will be utilized to produce increased buying power and to encourage private production. When a boom stage has been reached, emphasis will be placed on curtailing government expenditures to prevent overexpansion. Taxes, corporate and individual, will appropriately be heaviest during prosperity.

A central banking system (owned by government as in Britain or heavily controlled by government as in the United States) will, with its power over rediscount rates, its power to increase reserve ratios of member banks, and its right to engage in open-market operations, have substantial effect on the flow of credit and thus on investment.

(2) Flexible price policy. A strong program can be adopted to discourage price rigidities, much more widely prevalent among monopolistic industries.

Capital and labor can be encouraged to transfer from overcrowded industries by government contracts and by loans for capital and operating purposes.

(3) Social insurance. Unemployment insurance could be made universally avail-

---

14 Cf. also William Beveridge, *Full Employment in a Free Society* (New York, 1945); and British Government, White Paper on "Employment Policy" (May, 1944) and White Paper, Economic Survey, 1947. Cf. also French "Monnet" Plan, Chap. 24 below.

able, with effective employment services to help locate jobs, and special government projects to absorb the unemployed. Restoring consumer purchasing power would be one of the chief economic results.

Freedom to Kill Free Enterprise? What had been perceived was this: that too many, if not all, private entrepreneurs claimed freedom from government direction, that is, claimed freedom of enterprise, without always giving in return, fully competitive enterprise. They wanted to be free not to do as the consumers liked—namely, to have costs of production reduced to the minimum and to have all new efficiencies and inventions exploited for their benefit—but free to be lazy and obstructive and inefficient. After a certain point they were seduced by inertia, not tempted by profits. They used freedom to kill freedom. The very nature of the competitive system is to kill competition: for the motive of competition is private benefit, and, therefore, after a certain point of welfare and income and security have been reached by a successful businessman or manufacturer, the competitive factor works simply to cause him to bar competition from others. This is inherent in the nature of the competitive system of enterprise, whatever its claims. After a certain point the spur to industry and invention must come from outside. The state is then called on to regulate or break up the monopolies, or to take over their management. The essence of monopoly has been well stated by Chief Justice White in the American Tobacco Company Case, 1907: [15]

... its acts demonstrated from the beginning a purpose to acquire dominion and control of the tobacco trade [by methods] ruthlessly carried out upon the assumption that to work upon the fears or play upon the cupidity of competitors would make success possible.

It must never be forgotten that the laissez-faire economists implicitly or openly claim that competitive enterprise is a way of planning production: the mind of the producer being focused on the expressed wants of the consumers. The claim implies that the public benefit is the criterion. The question then is the practical one: does the system do its work better than a conceivable and workable alternative?

Thus, modern states have traveled exceedingly far in their economic and social activities since their origin in the sixteenth and seventeenth centuries, and very far indeed from their paucity of functions in the early part of the nineteenth century.[16] The next question has hitherto been chiefly a matter of intellectual wrestling and forecast: "Can work incentives and inventiveness and liberty be maintained at a high level compatibly with the self-control and social control implied in the state's provision of social security, the social services, the management of the basic industries, and the penetrating control of the monopolies it does not take over entirely?" It has still to be answered by the results of contemporary and future practice. For, though men demand much from the economy, they do not live by bread alone and they are not willing to surrender all spiritual freedom for a mess of pottage. They know, in the western world of Europe and the Americas and the British Dominions, that the true guarantee of personal dignity is to be found only in the system of democracy (if anywhere, and if imperfectly), where government which controls the economy is itself controlled by the people, and where voluntary association, and freedom of speech, meeting, and worship, are the sustainers of the popular power to determine the features of the community's way of life.[17]

15 *U.S.* v. *American Tobacco Co.,* 164 Fed. 700; 221, U.S. 106 (1911). Cf. also Final Report of the Temporary National Economic Committee, sections on monopolies. Cf. also H. Leak and A. Maizels, *Royal Statistical Society Journal,* for paper on "Concentration and Size of Business Units in British Industry," read in February, 1945.

16 Cf. J. H. Clapham, *Economic Development of France and Germany* (Cambridge, 1928); Louis Hacker, *Triumph of American Capitalism* (New York, 1947); Max Weber, *Deutsches Wirtschaftsleben* (Berlin, 1941).
17 Cf. Frank H. Knight, *Freedom and Reform* (New York, 1947) for the stressing of these latter considerations particularly—the attitude is philosophically laissez faire. Cf. also Karl Polanyi, *Origins of Our Time* (London, 1945).

The passion for material welfare could conceivably go so far as to induce men and women to yield their freedom to a managerial class. Burnham has suggested that this is indeed happening, and that this class will ultimately take over politics in the cunning guise of a single political party.[18] The world of the technocrats, also, who a few years ago offered to raise the standard of living and shorten the hours of work to some twenty or less per week for everybody, is one which is realizable only if all men and women being producers, submit themselves almost absolutely to the technocrats' commands.[19]

[18] *Managerial Revolution* (New York, 1941). The theme is grossly exaggerated, and the history and terms used are badly slanted.

[19] J. G. Frederick, *For and Against Technocracy: a Symposium* (New York, 1933).

4

State Activity: Analytical

THE STATE AS AN INSTRUMENT OF CONVERSION

AN act of government consists of the total process by which the desire of some individual or group in the society in question is converted into authorized social behavior by those people who are commanded by the government to act in that way. The process is divisible into two chief sections: politics and administration.

Politics and Administration. Before any government can successfully execute a program of planned action, it must gain popular support, keeping the opposition impotent or reducing its influence. Continual defense is needed to retain control of the governing process. It is this which is characterized as the political aspect. Administration, however, is the utilization of the hard-won power, the actual performance of the daily business of government, in accordance with the policy of the controlling group.

We may liken the state to a machine. Machines are contrivances which simply convert energy. Their use is to overcome the limitations of individual or collective power. Government is a machine in the sense that it is a converter of energy. Its ultimate force is composed of the psychological and physical qualities of the people, and their resources. There are phases in the life of society where local and national government is required to convert this force from what it is at any point of time into something more de-

sirable. But in the case of government the possibilities of conversion are immense, because human qualities are so many and diverse, and the processes are necessarily complex.

The state has no intrinsic advantage over any other social contrivance which is engaged in transforming its members' sentiments, energy, and resources, into more desirable products. It must necessarily submit to the laws of human nature and environment. No work is gained by using a machine. The product never contains more of the original material than was put in, though in its new form it may be more desirable. Indeed, work is lost in the process of transformation, for there is no perfect machine. Finally, "what is gained in force is lost in distance"—what is gained in one direction by the transformation is lost elsewhere because the transformation has taken place.

Factors in State Activity. The elements of the state as an instrument of conversion are:

(1) The initial energy: the first requirement. By this we mean the instincts, the sentiments, and the intellectual beliefs that certain courses of action or inaction are desirable or undesirable, and the mental and spiritual constitution which causes a movement of creation or destruction: as, for example, the desire to impose religious conformity, or to break up trusts, or to prohibit alcoholic liquors, or to establish workers' control in industry, or to avoid mass unemployment.

(2) However insistent the demands of the mind and the spirit, there must be present a sufficiency of material resources, because human energy by itself is often insufficient, however stimulated and encouraged, to accomplish what is desired. The recognition of this is one of the most powerful forces influencing modern man and government to discover and exploit physical resources, with heavy reliance on governmental action to secure such an advance.

(3) An administrative machine is necessary to apply the initial energy and the resources to their particular ends. This machine consists of the organization and the men especially engaged in formulating in detail the vaguer general wishes of the population, in converting the detailed formulas thus established into regulations, and in applying these to affect human behavior. It must be capable of understanding the general purpose, and steadfast in realizing it; it must be competent to know when, and where, and how much, its activity is required, and zealous in application; it must be honest; and it must be sufficiently powerful.

These three factors of energy, administration, and resources are observable in all forms of state activity, and upon their quality and combination depends the success of the undertaking. At the margin, where these factors cannot be produced, state activity fails. We shall, in the analysis which follows, explore the conditions which mold these factors in their special form, but first we shall analyze the valuable qualities which make possible the power of the state.

THE VALUABLE QUALITIES OF THE STATE

THE state is not necessarily or intrinsically abler for all things than other human groups or institutions. Statistics on the relative efficiency of state and private industry show, for example, that in various times and places the competition between them has been close (in such activities as telephones, telegraphs, railways, mining, and great hydroelectric schemes like the Tennessee Valley Authority). As a rule,

however, the state has certain qualities which bring it superior power. These are (1) age, (2) the vastness of ordered territory and institutions, and (3) stability and order.

Age. Age produces awe and veneration, and these, in turn, create a submissive, reverent, and obedient attitude; they stir inexplicable loyalties in the individual heart, and people are loath to destroy an ancient fabric, even though a new one is more useful and better satisfies the reason of their own day. In order that the ancestral temples, the quaint usages of their forefathers, and congenial memories and ceremonial may live on, they are reconciled to commands uttered in their name. When men say "the wisdom of our ancestors," the psychological emphasis is rather upon ancestors and ancestry than upon wisdom. Men will make sacrifices of energy and time for the modern state for the sake of its many generations, especially in time of war, but also in combating sedition or constitutional reform.

The interest of a generation does not cease with its regard for the past or for its own immediate comfort. The state is a continuing association. It is possible to appeal to men at work, and to appeal successfully, in the name of future generations. Some, indeed, find their own personal immortality in that of the state; others cannot deny the claims of their own children or those of their family in a wider sense, and they work to make the state a "better place" for them. To maintain the continuing association becomes so paramount a consideration with most men that they give money, energy, and obedience, and then regard the consequent burden as light in terms of the promised results. This is particularly true of war for the defense or increase of a country's dominions. Another aspect of it was interestingly observable in fascist Italy; almost the whole appeal to the people to suffer subordination and discipline was expressed in terms of the state's futurity, and the Corporative Constitution began: "The Italian Nation is an organism having ends, a life, and means superior in power and duration to the single individuals or groups of individuals that compose it." Likewise in nazi Germany the *Volk* and the race were manipulated to secure obedience, self-sacrifice, and abnegation, in view of the future of the *Reich*. The Soviet Union relies on much the same grounds for a considerable part of the obedience of its citizens in accepting basic conversion of the economy rather than plentiful consumption goods. They have even circulated the phrase that the present generation is "the manure of the future."

Democratic governments are equally influenced, except that their decisions between present and future are made by the developing choices of free citizens. Measures to defer consumption are not popular where they are severe, and democracies find it difficult though not impossible to entrust government with such powers. The keynote of such acquiescence is expressed in Burke's superb phrases:

Our political system is placed in a just correspondence and symmetry with the order of the world, and with the mode of existence decreed to a permanent body composed of transitory parts, wherein, by the disposition of a stupendous wisdom, moulding together the great mysterious incorporation of the human race, the whole, at one time, is never old, or middle-aged, or young, but in a condition of unchangeable constancy, moves on through the varied tenour of perpetual decay, fall, renovation, and progression.

Feelings like these are evoked in the majority of men and women by the modern state more than by any other institution of our day. There was a time when the churches lived by such sentiments and taught and succored the poor, as a result; and though those days have gone by, the churches seem to be entering into an era of knowledge of their application, through cooperation with the political parties of their choice. In virtue of these sentiments, the state acquires authority and power, for men will obey its commands when these things are recalled, though obedience might be otherwise distasteful.

Vastness of Territory. Then the state extends, as a rule, over a wider territory than other associations; it rules wherever territorial extent of authority is technically essential to effective and economical operation. The state has an advantage and so is obeyed. For example, it proved impossible to induce the United States Congress to allow any private enterprise to acquire power over so large a territory (two thirds the size of England) as that required to develop the hydroelectric resources of the Tennessee Valley Authority, yet it was essential that the whole of that territory be administered under a single hydroelectric and agricultural plan if it was to yield its maximum values.[1] The same idea is valid for the transfer to government ownership and management of the British transport, electricity, gas industries and iron and steel.

Stability and Order. Finally, the state is embodied in institutions and forms which, more than any others, are identified with the supreme guarantee of stability and order over the centuries. Now, struggles have occurred to decide which, among all the possible millions of rules, should be established. But all people have found the need for security. Whatever men's ultimate values, all require at least some calculable basis. Suppose social activities and obligations were as unpredictable and as uncontrollable as the weather, and you would obtain some small forecast of the misery of men's lives. The weather does not matter very much, for all ordinary purposes, in a manufacturing country, but it means life and death to an agricultural people. And men in the past have been alternately so disappointed and so elated at the hazards of the harvests that they have attempted to reduce them to order by making the elements into gods to whom they pray and sacrifice.

Man has plotted out time itself and charted the minutes and the days. The moment man becomes dependent upon others, even in the slightest degree, and as soon as social expectations are established, an order must be maintained in the recording and valuation of time. Only the

---

[1] Cf. Herman Finer, *International Lessons of T.V.A.* (Montreal, 1944), and Herman Prichett, *The Tennessee Valley Authority* (Chapel Hill, 1943), Chap. I.

unsocial beings have no order in time, such as infants and artists and tramps. But all others are bound to fix time. So with all other aspects of human behavior: some things must be fixed in order to relieve men of worry and anxiety, to act as a set basis for all the superstructure of industry, religion, and family life, and to be a measure of values and power. Men cannot bear the stress of encountering the unfamiliar. This is, in fact, what makes people save instead of at once consuming all they produce. Order is therefore natural to human kind. The state is one of the many institutions created, in part deliberately and in part unconsciously, to obtain the benefits of order, and it offers these benefits over a wider extent of human contacts than does any other institution.

The more complex the industrial operations of any society, the more complicated and refined its wants; and, as in our own day, the more that men dread economic and spiritual insecurity, the more the dependence on government and even the support of centralization and executive stability.

Nor is this all. The aid of the state is called for because, though a large number of people might act simultaneously, continuously, and similarly for the attainment of a desirable end, yet without a prearranged rule, there is possible at any time either too much or too little effort to assure the object. The state is regularity and associated effort, and it thus overcomes the waste caused by people giving in the wrong proportion at the right time or in the right proportion at the wrong time. Further, the moods of men are changeable from day to day, and their passions function intermittently. Intermittency of passion and alternation of moods render a common rule and a special instrument indispensable. Hence the cry for the state, which is a cry for the imposition and common acceptance of a rule ultimately controlling behavior, to regulate passion, moods, and attention, and to direct and apply them to an associated purpose.

Two illustrations are of eminent interest for our time. First, it has been found

unwise to rely upon individual acts of charity for the maintenance of public assistance and hospital care, so that it has been necessary for governments to organize and subsidize care for the poor and the sick. Hence, the central government of unitary states and the states in federal governments have assumed the administration of an enormous apparatus of public charity. Our second example came into being because provision by individuals against their own misfortunes in unemployment and sickness cannot be perfectly relied upon; because, also, the consequences of their improvidence will affect others; and because, again, a large proportion of the population finds it difficult to save out of their small income. Therefore all states have established elaborate schemes of social security which are dependent on universal or almost universal compulsory coverage. The universal coverage produces marked economies in administration and through the effect of averaging the risk.[2]

THE CONDITIONS OF STATE ACTIVITY

AGE, vastness of territory, stability and order: these are the qualities of the state which bring it great potential powers. But if the state is to use that power effectively in acts of government—if it is to be successful in both politics and administration—certain conditions must be fulfilled. The first of these is the presence of social conviction.

Social Conviction shows its importance in several ways:

(1) Only a good society makes a good state. The State's activity is never much, if at all, better in quality than the morality, the wealth, and the knowledge of the individual and groups which form the state. It often happens that the best brains and characters in society do serve the state, but the number of such minds is small

---

[2] The best survey is Abraham Epstein's *Insecurity, a Challenge to America* (New York, 1938). Also very enlightening is the International Labor Office Report, No. 4, *Principles of Social Security* (May, 1944); cf. also William Beveridge, *Report on Social Insurance and Allied Services* (New York, 1943); United States Social Security Board, *Annual Report*, 1948.

THE CONDITIONS OF STATE ACTIVITY

compared with the aggregate which remains in private industry, science, education, the churches, and elsewhere. Generally there is no higher level, more often a lower level in the cabinets and legislatures; and the incentives of officials take their tone, too often, from the social circles from which they are recruited. Whether there shall be competence, justice, and generosity in the activity of the state depends on whether these things are already present in society, and the state has no special additional qualities better than the level attained by its environment. On the whole it may be said that the state is much better off now in this respect than in the past and becomes increasingly better, owing to the establishment of methods of training and discipline which are considered in the chapters relating to parties, which select legislators, and to the civil services.

(2) Social forces make state activity. The state does not become active unless there are individual and social forces moving towards this end: spiritual forces, that is, which are productive of community and association. These forces are of many kinds. It is not absolutely essential that the forces should be articulately expressed —it is enough if they are felt—but they must exist if the state is ever to become active. These are the moral ultimates of individuals and associations, and they determine the scope and the direction of their energy. It may be said that these ultimates are not moral, but physiological, being dependent in the last resort upon the physical composition of human beings. Be it so! But men have called these things God or the Devil. Every man is a fanatic about something; he is convinced that something is of higher moral value or God-value than all other things, and it is this fanaticism which, at a certain temperature, involves the association of others to secure its satisfaction and social realization.

Zealots believe themselves providentially appointed to undertake crusades, and they regard plain occurrences as divine intervention. The best contemporary example of this relates not to existing state activity but only to that which is advocated. The most radical Bernard Shaw, the great divine, proposes the equalization of incomes. If the reasons for this reform are followed, step by step, back towards the ultimate moral basis, we arrive at the Life Force, that which is before reason and which causes us to choose and contrive. In *Man and Superman* his Don Juan exclaims that as long as he can conceive of some being better than himself, he is uneasy if he is not making efforts to open the way for it if not actually to create it. He was utterly at the mercy of this compulsion. Inside him the Life Force urged him on to become clearer-sighted, to more searching and comprehensive self-consciousness. After millions of years, of trial, this same Life Force had evolved the eye to enable human beings to progress by avoiding fatal dangers and exploiting things that could help them. Shaw's Don Juan held the religious faith that the Life Force was evolving a mind that, like the eye, could more clearly see the purpose of Life and so enable men to assist that purpose instead of obstructing it by shortsighted aims.

This Shavian ultimate finds its complex incarnation in concrete suggestions for the reform of human behavior and seeks to find its expression, if necessary, in the state. And so with two other such ultimates: the Nazi and the Soviet.

Hitler's first principle was *Deutschland über Alles*: it was the duty of the superior Nordic "race" to rule the entire world. Since the other great Nordic cultures—the Greek and Roman—had crumbled because of the addition of blood of alien people, the German state now had to maintain the purity of the German "race." It alone had physical and mental qualities of high enough caliber to be "culture-creative." Thus Hitler: [3]

What we see before us of human culture today, the results of art, science, and techniques, is almost exclusively the creative product of the Aryan. But just this fact admits of the not unfounded conclusion that he alone was the founder of higher humanity as a whole, thus the prototype of what we understand by

[3] *Mein Kampf* (New York, 1940), p. 398. Permission Houghton Mifflin.

the word 'man'. . . . Exclude him—and deep darkness will again fall upon the earth, perhaps even, after a few thousand years, human culture would perish and the world would turn into a desert.

Consequently, the Nazis established a pattern of world conquest to subordinate the inferior nations of the world.

The Soviet dictatorship has stressed the liquidation of classes, believing that as long as classes exist, unemployment and poverty are inevitable. The general principles of article 1 of the 1925 constitution of the Russian Socialist Federated Soviet Republic state its objective:

. . . to guarantee the dictatorship of the proletariat for the purpose of suppressing the bourgeoisie, of abolishing the exploitation of man by man, and of bringing about Communism, under which there will be neither division into classes nor state power.

And Chapter 1 of the constitution of the U.S.S.R. of 1936 redeclares the principle and reports progress.[4]

In the degree in which men are sanguine that their values should stand above all others, they will (like the Soviet rulers) force their rule on society through government by all means at their disposal, even the most violent and brutal. Even democracy once forced its own triumph by revolution, and in the last resort, contending with despotism, whether fascist or communist, it cannot be suicidal.

(3) Intensity of feeling creates activity. Now if the human and environmental forces operate at a certain pitch of intensity, there will be state activity whether the politicians and statesmen, all those officially occupied with politics, desire it or not. It depends upon the intensity of the feeling, and upon the insensitiveness of the official legislators, how long the transmutation of social forces into state activity can be retarded.

(4) Without social conviction the state fails. If the state undertakes any activity which is not based upon the necessary intensity of conviction in a sufficient number of people, it cannot be successful for long.

[4] Cf. Ernest T. Simmons (ed.), *U.S.S.R., A Concise Handbook* (Cornell, 1947).

The duration of successful state activity depends upon the duration of the convictional energy nourishing it, and as conviction flags, state activity deteriorates. Thus, it may be possible to get almost perfect success for a time, when the people are excited, as in a war or after extraordinary events like earthquakes or epidemics or upon the accession to power of a man or woman whose personality is abnormally compelling. But eventually, such conviction, born of excitement, dies. Again and again, the Italian Fascist government complained that the Fascist party and administration were lukewarm and lax. And the speeches of Stalin and other Soviet leaders to the Russian Communist party are full of reproaches that the Plans are not fulfilled in quantity or quality, that managers show lack of initiative, and that the building of categories of administrators by efficient promotion is a failure as the result of slackness or favoritism. When conviction does not naturally reach an intense pitch, and when it is short-lived, successful state activity is impossible without a special process of stimulating feeling and spreading knowledge, the latter being frequently a means to the first.

Those most sensitive to these latent forces are obliged to stimulate them to a point which will produce activity. To this end they try to disengage the lineaments of the forces to be promoted or controlled. As the common phrase goes, they are obliged "to bring home" the matter to those who have the psychological and physical power at their disposal. This process of stimulation, otherwise known as propaganda, promotes the disposition to obey when the orders are given as soon as the "movement" is under way, and thereafter when a settled administration is established.

Democracy itself is kept alive only by constant demonstrations in its support; a high percentage of voters is maintained only by canvassing and propaganda. People are worried into keeping the nation healthy by meetings presided over by prominent persons and by "Health Weeks," and, even so, thousands of lives are lost in each month (especially in the United States) despite "Safety Weeks." For this process there is a technique which is appropriate to the psychology of the people to be convinced and is based on the apparatus of propaganda. Experience has shown that no great branch of state activity has been advocated or resisted without this technique's including an armory of lies. But the agitator and the zealot cannot perceive that their arguments are so exaggerated that the truth is continuously suppressed, while they stigmatize beyond the true limit the untruths of their opponents. So always and today in all political parties.

There is a relationship between propaganda and education, but those interested in education are really saying: "In my father's house are many mansions and you may choose whichever you wish to dwell in. I have truthfully described them all." The propagandist's doctrine is: "In my father's house there is only one mansion, and it is ruled not by my father but by myself: and, in fact, I am my own father!"

Failing Conviction, Coercion and Reward. If the state commences to act before sufficient feeling has been generated, and before knowledge has adequately been spread, or if it tries to act when conviction has dissolved, it cannot be successful save by special coercion or special rewards. It has to fine or imprison or sometimes even to kill the dissentients, lest conviction be further weakened by imitation, and in the case of the dissentients themselves, it has to compel behavior by sanctions other than the intrinsic value of the conviction itself. As a rule, the convinced are so enraptured by the importance of their conviction that they go to great lengths; they shame, bully, ostracize, and often torture and kill, in order to make others conform. Indeed, given the nature of man and society today, government is impossible without some incidental violence. Thus, in the Nazi state, coercion was, and in the Soviet state is, used crushingly to the uttermost; the Gestapo in the one and the N.K.V.D. and "forced labor" camps in the other are the most conspicuous sign of homicide as

government.[5] In democracies there is still some coercion, but it is drastically limited. Theory does not condone it, and institutions reduce both its necessity and prevalence. In order to mitigate the pains of unconvinced obedience and yet obtain success, the state has often had to organize the education of its citizens by formal public teaching, and by the issue of proclamations, preambles to laws, instructions on official forms and cards, and detailed memoranda and orders to local governing bodies. Indeed, within the last quarter-century, the problem of public relations has become outstanding in public administration, and all governments are now equipped very elaborately "to project" to their citizens the nature of the work they are doing.[6]

Material Resources the Sinews of the State. If the factors already indicated are present in society, the state may still not be successful unless there are available for it the appropriate material resources. There is rarely an activity of the state which does not require material resources for its support, and this may mean one of two things, or both of them: either (1) there must be an adjustment of the constituents of expenditure, less being spent on other things in order to make a fund for the new; or (2) a greater aggregate amount must be somehow produced in order to pay for the new activity and yet maintain the other lines of expenditure unimpaired. In the former case, the material sacrifice will lie in the decrease of other satisfactions; in the latter case, in the need to work harder to produce more. We may be asked to spend less in our own spontaneous way in order that something called

[5] Cf. David Dallin, *The Real Soviet Russia,* 2nd edition (New Haven, 1946); John Fisher, *Why They Behave Like Russians* (New York, 1947).
[6] James L. McCamy, *Government Publicity* (Chicago, 1939); Francis Williams, *Parliament, Press and Public* (London, 1946). It is not surprising that in fascist Italy and nazi Germany (and still in the U.S.S.R.) this instructional or propagandist function of government was carried to the highest degree and was, of course, concentrated in various government offices or the parallel organizations of the one political party allowed to operate.

the Empire or the Commonwealth or the Republic or the Soviet State may flourish or be better prepared for war. The normal way adopted by the modern state to bear the burden is to tax—that is, to deprive us of part of our material resources. But this is not the only way in which members of the state are made to bear material burdens; for every activity of the state, even when there is no direct visible tax, alters economic conditions to the advantage of some and to the disadvantage of others. The tax, if we care to use that term, exists though it is not visible. The question is, can we, and will we if we can, give up other satisfactions for the satisfaction the state is to afford by its activity?

This question applies to democratic states, in which to a very large degree private enterprise and private property still prevail. In the Soviet Union practically all property and enterprise are under public ownership and management, and the decision is made by the central planning body as part of the annual or quinquennial arrangements of production. The quantities and qualities of goods and services to be produced by authority impose directly the material burdens the citizens must bear. The ability of the rulers to coerce the citizens is almost absolute.

The activity which demands more than the utmost amount possessed or borrowable must obviously fall short of perfection. Yet there are schemes of state activity occasionally suggested which are seen to depend for their efficacy upon more than society possesses or can acquire. But it is also true that some schemes, like the nationalization of railways or mines or hydroelectric power or housing or medical service, might cause an increase of the available resources. This is the uttermost limit of success which depends upon material resources. Further, society may desire not one but a number of state activities. In such a case, the resources to be spent upon any one activity are limited by the demand for resources for others, and this means that the success of one activity is limited by the intention to secure success in others. Those states are in the aggregate most capable where resources have been carefully portioned among the whole series of desires.

Definition of Purpose. Given conviction, coercion, and resources, success is attainable only in proportion to the clarity and precision with which the purpose of the activity is defined. The appropriate machinery and expenditure cannot be devised unless the aim is clearly defined; and the enterprise of officials either goes beyond the purpose or is stultified by uncertainty. In the modern state the following authorities are responsible for definition: the groups which advocate the purpose; the public, which is canvassed for its support; political parties, which organize the electorate and offer them satisfaction in return for votes; the legislative bodies, which discuss the proposal with more detail and state the intention in law; the cabinet, which initiates and guides this discussion; the technical experts like the civil service and special commissions of inquiry and official planning agents, who bring exactly recorded science to the solution of problems where these are soluble only by such application; and the civil service and courts of law, who must interpret the purpose in its relation to specific cases. If these define and fix the purpose well, state activity is successful; if not, their shortcomings are translated into its failure through confusion, ambiguity, inconsistency, vagueness regarding who is responsible, and so on.

The Executive Apparatus. Nor is this all. The state must have at hand an executive machine. It must solve the problems of (1) its personnel, (2) its technical apparatus, and (3) its territory.[7]

(1) It must secure officials sufficient in

---

[7] Cf. Dwight Waldo, *The Administrative State* (New York, 1948), for an uncommonly gifted treatment. Cf. also John M. Gaus, *Reflections on Administration* (Alabama, 1947); Woodrow Wilson, "The Study of Administration," *Political Science Quarterly*, 1941, pp. 481 ff. (a reprint from 1887); Leonard D. White, *The Federalists* (New York, 1948); and, currently, the journals *Public Administration Review* (Chicago) and *Public Administration* (London); Francis Hekking, *Refléxions sur la Mécanique Administrative* (New York, 1943) and *Point d'Administration, Point de France* (New York, 1944).

zeal, honesty, knowledge, and numbers, and it must establish material and spiritual rewards which will produce the qualities needed when they are not spontaneously available. Now, there are not many men or women in the world who have the ability to fulfil the extraordinary demands of the difficult offices; or, again, other satisfactions may pre-empt their energies. This is true of every branch of administration, and of all arts, crafts, and sciences. While we recognize in everyday life the truth that the world is a place in which the average of ability is low, and that genius is rare, we seem to expect more of these qualities in state activity than elsewhere, or, at least, we tend to expect such a quality of enterprise by the state that more genius than the world's actual supply would be required to produce it. It should not be forgotten, however, that there is no reason to expect more ability in the private administration of business than in public administration.

The great administrators have recognized the need of making their colleagues and subordinates in their own image, by embodying the results of their own inspiration in rules, and of adapting rewards and punishments to the incitement of those whose natures are unprompted by a native and undying flame. For it may happen that even a Hitler, a Mussolini, a Lenin, or a Stalin cannot transfer to his immediate followers, still less to the millions of average people throughout the territory, the intensity of his own convictions and the corresponding incessant devotion and activity necessary to their fulfillment.

Every activity requires its special technique, and the success of the administrator depends upon its possession. To secure the success of state activity, the same rule must be followed as in any other individual or social activity, officials who have the necessary technique or the capacity to acquire it must be appointed. It would not be necessary to insist upon this quite simple truth if it were not that the generality of mankind talk as if they believe that government is exempted from submission to this rule, and as if rulers had not for

centuries attempted to get along with friends, relations, kinsmen, coreligionists, or class comrades, instead of simply, with the able.

(2) The state must acquire the appropriate apparatus to overcome distance, time, force, and gravity—it must climb mountains, cross seas, receive and send messages, overtake runaway offenders, install natural-science laboratories and telephones, provide guns, organize armies, and shout with a radio voice.

(3) The state must properly dispose its officers, and distribute its powers territorially, at the center and at the extremities. Moreover, this machine must be properly adjusted to the organs of public opinion and lawmaking, in order that they shall propel and control it and that it shall be able to serve them with technical skill. The organization of public opinion and legislation themselves need to be delicately responsive, wise, and dutiful. The appropriate form of administrative arrangements for each activity, and their relationship to other parts of a system, require exceedingly subtle judgment for success.

Wholesale Administration and Efficiency. Finally, when all this is at hand, there is still a possible defect in the perfect scheme. Where all-inclusiveness is an essential condition of success, the state may not be able to treat every case upon its individual merits, making allowances for idiosyncrasies, aberrations, and abnormality. It may have to operate by one rule which, though it elevates the nature of the subnormal, incidentally wounds the feelings and depreciates the morality of citizens of average or more than average standard. For though size is essential to success and yields grand benefits, it has inherent possibilities of occasional maladministration. This has been seen where, in the large number of the social services the state has taken over, the responsibility was formerly fulfilled by voluntary societies—education or unemployment compensation, for example.

Yet, in the end, even these dangers may be avoided by devising a machine of the appropriate complexity and sensitiveness.

[63]

The Distant Result and the Immediate Success. Still there may be unexpected and unwanted effects of state activity, due to the imperfect prescience of mankind, so that its relative value may be much less than its immediate face value because it is being bought with costs which, though not immediately visible, are nevertheless expensive in the long run. For example, the imposition of uniformity of religious behavior in Spain through the Inquisition contributed to Spain's economic impoverishment, to the loss of its world status, and to the stifling of its scientific development. The mercantile system helped to impoverish and disaffect Ireland in the British Common-wealth, and partly caused the American secession. The Prohibition laws in the United States were put into execution at the cost of the creation of habits of violence and disrespect for law and majority rule. Social welfare administered by the state and paid for from taxation may sap individual enterprise and thrift if the known safeguards are omitted for the small proportion which investigation shows to be lax. The institution of measures to secure full employment must have some limiting effect upon certain civic liberties; the balance must be struck.

These large problems always lie in the background of state activity and ought to be counted in among its conditions.

Part Two

THE FUNDAMENTAL INSTITUTIONS OF GOVERNMENT

Yet this objection which the men of democracies make to forms is the very thing which renders forms so useful to freedom; for their chief merit is to serve as a barrier between the strong and the weak, the ruler and the people, to retard the one, and give the other time to look about him. Forms become more necessary in proportion as the government becomes more active and more powerful, whilst private persons are becoming more indolent and more feeble.
—DE TOCQUEVILLE

When we are dealing with words that are also a constituent act, like the Constitution of the United States, we must realize that they have called into life a being the development of which could not have been foreseen completely by the most gifted of its begetters. It was enough for them to realize or to hope that they had created an organism; it has taken a century and has cost their successors much sweat and blood to prove that they created a nation. The case before us must be considered in the light of our whole experience and not merely in that of what was said a hundred years ago.—JUSTICE HOLMES in *Missouri* v. *Holland*

5

Forms of Government, Especially Democracy

FORMS OF GOVERNMENT, ESPECIALLY DEMOCRACY

THE DEMOCRATIC SPIRIT

WE have seen that the state may be expressed in many activities and operate in many diverse forms; and also that the success of the activity depends upon the appropriateness of the mechanism to the purposes sought. In the countries which concern us, the social power relationship has embodied itself in a general form of the state called *democracy*. But this term, literally, conveys no more—but no less—than that government is, or ought to be, carried on *by the people*. "Democracy" has come to mean so many different things, some very hostile to each other, that it needs careful analysis if misunderstanding and idle controversies are to be avoided, and if the possible and quite legitimate differences of connotation and its very varied institutional arrangements are to be revealed. We intend to deal with the subject only generally and briefly, for the particulars are considered in subsequent chapters; and some, indeed, we have already casually described.

Political science has, since the earliest times, occupied itself with attempts to classify the forms of government, but to little purpose. For the facts to be classified were too many and too diversely combined to allow of a few simple and informative categories. Thinkers have, indeed, been sorely exercised by a difficulty which leaps to the eye: are we to classify upon the basis of the *legal* residence of authority, or upon our judgment of the *actual*

sources of power; and, whatever our decision, are we to qualify our classification by consideration of the actual manner, the purpose, and the temper of the governors? For example, is an intolerant exercise of power by the majority to be considered as democratic government? Such a difficulty already assailed Aristotle, for he thought it insufficient to say simply that the forms of government were three, monarchy, aristocracy, and the city or polity. He felt that he must go on to say that monarchy is tyranny, aristocracy is oligarchy, and the city is a democracy, when the purpose, instead of being the benefit of the whole community, is that of the individual, or the few, or the many, respectively. Hobbes thought this improper and wished to exclude the question of purpose and temper from the definition.[1] That difficulty has dogged political science throughout the centuries, and there are many today who urge that Rousseau, the great prophet of the sovereignty of the people, is no democrat but a pre-Fascist or pre-Nazi because there were no limits to the associated authority of this democracy over the individual!

We need not insist upon a consummate classification. It is enough if we know that such have been attempted and that they

---

[1] Cf. *Leviathan*, Chap. XIX: "There be other names of Government, in the Histories, and books of policy; as *Tyranny* and *Oligarchy:* But they are not the names of other Formes of Government, but of the same Formes misliked. . . ."

are not of much value owing to the different personal prejudices which have gone to their construction. Enough, also, if we remember that no monarchy or dictatorship has been allowed to govern, excepting *de facto*, for a short span of time (until some, or the majority, of the citizens have discovered the threat to their interests or beliefs), without the cooperation, control, or passive consent of the few rich or of the able or of the many poor.[2] An enormous apparatus of force had to be used by the fascist states and is still maintained by the Soviet government. Enough, again, if we recognize that the purpose of the governors and the consequences of their rule have ever been of the essence of the definition and title of the form of government, and that its mere machinery, ruled by one, or by an aristocratic council, or by all, has hardly ever been considered enough to deserve the name of government.[3]

Democracy as a Doctrine of Protest. Accordingly, democrats are united in principle but divided on most details. They were and are united in a negation: that is, in their antagonism to arbitrary government by a monarch or a very few. Positive proposals, however, find them widely divided; for some desire no government at all,[4] while the bulk, who admit the necessity of some degree of government, offer a large variety of solutions and patterns: ranging from the Whig ideal of a balance of authority and power between kings and lords and middle classes, to the German *Rechtsstaat* (explained below, Chap. 36), to the queer, alleged "democracy" of the Russian Soviet system.

The truth is that European monarchy was attacked and overcome by hosts who kept a rendezvous with different motives and aspirations. The task accomplished, the original interests continued to assert themselves, others arose by the way, and the machinery of each new government was cast in a mold fashioned by the peculiar and complex forces of those interests. These values were different; they are different; and they continue to differ; and since this is so, democratic institutions, hopes, and principles of criticism are necessarily of many kinds, so that democrats sometimes seem to each other either stupid or malevolent.[5] Yet all are right, granted their spiritual point of departure; and we must examine the phases of that process which has its end in democratic institutions and the democratic temper. We must find the ultimate spiritual values sought by democrats, the concrete social and economic changes demanded in the name of democracy, and the resultant machinery of government.

Liberty as an Ideal versus other Ideals. For the sake of convenient exposition, as also because the division corresponds broadly to the facts, I divide democrats into those who seek liberty as the main end of government, and those who seek other values, like equality, which have seemed to require the democratic form to produce them. If we follow out the meaning of these ideals from their origin, we shall find that quite different forms of government result from each. The ideal of liberal democracy is expressed in a variety of familiar phrases, such as "Just government is government by consent of the governed," or "Self-government," and it implies, in the works of various authors, voluntary association for unhindered establishment and operation of political parties, freedom of opinion, the subjection of government to popular control, the limitation of the sphere of government, and the universal possibility of active participation in the process of government. Essentially what is sought is, for its own sake, the possibility of unhindered initiative and self-developing enterprise, and an

---

[2] Cf. David Hume, *Essays* (London, 1875), Vol. I, Part I, Essay IV; A. V. Dicey, *The Relations between Law and Public Opinion in England* (London, 1905), Lecture I.
[3] Cf. James Bryce, *Modern Democracies* (New York, 1921), Vol. I, p. 176. De Tocqueville defines the form of government by reference to its temper. Montesquieu also defines by temper as well as by machinery.
[4] Cf. Kropotkin, *Mutual Aid* (London, 1904).

[5] For example, in the controversies regarding proportional representation and in the controversies between the Bolsheviks and the milder schools of socialism. Cf. Leon Trotsky, *Where is Britain Going?* (London, 1926).

element, more or less large, but self-determining, of dissociation from the groups who make and control the state: a No-State Land. In proportion as men have wanted this, for itself and for its unbounded inherent possibilities, they have insisted on those institutions, and those alone, which offer the measure of that liberty, and their central purpose has been to contrive limits to governmental action. They were not insistent upon universal franchise, provided there were a large enough measure of popular control to make government responsible; they did not press for *direct,* but only for *representative,* government; and it was enough if representatives were but generally and not minutely bound to follow their constituents.

Yet this ideal was never held for long by any man or class without other aspirations crossing it, which decelerated and deflected its original urge. Humanitarian feeling, patriotism, and loyalty to one's social circle shaped and limited the expression of the ideal, so that to the middle classes of the nineteenth century it was enough if such liberty were theirs and not the laborers', while in Russia since 1917, liberty is conceived as proper for rulers but not for middle-class businessman, free labor, or peasant.[6] In other words, the ideal was not and never is quite disinterested. It has been evolved, and is still in evolution, under the pressure of one class after another, each of which reinforces the assault upon sovereign power. Those who have been utterly convinced of the supreme value of liberty have been ready to take grave risks on its account; like Kant[7] and Herbert Spencer they have contemplated the prospect of misery and death, in the faith that human perfection would ultimately result. For what might come upon that upward path—oppression,

social inequality, and generations of human cruelty—they had small regard; they looked to the end, and believed that it would be so good that the rest must be stoically accepted. Such thinkers necessarily conflict with others who seek some such immediate good as economic equality, or what has been called a "democratic society," in which class privileges and distinctions have been abolished or murderously kept suppressed.

Passion in Government. Liberty, in short, is claimed by some on its own account, while to others it is a means to some other end. The end determines the means, and the end has not always been such as to produce democratic or freer institutions in the sense we have already assigned to them. The service of God in Calvin's sense, for example, required freedom of the church from the commands of the state, and was, therefore, in a sense democratic; it also required democracy within the church. Yet so passionate a conviction was expressed in the importance of deeds and of obedience to God, that government was supremely necessary to enforce them, and the civil authority was required to be very severe in its support of a comprehensive theocratic regimentation of transgressors. Not only at Geneva but in Boston, these very postulates formed the basis of veritable tyrannies, though the rulers (like John Cotton) governed for the good of the people. Calvinism gave birth to theocracy, the rule of the godly, and not to democracy, which came later with the tide of revolutionary feeling against Britain. For, ultimately, the Old Testament taught that only the elect are saved and the rest are damned; it inverted the order which really urges men to demand freedom, for it asserted predetermination and therefore excluded perfectibility, and if men are slaves of the Supreme Will and not masters of their own fate, what basis remains for a doctrine of political self-determination? Again, the ultimate moving force of Rousseau's faith was hatred of oppression, and therefore of economic inequality, and thus the belief that to secure harmonious, unoppressive, and "natural" civilization, economic equality was

6 Cf. F. R. Schlesinger, *Soviet Legal Theory* (London, 1943); Sidney and Beatrice Webb, *Soviet Communism* (London, 1941), 2 vols.; J. Towster, *Political Control in the U.S.S.R.* (New York, 1948); Andrei Y. Vyshinsky, *The Law of the Soviet State* (New York, 1948).
7 *Principles of Politics,* ed. and trans. by W. Hastie (Edinburg, 1891), Essay I, "The Natural Principle of the Political Order."

essential.[8] His democracy was made for this purpose, but to level men requires a mighty force, and this clearly threatened his freedom. Hence Rousseau's institutions culminated in the unqualified rule of the majority, with a perfect, unlimited sovereignty,[9] carried out by representatives who were strictly accountable mandatories of the people and intolerant of any gospel which conflicted with the end of the state as declared by the majority. Equality may be the result, but the liberty sought by Humboldt, Kant, Jefferson, de Tocqueville, and Mill is abolished unless men should, from that very equality, once more learn liberty's allurements.

Patience and Impatience in Government. We have arrived at the essence of the differences among those who say they hold the democratic faith, and who yet diverge at once when they propose or actually establish their institutions. The essence of the difference lies in two things: (1) the compatibility of the interests pursued with government by consent of all, and (2) the patience and toleration of those who govern (and let us always think not in terms of the government, but in terms of the individuals and groups who ultimately govern). The nature of the end of government may be such as to exclude such corollaries of the ideal of liberty as a limited sphere of government, freedom of opinion, meeting, and association, and dependence of government upon universal suffrage. These may not be altogether excluded; they may be qualified in various degrees. Thus when intoxicating liquors are prohibited, liberty is partially extinguished; no tuberculosis or diphtheria "contact," perfectly detected, can legally avoid quarantine; the parliamentary system can be maintained only if members limit their powers of invective and denunciation. In fact, examination of the tenets of various groups and classes who have demanded democracy reveals that their notion is largely (not wholly) the product of their values; they are willing to go to the margin needed to satisfy these and no further.[10] So much freedom, and freedom for such and such groups; beyond that, arguments are discovered to prove the unfitness of others to govern.

Further, and this seems to be the cause of modern anxiety regarding democracy, the governors or would-be governors or social philosophers urgently, passionately, immediately demand vast reforms. The inevitable result is to override the very things which democratic theorists, who regarded liberty as their principal purpose, have held to be the essence of the democratic faith: namely, government by discussion (that is, persuasion of the governed), and gradual concessions by the governing groups to the governed, with toleration for minorities, localities, and the individual and with a tender regard for conscience and property. Often between 1919 and the aftermath of World War II, men have been faced with the alternatives of a job or democracy.

Modern states are actually faced by this formidable task: to secure speedily, and thereafter to maintain, a number of reforms in the direction of greater economic and social equality, while excluding coercion and certainly bloodshed, and while still maintaining democratic institutions. There is the stress and strain.

The Social Contract. The roots of modern democracy lie in the Protestant Reformation of the sixteenth century, in the New Learning begun in Italy, in economic changes, and in geographical discoveries. The New Learning awakened the critical spirit by offering men the political models of classical antiquity with which to compare and condemn their own system, while scientific discoveries, if they did not yet make the old cosmogony and its religious superstructures quite unten-

---

[8] E. H. Wright, *The Meaning of Rousseau* (London, 1929).
[9] I am willing to allow that Rousseau was uncertain of this; but I would urge that the uncertainty arose from the desire to have the best both of the world of equality and the world of freedom without the surrender of the necessary hostages. Generous and emotional people often talk and write in this way; they are much more generous than Nature.

[10] For example, in France before the Revolution of 1848—the *pays legal*. Cf. Lowes Dickinson, *Revolution and Reaction in Modern France*, 2nd edition (London, 1927), p. 116.

able, at least raised doubts.[11] Economic changes, caused partly by catastrophes and partly by new agricultural and commercial pursuits, changed the balance of property. Geographical discoveries brought knowledge (or legends) of other civilizations, offered new outlets for adventurous energy, and set men marveling and thinking. The old certitude—incorporated in religious and social myths and popular ways, and thence subservient to government—was gone. Europe was dowered with Bibles in a tongue which the crowd could understand, and men like Erasmus, Luther, and Calvin thundered not only at ancient religious institutions —which were then almost indistinguishable from the other arm of society, kings and princes—but at beliefs.

The political essence of the Reformation was, on Luther's side, the equal worth of all Christians (not "all men"), the unique value of their individual consciences, and the freedom of the religious conscience and behavior from the dictates of the secular prince.[12] Calvin reinforced the doctrines of the priesthood of the laity, went some way toward government of the church and of the state (which in Geneva was only another aspect of the church) by a representative council of the more considerable of the citizens, and returned again and again to the theme of men united with each other and with God by a covenant. Here were all the materials of democracy: government *by* the people, because (quoting from various of Luther's tracts) each believer was "spiritually lord of all" and "faith is a voluntary matter which cannot be forced" by any one else, for "neither Pope nor Bishop nor any man has a right to dictate even a syllable

to the Christian without his own consent" and *for* the people but (in a Christian way), for "we may not become the servants of men." And what was the quintessence of the freedom of Christian men, the spiritual value behind all? It was the uncompromising, absolute conviction that since only the individual person can discover the meaning of existence, he ought to be free to live it, for his "inward sense of judging concerning doctrine is a sense which, though it cannot be proved, is nevertheless absolutely certain." I should rather say that precisely *because* it cannot be ultimately proved or disproved in any one, or by any one, it is accepted by the democrat to be as certain as any other person's "inward sense of judging." [13]

The Democratic Temper. This attitude may have either of two results according to the temper of the person: absolute certainty may lead to an attempt to impose it upon others, or it may lead to readiness to accept another's truth to be as good as his own, and therefore to enter into community, so far as it is possible, to secure a reconciliation.[14] The Certain have, in the flame of righteous indignation, created marvelous things, and they have broken states into bloody fragments (for example, in the American Civil War and the Russian Revolution of 1917) and have violently and remorselessly taken life. The Patient have maintained peace, harmony, and unity, but in so doing they have annihilated incongruous (perhaps creative) emotions, beliefs, and hopes. The one has caused battles between men; the second, battles of will within them. One may eradicate more than it intends; the other may kill, by its gradualness, the things whose survival and development it desires. This contrast of temper always arises, even on the rare occasions when men are unanimous as to their destination. Thus the democratic form of government—the simple idea of government by the people

---

[11] Cf. Jacob Burckhardt, *Civilization of The Renaissance in Italy* (London, 1945); H. O. Taylor, *Thought and Expression in the Sixteenth Century* (New York, 1920); W. E. Lecky, *History of the Rise and Influence of Rationalism in Europe* (London, 1865); A. Wolf, *History of Science, Technology and Philosophy in 16th and 17th Centuries* (London, 1935). [12] Cf. James Mackinnon, *Luther and the Reformation* (London, 1927-30), 4 vols. I do not forget Luther's part in the peasants' rising, or his hostility to the Anabaptists. He discriminated; but the people did not.

[13] On the political theories of Calvinists, see H. D. Foster, "Political Theories of the Calvinists before Exodus to America," *American Historical Review*, XXI, 481-503.
[14] Cf. R. B. Perry, *Puritanism and Democracy* (New York, 1944).

—is expressible in many different and complex ways. Let us remember, too, that the realization that life is short may have, broadly, one of two effects, according to the temperament: it may make men so impatient for reform and advancement that they even include assassination in their policy; it may cause resignation and a patient contemplative pity for the race of men and women condemned, alas, so soon to perish, while all is vanity.

Perhaps the best illustration of the difference of temper is to be found in the constitutional conflict of the seventeenth century in Britain, of which American development was a beneficiary as well as being a contributor (in the eighteenth century). The constitutional conflict began as a religious conflict between Nonconformist sects and the Crown as the head of the Church of England. But gradually there entered into that conflict considerations of taxation and property which sharpened the desire for control of the executive, and ultimately, the people who lent force to the claims of the parliamentary leaders, began to demand power for the common people. Though all professed much the same religion, and were brothers in arms to maintain the covenant of God, as soon as the question of the distribution of political power was raised, those who now represented the established and prosperous order—the middle- and upperclass landowners—were quick to detect and rebut the implications of complete democracy. The classic discussion of 1647 between Ireton and Cromwell and the representatives of the common soldiers of the army—the Levellers—reveals the effect upon democratic institutions of different tempers and aspirations. Broadly speaking, the soldiers (represented by John Wildman and Colonel Rainborow) maintained that the battle was "not to be enslaved"; Ireton that it was "against despotism," and Cromwell that it was for the "equality of consciences." The difference between the first and the latter two is vital, for the first meant abolition of enslavement of all kinds, political and economic, while Ireton's demand was consistent with the mere establishment of safeguards which would certainly redound to the religious advantage of everybody, but would redound more to the economic advantage of the prosperous than of the poor. Cromwell's formula was certainly a sound answer to royal pretensions and would make for some popular participation in government, but if consciences were equal, then those who possessed had an equal right to continue in possession, and the poor had not a better right to dispossess them.

The soldiers attempted, as almost all radical democrats have done (and, indeed, as almost all rebellious people, even the rich and powerful, do), to avoid the argument from the social consequences, and to insist only upon the argument from natural right—that is from the assumption that civil institutions did not yet exist—and that a primal sense of justice was consciously a political constitution for society. This way led to universal suffrage in the interests of the people.

To this Ireton replied, fundamentally, that he meant to enjoy his own property and to safeguard the institution in general. To this end only those with some property—a forty-shilling freehold, for example—not being domestics or servants of others, should be permitted to vote, for these alone could have an independent political opinion and a permanent "interest" in the country's welfare. But, to him, a kind of liberty was paramount even to property—"a peaceable spiritt which is suitable to the Gospell," a "Kingdom wherein I may live in godliness, and honesty, and peace and quietnesse." For these things he would yield his property, if all others desired it.

The ultimate issue then was this: should we move all at once from one constitution to another, on the passionate convictions of some men, or remain under the old state on the equally passionate convictions of others? Where was the spirit of God?—with the former or the latter? There was suffering either way if it were entered upon without regard for the other; for the first must cause the disruption of society as it was, and the second the continued misery of the poor.

The solution is that if national existence, the continuance of the sense of political community, is desired, the temper of both parties must be qualified by the recognition that the truth does not rest with either party, but in all together. God, Truth or the Ultimate Good, is discovered only in the assemblage of unique qualities in all persons. There is the ultimate axiom of the democratic system, for, men being different, conflict (perhaps breakdown) is inevitable if the temper or the intellect of self-governing individuals is permitted to work unhindered by conscious regard for, or partnership with, others.

Both Ireton and Cromwell—not uninfluenced, I think, by their social and economic position—urged this theory. Ireton said: "I thinke every Christian ought to beare that spiritt in him, that he will nott make a publique disturbance uppon a private prejudice." [15] Cromwell constantly intervened in debate to urge the cultivation of "a uniting spirit." [16] and when matters reached a point when it was decided that an adjournment for prayer might result in the return of the delegates with a fresh and more conciliatory idea of God's will, Cromwell asked "that they should nott meete as two contrary parties, butt as some desirous to satisfie or convince each other." That, experience has since taught, is the essential principle of democratic government by the party system. Cromwell pierces even further into the psychology of practicable democracy. True it is that God may speak through any man, high or low: "I know a man may answer all difficulties with faith, and faith will answer all difficulties really where it is." Yet there must be pause, for "we are very apt all of us to call that faith which perhaps may be but carnall imagination and carnall reasonings." [17] Difficulties must be considered. If any one is at liberty to produce his scheme of a constitution

founded upon natural right, "and not onely another, and another, butt many of this kinde, and if soe, what doe you think the consequence of that would bee? Would it not bee confusion? Would itt nott be utter confusion?" [18]

More, who knows God but all? Not *each,* let the term be marked, but all!

No! though we must watch for the manifestation of God in ourselves—and God is that which must move the conscience after earnest rational consideration [19]—we must beware lest we act precipitately. "I would wee should all take heede of mentioning our owne thought and conceptions with that which is of God." [20]

These two things are needful: (1) a tolerant watchfulness for the godliness in others, mixed with a strict interrogation of what wells up from our own inwardness; and (2) a disposition to live peaceably together. That is, there must be a readiness to create and utter the result of our creation—no passivity—and also a censorship of our own and other men's conceptions; and further, no temper of disunion.

Yet all men optimistically believe that their perception of God, or the Good, or the Best Self is a satisfactory dispensation for all. Wildman was as sure as Cromwell, and Lenin, the despotic Socialist, as Karl Kautsky, the democratic Socialist. And, thus, Cromwell asserts that God is not the author of contradictions, that these are more as to means than ends.

Even these optimistic beliefs, however, are proven wrong by daily experience, and democratic institutions become properly a compromise, with considerable conflict and suffering, between them all; for however sternly we restrain the impulses in us, which we call God, some of it will out—as in Cromwell's theses—in its own pristine character. The full impulse of the democratic temper might disrupt society; and to the extent that peace is desired, men produce liberalism by reducing democracy. This purpose has had to come about by the creation of institutions of restraint because men have not yet

---

15 C. H. Firth, *Clarke Papers* (London, 1891), p. 324.
16 *Ibid.,* p. 250.
17 *Ibid.,* p. 238. Cf. a similar train of reasoning in Junius Brutus, *Vindiciae contra Tyrannos,* historical introduction by H. J. Laski (London, 1924), p. 112.

18 *Clarke Papers,* p. 237.
19 Hegel's doctrine is similar.
20 *Clarke Papers,* p. 378.

learned enough, or deliberately do not choose, to set up the restraints within themselves. Democracy might operate perfectly if the condition laid down by Cromwell for satisfactory discussion were present:

that wee may all of us soe demeasne ourselves in this businesse that wee speake those thinges that tend to the uniting of us, and that we none of us exercise our parts to straine thinges, and to lett thinges to a longe dispute, or to unnecessary contradictions, or to the stirring uppe of any such seede of dissatisfaction in one another's mindes as may in the least render us unsatisfied one in another. I doe not speake this that anybody does doe itt, butt I say this ought to *become* both you and mee. that wee soe speake and act as that the end may be unison and a right understanding one with another.[21]

In proportion as this spirit does not exist, in proportion as it cannot exist owing to uncontrollable impulses in man's thought and behavior, a democratic form of government cannot but be turbulent, intolerant, violent.[22] The less passionate, willful, and fanatical reformers have recognized this, and have in the last two hundred years postulated certain institutions to act as restraints until the time shall come—if ever it does—when by some means, individual self-control shall be a sufficient guarantee of social creativeness and the satisfaction of appetites and interests, by the method of peaceful discussion.[23]

We shall now indicate briefly the fundamental spiritual impulses toward democratic government, the groups of people interested in this form of government, and the various devices suggested as proper to it.

The Spiritual Impulses. We have already spoken of the changes in the fifteenth and sixteenth centuries contributing to a movement of revolt against authority and to an assertion of individuality. It is interesting to search out what it was believed this liberty would produce, and we may do it by exploring the works of those who have contributed to the democratic tradition. Two things, to begin with, are clear. *First,* the great theorists took certain claims for granted, not seeking to justify them, perhaps because they were considered sufficiently ultimate as values to be impossible of justification. The spirit of this I think, is rather what one finds in such a passage from John Locke's *On Civil Government:* "Since a rational creature cannot be supposed, when free, to put himself into subjection to another for his own harm. . . .": [24] Consequently, only a bald statement, without psychological analysis, is made.

Secondly, the values were stated by people who, as a rule, were not in authority but fighting against it, and were therefore obliged to discover or invent some rule to justify their revolt and their positive claims. Or they were people who had acquired authority so recently, and usually by battle, that they still had to continue to encourage themselves and their followers. Once the battle for democracy was substantially won, as by the 1830's, even those—I might say, especially those—who were already in possession of its benefits and whose social predecessors battled in original terms, because, as it were, revisionists. That is, finding, like de Tocqueville, that liberty had not come with democracy but was actually threatened by it, they claimed safeguards against the product they had conjured up—impediments to produce *liberal* democracy. Thus, not all the views we shall presently read led necessarily to government of the people by the people for the people; to that they led only when the grouping of society, the character of its activities and its temper, were propitious.

Third, almost all felt resentment

---

21 *Ibid.,* p. 201.
22 Cf. Harrington, *The Commonwealth of Oceana* (edition of 1887), p. 67: "To the commonwealthsman I have no more to say, but that if he excludes any party, he is not truly such; nor shall ever found a commonwealth upon the natural principle of the same, which is justice . . . ," etc.
23 Ireton, as in G. P. Gooch, *English Democratic Ideas in the Seventeenth Century* (edition of 1927), pp. 139, 140.

24 Book II, para. 164.

against tyranny. Some, like La Boëtie, were sensitive to the cowardice of people who lived under it,[25] and compared their degradation to that of beasts.[26] Others, like Milton, inveighed against the results of a tyrant's power, terrible because it was "boundless and exorbitant." [27] Paine said that the principle of kingship caused man to become the enemy of man since royal ambitions incensed them to hostilities.[28] There was the ultimate unwillingness to be sacrificed unless for reasons which satisfy: "I am against the King or any power that would destroy God's people, and I will never bee destroyed till I cannot helpe myself. Is itt nott an argument, if a pylott run his shippe uppon a rock, or if a Generall mount his cannon against his army, hee is to bee resisted?" [29] Could any one person be relied upon, asked Junius Brutus, to safeguard another's life and welfare? Any one man was too mutable, too unruly and weak against his passions, to be so trusted.

(To perpetrate an anachronism, but a very useful analogy: observe that when, in 1924, it was proposed in the United States Congress to sell the Muscle Shoals hydroelectric development to Henry Ford, who would then use it to produce fertilizer, the proposal was resisted on the ground that although the first Henry Ford might be an administrative genius, there was no guarantee that when he died and his property passed to his heirs, they would equal or surpass their father in managerial ability. Hence, it was argued, let the public authorities own, manage, and appoint.)

A *fourth,* and a more powerful tend-

ency, was the denial that any one person or arbitrary grouping could be so certain of the righteousness of their values that control over their government was unnecessary. This tendency began with Lutheran doctrines and found its way, as a crude and nonrationalized enthusiasm, into the sermons and tenets of the new Nonconformist sects. They spoke of "conscience," "grace," and the "light of nature," which informed individuals and gave them a sovereign validity. But in the hands of men like Cromwell, Locke, and Milton, and afterwards of Paine, Humboldt, and J. S. Mill, the red-hot enthusiasms were molded by circumspect reason into weapons less cumbrous, if at once more destructive of tyranny and constructive of liberty, in their fine logic. Cromwell, as we have seen, urged "equality of consciences." Locke averred that every church is orthodox to itself: to others, erroneous or heretical. Whatsoever any church believes, it believes to be true; and the contrary thereunto, it pronounces to be error.[30] (The nazi and communist doctrines are strongly of this nature.)

But the quintessence of doubt, and therefore of the argument for freedom,

---

[25] *Discours de la Servitude Volontaire,* ed. by Paul Bonnefon (Paris, 1930), p. 57.
[26] *Ibid.,* p. 81.
[27] *Prose Works* (London, edition of 1900), Vol. II, *The Tenure of Kings and Magistrates,* p. 18.
[28] *Rights of Man,* ed. by H. B. Bonner (London, 1913), p. 75. According to Hobbes *Leviathan,* Part 2, Chap. 17 (Oxford edition, 1909), p. 130: ". . . amongst men, there are very many, that thinke themselves wiser, and abler to govern the Publique, better than the rest; and these strive to reforme and innovate, one this way, another that way" . . .
[29] *Clarke Papers,* p. 273.

[30] *Letters on Toleration* (London, Warde, Locke edition), p. 11: "So that the controversy between churches about the truth of their doctrines, and the fruits of their worship, is on both sides equal; nor is there any judge, either at Constantinople, or elsewhere upon earth, by whose sentence it can be determined. . . . The decision of that question belongs only to the Supreme Judge of all men, to whom also alone belongs the punishment of the erroneous. . . . There is only one of these [the ways of the Churches] which is the true way to eternal happiness. But in this great variety of ways that men follow, it is still doubted which is the right one. Now neither the care of the commonwealth, nor the right of enacting laws, does discover the way that leads to heaven, more certainly to the magistrate, than every private man's search and study discover it unto himself . . . if I be not thoroughly persuaded thereof in my own mind, there will be no safety for me in following it. No way whatsoever that I shall walk in against the dictate of my conscience will ever bring me to the mansions of the blessed. . . . Whatsoever may be doubtful in religion, yet this at least is certain, that no religion which I believe not to be true, can be either true or profitable to me."

toleration, and democratic government, is this: that men have not the faculties for perfect and unchallengeable conviction regarding their ultimate beliefs:

The articles of my religion, and of a great many other such shortsighted people as I am, are articles of faith, which we think there are so good grounds to believe, that we are persuaded to venture our eternal happiness on that belief: and hope to be of that number of whom our Saviour said, "Blessed are they that have not seen, and yet have believed." [31]

According to Milton, the truth is as divided among all men, who have no ability but to see according to the peculiar fashion in which they have each been shaped.[32] "Twenty capacities, how good soever" are insufficient to contain "all the invention, the art, the wit, the grave and solid judgement" of England.[33] "Neither is God appointed and confined, where and out of what place these his chosen shall be first heard to speak. . . ." [34] And yet in our own day, there are political doctrines and systems sanguine enough to locate this capacity for speech and government exclusively in a few self-chosen.

We could quote similar passages from the other authors we have mentioned, except that these belonged to an age when God had been replaced by Nature or Man or Science as a political standard; when, accordingly, politics were no longer discussed in Biblical terms. But religious feeling is indestructible: only the objects of worship are different, and behind all

lies the mystery which human faculties cannot understand; and hence for most men, the essence, if not the verbal vesture, of the arguments of Locke and Milton are of abiding validity.

The overwhelming tendency, however, moved not exclusively by resentment of tyranny and doubt of truth; it soared upon the wings of man's positive creativeness and was impelled by the overwhelming consciousness of individual worth. All other things might be doubtful, but this was certain, that God or Nature had implanted the seeds of good in every one and meant that they should freely bear their proper fruit. Evidence? Let each one search his soul and apprehend the message of his feelings, or cast the mind back to a time when government did not yet exist, or reason a little. There was evidence enough. And in truth, if that evidence did not suffice, let those who believed otherwise, supporting tyrants, find a sufficient rebuttal; for none of them could have been stupid enough to have desired the government under which they groaned. Thus La Boëtie:

All sensate things, as soon as they possess consciousness, feel the evil of subjection and run after liberty . . . what accident was that which was able to denature man, the only being born, really, to live in freedom, and to make him lose the memory of his original being and the desire to regain it? [35]

And so many others.

All this was systematized by John Locke —"a rational creature cannot be supposed, when free to put himself into subjection to another for his own harm"—and his *On Civil Government* exercised a tremendous influence upon the Continent and in the American colonies. Indeed, to quote Locke is with certain differences of style and passion to quote Rousseau, Patrick Henry, and Thomas Jefferson.

The early impulse which expressed itself in theological terms as the spirit of God freely moving and developing itself in human beings, which it was sinful to confine or injure, became gradually more rational: the ends in Locke are self-main-

---

[31] *Ibid.*, p. 292: "But we neither think that God requires, nor has given us faculties capable of knowing in this world several of those truths which are to be believed to salvation. For whatever may be known, besides matter of fact, is capable of demonstration; and when you have demonstrated to any one any point in religion, you shall have my consent to punish him if he do not assent to it."

[32] *Areopagitica*, in *Prose Works* (London, 1900), Vol. II, p. 66: "God uses not to captivate under a perpetual childhood of prescription but trusts him with the gift of reason to be his own chooser. . . . He [God] left arbitrary the dieting and repasting of our minds; as wherein every mature man might learn to exercise his own leading capacity."

[33] *Ibid.*, pp. 80, 81.

[34] *Ibid.*, p. 98.

[35] *Op. cit.*, p. 64.

tenance and development; in Rousseau, conservation and development of our "natural," our good, selves; and in Paine, development of the "dormant mass of sense."[36] In freedom Milton sought the value of fully developed virtue,[37] and the progress of faith and knowledge. Jefferson emphasized the involuntary nature of belief (a most mportant point, linking this discussion with the theme in chapter 1 concerning man's unconscious drives), and urged that uniformity of belief was as undesirable as uniformity of face and stature.[38] With Humboldt the joy in variety of human development was even more emphatically expressed and systematically treated. John Stuart Mill borrowed from him the motto, "The grand, leading principle, towards which every argument enfolded in these pages directly converges, is the absolute and essential importance of human development in its richest diversity," and then continued, but in a different age, its expansion and institutional form. To Kant, free activity was the only condition for a life at all worthy of man, for this alone, the separatist spirit—exhibited in his envious jealousy, his vanity, his insatiable acquisitiveness, and desire of power—awoke and fostered the development of his excellent capacities unto the day of the perfect society. Given liberty and equal conditions to what may not man aspire? There never was a social contract; but the legislator ought to act as though there were![39]

The essence of the democratic tendency to the end of the eighteenth century is a denial of inherent royal rights, the assertion of individual sovereignty, the growth of belief in equality of consciences and religious toleration, the development of the idea of beauty in variety, and the faith that nature, acting unimpeded in self-governing individuals, would produce works of the highest and holiest value. Only where this faith could reasonably be demonstrated to have failed ought authority to intervene, and authority could not be constituted except by the joint will of the people. We possess great goods, said men, of their mental and physical faculties. Why then should they not have their fullest development? All in all, the supreme good lay in liberty—that is, to interpret the many sayings, *the exemption of men from any burdens other than those imposed by the rationally proven nature of environment or men, assuming we were to begin life anew, with all the results of irrational tradition abolished.*[40]

Certain more immediate practical considerations weighed with democratic theorists—for example, the physiocrats or Harrington—who showed how a democratic form of government would draw the best talents into leadership, diminish the causes of sedition, promote eugenic marriage by the reduction of large fortunes, and give strength to empire. Others, like Paine, argued that popular government was the only form which could assemble the practical knowledge of "the various parts of society," while, also, it was often remarked how nonrepresentative government imposed the burdens of obedience and taxation upon those who had no say in government, since even when men knew all there was to know they could not do others justice owing to their "interest-begotten prejudices."

It is just to say, I think, that this evolution of political theory, and of sentiment, was protestant, revolutionary, and negatory, and only vaguely conscious of what would be established in the place of that

---

[36] *Op. cit.,* p. 92: "There is existing in man a mass of sense lying in a dormant state, and which, unless something excites to action, will descend to him, in that condition to the grave. As it is to the advantage of society that the whole of its faculties should be employed, the construction of government ought to be such as to bring forward by a quiet and regular operation, all that extent of capacity which never fails to appear in revolution."
[37] *Areopagitica,* p. 75: "For God sure esteems the growth and completing of one virtuous person, more than the restraint of ten vicious."
[38] *Notes on Virginia* (1781): "The error seems not sufficiently eradicated, that the operation of the mind, as well as the acts of the body, are subject to the coercion of laws."
[39] *Principles of Politics: Principles of Political Right* (trans. Edinburgh, 1891), Proposition 4.

[40] The student is referred to G. Ferrero, *The Principles of Power* (New York, 1942), an historical and analytical study of the nature of legitimacy.

which was to be swept away. It took the future of man, if he were free, on faith. It was thought sufficient to furnish a dissolvent of ancient irrational laws and institutions, and to insist on the criterion that all men ought to be free and equal according to the promptings and designs of nature. Freedom and equality were, of course, endowed with different meaning by the different men, social classes, and groups who used them, according to the interests of their time and place, for the question naturally arose: "When we admit the free power to evolve, what direction will each take?" The full drift of this question was not apprehended until about 1848, for until then the immediate tasks of demolition of privilege and absolutism fully occupied men's minds and energies. Then the far-reaching purport of the doctrines began to be perceived, and their force politically harnessed; and we may say that one generation after 1848, democracy as liberty only ended and socialism also took a seat on the throne.[41] We have treated this in the chapter on state activity and will come upon it again at a later stage. Let us now briefly consider what institutions the democratic theorists suggested.

DEMOCRATIC INSTITUTIONS

THERE were (1) a written constitution; (2) with a declaration of rights implying a limitation of the sphere of government; (3) majority rule, usually control of a government by an elected legislature; (4) the separation of the powers of government so that each power might check and balance the other; (5) public education to produce the knowledge and spirit appropriate to democratic government.

Written Constitutions. These naturally had their origin in the ideas of a state of nature followed by a compact among the natural individuals creating a political association. They followed either from the purely rational natural law associationism of men like Althusius, Harrington, Spinoza, Locke, Rousseau, Kant, Paine, and others, or from the covenants between men and God as elaborated from the material of the Old Testament by such thinkers as Junius Brutus and the Puritans.[42] Hence, too, the evolution of the idea of special constitutional assemblies, and popular ratification and a difficult amending process.[43] The end, as Harrington said, was a commonwealth, "a government of laws and not of men."[44] What was the result of this current, and the nature of constitutions, we discuss in Chapter 7.

It may be said at this point, however, that constitution making in the earlier part of the eighteenth century was a simpler process than it came to be in the twentieth century, when a longer experience of government, diversification, and marked rigidities of organized economic and spiritual groupings made a majority-supported constitution more difficult to attain.

Declaration of Rights. A declaration of rights laid certain positive limitations upon government. These were already formulated in a very broad way by the army in its draft treaties with Parliament in 1647.[45] Harrington urged the limitation of the sovereignty of the great association, asking "whether power, not confined to the bounds of reason and virtue, has any other bounds than those of vice and passion?" The whole of Locke's work reposes upon this notion, that only specifically transferred powers can be legitimately executed by the government. And we shall see how the constitutions of

41 For other discussions of the nature of democracy, see A. D. Lindsay, *The Modern Democratic State* (Oxford, 1943); Reinhold Niehbuhr, *The Children of Light and the Children of Darkness* (New York, 1943); Charles Merriam, *New Democracy and New Despotism* (New York, 1939); Max Ascoli, *The Power of Freedom* (New York, 1949).

42 Cf. Charles Borgeaud, *Rise of Modern Democracy in Old and New England* (London, 1894).
43 Cf. Charles Borgeaud, *Adoption and Amendment of Constitutions in Europe and America*, trans. by C. D. Hazen (New York and London, 1895).
44 *Op. cit.*, p. 42.
45 S. R. Gardiner, *The Constitutional Documents of the Puritan Revolution, 1628-60* (Oxford, 1889).

the independent American colonies, and hence most written constitutions, were based on the same idea: namely the greatest possible exemption of individuals from associative control.

It is not inappropriate to observe here that less happy countries, like the German states, which suffered absolute or almost absolute government until 1919, found a certain relief in the principles of the *Rechtsstaat*. The *Rechtsstaat* means a state in which the activities of the executive are permanently subject to legal rules that are implemented and safeguarded by independent and impartial law courts. Its great protagonists were originally Kant and Humboldt, but later and with more system the German liberals of 1848 elaborated it in their written constitution, the idea culminating in the work of the jurists von Mohl and von Gneist.[46] The substance of the rules is, of course, of as much importance as their guarantee, and many could have no validity unless they were not merely executive decrees but laws made with the cooperation of representative parliaments. Ideally, they would embody such limitations of governmental power as are implied in the rights declared in free constitutions, such as tolerance of religious differences, equality before the law, and others. But between the *Rechtsstaat* of the Germans (a notion of great value, as we shall see in discussing the idea of the separation of powers) and the constitutional limitations in free states there was this immense difference: In the *Rechtsstaat* the state was represented by the sovereign monarch and his bureaucracy; in the democratic state, the state was represented also by a popularly elected parliament. The limitation was thus drastically different in nature.[47] We

later examine the constitutions and the meaning of the rights they declare, and we shall see that strong modern forces constantly encroach upon them, in some cases to their utter destruction. This is, as we have noticed, because some freedoms of the individual have been found, in modern environment, to be on the whole noxious, not only to other goods but even to the general freedom itself.

Recently the idea of declaring rights superior to the parliamentary assembly, and therefore shackling the electorate itself, has been resuscitated by opponents of even mild degrees of state activity, of which one example, Hayek, will suffice (to Lippmann's *The Good Society* [48] we have already referred). Hayek, while admitting that "whatever form the [rule of law] takes, any such recognized limitations of the powers of legislation imply the recognition of the inalienable right of the individual, inviolable rights of man," [49] seems to believe that the purpose is to safeguard against a majority vote the system of capitalistic enterprise.

It is amazing also to see that two constitutions drafted in our own time—e.g., the U.S.S.R. constitution of 1936 and the French draft constitution of 1946 (the finally accepted one), widely divergent as they are regarding the basis of authority, the former being dictatorial and the latter democratic—contain long and substantial lists of rights. In the former the rights are given by grace of the Communist party and its leaders; in the latter they are guaranteed by the working of the majority principle in government.

Thus the new Soviet constitution in chapter 10 (Articles 118–129), "Basic Rights and Obligations of Citizens":

Citizens of the USSR have the right to work ... to rest ... to material security in old age as well as in the event of sickness and loss of capacity to work ... to education. ...

Women in the USSR are accorded equal rights with men in all fields of economic, state, cultural, social, and political life. ...

---

[46] Rudolf von Gneist, *Der Rechtsstaat* (Berlin, 1879). Cf. George Jellinek, *System der Subjektiven Richte* (Freiburg, 1902).

[47] The German doctrine of "auto-limitation," that is, of the self-control of the sovereign, goes some way in form toward the securing of individual rights; and a democracy might in fact be no better. Yet all depends on the comparative "temper" of a monarchical and a popular system. Normally the latter will be more moderate.

[48] Walter Lippmann, *The Good Society* (New York, 1936).

[49] F. Hayek, *The Road to Serfdom* (Chicago, 1944), p. 84.

The equality of the rights of citizens of the USRR, irrespective of their nationality or race ... is an irrevocable law. . . .

To ensure to citizens freedom of conscience the church in the USSR is separated from the state and the school from the church. Freedom to perform religious rites and freedom of anti-religious propaganda is recognized for all citizens.

In accordance with the interests of the toilers and for the purpose of strengthening the socialist system, the citizens of the USSR are guaranteed: (*a*) freedom of speech; (*b*) freedom of assembly and meetings; (*d*) freedom of street processions and demonstrations. . . .

In accordance with the interests of the toilers and for the purpose of developing the organizational self-expression and political activity of masses of the people, citizens of the USSR are ensured the right of combining in public organizations: trade unions, cooperative associations, [etc] . . . and, for the most active and conscientious citizens from the ranks of the working class and other strata of the toilers, of uniting in the All-Union Communist Party, which is the vanguard of the toilers in their struggle for strengthening and developing the socialist system and which represents the leading nucleus of all organizations of the toilers, both public and state.

The citizens of the USSR are ensured the inviolability of the person. No one may be subjected to arrest except upon the decision of a court or with the sanction of the prosecutor.

The inviolability of the homes of citizens and the secrecy of correspondence are protected by law.

The USSR grants the right of asylum to foreign citizens persecuted for defending the interests of the toilers or for their scientific activity or for their struggle for national liberation.

In the first-draft French constitution, rejected in the referendum of May 5, 1946, there is a lengthy list under the title "The Rights of Man." Twenty-one articles are noted as "The Freedoms" and eighteen as "Social and Economic Rights." In the new constitution, approved by the electorate on October 13, 1946, the preamble is considerably shorter. Reaffirming the Declaration of Rights of 1789 and the basic principles embodied in French laws, it states "as most vital in our time" these fundamentals:

The law guarantees to women equal rights with men in all domains.

Anyone persecuted because of his activities in the cause of freedom has the right of asylum within the territories of the Republic.

Everyone has the duty to work and the right to obtain employment. No one may suffer in his work or his employment because of his origin, his opinions, or his beliefs.

Everyone may defend his rights and interests by trade-union action and may join the union of his choice.

The right to strike may be exercised within the framework of the laws that govern it.

Every worker through his delegates may participate in collective bargaining to determine working conditions, as well as in the management of business.

All property and all enterprises that now have or subsequently shall have the character of a national public service or a monopoly in fact must become the property of the community.

The nation ensures to the individual and the family the conditions necessary to their development.

It guarantees to all, and notably to the child, the mother, and the aged worker, health protection, material security, rest, and leisure. Every human being who, because of his age, his physical or mental condition, or because of the economic situation, finds himself unable to work has the right to obtain from the community the means to lead a decent existence.

The nation proclaims the solidarity and equality of all Frenchmen with regard to the burdens resulting from national disasters.

The nation guarantees equal access of children and adults to education, professional training and culture. The establishment of free, secular, public education on all levels is a duty of the State.

In addition, there are some unique constitutional provisions about France's international and colonial relations (these were not included in the first draft of the constitution). "On condition of reciprocity, France accepts the limitations of sovereignty necessary to the organization and defense of peace." With respect to members of the French Union, the ultimate goal of democratic self-government is proposed.

The unaccepted constitution had contained not only the quoted statements but also these rights: sovereignty in the hands of the people; freedom as not acting contrary to others' rights; equal access to all rights; inviolability of home and correspondence; arrests only within the law; no *ex post facto* laws; "every accused person is presumed to be innocent until declared guilty"; right to justice regardless of wealth; "identity of jurisdiction" within a territory; "no one can be disturbed because of his origin, his opinions, or beliefs in religious, Philosophical, or political matters"; freedom of speech and publication and assembly; right to petition government; eligibility to hold public office dependent on capacity and ability; right to join an association; limitation on the suspension of rights in emergencies; maintenance of a public force subject to the people; "when the government violates freedom and rights guaranteed by the constitution, resistance in all its forms is the most sacred of rights and the most imperious of duties"; the right of "full physical, intellectual, and moral development"; state-supported health program; the right to just remuneration; "guarantee of [means of existence] is insured by the institution of public organisms of social security"; removal of private property rights only "by cause of public usefulness legally confirmed and on condition of fair indemnification fixed in conformity with the law"; "the right of ownership must not be exercised contrary to the social good"; progressive taxation; "no one must be placed in a position of economic, social, or political inferiority contrary to his dignity or be allowed to be exploited by reason of sex, color, nationality, religion, opinions, or racial or other origins." To protect all these rights, "citizens must serve the republic, defend it at the price of their lives, share in the charges of state, contribute to common welfare by their work, and aid each other fraternally."

The value to the citizen of the rights guaranteed in the French constitution depends on the continuing loyalty thereto of freely constituted majorities but in the Soviet system the rights are at the mercy of the dictators. Hence the proposals that the United Nations establish a court of appeal to which the aggrieved could repair against their own government, and the need for an executive power outside the dictatorship to enforce remedies.

Majority Rule. The philosophical basis of the democratic theory leads to government by all the people together: that is, unanimity. It was seen that however the "people" was defined, unanimity was impossible in practice, and therefore a majority must suffice. Thus Locke,[50] and thus also Rousseau.[51]

Some convention must be at the base of associated activity; upon what, then, is that of majority rule founded? *First,* waiving the impossibility of an objective measure of the importance of such person or group, it is clear that, normally and in the long run, the majority possesses overwhelming power, physically and mentally. (It always gets the army on its side in the end.) However, with the advent of modern arms and inquisitorial and repressive police with Gestapo and NKVD techniques, that end may be very hard to arrive at, and take a long time to reach.

Second, since, on the democratic assumption, every conscience is as worthy as any other, and there is eternal doubt as to who is right, the majority has a sound claim to rule. *Third,* unanimity is impossible to achieve. *Fourth,* to admit the right of a minority to rule involves the difficulty—*which* minority? It gives all minorities equal right—that is, it destroys the integration of society.[52] Majority rule serves as an integrative associative force—you must overcome your differences and unite in order to rule. *Finally,* there is enormous political power in the general tendency of the average person to believe that the majority must be right.

Yet minorities accept their situation

---

50 *On Civil Government,* Book II, para. 140.
51 Social Contract, Book IV, Chap. II. Cf. also Heimberg, "History of the Majority Principle," *American Political Science Review,* 1926, XX, 52-86.
52 Cf. Hans Kelsen, *Vom Wesen der Demokratie* (1929 edition); and Rudolf Smend, *Verfassungsrecht* (1929). Cf. also Willmoore Kendall, *John Locke and the Doctrine of Majority Rule* (Urbana, Illinois, 1941).

only on certain terms—(1) where the chance is open to them one day to become part of the ruling majority and to contribute to its dictates (permanent, unrelieved minority rule produces revolt), and (2) where they are not oppressed while in a condition of minority. It will be manifest that the minority, in conceding the right of the majority to rule, is surrendering the freedom of itself, and submitting to the goodwill and sense of right-doing of the majority. This is a very considerable act of self-abnegation, and it could not be expected to be accomplished or sustained unless it were on implied terms of forbearance by the majority, and unless experience showed that the terms were steadily honored. Of course, at no time did a minority make systematic pacts on this subject with the majority, and day by day the composition of the minority (as of the majority) undergoes internal change in its constituent groups, objects, and size. The democratic theory and system can be strained to death, and subverted by revolt, if the various temporary majorities do not compensate the minorities for the implied surrender to the majority of rights which are truly the rights only of the whole community in unanimity.[53]

It is, of course, extremely difficult to maintain the assumptions of majority rule in a state where there are obtrusive and persistent racial, class, or cultural differences, and where some groups—Negroes, Jews, Communists, or paupers—are excluded from political life.

The sacrosanctity of majority rule has, of course, been subject to the most violent and even corrupt challenges by men or groups who wish to dominate society for reasons good to themselves. Mussolini claimed that basic national necessities were concentrated in a single man, the Duce, he being one of the rare individuals whom nature had inspired with singular perception and responsiveness to historic reality.[54] Popular participation, therefore, would be actually harmful. Hitler's dogma, as expressed in *Mein Kampf,* was:[55]

The best State constitution and State form is that which, with the most natural certainty, brings the best heads of the national community to leading importance and to leading influence. . . . The State in its organization, beginning with the smallest cell of the community up to the highest leadership of the entire Reich, must be built upon the principle of personality. . . . There must be no decisions by majority, but only responsible persons . . . at every man's side there stand councillors, indeed, *but one man decides . . . authority of every leader towards below and responsibility towards above.*

Lenin emphatically stressed the virtue of the minority: the doctrine that a small, well-organized, and well-informed group, the party, should be the controlling power over the proletarian movement. Thus:[56]

We are the party of a class and therefore almost the entire class should act under the leadership of our Party, should adhere to our Party as closely as possible. But it would be smug and complacent . . . to think that at any time under capitalism the entire class, or almost the entire class, would be able to rise to the level of consciousness and activity of its vanguard, of its Social Democratic Party. . . . To forget the distinction between the vanguard and the whole of the masses which gravitate toward it, to forget the constant duty of the vanguard to raise ever wider strata to this most advanced level, means merely to deceive oneself, to shut one's eyes to the immensity of our tasks, and to narrow down these tasks.

In outlining the characteristics of the Soviet form of government, he noted:[57]

---

[53] Cf. Jefferson's *First Inaugural Address:* "All, too, will bear in mind this sacred principle, that though the will of the majority is in all cases to prevail, principle, to be rightful, must be reasonable; that the minority possess their equal rights, which equal laws must protect, and to violate which would be oppression."

[54] Herman Finer, *Mussolini's Italy* (London, 1935), p. 257.
[55] Hitler, *Mein Kampf* (New York, 1940), pp. 669-670. (Permission Houghton Mifflin Co.)
[56] Lenin, *Collected Works,* Vol. VI, pp. 205-206; quoted from *Short History of the Communist Party,* by a commission of the Central Committee of the Communist Party of the Soviet Union (Moscow, 1939), p. 46. See also Stalin, *Leninism* (New York, 1942), pp. 9-36, and M. Werner, *Stalin's Kampf* (New York, 1940).
[57] Lenin, *Selected Works,* Vol. VI, pp. 263-264.

. . . it provides a form of organization of the vanguard, i.e., of the most class-conscious, most energetic, and most progressive section of the oppressed classes, the workers and peasants, and thus constitutes an apparatus by means of which the vanguard of the oppressed classes can elevate, train, educate, and lead the entire vast mass of these classes. . . .

●

DEMOCRACY AND LIBERALISM

Now, democracy disturbs the liberals, for if the right of the majority is sacred, what becomes of the freedom of the minority? This question assumes a more critical importance in Rousseau's views than in Locke's; for, whereas Locke sets strict limits to the powers of the state, and checks them by the separation of executive from legislative power, Rousseau recognizes no limits to society's power once the contract is made,[58] and jeers at Montesquieu for pretending that sovereignty is divisible.[59] Government without safeguards for minorities has seemed to the fathers of the American constitution, and to men like Mill, the negation of liberty; indeed, to all who have some spiritual or material good which they would zealously retain, pure majority rule has seemed a peril. Hence comes the demand that the force of the rule be limited, by such devices as proportional representation, property and educational qualifications for the franchise, state representation in a federal state, local self-government, and, more recently, group or vocational representation, bicameralism generally, the separation of powers, and support of the rights of parliamentary or congressional opposition by a solid basis of procedure.[60]

In addition, as we have noticed, some strongly urge bills of rights to limit the power of majority rule. Calhoun supported his federal theories upon such a general basis, and his thesis is, essentially, that of all minority parties:[61]

There are two different modes in which the sense of the community may be taken: one, simply by the right of suffrage, unaided; the other, by the right through a proper organism. Each collects the sense of the majority. But one regards numbers only and considers the whole community as a unit, having but one common interest throughout; and collects the sense of the greater number of the whole, as that of the community. The other, on the contrary, regards interests as well as numbers; considering the community as made up of different and conflicting interests, as far as the action of the government is concerned; and takes the sense of each through its appropriate organ, and the united sense of all, as the sense of the entire community. The former of these I shall call the numerical, or absolute majority; and the latter, the concurrent, or constitutional majority.

Now, he says, in popular thought, these two kinds of majority are confounded, and this causes the rights, powers, and minorities of the whole people to be attributed to the numerical majority. This is not the government of the people; it is but the government of the major part over the minor. This is force, and the only way to meet it ultimately is force. Yet this, again, would produce anarchy. Then anarchy must be avoided by a balance of power provided in the constitution; only this is godly.[62]

---

58 Rousseau was contradictory on this subject. Thus: "As nature gives each man absolute power over all his members, the social compact gives the body politic absolute power over all its members also; and it is this power which, under the direction of the general will, bears, as I have said, the name of sovereignty." . . . *Social Contract* (Everyman edition), Book II, Chap. IV, p. 27.
59 *Ibid.*, Book II, Chap. II, pp. 23, 24.
60 Sir Henry Maine's phrase may be recalled: "Liberty is secreted in the interstices of procedure."

61 John C. Calhoun, *A Disquisition on Government*, ed. by R. K. Cralle (Columbia, S. C., 1851), p. 28. (Cf. Herman Finer, "Acton as Historian and Political Philosopher," *Journal of Politics*, August, 1948, for a discussion of the reservations of a Catholic liberal on absolute democracy.)
62 "Traced to this source, the voice of a people—uttered under the necessity of avoiding the greatest of calamities, through the organs of a government so constructed as to suppress the expression of all partial and selfish interests, and to give a full and faithful utterance to the sense of the whole community, in reference to its common welfare—may, without impiety, be called *the voice of God*. To call any other so, would be impious." —*Ibid.*, p. 39.

The Social Contract is an Unequal Contract. The experience of government in the nineteenth century, in short, rapidly and brusquely called attention to the fact that the mass of individuals, free and equal, did not, as Rousseau said and as Locke and others vaguely suggested, give to society an equal amount and receive from it the same amount.[63] That would have been true only if Rousseau had proved his hypothesis that all men were naturally equal. There is some excuse for such an abstraction where industry and agriculture are in a relatively primitive stage and where men are largely equal, if only in their misery. We know, however, that the differences between men's capacities are tremendous, and between their economic and spiritual values prodigious. We know also that government commends itself to them not on uniform grounds, but on grounds as diverse as their nature and interests. We know, or ought to know, what is much more important, that as a rule they attempt to subject each other in return for a price lower than the good they hope to obtain, and that their sovereign-subject relationship is not a predetermined, static, and authoritative one, but that the social contract between millions of diverse individuals and groups is overthrown and reformed every day and every minute, and that its terms are subject to the fluctuating fortunes of a ferocious and incessant battle. It may be that each man and woman gets from the state more than he gives, owing to the tremendous advantage given by associated action in so large a community. That, in fact, keeps it as stable as it is. Yet many give less in proportion to what they receive than others, while great multitudes contribute much more in proportion to what they receive than other people do. Some are plain exploiters, bandits.

One of the defensive and offensive weapons in that passionate scramble is the "special safeguard of the minority." In proportion as government has enhanced its mighty power, the safeguard is the more anxiously sought; and differences among citizens are championed rather than social uniformities. Both in practice and theory the legend of the sacredness of the majority is steadily being challenged. As a major expediency (Burke called it "violent"), interests always seek to subvert the majority principle: either by systematic restraints or by the convention that though it has the power it should use it with a sense of obligation to the minority. The theory of toleration, which began with religious differences, has now extended to general civil policy, for this has swallowed up religion. Men have, in the last few generations, become extraordinarily sensitive to the advantages of toleration for churches and for minorities of all kinds, of federalism, pluralism, and local self-government.[64] For they claim equality of consciences in a day when political conscience comprehends almost all of man's interests, and when inequality, therefore, is fraught with the gravest consequences. What has become of the principle of the majority we shall see in a later part of this work (Part III).

Separation of Powers. Next, a long line of theorists (including Locke but commencing principally with Montesquieu) have sought the liberty of the individual in the separation of powers—that is, in such an arrangement of the various institutions of government that each should prevent the other from having sufficient power to act tyrannically. Montesquieu suggested the separation of the legislative, executive, and judicial institutions, the American federal and state constitutions included it, and the French Revolution

---

[63] "Finally, each man, in giving himself to all, gives himself to nobody; and as there is no associate over whom he does not acquire the same right as he yields others over himself, he gains an equivalent for everything he loses, and an increase of force for the preservation of what he has."—Rousseau, *Social Contract,* Book I, Chap. VI, p. 15.

[64] Harold J. Laski (*The Grammar of Politics* and other works) was the foremost living exponent of this trend, until the influence of the development of the Soviet Union on him left his theoretical position too mixed for clear comprehension. Cf. *Reflections on the Revolution of Our Time* (London, 1941).

went so far as to say that without it there is no constitution.

Later liberals, like Benjamin Constant and his generation and de Tocqueville, and more recent theorists have elaborated Montesquieu's doctrine to include the division of power between the central and the local authorities. The object is plain: to render government as nearly powerless as is compatible with the most urgent dictates of associated activity. It is obvious that democracy thus organized has different intentions and consequences from democracy as the plain unchecked government of the majority. It is founded, in fact, upon a distrust of any sovereignty, of the one, the few, or the many, unchecked by formal restraints. The kernel of de Tocqueville is: "Forms safeguard Liberty." Seeking, ostensibly, the good of all individual men—namely, their dissociated, and therefore free, development—it denies the good of government by all, unless the counsels of government are protracted, and its will divided. This is a useful theory for those who have something to guard, but a wasteful obstacle to those who have urgent wants. Consequently, democracies based on universal franchise, especially those where the leaders are in a hurry of reformative passion, tend to overthrow the separation of powers, even that which is vested in the rights of a parliamentary opposition.[65] Naturally, neither the fascist nor the nazi nor the Soviet systems tolerate the separation of powers, and the Soviet has been particularly direct about its rejection. The Revolution dominates all the powers of government and the Communist party unites them.[66] The French Communist party in the Constituent Assembly of 1945 and 1946 fought bitterly against the separation of powers.[67] But the next chapter is devoted entirely to the study of the separation of powers, and we do not need any further to anticipate its conclusions.

The Spirit of Democratic Government. Finally, all save the earliest religious enthusiasts have recognized the need for the existence, even the inculcation, of a special spirit in democratic government. For, as we saw in our analysis of the debate between Ireton and the Levelers, if the principle of the independent grace of men is pressed, as it very easily is, beyond the principle that men are equal before the Lord, then the constant expectation prevails that men's hands will be raised against each other. This is also obvious in Calhoun's argument. Consequently, more circumspect thinkers have sought to define the spirit appropriate to the continuance of an association of individuals, and they are not concerned with continuance alone: they think, if they do not speak, of a creative continuance. Harrington says:[68]

A man is a spirit raised by the magic of Nature; if she does not stand safe, and so that she may set him to some good and useful work, he spits fire, and blows up castles; for where there is life, there must be motion or work; and the work of idleness is mischief, but the work of industry is health. To set men to this, the commonwealth must begin betimes with

---

[65] Cf. later chapters on parliamentary procedure, especially Chap. 20.

[66] In the program of the Communist party, adopted in 1919, it was stated: "The Soviet Government, guaranteeing to the working masses incomparably more opportunities to vote and to recall their delegates in the most easy and accessible manner than they possessed under bourgeois democracy and parliamentarism, especially the separation of legislative and executive powers, the isolation of the representative institutions from the masses, etc. . . .

"The aim of the Party consists in endeavor-

ing to bring the Government apparatus into still closer contact with the masses, for the purpose of realizing democracy more fully and strictly in practice, by making Government officials responsible to, and placing them under the control of, the masses."

And in the new Soviet constitution of 1936: "The supreme executive and administrative organ of state power in the USSR is the Council of People's Commissars of the USSR [Article 64]. . . . It has the right in respect to those branches of administration and economy which fall within the jurisdiction of the USSR, to suspend decisions and orders of the Councils of People's Commissars of the USSR." [Article 69]

See, especially, A. Y. Vyshinsky, *The Law of the Soviet State* (New York, 1948), p. 312 ff., for a characteristically perverse "history" of the separation of powers—a contemptuous denunciation.

[67] Cf. p. 106 below.

[68] Cf. Harrington, *op. cit.*, p. 202 ff.

them, or it will be too late; and the means whereby she sets them to it is education, the plastic art of government.

And he spends many pages discussing the appropriate education for the various orders in the commonwealth.

Montesquieu's discussion is perhaps more famous. Every form of government has its special principle, that is "that by which it is made to act—the human passions which set it in motion."[69] In a monarchy, the state is maintained by honor, ambition, glory, and love of applause; in an aristocracy, by moderation as between the aristocrats—that is, by a virile recognition of equality among the rulers, not indolence or pusillanimity. But in a democracy to maintain the state "one thing more is necessary, namely, virtue."[70] Why? Because here the "person who commands the execution of the laws feels that he himself is subject to them and that he must bear their burden." When a king is indolent or ill-advised, a remedy may be found; when the people are such, the state is necessarily lost, for the ill is general. What then is virtue? Montesquieu defines it first negatively, by imagining what happens when virtue is banished and later, positively:

When virtue is banished, ambition invades the minds of those who are disposed to receive it, and avarice possesses the whole community. . . .[71] It is in a republican government that the whole power of education is required. The fear of despotic governments naturally arises of itself amidst threats and punishments; the honour of monarchies is favoured by the passions, and favours them in its turn; but virtue is a self-renunciation, which is ever arduous and painful.[72]

This virtue may be defined as the love of the laws and of our country. As such love requires a constant preference of public to private interest, it is the source of all private virtues; for they are nothing more than this very preference itself. This love is peculiar to democracies. In these alone the government is intrusted to private citizens. Now a government is like everything else: to preserve it we must love it.

One thing alone has Montesquieu omitted: to preserve democracy we must not only love it, but sacrifice other things we love to its preservation. Democrats can maintain democracy only by renouncing some of the fruits of perfect freedom; for their machine, and the fruits also, may be destroyed altogether by too severe a strain. It means that some of our desires must be altogether suppressed, and some put off to the future; that we must be content with lesser mercies than we would like; that "gradualness is inevitable." Our impatience must be assuaged by the belief that in the eternal sweep of time, more good will come of this partial renunciation than from the demand that others shall be subjected to us. In proportion as such a belief is not natural to man, or is incapable of being inculcated, democracy may reign but not freedom, and, in its extreme form, democracy may become a form of government more intolerable than any other.

Rousseau treats of the subject, though not very profoundly, in the *Social Contract,* saying,

There is therefore a purely civil profession of faith of which the sovereign should fix the articles, not exactly as religious dogmas, but as social sentiments, without which a man cannot be a good citizen or a faithful subject.[73]

But then Rousseau only gives a bare indication of the content of this faith.[74] In an earlier chapter he admits that though the state, in making the laws, can do no wrong, yet the judgment of the people may be unwise. The inference is that to make the sovereign wise, a process of education is necessary. We have seen how the physiocrats came to believe in freedom plus public education. The line of such beliefs could be traced through the utili-

[69] *Esprit des Lois,* trans. by T. Nugent (London, 1878), Vol. I, Book III, Chap. III, p. 20.
[70] *Ibid.,* p. 21.
[71] *Ibid.,* p. 22.
[72] *Ibid.,* Book IV, Chap. V, p. 36.

[73] Montesquieu, *op. cit.,* Vol. I, Book VIII, pp. 118-22.
[74] *Social Contract,* Book IV, Chap. VIII (Everyman edition), p. 121. To be just to him, we ought to bear in mind his theories expressed in *Émile,* at least.

tarians down to the present, and it is a vital part of the democratic form of government, of urgent practical importance in our own day.

THE STAGES OF DEMOCRATIC DEVELOPMENT

ONLY one more task remains to be accomplished in this chapter, and that is, to indicate the stages of democratic development.

The Demand for Tolerance. The first stage was the demand for tolerance of nonconformity in religion and the rise of self-governing sects like the Independents, the Separatists, and the Presbyterians.[75] They cannot be entirely identified with the middle classes and the small commercial men. In the American colonies, the small and middling people who had torn themselves out of the English agricultural background formed the center of the movement. The very rich and the fairly rich held with bishop and king; they were the nobles, the great landowners, and the governors of their counties.

Though an undercurrent of social criticism, beginning with Wycliffe and John Ball, came out again in the Levellers and the Diggers, these were not the classes to triumph in the English Revolution. They helped the commercial classes of the towns and the prosperous yeomen to claim rights of Parliamentary control over taxation and regulation of trade, but they helped for the attainment of general liberties, "to assert and vindicate the just power and rights of this Kingdome in Parliament for those common ends premised against all arbitrary power, violence, and oppression, and against all particular parties or interest whatsoever."[76] They did not know

---

[75] Cf. Acton, *Essays on Freedom and Power* (Boston, 1949) Chaps. I, II, and V. Acton disposes of the most recent heresy of some laissez-faire economists—whose disposition to follow Marx in relating all human activity to an economic cause is amazing—the heresy that men of commerce first established modern liberty. Acton shows that religious belief played by far the most dominating part. Acton, of course, wrote first, before these economists.

[76] C. H. Firth, *Clarke Papers* (London, 1891), XXXV.

---

what the experience of two hundred and fifty years has since taught, that Parliamentary leaders might speak in the same terms as the common man, but that they necessarily meant something quite different, due to "interest-begotten prejudice." The peasants in all lands had sporadically revolted, and had been used by the Crown, the nobles, and the towns for their liberties; the day of the rank and file was not yet, for while their leaders were organized, armed, and disciplined, they themselves were not.

A potent impetus was given to the democratic movement by the revolt of the Netherlands and the creation of a republic, for English observers much envied Dutch institutions, and had, as they have today, especially jealous admiration for any country that is rich. In fact, freedom and commercial power are correlated, for commercial power depends upon the ability to buy and sell in the best market, regardless of religious or social differences.

The Demand for Representative Government. In France and England the townsfolk led the movement for representative government. Their commercial and industrial interests urged them to make of the legislature the executive instrument of their policy and social ambitions; and the very existence of numbers of people in close proximity and constant intercourse caused the growth of freer manners and a regard for the essential man. In Germany the proverb was coined: "The atmosphere of the town makes a man free." In France the Third Estate was a much more definite class than in England: not clergy, not noble, it stood between these and the peasantry. By the last *États Genéraux* in 1614 it had shown itself exceedingly pretentious; after their suppression it still held some governmental power in the *Parlements*—that is the semilegislative, semijudicial bodies which checked and controlled the power of Crown and intendant—and it permeated the bureaucracy with its sons. The French Revolution was its revolution, although as in the English Revolution the poor of the towns and the countryside followed them, partly for certain definite benefits (like fair taxation, guarantee of property, equality before the law, and the right to participate in government administratively and legislatively) and partly for the general benefits of free and settled rule. At a sad but perhaps unavoidable moment, the practical elaboration of the revolutionary principles was checked by the necessity of defense against the more feudal countries; Napoleonic genius was needed, but it converted France into a barracks, the opposite of a democracy, and later the forces of "legitimacy" triumphed. The main benefits of twenty years of struggle accrued to the returned nobility and the rising commercial and industrial families, who alone were the *"pays légal,"* and their leaders produced the philosophy of liberalism—namely, neither uncharted monarchy nor unlimited democracy, but government of Reason, represented by the wealthy, with a restricted franchise, restricted centralization, judicial restriction of the executive, and political parties balancing each other.

The balance of power seemed, as Harrington said, to follow the balance of property. Those who had the material means, or were nearest to their attainment, sought liberty for themselves, and having obtained it, by revolution or its threat, did not share it until they in turn were frightened or forced.

America,[77] a new country, settled (though not entirely) by people with strong democratic convictions, gave the first great opportunity for popular government. Even here, however, different spiritual and economic interests had been brought from Europe, and the path of democracy was neither open nor smooth. The nonexistence of remarkable inequality in estates made it very difficult to maintain other social distinctions for long, though wherever the influence of the British Crown penetrated, it brought swarms of aristocratic parasites around the governor's palace or the chief seats of the Anglican Church. Where, however, land was cheap and freehold, a property qualification was not a serious limitation upon democracy. Government of town and church were even more democratic. Little by little, however, a cleavage arose between the people of the coast and tidal rivers, interested in commerce, industry, and finance, and the yeomen of the hinterland, and by the time of the American War of Independence, this gulf was most marked, so that the constitutional .debates of the time are full of the difference between the agrarian and the manufacturing "interests." More, the Revolution had been very largely a war of trade and commerce, though we may add thereto the spirit of pride, independence, and, as James I once called it, the "gust of Government." The practical drive was there. But all classes were drawn in by cries like those of Patrick Henry—"Give me liberty or give me death!" Where people are excited by such talk and are flattered by those who need their help to fight battles, they are apt to continue to believe what they have been told long after their leaders have forgotten their promises. What were they told? This:

that all men are created equal, that they are endowed by their Creator with certain inalienable Rights, that among these are Life, Liberty, and the pursuit of Happiness—That to secure these rights, Governments are instituted among Men, deriving their just powers from the consent of the governed—That whenever any Form of Government becomes destructive of these ends, it is the Right of the People to alter or to abolish it, and to institute new Government, laying its foundation on such principles and organizing its powers in such form as to them shall seem most likely to effect their Safety and Happiness.

The royal executive and the nominated council had fled, and government was conducted by elected assemblies representative of agrarian interests. These began to govern in their own interests, putting off payment of debts and issuing paper money. The separation of powers and checks and balances suddenly became of vital impor-

---

[77] V. Parrington, *Main Currents of American Thought* (New York, 1927 and 1930), 3 vols. in one, especially I and II; Louis Hacker and others, *The Shaping of the American Tradition* (New York, 1947); and Merle Curti, *Growth of American Thought* (New York, 1943), and especially D. J. Boorstin, *The Lost World of Thomas Jefferson* (New York, 1948).

tance to those who feared such movements, and Montesquieu was acknowledged to be to political science what Homer had been to Greek literature. America expanded westward, and the equalitarian aspect of democratic thought was ever renewed, and constitution after constitution embodied the early Puritan principles, now vivified by the morality of the pioneers. The day has not yet come for the deliberate abandonment of the separation of powers, but it will come; to-day America is so well off that we see there the spectacle of a nation which has its cake, democracy, and yet eats it, by the separation of powers, in three slices.

The rise of manufactures in England urged forward the commercial and industrial middle class to obtain Parliamentary reform, and this they accomplished in 1832 with the aid of a threat that the working classes would revolt. These classes soon realized that they would get nothing unless they obtained it for themselves, and the Chartist movement was organized. Its political points are worth repetition. They were:

(1) Franchise for all adult men.

(2) Voting by ballot.

(3) Three hundred constituencies, divided as equally as possible on the basis of the last census; to be amended after each census.

(4) Annual Parliaments.

(5) No property qualification for Parliamentary candidates.

(6) Members of Parliament to be paid.

Similar things were happening abroad. In France and Germany [78] the upper and middle classes were enjoying the fruits of the liberal revolutions, especially since manufactures required laissez faire. It is true that the liberal intelligentsia furnished the theories which redounded to the ultimate advantage of the workers, but the power to move the bourgeoisie was beyond them; to do this required the exertion of one interest against another.

The Demand for Universal Franchise. By 1848 the interests below were already grappling with those above, but already a new element had entered, destined to end the struggle by a victory for universal franchise, and to change the nature of democratic government. The peculiar economic claims of the working classes, arising out of the nature of factory industry and the capitalistic system, resulted in the conversion of the claims for a rather abstract political freedom—the freedom of governmental negation or political dissociation—into the claims for economic equality. The Chartists in England, Lassalle, Marx, and Engels in Germany, and Fourier, Saint-Simon, and Proudhon in France preached more or less consciously, not *dis*-sociation, but its extreme opposite, socialism. No cry or demand could have been more effectual in an age of acquisitiveness (or, as Montesquieu expresses it, of the "desire of having") to call the nonenfranchised to the conquest of political power, and it brought the people in.

Further, the existence of the franchise for some citizens necessarily brought about an extension of it for all: for the enfranchised had different interests, and in order to win power by a majority of votes, they were bound to compete with each other for popular approval by campaigns of political excitement. They brought in outsiders to win their battles for them, just like the tyrants and parties in Athens, and the Catholics and Protestants during the wars of religion; and here as there, the strangers stayed, to become masters.

Finally, the liberal and the rational mind could not help, in the long run, admitting the right of women to political power.

Clarification through Conflict: Democracy. The foregoing institutions of democracy we have listed and explained were proposed over the centuries by the pioneers of the democratic movement, some of them being more interested in one or more rather than all of them as being the most certain guarantee of what their authors wanted in the social and individual results of government.

The years since 1917 have been full of a world-wide ideological debate of the most fervent and bitter kind, between the exponents and practitioners of fascism,

---

[78] In 1848 election manifestoes.

nazism, and communism (and specifically the official and unofficial defenders of the régimes of Mussolini, Hitler, and Stalin) and the defenders of democracy in the countries of western Europe and the western hemisphere. The result has been added clarification of the Lincolnian tenet that democracy is "government of the people, by the people, for the people," with the dividing line between the genuine and the imposters seen to reside altogether in the phrase, "*by* the people." The main principles for establishing this after World War II had to be formulated for the government of the German states in the American occupation zone. These are the principles the United States required the new constitutions to embody: [79]

All levels of German government in the U.S. Zone must be democratic to the extent that:

(a) All political power is recognized as originating with the people and subject to their control;

(b) Those who exercise political power are obliged to regularly renew their mandates by frequent references of their programs and leadership to popular elections;

(c) Popular elections are conducted under competive conditions in which not less than two effectively competing political parties submit their programs and candidates for public review;

(d) Political parties must be democratic in character and must be recognized as voluntary associations of citizens clearly distinguished from, rather than identified with, the instrumentalities of government;

(e) The basic rights of the individual including free speech, freedom of religious preference, the rights of assembly, freedom of political association, and other equally basic rights of free men are recognized and guaranteed;

(f) Control over the instrumentalities of public opinion, such as the radio and press, must be diffused and kept free from governmental domination;

(g) The rule of law is recognized as the individual's greatest single protection against a capricious and willful expression of governmental power.

[79] Cf. *Constitutions of Bavaria, Hesse and Wuerttemberg-Baden*, United States Office of Military Government for Germany (Berlin, February 15, 1947), p. 3.

German governmental systems must provide for a judiciary independent of the legislative and executive arms in general and of the police activity in particular. U.S. policy does not demand the rigid separation of legislative and executive powers. It has no objection to the cabinet or parliamentary type of government in which the executive and legislative branches are inter-dependent. Where a governmental system does provide for a separation of the executive and legislative, there must be no provision which would enable the executive to rule without the approval and consent of the legislative branch.

DICTATORIAL AND DEMOCRATIC LEADERSHIP

SOCIAL dissensions in the recent interwar period resulted in the severest trial democracy has undergone, forcing a restatement of its merits compared with totalitarian alternatives, and a reorientation of some of its social policy. Basically the two systems are antipodal in two respects —with respect to freedom, and with respect to the individual's prerogative in political activity.

In a political system where one man or group has created an omniscient image of itself, the individual is expected to receive guidance from the state, to follow, even submit to, the leader. Civil rights and freedom are excluded, for otherwise the position of the dictator might be challenged. Closely related to freedom is the question of responsibility; for without liberty for the individual, the ruling power is answerable to no one but himself. Democracy, however, challenges the infallibility of the dictatorial doctrine, which claims to be the transcendent and dominating truth. Rather, it desires and expects continuous enrichment of social life with equal opportunities for all citizens to contribute, recognizing the difficulty of discovering final solutions to the fundamental problems of human existence and destiny. Hence arises the requirement that the agents of government be responsible to the electorate, who must make the final decisions about the progress of their society.

Political participation in a democracy derives from the principle of equal rights. Since there are many alternative ways of discovering and achieving the best in public welfare, and since there is no objective way of determining which particular individual might most acceptably discover and utter them, all are entitled to formulate their opinions with equal right. This political equality gives the maximum encouragement to criticism of public officials, keeping them aware of popular needs and desires, and obliging them to answer. Equality also encourages, because it flatters, popular leadership in political affairs. Under a dictatorship, equality of rights is excluded; participation means carrying out orders without question.

Totalitarianism has four main features: (1) the use of propaganda, (2) the monopolistic party, (3) the "facade" legislature, and, finally, (4) a high degree of centralization.

Propaganda. Since the dictator acts as the mind and conscience for all his subjects, he must have an extremely well-organized, highly effective machine for implementing his orders. The device of attempting the complete and unquestioning transfer of conviction without regard to truth and its processes was highly developed by Goebbels.[80] A steady spate of words streamed from the Ministry of Enlightenment, serving up the same idea in many flavors (since so many varied publics had to be reached), oversimplifying, and resorting to a multitude of rational and irrational appeals. Such a technique is most effective over a short period of time, since truth, given time, has the unquenchable quality of being extricated from compromising situations. (In marked contrast are democratic attempts to educate—the presentation of alternative points of view, with the selection of the most satisfactory left to the individual.)

Role of Party. Next to and serving the leader, the party is the chief instrumentality of the dictatorship, supplementing the democratic executive and legislature. A small, extremely well-organized band of fanatically loyal members, it maintains national discipline, keeping the rest of the population emotionally aroused and obedient. Further, since it has at its command the monopolistic disposal of all positions in the country, and since it controls the entire social and economic as well as political life of the nation, not a single person can escape the weight of its authority. As the élite, the exemplars of the highest virtues of their particular system, the party members are expected to undergo severe self-sacrifice for the cause of the state, as interpreted by the leader, and to give him unquestioning obedience.

Within the Russian Communist party, however, an element of self-criticism is encouraged. "Democratic centralism" allows the local periodic election of the members of the executive units of the party. But centralization requires final and unconditional obedience to the orders of the top officials.

(In contrast, political parties in democracies are highly competitive agencies; the plurality of parties spurs each one continually to enlarge its membership, since a majority gives power until the next election. Here the democratic parties activate political thought and may convert the individual's political desires into law.)

The Legislature. In the police state, the parliament is merely a facade, since there is no spontaneous popular choice of candidates or free decisions by the electorate. The dynamic and only element of sovereign decision is the party. The party is above all so significant in democratic states, because at this level the conflicting aims of pressure groups become digested on their way to conversion into law.

Since dictatorial responsibility focuses in one individual, in conjunction with a few hand-picked lieutenants, a marked degree of centralization exists. The party is a vast hierarchy permeated by complete control from the top layers, and there is no recourse from the decisions imposed from on high.

Little pretense was made by the nazis that their government was popular government. They scoffed openly at "the people," and each individual was cheated by the device of causing him to think that the jeering was not at him, but at his neighbors! The Soviet, however, claims

---

[80] Paul Goebbels, *Diaries* (New York, 1948).

to be democratic. Stalin declared, in a speech reporting the draft constitution of 1936 to the Supreme Soviet: [81]

.. another group of critics ... accuses it ... of not granting freedom to political parties, and of preserving the present leading position of the Communist Party in the USSR. And this group of critics maintains that the absence of freedom for parties in the USSR is a symptom of the violation of the principles of democratism. I must admit that the draft of the new Constitution does preserve the régime of the working class, just as it also preserves unchanged the present leading position of the Communist Party of the USSR. ... We Bolsheviks regard it as a merit of the Draft Constitution. . . . In the USSR there is ground only for one party, the Communist Party. In the USSR only one party can exist, the Communist Party, which courageously defends the interests of the workers and peasants to the very end. ... They talk of democracy. But what is democracy? Democracy in capitalist countries, where there are antagonistic classes, is, in the last analysis, democracy for the strong, democracy for the propertied minority. In the USSR, on the contrary, democracy is democracy for the working people, that is, democracy for all. . . . That is why I think that the Constitution of the USSR is the only thoroughly democratic constitution in the world.

It will be seen that Stalin has accomplished the conjurer's trick by omitting the "individual" in his talk of "classes"; by suppressing the value of democracy for all individuals; and by arguing virtually that the one party which is "leading" can be trusted to reconcile all antagonisms as the antagonists would see them, and to give them the benefits which the party thinks they ought to have. This is a travesty of "democracy," and such chicanery must be exposed. Soviet government may or may not be "good" government and may or may not be historically explicable. But if we are to keep our thinking correct, it cannot be accepted as "democratic" in the sense of government *for* the people and *by* the people. The distinction between *for* and *by*, with all its consequences, must be firmly grasped. What

must never be forgotten, is that in a dictatorial system the good of the people depends on the accident of whether the dictator and his assistants *for the time being are* benevolent, wise, and responsive.[82] The democratic system alone offers the permanent guarantee of these values.

Doubt and Certainty. It will have been appreciated that deep inside the animating heart of the democratic idea is a feeling of doubt whether any man knows or can know enough about the past, the present, and the future to attempt to fasten his personal theory of the meaning of nature, the universe and human destiny on to other people, with so sanguine a temper as to be willing, and even more than prompt, to use coercion. Democracy admits reasonable doubt on these three decisive phenomena.[83] But dictatorial systems admit not such doubt, or at any rate do not admit it openly to those who are governed. They may joke about their own certainties, as proclaimed and enforced on others, when they are among themselves—my personal experience is that they do. This sanguine temper is the soul of Stalin's system, as it was of Lenin's and of Marx's. Similar certitudes governed the spirit of Mussolini and Hitler. Stalin's is very reminiscent of the century from which it sprang, the nineteenth, when the positivists and other schools of sociology and philosophy believed it possible to formulate the laws of society with the perennial firmness and precision found possible in the natural sciences. The monopolistic party is founded on a monistic and total creed with a temper of certainty.[84] Stalin's version is: [85]

Hence social life, the history of society, ceases to be an agglomeration of "accidents," and becomes the history of the development of

---

[81] Stalin, *Leninism* (New York, 1942), pp. 394-395.

[82] Therefore, see David Shub, *Life of Lenin* (New York, 1948); Boris Souvarine, *Stalin* (New York, 1937); and Bertram de Wolfe, *Three Who Made a Revolution* (New York, 1948).
[83] Cf. Benedetto Croce, *History as the History of Liberty* (New York, 1941).
[84] Cf. G. S. Counts and N. P. Lodge, "*I Want to be Like Stalin*" (New York, 1947).
[85] Stalin, *Leninism* (New York, 1942), p. 415.

society according to regular laws, and the study of the history of society becomes a science.

Hence the practical activity of the party of the proletariat must not be based on the good wishes of "outstanding individuals," not on the dictates of "reason, universal morals," etc., but on the laws of development of society and on the study of these laws.

Further, if the world is knowable and our knowledge of the laws of development of nature is authentic knowledge, having the validity of objective truth, it follows that social life, the development of society, is also knowable, and that the data of science regarding the laws of development of society are authentic data having the validity of objective truths.

Here is an iron law which, as Stalin's lieutenant, Bukharin (later executed) declared, furnished the party with "the sword of history." It is also the guillotine of democracy.

MYSTIFICATION VERSUS MYSTERY AND DEMOCRACY

Stalin's declaration of faith is a declaration that a few social scientists may take mankind into tutelage. By a remarkable paradox, it is the latest, but we must hope not the final, fruit of the empirical method in the natural sciences, which, in its early decades, was a most powerful stimulus to the rise of modern democracy. The amazing onset of the scientific method in the seventeenth century, whose potent and poetic champion was Francis Bacon, tended to the overthrow of socially functionless absolutisms and oligarchies, because it taught people that it was right to question all traditional authority, and to seek a pragmatic answer to the relationship between tools, instruments, modes of thought, procedures—and ends. From a consideration of the efficiency of instruments to doubt about the ends—that is, political authority and the churches—was only a short step. Political science (and the term comes from the seventeenth century) was pursued with an eye to a science complete in coverage of man's history and nature (Hobbes is an especially fine example of this) and in power of conviction.

In the long run a Karl Marx and an August Comte [86] were bound to arise to dot the *i*'s and cross the *t*'s, and make a continuous generalization of the uniformities in man's history, from his very beginning (though they could not find it) and passing on to eternity, with the same rigidity of cause and effect, as the chemist can know the properties and predict the behavior of sulphuric acid. They set on its head the tricentennial influence of the natural scientific state of mind on the liberation of man from tyranny: for it is that in man which is *not* subject to scientific generalization that entitles him to freedom and quashes the pretensions of irresponsible government. The search for a religious foundation of democracy is a search into life's mystery; the declaration of consummated discovery by dictatorships deliberately turns its back on mystery and exploits pseudo-scientific mystification.[87]

[86] It is time that attention was redirected to August Comte, *System of Positive Polity*, 4 vols. (London, 1875).

[87] John Stuart Mill's break with Comte is a most important part of democratic theory. He wrote: "I had fully agreed with him when he maintained that the mass of mankind, including even their rulers in all the practical departments of life, must, from the necessity of the case, accept most of their opinions on political and social matters, as they do on *physical* [present author's italics], from the authority of those who have bestowed more study on those subjects than they generally have it in their power to do . . . But when he exaggerated this line of thought into a practical system, in which philosophers were to be organized into a kind of corporate hierarchy, invested with almost the same spiritual supremacy (though without any secular power) once possessed by the Catholic Church; when I found him relying on this spiritual authority as the only security for good government, the sole bulwark against practical oppression, and expecting that by it a system of despotism in the state and despotism in the family would be rendered innocuous and beneficial . . . as sociologists we could travel together no further. M. Comte lived to carry out these doctrines to their extremest consequences, by planning, in his last work, the 'Système de Politique Positive,' the completest system of spiritual and temporal despotism which ever yet emanated from a human brain, unless possibly that of Ignatius Loyola . . ."—*Autobiography* (World's Classics, Oxford, 1924), pp. 179-80,

6

The Separation of Powers: False and True

THE theory of the separation of powers meant little to political science until the issue of political liberty became urgent. It began to acquire meaning in the seventeenth century; and in the eighteenth, with critical times, it came to the forefront of discussion. It is an important subject, for, like other things, it has fallen into the hands of partisans and needs rescue; and impartial analysis of it vividly reveals the nature of the modern state. Let us then attempt an answer to these questions: Who invented the theory? What is the theory? What does it mean? What was its historical setting? What was its derivation? What are its practical consequences?

Montesquieu's Primary Contribution. The theory of the separation of powers was first fully formulated by Montesquieu, and appears in *L'Esprit des Lois,* Book XI. But the full meaning of Book XI is obtainable only when it is read together with the rest of the work, for Montesquieu's own spirit appears in one continuous emanation all through the work. Further, the theory was Montesquieu's own, although there are traces of it in John Locke's *Civil Government,* for with him the theory was a conscious generalization linking the machinery of government to its purpose, while with Locke the theory was rather casual. Of that later.

The theory is this:

In every government there are three sorts of power: the legislative; the executive in respect of things dependent on the law of nations; and the executive in regard to matters that depend on the civil law.

This is not very intelligible, and the definition is therefore elaborated.

By virtue of the first, the prince or magistrate enacts temporary or perpetual laws, and amends or abrogates those that have been already enacted. By the second, he makes peace or war, sends or receives embassies, establishes the public security, and provides against invasions. By the third, he punishes criminals, or determines the disputes that arise between individuals. The latter we shall call the judicial power, and the other simply the executive power of the state.

Even this is not very clear, since the executive power surely includes more activities (and it did in Montesquieu's time) than are stated. So far Montesquieu has not sufficiently thrown off Locke's casual definitions. However, as soon as he gets into his own stride, Locke is forgotten, and he marches along entirely in his own manner toward political liberty, an object he had in common with Locke, but conceived somewhat differently. He says:

When the legislative and executive powers are united in the same person, or in the same body of magistrates, there can be no liberty; because apprehensions may arise, lest the same monarch or senate should enact tyrannical laws, and execute them in a tyrannical manner. Again, there is no liberty if the judiciary power be not separated from the legislative and executive. Were it joined with the legislative, the life and liberty of the subject would be exposed to arbitrary control; for the judge would be then the legislator. Were it joined to the executive power, the judge might behave with violence and oppression. There would be an end of everything, were the same man or the same body, whether of the nobles or of the people, to exercise those three powers, that of enacting laws, that of executing the public resolutions, and of trying the causes of individuals.

Montesquieu proposes two theses which are not in necessary combination: (1) that there are different *sorts* of powers in government; and (2) that to obtain liberty, power must not be concentrated. The first it is convenient to discuss at a later stage (Chap. 7). We are concerned with the idea that the separation of the powers will secure liberty. The whole of Montesquieu's work rests upon his profound persuasion that liberty is the highest human good. (I do not say passionate persuasion, for Montesquieu was more meditative than active.) To understand the separation of powers one must understand what Montesquieu meant by political liberty, and fortunately, he explains himself clearly enough. Once there is a state, "liberty can only consist in the power of doing what we ought to will, and in not being constrained to do what we ought not to will." [1] That is, liberty is behavior not outside the law but within the law. There, within the law, there ought to be no constraint, no unauthorized behavior by anyone. To be independent is not to be at liberty.[2] Does he not mean that independence from law is dissociation from other citizens? I think so; for his distinction between it and liberty is:

Liberty is a right of doing whatever the laws permit: and if a citizen could do what they forbid, he would be no longer possessed of liberty, because all his fellow citizens would have the same power.[3]

We may infer from this that all citizens must recognize the reasonableness of the restraints of law; if they do not, there will be the restraints of arbitrariness. We may go further. To Montesquieu, law is not only written law, or even written law with the addition of customary law and traditions. It is much more. It is the principle, the *spirit* of any particular form of government desired—even, we might go further and say, the spirit of the civilization desired. That spirit governs the customs and the traditions and should govern the written law. More, it should govern the form of government. Machinery does not make a government free. "Democratic and aristocratic states are not in their own nature free." [4] Where then is liberty secreted? In the spirit of government—that is, in something which is as fundamental as liberty in Montesquieu's system: in moderation. "Political liberty is to be found only in moderate governments. Yet it is not always found in these. It is there only when there is no abuse of power." [5]

Now comes a fresh contribution to the theory. Its presence can be detected throughout the *Esprit des Lois,* but it more frequently appears in the form of ancient history than of plain statement.

But constant experience shows us that every man invested with power is apt to abuse it, and to carry his authority until he is confronted with limits. Is it not strange that we are obliged to say that virtue itself has need of limits? [6]

How many philosophers and active statesmen, both before and after Montesquieu, have subscribed to this observation? It is, in fact, the central reason for separating powers. "To prevent this abuse, it is necessary, by a proper disposition of things, that power should be a check to power." Is this possible? Yes! "A constitution may be such that no one shall be compelled to do things to which he is not obliged by law, or not to do things which the law permits." [7]

What does Montesquieu mean? That bodies of people must be set up, the one confronting the other, with the implied threat that should any go beyond its prescribed sphere it will be challenged by

[1] *Esprit de Lois,* Book XI, 3.
[2] Cf. Locke, *On Civil Government,* Book II, para. 22; Hobbes, *Leviathan,* Chap. XXI.
[3] *Esprit des Lois, loc. cit.*
[4] *Esprit des Lois,* Book XI, 4.
[5] *Idem.*
[6] *Idem.*
[7] *Idem.*

the other; that each shall have a right to certain powers, which it will presumably, and out of its own desire for power, maintain against encroachment.[8] It means that before will can be translated into its ultimate application to citizens, all the bodies concerned must, at least implicitly, have agreed that the will is just. This is nothing other than saying that though sovereignty exists and must exist, yet it ought to consist in the agreed cooperation of several factors, none of which can exercise functions assigned to the other.

This theory does not depend essentially upon the nature of the power exercisable by each authority, or upon whether Montesquieu has accurately described that nature; and this is partly shown by the fact that he includes an extra check by dividing the legislature into two chambers. The distribution among possibly rival authorities is the virtue of his system.

Montesquieu's Purpose: Moderation. What will this system achieve? It will achieve, as in England, political liberty: that is, "a tranquillity" of mind arising from the opinion each person has of his safety. In order to have this liberty, it is requisite the government be such that one man need not fear any other. . . .[9] "It [political liberty] consists in security, or in the opinion people have of this security." [10] "When the subject has no barrier to secure his innocence, he has none for his liberty." [11]

Now, even as all governments, monarchic, aristocratic, or democratic, may be intemperate and may act despotically, so may any form of government, even a monarchy, be free in Montesquieu's sense if it observes the rules of separated powers, where none shall grow overmighty. There is nothing more in the separation of powers, and nothing less. So much did

[8] *Ibid.*, Book XI, 6.
[9] *Esprit des Lois, loc. cit.*; and J. Dédieu, *Montesquieu et la Tradition Politique Anglaise en France* (Paris, 1913). L. M. Levin, *The Political Doctrine of Montesquieu's Esprit des Lois* (New York, 1936) is an interesting general survey of his political thought, and relates it to the classics.
[10] *Esprit de Lois*, Book XII, 1.
[11] *Ibid.*, Book XII, 2.

Montesquieu say and no more, though he gave examples from the English constitution (see chapter 9 below) and from antiquity.

Certain points need completion and re-emphasis. (1) His riveted insistence is upon moderation, however sovereign power is divided. This is the ultimate object of the separation of powers. Separation is not necessary *per se*, but is a product of Montesquieu's desire, and his judgment of the measures necessary to shape human nature thereto.

(2) His judgment of human nature is that whoever has unrestrained power will abuse it. What does "abuse" mean? He does not say, but we may infer that he believes that men are inclined to exert more power than is really necessary with rational regard to the nature of the rights or duties prescribed by law, or that the power will be exerted along paths entirely unwarranted by the law. In other words, the sheer (not necessarily the malevolent) spontaneity of human life results in a ruthless urging forward until it is stopped. I repeat, the intention may not be bad; it may even be noble; but if it is unchecked, the result is too much of one man or body of men, and too little of the others. Is it not part of the liberal creed that all consciences are equal? Here is the everlasting difficulty of government which wishes to remain free: to admit the right and the necessity of spontaneous development, and yet to find the norms which shall provide regulation without suppression. We are back once again to the essence of the discussion on democracy.

Next—and this is exceptionally important of modern democracy—a secondary but essential use of all separation of power is that it imposes upon each power the need to explain itself; but this, again, is valued not simply because it illuminates the mind of those to be conciliated, but because, in the course of accounting for its attitude, an authority may discover flaws in its own information, logic, and principle and become convinced that a new synthesis is truly necessary. Nothing so imperatively causes a mind to question and remake itself as the obligation to account to someone else. (The lack of external compulsion on the will of the dictator in prewar Italy, in prewar Germany, and the Soviet system exemplifies this injurious deficiency.)

(3) The instruments of restraint sought for in Montesquieu's time could be no other than those within the machinery of government. There is no trace in his writings of the moderating effects of party government. There could be none. With all his leaning toward a republic, he never reckoned in terms of popular government; otherwise he would never have conceived of the people, even as Rousseau did (who copied out an enormous part of Montesquieu's best work), as a vast body of equal units acting either isolatedly or as a solid phalanx called the People. We know today, however, that outside the machine, the legislative body, the bureaucracy, and the judiciary, there are great organized bodies of electors in a permanent state of tension, mutually restraining one another, and that the problem of moderation is, in our own day, formulable and soluble only in terms of them.

Here again dictatorial governments, by establishing the monopoly of a single political party and forbidding voluntary associations, accentuate the consequences of a lack of separation of powers inside the internal organization of the organs of the state and render themselves at once capable of swift action and of arbitrary and irresponsible decisions.

Montesquieu, like the rest of that splendid line of liberal thinkers who preceded him, thought in terms of the state, or all the people, or the king, or an aristocracy, as a distinct entity confronting an individual, the citizen. This antithesis resulted from a temporary historical situation when governments were still in the coercive and exploitive states, and from the ascription to these badly understood entities of a power which, in fact, they mainly executed as the agents of other men and groups. Nevertheless, it was a convenient, a striking, and a useful antithesis; nothing could be better calculated to win the support of every man against despotism. But it had a bad effect, because of its untrue basis, in converting all discussion of government into one of despotism, and in making freedom from the state—*dissociation*—appear the beneficent ideal. It was an effective solvent, but as a creative agent it was deficient. It served well, however, in Montesquieu's time and for three quarters of a century thereafter.

The Historical Setting of Montesquieu's Theory need not occupy us long, although it invests the subject with more significance. France was a monarchy, in which authority was shared between a hereditary king and the *Parlements*. The *Parlements* were superior courts of justice with administrative functions, and they had the power to *register*: that is, officially to take cognizance of, royal decrees, as the basis of their judgments and executive acts, and to remonstrate with the Crown if such decrees, of general or fiscal nature, displeased them. The king and his friends insisted that the power of the *Parlements* was bestowed by, and held at, the royal grace; the *Parlements* argued that their power was at least as old as the king's, having been derived from the original meetings of followers with elected chieftains on the *champs de mars* or *de mai*. No one knew or knows the real truth, as with any institutions which have invisibly added power to power in the course of a thousand years and through vicissitudes during which other institutions have insensibly declined. Each of the pretenders caused its own history to be written, and it is enough that the *Parlements* were a check upon the Crown. The *Parlements* were not parliaments; that is, they were not full legislative bodies with the power to propose, discuss, and make laws or, as in England, openly to control the activities and purse of the executive. Nor were they popularly elected. They were, in the main, courts of justice and controllers of certain aspects of administration (like the censorship), with powers of protest against the Crown's legislative activities, but without the power to ask for an account from the Crown's ministers. Moreover, they were composed of judges, notaries, and other officers who had purchased their offices.

Now these were the only barriers between monarchy in Montesquieu's sense —that is, the moderate rule of one—and despotism—or the reckless willful rule of one. They were not quite so liberal as Montesquieu, they were not specially competent, they were not representative by election, and they had no general community of interest with the people, not even with the general body of the Third Estate. They were of the middle and the upper nobility—the Nobility of the Robe. But they were men fully conscious of their worth, of their power, and of the need for a restraint upon despotism, and they were the natural representative of the upper strata of the Third Estate, whose members gravitated from their rich bourgeois commercial and industrial life into a powerful, brilliant, and respected profession. As such, they, when fighting against the king, sometimes fought for the people, and at least promised the security and exemption from anxious uncertainty provided by a settled procedure based upon uniform, if not excellent, principles. Montesquieu's family was of the magistrature,[12] and he himself was presented with a "parliamentary" living.

Montesquieu was searching for means to limit the Crown; to make a constitution; to build canals through which, but not over which, power should stream; to create "intermediary bodies;" to check and balance probable despotism and yet he did not wish to fly to the extreme of democracy. Hence he saw great value in these *Parlements*, and especially defended the purchase and inheritance of offices, because they created a really independent body—independent in interest, not seeking to rise—but resolved upon its privileges. In these terms, also, did the magistracy defend themselves, liberally borrowing from Montesquieu when their privileges were attacked by Maupeou and Louis XV.[13] Montesquieu's spiritual need,

his environment, and his travels and study in England produced the solution we have just discussed. But a *threefold* separation was not essential to his plans; nor was he trying to discover scientifically the nature of each different power; nor did he define them once and for ever. As with all thinkers who are concerned to influence action, everything was grist to his mill, but the product was not of permanent value.

Indeed, we know that it was fostered by an inquiry into English government in the middle of the eighteenth century, and tinctured with Locke's theory of government. English government seemed to Montesquieu to offer the guarantees of individual freedom. Locke was devoted to it, and passage after passage of Locke and Montesquieu read word for word almost the same.[14]

Montesquieu follows Locke, but with more system, and it is important to observe that he never thinks to separate the powers completely, but rather to modify the concentration of powers. Moreover, to have insisted too emphatically upon complete separation would have meant, in his France, surgical action upon the *Parlements,* similar to that undertaken on the County Quarter Sessions by the County Councils Act of 1888 in England and Wales; a severance of judicial from administrative functions. But for Montesquieu, the executive convenes the legislature, states its duration, and restrains its encroachments; it may veto legislation lest it be stripped of its prerogative. The legislature has the right of impeachment: "If it has no power in a free state to stay the executive, it has the right and ought to have the means of examining in what manner its laws have been executed." It may not arraign the chief of state—but, "as the person intrusted with the executive power cannot abuse it without bad counsellors, and such as have the laws as ministers, though the laws protect them as subjects, these men may be examined and punished." He has thus not gone be-

---

12 A. Sorel, *Montesquieu* (Paris, 1921).
13 Cf. Ernest Lavisse, *Histoire de France . . . Jusqu'à la Révolution* (Paris, 1900), Vol. IX, Part I, Book I, Chap. I; E. Carcassonne, *Montesquieu et le Problème de la Constitution Française au XVIII Siècle* (Paris, 1926).
14 *Esprit des Lois,* Book XI, 6.

yond the idea of impeachment to that of the political responsibility of ministers.

Now Montesquieu had laid weight upon institutions: but he had equally declared that these were only the product of a free and moderate spirit. The institutions, however, were crystallized in a book, and indiscriminately adulated by liberty lovers. The object is addled, but people continue to adulate. Allowing twenty years for the general vulgarization of the *Esprit des Lois,* it would be in 1768 or thereabouts that educated people were reading it as a conscious part of education. To people born soon after that time, it would already be assuming the importance of a classic, without yet being left on the shelves as taken for granted. Small wonder that it had such an influence upon the Frenchmen of the Revolution and upon the Fathers of the American Constitution. They seized upon the institutional arrangement, but did not, and could not, recapture the spirit which had brought it to Montesquieu's attention and caused its creation in its native land, where it was supposed to work such daily wonders. Of this, more presently.

It seems to me that Montesquieu gazed upon his work and found it pretty rather than practicable. For he suddenly exclaims:

These three powers [here he means only the two parts of the legislative plus the executive] should bring about a state of repose or inaction. But since, by the necessary movement of things, they are obliged to move, they will be forced to move in concert." [15]

That second sentence sounds like an improvisation which skips many difficulties to save the trouble of disturbing a handsome scheme. Every honest political scientist will admit such temptations; and sometimes their very beauty utterly arrests thought. Let us observe that Montesquieu has avoided the problem of whether the speed and the direction of governmental movement will be appropriate to the needs of society. Nor does he explain exactly how the harmony among the powers, admittedly so necessary, will be produced.

[15] *Idem.*

Perhaps the small amount of creative governmental work of his time in comparison with our own did not raise these problems; and certainly he was a supporter of free industry and commerce. If that is a good excuse for his failure, it is also one for treating it very critically in relation to our time. For it drew the United States into a system of government of which one may say at the best that the people are happy in spite of it, and it has produced a crop of erroneous theories in relation to other countries. One thing we may add to palliate that abdication of Montesquieu's: at any rate he recognized that government must act "by the necessary movement of things."

The United States and Montesquieu's Theory. We shall never know whether the Fathers of the American constitution established the separation of powers from the influence of the theory, or to accomplish the immediately practical task of safeguarding liberty and property. They positively desired liberty in the sense enunciated by Montesquieu, and they also desired limits upon despotism; certainly they were permeated by his theory. And just as certainly property played a greater role with them than it did to the more spiritual and moderate Montesquieu, who had conceived of political well-being as based upon equal properties of small dimensions, used frugally. Whatever the respective weights of the influence of the antidemocratic and antidespotic tendencies in the Philadelphia Convention, the American constitution was consciously and elaborately made an essay in the separation of powers and is today the most important polity in the world which operates upon that principle.

As we shall presently indicate, the American constitution did not generally declare that powers ought to be separate. It had not, in the American phrase, a "distributing clause," [16] nor did it produce a

[16] As was done in some state constitutions of the time: for example, Maryland, Virginia, Massachusetts, New Hampshire. Cf. Massachusetts constitution of 1780, article XXX: "In the government of this commonwealth the legislative department shall never exercise the

clean severance, for that would have been to make government impossible. However, by certain internal checks and balances the constitution succeeded in making government next to impossible. The demands of those who believed they saw in the constitution the rise of a new despotism called forth a famous reply from James Madison, which we must analyze.[17] He pays his tribute to Montesquieu, "the oracle who is always consulted and cited on this subject," and then observes that in numerous and important ways, the departments of government in the British constitution are, by Montesquieu's "standard," not totally separate and distinct from each other, and concludes that a partial agency was permissible and not subversive of liberty, though a concentration of power in one body was. That "power is of an encroaching nature" was admitted; but in the present case was not the legislature to be more feared than the executive? In fact "the legislative department is everywhere extending the sphere of its activity, and drawing all power into its impetuous vortex." [18]

This is where the shoe pinched in the American states: this should be the object of fear and control. For a representative body can feel the passions which actuate a multitude and is small enough to be able rationally to make the plans to satisfy those passions.[19] The other powers, the executive and judiciary, can by their nature be carefully described; not so the legislature, for who can precisely define legislation? Further, legislatures can acquire power over executive officials through their control of the purse. Proofs are given from a number of states. Thus, there must be real, as distinct from mere paper, checks upon encroachment. What

can these be? Jefferson suggests an appeal to the people when any two of the three branches consider that there is need to correct a breach of the constitution. Madison, however, fears that frequent appeals to the people to correct defects in government must deprive it of veneration and stability, that ordinarily men acting in large masses will cause ignorant prejudices to rule, that the public tranquillity would too often be disturbed, and, finally, that the legislature would triumph in all contests by the same influences which won it its election.

What then? What expedient can be devised to maintain, in practice, the necessary partition of power among the several departments?

The only answer that can be given is, that as all these exterior provisions are found to be inadequate, the defect must be supplied, by so contriving the interior structure of the government as that its several constituent parts may by their mutual relations, be the means of keeping each other in their proper place.[20]

The principle to be followed is to contrive that "each department should have a will of its own." From this it follows that the members of each department should have as little share as possible in the appointment of members of the others. But this cannot be pressed too far; otherwise it will end in election by the people, manifestly bad in the case of judges, who, in any event, became independent by their permanent tenure.

The principal means against the concentration of powers is to provide the constitutional means and the personal motive necessary to each department's self-defense. The truth may grieve, but the truth is that ambition inexorably threatens. Nor can mere popular control suffice.

You cannot give each department an *equal* power of self-defense. As the legislative authority predominates, divide it, give the two chambers different modes of election and different principles of action! Give the executive a negative on the legislature, but not an absolute negative! It

---

executive and judicial powers or either of them; the executive shall never exercise the legislative and judicial powers or either of them; the judicial shall never exercise the legislative and executive powers or either of them: to the end it may be a government of laws and not of men."

[17] *The Federalist,* XLVII.

[18] This was a universal complaint of the time in America.

[19] Cf. *The Federalist,* XLVII (Everyman edition), p. 253.

[20] Cf. *The Federalist,* LI, para. 1.

must be remembered also that in a federal government, the associated governments control each other. More, a popular suffrage combined with the vast extent and varied range of the territory of the United States provided that different interests shall check each other and prevent the easy formation of a homogeneous, and hence a tyrannical, majority.

In a free government the security for civil rights must be the same as that for religious rights. It consists in the one case in the multiplicity of interests, and in the other in the multiplicity of sects. The degree of security in both cases will depend on the number of interests and sects; and this may be presumed to depend on the extent of country and people comprehended under the same government.[21]

Madison's argument has been proved true by the experience of the United States. Only one doubt arises: whether it has not proved to be too true; for it has, indeed, thrown government into alternating conditions of coma and convulsion. It is possible to have so many and various interests included in a single state that a majority can never be obtained, while forceful and cunning minorities always rule. This inability to act swiftly, and sometimes not at all, was one of the very effective arguments of the growing nazi movement against the Weimar constitution, to which reference is made further in chapter 8.

In the United States constitution, powers were thus distributed: legislative powers ("herein enumerated") were vested in Congress, the executive power in the President, and the judicial in the courts. Congress was divided into two bodies, each elected for different periods and by different modes, the first having a biennial tenure with complete renewal, the second six-yearly tenure with partial renewals every two years. Their powers are different and check each other. The executive was to be dependent upon neither the legislature nor the people, nor was it to be fortified by popular election: hence a special electoral college was created. His own sphere was not to be his alone, for

the Fathers feared the executive, especially a *national* executive. Hence, the power of appointment of the chief officials was to be shared by President and Senate. Nor was the executive to have a free hand in treaty making; hence the assent of the Senate was required thereto. War and peace were to be declared by Congress. Officers with a place of profit under the United States government were excluded from membership of Congress; and though the executive may appoint officers who may act as a cabinet to him, neither he nor they may, by a convention of the constitution, appear on the floor of Congress.

Not all the objects which the Fathers [22] had in view have been realized, but their main intention, effectively to separate the powers, has been achieved; for they destroyed the concert of leadership in government, which is now so important in the present age of ministrant politics. They separated the executive sources of knowledge from the legislative center of their application; severed the connection between those who ask for supplies and those who have the power to grant them; introduced the continuous possibility of contest between two legislative branches; created in each the necessity for separate leadership in their separate business; and made this leadership independent of the existence and functions of the executive. Legislative procedure has come to differ essentially from that in Britain and France; financial procedure is worlds apart; there is no coordination of political energy or responsibility; but each branch has its own derivation and its morsel of responsibility. All is designed to check the majority, and the end is achieved. At what cost? This we shall calculate, but not, unfortunately, in dollars, later.

UNITED STATES: PROBLEMS AND READJUSTMENTS

The problems arising in the United States as a result of the constitutionaliza-

---

21 *The Federalist*, LI, p. 263.

22 Cf. B. F. Wright, "Origin of the Separation of Powers in America," *Economica* (London, May, 1933), where American experience is correctly emphasized and theoretical influence perhaps overdisparaged.

tion of the theory of separation of powers have been very obstinate and have frustrated the modern social will. Particularly with the growth in extent and marked change in the technical nature of government control of the economy, have the legislative and executive arms of the government waged battles of jurisdiction. Congress, which in Franklin D. Roosevelt's administration was more cooperative than usual, constitutes a regular brake on executive policy. Where President and Congress are of different party or political philosophy, stalemates and compromises continually occur, the weapons being the executive veto power and Congressional refusal to legislate policies.

The independent regulatory commission [23] is the Congressional device to maintain a continuous expert appointed group in quasi-legislative authority over a specific segment of government economic control: for example, the Interstate Commerce Commission. Independent of the executive, the commission's purpose is to formulate in detail and enforce the standards set in the law, following its own uniform policy regardless of the President in office. Consequently, a President can be faced with a hostile commission which will stifle his plan of action or will frustrate his attempt to coordinate the commission's sphere with the rest of government policy.

Violent criticism and extensive litigation have revolved around the scope and powers wielded by these agencies and the departments. These administrative agencies, apparently, make their own laws, for in addition to rule making they have been empowered to judge and command individuals held to violate these same regulations. However, the courts have been particularly strict in requiring due process of law in procedural matters. They have considered as essential the parties' right to adequate notice, fair hearing, and the "findings" of fact as a basis for decision.

In addition, they have required "standards" to be established by Congress to limit the powers vested in administrative agencies. It is judicially considered unconstitutional for Congress to delegate the legislative powers delegated to it in article I, section 1, of the constitution. On this ground the Petroleum Code, for example, and, shortly afterward, the entire National Industrial Recovery Act, were declared invalid. The Supreme Court said in *Panama Refining* v. *Ryan* (293 U.S. 388) in 1935:

The Congress in section 9(c) [the clause held unconstitutional] thus declares no policy as to the transportation of the excess production. So far as this section is concerned, it gives to the President an unlimited authority to determine the policy and to lay down the prohibition, or not to lay it down, as he may see fit. . . .

And in the Schechter Poultry (NIRA) case:

Here is an attempted delegation not confined to any single act nor to any class or group of acts identified or described by reference to a standard. . . . This is delegation running riot.

However, the Court's subsequent policy has been to permit administrative rule making, provided the terms of the law are reasonably specific.

Such organizations as the American Bar Association, and commercial interests anxious to be free of government regulation, attempted to restrict administrative lawmaking and were influential in securing passage of the Walter-Logan Bill in 1940. Its main provisions were:

(1) Administrative rules were to be issued only after formal public hearings and were to be subject to judicial review through petition to the District of Columbia Court of Appeals.

(2) Regulatory agencies were to establish three-man interagency boards for formal quasi-judicial action on request of anyone aggrieved by any measure taken by an agency.

(3) Judicial review was to be expanded and systematized for all administrative orders.

President Roosevelt, who decisively vetoed the bill, declared that it would "place the entire function of government at the

[23] Cf. R. E. Cushman, *The Independent Regulatory Commission* (New York, 1941).

UNITED STATES: PROBLEMS AND READJUSTMENTS

mercy of never-ending lawsuits and subject all administrative acts and processes to the control of the judiciary." [24]

Nor did the Administration overlook the Supreme Court's adverse decisions on administrative procedures or the outcries of the industrial and commercial interests. The Attorney General's Committee on Administrative Procedure was appointed in 1939 to analyze current procedures and make recommendations, and published its report in January 1941. Later in this volume (Chap. 36) its proposals are noted, as well as the general significance of the Federal Administrative Procedure Act of 1946.[25]

About the time that the Walter-Logan Bill was being cogitated and discussed by Congress, Justice Harlan Stone, speaking for the Court majority in the first *United States* v. *Morgan* case (298 U.S. 468) in 1936, said:

In construing a statute setting up an administrative agency and providing for judicial review of its action, court and agency are not to be regarded as wholly independent and unrelated instrumentalities of justice, each acting in the performance of its prescribed statutory duty *without regard to the appropriate function of the other* in securing the plainly indicated objects of the statute. Court and agency are the means adopted to obtain the prescribed end, and, so far as their duties are defined by the words of the statute, those words should be construed so as to attain that end through coordinated action.

In the second case in 1941 (313 U.S. 409) Justice Frankfurter, speaking for the Court, said:

It will bear repeating that, although the administrative process has had a different development and pursues somewhat different ways from those of the courts, they are to be deemed collaborative instrumentalities of justice and the appropriate independence of each should be respected by the other.

This is very sound doctrine, and, perhaps because it seemed "that the Court now respected the finality of administra-

tive action" [26] the drive for statutory restraints of such action was resumed and to a large extent triumphed in the Act of 1946.

Perhaps no one has more clearly stated the case for the finality of action, and the immunity from judicial frustration, of the public official, acting of course in accordance with the statutes duly passed by an awake legislature, than President Roosevelt in his veto message on the Walter-Logan Bill. He said:

In addition to the lawyers, who see the administrative tribunal encroaching upon their exclusive prerogatives, there are powerful interests which are opposed to reforms that can only be made effective through the use of the administrative tribunal. Wherever a continuing series of controversies exists between a powerful and concentrated interest on one side and a *diversified mass of individuals, each of whose separate interests may be small,* on the other side, the only means of obtaining equality before the law has been to place the controversy in an administrative tribunal.

As the demands upon governmental machinery have changed since the end of the eighteenth century—and we have amply analyzed and accounted for that change—majorities instead of being detestable have become essential. As Montesquieu said: [27]

These three powers should bring about a state of repose or inaction. But since, by the necessary movement of things, they are obliged to move, they will be forced to move in concert.

The necessary movement of things in the United States has obliged the three powers to move. They cannot but move in concert since men abhor discord. And if concert cannot be obtained within the constitution it must—if movement is

---

[24] *Congressional Record,* December 18, 1940, 13943.
[25] See Chap. 36.

[26] For example, Justice Brandeis in *St. Joseph Stock Yards* v. *U.S.* (298 U.S. 38) said: "But supremacy of law does not demand that the correctness of every finding of fact to which the rule of law is to be applied shall be subject to review by a court. If it did, the power of courts to set aside findings of fact by an administrative tribunal would be broader than their power to set aside a jury's verdict. The Constitution contains no such command."
[27] *Esprit des Lois,* Book XI, 6.

really necessary—be obtained by something outside it, whether with complete or partial success. The indispensable institution has been found in the party system. That has tended to redistribute the authority divided by the constitution. Of its success and failure we speak later (part III).

Yet the mere existence of a separation of representative assembly, executive, and judiciary itself acts to disintegrate party government, which can never be sure of being in complete command of the three agencies of government at any one time. How much the party strains to achieve such a union of policy we have already observed earlier, in the close connection between political participation and the union of powers in the Soviet system.

The American system, which has been called "Congressional" government, is in very strong contrast to *European democratic systems, which have tacitly rejected the separation of powers, and indeed, deliberately coordinated them in the "cabinet system."* Briefly, the elements of the cabinet system are these. Functions are broadly divided between legislative, executive and judiciary. The judiciary is appointed, even as in the United States, by the executive, but on terms which render it practically an independent branch. The executive then falls into two parts—the ministerial or cabinet council, and the Crown or the presidency of the state. The latter has little independent political power. The cabinet is the creature of the legislative, but a creature which leads, nay, drives, its creator. It is not forbidden, but on the contrary is expected, to enter the legislature, and is often commanded to do so. There is thus a direct link between people, legislature, and executive: and as a rule they act in general unison, moved by the same tide of political feeling. The legislature is responsible to the people; the cabinet is responsible to the legislature and to the people. They are one body at different stages of leadership but in the straight line of ascent from the people. In the United States popular sovereignty operates by bifurcation and even trifurcation: it divides into channels which run parallel to each other but do not fully meet or mingle, but are connected by drawbridges.

THE SEPARATION OF POWERS: EUROPE AND BRITAIN

YET the Continent and England have not been and are not without an interest in the separation of powers. The theory began in France, and we can show that, though Rousseau moved the French towards revolution, Montesquieu governed the elaboration of France's early constitutions.[28] The French National Assembly of 1789 laid down the principle and divided the legislative from the executive power.[29] No compromises were permitted [30]—the decree-making power was refused to the executive—and it was resolved that no member of the National Assembly or future Parliaments should be made a minister within four years of the termination of his membership, or accept any office, gift, pension, salary, or commission from the executive. We need not, however, trace all the consequences of the principle in these constitutions. They broke down in 1793 before the onslaught of passionate revolutionary zeal which could not do its work quietly without a central control of all powers in the capital and at the extremities; they were readmitted in 1795; they fell at Napoleon's touch; and they were resuscitated in different forms in 1816, in 1830, in 1848, but not in 1875. But the revolutionary belief in the separation of powers has had one enduring result upon France—it caused her to deny, in her constitutions, the power of the courts of justice to declare a law made by the Chambers constitutionally invalid, and the power of the court to judge executive officials for a fault committed in and by reason of the public service; and the latter led directly to the creation of special administrative courts for such cases. Somewhat similarly in Germany; but quite otherwise in England.

---

[28] Cf. Robert Redslob, *Le Régime Parlementaire* (Paris, 1924).
[29] 1791, article III, 3, 4.
[30] Articles III, IV, VI, Sect. I.

Throughout the nineteenth century, there were those who argued that without the separation of powers there was no liberty. The clauses of the French constitution are not important to us, except that we may remember that in the constitution of 1875 the principle was no longer declared, and that in fact, that constitution adopted the cabinet system. The reason why the separation of powers was in various ways laid down until 1875, and the reasons why it is still demanded by some writers are, however, important. It is not that there was or is any special interest in the possibility of exactly and scientifically defining and severing the elements of governmental power. This occupation was strictly subordinate to the essential object: to secure such a balance and direction of governmental energies as comported with their social ideals. For let us be clear about one thing: the theories of the separation of powers are ultimately instrumental to some particular social design— the purpose of an individual reformer or of interested groups of classes—and theories of government, especially where they concern institutions, are the centers of will: desire produces will, and will is prior to institutions.

In France the idea of the separation of powers was soon used as a defense of the libertarians against the egalitarians. The difference between the consequences of the principle of liberty and of equalization forms the almost deliberate thesis of de Tocqueville's political philosophy. Considering democracy in America, he is tempted to this reflection: "Men desired to be free in order to be able to make themselves equal, and, in proportion as equality established itself with the aid of liberty, it made liberty more difficult for them." For equality being their principal care, they allowed the state to aggrandize itself, and men permitted their own degradation. How terrible the possible despotism! [31] Now, more than ever, is liberty the salvation of society,[32] not to destroy the democracy which reposes upon equality, for that is obviously the fulfillment of God's design, but to temper it, to make it a beneficent and not a fatal dispensation.[33] How secure liberty? Through legislature, liberty of the press, education, judicial independence, the recognition and guarantee of individual rights, and local and cultural corporations—institutions which will do in democracies what certain historical corporations had done in the old monarchy.

Nor has this strain disappeared from French political thought. The separation of powers has been demanded as a check upon the usurping tendencies of the parliamentary assemblies, which threaten both executive and society, but the arrangement is not now always called either independence or separation, but reciprocity. There was obviously a desire to exalt the executive in order to stay the equalitarian legislation of the Chambers. To another writer the problem appeared as that of the individual against the state, "that is to say, the great question of liberty itself," and the solution—the abolition of executive and legislative influence in the administration of justice, and the establishment of judicial control of the constitutionality of laws and administration (on the American model)—was reiterated after twenty-five years' experience of French politics.[34] Another, who was but a single example of many, deplores "parlementocratie" and the "confusion of powers"—and this was because parliamentary powers and behavior were feared as "anarchic," while the nonexistence of a popularly elected executive was said to offer no check to the "fatal enslavement of the people to the assemblies." [35] What was behind this? We once more come upon the struggle between economic equality and political liberty.

---

[31] Cf. A. de Tocqueville, *Democracy in America*, trans. by H. Reeve (London, 1889), 2 vols., Vol. I, Chap. XVI, p. 275, and Vol. II, Book IV. (There also is now available the Bradley edition, New York, 1946.)

[32] *Ibid.*, Vol. II, p. 301.
[33] *Ibid.*, Preface. Cf. also S. de Ruggiero, *The History of European Liberalism* (London, 1927), p. 197.
[34] Charles Benoist, *Les Lois de la Politique Francaise* (Paris, 1927).
[35] Jules Roche, *Quand Sérons Nous un République?* (Paris, 1918).

Nothing is more contrary to the spirit of the French Revolution, to the unanimous conception of the Republic, from its origin down to the recent times, when the retrograde spirit of Socialism commenced to pervert and ruin it, to substitute for the noble and fecund principle of liberty, of initiative, of individual responsibility, a truly collective regime, in anticipation of an absolute collectivist despotism which draws near.[36]

In the sessions of the constitutional committee and the debates of the constituent assemblies of 1945 and 1946, the French Communist party took an extreme course on every topic concerning the separation of powers, while the other parties were moderate on the subject, becoming strongly in favor with the M.R.P. and the Radical-Socialists, rightwards. On the supremacy of the party over its members, the supremacy of the legislature over the executive, the right to recall the deputies, the powerlessness of the titular chief of state, the right of pardon, and the supreme control over the judiciary, the Communist party expressed the most decided sentiments in favor of the unlimited domination of the legislative body, one and indivisible, not even accepting popular recall but leaving the latter to be exercised by the party's discipline over its members. The Communist party, with the aid of the Socialist party, was largely successful in securing the practical predominance of the National Assembly over all powers: its steady argument was reminiscent of the Russian Communist cry, "All power to the Soviets!", and its slogan was "All power to the people, through their party and the National Assembly!" The flavor of the majority's view, expressed by the *rapporteur,* a member of the M.R.P., may be gauged from this quotation from his report: [37]

To a presidential system founded on the absolute separation of powers [he was thinking of the United States constitution] is opposed government by the assembly established on the basis of the confusion of powers. It is said by some, that sovereignty is one; it resides wholly in the people: and as in so big a country as

France, the people cannot themselves possibly exercise their sovereignty; it is unavoidable that they delegate it to their representatives. Sovereignty being one, it cannot be delegated except in its entirety. Therefore, the three functions, legislative, executive, and judicial, must in their integrity be delegated to a single-chambered and sovereign assembly which the people is called on to elect.

"Such a system of government," as the rapporteur of the draft of April 19 wrote, "is adapted to the exigencies of revolutionary action because it is in some sort destined for revolutionary periods, and because France does *not* find herself in a revolutionary period, there cannot even be a question of proposing it to the constituent assembly. To repeat Robespierre's words, the France of 1946 needs a constitutional government."

Opposed to this is a phrase of the leading Communist member of the constitutional committee—he let it slip and wished later to retract. He said: "I think, differently from M. Capitant, who believes that certain principles exist over and above national sovereignty—that above this sovereignty there is nothing." [38]

It might be added here that in the Vyshinsky treatise on Soviet constitutional law (referred to above, p. 85), it is untruthfully asserted that in the United States and Europe, the separation of powers had always masked but never prevented the real predominance of the executive—a deliberate bourgeois trick!

When dealing with American practices arising out of the theory of separation of powers, we noticed the comparative recency of agencies (the independent regulatory commissions) which, not being law courts, have nevertheless been given a judicial kind of authority over the interpretation of the law. Yet it should be noticed that one consequence of the theory of separation of powers in France was the establishment of administrative courts culminating in the *Conseil d'État,* which for many decades have had exclusive jurisdiction over actions by citizens against misuse of official power by local or central officials, extending to *ultra vires* cases as

---

[36] *Ibid.,* p. 197.
[37] *Assemblée, Séance,* August 2, 1946, *annexe.*

[38] *Séances, Commission de la Constitution,* p. 36, December 5, 1945.

well as actions where the public authorities—for example, municipalities—are in conflict among themselves or with the central government. The subject is pursued further in later chapters.[39]

It is not necessary to multiply examples. The facts are clear. Many people and political parties [40] are afraid that without checks and balances in government, liberty will disappear. A similar development is apparent in German constitutional history [41] and in English. What caused the creation of the theory and the political demand? In every case there is a specific reason or group of reasons for fearing the intervention of government. Up to and in the eighteenth century it was fear of monarchical despotism, by the upper and lower classes. In the nineteenth century it was for the same classes in Germany the only hope of fettering absolute monarchy. In all countries today it is the desire of the economically prosperous classes or of private enterprise and its academic and other defenders to preserve themselves against the collectivist, egalitarian, and regulative tendency of democracy, and of the more patient, bourgeois, working-class leaders to attempt a synthesis of the liberal with the socialistic state. They desire at once dissociation from the state and an ordered regular procedure (preferably judicial) for the determination of the extent of their political obligations, whether merely imposed by the state or self-acknowledged.

But there is no such enthusiasm for checks and balances among those who are impatient to create a new social order, or sternly to maintain an old one, where, for example, the courts of justice show themselves imbued with a spirit of opposition to the executive. The bolshevik theory confounded all powers: so equally did the fascist system; so did the nazi system. The latter, like the Soviet system, destroyed the separation of powers by reducing legislation to a formality, by seizing power to make ordinances which had the force of law, even if such laws amended the constitution. Further, it seized the power of the appointment of and pressure on the judiciary and the complete subordination of the civil service system to the *Führer* himself.[42] All civil service associations were forcibly made a wing of the Nazi party. It is interesting to note that it was difficult for the Nazi government entirely to subjugate the judiciary.

Without any doubt, a powerful connection subsists between the economic and social status of the writer's group and his theories. Some people attempt to escape governmental control, and therefore demand the accumulation of courts of appeal of all kinds before they can be seized. Others, needing the help of government, can prove from that hypothesis that there ought not be any scruples about swift and immediate action. Everything depends upon what kind of moral sovereign good is worshipped. It is not necessary for the political scientist to have inquired into the separation of powers further than to have arrived at this result: whether we wish a separation of powers, and in what particular institutional form it is to be embodied, depends upon what general political needs we feel to be really urgent. That is to say, there is nothing absolutely inherent in the nature of different functions, nothing eternal and unchangeable, which will settle the question whether there ought to be a separation of powers, and if so, in what it should consist. The answer is relative to one's needs, and to the organization, procedure, and mentality of the institutions as they actually function. Yet even after conflict has removed hereditary coercions and privileges, by destroying or permeating the separated powers when these are hostile to those at a disadvantage, and even when society embodies more equal law, the newly desired relationship of the individual to the whole community will im-

---

[39] See Chap. 36.
[40] Henri Leyret, *Le Gouvernement et le Parlement* (Paris, 1918), and *Le Président de La République* (Paris, 1913); Charles Benoist, *La Réforme Parlementaire* (Paris, 1902), p. 201; Jules Roche, *op. cit.*
[41] Cf. S. de Ruggiero, *op. cit.*, p. 251 ff.

[42] See Chap. 25.

pose some newly appropriate separation of powers.

The Fall of the Triad of Powers. We cannot, however, leave the subject at this point, for there are two questions to consider. The *first* is the possibility of separating powers distinctly by reference to their specific qualities, and the *second* is, how are powers actually differentiated—not separated!—in modern democracies?

I will not answer the first question by detailed examination of the old triad of powers. In recent years the triad has been much attacked by theoretical writers, and has been proved by actual experience to be untenable. It has been shown, broadly, that the legislature does not always concern itself with the establishment of general policy, but often makes exceedingly detailed and specific rules concerning departmental and local organization and functions, and thus performs work to which only the technical knowledge of professional civil servants is adequate. Again, it is shown that the legislative body allows more and more scope to the executive to fill in large empty areas in the statutes, and that this rule making is no more or less than "secondary" or "subordinate" legislation—that is, general rules with the supreme binding authority of statute.

With the growth in the quantity and technical nature of the subject matter of legislation, and the need for flexibility and continuity in administration of the program, delegation of extensive powers to administrative agencies has become widespread. Quasi-legislation has two basic variants: the promulgation of general rules and regulations, sometimes called sublegislation or rule making; and the issuance of orders, entailing application of the standards to specific cases of enforcement.

The administrative departments are given judicial powers by statute—powers to judge of complicated situations of fact and public policy as they concern individuals and associations—from which there may or may not be appeal to the law courts. And, finally, the law courts add to or take away from the statutory law, or from the executive power, by their judgments. The analyses have proceeded to considerable depth, and we need not reproduce them.

The principal criterion is regarding the danger to individual liberty of allowing an administrative system—the servants of the chief executive—to undertake the functions of lawmaking and the administration of justice, with the finality which the responsibility entrusted to the administrative branch requires if the law is to become a social force.[43]

That is the sum and substance of the modern interest in the supremacy of law and in administrative law, and it is a direct consequence of the development of state activity since the 1870's. Originally the despotism of the Crown was feared and attacked; later the despotism of Parliaments and Congress was feared and attacked; now, in the twentieth century, the alleged enemy is the mighty corps of civil servants sometimes maligned as the "bureaucracy."

There is no longer any virtue in the triad, except as a provisional scheme. We must discover some other rough differentiation of the functions and organs of government. When we have done that, we may inquire briefly into their nature and into the extent to which modern policy demands their interaction. Let us always remember also that the political utility of any power—legislative or executive or judicial—does not depend upon its own nature but upon the mentality and procedure of the body which exercises it, and that this mentality depends upon its appointment, its training, and its working conditions.

---

[43] Cf. Milton Katz, *Cases in Administrative Law* (St. Paul, 1947), pp. 752 ff.; and James K. Hart, *Introduction to Administrative Law* (New York, 1940), Chap. 16.

7

A More Scientific Understanding of Powers

IF we observe the operation of modern government, regardless of any division of powers among different organs, we see that to a complete act of government two things are necessary: to resolve and to execute: that is, to determine that certain things shall be done and then to cause people to do them. If we apply this division to political activity, we see that the centers of the first—the resolving branch —are the electorate, the political parties, the legislature (Parliament or Congress), the cabinet, and the chief of state; and that the centers of the second—the executive branch—are the cabinet, the chief of state, the civil service, and the courts of justice. That is to say, there are seven main centers of political activity, the co-operation of which is necessary to produce a complete act of government.

The seven are, in practice, interlocking and essential to each other, though there may be jealousy and distrust among their actual personnel. Without the parties, the electorate would be a mass of men and women in a nasty state of nature, though I am far from saying that even with them the electorate is in any country as yet much beyond such a state. The electorate has its contact with the legislature through the constituencies, by-elections, lobbyists, and deputations. Legislatures today are little more than the political parties in conference specially organized by party meetings, caucuses, and the whips. The cabinet is, on the resolving side, interlocked with the electorate, with the par-

ties, and with the legislature, and obtains from the civil servants the expert material for initiating or handling discussions and resolutions. On the executive side, it is in touch with the chief of state; it controls, and is guided by, the professional administrators; and it appoints the judges of the law courts, having, also, its own legal counsel from bar and bench. The chief of state is (with the exception of Great Britain) in touch with the electorate, being elected either directly or by the legislature. The civil service is not entirely out of touch with the public: it is reached by deputations and aided by consultations, advisory councils, and its public relations departments. The courts of law are not entirely out of touch with the development of civilized needs, and for a very large part of their time they apply laws made by the factors we have already indicated; yet they also exercise a moderating effect upon the law, because they apply certain extrastatutory juridical principles, substantive and interpretary. In practice, the interlocking relationship we have sketched is even closer than indicated; but these are the main elements which cooperate in government.

The Electorate. This is an amalgam of individuals and groups, a seething mass of uncoordinated and often hostile wants. It is now recognized as the sovereign body in most constitutions and political theories; some deny that it ought to have limits, while others—the minority—urge that it ought not to be despotic, and they demand its self-limitation by reference to some moral standard. Whatever the literary theory of popular sovereignty, the power of the people is, in fact, limited by their ignorance, their conventions, their monetary resources, their apathy or their nonpolitical preoccupations, and the constitutional forms through which they operate, established before the advent of popular sovereignty and limiting it.

It is idle to speculate upon what this power—the electorate—would be without restraint and without the existence of party organization to lead, educate, and control it. This, however, is certain: democracy would be either impotent or destructive. And by destructive I mean that it would force men and things to actions which would cause their breakdown, so that not only would the objective not be obtained, but the energies and powers would be dissipated: the usual fate of ignorant attempts to use a complex machine. If we reflect upon the intricacy and worldwide range of modern government, domestic and international, we can understand at once that even the present amount of common sense and education in the majority, and even the present state of morality, including such things as popular notions of justice, decency, and prudence, need a remarkably long, careful, and intensive cultivation before the people will be able to do more than choose between two or three broad alternatives put before them in the form of party candidates. The demonic mightiness of the Sovereign People, combined with the relative incompetence of mere men and women, leads those who care for equity, order, and certainty to require specialized and skilled institutions to obstruct and sift the awful avalanche of its intentions. None more than the people themselves desire this.

Party and Legislature. The institution most immediately and continuously in contact with the people is the party. Its function is to organize the voters in the hope of a majority, or at least of a formidable opposition, and to control the creation and execution of policy, principally through legislature. Competition between parties already imposes upon them a certain amount of discipline and training for their task. In proportion as the plenitude of sovereignty is open to their acquisition, each vote is of supreme importance, none can be ignored, and since the achievement of power is frequently contingent upon the turnover of a small proportion of votes, here is a powerful tonic to political organization and energy. Conflict and contact with other parties fosters a knowledge of others and reveals one's self. Some technical knowledge of the whole field of government must be obtained. It is impossible to distort the truth either as to past services or future promises beyond certain bounds, for fear of public exposure. Reciprocity in debate leads to settled and rational rules of procedure. Corporate life and personal contacts in an assembly produce a conciliatory attitude, which is fostered by the traditions and usages of the assembly. The payment of members has made it possible for the less acquisitive to devote themselves entirely to their legislative duties. All these things promote party and legislative competence, and rational, considerate, and even tolerant principles.

Yet parties and legislatures are still in their infancy, and they have not yet solved those difficulties which now prevent them from being the proper center of all law and administration. The process of election depends upon the people, and despite the rivalry of the parties, which tends to lift the level of candidates, we are still far from a satisfactory solution of the main problem: to provide wise and competent representatives in a sufficient number and with sufficient time to fulfill their function as its technique demands. We have but said that within the electoral process of competition there are advantages obtainable by the operation of the party and the legislative system, but the level of the electorate and of the bulk of the members of different parties may cause, and in modern states in varying degrees does cause, such imperfections in the legislative body that if one more straw were put upon its back, disaster would follow certainly and swiftly.

What the elected representatives of the people may do, or ought to do, depends very largely upon what they *can* do. This is the clear lesson to be drawn from the hearings and report of the Joint Committee on the Reorganization of Congress, of 1945–46;[1] from the decade of the 1930's in France; and from the British Committee on the Procedure of the House of Commons of 1945.[2] To judge representatives now, and for a generation hence, they can no more than legislate by stating their personal, group, and local opinions of the projects of their leaders. Neither they nor their leaders are able to make the technical calculations and surveys upon which bills are founded, nor are they able to throw a bill into the form which will express their intentions with the least vagueness, having regard to the trouble which would follow if the clauses were not phrased conformably to other laws and the meanings already accepted by the courts and in common transactions. Nor, if the repeal of other laws is consequent upon the new statute, do members know enough about either the statute book or the state of the law, as made and administered in the courts or by the administration, to be able to act without skilled guidance. Further, it is of course possible within limits for representatives to inquire into administration: the function is important and possible, and one, furthermore, which can with advantage be extended beyond present limits, for to question is to alarm, and to alarm is to control and reform. They may also educate the public by their debates, and may express the doubts and aspirations of all interests. However, all this can be done only generally: for time is pressing, and numbers, for the sake of reasonable discussion in a full assembly, must be small. It is quite certain that when it comes to the constant and daily application of these general rules and intentions to a multitude of objects and citizens, the member has neither the necessary time, technique, patience, application, or interest. Some

other bodies must assist until such time as the legislature is appropriately constituted.

The chief function of legislatures is to establish statutes. A statute is a stage in the process of government, midway between the original desires of the people for social change and the governmental effectuation of those desires. If the statute concludes the legislative stage, it opens the administrative. A statute is a vital contribution to the process of administration, for it defines the permissible range of discretion and power available to the administration, and if it does not do this with clarity and precision, the administrative process itself is confused and both the public and the legislature may consequently be frustrated.

The Cabinet and President. The cabinet in the United States (the President and his advisers) or the Council of Ministers, as it is called in the Continental systems, consists of a small number of people: usually members of the legislative assembly (though not so in the United States system) and the leaders of the majority party or parties, acting as the supreme chiefs of the various administrative departments. It is at this point that the legislature comes into direct contact with the administration and with the law courts, exerting its guiding and creative influence freely upon the one and in a much lesser degree upon the other, superintending the conversion of laws into behavior in accordance with the wish of the majority, and using the administration as aid and counsel in the technical preparation of policy for introduction, explanation, and defense before the legislature and the country. Through this body the legislature and the electorate are improved by expert knowledge, and the permanent officials are energized and controlled.

The Administration and the Courts of Justice. On the other side of the cabinet looms the vast apparatus of administration, the machine for the concrete application of general principles to particular cases. There is nothing in the nature of administration which demands that it shall be divided into several departments or

---

[1] See Chap. 20.
[2] *Idem.*

that it shall be divided between the centers and the localities or, let us say, between departments and law courts—nothing at all, except considerations of utility depending upon the nature of the various subjects of administration, and the character of men's desires. Did we not observe that Locke's division of power was into legislative, executive, federative, the last being but executive action in foreign relations? This division was confusedly followed by Montesquieu, and the cause of his confusion was that he *wished* the law courts, much as he saw them in contemporary England and in France, to be bodies independent of the executive. Montesquieu's wish, however, cannot be our law, unless we find it convenient and proper for our own purposes. In fact, we see that the executive work of the state is divided broadly into the administrative and the judicial, but in no country was this (until the end of the eighteenth century in France and Prussia) the result of a conscious and systematic separation.

Our present institutions are the result of certain historical disputes about political power, in which the parties who wished to limit autocracy were able to secure, mainly by force or its threat, *first,* the creation of a special council of deliberation and resolution (the legislature) on a representative basis, and *second,* a special branch office to state the law when its meaning was vague or in dispute between individual and individual, and between individuals and the state. What was done is what some modern reformers wish to do: to institute special boards of appeal to which they may turn when they are troubled by the state (or by other people), and which are likely to be favorable to their claims, by virtue of their mentality, their deliberately designed opposition, their corporate conceit, and their forms of procedure. This was all the more necessary since the law is a special study, peculiarly difficult in the ages when practically all was customary law. We know why the executive grew so strong in the sixteenth century: men could not do without its strength, but they attempted—at least the powerful attempted—to confine the executive to what was strictly necessary to its admitted function. They could not allow the claims of policy—the *raison d'état*—to a fitful, uncertain, and secret prerogative. The executive must show due cause. How, and where? The answer was: before judges who were free from executive (royal) control.

It is clear that the execution of law involves two duties: judging the facts of a situation, and judging the relationship to the law. But what if the law is vague? Who shall judge between state and subject? That is one difficulty. A second is that the greater part of the law is concerned not with judging the state as a party, either as a recipient of duties from its members or as a donor of benefits to them, but with judging the claims of individuals and groups against each other. This was by far the largest part of the early jurisdiction of the courts, and is so even today.

Now, by a historical development which is of amazing interest but which is also so complex that we cannot follow it here, the courts in England and America (but not to such a degree in France or Germany) attracted to themselves: (1) all judgment between individual and individual, (2) judgments of crimes against the state, and (3) judgments rendered by the executive or by privileged corporations whenever these were challenged as outside their legal power. The courts obtained the power to challenge and rectify such judgments. The English method was extended to the United States, and even on the Continent, where the executive was much more resistant and where the administration had its own final jurisdiction, the courts of justice went far toward securing an extensive supremacy. This development proceeded until the last two generations, when the state assumed positive services and consequent duties were demanded from its citizens.

Little by little the latent and essential contest between the two branches of administration was revealed, for while the strictly administrative branch sought speed and efficiency, the courts were still the resorts of appeals, or the people—not yet having learnt that social duties are the price of social benefits—considered that they should be. By the "necessary movement of things" the courts were reviewing administration, and the administration was sitting in judgment, and each became resentful of the other's intrusion into a domain which had been existent long enough to be deemed "sacred," or which was considered so necessary to social salvation as to be "holy," while citizens were alternately terrified by stories of the "new bureaucracy" or the "new despotism" or "trial by Whitehall," and exalted by such policies as the demolition of slums, the stamping out of contagious diseases, and the extension of social services at lower than cost price.

What, in essence, is the dispute between the judicial and administrative branches?[3] It is a dispute about the comparative governmental merits of administrative action and judicial action, and the comparison (in England and America, at any rate) is usually made between the worst administrative and the best judicial practices. That, however, is not a scientific treatment of the problem, which is to compare the nature of the present work to be done and the best machinery which can be discovered to do it, and not to compare it simply with the machinery which has existed or now exists. Let us consider the two sorts of executive action as they now operate, and compare their merits and defects.

The administrative departments work within the broad limits set by the legislature, but these are today so broad that a large discretion resides in the departments. They exert a mighty power, for often the only appeal which can be made against the decision of an official is either to some higher official in the department itself, where the case may not be fairly judged, or to the courts, where the procedure may

be so complicated and costly in money and time that it is cheaper to the complainant to suffer the wrong than seek the remedy. Or, again, a question might be asked in the legislature, but lack of time, as well as ministerial equivocation fertilized by departmental ingenuity, may cause the denial of justice. An unaccountable power may be an unnecessarily cruel power.

What contributes to the possibility of departmental injustice? *First,* the personal desire to dominate, since what is to be done is a personal duty of the office and officers, to be carried through successfully. In their discussion of this question—namely, whether departmental powers and the rule of law were being strained—the famous British Report of the Committee on Ministers' Powers (1932), based upon an investigation into the charges of despotic behavior, made much of the potential trouble which might result from the very zeal of officials. Thus:

Indeed, we think it is clear that bias from strong and sincere conviction as to public policy may operate as a more serious disqualification than pecuniary interest. . . . No honest man acting in a judicial capacity allows himself to be influenced by pecuniary interest; if anything, the danger is likely to be that through fear of yielding to motives of self-interest he may unconsciously do an injustice to the party with which his pecuniary interest may appear to others to identify him. But the bias to which a public-spirited man is subjected if he adjudicates in any case in which he is interested on public grounds is more subtle and less easy for him to detect and register.

Second, the career depends upon success or failure, not quite so often as in private industry, but to an extent which is important here. *Third,* corporate defensiveness and sense of colleagueship take away from the value of an appeal to a superior officer. *Fourth,* administration is at present a rather secret process, some things not being recorded at all while other things are recorded but not published. Hence decision may be arbitrary, and secrecy, in any case, produces a reputation for arbitrariness. *Fifth,* there is

[3] Cf. C. K. Allen, *Law and Orders* (London, 1946); W. A. Robson, *Justice and Administrative Law,* 2nd edition (London, 1947); John Dickinson, *Administrative Justice and the Supremacy of Law* (Harvard, 1927); Charles E. Wyzanski, "The Trend of the Law and its Impact on Legal Education," *Harvard Law Review* (1944), p. 51 ff.; and J. M. Landis, *The Administrative Process* (Yale, 1938).

lacking a body of rules for training officials, and a code of duties and behavior, obligatory, certain, public, and enforceable, to secure the proper poise between efficient innovation and scrupulous regard for the rights of individuals and groups. The elaboration and establishment of such a theory and code is only in the process of being considered.

But those who sit in judgment, especially when there is no right of appeal, should be circumspect, wise, considerate, scrupulous in regard to every trifle of evidence, and personally disinterested, save to secure an equitable result as between complainants or defendants and the large body of citizens and social groups who, though they do not appear, are, in effect, the other party.

Finally, the judgment is often not made by the person or persons who have conducted the investigation of the evidence, but by some other officer, upon report.

The Courts of Justice. These qualities the courts of law have in most cases possessed and displayed, for their whole procedure has been built up on the basis of impartial umpireship between two parties. They have had no personal interest in the result, for they are irremovable, exempted from suit for any fault; there is little question of promotion; and the acceptance of gifts is forbidden. (Exception must be made for certain elective judgeships in the United States.) Procedure makes the discovery and presentation of all evidence fully possible, and gives all parties the opportunity of stating their case with expert help. Proceedings are public; reports are published; records are kept; and precedents have weight. Moreover, the principles of the law, as they are taught, include these things; they are revered; and though (in Britain, America, and the British Domains) there is no special training for judgeships, there is in the law. In the use of this law for attack or defense, counsel comes before a court with strict etiquette, presided over by justices who jealously guard the traditional morals of the profession. These things produce definite principles which all may know with considerable certainty, and a

process and convention of impartial and impersonal attention to the claims of the parties.[4]

When, however, the administration of justice is considered simply as a branch of government, these very advantages are observed to hide certain disadvantages. *First,* the courts move only as a remedial and not as a preventive machine, being concerned with cases when they arise and are presented, and not with the wholesale calculation and independent prevention of future contingencies. Control of trusts in the United States was weakened until recently by the attempt to administer control through the courts. In the judicial process, the initiative which sets the train for authoritative decision belongs to individuals and may never come or may come too late; in the administrative process, it is vested in officers definitely charged with forethought. *Second,* insofar as "public policy" is concerned, the court of law either may not be able to judge properly of the issues concerned, as it does not know the nature of various governmental factors involved, or may not be equipped to measure the facts with the quantitative exactness necessary for certain decisions. Chief Justice William Howard Taft, of the Supreme Court of the United States, believed he could find a "yardstick" to measure "unfair" competition; experience showed he was wrong. *Further,* the method is not sufficiently elastic, for it is bound overmuch by precedent and the need for uniformity (to secure certainty) and so cannot meet every situation which confronts it with specific appropriateness and yet maintain its great virtue: namely, continuous uniformity and equality of application. *Finally,* the substance of the law administered by the British and American courts, largely the common law, is the produce of a bygone age, when society did, and needed to do, much less with and for the life of the individual than it does today. Almost, the common law was born to resist government authority; in the United States it was deliberately set above

---

[4] Cf. Lord Chief Justice Hewart, *The New Despotism* (London, 1929), p. 25 ff.

the Congress and the executive to resist them; it still resists. That is precisely why it now meets with the favor of the groups who wish to be defended from the hand of the government.

It is not desired to suggest that judges have no bias in social matters. When Justice Oliver Wendell Holmes referred to "the inarticulate major premise," he had in mind the judges' personal outlook on life. That is the product of their social and economic class, their education, and the company they keep. Nevertheless, their judgments are to a large extent controlled by their training and the other factors to which we have referred. Professor Harold Laski has commented: [5]

They [the canons of historic method] make the task of considering the relationship of statutes, especially in the realm of great social experiments, to the social welfare they are intended to promote one in which the end involved may easily become unduly narrowed, either by reason of the unconscious assumption of the judge, or because he is observing principles of interpretation devised to suit interests we are no longer concerned to protect in the same degree as formerly. . . . Legislation construed by the historic canons of analysis which our courts adopt is too often so interpreted as to defeat the real intention of the legislature.

Cases which he cites from English practice to demonstrate a political bias in judges do not, on careful reading, show this at all. They show, rather, an insistence by the courts that public authorities will not be credited with powers to spend unless

they have indubitably been given the statutory power to do so and to raise taxation for the purpose. Furthermore, it is doubtful whether his suggestion that the control of judicial interpretation could be secured by a preamble to each statute stating its objects could be effective. If the words of the statute are insufficient to direct a judge, why should it be thought that the language of a preamble would do better? If the language of the preamble were more general than that of the statute, there would be much more opportunity for judicial discretion. If the legislature is clear in its intentions and accurate in its language, the judge loses his opportunity of bias.

From this study of the separation of powers, we have derived these conclusions: that the doctrine has ever been made to defend certain spiritual and material values from the control of government; that Montesquieu's division was but rough and depended largely on local and temporary circumstances; that he himself realized that it could not be carried out with any exactness, and that such exact and distinct severance would mean entire inanition; that since all government is a single process, its division into parts, and their relative power, depend upon the purpose of government and the relative technical capacity of the various bodies of men and women who are employed in its realization. As we proceed further we shall see more clearly, because in more detail, the real nature of the various instruments of government. And first, of constitutions.

---

[5] Annex V, "Note on the Judicial Interpretation of Statutes," pp. 135-137.

8

Constitutions—The Institutional Fabric of the State

THE state is a human grouping in which rules a certain power relationship between its individual and associated constituents. This power relationship is embodied in political institutions. The system of fundamental political institutions is the constitution. As we have already said, a constitution is the autobiography of a power relationship.

DEFINITIONS

THIS definition of "constitution" leaves open the question of its form and substance, and it is well that the question should be left open, for modern constitutions exhibit such a wide variety of forms, and so marked a difference in their substance, that no definition of reasonable length can include the main facts. The discussion is, for convenience, to hinge upon the two principal terms of the definition: *system* and *fundamental*.

"*System*." [1] The term *system* denotes that the fundamental political institutions are vitally connected with each other and vitally related to the nature of the society in which they exist. As for their connection with each other, it is clear that each

---

[1] Cf. Henry St. John, Viscount Bolingbroke, *Dissertation On Parties* (London, 1733), p. 108: "By Constitution we mean, whenever we speak with Propriety and Exactness, that Assemblage of Laws, Institutions and Customs, derived from certain fix'd Principles of Reason . . . that compose the general System, according to which the Community hath agreed to be governed."

institution lends significance to its neighbors. Institutions are obliged to cooperate, and in the long run their jagged edges are worn down until harmony prevails. What, for example, the legislature gains, it gains at the expense of the people, or of the executive or the courts of law.

When the Parliament Act of 1911 decreased the power of the House of Lords, the power of the House of Commons was relatively increased, but this gain was partly offset by a reduction of its term from seven to five years. In France, in 1934, the proposal to restore to the executive the power of dissolving the Chamber of Deputies was designed to reduce the personal power of individual deputies and parliamentary groups. Again, in the Weimar constitution, control wielded by Prussia in the old *Bundesrat* was greatly diminished in the *Reichsrat,* and the *Reichstag,* popularly controlled, became the chief legislative power. What the civil service gains, perhaps, legislative committees lose; what is taken from individual property may accrue to the social welfare; the institution which finally decides the appropriation of money goes far toward deciding the power of all others. Where, as in the United States, there is a separation of institutions which, for effective operation, should be in close contact, the political-party system secures value as a connecting link. Each part of a constitution, in short, must be read together with all the others if its real meaning is to be discovered; and all parts must, and do in practice, have regard to each other in the course of operation. The human energy which floods into them and makes them move abhors waste, and little by little reduces it to a minimum until they act as a system.

The fundamental political institutions are a system not only in relation to each other but in relation to their social environment. Every constitution is the product of the accumulated material and spiritual circumstances of its time. That lesson has been literally thundered out by Burke and Hegel. Although in its narrowly formal aspects it may (like the British constitution) be the product of an earlier time, or although, owing to the doctrinaire notions of some of its makers, it may (like the German constitution of 1919) seem to have application only to a possible or impossible future, its meaning in operation, as distinct from its meaning on paper, is fairly responsive to contemporary necessities. There is always an institutional lag in the state; it takes time, as we shall see, for institutions to overtake the necessity for them. But sooner or later that which is wanted is made in proportion to the intensity of the want, and that which is no longer wanted is dropped, formally or by simple disregard. That we learned, too, from a consideration of the conditions of state activity.

The working constitution will approximate what a written constitution would be if it were contemporarily established. Doctrinaire enthusiasms may adorn a constitution, but if they are out of tune with the existing power relationship, they are no more than an ornament. And by "power relationship" is meant not merely a situation where the naked force of so many people in the country could overcome that of the minority, or where an armed and more homicidal minority could dictate to majority, but also the spiritual values, awake or habitual, prevailing among the various groups which dwell together within a single nation.

"Fundamental." What is meant by fundamental? Is fundamentality a matter of detail or a question of which institutions to include? All countries insist that fundamental institutions do exist, and they have invented the word "constitution" or its equivalent. In Great Britain, at least since the seventeenth century, constitution has meant something more set and determined than ordinary law. In Germany, where *Gesetz* means law, emphasis is given to that which is even more basic, more "set," by the words *Grundgesetz*,[2] the ground or basic law, or *Verfassung*, that which is set, which grasps, holds together, causes coherence, fastens. Similar distinctions are observable in France (*loi: constitution*) and Italy (*legge: statuto*). We will leave the meaning of "fundamental" to unravel itself, but before entering upon that stage we may ask why, in general, men seek to establish certain institutions as fundamental.

They do so because they desire to reduce uncertainty to a minimum. The world is full of uncertainties, and to meet the problems which spring from them requires constant vigilance, constant effort. Physical and nervous strain are produced by uncertainty, and the more involved the complexity of human environment and human relationships, the greater the possible uncertainty, and, therefore, the heavier the strain.

The insecurity of human life is an inexorable factor in causing men to seek certainty and order. It is a matter of course that human beings should attempt to reduce the uncertainties, especially in the arena where these may cause conflicts of a radical and painful kind, that is, in political life. Your liberty, your property, your family, your religion, your town, province or country, the association of your fellow-workers—can these be put into daily jeopardy? It is enough, perhaps too much, in so short a lifetime of some sixty years, if they are endangered once

2 Cf. F. Lassalle, *Uber Verfassungswesen* (1863): *Reden und Schriften*, Vorwarts edition, Vol. I, p. 470 ff. Discussing the force of the term *Grundgesetz* he shows that its principal significance is that it is the *foundation* and that a foundation is based on *necessity*. "In the conception of a foundation there is the idea of a concrete *necessity*, and operative power, *which of necessity makes that which it supports that which actually prevails.*"

or twice, but it is intolerable not to know from day to day or year to year the conditions of your subordination or superordination in the community. We need not even add to this simple human sentiment the consideration of the obligations imposed by modern economic technique, or the mass of anxieties already confronting the professional politicians and lawmakers, to realize how important men feel it that limits should be set to the mutability of things, that stability be established and serenity bestowed. This becomes clear from a study of the form and substance of constitutions.

FORM OF THE CONSTITUTION

THE chief problems arising out of the forms of constitutions are three: (1) whether they are written or unwritten; (2) whether they are flexible or rigid; and (3) whether special arrangements secure their supremacy. Paramount over these technical questions is the essential one: what influence is exerted by these differences of form upon the political thought and behavior of the state possessing them?

Written and Unwritten Constitutions. The difference which has been paraded until the mind is tired of contemplating it is that between written and unwritten constitutions, and the difference is illustrated by contrasting the conditions of almost the only country in the world with an unwritten constitution, Great Britain, with those pertaining in all other countries. What is this difference?

The fundamental political institutions of Great Britain, those in which the very sap of authority flows, are not set down in writing in any formally accepted document or documents. They are regulated by (1) judicial decisions; sometimes founded on ancient promises of kings; sometimes founded on more or less vague "immemorial rights and liberties," such as freedom of public meeting and freedom of person and speech, which are corollaries of ordinary common-law rights; and sometimes founded on agreements, resolutions, and laws made by rebellious Parliaments. The occasions have been conflicts for power, and concessions have been made

or withheld by kings according to their personal character or according to monetary administrative and fiscal difficulties.[3] Then (2) there is a number of statutes made with more deliberateness and wider participation (like the Act of Settlement, the Franchise Acts, the Parliament Act of 1911, and The Crown Proceedings Act of 1947).[4] And (3) there is a series of understandings or "conventions," political usages of piecemeal growth, which regulate perhaps the most important part of the constitution: the sovereignty of Parliament, the responsibility of the cabinet to Parliament and so to the people.[5]

Judicial decisions form a body of written constitutional law; the statutes certainly do; and the utterances of Parliament on various supreme occasions are also authentically existent. These, taken together, are as explicit as, and usually more explicit than, the "written constitutions" of other countries. But the "conventions" are not so recorded by an institution with such authority as the courts of law or Parliament. Nevertheless, they are understood with fair exactness, and have been recorded by ministers in their correspondence and political speeches, accepted with inappreciable dissent by politicians and scholars, and even written down in great detail by such authorities as Hearn, Bagehot, Dicey, May, Anson, and Jennings.[6]

Where, then, is the difference between the British "unwritten" constitution and the "written" constitution of other lands? The difference, I think, is twofold. *First,* the British constitution includes impor-

---

[3] E.g. Magna Carta; cf. W. S. McKechnie, *Magna Carta* (Glasgow, 1905).
[4] Other examples are the Habeas Corpus Acts, the Bill of Rights, the Re-election of Ministers Act (1919), etc.
[5] Cf. A. V. Dicey, *The Law of the Constitution,* 9th edition (London, 1945), p. 24: "The other set of rules consists of conventions, understandings, habits or practices which, though they may regulate the conduct of the several members of the sovereign power, of the Ministry, or of other officials, are not in reality laws at all, since they are not enforced by the Courts."
[6] Cf. for example the position of the cabinet and the chief of state, Part V, below.

tant sections—the conventions—which are taken for granted, but not formulated, save occasionally by individuals; and does not include many of the fundamental institutions of the country, as, for example, trade unions and political parties, free public education, and religious freedom, which are formally included in the constitutions of other countries. *Second,* and more important, is that no body of people was deliberately called together and entrusted with the establishment of a constitution, as in other countries. Everywhere else there have been constituent assemblies or conventions,[7] but England has never possessed a formal *pouvoir constituant*—but only the ordinary legislature and executive. In England the constitution has not been the work of a specially designated body; it is the incidental accumulation of doctrines and practical arrangements formulated, piecemeal, for the righting of particular wrongs. At a point of time when a settled and deliberately planned constitution was appropriate—that is, after events had made possible the execution of Charles I— there was not sufficient homogeneity of opinion in the country to permit the establishment of fundamentals, for on the basis of religious authority and political authority the country was sorely divided.

Comparatively, then, and not absolutely, the adjective "unwritten" when applied to constitutions, in the chief example thereof, means: (1) that all is not included in writing which might be, while some things are altogether excluded which in other constitutions are included; and (2) that it is not the result of deliberate establishment and adoption as a whole, with the result that no external sign marks off a constitutional from an ordinary law. Let us again insist that the differences are not absolute, but relative; that they are a matter of "more or less" when compared with written constitutions. Dicey, for example, greatly exaggerates the differ-

ences when he fails to look behind the law at the social forces which sustain both written constitutions and the conventions of the British constitution.

The Rise of Written Constitutions. Written constitutions have developed from two causes. *First,* where an old social power relationship has collapsed, usually in violence, a definite and coherent assertion of a new power relationship has been embodied in written form. *Second,* where political and administrative waste and friction can be avoided, and where hitherto unattainable purposes are brought nearer realization, the conditions of united action among a number of states (as in the United States, the Swiss Federal Union, and the Commonwealth of Australia) are laid down in a constitution.

The Weimar constitution of 1919 arose out of both these causes: downfall of an old power, and recognition of the wisdom of better federal arrangements. The Soviet constitution of 1936 was formulated peacefully, but it represents the completion of a constitution following an overt change of an old power relationship in 1917. The difference between the 1925 and 1936 constitutions is marked: the tone of the one is belligerent; the other expresses acceptance of the new *status quo.* The RSFSR Fundamental Law of 1925, in stating the Republic's general principles, indicated that "its object is to guarantee the dictatorship of the proletariat for the purpose of suppressing the bourgeoisie, of abolishing the exploitation of man by man and of bringing about Communism, under which there will be neither division into classes nor state power." But in the new constitution the Revolution is an established fact: "The economic foundation of the USSR consists in the socialist system of economy and socialist ownership of the implements and means of production, firmly established as a result of the liquidation of the capitalist system of economy, the abolition of private ownership of the implements and means of production, and the abolition of exploitation of man by man" (article 4).

The first attempt at a written constitu-

---

[7] Cf. Charles Borgeaud, *Adoption and Amendment of Constitutions in Europe and America* (New York, 1895); and J. A. Jameson, *Constitutional Conventions,* 4th edition (Chicago, 1887).

tion was made in England in 1649 [8]—the Agreement of the People, a document drawn up and approved by the council of officers of the Parliamentary Army. Its purpose, as stated in its preamble, was to show why written constitutions are desired: "to take the best care we can for the future, to avoid both the danger of returning into a slavish condition and the chargeable remedy of another war." "We are fully agreed and resolved [there is the stuff of written constitutions!], God willing, to provide, that hereafter our Representatives be neither left to an uncertainty for times nor be unequally constituted, nor made useless to the ends for which they are intended. In order where unto we declare and agree. . . ." The Agreement never became effective.[9]

The one instance of a written constitution in England, the "Instrument of Government" made by Cromwell and his officers in 1653 was short lived, and the Restoration put an end to written constitutions in England. The very Parliament that was chosen under it repudiated it, alleging Parliament's supremacy, calling forth Cromwell's classic dictum on constitutions.

The country which was to be the most conspicuous example of an "unwritten" system was, however, the mother of written constitutions. For the religious and political struggle which had caused the Puritan Revolt caused many of the same antiepiscopal, antiroyalist citizens to forsake their native country and found colonies in North America. It was in these colonies that the written constitution had an infancy, not cut short as in England, but robust enough to determine the later political life of their surroundings and to be a very potent example to Europe. For two conditions existed in the New England colonies which did not exist in the old country. *First,* the people who founded

them were Puritans, and therefore they were predisposed in favor of democratic government. *Second,* since they had broken away from the old foundations and were in an entirely virgin country, a basis of cooperation had consciously to be formed.[10]

The immediate progenitors of modern written constitutions were, however, the constitutions made by the American colonies when they threw off the authority of Great Britain. The Congress of Philadelphia, organizing resistance, adopted this resolution on the motion of the New England representative, John Adams:

That it be recommended to the respective assemblies and conventions of the United States, where no government sufficient to the exigencies of their affairs hath been hitherto established, to adopt such government as shall in the opinion of the representatives of the people best conduce to the happiness and safety of their constituents in particular and America in general.[11]

This resolution was adopted in May, 1776. Already two colonies, New Hampshire, and South Carolina, had adopted such a constitution. In June, Virginia followed suit, and her constitutional activities are most famous because they set up the first declaration of rights, a model not only for America, but for Europe also.[12] By the spring of 1777, all states but Massachusetts

---

[8] Originally drawn up in October, 1647. Cf. S. R. Gardiner, *Constitutional Documents of the Puritan Revolution* (Oxford, 1889).
[9] Cf. J. Tanner, *English Constitutional Conflicts of the 17th Century* (Cambrdge, 1928); and D. L. Keir, *Modern Constitutional History* (Oxford, 1938).

[10] In 1639 Connecticut adopted the Fundamental Orders and in 1641 Rhode Island adopted a decree defining its fundamental institutions. The preamble to the Fundamental Orders clearly indicates the ultimate purposes of a fundamental law: the key words are "peace and union," "orderly and decent." For the other colonies, royal charters supplied constitutions. Cf. Benjamin Poore, *The Federal and State Constitutions of the United States* (Washington, 1877), Vol. I, p. 249; S. G. Fisher, *The Evolution of the Constitution of the United States* (Philadelphia, 1904), Chap. II, p. 41 ff.
[11] Charles Borgeaud, *op. cit.,* p. 17.
[12] See the Virginia "Declaration of Rights" of June 12, 1776. Its sixteen articles, including such basic concepts as human equality and the principle of separation of powers, should be known by all American students, as its reputation greatly influenced our own history and was well known in Europe. These are easy to find.

had promulgated new constitutions or appropriately amended the old. Massachusetts completed the series in 1780, and its constitution vies closely in importance with that of Virginia for the completeness with which it expresses the political theory of the day.

Here were deliberate acts to secure a firm basis for political life. The beliefs of the day as to what institutions were fundamental were written down and endowed with solemnity by their adoption by special conventions and by the grave declarations of intention and faith put at the head of the documents. The constitution of Massachusetts begins with an epitome of John Locke's *On Civil Government* and a thanksgiving to God—"the great Legislator of the Universe"—for the opportunity to form a constitution peacefully and honestly. Soon there were thirteen written constitutions, deliberately composed and recorded arrangements by which men declared their lives bound for the future.

The center of interest then shifted to France. That country had been ruled until the Revolution by a system which was arbitrariness itself. The elements which disputed for political authority— the Crown, the *Parlements* (half-judicial, half-legislative assemblies), the nobility, the municipalities, all the leaders of the Third Estate—all had need of something more bracing to their claims than the mere power to get themselves obeyed, and members of the bodies sought the sources of stable authority in so-called fundamental laws: laws which, for example, set bounds to the arbitrary authority of the Crown, or at least laws which should establish a set order in which this authority should predictably operate. This hankering after a *loi fondamental* is a most interesting phenomenon, and it is understandable that in the absence of a written constitution, men should pretend, with little authentic evidence, that fundamental laws did exist, which, when appealed to, would abolish confusion and terminate disturbing controversies.

Discussions of this kind were older than Montesquieu, but his *De l'Esprit des Lois*

stimulated discussion and contributed a historical analysis of French monarchy which led to the conclusion that the monarchy of France was limited, since authority must be certain and stable, and, that monarchy required limitation by "intermediary powers," the nobility, clergy, and magistrates. Two quotations from Montesquieu will make this clear. Monarchical government differs from despotic government thus: the former is "that in which one person governs, but by fixed and established laws; while in a despotism there is a single ruler, without law or regulation, led only by his will and caprices." And again: "The intermediate, subordinate and dependent powers constitute the nature of a monarchical government; I mean of that in which a single person governs by fundamental laws. . . . These fundamental laws necessarily suppose the intermediate channels through which power flows; for if there be only the momentary and capricious will of a single person to govern the State, nothing can be fixed." Montesquieu was only one, though perhaps the most eminent, of many who sought to establish the proper fundamental laws of the French monarchy, and the metaphor he used for the intermediary powers, namely, "channel," indicates very well the binding, restricting quality of a fundamental law. And though there were numerous conclusions reached, these varying with the interests and social class of the theorists, all sought guarantees.

The American Declaration of Independence and state constitutions phrased and legalized the aspirations of the French. Through the work of John Adams and Franklin, these constitutions were made known in France and were translated and published there before the American Revolution closed. The German scholar Jellinek has shown that the French Declaration of Rights of 1789 had its direct model and stimulus in American events: [13]

---

[13] Georg Jellinek, *Die Erklärung der Menschen-und Bürgerrechte*, 3rd edition (Berlin, 1919). On the whole, later research, even French research, agrees with the views expressed in this study.

that Rousseau's social-contract theory cannot have been the forerunner thereof; that mere natural-rights theories were insufficient, without a precipitating cause, to bring about their legal formulation. The very terms coined by the American revolutionists became part of French revolutionary vocabulary: declaration of rights, national conventions, committees of public safety, and so forth. Thus, on October 2, 1789, the French Constituent Assembly voted the Declaration of the Rights of Man and Citizen, and in its preamble is to be found all the essential reasons for a written constitution:

. . . in order that this declaration, being constantly present to the minds of members of the body social, they may for ever be kept attentive to their rights and their duties: that the acts of the legislative and executive powers of government, being capable of being at every moment compared with the end of political institutions, may be more respected [14] and also that the future claims of the citizens, being directed by simple and incontestable principles, may always tend to the maintenance of the constitution, and the general happiness.

This Declaration was declared to be "solemn" and the rights "sacred," while the timely and obliging presence of the Supreme Being at its acceptance was acknowledged and His blessing and favor solicited. In 1791 followed the first full written constitution: and then, at intervals until 1875, others, until by that year twelve immutable constitutions had vanished into the limbo of past years.

In 1875 the thirteenth constitution organized the Third Republic. Unlike the previous constitutions, it is not a compact and complete document headed by a declaration of rights, but three separate laws, together covering the main constitutional problems of the day—the status and authority of the executive, and the composition and relative authority of Chamber of Deputies, Senate, and the executive. It

is fragmentary—omitting a guarantee of rights, and any mention of the organization of the judiciary, the civil service, and the local government. But the "principles of 1789" were held by most constitutional lawyers to apply to the constitution of the Third Republic,[15] while the Fourth has supplied itself with a modern version.

France set the example of written constitutions in Europe, and the soldiers of the Revolution and the Empire carried the notion into Italy, Belgium, Spain, and the South German states. And the "Founding Fathers" welded by peaceful conferences and compromises the constitutional bonds that have held in "perpetual union" the mighty Republic of the West.

How Strong Can Twentieth-Century Constitutions Be? A new question is posed for the constitutions of the twentieth century: is a bill of rights, granting social and economic rights on a substantial scale, feasible?

The establishment of a written constitution by the free will of a democratic vote is a peculiarly difficult operation, because it concerns the assignment of fundamental rights and of the authority to use supreme power. Agreement on these matters, to be embodied in a document especially guarded against easy change, can hardly be secured in a measure which gives confidence in the endurance of the constitution. Some reflections on the experience of America, France, Weimar Germany, and the U.S.S.R. make this clear.

The United States was, indeed, fortunate to have established its constitution in the eighteenth century, for it enjoyed advantages not available to constitution-seeking nations in our own day. In the first place, it had the passion of a people recently emerged from ordeal by battle for their joint emancipation from alien rule. In the second place, neither political parties nor special interests had coagu-

---

[14] Cf. Baron Grimm's saying that all the rules of government could be put in a few pages. This, of course, is simply a reflection of late eighteenth-century optimism in general, the Age of Reason.

[15] Cf. Léon Duguit, *Traité de Droit Constitutionnel* (Paris, 1924), Vol. III, Chap. VI, p. 564; Maurice Hauriou, *Précis Elémentaire de Droit Constitutionnel* (Paris, 1930), p. 81; and A. Esmein, *Eléments de Droit Constitutionnel* (Paris, 1921), Vol. I. pp. 560-61.

lated into hard organizations. No one would wish to minimize the factional and ideological differences prevailing, nor the strength of the regional and economic interests in collision. They were immense, and almost disastrous. But it will also be admitted that American colonial society was simpler, the general spiritual outlook more unified, and the functional and party organizations less conscious and firm and pressing and insistent than anything like what would have been encountered within fifty years from that time, and even more so, one hundred and fifty years afterward. Even so, the great compromise between the small and the large states was made in a form which does injustice today (and could hardly be produced today, de novo), and made it impossible to settle the slavery problem inside the margins of the constitution.

Even so, it has to be remembered that the people of the United States did not in any real sense give themselves their constitution. "We, the people . . ." may be metaphorically true, but it is far from really true. For the delegates to the convention were chosen without any popular awareness of what they were to accomplish. As for ratification, it has been estimated that between a fifth and a third of the adult males were unfranchised in the states; [16] and, also that not more than five per cent of the population voted.[17] Beard has called the Convention's resolution that the constitution go into effect when nine of the states had ratified, a coup d'état, and his remark may well be compared with Hume's description of the making of the Glorious Revolution in England (1689) by "the majority of seven hundred." [18]

The revolutionary constitutions and governments of France were unmaintainable. When the National Assembly of 1871 met, it was composed of 738 members,

of which half had come from areas still under German occupation. A heavy conservative majority had emerged as the result of the conservative policy of ending the war—450 seats, including 200 noblemen. A constitutional monarchy on the British model was favored by a majority of the assembly. But the monarchists could not agree on which branch of the royal family to call to the throne, and the man they finally accepted refused to be king unless his family colors were established as the national flag. Month after month, with a provisional government of Thiers, various by-elections increased the republican strength. A law of 1871 used the title of President of the French *Republic,* without a clear majority intention then to install the republic; but it stuck. In November, 1873, a new President, Marshal MacMahon, was made President for seven years—hence the septennate came into existence—long enough, the conservatives thought, to keep the place warm for a king later. In January, 1875, a law was accepted further committing France to a republic, and a parliamentary republic at that: "The President of the Republic is elected by absolute majority of the Senate and the Chamber of Deputies meeting in joint session as a national Assembly." This fundamental commitment was adopted by a majority of one vote: 353 to 352. The majority had been made possible by the shift of 26 votes from moderate monarchists, who were afraid that further delay in installation of a constitution would provoke radical disorder in the country. A later vote on the same test brought the affirmative votes up to 425, though some of the converts voted in the hope that the republic would fail! Thereafter, various laws filled out the details of the executive power, the Senate, and the Deputies. But, significantly, no bill of rights was proposed, and none was passed. This constitution was "the constitution that divides us least."

It must be remembered that difficult as it was to get this constitution passed, and slight as was the loyalty to it, it was passed in an age when the masses were less conscious politically than they are today;

16 Cf. J. F. Jameson, *The American Revolution Considered as a Social Movement* (Princeton, 1940), p. 242; cf. also A. C. McLaughlin, *Constitutional History of the United States* (New York, 1935), Chap. XV.
17 Charles Beard, *Economic Interpretation of the Constitution* (New York, 1913), p. 16.
18 In *Essays,* "Of the Originall Contract."

when they were less organized in their interests and occupations than today; when the economy of France was much simpler; and when there was no referendum to follow the act of the assembly.

The latent insincerities and the fissures emerged with disastrous effect in May and June of 1940, and led to the overthrow of the constitution in July and its replacement by the Vichy dictatorship. When France, after World War II, set herself to making a constitution to replace that of the Third Republic, conditions were not propitious for a political consensus. The parties were firmly attached to ideologies nourished on the European battlefield of ideas between 1919 and our own day, and they were impassioned by the humiliating experiences of the capitulation and the heroism of the Resistance. The masses were more conscious of political realities than before. The economy was more complicated. The future had become a field of planned political life. The vote of the masses for a constituent assembly and a referendum on its work were taken for granted.

These were the strengths of voting for the respective parties for the Constituent Assembly of October 21, 1945: Communists, 26.1 per cent; MRP, 23.9 per cent; Socialists, 23.4 per cent; Left Association (including Radical Socialists), 10.6 per cent; Conservatives, 15.2 per cent . . . and various other smaller groups. Only about 80 per cent of the voters voted. A referendum on whether the assembly should be constituent gave 15.66 million for; over half a million against; and 8 million abstentions. We need not here dwell on other votes for the Constitutional Assembly of June 2, 1946—the scattering of opinion was roughly similar. But the first draft was rejected by 52.8 per cent of the votes at the referendum, with 47.2 per cent affirmative and 21.3 per cent of the electorate abstaining. At the referendum of October 13, 1946, the fresh, slightly amended draft was approved thus: 53.3 per cent of those voting were in favor and 46.7 per cent against, while 31.3 per cent of the voters abstained: thus actually only 35.9 per cent of the whole electorate favored the constitution. Out of a total of the register of 26.2 million voters, 9.25 million said "yes" to the constitution; 8 million said "no"; and 8.5 million did not even vote. What strength has such a constitution?

The Weimar constitution also suffered from this feebleness of sincere reception by the electorate. It was not submissible to a referendum, but the voting for the Weimar Constituent Assembly was ominous of troubles ahead. *First* of all, the extreme Left-wing, Communist-inspired groups, if not in a Communist party, were insurgent and had to be repressed by the Social Democratic provisional government assisted by remnants of the Right-wing Army elements. *Second,* the nationalistic groups were in a minority only for the time being. *Third,* the terror in Russia induced moderation in the German Liberal and Socialist parties, and took much of the virility out of their revolt against authority. The distribution of seats was: Social Democratic, 165; Independent Workers Party (left-wing socialist), 22; Democrats, 74; Center Party (based on Catholicism), 89; German People's Party, 22; German Nationalist Party, 42; various small parties, 9. The constitution was sponsored by the parties on the Left and by the Center. The vote received for the constitution was 262 in favor out of a total of 423—considerably more than one half, but still hardly enough to support with an ardent spirit so new and radically different a constitutional structure through the inevitable turmoils which the defeated nation had to undergo. The Right wing voted against it, as also did some of the extreme Left, and the rest abstained.

Thus, a modern constitution, however wise and reasonable it is, contains so many stipulations that a community, freely organized as it is into numerous self-assertive and self-protective groups, finds a sincere consensus difficult if not impossible to attain, against at least one substantial group's dissent from some important part of the document.

How much easier was constitution making in the Soviet Union between November, 1917, and 1936! Here there were a single leader; a well-knit political tenet: the abolition of classes combined with ownership of all the means of production and distribution by the state; the rights of the revolutionary minority; the denial that incompetent and nonrevolutionary masses were capable of exercising the highest political judgment and will; the right to overcome social contradictions and set the course by unlimited force, since the means justifies the end; the right to remake the consciousness by remaking the economy which, as Marx had said, determines the consciousness; materialistic reasons for denying the justification of doubt on spiritual grounds. How easy to make a constitution, aided by ruthless terror under these conditions! But under such conditions, what is a constitution?

It is a constitution somewhat in the same sense that Hitler's *Reich* was a constitution—the embodiment of the caprice of the dictator, which is no constitution, since it reposes on no explicit consent freely expressible by all. Hitler's theory of his state was that the Weimar constitution remained unless repealed by his ordinances and laws but beyond that by his speeches, which represented his will and therefore were incumbent upon the courts and the administration. He was able to establish this position by having received from the *Reichstag* of March, 1933, an Enabling Act giving him the power to make laws by cabinet decree, even if they amended the constitution; he obtained his two-thirds majority by the imprisonment of some Communists, the dispersal of the others, the terrorization of some Social Democrats, and the acceptance of his assurances by the Catholic Centre party, the Social Democrats voting against. The doctrine of the supremacy of his will was preached by his jurists, his political science teachers, and his attorneys before the courts.[19] Thus:

National life needs a container in order to be able to utilize forces active within it . . . this foundation of national being is the con-

stitution . . . the fundamental order in which a political people forms itself in a state. . . . A constitution is not a number (or assemblage) of individual constitutional laws but an enclosed whole made up of all the principles, the spirit and the nature of the national being. . . .

The Weimar constitution was no longer appropriate to the new idea. Therefore,

In the programme of the Movement, we possess a catechism of political world outlook which provides a criterion and principle in the decision of questions of constitutional law.

We are left to contemplate (not with envy, however) the ease with which modern dictatorships can establish "constitutions," as though by a magic wand, whereas free men find it almost impossible, through their heightened consciousness and freedom of conscience, freely to subject themselves to a mesh of basic rules of social ethics, which a constitution essentially is. Yet the democracies represent humanity in a more civilized condition, while the dictatorships are regressions to barbarism.

The Political Effects of a Written Constitution. The question we may now ask is: what is the political effect of the form of the constitution? Is the country with a written constitution capable, by that fact, of better government than the country with an unwritten constitution? Is there any substantial balance of advantage one way or the other? The comparison is necessarily between the British unwritten constitution and written ones which are otherwise universal.

If the effect of expression in writing alone is considered, the written constitution has little, if any, advantage over the unwritten.

First, the written constitution is not more revered as more solemn and fundamental than the unwritten constitution. In the countries of written constitutions people endeavor to stimulate reverence for them by urging their antiquity (none actually goes back before 1776), the dramatic struggles which gave them birth, and the character and ability of the men

19 Cf. R. Stödter in *Archiv für öffentliches Recht. Neu Folge,* Band 27 (Berlin), p. 166 *et seq.,* especially p. 178.

who promulgated them. But all these things with even greater force can be said of the British constitution; and if the essence of the constitution is its unalterable character, then written constitutions have the grave disadvantage of production by a deliberate and demonstrable—and therefore a disparageable—operation. All constitutions have a conservative effect, like all things, whether matter or concepts, which exist, but those which are written are not noticeably more or less conservative simply because of their expression in writing.

Second, are written constitutions more decisive of controversy than the British constitution? Is their meaning more certain and definite? Experience shows that they are not; or if they are, then only to a very small degree. For no constitution is so detailed that interpretation, or "construction," as it is technically called, is unnecessary. Only the broad principles can possibly be laid down by a constituent assembly unless it is to sit permanently; and were it to do this, its reputation would be no more exalted than that of the ordinary lawmaking body. Even the most detailed written constitutions like those of some American states and the German constitution of 1919 do not yield their meaning without much interpretation (every article of the 170 in the Weimar constitution gave rise to a voluminous literature). This occurs in various forms, chief of which are legislation and the decisions of the courts of law when cases raise problems. The latter is discussed presently in the analysis of the supremacy of the constitution. Yet we may say at once that the constitution of the United States is contained in the official edition in thirty-one pages; but the clauses when set down with the chief cases fought upon them need more than a thousand pages,[20] and then it must be remembered that in most cases there is a dissenting opinion; and finally, that students may even dissent from both the

majority and the minority (in all, over forty thousand actions have been fought).

What, then, does the constitution say? Statutes are made to give the clauses of the constitution precision and body. For example, the French Declarations of Rights contain explicit warnings that the articles shall have effect according to laws yet to be made. Freedom of opinion and the security of private property are instances of this. Then others—like the "career open to the talents," the position of the churches, and public education—mean little or nothing without concrete elaboration. So, too, in the German constitution of 1919 article after article ends with the phrase "a law shall state the details" or "within the general laws." Thus, the constitution cannot be accepted as the sole evidence of what is constitution—it must be taken together with the laws which further define it. The truth of this was emphatically exemplified in the unratified proposed French constitution of 1946. Its twenty-one articles of freedoms and its eighteen articles of social and economic rights raised at least as many doubts as they were intended to put down regarding the position of the individual in society. A written constitution, then, is the product of the constitution itself plus the laws and decisions subsequently made on its basis.

In Britain, however, constitutional principles are directly embodied, explicitly or as implied, in particular statutes. If it is desired to find the general principles of the British constitution, it is necessary to generalize from a vast body of particular legal decisions, resolutions, statutes, and biographies. A written constitution, however, yields up its general principles upon direct reading. But *only* its general principles; and they are, as a rule, so general that they are contradicted by the statutes defining them or by the behavior of political institutions apparently acting in virtue of them. If they are general, they are nebulous.

How, indeed, could agreement be reached on fundamentals were not those fundamentals so broad that most objec-

---

[20] *Constitution of the United States of America,* revised and annotated, 1938; Document 232, 74th Cong., 2d Session.

tions could be covered? Therefore, no written constitution, not the French, nor the German, nor the American, nor the Australian, nor any, can stand by itself. It needs completion: for the virtue of the law resides in its detail. And the laws which give it completion are not different from the laws passed in a country with an unwritten constitution.

Further, even though the constitution is written in some detail, and though it is completed by statutes and judicial construction, complete certainty as to its meaning is not attained. There is as lively a controversy over every article, even sentence, of the constitution in France, Weimar Germany, and the United States, as there is in Great Britain; perhaps more, because the British constitution consists of specific instances. The intentions of the founders, the social conditions of the country at the time of the establishment, the new problems which have arisen in a new era: all are explored with aggressive attention to every word and comma.

There is little advantage in mere writing or proclamation. Is there any at all? At the most, the written constitution is a standard of reference, and it is valuable only in proportion to its clarity and the extent to which it has not been altered by interpretation. As no constitution satisfies these conditions for more than a decade after it has issued from the constituent assembly, the advantage approaches nil.

A distinction, in short, must be made between the quality of a constitution as derived from its being written, and the difficulty of amendment, and these two things must not be confused.[21] It is not the writing which safeguards, but the obstacles to amendment.

---

[21] Such a confusion might arise from H. J. Laski's *Grammar of Politics* (London, 1925). He says (pp. 304-6): "There are notions so fundamental that it is necessary in every state to give them special protection. . . . It [the legislature] ought not, in a word, to be able to alter the basic framework of the state except under special conditions, direct access to which is rendered difficult. . . . This implies, I think, a written constitution."

INDEED, the essence of a constitution is its inflexibility as compared with ordinary laws. We might define a constitution as its process of amendment. For to amend is to deconstitute and reconstitute. That is the respect in which all other constitutions differ from the British constitution. Broadly speaking (and we shall have to make some modifications later), in the British governmental system any institution, whether or not it is considered to be fundamental and whether or not it is stated by past Parliaments or judicial decisions to be fundamental, is alterable to the extent of abolition—formally—by the ordinary process of lawmaking; that is, by a bare majority of the House of Commons and the ordinary collaboration of the House of Lords as laid down in the Parliament Act of 1910. An act to abolish important powers of the House of Lords, or to restrict the power of trade unions, may be passed by the same procedure as an act relating to widows' pensions or a minor field of public health or education. This is considered to be the extreme of flexibility. Other constitutions—those of the United States, France, Australia, Switzerland, Weimar Germany, and the U.S.S.R.—are rigid in various degrees.

Amendment in the United States. The United States constitution was purposely made most difficult to amend. The amending section, article V, prescribes two possible processes of proposal and two of ratification of amendments: (1) two thirds of both houses shall propose amendments; or (2) the legislatures of two thirds of the several states shall petition Congress to call a convention for proposing amendments, and ratification shall take place by (3) three fourths of the legislatures of the several states, or (4) by conventions of three fourths of the several states. In practice, only one amendment has been made by convention instead of by proposal by Congress and ratification by the legislatures of the states, and that was the 20th amendment, which repealed the 18th amendment which had prohibited the sale of liquor. Further, two thirds of Congress means two thirds not of the legal membership but of a quorum,[22] according to Congress and decisions in the national Prohibition cases.[23] Other questions of detail arise, such as whether there is any limit upon the time for ratification,[24] for, theoretically, the states could take a century over this;[25] or whether a state can withdraw once it has ratified action, which has several times been threatened.[26] These things serve to show that even a written constitution can cause as much perturbation and doubt as an unwritten one, and there is one even more important point: whether there are implied or intrinsic limits to the amending power. This we discuss later.

The main point, however, is this: What is the political effect, the effect upon the power relationship in society, of this amending process? It was intended to make change difficult; it has made change almost unattainable. It was apparently intended to make change difficult because in the fundamental political institutions were included these things: the indestructibility of the states, the strength of the federal authority, the central management of interstate and foreign commerce (the

immediate stimulus to the union), the maintenance of the sanctity of contracts, care for the soundness of paper currency, and distrust of democracy. These, and other considerations, in different degrees commended the constitution to the ruling classes: the men of big business (merchants, manufacturers, land speculators, bondholders), the lawyers, and the clergy.[27] But it was admitted that though "too mutable" a system was dangerous, the error of the previous Articles of Confederation, which made amendment well-nigh impossible, must not be imitated, since "extreme difficulty might perpetuate its [the Constitution's] discovered faults." [28]

The United States constitution has been formally amended twenty-one times. The last or 21st amendment, proclaimed as in force on December 5, 1933, repealed the 18th or the Prohibition Amendment: a novel instance. Evidence of excessive rigidity is that of the four thousand proposals [29] only twenty-one have actually been adopted, twenty by state legislatures, one by conventions of the states. But such

---

[22] *Constitution*, Article I, sect. 5, para. I: "A majority of each [House] shall constitute a quorum."

[23] *Ohio* v. *Cox*, 257, Fed., 334, 348 (1919); 253, U.S., 350, 386 (1920).

[24] Congress is coming to realize the need for time limits in completing the amending process. Accordingly the 18th, 20th, and 21st amendments provided a seven-year limitation. It should be noted that such a stipulation was held to be within Congressional rights by the Supreme Court. (*Dillon* v. *Gloss*, 1921). See also *Coleman* v. *Miller* (1939), 307 vs. 433.

[25] C. K. Burdick, *The Law of the American Constitution* (New York, 1922), p. 43. Another problem has arisen in the process of ratifying the proposed amendment: Can a state reject, and later ratify a proposal? In 1939 the Supreme Court in *Coleman* v. *Miller* (307 U.S. 433) ruled that the Kansas legislature's rejection of the Child-Labor Amendment in 1925 and approval in 1937 was a political question which was in the jurisdiction of Congress and not the courts. Congress took no action against Kansas; consequently it must have approved. This decision can also be applied to a Congressional refusal to allow a change once ratification has occurred.

[26] Burdick, *op. cit.*, pp. 43-44.

[27] Cf. Charles E. Beard, *An Economic Interpretation of the Constitution of the United States* (New York, 1939) and *Economic Origins of Jeffersonian Democracy* (New York, 1915); R. L. Schuyler, *The Constitution of the United States* (New York, 1923); Max Farrand, *The Framing of the Constitution* (New York, 1913); and O. G. Libby, *The Geographical Distribution of the Vote of the Thirteen States on the Federal Constitution* (Wisconsin, 1894).

[28] *The Federalist*, No. XLIII (by Madison). The theory that amendment was made intentionally difficult is founded upon the theory that the aristocratic and mercantile interests desired stability. Cf. J. A. Smith, *The Spirit of American Government* (1919), Chap. III. In fact, the records of the Federal Convention do not show the intention to make amendment difficult; rather the contrary. See *Documentary History of the Constitution* (Washington, U.S. State Department, 1894), Vol. III, pp. 64, 123, 403, 711 ff. Further evidence is to be found in Jonathan Elliot, *Debates in the Several State Conventions on the Adoption of the Federal Constitution* (Washington, 1901), 5 vols. Vols. II, pp. 169, 201; Vol. III, pp. 26, 304, 305, 629; Vol. IV, pp. 130, 178.

[29] M. A. Musmanno, *Proposed Amendments to the Constitution, 1889-1929* (U. S. Government Printing Office, 1929; and Halsey, *Ibid.*, *1926-1941*, U.S. Government Printing Office, 1941).

evidence is not entirely relevant to the problem of rigidity, for many resolutions were thrown out because of their intrinsic valuelessness [30] and would have been rejected in a country where amendment is easier than in the United States.

The twenty-one amendments which have so far (1948) been adopted fall into three main groups. The first includes the first ten amendments. They add to the constitution that which had been omitted by the businesslike convention of 1787: a bill of rights.[31] These ten were added while the constitution was still plastic and novel. They were accepted by the states almost at once and constituted a "strict constructionist" program of those who, in light of the first three years, were alarmed at the strength of the new government.

The 11th amendment, ratified in 1795, was to prevent the states from having their sovereignty challenged by being liable to suits instituted by citizens of other states of foreign countries. The 12th amendment cured the ambiguity of the constitution as to the election of the President and Vice-President. The second group—the 13th, 14th, and 15th amendments—being made between 1865 and 1870, registered the principal constitutional results of the Civil War.[32] Though mainly directed to securing the complete emancipation of the slaves, and the security of their citizenship on a basis of equality with all other citizens, these articles have been liberally interpreted and

have come to mean vastly more in the life of all Americans than was intended.[33] So much for the certainty of a constitution which is written! The terms which specifically apply to slavery had previously not been obtainable by the process of amendment, or by the voluntary action of the slave states. The regular amending process was insufficient to regulate such a great spiritual and economic change. Negotiation followed negotiation, and war was the only exit.[34]

It should be noted that due to the nullification of congressional legislation, there are several amendments effecting "Recall of Judicial Review," as when the 14th amendment repudiated the doctrines of the Dred Scott case and the 16th released Congress from the limits set by the Pollock case. The 16th amendment made possible a federal income tax. This, according to the Constitution (article I, sec. 9, par. 4, and sec. 2, para. 3), was impossible, and in 1895 a judicial decision [35] declared congressional legislation [36] on the subject unconstitutional. Thenceforward, until 1909, political agitation and congressional activity were necessary until the proper majorities were obtained, and in 1913 the clause was ratified.[37] The 17th amendment changes the composition of the Senate and establishes state-wide elections; this also was the result of long agitation.[38] Then came the 18th amendment, introducing national prohibition of alcoholic liquors, and, in 1920, the 19th amendment, establishing universal suffrage, especially to include women. The 20th amendment fixed the dates for the end of Presidential, Vice-Presidential and Congressional terms of office, and the 21st repealed the 18th (Prohibition) amendment. The long-pro-

30 The impractical nature of some of these proposals is evidenced by the following examples: a resolution frequently introduced since Repeal of Prohibition, banning alcoholic liquors and forbidding drunkenness in the United States; a prohibition on intermarriage of certain races; a limitation on the peacetime public debt. Many, however, have concerned fundamental rights. An "equal rights" amendment for men and women is now being discussed, and a referendum before war can be declared has often been suggested. It has also been proposed to abolish the electoral college.
31 Cf. *Documentary History of the Constitution*, Vol. II, p. 377.
32 W. A. Dunning, *Reconstruction, Political and Economic, 1865-77*, (New York, 1898), Chap. IV ff.

33 Cf., e.g., Rodney L. Mott, *Due Process of Law* (Indianapolis, 1926).
34 Arthur M. Schlesinger, *New Viewpoints in American History* (New York, 1922), Chap. III; and J. G. Van Deusen, *Economic Bases of Disunion in South Carolina* (New York, 1928).
35 *Pollock* v. *Farmers' Loan and Trust Co.* (157, U.S. 429; 158, U.S. 601).
36 28 Stat. 509.
37 Cf. *Hylton* v. *United States* (3 Dallas, 171 [1796]).
38 G. H. Haynes, *The Election of Senators* (New York, 1906).

posed Child Labor amendment has been ratified by only twenty-eight of the required thirty-six states, and since it was presented to the states by joint Congressional resolution in 1924, it is dubious whether it will ever be passed. By its terms, Congress would be empowered to control the labor of children under eighteen.

We have already indicated the means adopted to secure Prohibition. Enough political energy, in the special degree required by the constitution, was stoked up in the Congressional electorate and in thirty-six states to overcome the opposition of other electors and of representatives themselves. Extraordinary exertions, and abnormally powerful means of propaganda, were needed to overcome the obstacles to amendment: such excitation was practiced that the mind of the voter was unbalanced (and regret followed in saner moods), and the idea that power of any kind is properly employable in such a task was made current. To all action there is a reaction, and their strength is reciprocally proportioned. The difficulties of amendment being especially great, their conquest requires an intensity of application and therefore other things being equal an unscrupulousness beyond that which is normal in political campaigns. In this order of ideas, war, civil or international, is the extreme example. In the matter of woman suffrage, too, there was an undignified and ugly struggle, although to the leaders of the women's party, the campaign was heroic and the leaders heroines. The historian of that movement says: [39]

It is one way of describing their system to say that they worked on Congress by a series of electric shocks delivered to it downwards from the President, and by a constant succession of waves delivered upwards through the people. This pressure never ceased for a moment. It accumulated in power as the six years of this work went on. There were all the episodes of sensational misdemeanors for advertisement purposes, picketing, arrests, mass meetings, forcible feeding, the martyr's defiance of au-

[39] I. H. Irwin, *Story of the Women's Party* (New York, 1921), p. 31.

thority and suffering, and such a condition of excitement that strong men roared that they would burn jails! Tremendous pressure was exerted on the States, and none so great as that on Tennessee, when it seemed likely to be the thirty-sixth State to ratify. The campaign was, in the words of the campaigners, a whirlwind. The atmosphere of Nashville, the capital, grew rapidly more active . . . tense . . . hectic. Suspicions of bribery, charges, and fears that members were renegades; and then victory—by a majority of 49 to 47!

Presently we shall draw some conclusions regarding the difficulties of the amending process as it emerges from the theory and practice of the constitutions. But one point can be stated at once: that if one man—that is, the dictator—can stay an amendment, the impetus toward assassination is immense. But there is another result, the importance of which ought to be recognized. Amendment necessarily requires such political behavior as to bring settled, composed, and rational government under a severe strain every few years. It is this or quiescence. If the amending process were less difficult, it would not be necessary to convince people by methods which make opponents and even supporters of a change ultimately feel betrayed and cheated. Obedience is not likely to be given wholeheartedly when there is such a feeling; and the law loses its sanctity as a moral obligation, for this depends not only upon its being part of the constitution, but upon the sentiment of fairness in the process of its creation. Then, when the amendment is made, it is impossible to modify it as a result of valid second thoughts produced by experience, without the same quantity and quality of propaganda used to secure its acceptance.

There is, however, a measure in all things: and the more important each vote, the fiercer the strain on the passions. An amendment can be defeated if those against it control a bare majority in thirteen states. In the Prohibition, as in the Woman Suffrage, amendment, if the thirteen states with the smallest Senates had been selected, the control of those 159 state Senators could have blocked ratification. If the thirteen wettest states had been selected, the control of less than 250 state Senators could have defeated ratification. Each vote becomes of critical importance, for and against amendment. The logic of this argument reaches its extreme exemplification if 100 per cent of the voters—that is, all—were required for amendment.[40] There is a theoretical point where, since the vote is of permanent and unalterable significance, elections would cease to be fought by rhetoric and where murder would be instituted as the only effective electoral procedure under the circumstances. Too difficult an amending procedure necessarily requires, if not the killing of the body, then the killing of mind.

As we show below, since the constitution of a dictatorship is bound up with the physical constitution of the dictator, the only way to amend the constitution is to amend the dictator's constitution; that is, to get rid of the dictator. The closer the democratic constitution gets to being a millstone around the necks of a growing society, the more violent the impulses against frustration.

Amendment in Third Republic France, Australia, Switzerland, Weimar Germany, and the U.S.S.R. No other democratic constitution is so difficult to alter as that of the United States. In Third Republic France the method was fairly simple.[41] The Chambers proposed an amendment by separate resolutions, and by an absolute majority of votes (that is, an ordinary unqualified majority). Negotiations between the political leaders of both houses settled the form and scope of the propositions. The initiative could be Parliamentary, or Presidential. The resolutions voted, the Chambers met together in National Assembly. An absolute majority of the numbers—that is, in this case, the *legal* numbers composing the National Assembly—was required for acceptance.

The constitution went under revision thrice normally: once in 1879,[42] again in 1884 and again in 1926; and once in the abnormal circumstances of the downfall of 1940. In 1884 there were four amendments, of which only two have first-class importance. The organization of the Senate was deprived of constitutional character, a wise act.[43] The amending clause was itself amended: "The republican form of government cannot be made the object of a proposition to amend."[44] In 1926 sinking-fund arrangements which had hampered the government fiscal plans were amended.[45] On this occasion there was once more raised the question which agitates the theorists: is the National Assembly limited to amendments proposed by the Chambers, or once convoked, has it a general constituent power? There was disagreement on this question in France: Duguit argued that the Assembly could proceed without limitation,[46] Esmein that the Assembly was bound.[47] The only practical precedent on the matter was the revision of 1884, in which the Assembly went beyond the scope of the amendatory proposals and decreed that "members of families which have reigned in France are ineligible for the Presidency."[48] In 1926 people were much afraid that the executive power would be strengthened.

Subsequently France suffered under a strong executive. The Vichy regime of Marshal Pétain was a despotic government. Pétain had become Premier with the resignation of Paul Reynaud on June 13, 1940. After the capitulation, he called the Chambers to Vichy, and on July 9,

---

[40] Article V contains one clause in which this is actually decreed: "Provided . . . that no State, without its Consent, shall be deprived of its equal Suffrage in the Senate." If a time should come, and it is possible that it will come, when the rich and populous states like New Jersey, New York, Pennsylvania, feel that they cannot any longer yield equal authority in the Senate to smaller and poorer states, there is likely to be extraconstitutional violence to settle the question.
[41] *Law* of February 25, 1875, article 8.

[42] Disestablished Versailles as the seat of the executive and Parliament.
[43] *Law*, August 14, 1884, article 3.
[44] *Ibid.*, article 4.
[45] *Constitutional Law* of August 10, 1926. See Joseph Delpèch and Julien Laferrière, *Constitutions Modernes* (Paris, 1928), p. 13.
[46] Léon Duguit, *Traité*, Vol. IV, p. 530 ff.
[47] A. Esmein, *Éléments*, Vol. II, pp. 501-11.
[48] *Law*, August 14, 1884.

1940, their remnants voted a new constitution, subject to formulation by Pétain and ratification by the people. (The votes are given in Chap. 16 below.) By 569 to 80, the joint session adopted the following text:

The National Assembly confers full powers on the Government of the Republic under the authority and signature of Marshal Petain with a view to promulgating in one or several decrees a new Constitution for the French State. The Constitution must safeguard the rights of labor, family, and native land.

It must be ratified by the Nation and applied by the Assemblies which it shall create.

The method of amendment in Australia, Switzerland, Germany and the U.S.S.R. exhibits interesting variations on what we have so far observed of the United States and France. In each of these countries, with the exception of the U.S.S.R. arrangements are made for reference of the amendment to the people for ratification or rejection. In the first two countries, such referenda are obligatory; in Weimar Germany they were optional. In Switzerland and Weimar Germany, further, a proposal to amend could come directly from the initiative of the people, and in the case of the Soviet Union there are other phenomena which deserve notice.

In Australia the process is as follows: [49] the amendment must be passed by an absolute majority of each house of Parliament, and between two and six months afterward must be referred to the electors in each state. In order to overcome any difficulty arising out of disagreement between the houses as to the amendment (quite possible in France until the necessary coincidence of views is produced by informal bargaining), the house proposing the amendment may repass it after an interval of three months (in the same or the next session) with or without amendments offered by the dissenting house, and it is submissible to the people whatever the attitude of the other house. The ratifying vote is a majority of all the electors voting; and a majority of states must approve. This is a simpler process than that of the

United States, yet it preserves the quality of distinguishing the process of amending the constitution from the process of amending the ordinary laws, it provides for deliberate popular assent and state rights, and it makes for stability without stultification. It gives a fundamental quality to fundamental laws, yet avoids, by its moderation, the demoralizing effect of overmuch rigidity.

And yet, from the inception of the Australian Commonwealth in 1901 down to 1945, only three proposed constitutional amendments have been accepted of a total of nineteen put to the electorate by nine referenda. This is a most conservative use in quantity, and appears even more so when measured by the desperate unwillingness to allow the Commonwealth to assume powers in economic and social matters urgently needed for the welfare of all the states considered together. The clash of interests between the more sparsely inhabited pastoral areas and the more heavily populated urban commercial and manufacturing areas has obstructed beneficent centralization.[50]

The democratic element, which is also an element lending distinctiveness to the constitution, was in European constitutions first used by Switzerland, where the referendum is indigenous, and where more importance is still accorded to it than elsewhere.[51] The first Helvetic constitution (1797) made arrangements for ratification by the primary assemblies. In a few years, tragic events wrecked the Republic. Thenceforward to 1830 there was a slow building up which included the popular constituent power. It was merely a matter of time for this to be more thoroughly organized and embodied in the amending process of the cantons and the federation. To speak of the federation only, political evolution since 1848 has

---

[49] *Constitution*, Chap. 8, article 128.

[50] Cf. Gordon Greenwood, *The Future of Australian Federalism* (Melbourne, 1946); and Kenneth Wheare, *Federal Government* (New York, 1946).
[51] The history of the cantons and the Federation is sketched in detail in Charles Borgeaud, *Adoption and Amendment of Constitutions in Europe and America* (New York, 1895), Book III.

resulted in this method of amendment: [52] (1) A distinction is made between total and partial revision. Either council, by the ordinary legislative procedure, may pass a resolution for total revision, and if either council does not agree to the question whether there ought to be amendment, it is referred to the people; or the question is referred if fifty thousand voters demand a total revision. If the vote is in the affirmative, then new elections of both houses to prepare the revision take place. (2) Partial revision—i.e., amendment proper—is proposed by the two houses acting under their ordinary procedure, or by petition of fifty thousand voters. (3) The revised constitution, or amendments, must be referred to the people and accepted by the majority of voters, and by a majority of the cantons. The constitutional initiative may occur in the form of separate general suggestions or completed bills: if the former, then the Federal Assembly, if it agrees with the sense, must draft an appropriate amendment and refer to the people. If the Assembly disagrees, it must first refer the question whether there shall be a revision to the people; and if the answer is affirmative, the revision must be carried out by the Assembly. Should the petition be already fully drafted, the Federal Assembly may at once refer it to the people; or, disagreeing with it, may submit an alternative or a motion to reject, along with the petition, to a referendum.[53]

What is the net effect of this method of amendment? (1) It gives the Swiss constitution a majesty higher than that possessed by the ordinary laws. But the difference, when compared with Swiss legislative methods, is not so great as when this method of amendment is compared with that which prevails in other countries.

For the referendum and the initiative are an important part of Swiss democracy, frequently used for ordinary legislation: except that in federal constitutional matters the referendum is compulsory, but in ordinary legislation it is optional, while the initiative requires a support of fifty thousand voters for constitutional matters and only thirty thousand for ordinary legislation. That is to say, it is more difficult to interfere with what we considered the more fundamental law.

(2) Fifty thousand voters is about only one in eighty of the population of Switzerland,[54] and is not a large number to organize with modern methods of transport and communication. Thus there is combined with the extra majesty and the solemn consultation of the people, the organized possibility of easy change. Advantage has been taken of this, for, since 1874, fourteen amendments have been offered by the popular initiative, of which five have been accepted.[55] In the same time, some thirty amendments have been proposed and submitted to the people by the Assembly; and of these, twenty-four have been accepted. The possibility of the initiative has stimulated the enterprise of the Assembly, and the enterprise of the Assembly has reduced the need for the initiative.[56] Nor has the fear of constitutional rashness been warranted by Swiss experience. Though it has been possible to undo, as easily as to establish, an amendment, there has been no reversal and little modification. The process is deliberate, not difficult, and its value is partly created by a set of conditions peculiar to Switzerland: long experience in democratic institutions, comparative simplicity of its problems, and the smallness of the country, which sets much easier problems in propaganda techniques than in larger countries.

The use of the amendment in Switzerland is in marked contrast to the conservatism prevailing in the United States and Australia. Between the general re-

52 *Constitution of Swiss Republic*, 1874 (as amended in 1891 to introduce the constitutional initiative, Chap. III, articles 118-23).
53 The matter is discussed in some detail in F. Fleiner, *Schweizerisches Bundesstaatsrecht* (Tübigen, 1923), pp. 396-98. Cf. also Jacob Burckhardt, *Kommentar zur Schweizischen Bundesverfassung* (Berne, 1931) and W. E. Rappard, *L'Individu et l'Etat* (Zurich, 1936).

54 Fleiner, *op. cit.*
55 *Idem.*
56 Cf. F. Bonjour, *Real Democracy in Operation* (London, 1920), pp. 142-43.

visions of the Swiss constitution in 1874 and 1944 there have been eighty-three constitutional referenda; thirty-four out of forty-one proposals presented to the voters by the federal legislature were approved; of thirty-five plebiscites initiated by at least fifty thousand voters, seven became law; six amendments offered by the general legislature as substitutes for those introduced by initiative were passed of seven offered. Not only in numbers but also in enlarged jurisdiction over vital economic problems in particular was the central government strengthened. The taxing power especially was extended, and with it implications for further controls. Thus, the Swiss example shows how the alteration process need not act as a deterrent in effecting social and economic reform.[57]

The German constitution of 1919 was obliged to draw its amending process directly from foreign experience and reason, for the constitution of 1871 was based upon such a peculiar set of circumstances that it could afford no guide. The constitution of 1871 being designed to secure the hegemony of Prussia and at the same time to offer safeguards to the large states of South Germany (like Bavaria and Württemberg) and being, too, an arrangement of princes and not of peoples, the effective amending power was in the Federal Council, the *Bundesrat*. More particularly, the constitution ordained that:

Alterations in the Constitution take place by way of legislation. They are considered as rejected if they have fourteen votes in the Federal Council against them. Those provisions of the Constitution of the Empire, by which certain rights are established for separate States of the Confederation in their relation to the community, can only be altered with the consent of the State entitled to those rights.[58]

Since Prussia had seventeen out of fifty-eight votes in this *Bundesrat,* she was able always to veto any constitutional amendment, but several of the larger states could

also gather fourteen votes and so block amendments.

The constitution of 1919 had a strongly democratic character, acquired by the revolutionary manner of its foundation and embodied in its substance. It also contained a comprehensive bill of rights. It was necessary to provide for movement and also for stability. There were consequently mingled the ideas of special majorities in the representative assemblies, and of the initiative of the people.

Let us first consider the problem as it presented itself to the framers of the constitution. The essential problem still lay, as before, in the position of the states forming the federation. The first impulse of Professor Hugo Preusz, in his original draft of the constitution, was to make amendment slightly more difficult than ordinary legislation. While this required but a majority of a quorum (one half the legal membership of *Reichstag*), the amending process required a two-thirds majority in a quorum of two thirds of the legal membership of both houses: *Reichstag and State Council.* Besides this, amendments were to be ratified by a popular vote.[59]

After the representatives of the states had discussed this original draft, the amending process was slightly altered by the omission of the compulsory referendum, and its use was limited to cases of disagreement between the *Reichsrat* and the *Reichstag.*[60] This was apparently due to the attitude of the states which desired a less unitary system than Preusz had prescribed in his project, for Preusz had intended to overcome resistance to a future extension of federal power by providing that, in the ultimate resort, the decision should lie with the whole people. Two things in fact weighed with Preusz. The *first* was the necessity of greater difficulty in amending the constitution in a democracy than in an autocratic state: "experience shows that every people is the more jealous and cautious in the matter of constitutional amendments, the higher

---

[57] W. E. Rappard, *Government of Switzerland* (New York, 1936); K. Wheare, *op. cit.;* and Report of the Royal Commission on the Australian Constitution (1929).
[58] *Constitution*, 14, General Stipulations, Sect. LXVIII.

[59] Article 51, *Entwurf: Reichsanzeiger,* January 20, 1919.
[60] Articles 23, Part 4, and 54.

it sets the protection of its freedom by the constitution." The *second* was the federal relationship. The extra difficulty of amendment tended to thwart the grasping of more powers by the federal authority. Preusz patently regretted this: [61]

But on the other hand the National Assembly must not disregard the fact that those powers which are not now constitutionally transferred to the Reich will be more difficult of attainment later by the amending process. What, therefore, remains to the States in this constitution, is much more secure than hitherto. But it is also important for the Reich to keep in mind this difficulty of extending its powers when it now proceeds to lay down what powers it is to have.

Little more was said in the Assembly on the question, excepting that a few interesting remarks were made by Dr. Hans von Delbrück on the importance of easy amendment, for without ease the amending process, he said, became a *"manoeuvre de force."* [62] But the Eighth Committee on the Constitution took away from the *Reichsrat* (the Federal Council) equality of power with the *Reichstag* (the Popular Assembly) in the matter of passing amendments. The power was reduced to one of initiation, or of objection to a *Reichstag* resolution. But the *Reichstag* might override either the initiative or the objection of the *Reichsrat*. In the finally accepted form (article 76) of the constitution, it was arranged that if the *Reichstag* overrode the *Reichsrat's* objection, this body could press its objection within two weeks, and demand a referendum. This arrangement, giving the *Reichsrat* the power to impose a referendum, was introduced in the Assembly, whereas the Committee's draft had arranged to leave the President a discretion in the matter of the referendum. Finally, the Assembly, at the last moment, and hurriedly, voted the inclusion of the initiative for constitutional amendments, as, apparently, a corollary of the referendum and the initiative in ordinary legislation: "If a constitutional amendment is to be decreed by a referendum conse-quent upon the popular initiative, the assent of the majority of qualified voters is necessary." This provision made amendments by the initiative more difficult than the popular decision in ordinary legislation, since in that case no more than a simple majority of actual voters is required. The number of voters needed to initiate legislation, constitutional or ordinary, was one tenth of the total qualified.[63]

Thus, in fact, three things had been accomplished: (1) Additional difficulty and majesty were lent to the constitution. (2) A mobile element was introduced in the form of the constitutional initiative, whereby one tenth of the voters, that is, about four million voters, might legally put the *Reichstag* on its mettle, causing it, if it disagreed with the suggested amendment, *nolens volens* to put it to the country, though with a statement of its own views thereon. And (3) the constitution offered the states a special safeguard against federal encroachment.

This last element in the amending process is of special importance in a federal constitution, and all federal constitutions pay special regard to the fundamental nature of federalism by such arrangements.[64] We have already seen this in the case of Weimar Germany and in the case of the United States. Switzerland demands that there shall be a majority of cantons as well as of voters for constitutional amendments, and so does Australia.[65]

The Subversion of the Weimar Constitution and the Hitler Substitute. In order to gain control of the governmental machine, Hitler and his agents at the outset utilized tactics which were barely within the letter of the law. In 1928 Goebbels said: "We enter Parliament in order to paralyze the Weimar system with its own assistance. If democracy is so stupid as to

[61] *Heilfron, Die Deutsche Nationalversammlung von 1919,* Vol. II, pp. 698-99.
[62] *Ibid.,* Vol. II, pp. 954-55.

[63] Article 73, regulating the referendum and the initiative.
[64] Although the U.S.S.R. is regarded as having a federal constitution and even allows the right of secession, no special protection, as by a referendum, is provided for.
[65] *The Constitution of the Commonwealth,* Chap. VIII.

give us free tickets and salaries for this bears' work, that is its affair . . ."

When Hitler was appointed Chancellor in 1933 after a series of *Reichstag* dissolutions and coalition cabinets (nineteen in thirteen years), he came as leader of a firmly anticonstitutional party, and consequently Hindenburg's action was unconstitutional in effect. The questionable origin of the *Reichstag* fire one month later served as excuse for a decree suspending constitutional guarantees. Article 48, section 2,[66] permitting such a step in time of emergency, provided pseudoconstitutionality.

Constitutional Amendment in the Fourth Republic of France. Two changes have been made in the method of amendment of the Fourth Republic as compared with that in the Third Republic, and both changes tend to more rigidity:

First, it is not necessary for both chambers to meet together in joint session, but their concurrence is necessary—for without it a referendum may have to be appealed to. Thus, it is the Assembly that adopts the resolution to amend: it has the initiative. If the Council of the Republic also adopts the Assembly's resolution by an absolute majority, the resolution goes forward for second reading in the Assembly, and the bill is subject to the rules relating to ordinary legislation—that is, to the relationship between the two chambers.[67] If the Council of the Republic objects, then the Assembly cannot proceed, for at least three months, from its first resolution to the adoption of the bill on second reading. And then, unless adoption on second reading is by a two thirds majority of the Assembly, or a three fifths majority of both chambers, it must be submitted to a referendum. The text (arts. 90, 94) is as follows:

Amendment of the Constitution shall take place in the following manner:
Amendment must be decided upon by a resolution adopted by an absolute majority of the members of the National Assembly.
This resolution shall stipulate the purpose of the amendment.

Not less than three months later this resolution shall have a second reading under the same rules of procedure as the first, unless the Council of the Republic, to which the resolution has been referred by the National Assembly, has adopted the same resolution by an absolute majority.

After this second reading, the National Assembly shall draw up a bill to amend the Constitution. This bill shall be submitted to the Parliament and adopted by the same majority and according to the same rules established for any ordinary act of the Legislature.

It shall be submitted to a referendum unless it has been adopted on second reading by a two-thirds majority of the National Assembly or by a three-fifths majority of each of the two assemblies.

The bill shall be promulgated as a constitutional law within eight days after its adoption.

No constitutional amendment relative to the existence of the Council of the Republic may be made without the concurrence of this council or resort to a referendum.

In the case of occupation of all or part of the metropolitan territory by foreign forces, no procedure of amendment may be undertaken or continued.

The *second* important change is made by article 95:

The republican form of government may not be the subject of any proposal to amend the Constitution.

Amendments and the Establishment of the New Russian Constitution. Once the original draft of the new U.S.S.R. constitution of 1936 was completed, it was widely circulated for discussion and criticism. Approximately 527,000 meetings were held throughout the country between June and December of 1936, with the attendance estimated at 36,500,000 people. Altogether about 154,000 proposals for amendment were made, of which 43 were acted upon. The most important of these provided direct, in lieu of indirect, elections in the selection of the Council of Nationalities, and a right of inheritance. The remaining alterations were primarily in terminology.[68]

The Amending Process and Great Brit-

<hr/>

[66] See Chap. 25.
[67] See Chap. 18.

[68] Anna Louise Strong, *The New Soviet Constitution* (New York, 1937).

ain. The chief distinction, then, between constitutions, from the standpoint of form, is in the amending process. Who has the power to alter the constitution is master of the state, and the amending clause gives this power. Everywhere except in England this has been made exceptionally difficult; and difficulty is established to provide the advantages of conservation of a set order of social relationships, and to secure deliberateness, in the hope that from this will issue respect; and both respect and growth are sought for in popular ratification and initiative.

Is Great Britain the worse off for making no special rules concerning constitutional amendments? Now, any state in which care is not bestowed on the reform of fundamental institutions wastes its well-being, physical and spiritual. Care is fundamental: not writing, nor a difficult amending process. If care, a rational weighing of all factors, is possible and probable without artificial compulsion, then difficulty of amendment is unnecessary. None of the fundamental institutions is, in fact, treated without due circumspection. The great constitutional changes of the past century in Britain have, indeed, come slowly rather than rapidly, and what is more, they have all been preceded by long years of consideration and party maneuvers, and even by collaboration between the parties. In recent years this constitutional conservatism has even taken the form of a tentative convention. The reform of the House of Lords in 1911 was preceded by two elections, and in 1923 a special appeal was made to the country on the question of protective tariff. At other times, legislation of special importance has been introduced at the end of a session in order that the country might have the opportunity to reflect before the vital debates occurred: examples of this are the Health of Towns Bill in 1847 and the Education Bill of 1917. Further, other legislation, like the Local Government Act of 1929, is introduced only after all the interests have been consulted and have had the opportunity to urge amendments to the original project. The recommendations of royal commissions usually pre-cede the drafting of laws, and these recommendations are made only after exhaustive inquiries. All in all, by its practice the British constitution has gone far toward providing for extra deliberation in matters of fundamental importance. The Home Rule Bill of 1912 was, in some of its stages, the object of a round-table conference of the political parties; the Government of India Bill of 1936 was the subject of a joint select committee and special interparty conferences; the Parliament Bill of 1947 and the Representation of the People Bill of 1948 [69] were the subject of complicated extra-Parliamentary negotiations.[70] Finally, in many cases, especially those relating to the electoral system, foreign affairs, and imperial organization, the government of the day seeks the co-operation of the opposition.

In 1946, when it was necessary to amend the rules of procedure of the House of Commons in order to enable it to cope with the flood of reconstructive measures, the number of the standing committees was increased from five to seven. However, the rule (number 46) by which bills at committee stage were automatically sent to the standing committee included the proviso that bills of *constitutional importance* should remain with the whole House of Commons.

Thus, in the British system it is almost impossible to do damage to the "liberties of the subject" on the one hand, or disregard the "necessities of state" on the other, without so much advertisement and open discussion of a protracted nature that injustice and unwisdom are sure of detection, since it is a fundamental convention that no Parliament can bind its successors.

Yet the possibility remains that in abnormal times, when excitement has been roused to an uncontrollable intensity, unwise things may be done, or acts commit-

---

[69] Cf. on this for arguments about "the permanent will" of the nation, p. 418 below.
[70] Cf. especially House of Commons *Debates,* February 16, 1948, where Mr. Churchill charged the government with breaking the pledge made in biparty negotiation. See also *Debates,* March 16, 1948.

ted which sting by their injustice and leave a mood of smoldering resentment. Occasions may arise like the General Strike of 1926 which produced the Trades Disputes Act of 1927; the law was, in fact, repealed in 1946, but for the nineteen years it lasted it unjustly crippled the financing of the Labour party.

The advantage of the British constitution is that errors may be reversed by an ordinary majority. What is fundamental, in short, is left to the people to decide, and they are also left to decide whether this shall be amended. They are expected to control themselves rather than to be controlled by the constitution.

When, in 1945, the British Labour party was returned by a large majority with a program of quite extensive specialization, it was left to that party alone to gauge what was proper, subject only to its own sense of propriety, to the technical possibilities, and to the consideration of whether it could continue to carry the country with it sufficiently so as not to risk reversal of its measures in the future. Whether its program was wise or unwise is not the question. No external obstruction troubled the exercise of the government's wisdom.

It is as easy to remedy mistakes as to make them. Is it worth while, then, to (1) set up a special amending process which implies (2) a distinction between fundamental and other laws, which implies (3) a written constitution, which involves (4) the possibility of some external authority to declare Parliament's resolutions invalid? This would have serious effects upon the whole tenor of English political behavior and organization. And yet there are some people so obsessed with the need for securing some basic rights against the power of the majority that they would be prepared to go this length. My personal view is that it is not worth while to go to these extremes in order to safeguard against remote and rare possibilities. It is good that the responsibility

should rest squarely upon Parliament; that it should therefore bear heavily upon the political parties; and that it should therefore press sharply upon the people themselves.

Such an issue was raised during the debates on the Parliament Bill in 1910. The House of Lords, it was said, was the only existing defense against interference with fundamental institutions by a chance majority in the House of Commons. Since the powers of the Lords were reduced to mere suspension for two years in the case of ordinary laws and were practically abolished for money bills, no safeguard at all remained against the rashness of the lower house. Two alternatives were suggested: either the reform of the composition and fortification of the powers of the House of Lords or, failing that, the institution of the referendum.[71] It was said that until that time the House of Lords had, indeed, acted as an assembly for referring bills of fundamental importance to the people; for were these bills mutilated or rejected by the House of Lords, the result was their reinclusion in the party program and their further discussion in election campaigns. This argument did not prevail, since it was clear that the only fundamental institutions which the House of Lords had until then safeguarded were those attacked by the Liberal party as being unjustly fundamental and ripe for amendment, if not for abolition. The issue is still open. It is to be noticed that the House of Lords during the tenure of the British Labour party has used its power to modify slightly some of the nationalization proposals, particularly the Coal and Transport Nationalization Acts (see p. 416).

71 Cf. J. A. Spender, *Life of Sir Henry Campbell-Bannerman* (London, 1923), Vol. II, pp. 351-55. Cf. Sir William Harcourt's protest, on February 14, 1894, cited in A. G. Gardiner, *Life of Sir William Harcourt* (London, 1923), Vol. II, p. 256.

9

Constitutions: Supremacy and Contents

IF one element in the fundamentality of the constitution is its paramountcy as a regulator of political behavior, how is this paramountcy secured? The constitution ceases to be fundamental unless its principles are impressed upon the legislative, the executive, and the judiciary. How is this supremacy organized? States fall into two great classes, in one of which constitutionality is ultimately interpreted by the courts of law, while in the other, political institutions—of which the representative assembly is the most important, as the lawmaking and executive-controlling institution—themselves determine the constitutionality of their actions. In the first group fall, principally, the United States, Australia, Canada, and Switzerland; in the second, Great Britain, France, and Weimar Germany (although the latter showed, after 1919, a tendency to enter the first group). For the sake of convenient exposition, we will examine England and the United States as archetypes, and will introduce any consideration of other countries but briefly. We wish to know: (1) what is the nature of the difference, (2) how it arose, (3) what is its meaning in terms of political institutions, and (4) what is the effect thereof upon the general character of political behavior.

DIFFERENCE BETWEEN UNITED STATES AND BRITISH CONSTITUTIONS

Nature of the Difference. The difference, broadly, between the two countries is

this. In Great Britain, no body has legal authority to declare an act of Parliament or of the executive invalid, or to overrule Parliament's clearly expressed opinion as to its meaning; whereas in the United States, any act passed by Congress or any executive act, upon challenge by an interested party, is compared with the constitution and if in conflict therewith is declared unconstitutional, and, as such, of no effect.[1] In England (and France) there is in effect parliamentary sovereignty; in the United States the constitution is supreme, and that supremacy is maintained by the power of judicial review. Parliament is not legally bound to respect anything, but Congress must respect the limits set by the constitution: the eighteen articles giving it power and prescribing the rights of individuals and states. The ultimate guardian of these limits and rights is the judiciary, whose summit is the Supreme Court of the United States. How did this difference arise, and what are its effects?

How it Arose. It is easier to explain the manner in which American development began to diverge from English than to say *why* it did. It seems natural that where there is a written constitution, its binding power must be proclaimed and guarded by some institution; and if there is to be a binding force at all in a constitution, it ought to bind the legislature as well as

---

[1] Oliver Field, *The Effect of an Unconstitutional Statute* (Minneapolis, 1935).

[139]

other organs. Yet, in fact, this logic was not adopted in the French Third Republic, which possessed a written constitution, and though there were eager champions of it there were as vigorous opponents; nor were the courts of justice in Germany before 1919 permitted to review legislation. Nor does the Swiss Federation submit to judicial review, but only the cantons.[2] Why, then, the United States? In spite of the efforts of American historians and political scientists and constitutional lawyers, the matter remains a little obscure.

There are two main possibilities: that the courts at a certain point of time simply took this power and expediency caused its confirmation, and (or) the Fathers of the Constitution really intended that there should be judicial review. The first is demonstrably true. But the question of intention is still obscure; and the best that has so far been done to review the situation at the time of the framing of the constitution has yielded these results:

(1) Both the English constitutional conflicts of the early seventeenth century and the American colonial case against England rested upon the notion of a Fundamental Law. (2) In England, the struggle resulted in the establishment of Parliamentary supremacy, but, in America, constitutions were actually created by the people in whom sovereignty inhered; legislatures were the creatures of this sovereignty, and therefore subject to the law which created them. (3) The Constitutional Convention of 1787 was called partly—very largely, in fact—in order to create a defense against the crude state legislatures which were pursuing a jealous separatism, and which threatened, moreover, private rights like the keeping of contracts. (4) Some of the states had already tentatively commenced judicial review,[3] and the most notable figures of the

Convention actually desired it.[4] (5) Virginia had even suggested that the federal legislature should have power to review the constitutionality of state laws and to call forth the force of the Union against any state that failed to keep its obligations, and that acts of the federal legislature should be subject to the review of a council of revision composed of the executive and a part of the judiciary.[5] (6) The belief that the separation of powers would secure the liberty of the subject, by preventing either legislative or executive encroachment, was one of the most compelling ideas in American political philosophy, and it was given point by the fear of contemporary legislatures and the reputation of the courts, which, trained in the common law, were assumed to be dependable guardians of private rights. The judicial power was therefore a definite and separate power; and this definiteness and separateness were expressed in the words of a Massachusetts representative as a maxim than which none was better established: "that the power of making ought to be kept distinct from that of expounding the laws." This view was shared by the leading and most eloquent members of the Convention.[6] Yet in Third Republic France and Switzerland the same doctrine, the separation of powers, has been and is used as an argument not for, but against, judicial review.[7] (The law in

---

Cf. also E. S. Corwin, *Court over Constitution* (Princeton, 1938), Chap. 1; C. G. Haines, *The Revival of Natural Law Concepts* (Harvard, 1930), *The Role of the Supreme Court in American Politics, 1789-1835* (Berkeley, 1944), and *The American Doctrine of Judicial Supremacy*, 2nd edition (New York, 1932); and B. F. Wright, *Growth of American Constitutional Law* (Boston, 1942), Chap. II.

[4] Charles Beard, *The Supreme Court and the Constitution* (New York, 1912), p. 17 ff.

[5] Max Farrand, *Records of the Federal Convention*, Vol. I, *passim*.

[6] E. S. Corwin, *Court over Constitution* (Princeton, 1938).

[7] Cf. M. Hauriou, *Principes de Droit Constitutionnel* (Paris, 1929), p. 279. Hauriou, however, is in favor of judicial review. Léon Duguit, *Traité de Droit Constitutionnel* (Paris, 1924), Vol. III, p. 673 ff., is strongly of the opinion that the separation of powers theory requires judicial review.

---

[2] Fleiner considers this to be unfortunate. See F. Fleiner, *Schweizerisches Bundesstaatsrecht* (Tübingen, 1923), p. 442 ff. All federal acts are compulsory on the High Court.

[3] See E. S. Corwin, Note V, on "Alleged Precedents for Judicial Review," in *The Doctrine of Judicial Review* (Princeton, 1914), p. 71 ff.

Fourth Republic France is very different from before 1945—it is discussed presently.)

The argument has also been advanced that the overriding of colonial legislation by the Privy Council, and of the colonial courts by the Judicial Committee of the Privy Council, sustained the idea that the organs of government were not absolute. This may have been the case, though this kind of executive and judicial review is not on all fours with the review of constitutionality by the courts.[8]

No article whatsoever in the United States constitution expressly declares that it shall be interpreted by the courts, and by them alone. The only articles relative to judicial review are those on the constitution of the judiciary, and it is argued that the general principles of judicial review were so much a matter of course, owing to the various factors indicated above, that the articles *must be assumed* to embody them. When, therefore, the convention adopted article III of the constitution, vesting "the judicial power of the United States in one Supreme Court and such inferior Courts as the Congress shall from time to time ordain and establish," it must be regarded as having expressed the intention of excluding Congress altogether from the business of law interpreting.[9] Further, section II of the same article provides that, "The judicial Power shall extend to all Cases, in Law and Equity, arising under this Constitution . . ." Therefore it must extend to the lawmaking powers of Congress. And, finally, article VI, paragraph II of the constitution runs:

This Constitution, and the Laws of the United States which shall be made in Pursuance thereof; and all Treaties made or which shall be made, under the Authority of the United States, *shall be the supreme Law of the Land;* and the Judges in every State shall be bound thereby, any Thing in the Constitution or Laws of any State to the contrary notwithstanding.

The constitution is made supreme law. Even in the states, and even if state constitutions are contrary, the constitution shall prevail, its guardians being the judges! This latter section was proposed by the New Jersey plan, the project of the smaller states in the convention, as the alternative to the Virginia plan, which would have subjected the states to the Federal Congress, and it follows the New Jersey plan almost word for word. The constitution, then, is by this article, the supreme law of the land, and by article III the judicial power shall be vested in one Supreme Court, etc. It is argued that this conclusion was intentional. But all that we have today is a proof of the contemporary need for judicial review, and some proof of its desirability.[10] Unfortunately, no express resolution was taken on this matter in the convention: nor was there a direct discussion upon it. We are in the realm of conjecture: and all that can be said is that *probably* the convention desired it.[11]

In commending the constitution to the states for ratification, Hamilton is definite and emphatic about the power of judicial

[8] For an examination of the analogies, see E. B. Russell, *Review of American Colonial Legislation by the King in Council* (Harvard, 1915); L. W. Labaree, *Royal Government in America* (New Haven, 1930); and Arthur M. Schlesinger, "Colonial Appeals to the Privy Council," *Political Science Quarterly*, 1913, pp. 279 and 433.
[9] E. S. Corwin, *Doctrine of Judicial Review* (Princeton, 1914) p. 42.

[10] Cf. Charles Beard, *op. cit.*, p. 55. In P. L. Ford (ed.), *Pamphlets on the Constitution* (Brooklyn, 1888), there is hardly a mention of judicial review, and where it is mentioned there is no sign at all that the authors had in mind what it has come to be. But see the stalwart rejection of even this by L. B. Boudin, *Government by Judiciary* (New York, 1932).
[11] See the hearings in 1937 before the Judiciary Committee of the Senate on Reorganization of the Federal Judiciary (75 Cong., 1st sess., 1392, pts. 1-6), noting especially the testimony of Professor Corwin. With reference to judicial review he stated: "These people who say that framers intended it are talking nonsense; and the people who say they did not intend it are talking nonsense. There is evidence on both sides. Why not deal with the question as it stands in the year of grace 1937?" (Part II, p. 176.)

review.[12] Nothing could be clearer or more uncompromising than his statement. Its trenchant terms do seem to take for granted the law of the matter as implied in the constitution—and Hamilton was a delegate to the convention which made it —but that point is less important than his stern opposition to the "imprudence" of the people, his aversion from "the majesty of the multitude." Popular sovereignty he had been unable to check with his proffered but rejected proposals for a very strong executive and a senate appointed for life. His way to check the unsteadiness of the masses, and their almost certain attack on the rich, was the check of rights maintained by the judiciary, which was not elected by the people. Hamilton's theory reveals in the most graphic fashion the enormous gulf between the American and the British Constitutions.

Is it not an ironic commentary upon the supposed definiteness of written constitutions that the most characteristic feature in which the American is different from most other written constitutions—its radical distinction—is placed so uncertainly in the constitution and has to find its rightful position by an appeal to what *may* have been in the minds of those who framed it?

The law was hammered into its place in two famous cases decided in the Supreme Court under the chief justiceship of John Marshall, a strong supporter of the federation against the states, and a vigorous upholder of judicial review. The first was *Marbury* v. *Madison* (1803),[13] and the second *McCulloch* v. *Maryland* (1819).[14]

The opinion delivered in the first case deserves extensive quotation, because it is not merely an essential part of the development of this peculiarity of the American Constitution, but is also a commentary upon written constitutions. This case was an issue between Marbury, who claimed title to a commission of justice of the peace, and James Madison, then Secretary of State, who should have delivered the commission to him. Marbury asked the Court for a mandamus commanding the delivery of the commission. Marshall gave judgment, refusing the writ on the ground that the Supreme Court had appellate jurisdiction only, and that this action was original. The action had been brought under the Judiciary Act of 1789, passed by Congress and empowering the Court to issue writs of mandamus to any courts or officers of the United States. This clause Congress had not the right to make, for the constitution limited the Supreme Court to appellate jurisdiction excepting in four instances. Thereupon, Chief Justice Marshall asserted the supremacy of the constitution and the power of judicial review.[15] These are the weightiest passages:

Certainly all those who have framed written constitutions contemplate them as forming the fundamental paramount law of the nation, and consequently the theory of every such government must be, that an act of the legislature, repugnant to the constitution, is void. This theory is essentially attached to a

---

12 *The Federalist* (Everyman edition), No. 78, p. 397. "The interpretation of the laws is the proper and peculiar province of the courts. A Constitution is, in fact, and must be regarded by the judges, as a fundamental law. It therefore belongs to them to ascertain its meaning, as well as the meaning of any particular act proceeding from the legislative body. If there should happen to be an irreconcilable variance between the two, that which has the superior obligation and validity ought, of course, to be preferred; or, in other words, the Constitution ought to be preferred to the statute, the intention of the people to the intention of their agents."

13 *Marbury* v. *Madison*, I Cranch, 137 (1803).
14 *McCulloch* v. *Maryland, et al.*, 4 Wheaton, 316 (1819).
15 In view of recent attacks on judicial power, Marshall "welcomed the opportunity of fixing the precedent in a case in which his action would necessitate a decision in favour of his political opponents." Charles Warren, *The Supreme Court in United States History* (Boston, 1922), Vol. I, p. 243. "It must be noted that to contemporary opinion the importance of the decision lay in its alleged invasion of the Executive prerogative (i.e. that the Court might issue mandamus to a Cabinet official who was acting by direction of the President)." (*Ibid.*, p. 232.) Cf. also A. J. Beveridge, *Life of John Marshall* (New York, 1919), Vol. III, Chaps. 2 and 3.

written constitution, and is consequently to be considered, by this court, as one of the fundamental principles of our society. It is not therefore to be lost sight of in the future consideration of this subject. . . .

These principles were reinforced and applied to the supremacy of the federation over the states in a second famous case, *McCulloch* v. *Maryland*. But the principal importance of this case is its statement and application of the doctrine of interpretation known as "implied powers." The issue was this: Congress had passed an act in 1816 incorporating the Bank of the United States. A branch was established in Maryland, which imposed a tax upon notes issued by any bank or branch thereof established without its authority. McCulloch, the cashier of the Maryland branch, appealed against the judgment of the Maryland courts. The Supreme Court, speaking through Chief Justice Marshall, ruled that Congress had the right to incorporate such a bank, and therefore the states must not thwart the use of this power by taxation. There was, indeed, in the constitution, no specific power given to the United States to establish such a bank. But this was merely because everything could not possibly be expressly included in the constitution. Nothing excluded from the constitution "incidental or implied powers."

Thus leaving the question, whether the particular power which may become the subject of contest has been delegated to the one government, or prohibited to the other, to depend upon a fair construction of the whole instrument. . . . A constitution, to contain an accurate detail of all the subdivisions of which its great powers will admit, and of all the means by which they may be carried into execution, would partake of the prolixity of a legal code, and could scarcely be embraced by the human mind. It would probably never be understood by the public. Its nature, therefore, requires, that only its great outlines should be marked, its important objects designated, and the minor ingredients which compose those objects be deduced from the nature of the objects themselves. That this idea was entertained by the framers of the American constitution is not only to be inferred from the nature of the instrument, but from the

language. . . . It is, also, in some degree, warranted by their having omitted to use any restrictive term which might prevent its receiving a fair and just interpretation. In considering this question, then, we must never forget, that it is *a constitution* we are expounding.

Very well: of what general power is the power to establish a bank a fair corollary? Of the power of the sword, the purse, external relations, and the government of industry.

It may with great reason be contended that a government, entrusted with such ample powers, on the due execution of which the happiness and prosperity of the nation so vitally depends, must also be entrusted with ample means for their execution. The power being given, it is the interest of the nation to facilitate its execution. It can never be their interest, and cannot be presumed to have been their intention, to clog and embarrass its execution by withholding the most appropriate means. . . . It is then, the subject of fair inquiry how far such means may be employed.

Indeed, to the enumeration of Congress's powers is added that of making

all Laws which shall be necessary and proper for carrying into Execution the foregoing Powers, and all other Powers vested by this Constitution in the Government of the United States, or in any Department or Officer thereof.

Of the degree of necessity, said Marshall, Congress is properly the judge, not the courts.

Let the end be legitimate, let it be within the scope of the constitution, and all means which are appropriate, which are plainly adapted to that end, which are not prohibited, but consist with the letter and spirit of the constitution, are constitutional.

Well over a century has elapsed since these judgments were rendered. The doctrines were often disputed, but judicial interpretation survived them, and the power of the courts to review the constitutional validity of laws is the most striking feature of the American political system. From 1789 to the present over 40,000 cases have come before the Supreme Court, judgment upon which decided the validity of the laws and the meaning of constitutions. Of these, eighty federal laws were ruled unconstitutional.[16]

Schools of judgment have been synthesized in the brains of political and constitutional theorists: there are "strict constructionists" and "liberal constructionists," "conservatives" and "liberals," those who lean towards "states' rights" and those who subserve "national centralization." The doctrine of "implied powers" has given special scope to the discretion of the courts. "To make all laws which shall be necessary and proper . . ." has been called the "elastic clause," and where there is no warrant at all in the constitution, a doctrine of the "inherent powers" of government has been enunciated.[17] What, then, is the import of this political arrangement?

Consider the simplicity of the decision in the Butler Case,[18] invalidating the AAA, as set forth by Justice Owen J. Roberts:

Every presumption is to be indulged in favor of faithful compliance by Congress with the mandates of the fundamental law. Courts are reluctant to adjudge any statute in contravention of them. But, under our frame of government, no other place is provided where the citizen may be heard to urge that the law fails to conform to the limits set upon the use of a granted power. . . . If the statute plainly violates the stated principle of the Constitution we must so declare. . . .

The expressions of the framers of the Constitution, the decisions of this court interpret-

---

[16] No estimate of the importance of judicial review can be based only upon these or any figures. It can be judged only by the significance of the cases reviewed and reviewable. We show later that some of these are of supreme political significance. See W. C. Gilbert, *Provisions of Federal Law Held Unconstitutional* (U.S. Government Printing Office, 1936). For a careful examination of the "political" tendency of Supreme Court judges, see C. Herman Pritchett, *The Roosevelt Court* (New York, 1948). For the feelings which suffuse a Justice, Cf. Charles E. Hughes, *The Supreme Court of the United States* (New York, 1928), and Robert H. Jackson, *The Struggle for Judicial Supremacy* (New York, 1941).

[17] Cf. *Missouri* v. *Holland*, 252 U.S. 416, 40 S. Ct., 382 (1920).

[18] *U.S.* v. *Butler*, 297, U.S. I, 56 S. Ct., 312 (1936).

ing that instrument, and the writings of great commentators will be searched in vain for any suggestion that there exists in the clause under discussion or elsewhere in the Constitution, the authority whereby every provision and every fair implication from that instrument may be subverted, the independence of the individual states obliterated, and the United States converted into a central government exercising uncontrolled police power in every state of the Union, superseding all local control or regulation of the affairs or concerns of the states."

Justice Harlan F. Stone replied in the dissenting opinion:

The power of courts to declare a statute unconstitutional is subject to two guiding principles of decision which ought never to be absent from judicial consciousness. One is that courts are concerned only with the power to enact statutes, not with their wisdom. The other is that while unconstitutional exercise of power by the executive and legislative branches of the government is subject to judicial restraint, the only check upon our own exercise of power is our own sense of self-restraint. For the removal of unwise laws from the statute books appeal lies not to the courts but to the ballot and to the processes of democratic government. . . .

. . . interpretation of our great charter of government which proceeds on any assumption that the responsibility for the preservation of our institutions is the exclusive concern of any one of the three branches of government . . . is far more likely, in the long run, to obliterate the constituent members of "an indestructible union of indestructible states" than the frank recognition that language, even of a constitution, may mean what it says: that the power to tax and spend includes the power to relieve a nation-wide economic maladjustment by conditional gifts of money.

The so-called "Brandeis brief" was like a minister's speech or report recommending legislation to a legislature!

GOVERNMENT BY JUDGES

The United States. In the United States, the constitution is superior to the judgment of the authorities it creates, and the courts interpret the constitution: in other words, the courts are superior to the judgment of all other institutions, including Congress. Chief Justice Hughes once asserted: "We are under a constitution, but the constitution is what the judges say it is." Now, there is no set rule of construction which will unify the judgment of the nine men who at any one time constitute the Supreme Court, or the many inferior judges throughout the country. The logic of construction is created by the judges; it governs their mind and it is not something external to them. For logic is procedure and no more, but the decision of a judge depends upon the nature of the premises from which he proceeds. If by nature or the conviction of learning and experience the judge is individualist (as Herbert Spencer might have been) or favors small states (as William James might have done) or (like millions of socialists) believes that the community has large rights of control over the individual, or is conservative (as Chief Justice White and Justices Field, Sutherland, and Van Devanter were), these convictions enslave juristic logic and unavoidably emerge in the judgment. Thus, two things are of importance in the power of the courts: their rules of construction, and the nature of their membership.

There is no indisputably authoritative system of interpretation: nothing which is universally accepted. That which exists is a synthetic production of commentators and law schools. It is a collection of sayings and reasons extracted from judgments rendered. But the judges contradict each other. They contradict themselves—not always on different occasions. Their real motives do not always square with their expressed reasons. Obviously the rules are general and vague: and just as obviously their number complicates the issue and trammels the conscience. A fresh case is liable to call for a fresh rule, or such an application of an old one that it becomes unrecognizable without the services of intricate casuistry, as consideration of some of these rules show.[19]

British Judges No Authority over Parliament. It has already been suggested that in the British constitution, no body has legal authority to declare an act of Parliament or of the executive unconstitutional. In Britain there is in effect Parliamentary sovereignty. Parliament is not legally bound to respect anything, whereas Congress must respect the article giving it power, and the court will see to it that Congress does, and Congress acknowledges, even if it happens to be irked by the invalidation of its work. In the British constitution, when Parliament has indubitably stated its will in the unmistakable terms of a statute, that statute is sovereign, and the judges have nothing to do but to apply it to the case before them. If the words are unmistakable, no ground is left for judicial bias in interpretation, no loophole for the introduction of extraneous doctrine or philosophy.

Suppose, however, there is an ambiguity or vagueness in the language of the statute. Since the judges must fulfill their function of interpretation, how will they interpret? The principles of common law guiding the British judiciary on this question of constitutionality have been indicated by Keir and Lawson: [20]

(1) The state is not liable to suit unless by express legislative provision.

(2) Fundamental rights are not to be withdrawn by other than direct legislation; thus there is to be no deprivation of the common-law rights of individual freedom, or property without compensation, unless expressly stated, and penal and taxing legislation is to be strictly construed.

(3) Any change in the process of government which is the unintentional result of legislation on other matters will not be permitted.

(4) Wide latitude will be granted the executive in questions on the extent of its powers during periods of national emergency.

In 1610 Justice Coke introduced the

[19] *Annotated Constitution of the United States of America* (U.S. Government Printing Office, 1928), p. 57-77, "General Principles of Interpretation." Cf. also E. Levi, "Introduction to Legal Reasoning," *University of Chicago Law Review*, April, 1948.
[20] Keir and Lawson, *Cases on Constitutional Law* (Oxford, 1928), Chap. 1.

doctrine that the common law is above the House of Commons—in the celebrated Bonham's case—but the supremacy of Parliament prevailed. Note the statement of Justice Willes in *Lee* v. *Bude and Torrington Junction Railway Company:* [21]

I would observe, as to these Acts of Parliament, that they are the law of this land: and we do not sit here as a court of appeal from parliament. It was once said,—I think in Hobart,—that, if an Act of Parliament were to create a man judge in his own case, the Court might disregard it. That dictum, however, stands as a warning, rather than an authority to be followed. We sit here as servants of the Queen and the legislature. Are we to act as regents over what is done by Parliament with the consent of the Queen, lords, and commons? I deny that any such authority exists. If an Act of Parliament has been obtained improperly, it is for the legislature to correct it by repealing it: but, so long as it exists as law, the Courts are bound to obey it. The proceedings here are judicial, not autocratic, which they would be if we could make laws instead of administering them.

Thus in Britain, fundamental issues are decided by Parliament, which means they are decided almost by direct democracy.

American Judges and Statesmen. It will be seen how many opportunities occur for the personal prejudices of the judges to have effect as part of the constitution of the United States. Indeed, little else could be expected where a constitution of twenty-eight articles and some eight thousand words was made substantially to fit a ruder society and is expected to serve the highly complicated one of today.[22]

The transient problems of less than 4,000,000 people at the end of the eighteenth century seemed permanent and necessary, and the thirteen sparsely populated agricultural communities could not but be altogether blind to coming things. How shall a constitution chiefly made to serve such a small society serve a nation of forty-eight states, spreading over a diversified continent, with a 145,-000,000 inhabitants, and these not of a primitive agricultural but of an ultra-modern industrial and agricultural civilization?

Now, the lawmaking activity of parliaments in Britain and Western Europe in the nineteenth and twentieth centuries has been directed to three main ends: (1) to regulate commerce and manufactures; (2) to mitigate the evils arising from the reign of laissez faire in social and industrial relationships, and (3) to establish a new relationship between the legislature and the executive, in which the executive receives a substantial discretion to elaborate the law by the formulation of orders, decrees, and rules.

In all other countries but the United States, the scope and substance of state activity has been determined in general by the unchallenged discretion of representative assemblies. In the United States alone has it been defined and often seriously limited by the courts.

They have been untrammeled in their use of political power and in the making of social and economic legislation, and they have, at their own discretion, delegated sublegislative and judicial powers to the executive. What they could do and did depended rather directly on what the electorate desired and was prepared to stand, and not on what the judiciary would validate. For Congress has been obliged to respect constitutional clauses which were made before large-scale enterprise or capitalistic industry had shown its characteristic signs, and those clauses are peculiarly rigid, since the amending process is so difficult. The whole tone of the constitution is laissez faire and local government: it safeguards liberty and property and state rights, whereas the developments of the nineteenth century have been towards collectivism and centralization. All the chief clauses of the constitution have had to be interpreted under the pressure of these problems. But the three which have caused most anxiety,

---

[21] *Law Reports 6,* "Common Pleas," 1871, p. 582.
[22] Felix Frankfurter and J. M. Landis, *The Business of the Supreme Court: a Study in the Federal Judicial System* (1928); and see Association of American Law Schools, *Selected Essays of Constitutional Law* (Chicago, 1938), 4 vols.

most difficulty, and most controversy are the commerce clause,[23] the due-process clauses, and the general-welfare clause.

In the interpretation of the due-process clauses, the term upon which the courts fall back is "reasonable." If the law is "reasonable," the process of its creation is "due," and it is constitutional; if the law is "unreasonable," it does not represent a "due" process, and the law is unconstitutional. Here the discretion left to the Supreme Court is tremendous.

For many years it succeeded in emasculating federal and state legislation in which the police power was invoked for regulating economic activity, working conditions in particular. In 1905, in the case of *Lochner* v. *New York* (198 U.S. 45), the Court held

. . . that there can be no fair doubt that the trade of a baker, in and of itself, is not an unhealthy one to that degree which would authorize the legislature to interfere with the right to labor, and with the right of free contract on the part of the individual, either as employer or employee.

(However, in 1917, Oregon legislation providing for a ten-hour day for all workers in industry was upheld in *Bunting* v. *Oregon* [243 U.S. 426].) Justice Holmes, dissenting in the Lochner Case, had indicated that he thought "reasonableness" should be what a

. . . reasonable man might think a proper measure on the score of health. The Fourteenth Amendment does not enact Mr. Herbert Spencer's *Social Statics*. . . . A Constitution is not intended to embody a particular economic theory, whether of fraternalism and the organic relation of the citizen to the state or of laissez-faire. It is made for people of fundamentally differing views, and the accident of our finding certain opinions natural or familiar, or novel and even shocking, ought not to conclude our judgment upon the question whether statutes embodying them conflict with the Constitution of the United States.

The Court was even slower in admitting the constitutionality of minimum-wage legislation. In 1923, *Adkins* v. *Children's*

Hospital (261 U.S. 525) invalidated a minimum-wage law for women, saying:

If, in the face of the guarantees of the Fifth Amendment, this form of legislation shall be legally justified, the field for the operation of the police power will have been widened to a great and dangerous degree. A law to fix a maximum wage might one day follow.

The majority also objected to the fact that the minimum was supposed to be sufficient "to supply the necessary cost of living to women workers" and failed to consider the value of their services. Holmes stated in his dissent:

When so many intelligent persons (Congress, many States, and governments from which we have learnt our greatest lessons), who have studied the matter more than any of us can, have thought that the means are effective and are worth the price, it seems to me impossible to deny that the belief may be held by reasonable men.

In 1933, when New York State provided for a minimum-wage law for women and children, it stated specifically that the wage should be no greater than the reasonable value of the work. Again, in 1936, the Supreme Court held that the law involved deprivation of the liberty of contract as provided by the due-process clause of the 14th amendment (*Morehead* v. *Tipaldo*, 298 U.S. 587). Finally, in 1937, the Court upheld a Washington minimum-wage law; delivering the majority opinion in *West Coast Hotel* v. *Parrish* (300 U.S. 379), Chief Justice Hughes declared:

The Constitution does not speak of freedom of contract. It speaks of liberty and prohibits the deprivation of liberty without due process of law. In prohibiting that deprivation the Constitution does not recognize an absolute and uncontrollable liberty. Liberty in each of its phases has its history and connection. But the liberty safeguarded is liberty in a social organization which requires the protection of law against the evils which menace the health, safety, and morals of the people. Liberty under the Constitution is thus necessarily subject to the restraint of due process, and regulation which is reasonable in relation to its subject and is adopted in the interests of the community is due process.

---

[23] Article I, sect. 8, para. 3; Amendments V and XIV, article I, sect. 8, para. 1.

The future use of the due-process clause may well be confined primarily to procedural issues and questions of the power of administrative agencies, rather than to the constitutionality of laws. The famous "switch in time" in the Court's decisions in 1937 resulted in the upholding of far-reaching economic legislation on the basis of new and more liberal constitutional interpretations. National legislative power under the commerce clause was particularly affected. In 1937, in the case of *National Labor Relations Board v. Jones and Laughlin* (301 U. S. 1; 1937), upholding the validity of the National Labor Relations Act, the Court said:

When industries organize themselves on a national scale, making their relation to interstate commerce the dominant factor in their activities, how can it be maintained that their industrial labor relations constitute a forbidden field into which Congress may not enter when it is necessary to protect interstate commerce from the paralyzing consequences of industrial war?

(In the *NIRA* case it was held necessary to show direct effect on interstate commerce for the federal government to have jurisdiction.) In 1937 in *Helvering* v. *Davis* (301 U. S. 619), the Social Security Act was upheld as a proper exercise of the taxing power for the general welfare, since an evil, like unemployment, might spread from one locality and affect the general welfare of the whole national area: a far-reaching doctrine indeed. The Supreme Court's mind had, indeed, undergone a great transformation.

Thus, as we suggested, the three chief clauses of the constitution have been the focus of judicial policy making. There is an additional aspect, for which, however, there is no specific constitutional clause. It is the dictum *delegatus non potest delegare:* "When power is delegated, power cannot be delegated further by the delegate." These were not issues for the courts in other countries. There the legislatures were supreme in setting and defining law.

The commerce clause empowers Congress "To regulate Commerce with foreign Nations, and among the several States.

. . ." It is clear that in so far as interstate commerce is concerned, the elastic terms are "commerce" and "among the several States." What is commerce? Does it include telegraph messages which move, substanceless, through wires; correspondence sent by correspondence colleges; passengers on railways; women in white-slave traffic; manufactures not yet moved, but intended to be moved, into other states? At what point do commodities of commerce acquire the character interstate, and when do they cease to fit into this classification? Where is the margin between regulations which affect only interstate conditions and those which, in fact and with intent, govern the domestic industrial conditions within each state? [24]

The Political Consequences of Judicial Review. We are now in a position to realize the full distance between the American and British constitutions and between the former and European written constitutions. In America, there is a tribunal superior to Congress. In Great Britain there is none superior to Parliament. It may be and often is said that it is not the Supreme Court which is superior to the Congress, but the constitution. This, however, is only a verbal quibble, for the constitution does not speak; within the oracle are men, who construe the constitution. Nor do they know what the constitution originally meant—nor even were all its makers agreed upon what it meant.[25] It was, indeed, a favorite idea of the Fathers, excellently expressed in the Massachusetts constitution, that "this shall be a government of laws and not of men." Vain delusion! For whatever speaks through the mouth of man, speaks through his mind, and of all that molds

[24] W. W. Willoughby, *The Constitutional Law of the United States,* 2nd edition (1929), 3 vols., Vol. II, Chaps. XLII-XLVIII; G. C. Henderson, *The Federal Trade Commission* (1924); E. S. Corwin, *The Commerce Power versus States Rights* (Princeton, 1936); and J. E. Kallenbach, *Federal Cooperation with the States under the Commerce Clause* (Ann Arbor, 1942).
[25] Cf. the diversity of opinion about the nature of the federal relationship; see Chapters 10 and 26 on federalism and on the presidency.

it; and this, in a developing civilization, steadily supplants the original law.

What, then, is the fundamental difference between the American and the British constitutions? It is this. The British Parliament, democratically elected, is the ultimate authority over the appropriate principles of the constitution at any given time. The American Congress is only the court of first instance in such decision, and is overrulable by five members of a Supreme Court of nine, not democratically elected. The fundamental issues are decided by a body of lawyers neither appointable nor dismissible by democracy. (No article and no law provides for removal of the justices!)

The only remedy against these ultimate lawgivers who, by the way, invalidate a law without bearing the responsibility of establishing a workable alternative, is a constitutional amendment by a process difficult and dangerous. James Hart has said:

The only effective means of overcoming defect of constitutional power is to amend the amendable. . . . We should not abolish or curb judicial review as such. . . . The remedy to try first is so to re-define the spending and commerce powers of Congress as to leave the Court no room to substitute its discretion in such matters for that of the national legislature.[26]

Since the amending process is so difficult, and yet amendment is necessary, the courts will be relied upon more and more to bring the constitution up to date by interpretation. In 1940, Justice Felix Frankfurter, in *Minersville School District v. Gobitis* (310 U.S. 586) very effectively stated a progressive approach to the function of the courts:

Judicial review, itself a limitation on popular government, is a fundamental part of our constitutional scheme. But to the legislature no less than to the courts is committed the guardianship of deeply cherished liberties. To fight out the wise use of legislative authority in the forum of public opinion and before legislative assemblies rather than to transfer such a contest to the judicial arena, serves to vindicate the self-confidence of a free people.[*]

Comparatively, not completely and absolutely, Great Britain is governed by politicians and America by lawyers, but by lawyers whose function is that of the politician in the highest degree. The issues to be decided by the judges are not merely technical issues, nor such as can be subsumed under a perfectly clear major proposition accepted by all; but in the end, they are moral values, and to answer them requires that men shall always be asking the question, consciously or unconsciously, "What judgment will make for the best civilization, granted my ultimate convictions about God, the Devil, Humanity, Progress, and the rest?" These judges are statesmen—and the lawyers, politicians, and teachers have put their recognition of this into terse terms: they talk of Government by Judges, Judicial Oligarchy, the Aristocracy of the Robe, Covert Legislation, Judge-made Law. (We ought to say that the executive authority, which is separately empowered by the constitution, is also subject to the same judicial control, but we have preferred to emphasize the legislative aspect.)

Since what shall be the law depends upon a majority of five judges out of nine, it is clear that the appointment of each judge is of great moment. It is not surprising, therefore, to find that on the occasion of a vacancy, the organs of opinion—press, party managers, Congress, President, "political circles" just on the fringe of official politics, the Congressional lobbies, the hotels of Washington, the seminars and common rooms of universities, passengers aboard crack railway trains and airplanes—excitedly discuss the prospect. There is almost as much ado about a Supreme Court appointment in the United States as there is in the choice of a new party leader—a possible prime minister—in parliamentary countries, with perhaps just a little less overt noise.[27]

26 "A Unified Economy and States Rights," in *Annals of the American Academy of Political and Social Science,* May, 1936, pp. 108-09.

27 Cf. Warren, *op. cit., passim,* for the struggles regarding appointments at various times; and see the following lives: C. Fairman, *Mr. Justice Miller and the Supreme Court* (Harvard, 1939); H. F. Pringle, *The Life and*

The struggle for appointments has been specially urgent of recent years, for social legislation has been a source of keen dispute. In the matter of two appointments, at least, first-class political sensations were provoked.[28] For the appointments are made by the President by and with the consent of the Senate, and the President is under obligation to the party leaders in the Senate. The party "bosses" want the available offices for party friends.

Very recently leaders of the Republican party, for many years not having the power of appointment, hinted that the Supreme Court should not be controlled by members exclusively of one party. Perhaps (not certainly) in response to this, President Truman appointed Republican Senator Harold H. Burton to the Supreme Court. But three other considerations govern appointment; geography, professional fitness, and religion. The first is of considerable importance in a federation so extensive in area. The important religious minorities, the Catholics and Jews, are "represented" by one of their community: thus we have Butler followed by Murphy, and Brandeis and Cardozo followed by Frankfurter.

From 1897 to 1937, twelve of the twenty court appointees had served on other law courts, and twelve had had political experience in the federal administration or Congress. Since 1937, of ten appointments, only two had had some (little) judicial experience; all ten had been in "politics," and nine had held high office in the federal administration or Congress.

It is not surprising that in order to overcome the obduracy of judges who persist in deciding as they believe they ought, reforms have been broached of "recall;" [29]

of establishing a special majority for constitutional invalidity; [30] of giving Congress power to override the Court's decisions,[31] or limiting any President to three Supreme Court appointments.

The most significant example of attempts at reform occurred in the clash of Franklin Roosevelt with the Supreme Court. Law by law, the New Deal program to alleviate the depression was invalidated. The NIRA, the AAA, the Frazier Lemke Act, the Gold Clause repeal, the Bituminous Coal Act, the Municipal Bankruptcy Act, the Railroad Pension Act, part of the Home Owners' Loan Act, the federal tax law penalizing illegality in liquor-business operations—all were declared unconstitutional between January, 1935, and May, 1936. In his Congressional address in January, 1937, the President said:

The vital need is not an alteration of our fundamental law, but an increasingly enlightened view with reference to it. . . . Means must be found to adapt our legal forms and judicial interpretation to the actual present needs of the largest progressive democracy in the modern world.

Later, Roosevelt proposed that the Supreme Court should consist of as many as fifteen members, one additional for each justice who did not retire within six months after reaching the age of seventy, and such a bill was introduced. This provoked a Congressional tempest, in part due to the purported challenge to the independence of the court; the court handed down a series of liberal decisions,

Times of William Howard Taft (New York, 1939); C. Swisher, Stephen J. Field (New York, 1930) and Roger B. Taney (New York, 1935); and Lief, Brandeis (New York, 1936). See also Felix Frankfurter, Law and Politics (New York, 1939) and A. M. C. Ewing, The Judges of the Supreme Court, 1789-1937 (Minneapolis, 1938).
28 The reader may be referred to two sensational cases, those of Justices Louis D. Brandeis and Hugo Black. See also Robert K. Carr, The Supreme Court and Judicial Review (New York, 1942), Chap. X.

29 Taft, Message to Congress Vetoing the Arizona Bill, cited in William Howard Taft, Popular Government (New York, 1913), pp. 169-70.
30 See Charles Warren, Congress, The Constitution and Supreme Court (Boston, 1925), Chap. VI.
31 It has also been suggested that Congress shall prevail over a judicial decision in the following manner: If a statute is held unconstitutional by the Supreme Court but is enacted a second time by Congress (at least by a two-thirds majority), it shall therefore be held constitutional. This plan would make Congress supreme and would dispense with the necessity of submitting any amendment to the constitution to the state legislature. (Ibid., Chap. V.)

validating state minimum-wage legislation, the National Labor Relations Act, and social security laws, and the bill failed.[32]

Three problems are raised by the comparison of the American practice of judicial review with British and Continental practice. The American practice of judicial review of constitutionality undoubtedly transfers from Congress the fullness of sovereignty. What is taken from Congress is ultimately taken from the people, and whether this makes in the long run for good or bad government depends upon what value one attaches to democratic government. I may be permitted here to leave the general question open. But so much about the United States is certain:

First, that a great deal of substance and dramatic effect, as distinct from transient and superficial sensationalism, are extracted from American politics by judicial review, for no politician can make a promise of major importance with the ring of truth in his declaration. Short of promising the almost unattainable—a constitutional amendment—he has very little to offer. Nor, though he roar like a bull, has he much to deny. It is significant that nonparty organizations obtained the last three substantive constitutional amendments. When vital questions are taken from the hands of the party organizations, these are themselves devitalized. But in England and on the Continent, the plenitude of powers is in the hands of the legislature, the parties, and the people. Obtain a majority in the legislature and you may, legally, change the political and social fabric of the state. Burke, in his *Reflections on Revolution,* said:

A State without the means of some change is without the means of its conservation. Without such means it might even risk the loss of that part of the constitution which it wished the most religiously to preserve.

That is a spur to parties and a spur to the people to attack or to defend; and both receive an education in political thinking and self-control. In the United States, Congress is in a perpetual state of nonage, and the people likewise are bound by a testament made by their forefathers. In the British and Continental democracies the people are simultaneously father and son. In the United States, responsibility for political behavior may be shifted on to the courts and the constitution. There is no such escape from responsibility in Britain and Europe.

Second, in the same line of criticism lies the fact that in the United States, political questions are discussed by Congress, the parties, and the electorate not merely on their merits, not as to their social advantages and disadvantages, but as to their constitutionality. This stultification of political discussion does not occur elsewhere.[33] The prior interest is in the merits of the proposition, and it not infrequently happens that whatever shows a balance of advantage becomes constitutional, if it is not so already. The discussions of constitutionality are, in the United States, always an interference with the direct consideration of political issues, and not seldom they establish a screen round the real questions. We might, indeed, add another phrase to the catalogue of logical fallacies: the *argumentum ad constitutionem.*

Finally, like all authorities which have great power, the courts, and especially the Supreme Court, are alternately abused and applauded. But courts of justice cannot afford the charge of error or bias. For the courts of justice are not only concerned with constitutional cases but with other cases, in which states, individuals, and corporations are in conflict: where people sue one against the other, where the state

---

[32] Robert Alsop and Turner Catledge, *The 168 Days* (New York, 1938); E. S. Corwin, *Constitutional Revolution, Ltd.* (Claremont, California, 1941); James Farley, *My Story* (New York, 1948), Chaps. 9 and 10; C. Herman Pritchett, *The Roosevelt Court* (New York, 1948), Chap. 1.

[33] But something like it occurs. People often retreat from the immediate matters of argument to the broader basis that the "Senate" or the "Constitution" is either benefited or jeopardized. Cf. Jeremy Bentham, *Book of Fallacies (Works,* Bowring edition). However, in America the form of the constitution, the difficulty of its amendment, and the casuistical traditions of 170 years give a prior and principal importance to this method of argument.

sues citizens: where, in short, the whole mass of claims under admitted law is decided. The multitude does not minutely discriminate, and when it mistrusts for one thing it may mistrust for another, though the cases are poles asunder; especially, also, when political leaders are unguarded and intemperate in their legitimate business of acquiring votes.

Judicial Review Unusual Elsewhere: France, Switzerland, Canada, Australia, Weimar Germany. In general, Europe has not followed the American example. It was suggested in Revolutionary France by Siéyès and included in the constitution of the Year VIII, and later in the constitution of 1852 as a "conservative Senate" for constitutional vigilance. The Consul and the Emperor simply applied it to their own uses. But there was not a little advocacy for judicial review just before World War II, and the argument in its favor, however it may begin, always ends thus:

But these varied causes of resistance do not prevent the principle from existing and of slowly propagating itself, especially when one takes into account more and more the necessity of controlling parliaments, because their legislation, motivated by electoral purposes, has become a dangerous menace to liberties.[34]

This will be found even better expressed by the politicians of the Right than by the jurist. In Switzerland, the

34 *In favor:* Cf. Maurice Hauriou, *Principes de Droit Constitutionnel* (Paris, 1929), p. 270 and p. 288 ff.; Léon Duguit, *op. cit.,* Vol. III, p. 467 ff.; A. Esmein, *op. cit.;* H. Berthélemy (*Revue politique et Parlémentaire,* December, 1925) argues that control has already occurred in some cases. *Against:* Ferdinand Larnaude, *Bulletin de la Société de Législation Comparée,* 1902, p. 175 ff.; *Revue Politique, et Parlémentaire,* February, 1926; Gaston Jèze, *Principes Généraux du Droit Administratif* (3rd edition, Paris), Vol. I, p. 344 ff. Jèze is not a blind admirer of the French parliamentarian but he thinks that, politically, judicial control is too dangerous and inconvenient. Paul Duèz, in *Melanges, Maurice Hauriou* (Paris, 1930), p. 245, is against it for the interesting reason that "in spite of security of tenure the Government . . . holds the judges in its hands if they have not altogether given up promotion."

constitution of 1874 gave to the federal courts the power to review the constitutionality not of federal laws but of cantonal laws. The referendum acts, it is suggested, as a check upon the courts— but this is not the same kind of check as judicial review.[35]

Canadian constitutional issues are resolved by the Judicial Committee of the Privy Council, which is attached neither to the central government nor the provinces but sits in London and is a British court. (In January, 1947, the Judicial Committee said it would no longer entertain appeals from the Canadian courts.) This body has limited the jurisdiction of the Canadian central government through sections 91 and 92 of the constitution. According to section 91, the Dominion is granted power "to make laws for the peace, order, and good government of Canada" over those subjects which are not specifically assigned to the provinces, and an enumeration is made of the types of subjects which may be included within its jurisdiction. In section 92 a classification of the matters over which the provinces have exclusive powers is established. However, there is no clear dichotomy. Dominion laws "for the peace . . . of Canada" will undoubtedly influence provincial powers, and vice versa. The Privy Council, in the frequent disputes that have arisen as a result of the overlap, formulated the principle (1896) that section 91 could be utilized for powers delegated to the provinces in section 92 *only* where the enumerated topics of section 91 were concerned or when "such matters as are of unquestionably Canadian interest and importance" were involved. Otherwise, it was felt that provincial jurisdiction would be greatly whittled down.

Narrow construction of section 91 and

35 F. Fleiner, *op. cit.,* p. 410. Compare also p. 448: "This constitutional judicability fulfils a special duty in the life of the Swiss Republic. In a democracy the ultimate bulwark of the constitution and law is the judge. The feeling that the law is safe is based on confidence in him. If in the narrow sphere of cantonal affairs political passion is at the helm, then the lowest citizen in the State knows that the way to Lausanne is open to him."

wide construction of section 92 followed, and only war and disease as permitting emergency legislation were sanctioned. Any economic problem not stipulated in section 91 is beyond reach of the Dominion government. On the grounds that the depression was not so severe an emergency that the general power could be legitimately invoked, the Bennett New Deal laws were invalidated in 1937 (*Attorney General of Canada* v. *Attorney General of Ontario*, A.C. 326 and 355). The court ruled that power to regulate trade and commerce did not include intraprovincial trade. Thus, judicial review hemmed Dominion controls. When the alternative of amendment was suggested, the provinces balked. Only for unemployment insurance (1940) were the provincial governments willing to amend the constitution to allow the Dominion nationwide control of an economic problem.

Australia, on the other hand, has had a far more liberal court, which has enabled it to circumvent the difficulties imposed by the almost insurmountable hurdle of passing an amendment. The High Court has jurisdiction in constitutional cases concerning the division of powers and, with its consent, appeals can be made to the Judicial Committee of the Privy Council. (This has occurred only once.) Although from its inception in 1903 until 1920, the High Court adhered to the principle that the Commonwealth and the states should not legislate in the other's sphere, in 1920 the court changed its position to allow the Commonwealth wider powers. Only where the constitution expressly prohibited the central government was it to be hindered.

Weimar Germany was the European country where the subject of judicial review was most likely to become practically important. Under the old constitution, hardly anybody supported judicial review; nor were the courts held to be competent. But it was always agreed that the laws acquired validity only if they were passed as formally ordained by the constitution and that state laws could not override but must fit in with federal law—*Reichsrecht bricht Landsrecht*—and that orders could be invalidated by the courts if they were *ultra vires,* i.e. went beyond the statute. Anything further under the Bismarckian constitution would have been incompatible with the spirit of the constitution, for the supreme political authority—the body, indeed, which judged of interstate disputes, the disputes between the federation and the states—was the *Bundesrat,* and this could not acknowledge an authority higher than itself.[36]

The constitution of 1919 had various features which were more conducive to judicial review. There was popular sovereignty, there were fundamental rights, there was a well-expressed distrust of the legislature. Was the legislature, then, to be the ultimate arbiter of constitutionality? There was no express clause in the constitution establishing judicial review. The disputants were therefore thrown back upon hints obtainable from the proceedings of the constitutional committee of the National Assembly, and general, social, and political theory applied to German conditions. Meager results alone were obtainable from the proceedings of the National Assembly and its committee. In the latter the subject was debated by several of the most capable members, among them Hugo Preusz, the framer of the constitution, but it was impossible to secure agreement. Preusz was then in favor of judicial review, saying that it existed unconditionally wherever it was not expressly excluded, although some people had asked him for express exclusion and some for express inclusion of the power of judicial review, his own view was, and remained, that if nothing was said, then judicial review "went without saying." Preusz's opinion in favor of judicial review can be described as intending to secure the *Rechtsstaat,* that is, a government subject to the law as interpreted by the courts of justice. "And now I wish to say this, that I cannot conceive of judicial activity in the full sense, if the Court is to be forced to apply a substantially unconstitutional law against its clear conviction."

36 Cf. below, Chap. 10.

The constitution therefore said nothing at all about judicial review. From its advent, jurists were much occupied with this problem, and the courts were not able to remain aloof. Broadly, opinion was divided among the jurists, and the division was based ultimately upon whether the lawyers trusted or distrusted the democratic process of government. Those who opposed unlimited democracy and mistrusted legislatures argued that the liberties of the citizen and the efficiency of the government ought not to be left to the absolute mercy of politicians, party organization, and the modern electoral process. Nor, they said, was the bureaucracy what it once was, meticulously law-abiding and public spirited, for World War I and its aftermath had shaken its morale, and democracy would cause its corruption.[37] These arguments came almost unanimously from the conservative and liberal camps, and from socialists other than those who favored full parliamentary and direct democracy. The jurists, with rather more unanimity than in France, disbelieved in the possibility of justice emanating from legislatures, and with anti-autocratic impulses still passionately moving them, they demanded, at least as strongly as the liberal thinkers of 1848, the realization of the *Rechtsstaat*. The only guarantee lay in judicial review: nothing was to be hoped from "power-hungry" legislatures,[38] parliamentary "absolutism."[39] It was plain, however, that law had nothing to do with the question. The constitution said nothing about it. The issues were political issues, and the real question of justification was begged by the lawyers. So much, once more, for the clarity of written constitutions!

The courts themselves were not able to avoid the issue, and, indeed, assumed the power of judicial review, but without the confidence or militancy of John Marshall.

In 1924 the united branches of the High Court (*Zivilsenaten*) left the question open, since there was great disagreement upon it—and this, though one branch [40] had declared its permanent competence to review constitutionality. In the Revaluation Law Case (1925), the power was asserted, with only the foundation that, since the judge is independent and "only subject to the law," [41] he has the right and duty to give judgment about which legal provisions have the most commanding power: there was no attempt, as with Marshall, to found the utility of such a power upon the importance of maintaining the supremacy of the written constitution, because supremacy is a worthy thing. It seemed, however, that this declaration had, in the mind of most German lawyers at least, settled the matter affirmatively.[42] But opinion was opposed to the power of judgment being vested in the inferior courts: one supreme court for such cases was advocated to avoid uncertainty and waste of time and argument, both evident in the United States.[43]

The Fourth Republic Makes a Change. We have already observed that the French Fourth Republic came by its constitution by a difficult process, and that its basis of compromise was singularly precarious. We have noticed also that it has an extensive bill of rights, and that it has a fairly rigid amending clause.[44]

The Fourth Republic also introduced a special procedure for controlling the constitutional validity of laws made by the National Assembly. The terms of the constitution are:

Article 91. The Constitutional Committee shall be presided over by the President of the Republic.

---

[37] This is put very clearly by F. Morstein-Marx, *Variationen über Richterliches Zuständigkeit* (Berlin, 1927).
[38] Cf. Heinrich Triepel in *Archiv des Öffentlichen Rechts*, Vol. 39, p. 537.
[39] Cf. Theisen in *Archiv des Öffentlichen Rechts*, New Series, Vol. 8, p. 274.
[40] *Reichsgerichtzivilsenat*, p. 102, p. 161 ff.
[41] So runs article 102 of the constitution.
[42] Richard Thoma, in *Archiv des Öffentlichen Rechts*, Vol. 43, p. 272 ff., is a very good example of an opponent of judicial review on the ground that the constitution already contains sufficient guarantees.
[43] Cf. Gerhard Anschütz, *Die Verfassung des Deutschen Reiches* (Berlin, 1930), p. 326; *Verhandlungen des 33. und 34. Juristentages* (Berlin).
[44] Articles 90, 94, and 95. See above, p. 124.

It shall include the President of the National Assembly, the President of the Council of the Republic, seven members elected by the National Assembly at the beginning of each annual session by proportional representation of party groups and chosen outside its own membership and three members elected under the same conditions by the Council of the Republic.

The Constitutional Committee shall determine whether the laws passed by the National Assembly imply amendment of the Constitution.

Article 92. Within the period allowed for the promulgation of the law, the Committee shall receive a joint request that it examine said law from the President of the Republic and the President of the Council of the Republic, the Council having decided the matter by an absolute majority of its members.

The Committee shall examine the law, shall strive to bring about agreement between the National Assembly and the Council of the Republic and, if it does not succeed in this shall decide the matter within five days after it has received the request. This period may be reduced to two days in case of emergency.

The Committee shall be competent to decide on the possibility of amending only Titles I through X of the present Constitution.

Article 93. A law which, in the opinion of the Committee, implies amendment of the Constitution shall be sent back to the National Assembly for reconsideration.

If the Parliament adheres to its original vote, the law may not be promulgated until the Constitution has been amended according to the procedure set forth in Article 90.

If the law is considered to be in conformity with Titles I through X of the present Constitution, it shall be promulgated within the period specified in Article 36, said period being prolonged by the addition of the period specified in article 92 above.

This very complicated procedure was accepted as a compromise among various proposals made by all the political parties for some external control over the Assembly, excepting the Communist party and a few Left-wing friends. The broad choice was among returning to the position of the Third Republic, in which there was no constitutional invalidation of anything the Chambers might deem it right to do; or adopting some form of judicial control on the American model; or finding some other way whereby the Assembly should be kept within bounds. Some Rightist groups, of small dimensions, then, were advocating judicial review, as one of them said, by a "court of independent personalities." [45] This found little encouragement elsewhere: the United States experience was plentifully commented on, it being observed that the very intention of some of the laws made by Congress (for example, the Sherman Act) had been perverted by the Court's interpretation.

All the deputies, with the exception of the Communist party, admitted the need for an outside control over the Assembly. The Communist party argued thus: The only acceptable control over the Assembly might be the people themselves, consulted in referendum. But to the referendum, the Communists said, there was the serious objection that it was reminiscent of the *plébiscite,* which under the Second Republic had been abused by a would-be dictator, Louis Napoléon, who manipulated the plebiscite to convert the Republic into an Empire. The referendum, therefore, was totally inadmissible. This left the judgment of constitutionality either to the Assembly or to some outside body not the people itself. Further, said the Communists, there could not be conceived an organ outside the Assembly which could offer better guarantees of the constitution than the Assembly itself: any other organ would be at least as liable to violate the constitution as would the Assembly itself. All power to the Soviets! [46]

Both the Socialist party and the M.R.P. were strong for popular sovereignty, and the former, whatever its qualms about history, was willing to put its faith in the referendum. It seemed to both these parties that the Assembly ought not to be permitted to be judge in its own cause.

In comparison with the British and the United States constitutions, the notable features of the French guarantee of constitutionality are these. The National As-

---

[45] *Séances,* Commission de la Constitution, December 19, 1945, p. 133.
[46] *Ibid,* pp. 135 and 137.

sembly's interpretation of constitutionality is subject to challenge: it is not supreme as is the British Parliament. The President of the Republic and the President of the Council of the Republic (that is, the second chamber) are both given an *ex officio* status. The first is part of the executive; he is outside the Assembly; he holds office for a term longer than the Assembly. The second is also a person of authority independent of the Assembly, though less of political party organization than the former. The other members of the Constitutional Committee are members of the public outside the Assembly—but they are members of the party following, and therefore cannot be expected to have a view of constitutionality different from that of the Assembly and the Council of the Republic. They have not the independent status of the judges of the federal courts of the United States. But, at any rate, a delay is possible before the law becomes effective; and if it is declared to be unconstitutional by the Constitutional Committee, the procedure and the special majority required for the passage of an amendment to the constitution must be observed. And, finally, unless the special majorities in both chambers are obtained, the sovereign people will be called in to decide the issue. It should not be easy to obtain the absolute majority in the Council needed for a challenge, considering that the political parties dominate it as well as the Assembly.

The rules of the Council of the Republic require immediate action by the Council on a motion from any of its members to seize the Constitutional Committee with a challenge; within twenty-four hours its commission must report the matter to the Council; and debate follows swiftly. It will be noticed that the committee must first attempt a reconciliation between the Council of the Republic's view and the Assembly's, which means that whatever these three bodies acting together at this stage decide to be constitutional *is* constitutional.

It will be noticed that the scope of the Constitutional Committee is limited: the Preamble of the Constitution does *not* fall within its jurisdiction—this is the Bill of Rights and basic principles, that is, the very part which might have raised most challenges, as in the United States.

SURVEY OF THE GUARANTEE OF CONSTITUTIONALITY

IF we sum up the main differences in the forms of constitutions, we may say that they arise from the attempt practically to secure the *fundamentality* of the constitution, and this is sought in three things: in writing, in the amending process, and in judicial review.

Mere writing does not secure the supremacy of the constitution, because the terms of the supreme instrument are not, and cannot be, sufficiently precise in detail and scope. Government is dynamic, and the most detailed of constitutions cannot meet all the cases which arise in an evolving society.

Supremacy is shown and maintained chiefly in the amending process, which everywhere save in England, is made formally and really more difficult, while in England itself, convention tends to make the process more difficult than ordinary legislation. Difficulty in amendment certainly produces circumspection and makes impossible the surreptitious abrogation of rights guaranteed in the constitution; and where such rights, individual or state, are believed to be easily capable of annulment without a special safeguard, a difficult amending process has thwarted furtive encroachment. Yet, if this is pressed too far, the constitution ceases to be plastically responsive, and the rights of some are safeguarded at the expense of those who ask for the creation of new rights, while the strength of new social forces may compel a substantial evasion of the constitution and its amending clause, by popular refusals to obey and by governmental inability to enforce its terms. Further, even if slowly, the body which is the interpreter of the constitution—Parliament or the courts—stretches and must stretch the meaning of the constitution until it fits the advancing facts. Too difficult a process, in short, ruins the ultimate purpose of the amending clause, to maintain good government; causes the clandestine substitution of another fundamental law which is called by the old name; and, unfortunately, causes the demoralization of the electorate by propaganda, which, to overcome the obstacle to amendment, must be particularly ruthless. But the amending clause is so fundamental to a constitution that I am tempted to call it the constitution itself.

Finally, in the United States, and partially [47] and tentatively in other countries, the fundamental quality of the constitution is secured by the establishment of the judiciary as its interpreter. This device takes interpretation out of the hands of an elected body, which is liable extravagantly to assert its own supremacy over the constitution, and puts it into the hands of a number of judges, whose training and tenure do not, indeed, transform them into impersonal oracles but, in fact, secure the triumph of the general spirit of the constitution and the social theories of about a generation back. Where the constitutional issues are of grave import for the well-being of the state, the judges, doing the work elsewhere reserved to popularly elected statesmen, begin properly to be regarded as a unit in the struggle of partisans.

In other countries, the parliament and the party system decide how far the constitution shall be supreme over them and how far they shall be supreme over the written and conventional principles of the constitution. This places a dire responsibility upon parties and the electorate, and perhaps it is as well that these bodies should directly judge the gravest issues. The politicians are forced, at least, to think of improving their machinery and behavior. Thus Barthélemy and Duez in France sum up:

We think that the guarantees against parliamentary oppression should, in the existing state of our morals, be sought elsewhere than in the judicial review of constitutionality. We must organize Parliament so that we reduce the chances of the appearance of unconstitutional laws and develop the spirit of legality within it: since bicameralism, proportional representation, reform of procedure, the referendum, seem to us, in this respect, preferable to a too heavy arm put into the hands of an organ too weak to use it surely and securely.[48]

In England, the parties and the electorate have so far been quite as able to provide the needful political institutions as countries which have withdrawn the constitution from the direct judgment of the people: indeed, have they not done better?

Lastly, judicial interpretation has been for the American constitution the most effective way of making the rigid constitution flexible enough to work. The rigid constitution has lived only by judicial respiration.

The differences between democratic and dictatorial constitutions are particularly marked. In a democracy the constitution is established for popular protection, providing security along with guarantees of fundamental rights, at the same time enabling revisions. For a constitution in a democratic state may be defined as a pattern of applied scruples, an instituted philosophy of forbearance, a declaration of self-doubt. The constitution of a dictatorship, on the other hand, is entirely at the disposal and for the safeguard of the leader's monopoly powers, permitting changes to be made at his discretion alone, and placing the populace completely at his mercy. The amending process, although somewhat bloody, is by far simpler and swifter in a totalitarian state than in a republic, but it is more difficult for the people to find the opportunity to use it in the former since the government wields up-to-date means of physical repression.

---

[47] In Australia and Canada, the High Court decides questions of constitutionality only in so far as the division of power between the federal and state authorities is concerned; for the constitution does not limit the plenitude of some government's powers. In Australia the ultimate appeal may be to the Judicial Committee of the Privy Council.

[48] Cf. Joseph Barthélemy and Paul Duez, *Traité de Droit Constitutionnel* (Paris, 1933), p. 222; cf. also Paul Duez, in *Melanges Maurice Hauriou*, p. 213 ff.

WHAT have constitution makers considered to be fundamental political institutions? It hardly needs to be insisted that the catalogue has changed with time. The power relationship in that great amassment of human beings called the state varies with every change in human resources and material inventiveness, and with every addition to the stock of ideas brought to mankind by the extraordinary of their race. These precipitate themselves into the constitution. But there is the acknowledged body of conventions, long-wrought and accepted by several generations, and there are the claims of the hour and the particular interests of the men who assemble to establish the tables of the law. These things mingle, and in the supreme instrument of government there may appear, side by side, the permanent and the transient. Yet all have the same theoretical validity. Let us glance at the development of fundamentals.

To the Eighteenth Century. (1) The constant factor, since the Agreement of the People of 1649 in England, has been the question of political authority.[49] Who shall be supreme? Shall there be direct or representative government, and whichever is chosen, how shall it be organized? In representative government, for how many years ought the assembly to be elected? Questions such as these have always been deemed fundamental, and what, indeed, could be more fundamental than the definition of legitimate power? What was decided was the substantial sovereignty of the people; the strict control of the source of all past anxieties, the executive; and a short term for the legislature.

(2) The second most constant written fundamental, though I hesitate to place its advent earlier than security from arbitrary taxation, was religious freedom.[50]

This appears in the Agreement of the People; it assumed diverse and queer forms in the American colonies, and came to a well-nigh perfect maturity in the constitutions of the American states and the federation.

(3) The third is security of property. The earliest form of this fundamental was "no taxation without parliamentary consent."[51] It later assumed an importance, not as against an absolute king and in the form of taxation, but as the individual's right to do as he liked with his own, without regard to, and without control by, the community.

(4) There is liberty: meaning (a) freedom from arrest and detention unless on well-known principles and with safeguards against official arbitrariness;[52] (b) freedom of opinion, especially in the form of written utterances; and this was first proclaimed in the Virginia Declaration of Rights;[53] (c) trial by jury[54] and equality before the law.[55]

The French constitutions expanded

---

[49] If, of course, we go back as far as Magna Charta, we shall find that it is defense against arbitrary interference with property and personal liberty—of the barons in the first place.
[50] Cf. G. P. Gooch, *English Democratic Ideas in the Seventeenth Century* (London, 1927); John N. Figgis, *Studies in Political Thought from Gerson to Grotius, 1414-1625* (Cambridge, 1923).

[51] *The Petition of Right* (1628): "that no man hereafter be compelled to make or yield any gift, loan, benevolence, tax, or suchlike charge without common consent by it of Parliament."
[52] For example: the 39th clause of Magna Charta, the Habeas Corpus Act of 1679, and the amending act of 1816.
[53] The press had by that time given a new problem to political society: could Milton's noble plea, "Give men the ability to know, argue, and utter freely," be admitted where opinion could be spread so widely and so rapidly?
[54] Cf. W. H. Holdsworth, *History of English Law*, 3rd edition (London, 1922), Vol. I, pp. 312, 320; the development of the system is treated at length in the subsequent volumes.
[55] E.g. in *Danby's Case*, Vol. II, S.T. 599 (1679), it was decided that a minister of the Crown cannot plead the orders of the Crown as an exemption from liability for an illegal action. In accordance with the Bill of Rights (1688), the Crown can no longer dispense with the provision of Acts of Parliament in favor of individuals. By the Act of Settlement (1701), a pardon by the Crown is not a bar to an impeachment in the Commons. The argument of "state necessity" and the distinction between state officials and others were dismissed by Lord Camden, C.H., in 1765. (*Entick* v. *Carrington*, 19 S.T. 1067): "The common law does not understand that kind of reasoning, nor do our books take any notice of such distinction."

these fundamentals, including new ones and reshaping the old.[56] State honors and employments were opened to all without any other distinction than that of their virtues and talents; privilege was banished from the administrative as well as the legislative branch. Taxation ought to be divided equally among the members of the community according to their abilities. The right to property being inviolable and sacred, no one ought to be deprived of it, except in cases of evident public necessity, legally ascertained, and on condition of "a previous just indemnity." Finally, "The society in which the guarantee of rights is not assured, and where there is no separation of powers, cannot be deemed to have a constitution at all."

Eighteenth Century. Until 1791 the dominant note of these fundamental political institutions was individual resistance to oppression, and the guarantee of individual rights. This tendency continues for a while. But already in 1793, the community and the *duties* of man make their quiet appearance, not indeed to cry down that obdurate expression of individual claims, but as a friendly visitor, of whom much may yet be heard. "Liberty," says the French constitution of 1793, "is the power belonging to man to do everything which does not encroach upon the rights of others: its principle is justice, its safeguard, the law; its moral limit is in this maxim: *Do not do unto others what you would not have them do to you.*" The right of property is expressed in a confident form: it is the right to "enjoy and to dispose of his goods, his income, the profits of his labor and industry at his complete discretion (*a son gré*)." And freedom to labor comes as a reaction from the police state. "No kind of work, crop, or commerce may be forbidden to the industry of citizens." There was added the article that poor relief was a sacred debt, that society owed assistance to poor citizens, either by providing work or by giving relief to those who were unable to work. Public education was declared to be a social necessity and the state sworn to provide it.

Again came the harsh voice of duty into this fair land of fundamental rights: "There is oppression against the body social when one of its members is oppressed; there is oppression against every member when the social body is oppressed."

By 1795 the fundamental propositions included not only rights but duties; they were embodied in the Declaration of Rights and Duties of Men and Citizens.[57] All the rights we have so far read were reproduced, but attached to them was a little charter of nine articles entitled "Duties." They are, in fact, the indispensable basis of the rights if these are to be more than mere paper promises, but they fall with a leaden weight after the optimism of the earlier years.

Germany, 1848. Some extension of the scope of fundamental institutions was made in the abortive German constitution of Frankfurt, 1849. In the German states, individual freedom had been particularly repressed by the operation of the Metternichian system since 1815, and therefore the instinctive reaction of the Assembly and of various groups of liberals and republicans before the Assembly met was to declare those things which were more fundamental even than organs for the exercise of sovereignty. They were interested, first, in the substance of state activity, its direction and purpose, and only secondarily in the division of power between monarch and people, parliament and bureaucracy, states and federation; and so they spent the first six months— almost the only six months of their authority—in discussing and promulgating the Fundamental Rights of the German People.[58] The fact that there were 107

---

[56] The following are paraphrases from the Declaration of the Rights of Men and Citizens of 1789-91.

[57] Constitution of September 23, 1795.

[58] *Die Grundrechte des Deutschen Volkes* ("Grundrechte" being used for the first in this Assembly). The argument in the Assembly is naturally to be found without bias only in the *Stenographische Bericht Über die Verhandlungen der deutschen Konstituierenden National-versammlung zu Frankfort a. M.*, by F. Wigand, 9 vols. (Frankfort, 1849).

professors and teachers and 182 lawyers in an assembly of 541 doubtlessly determined the pedantic attention to these fundamental rights.[59]

Individual freedom and the need for civic order were very consciously balanced. The chief formulas were: free movement and equal civic rights over the whole territory of the *Reich;* the abolition of capital punishment; the inviolability of private dwellings; secrecy of post; freedom of opinion by word, writing, print, and pictorial representation; security of freedom of the press from censorship and denial of postal facilities; and trial by jury for press offences. Religious freedom was carefully defined; free education was publicly guaranteed, and the position of the churches thereto regulated; science and teaching were declared free; the rights of petition (for corporations as well as for individuals), of peaceable assembly without special permission, and of association, were guaranteed; intellectual property was to be protected; landed property was subjected to a most complicated set of clauses, to free land for use from ancient prohibition and obligations, and to rid small proprietorship of the feudal obligations. More freedom was to be given to local authorities, and administrative law was set about with proper safeguards by the appropriate differentiation of justice and administration.

The new things that entered into this constitution can be classed under four heads: those issuing (1) from the onset of capitalism, (2) from government by public opinion, (3) from the antibureaucratic trend of thought, and (4) from the growth of rationalism. It is interesting to see the constitution slowly catching up with developing civilization. Manufactures needed factory workers, and for these, combination was the first condition of freedom. The people and the press were becoming a power; they needed freedom to attain their fullest development. The antibureaucratic creed was based on local self-government, and as the powers of the

state grew, this was considered more and more important both for liberty and efficiency; and justice was considered in jeopardy while in the hands of departments whose professional bias and interest it was to judge in their own favor.[60] Finally, rationalism and the notion of progress made for the separation of church and state, religious tolerance, and public education.

The Assembly and its constitution were swept away; but some clauses were included in the ordinary laws of some of the German states, and many were put into the constitution of 1919. The episode is interesting in this context only for the instinctive recognition of the necessity of fundamental principles and for the evidence of responsiveness to the social life of the nineteenth century.

The Weimar Constitution. The next stage in the development of the substance of written constitutions took place after World War I, when old hierarchies fell and national entities embodied in alien states were withdrawn therefrom and given an independent state life. In the new constitutions could be seen the unmistakable impress of the Industrial Revolution and the political institutions which have issued from it, hitherto hardly noticeable, even if at all inscribed in the documents. The German constitution of 1919 was the fullest: it had the most complicated social life to serve.

(1) First, then, the organizatory parts of the constitution. The states which make up the federation were empowered, and in some cases obliged, to amalgamate in order the better to serve the economic and cultural welfare of the whole nation.

In Parliamentary organization the (three-generations-old) movement for the representation of minorities bore its fruit in the establishment of proportional representation for all elections, federal, state and local. A particular obstinacy is revealed in the declaration that members of the Parliament are representatives of

---

[59] Cf. L. Rosenbaum, *Beruf und Herkunft der Abgeordneten, 1847-1919* (Berlin, 1923), p. 51 ff.

[60] Upon this see further chapters 6 and 7 on the separation of powers, and chapter 36 legal remedies against public administration and administrative law.

the "whole people," and bound by their consciences and not by instructions. (This pronouncement first appeared in the earliest French constitution and has been slavishly imitated by most European constitutions since.)

Experience in other countries having shown that between Parliamentary sessions, the day-by-day administrative work is unwatched, a Parliamentary supervisory committee was established to sit between sessions to act as administrative invigilator.

Then, foreign affairs were controllable more closely than elsewhere by Parliamentary committees; cabinet government was regulated to an unusually fine degree; arrangements were made for a state of emergency when internal or external dangers threatened; direct government was introduced as a corrective of Parliamentary omnipotence; the budget system was elaborately organized; and exceptional attention was paid to the maintenance and administration of railroads and canals (subjects of importance to all modern countries, but of special importance to Germany owing to her position as the railroad station and seaboard of central and northwestern Europe).

A branch of the constitution which was elaborated with a detail and care seldom observed in other constitutions was the civil service, and this for two reasons peculiar to Germany: to preserve the capacity of the service, the best legacy of centuries of absolutism; and to make the service democratically sensitive and responsive. Incidentally, there was in article 130 [61] one of the very rare allusions to political parties, which in fact, though not in law, constitute the central engines of modern politics.

(2) The second part of the constitution, on the fundamental rights and fundamental duties of Germans was of exceedingly wide range, and was divided into five sections: I. The Individual; II. Social Life; III. Religion and Religious Associations; IV. Education and Schools; and V. Eco-

nomic Life. These were totally contrary to Hitler's *Reich,* and in order to establish the *Reich* it was necessary to destroy every one of the rights.

The principal novelties of Section I were the equalization of the status of women with that of men, the guarantees for cultural minorities, the extension of secrecy of the mail to the telegraph and telephone, and the uncompromising proclamation of freedom of opinion.

In the light of the later nazi régime, Section II is of special importance, dealing as it does with the whole matter of family life. The constitution made family health and the social welfare of the family a supreme obligation and a primary care of the state, but the nazis perverted this to their nefarious purpose. Of the same intense interest was Section III of the constitution, dealing with religious associations and guaranteeing freedom of worship.

Section IV was an educational code. It began with a declaration which was very dear to German teachers since it had so rarely been practiced: "Art, science, and their teachings are free. The State guarantees their protection and participates in their promotion." This was first declared in the Frankfurt Assembly's abortive declaration of 1849—very naturally, since its most eminent members were professors, lawyers, and journalists—when Treitschke spoke in its favor. Apart from its accidental relationship to German conditions, the aspiration is significant as an expression of confidence in the modern deities: invention and science.

The general aim of the educational system is peculiarly germane to a discussion of the modern state. When so many hostages are given to the individual and to religious and economic associations, some provision must be made for a consensus. It is not here maintained that these articles can achieve this, nor that the reverse may be the result: but the necessity is patent. Article 148 says:

All schools shall try to achieve moral training, civic conscience, personal and professional competence, in the spirit of the German people and international friendship. In educa-

---

[61] "Officials are servants of the community, and not of a party."

tion in State schools care must be taken not to wound the sensitiveness of the unorthodox. The curriculum must include instruction in civics and economic organization. Every student receives a copy of the constitution at the end of his school years.

Finally, Section V, on economic life, went further than any other constitution and was an interesting reflection of those fundamental aspects of modern economic life analyzed in previous chapters. The keynote was set by the first article in the section, 151, which ran:

The ordering of economic life must correspond to principles of justice with the aim of securing an existence worthy of human beings. Within these limits the economic freedom of the individual is to be secured. Legal compulsion is only permissible for the realization of threatened rights or in the service of the paramount necessities of the common good. The freedom of commerce and trade is to be guaranteed in the measure laid down by federal laws.

The tone was maintained all through this section, and the subsequent articles were instrumental to the first. There was in these articles more than a reaction from laissez faire: there was also a conscious acceptance of positive principles of collectivism, in some cases attaining to the point of nationalization of industry.

Throughout this whole program ran suggestions of the limited nature of private rights, of the conditional and limited right of property. All mineral resources and all economically useful natural forces were placed under public vigilance, and private royalty rights were to be transferred to the state. A uniform labor code for the federation was to be created by law, its essential principle being that labor power was especially protected by the state and by a complete system of social security.

Then followed the inevitable consequence, whether written or unwritten: "that every German has the moral duty to engage his mental and bodily strength so as to promote the welfare of the community."

The final article in Section V on economic life, article 165, created a scheme of representative bodies for the government of industry and agriculture, equally including employees and employers. All this was to find its summit in a great central body—the Economic Council—representative of workers, employers, consumers, and others.

France and the Soviet Union and an International Bill of Rights. We have already reproduced the elaborate bill of rights in the French Constitution of 1946 (p. 80) and that of the Soviet Constitution of 1936 (p. 79). The novelty of the latter is its apparent alliance of individual rights with submission to an economic system wholly authoritarian, resting on the almost complete community of the means of production and distribution.

It is of special interest to observe that apart from supporting the well-being of the individuals who compose the state, the rights and distribution of democratic authority, guaranteed in democratic constitutions, have an important value for international peace. For civil rights tend to break down the absolute solidarity of the nation; they make concrete the right to listen to the claims made by other nations and cultures; they allow of easy communication of ideas and moral feeling throughout the nation and across national boundaries; and by fortifying the right to associate voluntarily, to express dissent, and to press objections through the firm protections of procedure, they slow down the potentially precipitate decision of a government acting in the name of the nation as a unit.[62]

THE SIGNIFICANCE OF CONSTITUTIONS

WE have observed the development of the substance of the constitution from the time when there was no substance except the vague notion of royal absolutism to the point where it mirrors, if with some distortions and omissions, the multifarious convictions, habits, and social institutions of a very complicated civilization. Further emphasis of some aspects of this development is necessary.

[62] Cf. Herman Finer, *America's Destiny* (New York, 1947), Chap. XI.

First, what is fundamental is necessarily the result of evolving civilization. No fundamentals are capable of standing proof against time, except entities so vague as to be meaningless. If the principles which have been indicated were reduced by the abstraction of their temporary and local forms, we should arrive at the most primitive human instinct, such as the infant's hold upon its nurse for fear of falling, and the prerational resistance to physical constraint. Men will always search for the guarantee of the fundamentals in their own civilization, since these have insensibly taken on the urgent character of primary reactions. Stability and change, settlement and flux must then be expected, and men will constantly hover between the extremes and struggle for their fixture in constitutions. The lesson of it all is that there is nothing so fundamental that it may not change, and nothing so fundamental that it ought not to change; nor anything so fugitive that it may not be one day fixed and worshipped as an absolute dispensation.

Second, society does not wait until a constitution is written. In proportion as matters are urgent, it establishes fundamentals in the intervals between constitutions (when there is a series), by laws or by conventions; and what the written constitution does not include is provided outside its pages. The institutions created without constitutional benediction may be so embedded in the vital desires of men as to be able to persist as fundamentals, even when the paper fundamentals are swept away or even where these do not exist. In the United States the president has come to be elected directly by the people, and the party system is fundamental to democratic government; the former was virtually forbidden by the constitution, the latter is ignored by constitutions but nevertheless is everywhere the real center of government. British trade-union rights are not derived from any constitution, nor are freedom of speech, writing, and assembly; yet they are so fundamental that any attempts substantially to limit them meet with the strongest resistance. Constitutions do not include all that is fundamental, while many of the declared fundamentals are silently ignored.

Last, are constitutions fundamental in the sense of being perfect traps? Are they really indestructible and inalienable? No constitution has shown that "fundamental" means this. They are destructible, alienable, and escapable, and the people, the parties, the parliaments, and the courts of justice have destroyed them, alienated them, and escaped them. They have appeared to be all these and more to their framers, because of mankind's desire for order, the impossibility of living in constant flux, the belief that it is possible to express the government of society in a few wise pages covered with pregnant words, and the recurrent human confusion of that which is characteristic of their generations and the past with that which can properly be for all time.

Constitutions do acquire a special stability and reverence, but the latter passes with time and the former depends entirely upon the factors forming civilization (now one aspect of man's nature, now another) being awakened by some fresh property of the spirit or nature. Constitutions remain unchanged *first* in proportion as the basic elements in human nature are socially acknowledged as good; *second,* in proportion to the completeness with which these socially valid elements are embodied in the constitution, and *third* in proportion to the generality with which these elements are described, since if they are described in detail, amendments are often required.

Many of the clauses are so generally worded as to have no effect until they are interpreted by the competent authorities or until laws are passed to give them more precise meanings, and it has happened that the interpreters have even perverted the intentions of the fathers—thus, article 48 of the Weimar constitution.

In one sense, constitutions are eighteenth-century phenomena. When constitutions were established after the revolutions in America, France, and then (within a few decades) in all the European countries that followed France, they were set up in countries not having great bodies of statutes made by popular legislatures, such as have since been enacted. They were written replacements, in a revolutionary sense, of custom or royal ordinances. Today, nations are governed by vast codes of statutes regulating the substance and procedure of rights and obligations. They are more detailed, more intensive, more concrete than constitutions. Yet it is the principles that regulate their making, their interpretation, and their application. Hence, we may once again underline both the importance and the difficulty of creating constitutions by the democratic process, since their fundamentals rule all of our life.

Federalism: The Central-Local Territorial Fabric of the State

THE state necessarily occupies a territory. The problem at once arises how best to manage the area—whether to govern it undividedly from a single center or to disintegrate it and govern by a concert of central and local authorities; whether, also, the area of undivided rule should at any time be extended or diminished. These problems are not confined to the state; they arise in industrial and commercial concerns, in trade unions, in churches.

The problems have usually been discussed under the time-honored divisions of federalism and local government, but these are only subdivisions of the main problem of the territorial composition of the state. No issues different in kind can be raised in regard to the one or the other and, in fact, the same issues are traceable in and are determinant of such questions as regionalism, devolution (i.e., the transfer of powers from the center to the localities in a unitary state like Great Britain),[1] and international government. Here is a brood of difficulties and devices of state which are all of the same strain; they are differentiated by size, urgency, time, and place. Here we confine ourselves to the problem of federalism, which is at once a study in the efficiency of government, in the component factors of nationality, in the distribution of sovereign power, and above all, in the origin of

states. Interesting problems in world-federation analogies are suggested.

When the student contemplates a form of government such as the federal state, exhibiting a number of practical imperfections, his reforming zeal is aroused, yet he is faced with the fact of the historic realities out of which the federal state arose. Therefore, if he is critical of the federal state, which he may regard as a not yet perfected state, he may still be faced with the fact that his hands are tied. Yet, criticism began the federal state, and criticism may perfect it.

What we wish to discover is (1) the amalgam of motives and environmental factors which cause large states to be composed out of small ones, and (2) the organization adopted and its reasons.

The prevailing distinction between states is that between the unitary and the federal state.[2] In this distinction the

___

[1] Cf. for example, W. H. Chiao, *Devolution in Great Britain* (New York, 1926).

[2] James Viscount Bryce, *Studies in History and Jurisprudence* (1901), 2 vols., Essay IV; A. V. Dicey, *Law of the Constitution*, 8th edition (London, 1927), Introduction, Sect. III; H. Sidgwick, *The Elements of Politics* (London, 1891), Chap. XXVI: Siegfried Brie, *Theorie der Staatenverbindungen* (Stuttgart, 1886), and *Geschichte des Bundesstaates* (Leipzig, 1874); Georg Jellinek, *Die Lehre von den Staatenverbindungen* (Vienna, 1882); Hugo Preusz, *Gemeinde, Staat und Reich* (Berlin, 1889); G. F. Ebers, *Die Lehre vom Bundesstaat* (Breslau, 1910). The more up-to-date treatises are referred to in the course of the present discussion.

Cf. also *The Federalist* (Everyman edition or Max Beloff edition, New York, 1948); J.

unitary state is one in which all authority and power are lodged in a single center, whose will and agents are legally omnipotent over the whole area, whereas a federal state is one in which part of the authority and power is vested in the local areas while another part is vested in a central institution deliberately constituted by an association of the previously independent local areas. Neither has the right to take away power and authority belonging to the other.

Once a general name is given to a number of particular things in order to distinguish them from others, these things acquire a reputation for a discreteness they do not in fact possess. For all unitary states relax the severity of the central government, while in some forms of federalism there is more centralization than the name originally implied. There is, in short, in actual states and in their constitutions, a wide range of systems, never ending in a completely unitary or Federal one, but ascending towards the one or other extreme type.[3]

Federalism is of extreme modernity. Its theory and practice in the modern state are not older than the American federation, which came into existence in 1787. The federal idea—that is, the plan of government of a number of contiguous territories in association and neither in separation nor in one compound—was ancient and had been practiced in Greece.[4] Although the Fathers of the American Constitution referred to Greek theories and experience, the Constitutional Assembly well knew that it was building for the first time. The next examples of federalism were Switzerland in 1802 [5] and

Canada in 1837 and 1867 [6]; Germany in 1867 and 1871; the Commonwealth of Australia in 1902,[7] and the Union of South Africa in 1905.[8] Much scholarship has been expended on the history of the establishment of these federations. We therefore abstract the quintessential motives and events, with the simple warning that they were not so well-ordered or always avowed as they appear to be in an organized summary. Our examples are Australia, Canada, the United States, and Germany, more attention being given to the two latter as we are more concerned with the operation of their institutions.

FEDERALISM IN AUSTRALIA AND CANADA

Australia. The Australian process of federation was vastly different from the American and German. By 1863, when England had completed the territorial reorganization of the six Australian colonies, their seaport cities were in keen rivalry with one another. Since the local legislatures sat in these key cities, an especially virulent brand of particularism resulted. Each of the colonies was divided from the others by tariffs and frequently by railroads of different gauge. However,

---

Story, *Commentaries on the Constitution of the United States*, 5th edition (Boston, 1891), 2 vols.; and W. W. Willoughby, *The Constitutional Law of the United States*, 2nd edition (1929), 3 vols. Cf. Sobei Mogi, *Theory of Federalism* (London, 1931) 2 vols., for a history of federal theory; and Kenneth Wheare, *The Federal State* (New York, 1947).

[3] Hans Kelsen, *Allgemeine Staatslehre* (Berlin, 1925), Chap. VI.; see also his *General Theory of Law and State* (Harvard, 1946).

[4] E. A. Freeman, *Federal Government in Greece and Italy*, 2nd edition (London, 1893).

[5] Fritz Fleiner, *Schweizersches Bundesstaats-*

recht (Zurich, 1923), Introduction and Chap. I and bibliographies. For a dynamic survey see W. E. Rappard, *La Constitution Fédérale de la Suisse* (Neuchatel-Suisse, 1948).

[6] F. Bradshaw, *Self-Government in Canada* (London, 1903); W. P. M. Kennedy, *The Constitution of Canada* (Oxford, 1937); McGregor Dawson. *The Government of Canada* (Toronto, 1946).

[7] B. R. Wise, *The Making of the Australian Commonwealth* (London, 1913): W. H. Moore, *The Constitution of the Commonwealth of Australia*, 2nd edition (Melbourne, 1910); J. Quick and R. R. Garran, *The Annotated Constitution of the Australian Commonwealth* (Sydney, 1901); *Cambridge History of the British Empire* (Cambridge, 1929), Vol. VII on Australia, Chapter XVI; *Annotated Text Constitution of the Commonwealth of Australia* (Knowles, ed., Melbourne, 1947); S. V. Portus, ed., *Studies in the Australian Constitution* (Sydney, 1933); A. P. Canaway, *The Failure of Federalism in Australia* (Oxford, 1930); and Gordon Greenwood, *The Future of Federalism in Australia* (Melbourne, 1946).

[8] R. H. Brand, *The Union of South Africa* (London, 1909).

Victoria and South Australia, on the one hand, and New South Wales, on the other, had common interests.

Conferences on particular problems were held, but all proposals for federation were badly received. In addition to the economic rivalry, the small states were jealous of the large, and the poorer states feared increased taxes. Yet powerful forces encouraged federation. The need for defense was probably the strongest. France was attempting to expand in New Caledonia; a British war with Russia was possible; Bismarck was claiming part of New Guinea. Fearing a German neighbor, the eastern colonies were quite willing to contribute to the administrative expenses of British New Guinea. Britain refused to continue protection of the Australian colonies without cooperation from the colonies themselves. With the appearance of an imperial report discussing the exposed position of Australia in the event of a war and her inadequate defenses, alarm became widespread, and as a result of agitation led by the New South Wales premier, a general convention was held in 1891.

Economic issues also were involved. Some of the colonies were underdeveloped, because the expense of maintaining individual railroad systems made it difficult to bring new land under cultivation. Customs barriers discouraged commerce between the colonies. The economic issues were brought to a head in the panic of 1891 and 1892.

The general convention of 1891 produced a series of definite proposals: internal free trade, central control of fiscal and defense policy, and administration by a single federal authority. The urbanized states balked, however, and only after considerable crusading by the popular leagues to promote federalism in general, or for specific purposes, was another convention held—in 1897. Nor was the resulting constitutional draft accepted without amendment. But a second draft submitted to the legislatures obtained acceptance by all the states. Western Australia agreed only because it had been petitioned by its gold-field region for status as a separate state. Considerably more freedom had been obtained in relations with England by a collaborative policy.

The Commonwealth came into existence on January 1, 1901. The constitution enumerated substantial powers for the federal government, the residue remaining in the hands of the states. The Senate was federal; the House of Representatives popular and in control of the purse. The main taxation powers were given to the federal government, with three quarters of the revenues to be returned to the states during the first ten years.

As the Labour party had been long in office in the central government, it became increasingly an advocate of unitary power, while the Liberals, in power in the state governments, were strongly opposed to the relinquishment of state functions. The need for more centralization, as in the United States, is very serious even today, as the record of attempts at constitutional amendment demonstrates (see p. 132).

Canada. Canadian federation was produced by a different combination of factors. After the Durham Report of 1839, Lower and Upper Canada, the present-day Quebec and Ontario, were combined in United Canada. In Lower Canada, the English traders and officials and the conservative French Catholics had been in constant and vehement disagreement. The Ontario region, however, was beset by conflict between the independent frontier farmers and wealthy officialdom.

The direct cause of the federation movement was the persistent racial conflict between the British and French "national" groups. The Durham Report had lamented "two nations warring within the bosom of a single state." After 1858 legislature and administration were deadlocked. Each bloc sought special legislation for itself, and although the British majority was growing, its representation remained static. The French had retained not only their language and their religion but also their laws and customs, and they constituted social islands wherever they settled.

Economic problems also plagued a divided Canada. A reciprocal treaty with the United States, dropped in 1865, had been of great importance to the trade of eastern Canada. With the advent of English free trade, the Canadians lost their favored position in British markets. Union might make their bargaining strength far more effective.

Nor was defense unimportant. An undetermined boundary, together with an American policy of "manifest destiny," [9] put much land at stake. English influence was particularly active on this score.

Finally, in 1864, a coalition government took office, pledging unification. As a result of a simultaneous move among the maritime states, the Quebec Conference of 1864 was convened. United Canada had twelve representatives; New Brunswick and Prince Edward Islands had seven each; Nova Scotia sent five delegates; and Newfoundland, two. They were successful in producing a plan containing seventy-two resolutions. However, the propositions were rejected by popular election in Newfoundland and New Brunswick and by the legislature in Prince Edward Island; Nova Scotia strongly opposed them. Only United Canada approved.

In spite of the hostile reception a conference was called by the British government in London; it was attended by representatives from Nova Scotia, New Brunswick, and United Canada. The outcome was the passage of the British North America Act in 1867, containing sixty-nine sections, representing only slight modifications of the original draft. It was never presented for acceptance by the colonies, and became the law without it.

Accordingly, the Dominion of Canada was established in 1867. United Canada (redivided into Quebec and Ontario), Nova Scotia, and New Brunswick were the component provinces. By royal order, other provinces were to be admitted in the future; and Manitoba (1870), British Columbia (1871), Prince Edward Island (1873), and Saskatchewan and Alberta (1905) were subsequently added. Some notion of the readjustment between Domin-

ion and provincial governments has already been given.

THE RISE OF FEDERALISM IN THE UNITED STATES

The Colonial Period. Before 1789, the thirteen American colonies led an existence largely independent of each other; the colonies at the extremities of the Atlantic seaboard were months, and those between, weeks and days, away from each other. In 1776, it took about a week in good weather (not four hours as now) to travel from Boston to New York City.

The colonies were differentiated by their climate, by their commercial and industrial interests, and by religion, and these brought about secondary differences of culture.[10] But there was a substantial uniformity of cultural outlook and political tradition when compared with, say, the German states. The earliest tie was defense —against the Indians and European claimants to the "hinterland" of North America." [11]

Even in the late seventeenth century, William Penn wished to secure a common council to adjust differences and complaints among the colonies, as in commercial injuries and the mutual rendition of debtors and culprits who fled from justice, and to support the union and safety against common enemies. In Ben-

---

[10] C. and M. Beard, *The Rise of American Civilization* (New York, 1928); V. Parrington, *Main Currents in American Thought* (New York, 1929), Vol. I, "The Colonial Mind, 1620-1800."

[11] For example, as early as 1643 the New England confederacy was formed. Here was a solid block of colonies not overfar from each other and very similar in political organization and religious conviction. The union was "a firm and perpetual league of friendship and amity, for offence and defence, mutual advice and succour upon all just occasions both for preserving and propagating the truths of the Gospel and for mutual safety and welfare." (William Macdonald, *Source Book of American History*, New York, 1926, p. 45.) Cf. John Fiske, *Beginnings of New England* (Boston, 1889), Chap. IV; J. Scott Brown, *The United States: A Study in International Organization* (Oxford, 1920); A. H. Smythe, *The Writings of Benjamin Franklin* (Philadelphia, 1905-07) Vol. III, p. 210 ff.

---

[9] Cf. A. K. Weinberg, *Manifest Destiny* (Johns Hopkins, 1935).

jamin Franklin's scheme of the 1750's a further motive was the settlement of lands acquired from the Indians. The vast hinterland, full of disturbing penalties, was a factor of unique urgency in America as a problem whose menace demanded union for its peaceful solution.

The imperial theory, which assigned to the American colonies the position of plantations for the benefit of the mother country, was not violently challenged until it began to be applied with real energy by Grenville and Townshend.[12] Defensive resentment began to produce unity: "There ought to be no New England men, no New Yorkers known on the Continent, but all of us Americans."[13] England under Lord North persisted; war followed. The Second Continental Congress met in 1775 to conduct the struggle. The Declaration of Independence was promulgated.[14] The colonies drew together in common consciousness, and for defense of a righteous cause. They were now very self-conscious states and were not anxious to relinquish their government into the hands of a new central authority. The Congress, therefore, was lamentably weak.

Confederacy and Weakness. The Articles of Confederation were not ready until 1777 and were not ratified by all the states until 1781. Only extreme danger had brought them together, and the authors of the Articles apologized for the rickets of

their progeny.[15] The Confederation was announced to be a "firm league of friendship." It became a league of disgruntled independents. Sovereignty (legal supremacy) remained with the states; most illuminating was the fact that amendment of the Articles needed a unanimous vote. The powers conferred on Congress were few and strictly limited. Congress did not possess direct executive power over individuals everywhere to carry out its resolutions, but was obliged to rely upon the states for action. Most vital of all, Congress had no power to levy taxes or to regulate commerce.

The war ended, the remnants of the Congress silently dozed in an unheeded corner. But a few people, like Alexander Hamilton or Benjamin Rush, experienced the feeling that all America should be one—a feeling that was nourished on its own intrinsic merits and not on expectations of utility. "We are now a new nation," said Rush.[16] ". . . The more a man aims at serving America, the more he serves his colony. We have been too free with the word—independence; we are dependent on each other, not totally independent states. . . . When I entered that door, I considered myself a citizen of America." So also Hamilton.[17]

The weakness of the Confederation under the Articles and the failure of the attempt to govern by petitions, were invaluable in motivating the more effective scheme. Shay's Rebellion and virtual civil war over boundaries, the needs of organization in the western areas leading to the short-lived state of Franklin, and the Northwest Ordinance all argued convincingly that only a new federal system would supply a proper remedy.

---

[12] W. H. Lecky, *A History of England in the Eighteenth Century*, new edition (London, 1892), Vol. IV; see Adam Smith, *The Wealth of Nations* (Cannan's edition, 1904), Book IV, Chap. VII, part III; P. M. Trevelyan, *The American Revolution* (New York, 1907); Carl Becker, *The Declaration of Independence* (New York, 1922), Chap. III; E. H. Van Tyne, *The American Revolution, 1776-83* (New York, 1905); and H. C. Hackett, *The Constitutional History of the United States, 1776-1826* (New York, 1939).
[13] And see A. B. Hart, *American History Told by Contemporaries* (New York, 1924), Vol. II, pp. 394-412; see also Merle Curti, *Roots of American Loyalty* (New York, 1946); and John C. Miller, *Origins of the American Revolution* (Boston, 1943).
[14] Cf. Carl Becker, *op. cit.*; F. W. Hirst, *Life and Letters of Thomas Jefferson* (London, 1926).

[15] Official Letter Accompanying Act of Confederation in Congress, Yorktown, November 17, 1777; reprinted in J. Elliot, *Debates in the Several State Conventions on the Adoption of the Federal Constitution* (Washington, 1901). Cf. M. Jensen, *The Articles of Confederation, 1774-1781* (Madison, 1940).
[16] R. L. Schuyler, *The Constitution of the United States* (New York, 1923), p. 38.
[17] Cf. *The Federalist*, Nos. XV-XXII; and earlier in *The Continentalist*. M. Curti, *op. cit.*, gives many examples of such "American" sentiment. Above all cf. Weinberg, *op. cit.*

The actual existence of a confederation had already produced a literature of federalism, criticizing the old articles for their weakness and advocating a stronger union. The most brilliant and compelling series of essays, called *The Continentalist*, came from the pen of Hamilton in 1781–82, but there were others also. Exceptional men, like Hamilton, are always essential ingredients in the forging of states.

A few such men, foremost among them James Madison and George Washington, taking advantage of the unrest and distress and the growing expectancy of a "more perfect union," met in 1786 to consider commercial conditions and report an amendment to the Articles of Confederation.[18] The report read that:[19]

in the course of their reflections on the subject, they have been induced to think that the power of regulating trade is of such comprehensive extent, and will enter so far into the general system of the Federal Government, that to give it efficacy, and to obviate questions and doubts concerning its precise nature and limit, may require a correspondent adjustment of other parts of the federal system.

The invitation to a convention at Philadelphia in May, 1787, was now to consider not "commerce" but "the situation" of the American states. The old Congress, which was still the symbol of defensive fraternity and national independence, also recommended a convention "to render the federal constitution adequate to the exigencies of government, and the preservation of the Union."

The Work of the Constitutional Convention. We cannot analyze here the convention or the negotiations which produced the clauses of the new constitution. But it is of supreme importance that the finest minds and characters were then in American politics.

Little dispute was raised by the powers to be granted to the federal authority.

Their nature explains their ready adoption. Such powers as those over foreign and interstate commerce and commerce with the Indian tribes, over naturalization and bankruptcy; over currency and standards of weights and measures; over postal administration; over copyright; over crimes on the high seas and offenses against international law; over foreign affairs in general; over the declaration of war and maintenance of an army and navy —all such powers yield their greatest common utility with the least common effort when they are concerted over a large area. What that area shall be is determinable at any time by the existing state of invention, the organizing ability of mankind, and the strength of popular preferences for economic welfare and local independence. Uniformity in commerce brings the well-known economy of free trade; in currency it saves delay and the chaffering of exchange; in postal services it increases speed; in weights and measures it aids rapidity and certainty of calculation; in bankruptcy it enhances a sense of security; in copyright it facilitates protection, detective operations, and retribution. A single administration of diplomatic negotiations and the armed forces eliminates the waste involved in a number of separate armed forces, reduces the chances of domestic conflict, and adds weight and prestige in the world's balance of power.

These were the main utilitarian considerations that brought about the new union, as they have been of every federation since, and we shall later see that it was on the path of such utilities that the unitary element in federation afterward pursued its rapid way.

But just as decidedly, other powers were not transferred to the United States and remained with the states; indeed, the whole field of activity outside the transferred powers was left within their sphere.

The subjects of acute controversy were: state representation in the federal legislature; federal power to act directly upon the citizens instead of through the states as before; and the power to tax. The last two questions revolved almost entirely around the first. Supposing the power to

---

[18] Cf. Proposition of the General Assembly of Virginia, January 21, 1786 (reprinted in Elliot, *op. cit.*, Vol. I, pp. 115-16); and cf. Schuyler, *op. cit.*, p. 68.
[19] *Documentary History of the Constitution*, *op. cit.*, (U.S. Government Printing Office, 1894), Vol. I, pp. 1-8.

tax were granted, or supposing the central authority were given the power of direct jurisdiction. What would be the position of the states in that policy? Would the power to tax be limited by their counsel as separate entities with a guaranteed life? Would they be enabled to withstand the direct power of the central authority, which was to be so crushingly enhanced? No final decisions, therefore, were taken about other questions till the supreme issue—the place of the states in the union —had been settled. The small states were afraid for their identity and preferred disruption of the Union to attenuation of their own sovereignty. (Since the example of American federation is frequently used to argue for world federation, it is essential to emphasize the factor especially favoring union: that in 1790, 82 per cent of the population was English, 7 per cent Scotch, 1.2 per cent Irish.)

"The states and the advocates for them were intoxicated by the idea of their sovereignty." A compromise was reached, and its character is considered later (Chap. 18 below).

THE RISE OF FEDERALISM IN GERMANY:
TO 1848

IN the rise of the German federation, second only to the United States in federal importance, the problems to be faced were vastly different. Geography, economics, local culture, and political organization and traditions profoundly distinguished Germany from the United States and, more imperious still, cut off one German state from another. Evolution, therefore, one of stress and violence, led to solutions expressly rejected in the American system. The differences serve the better to show the basic nature of federalism.

Foreign oppression was the earliest stimulus to the formation of a federal union of the Germanic states; and its consummation came after war against France in 1871 and 1919.

Particularism. Before Napoleon and the French overran these territories, there were 1,800 independent political jurisdictions, including Prussia and Austria. Kings, spiritual and secular princes, imperial towns, imperial townships, dukes, abbots, divided up among them some twenty million subjects.[20] Within the loose tie of the Holy Roman Empire they were jealous and separatist. Critics of the small states (like Lessing, Schiller, Herder, Humboldt, Kant,[21]) sought the form of a large nation but world citizenship, *Weltburgertum.* The small estate owners in the country, the peasants, the urban citizens, and handicraftsmen—the masses in short— lived in and for their immediate surroundings; the civil servants lived for their royal masters.[22]

Nor were the facts of the German political system propitious for the birth of a national feeling. For at the core of that system was state "particularism," an obstinate force which neither civil nor foreign war, nor yet persistent governmental debility have yet cast out (even in spite of the Nazi attempt brutally to do so).[23] Every frontier was an economic barrier; systems of coinage were different;[24] each state had its own variety of political absolutism. Particularism has grown out of the gradual assumption of power over a territory by prince or church, as the result of gifts, thefts, marriage portions, and conquests. It was not a popular emanation, or entirely the product of race or of climate and different modes of livelihood. All these were in parts of particular-

20 Cf. James Bryce, *The Holy Roman Empire,* 13th edition (London, 1895) for the history of the political association of the German territories up to this time; and for an analysis of the situation at the beginning of the century, see Erich Brandenburg, *Die Reichsgründung* (Leipzig, 1922).
21 For a good account of these thinkers in this particular respect, see Friedrich Meinecke, *Weltbürgertum und Nationalstaat* (München, 1919), Part I.
22 Cf. Brandenburg, *op. cit.,* Vol. I, p. 55.
23 A very interesting and acute account of the rise of German nationality is to be found in the Royal Institute of International Affairs, *Study of Nationalism* (London, 1943); see also A. J. P. Taylor, *The Course of German History since 1815* (London, 1946).
24 Werner Sombart, *Die deutsche Volkswirtschaft in Neunzehnten Jahrundert,* 6th edition (Cambridge, 1928), Chap. IV.

ism, but it was more. It was the deliberately established separatism of princes anxious for the security of their own acquisitions and the maintenance of the power of their dynasties. The princes had won their way free of the imperial majesty, owing to the accident that the imperial authority was exercised by no one line for more than a century. Established in the states, they reiterated that their own race, religion, interests, culture were different from and superior to those existent elsewhere. The good life was made to seem founded upon the political independence of the dynasty—which, alone, in those days, was the state.

The Growth of Nationality. Then the French Revolution (in which the French *pays* was transformed into the French for *patrie* [25]) excited Germany,[26] and Napoleon swept away the Holy Roman Empire, reduced the independent principalities from eighteen hundred to thirty-three, and showed Germany how willing every dynasty was to accept his gifts of land at the expense of national independence and unity. A genuine national feeling was generated, not only among statesmen, poets, and philosophers but also among the people. All classes were affected in blood and property, in the War of Emancipation, and all shared the common sufferings and final triumph.[27] Fichte's *Reden an die Deutsche Nation* expressed the spirit of the time.

Men and women in the different states were permeated by a wider "consciousness of kind," which is the essence of nationality. Indeed, the social values and rewards, the esteem, the standards of right and wrong, the promise of immortality, which had hitherto been promised to men in the restricted area of the states, were now more brilliant and solid in the more extensive society! Vaguely, but effectively, their minds and feelings reached out to one another, to form the spiritual integument of a new fellowship. Old associations were revived with the inspiration of fresh meaning. Language and learning and religion were felt to be bonds that ought to produce a more general community. The very past—full of intellectual and artistic creativeness and of brave and golden events in men's physical struggles—urged men to remember that they had been of beneficial, if unconscious and unintended, service to each other, and that, though they were now members of separate political groups, their separativeness must not violate certain understandings of associated existence, and that Germany as a whole represented a standard of political good to which statesmen and people of all states must expect, of themselves and each other, to pay the homage of subordination. Their inward and ultimate reasons for subordination did not matter; each must expect from and render to the other the regard due to common citizenship.[28] But even when this spirit burned its fiercest, the monarchs returned to their particularism, lest any should obtain an advantage over the rest, and lest national feeling should destroy the pillars of their autocracy.

Nor were the unitary plans clear enough to unite a sufficient body of supporters. There was, as in the United States, substantial agreement about the powers it was desirable for a central authority to undertake;[29] but the question of conceding political authority to a unifying element was not so easily answered.

Prussia versus Austria—and the New Germany. The analysis of unitary plans

---

[25] Cf. also J. M. Thompson, *The French Revolution*, Chaps. 6 and 7 (Oxford, 1944).
[26] Cf. S. P. Gooch, *Germany and the French Revolution* (London, 1920).
[27] As Goethe said years afterwards (*Gesprache mit Eckerman*, March 14, 1830); "We have no town, we have not even a countryside of which we can say decidedly: This is Germany? Ask in Vienna and people will say, this is Austria; ask in Berlin and people will say, this is Prussia! Over sixteen years ago, when we finally wanted to get rid of the French, Germany was everywhere; a political poet could have been universally influential. But he was not necessary. The general sentiment of shame seized the nation daemonically; the inspiring fire which a poet might have lighted, burned everywhere of its own self."

[28] Cf. Fichte, *Reden*, trans. in R. F. Jones and S. H. Turnbull, *Addresses to the German Nation* (London, 1922).
[29] Cf. M. Lehmann, *Freiherr von Stein* (Leipzig, 1903), Vol. III, *passim.*

brought to light the second difficulty in German federal development: the existence, side by side, of Prussia and Austria, jealous competitors and the feared and hated superiors of the smaller states. These large and long-standing rivals were immensely greater in size and resources than other states, and recognized each other as rival claimants for Germanic power. Could the German problem possibly be solved by a division of the territories into two: a South German confederation with Austria at its head and the North German confederation with Prussia at its head? This was to court war between the federations. Could they work together? Austria could not tolerate equality. Could there be a balance, even an association, between three systems: a triad of Austria, Prussia, and a federation of smaller states? This was merely to increase the prospects of war, for the intermediate federation could not but be the diplomatic battleground of the two senior states, maneuvering to press loyalty from the smaller states. There was only one solution possible: the decisive exit of either Austria or Prussia from the field. For while both remained, the smaller states could and did play one off against the other, thus enjoying defense against their dreaded neighbors without having to make the sacrifice of independence implied in a federal arrangement. When one great defender, Austria, broke down, the mutual fears of the small states and their general fear of Prussia caused cohesion around Prussia.[30]

The advantages swayed more and more to the Prussian side. Prussia was almost entirely German in composition, whereas Austria was less than half so; Prussia's defensive plans were almost identical with those of the rest of Germany, that is, against Russia and France; her religion was Protestant and tolerant, whereas Austria's was Catholic; her absolutism was enlightened; and though her local and individual liberties could not be compared with England's, yet they were more generous than Austria's. Further, and this became plainer as the century advanced, Prussia was the dominant factor in the economic future of Germany, for she was planted where the lines of communication led to the great ports and river mouths of the north coast, and she was able to buy loyalty by the offer of roads and railway stations. Austria lay south, entangled in racial and national difficulties, and was almost landlocked.

Yet there were serious psychological obstacles to Prussia's march to pre-eminence. She had arrived at power by military violence; poetic, philosophic, and musical genius was less free and less warmly applauded than in other states; the pettier dynasties and courts looked with jealous disfavor upon the efficient hegemony; and the religious difference between her and the Southern states was enormous.

The military unity of the War of Liberation and the fears which persisted after its close had resulted in a queer kind of defensive confederation for "the maintenance of the external and internal security of Germany and the independence and inviolability of the individual German states." It was included in the Act of the Congress of Vienna. The Federal Act (Bundesakte) raised Prussia formally to equality with Austria (though Austria had the chairmanship of the Assembly) and seemed to give all that was necessary for the time being: external defense and the possibility of settling interstate disputes by peaceful methods.[31] It is hardly worth speaking of it except to mention that the votes of the states were differentiated according to their importance; that either a two-thirds vote or unanimity was required for resolutions; and that the small, though relatively larger, votes of Austria

[30] James K. Pollock, *The Government of Greater Germany* (New York, 1938); Arnold Brecht, *Federalism and Regionalism in Germany* (New York, 1946) and *Prelude to Silence* (New York, 1945).

[31] Cf. Brandenburg, *op. cit.*, p. 73; G. J. Ebers, *Die Lehre von Staatenbund* (Breslau, 1910), p. 50 ff.; Sir A. W. Ward, *Germany* (Cambridge, 1916-18), 3 vols., Vol. I; S. Brie, *Geschichte des Bundesstaats* (Leipzig, 1874) and compare S. J. Eber's short account in *Handbuch des Deutschen Staatsrechts*, ed. by G. Anschütz and R. Thoma (Tübingen, 1930), Vol. I, p. 26 ff.

and Prussia compelled them to trick intrigue in order to secure action. The Diet produced a sense of united government in Germany, and nourished the federal sense of liberals by their disgust with its actual reactionary character.

Confederation: 1815–48. Between 1815 and 1848, the lifetime of the Confederation, these lines of development are observable: the concentration of federalist aspirations upon Prussia, the evolution of political parties and national sentiment over state lines, the planning of constitutions for a federation, the growth of economic unity, the Revolution of 1848, and the end of the first open conflict between Prussia and Austria in which the latter was victorious. They all revealed by the credible demonstration of facts, more certainly than by theories, the real nature of the difficulties.

Early Plans for Federation. An expectation arose that Prussia ought to lead the federal movement. The summons, however, was conditional, and the condition was one which was inseparably attached to almost every similar signal to Prussia, made then or since.[32] It was that Prussia in creating Germany should dissolve in Germany. But the Prussian Junkers were afraid of the social consequences to their class of inclusion in a larger body; their interests required monarchical absolutism and the independence of their own provinces. Moreover, only a liberal régime would attract followers to Prussia from liberals all over Germany and weaken state dynasticism. Yet too liberal a system would cause those liberals to side with the dynasties out of fear of democracy.[33] The existence of a large state like Prussia —approaching two thirds of the total area and population of Germany excluding Austria—must either draw all other states to it or provoke their positive hostility. So narrow a channel had Prussia to navigate to become the instrument of union. Every plan for the peaceful unification of

Germany under Prussian leadership was caught in the toils of such difficulties.

The problem was thus left to students, liberal civil servants, governments, and a few convinced and enlightened politicians; and federal schemes thrown off between 1840 and 1848 were indeed many. The influence of political awakening and experience was just beginning (since the early 1830's) to tell in the most important way: parties and learned societies whose conferences and programs were concerned not only with the government of their own state but with the affairs of Germany were being formed,[34] especially in the South and Middle German states.[35]

The Economic Incentive. An advance towards unity was made in the economic sphere, by the creation of a *Zollverein,* or customs union. The Prussian Tariff Law of 1818 began a system of economic consolidation and free trade which ultimately included all Germany, but not without the most spiteful obstruction by the Southern states and even the creation of a rival *Zollverein* by them in 1828.[36]

GERMANY: FROM ECONOMIC TO POLITICAL
UNION: 1848 TO 1918

UP to 1848 the economic motive for union predominated. In fact, the *Zollverein,* being a Prussian invention, was now used by many particularists as a bogy to prevent full federalism. But the hopes of full union held by the liberals, to whom free trade was a fetish, were encouraged, especially in the Revolution of 1848, by this economic precursor.

From 1848 to Bismarck. Political passion now stirred in two directions. *Constitutional* monarchy, at least, was demanded; and the old Federal Diet, weak and conservative, impelled liberals to seek an alternative. Then, within a few weeks after the French Revolution of February,

---

32 F. Meinecke, *op. cit.,* pp. 33, 336. Cf. also Lehmann, *op. cit.,* Vol. III.

33 Even as at present the centripetal forces in Germany are nourished by the fear of Prussia's socialist bias.

34 Felix Salomon, *Die Partei Programme* (Berlin, 1920), pp. 3, 4.

35 See on this the short but pregnant remarks of L. Bergsträsser, *Geschichte der politischen Parteien Deutschlands,* 4th edition (Berlin, 1926), p. 17, and the bibliography given there.

36 Cf. M. Doeberl, *Bayern und das Deutsche Reich* (München, 1922).

1848, all state governments, even the Prussian, were being directed by Liberal ministers. Federal plans were busily canvassed. The princes, panic-stricken by the radicals, listened to them. Austria refused to join; and Bavaria consented reluctantly only when the Revolution had become victorious.[37]

A constituent assembly of 550 was elected on a very wide suffrage. Prussia had 141 delegates at this Assembly, Austria, partly owing to her difficulties with the revolution in Vienna, only two. Its success depended entirely on Prussian support. This would be of value only if Prussia were liberalized, if the King of Prussia was prepared to accept the leadership, and if Austria were to abstain. Prussia took the initiative, summoned the Diet (when Vienna succumbed to the Revolution) and declared the need for a federation.[38] But upon the slackening of the Revolution, the various Germanic princes called a halt to the King of Prussia. Revolutionary difficulties in Prussia put an end to her pretensions, for Frederick William IV simply dared not brave either Austria or democracy: the Junkers' desire for both political conservatism and Prussian separatism held them fast.

The Frankfurt Parliament lost itself in interminable discussions on the Fundamental Rights of Germans. It accepted a federal constitution which excluded Austria and provided for a Popular Assembly and for a Chamber of States with graduated voting power and a large sphere of federal authority. The constitution contained two other things of exceptional interest:

(1) In each large state the representatives were to be appointed, one half by the governments, the rest by the popular assemblies. And Prussia? Again, the motive to win Prussia for Germany, and Germany for Prussia: in any German state consisting of a number of provinces or counties with their own special constitution or administration, the representatives were to

be chosen not by the Parliament, but by the Provincial Assemblies or Estates.

(2) By a narrow majority (258 to 211) the chief executive was voted to be a German sovereign. Who this should be was not stated. But Prussia had the executive strength the federation needed. Frederick William IV was offered the supreme executive, but he refused because of the exclusion of Austria and the democratic source of the offer. Moreover, he desired unanimous invitation by the princes. Bavaria, Württemberg, Saxony, and Hanover ignored the movement and it collapsed.

What had it revealed? The *Gross-Deutsche* solution (which would include Austria) had been rejected by a small majority of federalists at Frankfurt in opposition to the Catholic South. Nevertheless, Austria did not accept this as a final judgment. Further, the South German states still wanted her guardianship, if from afar. Prussia had only two available methods of answering the call, each dangerous: to be liberal and risk domestic trouble and the vengeance of Austria and casual allies; or not to be liberal, and violently to expel Austria. There was a third way—to share power with Austria—but this Austria repelled.

Yet a number of states lay side by side, and each was the center of strong outward-running rays of aspiration and endeavor. Prussia had international interests and must reckon with France, Russia, and Austria. Austria had international interests and must reckon with Russia (for the Balkans), France (in regard to Italy), and Prussia. All the other Germanic states were reservoirs of men and money, and when combined, even as vague areas, were, as a friendly or a constitutionally associated unit, an asset in diplomatic relations. These, on the other hand, would have remained independent if they could: but if bigger neighbors had designs upon them, then they must play one off against another and attempt to obtain protection without loss of sovereignty. Yet all frontiers touch: and a touch upon sensitive frontiers injures, or appears to injure, the ganglia of spiritual and economic interests. The only alternative to warlike

[37] Cf. Doeberl, *op. cit.;* and for this and the following events cf. Brandenburg, *op. cit.*
[38] Ward, *op. cit.,* Vol. I, p. 437.

alarms is peaceful association. The federal association of Germany was impossible while Austria supported the South, and this prospect maintained the belief in all the middle and small German states that if ever an alarm developed into a real threat they could find a refuge. Association was possible only where none was secure without it. Then they would create their own security, not by looking to Austria or Prussia but by founding a federal state. Either Austria or Prussia must be excluded if international diplomacy were to be changed into federal cohesion. Given her geographical position and purely German composition, Prussia could not be excluded. Then Austria must be excluded. Why? Because some association was unavoidable, and the most feasible was prevented by Austria's presence.

The decision and deed were Bismarck's. From among all the plans he was able to choose the most feasible one. His courage and ruthlessness for his cause were perfect. Here was a man ready to sacrifice everybody and everything because his own sacrifice had lost all significance in face of the compelling nature of his ultimate aims. He who is without doubts is without scruples.

Bismarck's Policy to 1866. What did Bismarck believe about German federalism? He desired the greatness of Prussia. The conservative idea of the state was that it should be strong, dominant, and independent, and Bismarck shared this idea.[39] His congenital characteristics, his family history, the location of his estates, his friends, his caste (though he did not share in Romanticism), his country, and his king: all prescribed the channels of his energy. Prussia had to play a part in international affairs, independent of Russia, France, and Austria, all three hereditary and potential foes. For international power, Prussia needed united size. What rationality could be admitted to exist in this hodgepodge of states? Better for Prussia that there should be German unity; better for Germany that this should be so.

39 Cf. Meinecke, *op. cit.,* Chap. XII, "Ranke und Bismarck."

On what terms could unification be accomplished? The solution must be monarchical. The princes must be kept; they were repositories of political power.

In his *Reflections and Reminiscences,* Bismarck declared:

In order that German patriotism should be active and effective, it needs as a rule to hang on the peg of a dynasty. Independent of dynasty, it rarely comes to a rising point, though, in theory, it daily does so in parliament, in the press, in public meeting. In practice the German needs either attachment to a dynasty or the goad of anger hurrying him into action: the latter phenomenon, however, by its own nature is not permanent. It is as a Prussian, a Hanoverian, a Württemberger, a Bavarian, or a Hessian, rather than as a German, that he is disposed to give unequivocal proof of patriotism. It is not difference of stock, but dynastic relations upon which in their origin the separatist elements repose. . . . The preponderance of dynastic attachment, and the use of a dynasty as the indispensable cement to hold together a definite portion of the nation calling itself by the name of the dynasty, is a specific peculiarity of the German Empire.

Indeed, if Prussia assented to the downfall of a princely sovereignty outside Prussia, could there be any permanent security for herself against the same thing? Admit an indestructible sovereignty in the princes, and Prussia was saved as well as they. Further, it was, after all, not necessary at the commencement, at any rate, to secure more than that amount of associated energy and machinery which would make Germany a strong entity for the purposes of international diplomacy and the abolition of economic and judicial absurdities.

The dynamic elements were: Bismarck's convictions; the creation of a conquering army even by the destruction of constitutionalism; the belief that "blood and iron" alone would settle the German problem, and the excitement of the country by its declaration; the use of the *Zollverein* to persuade or browbeat any too-independent German states; the disarming of liberal opinion by the grant of universal franchise; the formulation of such constitutional plans as should exclude Austria; and, finally, the deliberate picking of a quarrel with that country in order that the test of arms might decide the German issue.

The *Nationalverein,*[40] the political party of liberal-unitarists under Bennigsen, though distrustful of Bismarck owing to his antiliberalism, declared its faith more in the Prussian constitutional proposals than in the Austrian.[41] This and the Austrian defeat over the *Zollverein* were preliminary skirmishes before the inevitable battle. The Schleswig-Holstein problem was deliberately reopened, and inflamed: victorious concessions were made by Austria. The middle states were disillusioned by Austria's capitulation; the small states were full of fear at Bismarck's friendship with Napoleon—for when had a Napoleon been respectful of the territory and sovereignty of the small German princes? Austria took fright that France would liberate her Italian possessions. Then Bismarck demanded a German parliament elected by universal franchise! This was genius in every sense of the word, even as far as the ultimate blindness of genius to the final, sometimes the suicidal, result of its own creative activities.[42] The immediate motives were: to generate a force in politics strong enough to overcome princely separatism; to make that force one which should, perhaps, counteract liberal majorities by working-class votes, which could be managed so as to benefit "national" candidates of any class; to inflame Austrian opposition; and, finally, to throw a sop to the great mass of opponents of autocracy in the states, in Prussia and in future Germany.[43] The

concession made easier Bismarck's way over Austria's body into the German *Reichstag.*

Finally, Bismarck proposed a widening of federal authority to include all economic and foreign relations, and the command of the German armed forces. The unanimity rule in the Diet was to be set aside. To this Austria could not possibly assent, because an increase of power and the possibility of majority decisions would mean—often, if not always—a Prussian success.

Then a new plan excluded Austria and the Lower Rhine states altogether. Austria was bound to refuse to be pushed out of Germany. The Prussian plan was rejected. Thereupon Prussia declared that she considered the Confederation disrupted and annulled. The war of 1866 followed.

The North German Confederation of 1867. The most difficult part of the German federal problem was solved: Austria was excluded. There were still difficulties to overcome, but only one magnetic pole of proven force now remained.

The North German states had found little security in time of war. Their Particularism had, in any case, been less stubborn than that of the Southern states. Out of their wartime association and treaties with Prussia emerged the North German Confederation of 1867,[44] the immediate precursor and model of the Empire of 1871.

The very core of Bismarck's constitution was this: the barest needs of unity, and no more, were satisfied, and a very large amount of independence was allowed, for Prussia's sake, as well as to coax the Southern states.[45] "One must keep more to the Confederal system in form, but in practice give it the nature of a Federation with elastic, innocent, but far-reaching phrases." To make a complete,

---

[40] Cf. Herman Oncken, *Rudolf von Bennigsen* (Berlin, 1910), 2 vols., Books II and III.

[41] Brandenburg, *op. cit.,* Vol. II, p. 79.

[42] Bismarck's grant of universal suffrage was ultimately to result in the creation of such strong opposition parties in the Social Democrats and the Progressive Liberals and so to awaken political consciousness in Germany that his whole system fell into danger immediately he ceased to be Chancellor, and within a score of years completely broke down.

[43] Brandenburg, *op. cit.,* Vol. II; R. Augst, *Bismarck's Stellung zur deutschen Wahlrecht* (Leipzig, 1917); Bismarck, *Reflections and Reminiscences* (Tauchnitz, Berlin, 1899), Vol. II, pp. 245-49.

[44] Cf. Treaty, August 18, 1866: Heinrich Triepel, *Quellensammlung* (Tübingen, 1926), p. 200.

[45] Brandenburg, *op. cit.,* Vol. II, p. 218; E. Kaufman, *Bismarck's Erbe in der Reicheverfassung* (Berlin, 1917). On Bavaria and the renewal of the Union see H. von Sybel, *Die Begründung des deutschen Reiches durch Wilhelm I* (München, 1901-08), 7 vols., Vol. III.

exhaustive scheme would take too long, nor was it desirable; the old forms could be used, if with some difficulty. Since Bismarck now sought association and not annexation, he kept the old number of votes, adding thereto only the votes of the annexed countries. This gave Prussia seventeen votes out of forty-three, and it could only be in a majority if it could control five more votes. Since a constitutional amendment, however, could be defeated by fourteen votes, a veto was given to the small states if they voted together, and to Prussia always. Military resolutions required the assent of the federal commander-in-chief—the Prussian king. Other main points were the sovereignty of the federal Council, not of the popularly elected *Reichstag,* and the responsibility of the federal chancellor to the federal chief alone, not to the parliamentary bodies; and the execution of federal laws by the states.

No state opposed this constitution, and it came into force in July, 1867.

Bismarck's Federal Reich. Bismarck had virtually made the German Empire. A feasible association had been created, giving unity in more things than had been hitherto possible in the Germanic states, and more things than, in the heat of the moment, Bismarck had thought immediately desirable. Fear had overcome the objections of princely separatists, and victory that of Prussian dissentients. Now, the economic and spiritual advantages of federalism issue in laws and they tend to heal old wounds and regrets and to make retrogression impossible. Free migration, common regulation of the locus of responsibility for relief of the destitute, freedom of industry from guild restrictions, freedom of association, factory legislation, the abolition of usury laws—all these were great economic and social boons and swept away many antiquated institutions. The industrial and commercial energy of the day were further regulated by a single bill-of-exchange law and commercial code, by laws relating to patents and joint-stock companies, and by the reform of consular representation. The federation was also knit together by

the social influence of a uniform criminal code.[46] The federation was as yet, however, only a fragment: the Southern states had not yet been included.

The South and the Customs Parliament. The first impulse of the Southern states —Bavaria, Württemberg, and Baden— was to make federal terms with the North German Confederation, for Austria had failed them and France was exacting. But particularistic motives revived; the dynasties were still popular, and anti-Prussian feeling was strong. The old fear of Prussian harshness and discipline, as seen in the civil service and the army and in Bismarck's roughness with Parliament, combined with the steady pressure of the Catholic Church [47] to keep them away from Prussia. Nothing more than a defensive alliance with these states could at the moment be achieved.[48] For all Germany, then, there was a federation for defense purposes, but the Southern states insisted on their independent judgment of a *casus foederis* (when the situation required their assistance).

It is impossible, in the long run, to discuss economic affairs alone, nor can the representatives of the states, when democratically elected, be always a unanimous phalanx representative of particularist interests. The free-trade and tariff arrangements had visibly favorable effects upon commerce. The ceremonial and the amenities of a common life in the same assembly had the effect of smoothing down the sharpest antagonisms. National political parties arose to extend the power of the union, and election campaigns were fought on the issue. On the other hand, the whole armory of political tactics was

---

[46] For an account of the North German Parliament's activities see H. Robolsky, *Der deutsche Reichstag* (Berlin, 1893).

[47] Cf. Karl Bachem, *Vorgeschichte, Geschichte und Politik der Deutschen Zentrumspartei* (Köln, 1927), Vol. II, Chap. VII. The Bavarian Catholic Party was particularist; the feelings of the Catholic majority in Bavaria were wounded by the assumption of some Prussians that the war of 1866 had been a religious war by which "the work of the Reformation had been completed" (*Ibid.,* p. 231).

[48] This secret treaty was signed in August, 1866, and published in 1867.

used to obstruct the road to unity now being trod by the great party of the National Liberals.[49]

Bismarck was not impatient; the result was inevitable. All must be done to attract the South German states; their peculiarities must not be mocked but genially suffered and even given institutional room and effectiveness.[50] Yet the federal movement slowed down, for Bismarck too well incarnated the Prussian spirit. The Southern states attempted to establish a separate federation, but their plans failed, for among equals there is neither fear nor gratitude nor reward which can overcome jealousy and sovereignty.

The War of 1871, and National Feeling. Some excitement, an upheaval, a scene, was necessary to give back creative control to Bismarck. Would a common war help? Yes; against a foe who aroused defensive reactions and memories of historic battles and common aspirations. It was evident that if the opportunity for war with France should arrive, it would be taken to make sure that Germany's unity, however produced, should not be subject to France's veto. Any quarrel would have to be braved out; for diplomatic defeat was federal retrogression, while military victory was almost certain federal progress. In 1868 Bismarck says:

---

[49] For this phase cf. Robolsky, *op. cit.*

[50] "Besides, is unitarism the most useful and the form? Is it so for Germany particularly? Is it historically founded in Germany? That it is not, is shown by the Particularist institutions which develop in all aspects of life in Germany. It has led to the German feeling completely comfortable only in a small area, and to the conviction that one is not doing well to deprive him of his domestic comfort any more than is necessary to keep the whole together and give it effectiveness as against outside countries. This Particularism is the basis of the weakness, but, from another standpoint, that of the strength of Germany. Give it enough time! . . . centralization is more or less a matter of force and is not to be carried through without a violent operation . . . I believe that one should ask oneself, in the Germanic states, what can be regulated in common? and that which need not be regulated in common should be left to local development. Thereby one serves freedom, and one serves welfare . . ." (Quoted in Robolsky, *op. cit.*, p. 85)

"A more extensive union of the majority of Germans could only be obtained by force—or else if common danger should arouse them to fury." [51] The occasion came; indeed, Bismarck made it.

In a few months the Second Empire had fallen. The Southern states had hardly hesitated to fall in line with North Germany—though in Bavaria the Ultramontanes were able for some time to stop intervention.[52] All troops had come under the Prussian supreme command. The war was felt to be a German war, and victory supported Unity.[53]

Union Completed. Bismarck had no desire to overpower the South, but the opportunity would perhaps never recur, and pressure was needed. After Sedan, Bismarck let his press loose. Elsewhere particularism had weakened, but in Bavaria the Ultramontanes and the peasantry were at odds with the nationally-minded people of the large towns and the population of the Palatinate and the Protestant districts. King, court, and liberal opponents of Prussia were still separatist. Bismarck's attitude was that the burden of proof was on those hostile to federalism. Germany was one, had been one in a great war, was naturally one. Yet this must be demonstrated. All diplomatic channels were opened and used: Alsace should become an imperial territory! The *Zollparlament* was convened—a forum of discussion just when the whole country was excited and eager for sensational events and policies. When, after Sedan, both Baden and Württemberg positively begged inclusion in the Federation, Bavaria's hand was forced: it would be shameful to be the last state in!

Protracted, subterranean and often angry negotiations between Bavaria and Württemberg, between these, separately, and Bismarck, and between Bismarck and Baden ensued, each state watching that

---

[51] E. Ludwig, *Bismarck* (London, 1927), p. 319.
[52] Bachem, *op. cit.*, Vol. II, pp. 242-43.
[53] In his *Von Wesen der Menschlichen Verbände* (Leipzig, 1902), the "pluralistic" Otto von Gierke confesses what an overpowering sentiment of identity with the nation he felt as the victorious troops came marching along Unter den Linden.

the others should get no more favored position than it received. The North German Confederation was accepted as the kernel of a new federation, but special concessions were demanded. Bavaria's principal demands were: complete independence of its railroad system, posts and telegraphs; taxation of beer and brandy; legislation in matters of settlement and citizenship, conditions of carrying on a trade, the whole of the civil and criminal code (with the exception of the law relating to commerce and credit instruments), and consulates; an increase of its votes in the *Bundesrat* to eight (it had six in the customs *Bundesrat*), a Bavarian representative in the *Bundesrat* committees for army and fortifications, tariffs and taxes, commerce and transport; independence of the Bavarian army while carrying out a reorganization uniform with that of other states; and subordination to the federal commander-in-chief only in time of war. Further, to the navy, which Bavaria considered to be of importance only to North Germany, she would make no contribution. All these exceptions inevitably led to the further demand for a separate budget. In foreign affairs, independence was to be guaranteed by separate ambassadors: the *Bundesrat* must assent to a declaration of war, and in peace negotiations Bavarian representatives should be present. Finally—and this was the most energetic claim to independence—Bavaria must have an absolute veto on any extension of federal power and against all constitutional amendments affecting its number of votes or its privileges, and it must have the presidency of the *Bundesrat* in the absence of Prussia. The more Bavaria wished, the more the other states demanded.

Bismarck, the Prussian fanatic, could realize what it meant for a state with a long independent history and a deeply founded individuality to surrender its sovereignty. Prussia had done this only because it was in a position to obtain much and give so little. The principle of graduated privileges was just and must be accepted. However, this graduation must be accomplished discreetly; neither must know what the other was asking or being offered. Negotiations, therefore, were conducted separately and privately. A tremendous amount of chicanery was practised; and even theft of territory was arranged by secret agreements with Bismarck!

Finally, Bavaria succumbed rather than risk the possibility of being the only state outside the Union; of individual war with France; and of exclusion from the *Zollverein,* which, in her peculiar geographical position, would have been a disaster felt every day and by every class. One by one her pretensions were surrendered: but she received considerable concessions, such as retention of her taxes on beer, her own postal administration, and separate military forces and command. Yet it was bitter to lose full military freedom and submit to federal inspection of the army, the federal oath, and federal determination of total military expenditure.

Had Bismarck used all his available force, the empire might have been more closely knit; but the powers of Europe were watchful and jealous. Nor did he desire anything much more unitary, for he was jealous of Prussian independence. Then the King of Prussia, swearing never to be "Emperor of Germany," became "German Emperor." [54]

The constitution was accepted with little opposition in Baden, Hesse, and Württemberg. In Bavaria the constitution was accepted in a few days by the lower chamber, by all except three votes. In the upper chamber the Ultramontane majority reported adversely.[55] Since there was no midway between acceptance or rejection and since the consequences of rejection were frightening, the constitution was ac-

---

[54] Bismarck had let go the title "Kaiser von Deutschland" on being convinced that the other princes might take his title to be a claim to sovereignty in their states, and Parliament had used the alternative title "Deutscher Kaiser." William I made this into an issue with Bismarck, out of temper at Bismarck's growing power rather than out of any rational discrimination between the one title and the other.

[55] Cf. Bachem, *op. cit.,* Vol. II, pp. 244-45.

cepted by 102 against 46, some Ultramontanes absenting themselves.

All things produce their proper symbols, but none was ever so appropriate as a coronation in a vanquished land to inaugurate this federation, reared to virility by the Prussian Mars, for only arms could expel Austria and exorcise that enemy of monarchical federation, democracy. Since the people could not win their way to political authority and to a federation based upon acknowledged utilities, fear and slaughter, ruthlessness, cruelty, and cunning were licensed. For the despotic prince of a sovereign state has all to lose, while the individual voter may believe that he personally loses hardly anything when he consents to give up a fraction of his morsel of sovereignty. The prince must be made to fear the consequences of his refusal. But every force in politics demands its price and is, in some way, paid for. The German Empire paid for its federal advantages by the burden of Prussian hegemony and the emasculation of liberalism. It was not until the originally needful operation had been performed—the transformation of the monarchy into a democracy, by a violent assertion of popular rights in November, 1918—that the empire at last arrived at a less strained, a more peaceful, and more unitary federation, distinctly more unitary in the scope of federal powers than Australia, Canada, and the United States, but less unified in common administration than the latter.

SAMENESS OF MOTIVES, DIFFERENCE OF FATE
IN FEDERATIONS

Thus, in the formation of federations the impulses have been given by spiritual ideals of national unity, by the prospect of the fullest extension of certain desired rights, by the economic motive, by a common language and literature, by considerations of defense and international prestige, by the peaceful settlement of fears produced by the contiguity of human groups which tend to form collective dislikes, by the amicable resolution of common problems, and by the energies and aspirations of specific leaders. On the other hand, racial, cultural, religious, and

economic differences obstruct the formation of the great state, while personal desires for prestige, which can be satisfied only in a small and separate polity, add to the separative force.

Before we turn to an analytical account of government institutions and ideas, let us compare and have before us the bare facts of their territorial extent.

Unitary States	Area, in sq. miles	Pop., in millions
Great Britain (excluding N. Ireland)	88,432	47.9
France	212,659	38.
Federal States		
United States	2,973,774	145.
Switzerland	15,940	4.3
Australia	2,974,581	9.9
Canada	3,684,723	11.5
Germany	182,741	69.6
USSR (this includes Carpatho-Ukraine, Baltic republics, occupied Poland, lands returned by Roumania)	9,619,791	193.5

There is a tremendous disparity in the size, density of population, and climatic and economic range. The United States, for example, contains nearly 34 times as many people as Switzerland and has an area about 180 times as large. The climatic and economic range of America, Canada, and Australia is enormously greater than that of Germany. Hence a wider effective and compelling diversity. Broadly we can say that, other things being equal, sheer size makes any governmental system difficult: the larger the area, the more diverse the interests and the greater the extent of decentralization; the sparser the population, the greater the decentralization; the smaller the area, the greater the contiguity and centralization, and the less the diversity of interests; the denser the population, evenly distributed over large areas of federation, the greater the centralization.

But athwart these facts lie differences of religion, secular culture, and the accidents of history, and these give extra and differentiating turns to the pattern. Of these differences, the most marked is displayed by the centralization of Russian government, whether under the Tsars or under the Soviet form. The centralizing forces of Kiev and Moscow, fighting against the Mongol invasion and two hundred years of occupation, left nothing but a centralized, absolute, and total régime, which swallowed the Church as well, and ideological fervor has in our own time made more drastic the authority of the capital.[56]

CONTRASTS BETWEEN AMERICAN AND GERMAN FEDERALISM

THE consequences of such marked difference between the territorial extent and the sociological history of Germany is a striking contrast in their federal institutions.

Relative Power of the Component States. Whereas, in the American union, all states were given an equal status, except for their numerical representation in the House of Representatives, in Germany some of the states received a particularly favored position. Most important was the fact that Prussia was hereditarily endowed with the office of chief executive—that is, the Emperor and Chancellor together, for the King of Prussia was always to be the German Emperor or Kaiser, and he appointed the Imperial Chancellor. Since these two were supreme in the conduct of foreign relations, and since also, the Emperor appointed as Chancellor the Prime Minister of Prussia, the predominance of Prussia was assured. Especially was this so since the sovereign power was not acknowledged to be in the people and therefore exercisable in the *Reichstag* for them. If it lay anywhere other than in the Emperor, then it must be in the *Bundesrat*—that is, the Federal Council, a second chamber like the United States Senate, but actually the sovereign representatives of the states' governments and avowedly representing their sovereignty. The *Bundesrat* had the final sanctioning power in the making of law; constitutional amendments could be passed only by a special form of vote within it; and it settled disputes between the *Reich* and the states and between the states themselves. But in the United States, the amending power lay with both houses and with the people (see Chap. 9 above), while interstate and nation-state disputes were in various forms subject to the jurisdiction of the Supreme Court, a judicial body. Thus in Germany, the hegemony of one state was acknowledged; not so in the United States.

Distribution of Powers. In the United States legislative powers were distributed by means of assigning a short but pregnant list of powers to the national legislature, while the rest were reserved to the states or to the people; and some, again, were denied to both the nation and the states. The first category allowed of a vast development of federal power, by judicial interpretation (see Chap. 9 above). Yet the distribution caused frustration and confusions due to the pressure of economic and social conditions and ideals when confronted with the various and unequal initiative of nation and states, and with their very diverse capacity, in area and financial ability, to make law and enforce it.

In Germany, the difficulty of inducing the states (mainly governed by kings or princes) to yield up their sovereignty caused the legislative powers assigned to the *Reich* to be very meager, and the residue to the states to be very great, though some of these were ludicrously small in population. Furthermore, some of the states were put in more favorable positions than others. Bavaria was allowed full power over her railways and her posts and telegraphs, and Württemberg over the latter; and both these states and Saxony had considerable though not complete autonomy over their armed forces and contingents for the *Reich* army. In the German system all powers were either assigned to the *Reich* or reserved, *ipso facto,* to the

[56] Cf. B. H. Sumner, *Short History of Russia* (New York, 1943); Edward Crankshaw, *Russia and the Russians* (New York, 1948); and the various works already cited on economic planning.

states: there were no limitations on the power of *both* governments, as described in the discussion of the American system in Chapter 9 above.

The Administration of the Laws showed also a marked divergence. The United States changed over from the Confederation's method of leaving administration to the states, to direct administration by the nation of all matters coming under its own legislative power and under the power of its president. However, the German method was tantamount to that which the United States had abandoned: namely, the administration of almost all *Reich* affairs by the state governments through their own public services. Thus there was *Reich* administration in foreign affairs, in naval and military affairs, and (with the reservations already noticed) in posts and telegraphs—but not in taxes and customs! In the United States, the nation merely required that its agencies and officers should not be obstructed in their administration as they applied it to individuals everywhere in the Union, and this assurance they obtained in several classic cases decided by the Supreme Court. In Germany, the *Reich* was obliged to seek good administration where it legislated by supervision—that is, a kind of inspection which was mainly applicable at the top management level and which only with difficulty penetrated on specific occasions to the lower levels. A diplomatic process of negotiation between *Reich* and state government was necessary to obtain results. A dispute could be finally referred to the *Bundesrat*. This, being a body of sovereign representatives, or ambassadors, could hardly secure enforcement. The larger states were immune from enforcement, Prussia above all, for in her case the supreme *Reich* executive and the supreme executive of Prussia, and some of the *Reich* ministers and Prussian ministers, were the very same persons. Further, the Chancellor had the constitutional power to make orders for administrative fulfillment of the laws. In the end, the logic of such a federal arrangement led to enforcement by punitive action, *Reichsexekution,* or "federal execution," direct

action upon a state. But such could not possibly be exercised, in fact, against a state so big as Prussia; and reciprocity therefore required that it be not threatened against any other. This weakened federal authority.

Distribution of Power within the Legislature. In the legislature, the United States House of Representatives and the Senate occupy an equal position of authority, except that financial legislation must be initiated by the lower chamber, conformably with traditional respect for the popular basis of a democratic system. But the Senate was endowed with extra powers in executive appointments, the conduct of foreign affairs, and the making of treaties. In the German system, though the *Reichstag* was founded on universal suffrage (ruined in effect by obsolete apportionment), final power of accepting legislation lay with the *Bundesrat,* an appointed body. Since the preponderance of representation herein was given to Prussia, and since in the government of Prussia the conservative Eastern parts dominated the rest because the system of representation designedly favored the country against the town and the East against the Center and West, Prussian conservatism limited the relatively liberal character of the *Reichstag.*

Power of the Upper Chamber. The special power and problems of the union of Prussia and the smaller states was revealed in the stark contrast of voting strength in the American Senate with that in the *Bundesrat.* In the Senate, by the Great Compromise of the Philadelphia convention, all states were represented equally. In the *Bundesrat,* the states were represented according to an impression of their size, population, and political weight, resulting in a very considerable diversity of representation. Prussia had a decided predominance. This had its effect in legislation: in the control of administration; in fear of or disdain for federal enforcement measures; and in constitutional amendment. The amendment clause provided that however the *Bundesrat* agreed upon an amendment (and the process would have to be one of negotiation among sovereigns), if fourteen votes were cast against it, it was defeated. As Prussia possessed seventeen votes in 1871, and later acquired more, her interests were safeguarded; so also combinations of the other states—especially Bavaria, Württemberg, and Saxony, who had, six, four, and four respectively—could protect themselves. Prussia in 1871 had five sixths of the total population of the *Reich,* and could have demanded forty-five votes or more out of the fifty-eight votes in the *Bundesrat.*

Powers of the Judiciary. In the exercise of judicial power, the United States assigned to federal courts, in inferior and appellate instances, the judgment of cases arising out of the constitution and the laws it passed, and the validity of state legislation and executive action under the United States constitution. It left to the state courts the rendering of judgment in cases involving state affairs and inferior suits involving the United States constitution on the way up to appeal. But in Germany, *all* judicial actions came before state courts only, though procedure was given uniformity by a *Reich* series of statutes, and, of course, the state courts were interpreting several *Reich* laws and codes, the detailed regulations and commentaries on which produced an assimilation of judgments. Judgment rendered in any state court was valid all over the nation. It was not till 1879 that the *Reichsgericht* was established, a supreme appellate court which heard appeals from the state Supreme Courts in all civil and criminal matters, but which was effective only if the state decisions had infringed a *Reich* law.

Financial Powers of Nation and States. Finally, in the United States, with small and removable limitations, both nation and states were given the enjoyment of independent powers of taxation. Once the constitutional limitation on the power of the nation to raise an income tax had been removed by the 17th amendment, the chief difficulty in American federal-state finances was the effect of growing competition between nation and states for mounting sources of revenue to meet social expenditures and to provide for rewards

and sanctions for the regulating effort of both governments. But in Germany, quite other difficulties dogged the federal finances. In the main, customs duties were assigned for the *Reich's* needs, while whatever more was necessary to meet its budget was supplied by proportional contributions from the states. This system gave the last word to the states. However, customs duties mounted with the increase in tariffs, and with the rise in the volume of commerce. A statute of 1879, therefore, was enacted which enabled the *Reichstag* from time to time to assign to the *Reich* a fixed sum out of the customs revenues: the excess went to the states! But the amount so assigned was such as to leave the *Reich* still in deficit; and so the states received a contribution from the *Reich* and crossed this with a contribution from their treasuries back to the *Reich!*

THE NECESSITY AND THE DIFFICULTIES OF FEDERALISM

THE historical conditions under which certain states came into existence, or the continuing large extent of the area under a single government, have forced some polities to be federal. In addition, up to a point, the virtues of decentralization merit perpetuation. They are: (1) experimentation; (2) limitation of damage to the area which makes mistakes, and the value of example where the innovators are successful: (3) clear acquaintance by the government with the local situation to be solved; and (4) the possibility of personal interest in day-by-day government and personal pressure for remedy of grievous situations.[57]

It cannot be denied that federalism has its disadvantages. (1) It is financially expensive, since there is much duplication of administrative machinery and procedure. It is wasteful of time and energy, in that it depends on much negotiation, political and administrative, to secure uniformity of law and proper administrative fulfilment thereof. It is also especially

---

[57] See H. Finer, *English Local Government* (London, 1949), Chapter 1.

difficult in the requirements for amendment.[58] It is, again, expensive because it does not allow of the full technical integration required in such services as transport, utilities, health, and employment placement. From this point of view, federalism is a premium on the irrational, in finance, area, and personnel. Government already has enough problems of decentralization and diversity, without this additional obstruction.

(2) Federalism is confusing to the public and has awkward results on personal rights and obligations. For example, in the United States the greatest fiscal confusion reigns: Who properly owes what to which authority? [59] So involved is this question that simplification and reason are baffled, even where vast tax-research bodies have been established to clarify the situation. One's rights in such matters as insurance, marriage, and divorce, the status of married women, bankruptcy, and social assistance, are most difficult to discover. So, also, regarding the acceptance of responsibility for social and economic regulation or assistance by the various authorities: [60] each waits on the other, often less to secure an opportunity for action than to deny it to the agency which has assumed it. It might be ventured that the quality of government at the center is a function of an integral nation-wide focus of attention upon it. This attention, federalism disintegrates.

(3) There are governmental tasks which federalism does not succeed in doing, because, being a product of bygone decades and even centuries, the distribution of powers resists the centralization essential to various modern large-scale economic and social needs. Crime, for instance, is especially difficult to control. A unified industry and society have overtaken a disintegrated power to regulate, control, and utilize them.[61]

The nation and the states are crisscrossed with lines of agreement and collaborative authority, designed to lace together what the constitution has put asunder. This we shall appreciate in particular by a mere glance at recent developments in the United States, it being necessarily assumed that the student is familiar with the general features of the system. And, in the next chapter, special attention is paid to federalism in Germany because it is a continuing problem in modern government.

MAIN TRENDS OF FEDERALISM IN THE UNITED STATES

THE United States, it is manifest, is moving swiftly towards a unified economic and social system, coextensive with its whole territory.[62] Economical administration requires large-scale operation (up to a point, if it is to be efficient). The advancement of health, labor, manufactures, commerce, and morals in one state can be frustrated by the backwardness of its neighbors—an unchallengeable example is unemployment-insurance systems. Higher taxes and better labor standards over the level of other states have been followed by the migration of employers and their industries to lesser-taxed places [63] (see the Supreme Court's acknowledgment of this in the social security cases). Free mobility of labor and capital to their best prospects can be and has been obstructed by state and local differences of taxation, by licensing, and, among other things, by an Employment

[58] Cf. Chap. 8 above. Cf. Herman Finer, "The Case for Local Government," *Public Administration Review*, Autumn, 1942; cf. also G. C. S. Benson, *The New Centralization* (New York, 1941); also Herman Finer, *English Local Government*, 4th edition (London, 1949).
[59] Cf. J. A. Maxwell, *The Fiscal Impact of Federalism in the United States* (Harvard, 1946), and Sen. Doc. 69, 78th Cong., 1st sess., *Federal, State and Local Government Fiscal Relations*.
[60] Cf. series published by Public Administration Clearing House (1313 East 60th Street, Chicago) on various federal functions.

[61] Cf. A. Millspaugh, *Crime Control by the National Government* (Brookings, 1937).
[62] J. K. Hart, "A Unified Economy and States Rights," *Annals, American Academy of Political Science*, May, 1936.
[63] Harold Groves, "Tax Differential and Relocation of Industries," 31st Annual Conference on Taxation of National Tax Association, 1935, pp. 557-61. Temporary National Economic Committee (U.S. Government Printing Office), monograph, *Interstate Economic Barriers*.

Placement Service broken into forty-eight parts, each without any concept of the opportunities or deterrents to be encountered in sister states, which are yet part of a single country. Some states have even established barriers to migrants and commerce from other states, such as the application of sanitary regulations for persons or commodities, or the imposition of special charges or of licenses for transport vehicles.[64]

Of course, whenever people and commodities are in "interstate" commerce, the federal government may legislate and has legislated uniform conditions: or, where it has the power, it can formulate and has formulated different principles to suit different geographical and social conditions. But what is to be done where the popular desire for a higher standard of living, keen as it is, beats vainly against the poverty, the ungenerosity, the ignorance, or the corruption of some state governments, yet where a uniform reasonable standard for all is a condition of the successful fulfillment of such desire? Must children born in poorer states be doomed to inferior education?[65] Must some states permanently suffer from inferior housing, corrupt insurance inspection, and business corporations whose charter has been obtained in complaisant states administered by officials of easy virtue? Must natural reserves, like water power, remain in the hands of do-nothing states legislatures? Shall the utilities which are not interstate but which are still part and parcel of the national economy be immune from regulation by the Federal Power Commission? How is a nationwide market to be assured its uniformities of freedom or concerted regulation? How can meats and other foods and drinks which are produced and distributed under interstate commerce, and so are subject to high standards of federal inspection, compete with commodities displayed side by side but produced within the state, possibly under the feeblest standards of cleanliness and purity? How can the moral interests of the states which prohibit or heavily regulate the alcoholic liquor traffic be defended? How can a national force assist the local agencies of crime control?

Is the agriculture of the United States to be treated as one unit, and, accordingly, is its policy of production and marketing to be uniformly regulated, especially in view of international agreements entered into by the federal government concerning the sale of certain primary farm commodities on the international market? Is the federal authority to say that the marginal lands within a single state are to be abandoned in keeping with a national plan of soil conservation?

New Deal legislation and the Supreme Court's attitude thereto have clearly drawn attention to the rapid development of centralization, but they have also strongly emphasized the recognition of the need for the reallocation of powers in a new balance, not excluding strong local organs of government.[66]

The United States constitution is, from this point of view, under tremendous strain, a strain even heavier than the similar pressures revealed by the Royal Commission on the Australian Constitution,[67] and by the Rowell-Sirois Report on Canadian Dominion-Provincial Relationships.[68] Devices have therefore been sought, and some applied, whereby the

---

[64] F. F. Melder, *Agricultural Quarantine as Trade Barrier* (Chicago: Council of State Governments, 1939) and *State Trade Walls* (New York, 1939).

[65] Report, President's Advisory Committee on Education, 1938, Tables 1 and 2, pages 225-26, on the differences in educational expenditure per child in the various states; see also Reports of the President's (Mr. Truman's) Commission on Higher Education in the United States, December, 1947; and subsequent volumes.

[66] Cf. David Fellman, "Ten Years of the Supreme Court: 1937-1947, Federalism," in *American Political Science Review*, December, 1947, p. 1142 *et seq.* and V. M. Barnett, *ibid.*, p. 1170 *et seq.*, "The Power to Regulate Commerce."

[67] Royal Commission on the Australian Constitution, 1929; cf. also defeat by referendum of attempt to increase Commonwealth powers, in August, 1944.

[68] Reports of Royal Commission on Dominion-Provincial Relations (the Sirois Report), 3 vols. (Ottawa, 1940); and the series of studies in appendices, 8 vols., 938-39.

federal government may assume the necessary additional authority. This has come about either by initiative where the states have not as yet used their own powers at all, or by extension of the federal sphere of "general welfare," or "taxing," or "interstate" commerce powers. There has been a kind of transference of power from the states where these have used their authority, but inadequately, wherever the services which require large-scale treatment for full efficiency for the state no less than for all its neighbors in the Republic; the most recent instance is insurance.[69] Remedies for excessive state disintegration of the national economy and society are necessarily incomplete and indirect, for they have to pass the censorship of a Congress composed of representatives who hardly dare (at any rate openly and avowedly) to prefer the larger loyalty to the smaller, and of the Supreme Court.

It is impossible here to do more than merely indicate the chief methods used to bring about a higher degree of governmental integration.[70] (1) There is a growing tendency to uniform state action, fostered by the voluntary Council of State Governments and the National Council of Commissioners on Uniform State Laws.[71] Yet action by the former is very slow and incomplete, admits of continued diversities, and is always uncertain since it depends on subsequent action by the state legislatures. Indeed, on the average, each of the uniform laws agreed upon (and it takes years to reach agreements) is adopted by only one fourth of the states,

while in important matters the Council's work is altogether jilted. (2) There is some slight influence exerted by the Conference of (State) Governors, sometimes meeting with federal officials.

(3) A much more important mechanism of the readjustment of federal-state powers is the federal grant-in-aid.[72] The federal government pays funds to the states, and sometimes directly to the cities and counties, to implement a federal statute.[73] The grants are given provided that federal standards are fulfilled by the state governments, in respect of the purposes and principles of the service in question, the structure and procedure of administration, the recruitment and management of personnel, the furnishing of reports, and submission to federal inspection. Either or all of these conditions are applied in varying measure according to the nature of the service to be administered by this developing and peculiar partnership between national and state governments, and according to the quality of feeling in each case about the independence of states as against the advantages to be derived from federal assistance.

(4) Sometimes free skilled assistance in terms of advice or collaboration is rendered by the federal government to the states. Here the action of the states is supplemented without obligation on their part, as for instance, by expert advice from the (now defunct) National Resources Planning Board or the Federal Bureau of Investigation, or by the training of local officers at the FBI's police school.

(5) There is the growing practice by the federal government of conducting its own administrative agencies (e.g., the Farm Security Administration) and those in which it collaborates with the states through grants-in-aid (e.g., the Social Security Administration) in large regions, which include several states, with more or less of a common economic or social character imprinted by their geographical re-

---

[69] U.S. v. South Eastern Underwriters Association; decision given in a court of seven by a majority of one. Cf. Thomas Reed Powell, "Insurance is Commerce," Harvard Law Review, September, 1944.
[70] For recent surveys of the problem and the growing solution, see J. P. Clark, The Rise of the New Federalism (New York, 1938); G. C. S. Benson, The New Centralization (New York, 1941); and A. W. MacMahon, "Taking Stock of Federalism in the U.S.A.," Canadian Journal of Economics and Political Science, May, 1941. Cf. also V. O. Key, The Administration of Federal Grants to the States (Chicago, 1941).
[71] W. B. Graves, Uniform State Action (Chapel Hill, 1934; and W. B. Graves, ed., "Intergovernmental Relations," Annals, American Academy of Political Science, January, 1940.

[72] Cf. Key, op. cit.
[73] Report, National Resources Planning Board, Federal Relations to Urban Government (U.S. Government Printing Office, 1936), Vol. I, part II.

lationships, by the character of their production, or by their contiguity.[74] But so far there is only one truly regional governmental agency of the federal government (perhaps two, if we add Boulder Dam, the product of a compact made by seven states regarding the uses of the Colorado River). It is the Tennessee Valley Authority.[75] Yet these regional arrangements are by themselves no substantial modifiers of state powers or of the divergencies in their use. The states are the weak links in the American system of government, so much so that the federal government has been tempted to by-pass them and cooperate directly with the great cities, or has sought, but hitherto not substantially found, a regional solution. It is improbable that the TVA can be a model for the rest of the country, for it came into existence to solve a precise local problem based upon more than usually specific features. Other valley regions, for example, the Missouri [76] and Arkansas, have been proposed, and they will certainly be of benefit in the solution of the two or three peculiar local problems of their area. But it is surely impossible to envisage American government conducted through a congeries of very diverse valley regions or of regions on any other geographical basis pure and simple. The way of the grant-in-aid to the states and the cities is at present discernible as the line of maximum progress in the readjustment of federal-state powers in an age which cries out for government yet understands the need not only for administrative decentralization but for considerable local autonomy.[77]

INTERNATIONAL FEDERATION

THE terrible results of World War I, and in part the weaknesses and yet in part also the promise of the League of Nations, produced impulses toward a "United States of Europe." The principal bid was made by the nation with the most to fear from isolation—France.[78] The effort was abortive. The idea lived on in the minds of some individuals and societies outside the groups of practical politicians in the League,[79] and was powerfully influenced by the miseries and devastation of World War II.[80] It was not difficult to formulate a plan of federal union. It is never difficult in matters of government to invent machinery; the question is, does the will to action exist?—without it machinery is doomed.[81]

What stood in the way of such proposals was nationalism, the spirit we have hitherto proclaimed to be unifying within the state. Such a "particularist" spirit we have seen to be at work within Germany, and such a spirit we saw had to be overcome in the American, Australian, Canadian, and other forms of federalism. But in these instances, deeply as state or sectional patriotism was felt, it was as nothing compared with the spirit of separation and contrast, rising to the plane of sustained hostility, prevalent in the relationship between nations. For those elements which produce a sentiment of commonalty within the nations are precisely those which sever

---

[74] Report, National Resources Committee, *Regional Factors in National Planning and Development* (U.S. Government Printing Office, 1935).
[75] Cf. Herman Finer, *Tennessee Valley Authority* (Montreal: International Labour Office, 1944); Herman Pritchett, *TVA: A Study in Public Administration* (Chapel Hill, 1943); and David Lilienthal, *T.V.A.: Democracy Marches On* (New York, 1944).
[76] "A Symposium on Regional Planning," *Iowa Law Review*, January, 1947.
[77] Cf. Report, *Federalism and Intergovernmental Relations,* by William Anderson, being "A Budget of Suggestions for Research" (Chi-cago: Public Administration Service, 1946), in the preparation of which the present author had some part. See also Dorothy G. Tompkins, *Materials for the Study of Federal Government* (Chicago, 1948).
[78] Cf. Briand's *Memorandum on the Organization . . . of European Federal Union* (New York: Carnegie Endowment for International Peace, 1930); and *Replies of 26 Governments of Europe to M. Briand's Memorandum* (same publisher, 1930).
[79] Cf. Edouard Herriot, *The United States of Europe* (New York, 1930).
[80] Clarence Streit, *Union Now with Great Britain* (New York, 1941); and Percy Corbett, *Post War Worlds* (New York, 1942).
[81] Cf. Ivor Jennings, *A Federation for Western Europe* (New York, 1940); and R. Mackay, *Federal Europe* (London, 1940); cf. also a truly great work, Lionel Curtis, *Civitas Dei* (London, 1934).

them. Every nation is a tough, persistent, corporate body, with a collective personality stoutly different from all others. As Hobbes said, each is "an artificial Man."

This confident nationalism is no capricious triviality, no fantasy, but something which has grown out of the location, climate, resources, economic occupations, and the vicissitudes of history peculiar to the locality. It has been influenced by the nature of the immediate neighboring national groups, as well as by isolation or semi-isolation, which was the lot of all of them, let it be well remembered, for long centuries before the very recent development of rapid and vivid communications. Each has formed a separate culture, compact of a different language, alphabet (in some cases), literature, songs, stories, manners, religion, proverbial wisdom, philosophy, everyday courtesies, standard of living and production and consumption habits, and—issuing from all and standing above all—laws and government and the spirit in which they are used. What was built in six hundred years cannot be abolished in six or in sixty; and some national differences are as desirable as the diversity we delight to see among individuals.[82]

It is of special interest to notice that the attempt at economic federalism—which was broached at the time the European Recovery Program was being considered by sixteen European nations, with the aid and comfort of the United States—could not go very far, not beyond the standing organs barely sufficient for implementing that plan. It is also noteworthy that fear of the U.S.S.R. succeeded in bringing about a union of Britain, France, Holland, Belgium, Luxembourg,—the so-called "Western Union"—in a fairly far-reaching pact of friendship and mutual assistance in the case of attack on any one of them. But the tenuousness of the authority of the United Nations Organization is proof positive, alas, of the present impossibility of more substantial advance towards a federation, even as unified and

internally peaceful and just as the German Federation of 1871, which was far from the more considerable union exemplified in the United States of America.

FEDERALISM AS THE GUARANTEE OF LIBERALISM

THE opinions of Lord Acton, a great liberal—so great a liberal, indeed, that he could scarcely applaud any action whatever taken either by governments or individual men—have given rise to the erroneous view that federalism is in itself a deliberately contrived guarantee of civil liberties. Thus, Acton said: [83]

Of all checks on democracy, federation has been the most efficacious and the most congenial . . . The federal system limits and restrains the sovereign power by dividing it and by assigning to Government only certain defined rights. It is the only method of curbing not only the majority but the power of the whole people.

Dicta of this kind are sweet as honey to dogmatic champions of *laissez faire* like Hayek.[84] And the *reductio ad absurdum* is to advocate the further disintegration of the nation, the state, and the great society. But the doctrine is wrong. *First,* federalism is not, historically, a deliberate decentralization starting from a centralized state: it is, on the contrary, a process of concentrating power by uniting previously independent and sovereign or almost sovereign states or provinces. *Second,* sovereign power is not limited and restrained by dividing it among states and national government: in some federations all the powers of government are, in fact, assigned to one or the other authority. What struck Acton was the experience of the United States: and he observed it at a time when she had not yet reached the point of heavy social and economic activity by states and federal government (he goes back to before *Munn v. Illinois,* 1877!). And, even more important, he seems not to have noticed that what re-

---

[82] Cf. Herman Finer, *America's Destiny* (New York, 1947), Chap. V.

[83] E.g., Acton, *Essays on Freedom and Power* (Boston, 1948), p. 163.
[84] Cf. *Road to Serfdom* (Chicago, 1945), p. 219 ff.

strained American government most was the interpretation of the Bill of Rights and the due-process clauses in both state and federal governments. It is the constitutional limitations, the prohibitions on certain activities by any government, that offers the minority and the individual the guarantees Acton considers to be essential to liberalism. Indeed, some federations have been absolutist: like the German *Reich,* from 1871 to 1918. We hardly care to adduce the Soviet *Union!*

The most that can be said is that if we omit the truly tempering effect of the Bill of Rights (which prohibits governmental power, reserving action, and therefore, if necessary, coercion, to the people) then

the distribution of powers, federally, is an obstruction to government, but it is not a really serious obstruction.[85] It is a guarantee of inefficient and expensive government rather than a guarantee of liberal government. Liberalism and responsibility are to be sought in other devices. It should not be forgotten that Acton was so intemperate about liberalism that, as a young man, he was prepared to condone the continuation of slavery in the Southern states rather than have the United States united by the compulsion of the North.[86] Nor was he anxious to see the disintegration of the Austro-Hungarian Empire to make way for the national self-determination of its subject peoples.

85 On this general theme see Roscoe Pound, C. H. McIlwain, and R. F. Nichols, *Federalism as a Democratic Process* (Rutgers, 1942).

86 Acton, *op. cit.*

Federalism — Germany, 1918-39

THE development of German federalism from the *Reich* of 1871 to that of Weimar in 1919, and beyond, to the nazi unification, exhibits features so different from other federal systems that the problems and answers must be reviewed. Nor can it be ignored that the problems have yet to be answered, since a post-World War II Germany will be reborn, on foundations still quite stubborn.

THE FOUNDING OF THE WEIMAR REPUBLIC

COMPARISON between the German empire of 1871 and that of 1919 reveals tremendous differences in spirit and organization. *Political Background.* Revolution caused the old powers to break down in November, 1918. The vital force of the union, Prussia's military prestige, had been destroyed by defeat. Democracy and socialism destroyed the dynasties. There was a momentary cry of "Free from Berlin," and murmurs for a South German republic. But the very forces which overthrew the old system established a new one—the unity of political parties across state boundaries. The Majority Socialists, Independent Socialists, Spartacists, Democrats, and Center were centralizers, in virtue of their social and economic aspirations. A torrent of projects for a new constitution poured forth, all centralizing.

The Council of People's Commissaries in Berlin had, from the first, extended its hand over the whole of Germany, in the name of the "German Socialistic Republic." [1] The states complained, and were invited to send delegates to Berlin, where the most generous devotion to German unity was expressed. [2] The central authority, however, had been warned that it could not go too far. The calling of a National Assembly required that the People's Commissaries should at once proceed to draft a constitution. For this purpose they made Hugo Preusz Minister of the Interior.

As a liberal and a professor of both constitutional and administrative law in centralist Berlin, Preusz had special qualifications. A democrat by temperament and by conviction, he was devoid of sympathy either for the princes or for the hegemony of Prussia. A zealous advocate of a more integrated Germany, his principles really became the new constitution.

Toward a Unitary State. The constitution of August 11, 1919, was strongly unitary. What were its dynamic forces? One was the abdication of the dynasties. Suddenly, forces which had for generations

---

[1] Proclamation of November 12, 1918 and announcement of November 23, 1918. Cf. F. Purlitz, *Deutscher Geschichtskalendar (Die Deutsche Revolution*, I, Berlin, November 1918—February 1919), pp. 48-49 for the proclamation.

[2] "The maintenance of the Unity of Germany is an urgent necessity. All German races stand united in the German Republic. They promise to work resolutely for the unity of the Reich and against separatist attempts."—November 25, 1918. Cf. Purlitz, *op. cit.*, Vol. I, p. 58 ff.

successfully acted as a drag upon unity disappeared, especially in Prussia. Further, Germany had attained a high degree of legislative and administrative unity during World War I. The process of integration had shown those who operated it that a great deal of former particularism was wanton waste. Moreover, the war period had not ended for Germany in 1918 or 1919: and the pressure for economy was immense. Therefore, that which appeared desirable in easier days to a rich people ceased to be worth its cost. Again, the National Assembly which made the constitution was elected by the whole people as an aggregate. There was no participation of the states as formal entities, but the *Reich* was divided into a number of constituencies with mere geographical significance. Quite expressly, it was as a collection of individuals uniting for the performance of a solemn political act, and not as states, that the people were asked to vote—at least by the vast majority of candidates. Social policy and democratic institutions were put into the foreground; greater unity seemed to be taken for granted. The National Assembly was the final authority: neither a body representing the states, nor ratification by the states, was to give validity to its work. (We show later how far the states *qua* states were consulted in the preparation of the constitution.) All these factors contributed to centralize the constitution. Yet one other element was quite as important as all of these put together: the position of Prussia.

Prussia's Position. Prussia had made herself master of Germany, but her mastership was not unchallenged. In particular, Bavaria's jealousy had never been stilled; nor were the states which had been absorbed by her—Silesia, Hanover, the Rhineland districts—quite happy within her conservative grip. Since 1917 the problem of Germany's future had become very largely the problem of Prussia's future, for a *Reichstag* with large, liberal and socialist elements in it accorded badly with a Prussian *Landtag* heavily conservative, and the whole *Reich* was vitally interested in the outcome of the problem

of Prussian electoral reform. For Prussia in 1914 constituted over three fifths of the total German territory and contained more than two fifths of its population. What was to be done with this great state? If the old system had continued, either Prussia or the *Reich* must have become increasingly dissatisfied. It was already within Prussia's administrative power to modify almost as she wished the effect of federal laws. Her position as the central war-making state had caused the exacerbation of separatist feeling, since all ills seemed to come from Berlin. Bavaria complained of *"Berlinerei,"* that is Berlin's clumsiness, inefficiency, and favoritism. The parts of Prussia began to shake the framework which contained them—not unaided by Allied propaganda. In the Rhineland and Westphalia, it was pretended that the disturbances at Berlin entitled them to form a separate state, and the bourgeoisie, the industrialists, and the Catholic Church saw great benefits in "freedom from Berlin." Both the Prussian and the *Reich* governments took a strong stand against such disruptive movements.

There was no doubt that something must be done in a new constitution to reduce the actual predominance of Prussia, even beyond the creation of a democratic basis which was to be common to the whole *Reich*. These separatist movements and the antagonism to Prussia gave Preusz his opportunity. Should the domestic institutions of Prussia be assimilated to those of the rest of Germany, her internal organization decentralized, then her own separatism was reducible and the unification of the *Reich* promoted. All the signs favored such a development.

The result of all the constitutional discussions and projects between November 9, 1918, and August 11, 1919, was the creation of a federal state of such a high degree of unity that constitutional lawyers and political scientists have found difficulty in giving it a satisfactory name. It was variously called.[3]

---

[3] Cf. the various commentaries to be referred to in future footnotes: Hans Nawiasky, *Der Bundesstaat als Rechtsbegriff* (Tübingen,

Original Published Draft. The original published draft of January 20, 1919, was completely saturated with unitarism. Preusz wanted the new German republic to be an entirely unitary popular state, founded on "the national self-consciousness of a self-organized people." Replacing the undemocratic dynastic divisions, local government would still be permitted to the states, allowing for some separatist spirit as part of the German political character.

Yet one state had far too much independence and weight: Prussia, with forty million out of a total of some seventy million people in all Germany. Her new destiny was to be fulfilled as somehow merged in the greater German nation which would stand above all the states. Preusz's original project provided for the division of Prussia into eight separate states, the others in the federation being consolidated to form eight additional states, regardless of traditional boundaries, to suit modern economic and administrative needs.

Separatism Cries, "Halt!" The draft evoked an indignant outcry. The temporary socialist rulers of Bavaria were anxious to make use of the widest possible powers for the realization of their social policies, while the bourgeoisie desired separate and more favored treatment of Bavaria at the peace conference. What became of increasing importance in the later tensions in the *Reich* was that the nonsocialistic Bavarians created the Bavarian People's Party to secure the economic and financial independence of their state. Baden and Saxony resented central direction, especially since this was carried out by radical elements in Berlin. A violent storm was unleashed against territorial reorganization. The states all highly approved of centralization—but none wished its own borders to be altered. Prussia, of course, having most to lose,

1920); G. Anschütz and C. Bilfinger, *et al.,* in *Bericht, Vereinigung der deutschen Staatsrechtsleherer* (Berlin, April, 1924); F. Fleiner, J. Lukas, *et al., ibid.* (April, 1929); and literature in *Handbuch des deutschen Staatsrechts,* Vol. I, ed. by G. Anschütz and R. Thoma (Tübingen, 1930).

was most reluctant. Therefore article 18, allowing area reorganization, was very considerably weakened, though not entirely emasculated.

The anti-unitarists also defeated Preusz's scheme for representing the states in a second chamber by representatives selected by the state legislatures, and secured, instead, selection by the state governments. The solution rejected would have tended to emphasize the peoples rather than the states as single-minded entities. In the *Reichsrat* the larger states attempted to maintain the proportionate strength they had enjoyed in the *Bundesrat,* but their defeat enhanced the feeling that the united Germans now counted for more than the states in forming the will of the *Reich.* Anschütz and Poetzsch, two of the foremost constitutional jurists, believed that "The victory of the idea of Unity over the territorial supremacy of the member states is patent." [4] We shall later see that the nazi régime found this altogether inadequate for its purposes.

It is now appropriate to analyze the federal institutions, and we shall do this in two phases, giving most attention to the Weimar Republic, then passing to the changes introduced by the nazi government. The subject is then concluded by a short consideration of the future.

THE WEIMAR REPUBLIC'S FEDERALISM

The Presidency. Instead of the Presidency being hereditarily vested in the Prussian dynasty, as between 1871 and 1918, it became, like the American, elective. This was a heavy blow at the moral and political authority of Prussia in the federation. Nor was the *Reich* Chancellor any longer the appointee of the President, but the creature of the popularly elected *Reichstag,* a body which took over the sovereign position hitherto occupied by the *Bundesrat,* the assembly of the states.[5] Prussia, then, though still a mighty state in the federation, found the former unity between her government and that of the *Reich,* in policy and administration,

[4] G. Anschütz, *Die Verfassung* (Berlin, 1931), p. 205.
[5] Cf. Chapters 23-26 on the executive.

sharply disrupted. This was a grave matter, for one political majority governed the *Reich* and a different one Prussia, in accordance with the changing fortunes at frequent elections, and in between them, the changing composition of the short-lived cabinets.

Since the Chancellorship and the Presidency were elective, it later became possible for Hitler, an Austrian, to attain those positions, for it was not stipulated that the candidate must be German born.

Legislative Powers. The special rights of some states (for example, postal affairs in Bavaria) were abolished. Such special rights had been necessary to secure their adhesion to the *Reich*, a situation unknown to federalism in the United States and elsewhere. All states were now equal in legislative power: Lippe with fifty thousand population or Prussia with forty million. The jurisprudence of the old constitution held that the *Reich* possessed only the powers expressly and indubitably transferred to it, while all else belonged to the states. The same rule was continued. Where the verbal grant of power reasonably entailed other consequential powers, the authority of the Reich was by so much increased, rather like the broad construction of the powers of the United States Congress and President, although the *Reich* constitution contained no "necessary and proper" clause.

The direct competence of the *Reich* was immensely extended, until the independent legislative activity of the states was almost entirely at its mercy—legally. *First*, both the *Reich* and the states were subject to the fundamental rights of the second part of the constitution, and many of these were fulfilled by federal law: for example, administrative jurisdiction, the law of property, and so on. *Secondly*, the *Reich* received powers of two kinds, exclusive and concurrent (so different from the distribution of powers in other federations, where a clean cut between exclusive federal or state is established)—and both make lists of formidable scope.[6] The lists

were so intricate that, especially through the concurrent powers, there was less clarity of distinction between federal and state functions than in any other constitution. The concurrent powers were exercisable by the *Reich* at its discretion: until then, state law was valid; but when the *Reich* legislated, state law on the subject was subordinate and had to be consonant. The exclusive and the concurrent together gave the *Reich* full authority over the whole economic life of the nation, to an extent far beyond the permissions and stultifications of the United States and other federal constitutions.[7]

The concurrent power to legislate fell into two classes: free and conditional. In

domicile, immigration, emigration, and extradition; military organization; the monetary system; the customs department, as well as uniformity in the sphere of customs and trade, and freedom of commercial intercourse; the postal and telegraph services, including the telephone service."

By article 7: "The federal government has legislative power as regards: civic rights; penal power, judicial procedure, including the carrying out of sentences, as well as official co-operation between authorities; the passport office and the police supervision of foreigners; the poor-law system and the provision for travelers; the press, trades-unions and the right of assembly; the population question, and the care of motherhood, infants, children, and young persons; the health and veterinary departments, and the protection of plants against disease and damage from pests; labor laws, the insurance and protection of the workers and employees, together with labor bureaus; the organization of competent representation for the federal territory; the care of all who took part in the war, and of their dependents; the law of expropriation; the formation of associations for dealing with natural resources and economic undertakings, as well as the production, preparation, distribution and determination of prices of economic commodities for common use: commerce, the system of weights and measures, the issue of paper money, banking affairs and the system of exchange; traffic in foodstuffs and luxuries, as well as articles of daily necessity; industry and mining; insurance matters; navigation, deep sea and coastal fishery; railroads, inland waterways, motor traffic by land, water and air, as well as the construction of highways, so far as this is concerned with general traffic and home defense; theaters and cinemas."

[6] By article 6: "The federal government has sole legislative power as regards: foreign relations; colonial affairs, nationality, right of

[7] Cf. A. W. MacMahon, "Taking Stock of Federalism in the U.S.A.," *Canadian Journal of Economics and Political Science*, May, 1941.

the first class were the powers enumerated in article 7, in which the *Reich* was free to legislate as it wished, and as it could, given the political conditions. In the conditional set of powers, in articles 9 and 10, the *Reich* was limited: in article 9 by the terms, "where there is need for the issue of uniform regulations the *Reich* has legislative power as regards the promotion of social welfare and the maintenance of public order and safety," and more particularly in article 10, where the *Reich* was given the power (unknown in other federations) to establish by law "general rules" (*Grundsätze*) on a certain number of subjects.[8]

Now, whether the *Reich* used its powers properly or not, as permitted by article 9, was not reviewable in any court of law.[9] These powers were very far-reaching indeed, and they were put into the constitution as the nearest possible compensation for not allowing the expansion of federal competence except by constitutional amendment. Soon, German financial difficulties—arising out of the need to pay World War I reparations out of the economic depression commencing in 1929—compelled the heavy use of all central legislative power to impose economy, to raise revenue, to regulate the conduct of state and municipal governments, and to unify the close control of industry, commerce, and agriculture.

The constitution further provided the *Reich* with a special veto over state "laws regarding the socialization (*Vergesellschaftung*) of natural resources and economic undertakings and the production, preparation, distribution, and price fixing of economic commodities for the commu-

nity's use" so long as the welfare of the community was affected.[10]

The hand of the *Reich* was everywhere, and this in the more fundamental of state activities. Economically, culturally, in her representative and administrative institutions, in the foundations of the educational system, in the matter of general civic rights, Germany was one, or far on the way to becoming one; and the battle provoked by the division of powers was, in theory, between the conception of the *Reich* as a federation and the *Reich* as a unitary state with decentralization to regions.

Doubts or disputes whether a regulation under state law was compatible with *Reich* law were decided by the Supreme Court of State at the suit of the competent *Reich* or state central department. This was very different from the situation under the imperial constitution, since no court was then entrusted with a direct decision on the compatibility of state with federal legislation; the ordinary courts determined this indirectly as an incident of a challenge to the validity of a rule. Under the Weimar Republic there was a direct challenge and a special court.

Nevertheless, the high degree of centralization of legislative power was, even by pro-monarchical, anti-socialistic, Catholic, and anti-Prussian Bavaria, generally acknowledged as nationally valuable. But what was desired was less administrative confusion, and the dissolution of Prussia. The existence of a different political party alignment in the whole *Reich* from that in Prussia caused frequent inconsistencies between the laws made for the seventy million of Germany and those made for the forty million of Prussia.

Whereas, before 1919, Prussia was more conservative than the *Reich* and Bavaria (because the three-class system of voting and the out-of-date apportionment of seats threw political power to East Prussia), afterwards, with modernized repre-

---

[8] Article 10 includes: the rights and duties of religious societies; public instruction, including universities, and the department of scientific literature; the rights of the officials of all public corporations; the land laws, the distribution of land, questions regarding colonization settlements, the tenure of landed property, the housing question and the distribution of the population; questions regarding burial.

[9] Cf. Anschütz, *op. cit.*, on article 9; H. Triepel, *Streitigkeiten zwischen Reich und Landern* (Berlin, 1923), p. 100; G. Lassar, *Handbuch des deutschen Staatsrechts* (1930), Vol. I, p. 307.

[10] K. C. Wheare, in *Federal Government* (New York, 1946) disqualifies the Weimar Republic as a federation because of the immense power wielded by the *Reich* over the states. He adduces as excessively strong the highly centralized financial powers.

sentation, she was distinctly more "liberal" and a striking contrast to Bavaria. The operation of parliamentary government in the medium and smallest states was very costly and brought popular government into ridicule through party tactics and instability of the executives. This was not only a legislative fault, but a serious administrative demerit for the state itself, and, as shown later, for the whole *Reich.*

Administrative Competence. Nothing like the clarity of the American and the British Dominion systems prevailed in the division of administrative authority. Whereas these use the "vertical" method—that is, they authorize the federal government itself to administer what it legislates—Germany used the "horizontal" method—that is, in general it permitted the states to administer *Reich* laws as well as their own. This method was a relic of state sovereignty, and had been a necessary condition of the *Reich* of 1871.

The articles which governed the power of the *Reich* to carry out its own laws were principally articles 14, 15, 16, and 77; and they attempted to combine federal strength with considerable flexibility, necessitated by the force of separatist sentiment and consecrated by the law and habits of the constitution of the German Empire. Let us consider the first three articles: They say that federal statutes shall be carried into execution by the state authorities, unless these same statutes decree otherwise, but that the federal government superintends the affairs which derive from its legislative power. It should be noted that under the imperial constitution, the power of superintendence where no law had been passed was disputed; but jurists held that the history of the Weimar article proved clearly that the *Reich* might superintend anything within its competence whether it had legislated or not.[11] Everything, of course, turned upon the machinery of superintendence ascribed to the *Reich.* This is roughly indicated in article 15.[12]

Quite a different system had replaced the previous methods of Kaiser and *Bundesrat.* Instead of disputes, as then, being arbitrated before the state-ridden *Bundesrat,* where the *Reich* accused a state of administrative default, administrative control was now to be exercised by the *Reich* cabinet operating through the departments and then inspectors, and disputes were settled not by a body like the *Bundesrat,* founded to maintain state independence, but by a law court appointable mainly by the central authority. How far this method of superintendence would be more effective than the old depended upon two things: the personal nature of the court to settle disputes and the extent to which the *Reich* had the power of direct contact with the inferior departments. The court granted the *Reich* the power to issue general instructions to state officials administering federal laws; sanctioned the dispatch of commissioners to state central departments and with the consent of state officials, to subdivisions of the state; and laid it down that whenever the central government desired changes in state administrative procedure concerning *Reich* legislation, the states must accede to its wishes. In the case of conflicting judgments, either *Reich* or state could refer to the Supreme Court for a decision.

Practice developed in three directions: the inclusion of detailed rules in various *Reich* statutes, the appointment of commissioners, and the establishment of authorities regularly to cooperate with and superintend the state departments. The financial laws, the civil service laws, the laws on unemployment exchanges, and others, laid down general rules within which the state governments must act, or fixed upon some special authority (like the *Reichsrat* or a special arbitration court) for the settlement of certain quasi-legislative matters like municipal loans or civil servants' salaries, or they associated the *Reich* departments directly with the state departments in the administration of certain subjects (e.g., in the case of social welfare) or required regular information from the states. The appointment of commissioners to inspect state admin-

---

[11] Cf. H. Triepel, *op cit.,* p. 58; Anschütz, *op. cit.,* p. 74.
[12] Article 15 of the constitution.

istration was rare and occurred only on exceptional occasions when civil disturbances occurred in a state, or when, as in Saxony in 1924, complaints were made about the administration of unemployment relief—but even this was due rather to a dispute on the interpretation of the statute than to incompetent execution. The *Reich* directly superintended many things (e.g., electricity, railways, canals), and, in the case of the regulation of the labor market and unemployment insurance and factory legislation, the entire administration went over to the *Reich*.

The administrative power of the *Reich*, in short, seems to have been exercised, either in the way, well known under the imperial constitution, of applications to the state government, or of the judicial settlement of disputes by certain courts, or the entire assumption of administrative power by the *Reich*. The judicial settlement of disputes (article 13, par. 2) operated through a special branch of the *Reichsgericht*,[13] and through the *Reichsfinanzhof* in twenty-three cases by 1931.

The power to assume detailed administrative responsibility was given to the *Reichstag* by article 77:

The general administrative rules needed to execute the *Reich* statutes were made by the *Reich* Government, unless the law otherwise determined. The *Reich* Government needed the assent of the *Reichsrat*, if the execution of *Reich* statutes belonged to the State authorities.

This power of the *Reich* was used for the creation or extension of *Reich* departments with their own local organization, as in social welfare, the coal commission, disarmament, the potato, wheat, and sugar departments, the labor exchange department, the juvenile welfare bureau, and the emigration department. Various of the activities of the Ministry for Economic Affairs and Ministry of Labor ramified through the federation in the same way. The administrative rules poured fast and furious from these departments.

All this was, of course, encouraged by the obvious necessities of each particular subject of administration for which large-scale organization and uniformity were essential. It was required by national financial stringency, and was enforced by the financial supremacy of the central government and its control over certain funds like those for the promotion of education.[14] The depression and its attendant problem of unemployment resulted in much closer ties between the state and the municipal governments and the *Reich*, particularly with regard to municipal finance. Partially because of the lack of constitutional ground on which to base this local control (which fell within state jurisdiction), Chancellor Brüning was forced to utilize article 48 (cf. Chap. 25 below), whereby under emergency conditions, civil rights could be suspended and government decrees enforced. The decrees, in this case, provided for control over local real estate taxes and municipal and state expenditures.

This, however, does not completely describe the extent to which the administrative power of the center increased. A number of subjects came directly and completely under the *Reich*. These were foreign affairs, railroads and posts, telegraphs, customs, cartel control, supervision of private insurance, and control of the potash and coal industries. Thus the distribution of administrative powers was very complicated, the location of administrative responsibility being in most cases (excepting for foreign affairs) not determinable without close inspection of the various *Reich* laws relating to the subject and the combination of powers given to the *Reich* by the constitution. This complexity was increased by two further principles: (1) that which permitted the states, by statute, to transfer to the *Reich* administrative competence over powers within their own field, and (2) article 16, which required that "officials entrusted with the direct

13 Cf. *Reichsgesetzblatt, 1920*, p. 510, *Gesetz zur Ausfuhrung des art. 13, abs, der Verfassung* (April 8, 1920).

14 Cf. Hans Nawiasky, *Grundprobleme der Reichsverfassung* (Berlin, 1925); G. Lassar, *Reichseigene Verwaltung unter der Weimarer Verfassung, Jahrbuch des Öffentlichen Rechts*, Vol. XIV (1926).

Reich administration in the states shall be as a rule citizens of these states." [15] The matter was even further complicated by the statutory devolution of administrative powers to the *Reichsrat,* which is discussed presently.

German judgment of this administrative system was almost universally adverse. *First,* for the public generally, its complexity baffled the understanding and thwarted the allocation of responsibility. *Second*—more technically—though the vast centralization of legislative power (especially over the economy) saved the nation from the wastes and frustrations of the division of power prevailing between Washington and the forty-eight states in the United States, Germany still suffered from the administrative incompetence of the smaller states, while the many boundaries caused much geographic and bureaucratic stultification of rational administration of economic affairs. The states could have cooperated by agreements, but with small exceptions, they did not. The enormous differences in area, the tortuous lines, the enclaves, resulted in the reverse of equal, manageable, economic regions.

Third, the *Reich* supplied the states with the cost of administration, in part directly, in part through a share in the income taxes levied by the *Reich.* This arrangement divorced responsibility for economical and efficient management from the disciplinary burden of raising funds. *Fourth,* the assumption of large administrative powers by the *Reich,* according to its constitutional rights—including even some concern for police, education, and the details of social assistance—alienated all the state administrative personnel as well as political personnel, above all in Prussia and Bavaria. But ill-feeling was not the only administrative sickness. Two authorities operated in each state. Especially obnoxious was this in Prussia: it involved an almost complete duplication of investigation and research, as well as actual operation in each. A *Reich* civil service paralleled a Prussian

civil service. Private interests, the public services, and local government units, interested in obstruction, found their abundant opportunity in the proliferation of authorities, which made easy the hiding of information and responsibility. There was no single career throughout the *Reich* for officials—transfer from state to state and to *Reich* was practically impossible owing to specialization in the particular laws and customs and administrative labyrinths.

Finally, the strength of particularist traditional feeling was revived and even more intensified by more modern political conflicts. Bavaria, which had gone antisocialist and antiliberal, was not prepared to submit to police action by the *Reich* when she was the incubator of antidemocratic forces, like Hitler's, preparing to overturn the Weimar constitution. She succeeded in securing an agreement that she would not be policed by the *Reich.* But Saxony, democratic, was disciplined by a momentarily hostile *Reich* Government; and Prussia, too, was in the end overborne by a dictatorial *Reich.*

It was clear that some day a cleaner, neater, simpler, better-ventilated administrative adjustment between *Reich* and states must be sought. This theme is resumed at the end of the chapter.

The Administration of Justice. In the distribution of judicial powers, the Weimar constitution (section VII, and articles 102 to 108) made little advance upon the imperial constitution. A weak attempt to take over completely the judicial powers of the ordinary courts was heavily defeated by the representatives of all states; and article 103, that "the ordinary administration of justice is exercised by the *Reich* Supreme Court and the courts of the states," was intended to continue the old system—i.e., the law courts were state courts, although their procedure was settled by *Reich* statutes and *Reich* law was so large a part of their subject-matter.

Two novelties appeared. *First,* the establishment by the constitution (article 107) of the administrative courts:

In the *Reich* the states administrative courts must be established, as regulated by law, for

---

[15] Cf. Lassar, *op. cit.*

the protection of the citizen against regulations and decrees of the administrative authorities.

The significance of this article is explained in Chapter 36.

The *second* was article 108: "A Court of State (*Staatsgerichthof*) shall be established by a *Reich* statute." This was a tribunal for the trial of constitutional issues of the first rank, these being:

(1) Impeachment by the *Reichstag* of the *Reich* President, the Imperial Chancellor, and *Reich* ministers for criminal violation of the constitution or statutes of the *Reich*. This follows from article 50 of the constitution, according to which the resolution for impeachment must be moved by at least a hundred members, and needs the assent of a majority as for a constitutional amendment, that is, a two-thirds majority in a quorum of two thirds of the members of the *Reichstag*: also similar impeachments in the states if they declare the court competent by statute.

(2) Differences of opinion regarding maladministration of *Reich* statutes by the states, suit being made by either *Reich* or state government, provided no other court is designated for the purpose by the statute. (This from article 15 of the constitution.)

(3) Disputes regarding property in cases arising out of territorial reorganization of the states (article 18, clause 7).

(4) Constitutional conflicts within a state in which no court exists for their settlement; [16] also conflicts of a nonprivate nature between states or between the *Reich* and a state (article 19).

(5) The rights of the *Reich* in disputes about its powers of expropriation and its authority regarding the railroad system; the conditions of transfer of the post and telegraph system, the state railways, canals and *seeziechen*, from the states which possessed them hitherto (articles 90, 170, and 171); and differences of opinion arising

out of the treaties relating to the transfer of these and similar institutions.

The constitutional article, 108, was followed by the law relating to the Court of State of July, 1921, which embodied the list of powers we have already indicated, and dealt with the composition of the Court for various classes of cases.

According as the Court applied itself to one or the other of its subjects, it included matters which were predominantly of parliamentary importance, and others the nature of which suggests their classification within a court of administrative law. Hence it was planned that this constitutional tribunal be part of the regular Supreme Court for such a purpose as impeachment; however, the connection remained theoretical, since impeachment proceedings were never initiated. In composition the constitutional tribunal could not but reflect the attitude of the Supreme Court, since the president of the latter served ex-officio as its chairman and since three of its associate justices were appointed from the Supreme Court. (The remaining three came from the supreme administrative courts of Prussia, Bavaria, and Saxony.)

The power of the Court to settle disputes between federation and states was an interesting and important innovation. Under the imperial constitution, the states were sometimes informally judged by the *Reich* without appeal to a properly constituted court of justice, or the *Reich* was successfully defied, since appeal to the *Bundesrat* was an appeal to a political body the members of which had a personal interest in the result. The character of the new federation made such a method impossible. A central authority to guard the spirit of the constitution was imposed by the facts of the situation.

In this court, the constitution added to its statesmen in parliament and the cabinet one more group entrusted with high decisions which, though couched in judicial form, were indubitably superlegislative. This function was not exercisable by the roundabout method of judicial review as in the Supreme Court of the

---

16 These were not disputes arising merely out of any violation of the constitution but only conflicts between Parliament and government. Cf. Lammers, *Gesetz über den Staatsgerichtshof*, p. 73, note 7.

United States, but by the direct claim of state upon *Reich* or *Reich* upon state.

One case of outstanding importance was settled by the Court. In October, 1932, it declared unconstitutional the action of Federal Chancellor Franz von Papen, in dismissing the Prussian government, and replacing its cabinet by himself and other federal commissioners. The *coup* had been undertaken in virtue of article 48 (see Chap. 25 below), ostensibly to restore order and safety in Prussia, which had for some time been in a state of uproar through Nazi and anti-Nazi rioting. Substantially the same issue arose when Hitler, on February 6, 1933, repeated von Papen's tactics. But this time the Court could not hear the Prussian challenge before Hitler's revolution swept away all constitutionality and scattered or killed the challengers.[17]

(In the Soviet constitution of 1936, which purports to be federal, no court guards the distribution of powers. Instead, the Praesidium, a body of thirty-seven members elected by the Supreme Council of the U.S.S.R., watches over the consonance of "state" administration with the superior authority of the Union. But *if* the constitution is federal, the Communist party is unitary, and that is quite enough to prevent disputes from occurring.)

Representation of the States. Here, more sharply than ever, the Weimar constitution diverged from the American and other federal systems, in its differential representation of the states. The tendencies towards unitarism were strong, but not strong enough entirely to overcome the demands for a body especially to represent the states and to obtain for them a power to influence the creation of federal policy. The reporter of the draft sent by the constitutional committee (in which mighty battles had been fought) to the full assembly said: [18]

The Committee has accepted the constitution of the *Reichsrat* to maintain the organic connection of the *Reich* with the individual states, and thus it has expressed the sense of historical evolution and the living necessities of the Federation. This *Reichsrat* is, however, not intended to be either a first or a second chamber, or a parliament or a house of states,[19] but a body to represent the German states in the legislation and administration of the *Reich*. The *Reichsrat*—recognized by all parties of the National Assembly as a necessary and useful organ—is at once an institution of the *Reich* as well as an organ of the totality of states with a constitutionally complete double status.

Before we turn to consider the composition and power of this body, a few words may be said in general about its political position in comparison with the *Bundesrat* under the imperial constitution.

(1) Though strong, it was distinctly inferior to the *Reichstag*—which emanated from popular election over the whole territory of the *Reich*—in political authority and constitutional power. The centers of importance lay in the government and the *Reichstag*, whose confidence was necessary to the former's existence. Under the imperial system the *Bundesrat* was predominant, even sovereign. Its legal and political status was far weaker than that of the powerful United States Senate, but politically it was much stronger than the weak Canadian and Australian Senates.

(2) The *Reichsrat* was no longer the center of the activity of an imperial chancellor working without substantial responsibility to anyone but the emperor, but it was dominated by the government, which, again, was a creature of the *Reichstag*.

(3) It had not the wide power to issue administrative rules and to arbitrate in disputes between the *Reich* and the states.

(4) It was not the representative of monarchs and princes but of governments (in the states) popularly supported and controlled.

Very clearly it mirrored the pronounced rise of unitarism; and its character was perhaps best expressed by the dictum that it was a body representing the states attached to the Federation for federal purposes and not at all an organization of the states for state purposes.[20]

---

[17] Cf. Arnold Brecht, *Prelude to Silence* (New York, 1944) p. 62 ff.
[18] Conrad Haussmann, Second Reading, Constitutional Assembly at Weimar, July 2, 1919.

[19] I. e., no doubt, equal in power and operating with a single view to benefit the states.
[20] Quarck, *Heilfron, op. cit.*, p. 1344.

Composition. Article 61 of the Weimar constitution said:

In the *Reichsrat* every state has at least one vote. The larger states have one vote for each 700,000 inhabitants. A surplus of at least 350,-000 inhabitants is taken as equivalent to 700,-000. No country may be represented by more than two fifths of all the votes. . . . The distribution of votes is regulated by the *Reichsrat* after every general census.

Until March, 1921, this article read:

The larger states . . . have one vote per million inhabitants. A surplus which at least equals the population of the smallest state is taken as equivalent to a full million.

against the federation and the varied dignity of each state, the new order made population a developing factor, the basis of present and future representation. The full significance of this is comprehensible only in the light of the fact that large territorial reforms were envisaged, and that a movement for such reforms was expected to take progressive effect. The representation and the population in 1933, given in Table I, also serve to show how petty were some of the states—which had all of the form and panoply of full-blown republican states. Prussia, which before 1919 had had three fifths, afterwards had only two fifths, of the total representation.

TABLE I—WEIMAR GERMANY: REPRESENTATION OF THE STATES IN THE REICHSRAT, AND POPULATION

State	Total Population	Number of Votes
Prussia	39,746,901	26
Bavaria	7,774,777	11
Saxony	5,196,652	7
Württemberg	2,696,324	4
Baden	2,412,951	3
Thuringen	1,659,510	2
Hessen	1,429,048	2
Hamburg	1,218,447	2
Mecklenburg-Schwerin	691,000	1
Oldenburg	573,853	1
Brunswick	512,989	1
Bremen	371,558	1
Anhalt	364,415	1
Lippe	175,538	1
Lübeck	136,392	1
Mecklenburg-Strelitz	114,000	1
Schaumburg-Lippe	49,955	1
Total	65,124,310	66

The amendment [21] was made in order to increase Prussia's votes so that the division of one half of them among her provinces would give them exactly one vote each. This we shall explain presently.

Preusz's attempt to group the smallest states and give them combined representation was foiled. The disputants slowly worked back to the graduation of the old system, except that instead of being a permanent arrangement, which stereotyped the results of the movement for and

The states were represented in the *Reichsrat* through members of their governments (whereas in the United States, Senators are elected at large) and could send as many representatives as they had votes.[22] Now, this closely followed the practice of the old *Bundesrat*, the delegates to which were chosen by the government of the states, though at that time the government consisted of forces not popularly controlled. Instead of popular election, which would have tended to weaken

[21] *Reichsgesetzblatt*, 440, March 24, 1921.

[22] Article 63.

the unity of state representation, the essential element in the previous situation was reproduced: the members of the *Reichsrat* were neither elected at large, like United States or Australian Senators, nor chosen by the members of the state legislatures, as in the United States before 1913, but, as before, they were directly appointed by the state governments. Although the article said that the states were represented by members of their governments, this meant only that ministers could be chosen, but it did not exclude representation by officials of the states, and, in fact, in most states the pressure of governmental affairs normally compelled the governments to designate high officials as state representatives.[23] But members of the governments spoke in the *Reichsrat* in support of their state's attitude on the more important occasions. There was still the flavor of ambassadorship about *Reichsrat* representation—the term *Hauptbevollmächtigter,* used to distinguish the "full plenipotentiary" from his deputies, and the title conferred upon these by many states, of "ambassador extraordinary" *(ausserordentlichen Gesandter),* supported the illusion.

Prussia. As a rule, then, all states cast their votes uniformly, although the constitution was silent on the subject. This arrangement, which conformed to the old practice, was, however, legally impossible for Prussia, for the constitution had attempted to serve the true cause of federation by disrupting the unity of this state. "However," said the constitution (article 63), "one half of the Prussian votes are accorded to the Prussian provincial administrations according to Prussian statute." The statute in question was passed in 1921.[24] Its main provisions were (1) that the thirteen representatives would each be elected by a provincial committee (the ordinary executive committee of the largest Prussian local government division), and (2) that all German citizens over twenty-five were eligible. Thus there was no obvious control of the Prussian government over the choice of these representatives. Yet the law was not unmindful of the need to reknit what the constitution had severed. For the law said (article 8) that in the committees of the *Reichsrat* (and the committee work was exceedingly important), the vote of Prussia would be cast by a representative appointed by the ministry, although any of the elected members could require a preliminary discussion of the matter with the ministry. Further, in the plenary sessions the elected members had a free vote: "Yet the items on the agenda shall be discussed in common by the appointed and the elected members for the purpose of producing a uniform vote." This was a clever device, and was certainly not in the spirit of the constitution; Prussia sought for every vestige of its lost inheritance. Yet Prussia was never certain that the thirteen provincial representatives would follow the wishes of the central authority; and, in fact, between March, 1922 and December, 1923, there were twenty-three important occasions when dissensions occurred,[25] and later similar events occurred in crucial matters, as for example, on the *Reich* School Law in 1927. At the end of the Weimar Republic, such divisions were particularly frequent, because of the vehemence of opposing parties in the western and the conservative eastern provinces of Prussia, and a German political cleavage at least as important as that between Northern and Southern Germany. This caused serious disquietude, for if thirteen votes were cast against fourteen, Prussia's influence upon the law in the *Reichsrat* was neutralized. This rarely happened, since some provincial representatives of the same party as the government voted with it; yet influence was

23 Cf. Anschütz, *op. cit.,* p. 203; Hugo Preusz, *Bericht und Protokoll* (Constitutional Assembly, 1919), p. 152; R. R. Held, *Der Reichsrat,* p. 23.
24 June 3, 1921. *Gesetzessammlung,* p. 379. Cf. *Preuszen und seine Provinzen in Reichsrat,* by Fritz Hummel (Berlin, 1928), which is a very capable and painstaking study of the law and partly of the practice.

25 Cf. H. Triepel, *Der Föderalismus und die Revision der Weimarer Reichsverfassung,* *Zeitschrift für Politik* (1924-25), XIV, 193 ff.

lost.[26] Prussia was, indeed, strait-jacketed, and only a constitutional amendment could release her. However, what Prussia could not achieve within the constitution she was in a fair way to obtain by direct influence upon the *Reich* government— for, after all, she was two thirds of the federation!—and by informal conferences with the states outside the *Reichsrat,* where the art of political reciprocity was carried to high, because necessary, levels. Prussia was still far more important than any other state.

The Government Presides. Prussia not only lost power by the arrangements we have sketched but she fell from authority because she no longer presided as of right over the *Reichsrat.* The power which she lost, however, redounded to no other of the states: the *Reichsrat,* was legally subordinated to the *Reichstag* and the *Reich* government, by the vesting of the presidency in the federal government, thus:

The *Reichsrat* and its committees are presided over by a member of the federal government. The members of the latter are entitled, and, if requested, are obliged, to take part in the proceedings of the *Reichsrat* and its committees. They must be heard upon their demand any time during debate.

Thus a regular and continuous reciprocal influence was made possible; the significance of this becomes the more apparent when we consider the power of the *Reichsrat.* The government had no voting power, but its representatives had con-

[26] Hans Nawiasky, *op. cit.,* p. 40 ff. Cf. also Hummel (*op. cit.,* pp. 84-85) who shows that the same provinces voted in contradiction to the government votes to safeguard their own local economic interests (tariff law, distribution of product of beer duty, wheat-production regulation, and rent law) as well as on spiritual issues.

K. H. Schoppmeier, in *Der Einflusz Preuszens auf die Gesetzgebung des Reiches* (Berlin, 1929), reports the following: Between June, 1921, and September, 1924, there were 2394 cases of division in the *Reichsrat.* Of these, there were 49 occasions when some Prussian provinces voted against their government. In 11 cases of the 2394, the Prussian government was in a minority. Of the 11 occasions, 4 would have occurred even with a united Prussian vote. In 7 cases, then, the division of the Prussian vote caused a defeat of that state.

siderable authority in the conduct of proceedings. The government, as well as any member of the *Reichsrat,* could introduce proposals.

The Rights of the Reichsrat. (1) The *Reichsrat* had the power (article 66) to establish its own rules of procedure, and this it did in November, 1919.

(2) The *Reichsrat* had to be kept informed, by the *Reich* departments, of the conduct of *Reich* affairs. The competent committees of the *Reichsrat* had to be called into counsel regarding important matters by the departments.

(3) In marked contrast to the United States Senate, the *Reichsrat's* consent was required to administrative rules made by the government when the execution of *Reich* statutes was carried out by the state authorities. The *Reichsrat* was given certain administrative powers by various laws passed since 1919.

(4) The *Reichsrat* had the right to initiate legislation and to challenge the bills passed by the *Reichstag,* and was required to be consulted before government bills were introduced in the *Reichstag.*

A few words must be said on points 3 and 4. The *Reichsrat's* consent to administrative rules was restricted to the cases where the states carried out federal statutes, and since this, according to article 14, was the rule, a wide scope of actual power was vested in the *Reichsrat.* It compared, in fact, not unfavorably with the *Bundesrat's,* because the field of federal power was so increased. In this matter the power of the *Reichsrat* was absolute, because it was not a mere power to challenge as in the case of legislation. The only remedy the government possessed was to convert the rejected order into a law; but that had its own political difficulties. The power was extensively used. The constitution amplified the general rule by the enumeration of certain special spheres of administration in which the *Reichsrat's* cooperation was required in details: so (according to article 88) regarding postal, telegraphic, and telephonic communication and the charges therefore; so too in railroad and canal transport (articles 93 and 98).

The *Reichsrat* was found a convenient body in which to vest certain other administrative duties; it was made a decision-giving body in a large number of disputes regarding land registration between a state and the *Reich* Minister of Finance, regarding resolutions of the Brandy Monopoly Council and its advisory committee, regarding the likelihood of municipal taxation prejudicing the income and prospects of the *Reich,* and so on. The *Reichsrat* sent representatives to the advisory committee of the brandy monopoly, to the advisory council for the *Reich* Electricity Administration, to the Committee for the *Reich* Debt and to the *Reich* Insurance Office. It elected and nominated members of the *Reich* Health Council, the Court of State, and many other advisory and quasi-administrative, quasi-judicial councils.[27]

All these powers tended to increase the authority of the *Reichsrat* much above the level to which it fell by the discredit of the *Bundesrat* and all that it stood for. Yet these powers would not be enough to satisfy the demands of the states for special representation unless they were merely the frills of something far more important—which served to give them a strength they did not inherently possess—namely, legislative power, which was given by articles 68 and 72. The most important clause—that which settled the respective authority of *Reichstag* and *Reichsrat* and served the certain and permanent supremacy of the former—was: "Federal statutes are passed by the *Reichstag*." This is in strongest contrast to the former constitution in which the *Bundesrat* had the decisive authority; it is in strong contrast to almost every other bicameral system, whether in a federal or unitary state. By law the *Reichsrat* was definitely excluded from coequality with the *Reichstag,* and the unitary, not the federal organ, exercised legislative sovereignty. The only position left to the *Reichsrat* was then, a subsidiary one: to challenge, to provoke an appeal to the people, to warn and advise. Did the facts change the law?

"The Introduction of Government bills requires the assent of the *Reichsrat*. If an agreement between *Reich* Government and *Reichsrat* cannot be reached, then the government can, nevertheless, introduce its bill, but must represent the objections of the *Reichsrat*." This provision included financial legislation, although this interpretation was challenged by the government in February, 1927. Now this clause (article 69, par. 1) left loopholes through which a government could reduce the power of the *Reichsrat* to a minimum: (1) no time was prescribed in the constitution during which the bill was to lie before the *Reichsrat,* and it could therefore be reduced to an impossible minimum; further, (2) the government could avoid the attentions of the *Reichsrat* altogether by getting a bill initiated by a private member of one of the coalition parties; and (3) its representation of the *Reichsrat's* views could be perfunctory. In fact, the government gave the *Reichsrat* ample time and negotiated until it obtained the assent of the *Reichsrat*—for it was persuaded, almost forced, to this course by the fact that the states would be the executants of many of its policies, by the desire to secure an amicable evolution of the Federation, and by the coincidence of the party membership of some members of the *Reichsrat* with its own *Reichstag* supporters.

A survey of all the bills before the *Reichsrat* from 1920 to 1933 shows a very great activity as a result of which the government gave way in a good many cases, while in other cases it and the *Reichstag* overruled all objections. Space allows us no more than to say briefly that the disputes occurred regarding the substance of the laws, but even more upon the *Reich*-state division of powers. There is no doubt that this power of the *Reichsrat* was compelling and was in regular use, and also that it gave the states *as* states the opportunity to resist encroachments upon their freedom, and the establishment of new *Reich* services which they believed they could furnish at a cheaper cost themselves.

The *Reichsrat* had a right of initiative: "If the *Reichsrat* resolves a bill to which

---

[27] Fr. Poetzsch-Heffter, *Jahrbuch des Öffentlichen Rechts* (1925), p. 202.

the government does not consent, then the government must introduce the bill into the *Reichstag* and represent the opinion of the *Reichsrat*." This power did not extend to financial legislation; and though it provided the *Reichsrat* with the opportunity of airing its opinions and securing their representation in the *Reichstag*, that representation was not given to its own delegate, as in the case of the Federal Economic Council, but was left to the tender mercies of the government. It made very small use of the initiative, and of five cases (until the end of 1928) where the government disagreed, only two became law, one of which was amended by the government. This was not one of the strengths of the *Reichsrat*.

"The publication of a statute may be suspended for two months, if one third of the *Reichstag* demands it." [28] This was one of the preliminaries to a referendum for the protection of the minority. But "when statutes are declared urgent by the *Reichstag* and the *Reichsrat*," the *Reich* president might override the resolution for suspension and publish the statute. The reason for the inclusion of the *Reichsrat* here is obvious: so solemn an action as the suppression of a minority right must be undertaken with due deliberation, and a multitude of counsel. Article 72 was used in 1925, when the Devaluation Act was passed, a statute which engendered the bitterest controversy as it settled the value of contracts and property calculated in depreciated currency. Both houses agreed upon the urgency of the act.

We come to the final and strongest power of the *Reichsrat* (article 74):

The *Reichsrat* has the right to challenge a bill passed by the *Reichstag*. The challenge must be made within two weeks of the final division in the *Reichstag* to the Government, and must be supported by reasons within, at the latest, two further weeks. The law must be put before the *Reichstag* to be revoted. If, then, *Reichstag* and *Reichsrat* still cannot agree, the President of the *Reich* may within three months order a Referendum on the subjects of disagreement. If the President does not use this power, then the law counts as of no

effect. If the *Reichstag* by a two-thirds majority, votes against the challenge of the *Reichsrat*, then the President is obliged to order a referendum within three months on the bill as voted by the *Reichstag*.

Let us examine this piece by piece. (1) The *Reichsrat* amply used its power of challenge,[29] and in most cases the *Reichstag* conceded its claims. (2) If the *Reichstag* had not surrendered, its chances of victory against the *Reichsrat* would, politically, have depended upon a two-thirds resolution—to bring in the people to overcome the *Reichsrat*. But in a chamber composed of many groups, this was difficult to obtain: several governments, indeed, were in a minority: and moreover, the *Reichsrat* was not a nonpopular assembly against which the corporate fury of the *Reichstag* could be summoned. Nor is that all. No government is, except in the most abnormal case, anxious to invoke a poll of the people. This is bound to be managed by the parties, which would fall into government and opposition; and an unfavorable result would wreck the government. Nor may we forget that governments do not lightly undertake an electoral campaign, or, indeed, anything laborious, when in the midst of a legislative and administrative program with all its attendant parliamentary difficulties. All this redounded to the advantage of the *Reichsrat*. It could suspend the bill or force a referendum. (3) The President had power to decide whether a bill should be destroyed, that is, whether he should at once support the *Reichsrat* (which was an unlikely contingency) or refer to the people to settle the issue. Long before this decision had to be taken, we can be sure that the government would have arranged things, on the warning of the President, with the *Reichsrat*.

As regards the budget—ways and means and appropriations—the *Reichsrat* had

---

[28] Article 72.

[29] Cf. Fr. Poetzsch-Heffter, articles in *Jahrbuch*, 1925 and 1929: twelve times between April, 1920, and May, 1927. Schoppmeier (*op. cit.*, p. 29) reports that in eight cases the *Reichsrat* won, and in only four cases was the necessary two-thirds majority obtained in the *Reichstag* to overcome the *Reichsrat*.

the same powers as in ordinary bills, since the budget is an ordinary bill in the formal sense. Here, however, the *Reichsrat* could exercise a partial, but ultimate, veto, for article 85 of the constitution said that the *Reichstag* could not increase or create expenditure without the assent of the *Reichsrat*. Or it could act simply, as in nonfinancial legislation, according to article 74, and challenge the whole of the budget. If assent was refused to an appropriation, then the Finance Law was published by the President of the *Reich* without that appropriation. The refusal of the *Reichsrat* could be carried out as a challenge under article 74. Both these powers of the *Reichsrat* were used, but not in vital matters.

Thus, originating in unwilling concessions to state sentiment and in an atmosphere of suspicion, the *Reichsrat* was first endowed with paper powers, which looked small compared with those of the *Reichstag* and the government, but the evolution of actual forces made it a fairly strong body. Its personal composition of distinguished officials (often connected with the *Reich's* own body of servants), its permanent sessions in relation to swiftly changing governments, the practical impossibility of a two-thirds majority of the *Reichstag* against it, and the administrative powers of the states—all furnished it with unexpected power. It also gained credit as an organ for the conclusion of agreements between states. In no case did the *Reichstag* ever pass a constitutional amendment over the objections of the *Reichsrat*. But a number of ordinary statutes were passed over its objection—and no referendum was ever called to challenge the *Reichstag*. Yet there were voices which called for large changes. We shall indicate their argument presently.

Finance. The financial strengths and weaknesses of nations and states in a federal system are simultaneously the products and the instruments of the real division of authority. If the other institutions expressed the tendency to centralization in the German *Reich*, none was so potent as the financial relationship between the central authority and the states.

Here the impulse toward a completely unitary political system almost achieved its goal, and it borrowed extra importance from its fundamentality to all else. Under the imperial system, the *Reich* neither had nor needed large revenues, since its sphere of legislative and administrative power was severely limited, and, moreover, the states had contrived at once to make a large part of the *Reich's* revenues depend upon a system of state contributions, while they received contributions from the *Reich*. All that was altered: the Federation had a large and easily expansible competence, and the reparations problem and general impoverishment inescapably imposed financial unity. This was embodied in the constitution, which was made at a time when these considerations were most keenly felt, and in a number of laws established as necessity revealed itself fully.

The ruling articles of the constitution were 8 and 11. Following directly upon the grant of legislative powers, article 8 said:

Further, the *Reich* has legislative power over taxation and other revenues, in so far as they are claimed wholly or in part for its own purposes. If the *Reich* claims taxes or other revenues which hitherto belonged to the states, then it must take into consideration the maintenance of the significance of the states.

Article 11 said:

The *Reich* can by statute establish principles regarding the permissibility and mode of raising state taxes, in so far as this is necessary in order to prevent (a) damage to the income or the commercial relations of the *Reich*, (b) double taxation, (c) charges for the use of public communications and institutions which are excessive or impede traffic, (d) tax discrimination against imported goods compared with home produce, in commerce between the individual states and parts of states, or (e) export bounties, or (f) for the protection of important social interests.

On the basis of these very wide powers —for the *Reich* obtained both freedom in its own sphere by article 8, and a regulatory power over the sphere of the states by article 11—a large number of laws and orders comprised a financial system [30] in which the *Reich* had a first call upon all revenues, and the states and the local authorities had a strictly limited freedom within permitted loopholes, and even here they were bound to follow procedure laid down by the *Reich*. The *Reich* could and did settle out of hand any problems of double taxation, and so avoided the confusions of the American system. For it was financial master.

The main features of the system were to be found in the financial settlement laws (*Finanzausgleichgesetze*).[31] They were: (*a*) The states and the local authorities could raise taxes only in so far as they did not infringe upon the *Reich* constitution and laws. (*b*) Where the *Reich* claimed a source of revenue, the states and local authorities were thereby excluded unless a *Reich* statute gave permission. (*c*) Additions to *Reich* taxes were leviable by the states and the local authorities in the measure permitted by *Reich* statute. (*d*) State and local taxation schemes had to be submitted to the *Reich* Minister of Finance in order that their compatibility with *Reich* necessities and the constitution could be examined. (*e*) The *Reich* Financial Court (*Reichsfinanzhof*) decided differences of opinion: whether state tax provisions were in consonance with *Reich* statutes. (*f*) The question of fact, whether state and local taxation was appropriate, or damaged the *Reich's* revenues, or was incompatible with the national interests, was decided by the *Reichsrat*. (*g*) Certain revenues were assigned to the states and municipalities. (*h*) Certain taxes raised by the *Reich* were transferred altogether to the states

on principles of distribution settled by the law, and the law also stated the principles upon which the states should transfer a portion to the local authorities. The income tax and the turnover tax were legislated exclusively by the *Reich*, which then turned over a proportion to the states along with legal rules regulating the further sharing of the total between state and local authorities. It is obvious that this controlling power of the *Reich* seriously affected state and local activities—hence the *Reich* was inevitably drawn in as a judge and provider where it required certain functions to be executed by these authorities.

Nor was this all. The change in the purpose of power resulted in a change in the administrative arrangements to achieve it: the *Reich* had, instead of a small group of officials, a large body, ramifying throughout the country, having absorbed most of the state financial officials.[32] Financial stringency even caused the *Reich* officials to take over the collection of state income and other taxes. This was not accomplished without difficulties, since the state officials were by no means happy to transfer to a new master in Berlin, and even then the new taxes were so many and the tasks of building a fresh administrative system so heavy that the *Reich* was very much understaffed. So, throughout the country, were thousands of federal tax officials and customs officers, controlled by *Reich* departments in the states, controlled in turn by the *Reich* Ministry of Finance. The *Reichsfinanzhof* acted as the final arbiter of the law in financial matters and as a unified interpreter of the law for the whole *Reich*.

This financial centralization was, of course, much criticized, but unavoidable. Further, the fact that each state's share of the income tax was measured by the income tax due in each state, hurt the poorer states.

Form of the State Constitutions. In other democratic federations, a certain minimum of uniformity in the govern-

[30] Cf. Hensel, *Finanzausgleich im Bundesstaat* (Berlin, 1922); Koch, *Finanzausgleichsgesetz* (Berlin, 1926), and 1928 Supplement. See for a statistical account Jessen, *Finanzbedarf und Steuern im Reich, Landern und Gemeinden; Handbuch der Finanzwissenschaft,* Vol. III (1929), pp. 53-67.
[31] The situations prevailing under the Weimar and nazi systems are to be found set out in a highly graphic fashion in *Tax Systems of the World* (Chicago: Tax Research Foundation, editions of 1934 and 1935). See also Mabel Newcomer, *Central and Local Finance in Germany and England* (New York, 1937).

[32] Cf. G. Lassar, *Jahrbuch des Öffentliches Rechts,* Vol. 16, "Finanzverwaltung."

ment of the several states is prescribed by the federal constitution. In Germany, the abortive Frankfurt constitution of 1848, democratic and influenced by American and Swiss experience, followed this principle, but the constitution of 1871, building from above, with the desire to tap the sources of cohesion existent in the monarchical states, did not concern itself with their constitutions at all. This was far from the propensities of Preusz and the surge of revolutionary feeling.

Even the opposition of the state representatives to Preusz's severe rules could not overcome the very strong feeling that unless there were some unity in political fundamentals throughout the *Reich*, the structure would be unsound and weak. Preusz said: [33]

If the *Reich* builds itself, appropriately to the structure of a popular state, from below upwards, and if, therefore, it rests, with the whole of its inward vital processes, upon the organic foundations of its municipal and state members, then a certain normative influence of the general will of the *Reich* upon the organization of the individual states and their local authorities is indispensable. But it must be limited to the indispensable, only assuring homogeneity between the structure of the *Reich* and its state and municipal constituents.

(The student of international relations, and especially world government, should take special notice of this idea.)

Preusz's wishes were challenged not only by the politicians who were hostile to any interference with their own constitution, but also on the juristic ground that to prescribe the principles of a state's constitution was to destroy its statehood, its "sovereignty." "A state which cannot even determine its own form ceases utterly to be a state. For its sovereignty is denied." [34]

Article 17, as finally passed, ran:

Every state must have a free-state constitution. The representatives of the people must

[33] *Denkschrift* (January 20, 1919), *Entwurf.* Constitutional Assembly, 1919.
[34] Kahl, in *Heilfron*, p. 1255. Cf. United States constitution, article IV, section 4. See *Luther* v. *Border*, 7. How. 1. (1849) and *Pacific States Tel. & Tel. Co.* v. *Oregon*, 223, U.S. 118 (1912), on the guarantee of a "republican form of government."

be elected by universal, equal, direct, and secret suffrage of all men and women of *Reich* nationality according to principles of proportional representation. The state government requires the confidence of the body of people's representatives. The electoral principles apply to elections of local authorities also. A state law, however, may declare the qualification for a vote to be conditional upon a year's residence in the district.

What does this mean? "Free state" is the equivalent of "republican," and implies that monarchy is excluded. The terms "representative" and "representative body" (*Volksvertretung*) imply the notion and institution of the Parliamentary system and exclude any sort of a dictatorial system, whether of one or a minority.

Then a government with the essential feature of the cabinet system—responsibility to the Parliament—was provided, but a variety of forms, including the government's power to meet a vote of no confidence with a referendum, was permissible. Was a bicameral system permitted? Preusz's original draft actually prescribed a unicameral parliament, but it was thereafter deleted, and in the constitutional committee it was admitted that a second chamber was possible; and commentators argued that if this were so, it was possible only in the form that the representative body, spoken of in article 17, was one, while at its side another organ existed which was not Parliament but only a check upon Parliament. Thus in Prussia there was a state council "representing the provinces in state legislation and administration," but its members did not enjoy the immunities given by the constitution to members of Parliament.

World War II, issuing from Hitler's abrogation of democratic principles and his destruction of democratic institutions in the *Reich* and the states (in some of the former, nazi governments arose earlier than 1933 and there enabled the movement to develop), taught the need of more specific guarantees of democracy in the states. This has already been discussed (p. 90 above).

Territorial Reorganization. The struggle

between the unitarists' desire for power freely to redistribute the areas of the states for federal utility, and to secure, at least, that no state should have a population smaller than two million, and the separatists' ardent desire to be left alone to make friendly arrangements should it suit them, resulted in a limited victory for the unitarists. Article 18 received this final shape: [35]

The composition of the *Reich* by states shall serve the maximum economic and cultural utility of the nation, with the fullest consideration for the will of the population concerned. Alteration of the territory of the states and the formation of states within the *Reich* shall be effected by a law for the amendment of the Constitution. If the directly concerned states assent, then an ordinary *Reich* statute suffices.

An ordinary *Reich* statute also suffices if one of the states concerned does not assent, but where the alteration of territory or reorganization is demanded by the will of the population and required by paramount *Reich* interests, the will of the population shall be ascertained by a poll. The *Reich* government orders the poll, if required by a third of the enfranchised inhabitants of the territory to be separated.

The clause, "When the states directly concerned give their consent, an ordinary federal law suffices," was used only in the union of Prussia and Pyrmont.[36] Only two changes of territory, the formation of Thuringia out of seven small states,[37] and the union of Coburg with Bavaria, took place by constitutional amendment, since the assent of the states could not be formally ascertained. In 1928, Saxony and Thuringia exchanged enclaves, and Waldeck merged with Prussia. From twenty-five in 1919 the number of the states dropped to seventeen by 1933.

Other attempts at reorganization failed: one attempt to constitute a separate state of Upper Silesia, was defeated in November, 1922, when a ten-to-one majority of the population voted in favor of remaining with Prussia, and in Hanover a good deal less than one third of the voters voted in favor of a plebiscite to separate from Prussia.

However, article 18 was as important for its continuous challenge to inquiry and rearrangement as for its immediate effects. While it existed, there could be no rest. It produced a law relating to its execution in cases where the *Reich* took the initiative, and it produced a *Reich* Bureau, which was dissolved in 1929. The law was never used, since the states exacted a promise that the *Reich* would not act without their assent.

The work of territorial reorganization fell into the sphere of the general constitutional reorganization desired on many sides, and began with the calling of the State Conference in 1928, culminating in the Democratic Reform Plan which we shall discuss at length presently (p. 214 ff.).

Reichs-exekution. Under the Weimar constitution the *Reich* President, that is, the government, had the power to compel a state to fulfill its constitutional obligations, thus (article 48): "If a state does not carry out its obligations under the *Reich* Constitution or Statutes, the President can compel it to do so with the aid of armed force." Such a power was unnecessary in the United States because the constitution was less a union of states. "We, the people . . . ." meant a more merged union, and the United States government was granted authority over all individuals directly wherever they dwelt, so long as the power had been granted to the Union. The power of federal compulsion was taken from an organ, the *Bundesrat,* which was not likely by its composition to force a state, and given to one which was less unlikely to do so, unless the President happened to be a native of the state which was to be forced. The decision of the President could be challenged by an appeal to the Court of State or other courts, where the constitution permitted an appeal in cases of disputes about interpretation, but this was hardly an obstruction to immediate intervention by the

[35] "In the case of union or separation, should any dispute arise on the question of arrangements as to property, the decision on such points shall be given, upon an application from one party, by the Court of State of the German Foundation."
[36] Law, March 24, 1922.
[37] Law, April 29, 1920.

President. We have already noted the two important cases in which the power was used.

Survey. The German *Reich* under the Weimar constitution was a federation in which the unitary element was very strongly marked. The constitution of 1919 conquered a good deal of the still-existing particularism of the states, but its attempts were met by a well-organized resistance. The result was that the anti-unitary elements were strongly stressed, much more so than in the United States, for the *Reich* was not able to obtain the plenitude of administrative powers. It is true, again, that it had a wider sphere of legislative power than the United States, but in such things as territorial reorganization, in which its unitary bias received pronounced expression, it was not able to make headway. The *Reichsrat,* which was not meant to be an independent body, gradually became more powerful than was originally desired.

The unitarists wished to see the many concessions to the states modified or entirely abolished, especially in regard to territorial reorganization, the administration of *Reich* affairs, the power of the *Reichsrat,* the power of the states to make treaties with foreign countries, and their claims regarding army organization. It was argued that the partial duplication of parliamentary and administrative machinery in so many states (seventeen), some with ridiculously small populations, was financially wasteful,[38] and, even worse, that the whole arrangement in states of this size made systematical administrative reform, with its consequent efficiency and financial economy, impossible. Especially wasteful was the coexistence of two great organizations—Prussia and *Reich*—in Berlin and over the whole of Prussia. Varying regulations broke up and made impossible the easy transfer of citizens from state to state in the great professions of

civil service and law, while ludicrous situations were caused by the intersection of great urban complexes (like Hamburg-Altona, Bremen-Wesermunde, Frankfurtam-Main-Offenbach) by state boundaries. The regional aspect of rearrangements of area was very strongly stressed.

On the other hand, anti-unitarist criticism was as comprehensive and perhaps as strong in political power. It came mainly, though not entirely, from Bavaria, which was too small to subject others, too large to accept subjection. It was argued that the constitution permanently endowed the central authority with a power won at an exceptional time, and appropriate for emergencies only, and that this has converted the "joy in the *Reich*" (*Reichsfreudigkeit*) into "grievance in the *Reich*" (*Reichsverdrossenheit*). The financial powers of the *Reich* took away all resiliency and strength from the states; the *Reich* officials only duplicated their already existing organizations, the various powers over the states wounded their patriotism, while centralization went far to reduce their power to pursue their own peculiar cultural development—especially so, felt Bavaria and Prussia.

At the end of this chapter the deficiencies of German federalism are resummarized indirectly in an outline of reform proposals.[39]

NAZI FEDERALISM

SINCE the nazi régime placed obedience above free comment, there is not yet and may never be available a realistic account of the highly unitary system by which it replaced Weimar federalism. Yet an outline of nazi practice is necessary. The transition is dealt with elsewhere (Chap. 25). The chief causes of the downfall of Weimar are not to be found in the federal arrangements, wasteful and confused as they were, but in other matters altogether. However, the rise of the nazi movement to power radically affected the relationship between the *Reich* and the states.

---

[38] Cf. Otto Braun, *Die Deutsche Einheitsstaat* (Berlin, 1927); W. Apelt, *Vom Bundesstaat zum Regionalstaat* (Berlin, 1927); Arnold Brecht, *Reich und Länder* (Berlin, 1928-30), Vol. 2 (1928), p. 349; Vol. 3 (1929), pp. 70 and 265; Vol. 4 (1930); Bund zur Erneuerung des Reichs, *Die Reichsreform* (Berlin, 1933).

[39] Cf. Arnold Brecht, *Federalism and Regionalism in Germany* (New York, 1945), for a most illuminating review of Weimar federalism.

The Nazi party program of 1921, and Hitler's *Mein Kampf* (chapter 10) favored the separate existence of the states. Even after January, 1933, confused talk about their preservation was continued. The "Roman pattern" of centralization was identified with "racial cross-breeding" and the "Jewish-democratic-socialist state"! However, the leadership principle could hardly be reconciled with federalism. And for Hitler the abolition of regional and local self-government was necessary as a means of scattering the landowning, military, and bureaucratic groups in state and local politics who might thwart his will. It was also a condition of full central mobilization of the resources of the *Reich* for military strength.

After the election of March 5, 1933, the Nazis controlled eight states, mostly in Northern Germany and including Prussia. They forced the resignation of the governments of the other six states, mostly in Central and Southern Germany, and of the three free cities of Hamburg, Bremen, and Lübeck. On March 31, 1933, they passed the First Coordination Act (*Gleichschaltungsgesetz*), "The Provisional Law for the Unification of the States with the Reich." By this law, *Reich* commissioners were appointed whose task it was to enforce the policies of the *Führer* in the states. The state cabinets were empowered to assume legislative authority and to ignore the state constitutions. The state legislatures—with the exception of the Prussian Diet elected on March 5, and all local legislative bodies except in Prussia—were dissolved and were reconstituted for four-year terms without new elections. The seats were allotted on the basis of the number of votes obtained within the states by each party in the Nazi-dominated *Reichstag* election of March 5. The Communist and later the Social-Democratic representation was canceled, and the other parties went out of existence "voluntarily." Then all but the Nazi party were prohibited by law.

The Unification of the States. On April 7, 1933, notwithstanding the provisions of the Enabling Act safeguarding the position of the *Reichsrat,* the *Reich* government passed the Second Coordination Act (*Reichsstatthaltergesetz*), "The Law on the Unification of the German States." This law vested the *Reich* commissioners, now called *Reich* governors (*Reichsstatthalter*), with permanent authority. It empowered the *Reich* President, on the nomination of the *Reich* Chancellor, to appoint governors of the states (except in Prussia, where the Chancellor would exercise the powers of the governor), who in their turn would appoint and remove the governments of the states, dissolve the legislatures, order new elections, make and publish state laws, "upon the proposal of the state cabinet" appoint and dismiss the higher officials and judges, and exercise the pardoning power. From time to time, the *Führer* convoked the national governors to acquaint them with national policies. It was their primary task to represent these policies and the authority of the *Reich* within the states. For this purpose, each was given the powers of a dictator, including the right to call out the army to preserve public order. Laws and decrees supplementary to the Law of April 7, 1933 (of April 25, May 26, June 1, June 18, and October 14, 1933) provided, among other things, that the Chancellor might transfer his powers in Prussia to the Minister-President, and that the governors might transfer their powers to the state governments. In three instances, two smaller states were placed under one national governor. In most cases the national governor was the party district leader (*Gauleiter*) of the district most closely corresponding to his state. As everywhere in the Third *Reich,* governmental and party offices were thus combined, preventing difficulties which could otherwise have arisen between governor and *Gauleiter* in the same area.

The Law of January 30, 1934, "for the Reconstruction of the *Reich*" (*Gesetz über den Neuaufbau des Reiches*), passed unanimously by both chambers without debate, was decisive for unification. Authority for this was taken from the plebiscite of November 12, 1933, on Germany's withdrawal from Geneva, which was alleged to prove that "the German nation has attained an indestructible unity superior to all internal subdivisions of a political character." This law decreed: (1) "Popular representation in the States will be abolished;" thus the state legislatures, which had in fact ceased to exist in October, 1933, were outlawed. (2) "The sovereign rights of the States are transferred to the *Reich*." (3) "The State cabinets are subordinate to the *Reich* cabinet." The *Reich* cabinet as a whole, and individual ministers within the jurisdiction of their ministries, could act through the state cabinets. State cabinets could still legislate, but only "by direction and in the name of the *Reich*." (4) The national governors of the states, who had until now been under the direct control of the *Führer*, were placed under the supervision of the *Reich* Ministry of the Interior. (5) The cabinet "may establish new constitutional rights [for states]."

By designating the governments of the states, the *Führer* had made a mockery of their representation in the *Reichsrat*. Hence, on February 14, 1934, this second chamber was finally abolished (*Gesetz über die Aufhebung des Reichsrats*). Though the existence of the *Reichsrat* had been safeguarded by the Enabling Act, this action could be considered valid, since the Law of January 30, 1934, had authorized the cabinet to pass new constitutional laws. After a series of laws and decrees, all state law courts were transformed into *Reich* law courts on April 1, 1935, so that decisions were rendered uniformly "in the name of the German people." Many other functions, such as the administration of forests, zoning, and public health supervision, were transferred to authorities under the direct control of *Reich* ministries during 1934 and 1935.

On January 30, 1935, any remaining individuality of the states was removed by an Act Relating to the *Reich* Governors, which largely replaced the *Reichsstatthaltergesetz* of April 7, 1933. This new law subjected the governors to supervision no longer by the Ministry of the Interior but by the various ministers of the *Reich* government in their respective fields of competence. The gradual reduction of the governors from immediate subordination to Hitler to direct responsibility merely to the specific ministries reflected the de-

cline of local authority and prestige. Although, according to the law, the national governor was not a civil servant, but occupied an office similar to that of a *Reich* minister, his actual role degenerated steadily to that of a *Reich* official. Their power was reduced: they no longer appointed the state cabinets, but merely made nominations to the *Führer* who nominated. Also, while by the decree of February 2, 1934, state laws needed approval of the governors, now their validity depended solely on approval by the *Reich* cabinet.

Furthermore, the nazi government vastly extended the range of nation-wide legislation: all civil service personnel, in nation, states, and municipalities were centrally regulated by the *Reich* Civil Service Act of January 26, 1937. So also were the basic norms of police, educational administration, and mining operation, nationally regulated. In most fields the states were only allowed a secondary or subordinate law-making power for adapting the centrally established laws to local circumstances in minor matters.

The Durability of Particularism. These nazi reforms were intended to remove all "dualism" between *Reich* and states. But the diverse state administrations were never eliminated, nor was a unified administrative machine ever developed, although the idea was current that the governors were merely "the agents-general" of the national government. For the total territory of Germany is too extensive, and the regional diversities too ingrained, for a swift and thoroughgoing change in a time of military and economic anxieties. In many instances, direct national authorities and state officials worked side by side, thus preserving a double administration but not wiping out the state administration. The subordinate lawmaking power was still of some substantial effect. Indeed, as it was impossible administratively to effectuate such drastic changes in a short time, Berlin even called on the states to act for a Berlin which had presumably abolished the states! In World War II, the nazi authorities in Berlin showed spiteful restiveness at the survival of the particularist spirit of some German states. This persisted in spite of the *Reich's* establishment at the center of the Superior Council of Defense and at the state and inferior territorial levels of civil commissioners of national defense to animate and control the normal peacetime governmental agencies now called upon to put forth all strength in a total war.

The particularist spirit even defeated the avowed intention of Hitler's government to resubdivide the *Reich* into entirely new administrative areas. The nazis talked much, in their early years, of plans for the establishment of economic-physiographic regions in place of the historic dynastic state boundaries, together with some return to ancient tribal regions (*Gaue*) as parts of the *Reich*.[40] On November 15, 1934, Dr. Frick, *Reich* Minister of the Interior, stated that in the near future the *Reich* would be reorganized into twenty regions (*Reichsgaue*) with three to four million inhabitants each. "These new regions," he declared, "and their governors will be instruments through which the *Reich* government will impose its authority on the humblest hamlet." These regions "will rest on considerations of an economic and geographic nature dictated by national interests." Earlier, Goebbels had enunciated a plan to set up thirteen tribal provinces, and other nazi leaders had propagated similar ideas. The matter was lost to view; it was probably never anything but romantic talk; military-economic tasks were far more important.

Little territorial reform was actually accomplished. On January 1, 1934, the two states of Mecklenburg-Schwerin and Mecklenburg-Strelitz were united into one state of Mecklenburg, and in 1937 the free city of Lübeck was incorporated in Prussia. Otherwise only minor boundary corrections were made between Bavaria and Württemberg and between Prussia and her neighbors, Oldenburg, Hamburg, Mecklenburg, Anhalt, Hesse, and Schaum-

burg-Lippe; these were made in 1934 and 1935, following a trend already apparent during the last years of the Weimar Republic. Exchanges of territory of somewhat greater importance occurred between Prussia on the one hand and Hamburg (1937), Oldenburg (1937), Bremen (1939), Brunswick (1941), and Anhalt (1942) on the other. The opposition to territorial reform came largely from two sources: (1) the Prussian aristocracy objected to any division of Prussia, which any through reform would involve; and (2) many nazi jobholders, headed by Goering as Prussian Premier, feared that their positions would be abolished by territorial change.

Prussia was incorporated in the *Reich*, but not fully. The *Führer* became the governor of Prussia; but on April 11, 1933, he appointed Goering Minister-President of Prussia and entrusted him with his powers. Goering was responsible, therefore, only to Hitler. By a law of July 20, 1933, the twelve provincial councils were changed from elective legislatures to honorary advisory bodies appointed by the Minister-President. The provincial chief presidents (*Oberpraesidenten*) were thus given all executive, legislative, and administrative power. By the decree of November 27, 1934, they were made nationally appointive and were given increased powers, so that they then occupied a status similar to that of national governors, that is, agents-general of the *Reich*, while as an inheritance of the older régimes they had detailed local administrative powers beyond those of the governors. Yet they were responsible to both the *Reich* and Prussia. All Prussian ministries, except the prime ministership and the Ministry of Finances, were amalgamated with the corresponding *Reich* ministries, so that for many years, Prussian government, laws, and budget, still prevailed. In September, 1944, Prussian finances were also taken over by the *Reich* "in order to set free additional manpower for the conduct of the war." The status of Prussia in the Third *Reich* was the reverse of that in the Bismarck constitution. Prussia was intermerged with the *Reich*: the *Reich* dominated, but did not abolish, Prussia. Yet the personal relationship between Her-

---

[40] Cf. Albert Lepawsky, "Nazis Reform the Reich," *American Political Science Review*, 1936, p. 324 ff.; R. H. Wells, "Liquidation of German Länder," *ibid.*, p. 350 ff. See *Nazi Conspiracy and Aggression* (U.S. Government Printing Office, 1946 and 1947).

mann Goering, the Prime Minister of Prussia, and Hitler, meant that Prussia was still a weighty, leading element in the *Reich,* with a power of independent leadership.

The thoroughgoing control of the *Reich* over all revenue-raising authorities that had developed in the Weimar period was carried by the nazi régime to a most pervasive mastery of taxation and expenditure in *Reich,* state, and local government units.[41]

Nazi Local Governments. Embodied in this highly unified "federal" system was the specialized instrument of heavily centralized local government, subjected to the Nazi party itself. This was introduced by the German Municipal Code of January 30, 1935.[42] All municipalities were subject to the supervision of the *Reich* Ministry of the Interior; their budget required advance approval by the *Reich;* the Ministry of the Interior appointed the mayors and councilors of cities with a population of over 100,000, while in smaller cities appointments were made by the *Reich* governors or other *Reich* officials. The burgomaster was chosen by the Ministry of the Interior or the *Reich* governor from among three candidates proposed by the local Nazi party delegate. Thus appointed, the burgomaster had full and exclusive responsibility for the government of the municipality. The councilors were a mere body of advisors, chosen by the Nazi party delegate (himself appointed by the *Führer's* deputy, usually the local Nazi leader) for their "political reliability, capability, and character." The burgomaster had to consult the council but did not have to be guided by the result. The councilors were supposed to maintain contact with the people and secure from them "a sympathetic understanding for the measures taken by the mayor." This function might have been a useful check on the mayor for the higher

authority, but it was difficult to fulfill in a despotic system; so the law went so far as to command the councilors to give expression to disagreeable criticism. The "leader" of the German League of Municipalities admitted the failure of the councilors; they had neither time nor will for their job.[43]

PAST AND FUTURE OF GERMAN FEDERALISM

THE future of German federalism is obscure because the future of the German state and democracy are as yet far from predictable in any clarity. But some factors are discernible, if dimly.

(1) It would seem that the Allied Occupation in four separate zones must encourage particularism, especially as elections were held in various states in 1946— states reconstituted and managed by reorganized political parties.[44]

(2) The difficulties in the way of interregional or interstate meeting of party leaders and followers assist the perpetuation of particularism, as parties based on common principles break down state and local particularism, but here their work is obstructed.

(3) Perhaps the Prussian problem will emerge easier of solution, for when the final distribution of population is settled (refugees from the eastern zone and from the areas taken by Poland, and some sort of permanence of adjustment achieved throughout the rump *Reich*), the proportion of Prussian population to that of the *Reich* will be considerably less than forty to seventy million. Moreover, the four zones have cut across Prussia, and for Allied administration her provinces are no longer as integrated under a common government as in the past, including the Weimar and nazi periods.

(4) The artificially induced division of

---

41 Cf. H. F. Abraham, *Intergovernmental Financial Relations in Contemporary Germany* (Bureau for Research in Municipal Government, Harvard Graduate School of Public Administration, February, 1943).

42 Cf. F. K. Süren, *Die Deutsche Gemeindeordnung, Kommentar* (Berlin, 1935), 2 vols.

43 Cf. K. Jesserich, *Zeitschrift für die gesammten Staatswissenschaften* (1938), p. 92.

44 See J. M. Pollock and A. Meisel, *Germany under Occupation* (Ann Arbor, 1947); and Office of Military Government for Germany, United States Constitution of Bavaria, Hesse and Wurttemberg-Baden (February, 1947). See also R. G. Neumann, "New Constitutions in Germany," *American Political Science Review,* June, 1948, p. 448 ff.

Germany, if long enough protracted, may produce a strong yearning for union as in the past, yet not be drastic enough to destroy "Germany," and may thus have powerful unifying tendencies.

(5) The United States Government and Great Britain have publicly declared their wish for the restoration of something like the Weimar federalism. The U.S.S.R. has declared for a unitary state,[45] but the Soviet idea of "unitary" is not defined in detail. A return to Weimar would satisfy the need to provide for reparations, for Allied control of German industry and general policy, and for effective demilitarization. It would be even more satisfactory if the areas of the states were evened out, and if financial unification were continued and reformed.

(6) The establishment of the constitutions of Bavaria, Hesse, and Württemberg-Baden by the people under the aegis of the Office of Military Government (American) for Germany accomplishes two things of definite portent for the future. These are: (a) the restoration of the several states, prior to the restoration of the Reich as whole, but of more rational area, as in Greater Hesse, and Württemberg-Baden, and (b) the deliberate establishment within them of the constitutional principles of democratic government much more specific, purposeful, and far-reaching than in the Weimar period, and emanating from the clarification of ideas during the world-wide ideological debates and the bitter European experience of the years from 1933 to the end of World War II.

(7) As to other future possibilities, in order to look forward we must look back to the proposals of the States Conference of 1928–32.[46] These also indirectly summarize the defects of Weimar federalism. In briefest paraphrase, they were:

(a) The Prussian provinces were to become states, with territorial changes, exercising a lawmaking power like the other states, and subject to the direct governmental powers of the Reich also, like

other states—no Prussian administration would come in between.

(b) No separate Prussian central government would exist: legislation for all-Prussia—that is, all the new states in common—would be undertaken by the Reichstag, perhaps by the members alone who were elected in Prussian states. A transition proposal allowed the existence of a common assembly for the Prussian states, whose laws would need the consent of the federal cabinet.

(c) The Reichsrat would be maintained, each state being represented by votes proportionate to its population, as in the Weimar constitution. The votes of each state would be cast uniformly. The Prussian states would cast their votes severally, as directed by their chief executive and a committee of the state assembly.

(d) The Reich would receive powers at least as wide as those developed in the latest practice of the Weimar system; the financial power of the Reich would be as unified and centralized. Moreover, in the field of federal lawmaking power, the direct pervading administrative power followed, with the exception of police, supervision of communities and professional organizations, industry and commerce, religious affairs, educational matters, and waterways, in the case of Bavaria, Saxon Württemberg, and Baden.

(e) But in the field of Reich legislative and administrative powers, it would be the duty of the Reich to delegate administration to the states, yet in the discretion of the Reich executive.

(f) A number of functions were assigned to the states, in addition to any that they might exercise because not assigned by law to the federal authority: they were social welfare, public health, juvenile welfare, public housing, state finance, agricultural affairs within and not interfering with the Reich power over the general economy, intermunicipal zoning, traffic. and roads within federal powers, and care of monuments. These rights were, for the

---

[45] Cf. Herman Finer, *America's Destiny* (New York, 1947), p. 203.

[46] See p. 214 above; and Brecht, *op. cit.*; also Gerhard Krebs, *The Problem of Federal Reform in Germany* (University of California, 1937).

Southern states already mentioned, to be guaranteed in the constitution.

(g) As for administrative harmony, it was proposed that within each state, the *Reich* agencies should be fused at the top, with power for the highest *Reich* official to supervise and direct in respect of administrative simplification. Several small states might be combined within single *Reich* administrative regions, and the *Reich* official at the top would supervise the whole regional establishment. He would keep close contact with state authorities, and it might be feasible even to appoint a state minister as the high federal official.

(h) The *Reich* could delegate its administrative powers to the states. When it did this, it could safeguard efficiency by a combination of general directions (and where necessary, directions in specific cases), these to be addressed only to the state governments and not to subordinates; disciplining of the states in their administration by appeal by the *Reich* to the Supreme Court for Constitutional Conflicts; the right to obtain full information, to make on-the-spot inspections, and to examine public records. In certain fields (especially labor, social insurance, and care of veterans), state and *Reich* administration at the regional level would require more cooperation than heretofore. Moreover, the power of the *Reich* over administrative courts, general administrative law, administrative structure, local government units, and public examinations, in the states, was greatly strengthened.

(i) The *Reich* should have the right to reorganize the territories so as to secure that the states should be of at least two million in population. This was not an official proposal of the conference, but the weighty opinion of experts of good will.

(j) In order to stabilize the states as administrative units, the reformers proposed that state cabinets should be appointed by the legislatures for a fixed term—say, four years—providing that only a two-thirds majority could overturn them within that time.

On all these matters, the delegates of the states at the conference were in agreement. But Bavaria's delegate objected in two vital matters: he wished to see the *Reichsrat* endowed with a legislative power equal to that of the *Reichstag*, and he rejected the Weimar powers of the *Reich* to make law on "principles" and "in case of urgency," and rejected also the increase of *Reich* powers newly proposed. What was of even more revealing effect was the Bavarian objection to the break-up of Prussia. The argument was that if Prussia were broken up, the resultant states would sooner or later be assimilated to the new states that were to be formed on more convenient territories, and that there would be a powerful impetus to reduce the special status of the Southern "old" states of which Bavaria was the chief! In other words, no Prussia, no Bavaria! Hence, Prussia ought to be maintained; and if she were not, then the new states formed out of her ought each to receive constitutionally guaranteed powers equal to those of the "old" states. The conference offered the four "old" states the guarantee that their rights would be unamendable if their combined votes were thrown against any encroaching proposal.

How complicated are the problems of German compared with American and British federalism! The latter have their complications also, deriving from the attempt to secure the supremacy of large-scale economic regulation over extensive territories which embrace strong diversities of climate, resources, occupations, and therefore of interests, and in the case of Canada, the additional obstinacy of a religion and culture and language in Quebec markedly different from that prevailing elsewhere. In Germany, additional confusion has been caused, and still exists, because in the little monarchies and free cities, the idea of sovereignty cast its sharp shadow forward; it claimed at the establishment of the *Reich*, as it still claims, a marked differentiation between states of legislative and administrative power, and a differential representation in the federal council. These differences, so engendered, have been continuously supported by real diversities of culture and religion. It does not look as though these have been seriously reduced by the bitter experiences of the last quarter of a century.

Part Three

THE SOVEREIGN MAJORITY

Decision by majorities is as much an expedient as lighting by gas. In adopting it as a rule, we are not realizing perfection, but bowing to an imperfection. It has the great merit of avoiding, and that by a test perfectly definite, the last resort to violence; and of making force itself the servant instead of the master of authority. But our country rejoices in the belief that she does not decide all things by majorities.—G LADSTONE

Governments therefore should not be the only active powers: associations ought, in democratic nations, to stand in lieu of those powerful private individuals whom the equality of conditions has swept away. . . . In democratic countries the science of association is the mother of science: the progress of all the rest depends upon the progress it has made. Amongst the laws which rule human societies there is one which seems to be more precise and clear than all the others. If men are to remain civilized, or to become so, the art of associating together must grow and improve, in the same ratio in which the equality of conditions is increased.—DE TOCQUEVILLE

12

The Electorate and Political Parties

RESPONSIBILITY AND REPRESENTATION

ANALYSIS of the idea of democracy has indicated that it may mean either of two things, which, however, are closely related in practice: a certain social purpose, or a specific machinery of government. Here we are concerned with the latter, and in this respect, generally speaking, democratic theorists have sought something labeled alternatively "responsible government" or "representative government." These are not coincident, but are very nearly so. It is not merely pedantry which requires it to be emphasized that responsibility is the chief and wider aim, and representativeness merely a convenient means to attain this. There are governments in which representative assemblies participate, but are so hampered in various ways that governments cannot be called responsible. The chief example before 1919 was the government of Germany. After that time the fascist government of Italy (commencing in 1922) had elections but not responsible government; rather the same thing was true of Hitler's Germany, and the distinction is still true of the government of Soviet Russia.

On the other hand, government may be responsible and yet not representative, because the people to whom it is responsible may act *directly* by popular vote. Of this there are no more examples in modern times, if we except the extraordinary procedure for ratifying constitutions (and this is to strain the example too much). The

desire for responsible government is paramount; people wish not merely to represent their views, but actually to make and unmake governments.[1]

The real question—and it is asked most anxiously of the Soviet system—is not whether the government deigns to take notice of popular criticisms and votes, but whether it can be voted out of office or forced by some machinery or procedures to change its policy, above all against its own will.

To whom, then, ought government to be responsible? Who ought to control the making of laws and their administration? Openly or silently men decide this by their general social philosophy. They ask, "What should I like to see government accomplish?" The answer generally dictates the desirable form of government, and this again settles for them the extent to which others should be represented. James Mill, for instance, desired the utmost perfection of society, and this was expressed for him in the principle of the greatest happiness of the greatest number. Thence it was simple to proceed to democratic government, and further, to representative government with universal suffrage.[2] But Macaulay was anxious for property, and to safeguard it he held that any franchise—that is, any system of representative government—which included the

[1] This was what so roused Burke's anger (in his *Reflections*) against Dr. Price and his friends.
[2] *Essay on Government.*

unpropertied working classes was ruinous.[3]

That question answered, there still remains another. How may the power to govern be best applied? Once it has been decided to have responsible government, the problem becomes whether the people shall act directly or through representatives. Now no modern state has faced this *ab initio;* every state, except the smallest, Switzerland, has found itself compelled to govern through the medium of a representative body. The reasons might be deduced from the nature of the work to be done by government. But we are fortunate in having the reasons put by a body of people —the French Constituent Assembly of 1789—who actually faced a situation spiritually favorable to direct government, and it is instructive to ask why representative was preferred to direct government. The reasons adduced were: that proper deliberation was impossible over a large area and with a large number of people to consult; that it was unnecessary to take the opinion of all citizens, sufficient direction being obtainable from a selection of them; that not all people had either the leisure or the instruction to judge capably of legislation; that tumultuous proceedings and demagoguery must prevail where no systematic procedure existed; and that, to secure the benefit of division of labor, it was good that citizens should allow representatives to exercise the function of government.[4] We may hazard a further reason: the deputies, as the debates plainly showed, enjoyed being deputies and were anxious to remain deputies; they relished their powers, and acquired a professional interest in maintaining that representative government was more feasible than direct.

The student may be referred to the results of the so-called unofficial "Peace Ballot" taken on the question of England's participation in the League of Nations and the problems of peace and disarmament.[5] It will there be seen (*a*) how easily it was possible for the questions to be misinterpreted unless they were debated for their meaning, and (*b*) how difficult it is to give meaning to the answers unless a series of alternative solutions are put for choice to the voter. The same conclusion may well be drawn from many of the Gallup Polls, where *Yes* or *No* is said to a proposition, but where, fallaciously, the consequent duties, responsibilities, and financial sacrifices are not brought into the picture.[6]

The arguments presented by the French Constituent Assembly—valid, we think— have prevailed, with the result that everywhere democratic government means, practically, a representative assembly in the center of the machinery of government. Nevertheless, representative government has not absolutely triumphed, for some countries seek to remedy its shortcomings by the addition of the initiative and the referendum.

In the main, however, modern government functions through popularly elected legislatures and ministers responsible to them and to the people. A qualification must, however, always be remembered: that owing to the existence and activity of special organizations—political parties —to influence the electors in their choice of representatives, even representative government without any formal admixture of direct government has been made substantially direct. Representatives are selected, catechized, pledged, supported,

---

[3] *E.g.,* Speech on the Chartists' petition. Bagehot was ready to have the working classes represented, in the sense of permitting their spokesmen to appear, but he would not allow them the full voting *force* of their total numbers. Cf. his *Essays on Parliamentary Reform* (written in 1859).

[4] All this is shown with a great abundance of learning in K. Loewenstein, *Volk und Parlament, nach der Staatstheorie der Französischen Nationalversammlung von 1789* (München, 1922).

[5] *The Peace Ballot: the Official History* (London, 1935).

[6] Cf. H. Cantril, *Gauging Public Opinion* (New York, 1944); and Lindsay Rogers, *The Pollsters* (New York, 1949).

See also Hearings, U.S. House of Representatives, "Campaign Expenditures," Part 12, December 28, 1944, on the Gallup Poll; and Social Science Research Council (New York), "Report of Committee on Analysis of Pre-Election Polls and Forecasts," released December 27, 1948.

and afterward controlled in their parliamentary activities by parties in close and continuous touch with the electorate, so that absolute differences between direct and indirect democracy do not exist. The question of which is the better instrument of government turns upon the comparative merits of the party organization of a state and any alternative organization which might be improvised for direct popular government. To this question we return, therefore, only when we have completely reviewed the subject of parties and legislatures.

The chief democratic theorists do not apparently diverge a great deal in their definitions of representative government. The most concise form in which Locke expressed himself on this subject is in this passage in *On Civil Government:*

It is in their legislative that the members of a commonwealth are united and combined together into one coherent living body. This is the soul that gives form, life, and unity to the commonwealth; from hence the several members have their mutual influence, sympathy, and connection; and therefore when the legislative is broken, or dissolved, dissolution and death follow. For the essence and union of the society consisting in having one will, the legislative, when once established by the majority, has the declaring and, as it were, keeping of that will. The constitution of the legislative is the first and fundamental act of society, whereby provision is made for the continuation of their union under the direction of persons and bonds of laws, made by persons authorized thereunto, by the consent and appointment of the people, without which no one man, or number of men, amongst them can have authority of making law that shall be binding to the rest.

Such descriptions of representative government are very general, and reveal few or none of the difficulties inherent in its nature, or, consequently, the wide gulf which actually separates people when the term "representative" is to be put into practice. Experience, however, shows that these vital problems are involved: (1) What entities shall the government represent? (2) How can the sovereign people be represented? (3) Who may choose representatives? These problems will concern us in the present chapter, and in the following two chapters we shall consider (4) how shall candidates for the assembly be chosen? (this is the problem of party government); and (5) how far is it permissible to influence others in the election of candidates? (this is the problem of public opinion and the parties). If we answer these questions by reference to the theories held at different times, and the practices based thereon, we shall discover more exactly what representative government means. Let it be remembered that it is not merely representation which is sought and accorded by democratic theory, but the actual selection and dismissal of the legislature and the executive.

WHAT ENTITIES SHALL THE GOVERNMENT REPRESENT?

AT THE PRESENT time, and in all the countries of which we speak, legislative assemblies are said to represent the "nation," the "country," "the people," or the "electorate," and these terms generally mean the whole body of citizens, considered as equally entitled to representation, and free of connection with each other except through their common residence in an area ordained by the law to be an electoral district. Representation is territorial, a vague image of the whole of the state's territory being conceived, this falling into districts convenient for registration and polling purposes.

It is largely convenience [7] which determines the size and nature of the electoral district, and not the local existence of a definite interest whose representation is considered to be desirable. It sometimes happens, in England especially, that an electoral district coincides with some ancient borough or rural area because for centuries it was a parliamentary unit, and it has come to be thought of, sentimen-

---

[7] It depends, in fact, partly upon the reasonable size of the legislature, partly upon the struggle of parties for special advantage in their own strong districts, and partly upon the desire to represent already existing entities like counties, cities, townships.

tally, as having a corporate existence. It happens also in all democratic countries that some districts are more or less completely in the area of some special industry or occupation—for example, coal mines, textile works, potteries, or corn belts—and to this extent there is a coincidence between territory and representation. The Soviet constitution of 1924–36 is said to have been based on occupational representation. Elections were held in the cities at each plant or institution, with such unattached groups as writers, artists, and scientists constituting individual units, so that the city soviets were composed of at least one delegate from each establishment.[8]

Within this territorial scheme the electors are supposed to be free and equal atoms. Continental writers have for over a century applied to this system the term "atomized" and "pulverized," meaning that the whole nation is split into sovereign fragments, all entitled to equal power in fashioning policy. This doctrine is not much older, politically, than the French Revolution, stemming chiefly from Rousseau's *Social Contract,* though it goes back, philosophically, to the rise of modern religious nonconformity and the Reformation. It replaced the old system of "community" representation, and "virtual representation," on the Continent and in England.

Past Theories: Community and Virtual Representation. According to the first theory, representatives were summoned not because government was based upon the sovereign authority of the people, but because the tenure of land was the foundation of order and political obligation, its products were the chief sources of taxation, and in troubled times it was easier for kings to collect taxes if they at least appeared to consult the taxpayers. Hence the growth of the idea that communities —bodies of people, constituent and substantial parts of society—were the proper units upon which to plan a parliamentary assembly.

The second theory (composed by the landed aristocracy who enjoyed political power) is most concisely expressed in Paley's words:

Before we seek to obtain anything more, consider duly what we already have. We have a House of Commons composed of 548 members, in which number are found the most considerable landholders and merchants of the Kingdom; the heads of the army, the navy, and the law; the occupiers of great offices in the state; together with many private individuals eminent by their knowledge, eloquence, and activity. If the country be not safe in such hands, in whom may it confide its interest? If such a number of such men be liable to the influence of corrupt motives, what assembly of men will be secure from the same danger? Does any new scheme of representation promise to collect together more wisdom, or to produce firmer integrity? [9]

The doctrine embodies two ideas—that of social bodies to be represented, but also the independence of the representative from the people to be represented. There were reformers, but as Macaulay said, speaking of the early part of this era, the object of the reformers was merely to make the representative body a more faithful interpreter of the sense of the constituent—it occurred to none that the constituent body might be an unfaithful interpreter of the sense of the nation.

Even Burke was only temporarily excited by the Wilkes' case, and he accepted virtual representation:

The virtue, spirit, and essence of a House of Commons consists in its being the express image of the feelings of the nation. It was not instituted to be a control upon the people, as of late it has been taught, by a doctrine of the most pernicious tendency. It was designed as a control for the people. . . . This change from an immediate state of procuration and delegation to a course of acting as from original power is the way in which all popular magistracies in the world have been perverted from their purposes.

---

[8] S. and B. Webb, *Soviet Communism,* Vol. I (London, 1936). In the 1936 constitution, however, selection of candidates is territorial, according to electoral districts.

[9] W. Paley, *Works* (London, 1825), Vol. IV, "The Principles of Moral and Political Philosophy," Book VI, pp. 392-93.

The "stake in the country" or "interest" theory of representation—that is, that wise laws could be made only by those sobered by ownership of property or pursuing a lucrative occupation—could not be surrendered by those who held it, for it was a product of their practical monopoly and part of the defense of that monopoly. Its natural fruits were the hideous maldistribution of seats, the queer franchises, and the electoral corruption which persisted until 1832 despite all debate about reform. Nor could theory and practice be changed until a hostile doctrine, claiming universal validity, violently challenged it. The attack was made in the name of the Natural Rights of Man, and in the vanguard were the middle classes, with the working classes acting as important allies in the two decades after the end of the Napoleonic Wars. The old tenets died a hard death, and to the last, in 1832 and even beyond, they were defended as wholesome for the commonwealth. Nor did France know the representation of individual persons until the Revolution. The system of three estates was possible only as long as graded social classes were not actively challenged; and that was possible only while the monarchy was absolute. When the monarchy fell, the question of who was to inherit the authority to govern naturally arose. The answer that nobility and clergy should be two to one against the Third Estate was ridiculous; for in that position, the Third Estate was indeed nothing. This was soon observed in 1788 and 1789, when the Revolution was brewing, and the holders of power held to their privileges until violence took them away.[10]

Sovereignty of the People—All the People—Triumphant. The substitute for divine-right government, based on a social contract of free and equal individuals, issued from the essays of Jean Jacques, to control administration and fill the pages of the new statute books. France under the *ancien régime* had known the free and equal voter less than England had; her policy was founded upon an almost untempered monarchy and graduated subjection. But it was in just such an environment that the new doctrine could spring up. In the Germanic states the practice of distinct Orders was usual where monarchy was at all tempered. In fact, Hegel's answer to the French doctrines was that representation of Estates was essential, for these, while supplying the informational advantage of representation, maintained the cohesion of the units in each Estate, whereas the free and equal vote inevitably disintegrated society. It is interesting to note that this part of Hegel's doctrine fitted in nicely with his idea that representatives should exist only to suggest ideas, but not to exert authority. Authority was the possession of the king and the aristocracy. It did not occur to him, as it did to contemporary Englishmen and

---

[10] Necker saw no way toward peace unless it were in convoking the *États*, to give the *Tiers État* a representation equal to that of both the others together. "The old-fashioned deliberation by Orders not being changeable, except-ing by the agreement of the three Orders and the approbation of the King, the number of deputies of the Third Estate is not, until then, anything but a means of gathering all the useful informed minds for the good of the State, and it cannot be denied that this variety of information belongs above all to the Order of the Third Estate, since there are a multitude of public affairs upon which it alone is instructed, such as domestic and foreign commerce, the condition of manufacturing industry, the best means to encourage these, the public credit, the rate of interest, and the circulation of currency, abuses of taxation, privileges and many other subjects within the experience of it alone. . . . The desire of the Third Estate, when it is unanimous, when it is in conformity with the principles of equity, must always be called the desire of the nation. . . ." (*Résultat du Conseil*, December 27, 1788. Cited in Ernest Lavisse, *Histoire* (Paris, 1912), Vol. IX, p. 371.

Later the Third Estate claimed to be the National Assembly. Siéyès declared: "This title is the only one which is appropriate in the present condition of things, as much because the members which compose it are the only representatives legitimately and publicly *known and verified*, as that, finally, the *national representation, being one and indivisible* [sic], none of the deputies, in whatever order he is chosen, has the right to exercise his functions separately from the present assembly."

The Germanic states, which during the nineteenth century had diets, based representation on the various estates.

Americans, that political parties would supply the cohesion.

The victorious principle was that every sane male citizen has a natural right to participate in government, that this right is normally represented by the right to vote for the representative assemblies, and that all are entitled to equal votes, none more, none less.[11] That right was independent of capacity and class, and was the direct issue of the humanity of man. This was a mystical dogma issuing from the affective qualities of those who held it, although they pretended that reason was on their side. This expression of the dogma contains practically all its essential features:

All the individuals who compose the association have the inalienable and sacred right to participate in the formation of the law, and if each could make his particular will known, the gathering of all these wills would veritably form the general will, and this would be the final degree of political perfection. No one can be deprived of this right upon any pretext or in any government . . . in every society the associated are essentially equal in rights, and the first of these is participation in the establishment of laws under the empire of which they consent to live.[12]

Common to all in the French constituent, it was gradually hammered out into the form contained in the Declaration of the Rights of Man:

Men are born, and always continue, free and equal in respect of their rights. . . . The nation is essentially the source of all sovereignty; nor can any individual, or any body of men, be entitled to any authority which is not expressly derived from it. . . . The law is an expression of the will of the community, all citizens have the right to concur, either personally, or by their representatives in its formation.[13]

[11] Cf. French Declaration of Rights, 1789, 1791, article 6.
[12] Pétion, Archives Parlementaires, 1788-1789, Vol. III, p. 582.
[13] An earlier form which shows the reasoning clearly was:

Article 17: "Since every man in the state of nature enjoys an absolute and universal right over himself, then society must possess over itself the same right, that is to say sovereignty resides in all the members of a society considered collectively."

The principle developed in England during the political conflicts of the seventeenth century; a mighty tributary joined it in the American colonies,[14] and later in the American states; [15] another flowed from the fount of the Contrat Social; [16] and all met, with the newer contribution of a few English radicals,[17] in the tempest of the Revolution and thence spread to become everywhere the ideal of the weaker and poorer members of society. In all countries—even in Soviet Russia—one can find a constitutional declaration of the

Article 18: "Thus any society incontestably possesses every kind of power. It has always that of revising and reforming its constitution, that of making laws, of executing them, and pronouncing upon their violation; that is to say, in virtue of its sovereignty, it possesses eminently the legislative, executive and judicial rights."
Article 22: "The general will is never so well expressed as when it is that of all the citizens; in default of this it must be expressed by the majority of votes."
Article 23: "Since all citizens ought to have an equal share in the advantages of society, they ought to exercise an equal share in public deliberations."
Article 25: "Thus one of the principal points in a constitution should be the manner in which a people should assemble in order that it may, wherever necessary, express its wishes freely, clearly, easily and promptly."—Gouges-Cartou, Projet, August 12, 1789, Archives Parlementaires, Vol. VIII, p. 429.
One practical reason did weigh strongly with the deputies: that is, the desire to get a just distribution of the burden of taxation. Just taxation is a driving incentive in the creation of the dogma of equal suffrage, e.g., Archives Parlementaires, Vol. VIII, p. 432: "Taxation, being a portion taken from the property of each citizen, he has the right of deciding upon its necessity, of freely consenting thereto, of following its employment, and of determining its destruction, levy, collection and period."
[14] Charles Merriam, American Political Ideas (New York, 1920).
[15] W. S. Carpenter, The Development of American Political Thought (Princeton, 1930), Chaps. III and V; Kirk Porter, History of Suffrage in the United States (Chicago, 1918); Harold Gosnell, Democracy: The Threshold of Freedom (New York, 1948), Chapters 1, 2, and 8; also Albert De Grazia, Theories of Representation (mss. of doctorate, University of Chicago, 1948).
[16] Book IV, 2 and 3.
[17] Cf. G. S. Veitch, Genesis of Parliamentary Reform (London, 1913).

principle—in all except England—and the declaration has its effects.

This conception of representation was necessarily entangled with the fundamental question of where sovereignty should reside. Since the governing classes were unwilling that sovereignty should go over to the people, every practicable obstacle was put in the way of full realization of the idea, so that only in our own day have universal suffrage and the free and equal voter become coincident.

It is essential to emphasize that it is only during the course of the last two or three decades that the whole body of the adult population has achieved sovereign authority in the nation. The importance of the observation lies in the fact that mass democracy is still in its infancy. If every infant has mighty potentialities, an infant is still deficient until these are realized, especially in relation to the extraordinarily intricate societies in which self-government is today to be practiced.

REPRESENTING THE SOVEREIGN PEOPLE

Now, here were a multitude of equal citizens. How were they to be represented? In some way a vast gulf had to be bridged —the palpable gulf between each individual and the nation.

According to the earlier German theorists, this gulf should never have been made; it did not really exist; and, even if it were tolerated, it should be overcome by representation in Estates which organically incorporated individual and group.[18]

---

[18] It is extraordinary how the nazis recovered this point of view, putting the *Volk* above and around each individual, or at any rate not admitting the right to existence of the individual. For example, Aurel Kolnai states in *The War against the West* (New York, 1938): "Individual rights are not encroached upon, they are deprived of meaning; the access to humanity is not obstructed, it is entirely cut off; humanitarian standards are not violated or disregarded, they are denied outright. Once the particular group has superseded humanity, then the individual, far from having merely to submit to stern governmental discipline, is philosophically considered and politically bound to live under the absolute domination of his own particular group over his wishes, mentality, and habits. It is no longer a ques-

But the disruptive, pulverizing philosophy of Locke and Rousseau had produced this gulf and had suggested that it was surmountable only by the social contract. The question still remained, how was the contract to be established in the everyday, continuous business of government? By what means could the reconciliation of all the particular wills be produced? As soon as this question was asked, and it was raised often and debated earnestly in the French National Assembly of 1789, statesmen were embarked upon a sea of troubles. There was the conflict we have already discussed, that of direct and representative government. There were the twin problems of the relationship between the constituencies and nation, and the electors and representatives.

If the nation were too large to be called together to deliberate, then the meeting must be reduced to manageable numbers, but nevertheless, there must be a proportionate expression of the will of the nation.[19] Mirabeau's metaphor, "a map to scale" (*carte réduite*), indicates the psychology of this form of representation. From each geographical point, a person or persons to speak for its people must be called. This was a simple and convenient solution, and seemed natural, for it was based upon the postulate that all wills are of equal value and therefore one, or ten, or ten thousand, or any group of citizens, or any fraction of the nation, was equal to any other, if it were numerically the same. Men do not seek out difficulties when their objects are obtainable without the burden of conquest.

Yet it could not be ignored that deputies coming from different places would have

---

tion of state reason, but of reason engulfed in the state; violence is no longer a means, it is the natural expression of the spirit underlying the new structure of the state; the voice of the ruler does not merely drown the voice of the individual soul, it entirely assimilates it." (P. 30.)

[19] Mirabeau, *Oeuvres* (Paris, 1819-22), Vol. I, p. 8: "When a nation is too numerous to meet in a single assembly, it forms a number of them. The individuals of each particular assembly give the right to vote for them to one person . . . the collection of representatives is the nation . . ."

different views. Were they, then, to hold out for those views? If the convention that a locality had sovereign rights were adopted, serious difficulties would follow: the locality and the deputy would be encouraged in their intransigeance.[20] Yet to deny sovereign rights was to fly in the face of revolutionary philosophy by minimizing the political importance of all the sovereign individuals locally resident.[21] A way out of the dilemma was found in a convention as subtle as Rousseau's discussion of the General Will, Hegel's metaphysics of the State, and Gierke's analysis of associations (and all these subjects are cognate to ours)—the convention that the representative of a locality must consider himself not as representing his district but as representing the nation.[22] But if he is

to do this, he ceases to be the representative of the district, unless, at the same time, the local inhabitants vote for him not because they are thinking of their district and willing the things which concern it, but because they have transcended the individuality which the philosophy of natural rights accorded them, and willingly vote as individuals who are part of a whole of which they are conscious. This, in fact, is the only practical way out of the philosophical difficulty raised by a political system which begins with individuals in a state of nature.[23] Individuals, in the terms of Kant, must be in a state of "unsociability," but of "social unsociability."

Now if it were admitted that representation of the locality was not really representation of this but of something else, called the nation—an image here invented to cause men to acknowledge an external authority—how was this something else to be known? Who should conceive the national interest or will the deputy or his constituents? In other words, how far was the deputy to be free, and how far bound by "instructions"? The constituents had a very important place in the scheme of things, for what was the national interest but some kind of combination of the interests of all the localities?

It is one thing to attempt to answer these questions as an "ought" in an ethical vacuum, another to read the answer

---

[20] *Archives Parlementaires*, Vol. VIII, p. 205: "If the system of imperative and limited powers were admitted, the resolutions of the assembly would be stultified by the recognition of a formidable veto in each one of the 177 *baillages* of the kingdom, or rather in the 431 divisions which have returned deputies to the assembly." Again: "If any *baillage*, or simply a division thereof, could govern in advance the opinion of the National Assembly, it could, on the same grounds, afterward repudiate its decrees, on the pretext that they were contrary to its own opinion." (Barrère)
[21] *Ibid.*, p. 204: "Each portion of society is subject; sovereignty resides only in the whole assembled: I say the whole, because the right to legislate does not belong to a part of the whole; I say assembled, because the nation cannot exercise the legislative power when it is divided, and then it cannot deliberate in common. This common deliberation can only come about through representatives; whenever I see the representatives of twenty-five million men, there I see the whole in which the plenitude of sovereignty resides; and if there exists a portion of this whole which wished to rise against the nation, I would see only one subject who pretended to be stronger than the whole. Protests and reservations are impermissible; they are attempts against the power of the majority" (Lally-Tollendal).
[22] *Ibid.*, p. 201: "Firstly, what is a *baillage* or a part of a *baillage*? [The reader should note our Anglo-Norman term "bailiwick."] It is not an independent state, a state united to others simply by a few connections, like any federal body; but a part of a whole, a portion of one only state, essentially submitted, whether it assents or not, to the general will, but having essentially the right to participate therein.— What is the deputy of a *baillage*? He is a man

whom the *baillage* charges to will in its name, but to will not as it would itself will if it could be transported to the general rendez-vous, that is *after having maturely deliberated and compared among themselves* all the motives of *the different baillages*. What is the mandate of a deputy? It is the act which transmits to him the powers of the *baillage*, which constitutes him representative of a *baillage*, and thereby representative of all the nation" (Talleyrand-Périgord).
E.g. *Constitution* of 1793, Vol. II, Chap. I, section 3, article 17: "The representatives elected in the departments are not representatives of a particular department, but of the entire nation and they must not be given any mandate."
[23] *Archives Parlementaires*, Vol. VIII, p. 593: "The deputy of a *baillage* is immediately chosen by his *baillage*; but indirectly, he is elected by the totality of *baillages*. That is why every deputy is a representative of the whole nation.

[226]

from history. When a desirable solution was being discussed, each party to the arrangement regarded the matter in the light of what was desirable to *him*. Representatives were not anxious to be bound by mandates; they desired independence and security of tenure.[24] They could not forget that, on the whole, they had a better education and more leisure than most of their constituents, whence some of them argued that they were better able to decide what was their will.[25] Further, it was asked, how could a constituency know what was the national will, and state its attitude thereto, until the deputies met and deliberated?[26] On the other hand, politically conscious electors desired to give instructions,[27] shorten the duration of the representative period,[28] and recall the members who dissatisfied them.

Such devices of the electors were the only means of controlling the representative assembly in an age which lacked two things which today exist in a highly efficient form: rapid transport and communications, and a party system—an organization specifically to connect the electorate with its representatives and the electors with each other. Hence, therefore, the importance of such communications as the letters which passed between Burke and the sheriffs of Bristol, and the strict views

held in America and France on the subject of the responsiveness of the representatives: in default of any intermediate body to whom to be responsive and responsible, either the locality was the controlling factor or the representative was virtually free. The development of communications and the party system has caused the representative system to change its meaning and forms. Of critical importance, further, to the meaning of representation has been the growth of great organized bodies of citizens in their economic callings and social pursuits. This subject is pursued further at a later stage.

Perhaps no short formula has ever better described the relationship between the representative and his district than Burke's address to the electors of Bristol in 1774.[29] So crucial is it for the present theme, and for that of leadership in a democracy that it must be quoted:

Their [his constituents'] wishes ought to have great weight with him; their opinion high respect; their business unremitted attention. It is his duty to sacrifice his repose, his pleasures, his satisfaction, to theirs; and above all, ever, and in all cases, to prefer their interest to his own. But, his unbiased opinion, his mature judgment, his enlightened conscience, he ought not to sacrifice to you, to any man, or to any set of men living. These he does not derive from your pleasure; no, nor from the law and the Constitution. They are a trust from Providence, for the abuse of which he is deeply answerable. Your representative owes you, not his industry only, but his judgment; and he betrays, instead of serving you, if he sacrifices it to your opinion. . . . if government were a matter of will upon my side, yours, without question, ought to be superior. But government and legislation are matters of reason and judgment, and not of inclination; and what sort of reason is that, in which the determination precedes the discussion; in which one set of men deliberate, and another decide; and where those who form the conclusion are perhaps three hundred miles distant from those who hear the arguments? . . .

Parliament is not a congress of ambassadors from different and hostile interests; which interests each must maintain, as an agent, and

24 *Ibid.*, p. 207.
25 Siéyès, in *Ibid.*, Vol. VIII, p. 594.
26 *Ibid.*, p. 594: "Here there is no question of drawing up a democratic survey, but to propose, listen, concert among ourselves, to modify one's opinion, finally to form in common a common will. . . . When we meet it is to deliberate, to know other people's opinions, to profit from reciprocal views, to confront particular wills, to modify, and conciliate them, to obtain a result common to the majority."
27 Monnier, in *Ibid.*, Vol. VIII, p. 560: "The people confides its sovereign power—in so far as it confides it it cannot exert it; but it can take it back whenever the depositories abuse it in order to oppress them; and when it recalls the power, it should return it as soon as possible with new precautions to assure its liberty and happiness."
28 Cf. Charles E. Merriam, *A History of American Political Theories* (New York, 1926); and cf. also the various declarations of rights in the American state constitutions of the Revolutionary period.

29 Cf. the interesting essay in Ernest Barker, *Essays on Government* (Oxford, 1945), "Burke and his Bristol Constituency."

advocate, against other agents and advocates; but Parliament is a deliberative assembly of one nation, with one interest, that of the whole; where, not local purposes, not local prejudices, ought to guide, but the general good, resulting from the general reason of the whole. You choose a member indeed: but when you have chosen him, he is not a member of Bristol, but he is a member of Parliament. If the local constituent should have an interest, or should form a hasty opinion, evidently opposite to the real good of the rest of the community, the member for that place ought to be as far as any other from any endeavor to give it effect.

In the program of the Communist party of the Soviet Union, adopted March 18–23, 1919, the theory of delegation is stressed to a point where the power to recall their delegates "in the most easy and accessible manner" is accorded to the electors. The constitution of 1925 stated (article 75): "The constituents who elected a deputy to a soviet shall have the right to recall him or her at any time and to hold new elections." And again in the constitution of 1936: "Every deputy is obliged to render account to the electors of his work and the work of the soviet of toilers' deputies, and may at any time be recalled in the manner established by law on the decision of a majority of the electors."

Actually, it will be seen from Soviet experience that the recall was used mainly as an extraordinary means of purging deputies disliked by the communist leadership at critical stages in the continuous revolution. It has otherwise been employed mainly at the city and village level. For the Soviet system has other ways—very effective—of "animating" its political class.[30]

The effects of the recall[31] on the government of a state in which not one monopoly party dictated but several par-

ties were in operation would be most chaotic, and furthermore would add to an instability of the parliamentary executive. As we have observed (p. 106) the Soviet Union denies the validity of the theory of separation of powers. It affects to replace checks and balances by such devices as the recall. It is noteworthy that in the French Constituent Assembly of 1946, the French Communist party declared for the "recall," but interpreted this to mean not recall by the people but cashiering of deputies *by their party!* Andrei Vyshinsky's sneering comments conveniently omit reference to the contrast between his own monopoly-party state and states with free parties.

As for the privilege of voting, the right to choose representatives was extended from time to time in the nineteenth century and recently, until now practically all males and females over twenty-one years of age are enfranchised. Over one hundred years of struggle were needed to secure this, although there was a widespread consciousness of the justice of the universal vote at the beginning of that time. But those in possession of political power realized that concessions would mean loss: only violence or the fear of violence could overcome this monopolistic attitude. This fear itself was of small effect while the disenfranchised were unorganized—and even when they were organized, so long as they were unwilling to act violently and the minority controlled the armed and disciplined forces. Therefore concessions were piecemeal and slow. In England the Reform Bill of 1832 was passed only after violence, threatened and actual, after a concerted attack on the credit of the Bank of England, and after a threat to dilute the blue blood of the peerage by "swamping" the House of Lords.[32] This was the consummation of a long and bloody skirmish begun in 1815. The Chartist movement with its warlike

---

[30] Andrei Vyshinsky, *Law of the Soviet State* (New York, 1948) pp. 719-23; and J. Towster, *Political Control in U.S.S.R.* (New York 1948).
[31] For the recall see: F. Bird and F. Ryan, *Recall of Public Officers* (New York, 1930). See newspaper accounts of the unsuccessful attempt to recall Roger D. Lapham, Mayor of San Francisco, in 1946.

[32] J. R. M. Butler, *Passing of the Great Reform Bill* (London, 1914); G. M. Trevelyan, *Lord Grey of the Reform Bill* (London, 1920); Graham Wallas, *Life of Francis Place* (London, 1898); J. Grego, *A History of Parliamentary Elections* (London, 1886).

demonstrations followed. Once the Act of 1867 was passed, politics were radicalized and the poorer classes naturally admitted their unenfranchised brethren. French development [33] was marked by actual and recurrent revolution. In Germany, the movement was pent up until the Revolution of 1848, which, proving abortive, accomplished no more than a declaration of universal suffrage. This was granted by Bismarck only as a price for support of his policy of unity.[34] This gift, however, was made to Germany and not to Prussia, and, until 1919, Prussia possessed a type of franchise especially designed to hold the masses in subjection; circumstances did not favor violent revolution until 1919, and this alone, under Prussian conditions, could produce universal suffrage.[35]

The Prussian system [36] contradicted the contemporary practice of the western world in so many points that it emphasizes (by contrast) those features now almost universally accepted. It explains, also, the queer nature of German policy before World War I, for Prussia was the dominant partner. The system was indirect and unequal, in contrast to direct and equal, suffrage. It was indirect in that the electors did not possess the right to vote immediately for their representatives in the House of Deputies, but the "original" electors (Urwähler) were only entitled to choose final electors (Wahlmänner), who then elected the deputies. The effect of organization by political parties, however, was to cause the election of those "final" electors. But the "original" electors had no equal right to choose the "final electors": their elective power was graded according to the amount of direct taxation paid. There were three classes of taxpayers. All in the constituency who paid the first one third of the direct taxes (in order of amount) comprised the first class; then came the second class, including the taxpayers in descending order until the line of two thirds in total was reached; and a third class contained the remainder. Hence the term "third-class system." This distribution of voting power caused, by the standard of equal suffrage, a serious distortion of representation,[37] for approximately, a voter in the first class possessed about four times the parliamentary power of a voter in the second and over sixteen times the power of a voter in the third class.

At one time, the Krupp family alone elected the whole representation of Essen. It is of special interest to notice the suggestion in a recent work, Hayek's The Road to Serfdom, that those persons who receive public assistance should have their civil rights limited. In nineteenth-century English poor-law policy, this meant deprivation of the right to vote. The resuscitation of the idea is interesting, as it seems once again to attempt to relate a defect in personal character, which is supposed to produce unemployment, to the right to a share in government.

A noteworthy effect of this inequality —equality is an incentive to all citizens because it encourages self-respect and self-expression and competition—was to reduce the electoral interest of all the three classes of voters, for the top class thought it unnecessary to go to the poll, while the other two thought it useless.[38] Even the oft-demonstrated electoral

---

[33] Léon Duguit and Henri Monnier, Les Constitutions, etc. (Paris, 1932), Introduction. Down to 1848 a distinction was made between the nation, which consisted of all the people, and "the legal nation" (pays légal), the latter being the small number of enfranchised adults.

[34] R. Augst, Bismarck's Stellung zur Wahlrecht (Leipzig, 1947).

[35] L. Bergstrasser, Die preussische Wahlrechtsfrage im Kriege (Tubingen, 1929). Cf. Arnold Brecht, Federalism and Regionalism in Germany (New York, 1945), p. 17 ff. Cf. also.

[36] Cf. H. von Gerlach, Das Parlament (Frankfurt, 1907).

[37] In 1908, for the whole of Prussia, the first class contained 293,000 electors; the second, 1,065,000; the third, 6,324,079. In 1913 (cf. Statistiches Jahrbuch für den Presüssischen Staat, 1914, Vol. XII, p. 634 ff.) the percentage of the electorate in the three classes was I, 4.43; II, 15.76; and III, 79.81. Cf. Schippel, Fort mit den Dreiklassen Wahlsystem (Berlin, 1890); Jastrow, Das Dreiklassensystem (Berlin, 1894); and Bock, Wahlstatistik (Halle, 1919).

[38] In 1913, Class I, 51.4 per cent; Class II, 41.8 per cent; Class III, 29.9 per cent of the electorate voted. This was in every case higher than at previous elections.

strength of the working class, even its services during World War I, failed to move the rulers to more than vague promises of reform, and, in fact, the people obtained electoral power only when they violently took it in the revolution of 1918. The defenders of the system used the subtle argument that only property owners ought to be represented because they alone had property: or, in other words, they could not risk the transfer of their property to others by being outvoted.[39] But this, again, was also a defense of the Hohenzollern monarchy, which could not have survived in a state based on universal franchise; and the monarchy was a bulwark of the social and political privileges of the upper classes, and these—especially the Junkers, the larger farmers, who obtained about one third of the membership of the House[40]— were most attached to dynastic despotism. The callous injustice of this system accounts for the ardent, even doctrinaire spirit with which the constitution makers of 1919 embraced all the known, if untried, devices, for equitable Parliamentary representation. From one extreme to another is one of the most frequent rules of political development.

WHO MAY CHOOSE REPRESENTATIVES?

Property and Educational Qualifications. The main qualification for the franchise in the nineteenth century, that which limited the numbers enjoying it, was the possession of property. Two main reasons were advanced for this. One was that the possession of some property was a trustworthy indication that its possessor was educated and therefore competent to pronounce upon public affairs. The other was

that if those who had no property were enfranchised there would be an end of private property. The first was advanced by such otherwise different minds as Hegel and Bagehot and Disraeli and members of the French Revolutionary Convention. That so crude and erroneous a test was acceptable to such minds (when in good faith) shows how difficult it is to measure political competence; but this acceptance is at least partly due to the difficulty of defining and applying a more accurate one to multitudes of people. Further, and from this point of view and this only, there was something to be said for it. Until about the year 1900, very few citizens in any country had the means of any substantial education, and the lack of private means implied a lack of education. Now, it is necessary to representative and responsible government that the electors shall be able to understand their own interests, the interests of the nation, the policy of a candidate for their suffrages, and the nature of parliamentary activity. For without this there is no judgment; yet the essence of responsible government is popular judgment. The real question, however, is whether people can exercise such a judgment without formal education. It is a mistake to imagine that formal education is absolutely essential, for we are often taught more by the informal (sometimes the chance) experiences of life than by schooling. This is not all. It is a fundamental fallacy to argue that political behavior has depended, depends now, or must depend upon instruction. It depends upon will, upon the passions, which are at the most modified by instruction, and men and women vote primarily for what they want and not from purely intellectual guidance. Thus, it is a fallacy to be-

---

[39] Cf. *Der Preussische Landtag Kein Klassenparlament,* by Julius Vorster, a member of the House of Deputies (Cologne, 1907).
[40] Cf. W. Kamm, *Abgeordnetenberuf und Parlament* (Karlsruhe, 1927). Cf. A. Rosenberg, *The Birth of the German Republic* (London, 1931), Chaps. I and II. The great change in representation was due partly to the redistribution of seats—until 1919 distribution rested upon a decree of 1867, when rural parts were more thickly populated than towns: a situation which changed remarkably after

1870. Cf. also W. H. Dawson, *The German Empire* (London, 1919), Vol. I, pp. 387-88. The shift in party strength from 1913 to 1919, with direct, equal, and proportional representation, was as follows (expressed as percentages):

	1913	*1919*
Conservatives	45.6	12.5
National Liberals	16.5	5.2
Democrats	9.0	16.2
Center	23.2	29.9
Social Democrats	2.3	42.1

lieve that the poorest, the most ignorant, ought not to vote because they will not know what to vote for—they know very well, even too well for some people's comfort. The real question, of course, is not whether people know what they *want*, but whether they know what is *possible*. There, education is vital; and we analyze the question in Chapter 14.

In most countries, then, the property qualification has been reduced to very small proportions or has ceased altogether, no more than mere residence for a short period being required as a preliminary to registration as a voter.[41] When

property qualifications were attacked, the defenders (in all countries) of the theory of government by the competent suggested the establishment of educational qualifications,[42] but it was found practically impossible to devise a valid scheme, and statesmen ultimately surrendered to the principle of mere citizenship. But a number of the American states have literacy tests for voting.[43] They are simple tests: some require mere ability to read; others require the reading of the constitution and the writing of the applicant's name; six Southern states require either the reading or understanding or reasonable interpretation of the state constitution. These tests were hardly established for the sake of an ideally good democracy but, in some states at least, to procure specific exclusions from the electorate.[44] In the Southern states the intention was to exclude Negroes—and this has been done, since the standard of success at an examination is set not by the candidate but by the examining registration officers, who are white. In the New England states the alien population fell too easy a prey to corrupt bosses to be permitted by the "forward- and upward-looking citizens" a

[41] In England, owing to the nonstatement of the rational theory of representation in constitution or statute, voters had as many votes as positive qualifications. This resulted in much plural voting. The Reform Act of 1918 permitted, at most, two votes per voter to be chosen among the qualifications of residence, occupation, and university degree. In 1945 it was estimated that there were 200,000 qualified to cast a business vote and 175,000 a university vote. Such a device is a defense mechanism for the more wealthy and educated, to protect them from the workers' vote. The Speaker's Conference on Electoral Procedure of 1944 decided to leave the subject alone, but the Labour government abolished the "plural vote" by the Representation of the People Act of 1948.

Before this Act was passed, there were in Britain twelve members of Parliament elected by the graduates of the universities. (This practice had commenced in the reign of James I). The Labour government proposed the abolition of the seats on the principle of "one man, one vote." To this the Conservative party and some independents strenuously objected. Their objection was not merely founded on the advantage they had possessed in almost always securing a victory in the universities, although no Labour candidate had ever been returned. They put forward the view that today, when the state is so extensively active, it was more important than ever to have members in the House who were independent of party, and the subsidiary argument followed that the university members were so unaffiliated. It is true that some notable members of independent views have come from the university constituencies: for instance, Eleanor Rathbone, the leader in the movement for family allowances, and A. P. Herbert—see his witty *The Ayes Have It* (London, 1937) and *University Member* (London, 1949)—who produced important changes in the law of divorce. In the Conservative argument there was still something of the ancient view that

representation was of communities and not of individual citizens grouped in areas—something of the corporate principle, as that principle had certainly prevailed when boroughs and counties were represented as communities. The Labour government's answer was that there was no more reason to represent the universities than the alumni clubs of the municipally provided schools anywhere in the land. Cf. *Debates* (February 16, 1948 onward).
[42] Cf. also G. Lowes Dickinson, *Development of Parliament in the Nineteenth Century* (London, 1895); J. Barthélemy, *L'Organisation du suffrage et l'Expérience Belge* (Paris, 1912); R. Smend, *Masstäbe der Repräsentation* (Stuttgart, 1912); and G. Leibholz, *Wesen der Repräsentation* (Berlin, 1919).
[43] Cf. Council of State Governments, *Book of the States* (Chicago, 1948-49), p. 96.
[44] R. R. Brooks, *Political Parties and Electoral Problems* (New York, 1933); E. M. Sait, *American Parties and Elections* (New York, revised 1948); F. G. Crawford, "The New York State Literacy Test," *American Political Science Review*, XVII, May, 1923; V. O. Key, *Politics, Parties, and Pressure Groups* (New York, 1947); and P. H. Odegard and E. A. Helms, *American Politics*, 2nd edition (New York, 1947).

place on the register without a test. At any rate, the tests are not any serious contribution toward the problem of electoral ability. They are pawns in the battle for social dominion, and exclude those who are considered heterogeneous on account of race or culture. Andrei Vyshinsky, in the treatise just referred to, alleges that the literacy tests are designed to reinforce the dictatorship of the bourgeoisie, everywhere!

The fact is that "political competence" is a very ambiguous term: it cannot be defined to the universal satisfaction, or even to the satisfaction of a majority of the people. Since it is not exactly definable, the prospects of difficulties in its administration stop those who are attracted by such a standard from its institution. Nor is the impersonal test which might be devised for intelligence and intellect any criterion by which to judge the moral excellence of an elector or candidate. This moral quality is entirely a subjective matter, itself in the very cockpit of politics; for what shall be considered "moral" in a nation's life is, in the modern state, to a large extent settled by law. It is difficult enough for the scientist to certify unsoundness of mind or prescribe the treatment for a juvenile delinquent, and when one arrives at the finer shades of moral rectitude one is baffled. I emphasize with all strength that it is exactly this uncertainty as to who is "right" and "good" in judging the direction society should take which has given birth to democracy and representative government: while the conviction of certainty has often given rise to minority and despotic government.

If we grant that those who are to elect and control government must justify their claim by their "understanding," then let us recognize two ingredients of political understanding. One is knowledge of fact, which includes history; and the other ingredient is values. When we use the word "moral" as we have used it above, we are referring to the fact that an act of political judgment is directed by a sense of values. The democratic theory is precisely that in the realm of values, each person must be presumed to have an equal

claim to speak, since there is no external objective test of value, that is, of the nature of the good life. This truth is denied by the dictators when they claim that government should be in the hands of those with special "competence." Its denial in a democracy implies the destruction of that democracy. The grave responsibility of placing even the queerest shade of idiosyncrasy beyond the bounds of potential validity has caused men both to offer and demand the inclusion of its opinion and weight in the lawmaking assembly.

Neither can there be an objective test of wisdom, which means judgment of the importance attachable to the various elements of a problem. This is certainly compounded of testable information, but its chief ingredients are intuitions, desires, and sanity of mind. But the democrat would say that such things are sacred. Knowledge, however, can be tested; and it is here that democracy is as yet most defective. A thorough knowledge of social affairs is fundamental to any real enfranchisement and sound decisions. Let us not pretend that uninstructed instinct can answer social and economic problems: it may be lucky or it may be disastrous, but it cannot be wise. Even then, we are unable either to teach or to test knowledge indefinitely. Science grows richer every day, but knowledge is still woefully lacking. When we reach that margin we inevitably shall, and do, set our course by large and imperfect socio-psychological generalizations—though science teaches caution. Equally, there is no doubt that tests based on knowledge now available, and indispensable to rational voting, would exclude some 95 per cent of all adults from the franchise.

These considerations throw into prominence two necessities: (1) the duty, for the future, of utilizing every social vehicle for promoting political knowledge: press, radio, periodicals, adult education, and so on; and (2) the dependence of the electorate upon a substantial number of rival leaders of wisdom and integrity, who may be sought through the selective filter of party organization. This still leaves much to hazard—the impediments and difficulties of the political party.

Other Qualifications. Thus, excluding race and sex discrimination, only the clearly distinguishable defects, like culpable pauperism,[45] certified mental deficiency,[46] and criminality, now bring exclusion from the franchise. Until recently, the armed forces were not permitted to vote, but the reason was far different from the other disqualification.[47] However, the value placed on the democratic army in the United States in World War II caused agitation for a federal law for military suffrage. Although it was defeated, the soldier ballot was enacted by state legislation. The Soviet government from the beginning enthusiastically enfranchised the Red Army, recruitment for which is draconically controlled by the Communist party.

Sex Qualifications. Female sex was an almost universal exclusion from the vote until a generation ago; the prohibition lasted longest (until very recently) in France, Italy, and many other, especially Latin, countries.[48] Female disfranchisement arose out of no rational consideration of woman's need to participate in political activity, but out of the general social position of women, as determined by sexual role, family life, and religious tenets.[49] It was assumed that man was, or

should be, the head of the family and the lord of women, and that woman's place was the home; it followed that women were "represented" in politics by their husbands. They were put off with cant about their beauty and modesty. But with the insistence of natural rights theories upon the uniqueness of individual experience, women found a way into political life. Among the pioneers of reform were men like John Stuart Mill and Charles Bradlaugh, not Christians in the ordinary sense of the word. The mass of men, securely installed in authority, were proof against argument until women formed militant organizations and worried and shocked them out of their domineering complacency. Some statesmen have ascribed their conversion to the efficient services of women in World War I. We cannot entirely exclude one other consideration: party competition to bid for the votes of the newly enfranchised.[50]

Our experience of universal suffrage is too short to enable us to say in what fashion the intervention of women has affected politics, or to make an accurate forecast. No country has general arrangements for keeping a separate record of the votes of men and women. Germany, from 1919, legally provided for separate ballot boxes, but left the power to the constituencies, and only an inconsiderable number used it.[51] The results showed that women's votes were almost identical in quality with those of men, except that women voted less than men (nonvoting is greater among the younger women), and

---

[45] In Germany including drunkeness, which endangers economic independence. The destitute are not disfranchised in England, France, or the United States.
[46] This is not easy to define and establish. Only this extreme limit serves to disfranchise; mental and moral weakness otherwise does not. Cf. J. Barthélemy and P. Duez, *Droit Constitutionnel* (Paris, 1926), p. 274 ff.
[47] So for France, Germany, United States; not so in Great Britain.
[48] In France, politicians were particularly afraid of the power which the clergy might win by their influence over the women—and the subject cannot be isolated from the struggle for political power between church and anticlerical statesmen. Cf. Leclerc, *Le Vote des Femmes en France* (Paris, 1929).
[49] Cf. W. E. Lecky, *Democracy and Liberty* (London, 1898); M. Ostrogorski, *Rights of Women;* John Stuart Mill, *The Subjection of Women* (London, 1869); Mary Wollstonecraft, *A Vindication of the Rights of Women* (London, 1792); E. R. Clough, *Mary Wollstone-*

craft and *The Rights of Women* (London, 1898); I. H. Irwin, *The Story of the Woman's Party* (New York, 1921).
[50] A critic of the German constitution of 1919, which enfranchised all women and men over twenty, raised the quaint protest that if it was difficult enough to accept the equality of voters (and hence the majority principle) when only men were voters, the convention entirely breaks down when one is counting women who have the vote, for they of a certainty are different from men. A. F. Freytag-Loringhoven, *Die Weimarer Verfassung in Lehre und Wirklichkeit* (München, 1924 and 1930).
[51] The power is derived from *Reichstimmordnung,* para. 5, established principally in order to make reference to voters' name easier.

that there was a slight bias to the parties of the Right, not least the Catholic Center party. This conservatism was also found to occur under the nazi régime, and in voting in Sweden, where a separate-ballot-box system was installed. Perhaps, too, the rise of the French Catholic party, the M.R.P., since World War II, is an evidence of this. One American study shows a definite inclination of women to the Republican party.[52] German politicians explain this conservatism by the aversion of women to the progressive and socialist parties, which on the Continent make of atheism and ungodliness a party religion.

In the course of legislative proceedings, women members have everywhere shown special interest in health, housing, temperance, social security, education, equality of economic conditions for the two sexes, international peace, and the abolition of the white-slave traffic. It is the intensity more than the direction of their interest which is important.

The wholesale entrance of women into politics must inevitably introduce complications, owing to the contact of different sexes. No one who has an experience of coeducation and cooperation in industry can avoid the conclusion that the minds of men and women are often diverted from objective considerations and are seriously affected by considerations of courtesy and the personal beauty and desirability of one of the opposite sex whose fate or interests are involved. Boys and girls tell lies for each other, and turn in work in some one else's name; pugnacity is aroused in the presence of girls, and discipline is audaciously rejected because it is humiliating. Time is wasted in philandering, and the mind loses itself in idle fancies. In business, women are often shielded from responsibility because of their sex; they are appointed because they are pleasing; they are dismissed or passed over in promotion because they are ugly. Women become extraordinarily devoted to their work because they are devoted to a particular manager, and work badly for others in the firm. We all know such facts, and they should not escape us in public life. And although the vast majority of people in a representative assembly, its committees, and the ancillary organizations may be married, and therefore presumably (but only presumably) less susceptible to the charms and wiles of the opposite sex, everyday experience teaches us to expect certain results.

Nationality Qualifications. Two other things are worth insisting upon in regard to qualification for voting. One is that all countries, including the Soviet Union since 1936, accord the vote only to their nationals: i.e., those who have acquired citizenship of a particular state by birth or naturalization. This is one of the directions in which nationality—that is, the sense of a collective whole with special rights and duties among its members and less tolerance towards alien collectivities— is expressed. In the Soviet Union the apparent liberality is possible because immigration is hardly permitted, least of all to non-Communists.

Race Qualifications. We must also notice the extent to which race affects the right to vote. In the Southern states of the United States, almost the whole Negro population [53] is excluded from the vote either by convention and fear of violence, by complicated and impossible requirements, or by administrative discrimination based upon "educational" tests. Other, more blatant means of exclusion have existed, but have been declared unconstitutional.[54] Exclusion of the Negroes from primaries is a question that has reached the Supreme Court several times in recent years. In 1932, to circumvent a previous high-court decision, the Texas Demo-

---

[52] S. Anderson and P. E. Davidson, *Ballots and the Democratic Class Struggle* (Stanford, 1943), p. 143.

[53] In 1940, with a total Negro adult population of 3,651,256 in the eight Deep South states (not including Oklahoma), only between 80,000 and 90,000 Negroes voted in the general election.
[54] Paul Lewinson, *Race, Class, Party* (New York, 1932) for a profound history and analysis; and G. Myrdal, *An American Dilemma* (New York, 1944), Chaps. 22 and 23. A certain number of poor, illiterate whites are accidentally excluded because they cannot come up to the residential, tax-paying, or educational standards.

cratic party ruled that the direct primary could be participated in solely by whites. The Supreme Court held that since the party was a private association, the state was not violating the 14th amendment, guaranteeing equal protection of the law by states to all. This decision of 1935 was reversed in 1944 in the case of *Smith* v. *Allwright* (321 U.S. 649). In Europe, national "minorities" lodged against their will in alien states were frequently obstructed in their rights to vote in spite of the guarantees of the minorities treaties; and in Germany, the nazi government withdrew the franchise from all Jews by race. The continual efforts by the Republican and Democratic parties to abolish or abate the poll tax in the Southern states —the present means of disqualifying Negro citizens—have been frustrated by the opposition of the Southern Democrats, especially by Senate filibusters.

In the Southern states of the United States, it has been necessary for the law to pursue the would-be discriminants against the Negro voter back to the primary elections, which were instituted to give the electorate the power of choosing candidates in each party. In these states, to secure nomination is tantamount to election. The Supreme Court said in *Smith* v. *Allwright*:

When primaries become a part of the machinery for choosing officials, state and national, as they have here, the same tests to determine the character of discrimination or abridgment should be applied to the primary as are applied to the general election. And, further, the privilege of membership in a party may be, as this Court said in *Grovey Vs. Townsend*, no concern of a state. But when, as here, that privilege is also the essential quality for voting in a primary to select nominees for a general election, the state makes the action of a party the action of the state.

(The bearing of this on international organization for peace and security is important and it is dealt with at some length in Lauterpacht, *An International Bill of Human Rights*, 1945.)

Hitler considered the vote as a defensive weapon of the *Volk*. Thus the Jewish people were not considered eligible to participate, since they were outside the classification of Germans or those "racially related," according to the nazis (not related by religion—for this the nazis held to be less detestable than "racial" features.) The Jews were subjects, not citizens, of the *Reich*. The victorious Allies under the impulse of their democratic theories, whether of the Western or the Soviet variety, accepting the doctrine of the equality of all men and women, abolished the nazi discrimination against Jewish citizens.

Age Qualifications. The age qualification for voting is almost everywhere coincident with that of the legal majority, though some countries set the age at lower than twenty-one (for example, the Soviet Union and Georgia in the United States, at eighteen, and Germany at twenty) and others higher.

I have nowhere met with a rational argument concerning the proper age to vote; it has been stumbled into without adequate consideration. Since natural-rights doctrines concerned the "citizen" and since the citizen was a man at his legal majority, the latter seems to have been accepted without examination. Argument has, in fact, been supplied only by those who take exception to the age of twenty-one. In the Soviet Union, where the age of eighteen was established, it was argued that economic productivity is a proper title to representation. Those who have set the age, or desire to set the age, above twenty-one, insist that the mind is not yet sufficiently mature to deliver a sound judgment upon political issues and that the youthful mind is too likely to vote for radical measures and enthusiastic but shallow-minded personalities. We can never know how far these theories are true, since the basis for statistical analysis is lacking. We *can* say that the official theory of the U.S.S.R. is that the democracies deliberately do not enfranchise at eighteen because they fear the political militancy of the young in favor of radical social change. Fascism in Italy was powerfully supported by young enthusiasts for Mussolini and that the Communist parties everywhere are a particularly powerful attraction to the young. The Nazi party in Germany found its most enthusiastic support in the youth of the country, but this may be partly put down to the unemployment that afflicted the country. Election figures for the United States in 1936 showed strong support of Roosevelt by the young voters—which was due partly to hero worship and partly to support of work-relief measures.

If experience may be held to teach, it seems to be a better arrangement to initiate youth into politics as early as possible; and the initial radicalism must be suffered in the hope that the extra period of voting experience will give a compensatory poise in later life.

No country in the world has yet thought of denying the franchise on the grounds of old age. The world grows kinder and wiser: some cultures starve their senile to death or bury them alive.

13

Representative Government Is Party Government

MODERN states, then, are ruled by the representatives of all their citizens, male and (often) female, of an age about twenty-one and over. These citizens are qualified by little more than their mere existence as indicated by residence, and practically no distinction is made on the grounds of property or ability. The voters are by law grouped territorially and in no other way, since representation of "interests" and Estates has been superseded by representation through equal electoral districts. The question now is what this system has achieved, and what its future is likely to be. This question cannot be answered without attention to others which arise out of it:

(1) Who nominates candidates for election as representatives?—the problem of this chapter.

(2) What influences are brought to bear upon voters and candidates in order to determine the result of election?—the problem of the next chapter.

There is no answer to these questions without an examination of the role played by political parties in representative government. It is difficult to analyze that role without the danger of losing a view of the integral function of party; but this difficulty attends all scientific analysis. We may say, then, that the function of political parties has two main aspects: (1) the organization of the electorate with the purpose of obtaining a majority, and (2) the maintenance of a continuous and responsible connection between representatives and constituencies from one election to another. It should be noticed that the better these two functions are fulfilled, the closer is the attainment of integration between political leaders and the masses. If an ideal standard were reached, then representative government would not need to be supplemented, still less replaced, by direct government: that is, by measures like the initiative and the referendum. Nor would it be necessary to include anything like article 142 of the Soviet constitution of 1936, which institutes the recall of deputies thus:

It is the duty of every deputy to report to the electors on his work and on the work of the Soviet of Toilers' Deputies and he is liable to be recalled at any time in the manner established by law upon decision of a majority of the electors.

These processes are intertwined: they have a common end. However, though not separate, they can be distinguished. Here we discuss the first, nomination and, in later chapters, the second, the influencing of voters in nomination.

REQUIREMENTS FOR NOMINATION

FIRST we should observe that various countries have required the age of candidacy as a representative to be higher than the age of voting. It is the distinction marked, on the Continent, between the active franchise (the right to choose) and passive franchise (the right to be chosen). The grounds are plain: legislators believed that greater maturity was desirable in the persons who actively govern than in those who merely choose representatives. (It will be recalled that eligibility for the United States House of Representatives is at age twenty-five, for the United States Senate at age thirty, and for the United States Presidency at age thirty-five. There is no similar age differentiation in England. In Soviet Russia the age of eligibility is twenty-three.) It seems to me, however, that if there is any validity in universal suffrage and representative government, there is no practical ground for the distinction. For if the people are to be truly represented, they must be able to judge of alternative policies and the respective capacity of candidates, and the mind—from the standpoint of age—that can do this can be trusted to do as much to make laws as the average member of a legislature in fact does. The rule goes too far, or not far enough. There are disqualifications (beyond those which exclude from the franchise) for candidacy: in France, *inéligibilité* extends to naturalized foreigners for ten years after naturalization, persons who have not satisfied military obligations, army and navy personnel on active duty, undischarged bankrupts, candidates and electors found guilty of corrupt practices, and officials (local and central) under varying conditions. In Germany, there was only one condition: naturalization for one year. In England, there are "incompatibilities" as the French say, which exclude certain people from Parliament but not from election: civil servants, the clergy, military personnel, and peers.

The law requires that a certain number of electors shall subscribe the nomination of a candidate, and it steers between the ideals of ease of candidacy [1] and preliminary assurance that the candidacy is not entirely frivolous. Both these points are of importance. But the latter has acquired special significance in recent years, because the efficacy of representative government has come to depend so much

upon the stability of the executive and, therefore, of party organization, that undisciplined candidacies which disturb party affiliations and upset "straight fights" between majority and minority are widely deprecated. In England, until 1945, candidates were required to deposit £150 with the returning officer, and this was forfeited if the candidate failed to secure one eighth of the votes cast in his constituency. It is doubtful whether this made much difference, though it probably had the effect of diminishing the number of Communist candidates, and candidates of various propagandist societies, who would stand not to win but to advertise their doctrines. In July, 1944, an all-party Conference on Electoral Reform and Redistribution of Seats recommended a change in this rule to make it easier for candidates to compete. The amount of the deposit was to be retained at £150 and was to be forfeited only if a candidate polled less than one eighth of the total votes cast where there were two or three candidates; or if there were more than three candidates, the deposit would be returned if a candidate polled one tenth of the total vote cast. The Conference rejected a proposal that the deposit should be reduced to £100, by eighteen votes to four.[2]

In other countries the law requires candidates to be sponsored by a number of electors who sign the nomination form: thus in England eight electors, in France one hundred, in Weimar Germany only twenty (provided that the party organization gave sufficient proof that it had at least five hundred supporters, and one such proof was the winning of at least one seat at the previous election.[3]) In the

---

[1] Bernard, *La Liberté de la Candidature* (Paris, 1925).

[2] *Cmd*. 6543: 1944.

[3] Cf. *Bergründung*, Law of August 24, 1918, article 6 (No. 1288 of 1928): "All proportional representation systems agree in the requirement that nominations must be endorsed by several persons, so that only seriously meant nominations shall be made and so prevent any casual adventurer or imperceptibly small group with inessential separate wishes from producing a harmful scattering of votes and thereby confusing and enhancing the difficulty of the electoral process." Severer regulations than this have been declared unconstitutional by the Supreme Court of State of Germany.

Soviet system under the constitution of 1936, no stated number of endorsements is required for candidates. The nomination is made by any of a number of social and economic organizations—above all the Communist party, which is assured predominance in the constitution itself. Soviet writers contrast the absence of need for endorsements in Russia with the need for them in other countries, declaring that the Soviet method is an evidence of a free democratic system of government!

NOMINATION IN ENGLAND, FRANCE AND GERMANY

The Local and the Central Caucus: with Special Reference to England. The main point, however, is: who actually nominates the candidates? The law, excepting in the United States, does not intervene, and nomination is left to the voluntary arrangements of the voters. Now it is clear that candidates are nominated because they and their supporters hope to win the seat, and, to do this, an organization to attract the attention of electors is necessary. As soon as the constituency becomes so large in area and number that a candidate cannot in person be known to all, a means of approaching the electors must be established. The necessity grows in proportion as the citizen's time available for political reflection is reduced by preoccupation with family duties and economic pursuits. For then the candidate must not only break through the barriers of territorial distance but also must overcome the resistance of the voter's fatigue, ignorance, and lack of interest. In the modern state, constituencies contain very large numbers of inhabitants [4] and are

extensive in area. In spite of the advanced condition of industrial technique and the means of travel between home and workplace, the voters' daily work exhausts them. They certainly show no signs of wishing to reduce their standard of living by absence from work for the sake of politics. This set of obstacles the candidate must overcome; but this he cannot overcome without an organization. Although such organizations first grew up to help the candidate,[5] they were later transformed to help the electorate also. But they were always established with a particular system of political principles in mind. Citizens founded local caucuses or local party organizations, and arrogated to themselves the power to select candidates. Their justification was their intention to serve their principles and their candidate. Selection by such bodies does not preclude other electors from acting similarly, but experience has shown that there are all too few citizens sufficiently conscious of their political powers to cause embarrassment by selecting excessive numbers of candidates. Still, with universal and equal suffrage, such embarrassment was and remains a possibility. A distinction between European and American parties must be remembered: the former fight chiefly for principles of public policy, the latter much more, though by no means entirely, for "spoils" (even though it is not desired to minimize the assertion of opposing principles by the American parties, especially since the New Deal). The distinction will become clear as the facts are unfolded throughout the rest of the book.

The local caucus desires to obtain the realization of its political principles—in

Cf. G. Kaisenberg, *Die Wahl zum Reichstag* (Berlin, 1928), pp. 8-13.

[4]

Country	Average Number of Inhabitants per Constituency
Great Britain (S.M.) 1946...	70,000
France (S.M.) 1946........	62,000
Weimar Germany (P.R.)...	1,800,000
U.S.A. (S.M.) 1946.........	320,000
Belgium (P.R.) 1946.......	40,000

(*S.M.* means single-member constituency; *P.R.* means proportional representation.)

[5] Cf. M. Ostrogorski, *Democracy and the Organization of Political Parties* (New York, 1908), 2 vols., for the United States and England; further, E. E. Robinson, *The Evolution of American Political Parties* (New York, 1924); E. and A. G. Porritt, *The Unreformed House of Commons* (Cambridge, 1903); J. Grego, *Parliamentary Elections in the Old Days* (London, 1888) and L. Namier, *The Structure of Politics at the Accession of George III* (London, 1929), 2 vols. For Germany, see L. Bergsträsser, *Geschichte der politischen Parteien Deutschlands* (Berlin, 1926).

other words, to govern other people. There is no certainty, however, that it will succeed unless its representative forms part of a majority of like-minded people. The need for a majority, therefore, causes candidates for office, local bodies of citizens, philosophers, and would-be leaders to seek each other out, to form a homogeneous policy, and to act in concert. In other words, they seek to discover the conditions of power before they proceed to fight for it, lest by not knowing them, they waste their efforts upon a representative who insists more upon his idiosyncrasies than upon his solidarity with others. The result is the creation of political parties—that is, the association of men and women who broadly agree upon the principles of government and their application, in Burke's definition of a party: "a body of men, united for the purpose of promoting by their joint endeavors the public interest, upon some principle on which they are all agreed," or in a modern German definition, "a battle fellowship established in the form of a permanent association, to obtain power over the State to realize political aims." [6]

It is essential to a party's objects that it should extend beyond the boundaries of a single constituency, and most modern parties do, in fact, spread over whole nations. This at once raises various questions of centralization and localization, an important one being that of the selection of candidates.

In England, about 1800, the choice was mainly local with small central interference, loyalty to party principles being secured both by a statement made by the candidate in answer to interrogations from the few sponsors, and by the judicious use of office and bribes. Gradually, after the Reform Bill of 1832, the large and continuous increase of the electorate compelled more deliberate and concerted or-

ganization, and the politicians of the Clubs (the Carlton and the Reform), the private secretaries to cabinet ministers and opposition leaders, and later, the central party agents, became the advisers of the local associations. The arrangement was convenient and useful, because in England, differently from the United States, neither law nor custom required or requires today that the candidate should be a resident of the constituency; so that a central reservoir of candidates was possible. The source being centralized, it was possible to compare candidates with one another and with the different needs of the constituencies. The central agent was then able to advise the local associations who had no candidate of their own. But it was advice only, and even now continues, in the main, to be only that, though it is very influential and often enforceable by appeal to the needs of the party for special talent and by an implied threat that political and administrative facilitation will be withheld.

The conditions under which such advice is given have greatly altered since the middle of the nineteenth century. For the party has acquired the character of a distinct and conscious nation-wide community. A feeling of unity now pervades the aggregation of local bodies. They recognize that they are ultimately parts of a single thing, deriving significance from a place in a system, composed of creative purposes and defensive and offensive impulses against hostile groups. What caused the growth of this feeling? Many things: the experience of corporate struggle, victory, and defeat; the exercise of governmental power; the influence of a succession of leaders whose personality and fame had that aura which produces loyalty and worship; the moving quality of significant causes; the growth and operation of centrally directed propaganda based upon large funds of money; the newspaper reiteration of creeds; and finally, the growing consciousness of the individual voter that the whole—the party—is mightier than its parts—the local associations. It must never be forgotten that the whole of Great Britain is relatively small. The

---

[6] Cf. H. Triepel in *Staatsverfassung und politische Parteien* (Berlin, 1930). The reader is also advised to study Max Weber's essay, "Politics as a Vocation," p. 77 ff. in his *Essays in Sociology* (New York, 1946), ed. by H. H. Gerth and C. W. Mills.

figures of the size of its constituencies in-dicate that but partially. The smallness of the island, and the density of its popu-lation, contribute more strikingly than can be imagined by outside observers to the rapid circulation of impressions throughout the entire country. This all contributes to a clear consciousness of issues and an association for political pur-poses about which, relatively speaking, confusion is not too confounded. British conditions always recall the observations of Aristotle on the need for an area small enough for *all* citizens to "know one an-other's characters"[7] and Rousseau's sim-ilar views.[8] Of course, we speak with the relationship between size of the state and the availability of excellent communica-tions in mind.

Victory is the first law of politics, and to this end all other laws are subordinated. If victory is more certainly attainable by centralization, then party organization is centralized. Centralization has triumphed, though this is far from meaning that local liberty has ceased to exist. The con-ditions of successful war are well known. Power must not be wasted, since how much will be called for cannot be exactly predicted. Therefore, there must be no quarrels within the camp, and pugnacity must never be turned inward, but always outward. Hence local supporters of the same party ought not to fight each other: one candidate for one seat is enough. To quarrel, especially on the eve of battle, is to discourage one's own supporters and to suffer defections, while encouraging the enemy. If, then, quarrels cannot be avoided, the intervention of a higher au-thority which can impartially represent the loss to the whole party community is desirable: it will ask for a sacrifice of the less to the more important, and a suppres-sion of the relatively undesirable to avoid the absolutely undesirable, namely, the defeat of the party by a victorious opposi-tion. Further, all strategy is one: forces must be concentrated where opposition is greatest and not wasted on gloriously

winning one's own strongholds. If this is to be accomplished, a skilled organization, a general staff, must concentrate informa-tion and material about the whole of the front and distribute it according to local need.

The party is a fighting organization, and it must obey the rules of successful war-fare. One of those rules is that the central directing agency must watch over the quality of the local candidates, and with the growth of party unity and the knowl-edge of the rules of success, the central office has acquired a good deal of power in the matter of nominations.

Local associations may insist upon their own candidates. Unless there is a really serious reason why they should not be adopted, they are "endorsed" by the cen-tral office.[9] Endorsement means that the central office approves of the choice and will help that candidate during the cam-paign. The local association may have no persons considered clever enough to meet its standard for a member of Parliament, or it may lack the special qualities needed to win that particular constituency. If this is the case, the central office is ap-proached. This already has a long list of people who urgently aspire to election,

---

[7] *Politics*, VII, iv; and *Ethics*, IX c.x, 3.
[8] *Social Contract*, Book 9.

[9] Cf. for the rule, the Labour party constitu-tion, 1944, clause IX. This clause requires, among other things, that the candidate accept and act in accord with the parliamentary laws of the Labour party, which subjects him to the discipline determined by the whole of the group in Parliament and therefore gives the leaders considerable power over him. There is no such clause or rule in the Liberal or Conservative party constitutions, but their practice is sometimes severer than that of the Labour party. For the Conservative party, see, e.g., the correspondence between the South Paddington Conservative Association and the headquarters in 1930, when the Association was excommunicated by headquarters. The constitutions of the Continental and American parties occasionally contain clauses on this question. It must be remembered that the local organizations, although composed of in-dividual members of the party or of trade unions, have affiliated with the party (this ap-plies to the Labour party), have accepted its policies, principles, and politics, and have promised to conform with the constitution and standing orders of the party and to sub-mit their political rules to the National Ex-ecutive Committee.

and of these several are suggested to the local association. They are invited before the nomination committee or the executive committee of the local association. The secretary of the association, or its agent, interviews the candidates beforehand, and experience shows that his judgment has much to do with the final choice. The reason for this is clear: the secretary and the agent have a vital interest in victory; they are employed (the agent, in fact, is paid) to engineer victory. They have, as a rule, had actual experience of organizing campaigns, and they are able, better than the committee, to calculate the chances of success for a candidate. Thus there comes about a certain abdication of judgment on the part of the amateur; and the permanent employee benefits from this abdication. In Weimar Germany, one even heard of the "party bureaucracy." [10] However, the will of the committee, if it wishes to exert it against the secretary or agent, is final.

What, then, is the composition and state of mind of the committee? The committee is no more than about a score of members of the local party association. This again is nothing but a body of voters, rarely running into thousands, who have formally joined the party, having formally attested their belief in the principles of the party, and who regularly contribute to the party funds. This body formally elects its executive committee, and the executive committee is the continuously active administrative authority of the party. It is the "machine" for selecting candidates. Its members are the politically conscious, aspiring, and energetic members of the electorate; they have read a little, attended meetings, learned the party jargon and, thought a good deal. They are capable tacticians, knowing their locality well. Some, perhaps, serve or have served as municipal councilors —such office being not seldom the crumbs from the rich man's table to reward them

for their services. Upon them falls the decentralized management of a ward in a number of streets preparatory to a campaign.

What considerations determine their choice of candidate? The dominating consideration is victory. It is true to say that a local caucus would rather send an inferior man or woman to Parliament than lose the seat with a superior one. For in Parliament all members are equal; the greatest number controls the law and its administration. However excellent the candidate, if he cannot win he is electorally deficient. Better a seat without a brain than a brain without a seat! The candidate who impresses the committee as a winner receives the nomination. First, then, the candidate must be loyal to the party. This means not absolute acceptance of every jot and tittle of its creed, but a satisfactory reply to the committee's questions, which may be, and often are, based (a) on partial ignorance of the party's program, and (b) on some disagreement therewith. The candidate must in this interrogation "satisfy" the committee. He need not do this by a parade of legislative wisdom or by proof of his moral qualities; he must, however, "persuade" them that either keeping within the bounds of party loyalty, or any deviation therefrom is desirable; and he must persuade them above all that he can win. For the local caucus is fond of a candidate who can add to the party's stock of policy: it persuades them of their independence and their own creativeness: but he must be a winner first. A detailed description of the methods by which one commends himself to others as a successful person is here not necessary: charm, manner, wit, humor, moral incandescence, along with more substantial qualities like wisdom, knowledge, intelligence, and a sincere, if crudely articulate, passion for social justice or for any other ideal. Any of these things and many others may win the committee's support. Sometimes these things will so affect the committee that they will miscalculate the speaker's party loyalty and chance of success. Other things, too, may affect the judgment: gratitude or hope for gifts of

---

[10] The position of the "bureaucracy" in the party is stressed in Max Weber, *loc. cit.*, and Robert Michels, *Political Parties* (London, 1915), who first emphasized the oligarchical tendencies of modern parties.

money or other property, conviviality in the party's festive meetings, deference to a hereditary title or large estates, admiration of success in literature, the theater, or philosophy, or respect for long years of work as a trade-union official or social worker. This represents the main features of nomination; the essence of which is the collaboration of the local with the central wills.

This is far from ignoring the activity and effect of sectional economic and social interests which are an outstanding mark of modern social life. For though the modern state has built upon the notion of free and equal citizens, it has not produced them in all the stark nakedness of the abstraction. The consideration that the peculiar interests of a special group should be represented has some weight in directing the nominations. For example, in coal-mining areas a preference is shown for employers and trade-union officials connected with the industry. Here and there in the shipbuilding constituencies a similar thing occurs, so also in agricultural constituencies. This occurs rather more in England than in France and the United States, where there are more "professional" politicians: that is, lawyers, journalists, and others who are prepared to represent any constituency, whatever its chief economic interest.[11] However, as between candidates of the same interest, the main generalizations regarding other kinds of candidates hold good.

This, however, is certain: that few, if any, of the selection committees in England and France (the United States varies only slightly) rationally analyze their own part in political life. If they did they would ask themselves the fundamental questions: What are the functions of a parliamentary representative in the modern state? How far ought he to think for himself, and deviate from the party's formally declared policy? What qualities are appropriate to a critic of one's own party; and what qualifications are required to participate productively in committee work, in the control of the civil service, in discussions on finance and foreign affairs? But to answer these questions, or even to know that they should be asked, requires a sense of public affairs and a knowledge of public administration such as exceedingly small numbers of citizens now possess. Because it lacks wisdom and knowledge, the local caucus becomes dependent upon the judgment of a few leading men and women at party headquarters. And even when their judgment is not accepted, they cannot prevent their nominee from coming under the influence and discipline of the central executive of the party once returned to Parliament, for he is not likely to be able to do or say much without the aid of the party's information service and handbooks on political questions. Now, since the party must, for its very life's sake, have a minimum number of experts of different kinds—good debaters, able committeemen, financial experts, some especially expert in each great branch of social and economic legislation and in international affairs—headquarters seizes every opportunity that offers to claim a comparatively safe seat for such candidates, and local caucuses rarely dispute such claims. Nowadays, the number of such experts is at least about one tenth of all the seats contested by a party. Again, England is more earnest and rational in this respect than either France or the United States, for the former has had an unstable executive and restiveness towards party leadership, while the latter is hampered by the "residence" rule.

One other thing: some of the candidates selected and returned are members of the central executive authority of the party and thus are tarred with its brush, although it is true that they have helped to make the composition with which they are colored.

It is enough, so far, if we have indicated how the idea of party unity and the effects of party organization overcome the atomization of the electorate. We shall later

---

[11] In 1935 at least 117 of the 166 British Labour M.P.'s were trade unionists. In 1945 it was estimated that 79 were trade-union officials—but the Labour members who were members of trade unions, manual and non-manual, is estimated to be about 231 out of a total Labour membership of 394.

observe the operation of other forces in the same direction. But we have described mainly English practice and the generalities regarding other countries. There are national deviations, due to different traditions, needs, and history.

Nomination in France. In France, local caucuses still play a far larger part in selecting candidates than in England, for neither the principle nor the organization of nation-wide political parties has been accepted as a controlling necessity. The principle of the second ballot forces the local organizations to pay special attention to the local situation, and their judgment has strong influence upon headquarters. A large number of parties exist, and so little possess the organizational qualities usually considered essential thereto, that even after the dreadful experience of 1940–45, they are frequently called *groups.* They have not the unbroken continuous history of the English and American political parties: the biggest and strongest are hardly more than four decades old. The *Parti Radical et Radical Socialiste,* the *Section Francaise de l'Internationale Ouvrière* (Socialist party), the *Parti Communist,* and the *Mouvement Republicain Populaire* (M.R.P.) have a fairly well-organized system of headquarters endorsements, called *investiture,* where the "federations" in each *département* which group the party members make the nomination which for parliamentary elections must then be ratified by the central directing committee. But there is still more forcefulness in the local committees than in England. The various parties of the Right in the past, as now, were less determined on securing discipline by insisting on endorsement. In 1930 the *Alliance Démocratique,* an election organization of Right groups, declared its repugnance to central endorsements, though it gave them. Criticizing the Left-wing parties, it said: [12]

The Alliance will not fall into these excesses. It requires discipline, but it does not impose the *perinde ac cadaver.* It is the great party of free men, masters of their opinion and sov-

ereigns of their own thoughts. . . . From the parliamentary point of view do we offer that solidly organized group, that center of attraction capable of drawing into its orbit the errant planets? No. We have only a nebulous group policy.

These Left parties managed considerable integration of candidates in their ranks before World War II. But there have still been weaknesses, more especially on the Center and Right. Numbers of candidates fight as quasi-independent or completely independent. The latter are run by local election caucuses, *comités,* which are self-constituted electors, sometimes including government officials directed by the *maire* or *prefet* or their close friends. They are free in their choice of candidate—that is, neither law nor custom binds them to the wishes of a constituent body, nor do these oblige them to obey a higher authority speaking in the name of a party. But their number has been sharply reduced since 1945. The extent of real party discipline is only imperfectly revealed by tables showing the numbers of "integrated" and independent candidatures. Before World War II this intraparty incoherence was a fundamental defect of French government; since then it has been considerably remedied because of the increased strength and resolution of the Left-wing parties (though this has its own evils) and the organized reaction to them. Its consequences are grave; the full import cannot be stated cursorily. Every part of the political machine suffers: the Parliament, the cabinet, the civil service, local government. Unless there is a cohesive force in the electorate, there can be no concerted arrangements for the nomination of candidates; unless there are such concerted arrangements, there is no cohesive force after the election campaign to hold the representatives together in a permanent and settled frame of mind and behavior. The initial cohesive force was almost entirely lacking in France before World War II except in the Communist, Socialist, and Radical-Socialist parties, where the influence of trade-union discipline, passionately held

---

[12] *Congrès Nationale,* 1930, p. 28 ff. and p. 116.

convictions, and capable leaders produced a sense of party community and loyalty.

Since World War II, when the immense social stresses were emphasized under German occupation, and the experience of organization in the "underground" was gained, all the major parties have become more integrated, including the new M.R.P., while the Resistance Party, or General de Gaulle's *Mouvement Unifié de Resistance* (a catch-all, but mainly Right), promises another political organization. Altogether this means that about five sixths of the membership of the French National Assembly has now come under well-integrated party organization. Yet we have still to see whether the individualism within each party can be so easily wiped out in practice, or the enmity between the parties.

Strong party organization used to be absent because, in the main, the French denied that the unit of government today is, or ought to be, the party. Almost incredibly, they still clung to the old dogma that the elector is sovereign and separate, and that the unit of political life is first the voter and then the representative. This was the result partly of character, partly of historical events; it is impossible to assess the proportions of each. But it is plain that there was little appreciation of the necessity of government, and indeed, government has not been kind to the French people. The majority (not all) of French people did not (perhaps still do not) wish to be governed, though they wish to govern; and the consequence is that they are badly governed. For some organization is indispensable and inevitably develops; but it develops in a hostile world, not in an environment of temperate control. Part of the energy which would otherwise be devoted to service the government uses to defend itself; and, since it has no friends, criticism makes it resentful and malicious. To a foreigner it was amazing, indeed, to observe the blankness of the French political mind in regard to party. In the literature of political and electoral reform there was much said about the electorate and its incompetence, but parties entered, if at all, as a minor

afterthought or as a lamentable misfortune. Indeed, it is impossible to refer to any French book—as it is possible to refer to scores of works for England and the United States—which specially handles the problem of party organization as the vital part of democratic technique, which it is. There are histories of political ideas and struggles, of crises which have thrown up organizations like the radical bloc of 1906–10 or the *bloc national* of 1919 to meet them—histories of outstanding men like Gambetta, Waldeck-Rousseau, Combes, Clemenceau, and Poincaré, who have embodied and proclaimed a sensational and transient cause. But that is all. This deficiency gnaws at the very vitals of French government, laming its every part. Its basic causes are indicated in Chapter 16—they are related partly to culture and partly to the predominance of the vast small-agricultural and petty-bourgeois element in the national economy.[13]

The French collapse of 1940 was due in part to this lack of electoral integration, since it weakened leadership. But it should be remembered that in the postwar elections the parties of negation, chiefly the Radical Socialist party, lost ground. With the strengthening of at least three parties

---

[13] These views are confirmed in Léon Blum's *For All Mankind* (London, 1946), e.g., p. 49: "The same congenital inability to create genuine and regular parties explains the distasteful and often revolting character of our parliamentary struggles, the persistence of personal rivalries, the impatient and often dishonest bitterness of the struggle for power. Politics is not a sport, but, like every other kind of struggle, it becomes degraded and is repulsive to the spectator if it is not governed by rules imposing a certain minimum of honesty and propriety. It is clear, I think, that impropriety and dishonesty in politics can be prevented only by stable parties, whose stability itself leads them to respect in opposition the code of behavior from which they in turn will benefit when they become the Government. Further reflection will reveal no less clearly that it is the lack of organized parties in France that makes the elected representative the agent of his electors, and that it is to the same cause, much more than to the undoubted weaknesses of our electoral system, that we owe the reduction of elected members to the role of representatives or custodians of local interests."

of major dimensions that advocate substantial social and economic change, the situation is altering. Indeed, the observer in the *Assemblée Nationale,* after 1946, recognizes a notable solidifying of party alignment, loyalty, and action.[14]

Nomination in Germany. Between the Prussian constitutional conflict of 1862–66 and the advent of World War II, strong, but numerous, parties developed in Germany. The renaissance of political parties after the defeat of 1945 shows the same characteristics as those we now describe. The largest parties, the Social Democrats, the German Nationals, the German People's party, the Center, and the Democrats, had organizations—central and local "machines" as thoroughly organized as the English and American—and often the organizations went down to details which were left unregulated by the latter. The parties were strongly centralized,[15] and the nomination of candidates was influenced by the central office, even more than in England. Since Germany was a federal state there was, formally, a separate political life in each of the component states, and this is the expression of certain real differences which still prevail in spite of the unitary movement and in spite of the nazi attempt completely to unify the country.

State politics required of the political parties two concessions in regard to nomination. *First,* they had to have regard for the special situation of the party in the state legislature. *Second,* the distinct political features of the country had to be "represented" by the nomination of those who knew them at first hand. German political literature is full of the admonition that geography should be regarded in representation. Certain parties, therefore, mainly the parties of the Right, which, more than those of the Left, insisted upon

state rights—were built up out of state party associations. The German National party was composed of 44 state associations. The Center (this Catholic party was, after World War II, replaced by Christian Democratic parties which include non-Catholics) was composed of 19 state associations and 16 provincial associations. The rest went mainly by electoral administrative districts: e.g., the People's party by 35 constituency associations, the Democratic party the same, the Social Democratic party by 33 secretaries, and so, too, the Communists. These culminated in *Reich* party conference, party committee, and executive committee.

Further, the peculiar electoral system which was instituted in 1919 provided for proportional representation, based on the "automatic" and "list" method,[16] and operating in 35 tremendous constituencies with an average of 1,500,000 inhabitants each. This system had the unforeseen effect of giving the parties more influence upon nominations than they possessed before.[17] Since the electors voted for party lists, the order of candidates on each list was vital to the chances of election: and after the fourth name on the list, further names need not have been given. The central machine felt bound to see that the "right" men were put in the "right" places. Further, a special list of candidates called the *Reichslist* (that is, the national list) had to be drawn up by each party in order (1) to obtain its proportion of the seats to which its surplus votes from the constituencies entitled it, and (2) as there were no by-elections, in order to form a reservoir from which representatives could be chosen when the party lost members of the *Reichstag* by death or resignation. The list was composed by the party leaders —the *Bonzes,* as they were called—and clearly the order of appearance on the list became essential. In the postwar period

---

14 Above all is the Communist party centralized as to candidatures, general discipline, policy, and a doctrine of obedience to the central machine. Cf. *Statuts du Parti Communiste Français* (Paris, June, 1945).

15 This in spite of the fact that the *Statuts* of the parties contain a federal organization, as they do also in France, Britain, and the United States.

16 That is, one seat is given to each party for every 60,000 votes polled; and fractions are gathered together to form a special national list, which benefits the parties. Voters vote not for candidates but for lists.

17 Cf. F. A. Hermens, *Democracy or Anarchy, A Study of Proportional Representation* (Notre Dame, 1941).

the German state constitutions have continued proportional representation.

NOMINATION REGULATED BY LAW: THE UNITED STATES

Now, in the countries of which we have spoken, legislative regulation of the selection of candidates is practically negligible. This is not so in the United States. The difference is so striking, and so important for the relationship between political cause and effect, that it must be discussed at some length. In the United States, owing to the excesses of political parties and groups of self-willed men, nomination has received close attention and has been submitted, one cannot yet use the word "subjected," to statutory regulation.

Machines: Their Rise and Reform. In the 1820's and 1830's the modern American party machine was created. As the decades passed, its chief elements became: (1) a democracy ignorant but strongly conscious of its sovereign power, (2) a monopoly of politics by men who made it a regular "trade," and (3) the availability of all the paid administrative offices, central and local, as "spoils" with which the victorious party could reward its supporters. Both the vast expanse of territory (soon to be over thirty-one times the size of England) which had to be covered by propaganda and drill if votes were to be turned to account, and the theory of the "rotation of office," which had as its object and consequence a multiplicity of elective offices and elections, made party organization at the same time essential and difficult; but, once party organization was established, it was even more difficult for dissentients to overthrow its rule. Oratory, graft, blackmail, deceptive demagoguery, and despoliation of public lands and resources welded the parts into an unbreakable machine obedient to the "boss." Stupidity, political conceit, and immigration prior to World War I caused the lower classes to fall into the boss's hands. The ruthlessness of his invincible tactics, combined with the people's haste after dollars, caused the wealthier and educated classes to abandon political competition. All nominations fell into the hands of professional politicians linked through ward, district, city, county, state, and country.[18]

This organization had (and still has, though in a much smaller quantity) remarkable commodities for sale. Through municipal government, it sold immunity from police interferences, contracts for all public works, leases for streetcar, gas, electric-light, and water service; through the state governments, contracts were obtainable, laws were passed for private benefit and others were weakly administered, joint-stock companies could obtain charters of incorporation permitting the spoliation of the consumer by monopoly rates, and ugly banking and insurance practices, and the evasion of civilized restraints in the pay, hours, hygiene, and safety of industry and commerce. "Booze, betting, and brothels"—the three B's, to which may be added a fourth, building regulations—were (and are) fertile fields of money and political pressure. The courts of justice could be "squared;" naturalization could be granted to or withheld from immigrants; from the Federal authority could be filched a share in the "pork barrel," that is, the mass of annual expenditure upon internal improvements; laxity of customs and tax administration prevailed; and the postponement of legislation needed in the public interest was obtainable. Moreover, hundreds of thousands of paid offices, legislative and admin-

---

18 Cf. E. L. Godkin, *Unforeseen Tendencies of Democracy* (London, 1903); Harold Gosnell, *Boss Platt and the New York Machine* (Chicago, 1924) and *Machine Politics: Chicago Model* (Chicago, 1937); James Bryce, *American Commonwealth* (New York, 1908), 2 vols.; M. Ostrogorski, *Democracy and the Organization of American Political Parties* (New York, 1908), Vol. I. Also cf. more recent studies: R. C. Brooks, *Political Parties and Electoral Problems* (New York, 1933); E. M. Sait, *American Parties and Elections* (New York, revised 1948); Frank R. Kent, *Political Behavior* (New York, 1928). On bosses see J. T. Salter, *Boss Rule* (New York, 1935) and *The Pattern of Politics* (New York, 1940); C. Van Devander, *The Big Bosses* (New York, 1944); E. Schattschneider, *Party Government* (New York, 1942); and E. J. Flynn, *You're the Boss* (New York, 1947).

istrative, were obtainable by the electoral voters.[19]

A famous American cartoon depicts some birds of prey upon a mountain crag. Anxiously they scan the heavens, full of the thunder, lightning, and rain of Justice. By their talons are the picked bones of the Treasury, Justice, and the Suffrage. The legend runs, "Let us Prey!" This injunction was executed largely by the sale of nominations of candidates for the benefit of private interests. In a democratic system, however, some show of public consultation is indispensable to the permanent reign of the "boss"; and, indeed, nominating committees of party delegates called *primaries* had a history going back to the Heroic Period of American history.

The primary is simply another name for the local caucus or local association of party members, the basic or original cell of party members who meet to designate candidates for the smaller authorities, and delegates to the higher or secondary conventions which select the candidates for the higher political offices. They are, therefore, vital parts of the democratic system; and until recent years they were thoroughly corrupt, especially in the large cities. The local politicians arranged primary meetings in such a way that their will destroyed the public's. The arrangements produced an expressive terminology. The "slate" was made up privately by the "bosses," good citizens being sometimes included in it. The party membership roll, inclusion in which gave the right to vote at the primary, was either falsified to exclude opponents of the slate makers or "padded" with false names. "Repeaters" voted several times, while the primary scrutineers or inspectors appointed by the henchmen of the "bosses" could not, curiously, detect impersonation. Date, time, and place of the meetings were arranged as inconveniently as possible for dissentient elements. The places chosen were sinister saloons in shady neighborhoods; and they were "packed" with rowdies.

sometimes lent by the organization of the rival party on the principle of "live and let live." The procedure was "cut and dried," the chairman with his henchmen tolerating no nonsense. Ballot boxes were "stuffed" with fraudulent votes, or more direct ways were taken with the count. "Snap" primaries were held, that is, meetings were fixed and held suddenly, without due notice; or sometimes, the chairman's watch being unaccountably fast, the meeting was held and over before the innocent voters arrived. This system exploited the power of the general will and destroyed its judgment.

About 1870 America began to awake to a consciousness of political degradation, and a stimulus was given to political reform.

Having defined the people so as to include women as well as men, the Progressive Movement aims to give to a majority of the people so defined an easy, direct, and certain control over their government. The first of the measures proposed by the Progressive Movement to give to the people greater control over the nomination and election of candidates is a direct primary law. It has long been the boast of politicians that they do not care who elect candidates to office so long as they have the power to nominate them.[20]

Direct primary laws were passed in most states during the ensuing years. While practice varies rather widely from state to state, the general intention is to take the powers of nomination away from the party managers and give them to the people, as directly as possible. This involves the establishment of a special meeting at which the nomination shall take place, and, further, the regulation of its procedure.[21]

---

[19] A rough estimate of the number of offices still so available is 770,000.

[20] B. P. De Witt, *The Progressive Movement* (New York, 1915), pp. 196-97.
[21] "Essentially the direct primary system is a system for making nominations by popular elections—the Primary held under state management. When applied to all offices it abolishes not only the state convention, but lesser conventions in districts, counties and cities, and popular caucuses of primaries as well. The convention system was a representative and indirect method of making nominations; the direct-primary election system is direct in that it places the nominating power in the hands of the voters themselves."—R. C.

The problems inherent in this system are obvious upon reflection. They are these: (1) Who has the right to attend and vote? This involves the definition of a political party and the test of membership of a party—assuming, as American theory and practice assume, that the primaries are to be based upon the recognized existence of political parties. Is the primary to be "open" to any voter, or "closed" to all but the communicants of the party officially in charge of the primary? (2) How is a candidate for nomination brought to the attention of the primary—how is he "designated," as the jargon goes? (3) What majorities are required for an effective choice of candidate?

Definition of Party. Parties are legally defined by the strength shown at previous elections, a minimum being laid down in terms of votes or percentage of the poll.[22] The New York definition of a party is a political organization which polled at least 10,000 votes (at one time 25,000) for governor at the last preceding election; in Texas it is 100,000. This number is so small compared with that usually polled that it is not unfair to the aspirations of new and rising bodies of opinion. The percentage tests are sometimes severer; in Maine 13 per cent of the total vote is required, in Illinois and Pennsylvania 3 per cent. But the large percentages of 20 per cent and 25 per cent are required in Kentucky and Alabama, respectively (and 50 per cent in Florida), the explanation here being that a large reduction of this minimum would involve the danger of specifically Negro parties. Some states, in order not to block the path to political expression, provide that recognition as a party may be obtained upon a petition signed by a certain number of voters, usually ranging from 3 to 5 per cent.

Now parties, thus defined, are obliged to obey the law regulating the procedure of the primary. Minority parties are not thereby excluded from the general elections, but nominate by petition, their nomination appearing on the ballot papers in those elections.

The definition of parties in these terms is not wanting in exactness. This cannot be said of the definitions of membership of a party. When a test of party affiliation is imposed by law, the primary is said to be "closed"; when no test is established, the primary is "open." Only Wisconsin, Montana, California, Minnesota, and Washington now have the open primary. In these states the voter is given the ballot papers of all parties together, secretly marks and returns them so folded that his choice remains undetected. With this system the party affiliation of the voter is not revealed; undue influence is thus avoided, which might subject the voter to concentrated electioneering by canvassers or might even obstruct his change from one party to another as his opinion changes. The open primary, however, has the serious defect that it is dissolvent of party: for members of other parties may press into the primary of the dominant party and interfere with its domestic politics, sometimes with the intention even of causing the election of the weaker candidate, while the managers within their own primary use the votes of people not strictly their own, to determine the issues in their own camp. This has occurred in both Wisconsin and Michigan.[23] In most states the open primary has therefore given way to the closed.[24]

The tests imposed in the closed primary system consist of declarations: these may be made either before or at the primary. Those made before the primary are classified under the "enrollment system"; those made at the primary, under the "challenge system." The voter makes a declaration of one of two kinds: (a) as to past allegiance and (b) as to present affiliation and intentions. The latter are much more frequent than the former.

In New York, the voter declares his

Brooks, *Political Parties and Electoral Problems* (New York, 1933), p. 260.
[22] Brooks, *op. cit.*, p. 264.

[23] E. M. Sait, *American Parties and Elections*, pp. 400-02.
[24] Cf. M. McClintock, "Party Affiliation Test in Direct Primary Election Laws," *American Political Science Review*, August, 1922, pp. 265-67.

general sympathy with the principles of the party and his intention to give its candidates general support in the next election. In some states enrollment takes place at the primary.[25]

May a voter, having enrolled, change party? Provision is made for this in most states; and it consists essentially in personal or written application to the registrars within a minimum time before the primary elections. In other states a change of affiliation is allowed only during the normal registration period.

Voters so enrolled may, in several states, be challenged at the primary to give proof of having previously voted for the party. Such challenge, however, is politically dangerous since it may drive the voter to support the opposition party at the general election.[26]

In the "challenge" system, the voter swears at the primary that he did not vote in the primary of another party for a period of so many years or, positively, that he voted for the party in the last election or, prophetically, that he will vote for the party at the next election. We discuss the effectiveness of these arrangements later.

Designation of Candidate. In the South and West, a large number of states permit candidacy by a simple declaration and by the payment of a fee. In others a petition is required, supported by a stated number or percentage of the party votes.[27] These qualifications must sometimes be accompanied by the payment of a fee. Further, the supporting voters are often required to belong, so many or such and such a percentage, to well-dispersed local government areas in the constituency. Some states, finding the primary elections difficult to run without previous concert among the party leaders and officials, arrange for "preprimary designating conventions." Here in the assemblies elected under rules determined by the respective parties, the delegates vote for the candidates: a certain quota of votes, for example, 10 per cent, entitling each candidate thus endowed to appear as a candidate in the primary.

Votes for Election. The primary elections for candidates are likely to suffer the same conspicuous difficulty as ordinary elections: namely, that if the ordinary rule of relative majority prevails, where there are more than two candidates for one place, a minority of votes may triumph. Remedies have been devised. In some states the alternative-vote system is accepted in order that the candidate shall ultimately achieve an absolute majority. Iowa has a plan which requires that when no candidate obtained more than 35 per cent of the total vote, the primary is dispensed with, a state convention taking its place. Other states having a specific percentage system abandoned it for the relative majority, since experience showed that while crucial issues resulted in a two-sided contest, only personal issues caused a many-sided contest, and these issues did not concern the public so much that a minority victory needed to be prevented by special legislation. Other states have adopted the second-ballot system or, as it is technically called, the "double primary": a second ballot being cast between the two top candidates when no absolute majority is obtained at the first ballot.

Value of the Direct Primary. By these methods American legislators have sought to break the power of the "party managers" and to give back to the people the power of choosing their representatives. Have the methods succeeded, and if so, to what extent?

(1) What has been the effect upon the party machine? It has been weakened, but not very much, for its organizing and campaigning services are almost indispensable to success in primary candidature and in the subsequent elections.[28] The candidate

---

25 Cf. also J. R. Starr, "The Legal State of American Political Parties," in *American Political Science Review,* June, 1940; C. Berdahl, "Party Membership in the United States," *ibid.,* February and April, 1942; and Louise Overacker, "Direct Primary Legislation, 1936-1939," *ibid.,* June, 1940.

26 Brooks, *op. cit.,* p. 269.

27 They vary with the importance of the office sought in each case.

28 F. R. Kent, *The Great Game of Politics* (New York, 1926), Chap. XXXV, also his

for nomination is not now so completely dependent upon the party managers for selection as before. He needs the support of the voters at the primary, and if he can obtain support he can dispense with the benediction of the bosses. He is then involved in two duties: he must induce people to attend the primary, and to vote for him. That is, the procedure to win a seat at a general election must be followed in order to win a candidacy, not always in so intense a manner, for the battle is within the party fold and not against an external opposition. But human nature does not, because it cannot, so easily solve its problems. Even as at a general election candidates seek anxiously for "wirepullers," for those with more than the ordinary influence, and even as they negotiate with interests and groups, so, at a primary campaign, they tend to gravitate to the party managers or to become the satellite of some more powerful man who himself seeks higher office.

Further, where there are acute personal differences within a party (which may happen anywhere in the United States), or where there are real political differences about state politics (as in parts of the South and the North and West), or where one party is so fast in the saddle (as in the South where the Democratic party has an almost exclusive hold upon office), then nomination is equivalent to election to office, and the primaries become the field of intense electioneering. Hence there arises a quantity of mendacious and spiteful publicity about the candidates (I, myself, have witnessed this in several elections) which is rare in European countries except when rival members of the same party fight each other. Thus the public is treated as the arbiter and is canvassed more sedulously, on the whole, than under the previous system.[29] The party managers are still important in this process, but, obviously, votes in a properly regulated primary campaign cannot be

"traded" quite as easily as before, though they are traded.

(2) Have normal party functions suffered under the direct primary? Part of the answer to this question is that the primary elections have affected the normal functions of party by shaking its foundations —hierarchy and discipline. This has come about in three ways: *First,* it has become less easy to distribute nominations among the orthodox and heterodox groups in the party. Just as political parties in France can be induced to "concentrate" in a ministry by the gift of a number of portfolios, so in the United States it was possible, before the primary laws, to keep the party together by dividing out the offices of the state among the various subgroups. The primary system enables the triumphant majority to behave despotically, but it still recognizes the value of some distribution of offices. *Second,* differences which were formerly settled in private can now be ventilated, but hardly settled, in public. Any dissentient element need not obey the majority or concede part of its claims for the sake of unity, since it is licensed to fight in public for its own candidate with its own policy. Nothing is so bitter as civil war, especially among professional warriors, and nothing is so difficult to quiet as its aftermath. That has been taught in England by the private and public conflicts of Lloyd George and his opponents in the Liberal party after 1924, the National Labour members (MacDonaldites) and the Labour party after 1931, and Churchill and the Conservative party in the period 1933 to 1940; and in Germany by the feuds between the Majority Socialists and Independent Socialists between 1918 and 1921. Imagine such conflicts made permanent and public! American observers emphasize the disintegrating effect upon party counsels, and the loss to parliamentary institutions, and to the public itself, which is asked to judge differences of opinion which it cannot really judge, since they are too many and often personal.

Finally, the "committeemen," that is, party officials and workers, are chosen at

Political Behavior (New York, 1928); and especially E. J. Flynn, *You're the Boss* (New York, 1947).
[29] Senator George W. Pepper, *In the Senate* (Philadelphia, 1930), Chaps. I, IV, and X.

the primaries also. Formerly such members of the hierarchy, particularly those at the top, were self-chosen and got themselves elected or ratified by the conventions, which were manageable. At any rate they had about them an air of authority— that is, the presumption of rulership with a title from an elevated source. They had a prerogative derived not really, although ostensibly, from election. Their title may have been morally bad, and its destined uses corrupt. It had, however, the quality of reducing the lower members of the hierarchy to obedience and, therefore, of making and keeping the party one and indivisible. All the ranks of committeemen and candidates now come from the same source: election by the sovereign people. This would, in any case, cause a weakening of cohesion and responsiveness throughout the body of the party: but there is the defect also that committeemen are sometimes elected before the candidates for whom they are to manage the election campaign, and since the party may be fluid in policy and membership, dissensions may and do arise.

It is not easy to say how far party disintegration has been caused by the direct primary. In the first place, quantitative measurement being impossible, observers differ widely in their estimation. In the second place, opinions differ not according to what is actually observed, but according to the observers' ideals, some desiring to discredit the primary because they believe that it threatens a well-integrated biparty system without which representative government breaks down, and others desiring to applaud it because they believe that, even with it, party managers will pursue, as in the past they have pursued, infernal plots against the people.

The truth seems to be that party organization has been endangered, that it has even suffered, but that the party managers have been able to adapt themselves to the requirements of the primaries singularly well.[30] They prepare their "slates" as before. They pull the strings as before,

with a little more difficulty and, to compensate for this, with more ingenuity. Though their power is decreased by the threat of a potential revolt against them, it has been increased by the addition of one more set of elections to the already great number upon which the professional politician must instruct the public. The system forces political leadership to come out into the open of the primary, but the vital needs of instructing the masses and of thinking and concerting before instructing still throws leadership into the hands of the "invisible government." And the ignorance of the public is proved by the necessary existence of primary laws which, to avoid the advantage obtainable by candidates with names first in the alphabet, provide for an order determined by rotation, or by priority of petition, or by lot.

Preparatory to the Congressional elections of 1938, Franklin D. Roosevelt intervened in the primary campaigns in Alabama, Florida, Oklahoma, Georgia, South Carolina, Maryland, Tennessee, and Kentucky. The intervention was more than a failure; it was damaging to the President.[31] The fact that most of the successful candidates were incumbents and in control of their local organizations was the potent factor. Also, Wendell L. Willkie in the 1944 preconvention campaign judged his prospects (unfavorably) by his failure to win in certain primaries; Harold E. Stassen, in 1948, made a general onslaught in the primaries for the party nomination, with mixed success. The results of the primaries in these cases were taken as indications of the prospects of the leaders. The action signified an attempt to create a steady party following at the earliest stage in the election process.

(3) Are the party tests valid? The answer is that the tests of party affiliation have proved to be the least satisfactory part of the primary system. Where the test is strict and elaborate, as in the South, no more has been accomplished than to cause the voter to reiterate current party jargon which he is apt to learn direct from the

---

[30] Cf. V. O. Key, *Politics, Parties, and Pressure Groups* (New York, 1943), pp. 340-72.

[31] Cf. James Farley, *My Story* (New York, 1949), Chaps. 13 and 14.

lips of the inquisitor, whose interrogation is lax for fear of driving away votes. The real purposes of the voters who take the test are beyond the scrutiny of the inspectors. It is said that the voters are impelled to register and some to participate in the primaries because they like the thought of having one more vote. Voting figures show quite clearly that primaries are invaded, and that voters register for one party and then vote for another. It is clear that a party test is practicable only under the following conditions: (*a*) if the parties are sundered by clear and definite programs of which the voters are entirely ignorant but which, having blindly accepted, they will maintain at the ensuing election; or (*b*) if the parties have clear and definite policies separating them, if they are sincere in wanting only the convinced voters on their register, and if the voters are so convinced by the program, which they fully understand, that they could neither enter the primary of another party nor vote for any but their own candidates at an election. Neither of these prerequisites exists. The voters are neither blind nor fully enlightened; the parties are neither certain of their own policies nor scrupulous in gathering votes. All are somewhere between, and consequently the party label may mean something, but it does not mean much for long.

(4) What has been the effect on campaign conduct?—in light of the fact that it is impossible that the primary election should take place without a preliminary campaign, which may be conducted in the open or in the dark? Open campaigns are necessarily conducted when the petitions are being pushed, and this process has raised two problems—that of fraud and force in the collection of signatures, and the public regulation of "publicity" and its cost. Apart from the costs to the state, which are considerable, the candidates' burden is exceedingly heavy.[32] Although

some states forbid party expenditure upon primary campaigns and although others strictly limit the expenditure, in fact the rules are evaded. The very process of appealing to the people inevitably returns the power to the place whence it was to be revoked: to the party, which possesses the instruments of publicity, the workers, and the money. (In the pursuit of equality, Oregon has arranged for the state publication and distribution of a publicity pamphlet for primary purposes. There is a pamphlet for each party, and each candidate may therein publish his portrait and reasons why he should be nominated. Any person or persons may file an opposing statement. A flat rate is charged for one page each to candidate and opponents.)

(5) Are the primaries actually free from party control? Actually, the instinct for preprimary control of the primaries cannot be smothered. Some states have set up preprimary conventions in order to give parties the opportunity of consultation and concerted arrangements. This is an inevitable development, whether the law recognizes it or not. For in a democracy nothing is to be done without a majority, and majorities do not come readymade. The existing parties, those with a history, do, in fact, privately conspire to help candidates and so let the public know whom they have chosen.

What is it that causes this flight from the party to the primary, from the primary to the preprimary, and from this, maybe, to the pre-preprimary—and thence back to the boss? It is the belief that somewhere there is the pristine voter, pure and undefiled, who, if properly informed, will vote as an ideal man for ideal parties and policies, without organization. It is the flight from men to man, from Americans today to Adam before the fall. Since man does not exist, the party still contrives to take his place.

(6) What are the effects on political participation? The numbers attending at the primaries are small, outside the South or elsewhere where one party dominates. Key has shown that in the South in 1942, from 10 times as many voters to an equal

---

32 Cf. S. Ervin, *Henry Ford vs. Truman H. Newberry* (New York, 1935), which reveals that $190,000 was spent by Newberry; C. H. Wooddy, *The Case of Frank L. Smith* (Chicago, 1931), which shows that over $1,000,000 was spent by Smith and his opponent in 1926.

number of voters participated in the primaries as in the general elections; while in all other states the participation ranged from 77 per cent in North Dakota to 43.2 in Wisconsin and 24.9 in Utah.[33] Yet the number of people participating in a choice of candidate, with the effective opportunity of choice, is far greater than the number who concern themselves even to this extent (which, at the minimum, is to ratify the choice of the party) with the selection of candidates in England, France, Germany, and other countries where nomination is unrestricted by law. This cannot but have a rousing effect upon the voters, if we admit at all that experience is capable of teaching.

(7) Can candidates and policies be coordinated? Experience shows that difficulty arises with regard to the "platform" or compendium of policies which the party puts before the electors. If a convention of a party frames a platform, it is not sure whether any of the adherents to that platform will be elected. If several candidates for nomination are put up, are they to suggest their own policies? But for the voters this means woeful confusion if the policies are set out at length. Therefore short, compendious pronouncements have been proposed, and, in one case, actually adopted.

To an English or Continental observer, nothing in politics can appear so quaint and dangerous to truly effective, as distinct from apparent, representation, as the choice of candidates with little or no continuous guarantee of a policy. In a large number of states, party conventions, voluntarily or by law, establish a platform —some before, some after the primary. But there is not that contact between candidates and policy which comes by their previous identification and selection on its basis. In other states, councils of candidates and sitting members formulate the policy. This is better than the convention system as a means of bringing the policies, the candidates, and later judgment upon their work, into close correspondence. But the more an automatic legal separation is

effected between candidate and policy, the more must party be relied upon to make them combine.

(8) Finally, has the direct primary system caused the choice of "better" or "superior" candidates? American observers speak with an uncertain voice in answer to this question. One says that it is impossible to prove that it has produced a superior type "in the absence of accepted standards of measurement to determine political ability and virtue." [34] The utmost he concedes to the primary is that "given a popular revolt against the machine of sufficient magnitude, it is possible to break the slate of the latter." He gives one example of this, and concludes: "No doubt the possibility of such untoward events induces a certain moderation on the part of political bosses that is doubtless salutary. On the whole this seems to be the greatest single advantage that can be claimed for direct primary elections after twenty years' experience with them." Another says: "Yet no judicious and impartial observer will contend that the new nominating system has revolutionized the character of candidates with reference to their ability, their integrity or their representative character. This is a part of the great problem of democracy, which cannot be so simply solved, and which will not be determined either by directness or indirectness in methods of selection." [35] A third says: "But there has already been no advance in the quality of public offices since the abandonment of the nominating convention." [36] A fourth says that "Doubtless some men have been nominated who would not have been nominated under the former system, or at least would not have been nominated so easily, but it cannot yet be affirmed that the type of man who is successful in politics has been materially altered." [37] And a fifth concludes that a really effective

_____

[33] Key, *op. cit.,* p. 362.

[34] Brooks, *op. cit.,* pp. 275-276.
[35] Charles Merriam and H. F. Gosnell, *The American Party System* (New York, 1940 edition), p. 280.
[36] Sait, *op. cit.,* pp. 419-420.
[37] A. W. Bromage, *State Government and Administration* (New York, 1936).

nominating system in the United States awaits a fundamental change, that is, the development of responsible government: that tinkering with the nominating mechanism is of small value.[38] Boss Flynn concurs.

NOMINATION AND ELECTION OF LEGISLATORS IN DICTATORSHIPS

THE characteristic mark of the selection of candidates in democracies is the openness and freedom of opportunity to all individuals to become candidates, and for any free grouping of citizens to propose them. The mark of candidacy in dictatorships is the reverse: the dictator or the ruling group and the dictator's party exercise the monopoly of nomination and conduct of the election campaign. To use the word "election" is, indeed, a misnomer, because the word implies a choice, whereas the dictatorial practice is the artful and forcible denial of choice—indeed, its deliberate seduction.

Fascist Italy. In the heyday of Italian fascism, the single-member election district was abolished: there were no local nominations. The system was that 400 candidates were placed on a single national electoral list, all together, and submitted for election *en bloc* throughout the nation. These 400 were selected from 1000 nominees presented to the Grand Council of Fascism by the legally constituted confederations of employers and employees and various social organizations. The council could and did include other "distinguished" candidates, thus displacing some of the others. Competing lists could, by law, be put up by any organization having more than 5,000 members, but no competing lists were ever drawn up,[39] and in fact, no organizations could exist without the permission of the fascist government and party. There was considerable competition within the party for nomination: only Fascists were nominated, and it was the object of all ambitious men to please the chiefs at the top of the hier-

archy. Loyalty and good works, within the interpretation of the régime, were the first qualifications.

Nazi Germany. The single-list system was also instituted by the nazi government, and though the details differed from Italian fascist practice, the end attained was the same: nomination by the party hierarchy, and the exclusion of freely-offered alternative candidatures.[40]

The U.S.S.R. In the Soviet Union, the nomination of candidates is vested in "public organizations and societies of the working people; Communist party organizations, trade unions, cooperatives, youth organizations and cultural societies." This is stipulated in article 141 of the constitution. Article 58 of the U.S.S.R. Election Regulations,[41] gives the right to nominate candidates to the central organizations and societies of the working people and their republic, territorial, regional, local and district bodies, as well as to general meetings of workers and other employees in enterprises, to general meetings of servicemen in army units, general meetings of peasants in the collective farms, villages, and so forth. The nominations are made to the "area" election commission. Such area commissions are formed of representatives of the various organizations already mentioned; they are appointed by the executive committees of the various Soviets, local, regional, republic, and upwards; and they manage the official side of the election. The nominations made by the various organizations are submitted to the area election commission along with the minutes of the meeting which designated him or her and comprehen-

---

38 Louise Overacker, *op. cit.*

39 Cf. Herman Finer, *Mussolini's Italy* (London, 1935), p. 258 ff.

40 Cf. *Nazi Conspiracy and Aggression* (U.S. Government Printing Office, 1946 and 1947), Vol. I, p. 220, and documents referred to therein.

41 Cf. *Information Bulletin,* Embassy of U.S.S.R., Washington, November 24, 1945. Cf. also R. Somerville, "The New Soviet Elections," *American Quarterly of the Soviet Union,* October, 1938. Above all cf. J. Towster, *Political Control in the U.S.S.R.,* Chap. X. A. Y. Vishinsky, *The Law of the Soviet State* (New York, 1948), pp. 711-12, admits the domination of the Communist party, but makes light of it while failing to give a full, realistic account of its pressure!

sive information about life and career of the candidate. The election commission of each republic and the central commission for the whole U.S.S.R. supervise every process from nomination to final registration of the elected deputies. By their power to consider complaints regarding "incorrect" actions of the commissions, they are able to influence beforehand, or amend after nomination, any proposal they consider against the public interest. Candidates have been replaced by others, even after their names have appeared on the ballot, by the area election commission or by higher authorities.

What stands out in this procedure is the role assigned to "organizations" or "collectivities," or "meetings," and their official nature. They cannot be called without the permission of the governing authorities. But all such authorities are dominated by the only political party permitted to exist: the Communist party. At the pre-election meetings this same party, and the Communist Youth, and the leaders of the organizations who are Communist, set the pace and direct affairs. Only those who have demonstrated their loyalty to the regime are nominated; only those devoted to the cause of Lenin-Stalin are considered worthy to stand for election. But the Communist party seeks to draw the non-party people—and about ninety-five per cent of the people are not members of the party—into the election process. They form with them the "bloc of the Communist party and non-party people." It is strongly desired, and enjoined from the top levels of the party downwards, that the people be not alienated, but on the contrary persuaded into union with the party. Many non-party nominations are made: many more, of course, in the local soviets than at the top, and more in the legislative branches than in the executive directorates of the various levels of government. This cannot be called a free election system, for it is dominated by the Communist party, and if there are non-party nominees and later deputies, it is by grace of and to the satisfaction of the party. The enthusiastic accounts which

the Soviet Government itself gives of the nominating process show genuinely that what may be called the élite of Soviet society are nominated: those who have rendered distinguished service in every sphere of life are honored by being made deputies: teachers from kindergarten upwards, skilled workers of all kinds, leaders of the nomadic communities, scientific workers, the organizers of the social services, physicians, engineers.

The ballot papers do not contain two or more candidates for each place: only one nominee for each office is agreed upon at the pre-election nominating meetings and negotiations. Thus, there is a rich representativeness of Soviet economy and society. But it will be remembered that between representative government and responsible government yawns a wide gulf. The efficacy of the Soviet election procedures may be gauged from the results: [42] in the elections for the Supreme Soviet of the U.S.S.R. on February 10, 1947, 99.7 per cent of the registered electors voted: while 99.18 per cent of the electors who voted cast their ballots for the candidates of "the bloc of Communists and non-party people." What *is* surprising is that even 0.81 per cent opposed the nominees. This they did, not by offering alternative candidates but by merely scratching out the names of those on the ballot. A little over 10,000 ballots were found invalid, either by reason of more than one candidate being left on it, or for other reasons.

Thus, the vast body of electors are not in fact free and equal, though they are in law and in political opportunity. They do not spontaneously move in an undifferentiated and incoherent mass. They are marshaled, and their candidates chosen for them, by those who have worked to acquire the controlling positions in the parties. It is in a sophisticated sense only that the people choose their representatives.

[42] *Information Bulletin*, Embassy of U.S.S.R., Washington, March 12, 1946.

Nor are the voters left to their own devices once candidates have been nominated. For the aim of a group or a party is to send its nominees to the representative assembly or the executive offices which are open to election. Therefore a continuous process of "education" is undertaken by the parties. It increases in intensity in the few months preceding an election, and becomes furious in the final fortnight.

Before the activity of the parties is analyzed, it is essential to consider the qualities without which sound representation —that is to say, public opinion—is impossible, and to ask how far the electorate possesses them.

14

Public Opinion and the Parties

THREE qualities are indispensable in any system of representation (if that word is to have its plain meaning, that is, the presentation of the will of the constituents in a common assembly where representatives meet representatives): the first is that those who are to be represented know what they want; the second, that they are able to express what they want; the third, that they are sufficiently interested to utter their wants.

THE NATURE OF PUBLIC OPINION

WE are in the realm of a subject which, though it has been made one of the cardinal studies in political science in the last twenty years, is still perhaps lacking proper analytical definition.

Most definitions of public opinion will, upon study, be found to reveal that one of three possible meanings is intended: (1) public opinion as a record of *fact;* (2) public opinion as *belief;* (3) public opinion as *will,* that which it is intended shall be done. It is important that the student should reflect upon the use of the term and distinguish which of the above three meanings is apposite in each of his particular contexts. It cannot be said that the professional writers have accomplished this clarification yet; and the failure vitiates their "public opinion" polls and problems of measurement.[1]

(1) By opinion as a record of *fact* is meant such a simple statement as "The price of bread has gone down" or "I know the United Nations exists."

(2) By opinion as *belief* is meant not only a record of fact but a valuation of the fact or facts involved, culminating in a prophecy of the probability of future events. For example, "The United States will not become socialist." It puts a weight on facts and constructs trends.

(3) Public opinion as *will* includes facts, includes the valuation of them to found a belief, and then goes beyond it to assert that it is worth while to pursue a course of action. Thus, "China should go to war with the Eskimos—Yes or No?" Or "Should the secret of the atom bomb be revealed to all—Yes or No?"

Politics is most concerned with public opinion as will—which typically eventuates in a statute and in administration. But in order that public opinion as will may be sound, it is essential for public opinion as a record of the facts to be sound, and for public opinion as belief to be founded on the facts and to be interpreted by the opinion developer according to a logical and reasonable social valuation of the facts. Now the last sentence raise serious difficulties which will be touched upon presently.

Belief will be created by two ingredients added to fact. One is the power of logical

---

[1] Lindsay Roger's *The Pollsters* (New York, 1949), published since this work was written, has addressed some very proper admonitions to the sounders of public opinion.

thought and inference, and the other is spiritual values. Few secrets any longer exist about the aspect of public opinion involved in logical thought, for the fallacies to which the mind can be victim have been thoroughly discussed from Aristotle onward and are to be learned from his *Rhetoric,* Hobbes's *Leviathan,* Bacon's *Novum Organon* and *Advancement of Learning,* Bentham's *Book of Fallacies,* and Hegel's *Phenomenology of Mind,* not to speak of many recent academic treatises on logic, such as the works of Morris R. Cohen and (of exceptional importance) M. Oakeshott's *Experience and its Modes.*

When the Institute of Propaganda Analysis lists the devices of propaganda, it is merely listing the well-known fallacies under a new slang or jargon: thus, name-calling ("rabble-rouser," "reactionaries"); glittering generalities ("democracy" used as a cover for carrying on faulty arguments); transfer (the use of symbols such as the flag or the cross or the clenched fist or the upraised arm to provide acceptance of a policy which, it is implied, is authorized by the virtues of the symbol); testimonials (using somebody else's recommendation and authority); plain folks (the confidence trick on the people you are talking to, known as *argumentum ad hominem*); card stacking, which means merely suggesting all the false points and suppressing the true ones (well-known for thousands of years as *suggestio falsi* and *suppressio veri*); and finally the band wagon ("140 million Americans can't be wrong"—join in).[2] These well-known logical errors, recoined, and sometimes merely

expressed in psychopathological terms, are almost all that public opinion analysis consists of. They have been known for centuries even before Francis Bacon expatiated on the idols of the Tribe, the Cave, the Market, and the Theater.

One thing more needs to be added. The premise, to observe the facts and interpret them, is also a question of: (1) interest in acknowledging all the phenomena, and (2) our moral attitude to man and society. The first is heavily dependent upon our economic and social position, and this is not a matter simply of class differences but involves the vertical occupational differences in a society and also our personal situation within the community or school or economic enterprise in which we happen to work. Both (1) and (2) at once involve what have been called *stereotypes, blind spots, codes,* and *myths* [3]—that is, limited versions of the truth, limited to selections from the booming, buzzing world of a million facts which will be of interest, use, and moral support to ourselves. Our symbols are created for simple, abbreviated thinking and for our determination to protect our interest and moral position, or to win what we want. They roughly correspond to Bacon's idols of the Tribe and the Cave.

Public opinion is compounded of perception of the facts, logical inferences from them, and moral interpretation of them. It is clear that between ourselves and the facts occur a number of processes which may distort our reception of them. Therefore, the process of distortion will determine our opinion as will, which becoming so distorted, may not solve the problem that we wish to see solved.

In any case, the facts of relevance to opinion regarding modern society are not the simple facts of everyday apprehension, but come necessarily from afar and through mediums of mass communication. Those means of communication are owned by a few people, who themselves have an opinion and therefore an interest in presenting the facts so that they are not

---

[2] *Propaganda Analysis* (New York), October-November, 1937, Vol. 1, Nos. 1 and 2. Cf. further on public opinion, Leonard Doob, *Propaganda* (New York, 1935 and 1948: the later edition contains a comprehensive bibliography); William Albig, *Public Opinion* (New York, 1939); Ruth Benedict, *Patterns of Culture* (New York, 1933); Charles Merriam, *The Making of Citizens* (Chicago, 1931), which is one of a series on the same subject as it related to several other countries (which see); Charles W. Morris, *Signs, Language, Behavior* (New York, 1945); Robert and Helen Lynd, *Middletown* (New York, 1932) and *Middletown in Transition* (New York, 1937).

[3] Cf. Walter Lippmann, *Public Opinion* (New York, 1922).

mere facts but belief, and even the suggestion of will. Hence, the citizen is deprived of the direct possibility of making up his own mind. This would seem to put him at the mercy of those who own the presses, the radio, and the films; and to some extent it does. Yet it must be remembered that of all the mediums of mass communication, the most important by far are individual human beings themselves, so long as they have legs on which to walk to meetings or to visit their neighbors, hearts to feel, brains to think, and tongues to speak.[4] And this accounts for the triumph of so many progressive movements over those defended by the owners of the mediums of mass communications.

Propaganda may be defined as the closure or coercion of the individual or mass will by the argument that only one way is available to accomplish a policy and that that policy is the best. It deliberately shuts the mind to all but one course. *Education* may be defined as the process which sets free the will because it opens the mind to all alternatives and does not insist on action. The difference between the two (as we have already observed) may so be put: the educationist says, "In our father's house are many mansions and it is your privilege to choose which of these is best suited to your values." The propagandist says, on the other hand, "In my father's house there is only one mansion, and in that one alone you are obliged to dwell; and moreover, there is no father but only a master, and I pretend not to be him."

Propaganda is not unlimited in effect; and in the interwar years, especially from 1933 to the outbreak of World War II— that is, the peculiarly Hitlerian period— its limits were more clearly exposed than ever before to students of public opinion. These limits will be mentioned at the end of this chapter, but it may be said at once that force was the bully who walked arm-in-arm with propaganda.

---

[4] Confirmed in Paul Lazarsfeld *et al., The People's Choice* (New York, 1944), Chap. XVI.

THE SOURCES OF PUBLIC OPINION

IF we closely examine the knowledge of the electorate, we must admit that it is sadly deficient, especially since the knowledge with which politics is concerned is mainly the control of the behavior of individuals and groups separated from the voter by vast distances, wealth, culture, and occupation. It is obvious that the citizen's knowledge is quite strictly limited to his personal daily experience. He learns the nature of the things which he does to others—and this but very vaguely when the effects reach out far into society—and almost nothing of the cause of the things which are done to him, especially by the distant Fates of industry and politics. We may divide the scope of his knowledge into that which he has at first hand and that which he has only upon report.

First-hand Information. At first hand there are his family relationships and the tangled skein of experience spun therefrom. He learns something, sometimes very much, of human character and its varied manifestations. He gets to know something of the medical profession, and of religion and the churches. He has some experience of the army or the navy, in some countries by family hearsay, in others, where there is conscription, from actual service. Most people come into contact with the police at one time or another, if only by a trivial attempt to square a minor misdemeanor.

The local mayor or prefect or member of the legislature occasionally reveals to the citizen that he is governed or that he is possessed of sovereign power, causes him to swear at public extravagance or to be inspired or amused by official regalia. The post office is known from childhood. The tax and rating departments become stern realities. As juryman he may even have assisted in the administration of justice. Thousands find places on local government councils. At home there is the eternal talk of prices and wages; at work that of wages and prices. There is the school with its routine and compulsions, its ambitions and opportunities. Transport is a daily preoccupation; theater, motion pictures, radio and sports offer an occasional excursion into a realm of experience in which the citizen plays neither a wholly active nor a quite passive part.

Even the most thoughtful man or woman cannot extract from this experience the knowledge needed to rule hundreds of millions of people with international connections. The field of facts is too narrow. If it is effective in stimulating wants, desires, and dreams, it has but little relation to (but because of domestic anxieties, *some* relation to) social possibility. Even in the stimulation of interests and desires, the daily round is not profoundly effective, and it has required a great deal of agitation, or exceedingly bad times, to teach political lessons, and to overcome the soporific effects of habit. How Lassalle, when founding the socialist party in Germany, in his anguish denounced the "cursed needlessness of the poor"!

The creation of public opinion—that is to say, fact, belief, and will in the family circle—has two important characteristics: it is compulsive and it is kindly. It is compulsive in the sense that, being formed from the early years of a child's experience and being continuous, the stereotypes and symbols—and every word is regarded as a "symbol" by the psychologists—of public opinion becomes ingrained. The opinion thus formed is difficult to penetrate and enlighten at a later stage. Social reformers have recognized the hard shell of the family as a public-opinion-making unit, and have accordingly either attempted to crush it, as was tried by early Soviet attempts (until just before World War II) to weaken family discipline, or as in the nazi and fascist movements, to destroy it by virtually kidnapping the children into youth movements.[5] The bitter complaints of the par-

ents in these countries are a testimony to this attempt at cracking the family unit. It is not here denied that unhappy tensions are set up in some family relationships with life-long results for the individuals and those he touches, near and far. But most benefit by kindness, assurance, and stability.

Family public opinion, however, has a vulnerable point: that it is kindly, because the family relationship, generally speaking, operates on a basis of special good faith as compared with the discipline and everyday competition of individuals in the outside world. This has made it easy for people like Hitler to take advantage of what they regard as the gullibility of the average man, woman, and child, that is to say, their amenability—their "full faith and credit"—to accept opinion stated by authority. This allowed the success of the

---

[5] Cf. George Zeimer, *Education for Death* (New York, 1941), and *Nuremberg Documents* (U. S. Government Printing Office, 1947), IV, *passim*.

This account of the relationship of the family to the formation of political opinion is deliberately simplified; for the depths and intricacies of which I am well aware (let the student read such novels as Edmund Gosse, *Father and Son* or Samuel Butler, *The Way of*

all Flesh) are purposely passed over, because the aim in my present context is one of relationships rather than the profundities of individual and family psychology, and still more, psychiatry. Many of the facts and hypotheses (more the latter than the former) are of the utmost importance to the psychiatrist and social welfare worker, but they have not the same kind of significance for the wholesale political *process.* The works of Schopenhauer, Nietzsche, William James, Freud, Adler, Jung, Flugel, Reik, Erich Fromm, Harold Lasswell, Geoffrey Gorer, Margaret Mead, Ruth Benedict, ought to be mastered by those who wish to make of this phase of political science a special feature. They might also see: R. G. Barker, J. S. Kounin, H. F. Wright, *Child Behavior and Development* (New York, 1943); K. Lewin, *Dynamic Theory of Personality* (New York, 1935); Jean Piaget, *The Child's Conception of the World* (New York, 1929); Ian Suttie, *The Origins of Love and Hate* (London, 1938); J. W. Haney's translation of Rudolf Otto, *The Idea of the Holy* (New York, 1939); J. S. Plant, *Personality and the Cultural Pattern* (New York, 1937); J. K. Folsom, *The Family* (New York, 1934); H. Ordan, *Social Concepts and the Child Mind* (New York, 1945); S. de Grazia, *The Political Community* (Chicago, 1948); a series of articles by P. Kecskemeti and N. Leites in *Journal of Social Psychology*, "Some Psychological Hypotheses on Nazi Germany," during 1947 and 1948, Vols. 26, 27, and 28; and "Round Table on the Treatment of Germany," *Journal of Orthopsychiatry*, June, 1945, p. 381 ff., on the relations between family life and national culture.

Hitler theory of the "big lie," which may now be stated: [6]

... [t]he size of the lie is a definite factor in causing it to be believed, for the vast masses of a nation are in the depths of their hearts more easily deceived than they are consciously and intentionally bad. The primitive simplicity of their minds renders them an easier prey to a big lie than a small one, for they themselves often tell little ones but would be ashamed to tell big ones. Such a form of lies would never enter their head. They would never credit to others so important a possibility as the complete reversal of facts. Even explanations would for a long time leave them in doubt and hesitation, and any trifling reason would dispose them to accept a thing as true. *Therefore something of the most impudent lies always remains and sticks,* a fact which all bodies and individuals occupied with the art of lying in this world know only too well, and hence they stop at nothing to achieve this end.

Nevertheless, the toughness of opinion formed over the years by the exchanges of views and experiences within the family produces an attitude which at least partially defeats propaganda as well as education. This attitude remains, therefore, an ingredient of the policy which cannot but be accepted. Much more must be done than the family does if the family is to appreciate the part that it should play in the government of a great community— that is, what conditions it may demand, and what obligations to the community it ought to honor. Modern American investigations attest the truth for at least the United States of Gilbert and Sullivan's wit concerning England:

> I often think it's comical
> How Nature always does contrive
> That every boy and every gal,
> That's born into the world alive
> Is either a little Liberal
> Or else a little Conservative.

Voting as the family has done is just as high as 75 per cent.[7]

Professional Knowledge. For men and women who earn their living in industry, commerce, and the professions, an additional source of understanding is open, and sometimes, in the most conscious and public spirited, it extends to deep knowledge of their work and its relationship to the situation of other groups. Of course, the development of employers' associations, cooperative societies,[8] and trade unions has done a tremendous amount in recent years to accumulate and spread knowledge which is of the very essence of public affairs. If their comprehension of fact is narrow, it is at the same time a critical microscope which defies deception in its own field. The great part played by such associations or interest groups led to a new theory of political representation: the guild socialist theory. This theory, which flourished shortly after World War I, avowed that men and women could not have a general political opinion and that this could not be represented. But these various opinions of producers and consumers could be woven together in a congress of guilds. The rank and file of employers and employees and of the liberal professions have, however, a rather limited personal experience. Think of the railroad conductor, the postman, the grocer, the bank clerks, of the bus driver, the miner, the textile worker, and multitudes of others who constitute the modern community, and ask, what would they know of any fruitful use to government, even of a rural district council, if no external agencies existed to discover and report to them the things they do not and cannot otherwise know? Save for the help of a few, we should be at a standstill. Wants which are largely the issue of instinctive dispositions could be expressed; the immediate self-regarding interests of each group would be well understood and claimed; but how to prevent these from causing collisions with undesirable consequences, how to attain them in an order of priority which would neither balk the desire nor kill the possibility of satisfac-

---

[6] *Mein Kampf* (New York, 1940), p. 313.
[7] Cf. Paul Lazarsfeld *et al., The People's Choice* (New York, 1944), p. 142 ff. Cf. also D. Anderson and P. E. Davidson, *Ballots and the Democratic Class Struggle* (Stanford, 1943), pp. 8 ff. and 317 ff.

[8] There are about 15,000 on the elected management committees of the British cooperative movement.

tion, whether the satisfaction is in any degree possible—these things are not to be learned in the appropriate degree from the common experience of the average man. It requires years of close and constant application to master even a single branch of public affairs.

Education and Publicity. Infinitely the chief part of knowledge of public affairs is obtained by report. All the modern instruments of education and publicity give this instruction and, further, dogmatize about the best way to satisfy wants. Without this the voters would be ignorant indeed, and utterly puppets in the hands of willful men—not that the puppets would always act, for they might be too wooden to do so. The apogee of the "governing class" lay in that era when certain families had much to obtain from governing the country and before either education or parties had influenced the voters.

The principal agencies of instruction in public affairs—other than political parties —are books, the newspaper press, schools, clubs, churches, the motion pictures, radio, and hearsay.

Books. The value of books depends upon their accessibility and the possession of leisure. Books have become easily accessible to those who really want them by the extension, in our own time, of public libraries, in spite of the parsimony practiced by many local councils.[9] Further, political parties, cooperative societies, and trade unions lend books, and one will find, in England and Germany at least, a small number of volumes at local party headquarters. An obstacle which is not entirely insuperable is the unwillingness of many municipal councils to provide books which shock their morals and political principles. There is an *index expurgatorius* in everybody's mind, and extremists of all kinds on local library committees apply it, to a degree which is, however,

limited by majority opinion and the democratic bias to tolerance.

There is much more leisure today than at any time since the Industrial Revolution took most people away from agricultural pursuits; and it consists of all the hours of the day which can be seized from rest and sleep, save eight or ten for work, besides one and a half to two clear days in each week. This would be clear gain were not economic pursuits extremely monotonous and fatiguing, and distances between work and home long and jading. Is not leisure, the average person will ask, for *living*? For conversation, music, the theater, the motion pictures, for one's family, for dancing, for dress, love making, sport, hobbies, drinking and smoking, and for the lethargic delight of armchair fantasies? The books are accessible, there are some hours, though not as many as appear on a surface calculation, for study. But does the mass of mankind read the books which will give them a clue to controversy and control of the sources of power? Common experience shows that they do not. It is calculated that even fairly popular books on public affairs costing two to three dollars cannot be expected to sell more than an average of five thousand copies in the United States. The advent of the cheap reprint at one dollar to twenty-five cents a copy is a very important and welcome political fact, but few are on public affairs. Novels are read, and the newspaper whiles away the rest of the time.

It requires a large amount of passionate interest, and the concentrated attention which comes of that, or intellectual power, or habit, to attempt the mastery of a serious study of a public problem. Few people have such a passionate interest, few have been trained in the habit of purposeful reading;[10] and even when these are present, the mind itself can only in rare cases hold out for the necessary time to master an argument. Every university teacher knows that only five or six out of every hundred students can show first-

9 The annual expenditure of local authorities in England and Wales alone is over one million pounds. Cf. *Annual Local Taxation Returns*, published by His Majesty's Stationery Office. Cf. also Report of Public Libraries Committee, Cmd. 2868; 1927. In the United States for 1943 the amount spent for libraries was $50,000,000.

10 Only a few people can be expected to follow the rather rigorous instructions by Prof. Mortimer Adler in *How to Read a Book* (New York, 1944), though they ought to.

class qualities, and fewer still originality, although students are helped in every way.

The conclusion is, then, that the masses of voters do not, and will not, until education has assumed new shapes, read for themselves—and that many will never be able to profit from it—although the opportunities exist and are improving. Any reader can think of twenty books in each country which all voters should have read as the absolute minimum necessary if they were to be able to select and check their representatives independently of the very parties themselves who recommend these representatives: are they likely to have read even one? Even then, in spite of conspicuous exceptions, how much real significance have the crude, unassimilated, distorted values of the self-taught man? It should be borne in mind, however, that so long as books and libraries which are comprehensive and not deliberately expurgated are available, there exists one potent source of opposition to dictatorship, and one more opportunity for democratic leadership.

The Press. The newspaper is not the most important feature of modern civilization, but it is among the most important, especially in regard to the electorate's opinion. Briefly, these are its qualities:

In every country, printed news and opinion, attractively written and produced, are purchasable at an exceedingly cheap rate, so that few people go a single day without reading a newspaper or conversing with somebody who has. It is the most widely disseminated single agent of instruction in the modern world. Newspapers can be sold at a ridiculously small price because they earn tremendous sums by carrying advertisements (from one half to three quarters of the revenue of a newspaper comes from this source). They are private property and are subject to no stricter measure of public control than the laws relating to libel, obscenity, blasphemy, and sedition.[11] Otherwise, no en-

actment, no public institution or official, regulates or challenges their veracity, for this kind of truth is private property. Upon public affairs the newspapers serve out news and opinion. A part of their material consists of plainly reported news or complete or reduced reproductions of important public documents. A part—the leading articles—consists of comments and short essays upon events and policies, and the reports of experts in some branch of public affairs. The "news" section, the representation of fact, varies among different countries and different newspapers in amount and quality. Several newspapers with a fairly wide circulation in each country give great attention to news, reproducing legislative debates in much detail; to government announcements; to judicial decisions; to the actions and declarations of representative bodies of industry, society, and the churches; to events abroad; to the findings of commissions of inquiry. There is more such attention in England and Germany than in the United States or France. In the Soviet Union there is practically nothing but this!

Another portion of the newspapers undoubtedly receives more attention: that is the plainly political, which here means the biased, part. Here fact and interpretation of fact—the past, the future, the hypothetical, and the prophetic—are mixed and served together. But each newspaper has a tendency and dogmas. Those who are conscious of them tend to become permanent readers of the paper whose bias is nearest their own; or some signed articles may hold them out of respect for the writer. The owners know the tendency they wish to spread and they can guess the circles where they will find support. There is such a close community of feeling between the directors of a newspaper

[11] The best descriptions of the law relating to the press are to be found in T. Dawson, *The Law of the Press* (London, 1927); G. Barbier, *Code Appliqué de la Presse,* 2nd edition (Paris, 1911-38). Cf. also Léon Duguit, *Traité de Droit Constitutionnel* (Paris, 1925), Vol. IV, Sects. 35-37; Mannheim, *Preszrecht* (1927); and Haentzchel, *Reichspreszgesetz* (1927); Z. Chafee, *Government and Mass Communications* (Chicago, 1947), 2 vols., for the United States. See also for a comparative treatment, I. Rothenberg, *The Newspaper* (New York, 1948).

and their readers that it is difficult to say how far the newspaper actually pushes opinion beyond the point independently reached by the readers.[12] Certainly the paper confirms and strengthens the reader's opinion and gives him confidence in it. Reasons appear there in plain words, while in the reader's mind they only float about, vague and unformed; and he is often convinced that what he reads is what he meant to say—although common experience proves that we may easily deceive ourselves about this when we have the habit of relying upon authority. At the same time, the proprietors and the editors are not unconscious of their constituency—the paper must not shock too much or the sales will decrease and revenue from advertisements will fall. Consequently, if the newspaper makes its readers it is also made by them. The newspaper, however, has a considerable power, for it may produce an effect upon the mind, and then raise a fresh issue to ward off the punishment which might have followed its deviation from what the readers expected.

Now all this would not cause the distortion of beliefs formed by independent experience, technical reading, and impartial teaching, if readers knew quite clearly that the papers deliberately hold and inculcate a biased attitude of mind. Then readers could agree or disagree, consciously. But in fact, a large proportion of the public is quite unconscious, and an even larger proportion is only dimly conscious, that they are the subjects of an everlasting mental operation conducted by unlicensed and sometimes venal practitioners.

The mass of readers is attracted to a newspaper not by its political tendency but by other qualities entirely.[13] Every conceivable domestic and social interest is catered to: we have an avid curiosity about our fellow creatures. All newspapers have succumbed to pictures, some carrying hardly any text matter. Their psychology is sound, though one may despise their ideals. For newspaper pictures appeal to the unimaginative, those unserved by their own wits and unable to read and think connectedly for a space of time. Tabloids have the greatest circulation. Important attractions are the news of crime and accidents, festival and ceremonial gatherings, preferably of those high in "society." Theatrical and Hollywood news (especially scandals), puzzles, and "comic strips" open the minds and mouths of millions. Most attractive of all, especially to men and boys, is sporting news, principally horse racing.[14] This social entertainment vastly preponderates over political news, and the headlines confess what is really attractive. Almost invariably they include the words "disclosure," "mystery," "sensation," "surprise," "startling." The gift of insurance benefits is another factor in the Delilah power of the press. All this blankets the eyes of the ordinary man and woman, and they swallow opinions at which they might pause if there were anything to give them pause. If they knew who and what interests were dictating the policy of the paper, or if policy were separated from news, they might be vigilant. But no law compels the regular declaration of the politics of the chief owners and editors of the paper.

Of graver importance is the practice of summarizing the contents and meaning of political events in headlines, that is, in a telling though ungrammatical sentence of anything up to ten words. Whether the distortion is intentional or not, distortion there is; and these reiterated distortions are too often the only

---

[12] On the closeness of the dependence on reader reaction see Robert M. Hutchins *et al.*, *A Free and Responsible Press* (Chicago, 1947); and Charles Merz of *The New York Times*, in *Annals of the American Academy of Political Science*, January, 1942, "The Press and Contemporary Society," p. 143.

[13] Cf. *Annals, loc. cit.*, p. 20, where it is shown that less than 27 per cent space is devoted to news.

[14] A good racing handicapper is an important asset of every newspaper which aspires to several editions a day and a wide circulation. During the general strike of 1926 in England my barber dolefully summed up the situation in regard to newspapers thus: "Terrible, ain't it, no newspapers! Why, it's like a day when there's no racing!"

political intelligence which the reader hurrying to work or homewards, or snatching his lunch, ever has the time to absorb.[15]

How then can the influence of the press of our own day be judged? (1) Few people use the newspapers consciously as a basis of independent opinion. (2) Many consciously subscribe to a paper because it preaches approximately the political creed they already hold. (3) The newspaper can develop these creeds and apply them to the events and policies of the day and take its readers along with it. It acts as a common worshipping ground, confirms opinions, and encourages resistance. Hence dictators suppress opposition papers, knowing that this will at least cause a dispersal of the mutually inspiring communicants.[16] The newspaper is able to tide over any unpopularity with its readers if it cleverly picks up and drops "stunts" and covers an advance or retreat with attractive "features." If, for example, after a newspaper has covered a political opponent with mud, the public decides that the real repository of the mud is the newspaper proprietor and not his opponent, the proprietor then assumes the pose of one who "takes his licking like a sportsman." Where he once fulminated he now fawns. (4) In the minds of the unsophisticated and unwarned (and large numbers of the electorate are so), ideas are silently and skillfully implanted, since, while unguarded, they consume untruthful "headlines." (5) Newspapers are most often avowed or unavowed tools of a particular political party, though the editors and proprietors may occasionally revolt owing to differences with the party leaders;[17] but their affiliations are not always known to the public.

The amount of objectively true information and balanced opinion is, on the whole, small, and the press has acquired an extraordinary dominance over opinion, aggravating rather than correcting its defects. A great deal of organization and education are required to overcome the power of the press over untutored minds, and such education and activity in fact falls to the political parties. That the power of the press is not so dominating as is supposed, that its effects are, as it were, suspensive of truthful opinion rather than quite destructive of it, can be seen from the steady and rapid growth of the mass parties of dissent—in spite of the daily opposition of newspapers—whose interests and political creed were entirely hostile to the majority of their readers. These continue to read the paper but vote against the paper's persuasion. The most widely read newspapers in the countries with which we are concerned—until recently in England and the United States, almost the only newspapers—were owned and directed by what may be broadly called the "capitalist" class. Yet mass parties and groups of dissent against their creed arose. The reader will recall how in France, Germany, and Britain the Social Democratic parties and the Labour party arose through thirty or thirty-five years of deliberate effort to organize their interests and ideals in a party, against the

---

[15] Cf. *Annals, loc. cit.,* p. 7, where an average reader is said to spend some 20 minutes per day on newspapers. Cf. also D. Waples, B. Berelson, and F. R. Bradshaw, *What Reading Does to People* (Chicago, 1940).

[16] Fascism claimed that Italy "is too poor to be able to afford the continual nervous strain and frittering away of energy. The formula was: Criticism is allowed, but not opposition." Moreover, the press "must be at the service of the nation, for the nation must be defended by all Italians without distinction." Cf. H. Schneider, *Making the Fascist State* (New York, 1928), pp. 96, 316; and cf. Herman Finer, *Mussolini's Italy* (London, 1935). As soon as the nazi movement took power, it seized newspapers and either suppressed or renamed and used them. (See *Nazi Conspiracy and Aggression,* U.S. Government Printing Office, 1947.) The Soviet régime is equally inhospitable to free newspapers. The government's absolute control of paper, the printing presses, and factory space is alone decisive. But in addition is the law relating to the practice of journalism and sedition, and control by the Communist party. In all three dictatorial régimes the journalist became a salaried officer of the state or of the monopolistic party, admission to the profession being officially controlled.

[17] Cf. the detailed analysis of the relations between the English press and the political parties in Hartman, *The Press and the Modern State* (unpublished thesis, University of London, 1930).

most persistent opposition of the "capitalist press." And it may be remembered that in spite of the almost universal hostility of the press, it was not possible to stop the electorate from choosing Mr. Roosevelt, not once, or twice, or thrice—but four times!

The limits on the power of the privately-owned press as an independent dominator of public opinion may be recapitulated. (1) Even where the press is "capitalist" there are rival capitalists, with marked differences of opinion and accounts of the facts in public affairs. (2) Even where only one newspaper circulates in a locality without a rival (and in the United States this occurs in nearly ninety per cent of the places), *given time,* it may be controverted by out-of-town papers, by the radio (even where this happens to be owned by the newspaper), by common report, or by reflection. (3) The special press —the periodicals of vocational and social groups, of the professions, the businesses, and the churches—carries alternative versions of the truth, confirming or denying the facts, beliefs, and policies of the general press. (4) The press is limited in influence by the receptivity of its readers. (5) There are institutes, like Brookings in the United States, or Political and Economic Planning in Britain, or university departments with publications, whose standards cut across the values peculiar to the general press.

Yet it must be admitted that the newspaper can and does enslave the uneducated; if not for always, yet for a time. And time is of the very essence of politics. Its battles are fought in terms of months, years, and generations. The general effect of the press is to uphold the *status quo;* it is on the whole conservative (less so in France, with its host of small newspapers of opinion). It does not assist dissident minority opinions. It defers their victories but cannot stop them. The strongest newspaper cannot, beyond a certain time, baffle the impetus of a group opinion founded upon the interests of that group. The group knows its own interests too well to be fooled by newspaper opinion. So that

we are back again in the making of public opinion to the conflict of groups.[18]

How complex a problem the better ordering of the press for modern society is, may be gathered from the recommendations contained in *A Free and Responsible Press,* already referred to.[19] A résumé of its principal points are as follows.

(1) What can be done by government: (a) Government must maintain freedom of the press, radio, and motion pictures, but as to the two latter, they must be subject to the kind of regulation conducted hitherto by boards of review and the Federal Communications Commission. (b) Government must foster new techniques and new ventures in communications and maintain competition through the antitrust laws—used with care. (c) Libeled persons should have a right to a retraction or a restatement or to reply. (d) Legislation prohibiting advocacy of revolutionary changes should be repealed where there is no clear and present danger of violence. (e) The government should inform the public of the facts respecting its policies and purposes through the mass mediums, and where private agencies do not permit this, the government should employ its own mediums.

---

18 For England, the reader is referred to Kingsley Martin, *Fascism, Democracy, and the Press* (London, 1938); "Report on the Press," by Political and Economic Planning (London, 1938); Francis Williams, *Press, Parliament and People* (London, 1945); and House of Commons Debates, October 29, 1946, on press control and ownership, a debate precipitated by the unfairness of the opposition press to the Labour government. The most penetrating analysis of the position of the American press and radio and movies is to be found in the report of the Chicago *Commission on Freedom of the Press* prepared by a body of eminent experts in political science and public opinion, published in 1947. The reader is also directed to the 1945 case of the *U.S.* v. *Associated Press* (326 U.S.1), in which the news-gathering agency was compelled to admit *The Chicago Sun* whose exclusion had been possible under the articles of the association permitting *The Chicago Tribune,* a member, among others, to exercise a right of objection. The reader may also consult the *University of Chicago Law Review* for April, 1946 and June, 1946, for articles on this decision.

19 *Op. cit.,* p. 79 ff.

(2) What can be done by the press: (a) The agencies of mass communication should be hospitable to ideas and attitudes different from their own—that is, accept the responsibilities of "common carriers" of information and discussion. (b) These agencies should finance new, experimental, activities of high literary, artistic, or intellectual quality which do not bring financial rewards, and they should do this out of their profits on the rest of their revenues. (c) The members of the press should engage in vigorous mutual criticism. (d) The press should use every means to increase the competence, independence, and effectiveness of its personnel.

(3) What can be done by the public: (a) Nonprofit institutions—like schools, libraries, colleges, universities, religious organizations, a chain of FM educational stations—should supply the variety, quantity, and quality of press service required by the nation, to give it diversity and elevation of ideas. (b) Academic-professional centers of advanced study, research, and publication in the field of mass communications must be established; and the schools of journalism must be converted into places of the broadest and most liberal education. (c) A new and independent agency to appraise and report annually upon the performance of the press should be established: to define standards, point out inadequacies, inquire into minority discrimination, etc., and foster publicity and public discussion on all phases of the service of the press to the nation and the world.

The School is of surprisingly small value in the creation of independent political opinion. Let us divide and discriminate. We may speak, broadly, of elementary, secondary, and university education—as it is.

In the elementary schools, attended by the mass of children until about the age of fourteen, what is taught? There are the introductory subjects like reading, writing, and arithmetic; elementary natural sciences and handicrafts; and—of sole importance as an approach to public affairs —history and geography. The chief features of this instruction are its scantiness

in terms of the time which can possibly be devoted to it, and the curious way in which the subjects have in the past been studied and taught. Even in the best schools in the most advanced educational systems, history has suffered from undue attention to battles, kings, and great men, with emphasis upon pretty-pretty stories about them, while the fundamental forces in the evolution of society—the economic, the social, the doctrinal, the technical— have been ignored. The "nation" is considered as a solid and homogeneous unit without internal troubles or conflict. Further, it is almost universally considered the sole standard by which the rest of the world should be judged. Geography has been too national, an enormous time being spent on learning trumpery natural features by rote, and long lists of products made or grown in different parts of the world. But the dynamic factors in race, the distribution of peoples, climate, migration, and commerce do not receive appropriate attention. At the very best the elementary school is a beginning; unfortunately, in the present context, it is for many the end of all disciplined schooling.

In the secondary schools, high schools, *gymnasia,* or *lycées,* history and geography are pursued further, and some attention is paid to the characteristics of other countries when the usual two modern foreign languages are taught. A little more than the few miserable stories of the elementary schools is recited. In some schools, where the headmaster and history and geography teachers are adventurous and wise spirits, the few good textbooks are introduced,[20] so that by the age of sixteen the pupil has learned enough at least to begin to inquire and read. How rare are such teachers and how rare such books; how inadequate, too, is the time

---

[20] For the situation in the United States, not likely to encourage complacency, see Educational Policies Commission, *Learning the Ways of Democracy: a Case Book of Civic Education* (Washington, 1941).

For an exceptionally fine high-school history see C. H. Firth, *History Secondary Series* (London, 1945-49), 5 volumes, each with a reference book. Cf. also B. Pierce, *Civic Attitudes in American School Textbooks* (Chicago, 1930).

for these studies! [21] The career approaches; and cramming for examinations is imperative. It is, however, interesting to note that during the last twenty years, almost all secondary schools have begun to teach a subject called "civics" [22] or "citizenship" or "American democracy," which is an introduction to public affairs. In the commercial secondary schools there is an introduction to economic theory, economic history, and "commercial" geography, and this, when taken seriously as a large part of the curriculum, is a useful step to a knowledge of the conditions of government.

However, generally speaking, any close and honest examination of the contribution of secondary schools in all countries clearly shows that three things stand in the way of an education which could fit pupils to grope their way to an independent judgment of public affairs: (1) the lack of teachers with the appropriate knowledge and skill; (2) the lack of proper textbooks and other equipment, such as motion-picture projectors, pictures, and books other than textbooks; and (3) the staring grim fact that children are not sent to school to become authorities upon public affairs but to learn to earn their living in some special vocation.

(1) We know that the national supply of good teachers is small; those who have the talent and the vocation are very few. Teachers are very badly paid, and so, often the timid and mild who are likely to fail at other things turn to teaching. The higher salaries now paid in some places induce the entrance of others who are not merely finding a refuge from a rough world. Yet it is impossible to find as many illustrious teachers in a nation as are required, given the large number of children at school. We are rather condemned to a large body of mediocre (many worse) teachers, with a few noted exceptions. It must be remembered also that teachers are not at liberty to devote themselves to one subject or a group of cognate subjects, but are expected to profess "subsidiary" subjects. This is all a question of cost. One improvement is noticeable: the more rapid acquaintance of teachers with recent research in the social sciences, yet even now far from adequate. Signs are not wanting that World War I and World War II and the interwar economic and ideological ferment have much vivified the curricula and the outlook of teachers.

(2) Secondly, owing to the short time available and the importance of obtaining examination results, textbooks form the principal reading. But even these summaries of summary summaries are not read all through, for heavy-leaded-type captions stand guard over the portals of the rest, crying out, "Read and remember me, if nothing else!"

(3) We come to the final count, and that is the prior necessity of earning a living. The standard of living lashes and goads the modern world. It causes parents to fling their children into school, whether they like it or not, and snatch them out again in time to get a job. They may stray a little to pick up some accomplishments, and, of course, if they insist upon straying altogether—there is nothing to be done.

It is relevant at this point to observe that in Britain, until 1946, the number of children going on to secondary education after the age of fourteen was only three out of ten. This is now changed by the recent Education Acts.[23] It would seem as though a body of citizens emergent from an educational system in which only so small a proportion had been educated beyond the age of fourteen would be an incompetent electorate. That this is not the case is observable from the political and social progress in Great Britain. The truth is that elementary education in Eng-

[21] H. G. Wells, in his *World Brain* (London, 1938), examines the number of years devoted at school to subjects which are a foundation of subsequent political understanding, and demonstrates how small is the proportion of time spent on the political-humanizing subjects. The reader is advised to study this book.
[22] In Germany, *Staatsbürgerkunde;* in France, *Instruction civique.*

[23] W. K. Richmond, *Education in England* (London, 1945, Penguin edition).

land has been of a rather higher quality than in the United States, in which attendance at high school is the reverse of the British proportion, that is, seven out of ten, and if the Southern states are excluded from the average, then the attendance is almost 100 per cent. The high schools in the United States have not been notable for adding preparation for political participation. However, whatever the quality of American high-school education, her system has the inestimable merit of opening the doors to all who want that education, and in the end her polity is certain to benefit immensely from this. In France and Germany the situation has been closer to that described for Britain than for the United States.

The mercenary is the chief motive to secondary education, and only those with expectations and the financial means of a political career, or the very few who are brave enough to dispense with expectations and financial rewards, can make the secondary stage the beginning of political understanding. Thus, of all the numbers of secondary students, only the moneyed "governing classes" and the mentally adventurous may pause to profit. Most of the rest rush helter-skelter out of the doors of school with some true and many false notions, and with the mind closed rather than made eager—to be governed, inevitably, not by their own qualities, but by other people's, or by their own, not too well.[24]

Owing to the expense and the necessity of finding work, only a tiny fraction of the population enters the college stage: in the United States about one in six of the population of university age; in England about one in forty; in France and Germany a little higher than the English figure. Those who do not enter do so mainly for a vocational purpose and specialize in a particular technique; only a very small proportion undertake studies which offer an approach to politics. Those

who learn history, law, political and economic theory, philosophy, and ethics are being fitted for comprehension of the political world, for they are learning something of human groups and their interpretations.[25] Even among these, there are stages of wisdom. The specialists in the social sciences are very few, though the present tendency is for a rapid increase in the numbers. That a college education may provide a man with a negligible endowment of political wisdom is to be observed from conversation with the average medical practitioner, engineer, clergyman, solicitor, bank manager, and, in a lesser degree, schoolteacher. People are often shocked when they observe for the first time that some of these very capable craftsmen are quite uneducated outside the narrow sphere of their own activities, necessary and humane as they are. Yet no one would expect, as of necessity, that a capable carpenter (or a nuclear physicist[26]) should *ipso facto* be a political oracle.

The net conclusion is that schooling, in its present state, may do much to prepare people to make a living, to exercise special skill, and even to enjoy leisure, but it does very little either to prepare the mind or train the mind to prepare itself competently to understand and judge social relationships in the nation and the world. No one, surely, would go to the other extreme and claim that schools turn out students highly efficient therein. There is ground for much constructive improvement in this respect.

So far, then, as schools are concerned, the irresistible conclusion is that the mass of mankind are destined to become what the Germans aptly call *Stimmvieh:* that is, voting cattle.

---

24 For a sensible, critical account of education for citizenship in American schools see D. Anderson and P. E. Davidson, *Ballots and the Democratic Class Struggle* (Stanford, 1943), Chap. V.

25 On the relationship between education and civic intelligence, compare the fallacious remarks of Hayek in *Road to Serfdom* (Chicago, 1943), Chap. 14, and my refutation of this in my *Road to Reaction* (Boston, 1946), pp. 112-13.

26 How far from political wisdom an eminent physicist can be may be learned from one among many similar cases from M. P. Blackett, *The Bomb, Fear and War* (New York, 1949).

This judgment, like others relating to the schools and political participation, must be tempered by the recognition that, however little the schools do accomplish, so long as the public has a clear economic or social interest to develop and defend, the domination of the press or political parties is limited.

In addition to the intellectual contribution of the schools to the formation of public opinion, as estimated already, certain other considerations are important. (1) The school is the earliest stage in the formation of the mind where the influence of the family is confronted with an alternative; it begins to put the family in a wider social setting. (2) The school contributes to the mind something beyond the range of the family's occupation, its locality, and its class. Manifestly, if properly improved it could render far greater services in these directions. (3) Yet one more truth is of tremendous importance: in preparation for political life, the school suffers from the vital defect that students are not living the full life of citizens but are sheltered, protected, and provided for by others, usually their parents. They have not to face the stern realities of self-maintenance, personal and economic protection, and advancement and security, in open, unassisted competition with others at least equally determined. But the conditions of personal existence and success, and full responsibility for these, are the essence of the political process and the public opinion which is its material. Hence the school, in the main, can do little else but supply theories or ideas. The realities come later, and for these, men and women need specifically contrived social arrangements—I refer to political parties.

Some slight headway is being made by adult education in evening courses, such as those provided by the Workers' Educational Association and Adult Education Association in England, the *Ligue de l'Enseignement* in France, the *Gesellschaft für die Verbreitung der Volksbildung* in Germany, and the Association for Adult Education in the United States.[27] An important opportunity is open for adult education to render a magnificent service for the welfare of democracy, that is, the kind which is not rendered by political parties. It is a remarkable fact that in Great Britain no less than one hundred members of Parliament on the Labour side returned in the election of 1945 were people who had attended the classes of the Workers' Educational Association. But this is a serious educational venture, requiring study, attendance, and paper work for a course lasting two or three years. Experience during World War II with the Army Bureau of Current Affairs in Britain, the Army Information and Education Division in the United States, and the "underground" in France has shown clearly what enormous avidity for political and economic education exists, and how quickly awakened are those who have made contact with it. In the United States, it is probable that a new lease of life in serious adult education is beginning with the efforts of Chancellor Hutchins of the University of Chicago in collaboration with the *Encyclopedia Britannica* to produce and circulate a series of humanity's mightiest classics and to have them discussed in regular classes by properly conducted and continuous groups.

Before passing on from this consideration of the schools and policy formation, one most important feature needs to be given high relief. If the teaching of policy in schools and colleges assumed important dimensions and a character of indoctrination, they could not possibly resist invasion in various ways by the managers, bosses, and officials of political parties. A narrow path must be trod—that of education, not party propaganda—and a high temperature will stimulate the attack of political disease germs from the outside upon the bodies academic.

The Motion Picture and the Radio.

27 Cf. A. Mansbridge, *An Adventure in Working Class Education* (London, 1920); cf. also the important report taken from statements made by adult students on this subject, in W. E. Williams, *Learn and Live* (London, 1936).

These two instruments have enormous potentialities, for at low cost they can reach almost everyone for long periods of time, and they do not exact the more difficult kind of attention necessary to master a printed argument. The cinema, owned by a few, has become almost exclusively a means of entertainment. It is enormously popular because it preaches with fanatical vehemence the ultimate and holy triumph of the Ten Commandments by showing with tropical imagination naked detail, and beautiful men and women, the attractive consequences of their disobedience. Of recent years there has been a conscious mobilization of "educational" films, and much may be done therewith. But even in the schools they are not as yet highly popular, and a theater manager takes a grave risk with an "educational week." The sound films are, I am sure, destined to become a most potent means of education, and all political parties possess portable apparatus.

The radio is of very unequal value. Its best development is in Great Britain, Germany, and France; in the United States the radio awaits more cultured public control. The policy of the British Broadcasting Corporation is to give about five hours per week to the discussion of subjects which may be called "political," and the intellectual standard is about that of well-expressed university and adult classes, not too high for large masses of people to profit from influence.[28] But so far the development is in its youth, and the time actually devoted to it is small compared with the long succession of plodding hours needed to master the vast range of complicated facts, especially in the form of organized discussion groups. The potentialities are enormous, and we are reminded of Carlyle's dictum that the true

university today is a library of books! Yes, for him who is by nature a part of the *universitas!* Shall we avoid again what we have seen in respect of the newspapers? The majority of minds attracted either by the crude, the sensational, and the vulgar, or by all that is sublime in artistic feeling and expression, but revolting from disciplined study of the science of government?

What has been said about the British Broadcasting Corporation also holds good for France and Germany. But during the nazi period, the amount of political education was enormously increased, not for the world's benefit. In the United States, because of the existence of several nationwide networks and hundreds of small stations, the amount of time during which a discriminating citizen may be regaled with political discussion is much larger than in Britain and France. This is, in part, due to the competitive effect of private enterprise, as each network must have some program of intense educational interest on the air. This, however, is enforced only by the most vigorous efforts on the part of the Federal Communications Commission, which is in control of the use of the air by the station owners and managers. News and talks during the daytime take about 11 per cent of the time. This includes talks which do not reach a good sober standard of quality and much which is futile.

On the whole, no country—whether, as in England, broadcasting is under government control, or, as in the United States, maintained by private enterprise, is really exploiting the educative potentialities of radio on the grand scale which is possible. This is one of the greatest of missed social opportunities.[29]

Churches, Clubs, and Social Intercourse.

---

[28] Cf. Adult Education Association, *Handbook and Directory of Adult Education* (London, 1928-29); on broadcasting policy see pp. 134-35. Cf. also Commission on Educational and Cultural Films, Papers Nos. 1 and 2, February, 1930, and July, 1930; *International Handbook of Adult Education*, published by the World Association for Adult Education (London, 1929), especially pp. 149 ff., 163 ff., 436 ff., and the Introduction.

[29] Charles A. Siepmann, *Radio's Second Chance* (Boston, 1946); *Public Service Responsibility of Broadcast Licensees,* Report by the Federal Communications Commission (Washington, D. C., 1946); "Radio: the Fifth Estate," *Annals of the American Academy of Political Science,* January, 1935; Llewellyn White, *The American Radio* (Chicago, 1947); and more sensationally, Frederic Wakeman, *The Hucksters* (New York, 1946).

It is not so much the moral pressure of the churches in politics that interests us, but their intellectual contribution to the understanding of political argument, not that the two can be entirely separated, for the fear of the particular Hell or the love of the particular Heaven of any church infallibly closes many minds to any argument at all which disputes the beliefs respecting the supernatural. Every church professes a body of ethics which consist of principles of human obligation and rights deemed to be universally valid. It is obvious that, in so far as the communicants have really mastered the verbal arguments addressed to them in schools and sermons and the history of their creed and group, and, in so far as they really believe what they have heard and read, there must be large bodies of opinion employable as a criterion of political problems. These bodies of opinion cut across each other, sometimes agreeing, more often violently disagreeing; and they are specific and often very rigid attitudes of mind.

Some even enter into questions of the day: for example, into education, temperance, marriage and divorce, the emancipation of women.[30] And in our own time the churches have begun sedulously to occupy themselves with labor conditions, with sporadic movements, called generally Christian Socialism,[31] commencing in the middle of the nineteenth century. The Papal Encyclical of 1891, for example, gave an impetus to Roman Catholics to occupy themselves with finding and embracing an industrial policy.[32] These tendencies are becoming strengthened, and

churches are now especially sensitive and proud of their answers to economic and social problems.[33] They are a little ashamed of one thing only: their inability always to preach the gospel of peace.[34] But this, of course, is the unfortunate fate of all who occupy themselves practically with man's actual lot *in the world where time is of the essence.* Christ himself brought a sword.

The teaching is, however, on the whole rather vague; the body of knowledge is small, and the people who may be supposed to be really influenced thereby are very few. Though for many the gospel of a church has still that commanding significance which only belief in an otherworldly scheme of values can give, their number is far outweighed by perfunctory attendants. The country is more "religious" than the town; the villages and townships of the United States, for example, still give a powerful impetus to its politics; and the Catholic strength in France and Germany is so formidable that pitched and long-drawn battles have occurred between secular politicians and churchmen. Their influence on education has been and is weighty. On the whole, however, the forces which would have drawn men to hear the social doctrines of the Church have become so weak that the churches have undertaken their study and instruction largely for their own preservation. Yet they are tortured and broken upon the rack of their followers' economic and local dissensions, as witness the difficulties of the Center (Catholic)—later the Democratic—Party in Germany and the *Mouvement Republicain Populaire* and parties of the extreme Right in France. For the exacting time-element spurs on to violence of feeling, word, and deed. Nevertheless, the churches speak when men are in a peculiarly receptive mood,

---

[30] Cf. the papal encyclicals on marriage and the family, and on socialism (1931), in J. Husslein (ed.), *Social Wellsprings* (Milwaukee, 1942), 2 vols.; and on atheistic communism (1938) and Hitler's and Mussolini's régimes (1931).

[31] Cf. C. E. Raven, *Christian Socialism: A History* (London, 1920); and the former Archbishop of Canterbury, William Temple, *Christianity and Social Order* (London, 1942); Philip Hughes, *The Pope's New Order* (London, 1943); H. Trommen, *The State in Catholic Thought* (St. Louis, Mo., 1945).

[32] Cf. reports issued by the I.L.O. (Geneva and Washington) on Roman Catholicism and economic welfare.

[33] Cf. reports by Federal Council of Churches of Christ of America, currently, but especially during 1946 to 1948, and the British Council of Churches, from time to time.

Above all, see *Man's Order and God's Design,* by the First Assembly of the World Council of Churches (New York, 1949).

[34] Cf. British Council of Churches, *The Era of Atomic Power* (London, 1946).

and there is no doubt that they are efficacious in creating a political mind independent of other and outside agencies.[35] They do not go far with the mass of people, but they can excite these when their privileges are attacked. In the Christian world, the paramount truth is, most probably, that in spite of the small hold of the churches on the externals of worship, men are much better citizens than they would have been had Christ never lived and died.

There remains the hearsay of clubs and social intercourse as sources of public opinion. More than at any time in the previous history of the world does man come into relation with man. Communication and transport are so rapid, and division of labor so takes people from their own homes and mixes them together at work and in their leisure, that, willy-nilly, they learn something of each other's experience, needs, aspirations, and values. It is true that these contacts are irregular, a little incoherent, often more trivial than the conversations reported in the novels of Sinclair Lewis, Thomas Wolfe, Aldous Huxley, and Jules Romains, but they take place over a long series of years and tend to cure purely personal preoccupations. There is force in the astonishing realization that there are other people in the world. It is idle to imagine that the knowledge and opinion thus diffused can possibly be gauged in any quantitative fashion, but it is obviously important. If we can judge by changes in fashion, in the vulgar tongue, in the spread of rumors, and changes of political allegiance which have been produced quite definitely *not* by the agency of printed opinion, it must be very important in quantity. Its quality, however, is crude: it is based upon all sorts of hearsay, evidence of the most doubtful value, complete nonsense, and logical op-

erations so crude and false that one would swear to their impossibility were it not for the direct evidence of one's senses. World War II, coming on top of ideological discussions, caused an enormous interpersonal stir—veteran interest was fostered, and the nations will surely benefit permanently.

PARTY IS KING!

WE have surveyed the extent to which the mass of voters are independently capable of judging public affairs, since only if they are capable can they know how they wish to be represented. We have seen that a number of agencies of instruction exist apart from the direct experience of the individual voter. We found that his direct experience in limited and special and produces desires but little knowledge of social possibilities. What can we say, in general, about the agencies through which experience of social events and problems are obtained at second hand?

The vast mass of voters are entirely innocent of objective knowledge of political possibilities. Their disciplined study is of the slightest. A few have a smattering, small in quantity, uneven in distribution, incoherent, without basic soundness. A very small number, indeed, go beyond this and obtain a sufficiently systematic and profound insight into the body politic. The general body of the electorate does not, and cannot under present conditions, contribute more to politics than some a smoldering, some a flaming, sensibility of their wants and passions. Even these are not clearly focused to themselves, and are hardly articulate without use of the jargon of propaganda. This holds good not only of the poor; it is just as true of the middle and upper classes who have not had a special training in the social sciences.

A consciousness of wants is the independent contribution of the electorate to representation: but not yet an adequate knowledge of what is possible. The electorate is not entirely devoid of an informed sense of the possible, for everyday contact inevitably teaches a good many things —all that is summed up in the terms mu-

---

[35] Cf. the papal protest against the fascist attempt to monopolize the education of youth in the interests of "the pagan state" (*Universe*, July, 1931). But consider also the failure of that church to combat Mussolini, and the obsequiousness of so many of its clergy to the fascist rulers, central and local. Nor did it speak clearly enough against Hitler's régime. See Herman Finer, *Mussolini's Italy* (London, 1935), Chap. XVI.

tuality, reciprocity, harmony, common sense, morality, and forbearance. But this can only be applied to the problems of government when these are known in all their intricacy, and when their remote, impersonal natures are "brought home" to the citizen. The power of generalization and abstraction, and of comprehending the significance of general laws, is of the rarest.

There is thus a field, which has always been vast, but which in the modern state is colossal, of which the average voter is ignorant and cannot help being ignorant. He is likely for several generations to remain so in spite of the specious and not disinterested observations of Lenin, hardly supported by the practice of the Soviet state.[36] It is the inescapable result of the peculiar civilization of our time, with its economic compulsions and ethical failures. It is not the result of capitalism but of something deeper, and that is economic acquisitiveness serving itself with modern sources of energy and the aid of a machine as vast and complicated as the great globe itself. The electorate needs help!

The Help the Electorate Needs. What is the help the electorate needs? (1) Since it consists of many small "publics", each with its own opinion, the voters need to be helped to see the consequences for themselves and for others of their self-regarding opinion. Some one, some agency,

must bring to them the vivid knowledge of the repercussions of the opinion of each upon others, and of others' opinion upon it. These repercussions, in the tangled, dense intricacy of modern societies, can be of the most desperate complexity in the number of interrelationships involved, and the extent to which they must be carried over successive stages of the future. Many of these interrelationships are world wide, concern the fate of foreign nations, and might involve war! Consider only the different interest of the various groups in a policy of full employment, and the variety, extent, depth, and future stages of the measures necessary to produce it! Or the pervasive, distant consequences of the control of traffic in alcoholic liquor! Hence, some agency standing *outside* the individual and the group is needed to render the all-round view possible, and simultaneously, it must stand at the pinnacle of knowledge in the state, so that to it may flow the total diversity of relevant facts.

Nor is this all. (2) Some one or some agency outside the groups must assume responsibility for presenting a public opinion which harmonizes all the little opinions as to *(a)* priority in time for satisfying their respective wants, *(b)* preference in *value,* how much satisfaction shall be accorded to each, and *(c)* a doctrine of *justice* by which to commend these to all who are virtually being asked to modify their little public opinions in the light of the wider one, a larger goal.

The Rarity of Native Aptitude. The attainment of political knowledge and wisdom is a faculty as special and rare as any other science and art. There are very few first-, second-, and third-rate political thinkers for the same reason that there are very few first-, second-, and third-rate poets, painters, sculptors, dramatists, composers, physicians, constructive engineers, actors, chemists, critics, and people of taste. For fruitful political initiative one needs, in addition to technical training, a native complex of qualities called "aptitude". Training and experience are alike wasted upon the inept: they can be given if society should set itself to the task, but

---

[36] Lenin, *State and Revolution* (New York, International Publishers, any edition since 1917): "Accounting and control—these are the chief things necessary for the organising and correct functioning of the first phase of Communist society. . . The accounting and control necessary for this have been simplified by capitalism to the utmost, till they have become the extraordinarily simple operations of watching, recording and issuing receipts, within the reach of anybody who can read and write and knows the first four rules of arithmetic. When the majority of the people begin everywhere to keep such accounts and maintain such control over the capitalists (now converted into employees) and over the intellectual gentry who still retain capitalist habits, this control will really become universal, general, national. . . The more complete the democracy, the nearer the moment when it begins to be unnecessary . . . the more rapidly does every state begin to wither away."

it is idle to imagine that the distribution of human talent can rise above itself. This is not to say that, given conditions we have earlier indicated, a great deal of ignorance and fallacious method could not be replaced by fact and sound knowledge. And that, obviously, on the democratic assumption, is most desirable and necessary. This would still leave the intelligence curve as it is, with only a few at its superior end, although it would cause the personal place on the curve of actual electors to be very different from what it now is owing to the operation of present-day factors. The student of government will make many mistakes in the analysis of political institutions and their operation unless he has in mind continually the broad results of certain well-known tests of intelligence.[37]

The Low Potential of the Mass. There is one thing more, of at least equal importance. The mass of men and women are not self-excitable except occasionally and for a few brief moments, and concerning one or two special interests. In regard to all other things they are permanently apathetic and bored. Even if they know, they do not feel. There are as few geniuses of emotion as of intellect or art. To use the language of motor transport, the mass of people are not "self-starters." Some agency is needed to excite them and, on special occasions such as elections, to concentrate a heavy and unrelenting bombardment upon them, enforcing their attention.

(To avoid any misunderstanding, I am anxious to affirm that the traits of the electorate do not commit one to the nazi and fascist, or even the Leninist-Stalinist claim, of the spiritual superiority of the leaders to the masses. For that claim is that their values are *naturally* better than those of the masses, whereas I have already shown that there is no test of the level of moral values that is objective and outside man: and that the surest long-run method

of discovering the most acceptable and livable level is to admit a right in all men to utter, and equally compel consideration for, what is revealed to them. This has little to do with knowledge of temporal facts, and does not lose in validity because the person is politically apathetic; see Chapters 5 and 38.)

Now what all the other agencies do not do—namely, teach—and what cannot be done without special organizations—namely, to gather the talented and stimulate interest—political parties set out to accomplish. They gather up the whole nation into fellowships, and they lead, in the sense of bringing to the individual citizen a vision of the whole nation, otherwise distant in history, territory, and futurity. They gather the knowledge and the capable practitioners, and we must now consider their methods and ask how far they are successful.

Let us make no mistake: political parties do not perform this function simply because they nobly want to; it is not entirely an elective virtue of theirs; they are in part compelled. For the first commandment of a political party is victory. Victory is found also written even unto the ninth of its commandments. The tenth, enforced by experience, the general sense of honesty, and one's personal integrity, may counsel other courses. By choice, the party would be victorious; virtuous it is only by compulsion. "Buncombe" is the homage which electoral virtue so often pays to electoral victory.

A Continuous Organization. The organization operates incessantly, partly because victory in parliamentary elections is otherwise impossible, but also because in the modern state there are many local elective offices to fill. In France, also, the Senate is partially renewed every three years, and in America and Germany there are state as well as federal elections. Although in the United States much has been done to bring about a coincidence of elections, the elective periods are too heterogeneous to perfect this. So the organization, the machine, the caucus, the workers, are always on the watch for movements of their opponents and for the opportunity to

---

[37] L. M. Terman, *The Measurement of Intelligence* (New York, 1916); L. L. Thurstone in *Psychometrica*, various surveys of "primary mental abilities," *The Nature of Intelligence* (New York, 1924), and *Multiple Factor Analysis* (Chicago, 1947).

"swing" over blocks of votes. There are slack periods, but none entirely dead; and informal talks and formal councils are always in progress. Reputations fluctuate as their owners legislate, administer, or conduct campaigns, and men and women are marked out for various positions.

This, the permanence of organization and activity, marks off the parties of the present from the parties of three quarters of a century ago, and the parties of England, Germany, and the United States from party organization in France until after World War II. For before the middle of last century, political parties were loosely organized and quiescent between elections, sudden mobilization taking place just before the election and demobilization after polling day.

More recently the parties have added another source of power: they deliberately set out to capture the young people, long before they are of an age to vote, and this is done by the creation of Leagues of Young Socialists, or Friends of the Children, or the Junior Imperial League, or Pioneers, or Communist Youth, Young Liberals. *Fascisti,* or *Hitler-Jugend* who are not so much taught as drilled. The impulses of human rhythm and harmony are exploited by demonstrations, processions, singing, and self-decoration. In this sphere Germany was first and most developed; England holds the second place, France the next, and the United States the last. (The Soviet state is, for obvious reasons, most interested in political youth organizations.[38]) Thus the party moves towards all-inclusiveness from infancy to senility, as well as permanency of organization.

How do the parties operate? We will not make a rigid separation between the all-the-year-round activity of the party and its activity in the few weeks preceding the campaign, but will point out any differences of kind that occur when the period

of organization and skirmishing merges into that of intensest battle. The parties operate through meetings, personal canvassing, the circulation of "literature," the creation and distribution of posters and slogans, the use of radio broadcasting, the manipulation of the press, demonstrations, and "pressure." These methods are common to all parties in each country, but in each the emphasis is differently placed.

Meetings are broadly of three kinds: at the party headquarters, in halls, in the streets. At the party headquarters only avowed members of the party and novices are entitled to be present. The meetings are regular and frequent. Here the serious business is speechmaking by nationally prominent members of the party and by the leading members of the local caucus. Questions and discussions follow the speeches. The speeches are naturally directed to strengthen the party's enthusiasm and numbers, and the tendency therefore is for the speaker to say that all things which the party considers desirable are possible. Only the hopeful may be alleged of one's party: electorally, to doubt is to die. The local members are more inclined to listen to doubts expressed by a considerable personage who comes from afar than from one, even a leader, among themselves. The local leaders also learn by such contacts three important things: (1) what the party can do as distinct from the full measure of what it would like to do; (2) the possible maximum accomplishment even if opponents did not exist; and (3) on what terms the various occupational interests and territorial sections can be reconciled with each other and with a conception of the "national" interest. The local workers learn the intentions of the national leaders, may apprehend that they are part of a nation-wide community, suffer a change of mind, and cause a change of mind in the speaker. By slow degrees, harmony and oneness are approached: it is never a perfect unison, but it is far from violent chaos. These meetings are important, too, for their cohesive powers, for they are accompanied by pleasant conviviality. One is the recognized member of

38 For the Soviet Union cf. Samuel Harper, *Making Bolsheviks* (Chicago, 1931); for Italian fascism, cf. Herman Finer, *Mussolini's Italy,* Chap. XV; for nazi Germany, *Nazi Conspiracy and Aggression* (U.S. Government Printing Office, 1947), Vol. I, p. 312 ff. and relevant documents.

a community! What does this not mean to otherwise rather humdrum and lonely souls? Here is significance, grace, justification, honor, even immortality—as well as utility! All these things warm the heart and provide the party with willing workers and preachers not too careful of the rational value of their gospel. Such meetings are more prevalent in England and Germany than in the United States and France, and less in France than the United States, where the parties have large competition from the churches and the Y.M.-C.A. (especially in the rural parts, which constitute nearly one-half of the whole country) and from its multitude of civic but nonparty organizations. They are less frequent in the parties of the middle and upper than of the poorer classes.

In all countries there are occasional meetings in halls. They are held on the occasion of some special national or party crisis, when a new policy is being debated; or when one of the great men of the party pays a visit; when a special fillip is needed to party organization—when a "rally" is required, or during an election when advertisement and the spectacle of activity are likely to arouse confidence and enthusiasm. They are open meetings, though usually the faithful form the largest part of the attendance.[39]

The objective merits of a policy are not explored with pedantic care. A cut-and-dried policy is artfully expounded. The art consists in appealing to the interests of the listeners while suppressing considerations of difficulty or making light of them or ascribing them to a moral defect in opponents; in drawing special attention to the noble personal character of the speaker and his colleagues; and, especially, in causing laughter. Usually the meeting is kept well under control by a chairman, and questions are allowed after the main speech. But it has become a well-established custom in England (not so well-founded, though practiced, in Germany

and France, and hardly attempted in the United States) to interject short sharp questions. The speakers are expected to answer this "heckling" good-naturedly. Nor are they everywhere expected to answer seriously and rationally. And much of a speaker's success depends upon his ability to glide over difficulties or to demonstrate, with wit, that the question is foolish and the questioner a congenital idiot. I have been astonished at the good humor and tolerance of audiences in England, at their ever-patient long-suffering in the United States, where they rarely "heckle," at their stern passionateness in Germany, and at their turbulence and pithy comments in France. Everywhere better and more questions are asked in the towns than in the country.

In the streets the local workers or paid speakers, the "party hacks" of the richer parties, gather audiences round them, especially during elections. This is practiced far more in Great Britain than elsewhere; in Germany and France previous permission of the police is required and freely granted. There are no rules of order, save those contributed by the ideas of fair play normally held by the majority. The meetings have the merit that they attract voters who might not go to a hall or party headquarters, and they give the illusion, by determined activity, that the party is out to win. (The activity of the Communist party and the Young Communists in the Soviet Union takes this form, very busily in election years, and also in between). Since the voice, even at its highest natural strength, will not carry far, the audience may drop off. The natural means to prevent this is to drop all subtlety of argument and to lay emphasis upon the sensational and the amazing. Consequently, these meetings, though serviceable to the party, are not of the same value to truth. There is no possibility of close argument and consecutive discussion. Both in the hall and in the street a "demonstration" is more important than technical and logical proof. The audience has neither the time, opportunity, nor wisdom to detect and challenge fallacies! (Some improvement in the speaker's rationality has re-

---

[39] In nazi Germany and fascist Italy such open argument was not possible. In the Soviet Union it is restricted to polite and "loyal" expressions on minor matters of government, but certainly not on high policy.

cently been produced by the invention of the sound truck with its public-address system.)

Personal Canvassing. It is the practice in England and the United States,[40] and to a lesser degree in Germany and France, for the party machine to organize personal calls upon the voters to discover their affiliation and induce them to promise their vote. All canvassing has for its object the production of the largest number of votes for one's own party on polling day, and it is then that it assumes its most intensive and desperate form. Canvassing is an ancient practice in the Anglo-Saxon countries, and has consequently been skilfully elaborated.[41] If the voter does not entirely close the door to conviction, the canvasser attempts the task of conversion. To be useful, the canvasser must have qualities akin to those of an expert salesman: the psychology of salesmanship is the psychology of canvassing. He must have a commodity for every taste and an answer to every objection; and these must be varied with the client. The canvassers usually learn from the party's handbook, or notes for speakers, or speeches at meetings; they also improvise. On the whole, voters are flattered by the attentions of the canvasser: their existence, it seems, is recognized: they are somebody: and they have a favor to grant which somebody actually begs. Some busy housewives are a little annoyed, and some voters, who are disillusioned with the promises of canvassers,

maintain a neutral and forbidding blankness which is disconcerting. But on the whole, canvassing is liked. The essence of successful canvassing is to be all things to all men, and the canvasser is so much tempted by personal contact with the voter, and the knowledge that perhaps a vote depends upon his talk, that it is exceedingly difficult not to promise too much. Much that is impossible is promised, much that is untrue is told, and there is a large element of nonrational persuasion, especially when the candidate himself canvasses. Men of great private integrity think it proper on such occasions to go along with their wife and their children especially dressed for the occasion. No doubt they are convinced that the end justifies the means. To say this is to emphasize the extent to which politicians themselves believe that the ordinary agencies of education have failed.

"Literature." Party literature is broadly of two kinds—that destined mainly for candidates and workers, and that to be broadcast among the electorate. In the first class are pamphlets upon special topics, a periodical, usually a monthly magazine or newspaper, sets of speaker's notes, and during campaigns, booklets full of "points" or "shot and shell." In the second class are leaflets and pamphlets and the literature distributed at elections—the "address to the electors" or *professions de foi*. (Material to be printed locally is distributed among several printers to attract votes from each, and at least cause the candidate to be discussed.) The mass of literature is immense; the greatest amount per head being circulated in the United States, the second place is shared by England and Germany, while France is far in the rear.

What are the chief features of this literature? It is inveterately dogmatic, and every fact adduced only goes to show that the party is right. It uses the fallacy known as "stacking the cards." Argument is mixed with facts and figures, the weak points of the opposition are paraded and ridiculed or denounced, while one's own promises are proclaimed as both desirable and possible.

Broadcasting and Politics. Broadcasting

40 Cf. F. R. Kent, *The Great Game of Politics* (New York, 1926); Charles E. Merriam, *The Making of Citizens* (Chicago, 1931), p. 316. Cf. also A. E. Smith, *The Citizen and His Government* (New York, 1935), p. 119 ff.

41 This is a laborious task, especially among the working class, for they are not accessible until the evening, and after they have washed and eaten. If a voter says he is of their party, their task is to sum up whether he is speaking the truth or not and, in any case, to see that he gets party literature; it is also to judge whether he needs to be called on before polling day, whether he can be trusted to go to the polling station, or whether he needs to be escorted by a party worker. Cf. F. Gray, *Confessions of a Candidate* (London, 1925). Cf. also R. B. Maccullum and A. Readman, *The British General Election, 1945* (Oxford, 1947), Chaps. V-X.

commenced as a casual auxiliary to the more personal process already described. Its importance swiftly increases. Millions of voters in their parlors can be directly reached by the party leaders! In the United States about one fourth of the campaign expenditures is for radio time. In Britain there is bitter interparty dispute for an "equal" time on the very few occasions allotted by the British Broadcasting Corporation, and the government is allowed little more than the opposition!

The effect is, on the whole, deleterious. Meetings and canvassing are partially supplanted. Immediate effectiveness of appeal tells far more than the truth, for time is short and the attention of listeners easily strained. Qualifying detail must be omitted in favor of exciting exaggerations. No personal meeting affects the speaker; there is no discussion; the effect of spontaneous interjections is lost. Attention is focused on immediate issues; the general program is blurred. The manner has some advantage over the matter. Worst of all, listeners cannot ask questions, make comments, or obtain elucidations. Thus we recede from rationality and approach the complete triumph of the good "debating point." The concentration of power in the party leaders is promoted, since they appeal over the heads of their immediate following, whose critical independence is thereby weakened. Let us remember that this is part of the process by which cabinets, the supreme governmental directorates, are selected.

Function and Effect of Political Parties. On reflection, then, it will be realized that political parties, whether they consciously intend it or not, and whether or not they are pleased with what they are obliged to do, perform a combination of six functions:

(1) They bridge distance, since the territorial area of nations and electoral districts is so wide that the electors must be brought into communion with each other. Party is the organizing intermediary. (2) Parties wrestle with the apathy of all citizens, and particularly of those who are least endowed with or convinced of an active interest in politics, the government of public affairs. The public opinion polls always register the numbers of those who declare their answer to the question as "Don't know!", and this is often translatable as "Don't care!". The parties work to make citizens care, and actively intervene. (3) Political parties seek to overcome ignorance: they penetrate social and economic complexity and make it simple; they investigate and report the territorially distant effects of local policies and bring home the results to the local district electors; they attempt the tasks of foresight, sometimes over generations, and confront the voter with the fact that a choice must be made between the short and the long run. Only a small number of citizens in democracies are as yet able to do these tasks for themselves without assistance.

(4) Political parties set a priority scale of values for the fulfilment of the will of the many diverse small publics of which the great national public is composed—who shall be attended to in preference to some other groups' demands, and what degree of the demands of each group shall obtain satisfaction in the law and administration. Parties also set an order of priority in time: what comes first for legislative attention. (5) They select spokesmen and leaders—indeed, they *are* spokesmen and leaders. Men and women select themselves as leaders in democratic countries, but for the victory of their ideas they need more men and women to accompany them. Hence an original process of self-selection, and then the selection of yet others, followed by a more organized method of seeking adherents and leaders occurs. It is done best where the party has dignity and prestige, and above all where it is founded on principles. (6) Parties assume responsibility for these services; they accept—indeed, they eagerly seek—the obligations of leadership. The status leads to authority, jobs in the vulgar sense as well as vocation in the nobler sense, and the satisfaction of realizing social, economic, and political ideals.

Professor Lazarsfeld has shown that political party campaigns tend to have three effects: they activate some voters, they reinforce others in their opinion, and they convert others. His figures are interesting, but their exactness as a generalization for the whole nation is not material to the present discussion. He concludes: [42]

In sum, then, this is what the campaign does: reinforcement (potential) 53%; activation 14%; reconversion 3%; partial conversion 6%; conversion 8%; no effect 16%.

By *activation* he means that campaign propaganda "brings the voter's predispositions to the level of visibility and expression. It transforms the latent political tendency into a manifest vote." [43] By *reinforcement* he means that though some people knew before the campaign how they would vote after it, "political communications served the important purpose of preserving prior decisions instead of initiating new decisions. It kept the partisans in line by reassuring them in their vote decision; it reduced defections from the ranks. It had the effect of reinforcing the original vote decision." [44] Lazarsfeld urges the importance of this, considering that where there are two strong parties confronting each other, party loyalties are constantly open to the danger of corrosion. As for *conversion,* he asks, "Were people actually convinced by campaign propaganda to renounce their original choice in favor of the opposition, or to decide upon a vote contrary to that ordinarily associated with their social characteristics?" [45]

If the Electorate Were Omniscient. What might be expected if the electorate were all-knowing and all-interested? What are the limits to the success of propaganda?

The first hypothesis is entertained simply to indicate the room for improvements in the public-opinion-forming bodies (like the schools) and political parties.

An omniscient electorate would choose representatives capable of carrying into the legislature a full and shrewd knowledge of (1) the human and environmental conditions requiring the making of law. It would understand the interest and

spiritual objections of dissentients in friendly ranks as well as the regular opposition. It would understand the obstacles and the means of surmounting or surrendering to them. The relationship between the social value and the time-order of legislation would be palpable. Citizens would insist on men who could fulfil such needs. They would therefore concentrate rigorously on the selection of candidates, and realize that this decision is their supreme contribution to the quality of the legislature and all its works. The electorate would not be deflected by arguments of transient strength as compared with the long-term values. It would not be seduced by meretricious but fallacious appeals. It would be much more *direct* in its seeking to be represented. It would not, that is to say, permit its convictions to be distorted by party organization or frustrated by party officials who amass special power by continually tending the machine, and by their disturbing conflicts over their own personal ambitions.

The Limits of Propaganda. Where parties can challenge each other constantly and in all districts, no falsehood can live for long, or long enough to be even a short positive influence on the laws. (The condition is notoriously unfulfilled in the Southern states of the United States.) More equality of wealth will solve many problems of "propaganda" that constitute anxieties to-day. Harder work by party rank and file can defeat almost any propaganda, though it costs leisure time.

In dictatorships propaganda is defeated, or at any rate limited by (1) people's biological proneness to certain ways of feeling and thinking; (2) common-sense discussion among men and women, which cannot be totally controlled; (3) memories of a former time; (4) reflection on events in one's own lifetime, and comparison between promises made, discrepancies between these and events, and inconsistencies in the arguments used by the propagandists. Libraries are always dangerous to dictators. Further, utilitarian values assert themselves strongly. And, above all, every scheme of human values, from metaphysics down to the pattern of our daily

[42] *The People's Choice* (New York, 1944), p. 103.
[43] *Ibid.,* p. 75.
[44] *Ibid.,* p. 87.
[45] *Ibid.,* p. 94.

duties, has somewhere a flaw for large bodies of people.

The propagandist can enforce obedience if force is at his disposal as the *ultima ratio,* and uses it to root out nascent dissent. He cannot make all the people believe by the (on the whole) trivial tricks used. To secure belief, he must deliver the goods. Otherwise the consumption of his persuasions is only temporary and more apparent than real. Even the most sanguine of propagandists, Hitler, could not transfer his fanaticism: only a handful died in the bunker with him. Nor can the Soviet rulers remake the consciousness of the Russian people in their own image; they continue to rule by enormous, unprecedented force, and yet still considerably yield to mass inertia. Mussolini's closest associates abandoned him in spite of his propaganda.[46]

The Burden of Electoral Responsibility. The modern democratic electorate is charged with a terribly heavy responsibility for the integrity, survival, and welfare of the society we call "the nation"— and when one says the "nation" one says "the world." That electorate is largely dependent on its leaders, because they are (or should be) men and women who devote themselves to getting to know "the nation," who have special aptitudes for such an enterprise, and who are especially sensitive to their representative function. To the vast social network of minds, characters, and interests—an incomplete and ragged texture without them—their service is to add coherence and riftless interweaving. But if they thus lead, they can do so only because informed and considered support is lent them by the rank and file of citizens, or because the job is abandoned to them out of electoral apathy, carelessness, or negligence. If the latter is the case, then the laws may not solve political problems as well as they might: a serious risk is incurred. At critical phases of world affairs, in economic depressions, during postwar readjustments, in periods of con-

flict between employers and workers, and between the workers themselves in their various occupations seeking each a larger share of the national product, disaster may occur. It can happen. It has happened. The condition of Europe and the United States is witness thereto. Falling short of catastrophe, but still seriously damaging, society may be afflicted with economic waste, underproduction, and injustice to large sections of the people.

When the student of politics is confronted with the problem of the "responsibility" of the German people for Hitler and World War II, or of the French people for their prewar governments leading to their dismal war effort, the quality of the electorate is at the heart of the answer. At the minimum, the voters were guilty of civic ignorance. To what destination did the road paved by their votes lead? It is not unreasonable to hold that the régime of political parties, as hitherto known, cannot satisfy the needs of democratic government—that is, achieve welfare and social justice and progress under the impulse of freely and actively cooperative citizens—without a marked improvement in the formation of policies, the selection of representatives, nation-wide discussion of the issues to be determined, and unremitting vigilance over the legislature. Britain's survival is, in part, due to the high degree of civic understanding of its people. Britain's solution of the problems of an extensively planned and socialized economy, beginning with the General Election of 1945, problems of incentive, loyalty, dissent, cooperation, is another test at least as exacting. The responsibilities on the shoulders of the modern electorate are, indeed Atlantean.[47] The Soviet rulers have denied that their people, at any rate, are able to bear them,[48] and hold them in the tutelage not merely of children, but mainly delinquent children.

---

[46] Cf. Piero Saporiti, *Empty Balcony* (London, 1947).

[47] Cf. Herman Finer, *America's Destiny* (New York, 1947), Chap. XII, "Destiny Follows Power."

[48] See especially, Finer, *Ibid.,* Chap. VIII, "The Soviet Despotism in Russia."

15

A Closer View of Party
and a Sketch of Dictatorial Parties

THE CENTRAL MACHINE

THE propaganda of political parties is not conducted by the unconcerted activity of the numerous local caucuses, for they have common interests, and not all have the information, money, speakers, and organizing ability adequate to their purpose. It is clear, too, that the central organization is in closer touch with the sources of information: the legislature, the political chiefs, the stock exchange, the government offices, the press agencies, spokesmen for the "lobby," and so on; and this proximity means exactness and promptness of reaction—which are essential to a campaign. Very broadly, the activities of the central machine, as regards the electorate, comprise the planning and execution of campaigns, policy making, and the accumulation and distribution of funds.

The planning and execution of an actual campaign is conducted with more deliberation in England, the United States, and Germany than in France; and it falls into a number of steps well known to close observers of the tactics of central headquarters. First comes the settlement of internecine disputes in the constituencies, the counseling of preparedness, and the determination of how many and which constituences are worth fighting. Second comes the discovery of an "issue" or "keynote" which will inflame the public and put opponents on the defensive and at a

disadvantage.[1] Campaign managers are not entirely free in this matter, for they cannot choose except from the more immediate subjects which affect national welfare. Experience has shown the remarkable effect of ingenuity, the best recent examples of this, in England, being the cry of "Free Trade" in 1923, "Bolshevism" in 1924, "Unemployment" in 1929, "Your postal savings" in 1931,[2] "Peace and collective security" in 1935, and "Socialism," "Let Churchill finish the job," and "Beware the Socialist Gestapo" in 1945; in Germany in 1930 "Revision of the peace treaties," "Strong and stable government," and "Domestic peace" against "Disturbers" (i.e. the extreme elements on the Right and Left): in 1932 the Nazi cry of "the shame of the Weimar system": and in the United States in 1928, "Prosperity" and in 1932 and 1936 "the New Deal versus free enterprise."

Search for an issue, and its formulation, fall to the leader of the party in Parliament, the chairman of the party executive committee (or its equivalent), the party manager or agent (as in England), or its secretary (on the Continent), or the

[1] Cf. F. R. Kent, *The Great Game of Politics* (New York, 1926), Chap. XLI; Raymond Moley, *After Ten Years* (New York, 1939); Charles Michelson, *The Ghost Talks* (New York, 1944).
[2] Cf. McNeill Weir, *The Tragedy of Ramsay MacDonald* (London, 1937).

especially appointed campaign manager in the United States. The connection between these and the Parliamentary leadership in England and on the Continent is very close, so that the Parliamentary leaders have every reason to be fully conscious of their undertakings and mandate. The connection is excessively loose in the United States, since the platform precedes the Presidential nomination and the manager is chosen even later than that. The discovery of the issue is, of course, preceded by careful soundings of the country taken through the medium of the local agents and secretaries, and sometimes circuits are made by the leaders for this purpose, as by Taft and Stassen during 1947. Such circuits are especially necessary in the United States, owing to the enormous size of the country.

The Program. The central machine is not only the energizing and strategic center of the campaign; it is also the creator of the program. The center is under the control of a committee, chosen by delegates to a conference who have been selected by the local caucuses. The various countries have slight variations of this machinery, as have the parties themselves. In England, Germany, and France (among the carefully organized parties), the creation of policy is strongly centralized, in spite of the fact that original as well as critical resolutions may be moved at conferences. The short time allowed for the conferences (five or six days at the outside), the necessity of preserving the semblance of a united front, the willingness to trust in the established leaders, the lesser information possessed by the critics compared with the party officials, and the superior knowledge and wisdom of those leading the opposition or the government in the legislature, and often their arbitrariness in using the procedure of the conference, most usually result in a decisive victory for headquarters.[3] The resolutions

become the party's policy. In the United States the resolutions committee of each party gets to work at the Presidential nominating conventions. Tremendous private battles occur for control of these committees. A distinctive feature is their "hearings" of the great organized economic and social groups—the "lobbies"—who want to insert a plank in the platform.

Now party conferences and conventions are demonstrations rather than organizations to think out policy, in spite of the fact that sometimes party conferences achieve success in this sphere, and that their temper may persuade the leaders of the urgency of change. Upsets are not infrequent in French party conferences, especially in the Socialist party and the Radical and Radical Socialist party. Hence the importance of unity in the conference. Where publicity imposes unity it is clear that some other way must be discovered of making terms with internal dissent before it becomes publicly disagreeable. This is done behind the scenes where the voters are never permitted to penetrate and the report of which they hear only, if at all, in a garbled form, and perhaps from a statesman's biography a generation or more after the event.[4] The political importance of this secrecy is twofold: it shrouds from the citizen the real source of policies, and it provides the possibility of a *rapprochement* between majority and minority groups and rival persons, and, by averting public strife, it works against the breakup of parties.[5] Policies are then set forth with the *imprimatur* of that joint anonymity, the party, or as though they were the personal contribution of its leader. Once again, then, the mass of voters is deprived of the knowledge without which control becomes an empty term. The prevention of the disintegration of

[3] Cf. also J. K. Pollock, "The British Party Conference," *American Political Science Review*, June, 1938, for an account of the British Labour party; and cf. above all, any report of the Annual Conference of Labour, Conservative, or Liberal parties.

[4] For example in Arthur Schlesinger Jr.'s *Age of Jackson* (New York, 1945); or J. Alsop and T. Catledge's *The 168 Days* (New York, 1938); or J. Morley's *Gladstone* (London, 1903); or J. A. Spender and C. Asquith's *Asquith* (London, 1932); and more recently, Keith Feiling's *Life of Neville Chamberlain* (London, 1947). [5] Cf. J. L. Garvin, *Joseph Chamberlain* (London, 1938) for the story of the tariff campaign and the Conservative party.

parties is, as we shall see in the chapters on legislatures and cabinets, good; but this good can be obtained only by a relegation of certain values and desires to a place far down upon the party program, and perhaps their utter surrender.

The Research of Policy. Now, for reasons explained in the preceding chapter when we discussed the limit of party rhetoric, parties tend to equip themselves systematically by research not only for propaganda but for legislation. This has developed best where a high level of popular common sense and political experience prevail and where the parties fight intensely about the application of serious differences of principle. The impulse comes originally from the need to answer sensible questions, and, in proportion as these are put either by the worker or by the rank and file of either one's own party or the opposing parties, a source of such answers has had to be created. Nor is this all. A party gets a decided advantage when it sets the pace with proposals, shows that it cares for the public welfare, and that it is busily occupied with this when it can put unanswerable posers to the other side. Further, some persons in a party are not satisfied unless all the possibilities of reform are explored by experts. Moreover, in countries where the parliamentary system functions well, with full publicity, a clear sense of responsibility, and a recognition of the importance of organized and continuous opposition, the need arises of putting questions and amendments to the government's proposals. It is clear that a good reputation can be obtained, and a sense of public duty satisfied, only if the proper means are established to make this possible in the best technical, not partisan, sense. One thing is sought above all by members of every party—to obtain for every move of their own, electoral or parliamentary, the repute that it is national in its intention and benefit, not partisan: and so fasten upon their opponents the vice of preferring party to nation.

The result has been the establishment, in varying degrees in different countries, of research institutions and schools for candidates and the rank and file. The principal experiments so far were in Weimar Germany; England comes next; [6] while France and the United States lag very far behind. (In France various organizations, economical and social, which are outside the parties but ancillary to them, provide information.) The full importance to this development is appreciable only when two things, which have yet to be discussed, are remembered: the plebiscitary nature of modern democratic government, and the controlling part played by parties in parliamentary discussion.

The first significant characteristic of the party research bureaus is that they are centralized—established and managed by the central machine in the capital. The second is that they were commenced by the socialist parties, followed at length by the liberals, and taken up last by the conservatives, the latter tending to the view that since all that is is good, and should be preserved, there is no need of research. Broadly, research is conducted continuously by an office organization of several permanent officials, of proven academic capacity, linking up with committees of members of the legislature and experts co-opted for special branches of inquiry; and it is stimulated, and its results spread (apart from the party's periodical press and handbooks) at occasional schools and institutes, usually held at Easter and in summer. The American practice is less party schools than university-sponsored institutes, or the adult schools of labor unions. European party schools are more intensive.

The results of this activity and organization, broadly viewed, are significant. All parties become more advised of the technical possibilities and impossibilities of their policies on subjects susceptible of quantitative statement and discussion (as, for example, socialization, the organization of certain staple industries, unemployment, and social insurance problems). Rhetoric and nonrational appeals are pushed far back, and a large measure of agreement can be and is reached before

---

[6] Cf. *The Labour Organizer,* a monthly journal of the British Labour party.

the inevitable clash of ultimate ideals occurs. The result has been to socialize the conservatives and to conservatize the socialists. That this is an advantage there can be no doubt: for parties are but means to ends, and where government can proceed without certain machinery and qualities, it is pure extravagance to have them. To disagree from ignorance is certainly waste, and to outvote a minority for the same reason is a deplorable addition to the necessary sum of human pain.

In the United States such developments have not occurred. The nearest approach thereto was the establishment of an advisory committee on policies and platform by the Republican party in 1919. But its report, of large bulk and wide scope, built up by about two hundred members, composed mainly of experts of the Republican party outside Congress, was swept away by that imperious and cynical campaign manager, Will Hays.[7] A subsequent attempt in 1937 had little more value.[8] So far, the central leadership of national and state parties in the United States has no place for scientific intelligence as distinct from campaign technicians. Both Republican and Democratic parties have, of course, a paid office staff, but they have nothing to compare with the research committee and schools of the British and German parties. The research is only the hand-to-mouth research of every political party; that is, the hasty discovery of fairly accurate facts to bolster up an argument during the campaign, not the steady application of scientific thought to problems with the view of providing a solution of permanent national benefit. The frame of mind does not exist in the public of the United States, with the exception of the unimportant Socialist party and the CIO's young Political Action Committee. Outside those groups it exists in a number of associations, which do the work which in England has come to be included in the normal functions of a political party. I refer to such organizations (to name but a few) as the National League of Women Voters, the Anti-Saloon League, the United Nations Association, the Women's International League, the National Child Labor Committee, the United States Chamber of Commerce, and the Committee for Economic Development.

These organizations are propagandist, research, and "pressure" organizations. They concentrate upon Congress, upon the electoral support of one or more specified "planks" in a platform, and work through candidates and parties who are the more amenable to their purposes. I shall say more about these organizations later in this chapter and in the discussion of legislatures, but it will be seen that they are outside, yet impinge upon, parties, and exercise an independent influence upon the electorate. The results of their research are not immediately embodied in party policy, as the results of party research are in England, but the parties are hounded down and driven from pillar to post until at last they become the vehicles of reforms they themselves have not fully examined.

Parties, through the activity of the central headquarters in the campaign and in the creation of policy, have become strongly centralized. Or, to put it in another way, the mind of the localities and that of the center are almost one and the same thing, and the response of the localities to any problem is likely to be much the same as that of the center even without prompting, of which the means is continually available. This condition is most fully realized in England and Germany, is most mechanical and spasmodic in the United States, and was the least effective in France until 1945. The belief in freedom plays a large part in slackening (but to a small extent only) the reins held by the central machine, and therefore in giving opportunities to the local caucuses to act spontaneously. In Weimar Germany the method of election (proportional representation) and the prevailing belief in order and discipline contributed to cen-

---

[7] Cf. E. M. Sait, *American Parties and Elections* (New York, 1947), p. 479; McCune Lindsay, "Political Platforms of 1924," *Review of Reviews*, LXX (1924), p. 193 ff.

[8] Cf. Ronald Bridges, "The Republican Program Committee," *Public Opinion Quarterly*, 1939, p. 299 ff.

tralization, but the social system, which was based upon some real local differences and more legendary ones, slackened central control, at least so far as the state-Berlin relationship was concerned. In the United States, state politics run on lines very different from federal politics, so that considerable decentralization (sometimes a complete annihilation) of national party organization occurs. But it is mechanically centralized because no profound differences of principle cause men to adhere to one machine or boss rather than another, and it is spasmodic because victory is more highly regarded than policy and because between elections policy making demands almost nothing of the organization. This is related to the Congressional system, which has been partly explained in Chapter 6 on the separation of powers and will be further considered in Parts IV and V on legislatures, cabinets, and chiefs of state. In France, for a number of reasons which have already been given (p. 244), the central authority of parties has been important only on a few outstanding occasions when the country has been deeply moved or involved in difficulties, and in normal times (today) four parties maintain an almost nation-wide organization supporting a common body of opinion.

FUNDS AND UNPAID WORKERS

WE have seen how the parties conduct campaigns. They can do little or nothing without a tremendous apparatus of printed material, canvassers, and speakers. There is a large party bureaucracy: permanent professional officials, secretaries, organizers, and agents, employed at central headquarters or in the locality.[9] This bureauc-

racy has attained the highest quality and status in Germany and Great Britain. Necessarily, therefore, they need as much money as they can get. There may come a time when paper manufacturers will provide all the paper called for by political parties, when printers will work with the slightest intervals for meals and rest, when speakers will find their own train fares, their own information, and their own cough drops free of charge to their party, out of enthusiasm and hope. Some do so now. But while voluntary services are appreciable during the excitement of an election and the imminence of success or failure (particularly so in the parties of attack and progress), the work is too exacting to be done by unpaid workers, even at election times. Then, we have seen, operations are continuous at a level requiring the establishment of a permanent body of officials and the aid of all the instruments of publicity. It is possible to live upon enthusiasm only a short time: a party marches upon its belly.

The problem of party funds has, therefore, always been of importance. There is no way of exactly isolating the effect of money in elections. It cannot be said that so many hundreds of thousands of votes were turned this way or that by an extra expenditure of such and such a sum upon posters, pamphlets, ribbons, party buttons, or speakers. The services of the formal and informal voluntary party workers must be accounted for. We know, however, that party managers have a high opinion of the importance of money and its influential products, and we may assume that, other things being equal, the parties gain votes in proportion to the spaciousness and excellence of their publicity, which depends largely on expenditure. That is an article of faith with every election agent, and with the candidates. A high American party official once declared: "We have lost continuously because we did not have money enough to present the issues. There is no question about that."[10] In spite of the

9 In England the agents have their own professional associations, and the association of Liberal agents provides a diploma for those who pass examinations in electoral law and organization. In Weimar Germany, the party officials were similarly given a special education; cf. Röder, *op. cit.*, p. 46 ff. Cf. also the *Conservative Agent's Journal*, the *Liberal Agent*, and *Labour Organizer*.
A noteworthy fact is that many of the Labour local agents were partially maintained by the central machine. See also a perennial

concern about agents, in the *Annual Reports*, Labour party.
10 W. R. Marsh, treasurer of the Democratic National Committee, *Hearings before the Sub-*

fact that much publicity is wasted—posters put in places where they can hardly be seen, pamphlets and declarations thrown away without perusal, canvassing, which falls on deaf ears, and speeches which are simply regarded as entertainment—yet there is a response to stimulation, the response being proportionate to the stimulus; for the voter has certain self-created defenses which need conquest.

Money is therefore of vital importance, and its possession has given the richer classes the power if not to nullify yet to defer hostile votes. The advantage has not been entirely overcome by the large amount of voluntary help enjoyed by the parties of the poorer classes, and they also have had to find sources of revenue. The amounts spent are very large but official figures are obtainable only for Great Britain and the United States; in the first, candidates spent £1,073,216 in 1945, and the second over 20 million dollars in 1944. Even these figures do not include all that is spent. In Great Britain the amount spent by the central headquarters is not included; and in America it is admitted that the official figures are far below the true amount.[11] Further, there is no reckoning of petty amounts spent by friends.

Money is spent by the local caucuses and the central machine. In the local caucuses it is obtained from the candidate himself and from contributions by the members of the caucus, the rank and file paying a regular but small subscription, while wealthy friends of the candidate give large sums. The central machines also obtain money from the affiliated caucuses and from various associations (industrial, commercial and social) as well as

from private individuals. The socialist parties in all countries have a more regular and wider circle of contributors owing to their adherence to democratic ideas. They receive publicly acknowledged contributions from their individual members, and affiliated societies, the trade unions and the cooperative movement.

The richer parties have never had to rely upon such means of raising money; they have been able to tap a few large sources. Nor have they, except until recently in the United States, been obliged to divulge the sources of their revenue. In the English Liberal and Conservative parties a small amount comes from the local caucuses paid by duly inscribed members, but by far the largest amount has come and still comes from private contributions. So also in France [12] and Weimar Germany.[13] It is very likely that Communist parties are financially assisted by the Cominform. In the United States, about which there is much more information than about England because publicity is required and politicians are frequently indiscreet, the Republican and Democratic parties draw their funds mainly from: (1) rich private subscribers, that is, individual persons or business firms; (2) assessments of office holders, though this is strictly forbidden by statutes, and (3) small subscriptions paid with some regu-

Committee of the Senate Committee on Privileges and Elections, 66th Congress, 2nd Session, I, 532. Yet how, then, can the victory of 1932 be explained? By 1936 and 1940, even less funds were really needed for victory by this same party.

[11] Cf. *Return of Election Expenses* (April, 1946). The American figures cited refer only to the campaign "to secure the Presidential nomination." The total includes the expenses of the various committees "operating in more than one state." Cf. especially Louise Overacker, *Presidential Campaign Funds* (Boston, 1946), p. 34.

[12] Candidates in the richer parties find their own means and obtain subsidies from great industrialists. Cf. A. Pilenco, *Les Moeurs du Suffrage Universel en France: 1848-1928* (Paris, 1930), p. 207. Cf. also M. Privat, *Les Heures d'André Tardieu, et la Crise des Partis* (Paris, 1935). Some French party leaders who favored the German Nazis were assisted by Hitler and Mussolini. Cf. C. A. Micaud, *The French Right and Nazi Germany* (New York, 1943); also observations in "Pertinax," *The Gravediggers of France* (New York, 1944), p. 417 ff.
[13] Consider the example of the German Nationalist party, almost entirely subsidized by Hugenberg, head of the great steel and other concerns, and also the example of the German Nationalist party. Not infrequently, a bargain is made between the money power and the party leaders for the inclusion of certain representatives on the party list of candidates. Herr Thyssen has told beyond any doubt the story of the forming of the Nazi movement by the industrialists. Cf. Fritz Thyssen, *I Paid Hitler* (New York, 1941), p. 32 ff.

larity to the local caucus or begged at meetings at election time. In 1944, 26.3 per cent of the individual contribution to the Democratic National Committee came from donors of less than $100; to the Republican, only 9 per cent.[14]

We later (p. 297) discuss legislative regulation of party funds. The sources of revenue, except the small contributions voluntarily paid, have in both England and the United States given rise to serious criticism in recent years. There are common problems, but each country has its special difficulties.

SALE OF HONORS

THE special but not really important problem of Great Britain is the sale of honors to contributors to the party funds.[15] Had not World War I and a production of honors-seeking profiteers degraded moral standards, it is very probable that this traffic would have quietly continued until the advent of a Labour government with a decisive and resolute majority. That some titles of honor were sold was well known in the political world of Parliament and the parties. World War I caused a break-up of the old parties and a coalition of ancient enemies. Henchmen of the new leaders acted as whips and party managers. The touts could not help making mistakes, and prime ministers were always too busy to purge the lists of improper nominations. The House of Lords was vitally interested in the value of its hold upon the public imagination; and it has never been slow to further the public interests when its own privileges have been threatened. The royal commission which was established as the result of this tremendous shudder did not recommend the abolition of titles for political services. It accepted the necessity for such funds,[16] accepted the necessity of reward,

and this in the form under criticism, and suggested arrangements to keep the lists pure of any man "whose antecedents, if properly known, would have precluded the idea of his being singled out for promotion." [17] Substantially "political" honors are still given as before, although greater care is doubtless taken to avoid the ennoblement of the infamous.[18]

The evil is less the increase of a party's power in the House of Lords, for a few more or less conservative votes there do not matter, than the social one of imposing upon the public, which cannot readily distinguish between virtue and title, and the political one of providing services and money for those who benefit politically through the magnitude of bought propaganda. Without any doubt there would be some diminution of political service if titles were not given—to deny that is to deny that honor and prestige, not to mention snobbery, are quite potent factors in English life. Now, there is nothing immoral in subscriptions for the support of a policy considered of benefit to the nation at large. It has been said that "money does not smell," but that, surely, depends upon the nostrils.

---

14 A closer analysis is made in Chapter 15, below.
15 Cf. Hilaire Belloc and G. K. Chesterton, *The Party System* (London, 1911).
16 Cf. Royal Commission on Honours, *Report*, Cmd. 1789 (1922), p. 8: "The existence of party funds is notorious and the necessity for such existence under modern conditions as to the

conduct of elections is equally so"; and p. 6: "The practice of giving honours for purely political service has been continuously followed ever since the growth and development of the Party System of Government."
17 A Committee of three Privy Councilors (not members of the Government)—"men of well-known character and position" appointed by the prime minister for the period of his government to scrutinize the lists as passed up by the patronage secretary or party manager and to report to the prime minister. An adverse report overruled by the prime minister is to be communicated to His Majesty.
18 Arthur Henderson, the Labour member of the Commission, declared: "In a democratic country it is a distinguishing mark of the good citizen that he interests himself according to his opportunity in the well-being of the community. It is indisputable that public service of great value has been rendered by men and women whose thoughts have never dwelt upon titled reward, and in view of the difficulty of keeping the honours list pure, I do not believe that the abolition of political honours would in any way diminish either the volume or the quality of the services given to the community by its citizens."

SPOILS

THE common difficulty of both England and the United States, and of Germany and France equally, is that of large contributions made by "interests." The trouble arises from the fact that such contributions arouse popular suspicion and cynicism about the democratic process. For they are used to buy radio, press, and pamphlet propaganda which is directed to nonrational judgment, especially when used and paid for by people whose economic interests are bound up with the subordination of the masses and the probability that contributions may be made in the hope of influencing a party to give special benefits to big interests at the expense of all, or virtually to buy ambassadorships and cabinet offices.

The atmosphere of suspicion and distrust is murkiest in the United States, owing to the immense gulf which separates the theoretical idealism of all from the politicians' cynical use of government for the benefit of "spoilsmen" and financial interests. The periodical tariff battles, and the continuous attempt to stave off government regulation of, and inquiries into, "big business," have attracted large fortunes into party funds, and more into the Republican party's coffers than the Democratic, since that party has been "regular" on these questions. Charles A. Beard [19] quotes John Wanamaker, the treasurer of the Republican National Committee of 1888, who said to businessmen: "How much would you pay for insurance upon your business? If you were confronted with from one year to three years of general depression by a change in our revenue and protective measures affecting our manufactures, wages, and good times, what would you pay to be insured for a better year?" The businessmen paid.

In a Senate investigation committee of 1892 it was admitted that the sugar trust contributed to the funds of both parties, regulating its contributions by the size of party votes.[20] Croly, in his life of Marcus Alonzo Hanna, who was chairman of the Republican National Committee for over sixteen years, gives many examples of this kind. The tariff and "sound money" were the sanctions for universal appeals to bank and industry, and the former were even taxed at 0.25 per cent of their capital. The Standard Oil Company gave a quarter of a million dollars. Enormous sums were raised in 1896, 1900, and 1904: it is rumored that in 1896 Hanna raised between ten and fifteen million dollars.[21] There is ample evidence that the contributors believed that they were to get a specific return for their money.[22]

Toward the end of Hanna's reign and with the advent of Theodore Roosevelt, a change came over the public conscience: it was part of the general progressive movement and in part due to Roosevelt's own initiative, for he was prepared to accept money from anybody, but not on terms.[23] He gave the impetus to the passage of the law of 1907 forbidding national corporations to contribute to any election and any corporation from contributing to federal election campaigns. But, of course, what a corporation is forbidden to do its officers as private individuals may do. Although public opinion now condemns large contributions and their danger is widely recognized, large total sums of money are still raised in this way, as the figures suggest, but the parties now make a conspicuous exhibition of getting a large number of small sums. Both parties have at various times fixed maxima: the Democrats in 1908, $10,000,[24] the Republicans in 1916, $1,000; but in order to bring the total sum up to a useful level, both parties carefully organized "drives" with paid collectors. Apparently all this apparatus was bothersome compared with

---

[19] *American Government and Politics*, 3rd edition (New York, 1920), p. 175.

[20] N. W. Stephenson, *Nelson W. Aldrich* (New York, 1930), p. 120.
[21] A. W. Dunn, *From Harrison to Harding* (New York, 1922), Vol. I, p. 194.
[22] Herbert Croly, *op. cit.*, p. 323; and J. B. Bishop, *Theodore Roosevelt and His Time* (New York, 1920), Vol. I, p. 312.
[23] Bishop, *op. cit.*, Vol. I, p. 329.
[24] *Hearings* (on *Privileges and Elections*, cited above, note 10), I, 535, 15668.

its fruits,[25] and the system was abandoned as the chief source of supply. In 1944, the big contributions came to the Republicans from bankers, brokers and financiers, from big manufacturers of the heavy industries, from oil, insurance, the press, radio, the utilities, mining. The Democrats were most helped by a greater but more even spread of contributors including office-holders, brewers, merchants, and labor.

In England we can only suspect that the great industrial and commercial associations and the captains of industry subscribe in much the same spirit as in America. But the motive of special advantage would operate as only a faint hope, owing to the comparatively high standard of English politics, the publicity of English parliamentary procedure, and the absence of that spur to intrigue, a general tariff. For years the Labour party has demanded the publicity of party accounts, knowing that this could disadvantage only its opponents, and this cry was raised most poignantly during the debates on the "political levy" clause [26] of the Trade Disputes Act of 1927. (This clause deliberately sought to hamstring the party funds which came as affiliation fees from the trade unions, by making it unlawful for a trade union to require any member to make a political contribution unless he first delivered a notice of his willingness to contribute. They constituted over 70 per cent of the party funds. The act caused a 35 per cent reduction in party funds from this source. The act was repealed in 1946 shortly after the Labour government took office.)

It cannot be expected that a reform such as publicity of party accounts will eventuate until the Conservative and Liberal parties are powerless, for secrecy of funds is part of their electoral strength. Their publication would without any doubt cause the loss of large blocks of votes as soon as the voters realized who were paying for the posters, pamphlets, and speakers.

Workers are obtained for political parties by the prospects of a share in the "spoils" and by appeals to their sense of self-importance and snobbery as well as by their zeal for the party cause. The term "spoils" (an American addition to political terminology) in its narrow and most usual sense connotes the distribution of governmental paid posts by favoritism and patronage, and not by technical tests of efficiency regardless of political affiliation. But in American minds its sense is widened to cover the "use of public office" in an illegal manner for personal profit or advantage.[27] It is now mainly an American phenomenon, thus summed up by a foremost American political scientist: [28]

Here we find the exploitation of the public by the official, sometimes assuming the most subtle and sinister form of class and personal discrimination, or of open challenge to the fundamentals of law and justice commonly recognized in civilized society, and of these elements arises the force which President Cleveland once characterized in his trenchant phrase as "the cohesive power of public plunder."

Outside the most benighted of South American countries, America has had the longest and most vicious experience of this political malpractice, and is still its chief playground.[29] First, then, we should know the extent of offices available for political distribution, and, second, the scope of political perversion of public functions.

From the beginning of the Republic both state and federal politics were nourished by the use of office as a political re-

---

25 Although these were quite large by English standards: between 1916 and 1920, 30,904 contributions were made, averaging a little over $90 each. (*Hearings*, I, 1103.)
26 *Trade Disputes and Trade Unions Act*, 1927 (Section 4).

27 Charles E. Merriam and Harold Gosnell, *The American Party System* (New York, 1940), p. 103: "But the term 'spoils' may be applied not merely to a patronage or favour system, but to use of public office in an illegal manner for personal profit or advantage."
28 *Loc. cit.*
29 Both Canada and Australia have similarly suffered, but have both gone far to purifying themselves (cf. *Report on the Public Services*, 1919; and Annual Reports of Public Service Commission). Cf. R. McGregor Dawson, *The Civil Service of Canada* (Toronto, 1929) and *Government of Canada* (Toronto, 1947), Part IV. Cf. also F. A. Bland, *The Government of Australia* (Sydney, 1944), Introduction and Chap. IV.

ward.[30] But the "spoils system" on a really grand scale began when Andrew Jackson became President in 1828, his victory having been made by the new states of the West. Then, for various reasons, chief of which were the wide diffusion of agricultural land and wealth, the self-reliance and equalitarian ideals of a pioneering society, and the lack of geographical or spiritual contact with the culture of the East and spite against the financiers of that section, a fierce belief in the democratic rights of the common man prevailed. De Tocqueville has said of this area and time: "In this part of the American Continent, population has escaped the influence not only of great names and great wealth, but even of the natural aristocracy of knowledge and virtue." The leveling spirit, and the cynical observation that here was a perfect means to obtain electoral victories and private wealth, conduced to the establishment of the system that all offices should fall to the victorious party. The classic statement of the doctrine and cult which gave the world a new political term was made by William L. Marcy, a United States Senator from New York, where the system had reached its most polished perfection: [31]

The politicians preach what they practise. When they are contending for victory they avow their intention of enjoying the fruits of it. If they are defeated, they expect to retire from office. If they are successful they claim as matter of right the advantages of success. They see nothing wrong in the rule that to the victor belong the spoils of the enemy.

It was not quite in this spirit that Jackson inaugurated the system for the nation. He defended his practice first on the

grounds that the service would be more efficient if there were frequent changes in personnel, since long and fixed tenure caused the growth of indifference—a loss not offset by the fruits of experience; and second on the grounds that the rotation of office "constituted a first principle in the republican creed." [32] From that time, with the development of universal suffrage, the growth of nation-wide parties, and the expansion of population, the "spoils system" more and more demoralized the whole of American government and administration: the politician promised office instead of policy, and the administration served the politicians instead of the public.

It is, indeed, a remarkable phenomenon that England and France (but more recently) have escaped the evils of "graft" that America has suffered. For why should the democratic principle stop short of administration? Why should it not, as it did in Greece and for centuries in Rome, go beyond the legislators and affect judges and civil servants? There has been, in fact, in both England and France, a deliberate self-denial of the absolute realization of the democratic theory, and not only a denial, but the assumption of a habit of mind and rule of political behavior culminating in great self-control on the part of politicians. That self-control is not so strong in France as it is in England, and it is only in its infancy in the United States. Germany as a republic saw the

[30] C. R. Fish, *The Civil Service Patronage* (London, 1905); M. Ostrogorski, *Democracy and the Organization of Political Parties,* Vol. II, p. 48 ff., and see MacDonald, *Jacksonian Democracy* in the American Nation Series (1906), Vol. XV, and C. J. Bowers, *Party Battles of the Jackson Period* (Boston, 1922); also L. D. White, *The Federalists* (New York, 1948).
[31] Cited in M. Ostrogorski, *Democracy and the Organization of Political Parties,* 2 vols. (London, 1902), Vol. II, p. 50; also cf. Fish, *op. cit.,* pp. 156-57.

[32] "The duties of all public offices are, or at least admit of being made, so plain and simple that men of intelligence may readily qualify themselves for their performance; and I cannot but believe that more is lost by the long continuance of men in office than is generally to be gained by their experience. . . . In a country where offices are created solely for the benefit of the people no one man has any more intrinsic right to official station than another. Offices were not established to give support to particular men at the public expense. No individual wrong is, therefore, done by removal, since neither appointment to or continuance in office is matter of right. . . He who is removed has the same means of obtaining a living that are enjoyed by the millions who never held office."—Jackson's *First Annual Message to Congress,* December 8, 1829. *House and Senate Journals,* 21st Congress, 1st session.

necessity of learning it and of proclaiming it in her constitution, because she suddenly turned from the calm three centuries of bureaucratic government to the turmoil of a party system: "Officials are servants of the whole community, not of any parties." [33] It would be missing the essence of modern government, its necessities, and its nature, to pass by the deliberate abnegation implied in the setting of administrative and judicial services beyond the bounds of party politics. Its full meaning is discussed, however, in the Chapters 27-37 on the civil service.

For a mass of offices this abnegation does not apply in the United States, and the great George Washington Plunkitt of Tammany Hall has supplied the reason with irresistible logic: [34]

First, this great and glorious country was built up by political parties; second, parties can't work together if their workers don't get the office when they win; third, if the parties go to pieces, the government they built up must go to pieces, too; fourth, then, there'd be the ———— to pay. Could anything be clearer than that? Say, honest now; can you answer *that* argument?"

The full number is not known, but there are some thousands of federal jobs available, and this is as nothing compared with the thousands of state and city "spoils," for which figures are given below.[35] Combined with the gift of offices is the assessment of their salaries—now prohibited by law. Less conspicuous, but more pervasive and mortal in effect, is the partisan perversion of law and administration. We need not pursue this in detail, for American students have themselves sufficiently analyzed the system.[36]

Against this portenous feature of American party life what has poor Europe to show? Administrative partisanship is, on

the whole, negligible. In England the only paid offices are a very few in the administrative service, post office, and some minor municipal offices. All these are insufficient to reward the small circle even of the most zealous party workers. Moreover, the standards are all against the use of office as party currency, so that patronage is dispensed shamefacedly. "Graft" is infinitesimal.[37] In France there is rather more party patronage than in England, the prefects and many local officials still being subject to "spoils," in spite of attempts in the 1930's at making the prefect a regular career, while recruitment and promotion in some of the central offices are rather badly tinged with party color. Further, the granting of tobacco licenses and such local governmental favors is influenced by political affiliations. Imperial Germany almost entirely rooted out "spoils" unless we are to say that her system was *entirely* "spoils" because some social classes and creeds were altogether excluded from the *Reich* and Prussian civil service. Even between 1919 and 1933 patronage was at a minimum. Under Hitler the nazi movement took all the "spoils" it wanted. In the U.S.S.R., the Communist party has the pick of all governing positions in the whole economy and all social organizations and the determination of all the rest. The Party Control Commission of the Communist party watches over this.

Why is there this sharp difference between the United States and the other democratic countries? The heavy demands made upon a party system which has to produce some coordination among so many agencies in a federal system occupying a continent is only one. Certain psychogenic factors stand out.

(1) The first is the idea, widely rife, that it is proper to acquire everything that one can afford to buy or which is obtainable by exploiting somebody or something. There are many people of that kind in

[33] Article 120, Constitution, 1919.
[34] W. L. Riordan, *George Washington Plunkitt* (New York, 1905), p. 24 ff.
[35] Cf. Chap. 33.
[36] Cf. C. E. Merriam and H. Gosnell, *The American Party System*, 4th edition (New York, 1949); E. M. Sait, *American Political Parties*, p. 357 ff.; Kent, *op. cit.*, J. T. Salter, *op. cit.*, and C. E. Merriam, *Chicago* (Chicago, 1929).

[37] Cf. Herman Finer, *Municipal Trading* (London, 1941). See also *Report*, of Tribunal to Inquire into Allegations . . . on the Official Conduct of Ministers of Crown and other Public Servants (Cmd. 7616), January, 1949 (H. M. S. O., London).

other countries, but not quite so many as in America. If a cause of this difference must be given, the best is that in the United States, millions of poor, oppressed, and ignorant people suddenly fell upon a tremendously rich land. We expect the starved to become gluttons, especially when they live in a land free as well as rich. A thoroughly predacious culture was created. It is considered highly laudable in America to "get by"—that is, to beat the competitor or acquire a commodity, by personal effort, no matter how questionable the moral quality of the process.[38] Then too, the never-ceasing waves of immigration brought a succession of people from lands where political authority was oppressive and where the only known ways of circumvention and propitiation are purchase, guile, and violence. Such people will never boldly and plainly assert a right granted them by the law, but always seek extralegal intermediaries who are believed to have influence.

(2) Next, the United States has, through a hypertrophy of the democratic theory, a tremendous number of elective offices—a matter we have already indicated—and this inevitably leads to two things: the parties have more grist and as mere managers are more indispensable than elsewhere.

(3) Lastly, there is not yet a wide enough intellectual participation in government insistent upon excellent administration—people are too occupied with other things.[39] However, it is making a gradual appearance. I have the distinct impression that the dictum reported in *Better Government Personnel*[40] that "spoils" is the

currency of politics, that "patronage is the price of democracy," is on the decline.

STATUTORY LIMITS ON PARTY ACTIVITIES

CANDIDATES and the organizing parties are so anxious to win that, especially in the heat of an election, they tend to forget sedulously established standards. They confuse the public good with their own policy, and feel that with their own victory is bound up every just solution of the problems of government. Moreover, many do not possess nice scruples about the roads to office. Consequently, the law has stepped in to purify the electoral process. It is significant that intervention began in a serious measure only after parties had developed a nation-wide organization and had begun to face each other as substantial and responsible rivals. Not until 1883 was a comprehensive and stringent law passed on this subject in Great Britain; not until after 1890 in the United States; while in France and Germany legislation is very recent.

Great Britain. In Great Britain,[41] the Corrupt and Illegal Practices Act of 1883, codified and added to the piecemeal legislation of previous centuries, making a code of admirable strictness. Corrupt practices include: (1) Bribery by gift, loan, or promise of money or money's worth to vote or abstain from voting; by offer or promise of a situation or employment to a voter or any one connected with him; by giving or paying money for the purpose of bribery, by gift or promise to a third person to procure a vote; or by payment for loss of time, wages or traveling expenses to secure a vote. The consequences are the same whether bribery is committed before, during, or after an election. (2) Treating, which means the provision or payment for any person, of meat, drink, entertainment, or provision, at any time, in order to induce him or any other person to vote or

---

[38] As a single example of dubious governmental practices, the reader is recommended to study the whole episode (1947) of the unsuccessful nomination of Edwin Pauley to office in the Navy Department, and his subsequent alleged speculating in grain, during his appointment in the Department of Agriculture.
[39] Cf. Edward J. (Boss) Flynn's almost contemptuous challenge in the title of his book *You're the Boss* (New York, 1947): "There are really 80 million political bosses in America."
[40] Luther Gulick *et al.*, *Better Government Personnel* (New York, 1935), p. 18.

[41] Cf. Rogers on *Elections* (London, 1928) 3 vols., Vol. II (20th ed.), *Parliamentary Elections and Petitions, passim;* Vol. III (19th ed.), *Municipal and Other Elections and Petitions, passim*. Also cf. J. K. Pollock, *Money and Politics Abroad* (New York, 1932).

abstain from voting—and such extends to the wives or relatives of voters. (3) Undue influence, i.e., the making use, or the threatening to make use, of any force, violence, or restraint, or inflicting or threatening to inflict any temporal or spiritual injury on any person in order to influence his vote, or by duress or fraud impeding the free exercise of the franchise by any man. (4) Personation: applying for a ballot paper in the name of another person, whether alive or dead, voting twice at the same election, aiding or abetting personation, forging or counterfeiting a ballot paper. (5) Unauthorized expenditure: that expenditure which is not authorized in writing by the election agent.

Illegal practices include paid conveyancing, advertising, and hiring, without authority, committee rooms; voting without qualifications; making false statements about candidates; disturbing public meetings between the issue of an election writ and the return of the election; printing, publishing, or posting any bill, placard, or poster not bearing on its face the name and address of the printer and publisher; illegal proxy voting. Heavy fines and withdrawal of the right to vote or be a candidate are attached to those offences.

The expenses of the candidates were limited by the Act of 1883 and, after the passage of the Reform Acts of 1918 and 1928, stand at 5d. per elector in a borough constituency and 6d. per elector in a county constituency. In some cases, therefore, it was possible to spend nearly £2000 in a single constituency. The average amount possible was £1200, but the average actually spent was only one half that. It was the general sentiment that the maxima should be reduced to give poor candidates a clear chance of election, and, following the recommendation of the Speaker's Conference of July 20, 1944, the Representation of the People Act, 1948 (Part III) reduced the legal maximum expenses per candidate to £450 plus 1d for each borough elector and 1½d for each county elector. This roughly halves the legal maxima hitherto prevailing.

In practice there is little corruption of a serious nature at election times. But neither law nor custom has stopped the practice of "nursing" a constituency; that is, of treating to entertainments, excursions, municipal gifts, and so on, from the time of "prospective" candidacy until the election period, as legally defined, has commenced. This practice still causes some nonrational bias in the election results and in party membership. Further, there is no easy means of inspecting whether the agents' returns are a true account of all that has been spent. A constituency, as we have seen, is a large place, and it is difficult for either the state or opposing parties to appoint officers who can light upon anything short of flagrant cheating. Nor are the parties as severe with each other as theoretical reasoning would teach, for though upon proof of illegality, the reward is the gift of the seat to the opponent, a denouncer risks unpopularity. Mutual tolerance on legal laxities is not seldom preferred by party agents. At any moment some worker may do an unwise and unauthorized thing and bring the law upon his organization.

The main evil from which British elections now suffer is the unfair contribution of motorcars and the occasional payment of party workers. Motorcars are lent by friends to candidates and the rich candidates [42] get more than the poor. Then there is also the pressure which is not sufficiently perceptible or fixable for prosecution. Tradesmen are intimidated into putting posters into windows—but who can litigate upon a smile, a wink, or a gesture? Agricultural workers, in particular, have not yet lost all fear of being dismissed from their jobs if they do not vote right. Canvassers of rural constituencies are full of anecdotes of those effective relics of feudalism, and everywhere the system of large estates and agricultural hired labor is accompanied by moral conservatism. But all this kind of influence is now very weak; the schools, the press and the parties, have practically killed it.

A final point. There is no penalty for the use at elections of the Union Jack—as

[42] Cf. the discussions of this subject in Parliamentary debates on the Electoral Reform Bill, 1931.

a "symbol"—on posters or unfurled over vans and speaking platforms. In France, neither white nor tricolored paper may be used for placards—because the former is reserved for official communications and the latter is the official color of the republic.[43]

France. The provisions of French law relating to electoral procedure are not vitally different from the English. The first serious attempt at statutory regulation of electoral behavior came with the Organic Decree of February 2, 1852, on the Election of Deputies to the Legislative Body, a decree following close upon the establishment of universal suffrage and Louis Napoleon's *coup d'etat.* Until that time a few dispositions of the penal law served to throw into relief the normal custom of electoral corruption; it could do little more, for the governments which managed France for the constitutional monarchy were themselves the supreme corruptors, their success being quite assured by the paucity of the electorate, and the firm centralized grip over local administration.[44] Nor were the governments of the Third Republic at pains to divest themselves of the electoral succor obtainable from the local officials: the prefects and the mayors in particular. In the early years of the Republic, the pressure of the government on the prefects and of the prefects on their subordinates was enormous. "Neutrality," said one prefect in a declaration to his staff, "is hostility which attempts to hide. As for me, I cannot be duped that way. I shall unmask it when I come across it, and mete out justice every time I can." [45]

Governmental pressure still persists, especially in the constituency of a minister, and through the practice of the distribution of administrative favors, like grants-in-aid, via favored candidates and members. But on the whole, the amount and intensity of governmental pressure is now quite small. It is clear from contested elections that much petty corruption still occurs, the main forms being an increase (promised or actual) or withdrawal of poor relief; considerable intimidation of leaseholders and laborers in agricultural areas; banquets held between the two ballots; food and drink given to electors who come from far away; small gifts of money; drinks on a large scale (the French form of canvassing); promises to bestow upon the constituency the whole or part of the Parliamentary salary; threats to stop a pension; and, in some constituencies, systematic distributions of goods and money. The laws of March 30, 1902, of July 29, 1913, and March 31, 1914 extend the scope and detail of the previous rules and make the penalties much more severe. But organized ecclesiastical pressure, very powerful in the rural districts, has not been overcome. The electors themselves are in many places always on sale. They enjoy the turbulence of the campaign and are imposed upon by pageants.[46]

Laws designed to produce equality of opportunity among candidates and to reduce election expenses were passed: the law of March 20, 1914, regulates placarding, and that of 1919 the free postage of circulars; while Title V of the Electoral Law of October 5, 1946, reaffirms these with some small modifications due to shortage of paper.

The reasons leading to the laws on placarding were: to stop candidates from swamping each other's posters by overposting and destruction, a practice which the law had attempted to regulate without success; to reduce electoral corruption by means of excessive payments to billposters; to reduce expenditure generally; and to reduce the bought competition which poorer candidates must face—this, the egalitarian motive, being the strong-

[43] See Étienne Pierre, *Traité de Droit Politique et Parlementaire,* Vol. I and Supplements 1919 and 1924, Chap. IX, "Des Crimes et Délits Electorales," and the full text in Léon Duguit and Henri Monnier, *Les Constitutions et les Principales Lois Politiques de la France* (Paris, 1932), p. 280 ff.

[44] Georges Weil, *Les Élections Législatives depuis 1789* (Paris, 1895), gives a good though brief account of the development of French electoral law and manners.

[45] *Ibid.,* p. 231.

[46] Cf. A. Pilenco, *Les Moeurs du Suffrage Universal* (Paris, 1930), Book II, Chap. I.

est. On the whole, candidates for the French chambers are poor men. They do not and cannot usually spend much on an election campaign. A large number are outside the parties which can afford to give help; hence the importance attached to equality. The administrative circular accompanying the text of the law runs: [47]

It [the law] proposes, by reducing electoral expenditure, to equalize as much as possible the means of propaganda which the different candidates may have at their disposition, in the course of the same electoral campaign and in the same constituency, and to prevent the wealthier from benefiting over their rivals by material advantages which hitherto have placed the poorer candidates in an unfavorable position. The legislator desires that, in placarding, the contest shall take place with equal weapons.

The law applies to all elections—for the chamber of deputies, the senate, local government bodies. No posters may, during the electoral period, be placarded anywhere excepting on special places reserved therefor by the municipal authorities. On each of these boards each list of candidates receives an equal surface. In order that there may be a proper distribution of boards through the constituency, their placing is regulated according to the size of the district. There is a categorical prohibition on placarding otherwise, even when it pretends to be an industrial or commercial advertisement, or a letter addressed by a candidate to one of his supporters. How careful legislators must be is shown by an amendment which the Senate made to the bill presented by the chamber. The chamber provided for "special sites and an equal surface . . . to each candidate." But this could mean each candidate or list being given a site, so long as the area was equal, but in different places in the constituency—some prominent, others unfrequented.[48] Hence the

Senate's amendment, whereby posters appear equally on each and the same site. Comparative study is thus possible for the electorate, and however little this is, the statesman cannot despise small mercies.

The law of October 25, 1919 was the result of a confused struggle to secure a diminution of candidates' expenses, and, if possible, to cause the state to take over some part thereof. A bill of July, 1912, voted by the Chamber, had even transferred to the state the printing and distribution of ballot papers and one election address for each elector. But the Senate killed the proposal. The project was taken up again in 1919 but was reduced to that of a sharing of expense between candidates (each to pay a flat rate) and the state. The law finally arranged for a kind of cooperative printing of ballot papers and one circular per candidate.

The law of October, 1946, carried this a stage farther. Each list of candidates is represented by a mandatory. He pays on behalf of each candidate of the list a bond of 20,000 francs (worth roughly $100 when the law was passed in 1946) for each constituency. The lists each receive the amount of paper from the local official electoral authorities, allowing for three big placards, three notices for meetings, envelopes, ballots, and two circulars. The lists designate their own printers to the electoral authorities and make up their circulars and placards as they themselves think fit. The circulars go out at separate short intervals before election day. Postage for these is government-franked. The state pays for the paper apportioned to the candidates, for envelopes, printing of the placards, ballots, and circulars. It also pays the cost of fixing the placards. It also pays for the gasoline used by candidates, according to the size of the district.

Then, let it be noted, the expenses of placarding and gasoline are not repaid to candidates, and the bond is forfeited to the state, whenever a list of candidates

[47] March 21, 1914; Pierre, *op. cit.*, Vol. III, p. 288, footnote.
[48] See Rapport, *Groussier*, March 9, 1914, Chambre des Députes, and Bérard, *rapporteur* in the Senate (March 5, 1914): "All boards reserved for candidates must be side by side,

in order that the electors may compare their 'professions of faith.' It would be arbitrary, unjust and disloyal to be able to sacrifice one candidate to any other by the location of the hoarding sites."

does not obtain at least three per cent of the votes cast in the district. In other cases, the bond is returned to the candidates. Here is a faint imitation, with additional features, of the British rule that the candidates put in a deposit of £150 which is forfeited if they do not get one eighth of the votes cast, the purpose being to deter frivolous candidatures.

The foregoing arrangements are administered by a local commission of the president of the civil court, the prefect, other local government officers, and representatives of the political parties putting up lists of candidates.

Outside of this, the candidates may spend as much as they like on their candidacies. In fact, the restrictions on placarding, and the saving of money on postage, have simply given rise to more expenditure upon meetings and the party newspapers. It is of the highest theoretical as well as practical interest that the Communist party, in the Consultative Assembly of 1945, resisted the equalization of electoral expenditure, thus reversing the historic trend—for it used to be the parties of the poor who were clamant for equality!

The United States. The law relating to electoral purity in the United States falls into the two divisions of federal and state regulation.[49] The federal authority has no jurisdiction excepting over electoral organizations which cover more than one state. Thus state and municipal elections are outside federal and only within state jurisdiction. Where possible, it has been attempted to prevent any mutually destructive legislation, though careful scientific coordination has been no more than occasionally mooted.

Federal law is now summed up in the Federal Corrupt Practices Act of 1925,[50] (which codified and expanded acts passed in 1907, 1909, 1910, 1911, and 1918) and the Hatch Acts of 1939 and 1940. Before

1907 the only law treating of corrupt practices was the Civil Service Act of 1883, which forbade political assessments and regulated several other incidents of the spoils system.

The broad features of federal regulation are:

(1) National banks and corporations organized by federal law many not contribute money in connection with elections to any political office; nor may *any* corporation contribute money for elections of the federal legislature and executive. Penalties of fines and imprisonment are established.[51]

In 1943, by a rider to the Smith-Connally Act to prevent strikes in wartime, it was made illegal for "any labor organization to make a contribution at which presidential or vice presidential electors or senators or representatives . . . to Congress are to be voted for, or for any candidate, political committee, or person to accept or receive any contribution prohibited by this section." (U. S. Statutes at Large; Public Law 89, 1943).

(2) All contributions and disbursements made to influence elections of representatives to Congress must be publicly declared. The treasurer of a political committee receiving and spending money and the candidates must file accounts before and after the election: quarterly, and in election years two reports between the fifteenth and fifth day before the election. The upward limit of a candidate's expenditure was put as $5000 for "nomination and election" for Representatives, and $15,000 for Senators. But personal expenses and expenses on objects previously exempted were not to be reckoned.

(3) In 1911 and 1918 the law was directed against the promise of office, money, or "anything of value" in consideration of votes or abstentions in elections. The filed declaration was to specify

---

49 Cf. J. K. Pollock, *Party Campaign Funds* (New York, 1926); E. R. Sikes, *State and Federal Corrupt Practices Legislation* (Durham, N. C., 1928).
50 Postal Salary Increase Act, Title III, *Federal Statutes Annotated, Supplementary Pamphlet*, April, 1925.

51 By the Law of 1907 (U. S. Statutes at Large: 34,814) corporations became liable to a fine not exceeding $5,000; any officer or director consenting to the contribution could be fined not in excess of $1000, or imprisoned for one year (maximum), or sustain both penalties. Cf. Sikes, *op. cit.*, pp. 191-92.

whether or not promises of appointment had been made.

(4) The Act of 1925 limited the law only to general elections.[52] Expense statements have to be made three times at intervals of five days before the day of election, and also after the day of election, within a period of thirty days.

(5) The Hatch Act of 1940 provided three major regulations. *(a)* No political committee may receive or disburse in any calendar year more than $3,000,000. The purpose was to limit the total expenditure of the political parties, with special reference to the two great parties. *(b)* No single person, committee, or corporation may contribute more than $5000 toward the election of any person in any calendar year. (This provision was not properly considered before it was introduced at a late stage of the legislative process, and its intention was actually to make the whole bill unworkable.) Nor may goods, commodities, or advertising be bought for the advantage of candidates. *(c)* To meet an unmistakable danger of a kind of intimidation arising out of the broad extensions of social security, work relief, and so on, severe limitations were placed upon the political activity of federal officials or state officials employed in the spending of federal funds (through the administrative device of federal financial grants-in-aid to the states). The purpose was to prevent political influence through the official denial of benefits or jobs to the seekers of relief.

Oaths or affirmations attest the honesty of the statements, an attempt thus being made, as in so many proceedings of state, to secure the truth by a special, if not a supernatural, solemnity.[53]

How have these laws worked? Let us consider, first, the group of rules designed to obtain publicity, for these seem to be the principal contributions of American law and experience to democratic government. Statements are filed and sworn to, as required. Not to do this is too obvious a breach of the law. Other committees, not political yet affected by the law, are sometimes recalcitrant, owing partly to ignorance and partly to their alleged honest belief that they are not affected. Thus, for example, the great champion of obedience to law, the Anti-Saloon League, did not in 1920 file its statement.[54] In 1944, the CIO Political Action Committee filed a statement, though contending it need not do so because it was not helping specific candidates.

The $5000 limitation is violated by the contribution of gifts from members of the same family, and to several individual candidates of one and the same party. The $3,000,000 limitation is violated by the establishment of numerous political committees operating for the benefit of a single party, the Democratic or the Republican, such as state committees, or "Willkie Clubs," or "the National Committee of Independent Voters." A carefully thought-out gentleman's agreement on who shall give how much to whom to spend upon what can and did make the aggregate go far above $3,000,000: to $6,000,000 for the Democrats, and $15,000,000 for the Republicans in 1944.[55]

All in all, the statutes have failed to have an appreciable affect upon American

---

[52] The constitutionality of the earlier law as applicable to primaries and conventions arose in 1921 in the famous case of *Newberry* v. *United States* (216 U.S. 232), in which five judges against four maintained that primaries and conventions were not elections in the sense of the constitution.

[53] Indeed, if their electoral and parliamentary eloquence is any index to the state of mind of American politicians, their oaths must have been as awful in effect as deep in substance. No politicians in the world have God upon their lips as often as the American.

[54] The decision of the Supreme Court in re the Anti-Saloon League of New York (188 N.Y. Supp. 605) in 1923 was as follows: "Many activities in connexion with elections are educational, but their motive is to affect the result, and to aid or defeat candidates or propositions submitted for a decision by the ballot-box. When money is received for such purposes, the law requires publicity to disclose its source and amount, and to test the sincerity for the public good of the means and propaganda employed. The law is predicated upon the truth that publicity will never hurt a good cause, and has destroyed many bad ones."

[55] Cf. Louise Overacker's analysis in *Presidential Campaign Funds* (Boston, 1945), pp. 32-35.

practice. There is neither restraint in expenditure nor full truth in the statement of its sources and destination. Such laws may make politicians either reform or hide; and American politicians have preferred to hide. Yet there is some restraint, and the spirit of the law establishes a standard, or at least the notion that there ought to be a standard, and this is not without value. The spirit of partisanship is stronger than the sense of state; and the vast apparatus of party requires an extent and quality of supervision to which American citizens have not yet awakened in sufficient numbers.

The limitations are designed to reduce the irrational befuddlement of voters, and to give an equal chance to all candidates, irrespective of wealth. But the former purpose may really require greater expenditure: the political results depend less on the amount spent than on its objects. Campaign propaganda matters less and less in a society dominated by occupational groups and better educated than generations ago. What is crucial is publicity of the source of funds. Here United States practice leads the world but could still be improved.

The individual states in the United States have a longer history of continuous occupation with electoral corruption, and many have gone along paths quite unfrequented by European nations in their attempts to purify electoral operations, not that they are anywhere more effective than in the federation.

(1) Publicity of accounts before and after election is adopted in many states. But in some there are no official forms. Where they exist they are sometimes not drawn with adequate detail; in other places, they begin to become revelatory by their classification or the attempt to differentiate clearly between pre-election and postelection declarations.

(2) States have, therefore, been compelled to go further. Some have public officials to review the accounts and report delinquents. Some require publication by the candidate in two newspapers of general circulation in the state as well as the usual filing. In others the accounts are marshaled in the annual report of the secretary of state; or parties and candidates must hold their accounts open for public inspection, and must notify rival candidates and parties of their revenue and expenditure. It is easier to hide from a public officer than from a rival in one's own trade. The only obstacle is that a "truce of God" between rivals of equal villainy may defeat the law. Yet there is the certain gain that the law gives the more honest candidates a weapon which costs them nothing and which may win them a good deal if they are vigilant.

(3) Limitation on expenditure is very common, but is evaded (a usual limitation is by percentage of the amount of yearly salary to be obtained from the office, a sum often quite inadequate for a statewide election).[56] Friends of a candidate spend what he is not permitted to. The exempted objects of expenditure are precisely those upon which much can be spent. If no single contribution of more than $1000 is permitted, then it is easy to ascribe part of the bigger subscription to any name taken at random. The politicians are merely embarrassed for a time. Nor is this all. American experience has shown that limitation of the total spent is not so effective as limitations of expenditure on special items. The success of this, however, depends on the practical ease of detection, and upon the difficulty of proper audit where money spent upon one object is wrongly classified.

(4) Several states forbid expenditure on election day. North Dakota even forbids electioneering on that day.[57]

(5) In most states corporations are forbidden to contribute, and assessments of public officials are prohibited. Further, careful distinctions are drawn between political and other committees and their respective rights clearly stated. The intention is to reduce the agencies of expenditure and propaganda and thus concentrate responsibility.[58]

(6) A general requirement is that all political advertisements must be plainly

56 Cf. Sait, op. cit. p. 558 ff.
57 Brooks, op. cit., pp. 340-46.
58 E.g., Utah (Pollock, op. cit., pp. 251-52).

distinguished by some such legend as "Paid advertisement," with a statement of the cost, the name of the candidate, and those authorizing the advertisement, and the name of its author.[59] Newspaper support may, in some places, not be purchased. This seems to be generally obeyed.

"But what is the constitution between friends?" Pollock's conclusions are not fully optimistic. He speaks of general agreement that the laws on campaign funds are of little use. He says that bribery laws are fully effective; limitations of expenditure innocuous; corporate contributions largely prevented.

Speaking generally, the whole tendency of state laws on the subject is toward raising the moral law of elections, and it can hardly be denied that they have not been of considerable value in this respect. They have been largely instrumental in producing better political conditions today and no amount of criticism should permit this fact to be covered up.[60]

Their efficacy, such as it is—and that an improvement has been caused is attested by a number of independent observers [61] —rests upon two grounds which issue directly from the democratic theory: first, that the citizen has the right to know what is being done in government, and second, that he has the right to revolt on the basis of this knowledge.

Weimar Germany. In Germany the law relating to the sincerity of elections was mainly embodied in the criminal code, but further rules were included in the general electoral law, the laws relating to meetings, press, and the secrecy of the ballot. We are mainly concerned with the contents of the criminal code once again effective for post-World War II Germany.[62] These are general and short, and their efficiency has necessitated parliamentary construction and application, especially since the clauses of the criminal law were before the Revolution of 1918 not seldom violated by the administrative authorities acting under the orders of the government. Whoever prevents a person from voting, either altogether or for a specific person, by a criminal act, is punishable with from six months' to five years' imprisonment. Officials employed in the collection of ballots or registration who intentionally produce a false or corrupt result are punishable by a week's to three years' imprisonment; others committing the same crime are punishable by imprisonment up to two years. The purchase or sale of votes is punishable by imprisonment of one month to two years and it may entail the loss of civil rights: "purchase or sale" here includes material reward of any kind. (Occasional gifts of beer are apparently not penal, but to swamp the constituency in beer is to invalidate the votes. However, where it is usual to provide free beer at election meetings, and this is fairly common, regard must be had for the custom.) The spreading of false defamatory facts about candidates is not a punishable electoral misdemeanor, whether actionable in the courts or not. Votes which are attended by improper practices are in some cases withdrawn from the total polled by the benefiter, and in other cases ascribed to the victim.

Systematic falsification entails the nullification of the election. Neither law nor practice limits the amount of money which may be spent in elections by either candidate or party (provided the articles of the criminal law are not violated); nor does the law require the publication of campaign funds; nor are there rules regarding the equality of placarding as in France, or the issue of publicity pamphlets as in various American states. Article 125 [63] of the constitution of 1919 stipulated that "electoral freedom and electoral secrecy are guaranteed. Details are to be settled by the electoral laws." This article has so far not been interpreted to include anything more than the law established in the criminal code (with which we have already dealt). And secrecy [64] is dealt

[59] Brooks, *op. cit.*, p. 346. Cf. also Sikes, *op. cit.*, Chap. IV.
[60] Pollock, *op. cit.*, p. 259.
[61] Brooks, *op. cit.*, p. 352; Sikes, *op. cit.*, pp. 246-47.
[62] Abschnitt, *Articles*, 107 ff.

[63] Cf. H. C. Nipperdey (ed.), *Die Grundrechte* (Boston, 1929-30), 3 vols., Vol. II.
[64] Cf. S. Kaisenberg, in Nipperdey, *Die Grundrechte*, Vol. II, p. 160 ff.

with by the *Reich* Electoral Law of April 1920, Section 27, and the Electoral Order of March 14, 1924. It is not an inconceivable interpretation of the article that freedom is not guaranteed where electoral funds are large and secret—yet this conclusion has not been drawn by the electoral court.

A SENSE OF PROPORTION

ON reflection, it is clear that much of the pother about election expenses arises out of the class inequalities in the state. But as previously explained, wealth can defer but not frustrate the advent of social control and equity. The abolition of expenditure on elections is impossible. A mere glance at the objects of expenditure is demonstration sufficient: radio, literature, overhead expenses like rent, postage, telephone and telegraph, travel, speakers. Another solution offered in the past was the payment of all election expenses by the state, proposed by Theodore Roosevelt in 1907. This would have involved very difficult administrative and political problems, and perhaps the eventual reduction of expenditures for reasons of economy. In democracies, it would threaten the freedom of political parties and electoral campaigns. In Britain, where the wealthier candidates obtained some advantage by the possession of cars in which to take voters to the polling booths, several legislative projects included the pooling of all cars, or the provision of these by the election officials. They failed.

The complete state assumption of electoral expenses obtains only in the U.S.S.R., where article 11 of the Election Regulations (Presidium, October 11, 1945) prescribes that the expenses of elections are covered by the state. This provision is feasible only in a dictatorship and it has its ulterior purpose as well as its declared one of making the campaigns "free," although the official apologists sneer at democratic elections as "commercialized."

The next possible solution is the reduction of expenditures to what is "reasonable," and that evidently is the intention of the various statutes we have reviewed.

In England, conservative candidates have been thought to gain an advantage by subscriptions to charitable, social, and sporting organizations in the intervals between the actual election campaigns— a practice known as "nursing" a constituency. This practice was deprecated in the *Speaker's Conference* (July, 1944), previously referred to, but was not abolished. It tends to favor the richer among the candidates of the wealthier parties, rather than hurt the rising progressive, mass, political cause. The same holds good for direct or indirect payments or promises of subscriptions to party organizations to influence the selection of prospective candidates.

Publicity, in which the United States at present leads the world, is the soundest antiseptic against democratic corruption,[65] although it must be confessed that some of the germs are decidedly virulent and hard to kill.

POLITICAL PARTIES IN THREE DICTATORSHIPS

DICTATORIAL countries have no political parties in the original sense of the word, namely, that they are parts of the state, for to be a part of the state would be to imply that there are other parts. The dictatorial party has attained its monopoly by the exclusion of other parties, either by positive law as under the nazi and fascist systems, together with a simultaneous liquidation and prohibition of others, or as in Soviet Russia, without the accord of a monopoly to a party but its *de facto* assumption by the Communist party preceded and accompanied by the forceful liquidation of all opponents of its leadership. Both in Germany and Italy, the parties by statutes or decrees were given a special status regarding their property and the dignity and physical safety of their membership. By being made public corporations they were assured that the use of their property, if challenged, would

[65] The student is advised to read the Green Committee Report and Hearings, 1944, *United States Senate, Special Committee to Investigate Presidential*, etc. *Campaign Expenditures*, 1944, Report No. 101 (79 Cong., 1st Sess., 1945).

receive from the courts and administrative agencies special consideration in relation to the ends the party performs; and party members, and especially functionaries of the parties, were granted various immunities from arrest, the right to use force, and protection by the law against insults.

In Soviet Russia, "antinational" (which can have a wide meaning) associations are not permitted, and since political parties are associations, the domination of the Communist party is assured. Further, article 126 of the Soviet constitution, which enumerates the organizations that may be established by citizens, sets up the Communist party as that in which "the most active and politically conscious citizens associate."

In contradistinction to democratic political parties, dictatorial parties are characterized by a sanguine doctrine. (From the sanguine to the sanguinary, the step is short and natural.) This faith springs either from a philosophy of history, expressing itself through a collective party leadership, or, as in fascist Italy and nazi Germany, from the dicta of a leader. There is a significant difference, as will be appreciated later, between the two. Since the leaders in either case are the repository of this faith, they claim and normally obtain unquestioning obedience. (Perhaps the best psychological analysis of such bonds is found in Arthur Koestler's novel, *Darkness at Noon,* and in his *The Yogi and the Commissar,* both treating the theme of loyalty to communism. For naziism, one among many illustrations is Dr. Ley's avowal, "The National Socialist Party is Hitler and Hitler is the Party." The Party Organization Book [66] contains the oath of loyalty to the *Fuehrer,* which runs: "I pledge allegiance to my *Fuehrer,* Adolph Hitler; I promise at all times to respect and obey him and the leaders whom he appoints over me." It was a regular pleasure for nazi leaders to declare, even when under extreme sentence at the war crime trials,

that they had no conscience but Hitler. Italian fascism showed a like absoluteness of declared submission.

In a democracy each party has every interest in securing for itself the largest possible membership and makes desperate efforts for success, for the size of its membership will directly or indirectly determine the extent of its control of the legislative and executive machines. Dictatorships deliberately practice the limitation of the membership of the dictatorial party, especially after they have achieved power. Thus, the Communist party of Russia probably has no more than five million members. The Fascist party in Italy had something like three million members. The Nazi party had nearly three million members. The restriction of membership is intentional, with various objects. (1) It is sought to maintain the militancy of the organization. With excessive numbers, a dilution of doctrine would arise, as the chance of internal dissent increase with every additional person recruited—he brings his individuality with him. Also, closeness of organization, discipline, a feeling of community are attained with smaller numbers. Nor can it be forgotten that a dictatorial régime founded on the will of a minority must rely—especially in times of domestic or foreign critical challenge—upon especially intense feeling, "fanaticism," as the dictators consciously say. But this needs activation by the leaders, and this cannot be successful except among a small number, and except that these do not move outside their artificial seclusion. (2) It is desired to maintain a sense, both in the public at large and among the members of the organization, that the members of the party are an *élite,* selected for their superior quality in comparison with the rest of the population. This serves to give them self-respect, to feed their confidence and pride, not to say their arrogance, and ultimately to supply that feeling of alienation from other men and women necessary to ensure the consistent and successful practice of hot persecution and cold brutality. (3) The restriction of numbers

[66] This is reproduced in the U.S. State Department publication called *National Socialism* (Washington, 1943).

makes it possible to claim that admission into the party is a privilege and a reward, and so secure a flow of gratitude and humility toward the leaders who have been so gracious. (4) None of the dictatorial parties offers membership primarily as a pleasure, except that of a duty properly performed; candidates join as members of a vocation, and indeed, especially in the Soviet system, there is heavy emphasis on the sacrifices they must make by voluntary unpaid work in the task of government and leadership.

It is important to re-emphasize the austerity of the vocation of party membership. On this the party documents are clear.

Any one who becomes a Party member does not merely join an organization but he becomes a soldier in the German freedom movement, and that means much more than just paying his dues and attending the members' meetings. He puts himself under the obligation of subordinating his own ego and to put everything he has at the service of the people's cause . . . readiness to fight, readiness to sacrifice, and strength of character are required for a good National Socialist.[67]

The introduction to the Nazi Party Organization Book goes on to stress the conception of servanthood of the movement and people; prohibits arrogance between party comrades; demands that each member should be a leader and promoter while on duty, and while off, a good comrade; prescribes simplicity and modesty of bearing; inveighs against vanity; applauds honesty and candor and constant solicitude for the humble members of the people. Festivities, honors, gifts, and drinking are deprecated for participators in the "unspeakably hard work" of constructing a better Germany.

The Communist party of the Soviet Republics expresses the austerity of the life of a party comrade all through its rules. Its preamble says: "The Party is a unified militant organization held together by conscious, iron, proletarian discipline. . . . The Party demands from all its members

active and self-sacrificing work. . . ." [68] A heavy list of duties follows.

It is well to reflect on the austerity (at any rate, as commanded) of party membership in the dictatorial as contrasted with the democratic countries. The difference is remarkable. In democratic systems, first, of course, almost anyone can join any party subject to practically no test whatever by the party. The joining of political parties may, by some people, be regarded as dedication to a serious public purpose, but it is also regarded by very many simply as a diversion or hobby, with dues unpaid and meetings unattended, an association which can be casually relinquished at any moment. Furthermore, in contrast to unquestioning obedience in dictatorships to the dictatorial leader, the follower in a democratic party is free, within very broad limits, to criticize the personal character, ability, motives, and policy of the leader. Indeed, in democracies the leadership is always on trial, and the displacement of the leader by some one more capable is the proper and the applauded object of political activity. In a dictatorship, the gain from discipline is militant strength and energy—for a time. But it is accompanied by the constant possibility of deadening the thoughtful and creative vital processes of both leader and follower, because there is no guarantee of mutual stimulation. Originality in the ranks is flattened by command from above. The creed that the leader is always right inhibits the movement of ideas upwards to him. Since his power to make or break political careers is absolute, and since any appeal from him is revolution and treason, he tends to become insulated from the views of the members of his own party who, paradoxically enough, have been commanded to keep in touch with the masses. In the democratic system, the open possibility of continued competition of ideas is kept alive. There is no stereotyped unbreakable hierarchy of value or

---

[67] *Op. cit.,* section, "Organisationsbuch," Para. 1.

[68] See Rules of the party published in *Land of Socialism Today and Tomorrow* (issued by the party and published by the Foreign Languages Publishing House, Moscow, 1939), p. 465 ff.

opinion. And though the democratic leader is not endowed with an extraordinary status to summon up the political energy of the party members, the mere existence of free contestants for the prize of a sovereign power that is accessible to all ensures the continuous renewal of the membership and, necessarily, as the continuing cost of success, of reasoning, reflection and the development of policies and programs of action.

Since the doctrine of dictatorial parties is one of already conceived perfection, and since this is fanatically embraced, and, since also the focus of party life and doctrine lies in a single person, the conditions are present for highly selective recruitment and for "expulsions" or "purges" or "liquidation" of those held to fall below the useful standard of mind, character, and physique. In the early days of the Fascist and Nazi dictatorial parties, a process of personal selection was conducted by members already in the party, careful account being taken of their general personal characteristics, readiness to assume responsibility, political dependability and firmness of character, their grasp of the party doctrine, their willingness to fight and sacrifice, their absence of self-seeking and ability to fulfil the various technical tasks. The party recruiting officials are enjoined to realize that this selection of members is a most serious responsibility. Soviet Communist rules for "cleansings" of the party indicate the positive qualities for retention of membership. Thus it provides against:

Double dealers who deceive the Party ... overt and covert violators of the iron discipline of the Party and of the State; ... careerists, self-seekers and bureaucratical elements; morally degraded persons who by their improper conduct lower the dignity of the Party and besmirch its banner; passive elements who do not fulfil the duties of Party members and who have not mastered the programme, the rules and the most important decisions of the Party.[69]

In their earlier days, the parties had recruited from among both old and young. After a time, graduation from the Youth Organizations became almost exclusively the source of recruitment. Choosing from organizations of school children and youth, the party had some guarantee founded upon several years of deliberate observation of the effect of its training upon the candidates.

The experience of these countries is far too short for conclusions regarding the efficiency of breeding a new political generation, except that they have been able to secure unconditional obedience and fanaticism within the fixed order from some, especially in Germany and Soviet Russia. Yet it left or produced apathy in others, especially in Italy. Not a few remain untouched and rebellious, while such obedience as was achieved can be to an important extent ascribed to fear of force, and to enjoyment or promise of the spoils of office.

The only formal discussion—not merely exhortations by party leaders—of the requisites of mind and character of party members known to the present author is one which occurred at the Eighteenth Congress of the Communist Party of the Soviet Union.[70] The inductions into the Communist party in Russia are governed by a well-conceived set of rules, the principal of which are as follows: From one to two years of candidature, admission to which requires recommendations from several party members of some years' good standing; followed by mastery of the program and rules of the party; or proven worth in the groups of sympathizers and youth organizations, and the Soviets, trade unions, and cooperatives.

At the Congress the question was the introduction of more vigor and life into the Communist party, and one of the principal issues was the intellectual preparation of candidates. Must the candidate be an adept at Marxian doctrine? If so,

---

[69] The exact source of this has been lost: but students will find it amply verified in the *Short History of the Communist Party of the Soviet Union*, 1939, available in translation from International Publishers, New York City, and in the speech of A. Zhdanov in *Land of Socialism Today and Tomorrow*, p. 173 ff.

[70] Cf. A. Zhdanov, *loc. cit.*, p. 199 ff.

the party would become a party of intellectuals and doctrinaires and filled with too large a proportion of university recruits. It was true that a mastery of doctrine was desirable on the part of some and perhaps of many; but what was also necessary was a membership which would show proven good will and reliability. Stout and decent believers, not philosophers, made a second party. The Congress abolished the rule that candidates must have thoroughly mastered the party program, must be a real Marxist, a tried and theoretically trained Marxist:

I do not know whether we have many members of the Party who have thoroughly mastered our programme, who have become real Marxists, theoretically trained and tried. If we continue farther along this path we should have to include only intellectuals and learned people generally in our Party. Who wants such a Party? We have Lenin's thoroughly tried and tested formula defining a member of the Party. According to this formula, a member of the Party is one who *accepts* the programme of the Party, pays membership dues and works in one of its organizations. Please note: Lenin's formula does not speak about *thoroughly mastering the programme* but about accepting the programme. These are two very different things.

To assist those who accept the program but cannot rise to a mastery of the theoretical basis, the "short histories" of the Communist party of the Soviet Union are employed, and every organ of the Soviet press is unflaggingly used to apply high party doctrine to every phase of social and individual life from art to zoology.[71] The problem, however, still remains: without a *full mastery of the grounds* of the doctrine and their acceptance, how can the rulers believe in the reliability of their followers in the long-run evolution of their state; how can they be sure that they are *followers*? While if, indeed, many do master the elements as propounded by the prophet, they may be-

come very inconvenient purists and proclaim the falseness of the leaders. Men have murdered kings out of patriotism. In a sense, the simplest way to provoke a schism is to discuss fundamental principles. Burke warned against too searching an inquiry into society's foundations. For a democracy this is no problem, for, in a way, dissent is what it exists to produce. Yet *mastery of the grounds* is the only reliable and durable foundation of life in the state, the national or world order; the democratic even more than the dictatorial. For if there is a gulf separating men's values, it ought to be seen, and then it ought to be bridged by voluntary conscious purpose; if not, coercion will assume the task of unity.

There is one very important difference between recruitment in the Soviet Communist party and in the Nazi and Fascist parties. In the former a process of free local election prevails, in which, though direction is by no means lacking, more free discussion and choice at the local party headquarters is permitted than in the Fascist parties which practise co-option by superior officials tempered by the collusion of favourites.

As for purges, these sometimes take the form of the expulsion, imprisonment, and execution of large groups of party members who, to use a Russian phrase, may have "deviated" to the right or left of the party line as laid down by the central organ of the party.[72] In Germany there was the Röhm massacre of 1934, when the *Fuehrer* claimed that he was the supreme judge for the well-being of the nation. But other than at revolutionary crises in the parties, the elimination of the infidels is not by such wholesale and therefore sometimes admittedly faulty treatment. In the Soviet Republics a return was made to the Leninist principle of "individual approach to people," especially because hostile elements could *en masse* cover their subversive activities by an outer show of agreement with the party line and deceitful practises designed to persuade people that they were militantly loyal, "creating

---

[71] This may now be clearly seen in the *Current Digest of the Soviet Press*, a weekly set of translations, made in Washington under the aegis of the American Council of Learned Societies and the Social Science Research Council.

[72] Cf. *Short History*, etc., pp. 264-346.

an atmosphere of flattery, uttering solemn speeches, greetings, and et cetera., in order to deceive and lull the vigilance of certain of our leading workers." [73] The "individual approach" was recommended also to stimulate Communist party members to throw off an alleged unwillingness to investigate charges, to avoid hedging and considerations of personal safety, and especially to depart from the assumption that a Communist is a good or bad Communist, not according to his own personal deeds, but to the actions of his relatives, even back to the "ideological stamina or social preference of a great grandmother."

Naturally, all those in dictatorial parties who deviate are covered with infamy and stigmatized by a spate of the choicest invective. Calumny, indeed, is one of the well-tempered instruments of punishment, of undermining independence of mind, and of political destruction. If the party doctrine were not clear-cut and presented with intense emotional force (honestly or otherwise), there would be no grounds for the tactics of calumny, since there could be no deviation to which one could point as the mark of infamy.

It is a simple consequence of what has been said that dictatorial parties are highly centralized, and at the same time that their central organs are deeply penetrative of society through their local offices down to the last cell in a block of a city or the floor of a workshop, the "capillaries," as the fascists say. There is no space for portraying the numbers of the hierarchy, beginning with the *Fuehrer,* the *Duce* or the Party Secretary at the very top of the pyramid, and then proceeding layer by layer, district by district, through the various governing bodies of the party. The important thing is that even the most disciplined party in the most democratic state does not begin to approach the intense centralization of dictatorial parties. Since there is such centralization, and since all movement must come from above, and since fidelity has to be maintained in all the ultimate organs of the party, there is

machinery at the top for inspections of the subordinate layers of the hierarchy, and at the same time for the appointment of the subordinate officials and trustees of the party going downwards.

In Russia, in characteristic contradistinction to the Nazi and Fascist parties, democratic elections in the lower councils of the party are permitted, but ratification by the party organization immediately superior is necessary. Neither in Germany nor in Italy was a democratic choice of executives the principle or the practice; the appointments are made from above by a process of delegation. In Soviet Russia—and this, let us re-emphasize, is a distinguishing mark of the régime—the principle and practice of so-called "democratic centralism" prevail. It arises mainly from the fact that a scientific (more or less) interpretation of history (more or less) dominates (more or less) the leaders, but also because those leaders govern an enormous area and have the good sense to know that achievement must depend upon local vitality. "Democratic centralism" means, according to the rules of the Communist party, the application of the elective principle to all leading organs of the party from the highest to the lowest, and the periodic accountability of the party organs to their respective organizations. That is the democratic side. But it also means the absolutely binding character— "iron discipline"—of the decisions of the higher organs upon the lower and upon all party members. That is the centralized aspect. The party requires a free and businesslike discussion of party policy in individual organizations or in the party; such discussion is declared to be the inalienable right of every party member derived from "internal party democracy." The declared purpose of this internal party democracy is to develop self-criticism, that is, criticism within the party itself, and to vitalize party discipline, which must be conscious and not mechanical. On this, the words of Lenin are always quoted: "All revolutionary parties which have hitherto perished, did so because they *grew conceited,* failed to see where their strength

---

[73] Zhdanov, *idem.,* p. 188 ff.

lay, *and feared to speak of their weaknesses.*" [74]

There is, then, a significant difference between the Communist and the Fascist parties: in the former's tolerated self-criticism—indeed, the stimulated self-criticism and even more, in the fact that it is regarded as a disloyalty to the party to undertake any action which diminishes—or be remiss in any action which maintains—the freedom and liveliness of local party life. We may refer again to the discussions at the Eighteenth Congress, where it was re-emphasized that the work of the party, which was the "remoulding of the people's consciousness," was frustrated by those who believed that all Communists were born free from prejudices and stood in no need of re-education. It was consequently necessary to restore the elective principle, to abolish the practice of co-option, to forbid voting by a list of candidates, to vote for individual candidatures, to guarantee all party members the right of criticizing and rejecting candidatures, to vote by secret ballot, and to guarantee periodical meetings of leading party workers. The revival of the elective principle of criticism and self-criticism was sought, in order to heighten the responsibility of party organizations to the party membership, and to intensify the activity of the members of the party. It was desired to develop and strengthen the feeling of contact between each party member and the party, and to enhance each member's sense of being a fully responsible unit. This was the meaning of "inner party democracy," and this would strengthen the unity of the party and its "conscious proletarian discipline."

The democratic element in the Soviet Communist party (but it is necessary that this be not *over*emphasized)—a quality distinguishing it from the Italian and German dictatorships—has two sources: the liberating purpose of the Bolshevist Revolution and the tradition of the party in its formative stage. In the first place, the bolshevist movement was founded to overthrow the Tsarist régime, one of the most horrible tyrannies in the history of humanity, and to bring freedom to the Russian people. It had a dual purpose: not only to inaugurate a free system of government, but to establish an equalizing and socialized economy—each purpose being enough to overtax the mind and energies of the mightiest statesmen. It proposed to progress from an inferior and practically primitive society of almost altogether illiterate members to a very highly civilized, most complicated and organized political and economic system. And it intended to progress with the greatest achievable rapidity in order to be able to withstand domestic and foreign hostility. Its animating force was liberty, equality, and fraternity. But the fascist and the nazi systems were founded on the denial of freedom and equality, and were erected or the corrupt destruction of existent democratic government. They were movements of decline from a superior to an inferior kind of society, even if there were marked blemishes in democratic practice. In the second place, under Lenin, freedom of discussion in the Bolshevist party was encouraged in order to stimulate vitality and to attract the sincere and the strong.

In the *Short History of the Communist Party,* the lessons of a generation of party experience are summarized. Among these are two which should be especially noticed. The first is the need for continual self-criticism; the second to keep in touch with the masses. On the first, the work says: [75]

A party perishes if it conceals its mistakes, if it glosses over sore problems, if it covers up its shortcomings by pretending that all is well, if it is intolerant of criticism and self-criticism, if it gives way to self-complacency and vainglory and rests on its laurels.

On the need of keeping in touch with the masses, it quotes Stalin: [76]

We may take it as a rule, that as long as the Bolsheviks maintain connection with the broad

[74] *Short History*, etc., p. 361.

[75] *Idem.*
[76] *Ibid.*, p. 362-63.

masses of the people, they will be invincible. And, on the contrary, as soon as the Bolsheviks sever themselves from the masses and lose their connection with them, as soon as they become covered with bureaucratic rust, they will lose all their strength and become a mere cipher. . . . I think that the Bolsheviks remind us of the hero of Greek mythology Antaeus. They, like Antaeus, are strong because they maintain connection with their mother, the masses, who gave birth to them, suckled them, and reared them. And as long as they maintain connection with their mother, with the people, they have every chance of remaining invincible. That is the clue to the invincibility of Bolshevik leadership.

Side by side, however, with the democratic virility of the Russian Communist party, there is the other aspect, namely, its centralism. The party will punish such discussion on "an all-Union scale" as would lead to the imposition of the will of an insignificant minority on the vast majority of the party, or cause the disintegration of its unity by factional groupings and attempts to split it. It is only if the necessity of an all-Union scale discussion is recognized by several regional party organizations, or if there is an insufficiently solid majority in the Central Committee on very important questions, or if a solid majority of the Central Committee wishes to test the quality of its policy by means of discussion, that such discussion would be permitted. These are the limits of internal party democracy, beyond which internal party democracy would be disintegrated. "The maintenance of party unity, the relentless struggle against the slightest attempt at a factional fight or a split and the strictest Party and Soviet discipline are the foremost duties of all Party members and of all Party organization." Since 1945 there is little doubt that hierarchical discipline overwhelms the democratic element in the Soviet Russian Communist party.

It ought to be added, in order that the power of the central leader or leaders of the dictatorial party may be fully comprehended, that since the dictatorial party controls a totalitarian state, expulsion from the party, as the leading officials

openly declare, is a question of life and death for those expelled. For the key positions in society, economic and otherwise, are held by loyal party members; and the conduct of the professions, and even ordinary occupations, can be made impossible on the mere fiat of the authorized party official. Thus, the disciplinary force is tremendous.

Another mark of the dictatorial party is its possession of a military organization. Within the Nazi party, there are the Storm Troopers *(S-A)* and the Elite Guards *(S-S)*, and the Gestapo or secret police; [77] within the Italian Fascist party, the Militia and the O.V.R.A.; [78] within the Communist party, the Red Guard and, acting with it, the O.G.P.U.[79] These organizations serve two purposes; first, of rooting out, as early as possible, the first faint stirrings of disagreement and opposition, and then, in the final resort, of defending the régime by force of arms. This organization of coercion is taken to the most minute point of detail, is well-equipped with all the best that technology and organization can offer, for investigation, record, and torture, and makes revolt practically impossible. These organizations are safeguarded against legal action by citizens or members of the party who have suffered maltreatment. They enjoy complete immunity from responsibility if their actions are in the interests of the party, and beyond where party comradeship and the maintenance of the power of the party requires it.

Now, it may be that many thousands, even hundreds of thousands, of members of dictatorial parties accept the party programme, even understand it, and even consciously and fanatically will it. It is difficult to read the mind and spirit of so many. Clearly, dictatorial party leaders are far from complacent. Experience shows

---

[77] O. Giles, *The Gestapo* (Oxford, 1936); and *Nazi Conspiracy and Aggression* (U.S. Government Printing Office, Washington, 1946), Vol. I and Vol. V.
[78] Herman Finer, *Mussolini's Italy* (London, 1945).
[79] Boris Souvarine, *Stalin* (New York, 1939).

that it is very difficult to maintain the flame of conviction, the permanence of devotion, and the fierceness of the party warrior simply by persuasion alone. The maintenance of cohesion and force in the party membership is promoted by two devices. One is the continuous emotional, ceremonial, and ritual procedures and evolutions designed to enhance the self-importance of party membership, arouse the feelings and appeal to the aesthetic element, agitate the sentiment of belonging to a great collective body, and this is accompanied by argumentative appeal. The second element promoting cohesion, though not exactly belief, is the vast "patronage" and "spoils" in the hands of the dictatorial parties, immeasurably greater than any democratic party has ever had. All the jobs, all the professions, all the occupations, all the symbols of social prestige are in the gift of the dictatorial party, and party members come first and necessarily hold the key positions in that society —so in the civil administration, so in the conduct of the national economy, so in the control and conduct of education, so also in the armed forces, though as to the latter there has been considerable resistance by the professional officers of the German army. With less spoils there would be less loyalty; take away the jobs and there would be smaller party membership and a less intense prosecution of its duties. It need not be laboured that Party and State are intimately linked. The leaders at the various levels of the Party machinery either had, as in Germany and Italy, by law an *ex officio* right to certain positions in the state, *de facto,* or, as in Russia, Germany, and Italy, held the key offices in the state, regional, and municipal government, and so, all through the apparatus of society and economy.

16

The Character and Policies of Modern Parties

THE nature of political parties is far from simple. Some are close to being little more than associations for economic purposes in a comparatively strict sense; others are almost like churches militant, embracing a complete religion or philosophy, high in temper and determination; others, again, are mixtures of a profound and all-embracing social philosophy with a special economic interest—with either an equal or unequal emphasis on the philosophy or the interest but not excluding the one or the other. Hardly a party anywhere exists only for a single narrow purpose, like some of the nonstate groups we have spoken about: parties are varieties of multipurpose associations, rising to some that have as their concern the totality of human existence.[1] But whether wider or narrower their outlook and objects, they have, almost all, a general view of right and wrong, a particular character of public conscience, a universal social creed, and this is exemplified in and implemented through specific policies and programs. At times, the policies and programs are more alike than the basic creeds are in themselves, or in logical inferences drawn from them; or they are jettisoned or bargained with in such wise as to make the observer affirm that there are, indeed, no creeds, and to cause the zealots of the party to cry out aloud against foul play while the party's opponents (who have done and

who will again do the same thing) twit their opposite numbers with patent insincerity at last publicly revealed! Some observers may even charge that political parties have no principles, but are merely logrollers for material gains, not least for office and power, power simply for the enjoyment of its use.

To all these, in part, we can return the answer already made to Acton,[2] who placed such emphasis on the "isms" alone as the determinators of political conflict and endeavor. In politics it is men who fight, not disembodied ideas. The transient, the utilitarian, the mundane goods must needs be tended within the brief lifetime of man, also. One cannot wait for perfection before living off an installment: for in the long run, it may be said, we are all dead. The surrender of what seem to be principles by compromise is essential to the attainment of something, or the best would get in the way of the good.[3]

What is attempted here, then, is just to sketch the more fundamental portion of the parties' creeds and suggest some of the temporal items of the contemporary program, not to be exhaustive regarding the former nor by any means complete in the later—for neither, in the compass of this work, is possible, and sometimes the two aspects are inextricably mixed up.

[1] Cf. M. Oakeshott, Political and Social Doctrines of Contemporary Europe (New York, 1947).

[2] Cf. H. Finer, "Acton," Journal of Politics, September, 1948.
[3] Cf. Morley, On Compromise (London, 1917, originally published 1877), and Notes on Politics and History (London, 1914).

England has three important parties, Labour, Liberal, and Conservative, and a small struggling Communist party. The United States has two major parties, Republican and Democratic, and some minor parties, notably the Socialist party. Weimar Germany had seven principal parties, German National, German People's, Center Party, Democratic, Social Democratic, National Socialist, Communist, and many minor parties. France of the Third Republic had a confused mass of parties from which emerge, with a history, *Action Francaise, Fédération Républicaine, Alliance Démocratique, Radical-Socialistes, Républicain-Socialistes, Socialistes,* and *Communistes.* Their fate since World War II, as that of the German parties, will be discussed later (p. 328 and p. 347).

The countries differ, then, in the number of their parties, and we shall study the effect of this upon the effectiveness of government and civic behavior. As remarkable is the variation undergone by the fundamental themes issuing from man's political nature. We shall see how at the contact of minds of different types with different problems, diverse solutions have come into being, causing men to group themselves in ways peculiar to them to find new methods of contest and cooperation, to acquire unique oddities of demeanor and a language all their own, gibberish to their opponents and to foreign countries, but shining like a vision for themselves.

ENGLAND: CONSERVATIVE AND LIBERAL PARTIES

MODERN parties appeared first in England, for here the revolution which was almost everywhere the prelude to democratic government came earliest. Differences were brought out from the private council of the king to become public confrontations. In the constitutional conflicts of the seventeenth century arose the two camps, Tory and Whig; but we have learned enough to know that men do not fight merely for a constitution, but for a good which it is to authorize and defend. The forces behind those conflicts pervaded the parties and caused their hostility, and down to our own day have continuously maintained a significant distinction between the parties which in time came to be called Conservative and Liberal.[4] Even as political feeling and thought produce variety of doctrine and behavior according to place, so do they according to time, and the history of Conservative and Liberal doctrines is necessarily one of digressions and deviations from their central character. But the central character is there, it does determine the solution in time and place, and, moreover, it is peculiar and clearly distinguishable. But we cannot follow out historic reactions: we can only attempt to penetrate to the sources. Early rivalry was not expressed as in the mass organizations of today, but in the leaders to whom different knots of men looked and in the rather vague general doctrines they held. The differences were recognizable if not constitutionalized, and the opposing faiths not seldom won away members from their previous allegiance.

Conservatism. The essence of conservatism is to be discovered in the social institutions of which it approves and its attitude to the idea of Progress. The social institutions favored by Conservatives are crown and national unity, church, a powerful governing class, and the freedom of private property from state interference. Each of these is desired both for itself, as an end, and also as a means to something else. The Crown is at once a glorious monument, a center of social life conferring distinction and prestige as one approaches it, a sign of the nation's age, a symbol and an instrument of political authority and unity, an evidence of the virtue of heredity, a link of empire. The depth of reverence for the Crown and the royal family is extraordinarily profound, and the fervor of the toast "The King, God bless him!" is so emphatic that, if the circumstances and the evidence did not demonstrate that the speaker was sincere, one would suspect caricature. This

---

[4] Cf. C. Hill, *Three Essays on the Revolution of 1640* (London, 1940), for an "economic" interpretation.

is an ultimate in human nature, issuing from reverence for the distinguished, especially when such distinction results from birth. Not that this is unprompted or comes from a vision of the ruler of the day. A long line of monarchs is dimly seen traversing centuries; each is clothed with qualities colossally virtuous; they are above the average, more even than humans. The response is awe and obeisance. Moreover, the Conservative has always applied and now applies, as we have reason to discuss in Part V on chiefs of state, all the contemporary means of publicity to creating the legend that the king, his wife, and children possess ideal virtues.

The fixation of the royal symbol has its uses: it enhances the sentiment of unity and order, and so tends to moderate economic and social grievance and to unite the nation in the world political struggle. Only a few romantic Conservatives like Churchill befriended Edward VIII; for the rest he was the principal civil servant of the nation, to preserve unifying social respectability or to go. Badly shaken in the crisis of 1936, the party nevertheless continued to hail the new king, of their making.

When such loyalty is attracted on a large scale, it is clear that proximity to the object thereof lends social prestige, and this again is valued tremendously by Tories, even attracting the more snobbish Americans, though their constitution was founded on a virile renunciation of kings and courts. Presentation at court and garden parties at the palace are satisfactions that reward many industrious, self-sacrificing home, foreign, and imperial officials. So, too, does a royal visit to slum neighborhoods have a conservative influence. The Crown, as the chief symbol of unity in nation and empire, is of immense importance in the Tory mind, sometimes on a par with Parliament. For, instinctively, the Conservative, though not wholly blind to utility for power, social status, and wealth, is enamored of national and imperial unity. There is a strong element of cooperativeness which, though its object may be restricted, is nevertheless stern

within its scope. This itself is founded upon an ultimately irrational, quite mystic, devotion to the national community, the community of race and history. Of this, obviously, a dynasty is an admirable symbol; it is, indeed, a part. It is understandable that though the origins of that dynasty may have been alien (William of Orange) and its accession bitterly contested by the forebears of the Conservatives of today, these facts should be ignored. At a certain point every practical thinker and leader becomes blind; and did he not do so, he would be irrevocably lost upon the sea of doubt. Rationally considered also, kingship is an efficient attraction for loyalty, for its hereditary origin impresses many and lends itself to the deliberate ascription of all those virtues to which most of us render homage. If not the king, it might be Hitler or Huey Long.

The Conservative sense of nationality is intense, and its most frequent judgment is that such and such a foreign country or sect is untrustworthy. It has faith in the superiority of the race to all other races, even its allies in war. It believes in the superiority of its own political institutions and traditions, and in the mission of the race to civilize other peoples, even aginst their will, and even with violence to the point of brutality. This feeling of nationality reveals itself in a glorification of all that makes for the defense or aggrandizement of the country; a grandeur considered rather in a material and warlike light than as artistic achievement. It shows itself unwilling to enter into foreign alliances and engagements except those absolutely necessary for the defense of what lies within the national boundaries. Its interpretation of obligations to the League of Nations and its looking to collective security was "strict," not "liberal." Empire is its very breath: for it betokens the potency of the race to extend its force and rule, and success gives the presumption of high spiritual value. Churchill's famous remark, that he had not become His Majesty's first minister to preside over the dissolution of the British Empire, was no accident.[5] Yet even the dominions and colonies are not quite the homeland: not quite the county or the town, the parish or the church which mothered their body and soul and actually planned part of itself abroad and still rules them from the "homeland." Nothing quite reaches the proud level of the indigenous: these are God's own, destined to be right whether they act or forbear, are consistent or inconsistent, slay or give life, break the Commandments or keep them. They echo—perhaps they inspired—the famous toast of Commander Stephen Decatur, United States Navy: "Our country! In her intercourse with foreign nations may she be always right; but our country right or wrong!"

Nevertheless, *noblesse oblige:* the station requires sacrifices. National unity, which is the first foundation of national strength, must be preferred to other goods; one must submit to heavy taxation and not actually revolt; one must see the House of Lords brought low in esteem by a crowd of newfangled peers and simply bite the lip; one must see the imperial services surrendered to natives and others no better, and must bide one's time; from 1945 one must even submit, accepting the principle of Parliamentary sovereignty, to a detested Labour government's policy of nationalizing the basic industries—but the nation must not be rent asunder. Yes! The Crown itself must be constrained to the service of national unity, even when that means the forcible retention of an alien population within the state, as when the Crown was dangerously counseled to use its veto power to overcome the Home Rule Bill. For behind all is the desire for dominion; and to lose Ireland was a prelude to weakening the bonds of the Empire. Moreover, how dangerous to national existence to have a weak, perhaps a hostile, power so near the English coasts! It is right to divest others of self-government if it will cause you any danger. Now aliens are always a danger: they have strange philosophies, necessarily issuing from their queer racial composition. It is not wrong to regard them with a tolerant and patronizing amiability when they are useful and amusing. After all, foreigners cannot be expected to know the English language or to understand English customs and "good form," but they can be useful and amusing. And if they are adequately kept in chains, or not taken really seriously, and if one is vigilant to detect and destroy the signs of corruption and treachery, then use may be made of them.

The recurrent motif of Conservative policy has been the need of a privileged governing class. They believe that there are people who have the skill and the right to govern independently of the popular will. They are suspicious of arithmetical majorities of the citizens *en masse,* and were in bygone times the advocates of "virtual" representation and the representation of "communities" rather than individual persons (See p. 222 ff.). To the last they defended the right of representation of the universities, as an offset against the dead level of mediocrity which the principle of "one man, one vote" would produce.[6] On their lips more than on any others is the assertion that there is something called the "real will" of the nation distinct from the transient will of the majority.[7] From the end of Elizabeth's reign they insisted that government is, of right, the possession of the king and, naturally, of the advisers he calls to his counsel. It is true that following Bolingbroke, many argued that the king was to be a patriot, a philanthropist, but this argument is remote from the doctrine of government by consent. It has, indeed, been used to bolster up the most nefarious tyrannies, as, of course, it is the standing argument to establish them.

When the Tories cried out for Parliamentary reform—as they often did in the seventeenth and eighteenth centuries—it was to spite their Whig rivals by excluding Dutchmen and Whigs from office by

---

[5] This attitude is well expressed in his subsequent speeches on Burmese independence. Cf. *Parliamentary Debates,* November 5, 1947, col. 1247 ff.

[6] Cf. p. 231 above.
[7] Cf. p. 418 below.

Place Bills, and, by shortening Parliaments, to appeal to the people more often, thus threatening the hold of the Whigs over Parliament and the Crown.[8] But when it came to any serious partition of political power with any body in the nation not sanctioned by long usage or controllable by wealth and influence, the matter was differently viewed. So fierce an opposition was engendered in 1832 that the country was all but wrecked, and, equally calamitous, the House of Lords all but swamped! Reason and utility challenged traditions long accepted and pleasant for those with hands upon the levers! A matchless and envied constitution was to be unbalanced! The mob was to be let in, under the name of Democracy, and it was quite clear from the experience of France that this meant disorder and a universal leveling! Property itself, no longer a stabilizing force, would be swept away! "I hold it as a maxim that every government which tends to separate property from constitutional power, must be liable to perpetual revolutions; for power will always seek property and find it." But the Tories have been swept along by the tide of time and necessity, and in 1867 they themselves forestalled the inevitable, trafficking time for popular gratitude. Yet they have followed, not led, the march towards universal suffrage, and with lamentations.[9] They, also, are the last to accept the doctrine of the member of Parliament as delegate,[10] especially if dependent on trade unions. They are the last to assert the possibility of an enlightened democracy, and insist more than any other party upon the ignorance of the electorate and its unfitness to govern, and more, the natural impossibility of its ever being able to govern, since this ability is,

apparently, derived from hereditary talent to be found only in the descendants of those who have so far enjoyed governing power.[11] This, again, leads back to a fundamental tenet—that there is virtue in heredity, more than a presumption, that he who is born of socially powerful and wealthy parents has qualities above the average, rightfully entitling him to govern others. They incline to independent executive leadership, as trustees for the people. Therefore, too, the inveterate defense of the House of Lords, and the belated search for utilitarian arguments in its defense in an age when everyday facts, as well as biological theory and historical research, have spread the view that the doctrine of "blue blood" is solemn nonsense.[12] Therefore, also, the disbelief in the right of self-government for other peoples, especially those within the Empire who are too weak to enforce their rights. Not that the Tory is always wrong in this view—but he insists on it with much greater emphasis as an inevitable and irremediable fact, than do Liberals and Socialists.

Other parts of this study have shown that in the nineteenth century, men became increasingly occupied with the pursuit of a high standard of living by new methods of production. Almost concurrently, equalitarian ideas became widespread, and social sensitiveness to the misery of the poor caused the commencement of a movement to establish a minimum of comfort, economic safety, security, education, and health. What was the Tory response? Two fundamentals were involved: private property and state interference.

Conservatives have been fierce defenders of private property, and this against the two main forms in which it can be practically attacked by the state—taxation and control of use. Conservative taxation theory has recognized the right

---

[8] Cf. G. S. Veitch, *Genesis of Parliamentary Reform* (London, 1913); Thomas B. Macaulay, *History of England* (London, collected works, 1866).
[9] So, too, in regard to women's suffrage and the age qualification for voting.
[10] Cf. G. Lowes Dickinson, *The Development of Parliament during the Nineteenth Century* (London, 1895), p. 77 ff.; cf. more recently, L. S. Amery, *Thoughts on the Constitution* (Oxford, 1947).

[11] E.g., Sir Henry Maine, *Popular Government* (London, 1886).
[12] Cf. A. F. Pollard, *The Evolution of Parliament*, 2nd edition (London, 1926), Chap. XV. Cf. also *Parliamentary Debates*, October 28, 1947, 715 ff.

of the state to take the least obtainable from private pockets, and has been the inveterate foe of direct taxation in all its forms, on income, land values, and legacies. It has attempted to create a circle which is sacredly beyond the reach of the state, for, as we have remarked, it will not have national unity and strength at any price. It has attempted to show, with some success, how the whole state suffers from the frustration of certain instincts, like acquisitiveness, enterprise, and family affection, by heavy taxation. It has ever been more friendly to indirect taxation, which tends to act degressively and to put the burden on those who least can bear it.

Further, Conservative taxation theory has denied the right of the state to limit the uses of private property.[13] It is true that a number of Tory philanthropists have devoted themselves to social reform [14]—early factory legislation being the first example of this, the promises of Tory democracy [15] its middle period, and comprehensive social insurance and pensions, the most recent tribute. All of these subjected property to state control. But for the most part they were conceded only after a period of electoral and Parliamentary agitation, not at all willingly from the conviction that a measure of justice might produce a better England, but out of a spirit of part surrender, part charity, when action had become inescapable. Even during World War II the Tories were obstinately unfriendly to social security and family allowances. In regard to the latter they preferred to offer school meals to the child rather than money allowances to be spent by the parents. The theory is plain: no one has a right to demand these things; it is better not to give, for this will sap the springs of individual enterprise and virtue, but if anything must be given, let it be given of charity and not of right. In our own day the defense of private property, which was once a principal tenet of the Liberals, has become vested mainly in the Conservatives. They remain its adamant defenders. This attitude was most clearly seen at work in the problem of the coal industry, and in that of municipal and private industry generally. It was found that the coal industry could not attain anything like its full efficiency without reorganization which, by reducing competition and amalgamating the private property units of production and distribution, would avoid tremendous waste. Conservatives were the constant and vigorous defenders of the inertia of the coal owners: [16] the pits were private property, hence no one had the right to interfere with their management. In the crucial election of 1945, the Conservative policy promised little more than investigation of monopolies, while its general theme closely followed Hayek's *Road to Serfdom*.[17] It has always been the curb on the power of the trade unions and is the strongest opponent of the "closed shop."

The Tory, at one time state interventionist, is now the defender of *laissez faire* and the "individual." Most people who are well endowed with all that they want of wealth, education, and pleasure are inclined to insist that they are better left alone, and if they resist statutes restricting individual rights for themselves, the rights are available to the poor and the middle class if they want them. It cannot be denied that Toryism is embraced and propagated by such people. They are not

[13] Cf. the fierce insistence on the game laws. The question of reform is commented on by A. V. Dicey, *Law and Public Opinion in England*, 2nd edition (London, 1914), pp. 87-88.
[14] Cf. A. V. Dicey, *ibid.*, p. 220 ff.
[15] Lord Hugh Cecil, *Conservatism* (London, 1912); M. Wilkinson, *Tory Democracy* (London, 1928), Chaps. 2 and 3; W. F. Buckle and S. E. Moneypenny, *Life of Disraeli* (London, 1929); and W. Sichel, *Disraeli* (London, 1904); Winston Churchill, *Life of Lord Randolph Churchill* (London, 1906); C. Driver, *Richard Oastler* (New York, 1946); Keith Feiling, *History of the Tory Party, 1640-1714* (Oxford, 1924); M. H. Woods, *History of the Tory Party* (London, 1924); and G. G. Butler, *The Tory Tradition* (London, 1914).

[16] Cf. evidence of the Duke of Northumberland before the Coal Industry Commission, 1919 Cmd. 360, Vol. II, Reports and Minutes of Evidence, pp. 621-31.
[17] Cf. R. B. McCullum and A. Readman, *The British General Election of 1945* (Oxford, 1947), p. 88 *et. seq.*

ungenerous in unprompted giving, that is, when they may do as they like to do; but state command is anathema. Hence the Tory hatred of officialdom, which it calls, and teaches others to call, bureaucracy: less competent than private people, usurpers, eaten up with routine, dangerous to liberties, extravagant.[18] Now all these things are true in their time and place; they are false as well. But to the Tory they are an almost unchallengeable creed because officials are the instruments of state activity. Is the state, then, to do nothing? The Tory does not hold this view. The state is to establish and not to disendow a church; it may call, by conscription even, for the lives of its citizens when danger threatens; it must protect property. Nowadays, it may by protective tariffs divert the whole natural course of industry and commerce in order that "national" ends may be pursued, nor must one let the condition of the people sink dangerously low. Nor ought one to give free play to disruptive tendencies within the state, like the trade-union movement, or permit the untrammeled advocacy of strange doctrines like communism. It was never the progressive party where education was concerned; and in the Education Act of 1944 it insisted on including religious teaching in the syllabus of the elementary schools.

In the elections of 1931 and 1935, the Conservative party, by astute electioneering tactics, managed to stave off a Labour government. It stayed in office to the end of World War II (from May, 1940 in coalition with Labour and Liberals), finally with Mr. Churchill, an unorthodox Conservative, as leader in place of Neville Chamberlain, who as a City man, whereas Mr. Churchill was an admirer of heroes rather than City men, was much more to the heart of the regular Tories.[19] In the election of 1945, its unpreparedness for war, its preference of the "dole" and the "means test" to great public-relief works to combat unemployment, and its tolerance of Mussolini and even Hitler, caught up with it. Wartime sufferings had sharpened the memories of the British masses.[20] It had lagged behind the times in its stubborn refusal to see the vast ideological and social changes. In that election the party received some 8.66 million votes and obtained 189 seats. But Labour won 11.99 million votes and 393 seats. The Liberal Party won 2.23 million votes and 12 seats. The Communist Party won 103,000 votes and 2 seats.

It is difficult to conceive a policy which, within some decades even, might win back for the Conservatives enough votes to support a solid government. A fortunate and timely exploitation of errors made by the Labour government might succeed; but a considered series of measures satisfactory to a majority of the people—no! This view leaves out of the reckoning the more sensitive social conscience of the younger men of the party: but the Labour movement gives abundantly already what these, at most thirty or forty of the Conservative party, are prepared to offer.

Yet two things are important. The difference between the Labour and the Conservative votes is roughly 3 million. A large proportion of these are fluid votes, especially of the "white collar" middle-class groups. They could fairly easily go Conservative, once they had obtained economic security and the increased social services promised and provided by Labour. Many Liberals could go Conservative and carry with them the middle class, politically fickle as it is. Further, the Conservative party has declared its intention not to repeal the nationalization of the Bank of England, the coal mines, inland transport, electricity and gas, telecommunications and civil aviation;[21] and it is fully committed to the social security and social service measures already instituted whether before or since the Labour government.

[18] For a moderate view, Lord Eustace Percy, *Government in Transition* (London, 1934), Chap. V; for an even more liberal view, see Eyre and Spottiswoode (publishers), *Some Proposals for Constitutional Reform* (London, 1946), by "A Group of Conservatives."
[19] Cf. Keith Feiling, *Neville Chamberlain* (London, 1947).

[20] Cf. "Cato," *Guilty Men* (London, 1943), and "Gracchus," *Your M. P.* (London, 1944).
[21] Cf. *The Industrial Charter*, statement by the Conservative party, May, 1947.

Liberalism. The Liberal creed is more an amalgam than the Conservative. This is easily comprehensible, for the party of conservatism and defense is not, like the party of attack, compelled to seek new weapons and justification. But the very essence of Liberalism is openness to new experience and the vindication of free growth. It began in the religious struggles of the Reformation when the right of individual judgment and testimony in matters of faith was asserted, and developed soon into an assault upon the notions of a state Church and arbitrary government. These have remained fundamental propositions in the latest history of the party, its new and radical elements of the nineteenth century supporting them by personal character and interests. The machinery of government has been a constant interest of Liberal thinkers because therein they have seen the potentialites of freedom or despotism. Their quintessential preoccupation, the axiom of their existence, has been the ultimate and transcendent value of the individual personality. This stands out clearly in the careers of Gladstone, Asquith, and Lloyd George and, in the time of Locke and the Revolution was expressed in the doctrine that individuals freely make their government and assign to it only as much power as they think good. The theory was the product not of experience but of a wish, and that wish has unified and determined Liberal faith and policy.

The individual is prior in importance to the state. Only in the individual appear the principles of growth, of initiative, of creation, and the possibility of really assenting to its validity in other people. The ultimate goal of existence is to produce the greatest number of perfect individuals. The pattern is not to be dictated by those with coercive power, but freely accepted by discussion, reasoning, and judgment, for no one can say for certain whose truth is more valid, more beautiful, more vitalizing. The only hope, therefore, of discovery, lies in an equal opportunity for all to utter and evolve. Organized restriction, which prevents the destruction of this opportunity, must be reduced to a mini-

mum.[22] Its life breath is the impossibility of knowing all that is latent in human nature, the strong hope that what is there is good and will prove so, and the belief that without freedom nothing valuable can arise and that variety which proceeds from liberty is productive of a more beautiful world than any imposed uniformity. How has this generosity and optimism been applied in English politics by the party which is founded upon it?

It has not denied nationality and race— their beauty and the necessity of their preservation. Patriotism is the opportunity of service and the motive to free collaboration. It is a support and stimulus to the full growth of that peculiar difference which inheres in each special ethnic portion of the human race. It deserves defense and encouragement, for none can understand and promote it so well as those who naturally and freely share its biological and cultural heritage. It may even transcend the limits of its own frontiers, offering a guide to those whose condition or reason leads them to accept it. Thus it can have a mission, but not an imperialist mission. It may teach but not coerce. And if it should mistake the point where education becomes coercion, or find itself burdened by an Empire made by others, then its duty is to prepare the subjugated peoples for their freedom. Nor is it right to safeguard one's own civilization and national strength by "unduly" placing bonds upon those of other nations. But "unduly" has not been interpreted in as liberal a sense as the general tenets would lead one to expect; it has rarely received the interpretation placed upon it by the Conservatives, but it has not seldom approximated to it. It was Liberals like John Morley who prepared India for freedom and advocated Irish Home Rule.[23]

Human salvation may possibly come from some source other than ourselves. The civilization of others is to be respected. When they threaten our own in the ex-

22 Cf. Chapter 5 on democracy; and also the attitude of mind expressed by William James, *Letters* (London, 1920), Vol. II, p. 100.
23 Cf. John Morley, *Recollections* (London, 1917), Vol. II.

treme we may be forced to self-defense. That is a tragic necessity and not one over which we can rejoice; and it does not justify the piling up of armaments. On the contrary, for two reasons it requires that every effort be made to establish machinery for world understanding in order that all the acts of compromise and the mutual promise of toleration may be exhausted first. Those reasons are, *first,* that to kill each other is not to settle anything except that one side has caused the other to surrender, that the aftermath in terms of human habits of force and discipline is evil, and, *second,* that armaments are costly and every pound spent upon them by the state is a deprivation of individual liberty. Every means of international understanding and harmony is to be adopted; and this end is served as much by free trade, which avoids economic friction, as by the machinery of conciliation and international justice.

From the rise of the new industry and commerce, Whiggism received the impulse which caused it to become Liberal and sometimes Radical, and to overthrow the monopoly of political power of the landed interests by the passage of the Great Reform Bill and the reform of the municipalities. The economists and political scientists who provided that impulse were not, and perhaps could not be, sufficiently aware of the difficulties inherent in the full gospel of laissez faire applied to industry and commerce. But their influence made for free trade on the ground that thereby every country produced what it could most economically produce. In other matters they saddled their party with a doctrine which was destined to be its downfall at the turn of the twentieth century— that is, the doctrine that the "invisible hand" of competition would produce a harmony of economic interests, the greatest happiness of the greatest number being thus securable. The accession of strength from the commercial and industrial middle classes, schooled by a long experience of ·the glorious result (for them) of self-help, further emphasized the force of the dogma. Liberalism had not faced this difficulty: awful misery, and even death, is a necessary incident of the state which is so designed as to let the strong win. We do not know what a really liberal civilization would produce in the long run, when the unsuccessful had been destroyed by the rest. It might be very fine, or not. No one knows; no one can guess; and even the greatest liberal philosopher, Kant, never made an attempt to find out. But we do know that men refuse to be trampled down, that onlookers are smitten with compassion, and the result is social control.

Bullied and preceded by the Tories, and harassed by voters, liberalism has become increasingly socialistic; once the promoter of competition, it has become its regulator. The scales must be equal to give the results which liberalism predicts. The good, in short, is to be obtained by regulation. The good, however, is still the greatest individual development of the greatest number, and the emphasis is still laid upon the fortune of the individual. This is the touchstone of all regulation; and the bureaucracy which is the necessary accompaniment of regulation must be popularly controlled, and liberalized by the nature of its education.

Property was once as sternly defended by the Liberal as by the Tory party; for each was the party of the propertied, and, if anything, the Tories were willing to recognize that property had some obligations, while the Liberals of the early nineteenth century believed that charity was demoralizing. Liberalism has, however, softened in this respect and, much more than the Tories, believes in the righteousness of considerable national expenditure for the provision of a minimum of amenities for the poor. Indeed, the years from 1906 to 1914 saw the introduction of important social legislation, the severe taxation of income and legacies, and the practical beginning of a policy of economic equality, social security (unemployment and health insurance, old age pensions, school meals), and housing. The Liberal government of 1906 gave strong status to the trade unions. It effected a major constitutional amendment by reducing the legislative power of the House of Lords. Sir William Beveridge, author of the 1942 report on social security, is one of the leading members of the party. In the 1930's it produced plans for full employment. By 1945 [24] the party came very close to Labour in all except "over-all planning," and it even favored nationalization of the coal industry—yet they disbelieve in the Conservative promise to curb monopoly, and would attempt regulation, failing which they would nationalize the industries.[25] This change is too late, however, for the party's survival as a significant force. It claims to be free of entanglements with vested interests, whereas the other parties are tied.

There is a clear and emphatic difference between the Tory and the Liberal creeds. Each stood and stands for a different view of human nature and its possibilities and the extent to which, and the reasons why, it should be free of control by the community. The desire to win victories for their general theories and office for themselves has sometimes caused them to carry out each other's policies, but this has never been done for long, or in any really serious matter.

Sources of Conservative and Liberal Support. Who have followed the Conservative and Liberal parties at different periods? The strength of the Tory party since the Reform Bill has always been in the rural counties and Scotland.[26] This does not mean that it has been badly supported elsewhere.[27] But the counties have been peculiarly Tory, for the land has been the source of both wealth and social prestige; it has bred rich men and attracted them. Further, the peculiar dependence of the church and the agricultural laborer upon the squire, strengthened by the laborer's ignorance and the belief that loss of employment would follow upon independent

voting, swept hundreds of thousands into the Conservative camp. Ignorance, charity, and snobbery cemented the workers in the country to the party of the rich men. Protection and the relief of local taxation were the gifts of the party to its supporters—and the maintenance of the Church of England. The issue of free trade once settled, the upper middle class of manufacturers steadily went over to the Tories, until nearly all the interests with property have moved into that party. Many were attracted, also, by imperialistic and aggressive foreign policy, for this appeals to many people, besides promising economic opportunities abroad, such as markets, concessions, and openings in foreign and colonial administration for sons who have been brought up on an income which they cannot earn in equal competition with others at home.

What interests now support the Conservatives?—banking, finance, investment, insurance, manufacturers, brewers, landlords generally and owners of large agricultural estates, the chief newspaper chains, the wealthier members of the professions, most high officials (especially those retired after imperial and military service), the middle and upper ranks of the Established Church, the shopkeeping groups, some working-class disgruntled voters not at ease with a trade unionism that includes the masses whether skilled or unskilled, and some who are authoritarian and imperialist. A substantial number of "white-collar" workers sway to and from the party, as each election raises hopes or reveals fears in the economic and foreign situation.

A vast number of people are attracted by the simple appeal of the stability and unity of the country. The suburbs—the home of superior clerks and the middling independent professional or business man, whose whole being is founded upon his inherited or acquired superiority—and the seaside resorts in the South are Conservative strongholds. They cannot admit the doctrine of equality. Thousands of working men and women are overruled by the splendor of the Crown, the history of the Union Jack, the deeds of the Navy. They

---

24 Cf. Walter Layton, *A Fighting Faith* (London, 1945).
25 Cf. Liberal Party Committee, *Monopoly* (London, 1945).
26 Cf. the geographic distribution of the vote, given in the form of a map by *The Times* (London) immediately after each general election.
27 Cf. H. Gosnell, *Why Europe Votes* (Chicago, 1930), p. 14 ff.; and Krehbiel, *Geographical Review*, December, 1916, pp. 419-32.

are nationalist without knowing why, because so many of us are proud without knowing why. Snobbery and charity win thousands. Others are disgruntled.

It should not be left out of account that the figures of voting themselves show that perhaps one third, perhaps even more, of the followers of Conservatism have no direct economic interest in the success of the party. But it is, of course, difficult to say how far the claim that employment and high wages are to be assured by Tariff protection brings followers. We cannot argue that the Tory party is a class party, if by class is meant a group founded entirely upon economic expectations. The Tory party is a spiritual party as well as an economic party: for a large part of its following genuinely seek satisfactions other than the mere increase or defense of their riches.

The Liberal party is, in the towns, followed by the middle- and lower-middle-class professional men and women—shopkeepers, small craftsmen, and the like—who are employers of labor on a small scale but who are not much affected by the economic policy of the Conservative party and cherish an affection for free trade common among those who are in fairly direct touch with their consumers. Many are Nonconformists. A working-class vote is presumable also, since the liberal and radical clubs still attract clerks and artisans who desire the schemes of social amelioration and economic renewal promoted by the Labour party, but are unwilling to leave the older party which pretends so much respect for individual freedom. A section of the people with much social generosity and considerable personal hope from state intervention think the Labour party dangerous and the Tories insensitive. The Liberal philosophy of self-reliance and toleration is a powerful attraction to those who have come, by experience or education, to realize the importance of human personality, freedom, and peace. Liberal strength is very evenly spread everywhere: it is most marked in Devon and Cornwall, Wales and Scotland (the rural areas), in the seaside resorts and pleasant towns, and in the big cities of the

Northeast and Northwest. To sum up, I should say that the Liberal following is now rather a residuary collection of elements which cannot find a comfortable home in either of the two extremes, much of its present strength coming from the traditionary allegiance once given to freedom and harmony as applied to the church, foreign affairs, tariffs, the franchise, and civil liberties. Until 1945 there was still a powerful attraction in Lloyd George, both as a fighting figure and as an advocate of the interests of the land.

The decline of the Liberal party may be seen from a comparison between its seats in the Commons in its heyday and in the last four elections: 1906—397; 1911—271; 1923—158; 1929—59; 1931—37; 1935—21; 1945—12. It is the passing of an age. The *humanitas* of the Liberal party in the twentieth century needs incarnation not in laissez faire but in positive governmental ways and means. The soul of the Liberal party has entered into the Labour party. It is also a tribute to the good parliamentary sense of the British electorate that it would not chance losing the effect of its votes by casting them for the Liberal party, whose powers (though it put up 300 candidates) were apparently insufficient to fulfill its promises; they mainly went Labour in 1945, and they might return and some be forced to the Conservatives by nationalization.

ENGLAND: LABOUR PARTY

THE Labour party was created as a challenge to both the old parties. Quite early in the nineteenth century, certain men had seen that to rely upon the existing parties for any great alleviation of the workers' condition was only to court disappointment. The Chartist movement was the first attempt of workingmen to lead workingmen to the assault upon political power. Why could they not leave the old parties to their own evolution, trusting to the competition of one party with another to give the workingman what they thought was his due? Manifestly all depends upon what was considered his due. The general theories of the older parties may have been valuable for all men, but the groups who controlled them kept the values for themselves.

Social Equality. What, then, was to be done? The front and center of social inequality and demoralization lay in economic inequality. They who had the material means controlled society and many of its spiritual manifestations, for man is a greedy animal and will sell his noblest hopes, will even marry and breed, for money. All socialist thinkers have insisted upon the economic determination of social development, but Karl Marx, in a thesis which has been named the materialist conception of history, made it totally determinative of moral and political consciousness.

An important truth resides in this, but it is not the whole truth—certainly not for the British Labour party, for this has its vital roots in the Christian religious faith, stemming from the Nonconformist Chapels and the Christian Socialist [28] groups of the nineteenth century. Its bible is the Bible, not Karl Marx's *Das Kapital.* Parties seize upon broad and vital truths first, and acknowledge the reservations later. Economic inequality was the most powerful argument upon which to build a party, precisely because its truth hardly needed any demonstration to great masses of men, women, and children who dwelt in a society, the livelihood of which was made by that combination of machinery, factories, and management by private property owners, called the capitalist system. That system must be abolished, or closely and rigorously directed, for while it exists there can be no real equality, no real self-determination, no culture free from distortion, no collectively determined creation of anything valuable.

It was quite clear that mere discussion and argument would not persuade the leaders of the old parties into approval of this conception of history or politics, and into teaching their followers that change was desirable. At the most, the ugliest forms of misery were cured by health and building regulations, which certainly cost money, and by occasional concessions of education, by the regulation of hours and conditions, by the payment of labor, and by the provision of public assistance. But all was done after a struggle, and not much, on socialist assumptions, even then. For the truth was that those who had a monopoly were not prepared to give it up until they were compelled. They could prove that they themselves had made some of their wealth, if not all of it, discounting the opportunities and the security maintained by the lawful behavior and the inventiveness of their fellow citizens. They could even show, with truth, that accumulation had vastly stimulated industrialization and economic development, and that this was of benefit to the whole country. They could persuade themselves that they were of a biologically superior stock, either by heredity, when the fortune had been inherited, or of themselves, when they had built their own fortunes; and their physical appearance and educated manner gave a semblance of truth to such a claim, for they ate more and better food. What! Give to other people's children opportunities as good as to their own? Allow their own children to go to publicly provided schools? Not pass to them those advantages of culture and cash that would protect them from the competition of the strong, and sometimes, if necessary, even from the full rigor of the law? It would be unnatural. So, indeed, it is: and every great reformer from the times of Plato and Christ has been dismayed by the granite crags of property and family, which, in other words, are nothing other than self-preservation and self-development. Few people will surrender these things out of rational reflection that the result may be a good society; society offers too few tangible securities for such a promise.

What we have so far described is the general attitude which caused socialist revolt against the existing state of society. But the organizers have not been able to lead vast bodies of men and women to an unqualified and immediate acceptance of all their tenets. For the Labour movement

---

[28] Cf. M. B. Reckitt, *Maurice to Temple* (London, 1947).

was born into an electorate already divided between the older parties, already organized in part to secure a measure of economic justice through its trade unions (waxing in strength in Britain since 1801 [29]), surrounded and impressed by imperial obligations and foreign connections assumed in previous centuries by the old parties and permeated by the general culture which these had supported.

Stern and uncompromising as the faith is, it was born in a country profoundly habituated to parliamentarism, highly gifted for compromise. Its leaders firmly rejected reform by revolutionary methods. Its leaders were not proscribed or persecuted, as in Russia, into becoming an outlawed class, irreconcilable altogether to the state in which they lived. The traditions and institutions of English political life, created very largely by the liberal party and its radical wing, favored fair play and tolerance. The church and the universities felt their obligations for social justice; they gave life to the Workers' Educational Movement.

The system, in short, was not impervious to the socialist movement; this could live and thrive in the atmosphere on condition that it should sacrifice time. Its leaders and organization have been such that time was willingly sacrificed to avoid the tragic possibilities of destruction implied in revolutionary conflict. Neither the materialist fatalism of Marx nor the hatred that possessed Lenin vanquished their self-control. The essence of the movement's policy was to admit the continuance of the present state so long as the possibility of its ultimate attrition was granted and the necessary liberty allowed for progress toward its goal. From the first, the Labour movement recognized not only the inevitability of gradualness, but even its desirability. In English politicians and, it may be said, in the people as a whole, a strong sense has ever held sway that the material of the body upon which they are operating may be changed, wholly

transformed, but it must not be destroyed. It is a recognition that, however strong the claim for change, something is owed to one's opponents. Most Englishmen have something of Edmund Burke in them: "Magnanimity in politics is not seldom truest wisdom; and a great empire and little minds go ill together."

Foundation of the Labour Party. As a result, then, of many factors—parliamentary traditions, political liberty, a sense of obligation to the existing social, foreign, and imperial commitments, resolute and sane trade unions, and even infiltration of the Labour party by members bred in the traditions of other parties—the Labour movement pursued the most opportune path. This was the creation of a bloc of special Labour representatives in Parliament, to be supported by a federal arrangement among the trade unions and socialist societies like the Fabian Society and the Independent Labour party. Until 1918, then, the Labour party was an electoral organization composed of representatives of various societies, but not of individual members, without an official body of doctrine, although it naturally drew this from extraparty sources, and from the Independent Labour Party and the Fabians. Its main concern was entrance into Parliament, when the old parties could be made to deliver immediate concessions to the working classes in return for votes.

By 1918, the importance of the party had grown beyond this, and the aftermath of World War I seemed to offer golden opportunities of social reconstruction. The old party system was badly shaken, if not destroyed, and the war had exposed all the defects of capitalist civilization. The party reformed its composition and sought to state its aims in *Labour and the New Social Order*.[30] The reform of its composition was shown essentially in its appeal to workers "by hand and brain," and by its admission of individual membership. It established its own research and propagandist organizations, not relying as formerly upon the work done in these directions by the constituent socialist bodies.

29 Cf. S. and B. Webb, *History of Trade Unionism* (new edition, London, 1920), and *Industrial Democracy* (new edition, London, 1920).

30 Published in 1918.

However, the membership and weight of the party is still largely composed of the trade unions. In this respect we observe a difference from the Continental and American socialist parties. On the Continent there is a close connection, because it is a frequent, though not a constant, occurrence that a trade unionist is a member of the Socialist party; but the parties are composed of individual membership organized by local committees mounting in a pyramid to the central conference and executive. A member enters as a socialist, and not as a trade unionist: it is always an act of faith, not, as often in England, a perfunctory incident of trade-union membership. This has an important effect upon the policy of the parties: for, where socialism leads the trade unions, only parliamentary exigencies limit the scope of socialistic doctrine and the speed of its realization; while when, as in England, trade-union money and interests in counsel are so powerful, their own policy and prejudices must be respected and their membership not shocked. This, however, does not prevent the British Parliamentary Labour leaders and the wise men of the party, from stating their aims in clear and uncompromising terms. Thus the doctrinal development during the interwar years and during World War II heavily socialized the thinking of trade unionists.

The marked contrast between England and the Continent is that in England a comprehensive and consistent sociology has never been made the basis of all minor deductions of policy and tactics, and, in especial, the blithe ignorance of the Marxian theory or its good-humored pooh-poohing. Marx was indigenous to Germany, and his and Engels' works appeared in the German language decades before they became accessible to English readers. Perhaps the Germans are especially fond of a theoretical justification of their actions. But English politicians, as the English people generally, can always justify what they want in the process of obtaining it, or afterwards. The English politician is less a theorist than a man of action, acting with the few materials necessary for the burden of the day, and no more. When,

finally, Marx was translated, his theories mastered and set on their way, the Labour party had come under the leadership of those versed in two or three decades of Parliamentary opportunism, or those who were capable of a sound refutation of the gospel. The men who have fallen under the domination of Marx are found outside the Labour party, among the small number of communists.

The Labour aims, then, consist of the fusion of two tendencies: the radical tendency entering from the Liberal party (the fundamentals of democratic government and civil liberties), and the socialist tendency. It would not be, at this moment, too misleading to say that the tenets of the Labour party consist of sincere liberalism, with the addition of very strong communal safeguards against the waste and miseries incidental to laissez faire in the economic sphere.[31]

Composition of the Labour Party. The Labour party is the offspring of the trade-union movement and a variety of "socialist" tendencies and groupings, some with an origin centuries ago. But at the end of the nineteenth and the beginning of the twentieth, the trade unions made the party. What is remarkable about it today is the extent to which the trade-union leadership and following have become pervaded with a sense of state which can be characterized as "democratic-socialist": that is, neither a mere class outlook nor the blinkered vision of any single group of workers, but a comprehensive attitude to all objects of state life, international as well as domestic. It is the result of a dual process of political education, education by and within the trade unions themselves, typified by the workingmen's colleges, which, in turn, were educated as well as supplemented by the non-trade-union organization, the Fabian Society, founded in the 1880's by the early socialists of the Independent Labour Party and made nation-wide by such men as the Scotsman, Keir Hardie.

---

[31] See *The Old Order and the New Society* (1942); and the short pamphlet *Let Us Face the Future* (April, 1945), which contains, in effect, the policy for the election.

Today the party is a full fusion of affiliated bodies—that is, mainly the trade unions—and individual members who have joined the local branches of the party. The National Executive Committee consists of 25 members: 12 trade unionists, 7 members of the constituency organizations, 1 member from the cooperative societies, and 5 women members, of whom 3 are from the trade unions and 2 from the constituency organizations. (In addition, the leader of the party, in opposition or prime minister, is a member *ex officio*.) The respective groups are elected each year by their own sections at the annual conference of the party, for the year, and are the chief executive authority of the party for that year. The separate nomination and election for each of the groups was instituted in 1937, up to which time the conference as a whole had nominated and elected, and therefore had allowed the overwhelmingly heavy vote of the trade unions to decide the non-trade-unionist representation. The party program is decided by the conference by two-thirds vote: but the conference is managed by the executive which receives and speaks on the resolutions submitted by its constituent bodies three months in advance.

In 1947, 73 trade unions provided a Labour party membership of 4,386,074; 649 constituency parties provided 608,487; 6 socialist and cooperative societies provided 45,738 members. The total membership was 5,040,299. Representation at the party conference is arranged so that each affiliated trade union has one delegate for each 5000 members or part thereof on whom affiliation fees were paid; so also for the constituency labour parties. They vote at the conference by casting one "card" for each 1000 members or part thereof for whom affiliation fees were paid.

Thus six sevenths of the party membership is trade-union membership. Taking the statement of receipts for the year 1947 the total was in round figures £315,000. To this the trade unions contributed in affiliation fees just over £96,000, and another £55,000 as party development dona-

tions and also, say, £30,000 for election purposes: in all £181,000, or about four sevenths of the total receipts.

The trade-union weight of voting and finance in the party is overwhelming. Therefore, the democratic sense, the drive for and loyalty to a planned, equalitarian, and productive economy, as well as a tenacious hold on civil liberties, are to be sought in the direct, original contribution of the trade-union members; but they have been enhanced, and the sense of obligation to the whole state is fostered by, the intelligentsia of the constituency Labour parties.

In the election of 1945, the Labour party promised to nationalize the coal mines, the iron and steel industry, fuel and power, transport, the Bank of England and the control of investment, to give comprehensive social security, to ensure full employment, to socialize medicine, to advance generous schemes of housing and education, and, where monopolies were otherwise unmanageable, to take them over. That program was rapidly and energetically fulfilled in the most reformative five years since the passage of the Great Reform Bill in 1832.

Followers of the Labour Party. Who follows and composes the party? It is not all of the proletariat. For millions must vote Conservative and Liberal in the towns, and large numbers in the country, considering that the electorate consists of some 32 million and that the "gainfully occupied population" numbers about 20 million. But it is substantially a proletarian body: that is, of wage earners in industry and agriculture. It also attracts the subordinate and middle ranks of the civil service, because it is favorable to state activity and bureaucracy and because it declares those general principles of cooperation and social justice which a civil servant already spends his life in applying, and to which he is morally, by temperament and profession, a subscriber. Since World War I, and even more since World War II, an appreciable number of higher civil servants are included. Then its generous hopes of a perfectible society attracts many members of both wealthy and middle-class families, with whom social justice is a strong passion, and who are the more firmly wedded to the party because they, as leaders, have the leisure and wealth to pursue and study argument, and even propaganda, without being required to make immediate and total sacrifice. The lower middle-classes, the white-collar groups, have found attractive the policy of equality of opportunity, especially in education and the chance of promotion in the public services, as well as social security. Agricultural laborers have also been pried loose from deference to the farmer and landlord.

A heterogeneous mass of followers has been collected by a number of special appeals: teachers by the emphasis placed upon education; pacifists by that on peace. Queer social misfits take refuge with the newer and hitherto pioneer party which contains so many eminent critics of life. Young men from the universities come for the thrill of social reform, and the ease with which office can be obtained. Many others enter simply because they think that "something ought to be done," and the older parties seem to have done so little.[32] The poorer white-collar workers sway to and fro, perhaps a million of them in 1945 to the party. Great strength comes from the 20 million people served by the Consumers' Cooperative Movement.

The England for which the Labour party appeals and works is not an England which would be of benefit to the wage-earning class only. There are many other ideals in its philosophy attractive to the small salary-earning groups, and others also. Indeed, it is uncertain whether the working class would follow with such force and number if the full social vision of such men as Owen, Morris, Webb, Shaw, or Bertrand Russell already came within the range of practical politics. It is because the party asserts that it stands for these things, and because its present fortunes and activity are at least the promise of a morally and esthetically better world, that many follow it who have no direct economic interest in its success. Numbers of Church of England parsons and curates are Labour, since they believe that the ethics of the New Testament receive more heed in that party than in others. Quakers have long assisted its chief counsels as well as voted for it. Nonconformity generally is tending rapidly away from Liberal to Labour. Roman Catholicism supports candidates according to the impression and promises they make locally: it tends, at present, to help the Labour party in the poor districts since its congregations are in need of succor,[33] but suspicions of atheism and birth control militate against a complete adherence. Poor Jews are generally friendly to the most "progressive" party, not only of economic interest, but because such parties have treated aliens generously and have not insisted upon serious obstacles to their citizenship. But middle-class and richer Jews of the second generation tend toward Conservatism, though Liberalism is the political home of many of these. The Jew has been particularly interested in, and affected by, the politics of the nation in which he is domiciled, but this has been more emphatic, especially for the socialist movement, in Germany than elsewhere (a subject we shall touch upon, p. 352 in the discussion of German parties). In England ease of assimilation has reduced the hostility and offensive-defensiveness of the Jew to the vanishing-point. There is less anti-Semitism, because there is less social cowardice, in England than in any other country in the world.

The Future of Democratic Socialism. A

---

[32] The members of the cooperative societies (that is, the female ranks of the proletariat, regarded from a consumer's standpoint) and the employees also furnish a good contingent of voters and party workers. Cf. F. Hall, *Handbook for Members of Co-operative Committees,* 3rd edition (Manchester, 1928). There are formal agreements between the party and the cooperative movement allowing the latter a say in candidatures.

[33] Cf. the Papal Encyclical of 1931, *Forty Years Have Passed,* and its fulmination against socialists. Yet the Labour party of Great Britain was treated more tolerantly than the parties of the Continent. For the development of the British Labour party see G. D. H. Cole, *The British People 1746-1946* (New York, 1947), and *History of the Labour Party* (London, 1948).

few further observations on the British Labour party are necessary. The party grew to the strength necessary to take power in twenty-three years, counting from its obtaining 63,000 votes in 1900, 500,000 in 1910, and 4,300,000 in 1923, the point where it first took office. Its increase in votes was steady since 1923 (with the exception of 1931, when some of its members followed Ramsay Macdonald, its then leader, to join the Conservatives and the Liberals in a "National" government). This tremendous achievement occurred in spite of the fact that all the media of mass opinion—press, periodicals, films, space for placarding, and so forth —were in the hands of the other parties, excepting for the one big Labour paper, the *Daily Herald,* the property of the trade unions but run for them by popular commercial publishers. Hard personal work by thousands of workers who spread the principles of the party in the homes of the workers, throughout the trade-union movement, into the cooperative societies, and from door to door, made this victory possible.

The crucial question still to be answered is whether the masses will be happy with the policy they have voted for when they see its concrete provisions at work, and when, above all, the equality they have asked for, or rather the degree of it they have asked, and the subordination and hard work essential to provide the social benefits they want, must be paid for by their own efforts. A modern government cannot operate at the dictates of the producers' associations which are most concerned in the particular nationalized industry which takes in their work and gives out their wages. The government is at the top to satisfy the nation as a whole. That attitude has already been assumed, in fact and in doctrine, by the Labour government. Will the workers be happier and at least as productive in such a régime compared with the régime of private businessmen? It already seems possible; but we have yet to see. Will the workers observe the sense of responsibility declared (in 1946) as especially necessary by Sir Walter Citrine, General Secretary of the Trades Union Congress? Above all, will they observe it by industriousness and by self-restraint in use of the right to strike? This is the testing time and place of problems which have hitherto been "solved" either by despotism, as in nazi Germany or in Soviet Russia, or only by hypothetical thinking. It will throw light on the adequacy of elementary and secondary education, and the formation of the public mind by the political parties, to the intricate new tasks of a body of voters who are at once the owners of the means of production and yet also workers, producers, with responsibilities to the whole community of consumers.

After some four years of the first Labour government with a substantial majority, two things were clear. (1) The party and the trade unions firmly maintained the right to strike, yet the latter had resolved to use their power to strike only with the utmost responsibility.[34] (2) In the nationalized industries, the producers had been given the right to enter joint management-workers councils for consultation and negotiations, but *not* for the conduct of the industry, except indirectly; and claims to representation on the directorates of the industries had been decisively rejected, though experience in the organization of workers was set down in the nationalization statutes as a qualification for appointment.[35]

The advent to power of the Labour party has been possible by the loyalty to democratic principles of the other parties. They have accepted the rules of the constitutional game. The Conservatives, it is true, have now and again tried to defer the day of Labour victory by "stunts," and have several times succeeded. Nevertheless, not the slightest doubt ever existed that when the time came they would behave as a normal parliamentary and constitutional opposition. Apart from

34 Cf. Chap. 35 below.
35 Cf. R. Dahl, "Workers' Control of Industry and the British Labour Party," *American Political Science Review* (October, 1947). Cf. Herman Finer, *International Review* (March and April 1947), "British Planning and Nationalization."

the Communist party, hardly more than one confused person affected to preach that Conservatives would sabotage the socialist efforts of a Labour government.[36]

The Labour party puts democracy above socialism. Indeed, it seeks socialism only by the democratic path: that is, by persuasion of a majority by free and open electoral debate. This is the point at which it parts most sternly from the Communist party of Great Britain and parties of this same name elsewhere. The social content of its program is roughly the same, though the Labour party would not socialize for the sake of socialization, and though its followers would accept the great change only on condition of the retention of their civil liberties, including the right to strike. But above all, the difference is their belief in the right and the ability of the citizen, that is the masses, to decide for themselves the extent and pace and conditions of socialization and the government which must continuously implement it. They do not believe, as Communists do, in the right of a minority of highly conscious leaders to decide the fate of the majority and force it on them on Lenin's and Stalin's plea that the trade unionist cannot, as they can, see what is for the good of society, or that the masses are incapable of independent political thinking.[37] This is the decisive cleavage between Labour and Communism: and this is what poisons the hatred of the Soviet

rulers for Labour's policy. The Labour government may give all the benefits of Communist policy, more efficiently and as far as the path of liberal persuasion allows, at which point it will stop. What the public can welcome of its own volition is what the government will give. This is why the Labour party has again and again, and in 1946 decisively, refused to accept the affiliation of the Communist party as a party: [38] the Communist party denies the rectitude of loyalty, obligation, a single standard of morality for all, and democratic self-government. Labour's small Left representation is not Communist, but idealist, in the sense that it wishes to make Britain self-sacrificial in foreign affairs at a far quicker pace than the economy—that is, the standard of living of the wage-earning masses—can tolerate in one dose in a highly competitive world.

FRANCE

FOR the United States, going back to the Civil War, there is no difficulty at all in making a table of electoral statistics, to characterize both justly and clearly the rise and fall of the fortunes of political parties. There is hardly any difficulty about English conditions for the last three quarters of a century, although the Irish and the free-trade problems cause certain complications. A little more difficulty is met in regard to Germany because the parties were many and fissiparous.

But for France most difficulty plagues us, for effective, nation-wide party organization was existent only in three parties, namely the Radical Socialists, the Socialists,[39] and the Communists, until the addition of the *Movement Républicain Populaire* [40] in 1945. Of these parties, the Communists and even more so, the M.R.P.,

---

[36] On this subject see E. M. Durbin, *The Politics of Democratic Socialism* (London, 1939).

[37] For example, Sir Stafford Cripps (then Minister of Economic Affairs), *Debates* (October 23, 1947). "It is not merely our economic survival with which we are concerned; it is something even more. We are in every sense fighting the battle of democracy as much as we were during the war. Our struggle is to maintain the decent standards and the freedom that our ever-expanding democratic experience has taught us, in circumstances in which it is only too easy for more violent and totalitarian methods to prevail. If our economy and that of Europe should collapse, our democracy will in all probability collapse too, and will disappear, and with it will go the last stronghold of Western democratic civilisation in Europe."

[38] Cf. Herman Finer, *America's Destiny* (New York, 1947), p. 214, for Herbert Morrison's speech of repudiation.

[39] This is the S.F.I.O. (*Séction Francaise de l'International Ouvrière*) but we shall normally use "Socialist," for simplicity's sake.

[40] Henceforth referred to as M.R.P.

are of recent parliamentary advent, the Socialists have had a checkered history, and the Radical Socialists do not and cannot thoroughly enforce discipline, and moreover, began to organize only at the beginning of the twentieth century. From election to election the names of the organizing groups and committees used to change. From constituency to constituency the labels of the candidates varied, though they may have been sponsored by the same Parisian headquarters and later met in the same group in the chamber. From election to election, the names and membership of the campaign *blocs* and *cartels,* the *unions,* the *fédérations,* and the *alliances* were transformed. From parliament to parliament the groups of the chamber freely changed their names. No wonder that the official electoral statistics have had an ever-varied classification since 1871. Moreover, it is difficult to compare the parties of before 1871 with those after. Not until 1914 was there a regular official grouping, when a rule of the Chamber of Deputies required the inscription of names in groups for representation on the parliamentary commissions.

As important as any of these factors is the rapid growth and change of French groups since 1900. At every election—1902, 1906, 1910, and so on, until 1936—new groups appeared. So also since World

War II. No one can tell beforehand exactly which groups will cooperate in the government of the opposition, and certainly not the terms of cooperation or the occasion of secession. For though they may run in loose harness for the purpose of defeating an opposition bloc—as did the *Cartel des Gauches* in 1924, or the *Front Populaire* in 1936, or De Gaulle's grouping in the municipal elections of 1947—the component groups are independent, and proud of their independence. Nor is that all: in every chamber a number of members are independent of any regular grouping. The characterization of French parties is therefore difficult, and one is almost compelled to choose between the simple dichotomy of Conservatives and Liberals, or, what is very frequent, Right, Center, and Left, and the bewildering task of comparing a dozen programs and histories whose shades of difference may be the product only of personal animosities or loyalties and one or two differences of principles among a score. Let us attempt a combination of these methods and always remember the phrase of a critic: "The members of parliament, in their general forgetfulness of principles, have become as subtle as cardinals and the scribes and teachers of the Talmud."

One can construct a rough table of the

TABLE 2—FRENCH ELECTIONS: 1936

Party	Number of Seats	Votes in Millions
Right		
Republican Independent	13	
Republican Federation	59	
Popular Independents	16	2.25
Independent and Agricultural Republicans	40	
Center		
Popular Democrats	13	
Left Republicans and Independent Radicals	44	1.94
Democratic Left and Independent Radicals	38	
Left		
Radicals and Radical Socialists	111	11.46
Socialists and Republicans	29	0.52
Independent Left Socialists	28	1.92
Communists	72	1.50
Nonparty	6	

fortune of parties since 1871: they pass from Right to Left. If we take the electoral results of 1936, the last pre-World War II election, we obtain the first general ground of distinction. The figures are shown in Table 2.

Right, Center, and Left Distinctions. (1) The groups in the Center and Right almost always cooperated as socially and economically conservative, though the Left-Central groups sometimes split. Left of the Center groups are the socialistically progressive, but with very strong reservations for the Radical-Socialists. Further discrimination is necessary within the Left:

(2) All the Left groups toward the Center are normally in agreement upon governmental authority and efficiency, private property, anti-Sovietism and severe anti-Germanism; the most sincere representative is Louis Marin. Within the Left there is a very serious Right-Left cleavage, for the Socialists look to rather strict and wide governmental authority while the Communists are far more extreme in this respect. Both would oppose a bourgeois government, at the present stage of social development, which attempted to use the strong hand for capitalistic purposes. Until 1936 the Socialists were not prepared to enter a government but, granted concessions, used to vote for a coalition of Left parties, which they abandoned on the first signs of forceful capitalism. The Communists would not enter a government, though they electorally and parliamentarily supported the Blum Popular Front government of 1936. After World War II they changed tactics, as we shall see.

(3) Then the main wings differ as to the parliamentary system: the extreme Right has looked even to a dictatorship (some members are monarchist), and always to the strengthening of the permanent executive power, i.e., the President. It favors the idea of the separation of powers to restrain the assemblies and increase the unchallengeable stability of the executive (General de Gaulle's doctrines on this idea bring him a large following on the Right). The Right bore the dreadful legacy of hatred of the principles of 1789—Liberty, Equality, and Fraternity—and carried into a new age the conservatism of the French royal dynasty, in combination with the royalism and nationalism of the *Action Française* and Charles Maurras.[41] Its young group, the *Camelots du Roi,* mixed with the anti-Communist, anti-Left, anti-Bolshevik movements. Others who found a spiritual home with the Right, afraid of the social tendencies of democracy, became admirers of Mussolini and Hitler and even accepted subsidies from foreign fascist and nazi sources. A fascist movement under Colonel de la Rocque stirred an uproar in the streets until the bloody climax of riot before the Chamber of Deputies on February 6, 1934, gladly risking the subversion of the Third Republic.

As the Popular Front election of 1936 gave an overwhelming victory to the Left, the extreme Right veered in their foreign policy toward Hitler and Mussolini and against the U.S.S.R. This intensified the division of France and the passion of the conservatism which, suspended throughout the century and almost victorious in the Constitutional Assembly of 1871, now surged forward with a nation-killing rancour. It had been defeated in its support of the army against the Jew Dreyfus, when for its own pride and power it had been perfectly ready to condone and assist an act of corrupt injustice. Closely allied with the Roman Catholic Church, it had been affronted and wounded at the end of the nineteenth century by the campaign against clericalism, so victorious in the early years of the twentieth. It preferred Hitler's victory to democratic socialism in France. It constituted the main encouragement of Pétain, and the main support of his Vichy régime when the German victory precipitated capitulation and the overthrow of the constitution of the Third Republic. It preferred the motto: Work, Family, Fatherland.

From these groups (sometimes stigma-

---

41 Cf. D. W. Brogan, *Development of Modern France, 1870-1939* (London, 1940); and *French Personalities and Problems* (London, 1946), chapters on Maurras, Bainville, and nationalism. Also cf. R. H. Soltau, *French Political Thought in the XIX Century* (London, 1931).

tized as *Black France*) leftward, through all shades of difference, the groups become more and more republican. In fact, if one goes back to the essential controversies of before 1871, groups even as far as the *Républicains de Gauche* must be included in the republican, anti-Monarchist camp. Yet still, on the extreme Left, appear the Communists, many of whom at least speak in terms of potential dictatorship, and foment extraparliamentary violence to cow Assembly and cabinet. Other elements disturb the simple division into Right and Left. Such are nationalism and internationalism, and Catholicism and secularism.

(4) From the extreme Right to the Radical Socialists there is a strong—at the extreme, a ferocious—nationalism. But in the middle of the Right this was, on the proper occasions, tempered by fascist ultramontanism; while, at the Radical Socialists, a rational recognition of the propriety of international peace—particularly a European Union, and therefore of reciprocal abnegation—begins to operate and finds its fullest expression in the internationalism of Socialists and Communists. The last-named, formerly affiliated with the Comintern, cherish a loyalty to the U.S.S.R. that has proved dangerous to the internal welfare and external security of France.

France, like Germany, is bound to have as a permanent rallying cry of the Right, and as a general permeation of all parties, the question of security. She has awkward frontiers, she has long, painful memories, she loves her own culture and people, and she is placed between other cultures and other peoples. Even as Englishmen are united regarding sea power, so are all French groups obliged to temper their liberalism by military defense. At any moment the "national" issue may take seeming and so-called republicans and radicals over into the camp of the Right and help either to support a "national" bloc which is also antirepublican and antiliberal, or to cause the downfall of a ministry founded on the Left groups which pursues a liberal policy at home and (alas!) abroad also. For economy's

sake a Rightist government may reduce military security, as that headed by Tardieu did in 1934; faced with military danger, the Socialists were split into militant and pacifist wings down beyond the defeat of 1940.

(5) Nor are the fires of religious passion extinguished. France still has a "religious" question to complicate her politics, unlike Britain, but like the United States in spite of the latter's rationalist constitution. The rational spirit of the eighteenth century sapped the foundations of the Catholic Church, the *societas perfecta,* the state by the side of the state, built on self-respect, general acceptance, and privileges established in the concordat centuries old. If liberalism had never come into the world outside the Church, the Church itself would have become (in part at least) liberal. But since liberalism grew up outside it, it was forced to react as an abnormally conservative institution and so vindicate tradition and the existing social order more than they deserved, and more perhaps than all the clergy in their heart of hearts believed that they deserved.[42] Liberals, then, were bound to think of the Catholic Church as the enemy of political and social progress; and, indeed, the life of the Church was bound up with the monarchy with whom it had made the concordat, and who, by the acceptance of religious ceremonies at the coronation and other state occasions, gave the Church an adventitious claim to public consideration and authority.

The Constituent Assembly dispossessed the Church and with violence incorporated it by making the clergy into civil-state functionaries paid by the state. But later the Convention and the Directory carried the secularization of the state to its logical conclusion and separated Church and state completely, partly from rationalism and partly because the Church was opposed to republicanism. Napoleon re-established the régime of the Concordat· the Catholic Church was once more recognized as an independent power, and the

---

42 Cf. J. M. Thompson, *The French Revolution* (Oxford, 1944), Chap. VIII.

clergy were paid out of the public treasury. Thenceforward, the Catholic Church was the established church of France. It was found always on the side of the monarchy and the monarchists; it was the permanent opponent of social and political liberalism.

The republican parties and sects regarded it a double enemy. *First,* it was an obstacle to the lay state in its doctrines and organization: a foe, that is, of the state, which alone has authority and comprehends equally all citizens without intervening associations, and which permits to all faiths equal freedom and privileges. *Second,* it was a powerful political obstacle to their programs of reform, with sanctions more compelling and less rational than those at the disposal of rationalists.[43] When Gambetta surveyed the causes of republican failures at elections, he saw that the *curé* in the villages had the power to nullify republican efforts: hence the cry *"Le cléricalisme, voilà l'ennemi!"* The republican form of government was itself outlawed by the Catholics until the *ralliement* of 1892, when Pope Leo XIII declared in his encyclical that to accept the powers that be was not only permissible but necessary. To separate state and church became, however, one of the urgent portions of the policy of the republican groups: i.e., to abolish the Concordat, to make the Church, equal with other churches, a self-governing association without official connection with the government. The Dreyfus affair, in which the Church and Catholic generals were the ferocious supporters of the army and hostile to revision and justice, added zest to the pursuit of this object.[44]

Moreover, *congregations,* which had been expelled by the Revolution, had established themselves again, and the monks had been particularly the enemies of the impious republican state; and both these and the regular clergy intervened in elections. Under Waldeck-Rousseau a *"bloc républicain"* of all the Left groups, in-

cluding the Socialists, was founded in 1899 to defend the Republic against the nationalists, militarists, and their Catholic supporters. Waldeck-Rousseau, himself a moderate radical, created this bloc for a defensive purpose, but could maintain it only by conceding social reforms to the more progressive groups. His ministry proceeded further to make the Law on Associations of 1901, which required previous authorization for the establishment of *congregations.* The radical Left pressed more extreme amendments, and the *congregations* were subjected to supervision.[45]

The contest was continued by the bloc under Emile Combes, which issued from the elections of 1902 somewhat radicalized. Relations between the government and the Holy See became exceedingly strained. The Socialists were, however, in 1904 detached by the noncooperation decision of the Amsterdam International Socialist Congress. The anti-Church policy was too severe for moderate republicans, and little by little they moved into opposition. Combes' ministry fell in January, 1905. The Law on the Separation of Church and State was passed some months later. The elections of 1906 were fought on the question of the execution of the law, and the groups fell into two blocs, the republican groups of radical tendency winning a remarkable victory. The radical bloc supported Clemenceau for nearly three years, while the law was executed, and then fell a victim to various disorders, postal strikes, and destructive strife with the extreme radicals and socialists. Church and state were separated. The wounds of the battle still smarted when World War II broke out. The strength of the Church, thus separated, had little diminished, for, short of complete suppression, its political influence must always operate, especially in the rural districts—and France is still far more of a rural than an urban society. The state is secular, but society is markedly religious and its religion is Catholic. While clerical influence prevailed, politics were not fully secularized.

---

43 Cf. Georges Weill, *Histoire du Parti Républicain en France, 1814-70* (Paris, 1900).
44 Cf. J. Reinach, *Histoire de l'Affaire Dreyfus* (Paris, 1901-11), 6 vols.

45 A. Débidour, *l'Église Catholique et l'État, 1870-1906* (Paris, 1906), Vol. II, p. 288 ff.

The parties of the Left were exceedingly sensitive to any movement, be it in education or otherwise, which might reintroduce the official influence of the Church.[46] Where that influence, which is generally socially and economically conservative, was desired, the Church was applauded by some parties—e.g., when the Church was opposed to votes for women (most political parties considered women to be peculiarly liable to clerical influence) or to egalitarian reforms. A numerous peasantry makes this possible, and the tendency is always in favor of conservatism; but a poor urban working class is also of its rank and file.

Although the Church had put the *Action Française* on the Index in 1926 and had disavowed its extreme antirepublican tenets (and it disliked its egoistic secularism), the effect of this on France's downfall was strong. The leaders of the Right Catholic nationalist groups were saturated with it; its essentially authoritarian doctrines produced a sharp and angry cleavage between them and the other political parties. They were constantly looking for revenge, for the day of church, army, and aristocracy—*les notables*—was inglorious and ending. The generals and admirals came of this stratum, Pétain and Weygand among them. The educational policy of Vichy attempted to reverse the laicization of the schools, not with complete success. Its "corporative" policy was in line with fascist development, and this had enough support, doctrinal and otherwise, of the Church, to produce unwholesome associations. Freemasons and Jews were purged from the Vichy civil service; not Catholics, as such. The Vatican did not denounce Pétain: it was, indeed, not unkind to him.

The Catholic trade unions and many individual antimonarchist, anti-conservative Catholics, and some lower clergy among them, resisted the Vichy administration and joined the resistance. The upper and older hierarchy of the Church was in bad favor with large masses of population. Its reputation was barely saved by the socially progressive Catholic political groups, the *Démocrates Populaires* and *La Jeune République*.

The M.R.P. As a result of the war and the occupation, most of the Right is still in disarray, parliamentarily. But a political party with strong Catholic, progressive support, the *Mouvement Républicain Populaire,* has come into existence. During the years of occupation and Vichy it began in the resistance as the *Mouvement Républicain de Liberation:* it carries on and enhances the *Démocrates Populaires* and *La Jeune République* and the *Jeunesse Ouvrière Catholic.* It is a Catholic party, supported by the Catholic trade unions (now numbering a million members and themselves strengthened by working-class revulsion from the Communists who had come to dominate the C.G.T.),[47] rather like the Christian Democratic parties that have gained strength or come into existence elsewhere in democratic Europe. Though a conglomerate, it is more fully Catholic than they except in Italy. It is led by left-wing Catholics: Bidault (once a professor of history), Schuman, Teitgen, and de Menthon. Their following is fairly large, comprising middle-class groups with a social-liberal outlook and accepting the democratic system, though this has no real or permanent countenance from the hierarchy. This intellectual leadership is closely followed and participated in by the Catholic trade unionists. Another group, by far the largest that follows the M.R.P., is the agricultural population, under the leadership, and not seldom the moral intimidation, of the local clergy. In the urban as well as the rural areas, the enfranchisement of the women, as was prophesied, has provided strong support for the party. There is, then, a hetero-

46 In 1929 and 1930, the Left upset the Tardieu and the Chautemps cabinets on the religious issue; an attempt had been made to include M. Pernot as Minister of Public Works in those cabinets—he was professor of law at a Catholic university. Cf. André Siegfried, *Tableau des Partis* (Paris, 1930), p. 151.

47 Cf. Notes Documentaires et Études, No. 420, *Le Syndicalisme Chrétien en France* (September, 1946).

geneous collection of Right-wingers who are, in fact, crypto-Rightist.

The M.R.P.'s policy is for wider social control, even in the shape of nationalization, than the Catholic groups of the interwar years would have come near tolerating: full social security, equitable taxation, developed social services, the universal encouragement of cooperatives in all industries and trades. It declares itself "anti-capitalist" and proposes the nationalization of monopolies, profit sharing, and joint management of all business. It also advocates the diffusion of private property—astute in a land in which a peasant proprietary has long flourished. In all these it is close to the socialists and the communists except for the accent on individual proprietorship and warnings against "excessive government." It is a Catholic democratic-socialist movement,[48] but it differs from these in wishing to restore religion in the schools. It is supported by intellectuals of Jacques Maritain's type. A leader described it to me as a party of *croyants,* that is, religious-minded.

Yet that it in reality harbors substantial numbers of Rightists is discernible from the fact that it was above all the party behind de Gaulle. His wishes for a strong executive above and even independent of parties was in the end too obvious and untenable, for the party has declared strongly for democracy. In 1947, the M.R.P. firmly declared its refusal to accept those who denied its anticapitalist program. A new Rightist grouping, *Parti Republicain Liberale,* conservative and even reactionary, has in many constituencies withdrawn (urged to, in many cases by the Catholic clergy) from the elections in order to give the M.R.P. its opportunity of victory.

In spite of substantial electoral victories, the status of the M.R.P. is insecure. It benefited in the immediate aftermath of World War II by certain transient strengths: its resistance under Vichy was strong and valiant; in times of sudden death and desperation, men, and especially the new millions of women voters, reach out for religious consolation. The parties of the Left had before the war opposed woman suffrage, though their general principles supported it, for fear of clerical domination of the women. The Soviet Union is to many, in the shape of French communism as well as the Kremlin, an impossibly materialist and despotic regime. While the Communists are extreme, the Vatican has an appeal. Since the M.R.P. *is* Catholic, it must be internally troubled—its membership will be swayed by the inclination of the Vatican now to the Right, now to the Left, now to Authority, now to Liberty. Many voters of the Right, even of fascist tendencies, have fled into this party: it is for them a waiting room until the Rightist trains come by again.[49]

Buffeted by the two hard forces on the Right (General de Gaulle with the renascent groups of the Right) and the communist Left, France has so far been driven on an uneven keel, but kept afloat and moving forward through a stormy sea of financial reconstruction and economic renewal, by a coalition of M.R.P., Socialists, and Center groups. It is clear that appeasement is once again urgently needed to recall to all Frenchmen the truth that if their nation is to be of any use to each group itself, let alone to attain national ends furthering the benefit and destiny of all, a loyalty must arise out of the individual and pervade, pass through, and tie his group to the nation. This is what the M.R.P. has sought, with the assistance of the Socialists, and in face of the intensified malevolence of Right and Left. Once again we are faced with the desire for unity expressed by all and, I am sure, truly felt by all; yet it is a desire for unity on the clear-cut, unyielding terms of each group, so inflexible that the state is disintegrated. It is meet to quote from speeches of M. Schuman, then prime minister, from de

---

48 Cf. C. Viatte, *La Sécurité Sociale;* P. Bacon, *La Réforme de l'Enterprise Capitaliste;* P. Pflimlin, *Perspectives sur Notre Economie;* A. Gortais, *Démocratie et Liberation;* all published by the party (Paris, 1947) as its policy. See also A. Spire, *Inventaire des Socialismes Contemporains* (Paris, 1945).

49 In the municipal elections of 1947, the train arrived—DeGaulle's new party—and the M.R.P. lost considerably to it.

Gaulle, and finally from M. Thorez, the Communist leader.

M. Schuman said: [50]

It was imperative then [when the government took power] and, no matter what happens, it is essential now, that the French people reacquire the desire and taste for authority, an authority freely accepted. . . We felt that our main task was to persuade Frenchmen gradually to resume the necessary practice of civic discipline. . . .

In these times the Government must less than ever be a syndicate of interests and a coalition of party politicians. . . . In order to achieve this must we, or indeed, can we, erase the differences between the various political tendencies? Are there only two alternatives: the standardization of all opinions or the erection of selfish and rigid barriers between the parties? . . . It is not difficult to reach agreement on objectives, but in the choice of technical solutions, we are naturally and legitimately swayed by our conception of the role of the state and its institutions. . . The existence of parties is not an evil; it is a logical and essential part of democracy.

However, any party pushed to extremes runs into error; a political organization that becomes an end in itself, that judges and weighs everything in relation to its own chances of winning and holding power, imperils the functioning of democracy. The party must serve the common good; even more than the individual, its duty is to educate the citizen, stimulate political life and guarantee the discipline that all parliamentary bodies must observe.

In thus justifying the existence of parties I am not attempting to defend our present political customs. We all agree that certain definite defects must be corrected. But the remedy is not the suppression of parties. That would only result in throwing minds, ideas and men into a dangerous confusion.

General de Gaulle's temper is far less patient. He holds: [51]

We shall not reach our goal by division into rigid opposing factions. The Republic of which we dreamed during the struggle must be based on efficiency, harmony, and liberty. Otherwise it will become nothing but impotence and disillusionment, waiting for the time when it will disappear into one swamp or another, falling either under dictatorship or into anarchy. . . . The time has come to organize, for the welfare of the nation and the reform of the state, above party differences and within the framework of the law, the *rassemblement du peuple français.*

M. Thorez' temper was perhaps even more determined: [52]

This program of national salvation can be put into effect only by a government of democratic union in which the working class and its Communist Party play a decisive role. . . . The French Communist Party calls upon all workers, all republicans, all patriots and all Resistants to unite in the Committees for the Defense of the Republic in order to check the plans of the instigators of civil war. It calls upon all the workers, technicians and manufacturers to unite in the Industrial Defense Committees organized to protect industry against the threat of American expansionism.

Recent Elections and the Old and New Parties. It is now convenient to exhibit the results of the elections held in France since the liberation and continue the discussion by reference to these, as well as to survey the movement of political opinion by a résumé of the *sondages* (soundings, or polls) taken by the *Service de Sondages et Statistiques,* the French Gallup polls. These results are shown in Table 3,[53] which does not include the referendum figures on the new constitution, as they have already been given on page 124 above.

---

[50] *L'Aube* (Paris), April 20, 1948. Cf. G. Almond, "The Christian Parties of Europe," *World Politics* Vol. I, No. 1, October, 1948.
[51] February 27, 1947; see also his *Le Fils de L'Epée* (Paris, 1944) for his political ideas more generally. Cf. *Partisan Review,* March, 1948, "DeGaulle; Dialogue between Burnham and Malraux."
[52] *Ce Soir,* April 18, 1948. The Defense Committees are reminiscent of, and indeed, resemble, the groups of men and women of the party, who in the Communist *coup d'état* of February, 1948, in Czechoslovakia, took direct action, wherever necessary by armed force, against those who resisted the seizure of power commanded by the Communist leader. The pattern has sprung up throughout western Europe since the establishment of the Cominform.
[53] Prepared from data in Keesing's *Contemporary Archives* (November 16-23, 1946) and the *New York Times.*

TABLE 3—FRENCH ELECTIONS: 1945–46

Parties and groups	October 21, 1945, general elections to Constituent Assembly of 586 members (final figures)			June 2, 1946, general elections to Constituent Assembly of 586 members (final figures)			November 10, 1946, general elections to first National Assembly of 618 members (some overseas districts not included)		
	Total votes[a]	Percentage of votes[a]	Seats	Total votes[a]	Percentage of votes[a]	Seats	Total votes[a]	Percentage of votes[a]	Seats
Communists[b]	5,004,121	26.1	159	5,203,046	25.9	153	5,475,955	28.2	168
M.R.P.	4,580,222	23.9	150	5,589,130	28.2	167	5,033,430	26.0	160
Socialists[b]	4,491,152	23.4	139	4,198,110	21.1	129	3,454,080	17.9	93
R. Gauches[c]	2,018,665	10.6	60	2,179,067	11.6	53	1,971,660	11.1	59
P.R.L.[d]	2,886,095	15.2	39	2,623,679	12.7	35	3,136,630	16.3	42
Independent Republicans	—	—	14	—	—	23	—	—	23
Gaullist Union	—	—	—	—	—	—	—	—	9
Peasant Party	—	—	11	—	—	9	—	—	8
Algerian parties	—	—	7	—	—	11	—	—	7
Minor groups and independents	—	—	7	—	—	6	—	—	—

	Number	Percentage of registered voters	Number	Percentage of registered voters	Number	Percentage of registered voters
Voters on register	24,680,981	—	24,688,750	—	24,387,315	—
Votes cast	19,661,515	79.7	20,199,202	81.8	19,153,756	78.5
Valid votes	19,126,093	—	19,883,138	—	19,148,744	—
Abstentions	5,019,466	20.3	4,489,548	18.2	5,233,561	21.5

[a] These figures include various minor parties and groups affiliated with or cooperating with the major parties.
[b] With minor affiliated groups.
[c] *Rassemblement des Gauches,* consisting of Radical Socialists, U.D.S.R. (*Union Démocratique et Socialiste de la Résistance*), and Left Republicans. The former two parties won the following number of seats in the three general elections:

	October 21, 1945	June 2, 1946	November 10, 1946
Radical Socialists	29	32	45
U.D.S.R.	31	21	14

[d] Republican Liberty Party: Figures for October, 1945, are for *Groupe d'Unité Républicaine,* which with other conservative groups later formed the P.R.L.

It will not be amiss if the parties from Right to Left are described at some length as they stood in 1928 before the great Depression and the accession of Hitler. Thence deductions can be made regarding their recent evolution. As shown in Table 4, the parties on the Right were:

(1) *Démocrates Populaires,*
(2) *Union Républicaine Démocratique.*

The parties in the Center were:

(3) *Action Démocratique et Sociale,*
(4) *Alliance Démocratique,*
(5) *Gauche Radicale.*

On the Left were:

(6) *Parti Radical et Radical-Socialiste,*
(7) *Parti Républicain Socialiste,*
(8) *Socialistes,*
(9) *Communistes.*

(1) The *Démocrates Populaires,* having established a grouping in November, 1924, were able to collect about fourteen members in that legislature. They claimed to be politically and industrially democratic, to accept the Republic as the dispensation of heaven. They supported liberty of conscience, free education, and liberty of press and meeting. They promised to educate the civic sense and to respect religious convictions. They were at once nationalist and supporters of international cooperation and the League of Nations. They appear to have been socially generous, matching the English Liberty party and the German Democratic party. They themselves declared that if the Chamber were divided into two, Right and Left, they

Table 4—DEVELOPMENT OF FRENCH PARTIES: TO 1928

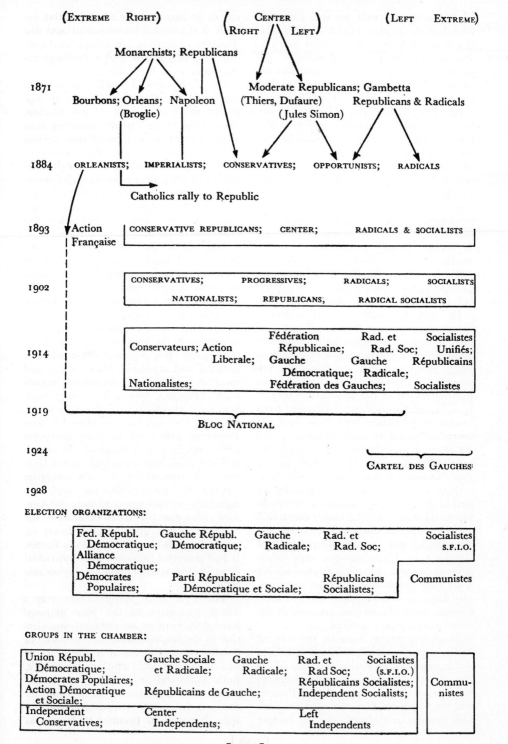

could be found well to the Left, yet French students placed them on the Right. (*La Jeune République,* founded in 1912, was a Christian-Catholic-democratic organization which could be found just on the left of the *Démocrates Populaires,* but it differed from these in its Catholic tinge.)

(2) The *Union Républicaine Démocratique* was the Chamber group of the party called the *Fedération Républicaine.* This was established in 1903 by a fusion of three organizations, with the informative motto of "Order and Progress," the maxim "Liberty, Equality, and Fraternity," and the policy of maintaining the principles formulated in the Declaration of the Rights of Man. It was antiradical; it became strictly conservative, in the modern sense; i.e., domestic individualism and international egoism. One of its past presidents was Charles Benoist; the present president is Louis Marin.

In 1920 the party received reinforcements in Lorraine. It insisted with remarkable obstinacy upon individual independence and guarantees for individual rights. Benoist's works emphasize the importance of the separation of powers and judicial review of the constitutionality of laws, in order to prevent Parliament from interfering by statutes with individual and corporate property and conscience, and the program included this. It was hostile to religious persecution. It ascribed the nation's financial troubles to state-socialistic activity and declared there could be no well-being unless the notions of retrenchment and respect for the family controlled society. Taxation ought not to be an engine of civil war. Nor should the guilt of Germany be forgotten—the only efficacious policy was that of "guarantees." No truck with socialism; freedom of testamentary disposition; abolition of estate duties! Citizens must obtain easy methods of defense against state services.

Much was to be done in the way of Parliamentary and administrative reform —the numbers of Parliament should be halved, professional associations were to collaborate constantly with Parliament and the *Conseil d'État,* the right to speak and propose amendments to the budget

was to be curtailed. In administrative reform, it demanded regroupment and distribution of services, less hierarchical control, decentralization, and a thorough reorganization of the cabinet.

The *Fedération Republicaine* strongly supported the Catholic Church: it supported the Catholics of Alsace-Lorraine, the embassy to the Vatican, the abrogation of the Law of Association of 1901 against religious congregations, the admission thereof to the benefits of the Law of Association of 1884, permission to such congregations to receive subscriptions and legacies, grants-in-aid to private schools (with state inspection), and the admission of the Holy See to the League of Nations.

This was the party of big industry and finance and landowners. It was harsher than the well-turned phrases of its philosophers suggest, and it seemed to be equivalent to the extreme English Tories. Though it insisted upon its republicanism, its spirit of social exclusiveness linked it loosely with the lost cause of monarchy. The party was a composition of new growths and revulsion from radical and socialist tendencies of its former republican colleagues. Among its leading members were Yves Guyot (died 1929), Arago, the Wendels, and François-Marsal (whom President Millerand in 1924 entrusted with a ministry in defiance of the constitutional objections of the Chamber of Deputies). It represented the new oligarchy created by industrialization, and was especially the spokesman of the "200 families" who ran the Bank of France, the Stock Exchange, and the great heavy industrial cartels like the Comité des Forges. It had powerful influence with individual deputies and senators and the higher officials.

The *Fedération Républicaine* was a strong supporter of the *bloc national* formed in 1919 as an electoral organization of the Right against the "menace" of Bolshevism and to see that the peace as well as the war was victorious for France. Both Millerand as president of the republic and Poincaré as prime minister received its steady friendship; and, in 1931, it preferred Doumer to Briand as

President of the Republic. It waned in electoral strength in the 1930's. This party was the full Rightist party and bears the heaviest responsibility for defeat and capitulation and Pétain in 1940. From this must be excepted Louis Marin and a small number of men who cared more for France than their own fortunes or fixed ideas; they are infiltrators into the Party of Republican Liberty of postwar France.

(3) A little on the left of the *Fedération Républicaine* (or *Union Republicain Democratique*) was the *Parti Républicain Démocratique et Social,* reorganized in 1920, but going back to a group of Left republicans of opportunist tactics, and claiming personal links with Gambetta, Jules Ferry, Sadi Carnot, and Waldeck-Rousseau. Such claims were made by other groups, also—and in fact may truly be made, for all the republicans and Left groups of the present day have at least the element of antimonarchism in them. It was peculiarly the party of Poincaré. It was marked off from its friends on the Right by its secularism (though it was favorable to resumption of relations with the Vatican), and from the Left by its economic tenets, by its irreconcilability with the Socialists, and by its affiliations with the commercial, industrial, and agricultural defensive associations of the capitalist system. Thus, it corresponded roughly to the Left of 1871–1900. It was the left wing of the *bloc national* of 1919, and in fact was its instigator.

The *Parti Républicain Démocratique et Sociale* fell into three groups in the Chamber of Deputies: the *Gauche Démocratique,* the *Gauche Indépendante,* and the *Républicains de Gauche.* But several cooperated with the *Groupe Radical et Radical Socialiste!* Such a division into groups was, in fact, not deprecated by the party, for it made easy the detachment of members from implicated groups. The Senators of the party belonged, in the Senate, to the *Union Républicaine* and to the *Gauche Démocratique.* Active in the party councils were Barthou, Chéron, and Doumer.

(4) In between this party and the *Fedération Républicaine* was the moderate Right group of the *Alliance Démocratique,* headed by Tardieu, Flandin (an appeaser of Hitler), and Reynaud (a member of this group who left it from antipathy to Flandin). Liberal with a Gladstonian flavor, it was composed of fluctuating groups.

(5) By the side of this party, formed by those who were expelled from the *Parti Radical et Radical Socialiste* in 1924 for voting with the *bloc national,* was the *Gauche Radicale.* It was opportunist, swaying now Right now Left, and could be described as Center Left. But a group of some fifty votes which sway here and there in a Chamber in which there are so many groups is very important and dangerous to the stability of government.

(6) Squarely in the liberal ranks was the *Parti Radical et Radical-Socialiste.* It was impiously anticlerical, supported the policy of uniform and secular public education and generous scholarship schemes, was genuinely concerned to secure international peace, and united a theory of private property with social services for the benefit of the poor and helpless. It insisted at once upon freedom and upon efficient administrative organization. Very spirited, it was antimilitarist, anticaesarist, the incarnation of the Jacobins, yet rather pallidly so. Its theorists and leaders have been Jules Simon, Gambetta, Clemenceau and Camille Pelletan, Bouisson, Edouard Herriot, and Daladier. Strong enough to urge, if not entirely to dominate, policy since 1898, it added to the statute book, in successive years, the Law of Associations (1901), reduction of military service (1905), separation of church and state (1905), workers' pensions (1910), and income tax (1917). It also championed peasant proprietorship and the *École unique.* The spirit of the party was well-characterized by Herriot, who indicated the sources of modern policy: the scientific attitude, unwillingness to be bound by nonevolving formulas, the hatred of oppression (which was especially awakened by the Dreyfus case), and social helpfulness of the state without bureaucratic routinization. Herriot's own words explain the party's differ-

[339]

ence from its Socialist neighbors on the extreme Left:

Is it possible to give to man his power of development, that which remains, according to us, the essential task of politics, if you refuse to him, in any object, and in particular in that which he has created, that right of property which, after all, given the brevity of life, can never be other than a right of use? [And yet] . . . radical socialists admit and proclaim the necessity of collective property for the profit of the communes or the state, cooperative societies or trade unions.

This political party most closely incarnated France prior to World War II. From 1885 to 1939 it supplied 16 out of 38 prime ministers. It had the major electoral following to 1932: 160 seats in the Chamber against the Socialists' 131. In 1936, the last election before World War II, it had 111 seats compared with the Socialists' 149. It was the broad-based "party of negation." It represented the better-off peasants, the shopkeepers, the petty doctors and lawyers, the middle and lower civil servants, the small urban bourgeoisie. They wanted to be left alone by government. Freemasonry played a considerable part in the party.

The party's main interest was in civil liberties, weak and do-nothing government, peace, and no taxes at all, if possible. Various internal groupings weakened it, even in its defensive negativeness: Herriot, Daladier, Chautemps jostled each other for leadership and influence. Its local committees showed much independence.[54] It was the chief single scapegoat of the *débacle*, for under Daladier, it led France to Munich and through the first six months of World War II. It was inadequately active in the resistance.

It is highly interesting to notice that France has rejected this "party of negation." Whatever the nation may do about governing with parties so different in their ethos as the big three, these, at any rate, are parties of governmental action.

54 Cf. A. Thibaudet, *Les Idées Politiques de la France* (Paris, 1932); Daniel Halévy, *République des Comités* (Paris, 1934); E. Berl, *La Politique et les Partis* (Paris, 1932); and "Pertinax," *The Gravediggers* (New York, 1946).

In the debates on the new constitution, the Radical Socialists insisted on a strong popular assembly, a weakish executive, a bicameral system, and made heavy claims for a Declaration of Rights, harking back to 1789. They especially stressed "Liberty." A poll (*Sondages,* March 15, 1946) shows that 8 per cent of the voters would have voted for the Radical Socialist party, the towns being rather more favorable to it than the country, the men less than the women, the older more than the younger, the wealthy twice as much as the people of small fortune. The Communists, if they had had a choice, would have given no votes to the Radical Socialists; the Socialists would have cast 2 per cent for them, and the M.R.P. would have cast 5 per cent.

It is possible that if the Communists and Socialists attempt to realize a large program of state activity, the electorate may well swing over to the Radical Socialists, particularly if the Communists disturb the nation by violence in industry and by parliamentary misbehavior. Indeed, in 1949 the prime minister and the presidents of both chambers were Radical Socialists.

(7) Between this party and the Socialists was the *Parti Républicain Socialiste,* more usually with the Radicals than with the Socialists. However, not all the members of the Republican Socialist group in the Chamber belonged to the electoral organization. Some of them voted with the *bloc national.* The principal leader was Painlévé, who sought a permanent alliance between all the Left groups excepting the Communists.

(8) and (9) We arrive at the Socialist and Communist parties. In the Chamber of 1936 there were 149 socialists belonging to the *Parti Socialiste, Section Française de l'Internationale Ouvrière.* Neither the Chamber group nor the party comprised all the socialist representation, for some of the group had certain affinities with some Radicals and some Republican Socialists. Moreover, there are socialist organizations and constituencies independent of the main body. The situation was the result of a long evolution of doctrine and organization, the year 1905 consti-

tuting a focal point. In that year the various lines of socialist evolution joined in a single organization: Rousseau's optimism about man if men were only equal; the class-conscious decentralization and self-aid in cooperative societies and the producer's syndicates of Proudhon; the revolutionary communism of Blanqui (drawing inspiration from Babeuf's "Conspiracy of the Equal" of the Great Revolution); the parliamentary state socialism of Louis Blanc; and the foreign but preponderant force of Marxism through Jules Guesde and Paul Lafargue. These tendencies had till then divided and wasted socialist efforts in a series of bitter animosities.[55] The "reformism" of Louis Blanc found its champion and developer in Jean Jaurès. The emergence of a unified party was no accident. From 1875 to 1905 was one period of the Third Republic, from 1905 to 1945 was another. In the first, the older, traditional, conservative, royalist, aristocratic, militarist, agricultural, and rural forces had been dominant though waning; after 1905 the urban, industrial, commercial, secularist, middle and working classes surged forward.

The new party, called the *Parti Socialiste Unifié,* accepted the basis of the revolutionary class war with the ultimate aim of a "collectivist society" but of immediate reforms, and of noncooperation with other groups in Parliament. Its electoral policy was not always so intransigent, its tactics often admitted transient alliances with bourgeois groups, its party discipline was severe. As in all other countries, so in France, World War I disrupted the Socialists, and the Bolshevist revolution set a seal upon the disruption.[56] In 1920, at the National Congress of Tours, a minority of the party formed the *Section Française de l'Internationale Ouvrière,* with a

doctrine and tactics similar to the British Labour party and the German Social Democratic party. The rest joined the Third (Moscow) International and formed the Communist party (S.F.I.C. or *Section Française de l'International Communiste.*) Since then other scissions have occurred: in 1923, the *Union Socialiste-Communiste,* a small group standing between the S.F.I.O. and the Communists, and moving toward the former; there is also a small group of socialists on the Right of the S.F.I.O. The leaders of the S.F.I.O. acquired a European reputation: Léon Blum, Rénaudel, Paul-Boncour, Longuet, Ramadier; so also of the Communist party, Marcel Cachin, Rappaport, Thorez, and Duclos. In 1924 the S.F.I.O. entered an electoral pact, the *Cartel des Gauches,* with the Radical Socialists against the electoral arrangements of the Right; the Communist party, although urged by Moscow to make a "united front" with other socialists against the Right, could not reach a complete agreement with the bloc. Until World War II, the Socialist party was supported by the reformist trade unions grouped in the *Confédération Générale du Travail,* and the Communist party by the *Confédération Générale du Travail Unitaire,* formed in 1922 and affiliated to the Communist Trade Union Internationale.

The stresses of the interwar years and of the ideological conflict and the Nazi occupation produced a serious change in the fortunes of the Socialist and Communist parties. The Socialist party under Léon Blum formed and led the so-called Popular Front government of 1936. The Communists supported this, since it was antifascist, but did not join it. The Socialist party, being democratic, was their firm opponent; the Communists harassed it and weakened its influence in their own fight for power, by the bitterest defamation. The Socialist party, like all such parties in Europe, had its own internal weakness, arising from two causes. One is the pacifism which brings many men into such parties. A group headed by Paul Fauré voted for the Munich Pact, and badly weakened the power of the party in

<hr>

[55] Cf. Paul Louis, *Histoire du Socialisme en France* (Paris, 1925); also J. H. Jackson, *Jean Jaurès* (London, 1943); also A. Zévaés, *Histoire du Socialism et du Communisme en France, 1871-1947* (Paris, 1947).
[56] Cf. M. Fainsod, *International Socialism and the World War* (Cambridge, Mass., 1935); and Henry Ehrmann, *French Labor from Popular Front to Liberation* (New York, 1947).

the face of European difficulties, just when a party in a national state needs to be strong. The second and more deep-seated cause of internal weakness is the inherent unwillingness of the party to act otherwise than in the spirit of democratic constitutionalism. In an age when the subversive feelings of masses of the electorate can be whipped up against undoubted social and economic miseries and injustices, this gives an appearance of impotence to such parties, for they cannot get a clear majority. They not only lose prestige, but the very thought is self-stultifying.

In such a situation, the Communist parties, whose sanguine faith and militant ardor blind them to scruples since Lenin set them the example, have a clear political advantage. They can decry everybody else's policy and actions, propose the most radical schemes, encourage the most revolutionary feeling, gain adherents—and yet know that probably they will not win a majority requiring fulfilment of their program. On a relatively quite recent memory of violent action, and the cult of revolutionary violence in 1789–95, in the Commune of 1871, and the syndicalist doctrines of George Sorel, they base subversive appeals to riot in the streets and industry against the duly elected government. In 1932 the party in France had 10 seats in the Chamber; in 1936, 72; in 1946, 168—that is, nearly a third of the representation, and had polled five and one half million votes in the country, making 28.2 per cent of the total.

In the interwar years, though France was faced with the dreadful threat of Germany across the borders, the Communist party pursued a policy which was in part dictated by the Communist Internationale, and in part spontaneously directed to favor the U.S.S.R. It sometimes made common cause with the French Right in order to discredit the Left-wing parties, and to keep the state in a perpetual condition of shock and instability. It was for military strength only when it suited the Soviet Union to have a strong France and not before. It organized and aggravated strikes in war factories. When the Nazi-Soviet pact was signed, it be-

came the enemy of French policy against Hitler. One fourth of the Communist deputies resigned from the party. The *Confédération Générale du Travail* expelled all Communists from office in its own organization and its affiliates. The government dissolved the party, and the Chamber of Deputies expelled its members by unanimous vote, including that of the Socialist party. It took little part in the resistance against Nazi occupation until Hitler's invasion of Russia. Thereafter it took a large and courageous part through *Le Front National* and the *Franc-Tireurs et Partisans*—keeping pretty strictly to itself and kept apart from other parties by their suspicion of it. It organized resistance even in districts in which it had hardly before been heard of. When Nazis killed hostages they were usually Communists. As the *parti des fusilés*, it capitalized on its part in the resistance, far beyond its undoubted services, since it has no scruples at all in making unverifiable claims.

In the constitutional convention of 1945–46, Socialists and Communists collaborated. Both were hostile to a strong executive, as a general theory, the Communists especially so, so long as they could not hope to be in sole power. They had their red eye on General de Gaulle. It was at the Communist insistence that the Chamber of Deputies was immensely strengthened, to the point of its formal choice of prime minister and cabinet. It also pressed hard for the long list of economic and social rights guaranteed by the constitution. It fortified its position by securing proportional representation, was hostile to the compulsory vote, opposed equality in electoral finances and propaganda, and preferred to deny the executive the right of dissolution. The first draft was defeated by the electorate: nevertheless Communist ideas are predominant, because the Socialist party needed to go along with them in order to hold off the M.R.P. and the Right. Yet the small positive vote for the constitution is a sign that Communist strength is not what it seems to be. *Sondages* has shown (March 15, 1946) that whereas 14 per cent of Socialist voters would give their votes to the Communists, if they had to choose between it and other parties, only 6 per cent of Communists would give theirs to the Socialists if *they* had to make such a choice.

The essential difference between Socialists and Communists is that the Socialists, unlike the Communists,[57] are suffused through and through with the conscience of democratic humanism, and acknowledge an imperative morality which stands above economic acquisitiveness and therefore the warfare among classes. To them, justice, rights, brotherhood, virtue, truth, loyalty, are something autonomous, and not the by-product of an economic war in which different standards prevail according to the fortunes of war and in which ethics vary with the side on which one is fighting: the conscience of man lives above economic production. Since this is so, some rapprochement and the transaction of political business is possible between them and such men as those who lead the M.R.P.[58] and the Radical-Socialists. Since this is so, also, they are hated by the Communist party. The best expression of democratic humanism, though it is no exception, is to be found in the life and theories of men like Jaurès and Léon Blum.[59]

The Communist party has the tremendous advantage of never having been in office, or at least, so predominantly as to incur the usual disappointment of the electorate. The Communist party is particularly strong in the industrial North and around Paris, and in the *Midi,* notable for its passionately Left politics. What has given it so much extra strength, however, is its undoubted appeal to the rural areas. This has come from two causes: (1) anti-Right and anticlerical feeling (and yet it has in places avowed tolerance for devout Catholics), strengthened by the antagonism to Vichy; and (2) the misery and resentment of what is now a large agricultural proletariat and small holders. There are, roughly, some eight million people in agriculture. Of these, less than one million own two thirds of the land privately cultivated. Nearly five million other owners have the remaining one third between them, in farms of from one to twenty-five acres. Nearly three million on the land are landless laborers. Finally, to the end of December, 1947, the Communist party enjoyed the support of the great trade-union organization, the *Confédération Générale du Travail,* which under Louis Saillant, a Communist, has been infiltrated and dominated by the Communist party, due to its tactics in the resistance.[60]

However, large as is the Communist party strength, it has its anxieties. It benefited abnormally from its part in the resistance, because it set up organizations before the other parties could do so, and because it shared in the vast wartime prestige of the Soviet Union. Both of these are wasting assets. Its physical and intellectual fight against the nazis was most vigorous. In times of turmoil the electors follow the virile and eschew the scrupulous. Yet the Communists are caught in the toils of the democratic principle while they remain a parliamentary party. They cannot avoid making a parliamentary record, which can be read by anybody. If it is obstructive, they will lose their more moderate supporters. They cannot avoid making a general public record, and so, since they are moving always towards the next election, they must tack and hedge. This takes away from their militancy, and loses them some of their militants. It also causes tensions within the party. If they are militant in the streets, as they were over their desire to defeat the Marshall Plan in 1947, they produce secessions of their followers who follow them for good economic conditions, for their action must

[57] Cf. A. Rossi, *Physiologie du Parti Communiste Français* (Paris, 1948), especially p. 375 ff.

[58] Cf. Jacques Maritain, *Les Droits de L'Homme et la Loi Naturelle,* and *Principes d'Une Politique Humaniste* (Paris, 1945).

[59] Cf. Blum's book, *For All Mankind* (New York, 1946).

[60] In the summer of 1948 it was commonly estimated that the C.G.T. numbers had been reduced to some three million; while the rival run by Jouhaux, the non-Communist trade union leader, had risen to one million, and the Catholic organization also numbered one million.

tend to thwart them. If they are militant in the trade unions, the more thoughtful workers—or the less idealistic, whichever way one cares to put it—will, feeling deceived, secede. In December, 1947, suspicions that the Communists were following the policy of the "Cominform," and strike after strike caused a revulsion against them, and produced a secession from the C.G.T. and the formation of the *Force Ouvrière*, a new confederation of trade unions, led by the veteran non-Communist leader of the C.G.T., Léon Jouhaux.[61] Thorez' declaration in March, 1949, that a war against the U.S.S.R. would be met with his party's refusal to obstruct the entrance of Soviet armies into France, is characteristic of the party and in time must sap its strength.

General Observations on French Parties. We may conclude the survey of French political parties with a few general observations.

As before World War II, no single party is in or near possession of enough seats to hold single and undisputed office. In fact, the prewar position is aggravated, because then, if no party were in the majority, at least some were so much stronger than others that they could take the lead in government. Now the Big Three—Communists, M.R.P., and Socialists—are too close to be anything but contenders for power and bad collaborators. A régime of impotence or chronic crisis would seem to follow. In December, 1946, the three were so jealous of each other that a government could not be formed, especially as it was felt necessary that certain cabinet posts connected with the security of the country could not be entrusted to the Communists. Léon Blum, for the Socialist party, was ready to join a Communist government. This not proving feasible, he courageously took office with a Socialist government only, but of course dependent on the votes of the Chamber. In January, 1947, under a Socialist, a coalition of the Big Three formed a government. It staggered along for ten months, expelling the Communists in May, 1947. In November,

1947, it was replaced by a coalition of M.R.P. and Socialists and other groups, headed by an M.R.P. prime minister. This is not wholesome for France, or for Europe. It may be that time will cause the further erosion of the Socialists and improve the fortunes of the Communists. That can happen only if the latter have become parliamentary and constitutional in procedure and speed. The forces in French society are too strong for a Leninist-Stalinist France; and the French are too intelligent for a materialistically based dictatorship.

The tension and confusion of French political parties is due, it will have been observed, not merely to the diversity of economic interests but to doctrines of society and government. Even if Thibaudet's designation [62] of six strands—Traditionalism, Liberalism, Industrialism, Social Catholicism, Jacobinism, and Socialism—exhausted the subtleties, and it does not, it would be complication disintegrating enough.

The Penalty of a History Full of Civil Wars. The many revolutionary and reactionary crises suffered by France since 1789 have left most political minds seared with historic thinking.[63] It is one thing to have party differences; it is another to push them to the point of civil war ten times in a century and a half. A viable party system requires that many past battles shall be forgotten. But it is difficult to forget the kind of battles the French have so recently fought with bloodshed among themselves. It is hard to decide whether this is the result of a passionate, doctrinaire state of mind, but many observers place much weight on this view.

Few countries contain so many cross-contradictions. Catholicism, and the place of the Church in the state, is one. It divides Left and Right, but not all the Left and all the Right, and yet it severs the

---

[61] Cf. Léon Jouhaux, *La C. G. T.* (Paris, 1937).

[62] A. Thibaudet, *Les Idées Politiques* (Paris, 1932); cf. also A. Siegfried, *France: a Study in Nationality* (New Haven, 1930).
[63] Cf. G. L. Dickinson, *Revolution and Reaction in Modern France*, 2nd edition (London, 1927); also David Thomson, *Democracy in France* (Oxford, 1946), a most brilliant treatment.

M.R.P. from both Left and Right. Monarchism and aristocracy divided the Right itself, and set some of the Right against the Republic as the form of government—and this would produce coalitions of the Left to defend it, but they again would be torn and severed by different social policies. Monarchist and aristocratic ideas and status produced contempt for parliamentary institutions, and helped to sponsor and inspire extreme nationalist and dictatorial groups and fascist formations. It found its way into the administrative services on the highest level at home and in the colonies—for the sake of France, but not the France of the Chamber of Deputies.[64] But this produced a tension between the Chamber and the officials; and the Left groups, not being able to control and use the administration, treated it as an enemy and so intensified its hatred of them. The higher administrative services did not adequately prepare for war against Germany, nor did the regular army; they were ready to cooperate with the nazis through Vichy.

Furthermore, the parties of the Left were always conscious of the legacy of "Caesarism" embodied in the *ancien régime,* and Napoléon, and Napoléon III, and later pretenders and swashbucklers like Boulanger. Therefore, though democratic, they were not energetic in social reforms which required a strong government. Liberty and equality were at loggerheads in values and timing. All the Left were afraid of Bonapartism, the glittering dictatorial leader using plebiscitary forms to bolster personal power. Hence, they were as jealous of a fierce Jacobin-like leader, Clemenceau, whose idea of democracy was a great surging solidarity of the people obedient to powerful government, as fearful of a Colonel de la Rocque, whose formations of fascists produced the antiparliamentary riots in February, 1934.[65] All parties as far as the

moderate Right had accepted democracy, but were seriously split many ways as to its governmental forms, the respective places of extralegal, forceful dissent and the coercion properly exercisable by government pursuant to electoral mandates. The socialist Left shared the common belief in democracy and social justice, but it was disintegrated by the varying emphasis placed on the legitimacy of majority or minority rule, and on gradualism against abrupt change. Here some of the more radical Socialists, and certainly the Communists, expressed the revolutionary tradition of the barricades; the right of the Directory to take full powers on behalf of the people, as their forbears Danton and Robespierre had done and as the Commune of 1871 had exemplified. All parties knew that national defense was an ultimate obligation, but they were divided on alliances, and on the extreme Left some members of the groups were pacifist, sometimes by persuasion, sometimes for fear of domestic militarism and hatred of monarcho-aristocratic Catholic military society. And even conservative leaders would cut down the estimates for economy's sake by reducing the size of the armed forces and the length of conscript service. Other groups joined in with such policies for their own purposes only, and then seceded.

Thirty or forty years of peace from about 1905 might have produced a forgetting of old rancors, and a forging of new reconciliations. But the pressure of ideas from outside, and the enemies on the frontier, fascists and nazis, two wars, and the world-wide ideological battle between the different interpretations of liberty, equality, and fraternity, democracy and despotism, and especially the brutal intransigeance of the Communist International, exacerbated all the contradictions, and kept fresh the sharp light and fierce heat that came from the past.[66]

[64] Cf. Chapter 32 below.

[65] A. Werth, *France in Ferment* (London, 1934), *The Destiny of France* (London, 1937), and *The Twilight of France* (London, 1942). Cf. also Francois Goguel, *La Politique des Partis sous la IIIe République,* (Paris, 1946), 2 vols.

[66] Cf. Herman Finer, *The Future of Government* (New York, 1946), Chap. IV, for a dynamic account of the decline and fall of the Third Republic, and bibliography. Especially worth consulting are: "Alain," *Éléments d'une Doctrine Radicale* (Paris, 1925); D.

TABLE 5—GERMAN REICHSTAG ELECTIONS: 1919, 1928, 1932, 1933

	January, 1919	May, 1928	November, 1932	March, 1933
Total number entitled to vote	36,767	41,225	44,374	44,686
Total number of valid votes cast	30,400	30,753	35,472	39,343
Per cent of valid votes cast	82.7	74.6	79.9	88.0
Parties				
(1) Nationalistic parties:				
Nazis	—	810	11,737	17,277
Nationalists	3,121	4,381	2,959	3,137
People's party	1,346	2,680	662	432
Several small parties combined (cf. below)	—	1,371	105	—
Total votes for nationalistic parties:	4,467	9,242	15,463	20,849
Per cent of total number of valid votes cast	14.7	30.0	43.6	53.0
Per cent of total number entitled to vote	12.1	22.4	34.9	46.6
(2) Nonsocialist republican parties:				
Democrats	5,642	1,506	336	334
Center	5,980	3,712	4,231	4,425
Bavarian People's party	—	946	1,095	1,074
Several small parties combined (cf. below)	275	2,472	259	498
Total votes for nonsocialist republican parties:	11,897	8,636	5,921	6,331
Per cent of total number of valid votes cast	39.1	28.1	16.7	16.1
Per cent of total number entitled to vote	32.4	21.0	13.3	14.2
(3) Labor parties:				
Social Democrats	11,509	9,153	7,248	7,182
Independent Socialists	2,317	3,265	5,980	4,848
Communists	—	—	—	—
Total votes for labor parties:	13,826	12,418	13,228	12,030
Per cent of total number of valid votes cast	45.5	40.4	37.3	30.6
Per cent of total number entitled to vote	37.6	30.1	29.8	26.9
(4) All other parties—10 to 20 parties, each receiving less than 100,000 votes:				
Total votes for all other parties:	210	457	860	136
Per cent of total number of valid votes cast	0.7	1.5	2.4	0.3
Per cent of total number entitled to vote	0.6	1.1	1.9	0.3
Breakdown of small nationalistic parties:				
Agrarian League	—	199	105	—
Württemberg Farmers' and Vineyardists' League	—	196	—	—
German-Hanoverian party	—	128	—	—
Saxony Country People	—	—	—	—
German Social party	—	—	—	—
German Country People	—	—	—	—
Christian National Farmers' and Country People's party	—	—	—	—
Conservative People's party	—	582	—	—
Popular National Bloc	—	266	—	—
Total	—	1,371	105	—
Breakdown of small nonsocialist republican parties:				
Bavarian Farmers' League	275	1,397	110	—
German Middle Class party	—	481	149	114
German Farmers' party	—	483	—	—
People's Rights party	—	—	—	384
Christian Social People's Service	—	111	—	—
Christian Social party	—	—	—	—
Christian Social People's Community	—	—	—	—
Total	275	2,472	259	498

The establishment by the law of 1945 of proportional representation for the election of the French Assembly is unfortunate, for that system perpetuates groupism, stimulates new parties, and does not throw upon the individual voter the responsibility of deciding one way or the other for a party which may become the government of France. It conduces to the continuation of cabinets which are the uncertain sum of several groups. In Britain, though the Liberal party in 1945 put up three hundred candidates, the electorate had the sense to give them only eleven seats. Under P.R. they should have had fifty or more—an embarrassment to the government. P.R. will further weaken the French executive which, being the committee of the Chamber, will not be able to take any successful initiative.

POLITICAL PARTIES IN GERMANY [67]

Between the Wars. A picture of the political strength of German parties at different periods in the interwar years must precede any discussion of the history, nature, and future of parties. The figures in

Halévy, *La Fin des Notables* (Paris, 1930), *Pour l'Étude de la Troisième République* (Paris, 1937); and *La République des Comités* (Paris, 1934); André Tardieu, *L'Heure de la Décision* (Paris, 1934); "Pertinax," *The Gravediggers* (New York, 1944); J. Fourcade, *La République de la Province* (Paris, 1936); M. Thorez, *France Today* (London, 1936). For the nascent Fourth Republic, see Paul Marabuto, *Les Partis Politiques et les Mouvements Sociaux sous la IVe République* (Paris, 1948).
[67] Cf. H. Finer, *The Future of Government* (New York, 1946), Chap. III; S. W. Halperin, *Germany Tried Democracy* (New York, 1946); Mendelssohn-Bartholdy, *The War and German Society* (New Haven, 1937); O. Braun, *Von Weimar zu Hitler* (New York, 1940); H. Rauschnig, *The Revolution of Nihilism* (New York, 1939); T. F. Abel, *Why Hitler Came to Power* (New York, 1938); Theodore Wolff, *Through Two Decades* (London, 1936); R. T. Clark, *The Fall of the German Republic* (London, 1935); R. D. Butler, *Roots of National Socialism* (New York, 1942); H. E. Fried, *The Guilt of the German Army* (New York, 1942); A. Rosenberg, *History of the German Republic* (London, 1936); Konrad Heiden, *The Führer* (New York, 1944); A. Hitler, *Mein Kampf* (trans., New York, 1933); A. F. Sturmthal, *The Tragedy of European Labor* (New York, 1943.)

Table 5 [68] refer to January, 1919, when the Weimar constitutional assembly was elected; to May, 1928, after some of the gravest of German adjustments to the problems of the Treaty of Versailles had been settled (including the almost complete lifting of reparation payments); to November, 1932, the last free election before the advent of Hitler; and to March, 1933, under the Hitler terror, with constitutional guarantees suspended.

Certain facts stand out immediately. The *first* is the multiplicity of parties, a serious confusion to the voter, not making for responsible choices of the government, but (as in France since 1875) only for the pieces of the mosaic that would eventually join together (out of his view) to form a government, on terms he did not know or endorse. *Second,* the small parties were kept alive by proportional representation. *Third,* it will be observed that some of the parties are definitely local parties, a result of the particularism of the German states going back centuries, and only partially overcome by the successive stages of federalization. Also, as the parties only acquired full authority in 1919, when the first democratic *Reichstag* was inaugurated, they were faced by the many well-organized economic groups and interests. They were harmful for their influence in narrowing the vision of the German people, so that the center of their *Reich* could get out of hand. Notice especially, for example, the Bavarian People's Catholic party and its steady strength.

Fourth, four great parties stand out as the pillars of the Weimar Republic: the Nationalist party (later largely merged but not completely identified with the Nazi party); the Center party, predominantly Catholic; the Social Democrats; and the Communist party. Together, in November, 1932, they mustered some 32 million votes out of 35.5 million votes cast.

Fifth, the practical erosion of the Democrats will be noticed, rather like the Liberal party in England in outlook, the last poor remnants of a great historic party, worn down by the extremes of militarism

[68] After S. L. W. Mellen, *American Political Science Review*, August, 1943, pp. 612-613, and *Nuremberg Documents*, V, 253 ff.

and conservatism, and by the parties of masses intent on social and economic reform.

The Nature of the German Parties. In view of the analysis of the content of party doctrines in other countries, it is here only necessary to offer some general observations on the German political parties.

(1) The nationalistic parties stemmed from the agricultural, authoritarian, Junker, Protestant, royalist strata that had made the absolutist Prussian state and pushed forward to the Prussianization of the German *Reich* of 1867 and 1871 to World War I. Their interests are clear from this characterization. But all interests are mixed. Accordingly, they were not merely Prussian; in other parts of the *Reich* there were authoritarian groups who cooperated with them. They were not entirely an economic interest, that is agricultural, though they were that predominantly. But with the industrialization of the *Reich,* especially from the 1870's, they were intermeshed with heavy industry: the Krupps, Hugenbergs, and Thyssens. They were imperialist, colonialist—they were for tariffs, for strong growth of cartels, for mighty German armies and navies, for the Kaiser's unqualified authority—they were antiparliamentary, antisocialist. Before 1919, they not infrequently joined with the Center party against the Liberals and Socialists, although there was the great religious cleavage between them. Their shining lights were Bismarck (though they had their doubts about him) and Wilhelm II. They nourished the German general staff, and formed the backbone of the twin pillars of the German state: the officer's corps and the civil service.

Though they were losing ground from election to election in the pre-World War I period, they persisted through it into the Weimar era, which they detested and never really accepted. Finally, they almost entirely lost their following to the Nazis. But a distinction must be drawn between them and Hitler's movement. They joined him not for everything he afterwards did, for some were conservative patriots with a sense of religious obligation and their anticommunism was inherently different from Hitler's. But, like the French Right, they preferred Hitler to the Social Democrats or the Communists. The so-called "baron's government" (there were so many *vons* in it) of 1932, paved the way for Hitler, who was indeed recommended to von Hindenberg, the President of the *Reich,* by von Papen. They opened the door to Hitler, in part because they were hostile to a proposed investigation into their use of subsidies granted by the *Reich* government to the hard-hit agricultural estates of their quintessential homeland, East Prussia. In the *Reichstag* of March, 1933, they voted Hitler full powers. World War II, the Allied war trials, and especially Soviet severity in East Prussia and the break-up of the estates, left but a handful of the old guard. Pastor Niemöller is an example of the purer of the German Protestant Christian conservative nationalists.

More will be said presently on the Nazi movement, which had affinities but not identity with the German Nationalist and Conservative parties. They were anti-Semitic before Hitler was born.

(2) The Center party, founded in 1852 to defend Catholic missions and university education from attack by conservatives in the Prussian government, consisted, in the immediate pre-World War II years, of a rank and file following of 56 per cent of all the Roman Catholic voters in Germany, the rest being divided among other parties. It has been estimated that of practising Catholics, about 80 per cent followed the Center party. It attracted many non-Catholics. Its strength lay in the Rhineland, Bavaria (the Bavarian People's party), Baden, Westphalia, Upper Silesia, and Hohenzollern.

The Center party had a Catholic outlook and policy: that is to say, independence for minorities, religious and local; a paternal labor policy; and a loose federal *Reich,* for this gave freedom to its communicants. It wanted at one time a declaration of rights in the Bismarck constitution; it withstood Bismarck's *Kulturkampf* against it, but joined him on tariff protection for decentralist concessions. It opposed the policy of aggrandizement and military expenditures in Bismarck's early years but later voted for them in return for concessions to the Church, that is, private education and no exceptional laws against Catholics. It supported the war of 1914, but seceded early from the militarists, and with the Left parties helped to bring the war to an end. It had supported advanced social legislation for the benefit of the workers, and continually stood for the maintenance of a strong middle class, the petty commercial and industrial bourgeoisie, and an independent peasantry.

It joined the Social Democrats and the Democrats (or Liberals) in establishing and supporting the Weimar constitution. Its chief distinction from the Social Democratic policy of world peace and social welfare lay in (1) its defense of private property and enterprise, and (2) its anti-centralization. In the interwar years, it was involved in many contradictions, which would seem to be unavoidable in a party which pretends the defense of Catholic Christianity and yet seeks secular power. It was an enemy of the Treaty of Versailles; it supported substantial armaments and forces for Germany; and it advocated protection for agriculture. Its trade unions attracted 13 per cent of the German organized workers and 33 per cent of the organized salaried employees. It was suspected of being democratic, not because it accepted the ideal of equality and freedom for all men but because it wanted protection for its own faith. Its leaders headed several cabinets, and just prior to the forceful incursion of the nazi movement, its chancellor, Brüning, had held office for some two years, ruling by emergency decrees. Through ineptitude and shortsightedness, its parliamentary leadership voted for Hitler's suspension of the constitutional guarantees in the *Reichstag* of March, 1933. But during World War II, some of its high dignitaries did much to maintain the faith of millions against nazi oppression. Its resuscitation in various forms is coming about in the various state Christian Democratic parties, which include non-Catholics. The similarity to the M.R.P. in France deserves notice. It may also be observed that such a direct complication of the party system as a party founded on Catholicism does not exist either in the United States [69] or in Great Britain.

(3) The Social Democratic party was organized in 1869 on the basis of smaller groups established earlier. It was a party for the defense of the workers' rights. It united the Lassallean and the Marxian strains of socialism, and in the days of the intensest crisis, in World War I and in the struggle against Hitler, suffered because of the mixture. From 12 seats in the *Reichstag* in 1877 it progressed to 110 out of 397 in 1912, and would have had more if the electoral constituencies had been redistributed with the changing occupational and territorial distribution from a mainly agricultural to a mainly industrial nation. Its general tenets need not be discussed: they are the same as those of all democratic socialist parties. But in Germany there was the peculiar need for changing the unfair three-class system of voting in Prussia; for securing real sovereign democracy of the electors in the *Reichstag;* and for resisting the Bismarckian and imperial determination to crush the movement altogether as a treasonable party. (From 1878-90 Bismarck attempted physically to crush it.)

The party was distinguished by the remarkable philosophical services it rendered to socialists everywhere through the work of Bebel, Liebknecht, Luxemburg, Kautsky, Hilferding, Bernstein. Broadly speaking, they were zealously Marxian as to ends, but decisively non-Leninist as to

[69] Yet it is interesting to notice the indirect effects in the United States: for example, its relationship to Alfred E. Smith's Presidential candidacy in 1928 and his failure to be nominated in 1932. Cf. R. V. Peel and T. C. Donnelly, *The 1928 Campaign* (New York, 1931), and cf. James Farley, *My Story* (New York, 1947), *passim,* for his continual preoccupation with the relationship between his religion and his desire to run for President in 1940. Though a Jew has been Prime Minister of England, no Catholic has been, nor most probably could he be.

democratic means.[70] They formulated the theory of imperialism and the economic causation of wars long before Lenin followed. But they were democrats, and they warned Lenin and his followers that their way of a small vanguard of revolutionary leaders must lead to the dictatorship of a small group over the workers and not the dictatorship of a mass workers' party —two vastly different things. For though the German Social Democrats tended to be agnostic or atheistic, they were not historical materialists.

The second characteristic of the party was its enormous administrative machinery for establishing policy, for running schools, and for promoting mass literature and leisure-time activities and social benefits of various kinds—its basis for an all-embracing and flourishing trade-union movement.

The Social Democratic Party was, *in excelsis,* the party of the Weimar Republic. It participated in many governments and led some. But, in the testing time it failed: failed to rid the government of saboteurs, failed to scatter the Right elements, failed to lead the voters against the combined onslaught of Nazis and Communists. It had shed its own Left wing by 1922. The Right had killed its brilliant agitators, Liebknecht and Luxemburg, as well as many smaller lights. It was steadily democratic in a land which was tempted away from democracy by other values (mentioned in the note on the Nazi movement to follow) and which was then so torn by the Right and Left extremes, that a viable majority government could not be found. It lost membership to the nazis when unemployment made men desperate and young people could be given no hope; it lost millions to the communists who could make the most irresponsible promises and even unite with the Nazis to bring the socialist leaders into contempt. A general strike at the right time (like that which in 1923 foiled a Rightist *putsch*) might have rallied more than the party's own supporters against the advent of Hitler's horrors, but appeasement and genuine democratic scruples had frittered away the party's *élan.* It did not vote for Hitler's constitutional measures, like the Center—and in the concentration camps and in the workshops, millions of its members kept their souls. Wherever the Soviet occupation ruled, its fate was bitter, as all pressures, including assassination, were used by the Russian-sponsored Communist leaders (brought out of Russia where they had found sanctuary for years) to compel a fusion of the Social Democrats with the Communists. Election results show that they have successfully resisted. It would seem that the future of German politics will be dominated by the Social Democratic party (especially since the occupation government will institute at least some of the socialism which the party did not institute when the mild revolution of 1918 occurred), and by the Christian Democratic parties.[71]

(4) The Communist party was strong and will always be a contender for power, because the German mind is inclined to socialized authority, to full philosophies, and is close to Russia whence comes the light, and because a peculiarly hard-and-fast social class system oppressed the nation. Karl Marx himself was born in 1820 not only of German parents but of German social and economic conditions at their most class-ridden epoch.[72] In the interwar years the party throve on economic depression; on laudation of and encouragement by the Comintern; on the impatient recognition that changes by the democratic method must inevitably be gradual; on the rise of fascism in Italy and the Hitler movement in Germany. It was a fighting creed, and its members took to

[70] Cf. Herman Finer, *America's Destiny* (New York, 1947), p. 237.

[71] The role of the various parties in the German resistance movement is estimated by W. Kraus, "The German Resistance Movement," *Journal of Social Issues,* August, 1946, and by Gabriel Almond, "The Resistance," *Political Science Quarterly,* March, 1947, pp. 27-61.

Cf. also Hans Rothfels, *The German Opposition to Hitler* (Hinsdale, Illinois, 1948).

[72] Cf. Isaiah Berlin, *Karl Marx* (London, 1938); and for the interwar phase see Ruth Fischer, *Stalin and German Communism* (Cambridge 1948), a splendid account of the Soviet's pressures and Machiavellianism.

the streets against the Right and the Nazis. This suited the Soviet rulers: so did the combination of Nazis and Communists to overthrow the Social Democrats and the liberals. The party for a long time after the advent of Hitler still declared that this was good for Germany because the fall of Hitler was imminent, whereupon *they* would take over office. Most of the conditions which favored the rise of the party are dissolving. Only artificial help from outside Germany is likely to keep it of any importance in the future, assuming the party does not seize power by force, and even that could not last.

(5) Were there then no liberal parties in Germany? In the nineteenth century, Prussia had a great Liberal party which spread over the whole of Germany. But it succumbed to Bismarck, who eviscerated it by creating through force the federal *Reich,* the unity, which was the Liberals' main purpose since unity would have widened the area of commerce, the free press, freedom of opinion. But Bismarck gave no really free constitution in return for the Liberals' votes of military credits and their condonation of his constitutional breach in 1863-65. He gave universal suffrage, but not to a responsible *Reichstag* and a responsible government.

Against the rising tide of social democracy and the traditional strength of the Prussian Right and the princely houses, these big and middle commercial men and manufacturers and *rentiers* divided into a Rightist conservative party—the German People's party—and the more liberal German Democrats. Both of these participated in the Weimar Assembly, the latter taking a leading part in the coalition which produced the constitution (one of its leaders, Hugo Preusz, drafted the constitution), while the former took part in the discussions but voted against acceptance of the constitution. Its strength lay in commercial, shipping, and financial groups, in the middle classes of the large towns, and in members of the free professions (officials, teachers, and lawyers in particular). It was anti-Prussian, and for private enterprise and civil liberties. In a Germany ridden by the devil of humili-

ation over a lost war, and never till 1919 with the experience of democratic government, and with ideological extremes mounting to ferocity, it had, alas, no chance.

(6) The Nazi movement [73] (the *Nazional-Sozialistische Arbeiter Partei Deutschlands,* the National Socialist Workers' Party of Germany) was the combined creation of Hitler's adolescent, prophetic patriotism and the forces of the Right who desired to use him for the restoration of their war-stricken agricultural and industrial wealth, and their imperial, military pretensions and social and political authority. His patriotic fanaticism, nourished by the intensest suffering at Germany's defeat in World War I, gathered around him elements of the Right, officers no longer employed, adventurers from the shock troops of the late war, men who could not find their way back into peaceful society. "The shame of Versailles" was not in reality the shame of the treaty but the shame of defeat for a proud nation whose history had been a glamorous succession of victories over other peoples but never over its own passions and civic docility.

The Nationalists had millions of followers in the postwar years, and in the end these almost *en bloc* went over to Hitler for reasons of national prestige and aggrandizement, and enmity to the Soviet Union. This must be remembered, as weight is usually and wrongly placed upon the economic depression of 1930-32 in bringing followers to Hitler from among the unemployed and the youthful unemployables. The Hitler movement made its

---

[73] Cf. *National Socialism* (U. S. Government Printing Office, 1942); *Nazi Conspiracy and Aggression* (U. S. Government Printing Office, 1947), Vol. I, and appropriate references therein to subsequent volumes; Joseph Goebbels, *My Part in Germany's Fight* (London, 1935); and Fritz Thyssen, *I Paid Hitler* (New York, 1941). T. F. Abel, *Why Hitler Came into Power* (New York, 1938), is the best sociological study of the subject.

An important light is thrown on the Nazi movement by *Joseph Goebbels,* ed. by Louis Lochner (New York, 1948), and *The Von Hassell Diaries,* by U. von Hassell (New York, 1947).

striking debut in the Munich uprising of 1923: thereafter the party pretended constitutional and democratic methods. Yet its propaganda genius Paul Goebbels later admitted that the claim of legality and democracy was designed only to make the approach to power easier, and that they entered Parliament only to destroy it.

Hitler's program was anticommunist, antiliberal, anti-social democracy, anti-Semitic. It was racial or national (or *völkisch*); that is, it saw the significance of the individual in his complete immersion in the objectives of the state, his significance in obedience to that social focus of human attainment. But it denied to the individual the right of democratic self-determination, on the ground that only one genius appeared to lead the nation from time to time, and such was Hitler. Only one nation (or race) in the world showed the highest human virtues, demonstrated by its domination of all others, especially in war: that was the Nordic, and of this the Teutonic branch; and, of this, again, the German *Volk* was the supreme élite. All liberalism, with authority coming upward to its leaders from the free people, must produce political chaos and destroy national cohesion, as it had done to Germany at the end of World War I. Hence, organization must be based on the principle of the inequality of men, on all authority downward and all responsibility upward.

This doctrine of utter contempt for average men, or of equal minds, where they disagreed with Hitler, would have been rejected for the corrupt nonsense it was, except that the leader, for parallel but not identical reasons, was supported by the Junkers, the industrialists, the militarists, the imperialists, the conservatives. The resurgence of Germany was what brought him his main support. But when the depression came, millions who had never been employed could not enter the disciplined ranks of labor, and millions of others could not find work. Thousands had been uprooted in the aftermath of the war and the inflation which followed. The ideological battle was fiercest in Germany—located between Russia and the

West. It is a morbid nation. The Germans sought salvation. It is not surprising that they capitulated to a quack. Yet only a small proportion could have had any inkling of what this leader finally intended. Hitler's following was weakest, relatively, among the urban workers; white-collar employees were heavily represented, and compared with their proportions in German industry, the skilled artisans, merchants, shopkeepers, professional workers, and officials were considerably overrepresented, while the peasantry were much underrepresented.

Extremism, irresponsibility, dramatic meetings and processions, riots in the streets, threats and manhandling of opponents, unscrupulousness, and *The Big Lie* brought hope and excitement and therefore belief in the leader (perhaps cynical damnation of all responsibility for the consequences to others and the state).

Yet even in March, 1933, Hitler's movement had no majority of votes.

The Political Context. Some additional observations are needed to complete the sketch of German parties. They were not sovereign parties until 1919, for though Germany had universal suffrage from 1867, she never had a government founded upon the parties: the chancellor (or prime minister) was chosen by the Kaiser. The parties had some influence, but no final power, and especially not the power to cashier and appoint the executive. While other nations were learning the art of popular government and of party cooperation, German parties, having no direct responsibility, could be doctrinaire, extreme, and divided.

In an age when the state needed to be strong and active, owing to the way of its economic life, these political parties did not create the state, as did the parties in the United States and Britain and even France: they succeeded the state already created by the royal oligarchy. They never learned the lesson of governing it, until the fission in German life, through occupational, capitalist-worker, and sectional interests, made a democratic majority control of the state impossible. Only Hitler appreciated the need, and his purpose was corrupt and antithetic to the collaboration of others in the formation of the state's will.

German parties did not operate in a society that felt the need of individual freedom and self-determination. In Britain, the United States, and France, kings had been beheaded or expelled for freedom's sake: never so in Prussia or Germany. What accounts for German political placidity when it comes to individual rights has not been decisively determined by historians. Hegel is really Germany's God. But the world is full of temptations, unbridled economic welfare, power, national prestige, sadism against political opponents, honors that society can bestow —and these are competitive with civil liberties (for others) and self-government, which is another word for self-control. If a people's tradition is long, it can survive hardships, and eschew seductions hostile to self-government. If self-government has never been in operation, or felt by the middle as well as the working classes, it stands no chance of surviving any hurricane of economic distress or fanatical leadership. Hard experience alone will re-educate Germany, and World War II is part of such experience.[74]

AMERICAN POLITICAL PARTIES

Indifference to the Choice between Parties. It will have been observed that the distinguishing mark of political parties in Britain and Europe is that they are parties of *principle:* that is, they profess the purpose of governing or of opposing government in the name of a general design of political values. They may represent an interest—economic or of an historic power-position in society—and may prosecute it; of course, being men, they

must and do. But over and above their special interest, they profess a broader social goal: that of conservatism, or liberalism, or communism, or Catholicism, or social democracy. Their interests are contained within a framework of value. They have made an order, or hierarchy, of items in their program—what shall be done, to what degree the relationships between individual and society shall be fashioned by law and administration, and what things shall come first, middle, and last. A long cultural history has obscured the answer to whether material or more spiritual values came first or which were more masterful. But there is considerable firmness in the definition of the pattern of social values. The absence of firmly defined and broad social purpose, consistently pursued over many decades, is the diagnostic mark of political parties in the United States.

It is not possible within the compass of this volume to sketch the history of American political parties throughout their long career. Their chances and changes may be found in many other volumes.[75] For long stretches they will be found saying the same thing, exactly, flatulent in phrase and combining the most inconsistent quasi-promises. So far is this the truth, especially for certain epochs, that cynical remarks have been made about the Republican and Democratic parties, the two which have held the field, gathering over 90 per cent of the votes cast, for about one hundred years. Bryce declared that they were like two bottles, each with different labels and both empty. Holcombe, American born

[74] Cf. *Facts about Occupied Germany,* by American Association for a Democratic Germany, January, 1947; Karl Mahler, *Die Programme der Politischen Parteien in Neuen Deutschland* (Berlin, 1945); R. Barzel, *Die Geistigen Grundlagen der Politischen Parteien* (Bonn, 1947); and *Aufsätze und Skizzen zu Fragen der Zeit* (Essen: Deutsche-Zentrums-Partei, 1947); and Heinrich Fraenkel, *A Nation Divided,* (London, 1949).

[75] Among others, W. E. Binkley, *American Political Parties* (New York, 1943); A. N. Holcombe, *The Middle Classes in American Politics* (New York, 1940); Charles Merriam and Harold Gosnell, *The American Party System* (New York, 1949 edition); E. M. Sait, *American Parties and Elections* (New York, 1948 edition). See also A. N. Schlesinger, Jr., *The Age of Jackson* (New York, 1945); E. E. Schattschneider, *Party Government* (New York, 1942).

These works among them furnish bibliographies covering the development of party organization, ideas, and conflicts, so that more specific references need not here be given.

and bred and a Harvard teacher for over forty years, says, some forty years after Bryce:[76]

Why, young men and women inquire of their elders and of one another with growing frequency, should a new voter become either a Democrat or a Republican? It is not easy—indeed, it is not possible—to give a convincing answer, if the reply is based upon no better evidence than is afforded by the planks of the party platforms and the declarations of the party candidates. Party platforms have tended to grow longer with the passing years, and less intelligible.

If the reader will compare two political biographies which came out within a year or two of each other, one English and the other American, they will appreciate the dismay with which American political parties may be regarded. In the biography of Neville Chamberlain they will find an intense concern and ambition for the highest office it is in the gift of the nation to bestow—but not a single page is without its deep anxiety about policy, the social purposes for which the premiership will be used. In the autobiography of James Farley they will see practically nothing but a concern for electoral victory, with hardly a trace of interest in a political program (except that the New Deal seems to jeopardize vote catching). In Mr. Farley's own cogitations about his ambitions for the Presidency, and in his estimates of his own qualifications, there is never a word about the Presidency as a medium for the national good. The difference is not altogether a difference between men.

Causes and Consequences of Political Indifference. For good or ill, indifference to the choice between parties could not possibly be postulated of British or European parties. This is the striking and controlling truth about American political parties, and the causes and consequences deserve some brief consideration. Somewhere in his *Age of Reform,* Professor E. L. Woodward, speaking of English political parties in the eighteenth century, likens them to "two rival stage coaches

spattering each other with mud, going along the same road to the same destination." This is true of American political parties today, except that it is a little difficult to discern the destination, even as it was, perhaps, in the eighteenth century in England.

(1) Let it be noticed that two parties dominate and organize American political life, not eight or ten. All the "occasional" parties, of a third- and fourth-party kind, have never, in any Presidential year, gained more than some 3 per cent of the vote.[77] Nor have many of them lived for more than ten years. This, at any rate, is an advantage to the nation, that its party organizations can gather the various sectional and occupational groupings into which the land falls into two opposed nation-wide confederations. Too many parties are confusing; the job of organizing the electorate must be done, the voters brought out, and provision made for a standing opposition of magnitude sufficient to threaten the government.

(2) The "third" parties have in the main been sectional or occupational groupings; that is to say, they have emerged from a fairly definite area of the country, or from an economic interest. For example; Free Soil, Know-nothing, Greenback, Populist, Labor, Farm Labor, and—if we go beyond occupation—Prohibition and Communist. They have beset the other parties with some intensely passionate ideas and claims, and have persuaded (the word "forced" would not be too strong) one of them to carry into law its desires. Examples are antitrust legislation in the 1890's; the Greenbacks and silver-purchase legislation; the Nonpartisan League and government assistance of many kinds to farmers; and again, the Anti-Saloon League and Prohibition during World War I. The Political Action Committee of the CIO continues the old story, to waylay candidates of the two dominant parties and hold them to legislative ransom.

(3) The two dominant parties have been

---

[76] E. B. Logan (ed.), *The American Political Scene* (New York, Harper, 1938), p. 5. By permission.

[77] Excepting Theodore Roosevelt in the Presidential campaign of 1912. But *is* this really an exception?

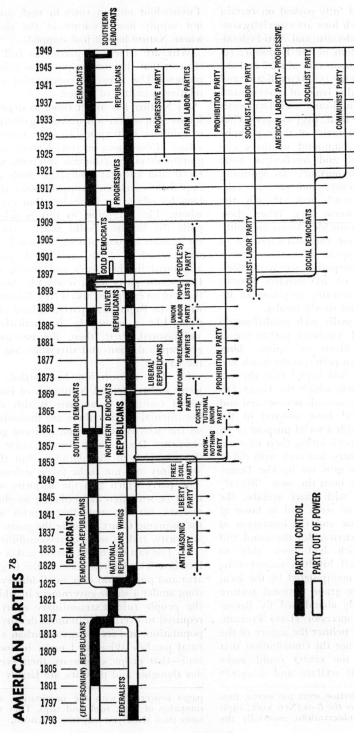

AMERICAN PARTIES [78]

[78] From J. L. Burdette, *Political Parties* (National Foundation for Education in American Citizenship, Washington, 1946), pp. 16-17.

round, firm, and fully packed on certain occasions of which four are especially conspicuous: (1) Federalist and Anti-Federalist at the inception of the Republic; (2) the Jacksonian Democracy of 1828 and the opposition thereto; (3) Republicans and Democrats on the issue of slavery and union; (4) Republicans and Democrats during the New Deal, 1933 to 1941. What were the characteristics of these periods? Each shows a compound of three elements: a moral and intellectual issue of the highest importance; an agonizing practical emergency; and on one side, at least, a "great" man, though the degrees of greatness vary. When these three elements coincide, American political parties assume the characteristics of British and European ones: they become for the time a purposive, partly ideological fellowship of like-minded persons throughout the country, inspiring an intense, sincere, and steady loyalty.

However, normally such conditions do not obtain, and American parties are at once without ideals or spine. They "straddle" in their policy, as the ironic saying goes. Many had hoped that the era of popular reform which the Great Depression of 1929 onwards necessitated and stimulated would have ushered in the rule of parties with a social purpose of an enduring kind, both loving their country, their whole country, but each with different but genuine gifts for it. The Democrats might have been the more "liberal" and concerned with mass welfare, the Republicans more stern and in favor of private enterprise and the limitation of governmental activity. But the mind and personality which had been able to attract to himself loyalties transcending those normally manipulated by the local bosses died. The grand national texture was involuntarily abandoned by Roosevelt's accidental successor, Harry Truman, who understood neither the nature of the weft and warp, nor the contribution that weaving from the center could make to the national welfare and liberty.[79]

Twenty-four million votes in 1948 could not supply moral stature at the point where Nature herself had stopped.

Why are American parties so full of electors that they are empty of sustained purpose? The answer is comparative and relative, a matter of degree.

(1) Neither has as yet come to depend for its support on a distinctive gathering of interests: both appeal to all sections of a land of enormous territorial range, geographic diversity, economic interests, and racial and cultural groupings. Both are impelled to seek their support, since they long for office, not somewhere but everywhere. The exception to this is principally the hitherto "solid South" where, for reasons bygone of race, economic interest, and a fairly accidental party alignment in the 1850's and 1860's, the Democratic party has a monopoly. Something of an exception also is New England, where the Republican party, without anything like a monopoly, is particularly well-favored. *First,* then, the enormous geographical span and diversification of the nation.

(2) The constitution has settled, or seems to have settled, a number of issues which continue to animate British and Continental parties: there are limitations on the activity of state and national governments. Declarations may be made on these subjects in the platforms, but they are empty and not to be taken seriously. The party which gets the majority will never be sovereign in legislating on these matters, for the amending process and the Supreme Court enfeeble the party, its authority, and its sense of responsibility.

(3) The vast size of the nation makes for localism. The United States is the largest area and population ever in all history to come under a single government in which the people rule. Extraordinary effort is required to overcome distances, density of population, and its variegated urban and rural patches. What do I mean by localism?—that people's interests, their everyday thoughts and pursuits, are largely fo-

---

[79] Should this reflection seem too severe, Boss E. J. Flynn's *You're the Boss* (New York, 1946) will justify the observations, especially the pages concerned with the nomination and campaign of 1932, 1936, and 1940. They tell more than Mr. Flynn may have intended.

cussed on and engaged by the life of their neighborhood. Since the constitution has considerably consecrated this by leaving to the states a very substantial range of authority, the natural localism is reinforced by elections, legislative authority and office and graft on the spot. This has two results:

One is to throw power into the hands of the local bosses—"machines" is no misnomer—especially those of the cities, from which their vote-gathering machine is operated—the Hagues, the Crumps, the Pendergasts,[80] the Rorabacks, the Vares, the Kellys, the Curleys, and so through many generations. For they can deliver the vote at the state and national conventions, the primaries and general elections. The second result is to some degree to confuse and take the mind off the national, and, in our day, even the international issues. Washington is very far away, and therefore the nation as a unit also when the screen of local bossism, irresponsible for the national vision, not versed in its national and international problems, is set between the everyday mind of the voter and the central problems. (I learned first to appreciate this when I lived for a year in Knoxville, Tennessee.) In other words, the centralizing function of party, and therefore its purpose - determining, coherent - making, integrating function is riddled, torn, and obfuscated. If loyalties are nurtured and harvested by the local boss, and political office is impossible without him, why should a loyalty to the center be developed? It may be expensive.

(4) The constitutional separation of powers and diverse terms of office break up the vision of unified purpose. Any vote cast at any election is not a vote which carries a total mandate. It is only a fraction of one, going to the House, the Senate, or the President. How it shall be cast is, therefore, not so momentous a consideration to a voter. So also, who shall be the trustee of its use at the center demands less searching of conscience and

less purposive loyalty to the party as a creative association. This cause is accompanied by the disintegrating element of the variety of terms for which the central legislative and executive body are elected, and the different election dates. If they were all elected simultaneously at least, and for the same term (say, four years), a unity of judgment and decision, stimulated by an enforced unity of program, would result.

(5) America has two assets as a polity which reduce party fever. Its people are materially acquisitive in a specially high degree and, compared with the size of its population, the vast expanse and rich resources of the land offer an optimistic sense of continuing opportunity. (The student must have lived in Europe to appreciate the tremendous power of these two factors.) Hence, the electorate is of a middle-class, bourgeois type, even if its members are impoverished farmers or unskilled laborers. They are not inspired by the heated winds of philosophic doctrine or transcendent ideology, which is more than wealth itself. They are moderate and good-tempered, generally speaking and omitting a Huey Long, a Bilbo, or a Father Coughlin. They do not take sides; and if the electorate does not take sides, there cannot be any sides.[81]

American political parties cannot therefore have much gristle though they may be fat. It is not possible to change this situation by constitutional fiat. And if the people are broadly content, why should there be more than virtually one all-inclusive party? Serious consequences must flow from this flabbiness of party structure. The parties being infirm of purpose, either party's legislative and executive policy and choice of men are rarely such as to meet the severe trials of modern statecraft. Laws are not passed in time; or they are muddled with riders; or they are kept till the last moment of a session; or confusion arises when a veto interposes itself between President and Congress and when party

---

[80] Cf. M. Milligan, *Missouri Waltz* (New York, 1948).

[81] Cf. *Fortune*, February, 1940, showing that 79.2% of the American people regard themselves as middle class, and January, 1946, for a poll on the hopefulness of American life.

voting is unclear; or Congressional voting cuts extraordinarily across parties, thus making for electoral perplexity; or coordination fails between legislation and its execution, or even between the departments of the administration. A clear stream of controlling tendency is lacking.

What is worse, there is no central responsible *thought* for the future and the relationships of the various governmental decisions to each other. The best examples of the latter are the immediate lifting of many controls on V-J Day, and the impossibility of recovering the controls; the fumbling labor-management, wage-price relationship as the war ended; the different doctrines published by Truman and Wallace on the same subject of wages; the fumbling with OPA; the failure in deliveries of promised food contributions to Europe; the rise in prices and the effect on wage demands of central fumbling; and the consequent damage to all those countries to whom the foreign policy of the United States require it to make loans —at one time, 50 per cent being the estimated loss in their value! [82] The position of labor in the nation—only a group, even if a very important group that deserves cherishing—is similarly the object of confused counsels, as the parties are morally flabby on this also. Labor is no homogeneous body, but a number of occupations. Each and all have a responsibility to each other, without the understanding and fulfilment of which they cannot fail to do each other damage by making claims incompatible with the welfare of all and each. For the wages of each constitutes part of the cost of production and the family budget of the others. And all of them have a responsibility to the nation as a body of consumers, a responsibility for using the investment of capital and invention in their industries to the maximum productivity and welfare of all. How can these responsibilities be explored and defined, and carried out, except through

political parties? Unless political parties have a mind compact of standards of social justice, what kind of order can there possibly be in the tempestuous world of industry? The tergiversation of chief executive and Congress on labor legislation in 1948 and 1949 will long be remembered.

If no national disaster follows from all this, great damage does, losses of production and justice to social groups who vainly demand what is truly theirs. Often when government should give only a reason for saying "No" it yields against its own reason.[83]

Possible Remedies For Political Indifference. Is there a remedy? For the discovery of purpose, there is none: time and vicissitudes, emergencies, and the chance of a born leader will settle what purpose shall animate a party by educating the popular conscience, beginning with the fifteen per cent of "opinion leaders" in the communities [84]—above all, time. Can constitutional changes assist? Yes, though they cannot solve the problem completely. It is useless to insist on the smaller gadgets, like questions in Congress to the heads of departments, for questions depend on the efficacy of the party organization outside Congress. But something valuable might well come of (1) fixed identical terms of office for House, Senate, and President, and election and commencement of office at the same time; and (2) abolition (by the power of Congress to fix the terms of its own election) of the traditional rule that members must be residents of their Congressional districts, and the constitutional rule that they must be residents of the state. These reforms would add weight to central leadership of the party.

How much government owes to the parties, and how weak American political parties are, may be seen from this quo-

---

[82] Cf. British House of Commons, *Debates*, August 7, 1947. Many other examples of incoherence in the practice of government will become apparent as the following chapters unfold.

[83] For example, the Truman speech in October, 1946, abandoning OPA.

[84] This is the percentage Paul Lazarsfeld found in his Erie County, Ohio, study, *The People's Choice* (New York, 1944). This is bigger than the immediate active leadership of the parties, which I estimate at about 2.5% of the electors, in Illinois.

tation from the *Report* of the Joint Committee on the Reorganization of Congress: [85]

The present steering committees, an informal and little-used device, seldom meet and never steer. . . . We recommend that these be replaced with the formal establishment in the House and the Senate of majority and minority policy committees. The majority policy committees of the two Houses would meet jointly at frequent intervals, as would those of the minority, to formulate the over-all legislative policy of the two parties. The majority policy committee of each House would also hold frequent meetings to consider its role in expediting consideration and passage of matters pledged to the people by the party.

It should be borne in mind that these functions are in British and European systems the normal functions of the parties. Then, the feet of clay appear in the Report, for it continues: [86]

No member of either party would be required to follow such announced party policy except as he chose to do so. Each member would be free to vote as he saw fit, but [oh, bathos!] the record of his action would be available to the public as a means of holding both the party and the individual accountable.

This proviso will kill the effective virtue of the reforms. The character of American parties is further underlined by the Committee Report when it says: [87]

Your Committee recognizes the need for freedom of action on the part of the individual Member of Congress and his right to vote at any time against the announced policy of his party.

If the parties are not marked by firm purpose, they are still organizations for the improvisation of legislative and administrative answers to emergent and unevadable practical difficulties of social and economic life. But, being such, they are very like each other in their organizational basis, and their appeal to all classes and occupations and areas. There is a differ-

ence in that rather more of the poor vote for the Democratic party and rather more of the rich for the Republican. The S.E.S. (social and economic status) [88] is a little different in each case, and the bias of their legislation attracts the appropriate beneficiaries, even as the would-be beneficiaries press the party forward in the direction they like. The writhing of the Democratic machines and local bosses against the policy of the New Deal in 1936 and 1940 is described with unconscious humor in Boss Flynn's memoirs—to keep their jobs, the men who tended the local machines—even had to do something for their voters! The likeness and the difference between the constituents of the parties can be seen from Table 6, showing voting over three Presidential elections, at a time when governmental problems were especially acute and reforms were markedly accelerated.

TABLE 6—COMPUTATION OF PERCENTAGE OF OCCUPATIONS VOTING DEMOCRATIC IN PRESIDENTIAL VOTE[89]

Occupations	1936	1940	1944
Professional	49	38	42
Businessmen	47	34	41
Farmers	59	54	48
White-collar workers	61	48	51[90]
Skilled workers	67	59	59
Semiskilled	74	67	62
Unskilled workers	81	69	65

[88] Cf. Lazarsfeld, *op. cit.*, Chap. III.
[89] Cf. E. G. Benson and P. Perry, "Analysis of Democratic-Republican Strength by Population Groups," *Public Opinion Quarterly*, September, 1940, pp. 464-73; and press release of American Institute of Public Opinion, March 3, 1945. Cf. also D. Anderson and P. E. Davidson, *op. cit.*, p. 143 ff. for similar tables; and Paul Lazarsfeld *et al.*, *The People's Choice*, p. 19 *et seq.*; also Ogburn and Hill, "Income Classes and the Roosevelt Vote," *Political Science Quarterly*, 1935, p. 186 ff.
[90] Anderson and Davidson admit that it is a puzzle "why people of no wealth and meager income should be arrayed against each other in opposing political parties." They hazard: "perhaps it cannot be explained in terms of their economic stake at all but is the result of other factors—such as the failure of either party to espouse their cause, subterfuge and chicanery impolitics, ignorance of their true economic stake, the party tradition in which they were nurtured, their social surroundings,

[85] Report of Joint Committee on Organization of Congress, March 4, 1946, p. 13.
[86] *Ibid.*, p. 13.
[87] *Ibid.*, p. 12.

Of course, the consequence of the all-inclusiveness and mental and moral fluidity of the main political parties is the incoherence of the parties in the legislative and administrative process itself. Lacking either the leadership of men or the leadership of ideas, the parties in Congress are undisciplined and vote across party lines. This was first shown by President Lowell of Harvard,[91] but more recently Stuart Rice [92] and others [93] have shown even more clearly the looseness of party discipline and cohesion in party policy. The Stuart Rice index of cohesion showed only 63.1 per cent for the Democratic Party and 66.3 per cent for the Republicans in the Senate in the Sixty-eighth Congress. The consequences for legislation and executive leadership are considered later. Table 7 (opposite) of some crucial votes in 1947 shows the disarray.

The upshot is both good and bad. It is good in that the surging social forces in the country have come within the bond of two parties, so that the nation is not torn by the kind of factions which Madison feared as a disintegrative force. This has occurred in such a way that millions of people have lived in peace in an enormous area which has had to adapt itself to the tremendous strain of swift, sometimes abrupt, and always massive, economic, technological, and social change: at any rate, wholesale violence has been avoided. Simultaneously, as the tax burden will bear out, government has been endowed with a great range and depth of regulative, remedial, conservational, and philanthropic functions. Yet it still must be remembered that "one-third of the nation is ill-housed, ill-fed, and ill-clad", and it may be added, ill-

provided with medical care. Perhaps the New Deal spirit will not be entirely lost to either party, and especially not to the Democratic; while the problem of social security, civil rights, and full employment may offer the opportunity for one or both to draw a sharper alignment of following and loyalty, and therefore of organization and purpose, than ever before.

CONCLUDING OBSERVATIONS OF POLITICAL PARTIES

THE intimate connection between political parties and the legislature and executive is manifest. Indeed, it is not extravagant to say that the legislature and the executive are hardly more than the formal, centrally organized, and authoritative assembly places and will-making agencies of the parties. The sounder the organization, the more cohesive its association, and the more defined its purpose, the more is it the soul of the legislature. The less so, the more the indecision, the derangement, the creaking and unserviceability of the lawmaking and executive bodies.

The contemporary mind cannot totally dictate to the institutions produced by history and geography. Yet it may well reflect that two parties are better for the happiness and duty of nations than many parties, and two parties contesting seats everywhere. For then lies and error may be in all places challenged, while distraction of will and disintegration of outlook are reduced.

If we regard parties as a kind of mountainous pyramid, with their broad base in the people and their summits constituting the legislature and executive, then the British system can be represented by a single mountain, from base to summit, all of one piece, including the opposition. The American system ends in three peaks, separate and of different dimensions, and awkward bridges are needed to allow to and from communication between them, not too successfully. In France, the mountain as it rises upward is cleft by a multitude of fissures. In dictatorial states, only one firm sharp summit arises, which weighs

the influence of party bosses, and others." *Op. cit.*, pp. 185-6.
[91] American Historical Association, Annual Report, 1901, pp. 321 ff., "Influence of Party upon Legislation in England and America."
[92] *Quantitative Methods in Politics* (New York, 1928), p. 211 *et seq.*
[93] J. M. Johnson, *Extent and Consistency of Party Voting in the United States* (mss. of Ph.D. thesis, University of Chicago, 1943), using more refined index on Stuart Rice's basis,

TABLE 7—Voting—By Party—on Some Key Issues in the United States Congress

		Total		Republicans		Democrats	
	Voting in the Senate, 1947	*Yes*	*No*	*Yes*	*No*	*Yes*	*No*
May 28	First income-tax reduction bill	34	52	2	45	32	7
July 18	Override veto on tax reduction	36	57	3	48	33	9
May 13	Omnibus labor bill	24	68	3	47	21	21
June 20	Override veto of labor bill	25	68	3	48	22	20
May 29	Hawkes amendment to increase rent 15 per cent	26	48	2	40	24	8
June 18	Reed-Bulwinkle bill	27	60	3	43	24	17
April 22	Greek-Turkish aid bill	67	23	35	16	32	7
April 30	$150-million foreign relief cut	64	19	32	12	32	7
June 18	Wool-tariff bill	38	48	12	36	26	12
April 3	Amendment to recommit Lilienthal appointment	52	38	18	31	34	7

		Total		Republicans		Democrats	
	Voting in the House of Representatives, 1947	*Yes*	*No*	*Yes*	*No*	*Yes*	*No*
March 27	First income-tax reduction bill	137	273	3	233	133	40
June 17	Override veto on tax reduction	137	268	2	233	134	35
July 18	Override veto on second tax reduction	108	299	2	236	105	63
April 17	House (Hartley) labor bill	107	308	22	215	84	93
June 20	Override labor-bill veto	83	331	11	225	71	106
May 9	Greek-Turkish aid bill	287	107	126	93	161	13
April 30	$150-million foreign-relief cut	165	225	36	190	128	35
June 16	Recommit wool-tariff bill	166	191	46	154	119	37
June 24	Overseas information, "Voice of America"	303	63	152	62	150	1
May 27	Agricultural appropriation cut	174	180	12	180	161	0
April 25	Interior appropriation cut	140	197	9	186	130	11
July 15	Civil rights for federal employees	133	248	33	191	99	57

down heavily upon the mass of dry powder beneath.

Modern parties must bridge the gap between the narrow range of factual observation, the self-regarding economic interests, and the special spiritual attractions of masses of diverse individuals and the small and larger groupings. For the comprehension of duty and the recognition of the interrelationship between the rights and welfare of the individual, the nation, and the world, demand the assistance of men who especially devote their time and particular skill thereto. In democratic government there is a proper vocation of leadership to which all can freely aspire: and leadership is essential. In our own day, the advent of great firm collectivities—in the occupations, in social groupings, in churches, and so forth— more than ever demands that parties shall

serve individuals, for it is there *at the individual focus,* that loyalties are engendered. If a reasonable and flexible unity in diversity is wanted, then the *party must penetrate through the associations, through the collectivities to the individual, and there teach its own doctrine of the relationship between its whole and its parts.* If not, as especially shown in the United States, parties become the sport of the lobby. The lobby exists everywhere, since interests exist everywhere, but it is chiefly in the United States that parties are unable to resist, as their superior loyalty is not sufficiently lofty or self-assured to fend off the lobbyists.

DICTATORIAL PARTIES

In marked contrast to these considerations concerning democratic political parties, we may recapitulate what has been said about the dictatorial parties.[94] In such régimes one party alone exists. Hence the legislature is emasculated, as it cannot be the forum of a confrontation of different wills. The legislatures are facades. As the party is in the service of a person or a doctrine (like the Marxist-Leninist) paramount, unqualified, final, to which possible alternatives are not admitted, and, above all, fanatically sanguine in temper, the single party acquires several peculiar characteristics. Its duty and discipline are severe—the cause is above all other loyalties, forever. To secure dynamic *élan*, the party is kept small relative to the population. To achieve the triumph of doctrine and to be assured of loyalty, a most careful process of selection compared with democratic parties is installed, with candidacy, endorsements, apprenticeship, formal preparation. To give the sense that this is a leadership of quality, an élite, the numbers are limited and purges periodically undertaken. Since no opposition is tolerated, the dictatorial party is used to challenge and destroy the opposition that mounts in the breast of any man or woman of common sense. In democratic systems, such opposition not only is expressible in parties and all other voluntary associations but is safeguarded by well-founded civil liberties. Since in dictatorships a spiritual following could not be relied on, not being spontaneous, and since only outward obedience could be enforced, the party is and continues to be cruel in its mental and physical attacks on a population which is simultaneously silenced and divided. Dictatorial parties are not parties, but doctrinal or personal despotisms; they do not spread and encourage leadership but monopolize it.

Parties are the power behind all thrones. Whatever the form of the state, parties govern by directing the energy which moves the machinery. Their peculiar power is that in their absence the political fires would run too low for activity, or the wheels would obstruct each other

instead of working smoothly in their appointed positions and functions. About forty years ago an American statesman referred to parties as the "invisible government" and contrasted the institutions and activities expressly permitted by the constitution with the real sources of power.

Party has ceased to be the invisible government, and has become not only the visible but the acknowledged government in democracies. Already it increasingly finds its place in statutes and written constitutions, and in the only example of a democratic unwritten constitution, the British, the acknowledged part played by party is enormous. When we have penetrated into the secrets of parliaments and cabinets, presidents, kings and departments of state, we shall have good cause to underline, and underline again, this judgment founded as yet only upon the party's electoral activities.

For without party the electorate would be "atomized," as it was intended to be, in the vague speculations of the school of Rousseau. Today it would be split not only into millions of personal fragments, but into groups and congregations: wherever there is an associated activity of man there is conscious organization. Without party there would be but churches, trade unions, employers' and professional associations, schools and universities, various kinds of consumers' associations, states in a federation, and municipalities—in short, all the organized human fellowship bands, seeking for all and for themselves that which their own ethic dictates. Modern political parties, not all in the same measure but all in some measure, absorb the members of these associations into their larger and wider fellowship. They act with an interest in, and a doctrine of, the state. The hard and fast line between them and smaller groups is not to be found. They cut across these groups, include them, marshal them, and form wider fellowships, seeking the solution of problems which arise altogether, or in part, outside these lesser groups—problems which may arise out of the relations between them, and which concern not only

---

[94] Cf. H. Finer, *Future of Government* (London, 1946), Chap. 2, and above, p. 302 ff.

those immediately affected but others away beyond, who may be affected thereby.

By degrees which to the ordinary citizen were imperceptible, these nation-wide fellowships have come into being and organized themselves with a gigantic and complex apparatus. They possess buildings and newspapers, printing presses and advertising experts, songs and slogans, heroes and martyrs, money and speakers, officials and prophets, feast days and fast days; like all religions, they disrupt families and ostracize heretics, and among their agencies of discipline and subordination are the novitiate and penance. They bear many resemblances to the churches militant, but their eyes and minds are directed more immediately to the legislature and the departments of state, for there lies the power and the glory.

It is apparent already, and the next chapter will more abundantly show, that in our own day political parties have partially usurped the power of the legislature. They make policies, create platforms, obtain seats in the legislative assemblies, and, if they attain a majority, their platforms tend to become laws. No sooner, in fact, did party organization in England suffer the change connected with Schnadhorst, Chamberlain, and the Birmingham caucus, than people coined the term a "Parliament outside Parliament." But, though in a different measure in different countries, the power more and more departs to parties. So far has this process gone that the English system has been deliberately characterized as "plebiscital." To the question of why the House of Commons has ceased to be a deliberative assembly (insofar as it has), the answer was given by Lord Robert Cecil in the 1930's: [95]

I should say that if you really looked into the real principle of our constitution now, it is purely plebiscital, that you have really a plebiscite by which a particular man is selected as Prime Minister, he then selects his Ministry himself, and it is pretty much what he likes, subject to what affects the rule that

he has to consider—namely, that he must not do anything that is very unpopular.

Indeed, the phenomenon of party government is, if we regard it at a distance, really remarkable. Does it not need an extraordinary restraint upon human passions to permit, as part of the ordinary machinery of government, an organized opposition which undermines the government of the day, enters upon weeks, nay years, of demagogy and militant electoral tactics, excites the people, and returns, perhaps, with the power of reversing former decisions, and in England, even of amending the basic institutions? It sounds, and in other days would have been judged, like treason, disruption, revolution, a battering at the foundations of the state. George Washington warned against it. James Madison was so terrified by party, or what he called "faction," that his concern is today difficult to understand. He said (in *The Federalist,* Paper X):

By a faction, I understand a number of citizens, whether amounting to a majority or minority of the whole, who are united and actuated by some common impulse of passion, of interest, adverse to the rights of other citizens, or to the permanent and aggregate interests of the community. . .

The change in manners in the Western world is immense for, though not every kind of tactics is allowed, the laws (written and unwritten) regulating them are equally binding on all the combatants and they are severe, considering the rather untameable disposition of man. Not all countries which adopted parliamentarianism were able to create and maintain these rules of electoral self-control. In some, as for example in Italy, parliamentary and electoral tactics were singularly corrupt and victory impure and simple, being the paramount consideration, victory for office the next consideration, and victory for policy the last. It was as though the morals of *The Prince* had been pawned with the parties, and the difference between one age and another simply an affair of the one or the many, the court or the caucus. Millions in Ger-

---

[95] L. S. Amery, also a Conservative politician, does not like to admit this in his *Thoughts on the Constitution* (London, 1946), and this constitutes the central defect of his whole thesis.

many could not stand it. Lenin and Stalin could not face the rigors of party strife. At critical times in the years between the world wars, French parties were so intent on stabbing each other that they almost killed their nation, which indeed was only revived by foreign arms.

Democratic government will not stand or fall, it is not efficient or inefficient, chiefly in the measure of the legislature's qualities: it rests, in its hopes and doubts, upon the party system. There is the political center of gravity. If the parties are divided upon sincere issues, fully conscious of their public duty as of their public power, equipped with the expertness which tempers zealous desire with calculated possibility, and if they conduct their campaigns with restraint, making the commonweal, and not victory, the standard of their rhetoric and militancy, then we may hope not only for the continuance of democratic government but for its improvement. If the divisions among men correspond to merely personal, factional, or sectional disputes, and, further, cannot be amicably assembled in parties not confusing to the electorate; if desire for complete victory wrecks temperateness and passion blinds to truth; if the men who form the organizations are not considerate and patient in their research and pursuit of policies and do not establish a permanent and generous reciprocity in matters electoral; if they cannot rise above the level of catchwords, office for office sake, and narrow-minded belligerency of phrase and tactics—in that measure not only is democracy despised by those who are the victims of party tactics, but a rot enters the vitals of the actors themselves. This is the testing time of democracy: and this means the testing time of political parties.

The remarkable thing is, as we have already mentioned, that there are so few parties, even in the countries where there are so many. Why are there not more? Any singularity of view is, by hypothesis, held by a small number, and a small number cannot by itself, and independent of the aid of any large party, carry through its

policy.[96] It cannot, as we shall show abundantly in Chapter 20, even obtain sufficient time to state its case in the representative assembly, so large is the amount of business, even the routine, of the modern state. The priority and the substance of parliamentary discussion is necessarily settled by the larger parties. The protestant then has the choice, either to maintain his principle and be forced into conscious political impotence, or to swallow his doubts and take them inside that party which is otherwise most favorable to his policy. From the outside the heterodox has rarely a chance of success: once inside the party he may, perhaps, barter his counsel, support, and services for some concession of his own demands. This practice has been commonest in England, and has gone to swell the chorus of Continental opinion that the Englishman is hypocritical. But in fact the Englishman's common sense is devoted to results in action, not the satisfaction of knowing that he is consistently supporting an entirely hopeless principle for its own sake. Even on the Continent, compromise must be and is practiced, for, in fact, men want government to continue, whether a majority is found or not. Principle, some might call it philosophic idiosyncrasy, is, however, not so easily sacrificed here to the necessary unity which is the prelude to power.

Another cause of the fewness of parties is the method of election, which by splitting up the country into constituencies, necessarily splits up the supporters of the small groups as well as of the big parties. This dispersal of the votes leads in the single-member constituency system to a loss, perhaps, of any representation: unless all the voters are sufficiently concentrated in one or more constituencies. Proportional representation, as we shall see, keeps them alive; but even so, the hopelessness of a small minority encourages adhesion to some larger entity. Though dissentients may be condemned to political exile, because of the tremendous difficulties in

[96] Cf. E. E. Schattschneider, *Party Government* (New York, 1942), an excellent analysis, especially on the relationship between class and groups and the major parties.

building a new party, this is, however, no justification for not clearly avowing opinions honestly held, nor any justification for the cowardice of not going into the wilderness to attempt the formation of a new party. For the gains of office, power, and half measures or promises, will be lost the possible effect upon opinion, whose strength can, after all, not be really gauged until one has staked one's career upon its exploration. Too often life is killed by office.

For the man of religion some are saved and others damned; for the teacher some are ethically right and others wrong; for the politician the world is divided into the righteous We and the wicked They. For if life is to be lived, it requires successful assertion; self-belief springs eternal and is fostered as realization demands it. But the scientist who seeks to understand and not to govern must be content with observation of the source of these differences. It is for him to say that all parties to a controversy are inspired, that what is considered ugly, vicious, and cruel by one side, is, for the other, all that it can know of the sublime, causing those who cherish it to experience here and now the delights which men have ascribed to Paradise, moving them to a sacred nobility and self-sacrifice, to a happiness immeasurable when ventures are successful, and, in the days of adversity, to sorrow and longing of overwhelming poignancy. Where men can live in harmony, then, let us be thankful, but when they war against each other, in parties, nations, or by "crime," let us understand first and judge afterward.

Along these diverse channels, men would move to the extreme boundaries of their faith were it not for the organized counter action of parties. For men are impelled to a complete establishment of their own good, and even its forcible fixture upon others. Parties mutually check and control the militant extension of ideals. In this organized interplay of forces, each learns the most important truth in politics: that in order to win one's way to development, some part of the way must be given up, either substantially, or in terms of time; that it is possible to destroy every hope by insistence upon all at once.[97] These organized bodies more easily find and hold to the terms of reciprocity than do dispersed, inarticulate persons. For they have the technical apparatus with which to accomplish this purpose, and they tend to acquire a sense of honor and self-respect: that is, a sense that promises given and accepted must be promises fulfilled.

---

[97] On the effect of time on political behavior see below, Chapter 38.

Part Four

LEGISLATURES

A political institution is a machine; the motive power is the national character. With that it rests, whether the machine will benefit society, or destroy it. Society in this country is perplexed, almost paralyzed; in time it will move, and it will devise. How are the elements of the nation to be blended again together? In what spirit is that reorganization to take place?—D I S R A E L I

The general will is always in the right, but the judgment which guides it is not always enlightened. It must be got to see objects as they are, and sometimes as they ought to appear to it; it must be shown the good road it is in search of, secured from the seductive influences of individual wills, taught to see times and spaces as a series, and made to weigh the attractions of present and sensible advantages against the danger of distant and hidden evils. The individuals see the good they reject; the public wills the good it does not see. All stand equally in need of guidance.—R O U S S E A U

17

Legislatures: General Problems

LEGISLATURES, assemblies, chosen as we have already described, meet to accomplish a variety of functions: to make laws, to control the executive, and to carry out a few judicial functions. In Chapter 6 we found that although there is no absolute separation of powers, there is a strongly marked distinctiveness of function, and that although each institution is occupied with a mixture of functions, its central occupation is different in kind from that of its collaborators. The function of legislatures is to apply the presumed will of the people to the creation of laws and the superintendence of their administration. Their judicial power is of small and residual importance, for it nowadays is almost wholly exercised by extremely specialized bodies.

THE MANDATE OF THE LEGISLATURE

THE relationship between the will of the electorate and the legislature has already been treated in some measure, but as we explained, that relationship must be viewed from the angle of the legislature as well as from the angle of parties. The candidates have been nominated, they and the party have associated, they have duly become members of one or other of the assemblies. Now what is their duty? How far may they proceed? What powers have they? Are they now free agents to do absolutely as their own discretion dictates?— or must they seek instructions from those who elected them?

These questions were raised as soon as legislatures began to meet on the express or implied assumption that they "represented" some body corporate or area. They were raised, for example, in relation to the *États Généraux* of France, where it was accepted that delegates could not think or act, *faute de charge spéciale* [1] they were raised in England in 1647 [2] in the Agreement of the People. They were raised in America with a special emphasis after the War of Independence.[3] The subject was

[1] Cf. G. Picot, *Histoire des États Généraux*, 2nd edition (Paris, 1885), Vol. V, p. 145 ff.

[2] Cf. S. R. Gardiner, *Constitutional Documents*, 3rd edition (Oxford, 1906, pp. 368-69: "That the Representatives have, and shall be understood to have, the supreme trust in order to the preservation and government of the whole; and that their power extend, without the consent or concurrence of any other person or persons, to the erecting and abolishing of Courts of Justice and public offices, and to the enacting, altering, repealing and declaring of laws, and the highest and final judgement, concerning all natural or civil things, but not concerning things spiritual or evangelical. Provided that, even in things natural and civil, these six particulars next following are, and shall be, understood to be excepted and reserved from our Representatives . . . That no Representative may in any wise render up, or give, or take away, any of the foundations of common right, liberty, and safety contained in this agreement, nor level men's estates, destroy property, or make all things common; and that in all matters of such fundamental concernment, there shall be a liberty to particular members of the said Representatives to enter their dissents from the major vote."

[3] Jefferson said that "all the powers of Government result to the legislative body" and

fiercely discussed by the French Constituent Assembly,[4] and in England, the claims to parliamentary representation of the new and powerful commercial interests first forced a famous opinion from Burke [5] and next compelled a reform of Parliament, and this, naturally, put the matter in a new light. The issue raised was, and is, that of the mandate of the member: is it imperative or is it discretional, and if discretional how far may discretion go?

Law and the Mandate of the Legislator. In English terms the problem has resolved itself into the problem of delegate as against representative. The British constitution offers no written guidance upon this, but where there are written constitutions (though not everywhere) a definite rule is laid down, which squares with Burke's reading of the British constitution in his own time and the general view rather vaguely held now by most members of Parliament. The Organic Law on the Election of Deputies of France (1875) [6] says: "All imperative mandates are null and void"; and that of Weimar Germany said: "Members are representatives of the whole nation. They are subject to their conscience only and not bound by any instructions."

These are counsels of excellence rather than rules enforceable in the courts, for no country has established practicable machinery for their enforcement. As regards Germany, it has been said that the rule belongs "rather in a catechism than in a constitution." [7] Once only has punishment

followed upon a definite acceptance of a mandate in France: invalidation of the election of the successful candidate who accepted a mandate, but, since the *bureau* of the Chamber which examined the case was composed politically, and not judicially, we may suspect that considerations of party advantage determined the issue.[8] Law and practice have since then inclined toward the freedom of the member, for the commission which prepared the law of November 3, 1875, deliberately refused to accept the grave penalty of annulment of the election.[9] It accepted the alternative, which not only gives the member his freedom, but gives him a statutory defence against exigent constituents: it declared the imperative mandate null and void. Virtually, the law says to the candidate: "Declare what you like, that business is between you and your constituents, and if you make any definite promise you will not be punishable by the Chamber; but whatever you have promised, know hereby that it has no effect. You are absolved!" The Chamber of Deputies decided against the nullity of an election contested because an imperative mandate has been accepted.[10] It decided also that article 13 of the Constitutional Law of 1875 prevents any penal sanction from confirming the nullity of mandates: for no member of the Chamber may be prosecuted for opinions or votes uttered in the exercise of his function.[11] Against those who clumsily obtrude the mandate (which, in fact, all members ask for and obtain, and to which they, in a certain degree, feel obliged, but which they pretend to ignore), a stiff though dignified protest can be made; for example, the president of the Chamber, the reporter of a commission, must protest when a mem-

"173 despots would surely be as oppressive as one." Cf. Charles Merriam, *A History of Political Theories* (New York, 1920), p. 110.
[4] Cf. E. Pierre, *Traité de Droit Politique et Parliamentaire* (Paris, 1924), Vol. I, p. 311; and Chap. 12 above.
[5] Address to the Electors of Bristol (1774): "Parliament is not a congress of ambassadors from different and hostile interests; which interests each must maintain as an agent, and advocate against other agents and advocates; but Parliament is a *deliberative assembly of the nation*, with one interest, that of the whole, where, not local purposes, not local prejudices, ought to guide, but the general good, resulting from the general reason of the whole."
[6] November, 1893.
[7] Pierre, *op. cit., Supplément* (1924), p. 437.

(This immunity from prosecution, detention, etc., is reaffirmed in the constitution of 1946, articles 21 and 22.)
[8] November 30, 1875, article 13. This stipulation does not appear either in the constitution of the Fourth Republic or in the election laws of 1946.
[9] Cf. F. Morstein Marx, *Rechtswirklichkeit und Freies Mandat, Archiv des Öffentlichen Rechts* (Berlin, New Series, XI), p. 435.
[10] Pierre, *op. cit.*, p. 312.
[11] *Ibid.*, p. 313.

ber refuses to withdraw an amendment because he says he has received a mandate to defend it.[12] There is thus theoretic freedom, but if, in electoral practice, the member is bound, there is no punishment. So do men play hide-and-seek with their consciences; for to admit the existence of a thing which does exist may, they believe, cause its pathological growth. There is much good sense in this view.

In Weimar Germany the constitution spoke, as we have seen, with uncompromising directness, and Anschütz said that "the exercise of this function [*Organschaft,* or action as an organ of government] should take place in complete independence of everybody: of party, social class, groups seeking special interests to which the member belongs, and even of constituents. That is the intention of the second sentence of the article." [13] He said further that it is a moral duty, but a legal one too: and one, moreover, which binds you to consider all your actions and connections in the light of their compatibility with the public welfare. It was even argued that one cannot be bound by a caucus of one's party.[14] It is clear, however, that these desirable things are not secured by the law, and in fact the whole discussion soon takes on that same negative character which it has in France. It all comes to mean that the member cannot legally be bound to instructions; that is, that he is free of them: for it is against the constitution to be otherwise. But the real political question was not answered: if the candidate makes promises, or if they are demanded of him as a condition of votes, is there an institution to uphold his constitutional independence? The law created no institution to deal with such a breach of the constitution, if we except the electoral court, which has never decided such a case. The law only provided that any such arrangement was legally null;

that contractual arrangements whereby gifts and other amenities were accepted to promote special interests could be punished as bribery. One important case occurred in which a Communist member of the Hamburg Parliament was caused to resign by the handing in of a declaration which he was alleged to have signed in blank as part of the regular procedure of his party, but which he denied he had done. He also denied any wish to resign. In debate the Communists argued that such blank-form resignations were regular features of their organization, justified because "the member held his mandate not as a person but as a member of the Party, and that therefore the Party could always exercise its influence upon the carrying out of the mandate [15] at any time, and also had the right to nullify his mandate." [16] The committee declared its indifference whether the signature was the member's or not; the Hamburg constitution included the terms of article 21 of the *Reich* constitution, and this settled the issue. For such a signed declaration would make it impossible for a member to act according to his conscience. Moreover, it deceived the voters, for they give their votes to the candidate on the assumption that he is not bound to an undisclosed obligation. Against this decision the spokesman of the Communist party argued that as Germany had a list-system of proportional representation and as the lists, rather than the individual members, were voted for, it was unavoidable, as well as desirable and proper, that the party should discipline its members and alter its list. Nor was that all. The democratic principle required that the party should have the right of removing a member who defaulted from the terms of their united policy!

The German *Reichstag* was peculiarly liable, for reasons noticed in our discussion of parties, to the entrance of representatives of special groups, and it attempted to control them by requiring di-

12 *Ibid.*, p. 437, footnote 9.
13 G. Anschütz, *Die Verfassung des deutschen Reichs* (Berlin, 1930), p. 115. The history of this subject for Germany is given in J. Hatschek, *Das Parlamentsrecht* (Berlin, 1915).
14 Cf. G. Anschütz and R. Thoma, *Handbuch des deutschen Staatsrechts* (Tübingen, 1930), Vol. I, p. 419.

15 F. Morstein Marx, *op. cit.*, p. 432.
16 This is an excellent though unintended illustration of the distinctive emphasis put by Communists on the superiority of party to the masses.

rectors of corporations to report their connections to the *Reichstag*. The British Parliament excludes government contractors and government officials; in France, officials and government contractors are excluded. This branch of politics and constitutional law has by no means received either the theoretical or practical attention it deserves.

According to English law, the Parliament is sovereign. The constitution knows nothing about the people. Therefore, in strict law, once a person has become a member he is free to act as his own mind dictates and is entitled to reject demands made by anybody.

In the United States the constitution also speaks in the words of the Bill of Rights of 1689: "and for any Speech or Debate in either house, they [Senators and Representatives] shall not be questioned in any other Place." [17]

Thus the laws, whether ancient or modern, incline to freedom of the member and ignore the actual nature of his present relations with his constituents. Yet in every country the facts deviate from the law, though the facts themselves allow the member considerable freedom. How much he is bound depends clearly upon the nature of the electoral process, and the part played therein by the local and the central caucuses of the political parties, a fact with which the law has not yet attempted to reckon. As the nineteenth century wore on, there was in England and America, and later in Germany, a gradual strengthening of the idea of delegation and a weakening of that of representation. This was due to the more conscious operation of democracy and the feeling that democratic government required active participation of the citizen.

Theories of the Mandate. Burke's theory (p. 228 ff.) gave the balance of power to the member. The movement of opinion leading to the franchise reform struggle of 1832 consisted, naturally, of the Whig claim for delegation and the Tory claim for virtual representation.[18] What was particularly in the mind of the former, and what gives the question its present-day importance, is the fact that it is manifestly impossible for legislatures to be dissolved and re-elected so often that their will and that of their constituents can be deemed to be in perfect harmony. To act with effect, even to act at all, in an age of inconsistent social demands for laws, legislatures must have such a length of life that the difficult problem arises of the connection between the constituents and the delegates during the time between elections. How can this problem be solved? It is soluble by strict instructions at the outset, and to this must be added the short duration of legislatures—and even that is not enough, for the people must exercise pressure upon legislatures through public meetings and other agencies in the interval between elections.

Tory doctrine rested upon two pillars: (1) the incompetence of the constituent to legislate for himself, and (2) the lack of the right locality to press its views to a conclusion against the interests of the country. We shall see that these are material elements of the problem not only deserving but commanding an important place in the final decision of the question. But the whole tendency during and especially after the Reform Bill struggle was toward definite pledges. Francis Place tells, for example, how the National Political Union decided that the opinions of all candidates on all the great leading questions should be accurately obtained and pledges on those alone demanded. The pledge became more and more acknowledged as a proper connection between members and constituents and more widely given. In the early days after Reform, the Whigs were not for strict pledges, and even James Mill was less radical on this matter than one might expect from the *Essay on Government*.

The last philosophical discussion upon parliamentary institutions written before the Reform Act of 1867 was John Stuart Mill's *Representative Government*, and Mill devotes a special chapter to the discussion of the question, "Ought pledges to be required from members of Parliament?"

---

[17] Constitution, article I, sect. 6, para. 1.
[18] *Edinburgh Review,* November, 1812.

The spirit of that chapter is as remote from our days as the Flood. And to explain why is to reveal the nature of the present political environment. Mill says that many members of Parliament, even apart from the prospect of re-election, solely as a matter of conviction, allow their constituents the power of judging them. Are they right or wrong? Mill tries to answer the question by the application of two principles: (1) that government must be responsible to the governed and, jointly therewith, and (2) that government shall acquire "the benefits of superior intellect, trained by long meditation and spiritual discipline to that special task." But how are the electors to decide which among a number of candidates can best give these benefits? Their judgment is unsound. Showiness rather than mind wins them; therefore they would be foolish not to exact a pledge. Nor can opinion be dismissed: Liberals ought not to vote for a competent Tory or Tories for a competent Liberal—the more competent, the worse for the constituents in such cases. Hence, again, pledges must be exacted, especially since in England the electors have no choice except between two or three rich people who are of a class superior to their own and who are certain to vote for measures in their own class interests. "This would not be needful under a political system which assured them an indefinite choice of honest and unprejudiced candidates."

It seems, says Mill, impracticable to lay down for the elector any political rule of duty. It depends on the general tone of the electors. Some look up to superior talent, some are distinctly without reverence. For the old politician, his record will guide the electors; for the untried one, a pledge should be exacted. Even when the electors seek wisdom and attainments, their own personal opinion must not be suppressed; but, apart from fundamentals, they should allow the member his freedom.

What is missing from this analysis? The factor which today is of the most importance: the political party. And much of the essay on *Representative Government* is stone-dead for the same reason: the omission of political parties.

Parties and the Mandate. It is clear that discussion after the rise of parties must proceed upon entirely different lines, for the whole relationship of the elector to the legislature has been altered. We have already displayed the nature of that alteration in the principal democracies of the world. The parties have become recognizable entities, secure of a large body of steady loyalty. These are the bodies which have applied themselves to the task Mill ascribes to the constituents; they search out qualities among men and ascertain the value of policies. They make or endorse the nominations. The caucus or the primary nominates on the basis of party membership and party program. The constituents expect the program to be followed. They expect the member to follow the instructions of the party whip. The party organization itself disciplines the member. If he does not vote with the party, then he ceases to receive the whip, or is expelled, or does not receive "endorsement," or does not receive aid in propaganda and funds—an important consideration. (However, it is true that the caucus is less authoritative in the United States and France than in Britain, where it is most authoritative of all, and Weimar Germany.)

The old-time discussion is, therefore, out of date. But its main considerations deserve recapitulation. The first was the need to overcome the gulf between isolated elector or electors and the assembly of the representatives. Hence the strong emphasis upon freedom of the representative at a date when communications were so rudimentary that the locality could not learn the views of others without a personal meeting between all representatives. It was the representatives who thus insisted, because they realized, as any person with experience of deliberative assemblies does realize, that it is impossible (1) to foresee all the points which may arise and (2) to know what is for the good even of the locality until the other representatives have fully stated their case and have revealed their emotional determination and social power of resistance. Identical considerations powerfully and almost unanimously moved the French Constituent Assembly, and essentially they remain true for our own day. *First,* the question arose, was the nation a unity, or not? If it were a unity, then its meaning lay in the power of the majority to will for all, after due deliberation. This is the test of corporate sovereignty. Unity was desired; therefore sovereignty lay with the whole nation, and not with any part. Hence, all the parts were subject to the will of the whole and could not prevail against the majority. The *interêt général* dominated the *interêt particulier.* The condition of unity was the condition laid down in debate: "*Il n'est pas permis de protester, de réserver; c'est un attentat à la puissance de la majorité.*" This condition is recognized generally today. *Secondly,* enlightenment on the general will was impossible without free discussion. For to bind to instructions is to destroy deliberation. Opinion cannot be known in advance.

When representatives from different parts of the country have to assemble and discuss in common objects which are as yet undetermined, which are neither foreseen nor known by the commissioners, it would be strange and absurd to shackle their wills by imperative mandates. Upon what could these absolute decisions be broken? They would necessarily be incoherent and destructive of all harmony; each district in occupying itself separately with different subjects, a general result on anything would not be reached.

Every constituency must have the nation in mind when it is choosing its representative: the theory of democracy is indeed, says Siéyès, that each deputy is chosen "in the name of the totality of constituencies; the deputy is of the entire nation." Who can know the national will elsewhere than in a national assembly? We must propose, listen, discuss and modify our opinions, and, in common, form a common will. When people meet it is to deliberate, to know the opinions of others, to profit from each other's illumination, to confront particular wills, to modify, to conciliate them, and finally to obtain a common result by a majority vote. The terms of the argument have changed radically in the last century: com-

munications have become abundant and almost instantaneous; indeed, party organization of the whole electorate became possible as this, along with the press, developed.

What then becomes of the constitutional clauses about mandates? They might be removed and no harm at all would follow; they cover up a patent fact. *The party gives a mandate to the member: he has his instructions from it; more, he generally carries them out.* As we shall presently see, even the speeches he may make, and other opportunities of activity in the parliament, are settled by the party, ultimately on behalf of the constituencies but immediately on behalf of the party itself. The imperative mandate was the constituencies' only safeguard in the days before party: and freedom was possible and desirable when the only means of meeting the minds of friends and opponents was in the national assembly. Those days have gone. Party is the great intermediary.

In the United States the power of the local mandate is consciously interwoven with that of the party. The practice of the British constitution before 1832 required that the candidate should be a resident of the place for which he sought election, although the statutes providing for this were very old (1414 and 1430) and were evaded. This no longer prevails in the British system, and more than half of the members are residents of districts other than their constituencies. The older practice was put into the American constitution in the fairly mild form that the member must be an inhabitant of the state in which he is chosen. It still applies, but it has been strongly reinforced by the statutory requirements of some states that the member must reside in the district which he represents, and convention supports the rule. This is based upon local patriotism of a rather predaceous kind, upon the interest of the local boss, and upon the general view that a member is a spokesman of local interests. The member is expected to further the special interests of the constituency in the matter of the "pork barrel": that is, expenditure upon public improvements in his district, such as river and harbor works, post offices, and the public jobs for his district or state. Further, as we have already remarked, the queer remoteness of the American Congress from popular needs—a separation produced by constitutional prohibitions and the separation of powers—makes the party less sensitive to public issues (though more vocal and apparently excited about them), and it is, therefore, not always so insistent upon party discipline as the English parties. The member is often prepared to hold up the legislature for some local advantage; there are always other members who are ready to support him for reciprocal benefits; it is a custom well known, to be taken good-humoredly and exploited with gusto. Therefore the constituencies can expect profitable "logrolling" by their members: and the electoral bargain is more than implied. This causes the mandate to be double: the local-predaceous and the party mandate. A member must bear both in mind: in regard to the latter, he knows that, owing to the Congressional weakness of American parties, he has more latitude than an English member; in regard to the former, he lifts up his eyes unto the "boss" of the state, whence cometh his help.

In pre-1939 France, the question played a more considerable part than in England or the United States, because there were few great party organizations to take the burden off the constituencies and assume responsibility for party discipline.[19] In 1871, Victor Hugo renamed the imperative mandate the *mandat contractuel:* "a contract between the mandate-member and the mandatories creates between the elector and the elected the absolute identity of aim and principles."[20] In 1881 a proposal was made in the Chamber of Deputies that the *"professions de foi"* of the members should be collected and reported upon, to demonstrate the difference between the promises and the achievements of members, and to cause pressure to be placed on the latter. The commission in charge of the proposal rejected it, the reporter saying that the electoral committees could not be considered as the faithful expression of the views of the country and that mandates may not be imperative since no one could foresee all questions which would arise in the course of four years. In 1894 a socialist project sought to make an imperative mandate really imperative by giving the justice of the peace in the constituency the right to declare breach of mandate and to annul the right to sit![21] This ridiculous suggestion, natural to a party in a hopeless minority, was refused consideration. Duguit appreciates the fact that modern parties have eviscerated the legal clause, and he remarks that even though we consider electoral districts a mechanical necessity and lacking specific character, yet they do play a part as the medium of expression of the electorate, and members are, in fact, rather closely bound to their constituencies.[22] Esmein, on the other hand, excessively formal, begins with the conception that representation is representation of the whole nation and concludes with the idea that there is no place for a mandate. History, which Esmein invokes, cannot, in fact, settle matters of this kind but only contemporary conditions.[23] *The mandate is, in fact, given by the party where the parties are strong, and where they are weak it is almost idle to talk of a mandate.*

Now, German doctrines on the subject were of a remote, metaphysical nature before World War I,[24] and devoted to the support of the constitutional clause which was borrowed from French constitutions. Support was widely given to it because the

---

[19] This is the burden of D. Halévy, *La République des Comités* (Paris, 1934).
[20] G. Weill, *Les Élections Législatives* (Paris, 1913), p. 271. This is an address to various electoral committees who asked him to stand for the National Assembly.

[21] *Ibid.*, pp. 272-73.
[22] L. Duguit, *Traité de Droit Constitutionnel* (Paris, 1921-25), Vol. II, pp. 504, 505, 510.
[23] A. Esmein, *Droit Constitutionnel* (Paris, 1921).
[24] Cf. J. Hatschek, *op. cit.*, and Paul Laband, *Staatsrecht* (Tübingen, 1876-82), Vol. I, p. 356 ff. But Laband says (p. 356, footnote 1): "On the contrary, there is a *political* responsibility which is demanded of the member of the *Reichstag* by caucuses, election committees, meetings, political clubs, the Press, etc. Such a demand cannot be legally enforced, neither is it legally denied."

[375]

whole system of government was unfree and the monarch was not anxious to assert popular power. After World War I there was a significant change in theory, but the upshot in terms of written law was the same. At the very moment when this change occurred, a system of proportional representation was established. That is, a system of election in which tremendous constituencies are combined with the placing of all the candidates for each party on a single list, that list to be accepted or rejected in its entirety. In other words, the method of voting for a single representative among a number of individual competitors was abandoned. Who now is the mandatory? It is, in fact, nobody but the party, and, indeed, the party in its least personal and most mechanical form.

The full significance of this cannot be discussed at this point, but it is treated in detail later. But this must be emphasized: the moment there is a departure from small single-member constituencies, the very question of an imperative mandate, of delegation or representation per member *to a constituency*, becomes highly unreal. There is no longer any direct apportionment of a member or members to a determinate group. All the psychological conditions of that relationship are disturbed by the size of the constituency, the predominance of the party doctrine, and the composite personality of several groups of candidates, each seeking a composite victory in a conjoint campaign. More than elsewhere, the party caucus is obliged to control the campaign and the nominations; and it does so. The members are bound in the first place to the dictates of the party machines.

Delegate and Representative. The conclusion, then, is this: that owing to the growth of party organization the question no longer is whether a candidate should hearken to his constituents, but how far he ought to obey the party. It is not in the legislature that the individual, sectional, or group mandate is so important but in the party councils, and it is there, indeed, that the relationship to the national interest is decided. There reconciliation takes place according to local urgency, the courage and talent of the members, and the ability and policy of the national leaders. But nowadays any local problem of importance which is capable of being settled by the party is looked upon as a national affair. As elsewhere in government, the distinction between local and national is being rapidly obliterated.

It is important to keep the parties alive to their duty. The electorate can do this through direct intervention, by deputations, through the lobby, by individual communications, or by mass appeals. Suppose a member of the legislature changes his mind in the course of a legislative term, or is negligent of his duties; what remedy ought the electorate to have? In Britain, the local party has sometimes called on a member to resign. It is the general theory that he should not. But sometimes he has done so. But in the Western democracies it is exceedingly rare for the member to be either politically unfaithful or negligent. If he is, the next election will remedy that. (So in the case of Sir Oswald Mosley in 1935, after he had formed *The New Party;* and the tension between Sir Stafford Cripps and his Bristol constituency on his expulsion from the Labour party in 1939, and in March, 1949, the Labour party's refusal to re-endorse Konni Zilliachus for the 1950 election.)

Would it be wise to institute the recall: that is, the right of the local electorate to request, decisively, the resignation of a member? At first sight this proposal seems attractive. It should, however, be repudiated. For its institution would be an encouragement to all minorities to offer petitions against the sitting member. At some time in the term of a legislature, its work could be disrupted by such a concerted onslaught. It is, therefore, of cardinal importance that, for the sake of the regular march of business, for stability, and for the assurance of being able to reckon on the governmental events of the near future, some surrender of the immediate will of the electorate must necessarily occur—for the nature of modern economy and welfare requires legislative and executive stability. The more urgent is the need, therefore, for close connections between constituencies, the legislature, and the executive through a continuing party organization in constant operation, and through access of all sorts of organized interests and petitioners to government.

(As we have already observed, in its anxiety to vaunt its affection for the people, the Russian Communist party declared for the recall.[25] The power has been used very rarely indeed; and where it has, it has been the instrument of the Communist party for removing representatives the party leaders have ceased to favor. It is interesting to find that during the debates on the formation of the constitution of the Fourth Republic the Communist party in France proposed—unsuccessfully —the recall of deputies *by the party;* no other party agreed with them.)

Functional Associations as Mandatories. Very rapidly in recent years, alongside the parties as mandatories have grown associations of citizens, often nation wide in their purpose and membership. These are always active, and intercede with the government departments and with legislatures by personal conference and written communications. They operate in elections (supporting candidates and supplying money) and in the legislatures; they exercise influence upon cabinet ministers and upon the administrative departments. We have much to say about their significance later (p. 458). Here it should be observed that their electoral business is the extraction of pledges from candidates when these are most susceptible. Deputations are sent to the candidate, but more frequently, elaborate pledge forms are sent to him for signature, and it is pointed out, more or less explicitly, that a block of votes in the constituency depends upon the answer. Many candidates throw these in the wastepaper basket, but some are intimidated.[26] Most give a "straddle" answer; that is, one specious enough to gain votes without committing the candidate. So in all democratic countries, but in the United States the practice has gone further than elsewhere. There are more "groups" formed, especially by women voters and church leaders, and more money available for printing. We are not now referring only to lobbyists. On the democratic assumption, associations are quite right in asking for pledges, and members must expect to rebuff them at their peril. Functionless or ill-willed frustrations by members of the legislature must be corrected. However responsive and capable the party system may be even where it is best organized, it is good that it should be stimulated from outside, as it usually is, by groups which feel passionately about some particular public affair. It would be highly dangerous to representative government to allow the parties a monopoly of political thought, for they—the party leaders and organizers —like all guilds, tend to be content with the minimum of thought that will obtain power, and when in office they have little time for thought at all. As the frank will admit, they begin to act not on information but on instinct. This is quicker and less troublesome. We shall show, further, how the party organizations are less the inventors than the brokers of policy, and that without independent philosophers and critics they would be wellnigh sterile.

THE GENERAL VALUE OF LEGISLATURES

The Multiplicity and Confusion of Issues. Legislatures are about to begin their work; the parties have accomplished theirs and have given pledges to the country. What is the meaning of these pledges? The parties carry a large basketful of projects. These are the things by which

---

25 Cf. p. 228 above.
26 "It is hereby agreed by the Headquarters of the Conservative, Labour and Liberal Parties that each shall send to all its respective Candidates a letter recommending them to refuse to answer all Questionnaires, received from outside the constituencies they are contesting, at the coming General Election, and also to decline to receive Deputations of persons other than electors in the particular constituencies which they are contesting . . ." (April, 1929). This agreement, together with the proposed letter, is reproduced in the *Report of the Labour Executive Committee,* 1928-29 (published in the Labour Party Annual Report, 1929, p. 10).

rational men would judge their worth in terms of votes. But owing to the desire for victory they parade these commodities not conscientiously, for experience of the electorate's mind shows that victory cannot thus be won. An issue embodied in a slogan is raised as the main object of the electoral struggle. One, two, perhaps three issues of relatively greater immediate importance than the rest are made the subject of contention. This procedure results in two things: first, cynicism of large numbers of people about the whole electoral process, and second, a heated discussion immediately after an election about what the voting really means, a discussion which may become particularly acrid and even grave when new problems arise and are dealt with by the government issuing from the election.

These are unfortunate results, and there is much to which the rationally minded may object in the practice of singling out issues for prominence and keeping others in the background. A mandate is incurred in respect to one thing or several things. Groups otherwise heterogeneous are brought into the same camp, and afterward some may feel cheated. Neither the government nor the people know exactly what they have done or engaged themselves to do. Exactly what proportion of the majority voted for what sections of the common platforms? But the answer to this is, if not entirely satisfactory, at least somewhat reassuring:

First, the *general* attitude of mind of the party and the character of its leaders are evoked in the course of discussing the special issues, and electors may be as much impressed by this as by the merits of the specific proposals. That is something they may rely on for the future. *Second,* the conduct of parties cannot be raised far above the level of the mass of the electorate, and until that is improved, chicanery is bound to prevail. In fact, in England, at least, the best of slogans and the most alluring of issues are modified in effect by the widespread if vague knowledge of party history and personalities. As to new problems raised in the course of a legislature, this is an inevitable occurrence

wherever they last more than a few minutes. The safeguard is complex: a reduction of their term, a party system with sensitive electoral antennae, a permanent party organization with its eye on the next elections, and a system of by-elections. In many places the referendum and the initiative have been not only widely advocated but adopted. It is also a good argument for decentralization to local authorities, and federal systems, that the more the authorities that participate in public affairs, the less is a confused complex of problems unloaded upon a single electorate at one stroke. (Up to a point: balance the advantages and disadvantages.) For it must be admitted that the mandate is confused and partly warrants the many letters written by unemployed clubmen to the leading newspapers after each election. It will appear as we go on that the evils can be and are mitigated by a good party and legislative system.

General Value of Legislatures: the Interpretation of the Mandate. It is at this point that an appreciation of the value rendered by legislatures in an age of high party organization begins. All legislatures, with varying quality, but all in an important degree, render three services, beyond the mere function of lawmaking and controlling the administration:

(1) When the members returned by election confront each other and compare thoughts and speeches, a sorting out of the generally confused mandate of the election is undertaken. A process of reflection occurs, in physical conditions more propitious than the stormy, wordy, nation-wide debate without detailed confrontations that is an election. An order of priority and values becomes more definite and settled: and sometimes has to be supplied afresh where the verdict was ambiguous.

(2) Numbers of votes do not tell all: they do not exactly indicate the duration of electoral opinion, and, above all, they do not register the intensity of the feeling of either majority or minority. This has to be discovered by meeting the other persons: there are vocal inflections and turns of phrase that can be met only in a small

assembly, where, also, expression of face and gesture will tell what a sacrifice it will be for some group to be forced to submit to a vote. This nonstatistical relationship must be heeded, if it be desired to obtain the maximum welfare by the law, with the minimum of avoidable coercion. The knowledge that some day the other side may be in office is a powerful support to such tolerance.

(3) And this leads to the final point, namely, that in a legislature common to all parties, close to each other, continuously with each other, engaged in common labors, appeasement takes birth and tends to grow. It is one thing to damn the other party's doctrines during an election in the crude, imprecise way that the enormous terrain of an election makes rather inevitable; it is another to look into the other man's face a few yards away. He now seems almost human: he has ceased to be a disembodied doctrinaire extremist. Many men have testified to this appeasing quality of common legislative service. Some men do not like it: they consider that their deputy is being seduced or that he sells out. This is usually not the case: legislators have learned that other men are not insincere or rogues, cowards, bloodsuckers, and that there is something in some parts of their philosophy that sometimes deserves support. To those who look to unity and mercy among men, such a function of legislative life is of importance; those who do not even banish their rivals altogether.

LEGISLATORS: THEIR GENERAL NATURE

WHETHER the mandate comes from the constituency or from an association or the party, its exercise requires the member to think, discuss, and determine—the last being expressed by his vote. We shall see that in modern legislatures everywhere, the large majority of members does little more than vote, that only a few discuss, and that a very small minority thinks effectively. The composition of these functions varies a little from country to country, but generally the emphasis is upon will or power—that is, upon the vote. This is a direct corollary of the majority principle; and it seems a parlous condition until we reflect that, after all, the real thought has already been accomplished outside the legislature and will yet be accomplished, completed, and applied to all points of practical detail by the opposing groups of leaders and the permanent officials. Fundamentally, a legislature is a forum where men may measure the strength of each other's will as expressed in their numbers and in other demonstrations of strength of feeling and purpose, and may either enter into agreements by mutual concessions or vote each other down.

Legislators as Policy Makers. Our survey of political parties gave this result: that, broadly, policies are made or adopted by them. This does not always or chiefly mean that the members of a party or its leaders are inventive, that they conceive and elaborate schemes of reform or conservation. They are certainly disposed to do this by character and the stimulus of their experience. Some, indeed, do discover the answer to problems and the means of fulfillment. Upon reflection, however, it will be seen that not many such inventions are due to party and legislative persons. The politician is a broker rather than an inventor. And not infrequently he must be prompted vigorously before he satisfies his clients.

Those who discover issues, and explore and plan the means of their settlement, are the thoughtful and sensitive among the population, though they may be, and in our own day usually are, voluntarily attached to some specific party. Consider the immense industrial and commercial associations, the social groups of all sorts with which every country now teems, the municipalities and their associations; consider the reformers and thinkers like Bentham and Chadwick, Tom Paine, Judge Lindsey, Henry George, Bernard Shaw, the Webbs, Lassalle, Mazzini, Raffeisen, Plimsoll, the Prohibitionists, the Bimetallists, Adam Smith, Rignano, Tolstoy, Marx, Marie Stopes, Veblen, Jane Addams, Octavia Hill, Florence Nightingale, Bellamy, Jevons, Keynes, Havelock Ellis, and others who first pursued lonely paths and were later joined by disciples who surged forward to harass, press, and sometimes to convince political parties. All these geniuses of sensitiveness and intellectual comprehension, these masters of history and moral value, are the true manufacturers of the politicians' stock-in-trade. This is quite natural, for to govern well has always required the rarest degree of knowledge and wisdom.

The application of this truth to our own day is especially important. Populations are vast, the division of function, economic and social, minute and complex. They are incomprehensible without long and patient study. Each individual has his own peculiar nature distinguishing him from all others and from human nature in the abstract. Abroad, in places so distant that the average person cannot even conceive that a full all-round life is lived there, are woven connections that will be beneficial or destructive in proportion as we learn to read the secrets of their mastery. The scale of society is so stupendous, the detail is so minute and manifold, the interests so special, the studies of the technicians so microscopic, that only the comprehensive mind, the patient, deep insight of the genius, and the vivid feeling of the fanatic, can master and reproduce their meaning for the purposes of philosophy or governmental control. Nor is that all. If states were indeed static, if humanity ceased to spin problems involved in the attempt to control the future, the larger half of the difficulty of government would be removed. Area and complexity can be mastered in proportion as they remain unchanged, but, since the idea of progress advanced to the center of civilized aspirations, the whole of futurity has become a building site, and the philosopher is needed to prophesy not only the important events and conjunctures of a year's time but those of a decade and even a century hence. The actual rapidity of change in the mechanical basis of our civilization and in fashions in thought, the swift increase of population in the nineteenth and early twentieth centuries, have encouraged this pioneering, which has ceased to be of the dream-like order of the old writers of Utopias, and has become the hard, directed foresight of people like H. G. Wells[27] or a Sir William Beveridge in social security and full employment, or the planning surveys of the United States National Resources Planning Board.

Leadership, then, comes first from the masters of thought, feeling, and moral apprehension. This leadership is the difference between man as a shortsighted beast and man as a noble, purposive human being of dignity. It is the duty of a democracy to cherish these leaders and allow them the first word: this does not deny the other principle, that the electorate has the final word.

The world of special groups, philosophy, and social speculation, then, furnishes the politician with his material. Nor must we forget that in that world the politician has his own salaried professional philosophers and contrivers—the civil service, which not only thinks and plans but also explores and formulates what the rest of the world is thinking and planning. It is a professional machine to acquire, to assimilate, to cut and dry the world's intellectual and emotional produce and put it up in the form which politicians may understand and employ. Of major importance is it also that, in our own time, international secretariats of the specialized agencies—first—in the League of Nations and now in the United Nations Organizations—have grown up to add to their carefully formulated thoughts and ideals.[28]

Politicians not Philosophers. The politician is not always chosen for his knowledge, nor always for his character. He is chosen because he represents the views of a certain party, and because he can win

---

27 When I once ventured to congratulate Mr. Wells on the success of his *Anticipations,* he answered: "That was easy. I merely had to project certain lines which were already visible. But now I have to go further; to find what is latent and then build upon that for an even remoter time." See *The Shape of Things to Come* (London, 1933) and *The End of Homo Sapiens* (London, 1939).
28 Cf. Herman Finer, *The Economic and Social Council of the United Nations* (Boston, 1945).

the seat (and this implies, quite naturally, that talented men without campaigning qualifications—kinetic, pachydermatic, confidence-winning—are rarely chosen as candidates). In other words, the policy has been largely made before he becomes a member. The party has already tapped the real sources of policy, and he becomes its representative. The only exceptions to this generalization are *first,* where the party may be weak, as in the United States, so that the politician, being less dependent, may himself, however unqualified to do so, compose or gather ideas; or *second,* where, the party being strong, a politician happens to be a person of abnormally creative mind. The party's character also continually grows.

Indeed, it is not the intention of the people or the parties to get philosophers elected; the prime object is *number,* the modern political medium of legitimate power. The member is a vehicle of the party, and the party is chosen because, fundamentally, it embodies the material and spiritual interests of the people who choose, and it is chosen to dominate the state, as far as it can, in the sense of its avowed and explained policy. As far as it can! In that phrase resides the virtue of legislatures and politicians! For in spite of the extralegislative activities of the parties—their researches, their considered formulations of policy, their crosscountry debates, and the incessant war in the press —the policy of each party is not complete and cannot be complete until the other side is heard. When members enter the legislature, were they conscious of anything but their electoral victories and the messianic programs of their "side" and the chances of reform and distinction, they would solemnly admit (1) that much in their program was tactical, included to "catch votes;" (2) that a good deal in heaven and earth had not been thought about at all; and (3) that they must expect the unexpected: events, contingencies, calling for quick thought and the improvisation of a policy. They would realize, upon a little reflection, that even when the policy was not tactical, but had been considered in all its facets with care and

with a calculation of their opponents' strength, not all could be foreseen, not every detail sifted, not every force truly evaluated until it had been discussed with hostile elements possessing the parliamentary power to enforce some at least of the drive of their opposition. Not until there is a personal confrontation in a small assembly, with systematic procedure, can the detailed expression of policy, which means everything, be considered, or the full spiritual force of majority and minority be measured and applied. Further, the good in dialectic is not only that it causes one person or party to triumph over another, but that it sometimes causes some truth to triumph over both by provoking the explanation of self to self.

Therefore legislatures and politicians still have their invaluable place in the modern state, and deliberations and debate still occupy a central place in their functions. The forms are mainly those of the age before rapid transport, fast communications, and party organization. They still take little account of these and so provide for ample debate, as though there had been no preparatory and even decisive stages in the country already; as though the legislature were the creator, not the creature, of discussion. We shall see that much is antiquated, wasteful, and dead in legislative procedure and forms. Perhaps this is, in general, of value in protecting debate so that the balance of welfare against coercion embodied in the laws may be thoroughly pondered.[29] The remarkable thing is that the minority is still allowed some opportunity of influencing the laws and administration— rightly in our opinion—and that, cleverly led, it can convert this opportunity into power.

The Politician as a Broker. The politician is, therefore, as near as any single term can signify him, a broker. His business is to apply the power resident in his constituency to convert desires into stat-

---

[29] *The Third Report of the Select Committee on Procedure, British House of Commons,* No. 189-91, 1946, exhibits very clearly the reluctance, for this reason, to depart from traditional forms in the quest of modern efficiency.

utes and administrative action by alloying them with the possible. He attempts to get as near the desirable as he can, and what is possible he will learn, whether he is in the government or in the opposition. The ways are many and devious. But let us attempt to paint a portrait in broad outline of the best type of member. The portrait will do for all legislatures. And we sketch, not the art of succeeding to high place or of obtaining favors—that will appear as we proceed—but simply the equipment of the member to convert his mandate (poor, poor word!) into governmental realities.

The Legislator as Scholar. He need not be a scholar, and indeed, this would entangle and embarrass rather than help him, for his function is to act, to fight, and to seize advantages, not to meditate upon them. Were he a scholar, an expert, he would be encumbered by doubts and details, and it is notable that scholars who have entered legislatures have either been silent or silenced (think of Acton, J. S. Mill or de Tocqueville); and Francis Bacon, a member of Parliament, and Lord Chancellor some 250 years before explained why this must be in his *Advancement of Learning* on the mentality of scholars. Or they have had to jettison their scholarship and become men of affairs, carrying the least baggage and allowing passion to vanquish their scruples. The legislator has no need to be a scholar, for he can get all the information he needs for debate in a desiccated preparation from the party pamphlets and newspapers (or, in the United States, from the Legislative Reference Division of the Library of Congress). Further, if he has to a sufficient degree the energy of reform, or the desire to shine in the legislature and the constituencies, the government printing offices turn out a spate of reports by official experts and investigating committees. Only the few more serious members make any pretense of trying to master these, for again the party and the press offer short versions (though it has been recounted by a witty member of the French parliament that a member has been known to sleep on the reports in a literal sense, owing to poverty so great that he could not afford a bed!).

Truth compels me to say that very many members are unable to master the meaning of a lengthy and complicated report by their own efforts, owing to insufficient native ability and education. A few, however, are able to understand the complex and technical information. Some, realizing the impossibility of being masters of all trades, wisely specialize. The specializers and others who are less fortunate may have friends who are experts; and then successful intervention in debate may be assured by persistent and acute interrogation, so that the most abstruse points are cleared up. Indeed, this is a very important part of the work of an able member—to discover the experts and philosophers and get himself coached by them. He may easily do this if he is a little energetic, for such people are usually good-natured and easily succumb to the flattery that they and their knowledge are of practical importance, and the belief that in this way they become the real sources of government, that "philosophers are kings." Nor are the hopes of these expert friends altogether vain, but they are imperfectly realized owing to practical exigencies—or, in other words, the confounded obstinacy of other people, and the fact that the advice of rival experts and philosophers has been taken by the other side.[30] But what the legislator cannot learn from print he may learn from verbal exchange.

The Legislator as "Politician." The member who has gone so far has gone very far, and it now behooves him to keep friendly with other members. Popularity on personal grounds is exceedingly important, for it takes the edge off sharp truths and opens a way for their acceptance. It is even more important to be popular with opponents than with friends, for they will grant concessions on that account, believing that such "a jolly fellow" could hardly be ill-willed or stupid: or at least the concession is granted before

30 Cf. T. V. Smith, *The Legislative Way of Life* (Chicago, 1940).

they come upon these truths, by which time they have lost the battle.[31] Hence the lobbies, the social life of the legislature, *la buvette,* and the political clubs play a large part in the evolution of the member and of policies. The full list of ingredients for success in this direction, universally valid, cannot be given—each person is born with his own way to the hearts of other people. The need to do social favors involves an incessant vigilance for friends who have social graces and power. Their value must be justly estimated—that is, their value in the political exchange—and they must be held in corresponding regard and offered corresponding respect and political favors. Friends must be made and dropped in accordance with this rule. If you wish to waste time on useless people you may do it, of course, but it should be recognized as waste. Here, in the activity of the man in politics, as everywhere in life, the function has its specific nature, and its commands are peremptory. On the political exchange, men and things are valued in terms of the desirable power which can be purchased with them: quite properly, for victory must not be jeopardized by giving way to a desire to gaze at the stars.

The Legislator as Parliamentarian. To the qualities already described, another is indispensable. It is a knowledge of the rules of legislative procedure. There the member will find all the permissions and prohibitions affecting his right to intervene in discussion. He will discover weapons to defeat his rivals and opportunities to advance his own cause, obstacles to his progress, and roads which will require a process of sapping. By adroit use of these rules he may exact concessions by threatening to obstruct his opponents' path with amendments; and in modern parliaments so much has to be done at the insistent call of the constituencies that men are willing to concede in order to proceed. He will also be able to obtain concessions by the intrinsic merits of his argument, his rhetoric. These together will

stem the tide of his opponents' policy by exhibiting to them its results, as the simple technical consequences they have not had sufficient imagination to foresee, and as the extent of human opposition which will be aroused and has been underestimated. Further, a speculative portrayal of results in terms of votes at the next election will help.

The Legislator as Party Member. Where the party is in opposition, the member's activity is favored by the leaders and it may bring him reputation and power (Senators Vandenberg and Taft in the first two sessions of the 79th Congress were outstanding examples). For then any stick is a good weapon; and the government must be unmercifully harassed. But when the party is in office, then the private member is sworn to cheer and vote, to cooperate and not to oppose. Even a trifle is a waste of time and may wreck the strategy resolved upon by the leaders. The party has many means of enforcing this unwritten rule, the principal method being to set officers to watch the conduct of the member, or to meet together and discuss and determine their course, and to threaten the refractory with expulsion or the withdrawal of aid at the next election.[32] The discipline is effective, for as we have seen, without the party there is no nomination, and no opportunity to play an effective part in the legislature, and the expenses of election are so great that most members must rely upon party help.

Thus it is an illusion, and a quite un-

31 Cf. D. Kirkwood, *My Life of Revolt* (London, 1935), pp. 202-307.

32 The British Labour party's Standing Orders, *q.v.* reproduced in each Report of the Party's Annual Conference, are particularly severe. Practice is far more lenient, though it is not possible to refrain altogether from disciplinary measures, as indiscipline spreads. In May, 1948, for example, two Labour members were expelled from the party: one for publicly denouncing the Labour government's intention to nationalize the iron and steel industry, and another for contumaciously leading a group of members against the government's policy of fighting against the Left-wing Socialists of Italy who were in company with the Italian Communist party during the crucial election of April, 1948. The expulsion took place after a long process of persuasion and a hearing at party headquarters.

necessary one, to believe that members of the legislature are creators of policy. They are parts of an embattled national host whose objective and strategy have long since been prepared, and they are needed for the purposes of minor tactics, which are not, however, without importance. Or, to change the metaphor, they are merchants buying votes in the cheapest market, the constituencies, and selling in the dearest, to the forces opposed to them, which is always the official opposition, and often to their own colleagues and leaders. It is not derogatory to the function and dignity of legislatures to say this; for we merely say that not in the members do the initiative and the need for thought reside, but in the party leaders. The work of the assembly is important, but the ordinary member cannot, does not, and need not, contribute much to its execution. To say that the average member was ever in a much (if any) better position, in a parliamentary "Golden Age," is to repeat legend, not history. Where, indeed, as in France, the private member has much independence and the parties are of small authority, *no* business is done, and the work of the legislature dissolves into an interminable series of oratorical skirmishes, with guerilla tactics and destructive ambuscades.

This is far from meaning that the quality of a legislature's work is independent of the ability and work of its members. We have seen by what methods and for what ends the member may become effective. But we are concerned to say that almost everything depends upon the leaders, and that is due to electioneering methods in large populations with universal suffrage, to the complex technical nature of modern civilization, and to the large amount of business which legislatures must get through. However, the better the followers the better (though the more embarrassed) the leaders. Above all, for the day-by-day supervision of executive policy in action, the work of the departments of government, the multifarious acts of administration by hundreds of thousands of career officials, and the diverse outlook and critical attentions of

the popular representatives are of the greatest value.

On the whole, then, in a country with well-organized and purposive parties, the constituencies do not cause much damage in returning mediocrities, but so far as such qualities are lacking—as in France and the United States (especially in the South)—their choice may be very damaging not only to their civilization but to the very notion of parliamentary government. Even this evil is partially overcome by that disbelief in the logical extreme of democracy which shows itself in the establishment of permanent, professional, career administrative officers. Now, if we examine the composition of legislatures, we shall see that no member is, in fact, likely to be expert in more than one subject of a rather narrow scope. Though all members taken together do have knowledge of most national and international interests, yet there is no distribution of members in arithmetical proportion to those interests.

The Representativeness of Legislators. The correspondence between members and the aspects of national life upon which they are expert varies in different countries as the accompanying tables (8, 9, 10) show.

The outstanding features of these tables are: (1) the small proportion of legislators who can, by the major occupation of their life, be expected to have an expert comprehensive opinion and make a useful contribution to general policy: hence, on each specific policy a large proportion of the assembly is bound to be silent and take things on trust; (2) that there is a spokesman for almost every aspect of national life; (3) the large number of teachers who find their way into the legislature; (4) the large number of professional politicians: authors, journalists, party officials, trade-union officials, "other professions," and "law." These, (3) and (4), usually have, in fact, the best all-round knowledge, but the knowledge is frequently superficial. The large number of "lawyers" is due to two facts: that so many men who have taken the qualifying examinations for the legal profession are incapable of earning a living in it, and

TABLE 8—OCCUPATIONS OF LEGISLATORS: UNITED STATES: 79TH CONGRESS, 1ST SESSION: 1945-46[a]

Occupation or profession	Senate	House	Total
Accountant	0	3	3
Agriculture	3	15	18
Author	0	2	2
Banking	2	10	12
Business and/or manufacturing	10	47	57
Dentistry	1	3	4
Editing, publishing, or journalism	10	24	34
Education	2	24	26
Investments	0	3	3
Law	62	241	303
Legislator	2	4	6
Medicine and surgery	0	7	7
Municipal officer	0	6	6
Pharmacy	0	2	2
Real estate and/or insurance	0	24	24
Secretary—Congressional	2	4	6
Social welfare	0	2	2
Union official	0	2	2
Miscellaneous	2	11	13
Vacancies	0	1	1
Total	96	435	531

[a] Sources: *Congressional Directory, Who's Who in America,* and *Martindale-Hubbell Law Directory.*

TABLE 9—OCCUPATIONS OF LEGISLATORS: GREAT BRITAIN: HOUSE OF COMMONS, NOVEMBER, 1945[a]

Occupation or Profession	Government	Opposition	Others
"Workers"	155	—	2
Cooperative movement	13	—	—
Journalists	28	6	4
Teachers	54	4	3
Medical	11	3	2
Barristers	27	43	4
Solicitors	14	5	—
Other professions	31	23	3
Business	31	46	4
Agriculture	4	4	—
Youths[b]	3	3	3
Army[c]	2	36	—
Navy	—	8	—
R.A.F.	—	3	—
Landed proprietors	—	3	—
No gainful occupation	12	27	5
Women[d]	8	1	2
Total	393	215	32

[a] Sources: *Dod's Parliamentary Companion* and *Who's Who.*

[b] The term "Youths" covers young men who before their war-service had not embarked on any professional career.

[c] "Armed Forces" refers only to men who before 1939 had been employed in the regular armed forces of the Crown.

[d] Twenty-four women were elected to Parliament in 1945. Those who can be described as having a profession are not included among the eleven women in the above list.

TABLE 10—OCCUPATIONS OF LEGISLATORS: FRANCE: ASSEMBLY ELECTED JUNE 2, 1946 [a]

Occupation or Profession		Comm.	Soc.	Rad.	M.R.P.	Right	Total
Forestry, agriculture, and fishing	Managers	12	4	—	21	10	47
	Workers	2	—	—	—	—	2
Industry	Managers	1	3	3	5 6	6	18
	Technicians	1	3	1	9	4	18
	Workers	41	5	—	12	—	58
	Employees	14	5	—	4	—	23
	Artisans	—	—	—	2	—	2
Commerce, banking	Managers	1	—	—	9	3	13
	Technicians	—	—	—	6	1	7
	Employees	2	—	—	2	—	4
Liberal professions	Law	3	16	11	21	15	66
	Medical	2	6	3	6	3	20
	Art, literary	8	9	5	13	3	38
	Technical	2	—	—	3	1	6
	Clerical	—	—	—	2	1	3
Civil servants	Active teachers	24	31	5	17	—	77
	others	18	7	2	13	2	42
	Retired teachers	2	5	—	—	—	7
	others	2	—	1	—	2	5
Miscellaneous		11	21	8	15	10	65
Total		146	115	39	160	62	522

[a] Not including deputies from the Empire. From *A Constitution for the Fourth Republic* (Washington: Foundation for Foreign Affairs, 1947), page 82.

therefore drift into the profession where a living can be picked up and prestige won —politics; and that there is a tradition that the man who knows the law can make the law.

The Qualities of a Representative Legislator. Is there a single royal road to the recruitment of the truly representative legislator? The answer depends on the qualities useful for his function. He needs sensitiveness to the life, difficulties, aspirations, and future emerging problems of the world outside the assembly. He needs not perfect knowledge, but knowledge enough to challenge and criticize the executive and the officials and opponents, and an understanding of where to go for more information if the situation requires. Any knowledge above this is valuable but excessive. He should have tenacity and stoutness of heart in advocacy as in criticism. He requires to be adept in the use of procedural ways and means. Above all, it is not special expertness that he needs to contribute, but wisdom, shrewdness, logi-

cal power, and an insight into human nature. He needs the general power of judgment, which enables him to say on all occasions, but especially on the most critical, "This course will in the long run be good or bad for the nation as a whole, and for this cause, such and such a sacrifice is meet."

It is clear, therefore, that no particular profession or training offers the royal road to the proper legislator, but that any way is eligible which has involved immersion in the life of the society and has required rigorous reflection and the use of mind. The more ample the variety in the legislature, then, the better. (Plato has some clues on this subject.)

THE DURATION OF LEGISLATURES

The Views of the "Federalist." We saw that those who desire a strict correspondence between the legislature and the will of the people believe that representativeness is to be produced by the frequency of legislatures, or, put in another way, by their short duration. What particular reasons have swayed men in their settlement of this question, and what should determine our judgment today?

In the United States the strength of democratic enthusiasm at once caused the new states to fly to such extremes as half-yearly and yearly elections,[33] and both John Adams and the author of the *Federalist* tell us that there was a current maxim running, "Where annual elections end, tyranny begins." [34] The constitutions explained themselves: that of Massachusetts, for example, saying, "in order to prevent those who be vested with authority from becoming oppressors, the people have a right . . . to cause their public officers to return to private life." The first urge, then, was to ward off tyranny; the claims of efficiency were naturally ignored. The federal constitution seems to have adopted a biennial term for the House of Representatives with little or no debate, but the *Federalist* supplies a sound set of arguments for two years rather than one, and, we might say, for a longer period than two, though it was speaking to the more limited brief.

What were the circumstances, as the *Federalist* saw them? *First,* there was less need to control the House since it was to be checked by the constitution itself, by the state legislatures, and by the other federal organs. "It is a received and well-founded maxim, that where no other circumstances affect the case, the greater the power is, the shorter ought to be its duration; and, conversely, the smaller the power, the more safely may its duration be protracted." *Second,* "No man can be a competent legislator who does not add to an upright intention and sound judgment a certain degree of knowledge of the subjects in which he is to legislate." *Third,* attainment of this was possible only by actual experience in the station that re-

quires the use of it. To settle the question, then, broadly, the *Federalist* asked the question, "Does the period of two years bear no greater proportion to the knowledge requisite for federal legislation than one year does to the knowledge requisite for state legislation?" The *Federalist* answered that the field of federal jurisdiction required a knowledge beyond that needed for the government of a single state. The condition of the states was diversified; the legislation of foreign trade demanded an acquaintance with the ports, usages, and regulations of the different states; taxation required a wide knowledge of internal conditions; so, too, regarding the regulation of the militia and foreign affairs. The *Federalist* argued (Paper LIII):

Some portion of this knowledge may, no doubt, be acquired in a man's closet; but some of it also can only be derived from the public services of information; and all of it will be acquired to best effect by a practical attention to the subject during the period of actual service in the legislature.

These, then, were the main grounds for a term longer than one year; time for business, and the need of expertness. The French National Assembly argued, generally, as the *Federalist* did and added the argument that a long duration was necessary to avoid the technical inconveniences of dissolution and re-election. However, short duration commended itself to them, also, as a means of overcoming the expression of transient feeling at any one election.

Actually, is it not tenable that if the House of Representatives were not of two years' but four years' duration, its laws would be better conceived, better drafted, better coordinated, perhaps even fewer per session, and its relations with the executive wiser, more reflective, effectuating more, and less sensational? Would not political parties be thereby stimulated to organize and plan policy more steadfastly? But more on this shortly.

European Thought and Law. The struggle has always been between a shortness of term—to bring pressure upon a monarch, or to prevent the legislative body

---

[33] Connecticut and Rhode Island were half-yearly, and the rest (save South Carolina, which was biannual) were annual.
[34] *Federalist*, p. 272; Merriam, *op. cit.*, p. 78. Cf. also the various declarations of rights in the state constitutions.

from becoming a corporation closed to the popular will—and the necessities of legislative technique. The English Act of 1641, calling for a parliament at least every three years "for the preventing of inconveniences happening by the long intermission of parliaments," was designed to intimidate the king by its simple presence. Then in 1716,[35] the Whig majority, taking advantage of disorders following the Jacobite rebellion, lengthened the duration of Parliament to seven years by the Septennial Act: this would avoid troublesome campaigns, "remove expenses" and disaffection. The arguments against this bill naturally pointed to the unrepresentative character of any house based upon such long tenure. The bill was naturally supported by all the placemen. The Septennial Act was not repealed until 1911, when the Parliament Act was thought to have so weakened the power of the House of Lords that more frequent appeals to the people were deemed necessary as a counterbalance to the power of the Commons.

The Parliament Act meant that the period of tenure had necessarily to be reduced. For, in accordance with the maxim of the *Federalist,* the greater the power of the House of Commons the stricter the need for its control; and the reform of the House of Lords certainly made the House of Commons the most powerful legislative body in the world. The idea that a slight majority—a transient majority—could override a large minority in fundamental matters naturally caused a search for safeguards. The referendum was proposed and rejected: the only thing that remained was a reduction of the term of Parliament, or, in other words, the greater frequency of necessary electoral appeals lest members

"outstay their mandates." This was fought by some among the Conservative opposition on the grounds that more frequent elections would increase the power of the party machine and further depress the already depressed condition of the private members, would increase the power of the cabinet because it decreased the power of the ordinary member, and would raise the expenses of a Parliamentary career. The arguments on the Liberal side were as irresistible as its numbers. Now the Parliament Act contains a clause, inserted upon pressure by Conservative peers, to the effect that the period of five years should never be lengthened by the exclusive action of Commons and king. It is easy to see that if any Parliament extended the term, the power, the "suspensive veto" left to the Lords, would be almost entirely swept away because, in order to suspend effectively, the opportunities of the House of Commons to propose laws must be restricted to a short term. Lengthen its term and the pressure ceases. The question now, however, is whether the period ought not to be less than five years?

France has a period of four years with, conventionally, no power of dissolution in the hands of the government. The Constitution of 1946 made no change in this respect, but the Election Law of October 5, 1946 (article 36) provides for election of members for five years. Weimar Germany very deliberately prescribed a period of four years,[36] with a right of dissolution which was exercised several times.

The Four-Year Term. What is there to be said for a period of four years rather than three or five? It is clear that frequency of appearance before the electorate is essential: not so much that the members be judged but in order to exercise a pres-

---

[35] In 1689 the introduction of an annual Mutiny Act and the granting of annual supplies added to the triennial frequency of parliaments the necessity of their annual session. The Act of 1694 positively provided for the discontinuance of any parliament after three years of life, and the motives at work in the passage of this Act were the House of Lords' jealousy of the Commons and the Whig desire to shackle the Crown. Cf. J. G. Randall, "The Frequency and Duration of Parliaments," *American Political Science Review* (1916), Vol. X, p. 665.

[36] Constitution, article 23: "The *Reichstag* is elected for four years." Similarly the Prussian *Landstag,* Prussian constitution, article 13. The old constitution (article 24) established a term of three years until 1888, when a law extended the term to five years. The law of 1888 was passed in order to avoid too frequent appeals to the people. Originally three years had been included in the constitution by the *Reichstag* instead of the four years proposed by Bismarck.

sure upon the party. The stronger the parties, in fact, and the weaker the individual member, the more necessary is it that the leaders be shaken in their convictions and out of their dogmatic self-satisfaction by an electoral shock. We have already spoken of the growth of a guild consciousness in the group at the head of each party, and the intensive research of Michels bears out the common observation that the leaders tend to become oligarchs remote not only from their constituents but also from their legislative following. The nearer the election, the more carefully they scan their own consciences and the movements of opinion in the constituencies.

This was most strongly urged by the Independent Socialist party of Germany during debates in the Constituent Assembly of 1919, and they were therefore in favor of a biennial term. Preusz and the Social Democratic party had suggested three years. Preusz refused to accept the proposal of a term of two years on the grounds that the shorter the period, the less favorable for the *Reichstag* since it is weakened as against the electorate and as against the cabinet. On the other hand, a large minority of the Assembly were in favor of quinquennial terms. It was remarked that a short period is incompatible with steady and good work and that, in default of this, the *Reichstag* must lose prestige. We think this argument sound. It was also rightly observed that a good deal of time is lost at the beginning and the end of each *Reichstag*—novices take time to find their stride—while, at the end of the term, deputies and parties are already busy with electoral plans and their thoughts are elsewhere. The longer the period, the shorter the proportion of time lost in this way. Further, it is necessary to avoid frequent excitement of the electorate. This argument is good only when it is measured: how frequently will excitement have a bad effect? No one can say this, and in fact elections are not so exciting and impassioned as is pretended. It is suggested, too, that the more elections, the greater the popular apathy and the smaller the number who vote. Again,

this is an unmeasured argument: and between four years and five years we venture to believe that there is no difference in this regard at all.

Thus a compromise must be made. For England I think three years is too short for the necessary novitiate and *expertise*, and five years too long. Four years might with advantage be adopted: for neither written constitution nor Second Chamber checks the power of the House, and the referendum has been rejected. Other countries have other problems: Weimar Germany, for example, had no by-elections in her system of proportional representation, and therefore lacked that impressive electoral weather vane [37] which is still of such intense interest in Great Britain.

There is one other argument for a reduction of the electoral period; it applies to all countries, and therefore to England. But so far we have not met in it any legislature. It is this: Since the electorate and the party are almost in direct touch and the main issues of government are thus decided outside the legislature, it has become all the more important that the electorate shall be politically capable. Political institutions may enable the electorate the better to fulfil its task or may have the reverse effect. A short duration of the legislature has the effect of consulting the people and causing the parties to renew their mandates after they have explained their case to the people and, to the degree we have previously analyzed, educated them. But shorter terms have a further effect quite as important as these: they make it possible for the elector to compare promises with achievements on a greater number of occasions. This constitutes his political experience, and it is important that he should have as much of it as is compatible with efficient government. At the present time an English voter who gives his first vote at twenty-one and his last, say, at sixty-six, has an electoral life

---

[37] Cf. Katzenstein (Social Democrat), National Assembly (*Heilfron,* p. 3113): "They are, as we all know, political weather vanes, the barometers by which one can tell the changes of electoral feeling." The occupied *Länder* follow the same system.

of forty-five years; that is, he votes a minimum of nine times—lives through nine campaigns, sees nine sets of leaders, nine sets of promises, nine Parliaments—and their results. If the duration of Parliament were legally four years, then the resultant electoral experience would be a minimum of eleven campaigns—and the rest. If experience teaches, we have the right to expect that this would be a gain in electoral wisdom: if experience does not teach, then the case for democracy is weakened. If this reform is of little moment, it can only be said that all reforms are but of small moment and that the great changes in civilization are produced only by an accumulation of trifles.

My judgment that a four years' term is a modern necessity is reinforced by reflection on the obvious mounting trend to national planning. A longer term than four years is inadvisable because the broader the activity of government, especially when it is (as much must be) still of an experimental nature, the more opportunities ought there to be for reference back to the citizens. The way back must be kept open. The more massive and complicated the administrative apparatus, the more ought it to be subjected to the periodical lashing waves of popular opinion.

Since the consumers in a planned economy have lost their direct individual influence, as customers, on the variety, quality, and cost of goods and services produced— an influence they exercised by buying or not buying at the prices asked—it is the more important that they be able to challenge and stimulate public enterprise (the national and municipal monopolies) through elections and all the turmoil of electoral will that goes with them, and to censure inefficiency and to exact improvements. The parties and their ancillary organizations will be the main directors of production, the agency of the consumers.

On the other hand, the government's need for ample time to carry through its pledged policy is well understood. It ought not be harassed into stupidities. It requires time to draft the formidable scores of clauses in its legislation. It must have time in which to negotiate quietly with the various groups who will have to bear the burden of obedience once the law is made.

Empirically, then, the duration might be set for four years, with earlier dissolution if circumstances require it in those constitutions which permit so valuable an arrangement.

THE SIZE OF LEGISLATURES

SINCE 1945, the British House of Commons has had 640 members; the French National Assembly 580; the United States House of Representatives 430; while the Weimar *Reichstag* had 500 or thereabouts. What number is advisable? The considerations are these. The bigger the number of representatives, the smaller need the electoral districts be. This conduces to heightened representativeness. For good law, representativeness is of cardinal importance; all men get the sense that they are being duly heard in the uses of authority. On the other hand, too large an assembly may be so unwieldy as to defeat effective procedure. In my own opinion, the claims of thorough representativeness have a very high order of validity. As for procedural clumsiness, since so large a part of legislative work is already done in committees, there is very little harm in increasing the size of the legislature. Indeed, I strongly favor the increase in size of the lower house to eight hundred in all modernized democratic states. This increase is to allow for more representativeness, and for the full manning of the many committees which a modern assembly must have to prepare the laws and, above all, to supervise the administration. I fully appreciate the need for a small, well-knit, coherent assembly, to attain coherence above all. But the other claims are powerful: it is the business of internal procedure to meet them, and to provide for coherence also. In a planning age, the legislature must be bigger. If time cannot be stretched beyond three hundred and sixty-five days in a year, then the legislature's burdens must be borne by multiplying its working members.

INCESSANT PRESSURE ON LEGISLATURES

IT is wrong to imagine that the proximity of dissolution and re-election is the only check upon the enterprise of legislatures. This would be to allow to modern party organizations only a fragment of their actual effectiveness. Party organization is permanent, and the central machine and the legislative leaders are linked to the localities by continuous ties. It has the means of knowing what people feel about its legislative activity, through the local caucuses and election agents. The private member is sensitive to the views of his local committee and the local press, and this is not slow to complain when there is cause. Further, in times of crisis, members are approached by letter, telegram, and deputation, and they cannot avoid a response if they value re-election. Since the rise of the caucuses, these are a natural vehicle for the expression of constituents' opinion. The effect is that the electorate functions between, as well as during, elections. Moreover, all the vocational, cultural, and local associations are incessantly vigilant and clamant. Modern development has given the lie to Rousseau's criticism, sound in its time: [38]

On this point I cannot but admire the negligence, the carelessness and I dare to say, the stupidity of the English nation which, after having armed its deputies with the supreme authority, demands no check whatever to regulate the use which they can make for seven whole years of their commission.

And again: [39]

The English people thinks it is free; it makes a great mistake, it is not free except during the election of members of Parliament; as soon as they are elected, it is a slave, indeed nothing. In the short moments of its liberty, the use it makes thereof deserves that it shall be lost.

That state of affairs, as we have seen, has passed away, and all representative assemblies are tethered to the people by thousands of living ties. The connection was weakest in Third-Republic France,

for the lack of parties gave full rein to a personal connection founded upon the changeable opinions and fortunes of individuals and the personal and local favors which the deputy was able to obtain for his constituents. There is in a party an impersonal force and stability, a loyalty, which comes of the belief of each individual member that he is accountable to a large and powerful entity, that he cannot change his mind without the consultation and consent of others. This constitutes the essence of any membership, and it prevents change for narrowly personal reasons. Parties of this kind—of varying quality, however—exist in England, in the United States, in Germany, and in the Fourth Republic in France. This type of association results in fairly continuous accord between the central authority and the members. Sometimes, however, especially in the United States, the impulse from the localities is fictitious, emanating from some interested association which urges the constituents to send special instructions to their members. Examples of this are to be found in the policies for Prohibition, woman suffrage, labor relations, and price control. Thus again we are in the circle of influences which makes the center think with the mind of the localities, and the localities think with the mind of the center. [40]

DISSOLUTION—AND BY-ELECTIONS

LEGISLATURES have a legal term, at the end of which they are dissolved. In the United States Congress, that term is not curtailable by dissolution but is fixed. In England, France, and Weimar Germany, the law permits an earlier dissolution, if necessary, and practice has so far kept the law alive. In England, the quinquennial period is a maximum, but the Crown may dissolve Parliament, and has often done so, before the end is reached. In pre-1946 France the Chamber could be dissolved by the President (with the consent of the Senate),[41] but convention worked against

---

[38] *Gouvernement de Pologne*, Book XV.
[39] *Social Contract*, Book III, Chap. XV.

[40] Cf., at once, the diagram, "The Viscera of the Modern Leviathan," p. 546.
[41] Law of February 24, 1875, article 5.

the practice and the Chamber had, practically, a fixed term of four years. The new dissolution provisions of the Constitution of 1946 are discussed in Chapter 24 on the French cabinet. We are, therefore, concerned with the intentions and effects of dissolution in England and Germany and the causes and effects of the convention which grew up in France.

England. In England the right of dissolution lies with the Crown. In earlier times it was used by the Crown to get rid of an uncongenial Parliament at a moment favorable to its own friends' prospects of success. But with the democratization of the constitution and the rise of the convention that the cabinet requires the confidence of the House of Commons, it naturally happened that the initiative in this matter passed into the hands of the prime minister. Not that the Crown was not in earlier days advised by its ministers, but now the advice is given not in the personal interests of the Crown, but "in the interests of the country." This means, of course, that the party view of the national interest rules. Thus, then, authority to dissolve is located in the cabinet.[42]

By what motives have cabinets been moved, and what is the generally expected rule of dissolution, which will govern the advice tendered to the Crown? The history of the nineteenth century shows that on one occasion only did a Parliament run its full seven years: the Parliament of 1867-73, when the Liberals, led by Gladstone, had a large and homogeneous majority[43] gathered from among the new voters by going "on the stump." Before this Parliament, parties were either so evenly divided after elections, or so cut across and heterogeneous, through religious issues and sudden foreign contingencies or by the protectionist—free-trade struggle, that frequent changes of ministry occurred without, however, adding any strength to the new government. So great was the need to end parliamentary stagna-

tion, and the uncertainty of balanced opinion, that both parties agreed upon dissolution.[44] Majorities and minorities of less than a score of votes marked this time, their composition being different on each division. And after the Parliament of 1867-73 the serenity of majorities was troubled by a new difficulty: the parties were split by Irish Home Rule and Coercion, and the House rejoiced in a solid block of some sixty Home Rulers who derided the calm and stability of English politics. The impasse of 1885 could be escaped only by an understanding between the Liberals and Conservatives to dissolve. A year later it was necessary to consult the country, for the Liberal Unionists went over to the Conservatives to defeat the Home Rule Bill. A fairly long parliament was the result, during which the Liberal opposition was excogitating the Newcastle program and the Conservatives strangled Ireland. The election of 1892 gave the Liberals a majority only with the help of the Irish; it could not last and was defeated on a minor matter of supply. In 1895 another election occurred, and a seven-years' Parliament followed the Conservative successes.

The "khaki election" of 1901 was fought on the Boer War issue. The Conservatives obtained an enormous majority. The Balfour cabinet succeeded to the boredom which is the aftermath of war excitement, when victory has to be paid for, and it was smitten with intestine strife when Chamberlain began his tariff reform movement. Prominent members, including Chamberlain, resigned from the cabinet. The issue of Chinese labor and the Taff-Vale judgment arose. By-elections were disastrous.[45] Irish troubles beset a government which could neither leave Ireland nor crush her, and in December, 1905, two years before it was legally necessary, Mr. Balfour resigned. The govern-

---

[42] This subject is treated further, and from a slightly different angle, in Chapter 23 on the British cabinet.

[43] A majority of 120. T. E. May, *Constitutional History* (London, 1912), Vol. III, p. 73.

[44] E.g., in July, 1852, after Palmerston's exit from the weak Russell government. Cf. Spencer Walpole, *Life of Lord John Russell* (London, 1889), Vols. II, XXII, and XXIII.

[45] Cf. J. A. Spender, *Life of Sir Henry Campbell-Bannerman* (London, 1923), Vol. II, Chap. XXV.

ment felt that it was not wanted, that its mandate had been outstayed. What is of even more importance than these events and doctrine was the fact that Balfour, faced with a new policy of a rather fundamental kind, had declared that it would be neither possible, nor right, for the government to adopt any system of fiscal reform unless it had first been submitted to the country.[46] Resignation was one way of clearing up the internal difficulties of the party.

The next dissolutions of interest were those of 1910, in January and December. They were deliberate invocations of the electorate to decide upon two issues, the social and fiscal reforms of Lloyd George, and the consequent reform of the House of Lords. In 1918, after the Armistice, a dissolution took place; Parliament had sat since 1910, through the war, and Mr. Lloyd George now sought a mandate for his policy of peace and reconstruction. Four years afterwards, in 1922, the coalition government dissolved owing to the difficulties of continued cooperation between the Conservative and Liberal elements of the cabinet, neither side feeling satisfied with its share in making policy. A Conservative majority followed, but in 1923, the question of Protection becoming once more acute as a remedy for unemployment, Mr. Baldwin resigned on the ground that so great a reform ought not to take place when his predecessor, Bonar Law, had given a pledge against it at the election.[47]

Then began a period of parliamentary difficulty. The Labour party, which had been a third party, suddenly developed great electoral and parliamentary strength, while the Liberal party did not disappear. No single party then obtained a clear majority over the other two. The Liberals helped the Labour party to overturn the Conservatives, and did not vote the Labour party out of office until nearly a year had elapsed. When the inevitable defeat occurred, the question arose, "In such a state of parties what is the rule for disso-

lution?" When there is no certainty that a majority government is attainable, ought the minority in office to advise the Crown to dissolve in order to escape from parliamentary difficulties and perhaps improve its electoral position? The vista of a long and indecisive series of elections at short and disturbing intervals appeared. The ostensible question revolved around the position of the Crown: could it reject the advice given by the cabinet of the day? In its proper place we discuss that aspect of the problem, but the real question was: what rule should guide the party in advising dissolution?

Again, when in August, 1931, through the defection of Mr. Ramsay MacDonald, the Labour prime minister, a coalition government, so-called "National," of Conservatives, Labour, and Liberal members were formed, they found themselves in difficulties of conscience and interest, though they had made a so-called "agreement to differ." The free trade *versus* protection issue, with the latter as a conservative principle for trade revival and device for balancing the budget by tariff receipts, destroyed the agreement and aggravated differences. It was, therefore, decided to dissolve and seek from the electorate a "doctor's mandate," that is, governmental latitude to find a policy and some condonation of the coalition.

History gives no precise authoritative answer, but, as we have seen, it tells us in what circumstances dissolution was thought advisable. Those circumstances are:

(1) When the position of parties is such as to produce deadlock, preventing legislation which any party liable to be called on to be a government conceives necessary, or when criticism of the administration is so emphatic that the government can no longer preserve its dignity.

(2) When a government sees convincing signs that it is no longer trusted by the country or is unsure of its authority and following.

(3) When a policy of fundamental importance is newly evolved and there has yet been no opportunity of plainly consulting the country upon it.

The psychology of average members of

[46] J. A. Spender, *op. cit.*, Vol. II, p. 168. Cf. also Sir Almeric Fitzroy, *Memoirs* (London, 1925), Vol. II.
[47] See p. 137 above.

Parliament indicates the effect of a threatened dissolution. It throws them all into a state of frightened self-inquiry which is followed by a tightening of party discipline. If the opposition is sanguine of its chances at the next election, it closes its ranks and becomes less yielding. If its chances are weak, the threat of a dissolution—which need not be actually made, for it is known by all that such must occur upon any first-class defeat of the government—will cause it to search its mind once more and, as with the Liberal party in recent years, to yield more than it would do in independence. As for the followers of the government, the threat of dissolution is a means of consolidating them in support of the cabinet—for to expose one's own party to the risk of overthrow, to surrender one's own seat, and to invite the anxiety and expense of fighting to regain it, to take the risk that the other side's policies may be triumphant, is more than most members will do. Dissolution thus throws power into the hands of the leaders, for they are in the best position to ascertain when it will be most advantageous to their side, and they are able to decree that electoral aid shall be given or refused to a candidate in proportion as he has served his party well.

Weimar Germany. The German constitution of 1919 contained a clause (article 52) empowering the *Reich* President to dissolve the *Reichstag,* but only once for the same cause. What did this mean? The spirit of the Constitution was strongly democratic. Now the experience of France influenced Germany very powerfully—but by its pathological qualities. The Germans were anxious to avoid the evils inherent in French parliamentarism. Therefore, in giving the cabinet large powers, safeguards were created against developments like the barren and even harmful activity of the French Chambers. The referendum and the initiative were introduced. So, also, was a President, elected directly by the people to act as a counterweight to the *Reichstag.* The instrument of his power in this particular respect was the power of dissolution. At once difficulties arose; was the cabinet to countersign the order for dissolution, or

not? If this was affirmed, then the cabinet would have at least as much authority to order a dissolution as the President, and, then, the President's power would be smaller than the Conservatives, and even the Liberals and some Social Democrats would have the power to intervene, and the center of political gravity would be shifted from the political parties to a single person—a proposition unacceptable to the majority of the Assembly. Although popular election of the President reduced the opposition to his independent power of dissolution, ministerial responsibility was adopted. The result, then, was that the President might declare himself dissatisfied with the parliamentary situation and suggest to the cabinet the desirability of a dissolution; or he might refuse a dissolution asked for by the chancellor. The first case never arose in practice. The second did. Ministers might desire a dissolution and could resign in order to get it—but they could be successful in their demand only if the President could not find another practicable set of ministers. This might easily occur owing to the large number of parties, and the size of the extremes who might join in overturning a government but could not cooperate in a new one. In fact, not all cabinets which threatened dissolution were able to secure it. It was granted them on three occasions of parliamentary impasse. It was also refused by President Hindenburg, who preferred to urge the cabinet to continue in office and carry through its less controversial business. Let us consider (1) the circumstances in which it was conceived dissolution was appropriate; and (2) those in which it has already been used.

The first occasion was in March, 1924. The Marx cabinet was based upon a coalition of the middle parties (Democrats, Center Popular party, Bavarian People's party, and two ministers not in the *Reichstag*). These together mustered about 189 members; and the potential opposition was, therefore, 270 members. The German Nationalists with 71, the Social Democrats with 102, and the Independent Social Democrats with 84, could, between them, overturn the cabinet at any time. The government, therefore, lived on sufferance. This was already the eighth government since the elections of June 1, 1920. One had fallen owing to the London ultimatum; another fell through its own internal weakness and the impossibility of forcing the German People's party to coalesce with it; the irruption into the Ruhr caused a reorganization; a sixth fell when this combination failed to survive the antipathies of the coalition parties; and the seventh shattered upon the difficulties between the *Reich*, Bavaria, and Saxony. And now the minority government expressed the desire that certain decrees based upon the Emergency Powers Acts (October and December, 1923) should be continued. It was folly, however, to create a new ministerial crisis which would produce a fresh ministry when the general elections were only three months away. Perhaps the elections would settle the question? They did not. The parties came back as ill-assorted and each as weak as before. Within six months it was found to be impossible either to maintain the existing government (the Marx coalition as before) or to found a ministry with any better prospects of life. In October, 1924, therefore, the *Reichstag* was dissolved again. In July, 1930, the Brüning government, a coalition of minority parties, dissolved in face of a coalition of extremes.

The object of the dissolutions was clear and laudable. Parliament was impotent, and it was believed that reference to the electorate would produce a shift of votes sufficient to break the deadlock. Doubtless if there were numerous general elections the disturbance would in time produce a pre-parliamentary coalition of parties or voters and thus provide stability for the government.[48] The parties and the people would be continually faced with the problem of instability in government caused by small, numerous, and irreconcilable parties, and the question would arise: why not sink your minor differences for the sake of good government? Germany might have learned the proper lesson that the power

of dissolution is a wholesome and necessary one if Parliament is to learn a proper dependence upon the people.

But disaster to democracy in Germany, from the parliamentary coalition of the extremes—Nazis, Conservatives, and Communists—overwhelmed the experiment in dissolutions. Brüning, after two years of masterly balancing of Center and Social Democrats and casual allies against the extremes, was pushed out by President Hindenburg, who, persuaded thereto by his Junker friends, used his power of withdrawing his confidence from the chancellor and asked Brüning to resign, May 29, 1932. He acceded. The new "barons'" cabinet advised Hindenburg to dissolve: he did, and the July elections were held in a quasi-terroristic uproar. The President continued the barons in office as he had once supported Brüning. Without a standing in the *Reichstag*—for the elections were still unable to appease and unite the contenders for power—the new chancellor, von Papen, was given a blank dissolution order by the President to use when he thought fit—it was to be a weapon against the Nazis, now on the threshold of power and afraid of dissolution lest their strength be reduced. The von Papen government received a vote of "no confidence," 512 to 42, and, remaining in office, dissolved the *Reichstag*. The next elections took place in November, 1932. The electoral returns left the *Reichstag* still so divided as to be impotent. A Hitler government followed in January, 1933; and then came the dissolution, granted February 28, 1933. This was accompanied by the use of article 48 of the constitution to suspend the constitutional rights of civil liberty and political-electoral freedom. The dreadful part played by an overstrong Presidential counterbalance to the cabinet may be pondered, and ought not be repeated.[49]

---

[48] Such as that attempted by the German Democratic party and a number of small groups in the election of 1930—they formed the *Staatspartei*.

[49] Perhaps the new constitution of Bavaria, October, 1946 (under American occupation) foreshadows a move away from an executive divided into rival cabinet and President. There is no separately elected President but only a Minister-President—that is, a Prime Minister—and he is elected by the legislature. Dissolution of the *Landtag* is possible only (1) by majority decision of its own members;

France. In France, the constitution of 1875 [50] gave the President, with the assent of the Senate, power to dissolve the Chamber of Deputies. The debates of the National Assembly show that this body (which was strongly monarchical) was mainly influenced by the desire to give the Presidency, which they had designed as nearly as they could to be the niche for a king, a weapon of defense against encroachment by parliament. Prévost Paradol in his *La France Nouvelle,*[51] which had a great deal of influence upon the more thoughtful members of the Assembly, had argued that the greatest peril to liberty and order in parliamentary government was a discordance between the constituted authorities and public opinion. In a country with a ministry based upon parliament and the people, this danger was produced by the gradual or sudden loss of support, and the stubborn retention of office, by the ministry. Dissolution and new elections are the only sound remedies. Could you give this power to a president who was himself elected by a party? Dependent upon its friendship after his term, his sense of duty would hardly be strong enough to force it to the country. "It is to count too much on the idea of duty. It is to demand too much out of pure love for the public good, and when institutions sin by this noble excess, human weakness has its revenge by leaving them unused or destroying them.[52] The power of dissolution may well be given to a king who stands above parties and has an independent love of his country. It is useless to give it to the cabinet, for this will never utilize the power against itself or its followers. But a king supported by an upper chamber could, with public advantage, exercise such a power.

We must observe that Prévost Paradol

imagined no other case than the loss by the majority of its support in the country. But he did arrive at an inkling of what has actually become the stumbling block of French parliamentary life: too many parties, violent intransigeance, a surplus of personal advertisement, an excess of histrionic tactics—factors which have not only deprived the parliamentary majority of social support in the country, but have prevented a stable majority with an appetite and ability for work from ever coming into existence. The National Assembly followed Prévost Paradol and its own desire to strengthen the executive and vested the right of dissolution in the President, with the consent of the Senate.

The right was used once, in circumstances so unfortunate as to cause the destruction of the power. The Chamber of Deputies of March 8, 1876, contained a large republican majority. Marshal MacMahon, monarchist, elected President by the monarchist National Assembly upon the fall of Thiers, sought to overcome the anticlerical and republican impulses of the Chamber. He caused the resignation of Jules Simon on the *Seize Mai* ("the sixteenth of May," 1877), and, faced with an exceedingly restive Parliament, asked the Senate to support a dissolution. By a small majority (149 to 130), and after grave debate, consent was granted, and this in a Senate one quarter full of life members appointed by the monarchist Assembly. A constitutional right had been used in an unconstitutional spirit, not in order to serve the electorate but directly to thwart it.

The power to dissolve fell into disrepute, and has never since been used. France has seriously suffered in consequence. As Leyret has put it: *"Le Parlément est tout: la nation n'est rien."* [53]

Discussion of the question in pre-1945 France proceeded, however, on rather unreal lines: as part of the theory of the separation of powers. It assumed that liberty cannot be secured unless powers are separated. If, therefore, the Chamber attempts to control too much, and thus in-

(2) by popular recall on petition of one million citizens; or (3) when a Minister-President has resigned or died and the *Landtag* has not elected another within four weeks, in which case its own presiding officer must dissolve it. (See articles 18 and 44.) Cf. R. G. Neumann, "New Constitutions in Germany," *American Political Science Review,* June, 1948.
[50] Law, February 25, 1875, article 5.
[51] (Paris, 1869), pp. 143-47.
[52] *Ibid.,* p. 144.

[53] Henri Leyret, *Le Président de la République* (Paris, 1935), p. 196.

fringes the rule of separation, the power of dissolution is required to free the executive from encroachment. But such matters ought rather to be judged by their direct results than as a corollary of a general proposition in government. The fact, radical and striking, is that no cabinet in France until the constitution of 1946 had the power to counterattack an insurgent Assembly. The members could and therefore did allow themselves all liberties until the proximity of an election. They wasted time, overturned ministries, staged interpellations, and, as Faguet has said, labored without accomplishment. It is not the cabinet which was so much at fault (as Prévost Paradol calculated) but Parliament; the executive needed defense, but never so much as the country itself. Though a government might be busy with the most urgent affairs, its work could be stopped by an interpellation, for the interpellation was a threat to its existence. Nor could it, by making the subject a question of confidence, permanently quash the interpellation and frighten the errant deputy by the thought that the cabinet would fall and crush him as well as them. If the Commission on the Budget played with the finance bill all the year round, the cabinet could not reduce it to order. If its program was disturbed by purely obstructive amendments and discussion, it was forced either to sit by (vociferous, or sighing, but idle) or to resign—which is exactly what the attacking aspirants for office wished. There was no power to secure the working strength of the government, or the correspondence between public opinion and parliamentary activities.

It must not be forgotten that the power to dissolve was less employable because of the part the Senate was required to play in it. Though the Senate had few enemies, it was barely tolerated, for its powers were considerable, and its emanation from popular election, although by an indirect route, gave it a conceit of which the Deputies were jealous.

The Significance of Dissolution. To 1934 the true importance of dissolution was misunderstood by French thinkers. Professor Redslob's then current views [54] were these:

To dissolve is to demand arbitration by the people between the ministry and the Assembly: but arbitration is possible only as between two equal subjects, not between subjects of unequal strength, and the Chamber is necessarily weaker because it has to be destroyed before the arbitration can take place; that is, the ministry is stronger, and is for a short time even free from the competition of its rival. To destroy the Chamber is an act of authority: only a strong institution can do it. But the President is a weak institution, derived as it is from Parliamentary election. Hence there cannot be a dissolution, especially since the cabinet is itself appointed by this weak institution.

The whole attitude is erroneous. The principal fallacy resides in the notion of arbitration and the assumption that equality is necessary for it. Even if this were right—which it is not—this has no application to the case considered. The real issue is between an appeal to the people to remedy internal conditions in the Chamber, or omitting it, to leave the Chamber free for the display of disorganized and incoherent animosities. If the latter is preferred, and it has been since 1876, then the cause is no solemn nonsense about arbitration and its supposed nature, but that the Chamber and the government knew and know that the people do not care enough about regular and systematic government to support either the one or the other in any action they may take. The Chamber is still regarded with cynicism, the ministry with suspicion, the President with humor. The causes are the experience of former régimes and national character. In 1934 it was vainly attempted to revive the power of dissolution; in 1945 the new constitution contained a qualified power to dissolve. The subject is considered further, below.[55]

In England dissolution is permitted because all are convinced that, whatever party governs, there must be government. Deadlock and verbal contests are insufficient as fruits of parliamentary endeavor. They must be ended by an appeal

---

[54] *Le Régime Parlementaire* (Paris, 1924).
[55] Chap. 24, below.

to the people, which it is better that the government should make than that it should not be made at all. Though it pains the government and members of Parliament to give up office and a seat in the House, these are felt to be necessary and proper, if reluctant and belated, sacrifices. What Chamber of Deputies or French cabinet has, since the rise of the French Republic, been imbued with such a spirit? Has even the new National Assembly? No French President can do what these bodies are unwilling to do. That which has obstructed good party organization is equally the cause of this—a lack of practical governing sense in the people, which is content to do without results in action and behavior, but to "unpack its heart with words" and gestures. It is true that the British Crown, by its hereditary position, presents, in a dissolution, an appearance of impartiality and national concern which is not reproducible in France where the chief of state is elected—but this is not why dissolution is possible in England and impossible in France. All these institutions are founded on the national character, and Redslob only begins to touch the problem at the close of his discourse, when he says: "Finally, the current of opinion hostile to the executive which characterizes France and derives from the vicissitudes of its history does not exist in England." [56] The question is not really one between chief of state and Parliament, but between Parliament and the cabinet. It is whether the cabinet shall have the right to challenge a fractious parliament, and say, "Now consider well: is your attitude dictated by personal considerations or by considerations of benefit to the state; are you thinking of yourselves or of your constituency? Compare and choose! If you choose to overturn us, you

must answer to the people for it!" This often gives the cabinet a coercive power over its followers and the opposition; but government is not perfect. The problem receives further attention in Part V on *Cabinets and Chiefs of State.* Let us add that Redslob's doctrine influenced Preusz in his drafting of the German constitution of 1919.

By-elections. When sitting members die or retire, an election is held in the district concerned, though not for the United States Senate—and not where P.R. prevails, for there, usually, the member's party appoints to the vacancy. In Britain the by-election is regarded as an important indication of the popular will. Despite the fact that in the vast majority of cases the same party is victorious (and despite statistical studies [57] to show that this has been so in the past), British parties do not know for certain that they will win. Therefore, past figures notwithstanding, the government and the opposition are very excited, attach considerable significance to the election, and scan the slightest change in the voting figures for signs of the times. Did more voters come out? What issue most stirred them? What arguments were circulated about the contest? How did the results for the contestants compare with those at the general election?

Thus mandates, and the frequency and dissolution of legislatures, formally maintain the correspondence between people and legislature. But we are not yet free to observe how legislatures use their powers, for they themselves are not organized upon the simple basis of one chamber, but for various reasons and from diverse causes are divided into two. We must, therefore, pause for an inquiry into bicameral arrangements, and having discovered how power is divided between the assemblies, we then can proceed to a discussion of the procedure and activities of the more popular chamber.

---

[56] Robert Redslob, *Le Régime Parlémentaire*, p. 181. Both Esmein (*op. cit.*, Vol. II, p. 180 ff.) and Duguit (*op. cit.*, Vol. IV, p. 572 ff.) incline away from the treatment of the subject as a branch of the separation of powers (i.e., the right of dissolution as a defense of the executive) and recognize the importance of the right of dissolution as an instrument for clearing away difficulties in the Chamber of Deputies and in the relations between this and the cabinet.

[57] J. K. Pollock, "British By-elections Between the Wars," *American Political Science Review*, June, 1941. The student is invited to consult the British press on the Gravesend election of December, 1947.

18

Second Chambers

ORIGINS

WE must distinguish. Legislatures are bicameral for two broad and different reasons: as part of federalism, and as the result of a desire to check the popular principle in the constitution. This does not mean that in federal states the second chamber was designed only to represent the states. If we take the records of the constitutional conventions as evidence, it is likely that there would have been some sort of second chamber, even if it were not required by the federal principle. There is not absent from the United States Senate and the German *Reichsrat* of Weimar the intention or spirit of a curb.

A Multitude of Counselors. If, then, we contemplate the history of government, we find that two basic motives have contributed to the establishment of bicameral systems. The first is, perhaps, the more universal, and is likely to be the more enduring. Most human beings desire a multitude of counselors and all the advice they can obtain: whether from self-doubt, the fear of taking responsibility and the desire to absolve themselves from blame if matters go awry, or from the wish to repair their lack of knowledge or judgment. It is not that others need to be convinced, but that the mind is clarified by talking out, which implies thinking out the issue. Indeed, for most people, to talk is the only way to think. This tendency will be found everywhere operative and particularly in proportion to

the gravity of the object: in cases of real urgency, such as dangerous illness, the number of counselors is limited only by the resources at the patient's disposal. It is not a question of courage or fear to innovate, but a sound sense of self-preservation, which leads men to take counsel before proceeding: it is not merely a question of *whether* but of *how* to act. Generally, then, men are circumspect, especially in acts of government, whose burden is heavy and difficult to reverse, and therefore they establish institutions which compel judgments to be deliberate. They establish delays and adjournments, notices of resolution, and a multitude of advisory bodies. But in affairs of state the result of any resolution is widespread: hence even greater care to prevent abuses of power. Further, deliberation and solemnity strengthen the prospects of obedience and acceptance. They seem to have exhausted the possibilities of error and of the arbitrary, and assume the air of the inevitable, the decree of nature, and, since it is useless to rebel against nature, adaptation is the only road to relief. These motives are the constant and essential nucleus of most arguments in favor of more deliberation—or in other words, a second chamber. But the phrases in which arguments are couched are usually less conscious, more conventional, and often more picturesque.

The Defense of Possessions. Secondly, quite apart from the need for mature deliberation, second chambers have come into existence for the same reason as so many other institutions: those who have power and possessions create all possible barricades to prevent their loss. Revolution is not the only movement of the human spirit to produce barricades: conservatism has produced more. Indeed, all second chambers have been instituted, and are maintained, not from disinterested love of mature deliberation, but because there is something their makers wished to defend against the rest of the community, especially inherited possessions and status. It is not always difficult to trace this motive to its sources and channels. The diminution of social inequality, and the downfall of social monopolies, may in time cause the disappearance of this protectiveness, but the spontaneous desire for careful unhurried deliberation in a vast complex society will not easily fade or lose its need for institutional embodiment, particularly as the community's functions expand through the state. The final question is, what form ought this best take?

We are concerned with the British House of Lords, the United States Senate, and the French Senate. The German *Reichsrat* has been discussed already.[1] We shall consider, first, the general conditions of their origin, and second, their composition, power, and political effect.

Origins in England. The House of Lords came into existence in the first blithe unconsciousness of political development.[2] It was perfectly natural for conquerors and the owners of large estates to give counsel to the Crown—natural, too, for the learned and propertied ecclesiastics to form part of the empowered circle of the great council. Soon the lesser property owners were excluded and, individually insignificant barons that they were, relegated to a class below the peers. The magnates even compelled the Crown to accept them as participators in government, on the basis of a right inherent in their position and not created by the Crown. They obtained safeguards against

the king's own judges in the institution of *judicium parium*, judgment by peers, which extended beyond the confines of law into the legislative acts of Parliament —the distinction in the fourteenth and fifteenth centuries being not yet as clear as it became when Parliament had become a body representative against, rather than a council with, the king. We cannot enter into the rights and wrongs of the learned controversies regarding origins. All we need to know is what all scholars accept; namely, that feudal land tenure, the hereditary principle, and peerage, a complex of political and legal privileges, became indissolubly associated, and associated by the forceful pressure of landed proprietors and their descendants.

It is interesting to observe that until Parliament had evolved so as to become a potential challenge to the king's will, and an independent source of authority, the magnates preferred to stay at home, "lording it" in their territories. They had the estates; and to prevent their undue conversion into royal revenue was a virtue. Further, a power threatened is a power which arms. So when the Crown found itself surrounded by a customary circle of peers outside of whom convention dictated that none others should be summoned, it (Richard II, *circa* 1380) began the practice, which has had such remarkable effects in recent generations, of creating peers by letters patent. The presentation of estates (or a title indicating estates) followed in keeping with the ancient association.

Lastly, the House of Lords came to be founded not only upon the hereditary principle, but upon a particular application of this principle: of primogeniture. For this principle preserved the size of estates and had become a cherished rule of succession. Here, then, in this branch of the council were concentrated lords territorial and hereditary, lords created and hereditary, and lords spiritual but not hereditary. At first Commons and Lords met in common council. Towards the end of the fourteenth century, burgesses and knights drew more definitely and continuously together as one body, consulted

[1] Cf. Chap. 11 above.
[2] Cf. A. F. Pollard, *The Evolution of Parliament* (London, 1922); J. A. Jolliffe, *Medieval Constitutional History* (Oxford, 1938).

and acted in common, and separately, in a special place: the king, the lords, the chancellor and judges remaining, as it were, as a single body in possession. Little by little, two houses emerged in one Parliament, each with its own characteristic and now familiar offices and body of usages, while individual petitions requiring the judgment of Parliament as a high court had changed into general petitions. But general petitions are politics, and their result is law, for more clearly they represent the demands of one part of the population upon the rest.

This division into two houses was, then, the simple result of (1) the appropriation of governmental authority by those who possessed economic power and the prestige of conquest and social leadership and (2) the unavoidable consultation of representatives of the rest of the population, since the threat of unrest and fiscal resistance was ever emergent. The division was a division of interests, as the articles of Magna Carta show, and not the consequence of a desire for mature deliberation and a check upon a tumultuous and self-willed democratic assembly. That came later, much later, in the middle of the nineteenth century, when a powerful and self-conscious democracy began to ask the question *quo warranto?* of a House of Lords founded upon every sort of title except democratic functional utility.[3]

Origins in the United States. The modern political theory of a second chamber was, in fact, first developed by American statesmen in the convention of 1787, and is to be found in its *Records,* and, more systematically, in the *Federalist.* The convention was impelled toward the establishment of the Senate not only by the necessities of federalism, but by the practical and immediate fear of tumultuous democracy which, in the few years since the end of English rule in 1776, had acted very intemperately. Nearly all speakers who discussed the topic did so with reference to events in the states. McHenry of Maryland, for example, said: [4]

Our chief danger arises from the democratic parts of our constitutions. It is a maxim which I hold incontrovertible, that the power of government exercised by the people swallows up the other branch. None of the constitutions have provided sufficient checks against the democracy. The feeble Senate of Virginia is a phantom. Maryland has a more powerful Senate, but the late distractions in that State have discovered that it is not powerful enough. The check established in the constitution of New York and Massachusetts is yet a stronger barrier against democracy, but they all seem insufficient.

Madison took a large part in the debates relating to the Senate. The ends of a second chamber according to him were: (1) the defense of the people against their rulers—which might be secured by a "division of the Senate between different bodies of men, who might watch and check each other," and (2) the protection of themselves against their own transient impressions. The latter end was important since temporary errors were liable to result from *(a)* want of information as to their true interest, this being shared by representatives who were elected for only a short term and occupied, perhaps, with other affairs, and *(b)* fickleness and passion in themselves and a numerous representative body. Therefore, a fence was required, and this must be a body, enlightened, of limited number, and with the "firmness seasonably to interpose against impetuous counsels." [5]

Madison's thought, however, reached further than this. Liberty means the development of diversity. The constitution was designed to secure liberty. Then, said Madison, different interests may clash, for in all civilized countries the people fall into different classes having a real or supposed difference of interests.

We need not pursue the topic to the point of exhaustion. Members were agreed on these general principles.[6] The only

---

[3] Cf. Pinckney's analysis of the English constitution in the American Federal Convention, in Max Farrand, *Records of the Federal Convention* (New Haven, 1911), 3 vols., Vol. I, p. 410.

[4] *Ibid.,* Vol. I, pp. 26-27.
[5] *Ibid.,* Vol. I, p. 422.
[6] Sherman: "steadiness and wisdom"; Gerry: "stability of efficacy" of government; Mason:

controversy was regarding the composition of this assembly: its selection, the age of its members, its duration, and so on. After discussing the changes that might come in the course of time, Madison held that nine years were not too long; and it should come so late in life that the senator would not mind on public or private grounds if he were not re-elected. The opposition to a Senate of long duration was "that it might by gradual encroachments prolong itself first into a body for life, and finally become a hereditary one," [7] and that long separation from constituents would cause "attachments different from that of the State." [8] But Hamilton's plan went furthest. In that famous intervention in debate which earned him the credit of being a monarchist, he scornfully rejected Randolph's proposition that a Senate of seven years was enough.[9] Could it save the few against the many, or the many against the few? No. Neither had a defense. But observe the British House of Lords!

It is a most noble institution. Having nothing to hope for by a change, and a sufficient interest by means of their property in being faithful to the National interest, they form a permanent barrier against every pernicious innovation,[10] whether attempted on the part of the Crown or of the Commons. Gentlemen differ in their opinion concerning the necessary checks, from the different estimate they form of the human passions. They suppose seven years a sufficient period to give the Senate an adequate firmness, from not duly considering the amazing violence and turbulence of the democratic spirit.

Did not the experience of the New England states prove that popular passion spread like wildfire and became irresistible? . . . etc., etc. . . . . "What is the inference

from all these observations? That we ought to go as far in order to attain stability and permanency as republican principles will admit." How far? "Let one branch of the Legislature hold their places for life, or at least during good behavior. Let the Executive also be for life." Indeed, this would have produced what was claimed for it—a permanent will, a weighty interest! His suggestion was, then, a Senate of persons elected to serve during good behavior; election to be indirect. A later edition of the suggestion required that candidates should have an estate in land.[11]

In the *Federalist* [12] the Senate was defended. The age of thirty was proper since the Senator's duties required a "greater extent of information and stability of character." Choice by the state legislature constituted "a select appointment." The number would always be far smaller (two from each state) than the House of Representatives: this would counter "the propensity of all single and numerous bodies to yield to the impulse of sudden and violent passions, and so be seduced by factious leaders into intemperate and pernicious resolutions." A long duration (nine years) would promote "great firmness." A bicameral system doubles the security to the people against schemes of "usurpation or perfidy" where the ambition or corruption of one would otherwise be sufficient. A due acquaintance with the objects and principles of legislation is not to be expected from people called from pursuits of a private nature, and in office only for a short time. Recent experience showed this. A rapid succession of new members of Congress would cause "mutability in public councils"; but change of opinions and measures is desirable only in a temperate form. The effects of instability are loss of foreign confidence in the country, uncertainty of the law, opportunities to speculators, and perils to prudent producers, but most important of all is the loss of reverence for governments which are infirm and dis-

"weight and firmness" to "secure the rights of property." Therefore, also, a qualification of property should be annexed to the office.
[7] Wilson, in Farrand, *op. cit.*, Vol. I, p. 426.
[8] Pinckney, in *ibid.*, Vol. I, p. 430; i.e., distinguishing the states from the federation.
[9] June 18, in *ibid.*, Vol. I, p. 282 ff.
[10] Query: Does this mean that every innovation is pernicious, or did the House reject only innovations which were pernicious?

[11] *Ibid.*, Vol. I, p. 291, and Vol. III, Appendix F.
[12] Essays LXII and LXIII.

appointing to men's hopes.[13] Further, only a "select and stable" body can become sensible to the opinion as to the qualities of foreign countries—in a small body, it is argued, the praise and blame, pride and consequence of each member are involved. Not so in large bodies. Moreover, the longer the tenure, the keener the sense of responsibility for long-period plans, like a "succession of well-chosen and well-connected measures which have a gradual and perhaps unobserved operation." Only those enjoying the result will care to create its possibility and watch for its advent with concern.

Origins in France. In France the fury of the revolution against inequalities of all sorts, and the burning, reckless belief in popular sovereignty, overcame both the wishes of some of the *cahiers* and the theories of Delolme and Montesquieu, which suggested a bicameral system of commons and lords. The ideology of Rousseau was accepted as a true description of the facts of the time: the constituent assembly accepted the argument that sovereignty was indivisible and the nation was sovereign, and hence that its representative body could not but be one.

This pedantic eloquence was the necessary consequence of two causes: the need of the revolutionaries to prove that sovereignty lay with the people, and their need to deny the inequality of men.[14] What possible second chamber could be established save on a basis which admitted that there were natural differences among men? To admit this was to return to the principle of aristocracy, which God forbid! [15] This argument is to be found in Siéyès' classic dilemma: "If the two assemblies agree the second chamber is unnecessary; if they disagree it is obnoxious." [16] It is developed further in the argument of Mathieu de Montmorency, thus: [17]

If the two chambers have the like composition, one of them becomes useless, because it can no longer be anything other than a body necessarily always influenced by the other. If the composition is not the same and the idea of a Senate is adopted, it will establish aristocracy and will lead to the subjection of the people.

A second-chamber system was suggested by Lally-Tollendal, with the already familiar arguments: that it stops too-hasty decisions; that a single body would be amenable to nonparliamentary influence; that a senate of elders adds wisdom to decisions, that two chambers in agreement have great authority, especially against popular turbulence. These arguments could not prevail: [18] revolutionists do not want obstructions.

Since Siéyès' dilemma has been accepted so easily by generations of later students, it ought to be demolished: not because a second chamber may be found to be ultimately unnecessary, but because it is one of those phrases which stop thought by stunning the mind. The answer to Siéyès' dilemma is this: "If the two assemblies agree, so much the better for our belief in the wisdom and justice of the law; if they disagree, it is time for the people to reconsider their attitude." Further, he provided otherwise for many checks and balances.

Elemental forces, other than doctrine, swept the members of the constituent assembly along. There was, therefore, no second chamber in 1791. Nor in the constitution of 1793 was a bicameral system established, but to the electoral colleges a right of challenge within forty days was given.[19]

---

[13] "No government, any more than an individual, will long be respected without being truly respectable; nor be truly respectable without possessing a certain portion of order and stability."

[14] Cf. Necker, *Le Pouvoir Éxécutif dans les Grands États* (Paris, 1792), p. 68.

[15] It was argued that nobles were made not by the sovereign people, but by the king who had no right to be sovereign.

[16] Cf. J. H. Clapham, *Abbé Siéyès* (London, 1912), pp. 128-131.

[17] *Archives Parlementaires,* Premier série, VIII, p. 585, also pp. 580-600.

[18] Cf. R. Redslob, *Staatstheorien der Französische National Versammlung* (Leipzig, 1912), p. 178 ff.

[19] Cf. M. Billecard, *De la Mode du Recrutement du Sénat* (thèse, Paris, 1912), p. 24 ff.

The constitution of the Year III showed the result of the terrible experiences through which France had passed and was passing. Terror, intrigues, foreign danger, the dictatorship of the Commune of Paris —of the Mountain—of Robespierre: all pressed the convention toward any port which promised refuge. The experience of America was now invoked. A *"Corps législatif"* was created, of two chambers, the lower, the Council of Five Hundred, and the upper, the Council of the Ancients, numbering two hundred and fifty; the one was the Republic's "inspiration," the other its "reason." [20] The suffrage was already limited,[21] and both bodies emanated from election, one third being renewable each year. The lower house initiated laws and the upper house had the right of rejection when the law could not be represented until a year had elapsed, but the lower house could present another law in which the rejected one appeared as a part. Thus the upper house could provoke amendments. Napoleon dispersed these bodies.[22]

At the Restoration a Chamber of Peers established itself. The Revolution of July broke the hereditary principle: the king nominated to the Chamber from among select groups of notabilities, mainly civil, judicial, and military administrators and the eminent among the great bourgeoisie.[23] This body was so meek that the revolutionists of 1848 did not bother to disperse it; it was said that had they done so they would have flattered it.[24] The constituent assembly of 1848 rejected the bicameral system. The argument on both sides contained nothing new. Were they to return to aristocracy? No. Had the recent experience of notables been satisfying? No. Then 530 against 289 decided for a single body [25] and significantly agreed to (1) a more settled and deliberate form of procedure for the creation of laws,[26] and (2) the short tenure of three years.[27] Further, a Council of State was established, elected by the assembly for six years (renewable), one half every three years. This body was to be consulted by the assembly in its projects for examination previous to discussion.

During the Second Empire a single-chamber National Assembly faced Napoleon III.

We have arrived at the Senate of the Third Republic. What was to be done? France had had a most disastrous constitutional experience. The neatest imported American doctrines had come to nought upon contact with the realities of character and existing social institutions, and seemingly every argument which had been made on the one side or the other in the perennial controversy had at some time been ridiculed by unexpected events. Two chambers had been unsatisfactory; one chamber had been unsatisfactory. The constitution was made, as all constitutions are made, not by the molding power of pure reason so illuminating that all could accept its direction, but by the power of numbers emergent from the immediate action and counteraction of social forces. The vital fact was that about 400 members of a total number of 630 were monarchical, and were determined that if they could not re-establish a monarchy, they must at least set up institutions into which its spirit might return at a propitious date.[28]

As for the composition of the Senate, there were three possibilities: hereditability in certain privileged families; nomination for life by the sovereign either entirely at his discretion or with certain restrictions; or election in a manner differ-

[20] Boissy d'Anglas: *rapporteur:* cited in A. Aulard, *Histoire Politique de la Révolution Française* (Paris, 1901), p. 559.
[21] See L. Duguit and H. Monnier, *Les Constitutions de la France* (Paris, 1930).
[22] Cf. Edmond Blanc, *Napoleon I* (Paris, 1888), Chap. II.
[23] Duguit and Monnier, *op. cit.*, on Law of December 29, replacing article 23 of the *Charte*.
[24] Billecard, *op. cit.*, p. 31.

[25] Constitution of 1848, Chap. IV, article 20.
[26] *Ibid.*, Chap. IV, article 40: a quorum was to be half the membership plus one; article 41: three deliberations at intervals of at least five days for the valid making of a law.
[27] *Ibid.*, Chap. IV, article 31.
[28] Cf. Gabriel Hanotaux, *Histoire Contemporaine de la France* (Paris, 1913), Vol. I, Chap. I (for figures quoted) and Vol. II, Chap. IX.

ent from that of the lower house. The democratic state could not accept the first; the second could not be recommended since it would not have the necessary authority, and it implied a monarchy. Election was left; and, in Prévost Paradol's opinion, it was good that this should be based on the local governing bodies. Supposing these (the *Conseils Généraux*) elected 250 members, the intelligence, the knowledge, the substantial position, and their conservative spirit would produce a first-class body of the type needed. Election for life would cut them off from touch with public opinion; hence election for ten years should be adopted. Since the chamber might well have 300 members, the remaining 50 seats could be given as of right to certain high civil and military officers. Thus, then, a place would be made for men useful to the state but not able or willing to run the chances of election to the lower chamber.

The Senate was established, by the first of the constitutional laws of 1875, as a carefully concocted compromise between the parties of the Left, which were in a minority, and the parties of the Center and Right (excluding the extreme Right), brought about by a series of subtle maneuvers. Although it was not the institution the monarchists would have liked to get, its very existence was compelled by their numbers in the Assembly, and, although the Republicans of the Center and the Left had obtained concessions and had good reason to be satisfied that their tactics had averted a Chamber of Peers, yet the Senate was not in keeping with their philosophy.

Let us consider the composition of the Senate down to its supersession in 1946 by the Council of the Republic. To 1884 it had 300 members, of which 225 were elected by the *départements,* and 75 by the National Assembly. The age qualification was forty. The elected senators in each department were elected by a body thus composed: *(a)* the parliamentary deputies of the department, *(b)* the members of the *Conseil-Général,*[29] *(c)* the

members of the *Conseil d'Arrondissement,*[30] and *(d)* one delegate chosen by each municipal council. Election was for nine years, with triennial renewal. The powers of the Senate were to control ministries, and to initiate and make laws in cooperation with the Chamber of Deputies; but financial bills were to be presented to and voted by the Chamber of Deputies first. Sessions of the Chambers must be simultaneous.[31] Before we consider the consequences of this manner of composition, and the political results of the powers, we must dwell a little upon the later constitutional history of the Senate, for it suffered amendment in 1884, as soon as the Republic was well established and the parties of the Left were strong enough to undertake a revision.

The Left Republicans set out to destroy the life membership of the Senate, and to reduce the overrepresentation of the small communes. By this time most of the Left had rallied to a second chamber, though they desired revision. In the election of 1881, revision played a principal part. The Senate, partially renewed in 1883, gave the Republicans large gains. The Senate was adroitly won by the suggestion of Jules Ferry that the law on the organization of the Senate should be deconstitutionalized, whereby the Senate obtained the assurance that in the future it would not be swamped by the Chamber's superior numbers in a constitutional assembly having for its object an uncongenial change of composition. The composition of the Senate was transferred to an ordinary law. An elected Senator was to replace each deceased life member. Finally, a certain proportionality was established between the communes in the matter of their representation. In 1919 the number of the Senate was increased to 314, as a redistribution of membership among the departments on the occasion of the inclusion of Alsace-Lorraine in the French state.

---

[29] The *Conseil-Général* is the locally-elected local authority of the department.

[30] These are the locally-elected local government authorities in the next smaller area of local government after the department.
[31] Law of July 16, 1875, article 4.

ENGLAND: HOUSE OF LORDS

UNTIL 1832 the existence of the House of Lords raised no critical problems; disputes concerned personal and corporate dignity in relation to the House of Commons. The lower house was, indeed, until toward the end of the eighteenth century the *lower* house, in spite of the convention that its authority over finance was superior. In every aspect of government—legislative, critical of policy, formative of ministries—the House of Lords was superior to the House of Commons.[32] The houses were often in disagreement, but this was merely because alignment of personal and party forces in the two houses did not happen to agree, owing to the results of elections or the ambitions and intrigues of faction and court.

The main difficulty of recent generations, however, did not exist—that is, disagreement between the two houses as units, arising from the diversity of their very composition and character. On the contrary, the social elements which begot the constitution of the eighteenth century enabled the House of Lords, without any strain, to control the House of Commons, for two reasons: the personal position of the aristocracy, and the lack of constitutional challenge. The aristocracy dominated both houses because they acquired dignity (1) from their landed possessions —they possessed much of the territory of England, Scotland, Wales, and Ireland— which gave them the position of local sovereigns and the prestige of wealth; (2) from their ancient standing in many cases; and (3) in all cases, from the ennoblement by the Crown. "The King of England," said Disraeli, enamored of the *jeunesse dorée*, "may make Peers, but he cannot make a House of Lords. The order of men of whom such an assembly is formed is the creation of ages." These had always possessed the superiority in government; neither powerful reason nor force threat-

ened this legacy; hence they continued "naturally" to form ministries, with the occasional adjunct of a great commoner or learned judge. Moreover, a very large proportion of the constituencies of the Commons were in their pockets: [33] they were the all-powerful "bosses," who dispensed local and central patronage, bribed and intimidated the voters, to form their "connections." The House of Commons responded. Hence the real political struggle was hardly between two houses. It was between the inarticulate country and Parliament; and between king and Parliament. And, to come to the second reason why there was no strain between the houses, there was no continuous challenge from the people—at least until the era of reform which began about 1780 and ended its first phase in 1832. There was as yet no economic challenge; Lords and Commons were much of the same class and united by family ties—"cousins." There was a religious challenge, but it was damped down with the tacit and spasmodic connivance of the ignorant and bigoted multitude. There was no widespread sentimental challenge for freedom of opinion and self-government.

By 1832, the forces of an entirely new era had matured; they no longer "pitied the plumage and forgot the dying bird." The struggle over the Reform Act revealed their strength, and ended with the violent defeat of the House of Lords and the adoption of an electoral system for the Commons which was bound to make the House of Lords permanently hostile, continually defensive, and ultimately powerless. The foundations of authority had shifted, and whereas they ever more soundly buttressed the House of Commons, the House of Lords declined into a conscious excrescence. The representative principle continuously renewed, invigorated, and adapted the Commons, which

---

32 Cf. C. H. Firth, *The House of Lords during the Civil War* (London, 1910); A. G. Turberville, *The House of Lords in the Reign of William III* (London, 1913), and *The House of Lords in the Eighteenth Century* (Oxford, 1927).

33 Cf. L. B. Namier, *The Structure of Politics at the Accession of George III* (London, 1929). In Volume 1, pp. 176-81, it is shown that a total of 51 peers nominated members of the lower house (or influenced their election) for 101 seats. Cf. *England in the Age of the American Revolution* (London, 1930) by the same author.

became the rightful bearer of power. That same principle was, and is, a continual reprimand to the House of Lords. It is suffered to exist—suffered, why?

Present Composition. At present (1949) the House of Lords is composed of four classes of members: (1) hereditary peers, about 779; [34] (2) Scottish representative peers (elected for each Parliament), 16, and Irish representative peers (elected for life), 8; (3) archbishops and bishops, 26; (4) ten law lords, or lords of appeal, appointed for life.[35] Class (3) become legislators by virtue simply of professional success in the ranks of the Church of England. They are not excluded from the legislative and executive functions of the House other than religious affairs. They may be said to represent the spiritual and proprietary interest of the Church of England in government, but vast numbers of religious people outside this church receive no representation as such. Class (2), the Scottish and Irish [36] peers, are elected by their fellows, and the peer members of governments have occasionally managed the elections to secure the success of the capable and those likely to support their policy.

Class (1), the hereditary peers, consist of two groups which must be distinguished: the "accidents of an accident" as Bagehot has called them, and those honored for proven or presumed virtue. The first group forms the great bulk of the House of Lords—their rank and title to sit and exercise power arises from the fact that they are the eldest sons of their fathers and mothers. All may, and some do, have the makings of capable legislators; but no test of their aptitude is applied, and even if ability were positively proved, the modern world has rejected the application of ability to government unless it is representative of the interests of those expected to obey the law. With the exception of about a score, these hereditary legislators are usually absent from the proceedings of the House, whose benches are conspicuous by their red-plush vacancy. But the right to attend, speak, and vote exists: and it is used by large numbers when the interests of the country, in the estimation of the party managers, are in danger. We return to this presently. The second group, quite large in recent years, is, in the first generation, composed of those ennobled for political and social services. These services are of three kinds: (a) those securing the benefit of the nation by political office (as in the case of such men as Wellington, Disraeli, Iddesleigh, Sherborne, Rhondda, Asquith, Birkenhead, Banbury, Curzon, Balfour, Beatty, Reading, Ullswater, Samuel, Beveridge); (b) those more immediately benefiting a party, or its organization or finances; (c) charitable works or gifts, or eminence in science and art. Perhaps there should be added to class (2) some, of decent talent and certain loyalty, who are elevated to the peerage because the government of the day needs spokesmen in the Lords or must fill Household appointments: for example, Passfeld (Sidney Webb) in the first Labour government, and nearly a score in 1945-46.

Thus there is no popular—or occupational—elective principle in the composition of the House of Lords. How far the mentality of the House divides according to the main divisions of public opinion is determined only by the interests and the individual mentality of the peers, and, in the case of recent creations, by the party to which the new peer belonged. Of those whose party membership is known, it is computed that some 600 members belong to the Conservative party, between 80 and 100 to the Liberal party, and about 20 to the Labour party.

Beneath their robes of red and ermine, the peers are predominantly an economic interest: they are not so much the representatives of, as they *are*, big private enterprise. Over one third of them are directors (some multiple) of the staple industries of the nation. One third of them

---

[34] Cf. also Debrett's *Peerage, Baronetage, Knightage and Companionage* (London, editions from time to time).

[35] Appellate Jurisdiction Act, 1876.

[36] The 11 Irish peers are the survivors of 26 who were elected for life under the Act of Union of 1801. The Irish Free State Act, 1922, abolished the machinery for electing these peers.

also own very large estates. Many of them are related by marriage, birth, and business connections with Conservative members of the House of Commons.[37] The existence of the House of Lords is a gross anomaly, without justification in this era.

Writing to Gladstone's daughter, Lord Acton said, in 1881 when the Lords opposed the Irish Land Bill [38] (to make tenure less unjust to the tenants):

But a corporation, according to a profound saying, has neither body to kick nor soul to save. The principle of self-interest is sure to tell upon it. The House of Lords feels a stronger duty toward its eldest sons than towards the masses of ignorant, vulgar, and greedy people. Therefore, except under very perceptible pressure, it always resists measures aimed at doing good to the poor. It has almost always been in the wrong—sometimes from prejudice and fear and miscalculation, still oftener from instinct and self-preservation.

The Power of the House of Lords. The House of Lords had, until the Parliament Act of 1911, four branches of power: judicial, legislative, financial, and executive. We cannot here treat of the first, the judicial, except to say that the House is the supreme court of appeal in civil cases for Great Britain and Northern Ireland, and that in this function the Lords of Appeal and the Lord Chancellor alone participate.[39] That work continued, untouched by the Act of 1910.

As regards ordinary legislation, public and private, the House of Lords was on a par with the Commons, having as full a right of initiative and amendment and rejection.[40] In fact, few bills were introduced in the Lords, since the political center of gravity had shifted to the cabinet based upon the Commons, and the cabinet was able to control the timetable of that House. No arrangement existed to break deadlocks. The important question is how the House of Lords used its legislative power, and upon what theories it proceeded.

Somewhat similarly in regard to the financial power. In 1614 the Lords admitted the exclusive right of the Commons to initiate money bills. In 1671 the Commons successfully challenged and denied the right of the Lords to reduce taxes, while the convention that the Crown asks for supplies came to mean that the cabinet alone, and not ordinary members, could increase expenditures or taxation. The general convention that money bills could not be amended by the Lords, but only accepted or rejected "without diminution or alteration," was obeyed until the budget of 1909, but with some slight deviations concerned with customs duties, upon which occasions the Commons saved their privilege by introducing a new bill incorporating the amendment. The power to reject a money bill was used once, in 1860, when the Paper Duties Bill, repealing the duty, was thrown out after the enactment of a property tax and stamp duties which were intended to provide the revenue lost by repeal of the paper duties.[41] A furious controversy arose, the majority of the commons contending that the power ought not to have been used, or as Erskine May has it, "If the letter of the law was with the Lords, its spirit was clearly with the Commons." The House of Commons voted a solemn protest,[42] the import of which was that the Lords had no authority to touch bills to "grant supplies—to provide the ways and means for the service of the year." The paper duties were later repealed by the inclusion of the enactment in the Finance Act of the Year —by "tacking"—and the Lords could not fail to accept this, since rejection would have involved a further dispute of a more serious nature, directly concerned with the annual finances. A time came when the confusion of policy and finance raised

[37] See Simon Haxey, *Tory M.P.* (London, 1939).
[38] *Letters of Lord Acton* (London, 1904), p. 102.
[39] Cf. S. Jackson, *The Machinery of English Justice* (London, 1938).
[40] Cf. W. R. Anson, *The Law and Custom of the Constitution*, 3rd edition (Oxford, 1907), Part I, Chap. VII, p. 260: "The House of Lords is, for legislative purposes, coordinate with the House of Commons."
[41] T. E. May, *Constitutional History of England* (London, 1912), Vol. II, pp. 104-12.
[42] *Ibid.*

fatal issues for the Lords, and their temerity drew upon them the wrath and destruction of the representative principle—in 1911; to that we return presently.

Finally, the House of Lords questions the government and debates its policy. It does not in any way control the executive in the sense we shall see to be true of the Commons, for this body is immediately in touch with the electorate and the parties, and is of the same flesh and blood as the cabinet. The Lords contributed members to the cabinet during the nineteenth century, but in an ever smaller proportion, and never overthrew or thought to overthrow a cabinet. They raised and may raise issues, as does the Commons, but they were never answered with the same earnestness.

The Spirit of the House of Lords. How were these powers used during the nineteenth century? The works of the House of Lords in the nineteenth and twentieth centuries are accompanied with a note of apology or of excessive defiance, as though that House were not only upon sufferance, but knew it was. It must find a reason for existing, and therefore it finds a reason in the only thing now considered capable of being reasonable: namely, the representative principle. It now claims to save the people from their own elected parliamentary representatives, by revising, amending, and rejecting bills sent up by the Commons, until such time as it is sufficiently clear that the people really desire the laws. (Thus the Duke of Wellington, and so, also, in various phrasing, all subsequent apologists.[43]) That is to say, while remaining in existence, anxious and prepared to use their powers, the Lords suffered an inner conversion. They conceded, under pressure, it is true,

their eighteenth-century superiority, some out of regard for the public welfare, others out of the last cry of their reason; and to justify, and maintain, a remnant of power, they were compelled to use an argument ultimately quite fatal to it.

The House of Lords, with such a mentality, had a large reserve of strength founded upon its social position and upon the extensive belief that there was something really virtuous in hereditary aristocracy and titles. How could, and how can, the inexperienced peasant or working man and woman, discern real merit apart from its wonted trappings? As Pascal says: "We need a highly refined reason to regard as an ordinary man the Grand Turk, in his superb seraglio, surrounded with forty thousand janissaries." Estates, money, society, intimacy with the court, commissions in the army and the navy, conspicuous and brilliant position at home and abroad, fine clothes, beautiful women, and thoroughbred horses—the consciousness of ancient authority, the conceit of family and a strong, if narrow, love of "country"—all these contributed to strength of purpose and safety from a direct and doctrinaire assault by Commons and people. Moreover, democracy was unpracticed. This was the strength of the House of Lords; and it proceeded to use it.

Almost every Liberal measure was amended or rejected, while Conservative measures which most accorded with its interest-begotten prejudices received usually a safe passage, until even Gladstone was moved to become the herald of the ultimate storm against the profession of the House of Lords that it represented the permanent opinion of the country.[44] The landlords' position in re-

---

[43] Referring to the Reform Bill, the Duke of Wellington wrote: "We here think that there is reason to believe that there is a very prevailing change of opinion in the country upon the subject of the Bill. At all events we think the House of Lords ought to give the country a chance of being saved by affording further time to consider the question" (Correspondence, Letter to the Marquis of Bath, Vol. VII, p. 531); cited in T. A. Spalding, *The House of Lords* (London, 1894), p. 155.

[44] August 30, 1884. Cf. John Morley, *Life of Gladstone* (London, 1903), Book VII, Chap. VIII. He says that since 1832, there were twelve Parliaments; ten Liberal, one divided (1841-47), and one Tory (1874). "Well, here are ten parliaments on the one side; here is one parliament on the other side . . . The House of Lords was in sympathy with the one parliament and was in opposition to the ten. And yet you are told, when,—we will say for forty-five years out of fifty—practically the nation has manifested its Liberal tendencies

gard to tenants' improvements was defended; religious and political equality was denied, the universities were kept closed to Dissenters; army privileges were maintained; counsel for poor prisoners refused, Ireland maltreated, municipal improvement thwarted; parliamentary reform (bribery and ballot laws) rejected or mutilated; humane measures (like the Deceased Wife's Sister Bill) held up for years; the first Employer's Liability Bill decisively rejected. The House of Lords bolstered the Church of England at the expense of Noncomformist rate-payers, and then, in the Liberal era of 1906 to 1914, they well-nigh stultified its great majority by defeating the Education Bill, the Licensing Bill, the Scottish Land Bill, and the Plural Voting Bill of 1912. The methods adopted were ingenious: principles were destroyed obliquely, without the enunciation of the true motives which caused their destruction; it was pretended that bills had come up to the Lords too late in the session for due deliberation; so many impossible amendments were added that the purpose and efficacy of legislation were frustrated (forcing a compromise).

Nineteenth-Century Attempts at Reform. The theorists of the Victorian era had not reckoned with the ultimate effects of such legislation as the Franchise Acts of 1867 and 1884. Its consequences in reform, especially social reform, speedily became apparent after these dates. The House of Lords could not but attempt to defeat them. Its leaders, however, saw that this must result in self-destruction, unless the House could improve its claim to conduct, which became only a representative body. Hence proposals began to be made for reform—all in the direction of denying the simple claim of inheritance to govern and admitting the validity of the representative principle. The first of these was in 1869, when Lord Russell's Bill

provided that the Crown should be authorized to create life Peers, but only up to the maximum number of twenty-eight and not more than four in any one year, and these life peers were to be taken from any of six given categories, namely: *(a)* Scotch and Irish nonrepresentative peers; *(b)* persons who have been members of the House of Commons for ten years; *(c)* officers in the army and navy; *(d)* judges of England, Scotland, or Ireland, and certain other high legal officials; *(e)* men distinguished in literature, science, and art; *(f)* persons who have served the Crown with distinction for not less than five years.[45] This timid proposition was defeated, because of its terrifying implications, by 106 to 76.

Two admissions made by Lord Salisbury in the debate reveal at once the view of the House which was shaping in the minds of some peers, and the palpable insufficiency of the House as a partner in modern government.[46] Lord Salisbury declared that the Bill would

tend to meet all the large advances of democracy as the third power of the State, as we must meet those advances by making this House strong in the support of public opinion, strong in its influence in the country, and strong in the character and ability of those who compose it.

And again,

We belong too much to one class, and the consequence is that, with respect to a large number of questions. we are all of one mind. Now that is a fact which appears to me to be injurious to the character of the House as a political assembly in two ways. The House of Lords, though not an elective, is strictly a representative assembly, and it does in fact represent very large classes in the country. But if you wish this representation to be effective you must take care that it is sufficiently wide, and it is undoubtedly true that, for one reason or another, those classes whose wealth and power depend on commerce and mercantile industry do not find there representation in this House so large or so adequate as do those whose wealth and power depend upon the agricultural interest and landed property. . . .

by the election of Liberal parliaments, and once only has chanced to elect a thoroughly Tory parliament, you are told that it is the thoroughly Tory parliament that represents the solid and permanent opinion of the country."

[45] Cf. T. A. Spalding, *op. cit.*, p. 108.
[46] *Ibid.*, p. 114.

We want, if possible, more representations of divers views, more antagonism. There are a vast number of social questions, deeply interesting to the people of this country, especially having reference to the health and moral condition of the people, and upon which many members of your Lordships' House are capable of throwing great light, and yet these subjects are not closely investigated here because the *fighting power* [my italics] is wanting, and the debates cannot be sustained.

Other attempts at reform were made in 1874 by Lord Rosebery, and in 1888 by Rosebery and Salisbury. In the first, Rosebery observed that the House did not command respect because it did not represent dissenters, medicine, science, literature, arts, commerce, tenants of land, the colonies, the laboring classes—a truly sufficient damnation. He suggested the institution of life peers, presumably from the categories of the hitherto unrepresented. The motion for an inquiry was defeated. Again in 1888 Rosebery made proposals. "The House of Commons rests upon the votes of some 6,000,000 persons. What we represent is not so easy to divine." He proposed that the House be decreased in size by the election of representatives of peers by their fellows: then there were places for members chosen by the county councils (then newly created), the larger municipalities, and by the House of Commons; and for life and official peers; and for representation of the colonies. Salisbury proposed the addition of fifty life peers, not more than five to be created in any one year. Of the five, three were to be chosen from certain categories and two from outside.[47]

No more was heard of House of Lords reform until 1907, for until then Conservative governments ruled the country. Is it not true, and true again, that few people possessing power will relinquish it out of simple consideration for the public good, and that only force or the threat of retaliation has produced concessions? In 1907 the House set up a select committee to consider the suggestions made from time to time to increase the efficiency of the House in legislation. The report[48]

suggested a new constitution for the House: *(a)* peers of the royal blood (a class always included hitherto); *(b)* the lords of appeal in ordinary; *(c)* two hundred representatives elected by the hereditary peers; *(d)* hereditary peers possessing special qualification; *(e)* spiritual lords of parliament; *(f)* life peers.

The Struggle of 1910. It was too late:[49] only under the pressure of attack of imminent and serious threat did the peers propose a new plan.[50] Too late! for they attempted to use their power of forcing a government to take its measure to the country, in relation to the Finance Bill of 1909. The House by a vote of 350 to 75 rejected the Bill.[51] This was to employ a power which had never been used since the modern budget system had been developed, which the House of Commons had solemnly claimed ought not to be used, and which was a direct challenge to the authority of the cabinet. The Bill was certainly provocative, for it introduced a steeply progressive income tax and death duties, a tax upon mineral royalties, and land-values duties. It was bound to provoke those whose estates and fortunes would be immediately affected. The

---

[47] *Idem.*

[48] Report from the Select Committee of the House of Lords. Appendix A (234), December, 1908.

[49] Note the Commons' resolution, on the motion of the Prime Minister (June 26, 1907): "That, in order to give effect to the will of the people as expressed by their elected representatives, it is necessary that the power of the other House to alter or reject Bills passed by this House should be so restricted by Law as to secure that within the limits of a single Parliament the final decision of the Commons shall prevail."

A second Commons' resolution (December 2, 1909) ran: "That the action of the House of Lords in refusing to pass into law the financial provision made by this House for the Service of the year is a breach of the Constitution and a usurpation of the rights of the Commons." Cf. also J. A. Spender, *The Life of Sir H. Campbell-Bannerman* (London, 1923), Vol. II, Chap. XXXV.

[50] Cf. J. A. R. Marriott, *The Mechanism of the Modern State* (Oxford, 1927), Vol. I, p. 427.

[51] At the time the House of Lords consisted of about 554 members, so that an abnormally large proportion of the membership was present.

Commons dissolved and a general election took place in January, 1910, the government returning with a majority, though a depleted one. The Bill was reintroduced and the Lords yielded. The Commons proceeded to the next logical step: the Parliament Bill of 1910. All-party conferences attempted to produce an agreed scheme. It was impossible.[52] The government dissolved, and a fresh election took place in December, 1910, the main issue being reform of the House of Lords. The balance of power in the Commons was unchanged. The intentions of the government were carried, but accepted by the Lords only after the declaration that the king had consented to the creation of sufficient peers to overcome obstruction. Various maneuvers followed, resulting in some queer crossvoting, but by 131 to 114 the Bill was passed.

The Parliament Act and its Effects. The Act [53] was declared to be only a stage toward a more fundamental reform, and confined itself to immediate tasks. It took away financial powers from the Lords, by providing that money bills, after passage by the House, must be sent up to the Lords at least one month before the end of the session, and if not passed without amendment within a month shall become an Act of Parliament with the royal assent and without the consent of the Lords. Money bills are defined, but not in such detail as to avoid possible conflict, and the speaker of the Commons is the ultimate authority for the certification that a public bill is a money bill.[54] Broadly, the Lords have lost all powers over taxation and appropriations for expenditure.

As regards other public bills, the absolute veto power of the Lords was converted into a suspensive veto of the uttermost limit of two years: a bill passed three times in three successive sessions, two years having elapsed between the second reading on the first occasion and the third reading on the last occasion passes for the royal assent without acceptance by the Lords. This is the extreme power of the Lords—to hold up a bill for such a time. Within this time, it may amend as it will, with the possible pain of having amendments rejected if the Commons can hold out for the two years and find the time for repassage as demanded by the Act.

From the plain terms of the Act, and the general nature of political forces in the country, the following deductions could then be made as to the parliamentary results of this reform:

(1) That in times of Conservative rule the Lords would use their power of amendment on details, excepting where the government was swept along by electoral forces to undertake social reforms, but that ordinarily the Lords would be nothing but the stage on which verbal amendments, and the government's own voluntary amendments, were undertaken.

(2) That in times of Liberal or Labour governments the Lords would not hesitate to use their power when a serious clash of opinion would (a) put the government to the almost impossibly difficult task of finding time to do its work thrice over, and (b) obtain concessions where the government urgently needed the bill and could not find the time or did not wish to wait three years.

(3) That in times of Liberal or Labour governments the House of Lords would virtually be the supporter of the Conservative opposition in the House of Commons and work hand and glove with its leaders. As Lloyd George once said in reference to the past, the Lords would not be the watchdog of the constitution but the Conservative leader's poodle.

Experience since 1911 has amply borne out such deductions, but two subjects need special emphasis. The *first* is that the House of Lords has been used by all governments as a stage on which they themselves have introduced technical or

---

[52] The Constitutional Conference of 1910 numbered eight members including the Prime Minister (Asquith). It broke up without reaching any agreement. Cf. A. Fitzroy, *Memoirs* (London, 1925), Vol. II, p. 423.

[53] Parliament Act of 1911, 1 and 2 Geo. V, Ch. 13.

[54] The definition focuses on the hitherto normal budgetary provision—the expenditure and ways and means. A serious situation would arise if an attempt were made to enact socialist measures via the form of money bills.

political amendments suggested by the influence of the sense of the House of Commons, recommended by experts, or solicited by interested groups. It has offered the occasion and agency to the government for second thoughts and verbal clarification—a function of no mean importance. Yet it is obvious that any democratically composed body, a committee of the House of Commons itself, could serve this function. For the amendments we speak of, if rarely initiated by the Lords or by members of the Government, are plentifully suggested by independent members.

Second, the existence of a minority government, unsure of parliamentary support though normally possessed of it, becomes the sport of the House of Lords. It can be squeezed successfully, especially where a bill is urgent; and where a bill is urgent, any government makes concessions rather than enter upon a time-wasting constitutional conflict. Only the Home Rule Bill of 1912 and the Welsh Disestablishment Bill of 1912 were forced through the procedure of the Parliament Act. A survey of the legislative behavior of the House of Lords since 1919 to the present serves, further, to show the social groups to whom it has been generous and those to which it has been ungenerous. In the first class are landlords, the clergy, the taxpayers generally (where administrative institutions requiring the expenditure of money, have been rejected), employers, rentiers, agriculturists, agricultural-machinery manufacturers, landlords who wished power of eviction from their property, criminals in the course of trial (regarding evidence, witnesses, grand juries, etc., but not sentences), private electric-power enterprises,[55] ordinary jurisdiction (Landlord and Tenant Bill, 1927), individual rather than governmental or municipal enterprise. It has

been positively unfavorable to state control over private enterprise and activities, local and central government expenditure, public libraries, housing efforts, agricultural laborers, the unemployed insured, allotment holders, education, and trade unions. In 1930 it once again killed a bill against plural voting, and rejected the restriction of the use of cars at elections. In 1931 it killed the Education Bill which would have raised the age of free education—the House took three months to handle it; the Lords killed it after four hours' debate. When, in 1933, a Conservative government proposed the abolition of whipping for juvenile delinquents, the Lords reinserted the power.

Moral Position and Future. On the whole, the Parliament Act, by its very existence as the embodiment of protests against the House of Lords, has tremendously weakened the moral position of that House. It is more on sufferance than ever.

One half of its membership has perhaps never spoken at all in the Lords. The number who have spoken several times is something like one in eight of the entire membership. Normally eighty or ninety participate in its divisions, which are rarer than divisions in the Commons. They bring up the big battalions, however, when the defeat of a progressive measure is desired—the "backwoodsmen."

Then why does the House of Lords still exist? For several reasons. (1) A second chamber, *any second chamber,* has some utility where legislation is complicated and only time and many minds can secure the soundness of its substance and the excellence of its drafting. (2) Next, the House of Lords is still a forum of debate on the administrative activity of the government, and lack of time in the Commons gives the other House an opportunity of useful service. (3) Again, the Lords contain a number of able legislators and administrators whose ability serves to weaken the full force of arguments against the existence of the House. It is helpful in the passage of private bills. (4) Further, no non-Conservative govern-

---

[55] In the Electricity Act of 1919, the Lords rejected the provision for compulsory amalgamation of small electric-power enterprises. The Conservative Lord Chancellor, Birkenhead, openly derided the Lords who did not read the bill or hear or understand the debate but voted solidly for their brother directors of electric-power corporations.

ment has yet come into existence with a sufficiently strong majority to make away with it (even including the Labour government of 1945), and the difficulties of mere reform are enormous. (5) Finally, it must be remembered that though the House does not issue from election, its opinion nevertheless coincides with that of some millions of people. It defends what they are glad to see defended. Yet there are Conservatives who see the need for reform. Some demand the strengthening of the power of the House, but that would certainly invite its abolition. Others seek to alter its composition, so that in the future it will be able to justify its power by popular elements.

If we treat the Conservative idea of a second chamber as impossible nowadays, there is hardly a halt to abolition, for reform of the composition of the existing House is impossible. It is this House by sheer inertia, or none at all by abolition, for almost every plan suggested since 1911 is impracticable.

Reform Plans: 1911-34. The Bryce Conference on the Reform of the Second Chamber,[56] which was the most scientific and careful inquiry, fell into two difficulties, each unanswerable: (1) the powers proposed were too great for progressives [57] and too small for conserva-

tives; (2) the indirect method of election was cumbersome,[58] too undemocratic for progressive politicians and not aristocratic enough for conservatives. Other schemes have come from the Conservative party, some in the House of Commons and others in the House of Lords, but they have been based on the principle that the House shall keep substantial powers as at present, or obtain even more, and upon a large element of hereditary representation.[59] But no Conservative government

---

56 Conference on the Reform of the Second Chamber. Letter from Viscount Bryce to the Prime Minister, 1918, Cd. 9038.

57 The powers proposed by the Conference were:

(a) In the case of money bills, a finance committee composed of about seven members of each House, chosen at the beginning of each Parliament, to determine what constitutes a money bill. (Under the Parliament Act the Speaker is the arbiter.)

(b) A "Free Conference" composed of sixty members ("thirty chosen by each chamber, twenty members being selected for the lifetime of the Parliament, and the remaining ten *ad hoc* for each particular Bill") to consider a bill on which the two chambers disagree. The Conference was to sit in secret and to be empowered to reject or amend the bill. In case of rejection, the bill would die. In the more probable case of amendment, should either House reject the amended bill, a delay of one session would follow. At the end of this period the Conference could either fail to report the bill back in the same form (which would en-

tail the death of the bill) or return it without amendment, by a majority of not less than three. In the latter instance, acceptance by the House of Commons would enable the bill to become law even if the House of Lords should disagree.

58 The indirect method of election involved the division of Great Britain into thirteen areas and invested "the election of the representatives for each area in the hands of the members for the House of Commons sitting for constituencies within the area." Secondly, there were to be eighty-one members of the existing peerage (a number to be eventually reduced to thirty). The method proposed was election by a "joint Committee of ten members, five to represent the new Second Chamber, chosen by the Committee of Selection for that Chamber, and five to represent the House of Commons chosen by the Speaker." The vacancies created by the gradual reduction in the number of peers were to be filled by the same committee, but without restriction to the peerage.

59 The government resolutions of July 11, 1922 provided that "in addition to Peers of the Blood Royal, Lords Spiritual and Law Lords" there should be "(a) Members elected, either directly or indirectly from the outside; (b) Hereditary Peers elected by their Order; (c) Members nominated by the Crown, the numbers in each case to be determined by Statute." The reconstituted House was to consist of approximately 350 members. The decision as to whether or not a bill was a money bill was to be referred to a joint standing committee, appointed at the beginning of each Parliament and composed of seven members of each House, in addition to the speaker (ex-officio chairman). The Parliament Act of 1911 would be maintained with exception of "any Bill which alters or amends the constitution of the House of Lords as set out in these Resolutions, or which in any way changes the powers of the House of Lords, as laid down in the Parliament Act and modified by these Resolutions." The term of office of members under (a), (b) and (c) was to be fixed by statute, re-election being permissible. Cf. Lords Debates, 1922, Vol. 51, col. 324.

really attempted reform: who knows where a war will end? In fact, the party leaders even deprecate discussion at party conferences. Progressive opinion inclines to the creation of a small body chosen by the House of Commons from among its own members or from outside at its discretion, with a revising power over ordinary bills to include (a) drafting amendments, (b) amendments of substance, and (c) power to require a short suspension, and then reconsideration by the Commons. But the Commons are supreme, and carry that supremacy even to the challenge of the rules of procedure of the revising committee.[60]

In December, 1933, in the heyday of the National government, the Salisburys were at it again. The Marquis introduced into the Lords a bill for the reform of the House. This time, the House was to be greatly strengthened! Thus, the definition of a money bill was to be more restrictive than hitherto, and was to be interpreted by a joint select committee of both Houses, with the speaker as chairman. No bill, other than a money bill, should be passed under the Parliament Act until after a dissolution. This would have meant that any substantial liberal or socialistic legislation, in the definition of the House of Lords, would have been obstructed and held up pending an election on each measure! To exercise this enhanced power, the peers were to select 150 from their own order, adding another 150 from

outside by a method to be prescribed by both Houses of Parliament. The bill was passed by the House of Lords by 84 to 34 on the first reading and by 171 to 82 on the second. Mr. Baldwin, leader of the Conservative party, brought about the discontinuance of discussion.

Reform by the Labour Government. In 1934, the Labour party, having suffered badly at the hands of the Lords when it was a minority government in 1929-31, adopted the following resolution: [61]

A Labour Government meeting with sabotage from the House of Lords would take immediate steps to overcome it; and it will in any event, take steps during its term of office to pass legislation abolishing the House of Lords as a legislative chamber.

If the Party obtained a mandate from the people in support of its policy, the Labour Government would regard it as its duty to carry that policy through by necessary legislation and administrative action. The Party will therefore at the next General Election, make it clear to the country that in placing its policy before the people, it was also asking for a mandate to deal forthwith with any attempt by the House of Lords to defeat the will of the people by rejecting, mutilating or relaying measures which formed an essential part of a program approved by the electorate.

Since that time the Labour party has obtained its majority. It was immediately asked whether it would proceed to abolish the House of Lords. The question was idle. So long as the House was not obstructive, no Labour government, with a full program of social security and socialization measures, and only five years to carry through the immensely elaborate legislation, means to waste its time on a frontal constitutional battle against the Lords. It would proceed with its program. If, on an issue stirring the people, it were obstructed, then it would be twice-armed to make short shrift of the House of Lords. The attack, then, if it came, would be oblique and two-armed.

Until the middle of 1947, the House of Lords had maintained an exemplary silence and acquiescence—not without a gentlemen's agreement with the Com-

[60] Cf. H. B. Lees-Smith, *Second Chambers in Theory and Practice* (London, 1923), p. 246 ff. This scheme is based on the Norwegian system, which is as follows: The newly-elected *Storthing* elects one quarter of its members to form a second chamber (*Lagthing*) whilst the remaining three fourths (*Odelsthing*) constitute the first chamber. The *Lagthing* may consider only ordinary legislation (i.e., neither finance nor constitutional bills) and may not initiate any bills. Its right of amendment is restricted: if it returns a bill with amendments already once rejected by the *Odelsthing*, a full meeting of the *Storthing* is required and a two-thirds majority necessary for the passage of the bill (cf. *ibid.*, p. 192 ff.). Cf. also H. J. Laski, *The Problem of a Second Chamber*, Fabian Tract No. 213 (London, 1925); S. Webb, *The Reform of the House of Lords*, Fabian Tract No. 188 (London, 1917).

[61] *Report*, Annual Conference, 1934.

mons' Conservative leaders—with the exceptions of the Coal Mines Nationalization Bill of 1946 and the Transport Bill of 1947. It is impossible in the present compass to traverse the sections of these Bills the Lords criticized and amended. The student is advised to see the Commons' debates on the Lords' amendments. There he will discover that on several matters, the process of second-chamber discussion did the Bill good. In the Coal Bill, it enabled the introduction of a proviso that the government in selling coal should not discriminate between the same class of users; that accounts should be kept in best commercial form; and that contracts made by the corporations after the advent of the Labour government, but not those before it, might be reviewed and terminated by the Coal Authority. It also made extra provision for workers' participation in the management of the collieries, and for representation of individuals of expert knowledge in the nationalized industry's advisory bodies; and it provided that the minister should be second in priority to the Coal Authority in managing reserve funds.

All these things were valuable. They would almost certainly have been done by the Labour administration. But it is just as well to have clarity on the subject. The Conservative opposition in the House of Commons smacked their lips over the amendments, some of which they had arduously urged in the House, only to be refused. They praised the work of a second chamber. They observed how necessary it was to have high-class legislation, and not mass legislation. All these things were true: though those who said them were thinking mainly of power.

Why did the minister accept them from the Lords when he had not wished to accept them from the opposition in the Commons? He could have resisted them. If so, it would have been necessary to go through the stages of the Parliament Act. If he had elected to do this, then (a) he would have lost most valuable time in a House already overcongested, and (b) the House of Lords would have played the devil with them on the government's

other socialistic legislation. All the bills would have had to go through three times, and these are bills, running into scores of the most complicated clauses. Or he could have taken a different course. He could have gone to the king for the appointment of enough peers to outvote the six hundred or more potential last-ditchers. Precedent would seem to require that the king not make these peers, unless after a general election in which the party were returned with a clear mandate on the subject. This would have blocked the party's program for a time. Or, they could dissolve on the very issue of the abolition of the House of Lords—and again be frustrated on their immediate program, until after the election. It is much wiser to accept some amendments. But this means also that the House of Lords runs risks:—it has a power arising out of its suspensive veto, which can compel progressive ministers but not compel them too much. Above all, the House of Lords dare not offer any amendment which is too clearly the object of its own special interests: that would lead to its mending or ending. Indeed, as we shall presently see, this sequence occurred in 1947.

When the reform does come, the importance of public-spirited and appropriately organized and regulated political parties will become even more essential than it is today. At present, the glaring and amazing truth is that Britain is formally governed by only a quasi-democratic assembly, for the House of Lords stands in direct and practical opposition to the principle of majority rule. This, whether for good or ill, is the result of Britain's nonrevolutionary development of political institutions, and the consequent lack of a declaration of absolute principles like those which appear in Continental and American constitutions.

Two other observations must be added. (1) The House of Lords conducts debates on administrative and foreign policy. It is hardly fair that a non democratic assembly shall have an authoritative status for its unrepresentative and irresponsible utterances. However, its wisdom may be considerable; for even if it is different from that of the government in the Commons, it is nevertheless of popular interest simply by being different. Nor can it be ignored that the House of Lords contains, for the purpose now under discussion, many former officials—military, colonial, civil—former members of the House of Commons, men of abundant experience and marked sagacity who are valuable assets to the state. Yet there are alternative ways, besides an hereditary assembly with legislative power, to provide for the continued utilization of the elder statesmen, which should be the object of good policy. We must not lose sight of the fact that the leaders of the nazi movement were misled regarding Britain's staunchness against aggression by an excessive confidence in the special attachment of the Lords to appeasement. Rudolph Hess, it was said, was sent to Britain to make contact with Joachim von Ribbentrop's friends in and around the House of Lords. (2) The Lords possess the power, equally with the Commons, of rejecting rules and orders submitted to them by the Government when these have been made pursuant to statute. This power is not merely suspensive—it can entirely kill, and, indeed, a Conservative speaker, during the 1948 debates to be referred to, declared that this power if fully used, "could reduce government to a nullity."

On November 10, 1947,[62] after a rather abrupt announcement in the King's Speech in October, the Labour government introduced the Parliament Bill of 1947 to amend the Act of 1911. It left the statute intact, with one exception: in future, ordinary legislation would go through the procedure prescribed by it, but instead of a bill to which the House of Lords objected having to pass the Commons in each of three successive sessions, only two would be necessary; and instead of a two years' span between the second reading in the first of such sessions and the final passage of the bill, only one year

would need to elapse. In other words, the suspensive veto of the House of Lords was reduced to one year, while the House of Commons stage was made easier.

The project caused the fiercest storm in British political life for many years—and indeed, it seemed to come out of the blue. Two things are of interest here: the reason for the project, and the arguments advanced about it in debate.

All that the Labour party has said in its election platform, *Let's Face the Future,* was, "We give clear warning that we will tolerate no obstructionism to the people's will by the House of Lords." Government spokesmen had several times paid tribute not only to the generally good and unobstructive behavior of the House of Lords, but to the positive value of the many amendments it had offered to improve the government's own legislation. Why then the sudden change? Two problems arose. *First,* some of the government's supporters had been demanding the nationalization of the iron and steel industry: while some in the cabinet resisted this on account of the economic short-term difficulties the country faced, and the intricacy of the problem of nationalization. Therefore, to appease the former the reform of the Lords was offered; while, if the iron and steel plan could be worked out, the government would be nearing the last two years of its term before it was introduced, and therefore it was necessary to defeat the power of the Lords to suspend a bill for two years. But there was a second reason for the change. After the Commons, in August, 1947, gave the government strong powers to deal with the economic crisis, it adjourned for the summer, and thus the opportunity of immediate debate on the government's rules and orders was postponed. The House of Lords decided that it would sit in September, by itself if necessary, to debate the government's measures. It could, using its own rights, have vetoed the rules and orders. This raised important constitutional issues and was a direct challenge to the government. It may have been in the national interest; it certainly was in the party interests of the Conservatives. The

[62] See Commons Debates, November 10 and 11, Cols. 36 ff.

government did not forget this. Hence the introduction of the bill.

The arguments for the reduction of the veto power of the House of Lords were these. The will of the people must prevail, as expressed in the general election. For its economic policy, and even for overcoming the obstruction of the House of Lords, the government had a mandate. The economic and social planning on which the government was embarked required orderly sequence, and the various measures were urgent and contributed to the effectiveness of each other. Therefore the government could not tolerate a disruption in time or substance of its program. Suspense was dangerous; hence the period of delay must be curtailed. In a democratic system there was no place for a second chamber which steadily favored one party only—the Conservative party —and was prompted by its leaders. In a sense, the constitution had become unicameral, since the House of Lords always sided with the Conservatives. It was monstrous that great power should be in the hands of a body that was not subject to dissolution and election like the House of Commons. Why should a progressive government have an effective and assured life of only three years, and a Conservative five years? It meant that a minority had, when it wished, the right of government over the majority. It was the business of the Conservatives who had been in office for the major part of the nearly forty years that had elapsed since the Act of 1911 to have reformed the Lords long ago, as envisaged in the preamble to the Act. If it was true that in a democracy a revising chamber was valuable, and indeed, necessary, no case could be made for the exercise of a power to obstruct the government by a body founded on heredity. In any case, twelve months' delay was ample time for the Lords to revise and amend. All democratic countries had bicameral systems.

The Conservatives complained, in opposing the bill, that the work of the Lords had been valuable and so acknowledged.[63] They pointed out that the Parlia-

[63] Cf. especially *ibid.*, Cols. 56, 57.

ment Act allowed a Government to resume the stages of a bill, if after termination of a Parliament, or resignation and dissolution, they were returned by the general election. Hence, if their iron-and-steel project should have merit in it, and the people's will should endorse it, then a Labour government would have lost no time, by having been held up for two years followed by an election. It was emphasized repeatedly that elections in Britain permit great fluctuations of party fortune, and that a very small majority of votes in the country could return a disproportionate majority of members in the House. Some check on behalf of the people was therefore necessary to see that the "real," "permanent," "persistent" will of the nation was behind the legislation. This argument was a massive part of the Conservative case, and Mr. Churchill, leader of the opposition, made particularly strong play with it. United with this contention were its analogues, that the power of government was today so wide and pervasive of the national life that checks, revision, delay, and deliberation were needed before such power were utilized. It was further urged that pressure groups might dominate a government from inside or outside, so that what appeared to be the majority's will would, in fact, be a minority view, which happened to possess strategic strength at a given moment. Nor was this all. It was stressed heavily that in the last two years or so of a government's term, whatever the will of the people at the beginning, the effectiveness of the mandate begins to peter out. Therefore, it was essential that some institution in the state should be able to challenge the government, and if necessary force it to seek a new mandate in an election. For such a purpose a twelve months' delaying power was insufficient.

Most of the speakers on all sides agreed on the need for a revising chamber. But the Conservative arguments were weakened by a universal admission that the hereditary principle was untenable. Who were they to decide, as against an elected government, when that government was not reflecting the people's will? But when the attempt was made to discover a more acceptable basis for the composition of the second chamber, all political leaders were nonplussed. As for the argument that the engine of the popular will must be refueled by popular re-election, and forced into the process by a brake from the Lords, the Prime Minister, Mr. Attlee, concluded the second reading debate by saying: "He [Mr. Churchill], regarded that brake as essential, and the engine had to go to be repaired every five years for a Conservative Government and every two years when a Labour Government was in power."

The Conservative and Liberal parties strongly pressed the claim that a constitutional reform as important as that of the Lords ought not to be pursued by the Labour government by the sheer use of its voting battalions. The matter ought, as in precedents for constitutional change (see p. 137 above), be submitted to an interparty conference for the exploration of an agreed solution. This, if achieved, would avert a conflict between the two Houses. The Labour government were responsive, of course, to this argument. An interparty conference, under the chairmanship of the Prime Minister, was convened early in 1948, the issue being the relationship of the composition to the powers of a second chamber. The conversations were arduous, inventive, in good faith, and in vain. An "Agreed Statement" was published (*Cmd. 7380*) on May 4, 1948. The Liberals had, on the whole, sided with the Labour party.

The Labour leaders had been prepared to concede more time to the Lords for the use of their powers of revision, the "period of delay," as the phrase went. Instead of insisting on a span of time for complete passage of a bill over the heads of the Lords within twelve months from its second reading in the Commons, they offered a period of nine months from the end of the third reading. This was a considerable concession, since the second reading and the committee and report stages on a controversial bill (to be twice enacted) might be quite long, and in the fourth and fifth year of a progressive

government's term might cause it considerable parliamentary anguish. But the Conservatives demanded a halfway period between the two years of the Parliament Act and the one year of the government's bill, that is, eighteen months. They were prepared to reduce this period, if they could have obtained the kind of reformed second chamber they had in mind.

However, when it came to formulating the details of the agreed general propositions regarding the composition of the reformed chamber, agreement was impossible on the Lords' terms which contemplated some partial survival of hereditary rights. Nor could a way of implementing the proposition that "the revised constitution should secure that a permanent majority is not assured for any one party."

The irresoluble conflict came over the powers of a second chamber: for Labour, a revising power, a short period of second thoughts, a body in which some legislation could be introduced, were genuinely appreciated (see, for illustration, Herbert Morrison's speech at the annual conference of the Labour party as reported in the official report, commencing page 211). But for such functions twelve months were enough. For the Conservatives, the function of a revising chamber was much further reaching: it was to check the Commons' majority, to delay its work while public opinion was called in to defeat or modify the will of the government of the day. Labour could not accept such a period of delay, which would ruin the fourth- and fifth-year program of a progressive government. Hence, the conference did not achieve the modification of the Parliament Bill of 1947 and the government's intention to carry it through under the Act of 1911, against the will of the Lords, if necessary. The Bill was introduced for the second time on September 20, 1948.

It is necessary now to restate the proposals regarding a reformed composition of the House of Lords, and then to conclude this account of an episode not yet itself concluded with some reflections.

The proposals (dependent on agreement on powers!) were as follows:

The Second Chamber should be complementary to and not a rival to the Lower House, and reform should be based on a modification of the House of Lords existing constitution as opposed to establishment of a Second Chamber of a completely new type based on some system of election.
The revised constitution should secure that a permanent majority is not assured for any one party.
The present right to attend and vote based solely on heredity should not by itself constitute a qualification for admission.
Members should be styled "Lords of Parliament" and would be appointed on grounds of personal distinction or public service. They might be drawn either from hereditary peers or from commoners who would be created life peers.
Women should be capable of being appointed Lords of Parliament in the same way as men.

The foregoing study of the status and problem of the House of Lords was deliberately pursued in detail in order to show the intractability of a situation in which a number of starkly contrasted conditions have to be given rational accommodation in an age as distracted in its social tensions as we have seen other constitution-making nations to be (p. 122 ff. above). Here is an attempt to re-devise a second chamber where there is no federal-state basis for it, right or wrong as that basis may be. It is then proposed to leave the present basis, which is heredity, and is untenable since the contemporary justification of political authority is representative and responsible. But some lords still demand heredity as at least a claim for an elected number of their own peers to be members of the second chamber. If, again, the elective principle is suggested, it is feared that a body with rival authority to the first chamber will arise, and confuse the public in the inevitable controversies, as well as play havoc with the conduct of government and the enactment of promised legislation. If the government of the day is given the power of appointing life peers, it is not difficult to guess the untenability of the principle, in the long run, of not

shaping the second chamber to the advantage of one rather than the other party. Finally, though the reign of political parties and public opinion and the organization and spirit of parliamentary procedure, together, furnish guarantees of deliberation, care, and fairness to the minority, all parties in an age of vast legislative activity acknowledge the possibility of error or haste in the first chamber and would like a second: the question is still, how composed and with what powers? For long it will probably remain the present Lords, with powers reduced as in the Bill of 1947, and in some years' time there may come an exclusion of all but a few hereditary peers and inclusion of many life peers appointed by the government up to a certain number by each government in turn.

THE UNITED STATES SENATE[64]

SOMETHING has already been said on the reasons for the foundation of the United States Senate. It is necessary to add only some remarks on the problems arising out of its operation.

(1) It is substantially more powerful than the House of Representatives (though its members, one third every two years, are elected for the period of six years as compared with what is always thought to be the more popular House, elected at intervals of two years). For it has not only the power of legislation equal to that of the House. Its authority to amend financial legislation which, by the constitution, must commence in the House, has been construed by it to be a plenary power to remake the budget sent up to it. By substitutions for original proposals made by the House, it is as much master of the financial provision of the nation as the House. And owing to its composition and operation, it is even more powerful.

Besides this, it has the power of assenting to or rejecting the Presidential nominations for offices not subject to civil ser-

[64] G. H. Haynes, *The Senate of the United States: Its History and Practice* (Boston, 1938), and p. 183 above.

vice.[65] These are still very many: and all the high appointments, the heads of departments, judges, ambassadors and ministers, are in its hands. In the balance of power which establishes itself between the two assemblies, and between the Senate and the President, this appointive power not only governs who shall be entrusted to administer the laws, but is a pawn in the give-and-take which decides policy. The Senator with patronage has influence with the House of Representatives' contingent from his own state and party. In addition, the prestige and power stemming from the authority to accept or reject treaties, with access, therefore, to a part in the President's conduct of foreign policy, is also of special potency in the status of the Senate.[66]

(2) Being so much smaller than the House, the Senate has not been obliged to swathe and tangle itself in limitation of debate or closure. Unanimous consent is required to stop a Senator from obstructing the work of legislation and administration. By continuous talking, without discipline for irrelevance, filibustering is possible.[67] This enables any individual or sectional minority to block legislation by the simple device of seizing on a time when the majority are keenly intent on passing important and urgent legislation. Thus the year's appropriations and various war measures have been held up, in order to prevent the reduction or abolition of the poll tax used by Southern Democrats to prohibit Negroes from exercising their constitutionally guaranteed right to vote, and more substantially to establish all the civil rights for the Negroes. Amplitude of debate does permit the Senate to debate at any time

the every day actions of the executive,[68] a necessary and useful function, but not one that needs to be accomplished by this forum in this particular setting of procedure.

(3) In view of these extraordinarily considerable powers, the composition of the Senate has been frequently assailed. In the first place, to placate the South, and effect the great compromise between the small states (then) and the large states (then), all states were given an equality of representation—two each—in the Senate. It was stipulated that no state might be deprived of its equality, even by means of amendment, without its consent. The growth of the Republic from thirteen to forty-eight states has produced some very serious anomalies in the balance of power. Thus, Nevada (favorite case) with 110,000 population has the same representation as New York with nearly 14,000,000. New York, Pennsylvania, Illinois, Ohio, Texas, and California have together over 50,-000,000 people, but only twelve Senators together, or, with 12 per cent of the representatives, they have 40 per cent of the population. New England has 1,500,000 less inhabitants than Pennsylvania: the latter has two representatives to that region's twelve. And so on.

This produces a very disproportionate representation of economic and social groups. Can this be defended? Not very strongly, though a case may be made out. If the richer parts of the nation were not as rich as they are, they would not take the risk of carrying the sparser and poorer states along with them, with the power of taxation equally in the hands of the latter. They can afford it, though they may grumble at the charge put on them by the silver-producing states, whose Senate votes forced the United States Treasury to buy their silver. No one has yet adequately analyzed the real effect of the strategic application of the disproportionate vote of the minority-population states. But it seems not to have been seriously aimed at the disadvantage of the rest. It is

[65] Cf. A. W. Macmahon, "Senatorial Confirmation," *Public Administration Review,* Autumn, 1943.

[66] Cf. Q. Wright, *The Control of American Foreign Relations* (New York, 1922); W. S. Holt, *Treaties Defeated by the Senate* (Baltimore, 1933); D. F. Fleming, *Treaty Veto of the American Senate* (1930); E. E. Denison, *The Senate Foreign Relations Committee* (Stanford, 1942).

[67] F. L. Burdette, *Filibustering in the Senate* (Princeton, 1940).

[68] Lindsay Rogers, *The American Senate* (New York, 1926).

à fact, also, that the representation of some of these states is split by parties—one Senator Republican, one Democratic—which reduces the effect of their votes as states. So far, habit has closed the eyes of people in the states that pay in taxes and moral forbearance for the overrepresentation of the puny states.

If something is lost in equity to the populous states by equal representation, it must still be considered that, perhaps, their voting power gives to the less populous ones a lever against their being ignored in so extensive and diverse a land, the parts of which are not known personally to the representatives from other states. With so vast a territorial span, there is a strong case for the power of a state to protect itself from complete misunderstanding or roughshod treatment.

(4) What is more parlous is the inability to break a deadlock between the two Houses except by the appointment of conferees to negotiate and report back an agreement. In secrecy these conferees arrive at bargains so late in the session that the full representative bodies themselves cannot redebate the issues.[69] This is far from representative and responsible government. The law of August, 1946,[70] to amend the procedure and committee practices remedies this to the extent of setting up a joint committee on budget (sec. 138), and of not permitting conference committees to report on matters not committed to them by either House.

THE FRENCH SENATE

WE saw earlier in this chapter that the recruitment of the French Senate in the Third Republic embodied a triple basis: (1) a higher age qualification for senators than for members of the lower house; (2) a long term of office—nine years compared with the four years of the Chamber of Deputies; and (3) indirect election based on local government bodies with the representation designedly favoring the villages and small towns.

What were the effects of this mode of recruiting the Senate? On the whole, it produced what was intended by the Center parties: a body, not antirepublican, yet of a conservative nature. Every one of its ingredients served to produce this result.

Age and Conservatism. It has ever been the belief of legislators that age will produce maturity of judgment and obstruct rash innovation.[71] We shall later see in what respects this object has been attained. It is more difficult to show a direct causal relationship between age and behavior, for there were other causes of the French Senate's deliberate slowness. We cannot isolate the effects of age, but we can say that age was more represented in the Senate than in the Chamber of Deputies. The minimum age was 40; available statistics to 1939 show that the actual average age of senators was a little over 60, while the deputies appeared to be an average of 50 years of age.

There are certain usual accompaniments of age: marriage, family, profession, property, experience, and physical change. Older men and women come to be satisfied with themselves: this is a powerful influence on their social complacency.

Whether the main cause is to be found in experience or physical change, there is no doubt that legislators act rightly in establishing a higher minimum age for senators than for members of the lower chamber, if their intention is to secure conservatism. But the gap in age must be large, at least a score of years. Yet there is no exact correlationship between age and conservatism in each case or in general; and it must be remembered that the age of members of any lower house is itself apt to be rather high.

A Long Term. Election to the French Senate of the Third Republic was for nine years. The senator did not need to be

---

[69] Cf. A. C. McCown, *The Congressional Conference Committee* (New York, 1927).
[70] Public Law, 601: Legislative Reorganization Act.

[71] For example, the following countries have a minimum age-limit for members of the second chamber: Czechoslovakia, 45; Poland, 40; Belgium, 40; Canada, 30; South Africa, 30; Irish Free State, 30.

constantly concerned for the views of the electors, and though many strokes of his authority might be unpopular in nine years, they would be forgotten; nor was he, like the deputy, compelled even at intervals of four years to prepare an electoral profession of faith. Now it is impossible to argue directly from this duration of the mandate to conservatism: the better generalization is that the Chamber of Deputies and the Senate were never in exact accord in their opinions, since each had been constituted by different states of mind in the country. A senator at the end of his term was already five years behind a contemporary deputy at the end of his: and there was a nine-years' difference between the end of a senator's term and the beginning of a deputy's. The distance was even greater, for the senator did not owe his election to an immediate canvass of the people, but to bodies who themselves might already have been in office three or four years. But this is an eternity. In social legislation in particular, our time moves rapidly, and where popular election exists, even the most conservative political parties have been obliged to outbid the progressive parties. We can safely conclude that the nine-years' term, together with the leeway in time contributed by election by elected bodies, accounted for the divergence of opinion between the two chambers. That is not all. There were important "landslides" of votes for the first chamber from one election to another. These affected the composition of groups and cabinets; and it was often upon a subtle difference in composition, to the extent of a few votes, that differences between two elected chambers depended. Only by a rare accident, then, was there a coincidence of strength in the Chamber and the Senate. The normal condition was dissonance; and the method of election of the Senate, together with the weakness of party organization in its elections, aggravated this dissonance. But this did not always mean the conservatism of the Senate and the progressivism of the Chamber: it meant only dissonance, and sometimes the Senate, as between 1920 and 1930, was on occasion (during the time of the *bloc*

national and after 1924) more liberal than the Chamber.[72] Until World War I, however, it was more conservative, and this persisted almost entirely through the interwar years.

Nor is that all. Senators were frequently re-elected, as a matter of course, and some served for very long periods, with two results: increase in the distance in opinion between the Chamber of Deputies and the Senate, and enhancement of the knowledge of affairs and prestige of the latter.

Indirect Election. The Senate derived from indirect election: the public at large had little contact with the senator. The bodies which elected were small compared with the open constituencies of the Chamber of Deputies, and they were scattered —a handful in a large area, an average of something over one thousand.[73] The senators were themselves men of some experience in government, and acquainted with the arts of electioneering. There was, therefore, no question of crowd rhetoric or the undue predominance of the desirable over the possible. As a rule, speeches were made to the electoral body assembled, only on the actual day of the election, and then by the various candidates in turn. Their experience, in fact, tended to make them more conservative, more official-minded and negativing, than the ordinary conservative citizen. Eminence of a kind was required; there had to be more than the average qualities which impress the average voter. Persons elected in such wise and on such assumptions are certain to insist upon their power and dignity. The campaigns of a senator were restrained and continuous; as a mayor, or departmental councilor himself, or as a deputy or, already a senator, he won little favors for the communes, was festive and

---

72 Cf. J. Barthélemy, *Le Gouvernment de la France* (Paris, 1919), p. 67, and compare the defeat in December, 1930, of the Tardieu ministry, which was not upset in the Chamber of Deputies.

73 E.g. in 1927, the smallest was Alger, with 280 delegates from the *communes*, and 33 of the other classes of electors; in Hautes Alpes, 276 and 58 respectively; in Gironde, 1187 and 120; and Nièvre, the largest, 2346 and 160.

generous with the kind of treating which cannot be brought home on so considerable a scale and so directly that the election will be invalidated. Since the electoral body was comparatively small, all, or at least the more influential, could be personally canvassed. Each vote was very important in such a body. An absolute majority was necessary to election: and on the occasion of second and even third ballots, the maneuvers and intrigues offered an extra entertainment, *vin compris*.[74] Thus when Pierre Laval had been rejected by his constituency for the Chamber of Deputies, his more refined qualities of "politicking" secured him a seat in the Senate—the price, persistent button-holing.

The constituent of the Senate which gave it the surest proclivity toward conservatism was the distribution of votes in the electoral bodies. The composition was revised in 1884 in order to avoid the predominance of the smallest rural communes. But the Chamber of Deputies and the Senate were not prepared to endow radicalism with more power than could be helped. In other words, they chose a way between, putting the chief power into the command of the townships of between 4000 and 5000. This is easily seen from the distribution.

No place could send more than twenty-four delegates, save Paris. But any commune with over 60,000 inhabitants and more had only four times as many delegates as communes with between 2500 and 3500 inhabitants, and not quite three times as many as places between 3500 and 10,000. For larger rises in population from 2500 and upward, there was only a uniform increase of three delegates per stage, even where that was as many as 20,000 (at the point 10,000 to 30,000). Barthélemy has shown, statistically, how unfair this method of election was, judged by the principle of the equality of voters. Lille, for example, had 216,000 inhabitants and sent twenty-four delegates, while twenty-four villages near it had together 4000 inhabitants and

sent twenty-four, and this with the twelve contributed to by twelve places with 6600 inhabitants, caused Lille to be quite outvoted. Of 945 senatorial electors in the Department of the Seine, Paris has but 110. This resulted in the predominance of about 75,000 (the total number of senatorial electors) middle *bourgeoisie*, officials, proprietors, merchants and manufacturers of middle-class status, and publicists.[75] Its adversaries were able to say that it constituted an assembly without the principle of life and without a sense of authority. Hence the importance which French politicians attached to the municipal and departmental local elections: hence also the special attention paid by Socialists and Radical-Socialists and later the Communists to the municipal authorities. The composition of the Senate was the fruit of a compromise between opposed theories, the result of an empirical transaction. Parliamentary critics have blamed the Senate's derivation for its slowness in economic and social legislation.

Owing to various circumstances, the Senate was a goal that forcefully lured the ambitious deputy. The senatorship rounded out a political career. In 1910, thirty-two ministers and ex-ministers sat in the Senate; in 1925-26 and in 1928 there were fifty-two. Despite its membership and constitution, the Senate still claimed close alliance with the people. Though somewhat removed from the people, the Senate held a tight grip on the constituents, and senators compelled the deputies to pay tribute to them by concessions in policy.

Further, its origin in electoral colleges consisting mainly of local government councilors made local government itself a channel of access to the Senate: thus, in 1930, 137 senators had been councilors-general (i.e. of the department), and 104 had been mayors of communes.

The Senate, then, had a constitution which gave it a curbing, deliberate, de-

---

[74] 1927, 112 serving the first term; 147 the second; 36 the third; 12 the fourth; and 3 the fifth.

[75] J. Barthélemy, "Les Résistances du Sénat," *Revue du Droit Public* (Paris, 1913). Other figures and facts to the same effect are given in M. Billecard, *De la Mode du Recrutement du Sénat* (thèse, Paris, 1912), p. 84 ff.

celerating bias and the substance as well as the consciousness of power. Whether it is more conservative, or for the time more liberal, it is different from the Chamber.

The Powers of the Senate. What were its powers and how did it use them? Apart from its position as a high court of justice, the Senate's constitutional powers were three: the partial or total revision of bills emanating from the Chamber of Deputies and the initiation of bills; cooperation in finance bills which must be introduced in the Chamber of Deputies; and control over the government.

Now, these were powers of real moment and exercised with decision and effect. For the ultimate fact was that the Chamber of Deputies had no power to compel the Senate to send back its bills in the shape it desired unless it could persuade that body that the electorate was, by a majority, continuously favorable to and even insistent upon its policy, *or* unless it could throw over into the Senate the grappling irons of party. It was only possible to do the first after the lapse of something like a decade from the original introduction of a bill. As for the second, party—which meant so little in the definition of attitude in the Chamber itself—this did not establish a discipline causing deputies and senators to march along a common legislative route. Even a small disparity between the strength of the parties in both chambers—ten votes in one or two groups—could do all the damage. No government could, therefore, be sure that the Senate would not reject or mutilate its bills, and none could be sure that when its administration satisfied the Chamber it would equally satisfy the Senate. Further, owing to the fact that the Senate had not relinquished its power to reverse governments, and owing also to the strong element of individual careerism in French politics, senators were ready to join ministries not supported by the rest of their party. Yet such a ministerial senator had no power to get the government's bill accepted, for he had no party supporting him. The party relationship of Senate and deputies, then, was: a series of groups not firmly tied by agreement upon policy, but associating and falling apart on issues of the day.

Now in other countries where senates exist—the United States, as we have shown, and Australia—a real duality between the two chambers is overcome by the agency of party organization: a common electoral fight is fought. Or, as in Canada, the ruling party nominates enough members to overcome the recalcitrant nominees of its predecessors.[76] Some duality may yet exist, because no two bodies of men sitting separately, endowed with real power (be it ever so small) and having even the smallest diversity of composition, produce the same legislative result. But such duality is not insuperable, or at least, it is superable in a comparatively short time. The duality of the legislative assembly in France could not be overcome easily, or in a short time. For it reposed upon a basis of group independence so strong as to be almost indistinguishable from personal independence. This personal independence was of such a quality in the Senate as to be readily converted into that kind of group esteem which is eager to make its authority felt—in this case, as a spirit which almost always denied.

There was very little, then, to bring the Senate into consonance with the Chamber: only a strong government, its long persistence in a policy, and the clear verdict of the polls [77] at recent elections of the Chamber and the Senate could do this. And there were cases—like that of the fight for electoral reform until 1913, and of women's suffrage until World War II, and many proposals for social security—where no effective consonance was possible. But we must not forget that French cabinets contained on an average three or four members (in a total of about twelve) from the Senate.

Ordinary Bills. Let us see how the Sen-

[76] Cf. R. A. Mackay, *The Unreformed Senate of Canada* (Oxford, 1928), Chap. IX. Cf. R. McGregor Dawson, *The Government of Canada* (Toronto, 1947), Chap. XV.

[77] Relatively, of course, to French conditions. I am conscious of the disillusioning and disconcerting realities latent in this customary phrase.

ate works in each of its three main functions. All depended on the power of the Chamber of Deputies to cause the Senate to bring the matter to debate and decision. But the Chamber of Deputies had no legal power to compel the Senate to proceed to the discussion of a bill.[78] It had only the psychological power of demonstrations in the Chambers and in the country, and the influence of those ministers, perhaps of the prime minister himself, who belonged to the Senate and could exert it.

Further, ministers, whether members of the Senate or not, had the right to speak in both Chambers. While neither chamber had the right directly to criticize the work, the procedure, or the members of the other,[79] it might pass resolutions begging the government to urge it onwards. Pierre sums up the experience of the Chamber of Deputies in regard to attempts to praise or blame the Senate in a manner which makes very plain the gulf between Chambers:[80]

The mechanism established by our constitutional laws would be falsified if each of the assemblies which divide between them the legislative power did not deliberate in full independence, if the acts of the Senate or of the Chamber could at any time be cast into the balance of the votes of the Chamber or of the Senate. For the assemblies as for individual persons, there is an interior as well as an exterior court of conscience. In the interior one, Senators and Deputies can place whatever importance they wish upon projects which have been introduced or resolutions passed in a body other than that in which they sit. In the exterior court the Senators and the Deputies must regulate their conduct entirely according to the manner in which they conceive the public good. The balance of power would be upset if arguments drawn from the attitude or resolutions of one House were used in the parliamentary debates of the other: one would

cultivate the habit of voting by complaisance or by hostility, instead of voting in the sole interest of the community.

So much for form. But, in fact, the Chamber acquired the power to press the Senate, by resolutions of this nature: "The chamber, *the issue of universal suffrage,* faithful to the principle of the representation of minorities affirmed by its votes of 5th July, 1911, and 1st July, 1912, and rejecting any adjunction thereto, adjourns until Tuesday." The rule that one chamber could harass the other by debates on the same subject as those under its consideration was overcome by resolutions which could be debated, apparently directed to the government but in reality intended to impress the other chamber. Thus: "The Chamber invites the government to sustain before the Senate, in the matter of the personnel of workers and employees of the railways, the solutions which approximate closest to the votes already given on several occasions by the Chamber of Deputies, especially that of the 14th November, 1901." [81] It might also urge the Senate to continue its good works, lest it fall from grace. The Chamber might be more urgent and invite action.

The Senate did not allow its constitutional right of revision and rejection to lapse. It even converted a power originally used only for financial bills, which contained so many unwise and disconnected clauses, into a weapon for dealing with ordinary bills: "disjunction." The obnoxious clauses of a bill are simply disjoined from the text by the Senate: they are not commented upon, but are ignored: thus they are neither accepted, nor rejected, nor amended.

To what effect did the Senate use its powers in ordinary laws? Great governmental measures were fully amended and rejected and this in a particular direction which we may, remembering the distinctions established in the analysis of party policies, call conservative. It retarded the projects for the weekly holiday for workers, for reducing the legal hours of labor,

---

[78] Cf. E. Pierre, *Traité de Droit, Politique et Parlémentaire* (Paris, 1922, and Supplements), Vol. III, p. 1609: "The right imparted to each assembly of rejecting a proposition or a project of the law adopted by the other assembly is not limited by any constitutional or procedural text; in consequence, a project often voted by one of the two Chambers can be indefinitely repulsed by the other."
[79] *Ibid.*, Vol. I, para. 681.
[80] *Ibid.*, paras. 826, 827.

[81] *Ibid.*, Vol. III, para. 1015.

for workers' pensions, for state railroad-men's pensions, for income tax, for pro-portional representation; it sternly re-jected woman's suffrage, projects for taxes on business, rent restriction; it was ada-mant against the recognition of civil ser-vice syndicates. It rejected a woman's suf-frage bill on November 21, 1922, and also a bill of minor importance, creating an unpaid High Commissioner to deal with housing. Under the pressure of emergency and electoral trends, it accepted the Blum Popular Front "New Deal" measures: the forty-hour week, collective wage agree-ments, paid vacations. But it weakened the law to control the Bank of France. Finally, after a year of determined hostility, it overthrew the Blum government in June, 1937, by refusing to grant the strong finan-cial powers necessary to deal with the con-sequences of the former reforms and the critical economic situation: exchange con-trol, government loan, change in the par-ity of the franc, nationalization. Blum was again overthrown in April, 1938, when his finance bill was rejected.[82]

It is rather difficult to place the actions of the Senate crudely in the "conservative" category. Their aspect is dependent on the character of the Chamber of Deputies for the time being, and the commotion of ideas and personalities in the nation. Thus, between the advent of Hitler and World War II, the Senate was more amenable to social legislation than ever before, though with reluctance. But in the earlier part of that period it was a center of resistance to fascist and communist ex-tremes. Is it "conservative" or is it "lib-eral" to be anticommunist? When it emas-culated M. Blum's bill for the limitation of the libellous and violently defamatory tactics of the French press (a reform long overdue), was it "liberal" or "conserva-tive"? Furthermore, in the field of foreign policy, the Senate was rather more na-tionalist than the Chamber, which was more flexible. In particular, the social divisions of the French between the rise of Hitler and 1940 were aggravated by the

Senate, which, when that dreadful choice was thrust on France, more and more favored Hitler, and less and less the Franco-Soviet alignment. When a robust answer was made to Mussolini's territorial claims on France at the beginning of 1939, 156 Socialists and 72 Communists voted against Mussolini in the Chamber, but the Senate had only 13 Socialists and 2 Com-munists to stand up against the 287 votes in favor.

Finance Bills. The financial powers of the Senate were just as important as its power in ordinary legislation except that it had no right of initiation, a power which, as in every democracy, was re-served to the lower house. As the most eminent of all French constitutional law-yers and political scientists, Jèze, says—the real question was not one of the interpre-tation of the text, but a question of po-litical and social power (force). The text runs: "The Senate has, concurrently with the Chamber of Deputies, the initiation and the confection of laws; however, finan-cial laws must be, in the first place, pre-sented to the Chamber of Deputies and voted by it." This only meant, argued those who wanted a powerful Senate, that priority alone was given to the Chamber, but not decisive power: the Senate had a complete amending power—authority to amend so severely as to reject, or entirely to remodel. Further, the elective origin of the Senate gave it a right which perhaps might not be accorded to nonelective bodies. However, its mode of election gave the advantage to the propertied classes, and caused a large opposition not to trust its maneuvers, and certainly not to accept its economic and fiscal doctrines. Never-theless, the Senate became the defender of republicanism against other forms of rule, and the repetition of the *Seize Mai* never occurred. Deputies and ministers have found their way into the Senate: consider such names as Bourgeois, Méline, Dupuy, Clemenceau, Ribot, Pichon, Poincaré, Barthou, Doumer, Millerand, Laval, Ley-gues. Finally, the Chamber of Deputies was not fully trustworthy alone in matters of finance—it had not the *expertise* or the self-control to make a proper budget in

[82] A. Soulier, *L'Instabilité Ministerielle* (Paris, 1939), p. 184 ff.

the proper time. Naturally, when the Senate was obstinate, the Chamber usually gave way, for it was not strong enough in the country to insist successfully, and knew it. When M. Blum was overthrown, he argued that the will of universal suffrage ought to be respected—but in vain. The Chamber was not sufficiently solid for him. Governments have not seldom induced the Senate to insert or omit appropriations which the folly of the Deputies, not held in check by suitable rules of procedure, had mishandled.[83]

The Senate therefore acquired important financial powers, extending not only to the actual budget but to laws with immediate financial consequences—as customs laws, and laws imposing any kind of taxes or regulating loans. The rule did not include laws causing expenditure, and thus the Senate had a power to initiate such legislation.[84] In financial laws other than the budget, the Senate had complete rights to modify the projects of the Chamber; that is, it could accept, reject, reduce, or increase the credits voted by that body. For example, in 1920 the Senate seriously amended the income tax proposed by the Chamber of Deputies. The Chamber conceded the right to reject any expenditure, and the right to reject any tax which appeared excessive. But it denied the right to substitute its initiative for that of the Chamber or the government in order to vote increases of any expenditure or taxation.

The Senate seized the opportunity to vindicate its rights. Its protest is of first-class importance:[85]

Not only do the constitutional laws assert nothing of the kind, but jurisprudence, more rigorous than the texts, has never reduced the financial prerogative of the Senate to this point. . . . The importance and the complexity of the laws require that they shall be submitted to the free deliberation of the two Chambers. . . . It is necessary today more than ever, for there cannot be too much labor or ability of all the representatives of the country to bring to the budget the considerable resources of which it has pressing need and to divide the burden equitably among the body of taxpayers.

The Chamber of Deputies had the initiative in the matter of taxation laws; but the Senate cannot transform a tax voted by the Chamber "in such a fashion that it becomes in reality a new tax affecting taxpayers other than those included in the text of the Chamber of Deputies." [86] There were no other restrictions upon the Senate's rights regarding fiscal laws.

This report was drafted by Doumer and, having regard to his financial ability and substantial political talents, not to add his fine character,[87] we can understand why, when such men were in the Senate, the Chamber could not win and made concessions to Senatorial claims. However, the Senate's power was the subject of a battle in which the fortunes swayed now to this side, now to that, from 1875 to 1940. It favored the Senate: but the issue was still open.

Control Over Administration. We come to the third of the Senate's functions: its control over the administration, exercised through the medium of its control over the ministry. Its authority was derived from the constitution:[88] "Ministers are collectively responsible before the Chambers for the general policy of the government and individually for their personal acts." On a number of occasions the Senate was able to enforce its will by the threat to use the power implied in this clause, and sometimes it actually overthrew governments. If the power rested it never slept; it was always one which governments had to take into their serious calculation. It gave the Senate the sanction requisite for the insistent claims of its commissions to

[83] Gaston Jèze, *Le Budget* (Paris, 1922); Pierre, *op. cit.*, Vol. I, p. 605.
[84] For a more detailed discussion see F. Goguel, *Le Rôle Financier du Sénat Français* (Paris, 1937). See also L. Rogers, "M. Blum and the French Senate," *Political Science Quarterly*, September, 1937.
[85] Report, June 9, 1920, D.C. No. 1032, and Chamber debate of June 15, 1920, *Journal Officiel, Débats*, p. 2134.

[86] June 18, 1920, Sénat, *Documents*, No. 250.
[87] Some account of Doumer is given in (anon.) *Ceux qui Nous Mènent* (Plon, 1922). He was afterwards President of the Republic.
[88] Law of February 25, 1875, Article 8.

question ministers and officials, and even to arraign them. True, ministers appeared less often in the Senate than the Chamber; true also, that the premier was but rarely a senator. But a power resided in the Senate, and ministers could not reduce their presence beyond a safety line. And, further, a senator was usually made *Garde des Sceaux,* which office carried with it, conventionally, the vice-premiership.

The early republican chiefs like Gambetta and Ferry had emphatically enunciated the doctrine that only the Chamber had the right to cause a ministry to resign.[89] The question came to a head in 1894 in an interesting situation. The election of 1893 had caused a defeat of conservative groups and a large victory for radical and republican (that is, the liberal-conservative) groups. But the situation of the Chamber and the country caused considerable parliamentary difficulties. Attempts to govern with center groups or liberal groups failed, owing to the strength of the radicals and the socialists. These in common sought to obtain a progressive income tax, while the socialists sought to safeguard anarchists and socialists who were then urging the "propaganda of the deed" from too rigorous prosecution. The Senate, full of conservative elements, was profoundly disturbed. Then a bomb was thrown in the Chamber of Deputies, Carnot was assassinated, and Casimir Périer forced to resign the Presidency by reason of a virulent personal campaign against him in the press and at meetings of the extreme Left. A petty judge was removed from his duties by the Minister of Justice of the Bourgeois (Radical) cabinet, on the suspicion that he was not properly pursuing the guilty in the scandal of the Southern railways.[90] The legal forms necessary for the withdrawal of the case from him were not observed and the Senate took the offensive. It voted a resolution of censure

against the government by 156 and 63. Bourgeois answered that this was aimed at the government's general policy (in particular the progressive income tax). The Chamber supported him by 314 to 45. The Senate repeated its censure; and raised the question of its constitutional rights. The Chamber gave the government its confidence by a large majority, though some who had previously abstained from voting were now found ranged against Bourgeois. The Senate replied by a vote of 175 to 59 in favor of the declaration that

the Ministry argues that it may govern without the Senate. . . . It assumes that ministerial responsibility cannot be involved before the Senate. We protest against this attack upon the clear dispositions of the laws of the constitution. . . . We affirm our right of control and the responsibility of ministries before the two Chambers.

But the Senate, nevertheless, did not sever diplomatic relations, as it were, with the ministry.[91] This showed that the Senate did not really believe in its claim, for if it had, it would not have scrupled to force an open rupture, and to trust to law and opinion to support it. The struggle divided the country into those who were for conservatism in government and those who supported a policy of social reform. The cry was on the one side *"Vive le Sénat!"* (at the fashionable Auteuil race course) and *"A bas le Sénat!"* in the Southwest of the country. Then the cabinet asked the Chamber to vote credits to send troops to Madagascar. They were accorded, and the Chamber was adjourned for the Easter recess. The Senate, now by itself, voted no confidence in the government, and adjourned without voting the credit. When the Senate returned, the leaders of the three majority groups declared:

Three times has the Senate refused its confidence to the Ministry, and that by considerable majorities. However, in violation of the law of the Constitution, this Ministry has kept itself in office . . . we will not refuse the credits, but we cannot grant them to the present Ministry.

---

[89] Cf. A. Soulier, *op. cit.,* Part II, Chapter II; J. Devaux, "Le Rôle du Sénat et la Résponsibilité du Ministère," *Revue du Droit Public* (Paris, 1925), p. 653; L. Hubert, "Les Ministeres devant le Sénat," *Revue de Paris,* April, 1931.

[90] Cf. C. Seignobos in E. Lavisse, *Histoire de France Contemporaine* (Paris, 1921), pp. 184 ff.

[91] Cf. *Déclarations Ministérielles* (Paris, 1914), p. 82. The cabinet then included Senators.

And the Senate adjourned its vote until it should have before it a constitutional ministry possessing the confidence of both chambers.

Upon this, Bourgeois gave up the struggle, knowing that he had no large compact majority: in fact, his declaration on the whole subject was received in a fashion which illustrates the nature of French parliamentary life as few single episodes do. The general principle of "the preponderance of universal suffrage" was voted by 282 against 28; the resolution to prosecute democratic reforms by 379 against 31, but the resolutions together, which meant support of the existing government, suffered 324 abstentions from voting. The government's majority was 256 to 20. The cabinet fell through the abstentions, to its own satisfaction as well as that of the deputies hungry for ministerial opportunities. Nothing of principle was settled: only this was proved, that a division of interests in the Chamber of Deputies automatically redounds to the advantage of the power of the Senate. The principle of universal suffrage was sold by deputies for the chance of ministerial office.

The afterhistory of this episode also illuminates the shifting shadows of French politics. A moderate government followed, under Méline. This cabinet skimmed over the constitutional issue; its declaration [92] to the Chamber of Deputies on appearing before it recognized that it was "impossible to legislate and govern without the cooperation of the Senate."

What is the meaning of this history? As for authority, the plain text of the constitution seems to be clear. In addition, there was a genuine belief of the groups, from the Right Center to the extreme Right, in the political necessity for a second chamber. Right or wrong as it may be judged in any specific use of its power, these groups will always tend to be in favor of the Senate, because though it is an institution which may from time to time err in judgment, it can never lack ultimate justification. Then too, recognition of senatorial power issued from the opportunism of large numbers of deputies who supported or deserted a government in conflict with the Senate because they rated the immediate gain above the importance of the ultimate position of the Senate, and too often considered only the gain for their own careers. Recognition came from popular unwillingness to support those governments and those deputies who stood out against senatorial powers. Much of this is derived from the belief that, given the nature of its members, a check upon the Chamber is necessary. These are the ultimate sources of authority; and the Senate enjoyed their fruits. But they were clearly uncertain factors: no one could predict their quantity and their quality and, therefore, the meaning of the constitutional clause was not precise, though it seemed clear.

Hence, the Senate exercised, as the Chamber did, a daily supervision over the government, by means of interpellations and through its commissions. Generally speaking, the ministers were called upon to answer for their day-by-day conduct of the administration, and through this medium, the will and the ability of the Senate were brought to bear upon the actual work of government. Now, the Senate commissions were usually headed by men of experience in high office—some had been premiers. The minister who was in charge of a bill or was asked to explain some administrative history or to defend a vote of money, was not always a man of longer experience, either in Parliament or in a ministry, than his inquisitors. Some senatorial commissions [93] have been of greater effect than their counterparts in the Chamber of Deputies, and they had better organization and secretarial and advisory personnel than the Chamber of Deputies. During World War I, especially, the commission of the army, foreign affairs, and finance of the Senate acquired a mastery over the conduct of the war, transcending that of the government

92 *Déclarations Ministérielles*, April 30, 1896.

93 See Pierre, *op. cit.*, for the composition and power of commissions in the Senate.

itself.[94] The reasons for the pre-eminence of this Senate commission are given by Mermeix, in an interesting work.[95]

There was this difference between the work of the two Assemblies, that in the Senate members were more severe; vehement, if not more vigilant than in the Chamber, and that public opinion interested itself much more in the work of the Commission of the Senate . . .

More: no one in the Senate commission could be charged, as some of the deputies could be charged, with prewar pacifism and policies of unpreparedness. Since 1908, the Senate commission of the army had taken the lead in harassing ministers for more guns and munitions.

Conclusion: the Senate to 1940. Thus, the Senate of Third Republic France largely fulfilled the intentions and justified the hopes of its creators: a check upon the pure law of Number. It seems clear to us that the cause lies in two things: the bad conduct of the deputies, which lost them the confidence of the country. Partly arising out of this, strong party organization in each chamber and in the country did not unite the two chambers by a policy and a program made by the common advice and consent of the deputies and senators in party caucus assembled, prior to their separation into the two legislative bodies.

Let us observe, too, that the Senate was content to remain a center of revision and resistance, and rarely and only in relatively unimportant matters attempted to take a lead in initiating laws. Its numbness to popular drive is shown by its tardiness in accepting the political groups as the nominators of its commissions. While this was accomplished in the Chamber in 1910, it was established in the Senate only in 1921. It has left the initiative to the Chamber of Deputies and the government, so that energy resided principally in the Chamber of Deputies. The Senate often converted this energy into

waste. It was all the more effective for not attracting the public attention. Every minister had a few good friends in the Senate among his entourage, and their influence was always operative. Only the Socialists and the Communists really intended to reduce its powers, though other reformers proposed direct elections, or smaller representation for the small communes, or "functional" representation.

The Senate voted for the establishment of the Vichy regime by 225 to 1; thus, about 70 per cent of its total membership voted for Vichy. The Chamber of Deputies' vote was 395 for and 3 against, but as the total membership was 618, only about 64 per cent was in favor. If not a great, it is a significant, difference.

The New Beginning. The National Constituent Assembly of October 21, 1945, was a single-chamber body. In the first flush of postwar political feeling, the Socialists and the Communists were able to provide for an almost powerless second chamber. They could not entirely carry their own theory of single-chamber power to the extreme, because they needed at least the M.R.P. votes to carry the constitution. What they provided was this: [96] By the side of the National Assembly (to take the place of the former Chamber of Deputies), there would be established "the Council of the French Union," elected by departmental councilors in France, and the assemblies of the departments and the territories overseas. Note that the municipal councils were excluded. In this draft, the Assembly was to be elected for five years while the councilors were to sit for only four years.

Note this exercise in subordination. The Council's power was to be one of advice only, upon the drafts of law sent to it at its request or by the cabinet or the National Assembly. It would have to render its opinion within a month after the text was sent to it by the Assembly. The Assembly might declare urgency—in which case the Council would have to give its advice within the time limit laid down by the Assembly. If the Council agreed with

---

[94] From 1914-16. The powers of the commissions, excepting that of the army, were prorogued after 1916.
[95] Cf. "Mermeix," *Au Sein des Commissions, Fragments d'Histoire, 1914-19,* 2nd edition (Paris, 1924), p. 210 ff.

[96] Draft constitution, rejected May 6, 1946, articles 71 ff.

the Assembly, then the latter would pass the bill. If the Council gave no opinion, then the Assembly would pass the bill. But if the Council disagreed with the Assembly, the Assembly would give the bill a second reading, and having done this, decide in its own right how much regard to pay to the advice of the Council, without further ado. Clearly, a very weak body.

Against such a solution, the M.R.P., the Radical Socialists, and the Right and Center groups fulminated: being minorities in an age of socialist trend, they demanded a powerful second chamber as an antibody. The M.R.P. and the Radical Socialists contended also that a bicameral legislature would be stronger than a unicameral—stronger in popular acceptance and in its relations with the executive—and that, by slowing up action, it would compel a search for compromises. The draft constitution was rejected; the second-chamber problem playing quite a part in the negative vote. "The régime of a single Assembly," it was declared, "was an open door to adventure."

The second draft was accepted (dubiously, see p. 124 above), and it gives to the "Council of the Republic" a more substantial status. However, the general report of the Commission on the Constitution clearly broke with the former powers of the Senate over the executive. Its report, presented to the Assembly by the *rapporteur* (M.R.P.),[97] rejected the idea of ministerial responsibility to *both* houses, because this had produced additional ministerial instability in prewar France—"one of the principal vices of the Third Republic."

Legislatively, the Council has a certain degree of power. Instead of the Parliament's being, as in the unsuccessful draft, the National Assembly only, the second draft declares (Title II, article 5): "The Parliament shall be composed of the National Assembly and the Council of the Republic."

It may have a membership of between 250 and 320, and according to the Election Law of October 27, 1946, it is 315, of which 50 are elected by the National Assembly,

200 by metropolitan France, and the rest by Algerian and overseas regions. In metropolitan France, electoral colleges are composed of deputies of the department, the departmental councilors-general, and, by universal suffrage, the voters elect by proportional representation one delegate for each 300 voters in each canton. To be a candidate it is necessary to be at least 35 years old, and to be a municipal councilor or a voter, or domiciled in the canton for at least five years. These colleges are elected two weeks after the National Assembly is; and two weeks later they choose the councilors. This choice is made part by majority vote and part by proportional representation. Each electoral college elects one councilor for each half million inhabitants, or fraction thereof. There are further complications into which it is only a nightmare to enter. The main point is that the former basis of indirect election has been kept; but the heavy preponderance of the rural and smaller urban areas has been drastically ended. It should be noticed that this method of election is established by an ordinary law, and for the first Council only. It may be continued, or it may be modified, as experience shows. This was intended by the Constitutional Assembly. All that the constitution says is that the Council of the Republic shall be elected by "local and departmental bodies, by universal indirect suffrage" (article 6), and that it shall be re-elected one half its membership at a time.[98] The Communist representative wanted universal suffrage operating to choose electors who would choose the councilors—but not departmental electoral colleges of the kind actually adopted in the law. He thought that since, under his scheme, the men chosen would be other than the members of the Assembly, and probably older, that would be enough differentiation for the Council's revising function, and yet would avoid political obstruction by the Assembly. The Communists believed that the local-government-body type of election would produce a "reactionary" Council. The Socialists combated this view. They wanted

---

97 *Journal Officiel*, August 2, 1946.

98 Law of October 27, 1946.

a "chamber of reflection" which would "express the more profound, the more durable, the more proportionate views." This would be obtained by taking the local-government basis. It would entail changes in the law relating to the election of the departmental councilors-general. At any rate, there must be a period of experiment. The spokesman was M. Ramadier, later premier.[99]

Only the Assembly votes the laws. Any bills initiated by the Council of the Republic are merely transmitted to clerical officers of the Assembly. The proposal that the Council's spokesmen should appear before the Assembly was rejected. Bills initiated by the Council are not acceptable if they would lead to a diminution of revenues or create expenditures. No obligation lies on the Assembly to do more than study such bills. Financial legislation is initiatable by the Assembly alone. When the Assembly has voted a bill, it must be transmitted to the Council. This must give its opinion on it within two months. The budget, however, need not be submitted to this two months' delay, if the Assembly has itself taken less to discuss and vote it: then the Council has only the same span of time for its observations. Whenever the Assembly adopts an urgency procedure, the Council must limit its term for giving its opinion on the bill to that which the Assembly has fixed for itself.

If the opinion of the Council is in agreement with the Assembly's bill, or if it is not rendered within the time limits already mentioned, the Assembly's text is promulgated as law. If the Council disagrees, then the Assembly must give the bill a second discussion, but then decides "finally and in sovereignty" on the amendments proposed by the Council, accepting or rejecting in whole or in part as it thinks fit. However, in the case of partial or total rejections, the vote on the second discussion of the law must take place on a public roll call, by absolute majority of the membership of the Assembly, if the vote on the bill as a whole by the Council was public and by absolute majority of the Council.

[99] *Journal Officiel*, September 12, 1946.

Let it be noticed that two proposals to increase the power of the Council were rejected. One, by M. René Coty (Right), required the Council to address to the Assembly reports on the administration of the public services. His idea was that the Assembly would be too busy itself to be able to accomplish all the supervision of public administration that was desirable. Another deputy, M. Delachenal (Right), attempted to get the vote of the Assembly overruling the Council's opinion raised from an absolute majority to a three-fifths majority. His point was that "a law might have a heavy majority of the Council of the Republic against it and yet have only a very small majority in its favor in the Assembly," and that this "would not correspond to the will of the nation." [100]

The Council of the Republic's opinion is required before war can be declared; but it is the vote of the Assembly that is the decisive condition.[101]

Thus, the audacity of the Senate of the Third Republic has been avenged. The power of the Council of the Republic lies in its power to delay for some time, and to require a special majority (not a mere plurality of members present) where the Assembly wishes to reject its advice. Given the fluid nature of French political parties, it is a substantial obstruction. M. Ramadier, whose opinion on the need for a second chamber with a power of delaying the Assembly has been noticed, used an adroit method to overcome its delaying power in his ministerial difficulties of August and September of 1947: he piled many bills on the Council, all under resolution of urgency. It bitterly complained that it was too overwhelmed to do its job properly.

Since the Council has obstructive power and especially as regarding amendment of the constitution, all parties took an eager part in the election of the first Council in December, 1946. They also took as eager a part in the municipal elections of November, 1947.

In both Canada and Australia, the gov-

[100] *Journal Officiel*, September 13, 1946.
[101] Title II, article 7; and discussion in *Journal Officiel*, September 3, 1946.

TABLE 11—FRANCE: ELECTIONS TO THE ELECTORAL COLLEGE
FOR THE COUNCIL OF THE REPUBLIC, NOVEMBER 24, 1946

Parties and Blocs	Number of Electors[a]	Percent of Electors
Communist	24,544	29.2
M.R.P.	24,151	28.8
Socialist	14,244	16.9
Radical-Socialist bloc	11,056	13.1
Rightist bloc	9,827	11.7
Minor parties	256	0.3

[a] These figures were published as the final, official ones for 89
out of 90 departments, but several minor revisions were made
later, following M.R.P. and Communist claims and counter-
claims. The outcome was very similar to that of the general
elections to the National Assembly held two weeks earlier.

ernment (that is, the lower house) can
break a deadlock with the Senate by dissolution. This can, drastically otherwise,
be done in Britain. France and the United
States remained the lands without an electoral way of breaking a deadlock—until
1946, when the second French constitution of that year left the United States
alone in this position.

*Fourth Republic France: Four Cham-
bers.* Actually, it is not altogether accurate
to say merely that France is a bicameral
system of government, since four representative chambers have been established
by the constitution of the Fourth Republic. Two have already been discussed:
that is, the Parliament, falling into the
sovereign National Assembly and the subsidiary Council of the Republic. Another
body, composed of delegates from the vocational groups of the nation, is the *Conseil Économique Nationale,* or the National Economic Council. It has an advisory status, it being chiefly voluntary
for the government and the assembly to
consult it, and yet there is a quasi-com-
pulsory character about it. Its status and
powers are discussed later.[102]

In addition to these three assemblies,
an Assembly of the French Union was instituted. The first conception was to establish a legislative body in which the
overseas possessions of France as well as
metropolitan France were represented,
and the purpose was to draw together all
the parts of France and above all to give

colonial peoples a long-denied share in
the building of the political will of the
nation, indeed, to make them equal parts
of a single nation. This original proposition was supported by the Communists
and the Socialists, but was more and more
contested by the Center and Right and the
M.R.P. The final result was Title VIII of
the constitution, comprising articles 60 to
72. Briefly, this creates a Presidency of
the French Union, who is the President
of the Republic; the High Council; and
the Assembly. The High Council is composed of delegates of the government of
France and of the various overseas territories accredited to the President of the
Union. Its function is to assist the government in the general conduct of the
affairs of the Union. The Assembly is
composed of half the members representing metropolitan France, and the other
half of members from the overseas territories. The latter are elected by the regional assemblies; the former, by two
thirds by the National Assembly and by
one third by the Council of the Republic.
The Assembly meets when convoked by
the President: it must meet when one half
of its membership request it. Its function
is to examine bills and proposals submitted to it, for its advice, by the National
Assembly, or the government, or the governments of the associated states (that is,
the various states under the suzerainty of
the Republic). The Assembly has the
power to express its opinion on resolutions submitted to it by any of its members, and if the Assembly approves, to

---

[102] Cf. p. 547 below.

instruct its secretariat to send them to the National Assembly. The Assembly of the Union may also submit proposals to the government and the High Council of the French Union. All the resolutions referred to must relate to legislation concerning the overseas territories. All law made by the Parliament is applicable to the overseas territories so far as penal law, civil liberties, and political and administrative organization are concerned. In matters outside this—for example, economic and social affairs—an express provision is required in the law that it is applicable to the overseas territories; or the extension to them takes place by decree after consultation with the Assembly of the French Union. As an exception to the constitutional provision (article 13) that laws may be passed only by the National Assembly, special provisions for each territory may be enacted by the President of the Republic in the Council of Ministers after consultation with the Assembly of the Union.

CONCLUSION

BEFORE we pass to a consideration of the power and procedure of first chambers, we must ask what our survey of second chambers teaches regarding them. We have seen that when there are two houses there necessarily follows a contest for power. Each house gets and keeps whatever it can. No exact prediction can be made of the final outcome of any specific constitution, for this is settled by the balance of power (social, economic, moral) in the community, and this is so complex and so unfixable for any length of time ahead, that the nicest predictions are bound to be upset. If the houses are built on different foundations, the differences inevitably produce consequences in the balance of power, whatever the intention may have been. Only party can overcome the difference, but the very differences strain and break the unity of parties, by introducing a new corporate loyalty which collides with party. Even the same party, divided into two assemblies but stemming from different modes of election, supplies two different angles of vision.

The question, then, is whether the com-plication of the constitutional machinery, the obscuring of ultimate power relationships, the disturbance of the unity of party, and the checks and brakes upon government, are together worth the security given by a second chamber. That security is of no value unless it implies the introduction of sobriety and wisdom into government. Suppose, however, that it is possible for the lower chamber to provide good sense, adequate representativeness, sober and conscientious debate and procedure, mature reasoning; then where is the need for a second chamber, at such a cost?

Of all political maxims, one is sound; it has the keenness of Occam's razor: never create an institution when it is not necessary. If other institutions fulfill the conditions of good government, a second chamber is not necessary. Whether such an institution should be set up obviously depends upon the answer which each country can give to these questions: Are the deputies wise? Do the parties think out their programs adequately, and are they sincere in their intentions? Is there a parliamentary sense of justice and tolerance which will prevent persecution? How far is the lower chamber aided and rescued from the blunders of ignorant benevolence by the expert, professional, but democratically-minded civil servants? How far does the lower chamber possess and master adequate sources of information about the state of the country, domestic and foreign? How far does it command a procedure which passes the laws after adequate thinking and debate, and in such style as to avoid internal contradiction or erroneous record of legislative intention?

These questions are answerable for each country from the facts we have already recounted; they will be even better answerable when we have analyzed the manner of action of the lower chambers. We may be sure, however, that wherever there are material or spiritual interests which desire defense against the grasp of the majority, a bicameral system will be claimed; for even the mere deferment of an undesirable policy is already a gratifying deliverance.

[435]

19

First Chambers: The Functions of Legislatures

LOWER chambers occupy themselves with three main functions—lawmaking, control of the executive, and the development of policy [1]—which will be treated in this chapter and the two following, where we shall observe how the rules of procedure, written and conventional, provide for them.

Lawmaking falls into two main processes: the making of laws of general concern, or public bills; and the making of laws of private concern, or private bills. The latter are not treated in this work: [2] we deal only with public bills. Lawmaking is often considered under two separate heads: ordinary statutes, to be discussed in this chapter and the next, and the budget (or the provision of funds and determination of expenditures), to be considered in Chapter 21.

---

[1] The reader may compare this statement with that made by the clerk of the House of Commons to the Select Committee on Procedure, *Third Report*. October, 1946, p. xxii: "The main functions of the House are: 1. Representation of popular opinion. 2. The control of finance. 3. The formulation and control of policy. 4. Legislation. Though the list could be added to, these are at any rate the main functions of the House. But it will be readily perceived that the first function, representation of opinion, is not commensurate with the other three, since it cuts across the classification and pervades every form of proceeding." Query: does not the same hold good of "formulation and control of policy"?

[2] For the treatment of private and local bills in Great Britain, see Herman Finer, *English Local Government* (London, 1949), 4th edition, and *Municipal Trading* (London, 1941).

Lawmaking assemblies find themselves in need of (1) guidance in regard to the time they may spend upon particular subjects of deliberation, and the priority in which they are to be considered (pp. 437-446); (2) guidance by experts upon the substance and drafting of the law and instruction on its probable results (pp. 446-458); and (3) appropriate rules of deliberation (Chap. 20).

TIME AND PRIORITY

IT is clear that there must be some regulation, the minimum of which is to divide the time between majority and minority, and to settle which business is to come first. Further, there is need for setting a limit to the time allowed to each speaker and the proportion of time to be spent on each subject. The necessity arises from the size of the assemblies, the complexity and amount of legislation, the constitutional equality of every deputy's mandate, and the majority's ultimate need of decisive action. It is unnecessary to insist upon the amount of work with which modern assemblies are faced: some indication has already been given in the chapter upon state activity. But all of them are more than busy: they are pathologically congested, and this in spite of repeated attempts to relieve them by procedural reform. Business must be treated in order of urgency. Who is to decide that order, when all mandates are equal? That question is not answered by leaving the matter

TABLE 12—HOUSE OF COMMONS: DISTRIBUTION OF TIME
AMONG FUNCTIONS

	Average Number of Days Annually, 1906–38	Average Annual Percentage, 1906–38
Control of finance	15	10.3
Control and formulation of policy	58.5	40.
Legislation	—	—
Public bills	67.9	47.
Private bills	2.4	1.6
Delegated legislation	1.6	1.1
Total per session	145.4	100.0

to the free decision of all the equal mandates, for then the answer would be the anarchy of a mob of uncompromising equals. It is answered by the need to secure a majority if anything is to be accomplished. This need gave rise to party groupings; today it is one of the forces necessitating party organization. The paramount necessity of a majority causes subordination; and in our own day that subordination is to the leaders of the parties. It is a remarkable subordination, and, when disputed, as it incessantly and desperately is, it is in the manner of those who sigh for a mythological Golden Age. The marshaling of voters into parties, the exchange of votes for programs, are the bloom of the majority principle. No government can escape from the clutches of its own program, and continue to be a government. The need for the regulation of time is intensified to the utmost by the large amount of business.

Little Time for the Private Member. The private member has an exceedingly small proportion of legislative time used at his discretion, or for business initiated by himself. In England the amount of time allowed by the rules is about 85 per cent for the government, and 15 per cent when added together at the initiative of private members. I am more than gratified to find that my estimate is very closely corroborated (14 per cent) by the evidence of the clerk of the House, Sir Gilbert Campion, since he had at his disposal the clerks of the House to research into many sessions. (It may be added that sessional rules dur-

ing the Labour government's term since October, 1945, sharply reduced this proportion of private members' initiative.) His evidence on the utilization of the time of the House of Commons was based on careful analysis.[3] His tables are based on two separate but related principles: the first (Table 12) is the general distribution of time between various functions, and the second (Table 13) is the general distribution of time among the government, private members, and the opposition.

It will be observed in Table 12 that the control of policy occupies no less than some 40 per cent of the total time. Also, in the last ten years some 24 days per session were devoted to motions for debate of government policy as compared with 18 in ten years before that. Note too the distribution shown in Table 13.

In France, the proportion allowed to the private member is much higher, owing to the time for interpellations, the weakness of the executive, and the intransigence of the parties: in Weimar Germany, the proportion was much as in England; the United States House of Representatives is perhaps more in the hands of the dominant party than in England. In all countries the power of the private member has deteriorated. He has the power only to worry his party, and the power to worry is effective according to strength of personality and representative argument.

Who, then, steers the work of the assem-

[3] *Third Report,* Select Committee on Procedure, Nos. 189-91. October 31, 1946, pp. 29 and 31.

TABLE 13—HOUSE OF COMMONS: DISTRIBUTION OF TIME AMONG
GOVERNMENT, PRIVATE MEMBERS, AND OPPOSITION

	Average Number of Days Annually, 1929–38	Average Annual Percentage, 1906–38
Private members' days (Including bills, motions adjournment)	21.8	14
Opposition time	46.5	31
Indeterminate (Budget and finance bills, private bills)	19	12
Government time	70.4	43
Total per session	157.7	100

blies and decides upon the priority of debate? It is, of course, in all countries, the leaders of the dominant parties.

Parliamentary Pilotage in England. In England,[4] the government decides upon the allocation of time for particular bills; the opposition may challenge this allocation, but it cannot overturn the government's decision because it cannot muster a majority against the government, and if it did it would itself decide upon priority. Being in a majority, the government party is able to secure the alteration of the Standing Orders of the House, which already give a substantial priority to government business, and to ask for convenient sessional orders. But serious changes are by custom first reported on by a select, all-party committee of the House. However, it is one of the strongly recognized customs of Parliament that the government of the day shall meet the opposition as far as it possibly can: or in other words, that it shall not use its power intolerantly.[5] This is an ideal pursued for its own democratic value, but governments are also led to this by the unpopularity which meets a

government when it uses its right in a narrow spirit. For "freedom of speech," the "rights of minorities," and "careful deliberation" are powerful ideas. They embody objects of worth which can be offset against the good in the substance of the laws passed by their suppression; and a government is constrained by honor. Oppression also brings revenge; a government which uses it may later suffer from it; and in debate the opposition may convey this possibility and also point to their own liberality in the past. Oppositions have always favored the idea of a committee of both sides of the House to allocate time; governments are naturally less favorable thereto. Until the present the arrangements between both sides of the House have been made by informal talks of the whips—referred to as "the usual channels"—and ultimately by the fiat of the government. When the government is not in a majority, it is interesting to observe, it tends to lose its power over the timetable.[6] When it has both a large majority and a weighty mandate to legislate (like the Labour government of 1945), it is severe about the timetable, in spite of opposition protests. The government's sense of its mandate (referred to in the previous chapter)—its sense of responsibility for the fulfilment of recent promises and the promises made over the years

---

[4] Cf. T. E. May, *Parliamentary Practice* (London, 1946), 14th edition; G. Campion, *Procedure of the House of Commons* (London, 1937 and 1947); *Manual of Procedure, House of Commons* (annually); Reports on Procedure, Select Committee on Procedure, House of Commons, 1932 and 1946 (Nos. 189-91).
[5] Since the rise of closure, several suggestions have been made for the establishment of a committee of both government and opposition to allocate time for debate.

[6] It is only necessary to point to the fate of the Labour government of 1923 and 1929 in England and the Brüning cabinet in Germany in the summer of 1930.

by the party—is intense; and it expects the electorate to judge it by its fulfilment.

How differently the government's control of the time of the House looks from the private members' point of view (and from the whole opposition's for that matter), and from the position of the government, can be seen from observations made during the discussions on the reform of the procedure of the House of Commons: [7]

He [the government spokesman] showed a tendency merely to consider this House as a gearbox, on the lever of which the hand of the Government must always rest; and that the transmission of power and action must always reside in the hands of the Government and their supporters, thereby showing an inherent desire on the part of the Executive always to impose their will on the House.

But a government statement said: [8]

The Government must be constantly mindful of their legislative requirements, and proceed with the main objective of facilitating through Parliament of legislation which the Government regard as necessary for the well-being of the nation.

Two other remarks throw great light on legislative leadership and the modern position of the rank and file of members. A Labour government spokesman declared, "My honorable friend said that democracy means debate and discussion, but it also means decision; it must be debate and discussion leading up to a decision." [9] Finally let us notice the implications of the following question and answer: [10]

Does it [the government's theory of the position of the private member] not involve . . . that a Private Member of the House could never have any scope whatever for initiating

anything unless he could do it within the councils of a large party, forming either the Government or the official Opposition?

The answer was:

Not too much, I agree, unless he can influence either the Government or the Opposition. But, broadly speaking, it is a two-party country. Broadly speaking, it is Government and Opposition in Parliament, though the others are, of course, taken account of, and I personally think it is a good thing it is a two-party country.

In a typical parliamentary year before World War II, the government initiated and secured the passage of fifty-nine public general statutes, including the financial legislation of the year, while private members had the time in which to initiate a number of measures, but were only allowed enough time by the government to persuade the House to pass eleven. In addition to such legislative time, the private member, whether on the opposition or the government benches, has time for introducing motions of various kinds (practical or theoretical) for debate, and has the opportunity of putting amendments to bills. And the opposition, as a body, has the choice of the estimates it would like to debate, since there is not time for discussion of them all. It is by no means an ungenerous division of time between majority and minority.

The Legislative Timetable in France. In pre-1945 France, the government struggled valiantly, often vainly, with the arrangement of a timetable. There was entirely absent from the rules of procedure of the Chamber of Deputies any such rule as those which, in the Standing Orders of the House of Commons, give so much time to the British government. But—and the exception is important—the constitution of the Third Republic recognized to the government a right of initiative (article 3; February 25, 1875), gave the President of the Republic the right of initiative, and, since Presidential decrees require ministerial countersignature, there was the warrant for governmental initiative. Duguit says that this gave the govern-

[7] A Conservative member of Parliament, Debates on Procedure, November 4, 1947, col. 1630.
[8] Report, Select Committee on Procedure, House of Commons, 1946, Nos. 189-91, p. 97, Memorandum by His Majesty's Government.
[9] Debates, *loc. cit.*, col. 1607.
[10] Report, Select Committee on Procedure, House of Commons, 1946, Nos. 189-91, Question 3612, by a Labour member; answer by Herbert Morrison, then Lord President of the Council, and leader of the House of Commons.

ment the largest freedom; [11] and there is no doubt that for the reasons given by him,[12] the French government obtained a large measure of parliamentary predominance. While the government's projects obtained immediate introduction before the House, bills initiated by members, equally acknowledged in the constitution, had to go to a special commission for report before appearing in the Assembly. Such an initiative is given directly to the government by the constitution of 1946 (article 14); and the right to be heard at any time goes to the ministers (article 53). Governmental bills received the dignity of being called *projets,* while the bills of members were mere *propositions;* the terms are indicative of a real difference in constitutional significance. Before World War II, ministers introduced slightly fewer bills than did individual deputies; but secured the passage about four times as many.

Until 1911, nothing but informal pressure of the government upon groups provided security for a regular current of business. The rules of the House provided only that the president of the Chamber had authority to set up the Order of the Day after consulting, and securing the agreement of, the Chamber. Certain days were regularly allowed to commissions to report; but they were often put off by the Chamber and its president when the government or nongovernmental groups were interested in something else. Further, the doctrine that "the Chamber is mistress of its procedure" gave legitimacy to sudden demands in the middle of a sitting for changes in the timetable. Thus the government had no privileged position, excepting the rule that a minister must be heard at any time he wished, which had its obvious limits. The government was compelled to bargain with its component groups and its rivals, working with little more strength than theirs. Further, it was not difficult to upset the Order of the Day by pleading urgency for some bill or resolution, though it was the custom to warn

the government that a request for urgency was to be made, and the president of the Assembly could hold up the discussion until the competent minister attended. The position of the government and of the Chamber in general under such a system was intolerable, and the abuse of these opportunities of upsetting the Order of the Day forms a principal ingredient in the criticisms of French parliamentarism before 1914.

The phrase "the Chamber is mistress of its procedure" is parallel to the English political dictum, "the House can do as it likes"—but remarkable differences in practice result from the facts of party organization, loyalty, and discipline. In the House of Commons, it is difficult to distinguish the House, the executive, and the parties as separate entities.

The Chamber set out to cure itself, and some improvements were produced by the wholesale reforms of procedure in 1911, 1915, and 1920.[13]

The presidents of the great commissions, the presidents of the groups, or, in their default, a member nominated by the bureau of the commission or the group, the vice-presidents of the Chamber, are convoked by the president of the Chamber, each week if it is necessary, to examine the state of business of the Committee. Their conference gives rise to motivated propositions concerning the order of business and the work of the Chamber and the regulation of the daily timetable. The Government, specially warned by the President of the Chamber of the day and hour of the conference, can be heard. The proposition presented by the conference is read during a session by the President, who submits it to the approbation of the Chamber. The timetable as fixed by the Chamber is put up in the precincts of Parliament and published in the *Journal Officiel.* It cannot be modified except by a vote taken either upon the initiative of the Government, or upon a demand signed by fifty members.

This system is reconsecrated in Chapter IX of the Procedure of March, 1947, except that groups with less than fourteen members cannot be represented, and a

---

[11] *Traité du Droit Constitutionnel* (Paris, 1921-25), Vol. IV, p. 308.
[12] *Ibid.,* p. 305.

[13] Résolution, May 24, 1920. Cf. R. Bonnard, *Les Réglements des Assemblées* (Paris, 1926), p. 535 ff.

commission can propose a change in the order.

What did this mean down to 1940? At the conference were assembled the knowledge of pending business possessed by the heads of the commissions, the desires of the different groups, and the policy of the government (which was, of course, also strongly represented in the groups). The government groups could, if strong and loyal to each other, win their way, if not by a vote in the conference at least by a challenge to the Order of the Day in the Chamber. The government derived a certain strength from the fact that it could challenge and perhaps overturn the Order in the House. It was obviously better for it to bargain with the opposition groups in the conference than try its strength in the open Chamber—always a dangerous encounter. The government was not put upon better terms than the other groups; it was on equal terms; it was not in a position, as in England, to extend mercies; happy was it if it could obtain them. So pressed was the government that, in 1922, all presidents of commissions were asked by the presidents of both chambers to try to send forward a notice of matters to be put down on the agenda at least the evening before the conference, in order that the government might have time to look over the dossiers before the meeting.

Other things are worth observation at this point, which will be seen in the full light of their significance later. The president of the Chamber and the presidents of the commissions were parts of this steering committee, and it was not in nature that they could be parts of such a conference without being able to exercise an influence upon its decisions. No government will make trouble for itself when constitutional rights have been accorded to certain officers. The knowledge and experience acquired by these officers made their consultation by the President of the Republic at a ministerial crisis important. Their importance then gave them power over the government. Hence these positions were sought after, and one way of obtaining them was to form a group and

become its leader. In their due place, these facts light up the obscure labyrinths of French politics.

The conference which regulates the Order of the Day is concerned not only with law but also with interpellations. The National Assembly of 1946 follows in general the old procedure; and the leadership is once again weakened by a restive following.

Time and Priority in the House of Representatives. The United States House of Representatives is bound hand and foot by rules which tie it to a program determined by the majority party.[14] No government, in the English or Continental sense, is responsible for the distribution of time and the decision of priority. No such smooth seamless connection between executive and legislature as in Britain reigns in the United States. The shortness of the legislative term—two years—and the lawmaking propensities of the American people, coupled with the procedural confusion between public and private bills, develop such an urgent pressure that the dominant party controls almost every second. In the 78th Congress, that is, in a space of two years, 7845 bills were introduced in the House and 5628 in the Senate. The laws enacted numbered 1157, of which 589 were private and local acts. This still makes the total of public acts nearly three times the number of those passed by the British Parliament. Some of the discrepancy is due to procedural consolidation in the British system. In Congress' mechanical debates, American party organization reaches its perfection, no pliability being admitted

---

14 Cf. D. S. Alexander, *History of Procedure of the House of Representatives* (Boston, 1916); G. R. Brown, *Leadership of Congress* (Indianapolis, 1923); P. D. Hasbrouck, *Party Control of the House of Representatives* (New York, 1927); M. P. Follett, *The Speaker of the House* (New York, 1904); and C. W. Chiu, *The Speaker of the House of Representatives since 1896* (Boston, 1917); and, for the formal rulings, A. C. Hinds, *Parliamentary Precedents* (Washington, 1907); F. M. Riddick, *Congressional Procedure* (Boston, 1941); G. B. Galloway, *Congress at the Crossroads* (New York, 1946); and R. Young, *This Is Congress* (New York, 1943).

at all. The power wielded abroad by the government, came, until 1910, to be here wielded by one man: the speaker of the House, who was, and remains, a deliberate and acknowledged partisan, almost to the complete opposite of the speaker of the House of Commons. He led the majority forces and secured discipline by his power, individually, to nominate members to committees. As the committees are the decisive stage in lawmaking and executive control in America, the speaker's power was that of political life and death over the members. By the assignment of bills to appropriate committees, and by the power of "recognition" of a member in debate, the speaker enhanced this power. He and his leading party friends controlled the time of the House. Control was exerted through the formal power of the Committee on Rules, which had the singular power of reporting to the House and changing the procedure and course of measures at any time; of this committee of five, the speaker, who nominated the rest, was chairman.

A revolt occurred against this system in 1910; the speaker was deposed from the Committee on Rules; and all committees were henceforth to be chosen by the House Committee on Committees. The party leaders (in caucus) control the nominations to this committee, and usually get themselves appointed to the chairmanship of all other committees by intraparty jockeying. This process is tempered by the rule of seniority. The speaker's power was thus disintegrated, and given to the controllers of the party caucuses. These leaders decide who shall be speaker (just as he contributes to the decision as to who shall lead in his party). They select a floor leader: that is, a manager of debates and tactics (in the Democratic party he is chairman of the Committee on Ways and Means, and chairman of the party's committee on committees; in the Republican party he is *ex-officio* chairman of the party's committee on committees, and of the informal steering committee). They settle also the composition of the committees and appropriate the chief positions thereon, and they (the Republicans)

settle who shall compose the steering committee.

The controlling power over the time and procedure of the House, then, is in the majority party, the speaker (whose aid in controlling the House is indispensable), the floor leader, the chairman of the Committee on Rules and the chairman of the Committee on Appropriations, and several other party personages who together form the steering committee—the name of which is sufficiently expressive of its function. These lead, control, and do business with the little clique of leaders on the other side; they settle the legislative program with the President when the party controls the executive branch also; they direct debate, and get the laws passed. Party caucus decisions supplement their personal influence. The steering committee is appointed to superintend generally the operation of the rules of procedure; but its special political business is to appear before the House when the majority party is in distress, and propose a rule that such and such a bill be given priority over everything else. It does not follow that the steering is steady and well considered. The party is volcanic and offers uncertain foothold. The steering is itself eruptive and opportunistic. Not all the followers follow.[15]

Another important aspect of the legislative activity of the United States House of Representatives deserves emphasis here. This is the role of the United States President in legislation. Although the legislative power is vested in the Congress of the United States, the President plays a very important part in making the laws, when he wants to do so, has the ability, and is not faced either by a politically hostile Congress or by a politically friendly one that contains personal enemies. He cannot, for reasons which will become much clearer in a following chapter,

---

[15] Henceforth the facts about United States Congressional behavior are founded largely in the hearings, the symposium, and the report of the Joint Committee on Reorganization of Congress, 1945 and 1946. Notice that the House of Commons was simultaneously re-examining its procedure!

exercise a legislative leadership on anything like the scale of the British cabinet or with its undoubted authority over the legislature. But he has four qualifications which enable him to take a not inconsiderable part in adding to the statute book. (1) First is the requirement of the constitution that he give messages to the Congress on the state of the union, both regularly and at his own wish. (2) He may veto legislation passed by Congress. (3) He has acquired something like nation-wide party leadership. (4) Being in actual control of the day-by-day active government, he is stimulated by his own official advisers to amend and extend the laws in their particular provinces, and the clients of the various departments urge this upon them, and so upon the President.

Many Presidents have used their message-making and veto power as vehicles of lawmaking. But there is no virtue in the vehicles themselves: the state of mind of Congress, the parties, and the nation settles whether there is to be creative force in the Presidential instruments. The odds are usually against him: and he must triumph over them. In Britain no cabinet can ever assume the power to write a message until it has acquired the power to embody its contents in law and administration: that is the essence of the cabinet system. Men like Theodore Roosevelt, Woodrow Wilson, William Taft, and Franklin Delano Roosevelt used their opportunities with some success (the last-named especially). They bored into the precincts of Congress, and by all the arts of management pushed their suggestions to a legislative conclusion. They sent messages to the Houses and letters to party friends, held conferences and breakfasts in their room adjoining the Senate, and invited the chairmen of Congressional committees and the "floor leaders" to the White House. Their most trusted and astute cabinet officers were often sent to whip up support, and to exert the influence of the personal representation of the president. "Trouble-shooters" were sent up to the "Hill": men of the "brains trust" or the White House staff or party friends or confidants of the "kitchen cabi-

net." Heads of departments attended caucus meetings; information was poured into Congress through the attendance of officials at Congressional hearings, and sometimes less publicly—to a point where some Congressmen even complained that the restrictions on lobbying should be made to apply to the executive! Party friends were provided with drafts of bills and vindicating briefs. Many a bill was drafted in the departments; [16] many a Congressman turned to the executive departments for this assistance; and since 1921, by the Budget and Accounting Act, in order that the chief executive should know what is going on in his own house and to secure a minimum of coordination, the projects emanating from government departments were to be cleared with the Bureau of the Budget.

What has been the net result? We are indebted to Dr. Chamberlain [17] for illumination on this subject. In a most painstaking and objective study of the ninety major laws passed between 1890 and 1942, he shows that about 20 per cent fell to the credit of the President, about 40 per cent were mainly the fruit of Congressional initiative and industry, some 30 per cent were the joint work of President and Congress, while rather less than 10 per cent were initiated and carried through under the pressure of outside groups. Dr. Chamberlain had taken the greatest care in tracing to their roots the enterprise and original impetus which gave birth to the statutes, and, of course, they were complicated, interest sometimes commencing with a Congress or a President, the initiative being dropped by either and then resumed later by some other person. The President was strong in legislation concerning national defense and the control of business, but weak in regard to agriculture, immigration, labor, natural resources, and railroads. Congress evinced a major

---

[16] Cf. E. E. Witte, "The Preparation of Proposed Legislative Measures by Administrative Departments," in Report, President's Committee on Administrative Management, 1936, p. 361 ff.

[17] L. H. Chamberlain, *The President, Congress and Legislation* (New York, 1946).

influence in the regulation of banking, currency, immigration, labor, and conservation. Four out of a total of eight tariff statutes were passed under the steam of lobby pressure; two had their inspiration in Congress; and two (the Underwood and Reciprocal Trade Agreements Acts) were initiated and thrust through by the President.

Legislative Priority in Weimar Germany. The German constitution of 1919 accorded the right of initiative to the government or to the members of the *Reichstag*.[18] This terminology indicates the priority of the government;[19] and tradition, party organization, and necessity substantiated their priority.

German parliamentarians described the process of legislation without a mention of any other initiatory activity than that of the government, except that the private members' own initiative was often used for urgent laws of minor importance to help the government evade the need for consulting the *Reichsrat*. German rules of procedure provides for a Council of Elders (*Ältestenrat*): that is, a council representative of all parties, to plan out, but not enforce, the order of business. This arrangement had existed in the old constitution, and it was found to be particularly useful in a system where so many parties abounded. (We have seen that in the French system there is an analogue to this.) The Weimar rules (section 3, articles 10, 11, and 12) provided for such a council, composed of twenty-one members, representative of the parties, "to support the President [of the Assembly] in the conduct of affairs, and especially to bring about an understanding among the groups regarding the order of business. It also regulates the distribution of Committee Chairmanships and their substitutes." The report on these articles says that it was considered impossible to give the Council of Elders compulsory powers, and the old practice had to be followed: that is, advisory power only, in which, "after long discussions on a question, nothing came of it if even one member stood out." Naturally! for that member might be the government or a minority which hoped for better treatment in the *Reichstag*.

Government Commands Time. Governments cannot avoid some time's being taken by the opposition, as an official body, or by private members on either the government or opposition side. But most of the time is commanded by the government, and where the cabinet system prevails, priority is settled by the cabinet, even though, as we have seen, the cabinet's authority in this respect varies in degree in different countries. What is important is the general acknowledgement of supremacy of the government (or, for the United States, the majority party), and the general recognition that the private member's role is subordinated to his group's leadership and the group's role to the government's. Even the generous desires of leaders to allow members independent headway is not—and on occasions when it was declared, could not—be fulfilled.[20] The results are, on the whole, good. It has often been said that to disperse power is to obscure responsibility. Representative government develops into a farce when power is divided minutely, for the electorate, when called upon to judge, is muddled. We have already seen to what a small extent the electorate can intervene with an independent and positive judgment, even under the conditions where power is divided among and contested by two or three well-known entities, like parties. No subtle argument is needed to demonstrate the necessary

---

18 Article 68.
19 *Vorlagen.* Members' bills are again distinguished by a less important title, *Anträge*—which is little more than a suggestion, and is almost synonymous with the French *proposition.* W. Lambach, *Herrschaft der 500* (Berlin, 1926), Section: "Wie eine Gesetzvorlage entsteht." Cf. also Hauffe, *Der Reichstag hat beschlossen* (Berlin, 1931).

20 This historical generalization is still substantiated by contemporary argument and practice. Above all see Minutes of Evidence of Third Report of Select Committee on Procedure of House of Commons, Nos. 189-91 of 1946; particularly evidence of Herbert Morrison and Mr. Glanvil Hall, Chief Government Whip.

failure of the electorate when these political parties are many, without a past and very probably without a future.

It is a disadvantage of modern legislative practice that the ordinary member is excluded from the power to determine the course of business, of legislation, of control over the government. Every member has something unique (if, in our opinion, silly) to add to discussion, and when the dictation of a government is regularly unchallenged, it may fall into error. The question, however, is, whether, on the whole, representative government functions better or not without every member's contribution. We have already seen that not all members, as a rule, have a vital contribution to make to discussion; neither special training nor formal profession nor conspicuous general sagacity fits them for it. Nor is there anything so special about the locality they represent that its voice ought to be heard. When it is, indeed, the party caucus knows it, and promptly includes it in the ingredients of the party's policy. It is enough if men of exceptional talent and character, evinced in open competition and without privilege, are guaranteed by procedure the opportunity to denounce the misdeeds of government and opposition when the occasion demands, if a right of criticism remains. We shall show, later, that for this there is ample—sometimes too ample —freedom, though it is not always used capably. The major necessity is a clear and decisive lead given by a plainly identifiable body which can be judged both during and after its actual tenure of office in government or opposition. Again we see that modern democracy demands a great deal of political parties. Without them, representativeness and responsibility are denuded of meaning. If able, forceful men are elected by their districts, they will have enough individual and collective kick in them to compel merit and wisdom in the leadership or its change. Within each party prevails a constant competition by which political talent rises and falls to its own level. Those who get to the top get access to other men's time.

EXPERTNESS AND INTERESTS

EXPERTNESS in making laws consists of two main qualities: a command of the knowledge of their substance, and ability to formulate the results with the minimum of vagueness and unintentional contradiction of other parts of the statute book. Here again, certain technical necessities have thrown the power into the hands of the executive, though arrangements are possible, and do exist, whereby the members of the houses may act independently and efficiently. In the United States, with its separation of powers, the actual dependence of Congress on the chief executive is less in fact and also less obvious— yet it is considerable, as we shall see, and ought to be still greater in fact.

The difficulties of modern lawmaking are colossal. The knowledge required for the simplest statute is complex and special. Even when that knowledge is available, it does not follow that the same person knows how far existing legal and administrative institutions can be used to obtain the desired results, or how far existing rights will be injured by the new law. The creation of good law involves the careful combination of (1) technical knowledge, (2) an understanding of the law as it is, (3) an ability to make sound estimates of the expenditure of money and the administrative energy, procedure, and machinery required to accomplish the necessary tasks, and (4) an appreciation of the general disturbance to be caused. This implies the cooperation of a number of technically competent authorities. If, indeed, one single member or a group of members could muster these requirements, there would still remain a condition which only the executive branch can fulfill in the modern state: that is, to scrutinize the obvious constituents of the policy and take responsibility for their soundness, and to decide upon their timeliness and harmony with all the other parts in the general plan of legislative, administrative, and fiscal evolution. This can only be done by trusted persons; such people as have won the public confidence in a major degree. That, at least, is what evolution of the democratic theory and practice amounts to.

Experts within the Government. It is true that there may be experts outside the government ranks, and there are. But in government the people ask not only for an expert but for an expert upon experts, even as ordinary men and women tend to seek the opinion of those who know the possible shortcomings of the experts in law or medicine or architecture whose services they contemplate employing. Those who are trusted in this matter are, naturally, those who have had long experience of government, whether inside or outside of the legislature, and those, too, who have won confidence in a high degree by other qualities. This is no other than the government, in the first resort, and the administration or the civil service, in the second, and we shall see later that it is upon the civil service that the government itself relies very largely for its judgment upon the substance of legislation. This is the robust second line of defense—the real "second chamber," as Graham Wallas has called it—of our own day. Without it, confidence in parties and their leaders would necessarily suffer serious shocks from time to time. For the civil service is a body of men and women professionally occupied for life in executing the law, in watching its effects, its merits, its failures, and in observing the reciprocal influence of government and society. This is true of all the countries of which we speak (even, perhaps especially, of dictatorships). It is to this court of judgment that the proposals of the public, of members of the legislature, of party leaders, and of ministers ultimately come, and it is from here that proposals not seldom emanate. I strongly re-emphasize this phase of the importance of continuous career statesmanship — the responsible civil service—to modern government, especially in planning.

Outside Experts and Representatives of Interests. The sources of law are, however, far from being confined to the legislature, to the ministry, or to the civil service, for neither their range of knowledge nor their range of interests is as comprehen-

sive as society itself. Legislatures possess the authority to make laws, but as already seen, in a varying degree, they only partially represent the occupational and spiritual composition of the nation; the men in the cabinet rise a little, but not much if at all, above the level of talent in the legislature itself. Indeed, these have not come into office entirely on their merits as governors; they express desire, will, claims. Nor can the civil service itself do its work unaided. All are obliged to seek the aid of outside experts and representatives of interests, lest they fall into serious mistakes not only regarding the particular interests, but lest, too, they do an injustice to that vast unseen intricacy called the public, which remains a phantom while it is unaffected but suddenly becomes a frenzied monster when molested. This is not an entirely new phenomenon in government; the ancient and the medieval state exhibited the same features. It is impossible for the ordinary institutions of government to penetrate the depths, and master the complexities, of any modern branch of society and law without the special aid of those to whom the matter is one of lifelong and intimate acquaintance, and to whom all things are revealed owing to the vitally felt quality of their interest in the result, "the felt necessities," as one of Justice Holmes' opinions has it. Nor is it necessary that government shall ask for aid: it is continually pressed by those who observe that the normal political institutions are ignorant or uncomprehending, or that their interests are inadequately represented and likely to be treated with insufficient care.

Hence modern governments—legislature, ministry, and civil service alike—have come, on the one hand, to depend to an extraordinary degree upon a variety of institutions to gather information and recommend policy, and, on the other, to be pressed by organized social and occupational groups. To leave these out of account in the analysis of modern lawmaking and government is entirely to miss its nature, to place an undue importance upon legislative creativeness, and quite to mistake the character of modern methods of popular representation.

In the *first* category—that of institutions gathering information and recommending policy—are such institutions as royal commissions, departmental committees, and select committees in Great Britain; investigating committees and departmental committees in the United States; inquiry commissions and the Economic Council in Germany; the *Commissions Extraparlementaires* and the *Conseil Nationale Économique* in France. To these must be added regular departmental advisory boards which have been set up in various countries, principally in Great Britain,[21] Weimar Germany, and France. Finally, there are the technical aids in the legislatures, like libraries, and more important to nascent American development, the Legislative Reference Bureau and the legislative counsel. In the *second* category are the private representative organizations which push an interest. These operate by deputations to departments at the request of the latter, deputations to ministers, and special "pressure" organizations located in the neighborhood or precinct of Parliament or Congress and the departments, and called by the American name of "the lobby."

Now all these are simply expressions of the extent to which governmental action affects the life of the citizen, and of a social life which far surpasses in scope and depth that for the regulation of which legislatures originally came into existence. No metaphor can adequately convey the clamancy of these huge diverse surging waves of life and desire which are now forced forward to pass, filtered and controlled, through the narrow channel of the simple institutions of our simple immediate past. Lower chambers, upper chambers—they are miserably incompetent by themselves to accomplish a tithe of what is needed. They still seem to be important because the new ways require time to establish their repute and organization for

service, while the old are still ceremonial centers which invite pilgrimages. The real machinery is elsewhere, not occult, yet not in the center—and with good reason, for in the center is universal suffrage and its incidental ideology and trappings; it waves the Urim and the Thummim. It is authority. Life and movement, however, stir in the wings.

Hence, as we shall more amply show later, all controversies about the decline of legislatures and the need for a second chamber are unreal without a recognition of the actual, often the legal, significance of these accessory institutions. Moreover, these extralegislative institutions themselves, having grown up piecemeal in response to the special demands of casual events and needs, are now in need of co-ordination, and suggestions are plentiful to this end. Among them is the conception of industrial or economic parliaments or councils, and this we shall discuss later with particular reference to the experience of Germany and France. But before we do that, we ought to indicate (we cannot treat in detail) the principal types of institutions which now exist to make representative government more adequate to the demands upon it.

Inquiries: the Social Microscope. The form of inquiry employed in Great Britain to cover a wide scope of first-class political importance is the royal commission of inquiry. We are less concerned with its legal form [22] than with its service. A royal commission is usually established when Parliament or the government or the department within whose purview the subject falls has become convinced that more information and guidance upon policy are necessary; when a government which has been advocating a reform for years (when in opposition) is suddenly shocked by the realization that it is not omniscient. It is, of course, needless to say that some inquiries are commenced by a government in order to avoid the difficulty and responsibility of dealing with a subject at once; it is hoped that public

---

21 Cf. R. V. Vernon and N. Mansergh, *Advisory Bodies* (Oxford, 1940).

22 Cf. A. Todd, *Parliamentary Government* (London, 1892), Vol. II, Part V, Chap. 4, sect. 6.

opinion will be lulled by the assurance that the question is under consideration.

Every few years the opinion of the few thousand people intensely interested in politics reaches a point where it is generally agreed that something ought to be done. A departmental committee of the Treasury, reporting on the procedure of royal commissions, deprecated the appointment of royal commissions on subjects on which there is no reasonable prospect of early legislation.[23] This disapproval concerned only the expense involved. But there is another consideration. Urgency of the result is a spur to inventive thought—and some commissions have languished into a kind of somatic impotence owing to the lack of this spur. Legislators cast about for a policy, and since 1832 they have more and more come to rely upon the results of investigation by royal commissions.[24] The commissioners are experts or interested persons, with a chairman, usually of long and distinguished administrative, legislative, or judicial experience. The chairman is of importance to the success of a commission, since he can direct its inquiries fruitfully, can cause members to cooperate harmoniously, and can save its time by the conduct of its sessions, as his experience and personality determine. If he is like Lord Tomlin, chairman of the Royal Commission on the Civil Service (1930), an expert in excluding irrelevant evidence, he is particularly useful; yet, as the report of that commission ultimately showed, his legislative creativeness and doctrinal boldness may fall far short of his management of procedure.

It is not an easy thing to choose commissioners: are they to be disinterested experts or representatives of interests affected? Is it possible to find experts unconnected with bodies affected by the inquiry? In order that the truth may be discovered, the advantage on the whole lies with commissions of disinterested experts, or as near to this as one can attain in practice.[25] But governments are obliged to remember that what they are seeking is a policy, not the objective truth. They seek a practicable plan, given the existing interests which will try to resist any change calculated to damage their situation. Governments, therefore, believe it is better to consult those interests beforehand, in the hope that they will define the extent of acceptable reform and the concessions they require. Hence, representatives of interests are often put on the commission; and since they cannot agree with each other, they compromise, making mutual concessions not always for the public good. Governments have lost great opportunities to hear recommendations made on a national basis, through their desire to find an immediately viable plan: for example, in the Royal Commission on Local Government (1923). It would undoubtedly be best for widest exploration if the interests were excluded, but it is difficult to see how this course can be pursued, for once it has been admitted that government is by the consent of the governed, the representation of interests upon the commissions is an unavoidable conclusion. I, personally, agree with the opinion of the Committee on Royal Commissions, and I think its way would ultimately be the way of happiness for the general body of the people, but, on the present foundations of government, it can be accepted only by governments with exceptional

---

[23] Cf. Report of the Departmental Committee on the Procedure of Royal Commissions, 1910, Cd. 5235, p. 6.

[24] A picture of the work of royal commissions of inquiry is to be constructed from Parliamentary Returns: Accounts and Papers, 1856, Vol. 38; Parliamentary Papers, No. 720 of 1850, No. 317 of 1862, No. 342 of 1885, No. 338 of 1896, No. 315 of 1904, No. 159 of 1913; also, Cd. 7855 of 1914-16; Cd. 8526 of 1916; Cd. 8916 of 1917-18. Cf. also H. M. Clokie and J. W. Robinson, *British Royal Commissions of Inquiry* (Oxford, 1938); and see also S. and B. Webb, *Methods of Social Study* (London, 1932).

[25] Cf. Report, Departmental Committee on Procedure of Royal Commission, Cd. 5235, p. 6: "And it is of equal or greater importance that those selected as Commissioners should, as far as possible, be persons who have not committed themselves so deeply on any side of the questions involved in the reference as to render the probability of an impartial inquiry and a unanimous Report practically impossible."

courage which are prepared to fight hard against the interests controlling many votes. However, a large admixture of independent experts is possible only in the rare cases when the interests have not wide territorial ramifications. When, moreover, a matter is of high urgency, and the parties to it have hopelessly disagreed, as in the coal-industry disputes of 1926, the way is open for a commission of experts only.

Commissions function by calling before them independent experts and representatives of interests who give written and oral evidence. Commissions sometimes employ special investigators, as in the Poor Law Commission of 1909; or send assistants, or go themselves, to various parts of the country to obtain evidence by direct observation. A fault of the procedure is that the witnesses never confront each other to debate their differences before the commission. Another perhaps unavoidable defect is the truly awful ignorance of some of the chairmen and commissioners. The appointment of commissioners who are interested in and know, if anything at all, only one branch of the subject seriously wastes time, for the commission spends day after day in acquiring the most elementary facts, until such time as witnesses have coached them in the problems which they should already have come prepared to investigate. Meanwhile, they lunge about in the hope of coming upon a "revelation." Nor have commissions succeeded in working out a code of procedure with principles at once sound and always adopted. The way to authority is behavior based upon a systematic recognition of certain principles of inquiry.[26]

However, it cannot be denied that royal commissions have been of basic importance in the country's legislative and administrative progress. For even when they have split into majority and minority, they have put the issues clearly. It may be that only a unanimous report is a policy. But again a divided report is a record, and that also has its usefulness. Even when recommendations have been foolish, and selfishly established at the expense of the general public, the evidence gathered in the interesting and revelatory form of question and answer has been of immense value. It is a bad mistake to attempt to state the value of royal commissions by an *obiter dictum* on the length of time which elapses between the recommendations and their realization. It is commonly retailed that this length of time is ten years. But what does ten years mean? That all the recommendations or some of them have been put into practice? Why, indeed, should they be put into practice at all, if they are deemed to be politically bad? All the great pieces of social legislation of the nineteenth and twentieth centuries have been made by royal commissions, or the other forms of inquiry, such as select committees or departmental committees.

In other countries also, similar bodies of inquiry are set up from time to time, and of much the same nature as those in England. In France, Germany, and the United States much more is done by the regular legislative committees and commissions which are normally concerned with legislation, and here the investigations and reporters are purely parliamentary, but evidence is obtained also by written communications from interests concerned (in France and Germany) and by personal hearings (in the United States). In these last three countries there are departmental inquiries, instigated by the executive, or especially comprehensive investigations, where not only officials or former officials cooperate, but where outside experts and members representative of interests participate. Consider, for example, in Germany, the great Economic Inquiry (1928); in France, the Committee of Financial Experts (1925 and 1926); in the United States, the Hoover Commission on Unemployment (1930), the President's (F.D.R.'s) Commission on Education (1938), and Mr. Truman's Committee on Civil Rights (1947).

26 The student would do well to study the royal commissions on population, and on the newspaper press and on monopoly, established in 1945, 1947, and 1948: their procedure in organization, research, and mass observation.

German experience has given rise to the lessons that for success, commissions of inquiry, whether set up by the legislature or the executive, need to have a regular though flexible procedure; that the objective must be clear, for often, the clear formulation of the question is halfway to a valid answer; that the inquirers must be free from obligation to the appointing authority and the witnesses; that the commission should not be large; and that when the report is published, the evidence should be published with it.[27]

In the United States, there is a clear-cut distinction between Congressional committees of investigation and Presidential commissions, and in both cases they fall into the two broad classes of being narrowly departmental in their objective or being concerned with a big field of policy. In the Congressional committees of investigation the object may be to discover facts auxiliary to the formulation of law;[28] or it may be to understand and control the executive or to worry the executive so as to secure control over it; or it may be to draw public attention to fields of policy. Presidential commissions may be established to find fact, to formulate policy, to lead up to legislative proposals or administrative reform, or to defend the executive against some criticism made by Congress or the public. Whatever the motive or the purpose of either class of investigation, information is presented, and as a by-product, sometimes extraordinarily valuable facts are unearthed. The motives, of course, affect the facts presented, because they affect the extent to which they are unearthed, the form in which they enter into the report or the hearings, and the slant they are given when the evidence is weighed in the report. But even when the investigations are highly corrupted, they serve a useful purpose. American students have deplored

the separate appointment of investigations by legislature and executive, with no relatively impartial agency in between, because they hold that in too many cases the legislative members speak as the legislature wants against the executive, while Presidential commissions are very inclined to Presidential values. On the other hand, they observe, British royal commissions have no "employer", and are much more detached, objective, and "public-minded."

The congressional investigating committees are manned by Congressmen, and more latterly, assisted by expert counsel—expert, that is, either in handling the procedure of an investigation, or in the subject matter to be investigated, or in both. Notable examples are the Tennessee Valley Authority investigation of 1937-38 and that continuous body in wartime, the Senate National Defense Committee, under the chairmanship of Harry S. Truman until April, 1945. The Presidential commissions are manned by departmental and outside "experts." Some famous Presidential commissions are the Taft Commission on Economy and Efficiency of 1910-13; Hoover's Wickersham Commission on Law Observance and Enforcement of 1929; the Roosevelt St. Lawrence Waterway Survey of 1939; Hoover's Research Committee on Social Trends of 1930-33; the Theodore Roosevelt National Conservation Commission of 1908-09; Franklin Roosevelt's Committee on Administrative Management of 1936; and the Truman Committee on Civil Rights of 1947.

There seems to be an increasing use of commissions which contain a mixture of Congressional and executive appointees. Two are conspicuous: the Temporary National Economic Committee, and the Commission on the Organization of the Executive Branch of the Government. (1) The former was authorized by Congress in response to a request by President Roosevelt in 1938, to study the concentration of economic power on American industry and its effects on competition. The committee was joint executive-legislative: three from the Senate, three from the House, six from the executive branch. It

---

[27] F. Morstein-Marx, "Commissions of Inquiry in Germany," *American Political Science Review,* December, 1936.

[28] For example, the Senate's Special Committee on Post-war Economic Policy and Planning (1944) or the Senate Committee on Housing (1945).

did a mighty work—thirty-two volumes of hearings, forty-four expert monographs (some invaluable)—and its impact on the mind of the nation, through its impact on the minds of the several thousand who deliberately think in order to lead opinion, has on the whole been immense. (2) The latter was established in July, 1947 "to make a thorough study of the organization of the government with a view to securing the maximum efficiency in the performance of essential services, activities and functions . . . and to generally improve the Federal service and reduce the cost thereof. . . ." Its membership consists of four members, each appointed by the President, the president of the Senate, the speaker of the House; and in each case two are appointed from private life, and two from the executive branch, the Senate, and the House. Not more than one commissioner in each case is to be from either of the two major political parties. Ex-President Hoover was appointed chairman. The original appropriation was $750,000; it spent about $2,000,000. (See below, Chap. 26.)

Criticism of the form and methods of these investigating, fact-finding, and quasi-policy-producing bodies would not be appropriate here, since it would necessitate examination of the several varieties of each and their adequacy for their special purposes. Fortunately, attention has been given to this by other students.[29] The present author's own preference where the purpose is the eventual shaping of policy and the making of law is for the mixed legislative-executive type, with a chairman notable for brain and drive. For the rest, one is in the hands of the everlasting logical consequences of the separation of powers: to each his own.

Principal Defects of Inquiries. A larger view of these investigating bodies, especially the extraparliamentary bodies en-

trusted with important inquiries, reveals three qualities which have their advantages but also have disadvantages. (1) Inquiries are arranged for only when they are urgently required; (2) their terms of reference are narrow (an exception was the Temporary National Economic Committee); and (3) they cease to exist as soon as they have made their recommendations.

We have already suggested that urgency is a constituent of successful inventive thought; it prevents rambling, waste of time on unimportant details, excessive subtlety. And narrowness of the terms of reference is necessary to limit and concentrate attention; the particular question determines these limits. However, these advantages have their reverse side. Urgency may sharpen attention and inhibit preoccupation with the relatively unimportant, but it may also check exploration. The terms of reference may be too narrow: indeed, social and economic relationships are so much parts of one far-spun web that the whole difficulty of economics and sociology is to know at what point to penetrate and how much to include. If the inquiry is for immediate use—or is said to be—and if it is conceived as subordinate to a particular piece of legislation, only the immediate threads connecting it with cognate subjects are examined. It might be of public advantage, in the long run, if the terms were wide and if the commission were larger and sat longer. Finally, since the commission is not a permanent body, there is no one to watch the reception of its recommendations on its behalf, to give an authoritative answer to difficulties of interpretation, or to answer questions which have escaped attention.

Considerations of this kind—the belief that a permanent body of wide membership and large scope would be a useful supplement to existing institutions—contributed to the growth of the theory of an industrial or economic council, and even contributed to their establishment in Germany and France. It may be said at once, though the further analysis is reserved for later pages, that in Germany at any rate the council disintegrated into

29 Cf. M. N. McGeary, *The Developments of Congressional Investigative Power* (New York, 1940); C. M. Marcy, *Presidential Commissions* (New York, 1945); and Hearings of the Senate Committee on Establishment of Commission on the Organization of the Executive Branch of Government, 80th Congress, 1st session, S. 164.

a number of special committees of inquiry, though permanently linked and functioning, and chosen, by an autonomous procedure, from a large body (two hundred) of representatives of interests. This is not what was intended, but was the result of practice.

Whether or not the bodies which already exist to inquire and recommend are organized in the best conceivable manner, their value is indisputably vital to representative government. They provide *expertise* very rarely possessed by the members of the assemblies, and they virtually add the representation of interests not otherwise adequately included by modern territorial representation. They lighten the task of legislatures, as to quantity, and prepare for their final decision, sometimes only for their information, the measured considerations on both sides of legislative proposals. This division of labor leaves to members the application of their political mind and will: that is, the pure assertion of their power in the direction they think best for the life of the state. The principle of number, authority, and valuation still operates, but only after the influence of science and the pleading of interests have been brought to bear on the confronted multitudes. Here, again, are things undreamed of by Rousseau, Jefferson, Madison, and the elder Mill. The process of education of parties and electorate never ceases while the legislature is in session and the executive (parliamentary or presidential) is in office, and in the intervals, a constant stream of scientific knowledge and declaration of need flows from commissions and committees, the parties, and the civil service. The professional and independent publicists and thinkers seize upon it, analyze it, break it up, and, according to their political lights, endow it with meaning. Their values are modified, their claims deferred or permanently suppressed, as their partial or complete impossibility is rationally demonstrated. Philosophers cannot be kings, but in our own day they advise and impress rulers through institutions such as we have examined.

Departmental Advisory Councils. A development which has accompanied that already described is the growth of permanent advisory councils of experts in the government departments. This is clear recognition that legislative and administrative initiative lies with the executive; an aid to sound thinking has been established at its most frequent source.

On a major scale, and as part of the regular administration of the state, this development first occurred in France. It was, perhaps, a product *first* of the fact that the French civil service was not until recent years recruited for its efficiency, but was largely a creation of political favoritism. Sound sense must necessarily be procured somewhere: even an oligarchy has an interest in the efficiency of its own monopoly. *Second,* and this is more important, since it is a more permanent feature: the French have—at least since the time of the physiocrats, and it could be even maintained since the time of Louis XIV and Colbert—insisted that experts, the intellectual *élite,* shall provide their lawmaking. It was observable in the economists who thronged the court of Louis XVI,[30] in the galaxy of intellectual stars who shone in the firmament around Napoleon, and in the continuous deference to the *Conseil d'État* (as a supreme court of governmental intellect). It was also observable in French political theories of vocational representation and democratic competence,[31] rife before World War II.

Various departments [32] of state are aided by consultative councils, some of which are already over a century old, although naturally their composition and

---

[30] Cf. G. Weulersse, *Le Mouvement Physiocratique en France* (Paris, 1910), Vol. II, pp. 155, 249-53.

[31] Its general aspects are discussed in S. de Madariaga's *Englishmen, Frenchmen and Spaniards* (Oxford, 1931). It is further to be observed in the program of practically every political party, especially the great study groups. See also the works of Léon Duguit.

[32] Cf. P. Pic, *Traité Elémentaire de Législation Industrielle* (Paris, 1930, and Supplements, 1937), p. 107. Cf. also H. Berthélemy, *Traité Elémentaire de Droit Administratif* (Paris, 1933).

function have been amended from time to time. I do not propose to enter into a detailed analysis of these features, but I wish to point out only their general character. They are composed of two elements: (1) the purely expert, when they may be officials (in service or retired) of the various departments combined for effective survey of the whole field, and (2) representatives of interests, though this does not necessarily exclude an expertness which would entitle them to be heard on this ground alone.[33] Thus the *Conseil Supérieur de l'instruction Publique* began in 1850 as a body representative of groups whose vital aims would be affected by state control of education: along with professors and professions, which would combine the opinion of an intellectual and judicial *élite,* there was a majority of ministers of different religions, members of the Institute, councilors of state, judges; moreover, these members were chosen by their own groups. In 1880 the *Conseil* was converted into a body formed by members elected by the various groups within the teaching profession. Of fifty-seven members thirteen were chosen by decree, which means by the Minister of Public Instruction. Nine of the thirteen were members or past members of the administrative or professorial staff of the universities, and the other four were chosen from among non-state-supported education. Forty-three members were elected by the Institute and the teachers.

The work of these committees is substantially the same: to advise the government upon its projects of law and the orders which are designed to give detailed effect to the law. They have done important work preparatory to the passage of legislation and have cleared up difficult questions of law which have been raised in the course of administration. Since they are fairly large bodies, and since to convene them often would mean a disturbance in the ordinary administration in which they are engaged, they meet

rarely, and current work is left in the hands of a permanent sub-committee. An acute critic, Chardon, once observed that at the Ministry of Public Works great services had been rendered by the committees, but that there was always the danger that such institutions might be abused when they were made the means of replacing an urgent act by discussion; when the more instructed members were reduced to giving lectures to the rest; when instead of light proceeding from discussion there proceeded an illegitimate child of compromise; or when number triumphed over reason. Other criticisms of waste of time have been made.[34]

Conseil d'État. There was a time when the *Conseil d'État* was a sort of grand initiating legislative body. This was under Napoleon.[35] Its very success in those years, when it included men like Cambacérès, the Tronchets, Roederer, Portalis, Merlin de Douai, Molé, made it anathema to the Restoration. It fell, to rise again in the constitution of 1848 as the consultative body for all laws except financial and those which were declared urgent, and then it was elected by the National Assembly. Under Napoleon III it became an imitation of its former self at the beginning of the century, but the Third Republic, while making it the heart of the French administrative and judicial system, reduced its lawmaking powers. It must be remembered that it is composed of career officials.

The government must submit its projects of laws to the *Conseil,* which gives its opinion on them and proposes the amendments of drafting it considers necessary.[36]

---

[33] Cf. Jean Cahen-Salvador, *La Représentation des Interêts et Les Services Publics* (Paris, 1935): the most complete and intelligent.

[34] Cf. *Annales de l'Académie des Sciences Sociales et Morales,* "Les Réformes Administratives" (Paris, 1929).

[35] Cf. Léon Aucoc, *Conferences sur l'Administration* (Paris, 1882), Vol. I, p. 132, and Edmond Blanc, *Napoleon I* (Paris, 1888), Chap. III.

[36] Law of May 24, 1872, on the reorganization of the *Conseil d'État,* Part II, article 8: "The *Conseil d'État* gives its advice: (1) Upon projects of law initiated by Parliament which the National Assembly (then a single Chamber) decrees should be sent to it. (2) Upon the project of law prepared by the Government, and which a special decree orders to be sub-

It prepares and drafts the texts of law when asked to do so. Its vice-president may at the request of a minister nominate a member of the *Conseil* to help their department in the elaboration of any particular project. The *Conseil* may, on its own initiative, call the attention of the departments to reforms of a legislative, rule-making, or administrative sort which appear to it to be of public interest. All this leaves the government free to take or reject advice and assistance.[37] But it must be consulted on decrees with legislative force that the government has been empowered to promulgate, as well as the rules of public administration and decrees taking such a form.

Ministers rarely consult it as regards the subject matter, the policy, of a bill; that, as we have seen, has been devolved upon special councils attached to each government department. It can, however, advise upon the form of the law and upon the effects of new legislation upon the existing codes.[38] a very important function in the modern state, where a legal link added or subtracted vitally affects the character of the whole chain; where security of existent rights is a part of the incentive to continue to make them fruitful; and where the economic and social edifice is so nicely composed of anticipations that a multitude of forces will act and interact in a certain way, and any brusque and careless movement may cause disturbances far beyond the range of immediate vision or control. We shall have occasion to discuss the administrative work of the *Conseil d'État* later. We may at this point, however, make this observation. Every country has produced something of saving excel-

lence in its machinery of government. Perhaps at those points the student will find the best means of exploring the characteristic governmental genius of each nation. In France the effective prop is the *Conseil d'État*. Indeed, its brilliant history has caused a number of critics of French parliamentarism to seek relief by a return to the obligatory consultation of the *Conseil* on all laws.[39] However, after the not-too-helpful services of the high administration in general in the events leading up to World War II and the Capitulation, the political parties emerging at the Liberation were politically too self-confident, rightly, to submit to a body of officials, however expert, some of whom had been monarchist or quasi-fascist.[40]

What we have said about France in regard to consultative councils does not require much modification to be applicable to the other countries of this study. But there are some differences of detail respecting the length of time for which such bodies have existed, their composition, and their functions. Of all of them we can say broadly that the representative element is only of recent inclusion, and that it is the result both of the maturity of the representative principle in the modern world and of the recognition that though legislatures may have the plenitude of authority, they have not the plenitude of wisdom.[41] Nor should one omit the advisory work done by such bodies as cham-

mitted to the *Conseil d'État.* . . ." And cf. E. Pierre, *Traite de Droit Politique et Parlementaire* (Paris, 1922), Vols. I and III, paras. 82-85, for a commentary on this article. Cf. also *Ordonnance* of July 31, 1945, on the *Conseil d'État,* Titre II; also *Decret* of July 31, 1945, *Règlement Interieur du Conseil d'État,* contained, also, in *Conseil d'État, Études et Documents* (Paris, Imprimerie Nationale, 1947).
[37] Pierre comments: "They [the Government] are not bound in any degree by the collaboration which they have requested" (*op. cit.,* Vol. I, p. 85).
[38] Cf. Aucoc, *op. cit.,* Vol. I, p. 146.

[39] These will be found summarized up to 1898 in L. Michon, *L'Initiative Parlementaire* (Paris, 1898), p. 310 ff.; and the trend of ideas since then is to be found in the party programs, and in such articles as those by A. Lefas in the *Revue des Sciences Politiques* for 1929-31.
[40] Cf. the characterization of the *Conseil d'État* by one of its former members, Pierre Tissier, *I Worked with Laval* (London, 1942), especially p. 7 ff.
[41] For United States advisory committees, see J. P. Comer, *Legislative Functions of National Administrative Authorities* (New York, 1927), Chaps. VII and VIII; E. P. Herring, *Public Administration and the Public Interest* (New York, 1936); Report of Attorney General's Committee on Administrative Procedure (1941), Chap. VIII. Regarding Germany, cf. my article, "Officials and the Public," cited in *Public Administration,* January, 1931.

bers of commerce, agriculture, etc., which in Europe have a public status.[42]

Libraries and Reference Bureaus. No results of a specially fruitful kind are to be obtained from a special analysis of such aids to the legislator as mere libraries. All legislatures have collections of books and documents and places where fairly quiet study is possible, and the librarians are usually persons able to indicate references and furnish material. But all legislatures seem to be cursed with the same vice: it is impossible for the member to find a convenient and comfortable solitude in which he may work in undisturbed quiet. Only the United States Congress has approached a dignified and useful accommodation for its members. Of the rest, the English politician's judgment is true: "The House of Commons is a place where you can't rest and you can't work." (Yet members do!)

In the United States special arrangements are made in Congress and in many of the states for expert aid to the legislator, not only for the form of bills but also for their material. Congress itself has created a special branch of the Library of Congress (the equivalent of the British Museum Reading Room) to which members may send questions and whence information and references are sent to them.

Until recent years the principal experiment of the United States in this respect was to be found in some of the states, following the lead of Wisconsin. (But the growth of the work and influence of the Legislative Reference Service of the Library of Congress, culminating in its reorganization in 1946, gives it the palm.) The Wisconsin Legislative Reference Department was established in 1901. It was a part of the Wisconsin Library Commission especially designed to help legislators. Its efficacy of course depended upon the intelligent anticipation of the staff and, while this was under the founder, Charles McCarthy, its work became the wonder of America.

The essentials of the scheme were: a carefully selected library conveniently placed; a talented librarian and indexer; compact and accessible arrangement of the material ("legislators have no time to read large books"); complete index of all past bills; records of all "political" as well as scientific arguments on bills ("we must remember that he often relies as much upon political or unscientific arguments as we do upon scientific work"); digests of laws, accounts of their operation, bibliographies; a nonpolitical and nonpartisan staff; a head of the department trained in the social services—with tact and knowledge of human nature; a trained legislative draftsman; and complete devotion as to hours of labor, quick work in an emergency, and continuous anticipation of the legislator's needs. Other states have adopted similar schemes.

The Legislative Reference Service was organized in 1916, after the Wisconsin model. It answers Congressional requests for information. In 1925 those inquiries totalled 774; in 1945, about 16,000. They fall into inquiries for the citation of laws, for compilations of law on various subjects, for information on whether laws exist on certain subjects, for facts (some very trivial), and for preparation of speech material. The Service maintains newspaper clippings, digests of Congressional reports and hearings—"to save the Congressmen's time"!—and an index of federal and state laws. It answers many questions on international affairs. Beyond this, it has occasionally made "basic data studies": for example, the pros and cons of problems relating to Indian affairs, cartels, strikes in war industries, workmen's compensation, the regulation of trade unions, the constitutionality of the poll tax, and Communism in Action (the government of the Soviet Union). It prepares bibliographies. It is in telephonic communication with the Congressmen.

In the session of 1943, every member of the Senate and all but 20 members of the House of Representatives made use of the Service at some time; the Senators averaged 45 inquiries each, the Representatives, 18.

---

[42] Cf. Gény, *La Collaboration des Particuliers avec l'Administration* (Paris, 1930), pp. 180 ff.; E. Tatarin-Tarnheyden, *Die Berufsstände* (Berlin, 1923).

The Legislative Reference Service is organized as a branch of the Library of Congress but functions autonomously in its service of Congress. In 1945, it had 45 professional and 18 clerical and administrative employees and its appropriation amounted to about $200,000.

The Chief Assistant Librarian of Congress and the Director of the Legislative Reference Service gave evidence to the Joint Committee of the Organization of Congress in May, 1945. They proposed a large increase in staff (to cost some half a million dollars a year) and a specialization of the services they could render to Congress. Their aim was, indeed, to have [43]

at least one person of front rank in each of the major fields of Congressional interest available to prepare studies of this type [the "basic data studies"] for the appropriate committee at the request either of the chairman or of the ranking minority member or of the committee as a whole. Such studies would be completely impartial, the pros and cons would be set out, and the basic data summarized. They would be authoritative analyses of the problem; they would not be mere compilations.

The attitude of such a legislative reference service to its work is of conspicuous interest as an indication of the nature of American government:

(1) It would not give an opinion unless asked for it; it would volunteer no recommendations; it would offer no opinion at all beyond the field of its expertness.

(2) Congress "should be able to call upon scholarly research and counsel at least equal in competence to the research and counsel relied upon by those who appear before congressional committees.[44] Neither the representatives of American business nor the representatives of the various departments of government should be able to draw upon expert opinion superior to the expert opinion available to Congress." [45]

(3) The relationship to the executive

is of peculiar importance. The director of the Service observed on this subject:[46]

It is largely, but not entirely, the function of the executive researchers to gather facts initially; it is their function to draw conclusions which their political chiefs may then decide to advocate before Congress and its committees with their help.

On the other hand, Congress is entitled to have before it on a given issue much more than just the presentation from the Executive. Congress must know what alternative proposals there are; what facts have been ignored, suppressed, or underrated; what criticism of one or another of the proposed solutions may be anticipated.

The central function of a research staff attached to the legislative branch is to analyze, not only the research findings and recommendations of the Executive branch, but the findings and recommendations of other research organizations and individuals . . . This will promote understanding and avoid duplication . . . the staff of the legislative branch must at all times maintain an attitude of complete independence and objectivity . . .

The executive has a right to expect from the legislative staff member that the former's facts and contentions shall be fairly and clearly represented. The legislative researcher has a right to expect from the Executive reasonable candor in warning against particular flaws in research done by others . . . the researchers in the legislative branch must not reveal information as to congressional attitudes or action secured because of their privileged position unless the member or members in question desire it.

(4) In the preparation of basic data studies on controversial questions, it was the policy to have them read by persons holding opposite political views, so as to be certain "that they are completely dehydrated politically."

I draw particular attention to the atmosphere of political aloofness and objectivity and impartial service it was believed should be rendered by the reference branch. Its terms are those in which it is properly customary to describe the "brains-trust" function of the highest branch of the British civil service. But whereas the latter serves both the executive and the legislature as these are

[43] *Hearings*, Part 3, p. 435.
[44] This is an attempt to limit the influence of "the lobby" by a method different from that discussed later, p. 458 ff.
[45] *Hearings*, Part 3, p. 432.
[46] *Ibid.*, p. 434.

severed, in the United States system of government, Solomon the Wise, and not the baby, is divided between Congress and the executive.

Study of the Legislative Reference Service of the Library of Congress shows that no other democratic government has come anywhere near the establishment of such arrangements—not Great Britain, nor Continental systems. The reasons for this contrast offer enlightenment on the character of the different forms of government. The need which in the United States is supplied by the Legislative Reference Division is in Britain supplied by the combined efforts of the political parties' research organizations, the government, and the civil service. Normally, a member of Parliament who wants assistance in finding facts, or a line of argument, or the sketch of bills or policy, can get very valuable help from the party headquarter's research and library staff. We have already noted that these are continuous agencies, commendably efficient. But above all, the leadership of the Parliament—that is, the government (roughly equivalent to the majority leaders and chairmen of committees in the United States Congress)—is served faithfully by its top civil-service career officials. Indeed, the language used before the Joint Congressional Committee in advocacy of the services of the Legislative Reference Division is almost identical to that which is so often used by the British to characterize the services of impartial advice and analysis of alternative ways and means and objectives and methods, rendered to the ministers (and through them to the Commons and people) by their civil service experts. I quote:[47]

They would give an opinion only if they were asked to do so, and they would not volunteer advice or recommendations, and beyond their field of expertness they would refrain from expressing an opinion . . . The staff of the legislative branch must at all times maintain an attitude of complete independence and objectivity.

Since this service is not directly provided by the United States executive to the Congress, it must be sought elsewhere. If the institution does not exist, the need for it does, as in Britain, and the method sought is characteristically American. It must be obtained from an agency which seems to have nothing at all to do with the government, especially the executive. For Congress does not trust the executive. It occasionally uses the administration's experts, lent to it for limited, specific purposes, but it insists on independence. Again, the executive is not in convenient and continuous contact with Congress. It could be if the distrust were not there. But that could only be overcome if party united them in one fellowship, or if the separation of powers did not exist to give each side, Congress and the executive, a corporate temper, setting one against the other. Once more, it is not only the chasm between Congress and the executive that is of importance, but also the independence that the follower of either of the great parties insists on from his own leaders. He, also, wants an independent channel for his own personal effectiveness, so that he may make his own contribution. Finally, the parties themselves have no research organization to which leaders and rank and file could turn for help. They have, therefore, come to look to the Legislative Reference Division. And this has through its spokesman abjured any concern for party policy—it will serve all, "objectively."

The upshot of the Congressional reorganization of 1946 [48] is the establishment of special expert staffs for each Congressional committee, and, in adition, the expert staff of the Legislative Division: the former being more narrowly specialized, the latter of broader scope.

In Weimar Germany an experienced parliamentarian said:[49]

All of this [the four-storied, well-stocked library] is at his disposal. He should use it. Should speak not a word and make not a decision before he has consulted every aid in

---

[47] Cf. Dr. Luther Evans and Dr. E. S. Griffith, Hearings, Joint Committee on Organization of Congress, 79th Congress, 1st session, Vol. III, pp. 445 and 448.

[48] Public Law 601: 1946: Secs. 202, 203.
[49] Cf. W. Lambach, *Herrschaft der 500* (Berlin, 1926), p. 91.

the archives and the library to test and explore his judgment. Poor Müller! The pressure of the vocation does not allow you so much as to take thought of, let alone come to, any profound research of the truth!

In France there was bitter complaint of the lack of library facilities and other help even in the commissions. The help of the civil service is available only for the government, and not for private members. If the rank and file are ever again to add to the wealth possessed by the party, instead of living upon it, only institutions of this nature (party research pursued seriously, and official but independent reference agencies) can rouse them from their slumbers interrupted only by the division bells. For committee work, particularly, is aid of this kind important.

THE "LOBBY"

So far we have been concerned with the influence upon legislatures of information procured by officially constituted bodies which serve fairly in a scientific spirit. In so far as these have influence, it is the influence of fact upon desire. Even when experts are representative of groups whose power affects the legislature, the intention of the fact-finding and policy-reporting bodies is, in the first place, to educe and express the facts apart from considerations of how many would vote for or against the recommendations based upon them. They are the evidence and policies of the disinterested, as near as can be in a political world. But men are fearful for their interests, and do not easily trust advocates so far removed from them as political parties, members of the legislature, civil servants, and experts. The tendency to scramble for the goods of life and to defend one's personality against attack never relaxes. Consequently, various groups with well-defined interests specially organize to influence the legislature and the executive. They are not satisfied that government knows enough about them to be fair when subjecting them to the burdens of citizenship. They feel that they must inform members of the true state of affairs, must call their attention to the numbers of peo-

ple who will be affected and to the opinion of these people upon the suggested measures. They cannot resist the desire to follow the legislator vigilantly and solicitously from the days of his candidacy, into the legislature, and thence through the various stages of legislation, teaching him the factual and justifying foundations and consequences of their claims. In an age of advancing specialization and conscious organization of interest groups, this sets democratic government a very serious problem.

All goes back to the vast scope of modern state activity and the fact that it is impossible for the existing organs of government themselves accurately to know the substance and the strength of the various claims in any given legislative and administrative situation. We should expect to find political self-help where help is otherwise not forthcoming: wherever the ordinary representative institutions are weak in their representative qualities, and wherever groups do not trust these, either because they are weak or because the groups are voracious. The two, of course, go together, but there are differences of emphasis in different countries. We should, however, notice, before we proceed to discuss the different countries, that all of them have been moving in the same direction in recent years: that is, in the direction of what in the United States is called the "lobby," or "third house" all, of course, because industry and social feeling have everywhere shown the same tendencies. Let us first discuss group representation before the Congress of the United States, since this country has developed furthest. Both the pathological and the healthy features of that system afford good criteria of the theory and practice of group representation.

The United States. The practice of "lobbying" is far from new.[50] From the begin-

[50] E. P. Herring, *Group Representation before Congress* (Johns Hopkins, 1929) and *Public Administration and Public Interest* (New York, 1936); T. C. Blaisdell, *Economic Power and Political Pressures*, Monograph No. 20, Temporary National Economic Committee, 1941; Kenneth Crawford, *The Pressure Boys* (New York, 1939); M. E. Dillon, "Pressure

ning of Congress there were people, not elected representatives, who understood and employed the means of influencing Congressmen to pass or obstruct legislation favoring specific interests. With the increase of state activity, and, therefore, of legislative power, the "lobby" of Washington became more and more the center of such business. Friends of Congressmen, hangers-on of the departments, former officials, Congressmen who had failed of re-election, lawyers and journalists, and members of Congress themselves, promoted special interests. Women were employed to trim the locks of Congressional Samsons. The terms "lobby" and "lobbyist" became expressions of contempt and vituperation.

Today the lone wolf has vanished; and there is no slinking about upon unsavory errands. Contempt is not entirely dissipated, but fear and respect have taken its place. For the "lobbyist" has come out in the open, advertises himself to the public rather than hides from it, and has sources of revenue which are cheerfully, if not fully, disclosed and even vaunted. The groups have vast territorial organizations, some of them nation-wide. They concentrate in Washington, in large suites of offices filled with trained officials and experts, executive staff, and all the modern equipment of research and propaganda bodies, rivaling the minor departments of the government.

Over four hundred such groups have representatives in Washington, and this does not include volunteer spokesmen who come to the capital from time to time on special deputations to the departments. Yet only about one out of five are really effective and "recognized" by Congressmen as being authentically representative of interests in the country and worth a careful hearing. The delegations represent an enormous variety of interests, and every part of the country. To give a summary view of these interests is almost to reproduce a census of production, every

plank in all the political platforms, and a register of social interests. Broadly, the delegations are of two kinds: those whose primary interest is to secure immediately selfish benefits, and those whose primary interest is to furnish themselves and others with some material or spiritual blessing. In the first category, we find such organizations as the National Association of Manufacturers, the Chamber of Commerce, the Farm Bureau Federation, the Association of Life Insurance Executives, the Motion Picture Producers and Distributors of America, the American Medical Association, the American Newspaper Publishers Association, the American Federation of Labor, and the CIO. Among the latter are the League of Women Voters, the American Legion, the National Catholic Welfare Conference, the Federal Council of Churches of Christ in America, and the Daughters of the American Revolution.

These organizations were founded and are maintained because they deem—each in its own interests—that popular electoral action every two or four years was and is insufficient to direct the activities of government in the direction they think right. As a well-known practitioner has observed:[51]

In Congress, from my experience, the fellow that makes the most noise, and the fellow that makes the most demands, that keeps his problems in front of them all the time, he gets service. If he doesn't; if he depends upon somebody else to do it for him, he is going to get what we all get when we don't go after the thing the way we ought to—nothing.

Their purposes concern not merely domestic policy but also America's foreign relations, affecting peace and welfare and justice all over the world.[52] They have elaborated all the technical means they require, they have become experts upon the sources and channels of legislative and administrative power, and they harness the

[51] Cf. E. E. Schattschneider, *Politics, Pressures and the Tariff* (New York, 1935), p. 219.
[52] Cf. Crawford, *op. cit.*, Chap. 9; Herman Finer, *Road to Reaction* (Boston, 1945), pp. 9 ff. and 199, and *America's Destiny* (New York, 1947), p. 370 ff.

Groups," *American Political Science Review*, June, 1942, p. 471 ff.; also V. O. Key, *Politics, Parties, and Pressure Groups* (New York, 1947).

aims and impulses of a coherent mass of citizens. They have acquired the name of the "third house," the "assistant government." They have emerged into a public and recognized position, because of the appreciation that parties in a country so vast as the United States cannot possibly, and certainly do not (for reasons we have advanced), do the necessary work of representation of so many different purposes, and Congress has itself admitted the groups into its counsels through the doors of its committees, where the effective work of legislation is done. The "muck-raking" period caused the institution of better traditions of government, and made it more difficult for Congressmen themselves to accept the briefs of special interests, while by the 17th amendment, Senators were subjected to a purified process of selection. A thorough investigation of the "lobby" took place in 1913 after certain scandals had alarmed and disgusted the Congress and the public. The conclusions of the committee of investigation recognized the need for public access to Congressmen, but they show that the committee was rather overawed by this huge growth. Its severity, though veiled in disarming phrases, was reserved for the "lobby's" threats against upright Congressmen to contrive their defeat at the next elections, but the propriety of "lobby" activities was admitted.

The note of the sinister has not passed away from newspaper or Congressional descriptions of the "lobby," [53] but it is in part palliated by the openness of the lobby's activities. The organizers and the negotiators are naturally those with a special knowledge of the byways of legislation and the habits of Congress; and they are recruited from "lawyers," journalists, self-constituted agents and touts, "public relations counsellors," former civil servants, and ex-Congressmen. Many of the members of either House are professional politicians. Hence, the majority are dependent upon re-election or upon an administrative appointment. Not all can find a berth. But their services are of the highest value to the groups. They know their way to the offices and committee rooms of Congress. Up to 1933 "lame ducks" were especially amenable to pressure. All in all, these "legislative agents" are rumored to be abler than the average Congressman.

While the public in general is thus made pliable, and when a sufficient following can be counted upon, the lobbyist concentrates upon the Congressman. Every interest has a sympathizer in the seats of power, and he forms the permanent open door for successful prosecution of the special claims to accommodation in the law and its administration. It has even been said that "Many a seat in Congress is no more than a prosperous law firm's business-getting equipment." [54] A Congressman can give aid by reading into the *Congressional Record* whatever articles he may compose, so that copies may be obtained at cost.

With the sympathetic Congressman no difficulty arises. But the unsympathetic Congressman must be persuaded; and persuasion takes two forms: technical argument, and the threat that, since he misrepresents opinion, opinion will retaliate. Argument has a double virtue: it is intrinsically effective, and gives the Congressman the material for intervention in debate. These virtues, however, are insufficient to move the mind, and besides, Congressmen are so deluged with information of all kinds that the original evil has returned: the solicitous interests are too many for their time and legislative capacity, and, further, Congressmen tend to distrust the information on the grounds that it is uncertified and without counterargument. (They are, of course, incapable of discovering the technical counterargument themselves; and this is often provided by an opponent group.)

Success lies with those who get in first, and most forcibly. Hence the voice of the people must be conjured up. The method

---

[53] Crawford, *op. cit.*, demonstrates this. So also Hearings, Senate Committee to Investigate Lobbying Activities, 74th Congress (1936). Nor is the Howard Hughes' investigation by the Senate in July and August of 1947 a sign that matters have improved.

[54] Crawford, *op. cit.*, p. 19.

adopted is almost the same in every big organization. The local groups are consulted, and a policy is produced in Washington; the policy is compared with the attitude of Congressmen; the local groups are informed of the discrepancies; these begin to press upon their members by post, wire, and meetings. A steady fire from the constituencies is concentrated upon the member. He is warned that re-election is impossible if he does not alter his mind. His legislative record is ransacked and, with the exaggerations of politics, thrown into the balance at primary and general elections. One lobby helps another, unless they happen to be directly opposite in interests (which is infrequent), since coercion is more effective when the strength behind it is apparently overwhelming. The method is based upon the general truth that in a democracy no elective office is permanently safe: every vote may ultimately count, and therefore all must be canvassed. Through the Congressman's mind flashes the fact that the active groups may be small, but that they are more effective electorally than the apathetic mass, that unless they are placated they will continue to worry him.

The procedure of Congress gives the lobbyist good opportunities. The most important are the hearings before congressional committees. Decisions on bills are made in committees, and not in the full assembly, and it has become the practice for committees to take evidence from all interests concerned by any bill. (The reasons for this procedure are discussed later, p. 498 ff.) The lobbyist puts written and printed information before the committee, selects and sends up witnesses, argues his case. It is here, of course, that Congressmen are able to sift the evidence and to guess at the truth about the public support alleged by the lobbyist, and here that weight is given to the evidence in rough proportion to its authenticity. Congressional procedure is very intricate and offers many opportunities of destroying or deferring a bill: the lobbyist concentrates upon these points either for attack or defense. But there are occult approaches to

chairmen and other committee men with unusual influence.

How effective is the lobby? This is difficult to answer. It is possible to point to some very important pieces of legislation which result from lobbying activity.[55] Yet of all these it may be said that the full desire of the lobbyist was not granted, and that in some cases, it was only when public opinion was thoroughly roused that Congress actually legislated. But this last argument glosses over the fact (observed in detail in the Prohibition movement) that public opinion was roused or chloroformed or confused (as the case required) by the lobbyist, and that simultaneously with these operations upon the public, operations were conducted upon Congressmen.

Party organization is placed in a rather curious position by the lobby. Party has the ultimate control of policy and priority of business in Congress. It cannot ignore either the threat of a secession of a block of voters or the promise of support. Yet there are so many interests strongly and separately organized that the parties cannot possibly satisfy them all, and can only choose from among them from time to time when it is judged that legislation is inevitable in the near future. Then, as a rule, both parties are found on the same side. Usually they "straddle" to satisfy as many aspirations as possible, which means that none is completely satisfied, even in the program. We have already noticed that committees do most of the legislative work of Congress. The more important of these are seized, in the heyday of the session, with measures espoused by the party. Yet all committees have a large degree of freedom from party domination; that is to say, the party has not made up its mind and has made no promises about a good many things which arise, and does not see the necessity of adopting a party attitude. Here both sides are malleable and open to argument. Since, also, the committees at their largest contain only twenty-one members, influence upon them is fairly easily

55 Crawford, op. cit.; and for New York state, Belle Zeller, Pressure Politics in New York (New York, 1937).

won. Moreover, we have seen that priority before Congress is determined by a small knot of party leaders; it is upon the pliability of these that ultimately depends the success of the lobbyist.

It is clear that the lobby in its American form and efficacy is a direct product of American conditions. What is elsewhere accomplished by the partial dissolution or blending of interests in parties and the legislature is accomplished in America by the explosive approach of two almost exclusive bodies: party and lobby. It is all that parties can do to overcome the checks and balances, the obstacles and separations of American politics; they have no time or energy left for further integrations. And the lobby is the necessary adjunct to the American party system, for it makes the policy while the parties are necessarily occupied with other functions. It is possible also that if the nation were less wealthy, the fight for a share of the wealth would be fiercer in Congress and the lobby interests would not be able to win their separate victories so easily. Whatever each takes, however large, is a very small proportion of the total wealth; their millions of dollars divided by the total population is small, so that the amount by which each individual citizen is thereby deprived does not matter enough to produce a real reform. The injustice and impropriety perhaps matters more, but the public is scattered over too wide an area to establish adamant standards of social justice.

It is gratifying that Congressmen have shown increasing and substantial restiveness about the lobby. The next step after the creation of a powerful institution is for the state to attempt to control it. In the case of the American lobby the state is represented in the first place by Congressmen. Their attack upon the lobby results from their fear of it, and from their recognition that it may acquire power to which it is not entitled either by its representativeness in terms of genuine numbers, or by the scientific reasonableness of its claims compared with those of the rest of the nation. Congress has had to steer between prejudicing the rightful freedom of any group to approach it for a hearing, and

undue pressure for privileges. Various proposals, whether in the form of statutes or as amendments of the rules of Congress, have included those (1) to define lobbying, (2) to compel lobbyists to register and disclose their purposes, their employers, and accounts of expenditures, and (3) to prohibit former members of Congress to lobby, "for money or other emolument," within two years of their term as members.

Such proposals for reform culminated in the recommendation of the Report of the Joint Committee on Reorganization of Congress and the measures to implement it. The committee recommended:[56]

That Congress enact legislation providing for the registration of organized groups and their agents who seek to influence legislation and that such registration include quarterly statements of expenditures made for this purpose.

The committee thus relied on publicity and on evidence of the origin, sincerity, and strength of the groups—a reasonable attitude. The Federal Regulation of Lobbying Act, 1946, provided as follows: Any person, individual, partnership, committee, association, corporation, and any other organization or group of persons

who by himself, or through any agent or employee or other persons in any manner whatsoever, directly or indirectly, solicits, collects, or receives money or any other thing of value to be used principally to aid, or the principal purpose of which person is to aid, in the accomplishment of any of the following purposes: (a) The passage or defeat of any legislation by the Congress of the United States (b) To influence, directly or indirectly, the passage or defeat of any legislation by the Congress of the United States

must file quarterly statements to show who has contributed $500 or more and who has received any expenditures of $10 or more, with the amount, date, and purpose of the expenditure. Persons engaging themselves for pay or other consideration for purpose (b) above must register with the officers of the House and Senate, with full particulars of their employers, purposes, duration of employment, pay, and expenses. Cumulative quarterly statements

---

56 P. 27.

of activities, with expenditures thereon, and action through any form of the press are required from the Lobbyists, under oath. Appropriate forms are provided by the Congressional officers for purposes of registration and return of information. The officers of the Congress responsible for the administration of the act, so far as the filing and compilation of the information are concerned, jointly prepare an annual report compiling the information, and this is printed in the *Congressional Record*. The statements, preserved for two years, are open to public inspection. Violation of the law is punishable by a fine of not more than $5000 and/or by imprisonment up to twelve months. Convicted persons are debarred from influencing, directly or indirectly, the passage or defeat of legislation. Debarred persons who continue to lobby are guilty of a felony.

In its first year of operation, the act showed some little success in achieving its main purpose, publicity. But it was very far from a full success, judging by the small number of organizations filing registrations and the paucity of information they supplied. Many were palpably withholding information that they could have given and which the law in terms, let alone in spirit, requires. Many powerful organizations did not file, either with no plea at all, or on the plea that they were not *principally* engaged in lobbying, or that their *principal* purpose was not lobbying: an opening for evasion supplied by the statute, provided by Congress in a fit of bad drafting or of confused intentions or of curious inability to prophesy how lobbying organizations might act. It is clear that all organizations ought to be included —not merely those that think themselves to be qualified by the adjectives used above; and that a far deeper fund of information, to disclose the internal set-up and composition of the policy leaders in the organizations, is required, Moreover, distinct responsibility for enforcement needs to be placed on the Attorney-General, since the Congressional officers have neither the authority nor the staff for the purpose. It would be as valuable to proscribe lobbying when exerted on adminis-

trative agencies and officials as when applied to Congressmen.[57]

England. The social relationships and the group life of England are almost as complex and subdivided as those of the United States if less extensive territorially, and there are consequently as many interests seeking for representation. On the whole, however, an organized lobby of the size, importance, and system of the United States does not exist. A large number of groups have headquarters near Parliament Street in order to influence the process of government. They are of the same general character as those in America; they approach members of Parliament and send deputations to the departments. But they cannot appear in Parliament, before committees or otherwise, though they are asked to give evidence before royal commissions of inquiry or to act as commissioners; they are normally confined to the lobby. Their electoral work is not propaganda in certain constituencies to secure a stream of communications from constituents to representatives, but questionnaires during elections, and the rather informal promotion of candidatures of members. Party is too strongly in control of English politics for members to be liable to influence by lobbyists. The Commons' committees are large and their work is dominated by the parties and led by a minister. They do not possess the power of Congressional committees. There is hardly a loophole between the constituencies and Parliament through which the lobbyist can slide to extort concessions. The doctrine of ministerial responsibility and its organization—such that the fullest light of publicity beats everlastingly upon the smallest number of answerable ministers, leaders of parties with high traditions—makes impossible transactions not

[57] For a remarkably cogent and thorough account of the operation of the law and suggestions for reform, see Belle Zeller, "The Federal Regulation of Lobbying Act," *American Political Science Review*, April, 1948; and her evidence before the Committee on Expenditures in the Executive Departments, U. S. Senate, 80th Congress, 2nd Session, on "Evaluation of the Legislative Reorganization Act of 1946," p. 98 ff.

publicly advocated, discussed, and authorized.

The lobbyist is obliged to influence the electorate by press propaganda. Or he must appear in the ranks of a party and operate as a member of Parliament, under all the restraints of party and parliamentary discipline, and this often happens. His doctrine must stand a severe test, and even if a clever Parliamentary representative of a special branch of industry, or of prohibition, or of divorce reform, found himself upon a committee with that very slight access of power which the private member enjoys in committee, he would need to persuade not only his colleagues, but the minister, and not only the minister, but the civil servants who stand at the latter's elbow invoking the claims of the country as a whole.[58] In fact, the representatives of the groups are usually members of the House of Commons, which is peculiarly rich, as we have seen, in the representation of the great vocational groups. The House listens with sympathy to an informed and reasoned case,[59] but any obvious advocacy of a brief in the House results in loss of influence, since the House has learned to beware of special pleading. The English "lobby" is more effective in Whitehall where deputations are received, and where advice is frequently asked for from interested groups, before legislation is put into a final draft. Such information suffers a quadruple sifting: once by the permanent officials, once by a cabinet committee or its secretariat, a third time by the cabinet, and another, also, by the House of Commons.

These, then, are the three hopes of English groups: to teach the public, to obtain direct parliamentary representation, and to persuade the government. The publicity attending these processes causes the narrow and disreputable groups never to attempt organization, for they know that their chance of success is nil. Further, the rigid separation between public and private bills, with a procedure of judicial examination for the latter, marks off English from American habits, for it gives, even requires, the open appearance of interests and their counsel, to state the nature of the interest. And it takes away the remotest hope of success from any interest which is antisocial when tested by judicially sifted evidence of the balance between the public and the private benefit. The smallness of the country, the cohesion and intermixture of locality and interest, the nation-wide circulation of several metropolitan newspapers, the central quasi-governmental management of radio—all cause a whisper to be heard everywhere and make a fierce light beat upon the throne. (In the United States, the distances and diversity of interests, and confusion of responsibility at the center and in the localities, defeat the subjection of the lobbyist.) Until 1931 in Great Britain, the nonexistence of tariffs reduced the capacity of special interests to prevail against the common good. Digested in parties, the interests there sought mutual accommodations.

The labor unions, of course, constitute one of the lobbies. When the Labour government of 1945 took power, it was one of the first truly democratic systems to face the pressure of the unions, which in their political form had brought a party into power. The coal miners' union asked for a charter of ten points to be included in the nationalization law, or at any rate, to be promised them by administrative measures. Among these were a guaranteed week with a minimum wage, special welfare concessions, and representation on the National Coal Board, the everyday administrative authority managing the mines. The government refused any commitment. It was a Labour party government, but it was a government with a national outlook and responsibilities to be discharged to all occupations and all individuals within the nation. It did not even provide for representation of the coal workers on the board, though one mem-

---

[58] Cf. this point with the argument made by the United States Legislative Reference Service on page 456 above.
[59] Cf., for example, debate on Wool Price Orders, *Debates*, December, 1946. Cf. J. S. Ross, *Parliamentary Representation* (London, 1943), especially Chaps. VII and VIII; Simon Haxey, *Tory M. P.* (London, 1939); and 1946 Report, Annual Conference, Labour party.

ber is appointed with the qualification of "experience in the organization of labor." [60] "The nation" is a good card to play by any party, which has the courage to use it against the claims of any special group, whenever it is played sincerely and wisely: for millions of voters respond to its essential appeal—fair play for all.

The House of Commons has never, like the United States Congress, been clearly faced with the starker problem of lobbying. It has on several occasions affirmed it to be a breach of privilege of Parliament, punishable in various ways, if, to influence their Parliamentary conduct, members were subjected to bribery, threats of violence, abuse, loss of occupation or emoluments, or withdrawal of various social privileges (like membership in a club).[61] It is well known and officially admitted that some members of Parliament are paid by outside bodies.[62] But it is a rule that where a member has a private interest, he will admit it in debate, and allow the House to discount or put a premium on what he says, and in some cases he must refrain from voting. The rule on bribery and disclosure of interest might, if stretched far enough, include members who are paid wholly or partly to represent bodies outside the House, not being their electorate. But the rule has never yet been so extended, presumably because it has not been necessitated by undue violation of the conscientious duties of members.

An aspect of lobbying, though not on an exact par with the problem as it appears in the United States, was considered in 1947 by the House of Commons.[63] A member of the House claimed the protection of the House because the Civil Service Clerical Association—a labor union—had attempted to get him to terminate a life-

tenure appointment he held as their Parliamentary General Secretary. His agreement (made in May, 1943) paid him for dealing with all questions arising in the work of the Association which required parliamentary or political action, and for using his best endeavors to promote the work and objects of the Association. He was, especially, their spokesman in Parliament on civil-service matters. It was agreed that he should "be entitled to engage in his political activities with complete freedom," but on the other hand, should not be entitled in his political and parliamentary activities to purport to represent the political views of the Association, if any; and, should "only represent the Association" so far as civil-service matters were concerned.

In the course of time the general political views of this member clashed with those of many members of the Association, since it was largely Labour, while on the "closed shop," affiliation with the Trade Union Congress, and some other matters his views were seriously different. The Association's officers therefore attempted to persuade him to retire on full pay and a bonus, as it found a widespread misunderstanding among its own constituents that a paid officer of the Association should be at serious variance with it on public issues and in public discussion, and as, also, the Association suffered grave embarrassment at meetings of the trade-union world. To protect himself from the Association's persuasions (not to change his opinion, but to agree to retire), he prayed the House to declare that the Association was violating the Commons' privilege that members should not be put under pressure to speak otherwise than they freely felt they ought. The Committee found that the Association had not committed a breach of privilege. Its essential doctrine is not only important as a pronouncement on the main theme, but is also of conspicuous interest as an expression of British parliamentarism.[64]

Not every action by an outside body which may influence the conduct of a Member of

---

[60] Cf. D. R. Grenfell, *The British Coal Industry* (London, 1947), Appendix; also R. A. Dahl, "Workers' Control of Industry and the British Labour Party," *American Political Science Review*, October, 1947.

[61] Cf. Report, Select Committee of Privileges, and Minutes of Evidence, No. 118; June 17, 1947; memorandum by the clerk of the House, p. 83 ff., and cases there listed.

[62] *Ibid.*, Question 83, and Report.

[63] *Ibid.*

[64] *Ibid.*, p. xii.

Parliament as such could now be regarded as a breach of privilege, even if it were calculated and intended to bring pressure on the Member to take or to refrain from taking a particular course. Thus a Resolution passed by some national organization, or a town's meeting in a Member's constituency urging him to speak or vote in one way or another would not normally involve any breach of privilege, even though it expressly or by implication indicated that political support would be given or withheld according to the Member's response . . . In Your Committee's view the fact that a contractual relationship does exist is not in itself one which must completely tie the hands of the outside body if it desires to criticise or comment on a Member's activities.

The relationship between a Member and an outside body with which he is in contractual relationship and from which he receives financial payments is, however, one of great difficulty and delicacy in which there must often be a danger that the rules of privilege may be infringed. Thus it would certainly be improper for a Member to enter into any arrangement fettering his complete independence as a Member of Parliament by undertaking to press some particular point of view on behalf of an outside interest, whether for reward or not. Equally it might be a breach of privilege for an outside body to use the fact that a Member had entered into an agreement with it or was receiving payments from it as a means of exerting pressure upon that Member to follow a particular course of conduct in his capacity as a Member.

It would also be clearly improper to attempt to punish a Member pecuniarily because of his actions as a Member . . . Your Committee regard it as an inevitable corollary that if an outside body may properly enter into contractual relationships with and make payments to a Member as such, it must in general be entitled to terminate that relationship if it lawfully can where it considers it necessary for the protection of its own interests to do so. What, on the other hand, an outside body is certainly not entitled to do is to use the agreement or the payment as an instrument by which it controls, or seeks to control the conduct of a Member or to punish him for what he has done as a Member.

. . . It must be assumed in the Member's favour that having voluntarily entered the relationship he has put himself beyond the reach of any improper influence to which either its continuance or its threatened termi-

nation might give rise. None the less your Committee consider that Parliament must be jealous to see that relationships of this kind are not allowed by Members or used by outside bodies to influence Members in their course of conduct.

Only three other things need be added. *First,* Mr. Churchill, who was a member of the committee, said, "We are very greatly interested in whether in fact we have a Member here who can give his conscientious service to the House or is regulated by an outside body." *Second,* it could, on even a strict construction, have been argued that some of the general political matters on which the Association was aggrieved at its agent's opinions and votes were "civil service" matters: thus the repeal of the Trade Disputes Act, affiliation with the Trade Union Congress, and even the "closed shop" are matters of moment to civil servants as civil servants, and not merely as citizens. *Finally,* though it is clear that Parliament had never yet decided whether it was or was not a breach of privilege for a member on the one hand, and any body of persons outside his constituency on the other, to enter into an agreement by which the member should pursue a certain line in Parliament, the privilege of freedom of speech is more than the individual right of a member which he is free to sign away in part, for the right is a collective right of the House as a whole.[65]

This particular case was followed by a government resolution accepted by the House after earnest debate:[66]

That this House agrees with the Report of the Committee of Privileges, and in particular declares that it is inconsistent with the dignity of the House, with the duty of a Member to his constituents, and with the maintenance of the privilege of freedom of speech, for any Member of this House to enter into any contractual agreement with an outside body, controlling or limiting the Member's complete independence and freedom of action in Parliament or stipulating that he shall act in any way as the representative of such outside body

---

[65] Select Committee Report, Clerk of the House Memorandum, *ibid.*, p. 87.
[66] July 15, 1947. Cf. Debates.

in regard to any matters to be transacted in Parliament; the duty of a Member being to his constituents and to the country as a whole, rather than to any particular section thereof.

The possible punishment of lobbyists in Britain can be inferentially deduced from a further case of privilege. Two members of the House of Commons were found guilty of disclosing information to newspapers of the proceedings at a Labour party meeting of Labour members of the House of Commons, held in the House.[67] The meeting had been discussing matters directly related to the transactions of the House of Commons, past, present, and to come. The facts were discovered when one of the members wrote an article on the way in which news about parliamentary and party transactions "leaked" to the public. It was alleged that members gave information for pay, or while in a semi-drunken state, or in return for favorable attention in the press. This article was held to be a gross libel on the House. It was found by the select committee which inquired into the libel that the very member who had thus accused others of giving information was himself the author of disclosures to the press, for pay (he had been a journalist for many years). Another member became implicated as the result of evidence given during the inquiry.

Several very important matters bearing on the conduct of democratic government were ventilated or effectuated by this episode.[68] The members were condignly expelled from the House of Commons after making a humble apology for their libels, and above all, for corruptly receiving money for the disclosure of information about matters to be proceeded with in Parliament. The payments were regarded as being in the nature of bribery. It was then thought by the government that this scandalous case and the severity of the action of the House, memorable as they were, ought to be supplemented by a resolution of the House, as a clear warning to potential offenders. Therefore the following resolution was proposed,[69] and after strenuous debate accepted:

That, if in any case hereafter a Member shall have been found guilty by this House of corruptly accepting payment for the disclosure and publication of confidential information about matters to be proceeded with in Parliament, any person responsible for offering such payment shall incur the grave displeasure of this House; and this House shall take such action as it may, in the circumstances, think fit.

It is clear from this resolution that in future, any lobbyist attempting to influence the course of Parliamentary business by paying a member of Parliament would be taking an extremely grave risk of punishment by the House. And there being no definition of the word "payment," the risk is the greater. The House was warning the tempter, as well as the tempted, for in this case, the buyers had not been punished.[70]

Of more than passing interest are three ideas evoked by the case: (1) that meetings of a party in the House of Commons are entitled to the protection of privilege, (2) the duty owed by members to the good fame of the House and the House to the nation, and (3) the drastic nature of punishment by the House of Commons.

A majority of the Select Committee held that party meetings in the House had become so integral a part of the general functioning of Parliament that they ought to be regarded as conducting Parliamentary business. Therefore, members attending them ought to be punished in the same way as Parliament would punish a member who disclosed official transactions in the Chamber itself, and in the committees of the House itself. The report said:

In modern times the practice of holding private meetings in the precincts of the Palace

---

[67] Cf. Report, Committee of Privileges, H.C. No. 138; July 23, 1947.
[68] Ibid., and Debates, October 30, 1947.

[69] December 10, 1947, Debates.
[70] One paper paid thirty pounds a week to a press agency to whom one of the members gave information: the agency acted for the member; the other received five pounds a week direct from a newspaper. The first member claimed this was his regular journalistic work. (Report, para. 17 ff.)

of Westminster of different parties has become well established and, in the view of Your Committee, it must now be taken to form a normal and everyday incident of parliamentary procedure, without which the business of Parliament could not conveniently be conducted. Thus meetings held within the precincts of the Palace of Westminster during the parliamentary session are normally attended by Members as such, and the information which is given at such meetings is, in Your Committee's view, given to those attending them in their capacity as Members. Your Committee therefore conclude on this matter that attendance of Members at a private party meeting held in the precincts of the Palace of Westminster during the parliamentary session, to discuss parliamentary matters connected with the current or future proceedings of Parliament, is attendance in their capacity of Members of Parliament. . . . It follows that an unfounded imputation in regard to such meetings involves an affront to the House as such. Your Committee consider that an unjustified allegation that Members regularly betray the confidence of private party meetings either for payment or whilst their discretion has been undermined by drink is a serious contempt.

. . . The information has come to him confidentially as a member; it is only as a Member that he can part with it. In Your Committee's view, therefore, the making of a payment in order that a Member should specially note what took place at the meeting and should disclose information about it, or the acceptance of such payment, constitutes a transaction in the nature of bribery of a Member in regard to what is part of his work in Parliament and is a breach of the privileges of this House.

In debate it was argued: [71]

To me this is not a question of punishing or not punishing the hon. Member for Gravesend. This is a simple question of our duty as Members of the House of Commons, with all that long tradition which we have been taught to respect and observe. The hon. Member for Gravesend has been proved by practically everything that has been said here today to be the wrong kind of person to be here representing any section of the British people. We are here primarily to act on behalf of the people as a whole, and not any particular constituencies . . .

It was further contended: [72]

I feel that I have a duty not only to this House of Commons of which I am a Member but also to my own political party, and, whatever the crime may have been of the Member for Gravesend against this House, as a strong party member I view his crime against his own party as being, at least, equally strong. . . . There is another side to this question to which I think we Members of this House of Commons have to give attention. This is the central governing authority of this country, and this question is being watched in every part of the country with very close attention. Difficulties of this sort arise in all sorts of Government Departments and in all sorts of local government departments, and if we are going to countenance an offence of this sort, which we have condemned to the uttermost degree, and not deal with it by the right sentence of this court, we shall be encouraging all sorts of difficulties, all sorts of wrong action, in local government and other types of organisation in this country.

Mr. Churchill, in suggesting that rather than a temporary suspension the members should be expelled, said, "It [suspension] simply means that, after an interval, the Member will return here, without in the slightest degree having lifted from himself the terrible stain, the indelible stigma, the House has inflicted upon him. . . ." [73] Another Conservative member, speaking on the motion to make the tempter punishable as well as the tempted, observed, "They [Labour members] feel, perhaps we all feel, that the two honourable Members should not have been so cruelly and harshly punished—for it is a terrible punishment, nothing could be worse, and we can imagine what a terrible situation it is —and that there should be no broad censure on those who have been equally guilty in having tempted them to fall into this error." [74] (The student may wonder, "What! mere expulsion from the House of Commons is so terrible a punishment?" In England it is thought to be so.)

It ought to be noticed that there was much division in the House of Commons

---

[71] A Labour member, Debates, October 30, 1947, col. 1189.

[72] A Labour member, Debates, same date, col. 1190.
[73] Debates, same date, col. 1164.
[74] Debates, December 10, col. 1147.

on the question whether private party meetings in the precincts of the House ought to be covered by parliamentary privilege, though the Select Committee reported on this affirmatively. Of course, no precedent could be found to fit, because it is only in recent years that political parties have come to be so intimately a part of the structure and functioning of legislatures.[75]

Germany. I have, in another work,[76] made a detailed analysis of the organized interest groups of Weimar Germany. In number and size and technique of organization, they are at least on a par with those of America. They had their roots in the German love of organization, in the rapid changes in German industry after 1870 (when all branches of economic life were in a process of both natural and statutory evolution and before political parties were actually sovereign), and in the need for organization where the civil service was a body of jurists and where Parliament had less to give than ministers and the emperor. Before Hitler, they operated directly upon the *Reichstag* by supporting candidates, and upon the departments of state by deputations. Their pressure upon the departments responsible for their particular branch of interest was continuous and intense. It was welcomed for its usefulness. Their representation in the *Reichstag* was made easier than in other countries because proportional representation enabled them to influence party leaders (they were themselves sometimes party leaders) to put them upon the electoral lists in safe constituencies. These influences were largely controlled by the parties, which were strong in discipline and conviction. But one must observe the growth of a number of specifically "interest" parties, with which we have already dealt in Chapter 16 on parties. An attempt was made to conduct group interests and *expertise* into formal and open channels in the Economic Council (the *Reichswirt-*

schaftsrat), discussed later (p. 546). Complaints about members who too specially represented certain interests were frequent, but no bill to cope with the matter, whether by the Rules of Procedure or the general law, was successful.

The nazi régime, which replaced statute-making by ministerial ordinance, set up corporate representation of business and labor, though not in the legislature, which was merely a facade. Nazi Germany was ruled by the Nazi party, which meant the immediate relationship of the party hierarchy with the occupational groupings of every kind and at all levels, national, state, regional, and local. It even meant collaboration—but in the interest of the Nazi government's military-economic plans—in the very workshops and offices of the groups, and sometimes the acquisition of special advantage by leaders of groups who were personally befriended by Nazi leaders. The proceedings of the war-guilt trials, especially concerning the industrial and banking leaders, luridly reveal this situation. The legislature was no intermediate body between Nazi party and Nazi government and the interest groups: they starkly confronted each other.[77]

It is interesting to observe that the Senate of the postwar Bavarian constitution (Part III) is composed of representatives of economic and social groupings.

France. France is rich in the theory of group influence upon government (as witness the names of Benoist, Durkheim, and Duguit, to name only the most distinguished), but until recently was poor in actual organization. The notion of national sovereignty and the equality of citizens seems to have acted as an obstacle to it. There are, however, other causes. Until very recent years, state activity was small, for all the French outcry about *étatisme*. The chambers were intensely occupied

---

[75] Cf. Report, Select Committee, *loc. cit.*, Appendix and Evidence of Clerk of the House of Commons.
[76] Cf. *Representative Government and a Parliament of Industry* (London, 1923).

[77] Cf. Franz Neumann, *Behemoth*, 2nd edition (New York, 1945); Robert Brady, *Spirit and Structure of Nazi Germany* (London, 1939); M. N. Sweezy, *Structure of the Nazi Economy* (New York, 1941); L. Hamburger, *How Nazi Germany Controlled Business* (Washington, 1943); and Frank Munk, *The Legacy of Nazism* (New York, 1943).

with issues for which political groups are the better middlemen. The best thing for the interest, especially economic, was to have nothing at all to do with politics. Then, in so far as influence upon the chambers was necessary, this was exercised through ministers, and implemented by social gratifications. The advisory councils, of which we have already spoken, could be approached, and their members influenced, by powerful individuals, and little more than this was attempted. The state itself had created in its local Consultative Chambers of Arts and Manufactures, in the Chambers of Commerce and the Chambers of Labor, the normal means of communication upon industrial and commercial matters.[78] That is the Continental fashion (Weimar, nazi, and post-nazi Germany has it also): to put the mark and the discipline of the state upon such representative bodies. Further, the proportion of industrial and commercial interests, compared with those in other countries, to agricultural interests, which needed on the whole less state intervention, was and is small.

Since World War I, economic development stimulated the growth and pertinacity of a number of large associations like the *Comité de liaison des Grandes Associations,* and the *Union des Intérêts Économiques,* and the C.S.T. These organizations openly sought to influence legislation, and in election campaigns they sought to bind members to their program. In their directorates were often found distinguished deputies, more particularly senators, and there are connections between the parliamentary commissions and the associations. Neither French political logic nor the conditions of the day have allowed these voluntary organizations to remain masters of the field, for, following the example of Germany, and much influenced thereby, a comprehensive Economic Council was formed in 1927. We later compare its composition and effect with the German Economic Council, but may now note that it was regarded as sufficiently valuable to be resuscitated in the constitution itself of the Fourth Republic (title II, article 25).

The rules of procedure adopted by the National Assembly in March, 1947, forbid the establishment within the Assembly itself of groups bearing titles "for the defence of individual, local or professional interests" (article 13). Moreover, the rules (article 116) prohibit a deputy, "under penalty of suspension or expulsion, from taking advantage or allowing use of his status in financial, industrial or commercial enterprises or in the exercise of liberal or other professions, and, in a general fashion, using his title for other motives than the exercise of his mandate."

We have now briefly reviewed the existing means whereby legislators supply themselves, and are supplied, with the expertness necessary to the creation of law. We may conclude that were it not for these agencies, parliamentarism would be incompetent to the tasks assumed by the modern state. We may also conclude that were it not for the civil service and modern parties led by a few talented men and helped by their research bodies, it would be necessary to demand of the ordinary elected deputy a critical ability which he does not yet possess and which he could not acquire without years of careful study. Nor can it be omitted that without parties, and the centralizing, national authority of legislatures, modern states would be disrupted by the schismatic demands of the group interests. (In the government of the Soviet Union much nervous energy is saved by the fact that all special interests are consciously and resolutely domesticated by the only party, the Communist party. Yet it is observable that the Russian people, grouped in factory and farm, do, through meetings and other contact with the party, bring home to the latter what they would like, how much they can endure, and the limits of their obedience. "Lobbying" is in the Soviet

---

[78] P. Pic, *Traité Elémentaire de Législation Industrielle* (Paris, 1937), p. 122 ff.; and article by Herman Finer, "Officials and the Public," in *Public Administration,* January, 1931; cf. Gény, *La Collaboration des Particuliers avec l'État* (Paris, 1930). Cf. also K. Bopp, "The Government and the Bank of France," in *Public Policy* (Harvard, 1941).

Union an incessant contest between the officials at the head of bureau, trust, mine, factory, and collective farm.[79])

When we hear the current slogans, "the decline of parliaments" and the "crisis of democracy," we have to recall that it is an apparent decline only. New tasks have been imposed upon institutions which have not declined but remained the same. Other representative institutions, some with good credentials, have not yet been properly shaped and accommodated and granted a fully acknowledged place in the court of the sovereign.

DRAFTING OF THE LAW

It is not enough to have rightly determined the substance of the law, for it may be entirely ruined by the manner of its formulation. Both Montesquieu [80] and Austin [81] placed the highest value upon the technical drafting of the law, quite properly when one considers the problems it raises:

(1) No law can be made without affecting, by contradiction or amendment, other parts of the statute book or case-made law. The new law must be formulated with due reference to these, else inconsistencies and litigation will follow.

(2) The law requires careful definition to embody the intention of the legislator with the least amount of ambiguity, for the law courts interpret mainly by following the letter of the law and not by reference to the intention of the legislator. For how should one discover that intention? By parliamentary debate? (It is vague and one-sided); by numbers voting? (many may not have heard the debate and some may not have understood it). The judges are wise in looking only to the letter of the law, but we have already learned that this is an epoch of statutory revolution regarding property, civil liberties, and morals, an epoch bursting with the gravest problems. Moreover, it is desirable that the law should be as simply, that is, as economically, worded as possible. If then, it is badly formulated, the very intention of the legislator may be reversed; and *casus omissi* are the regular bread and butter of law courts. Serious accidents have occurred; ludicrous inconsistencies are reported from all countries, and to avoid them requires great care and skill.

(3) Last but not least, if a statute ends the legislative process, it begins the administrative. The administrators must have clear instructions. If not, they may either exceed their powers or be timid and confused, or public recrimination and litigation may result.[82]

Hence the tendency to place bill drafting in the hands of specialists, who become skilled with practice, who are able to use terms which have already acquired a settled definition in the courts of law,[83]

---

[79] Cf. A. Baykov, *The Development of the Soviet Economic System* (New York, 1947); V. Kravchenko, *I Chose Freedom* (New York, 1945); and *Communism in Action*, U. S. Legislative Reference Service (1946).
[80] Cf. *Esprit des Lois*, Book XXIX, Chaps. XVI-XIX.
[81] Cf. *Jurisprudence*, 1136: "I will venture to affirm, that what is called the *technical* part of legislation is incomparably more difficult than what may be styled as the *ethical*. In other words, it is far easier to conceive justly what would be useful law, than so construct the same law that it may accomplish the design of the law-giver."

[82] As, for example, in the Rating and Valuation (Apportionment) Act, 1928; in the definition of "industrial" hereditaments, which were to be derated; in TVA's "planning" powers, and power to make "studies"; in NLRB's definition of "employed" (was it to include foremen?); in the "portal-to-portal" suits. An especially apposite case study of faulty drafting and the consequences on the deficient administration of the law is to be found in the Legislative Reorganization Act, in the part referring to lobbying: relating to the word "principal" (cf. p. 463 above).
[83] F. T. Lee in "The Office of the Legislative Counsel," *Columbia Law Review*, April, 1929, p. 390: "The essential and the time consuming elements are analyses of the problems and of the existing law and the administrative and technical details—in order that the general substantive policies may be built upon a sound understructure that will make practicable the accurate execution of the policies . . . It is the rare exception when a simple policy cannot be simply expressed. Usually the explanation of complex, indefinite, disorderly statutes is attributable to the existence of a complex policy, whose ramifications cannot be definitely ascertained, or else is attributable to political or parliamentary exigencies."

and who, by centralizing the process, are able to exclude unintentional and mutually destructive provisions.

England. In England, for government measures only and for private members' bills befriended by the government, a special office of draftsmen, Parliamentary Counsel to the Treasury, is employed. The office has had a distinguished history since its creation in 1837 (Lord Thring and Sir Courtenay Ilbert were its incumbents for years [84]). The minister and the leading officials in the department responsible for the bill cooperate with Counsel in the inception of the bill, and then continuously with amendments which arise during its passage through Parliament; indeed, they are conveniently present during debates in the House and in committee. Moreover, Counsel provide memoranda on the clauses for the instruction of the minister, and search out and make plain the history, and the connection with other departments of state, especially of the Treasury. It is a vital, and an intricate, and a highly technical business. The value of the office of draftsmen has been thus assessed by Bryce: it produced harmony in the laws; a form at once shorter, clearer, better expressed, and less likely, all things being equal, to provoke litigation; and a means for consultation on the probable legal effects of contemplated proposals, and for reports upon existing law.[85]

Germany. In Weimar Germany no special draftsmen but the leading departmental civil servants were responsible. Indeed, this is why legal studies formed so large a part of the German civil servant's training. This dispersion of drafting responsibility was criticized as leading to ambiguous clauses and unnecessary additions to the law.

United States. In the United States until 1915, there was only the very casual help of the administrative departments with their legal advisers when "administration" bills were being pressed. In 1918 [86] special officers, called legislative counsel, were created, one each for the Senate and the House of Representatives, with adequate assistants to "aid in drafting public bills and resolutions or amendments thereto on the request of any committee of either House of Congress."

When the work of the offices of legislative counsel, in House and Senate, was reviewed by the Joint Committee on the Reorganization of Congress in 1945, it became clear that only about one quarter of the bills introduced into the Houses (if indeed so many) came to counsel for assistance. Many of them were not dealt with completely. Much time was spent—and, from a legislative point of view, wasted—on assistance to individuals instead of services to the committees as such. The recruits to the service were not of the highest possible quality, partly because of the rather low salaries offered. There was considerable turnover in the employees, hardly conducive to the proper exercise of this delicate and abstruse drafting function. Counsel frequently were at sea in ignorance of the subject matter on which they were expected to draft law. In fact, a very substantial proportion of the statutes had come from the executive departments, and in many cases, were adopted with sighs of relief by all concerned, almost exactly as they arrived from the departments that drafted them, it being recognized that Congress was unable and ill-equipped, through lack of knowledge and active experience in the subject, to formulate a sound law.[87]

The Reorganization Act of 1946 provided for more counsel and higher salaries. Congress cannot but still suffer from inadequate inwardness of connection with the administration, and so either must continue to produce rough-and-ready laws (a trouble to the public, the interests, and the officials who have to administer them, and a frequent source of con-

---

[84] Cf. C. P. Ilbert, *Legislative Forms and Methods* (London, 1901) and *The Mechanics of Law Making* (London, 1911); Lord Thring, *Practical Legislation* (London, 1877 and 1902); and Harrison in Minutes of Evidence, Committee on Ministers' Powers, 1932.
[85] United States Senate Report, 62nd Congress, No. 1271 (1913), "Legislative Drafting Bureau and Reference Division," p. 74 ff.

[86] Cf. Lee, *op. cit.*
[87] Cf. evidence of Counsel, Hearings on Reorganization of Congress, 2413 ff. and 3455 ff.

fusion, litigation and re-enactment) or must accept the assistance of the administrative agencies.

France. In France, consultation of the *Conseil d'État* was made permissive, instead of compulsory, in 1878, and this, we have seen, is continued by the decree of July 31, 1945. Governments have relied upon the unsystematic aid of departmental officials, ministers' private secretaries, academic experts, commissions of inquiry, and experts who happen to get on to the parliamentary commissions. In one or two departments, some officials are especially

entrusted with bill drafting, but this is not common.

In so far as the operation of lobbyists is pernicious, it might be reduced to more reasonable proportions by the lengthening of the duration of legislatures which are now fixed at less than four years: the chief example is the House of Representatives. Also, an increase in the size of the legislature, important for other reasons also, might make it difficult for the lobbyist to sway its mind, and this might be followed by an increase in the size of Congressional committees.

20

First Chambers—Deliberation

THE law has been conceived; it is drafted; outside influences have been at work and remain vigilant. How does the legislature proceed to convert it into law? What rules does it impose upon itself, and for what motives?

Rules of procedure have always been considered with peculiar regard by parliamentarians. For long, the right to make rules free from intervention by the monarch was regarded as a test of the independence of parliament and was one element in the battle for self-government. It was possible for a parliament with such rights to bind the Crown and its ministers to its will, since a price could be exacted for the lowering of each obstacle. But in our own day, procedure has an even more solemn meaning: it is the self-control of the sovereign people, the voluntary surrender of all parties to common considerations of utility and justice. This meaning is implicit in the rules and habits of the various legislatures and can be generally thus summarized:

(1) Deliberation should be so arranged as to avoid members' being taken by surprise.

(2) There must be sufficient deliberation.

(3) The majority must have the ultimate power to pass the law and administer.

(4) The minority must not be oppressed.

(5) Deliberation must be orderly, earnest, and genuine.

(6) The good faith of all speakers must be assumed.

(7) The system of government by parliamentary discussion and decision is accepted as proper and incontrovertible.

It is obvious that the use of the rules depends on the general sense of justice existent in the majority and in society at large, and, of course, on how far these are aware of the nature of the task to be performed. Upon the decision depends, in part, the general repute of the legislature and also, as has been shown, the extent to which people come to believe that one assembly ought to be checked by another, whether parliamentary or extraparliamentary. Thus the House of Lords has been defended by some because there is insufficient deliberation in the House of Commons, and the American Senate is defended as the only governmental place in which a minority can speak without restriction.

THE PRESIDING OFFICER

ESSENTIAL to the operation of all the rules is an officer to preside, interpret them, and put them into effect. A presiding officer needs many qualities; for instance, tact and sufficient alertness during hours of speeches to detect and stop any disorder. The prime qualities are decision and impartiality. The need for a knowledge of the rules is obvious. Impartiality rests upon less obvious bases, since we find legislatures—for example, the French National Assembly and the United States House of Representatives—where it is almost a rule that the presiding officer shall *not* be impartial. Partiality results in waste of time by the challenge of the chairman's ruling. What is much worse, the more that government intervenes, the more likely is it that after the passage of the laws, the claim may arise that they were unfairly passed. Laws made under such conditions lose part of their authority. To these effects of partiality must be added the tumult which comes from enraged spirits, or resignation to a condition of apathy. The English Parliament has contrived to establish the conditions of impartiality better than any other legislature.[1]

The British Speaker. By convention, the speaker is elected by the House for the duration of a parliament, and once elected he will be reelected as often as he cares to stand, without competition.[2] This provides both continuity of practice, the authority of permanence, and the minimum of controversy. Although the House is at liberty to propose several candidates for the chair, the party leaders and whips attempt to arrange to avoid party competition and to secure unanimous election. This has usually been achieved, since 1839, by the forbearance of the opposition and the care of the majority not to propose a virulent partisan. The power of speakership issues from tradition, ceremony, and the possession of present-day rights by practice, rule, and statute. The office is of unbroken continuity since the fourteenth century and is actually connected with the grandest creative events of national and parliamentary history. The elaborate ritual of bowing to the chair and manipulating the mace adds to

this as a factor striking reverence and awe in the breast of the average member of Parliament, causing him, as he approaches, to feel, as someone has recorded, like a schoolboy before the principal. Moreover, the speaker enjoys high state precedence: silk-stockinged, gowned, and wigged, and frequently selected with an eye to his own physical impressiveness, he himself renders obeisance to the chair at the opening of every sitting of the House.

For centuries the speaker has been denied the right to speak and vote in the proceedings of the House. A casting vote he has, but its occasion is necessarily rare, and practice has defined that the casting vote be used to vote no change of the existing situation. It is the convention that he shall cease to have connection with political parties or membership of a political club. His constituency was never contested from 1895 to 1935, when the Labour party was ill-advised to contest Speaker Fitzroy's seat, unsuccessfully.[3]

Thus the speaker is insulated from politics, and this is, indeed, the condition which underlies his usefulness to the House and his authority over it, which are intimately related. The speaker's dignity is supported by a large salary (on the Permanent Appropriations Act), an official palace, and, unless he objects, a peerage on retirement. The speaker presides over the house, applies the rules of debate, and settles questions of order. He is, as near as a human being can be, the rules and practice of the house come to life without interposition of his personal or party view. He regulates the order of speech, puts the question, and announces the House's decisions. He revises notices of motion and questions. He is the safeguard of private members against the abuse of the powers of the leaders in government and opposition and is their mentor in procedural difficulties. Most important is the understanding that if in giving a ruling the speaker chooses to insist, the ruling prevails in the situation,

---

[1] Cf. T. Erskine May, *Parliamentary Practice* (London, 1946 edition), *passim;* Joseph Redlich, *The Procedure of the House of Commons* (London, 1948), Vol. II, p. 131 ff.; and Michael Macdonagh, *The Speaker of the House* (London, 1914); cf. also John Evelyn Dennison, *Notes from My Journal* (London, 1900); Lord Ullswater, *A Speaker's Commentaries* (London, 1925), and G. P. Gooch, *Life of Lord Courtney* (London, 1920). Such biographies as Disraeli's, Gladstone's, Harcourt's, and Campbell-Bannerman's must be consulted for ministerial attitude to the speakership.

[2] The practice began with Speaker Compton in 1722.

[3] Spanning eleven elections. From 1714 to the present only four contests occurred.

although the ruling may be challenged in a vote of censure.

His powers include the following weighty controls over the pressure of party against party. He can prevent the putting of the previous question until he is satisfied that the minority has had adequate opportunity to put its views to the House. He can accept or refuse a motion, put just after the question period, that the House adjourn on a matter of "definite urgent and public importance"— the application of this definition to the matter which a member wants to get debated by the House is in the discretion of the speaker.[4] Furthermore, when the House in 1947 was discussing the extent to which ministers were prepared to answer questions about the everyday administration of the nationalized industries, and the government declared for the maximum restriction, the speaker informed the House, at the urging of some members, that he and not the government was the authority to settle what questions were admissible. He recognizes the right of members to speak, and as such assumes the responsibility of seeing that all representative views get their fair share of available parliamentary time, even if this means that the leaders of government and opposition are irked by speeches from

men in their own following whom they do not like. He is empowered to stop irrelevance and frivolous repetition in debate. Questions to ministers are regulated by him as to their admissibility, and the amount of time allowed to supplementary questions is settled by his ruling. He has the power of choosing amendments among those offered; since all cannot be debated, he exercises the power of jumping over the less important and controversial—this is the "kangaroo closure." Finally, he has the very important power of certifying money bills.

When the Labour party contested his seat in 1935, all other parties rallied to Speaker Fitzroy's support. One of the arguments, namely that because the speaker has become impartial his constituency is disfranchised, is, in view of the nature of British political parties, ridiculous. The action of the Labour party precipitated the submission of the question to a select committee of the House of Commons. Its historical and comparative researches led to the conclusion that well enough should be left alone. The speaker, it thought, ought to be elected like other members of Parliament—this gave him something in common with them. If the speaker's seat were then liable to contest, the undesirability of contest must be met by "fuller education of the electorate toward the recognition and increased understanding of those vital democratic safeguards which it is the duty of every speaker to defend."[5]

It has been my constant experience in explaining to American students the nature of the speaker's status to meet with incredulity that he could possibly be impartial. This is a reflection of the designed and necessary partisanship of the speakership in the United States House of Representatives, and is an act of homage to a system of government which is mature enough to have freely and consciously established such an arbiter in a whirlpool of party politics. It is an important index to the self-control of the British in political action that the present

---

[4] Cf. the speaker's view on the gravity of this responsibility in reply to suggestions by members that speakers, especially since 1923, had so strictly interpreted the phrase as to reduce almost to nonexistence the right of the rank and file to challenge the government by such a motion. Cf. Third Report, Select Committee on Procedure. Evidence, H.C. 189-91, 1946, p. 88. For illustration: "Mr. Speaker, your criticism of this proposal [to allow members to interpret the phrase] is that if the question of urgency and public importance were left to the House, in effect forty members could continually obstruct the business of the Government?" "Yes.". . . "My point is this, that I suppose in nine cases out of ten the motion which is put to the House arises from something that appears in the Press, and you invariably see it as well as the Members, and are able to judge whether it is a matter of public importance equally as well as the House?" "Yes. Personally, I think it is a responsibility which the Speaker has to accept and to exercise in the interests of the House of Commons and all parties." (Questions 3064 and 3077.)

[5] See Report on Mr. Speaker's Constituency, No. 98, 1939.

(1949) deputy speaker was formerly a Labour member of Parliament and the present speaker a former Conservative. Each agent of government, in any system of government, is the epitome of all that is significant everywhere in that system: "the universe in a grain of sand." The student will recall the discussion of the meaning of the word "system" in the first paragraphs of the chapter on constitutions (Chap. 8).

The Speaker of the United States House of Representatives. In the House of Representatives the speakership, although originating in the conventions of the British eighteenth-century speaker,[6] is an entirely different institution. Whereas the speaker of the House of Commons simply utters the rules of the House, whether they are to the advantage or disadvantage of minority or majority, the speaker of the House of Representatives has often made the rules of his House by wide discretion in interpretation or in the appointment of committees with power over the procedure of the House. Some of the steering and program-making powers customarily exercised by the government in England are exercised by the speaker in America.

In the United States, the speaker is not impartial and is not intended to be by the majority; nor, if we judge by experience, does he intend to be, although he is expected to be fair both to the minority and to the rank and file of the majority's followers. He is today one of the majority party leaders; before 1911 he was *the* party leader in the legislative branch of government, and not seldom a rival in political pre-eminence of the President of the United States.

The speakership is established in the constitution,[7] where it is provided that "the House of Representatives shall choose their Speaker." In fact he is chosen by the caucus of the majority party and then the House proceeds to his election. No minority party when it becomes a majority will, as in Great Britain, take over a speaker previously selected by the former majority. Within the caucus the fight rages between various sections of the party for this great tactical position of leadership and control. When the speaker is chosen he does not cut off connections with his party—on the contrary, they are even more sedulously cultivated. He occasionally promotes bills of great and sometimes of general importance. He speaks in debate, although the written rules of the House deprecate this.[8] He votes, although the rules of the House do not encourage him to vote except in certain circumstances.[9] He is in constant consultation with the executive and the leader of the Senate when of the same party as his, so that the executive's policies may be effectuated and the latter's collaboration cultivated. He is one of the small knot of policy-makers and campaign leaders—partisan in the profoundest and most vociferous sense. His seat is contested, and therefore he must nurse his constituency by tidbits from the "pork barrel" and by declarations of policy, and he must frequently harbor a certain resentment against his opponents. He promotes by positive strategy and intervention a legislative and executive policy.[10] Thus the speaker of the House of Representatives is the avowed agent of the majority; he is involved—often he leads—in the party councils. Before 1911 he was the supreme party leader. In entering into the analysis of these functions we concern ourselves, also, with the general arrangements for governing the work and time of the House.

The House of Representatives is specially obliged to make detailed arrange-

[6] Cf. M. P. Follett, *The Speaker of the House of Representatives* (New York, 1896), Chap. I, and A. C. Hinds, "The Speaker of the House of Representatives," *American Political Science Review*, May, 1909, Vol. III, p. 116 ff.; and C. W. Chiu, *The Speaker of the House of Representatives since 1896* (New York, 1928).
[7] Article I, sect. 2.

[8] Cf. Jefferson's *Manual*, xvii; Chiu, *op. cit.*, p. 44.
[9] Rule I, 6.
[10] Cf. Congressional Record, 62nd Congress, 1st session, p. 7. Cf. also Congressional Record, 69th Congress, special session, 1st session, p. 379 ff, the debate on election of Speaker Longworth. Cf. also the course of events between March, 1933 and April 23, 1945, and the remarks of Speaker Rayburn.

ments for the conduct of its proceedings (1) because it has a large membership, the individuals of which hunger for a part of its time (especially, too, since bills of a private character are promoted in exceptionally large numbers); (2) because the total amount of business is large; [11] and (3) because the executive, under the rule of the separation of powers, does not lead and serve the assembly, as in the cabinet system. But why should the power of leadership and discipline have found its way to the speakership? For three main reasons. *First,* the spirit of majority rule is exceptionally strong in the United States, and this has produced the disposition to vest very great power in someone. *Second,* power tends to go first of all to the person in a conspicuous position with an already acquired prestige. *Third,* the separation of power between legislature and executive requires the bridging of the gap by personal arrangement between the formal spokesman of the House —namely the speaker—and the President (when they are both of the same party), and sometimes produces a contest between the speaker on behalf of a majority party in the House and a President who happens to have been put in power by the party which is in a minority in the House.[12]

From the beginning of the Republic these tendencies were at work. When, after

the Civil War, the economic and social development of the country began to force a mass of new work upon political institutions, the parties were compelled to promise much, and, in order to keep some part of their promises, to submit themselves to a systematic and rigid discipline. This involved both Congress and the executive. A combination of personal character (as embodied in speakers like Blaine,[13] Randall, Reed,[14] and Cannon,[15] who were forceful and capable leaders of their parties) with the novelty of the problem of positive governmental leadership gave the power, with remarkable absoluteness, to the speaker.[16] There it remained until, by 1911, Congressmen realized that, after all, this was not the only possible way of providing for the leadership that was needed. There were alternatives; and such alternatives might open the way for a share in power by those who dissented from the policy of the party leaders. Moreover, a new generation, especially from the West and Middle West, were insurgent against the "old gang" who had made the rules to suit themselves. Hence the Congressional revolt of 1911, and a slight decentralization of the speaker's power.

Several questions require discussion: first, the formal sources of the speaker's power 1911; second, the formal changes made as a result of the revolt of 1911; third, the practical results of the revolt.

The speaker's strength before 1911 issued from his right to the exercise of three main powers: (1) the appointment of committees (2) his chairmanship, *ex officio,* of the committee on rules, and (3) the "recognition" of a member to address the House.

<hr>

[11] From January 3, 1941, to December 16, 1942 (77th Congress), 7869 bills were introduced in the House, and 1018 House bills and 476 Senate bills were passed. Cf. Joint Committee on the Reorganization of Congress, *Symposium,* p. 41 and pp. 210-238.

[12] Cf. G. H. Brown, *Leadership of Congress* (Indianapolis, 1923), p. 52: "Perceiving a possible danger to the security and stability of legislative government, the House of Representatives, the body peculiarly the bulwark of popular liberty, put itself in a posture of defense to meet its two deadliest enemies, fortifying itself on the one hand against the possible encroachment of the Executive, from an instinctive fear of despotism, and on the other against forces within its own membership likely under exceptional circumstances to seek the destruction of the party system for the sake of immediate selfish interest, as a thoughtless boy might fell a splendid tree to obtain a kite caught in its branches."

[13] Cf. J. C. Ridpath, *Life and Work of James G. Blaine* (Boston, 1893); J. G. Blaine, *Twenty Years in Congress* (Boston, 1893).

[14] Cf. S. W. McCall, *Life of Thomas Brackett Reed* (New York, 1914).

[15] Cf. L. W. Busbey, *Uncle Joe Cannon: The Reminiscences of a Pioneer American* (New York, 1927). Sidelights on Cannon's powers are to be found in N. W. Stephenson's *Nelson W. Aldrich* (New York, 1930).

[16] They claimed that if they were "czars," it was only if the majority supported them.

(1) The appointment of committees was a tremendous source of strength, because in the American Congressional system, as we show later, no bill is considered by the House unless first reported by a committee. Committees have authority not only over the bill in all its essence and parts but also (in practice) as to whether it shall ever arrive before the House at all. Hence, the power to appoint committees was a plenary power to determine policy; it was not only leadership but command. Though certain rules, like that of seniority and geographical distribution, were conventional restraints upon the discretion of the speaker, they could still be overcome by determined speakers, and they were. If the committees had such power, not only over bills of general importance and of appropriations and taxes, but over those of a private and local nature, giving benefit to specific districts, then they were obviously the key positions for political influence. The speaker therefore had the distribution of the political prestige, of the chairmanships which gave the holders thereof a claim in party councils and in the patronage which fell to the party under the "spoils" system. He also had the wherewithal to please and attach his constituency, territorial or group, to himself. This was a formidable power; the speaker could make or destroy the careers of Congressmen. Hence their humility and subservience, which again added to his power. Hence also their readiness to revolt as soon as cleavage within the party should offer the prospect of throwing off the yoke. Especially bitter were the personal controversies relating to chairmanships of the committees. The speaker ruled in the name of the party;[17] he ruled, however, with the cooperation not of the whole party but of a half dozen principal henchmen. The House was guided and controlled in its debates, its legislative output, and its executive investigations by the speaker and the chairmen of the half dozen principal committees.

Nor was that all. (2) Among the committees of the House was and still is the Committee on Rules. This was first appointed in 1858 to revise the rules of the House and report the revision to the House.[18] The committee, in 1880, became permanent. The pressure of business and of the constituencies upon the House increased. New powers, calculated to help the House to cut through the thick jungle of legislative proposals, were given to the committee. It acquired the power to make a way in the business of the House for the consideration of any bills. This was done by giving the Committee on Rules the right to report at any time[19] that the rules should be changed, and the change of rules permitted any other committee to report its proposal only at the time stated by the Committee on Rules. True it was that a majority of the House had to accept this report—but when has a majority party ever refused to follow its leaders? Dilatory tactics against the Committee on Rules were swept away by the speaker's ruling,[20] and it was allowed to report without previous notice.[21] These "special orders" were thus used to give priority to legislation which the committee and the speaker believed to be entitled to it.[22] Notice well that they are Congress' equivalent of the power of the cabinet in the British House of Commons to ask for, and obtain, by majority vote, the settlement of the timetable of the House. Before 1911, the speaker was chair-

---

17 Cf. G. H. Brown, *op. cit.*, p. 160: " 'The appointment of the committees,' said the Speaker, 'is made by the Speaker under the rules, unless the House should otherwise specially order. The Speaker of the House in the exercise of that function is responsible to the House and to the country, this being a government through parties and the Republican party has placed power in the Speaker as to the appointment of committees.' "

18 Cf. A. C. Hinds, *op. cit.*, Vol. IV, sect. 4321; D. S. Alexander, *History and Procedure of House of Representatives* (Boston, 1916).
19 Cf. M. P. Follett, *op. cit.*, p. 275; D. S. Alexander, *op. cit.*; S. W. McCall, *The Business of Congress* (New York, 1911).
20 Hinds, *op. cit.*, Vol. V, sect. 5739.
21 M. P. Follett, *op. cit.*, p. 276.
22 Cf. *Congressional Record*, 60th Congress, 2nd session, pp. 588-89; Hinds (clerk at the speaker's table) on *Order of Business in the House*.

man of the Committee on Rules, and he appointed its two majority members, while the two minority members received scant grace. Thus the triumvirate ruled the House; and of the three the speaker was first and all.[23] He benefited from the admitted need to disentangle the thousands of threads of Congressional business and to give preference to the business which the party leaders, whether in the Congress or in the presidency, considered indispensable. What the speaker decided in committee, the speaker would facilitate from the chair.

(3) Yet in order to overcome obstruction, the right to "recognize" a member needed to be vested in the speaker. This was done by a succession of developments which led to a singular absoluteness of his power. No one could address the House unless by previous arrangement with the speaker.

This system was attacked and formally destroyed in a campaign which began in March, 1910.[24] Two vigorous tendencies sought their outlet: the Republican "insurgent" movement invigorated by the political forces in the western states, and the individual dissatisfaction of Congressmen, ostensibly with the injustice done to their constituencies by an unrepresentative system. The result was the establishment of certain new rules: (a) making the Committee on Rules elective by the House and of an increased size, and depriving the speaker of the right to a place upon it; (b) making the committees of the House selective no longer by the speaker but by a Committee on Committees, and (c) establishing by the rules of the House definite times for certain business which the speaker must respect—

---

[23] Congressional Record, 56th Congress, 1st session, p. 7: "To say that the Committee can be controlled by the majority is not candid, because the Committee is considered the Speaker's official family, and no gentleman of the Speaker's party would serve upon it unless he could support the Speaker's policy."
[24] Cf. Chiu, op. cit.; also, C. R. Atkinson and C. A. Beard, "Syndication of the Speakership," American Political Science Quarterly, Vol. XXVI (1911), pp. 381-414; Brown, op. cit., Chap. X ff., especially p. 159 (speech of Nelson of Wisconsin).

such as Calendar Wednesday and the Discharge Calendar.

What have been the results of this evolution upon the speakership? He still remains in intention and practice a party man. He is still one of the very small knot of Congressional leaders who treat with the president for passage of "administration" measures. He is still consulted by, and has great sway with, his party "steering" committee and the floor leader of the majority party. He is still a major factor in deciding assignments to committees and the priority of business, because he is one of the most eminent, usually the most eminent, of his party: that, indeed, is why he was elected speaker. Order and system in a House of four hundred and thirty-five members there is bound to be, and the power of leadership must somewhere be lodged. While, until 1911, it was concentrated in the speaker and his friends by grace, it is now concentrated in the speaker's friends and the speaker. Leadership has been "syndicated" or put into "commission," but the speaker is still the predominant member of the syndicate. The contrast with British procedure is remarkable: each speakership epitomizes a whole political system.

Instead of losing his political partisan character on becoming speaker, he becomes speaker in order to be more political. Having helped his party to power by electoral leadership in company with the other party leaders who are out to obtain victory in Congressional elections and in the nomination and election of the President of the United States, he continues to help the party to carry through the program desired by the leaders. As former speaker, John Nance Garner is said to have declared in 1931 when a Democratic House confronted a Republican President: "I hold the most powerful position in this government excepting that of President of the United States. I accepted the proposed Vice-Presidential nomination with much hesitancy."

France. The president of the Chamber of Deputies, now the National Assembly, is, of course, like the British speaker and unlike the American speaker, the product of a parliamentary system in which the guiding and controlling authority is a responsible ministry. The presidents have little extraneous cause, therefore, to become partisans. Yet the conditions of effective technical excellence or impartiality are not present in the same measure as in England. In France [25] the president of the Chamber was elected anew at every session, and in the procedure of the Assembly of the Fourth Republic the rule is continued.[26] This is part of the tradition of distrust against constituted authorities. It is a grave fault from the standpoint of legislative efficiency, as with each contest in every session there is a stirring of all the passions of party, and objections are urged to the incumbent as well as his merits. Nor is there sufficient time for the president to dominate his electors: the sense of his recent arrival is always there, and he cannot acquire the aspect of doom which permanence gives. Whereas, between 1872 and 1945, the House of Commons had six speakers, France had fifteen, and between them Paul Deschanel and Henri Brisson held office for one third of the time, the latter very intermittently. The uncertainty of election produced by the large number of groups is also a factor which prevents the president from towering above them all, especially since the need for an absolute majority produces the second ballot system. Nor is that all. The presidents of the Chamber and of the Senate (now Assembly and Council of the Fourth Republic) have become part of the regular machinery of state with the President of the Republic in the formation of ministries. They are opposed in their constituencies. They remain attached to their parties (though not in sittings of the Chambers), cooperate at group meetings, sometimes enter into press controversies. They pass into ministries, then back into the chair [27] and, although they do not intervene as partisans in debate, their frequent hortatory remarks are necessarily biased and provoke partisan passions. In July, 1926, there occurred an incident in the Chamber of Deputies, unthinkable in England. M. Herriot, then president of the Chamber, suddenly determined to prevent the government from obtaining powers of legislation by decree. Without notice he quietly and suddenly appeared in his seat in the Chamber, and his speech overturned the Briand government. Hereupon he was called by the President of the Republic to form a new ministry.[28] In June, 1935, M. Fernand Bouisson, Socialist, president of the Chamber since 1926, resigned to become premier. Within a few days, the Chamber overthrew his cabinet. It then elected him to the chair! The presidency of the Chambers is a steppingstone to Presidency of the Republic.[29]

The presidents of the French Chambers have powers in regard to the regulation of business similar to those possessed by the English speakers, though perhaps more complicated by virtue of the many groups, the parliamentary commissions, and participation in the council which settles the order of business. It is somewhat simplified by the fact that the order of speech is settled by the rules. The task, moreover, is made very difficult by the tradition of the office, its connection with politics, but most of all by the restiveness of the Chambers. Calls to order are unheeded or are challenged with invective. The House may, and often does, reverse by its vote a ruling of its president. Irrelevance when reprimanded turns sour and becomes sarcastic expostulation. Suspensions of the House for a quarter hour are frequent to quiet the irate. At the root of all this is the notion of the deputy's individual sovereignty, the

[25] Cf. *Règlement*, March, 1947, Chap. IV.
[26] Cf. E. Pierre, *op. cit.*, Vols. I, II, and III, paras. 407 ff., and sections on his various attributes; Ripert, *La Présidence des Assemblées Politiques* (Paris, 1908): for history and evaluation.
[27] For example, Paul Deschanel, Charles Dupuy, Casimir Perier, Henry Brisson, Léon Bourgeois, Painlevé, Herriot, Fernand Bouisson.
[28] Cf. for an account of this incident Georges Suarez, *De Poincaré à Poincaré* (Paris, 1928), p. 138 ff.
[29] For example, Deschanel, Casimir Perier (Bourgeois and Painlevé were spoken of), and Doumer (1931). But Herriot was unsuccessful in 1939.

petulant party divisions, and the lack of a sense of state.

The rules of the National Assembly of the Fourth Republic have rendered the position of the president of the Assembly even more difficult by adding powers and subtracting authority. His power to convene the commissions and transmit bills to the Council of the Republic and to the president of the Republic for promulgation; his right to promulgate laws if the president of the Republic does not do so within ten days of their submission to him for promulgation; the power to impose disciplinary penalties on disorderly deputies and to control the military forces guarding the assembly—all these can be used by men of ill-will to obstruct the government of the nation at crucial times. In the hands of antidemocratic men it would be easy to do more damage than merely upset the shaky coalitions which constitute the cabinets of France in subrevolutionary times.

Nor is that all. In seeking to strengthen the Assembly as the unrivalled center of political power in the nation, the president of the Assembly is vested by the constitution of the Fourth Republic with immense responsibilities of an order quite distinctive from those of other presiding officers of legislatures. When a cabinet decides on dissolution of the Assembly it must first ask the advice of the president of the Assembly (article 51, and see p. 396 above and p. 643 below). When a cabinet has dissolved the Assembly, the premier steps down from the cabinet, which remains, and the president of the Assembly becomes premier. He takes care of the government until the elections, meanwhile adding a new Minister of the Interior and adding ministers of state from the groups not so far represented in the cabinet (article 52). Finally, in case of obstruction duly verified by a vote of the "parliament" (the two houses?), or in case of vacancy through death, resignation, or any other cause, the president of the Assembly assumes the functions of the President of the Republic in the interim until the election of a new President (article 42).

The rules have imported proportional representation into the voting for president of the legislature and the six vice-presidents (the *bureau*) who would take the place of the former, one by one, in the order of their precedence if he were incapacitated or absent. Article 9 of the rules requires the selection of the *bureau* of the Assembly each year "by proportional representation of the groups." Who is to be second and third vice-president is a matter, then, that might shake the foundations of the Republic, especially in a day when the Soviet Union has strong friends in the Communist party of France. And already the non-Communist groups have interpreted proportional representation in a way—quite legitimate—to exclude a Communist leader from second and third place.[30] Is it to be expected that a session which begins with a riot over the President will deliberate calmly thereafter? Again let it be said that the presiding officer of the legislature is the epitome of the political character of each country.

DISCUSSION

WE have no means of knowing the earliest history of the establishment of the number of readings of a bill in its progress toward law, because British practice, which has been of such influence upon other countries, began at a remote and unreported time. We can only guess at the motives from the remarks of commentators who have rationalized the processes at whose birth they were not present.[31]

---

[30] For the riotous scenes at the opening of the session of January, 1948, see *New York Times*, January 14, 15, 16, 1948. The Communist party appealed to the President of the Republic, since the rules require that he be notified of the formation of the *bureau*. As we have already noticed, the Communist party representatives on the constitutional committee of the assembly to draft the new constitution held as fast as steel to the principle of proportional representation electorally and of its extension throughout the apparatus of government. Proportional representation is the barricade of minorities.

[31] Cf. Sir Thomas Smith, *Re Republica Anglorum* (Cambridge, edition of 1906), p. 54: "All bills, be thrice, in three divers days, read

Three readings of a bill have become an unquestioned dogma in England, though, of course, today the dogma is hollow and practice is far different from anything that the term suggests. But the notion of three readings was carried into the United States through the early legislative assemblies in the colonies and Thomas Jefferson's *Manual of Procedure*,[32] and into France and Germany by the influence of Bentham.

No Longer Three Readings. No constitution can escape the molding effect of the necessities of character and environment, and today in England the three readings are not what they seem, while on the Continent and in America, vital differences from the English system have been instituted. The great changes which have occurred in English practice are: the change in the public significance of the first reading, the increased importance of committee discussion, and the reduction in the seriousness of the third reading.

On the Continent and in America a system of deliberation has been developed, the features of which are direct contradictions of all for which English parliamentarians seem to strive. For, in England, in spite of the increasing importance of committees in parliamentary procedure, the theory is still maintained that the House itself, as a whole, is sovereign over the principle and the major applications of a bill. The Continent and America have abandoned this practice if not the theory, and their committees are made if not the sovereign then the principal masters of the bill. Regard, for example, Pierre's great treatise on French parliamentary law; the parliamentary commissions must be treated of first, for they are so much the masters of the chambers, and have rights of intervention and decision to such a degree, that if their composition and functions are not well grasped, the whole

meaning of procedure in the chambers is misunderstood.

We may briefly say now the demonstration will follow later that in America and on the Continent the proceedings of the full legislature are mainly (not wholly) directed to impressing the public, while the real work is done in the commissions; and England maintains the House as still an effective place of thought, deliberation, and decision only by the most desperate effort. For, hard and unchallengeable in their power, the dictates of the party system have impatiently torn the power of government away from the legislature as a body of individual members, and have firmly vested it in the leaders of the major parties. Of the full assembly a kind of essential committee has been formed, consisting of the leaders of the government and the opposition, and these—with their immediate confidants and officers and with others drawn from time to time (as required) from the body outside to help them in special matters—draft bills, lay down the limits of discussion, bargain for compromises, and fix the date and time of a vote. In England, if we went by the historic declarations, the standing committees are supposed only to edit the bill and the amendments resulting from this process: they are supposed to be noncontentious but in fact, their work is taking them more and more into the fields of the struggle for power. Elsewhere the parliamentary committees or commissions share the power of decision with the little knot of party leaders. Mindful of these general conditions we can approach the stages of parliamentary deliberation.

English Practice. In England the first reading is almost entirely a formal and nondeliberative state. A bill may be introduced either by its simple presentation at the table[33] or with a brief explanatory statement from the member who moves the motion for leave to bring in the bill.[34] In the first case, the first reading

and disputed upon before they come to the question . . ." Cf. Blackstone, *Commentaries*, Book I, Chap. II; J. Redlich, *op. cit.*, Vol. I, p. 6 ff.
[32] This is still a part of the rules of procedure of the House of Representatives, and the official edition of these rules begins with the manual.

[33] Standing Order (2); cf. T. E. May, *op. cit.* (14th edition), p. 485.
[34] Standing Order. Cf. May, *op. cit.*, p. 484. "The practice of introducing bills under this procedure is frequently adopted, more espe-

has taken place without any debate at all, and perhaps without members realizing that a bill was being introduced. In the second case, a brief explanatory statement is allowed to the mover and the member who opposes introduction; and the rule has come to be called the Ten Minutes' Rule. The Ten Minutes' Rule is usually employed for government bills where a deliberate public announcement is deemed necessary, as in the Education Bill of 1917, but it is now rare. Simple presentation is adopted by private members who wish to impress their constituents with their zeal, and who know very well that their chances of getting a bill made into law are almost as remote as the moon. It is also adopted by the government. This undebated introductory stage is purely one of preliminary formal advertisement that the subject is about to be treated by Parliament. For the first time, a formal draft is presented of the detailed form in which principles discussed at previous elections are to be made law, or, sometimes, never discussed before.[35] It is a notice of intention not only to Parliament, but to the press, the party caucuses, and the organized interests. While it is the beginning of one process, it is the end of another: for from the moment that legislation becomes possible, and the draft is in preparation, the most important interests scan the press for signs of its progress, and exert every means to influence its shape. So also does the department responsible for composing the bill call in to its aid experts and representatives of interests. Kites are also flown in order to give the government the opportunity of discovering its strength or weakness.

A day is fixed for the second reading by the member proposing the bill. In England no difference is made, formally, between a private member and a member of the government for this arrangement. But practically there is all the difference in the world, for the government commands the time of the House, and fixes the day, usually after conversation through its whips—"the usual channels" —with the opposition. The rules of the House do not provide for an interval between the first reading and the second. In olden times, the rule was on "divers days"—undoubtedly as a safeguard against surprise. This is hardly necessary in England, where rather strong principles of fairness are shared by all parties and the electorate, and in fact plenty of notice is given to the opposition. Jefferson's *Manual* provides that the second reading must regularly be on another day.[36] (On the Continent there are regular, but short, intervals.[37]) The second reading is not the time for detailed amendments or for any discussion and vote upon the clauses. (It corresponds almost exactly to the Continental practice of *"discussion générale,"* which usually precedes passage to the specific articles.) The supporters of the bill agree why *in general* such a bill, and even this specific bill, is necessary—not to insist that every clause is either perfectly adapted to its purpose, or that every purpose is incontestably good. It is true, indeed, that ministers would and do speak in this sense, but more out of the tactics of bargaining than out of an unqualified belief in their charge. The opposition, on the other hand, moves formally that the bill be put off to some impossible time,[38] or in a "reasoned amendment" that for various reasons it ought to be rejected. Its attack is to show that the details of the bill do not carry out its main intention, and that the intention itself is unjust or inexpedient.

The words of Erskine May, former clerk of Parliament, are carefully selected but still convey a slightly erroneous impres-

cially by private members, as it gives early publicity to a controversial measure or one of general interest . . ."
[35] Though, indeed, the bill may be merely presented in "dummy": that is, there is the title, and a bare explanation of the objects of the bill, without argument.

[36] P. 156, section XXV.
[37] Thus Germany and France.
[38] This locution is thus reasoned (May, *op. cit.*, p. 498): (*a*) Such a form of amendment is more courteous than a point-blank rejection; (*b*) a mere negative would not prevent the repetition of a bill on any subsequent day.

sion. He says that "The second reading is the most important stage through which the bill is required to pass; for its whole principle is then at issue, and is affirmed or denied, by a vote of the House." [39] Now this may have been true of the House of Commons up to 1870, but it became less and less true from that time. It cannot be gainsaid that any other stage in the full assembly is less important; it cannot be denied that the House divides. It is true that members (the few who are interested and instructed in the matter of any specific bill) fervently applaud or denounce the bill; but we must not forget the saying which is proverbial in all parliaments, "I have heard speeches which have profoundly moved members; but none which has even turned a single vote." The principle has already been affirmed or rejected in the electoral process which put some men in a majority and others in a minority. Neither does the opinion of the great clerk of Parliament adequately include a consideration of the part played by the committees of the House. Decisions are made there: but not in the second reading; though it is true that argument during the second reading may and frequently does influence the government and cause it to make promises of amendment. What is more, the organs of opinion of party and interested groups are extremely vocal from now onward and seek to exert influence upon the minister in charge of the bill. These obtain their opportunity for concrete amendments in the states of cogitation which immediately precede, and operate during, consideration in committee.

It will be seen on close inspection that actually there are five stages in the normal progress of a bill: the first reading, the second reading, the committee stage, the report state, and the third reading. If these five stages were each of adequate length, there would be no question of the care with which the House discusses a bill. But we shall shortly see that in fact these stages are short, sharp, and vehement; that not all clauses are dis-

cussed; that not all amendments are considered; that not all the loose ends are tied up; that not all obscurities are clarified. Disaster would entirely overcome the House of Commons if it were not for strict rules. An even worse fate would overwhelm Parliament were it not based, as it is, upon the assumption that parties and not the individual members are the appropriate managers of discussion. In fact almost the whole process of discussion and amendment is carried through by the initiative, the expertness, and the drive of some ten leading members, who are particularly expert upon the given subject, and who are aided by private experts, or members of the parties' research staff, or even specially briefed assistance. There must be a continuously attentive and expert body which assumes the responsibility of discussion: a small body which can sift from the numerous objections those which are most important and for which there is time. That small body is in all countries the party, which, for the time being, is represented by a specially designated member from among the ranks. In England the party operates in the House and in committee; in France, Germany, and the United States it operates more forcefully in the committees. Let us then turn to the procedure of these countries; sketch their general manner of handling bills, and then concentrate particularly upon committee procedure.

France: the Power of the Commissions. Following Jeremy Bentham's "Tactics" [40] the French constitution of 1791 required three readings with intervals of eight days between them. Under the Consulate, the Empire, and the following régimes, one reading only was required; but this was in assemblies which were not sovereign and to whom the bill was sent in its ultimate form by the *Conseil d'État.* The short-lived Second Republic, being founded upon a single-chamber system, provided for three readings. The first impulse of the Assembly of 1871 was to decree three readings; but since a biennial

[40] Cf. C. P. Ilbert, *Legislative Forms* (London, 1901); and cf. Pierre, *op. cit.,* Vol. I, p. 971, footnote.

[39] May, *loc. cit.*

system then prevailed, the readings were reduced to two, with an interval of five days between the vote of each reading.[41] The system that prevailed to 1946, and has since then been continued, is as follows. Owing to the looseness of party control, discussions tend to become interminable; and the tendency, therefore, has constantly been to curtail the formal stages of debate, which would give members an opportunity to raise questions and offer objections. Indeed, as we shall later see, parliamentary self-control was so weak that financial legislation was rarely passed within the proper time, given the date of ending of the financial year, and the rules of procedure went so far as to reduce the deliberation upon money bills to one stage.[42] The urgency of such bills dictated the discarding of the safeguard of debate, whereas in England the gravity of such bills has caused the creation of additional safeguards. But whether this itself is wise we discuss later. Further, in recent years a time limit has been put upon speeches.

Now it has been decided[43] that normally there shall be only one deliberation in the Chamber—unless a second stage is moved by a member at the point where the bill as a whole is being voted on after all discussion is finished, when the Chamber decides what should be done and whether to recommit the bill to a commission. This would seem a strange and dangerous procedure were it not for the fact that the bill has already been thoroughly threshed out by commissions whose report has been distributed in advance of the debate. The constitution and function of these commissions we shall study in a moment. Let us now sketch only the broad lines of procedure. The reading falls into two parts: the *"discussion générale"* and the *"passage aux articles"*; as a rule the first precedes, but the order is sometimes reversed. Amendments may be put, of course, only in the discussion of the articles. Before the final vote is taken

on the whole bill, directly after the articles have been discussed and passed, the parties are allowed a Parthian shot. Deputies may "explain" their vote in a five-minute speech.[44] It appears that these *"considérations générales"* may be the collective declarations of groups.[45]

Amendments must be offered before the discussion commences; and they are examined by the commission which states its attitude to them. Later amendments tabled before the discussion begins are the subject of a supplementary report. The commission is thus the master of the bill and amendments of it, for its jurisdiction extends even into the debate. Amendments offered during debate may at the request of the president or the reporter of a commission or a minister be sent to the commission for study. When the amendment is not challenged in this way, the motion is put to the House, "Shall we consider this amendment?"[46] and upon this there is a brief speech by the author. When the chamber has decided that it shall be taken into consideration, the amendment goes to the commission for consideration; of course, to save time and to avoid the interruptions of debate, the commission often deliberates at once in the House. The discussion is suspended only if the articles following are affected by the amendment; for then the commission requires more deliberate study before it can give the chamber a proper account of the effect of the amendment. Before the vote on the whole of the bill, the chamber may send it back to the commission for revision and coordination. The commission has the right to require this reference back.

The constitution of the Fourth Republic has introduced a slight complication into this relatively simple method of deliberation. If the bill happens to be one of those on which the Economic Council has had the authority to offer an opinion, then before the commencement

---

[41] Pierre, *op. cit.*, Vol. I, p. 972.

[42] Pierre, *op. cit.*, Vol. I, para. 816.

[43] *Règlement*, Third Republic, Chap. X, article 82; Fourth Republic, article 56 ff.

[44] Pierre, *op. cit.*, Vols. I and III, para. 820.

[45] Pierre, *op. cit.*, Vol. III, p. 822.

[46] *Vote de prise en considération* (Pierre, *op. cit.*, Vol. III, paras. 830-38) and *Règlement*, Chap. X, articles 85-7.

of the *discussion générale* the opinion is read in the Assembly by the *rapporteur* (report-maker and spokesman combined) of the Economic Council or by the *rapporteur* of the Assembly's own appropriate commission. Again, when the Council of the Republic disagrees with the Assembly, the Assembly must undertake a second deliberation on the bill. Finally, in the case of a proposal for amendment of the constitution, there are two stages of deliberation: an interval of three months must separate the second from the first. After the second deliberation, the Assembly formulates a law based on the broad propositions accepted in the two deliberations, and then the ensuing bill is dealt with as ordinary laws are dealt with.[47]

This is a picture entirely different from the English: the commission predominates, the House cannot discuss before it reports, it selects and amends amendments, it watches the whole of the debate, guides it, intervenes as a specially authorized body, and can take the bill away from the House and reconsider it when amendments are being offered and after the House has done with it. The English committee has no such decisive rights of intervention: it works within the limits settled by the House. Parliament as a whole dominates it in theory and, still, in practice, although the superior ability of the committee wins it important authority, for the House has neither the time nor the knowledge to review all its decisions.

The German Reichstag. The formal march of a bill in the Weimar *Reichstag* was through three readings. The first reading was usually one of simple announcement without debate. If there was debate it was a short discussion of general principles.[48] But before the first reading of any bill was undertaken, it went through a number of stages outside the *Reichstag*. These which are discussed more fully on the proper occasion were important preparatory stages. When the draft left the

ministry (which normally obtained an expression of public opinion by publication of the draft), it went, as in other countries with cabinet government, to the cabinet. In Germany it passed always through one more preliminary stage at least—it went to the *Reichsrat* (the State Council), and there was subjected to a very close scrutiny from the standpoint of the various state governments which gave their delegates general instructions.[49] Then, if the bill was of outstanding social or economic importance, it had to pass through the *Reichswirtschaftsrat* (the Economic Council),[50] and sometimes, to save time, the bill appeared before these two assemblies simultaneously. Only then, with the amendments accepted by the government or put down as objections or advice, was the first reading reached. Between the first and the second readings an interval of at least two days had to elapse. The intention is obvious; it was to avoid surprise and inconsiderateness. But the rule was surely one for times of emergency only (when the minority was in danger) and when, in fact, it could be set aside;[51] for between the first and the second reading there was the committee stage which lasted many days.

The next stage was the most important one—it was the committee stage. It was possible for the *Reichstag* not to send the bill to a committee.[52] But the practice in every case was to make the committee the court of judgment within the very wide limits of whether or not the bill should be passed at all. We shall return to the meaning of the committee stage soon. The second reading followed two days after the report of the committee, an important advisory document, had been distributed. This reading was, as a rule, confined to the articles, and is not spread, without special permission, into general discussion except for the speech of the reporter of the commission. Amendments

---

[47] *Règlement*, article 56.
[48] G. O. (*Geschäftsordnung*) 37.

[49] See Chap. 11.
[50] See p. 546.
[51] *Geschäftsordnung* 47. Cf. F. Morstein-Marx, *Problem des parlamentarischen Minderheitenschutzes* (Hamburg, 1924).
[52] *Geschäftsordnung*, article 38.

were freely put. An interval of two days was the minimum between the second and the third readings.

The third reading was a rather formal editorial stage, with little debate, though by the rules the general principles would be discussed, and amendments could be offered when supported by fifteen members.

The United States. The House of Representatives has the system of three readings, but debate is so closured, so cut and dried by the parties and the speaker, that it is hardly worth while speaking of these stages. The committee is here more than anywhere else, everything; the House, nothing. The first reading is merely one of notifying the House in the *Journal* and the *Record* that a bill has been introduced bearing such and such a title. Then the bill goes to committee, which always amends and often kills the bill. If it ever emerges, its second reading is the occasion for a discussion of the articles and amendments thereto. The actual reading of the text may be and not infrequently is demanded, to the waste of considerable time. The third reading is almost purely an automatic and undebated acceptance of what has resulted from the previous stages. The broad forms are those of the English Parliament in Jefferson's time, but American experience has charged them with such a different meaning and balance that the two systems have ceased to bear any resemblance.

The Value of Several Readings. Why are these stages still existent, when parties and the committee system are so vital to the procedure, and so strong in their influence over the evolution of a bill and its discussion at each turn?

Apparently, because when stages are named they give the impression of orderly progress. Each one implies notice and advertisement to all who are concerned: and this adds to the authority of the law. As long as successive and separate forms are prescribed, any one of them may, in the case of need, be used with all emphasis upon their obstructionist possibilities. They are possible safeguards against potential coercion of the opposition by the

government, and of the rank and file by their leaders. They also look back to the days when parliaments needed every means of obstructing the Crown and its friends. Today, in the United States, they are used to obstruct the friends of an uncongenial President. Few are the decisions which are born of the discussions. The Parthian shot allowed in France, and the general discussion allowed in all countries on the final reading, are indicative of the modern meaning and practice of parliamentary debate. It is a conscious address to the world outside the House. It is speech for *Hansard* and the *Congressional Record*, for *Le Monde, Der Tageblatt, The Times,* and *The Herald-Tribune.* Here is the chance to inform the country, agitate minds and consciences, and have a mutual exhibition of the excellences and deficiencies of government and opposition parties. In England the government, in France the government and the commissions, in Weimar Germany the government and the commissions, in the United States the party leaders and the committees, decide and debate: the rest is advertisement, explanation, electoral strategy, the joy of talking, and sealing wax.

Absenteeism and the Private Member. It is a well-known fact that during legislative debate the chamber is attended by a mere handful of members, unless upon the general discussion. When technical points, perhaps of very great importance, are under discussion, members are in the libraries, the buffet, the smoking room, or are present with ineffable boredom and imminent sleep on their faces, wondering why on earth he or she *will* go on talking. It is notorious, also, that members vote without having heard the discussion. In France, which is an exception in this matter, voting by proxy is allowed; members may not hear even a single word said for or against the bill in all its stages. Their party friends have the little blue or white counters with which to say "Yes" or "No" to a bill or a policy or a treaty.

The truth is that parliamentary power is, in the matter of legislation, only exercisable through the party or in close concert with a small number of colleagues who are entrusted with the duty of advising the house. The unattached member has slight place in this scheme. A one-six-hundredth or four-hundred-and-thirtieth part of the time cannot be meted out to him. He cannot stand against the power of united officialdom, government opposition, leaders, and committees.

We shall gain an important insight into the vital mechanism of legislative bodies if we now turn our attention to the constitution and functions of the committees of which we have been speaking.

PARLIAMENTARY LEGISLATIVE COMMITTEES

This difference between England and other countries must be remembered: in England the opportunity of substantial amendment is granted or denied by the government in full house rather than in the committees. The committees are only secondary amending bodies: the House itself decides main principles and major corollaries. In committees elsewhere the bill is totally malleable.

England. The modern history of the committees of the House of Commons began in 1885. As a result of the increasing pressure of business on the House, and the obstructionist tactics of the Irish members using the opportunities of ancient procedure, a way had to be found to relieve the congestion. In 1888, two standing committees were put into operation to take the committee stage. In 1907 their number was increased to four, one to deal with Scottish business only. The normal practice became to send all bills after second reading (except finance bills) to committees, unless the House otherwise ordered.

In 1919 the House found itself in arrears with its work: legislation had been stimulated by the war between democratic principle and economic acquisitiveness. Among the changes the committees were increased to six—five general and one Scottish.[53] The members on the commit-

tee were reduced from between sixty and eighty to between forty and sixty. Further, it had previously been the practice to constitute these committees on the basis of party strength in the House so that the committees became its microcosm. For any specific bill requiring special competence in committee, a committee could take on as many added members as had comprised its original membership. The representative number of the committees was reduced in the change of 1919 and the number of special members limited to between ten and fifteen. The committees were no longer limited to sessions before 2:15 P.M., as up till before 1907, or 4 P.M., as between 1907 and 1919. They could meet at any time they decided, except that their discussions were to be suspended during divisions in the House (illuminating rule!). The committees were reduced to five in 1926 and their minimum number reduced to thirty, and their maximum to fifty, while their optional auxiliary element was increased to between ten and thirty-five. It has for long been the practice for the committee on selection to change the membership of the entire committee as a bill is discharged. In 1946, the number was increased to six in all, with twenty as the permanent nucleus and up to thirty additional members.[54] To 1939 it was the practice for committees to sit in for four days a week between 11 A.M. and 1 P.M. The change of 1946 allowed them to meet three days a week for two and one-half hours each morning but also in the afternoons, if the House is not considering important business at a time when its committees are heavily laden.[55]

How do the standing committees operate, and what is the opinion of the House upon their value?

Standing committees are nominated by the Committee on Selection, which is itself

---

[53] *Hansard,* February 18, 1919, cols. 815 ff. These changes followed in the wake of the

Report of the Select Committee on House of Commons (Procedure), 1915, p. 378.
[54] Which meant in practice, very often, those who were specially interested, from local or group considerations.
[55] Cf. First Report, Select Committee on Procedure, House of Commons, No. 9, October 16, 1945; and May, *op. cit.,* p. 614 ff.

established sessionally. The Committee on Selection consists of eleven members, who by the practice of the House are experienced members nominated by the leaders and whips of the parties in accordance with the numerical strength of the parties. In the composition of the committees, the Committee of Selection is directed by the Standing Orders to have regard to the "composition of the House, the classes of bills committed to such committees," and to "the qualifications of the members selected." This means that as regards the ordinary standing committees the dominating considerations are party strength and loyalty, the geographical distribution of membership (rural-urban, North-South, etc.), and expertness, especially in the matter of auxiliary members. In the case of the Scottish committees all Scottish members sit, together with between ten and fifteen members nominated by the Committee of Selection, with an eye to the balance of parties in the House. When a bill relates to Wales only, all Welsh members are put on the appropriate committee. Further, the Committee on Selection nominates a panel of between eight and twelve chairmen of committees, and these appoint the chairmen of the standing committees from among themselves. The chairmen are naturally supporters of the government of the day.

Upon important bills extended amendments were not customary, but in fact, as soon as the committees went beyond verbal and minute emendation, they became the scene of party battles like those in the House, and the same problems of decorum, order, and obstruction confronted them.[56] In 1905, when the need of the committees had become so urgent, and experience was already sufficient to permit a judgment, the chairmen met and reported many complaints. Bills were being referred to committees for which they were not adapted; they aroused fierce controversies or excited acute religious susceptibilities, or the House referred them with a very divided voice. The operations of the committees became stormy, and the minority felt bound to obstruct. If bills of this kind were to be referred, then the committees must get powers of closure equivalent to those of the speaker. This indicates quite clearly how congested was the House, which, in fact, found itself obliged more and more to seek the aid of the committees. It began to be pointed out that the representative character of the House was decreasing; for it was argued, if six hundred members are already but a minute and distorted mirror of a great country, is it not certain that a committee of sixty still less represents it? (Compare this with the smaller size of Congressional and European committees.) This feeling caused both members of committees and the House in general to be jealous of legislation—with the natural consequences:

(1) The minority on the committees began to obstruct by calculated absenteeism, often standing outside the committee-room until the majority made a quorum, or attempted to maneuver into a position of majority for the time being. This has caused serious annoyance to chairmen and the majority, and results in a heavier party pressure upon members to assure a government majority. The time of members is claimed to an excessive degree.

(2) The report stage in the House began to lengthen out, the members not on the committee wishing to re-exert their control.[57] However, the rules of the House have checked this practice. The report stage consists of the House of Commons' going over the bill in ordinary procedure of discussion. New amendments may be moved, and attempts may be made to restore the original text of the bill by canceling out the amendments in committee. But the House has saved itself from undue prolixity by giving the speaker the power to select amendments

[56] Balfour, *Debates*, July 5, 1905, col. 1156: "Party spirit has penetrated even to the Grand Committees. . . ." Cf. Minutes of Evidence, Select Committee on Procedure, 1915, p. 13; "The Government have got their supporters to support their Bills in Committee as a matter of confidence in them, and therefore there has been less latitude."

[57] Balfour, Select Committee on Procedure of 1906, pp. 14, 15; Ilbert, *op. cit.*, p. 37; Wortley, *op. cit.*, p. 47 ff.

to check the excessive repetition of debates in committee, and this power is exercised quite freely and usefully. There is unyielding resistance to various proposals either for taking the report stage away from the House or seriously modifying it, as the House wishes to remain master of the bill when it has returned from committee. Moreover, the House has much tenderness for the rights of minorities, and it holds to the report stage in order that minorities who may not get really effective representation on a standing committee, by reason of the smallness of the committees, may be able to state their mind in the House itself.

Nevertheless, the consensus is overwhelmingly in favor of the committees. For, in the *first* place, at least one generation has already arisen which knew not the more leisurely and easy ways of the past, and many of the new generation have graduated in the school of local government, which, in England, is committee government. *Second,* it is realized that the committees save the time of the House to such an extent that without them Parliament could never satisfy the legislative needs of the modern electorate.[58] Yet it is computed that in every fifty-six days spent on government bills (allowing for finance and constitutional bills) at least sixteen are spent in Committee of the Whole House and on report stage. *Third,* it is universally admitted that committees do beneficial work, considerable emphasis being placed upon the fact that they vote after hearing the arguments (this is less usual in the House) and that the government is prepared to make concessions as the argument goes and not use the power of the whips so much. (But no serious concessions of principle are made.)

These are great gains; but certain losses are suffered also. Complaints have been raised that there is insufficient publicity of committee proceedings. In fact, there

are some official reports (of recent years only) but only for the bills which cause the acutest political differences. The press reports are very summary. The result is that the country tends to lose what Parliament alone can offer if it is to be true to its name, and what it is important that representative government should provide: publicity of authoritative debate. Besides, attentive members of the House may get to know wherein the bill as reported differs from the bill as read a second time, but they are not informed of the reasons. These things, however, can easily be remedied. The House of Commons' reported bills could approximate in form to those of the French and Weimar German Parliaments: they could contain the original bill, the amendments to it, and short memoranda explaining the motives for the acceptance or rejection of amendments. This defect is aggravated by the numbers of the committees, and the extent of their labors. This enforced ignorance could be easily counteracted if the House added to its usual printed material a weekly or fortnightly periodical giving a conspectus of the work and proceedings of committees. This will probably be of no avail for the lazy member: but in all aspects of life we create devices accordant with the spirit of our purpose, in the hope that at least some of its servants will have the means of fulfilling the necessary tasks. Is it vain to trust that members will rise to the moral level of the institution?

Instead of the committees maintaining a permanent membership, which might constitute an expert and perhaps impartial jury, members who have exhausted their interest in a bill get discharged. Hence, there is a constant renewal of members, with those coming on who are prone to take an expert or interested attitude. Is the Continental and American system, which gives to committees a permanent interest in specific branches of government, the only way to make the committees work effectively (that is, expertly), and of making the member capable of intelligent criticism? Even in local government where the field of work

---

[58] In the sessions from 1919 to 1939, standing committees sat on an average of 95 days per session; in 1930-31, the highest was 152 days; in 1945, the Education Bill took *14 days* for committee alone on the floor of the house!

is different, experience has shown the answer to be in the affirmative.

Altogether, we may frame this judgment of the committees of the House of Commons: Designed to relieve the House of work for which it had no time, they have done this, and the House is ceasing to fret over this loss of its power yet the House believes too little in the committee system for a more substantial economy of its time. The incidental advantage of committee work has been technically better legislation coupled with a moderation of the crudeness of party political judgments, especially as expressed before the electorate.

In 1946 the clerk of the House of Commons proposed a radical reform of committee and report stage. He proposed to delegate the report stage from the House itself—by giving the committee stage of bills not to the standing committees as usual hitherto, but to subcommittees of these standing committees, then allowing the standing committees to undertake the equivalent of the report stage usually undertaken by the House itself. His subcommittees would be different in size and membership according to the particular bill with which each was to be charged from time to time. He would have provided only two standing committees, with 75 or 100 members each, with three subcommittees of each. The two standing committees would be, in his scheme, "efficient substitutes for the House itself for the work of reviewing the results of the amendments in committee." [59]

The Select Committee on Procedure rejected these proposals, though they recognized that they would save the time of the House. Their reasons are significant: [60]

The removal of the report stage of bills from the floor of the House would be, in the words of Mr. Speaker, "a drastic interference with the rights of private Members", and would also adversely affect any smaller parties who could not receive adequate representation on the committees and sub-committees . . .

[59] Report cited, p. xi.
[60] *Ibid.*, p. vii, paragraph 11.

It should be emphasized that revenue and appropriation bills never go before standing committees; they are dealt with by committees of the whole House, that is, by the House as a whole resolving itself into committee, which means that the procedure is less formal and that members may speak more than once. Nor do standing committees deal with Provisional Order Bills; that is, bills which include a number of acts of minor legislation drafted by the departments and subject to blanket submission to the House for approval. It has been the steady practice to keep much important legislation on the floor of the House, as a committee of the whole. Here the government and the House have weighed the time to be saved and the burden of business downstairs and upstairs, against the political significance of the bill, and have given the latter major value.

Thus, the House of Commons has not delivered itself over to the mercy of its own useful instruments. It retains the second reading and the report and third reading stages as vital debating stages, so that the country may focus its attention on a fully representative and wide-open forum, where principle is openly debated and accepted or rejected. This is sound democratic practice.

Some changes of 1946 have been referred to. Something more should be said on these. The increase in the number of the committees and the increase in the time of sittings resulted from the realization by the wartime government, that, whoever was in power after the war, much legislation would be needed. Hence a substantial agreement that the sessional orders should allow for latitude, session by session, experimentally. The Labour government in asking for the change (it fell to it to do so, and it needed parliamentary time for its planning program) prescribed three exceptional practical rules for keeping bills before the whole House. It is interesting to see the bills to which the rules apply: *(a)* any bill which it may be necessary to pass with great expedition; *(b)* "one-clause" bills not requiring detailed examination in committee; and *(c)* bills of "first-class constitutional importance," of the order of the Statute of Westminster. Of course the regular exceptions also apply, and any member may move the retention of any bill on the floor of the House. The government thought that these reforms would yield some 700 committee hours of work as compared with the old average of 190 committee hours in the past.[61]

France. Since the Revolution, French parliaments have always had committees as part of their organization, to explore social conditions prior to the creation of law or to revise the work of the Assembly. The difficulty was to prevent the committees from getting too strong and setting themselves in direct touch with the public. In 1848 (in the Republican constitution) it was arranged that the committees, each of some sixty members, should each correspond to a particular ministerial department, and though that desideratum has not been entirely realized, present organization has approximately reached that point. Already in 1848 controversies arose which have reached down to our own day: whether it were better to have permanent committees parallel with the ministerial departments (rather like the American Congressional committees), or special committees which should last only so long as a specific piece of work (like the British House of Commons committees). The former method was, and has since been, attacked on the ground that the committees so organized began to interfere in the work of administration, their interference being fostered by their permanence and their growing expertness.[62] For decades, until recently, permanence and speciality were taboo: but little by little the nature of parliamentary business, and of the deputies themselves, compelled a re-entry on old paths, though of course, with modern improvements. In 1898 there began the practice of creating commissions (committees) to last through the entire term of a parliament—that is,

for four years—and the projects for a systematic organization of their work became very numerous.[63] Permanent commissions were demanded because under the existing system the committees, like the British committees, could develop no traditions and could not devote themselves to a continuous study of a special subject, and because energy was wasted in the dispersal of members among new committees. All this was aggravated by the queer method of constituting the committees. This did not repose upon a party basis, but upon a principle calculated to stultify party leadership and control.

The method of action by *bureaux* (small official groupings for parliamentary business) dating back into *États-Généraux* times and to the Assembly of the *Tiers État* served to defend the Chamber against summary action by the commissions. They were not unlike United States Congressional committees which took the place of party organizations in experimental days. Chosen sometimes by the hazard of the lot or of the alphabet, the *bureaux* were never formed on a party basis! The *bureaux* chose the commissioners.

This haphazard method could be allowed to exist only until legislative business began to be important, and parties to be organized. Often the most competent members on a particular question were thrown together into the same *bureaux,* so that some were necessarily excluded from commissions for which they were especially apt. Chance ruined careers. A deep gulf existed between the commission and the Chamber, because the former grouped men on an entirely fortuitous basis. Sometimes there would be two commissions with cognate propositions studying them in an absolutely opposed sense. The government could never be sure of a clear path for its proposals.

The commissions were made permanent in 1902, and systematized by subsequent amendments of the rules of the Chamber. In 1910 the method of estab-

[61] See First Report, Select Committee on Procedure, October 16, 1945.
[62] Pierre, *op. cit.,* Vol. 1, para. 737.

[63] Cf. Bonnard, *op. cit.,* "Notice Historique," p. 87 ff.

lishing the commission by the *bureaux* was abolished in the Chamber. It was not abolished in the Senate until 1919.[64] By these two reforms the modern basis of the parliamentary commissions was established: party composition and permanence. Not till 1946 were the commissions mentioned in the constitution. Yet to 1946 many deputies still maintained that group election is disadvantageous because the group may be very small and contain no one of proper competence for a commission. While permanence in 1902 meant for a whole legislature, reforms of 1920 reduced the permanence to one year. An attack was made on the system of 1920, but was repulsed. The rules of March, 1947,[65] continue the annual term. In practice, members remain for long terms upon the same commission. The commissions now number nineteen, being almost parallel with the great ministerial departments, though some cover activities included in more than one department.[66] For reasons of expediency, complete parallelism was rejected in 1920. Parallelism, said the commissioners, would mean the organization of conflict resulting in the "effacement, to the country's great damage, of the responsible ministry by the irresponsible Commission." [67]

These commissions, appointed by general vote of the assembly, are composed of forty-four members each. Members are nominated by the parliamentary groups in proportion to their numerical strength, but no group with less than fourteen members can get representation. This proviso was introduced after World War II in order to deter the disintegration of party groupings. Smaller groups may negotiate representation by affiliating with other groups. Each commission elects a president, vice-president, a *rapporteur,* and secretaries. The president is chairman and the official channel of ordinary communication between the members and other official bodies like the assembly and the ministries. The position is much sought after since it is one of authority and influence and has a prestige value. (The president is a member of the conference which sets the assembly's business each week.) It is never held by a member of the government of the day, and that for various reasons: the desire of deputies to keep a check upon the government and to establish offices rivaling the ministers (since there are not enough ministerial offices for all the deputies), and the desire to support men of experience and expertness, former ministers, former prime ministers, perhaps future ministers. Similarly with the *rapporteur.* This is an onerous office, for the *rapporteur* is responsible for guiding the work of the commission from the standpoint of policy, while that of the president is to guide it from the standpoint of domestic order and its relations with the outside world. The *rapporteur* reports the views of the commission to the assembly (and to the outside world) and then guides the discussion in the assembly, a function undertaken in the first place by the president and then by other prominent members. The position of the *rapporteur* is one much sought after, for it offers the opportunity to acquire prestige in the assembly and with ministers. The name of the *rapporteur* is published in order that those who wish to know how the work is progressing may know to whom to apply. Better to be a *rapporteur* of a commission which has much to do than the president of a commission not in the public eye. The choice of *rapporteur* is determined by the considerations we have men-

---

[64] Pierre, *op. cit.,* Vol. III, para. 711.

[65] Articles 14 ff.

[66] They are the commissions of: economic affairs (customs and commercial treaties); foreign affairs; agriculture; national defense; national education (arts, youth, sports, and leisure); family, population, and public health; finances; interior (Algeria, general administration, and communal and departmental administration); justice and legislation; merchant marine and fisheries; means of communication (railroads, airlines, posts, telegraphs, and telephones); pensions (civil, military, and for victims of war and oppression); the press (radio and cinema); industrial production; food; reconstruction and war damage; universal suffrage; the Assembly's rules of procedure and petitions; overseas territories; and labor and social security.

[67] The student may be referred for an extensive alternative treatment to R. K. Gooch, *French Parliamentary Commissions* (New York, 1935).

tioned in reference to the presidents. Most often the recognized experts are chosen, sometimes ambitious young men. Upon government bills it is clear that the government can secure a *rapporteur* favorable to its own attitude—he has been called "naturally the organ of the majority"—for the commission is based upon party. But it must be noticed that as the tenure of the commissions and the cabinets do not coincide, their respective party composition and policy can and do contrast with each other, with effects of collision and confusion.

Every bill, whether governmental or otherwise, goes to the appropriate commission; this being settled by the president of the Chamber. Where it is uncertain which commission should be asked to report upon a bill, or where it is desirable that two commissions with cognate fields of interest should be consulted, this is easily arranged by a vote of the assembly: they may deliberate in common, or the principal commission is instructed to seek the advice of another. The presidents of commissions may request powers of joint deliberation of the assembly. Most important of all in these intercommission operations is the rule and practice that where finance is involved, the Commission of Finances send its special *rapporteurs* to the principal commission, where they take part consultatively in its work. Also, each commission may send a representative to participate in the Commission of Finances during its examination of the credits concerning it.

By what in the United States is called a "discharge rule," the commissions must report a measure within three months at the latest. Normally the assembly at the committal of the bill states the time allowed the commission. In default of action, the government or fifty deputies may move to discharge a bill. During these months these commissioners deliberate and hold numerous conferences. They must hear the authors of a bill, and the authors of amendments, if they wish—and of course the commissions may and do call them. Members so appearing before the commission can only support their own proposals, but not express their opposition to other parts of the bill, though where the subject under discussion is difficult, the commissions allow considerable latitude in order that subsequent proceedings in the Chamber may be facilitated. Ministries have access to the commissions at any time, and must be heard.

The reports issued by the commission are printed and circulated to members before debate by the assembly. They are usually composed of the following elements: a carefully written history of the problem; an analysis of the immediate social situation which has evoked parliamentary action; a critical description of earlier legislative proposals; a critical examination of the project before it; and its recommendations. There is no doubt in my mind that the French deputy has in this report, if he cares to make use of it, a far better basis for participation in debate than anything available to his British and as good as his American colleague. He has not only the record of work but also the reasoning upon which it is based. The minority has, however, not been given the right to present a separate report. The commission reports as a single entity. How far the dissentients whose views have not been given systematic expression in the report obtain other opportunities in the assembly we shall now see.

At a date fixed by the president of the Chamber and his colleagues for the settlement of the Order of the Day, the bill is debated unless the assembly decides, as it may, on a vote without discussion. The members of the commission occupy special seats to enable them to act together during the sitting. The *rapporteur* takes the lead in debate and is usually the first at the tribune. The rules give the *rapporteur* and the president of the commission the right to intervene at any time in debate, at their own discretion; that is, they may begin if they wish, may interrupt whenever it suits them, and may make their chief contribution at a point favorable to the success of the debate and the work of the commission. The time of speaking of other members is considerably curtailed, but not of *rapporteurs* or the presidents of commissions. The minority has no official organ, and no special priority in debate; but the convention has been established that a member who speaks in the name of the minority of a commission may be accorded a place out of his registered turn, if the assembly agrees, and it is a courtesy the assembly rarely denies. Further, the minority may have its opinion summarized and published in the *Journal Officiel* at the end of the report of the debate.

The establishment of the Economic Council and the Assembly of the French Union [68] brought changes in the rules regarding the work of the commissions which were designed to produce proper cooperation. Every commission that handles a bill that has been before the Economic Council or the Assembly of the French Union must extend to their *rapporteurs* a hearing, and if those bodies were not unanimous must hear minority as well as majority views.

Further, the new restrictions on the former powers of the deputies to propose expenditures or reduce taxation (discussed later [69]) have required new stipulations regarding the relationship of the Commission of Finances and the deputies during debate in the assembly. If the consequence of a bill or an amendment is to increase public expenditures or decrease revenues of the nation or of the departments or local government bodies, it cannot be debated until eight days after submission to the president of the Assembly in order that the Commission on Finances may be consulted. Such bills or amendments cannot get on to the order of the day at all unless their author can offer a means of meeting the increased expenditures or making up the loss of revenue. If the president of the Commission of Finances, the *rapporteur général,* or one of its *rapporteurs specials* (for the specific appropriation or revenue) declares that the condition is not fulfilled, it is enough to keep the proposal off the Order of the Day.

Thus the commission system provides a bloc of twenty or thirty fairly expert members before the principal debate commences. Their leaders have a special priority in debate. The time of the Assembly is saved: the possibility of informed debate is provided. Technical questions have been threshed out beforehand, and the principal amendments have been considered. Moreover, as we have already indicated, the commission is vigilant all through the debate, especially in that on the articles, for no new amendment can be put without its assent and in many cases its report. Before the discussion opens, the commission may announce that it has modifications to make to its own reported bill. It may make up its mind upon amendments in the Assembly, or if it requires time or wishes to delay, may ask for a suspension of the sitting. Any article may be taken back by the commission (a majority of the members) from the Assembly, when it perceives amendable faults. Although this power is exercisable only on the article and amendments, the Assembly rarely refuses a recommittal when asked for even during the general discussion, since it is deemed that the commission is a better judge of the necessity. When all the articles have been voted, the commission may obtain a recommittal of the bill, since it is agreed that after amendments have been made, some repairs will be required.

Throughout the debate, the bill produced by the commission is the basis. If its principle is denied it is recommitted. When the commission nods its head, an amendment put in full session does not require to be formally commended to the Assembly in order to be considered; and that amendment may be modified verbally, accepted with qualifications, or rejected altogether by the commission. The *rapporteur* or the president can, in the name of the commission, demand the committal of an amendment. This large power was granted because it has sometimes happened that a quorum of commissioners could not be obtained quickly enough during a session. Any commission which thinks it is competent to give an opinion on any bill which does not come to it

---

[68] Cf. p. 547 below.
[69] Cf. p. 517 below.

may ask the president of the Assembly for the opportunity to send representatives to the commission in charge of the bill, and its own reports are circulated to the Assembly. We do not need more information to realize that the legislative power of the commissions is very extensive.

The power and influence of the commissions are far-reaching. They have often become powerful enough to challenge the leadership of the government, but their power has there been exerted more through their powers of administrative control (yet to be discussed) and through the annual challenge to the cabinet's budget, than on ordinary legislation. The commissions help to compensate for the lack of party instinct in France. It must be remembered that French ministries are swift-changing coalitions of groups. It is partly to overcome the weakness of this situation that such a system of commissions has grown up. The commissioners provide the machinery for parliamentary leadership in legislation, and supply a continuity and stability—and therefore an expertness—which short-lived cabinets have not done. Whatever the faults of the deputy, the machinery is good, for it supplies expertness and links the members with others in an active and effective group.

This machinery differs very much from that of the British House of Commons and chiefly in these features: consideration of the bill in the House is preceded, not succeeded, by consideration in committee; the examination and report extend to the principle of the bill; the House is guided by the commission and the government, not solely by the government; the alignment on the bill is less a party alignment than in England.

Committees in the United States. The committees are in fact the real legislative bodies of the House of Representatives. They have been called the "little legislatures" by the critic [70] who first startled the country with a realistic study of their activity. A famous speaker of the House,

Thomas B. Reed, has called them "the eye, the ear, the hand, and very often the brain of the House." [71] The "very often" has, since Reed's time, been changed into "with inappreciable exceptions."

All bills go to committees—and this means the standing committees, since the Committee of the Whole is hardly used for nonfinancial bills, and even when it is, the business is previously reported upon by a standing committee. The committees are inevitable stages [72] in the progress of the bill; custom has converted them into the chief judges of the substance and forms of legislation. The President's sessional message is divided into its component parts and scattered among the committees; all bills go to them. They have full power over bills committed to them "except that they cannot change the title or subject"; but amendment of a project may essentially change it.

The committee sorts the proposals which pour in and selects those of importance and with a chance of acceptance within the time limit imposed by their short term of office and the necessity of the Senate's consent. Those upon which the party in power insists, or those recommended by the President when he and the majority are of the same party, get priority. The rest are left in the "morgue" (otherwise known as the "inactive list" or "calendar")—the archives which harbor stillborn projects, and this consignment is decisive. Long and ardent controversies against the old rule of unanimous consent for the forced reporting-out or "discharge" of a bill, which placed despotic power in the hands of committees and the speaker, have resulted in some amelioration, but not much. For in spite of the spokesman of the more independent groups within the great parties, the House maneuvered toward very onerous requirements; if a bill has been held thirty days or more, then on two Mondays a month it may be moved that a bill be reported out; the motion must be seconded by a majority of the

[70] Woodrow Wilson, *Congressional Government* (Boston, 1885).

[71] Jefferson's *Manual and Rules of the House of Representatives*, p. 59.
[72] *Manual of Procedure, House of Representatives*, sects. 439, 667.

membership of the House, that is, by 218 members. If this requirement is fulfilled, there is a twenty-minute debate on the motion.[73] The bill can then at once be debated or set for a given date. However, there are rarely as many as 200 members present on Mondays; and even when the motion is successful, time cannot be found by the house to debate the reported bill. Legislation is, therefore, by permission of the committees. Between 1923 and 1939, although thousands of bills were introduced and sent to committee, only 134 discharge motions were ever filed, of which 19 reached the discharge calendar, 13 came up for hearing, and only 8 recalled bills from committee. Of these 4 were passed by the House, but only one passed both Houses and became law—the Fair Labor Standards Act! In the debates the chairman or, if he is not in favor of the bill, the foremost member who is—has a right of recognition prior to all others in the House, and members of the committee are prior to others.

But the committee has no such jurisdiction over amendments as have the French commissions. Nevertheless, the real power lies with the majority party's members of committee, aided and guided by the party floor leader.

The Government of the United States Congress. It is manifest that in its committee arrangements Congress has discovered and lodged the true practical leadership of the legislature, if we think of leadership as composed of those who decide whether bills shall be killed or sent forward for debate, what shall be their substance, what recommendations shall go forward with the suggested draft, and when (in collaboration with the Committee on Rules) the bills shall go from them to the House.

Most bills recommended by congressional committees become the law of the land, and the content of legislation finally passed is largely determined in the committees.[74]

---

[73] The development of this system, with some interesting references to the issues involved, is traced in Chiu, *op. cit.*, p. 258 ff.
[74] Report, Joint Committee on Reorganization of Congress, 1946, p. 2.

The figures previously given (above, Chap. 17 and page 441) indicate the extent of the sifting process fulfilled by the committees.

Hence, the nature of the committees is of crucial importance in the problem of legislative leadership. Four factors have been singled out as critical: (1) the numbers of committees, (2) their size, (3) their expertness or otherwise, and (4) the manner of appointing their chairmen.

(1) The standing committees have been too numerous: forty-eight in the House, and thirty-three in the Senate. Thereby they violated certain criteria of good government. An excess of numbers means that the work of government is disintegrated into unnatural segments, considering that there is a natural unity in all government work. Their terms of reference are therefore too narrow: they needed extension at their margins, to do their work properly. The more committees the more the overlapping, and, therefore, the more the controversies as to the committee which should be seized with a bill. Further, a high degree of parallelism of committees with executive departments is desirable— an even wider field than departmental is desirable in order to coordinate them by Congressional supervision. It is a serious defect also that some members have served on as many as from six to ten committees at one time.

(2) The committees are too small for due national representativeness. They contrast with the legislatures of other countries in this respect: 21 compared with 44 in France and 50 in Britain.

(3) Though some of the committees have had expert staffs to counsel them and arrange their business (for example, the House Appropriations Committee), they have hitherto been understaffed and inexpertly served. If the committees call upon experts from the executive departments, they do so reluctantly and out of the direst need. If they insist on the independence of Congress in legislative leadership, as the constitution provides, they need expert assistants not inferior to the career civil servants.

(4) The chairmen are almost invariably

appointed according to seniority of service in the legislature, provided they have risen in the party ranks. Seniority is no guarantee of ability and still less of sympathy with the times and with the Presidential policy. Yet it is extremely difficult to find another principle of selection. If it were ability, who would define it? It would be definable no doubt by a caucus vote—but this would make the caucus as a whole the master of the assembly. Actually, it would be well if it were so, but as we have seen, the political parties are not cohesive and associational enough to perform this organizing function capably.

If the committees were bigger they would be more restive in relationship to the small gerontocracy. As it is, the seniors of the party become chairmen, while the able young men are almost inevitably put on unimportant committees. The seniors have the patronage; they have acquired positions in the hierarchy of the party machine. Though Congressional rules give them no powers to dominate the committee, the usual powers of chairmanship extend to fixing the time of meetings, the agenda, the calling and interrogation of witnesses, and the latitude allowed the committeemen to ask questions. Above all, the chairmen have power in the off-the-record meetings to shape the report to Congress, backed by the power to recommend to the floor leaders who shall be allowed to speak in debate.

If American political parties were associations founded on principle, if they were more stable, and their sectional interests more harmonized, then the fact that the older men in the party were at the top would not matter. Indeed, in the natural order of things this would be as almost all human institutions are. But the parties are not fellowships of principle. Therefore the seniority of chairmanship actually introduces another obstacle to the development of proper parties. It breaks the potential unison of chairman and followers, and party connection between committees and Presidential legislative leadership. Above all, it obstructs the control of the chairmen by the majority members: they cannot get a chairman removed and

re-elect another. The chairmen of the committees are an incipient, defective, and so far arrested form of legislative cabinet leadership. As such they could be more effective and responsible if party loyalty were stronger, and if they were fully elective (even if not formally) according to party temper and the needs of the time, without the intrusion of an irrelevant but enforced restriction on choice.

It is not easy to discover why the younger members of a party tolerate the rule of seniority. But careful inquiry seems to point to a combination of several factors: (1) The neophyte in Washington does not know his way about; does not know who is powerful in the delivery of administrative and legal favors and who can get bills passed; and does not know the canny uses of procedure. It must be remembered that nearly fifty per cent is the index of turnover at each election in the House, while two thirds of the Senators in 1933 had served more than twenty years in the Senate. (2) The older member of the Congress are also the elders of the party organization. They attract some loyalty for this reason, and in their own states they are powerful in the political machines which may make or mar the career of the younger men. (3) Many of the members of Congress are seniors, and the slightly less senior members support the more senior in the hierarchy so that in time they will be sure of their own rewards. (4) Finally, a custom that has lasted several scores of years is, in itself, powerful.

The reorganization of Congress of 1946 was able to reduce the committees in number, the objective being sixteen in the Senate and eighteen in the House. However, it did not touch the size of committees, which still remain small. It established staff experts for each committee, on a merit and permanent tenure basis. But it could not change the seniority rule, though it sought to reduce its impact by making more regular the procedure of public hearings, their records of business and attendance and votes; and by requiring committee chairmen to report promptly all bills approved by the committee and seek to bring them onto the floor for consideration.[75] Also, it is possible that the Legislative Policy Committee of Majority and Minority as recommended, if meeting frequently, would tend to subject chairmen to the consensus of caucus opinion.

It is regrettable that the passage of the law was followed by only imperfect obedience so far as the number of committees was concerned.[76]

Hearings. The most notable difference between the Congressional committees and those of the British and Continental parliaments is that the former may institute hearings in any place where their information is to be found, and they may open their "hearings" to receive witnesses of all kinds. As we have already shown in the analysis of the "lobby," the hearings do speedily attract people with an interest and with knowledge useful to the committee. When the hearings are concluded, the committee proceeds to make its report. The minority has whatever chance of actual concessions the majority is prepared to give it, but it has an unrestricted right to expression and publication of its full opinion in the report.[77] Much more is, however, claimed for these committees: that they cut across party lines in their judgment and drafting of bills, and that party rules less than economic and sectional constituencies. Only the revenue-raising committee, the Committee of Ways and Means, and the Committee on Rules seriously divide according to party: here, the minority is expected not to appear.[78]

"If a department or bureau is involved, its head or his representative usually comes upon request, and in that way there is maintained a much closer contact between the legislative and executive branches than is commonly supposed." [79] Indeed, some Congressional committees habitually refer their bills to the appropriate government departments for comment, which is not seldom highly effective. Civil servants are called before the committees. Committees have their drafting experts. The President and the heads of departments are in constant touch with the appropriate committees. Also, the committees are permanent accumulators of letters and other communications from the public and the organized interests.

It will be recalled that the Report of the Joint Committee on the Reorganization of Congress recommended (and the Legislative Reorganization Act provided for) expert staffs for the committees not inferior to those sent by the lobby and the executive to influence the hearings.

It might almost be said that the Congressional committee offers, in this respect, one remedy for the unwholesome effects of the separation of powers. How the executive contrives to penetrate the legislature through the medium of the committees is discussed in Chapter 21 in the section relating to the legislative leadership of the chief executive. It should be remembered that the committees wielding the power of the purse have a supervisory power over the administration. This once more distinguishes them from the British committees and likens them to the French. The topic is pursued later.[80] The American committees are still surely too small, especially when we remember the geographical and occupational diversity of the country, and the unrepresentative character of the parties. If, as is true, they are the real legislatures of America, then they ought to be more representative.

CLOSURE AND ORDERLY DEBATE

Closure in England. Let us consider the situation in England first.[81] Until 1881 closure of debate was left to the speaker and the good sense of the House, and debate was terminated by a simple putting of the question when the speaker considered that it had been suffi-

---

[75] Public Law 601; sec. 102, 103, 133.
[76] For an interim appraisal, cf. testimony of George B. Galloway, Hearings, Committee on Expenditures in the Executive Departments, U. S. Senate, 80th Congress, 2nd session, Evaluation of Legislative Reorganization Act, 1946, p. 117 ff.
[77] *Manual of Procedure, House of Representatives,* sec. 730.
[78] R. Luce, *Congress* (Cambridge, 1926), p. 13.
[79] *Ibid.,* p. 12.

[80] Page 539 ff.
[81] Redlich, *op. cit.,* Vol. III, Part IX, Chap. II; May, *op. cit.,* Chaps. XVIII and XIX.

ciently discussed. Indeed, if we consider the procedure of the House in the middle of the nineteenth century, it was directed rather to prolonging than to limiting debate. But already, from 1848 onward, complaints are made in the House that the burden of legislation is so great that limitation is necessary.[82] That is to say, the problem of obstruction of business arose as soon as Parliament was consciously made the instrument of far-reaching social reforms, and "obstruction" was fraught with serious effects. Now, "obstruction" is a relative term, depending for its meaning upon the number and urgency of measures a government wishes to pass compared with the time available. It is used to hold up a specific measure, or a measure is discussed at inordinate length in order to derange the timetable of the House and prevent other measures from ever being discussed at all. This is practiced everywhere.

Yet it was not until the willful obstruction of the Irish Parliamentary party in 1881 that the government began to acquire drastic powers of closure. In that year Speaker Brand, with the connivance of the government, suddenly terminated debate, although there was a large minority against such a procedure.[83] In 1882 the rule was added that the closure could be moved if 200 voters were in favor; or, if only 100 were in favor and 40 only were against, it could be carried by a simple majority. Even then this was regarded as a provisional concession to emergencies, and until 1887 the government demanded closure only twice. In 1887 a rule more in keeping with the pride of the House was established. This was the rule of simple closure, whereby any member might claim to move that the question be now put, when—unless it appeared to the Chair that the motion was an abuse of the rules of the House, or an infringement of the rights of the minority—it was put forthwith. In 1888 the rule of 1882 was abolished, and the new one was amended by the addition that in a division, at least 100 members be in favor of the motion. This put an important trust in the hands of the speaker, and it has been carried out against the government, though not often.

Since 1887 more coercive forms of closure have been invented which give the government a very strong position. They are known as the "guillotine," and the "closure by compartments" or "the allocation of time." In the first, the "guillotine," the method is to resolve the number of days for debate upon a bill, when, the time being arrived, and notwithstanding the state of discussion or the amount of the bill discussed, the "guillotine" automatically cuts off debate. This was first used in 1887. Closure by compartments or the allocation of time is a procedure at once drastic and yet permissive of a certain latitude to the opposition. For here the government considers the whole of the bill as one plan requiring so many days of discussion, and then offers such and such a proportion of the time for groups of clauses. In this method, if the government is tyrannical, it is possible for it to jump over the clauses which it would rather not have discussed—but, as a matter of fact, the traditions of English parliamentary life, regard for the authority of law, and the fear of future reprisals cause the government to come to some arrangement with the opposition as to the amount of time to be spent on the various groups of clauses. Closure by compartments was first used in 1893. Finally, in 1911, for the committee and report stages it was found necessary to introduce the type of closure known colloquially as the "kangaroo," and officially as the "selection of amendments." [84] This permits the speaker, the chairman of the Ways and Means Committee and the deputy chairman to decide which amendments offered to a bill

[82] See "Report of Select Committee of House of Commons on whether Any Alterations in Forms and Proceedings in this House are Necessary." 1861.
[83] Cf. Redlich, op. cit., Vol. I, pp. 153, 155-59; John Morley, Life of Gladstone (London edition, 1911), Vol. II, pp. 291-93: A. G. Gardiner, Life of Sir William Harcourt (London, 1923), Vol. II, p. 423.

[84] Standing Orders, May, 465. In 1919 the Chair was given permanent powers, whereas the Standing Order of 1909 allowed the House to impose this duty only by a special motion of the House. Cf. Debates, February 19, 1919.

shall be debated by the House. This at once gives the speaker the opportunity of ruling out frivolous and obstructive amendments and of discovering, by questioning the mover, how far the amendments raise serious and comprehensive issues.

The introduction of these rules was not accomplished without protest from the private member, the demand for liberty of speech being in the earlier stages most poignant, and the battles long and stern. The answer which was made to their claims seems to me to be incontrovertible. It was:[85]

The principle of closure is an assertion of the principle that the privilege of speech is a privilege which the House permits to be exercised for its own instruction, for its own information, in order to form its own opinion, and that it is not a personal privilege to be used irrespective of the convenience and efficiency of the House . . . If it is true that the privilege of speech is a personal privilege, it belongs, I presume, equally to every member of the House. Every member of the House has a right to make use of it in an equal degree when he pleases, and if every member of the House were to make but a very sparing use of that privilege, the question would very soon be brought to a *reductio ad absurdum*. Well, if the right can only be exercised by a few and by the forbearance of the vast majority of the House, I should like to know on what ground it can be contended that such a right as this is a personal right at all? . . .

On a more recent occasion the argument took this form:[86]

My honorable friend also said that democracy means debate and discussion. That is quite true, but it also means decision; it must be debate and discussion leading up to a decision . . . There are 640 members in this House, and I do not imagine that anyone would propose that rationing should be carried to such an extent that everybody should be entitled to one-640th part of the time of the session, because that might lead to a black market in coupons.

The criticism of such doctrines as these was forcible until about 1902, when the rules of the House were remodelled and what had been, it was thought, temporary expedients were made permanent principles. By that time, both government and opposition had experienced the need for the use of the closure, though the opposition always used the argument of freedom of speech as part of their general strategy. Again and again it is pointed out in the *Parliamentary Debates* that the choice before members was the "guillotine" or the "rack": that is to say, either the sudden termination of debate or the agony of all-night sittings. By 1908 Parliament had sickened under such limitations, it being urged that there was no reality in debate. Further, a Liberal ministry had been returned after nearly twenty years in the wilderness, with a large array of projects of social reform and, therefore, in need of every minute of parliamentary time. Naturally, the Conservative opposition immediately began to inveigh against the immorality of the closure. Balfour observed that between 1886 and 1905, closure by compartments had been used seven times, whereas in two and a half sessions, from 1906 to 1908, the government had used it for as many as ten bills,[87] and Lord Robert Cecil [88] observed that "the future historian of the Constitution would find no more interesting topic than the gradual decay of the corporate self-respect of the House of Commons."

The retort to these criticisms was the inevitable one which Mr. Asquith made, namely, that the government was overtaking arrears of legislation; that it was impossible to work without the allocation of time (and the experience of the last twenty

---

[85] Marquess of Hartington, Commons Debates, 1882.
[86] Chester Ede, Commons Debates, November 4, 1947, cols. 1607-08.

[87] July 17, 1908, col. 1242. Cf. Lord Hugh Cecil, Debates, March 17, 1913; "It used to be a scandal that the Government proposed these Motions; it has now become a joke. There is a certain significance in that. When you have got to the point when nobody is very angry about it and the thing excites no feeling, the House of Commons must be recognized as having gone one step further down to that abyss of impotence and subservience to the Government of the day which seems every day more ready to swallow it up."
[88] July 17, 1908, col. 1255.

years had taught that common lesson to all governments); that as much justice was done to a minority as was possible, and this by permitting the opposition to discuss the things they most desired.

Perhaps the most serious result of the closure is that Parliament loses the nature of a thought organization and tends to become so plainly a will organization that the opposition and many people in the country are prompted to deny the moral authority not only of the government of the day, but of government in general. For if matters are to be settled merely by superior members, then what is the use of Parliament? Yet the majority could find a reply:[89]

We honestly and sincerely think that these are good bills. We have put them to our constituents, and we believe that our constituents agree with us and that we have a mandate to carry these bills into law. . . . We believe that we have done Hon. Members opposite more than justice in the opportunities which we have given them to oppose the policy which we were returned to carry into force.

Apart from the injurious effects of closure upon the creativeness and interest of the ordinary member, and upon the tendency to undebated and uncontrolled rule on the part of the government, closure has the defect of adding to the difficulties of the speakership. As we have shown, the orderliness of the procedure of the House depends very much upon the impartiality of the presiding officer. But it is difficult to preserve impartiality or the belief in impartiality when so onerous a burden as the choice among amendments is placed upon one man, and when the passions of the House, strongly aroused by modern controversies, are inflamed by limitation of debate. A similar evolution of obstruction, congestion, and closure is observable in the standing committees of the House of Commons.[90] Whether there is any way out of this we discuss presently.

[89] MacCallum Scott, Debates, June 23, 1913, col. 882.
[90] Cf. Debates, June 19, 1931, debate on the power of the chairman of the Committee on the Consumers' Council Bill to select amendments.

Closure in the United States. In the United States a similar process has occurred, and it operates with more tyrannical force because the amount of legislation is so much greater, the division of the session is less rational, and party spirit is less tolerant. The rules regarding the limitation of debate were developed between 1880 and 1890, Speaker Reed in the latter year bringing about a veritable revolution in the rather lax methods used against obstruction until that time. The spirit of the changes was explained by Reed when he said: "The object of a parliamentary body is action and not stoppage of action. It is then the duty of the occupant of the Speaker's Chair to take, under parliamentary law, the proper course with regard to such matters."

There appear to be five principles which give the majority the power, at any time, of overcoming an obstructive opposition. They are: (1) The Speaker may in his sole discretion refuse to put a motion which he regards as dilatory, as for example, to adjourn for a recess or to recommit. As the speaker is the avowed supporter of the majority, this discretion is very liberally interpreted. (2) When a roll call is taken to determine the presence of a quorum, members shall be counted present even though they do not answer to the call. Prior to 1890, refusal to answer to the call was a regular form of obstruction, since the answer was the only accepted evidence of presence, even though the member stood grinning on the floor. (3) Only by unanimous consent can any members speak for more than one hour. (4) The previous question can be moved, and if the majority supports the Committee on Rules, it can be moved at any time! (5) Finally, the Committee on Rules, upon which the majority has a decisive number, can report at will to the House arrangements for reordering debate and distributing time, and its report is immediately considered if two thirds of the members voting agree; otherwise another day is found. The minority have no liberties excepting those accorded to them by the good grace of the majority. Further, the leaders of the majority party (that is, the speaker, the Steering Committee, and company) possess the power to decide which of the rank and file shall be permitted to speak. There is ample testimony both from within and from outside the House of Representatives that debate is devitalized. We must add to this account, also, what we have said above regarding the enormous hold of the committees upon the time of the House.

Closure in France. In France the closure is of long ancestry, but as in other countries its use has become of serious moment only in the last two generations. It is left to the president of the Chamber or any member to demand closure.[91] Then it must be put to the vote, but at least two opposing speeches must have been given on the issue before the Assembly. Upon a motion to vote on closure on the general debate, one member is allowed to speak against it for five minutes, the intention being to give the minority an opportunity of saying why the discussion should still proceed. No debate is allowed on motion for closure on matters outside the *discussion générale*.

The government, which, according to the constitution, has the right to speak at any time, has frequently claimed the right to speak after closure has been voted. And this, in view of the superior authority of the constitution to the rules of procedure, has been permitted, but with the proviso that such permission involves a reopening of debate. After closure has been voted, members may speak each for five minutes in explanation of their vote. In judging of the extent to which debate is limited, we must remember the priority given to speech by the government and members of the commissions. Further, when the Assembly, at the request of the government, or the author of a bill, or a commission, votes a matter urgent,[92] the whole procedure is shortened before the commission, and the closure comes into effect as soon as the *rapporteur* and one member has spoken against it. The author

of a bill needs fifty supporters to get his urgency motion before the assembly.

The Order of Speech. In the House of Commons the speaker has the power to permit members to speak, and the question is, by what rules he guides his discretion. The dictum goes that he who catches the eye of the speaker has the floor. This is now substantially untrue, being inherited from the time when there was no party organization. Although speakers have defended themselves against the charge that their recognition of members is regulated by the parties, the party whips, in fact, arrange who shall speak because they contrive to get consulted by members, who then inform the speaker of their desire to speak. Naturally, if a debate peters out and exhausts their lists, the speaker then uses his unfettered discretion, calling upon supporters and opponents of the bill or resolution alternately. In recent years the practice has been admitted—at least for what are called "full-dress" debates—and the reasons which have been given are quite comprehensible and not at all sinister. It is convenient for the speaker to know what members are prepared with speeches, and as time is limited, the "most representative men" of different sections of the House may be heard. There is, however, one drawback to the practice. The party leaders would seem to attempt a certain power to ostracize heretics within their own ranks, and this means that perhaps fruitful criticism is obstructed and the authority of the party leaders becomes excessive. Yet the speaker's reserve of power to disregard the whips—and his authority is plenary—is an important guarantee that the voices of the independent rank and file shall be heard, however unpleasant to the leaders.

In France, members who wish to speak on a measure give in their names personally to the president or the secretaries and are inscribed on one or the other of two lists, *pour* and *contre*, and speakers are called upon in the order of their inscription on the list.[93] It must be remembered

---

91 *Règlements*, 1876, article 108 (and Pierre, *op. cit.*, Vol. I, p. 918 ff.); 1915, article 48; 1947, articles 45 and 92.
92 Articles 61 to 67, *Règlement*, 1947.

93 Article 43, *Règlement*.

that the government has the right to speak at any time, and the presidents, the *rapporteurs,* and the members of the commissions whose report is under discussion are given priority.

The Duration of Speeches. It has often been suggested in the House of Commons that a remedy for congestion is to shorten individual speeches. In 1919 it was calculated that on the first and second readings of the Home Rule Bill, 97 speakers had occupied an average of 41 minutes each, largely spent in repetition of previous arguments.[94] Members have been afraid to take this last step in apparent degradation. They have preferred to rely on good sense. The House regularly shows its annoyance with members who speak for more than 20 minutes, unless they have important material of fresh value. But other parliaments have formally limited speeches. In the Weimar *Reichstag* the maximum was one hour, which could be lengthened for special occasions.[95] In 1926 the French Chamber of Deputies carefully graduated speeches according to the status of the speaker, minister, chairmen of commissions, mandatories of parties, and ordinary members.[96] Observe! The reform was carried when financial disaster threatened. It has not been continued in the procedure of the Fourth Republic.

In America the quality of parliamentary oratory is different from that in England. Congressmen love fine-sounding phrases with which American history, especially of the era of the Declaration of Independence, is full, and love to gush grand principles. Moreover, the size of the House, which is tremendous, and the constant coming and going of members through the swinging doors, give the impression that the member is bellowing in the middle of a noisy fairground. No one takes notice of what a member says, partly because he cannot be heard and partly because the shape of the law has already been determined in committee. This, perhaps, is one of the causes of the flights of oratory, the principle being that if you cannot say something useful you may as well say something stupendous.

In Weimar Germany discussion tended to be quiet and businesslike, save for the grim gusts of class passion which swept across the assembly from the Communist and National Socialist benches, but it is admitted on every hand that discussions in the full assembly were mainly demonstrations for the electorate and were not directed to changing votes.

In France, oratory still has a great appeal and is more frequently denunciatory than helpfully directed to the improvement of its resolutions.[97] This hardly matters so far as legislation is concerned, for, as in Germany and the United States, the principal work is done in the commissions, but it is a serious deficiency in the debates on control of administration. Owing to the lack of party discipline and loyalty, votes are changeable by an apt speech and can be lost by a stupid one. Briand [98]

---

[94] Morrison-Bell, Debates, February 19, 1919, col. 1057.

[95] Five minutes before the hour, a yellow light-signal flashes out *"Noch fünf Minuten!"*

[96] Cf. *Résolution,* July 15, 1926: article 41, *Règlement (Rapport,* Barthélémy, *Chambre,* 1926, No. 2945); *Debates,* 2883 of July 15, 1926). An important commentary is the article by J. Barthélémy, "La Réforme de Methodes Parlementaires," in *Mélanges pour Maurice Hauriou* (Paris, 1929).

[97] Cf. L. Barthou, *Le Politique* (Paris, 1923), p. 48: "For a speech pronounced at the tribune should be an act; when the discourse or the act has commenced, emotion has already taken another form. A battle is begun, one must win; one has thrown oneself into the water and one must swim towards the bank. Some go under beneath applause, others beneath sarcasm, but the success of an act is not a judgment of its value. The idea vanquished today will perhaps be triumphant tomorrow, and perhaps tomorrow's events may make the orator acclaimed yesterday pay dear for his passing triumph."

M. Barthou (*op. cit.,* p. 62) gives six precepts for speaking in the Chamber of Deputies: (1) Not to abuse citations and not to make excuses for them. (2) Not to affirm one's frankness too frequently. (3) Not to say one does not wish to be a minister. (4) Not to interrupt except necessarily, discreetly, and prudently. (5) Not to hear interruptions and not to reply to them except in the measure in which one may gain from them, (6) Never to strain the voice to enforce silence: wait!

[98] *Ibid.,* p. 50.

owed his ascendancy to his eloquence, and Clemenceau once fell from the prime ministership by oral clumsiness. The temperament and traditions of the French chambers produce excitable, restless discussion.[99]

In England and the United States members speak from their places. Being on the floor, they are simply on a level with other members and therefore receive no physical stimulus to speak otherwise than as man to man. In Germany and France the orator may mount a tribune, and there he sees below him and around him an arena full of spectators, and it is generally agreed that this stimulates the speaker to attempt to "show off." Who can avoid self-consciousness (at least) in such a situation?

Further, in England the seating arrangement, by accidental evolution, groups the government on one side and the opposition on the other, a very clear mark being thus made in the "for" and "against."

The House is only seventy-five feet long and forty-five feet wide, which means that the front rows are within little more than an armslength from each other. There is a drawing-room proximity of all members. The student will enjoy Mr. Churchill's plea for retention of the "oblong" shape of the House of Commons, in rebuilding the bombed assembly. It is true architec-

ture, that is to say, it is political psychology.[100]

In the other countries, the seats are arranged in a semicircle, in France and Germany special seats being given to ministers facing the assembly, while in the United States the floor leaders occupy certain seats by the gangways in the semicircle. In the Continental assemblies this arrangement makes a little for confusion and theatricalism, but it is a rather natural result of the group system. The Continental arrangement of writing desks is very bad: it tempts members to conduct their correspondence and write articles or novelettes for the press in shelter, while the flaps of the desks can be used to outrattle speakers. Perhaps consideration for the convenience of orators goes furthest in America, where spittoons (or cuspidors) are arranged along the gangways at proper intervals.

The result of this discussion is, I think, to show very clearly the great extent to which party organization has made itself master of parliamentary activity, ordaining debates and speakers as it thinks proper, so that it may fulfill the promises made during the election campaign. This was foreseen by some, and defended, a generation ago and even earlier, when parliaments became so obviously the vehicles of popular opinion.[101] And now, in

---

[99] Cf. *Ibid.*, p. 71: "The tribune is a great peril, because it is a scene where one plays a part in a hall where the spectators take their part in the piece. Different from a play in this: all is unforeseen—one does not always know how it will open because the Government has the right of intervention at any moment, and may—by an initial declaration which may even bring about an adjournment or the closure—disturb the order of the spectacle; still less can one foresee how it will finish.

"There is an atmosphere whose extremely variable pressure can be registered by no barometer. A breath is enough to make everything change. . .

"These tumults, spontaneous or concerted, this fever, these agitations, these surprises, these incidents, explain why those accustomed to the conditions of the Bar where the dossiers have been exchanged . . . before the blows—why celebrated barristers have failed at the tribune.

"At the Bar there is a discussion, an ordered dialogue, known conditions which fix the debate—at the tribune there is a battle."

[100] See Churchill's Speech, Debates, October 25, 1944.
[101] Sir William Harcourt (during the debates on the closure rules in 1882, column 1762): "I believe the Government of this country can only be conducted by Party. If you have not organized Party, what have you got? You have got the caprices and fancies of individuals in a chaos, and the public good perishes in the midst of it. The organization of Parties is nothing less than the predominance of the counsels of those who are chosen by the Party to advise them, because they think they are the fittest advisers. . . The Party which expects to hold power, or accomplish anything, always must accept the advice of those whom they have placed in the position they hold for the express purpose of advising them; they have made them their leaders for that purpose. To talk of coercion seems to me the most absurd thing in the world. Why, a Leader of a Party—and especially the Leader of a Government—is there by the free choice of those with whom he acts. At any time their

our time, it is an argument for the most sedulous thought on the improvement of parties.

Parliamentary Language. One other thing needs consideration. It is impossible to continue parliamentary discussions except on two bases: *first*, that there shall be quiet during discussion, and *second*, that members shall not use expressions which rouse the temper of the House or impugn the good faith of other members or challenge the fundamental validity of parliamentary institutions in the form created by the constitution.[102] All countries, therefore, have rules to secure these objects. We need not spend time in discussing the details relating to the first, namely, the prevention of disorderly conduct, except to say that at a certain point sessions are suspended or disorderly members expelled from debates.[103] And further, such disorderliness is naturally present wherever differences among groups are deep-rooted, as, for example, in all countries where economic inequality inflames

passionate resentment of its attackers and defenders, and further, where racial or religious difference are strong.[104] Sometimes these and other differences may be so drastic as to make the parliamentary method entirely impossible, as for example, in the Weimar *Reichstag* when Nazis and Communists attained great strength. Or personal vanity or uncontrollable natural impatience may sometime be too sensitive to permit quiet discussion, as in France and Italy.

As the inevitable time comes when the majority throws off its bonds and enforces its social policy, "unparliamentary" expressions become more common. What concerns members is not so much that they are uttered, but that they are often true. Yet the truth may often be thought, but not be told; for the whole of parliamentarism is an edifice of conventions erected on a very fragile basis of civilization. This theme recalls the right of revolution which has been denied written expression in the constitution by most political scientists, lest men should fly to that as the first, and not the last, resort.[105]

---

breath can unmake him, as their breath has made him. He is their champion, it is true, but he is also their creature."
[102] Cf. May, *op. cit.*, p. 431.
[103] Cf. May, *op. cit.*, p. 440 ff., and Standing Order 19. Cf. Vogler, *Die Ordnungsgewalt der deutschen Parlamente* (Hamburg, 1926); Zschucke, *Die Geschäftsordnungen der deutschen Parlamente* (Berlin, 1928), *Gesdräftsordnung* 89-94; Pierre, *op. cit.*, para. 484 ff.; *Manual and Rules of the House of Representatives*, section 359 ff. On the Continent, suspension of sessions is frequent; in Anglo-Saxon countries, it hardly ever occurs.

[104] E.g., in Poland and Serbia; while in the Southern states of the United States, racial prejudice is so strong that it has excluded the Negro race from discussion altogether.
[105] E.g., Kant, *Principles of Political Right* (trans. by Hastie, 1891), p. 50: "For, such resistance would proceed according to a rule which if made universal would destroy all civil constitutionalism, and would annihilate the only state in which men can live in the actual possession of rights. . . The prohibition of them [insurrections] is therefore absolute."

21

Financial Legislation; Delegated Legislation; Legislative Control of the Executive

FINANCIAL LEGISLATION

So far, we have concerned ourselves only with legislation on ordinary matters. There is still something to add in regard to legislation where finance is directly involved. Here let us enter one warning. Recent discussions of legislatures have placed more importance upon what is called "financial" legislation—meaning the laws which directly vote supplies or affect taxation—than upon other laws. Yet it is clear that bills of the former character are only the logical consequence of ordinary bills which create services and institutions for which payment must be found, especially in an age of drastic economic reconstruction and a governmentally planned economy. Consequently, there is no fundamental reason why these bills should be differentiated, since it often happens that ordinary legislation imposes the burdens. However, in the historical evolution of parliamentarism, procedure upon financial bills was conceived not simply as a method of securing economy but also as a means of checking the power of Crown or ministers and of vesting in Parliament the power to stop the whole machinery of government should its will be thwarted.

It should be noticed that contemporary financial legislation is simultaneously and often deliberately used as a legislative instrument for controlling administration

and the executive, being the most powerful one among the instruments used to effect this control.

British Financial Legislation. The British system rests upon law, practice, and the rules of the House of Commons,[1] and its foundations are: (1) that no one except the responsible ministers of the Crown may originate a new charge or increase an existing one; (2) that the House will not grant money unless the demands are initiated in committee of the whole house; (3) that these stages are complex, not simple; (4) that debates upon the regular annual financial legislation take place within a space of time allocated broadly but definitely by the Standing Orders; (5)

---

[1] Cf. T. Erskine May, *Parliamentary Procedure* (14th edition, London, 1946), Chap. 24; A. J. V. Durell, *Parliamentary Grants* (London, 1917); W. F. Willoughby, *Financial System of Great Britain* (New York, 1917); E. Hilton Young, *System of National Finance* (London, 1936). For historical account: House of Commons, Eleventh Report, Select Committee on National Expenditure, 1944. For simplicity I omit the discussion of the supplementary votes and votes on account; also the distinction between Consolidated Fund and Supply Services. Nor do I enter into the question of the proportion of annually variable taxation to that which is more permanently settled. The general theory of budgets is best treated in G. Jèze, *Cours de Finances Publiques: Le Budget* (Paris, 1922); and, further, in other matters regarding public finances, in his *Cours des Finances Publiques* (Paris, 1935-36). In English there is C. F. Bastable's *Public Finance*, 3rd edition (London, 1917).

that appropriations made by Parliament are specifically assigned to object and time; (6) that there is a retrospective survey of the legality and economy of the appropriated amounts. Let us consider each of these a little more closely.

(1) Around the rule of government responsibility revolves almost all the excellences and all the defects of financial procedure. It is the residual deposit of all the constitutional currents which, in the course of centuries, have transformed a monarchy into a virtual republic.[2] A compromise has retained the name of the Crown to support the independence of the cabinet and to limit the chaotic results of parliamentary initiative, and at the same time has transferred to the popularly responsible cabinet the real initiatory power. The Standing Orders of the House (Numbers 63 to 70) embody this. Standing Order 63 reads:

This House will receive no petition for any sum relating to public service, or proceed upon any motion for a grant or charge upon the public revenue, whether payable out of the consolidated fund or out of money to be provided by parliament, unless recommended from the Crown.

Perhaps the most noteworthy feature of this arrangement is that it is pure usage and self-control upon the part of politicians: no external authority, no statute, ordinary or constitutional, imposes this rule of behavior, which differentiates the British system from all others.

How is the rule implemented? The responsibility of asking for money is put upon the government: it is the spender. It produces annually a complete set of proposals for expenditure, known as the Estimates, and proposals to cover the total sum by taxation, in the Budget, where the expenditure and revenue are balanced. Very complicated and important processes precede the government's advent before the Commons. The Estimates begin to appear before the Commons in February preceding the April 1 which begins the year for which they have been calculated. They have undergone long gestation, and

it is true to say that although the final battles and establishment have occurred in autumn and winter. they have been the subject of a continuous year-round process of excogitation and arrangement within the Treasury, for they are far too involved, and too large and too disturbing, to be improvised: £800,000,000, in 1938 (and £3,181,000,000 in 1947–48) and thirty large and voracious departments!

If the ultimate net effect is to be that every penny is spent to the maximum social satisfaction, it is clear that there must occur a process of adjustment among the departments and a process of adaptation to economic circumstances and the relationship of political forces. Especially urgent is this budgetary planning in modern nations which raise a vast sum from the economic product each year, thus powerfully influencing the whole economy, labor and investment incentives, and consumption habits. Further, the fiscal instrument is now used to combat depressions.[3] This necessitates three things: considered comparison of diverse claims for expenditure; considered relationship between the total of admitted claims and the total available resources; and, as an inevitable corollary in a day of highly complicated and extensive state activity and changing ministers and parliaments, a permanent organization to secure the first two factors. These three are provided by the institutions of review and control of the estimates of the spending departments by the Treasury, with the Chancellor of the Exchequer at its head; by the Chancellor's power of censorship, with the departments' ultimate appeal to the cabinet; and by the Treasury, the department of finance. Moreover, upon these is fixed, clearly and ultimately, the responsibility for financial soundness: for the House of Commons can only directly interfere to reduce, not increase, the estimates produced by the government.

[2] Best described in A. J. V. Durell, op. cit., Chap. I.

[3] Cf. Alvin Hansen, Economic Policy and Full Employment (New York, 1947); Employment Policy, British White Paper, May, 1944; Economic Reports of the President (published by the U. S. Government Printing Office annually, in January and June).

(2) It is the second fundamental practice of the constitution that financial legislation originates in the House of Commons, and, further, it is a settled observance to resolve upon grants of money and impositions of taxes only in committee of the whole House. The House once tried the experiment of sending estimates to a standing committee by rules adopted in 1919, but the practice was dropped after one session because it was generally felt that the estimates were too important to devolve to a committee.

The proceedings in committee of the whole House possess three qualities, which may be considered merits or defects according to the angle from which they are viewed: the House has slightly easier rules of debate; the whole House is formally in charge of such vital matters as grants of money; and the necessary resolutions that the speaker leave the chair give the opportunity for general debates on governmental policy. The most important characteristic of English procedure at this stage is that it does not entrust the estimates or the tax proposals to standing committees as do the legislatures of France, Germany, the United States, and other important countries, but insists on their consideration by the whole House. Moreover, owing to the English party system and the existing body of tradition, the government as a whole, the various ministers during discussion of the estimates, and the Chancellor of the Exchequer at the tax-proposal stage are in charge of the House and are, invariably, its masters. No one is strong enough to compete with them—neither an independent parliamentary commission of finances as in France or Germany, nor the members considered individually. The House, organized as the Committee of Supply, discusses the individual estimates, votes a sum of money "not exceeding" so many pounds, and this is afterward converted in the ordinary procedure of the House into a vote. All the votes together are gathered annually into a single Appropriation Act. The Committee of Ways and Means comes into existence about the same time, but a little later, to give effect to these grants

by authorizing the government actually to spend the money granted and to designate and provide it with the sources of revenue. Thus there is a dual control by the House, and its work is summed up in one Finance Act, which includes the annual taxes and the changes in the permanent ones, and one Appropriation Act which enacts the grants, authorizes the expenditure, and assigns the money required to each item.

(3) and (4) What are the main features of this process? *First*, it is clear that if the estimates were left to the tender mercies of the opposition, the House might never cease debating them, and, indeed, until 1902, the arrangements obstructed rather than facilitated the work of the House. Since 1902, twenty days were allotted to the Committee of Supply (before August 5), though an extra three days might be added. In October, 1947, after much discussion by the Select Committee on Procedure, the House decided on a total of twenty-six days, but no longer allowing certain extra days available before.

Second, the House sees the estimates only very shortly before the day of discussion.

Third, the House may vote a decrease of the estimate but not an increase, though it may "suggest" extra expenditure. The consequences for the individual members of the House are serious: members can do no more than enter upon a general, scrappy, and rather vague discussion of the government's proposals. To offer to decrease an estimate is tantamount to a vote of no confidence, and is, indeed, the formal resolution upon which discussion turns. It cannot be carried, and therefore the discussion loses its sharpest sting. To offer the increase of an estimate might be desirable but is legally impossible, and perhaps, on the whole, it is best here that the government should have considerable independence.

Next, the members are incapable of any significant control of the estimates in the sense of "value for money," owing to the shortness of time available for their examination and also the form in which they are couched. Even if the estimates were put into a clearer form, they are so voluminous, and each item represents so highly technical a set of circumstances and inwardly technical relationship with all other items, that the discovery of the true connection between the figures stated and the real nature of the values represented would demand years of application and expert tuition. But only days are available, and of them but a few.

After various experiments aimed at more effective control of the expenditures through parliamentary committees, a Select Committee on Estimates, annually reappointed, was established in 1920. It consists of twenty-eight members, may work through subcommittees, may examine any estimates presented to the House, and may report "economies consistent with the policy implied in those estimates." In 1926, it was given the assistance of a Treasury official. Though its work has been useful,[4] it still suffers from

[4] Its World War II counterpart, the Select Committee on National Expenditure, issued a long series of very valuable and effective reports on the multifarious problems of administration in time of war. It secured much the same range of power as the Estimates Committee, but since the financial votes were blank, for security purposes, the House was the readier to support its power of investigations into what its chairman, Sir John Wardlaw-Milne, habitually calls "seeing that the nation gets value for money." It consisted of thirty-two members, and worked through subcommittees. It paid visits to the government's field agencies. Its success largely depended on the time it spent on its work, and the specialization and businesslike methods of its small subcommittees. In six years it held 1740 meetings, that is, about 300 per session. (As a contrast, the Estimates Committee sits twice a week.) Its success was due also to the fact that the House of Commons supplied it with a staff of clerks who became expert and who were able to cooperate smoothly with the officials of the departments that were investigated. The present author testifies to the enormous public value of the many reports. The committee scored many successes that were not known to the public, because it disclosed findings to ministers privately in order that military secrets should not be divulged, the government hampered, or public morale depressed while administrative improvement was being secured. For an account see Third Report, Select Committee on National Expenditure, October 31, 1946, evidence of former chairman, cited p. 206 ff.

certain natural results of the parliamentary cabinet system. It has not the time, even superficially, to examine more than two or three departments each year: therefore it can only be of small use to the House, and only of occasional effect in frightening a department into economy. Not all of its members give the service to it that is desirable. It has not used subcommittees. It cannot take retrospective views. It sometimes makes recommendations which omit elementary facts. It cannot secure settled days for the discussion of its reports, for an important reason already observed: that is, that the discussions on policy and the courtesy of Parliament have given the opposition leaders one of its all-too-rare privileges of choosing the subject of discussion. Are these to be limited?

Thus Parliament is still largely undirected in financial legislation. Nor is it helped by the form of the estimates. Until 1927, indeed, the votes were put together without any uniform principle; the subject matter of the vote was the original principle, but this was not always followed when innovations were made. In 1926 the Select Committee on Estimates recommended a grouping into a number of services,[5] each containing the appropriate departments, and advised that services done for the departments by others should appear as a footnote. This was adopted and has promoted clarity. Yet other proposals—such as those of Sir Charles Harris of the War Office, to produce estimates of units of cost in the various departments (say, a hospital, a horse, a lorry driver, etc.) and thereby facilitate comparison and therefore understanding and criticism—have only a very limited application. For in the first place, units are not so easily discoverable, and when so, they are only formally the same, for it is the vast hinterland of many subtle but concrete differences that makes the difficulty of financial control.

The plain truth is that members of the House of Commons lack the two things

[5] Cf. First and Second Reports from the Select Committee on Estimates, Nos. 59, 119 of 1926.

which would give them financial control: time, and a great deal of it, and expert knowledge of the details of everyday departmental administration as well as financial insight. The Treasury has both of these, as it is permanent and professional. The time of the House can only be increased by reforms such as those discussed later, and principally by the multiplication of committees. Its expertness may be increased, but only to the point of spurring and curbing the administration, and even this very weakly. The amount of time available in the Committee of Supply for discussion of the estimates has certain necessary results: discussion must be superficial, and it can touch upon only a fraction of the total estimates, while others are simply accepted in the division lobby without a single word of discussion. Debate has, of course, become merely a general challenge of the main policy, its principle and general features, pursued by the government, and the government's general answer thereto.

This means that the Treasury is the first-line controller of economy in government: government, a vast apparatus employing nearly one million people and spending over three billion pounds a year after World War II.

Another basic principle of the British financial system is that (5) the Appropriation Act does not compel the government to spend the money granted, that is, merely their maximum. But any unspent balances cannot be used at the discretion of the department which has received the grant, but is returned to the Exchequer. This *annuality* secures the control of the Commons if it should ever be in a situation where such a drastic control were necessary. Further, since 1689 there has developed with more and more minuteness, the principle of the specialty of appropriations.[6] The Estimates appear in a detailed classification of classes, votes, and subheads, and, except under conditions, this classification regulates upon what things the department may legally spend. Yet, what if calculation could not exactly

estimate the amounts required in each unit? May there not be a diversion of funds from one to the other? Such a course is dangerous, as it may open the way, if uncontrolled, to a flouting of Parliament. Diversion, or *virement*, as it is technically called, is permitted on condition. In the case of votes for Civil Estimates no virement between them is at all possible: in that of the army and navy, the Appropriation Act annually lays down conditions of virement between votes with the sanction of the Treasury.[7] As regards subheads, these are purely informatory and the House resolves only the votes. The departments are therefore free to divert from one subhead to another, but in order to avoid undue liberties and the mystification of Parliament, Treasury sanction must be obtained, and the Treasury acts strictly, sanctioning only allied subheads in the case of the Civil Estimates.

(6) The control of the executive, and to some extent even of the Treasury, is served by two institutions: the Office of Comptroller and Auditor-General, and the Public Accounts Committee.

The Comptroller and Auditor-General, whose office was created by the Exchequer and Audit Act of 1866, serves two functions: the control of monies from the Consolidated Fund, and the audit of accounts. Pursuing the first function, the Comptroller permits issues to the Treasury (which then permits the money to pass to the paymaster-general and thence to state creditors) only after review of the authority for such issue. This is a power, which not altogether, but almost so, prevents the misapplication of money. Pursuing the second function, he audits the accounts of issues made yearly, certifies the accounts, and reports to Parliament. He is concerned with the proofs of payment and with the proper expenditure of the money. Further, the Comptroller reports not only upon legality but upon the wisdom and economy of expenditure; that is, he is concerned with waste in so far as it is to be detected:

---

[6] Cf. Willoughby, *op. cit.*

[7] Durell, *op. cit.*, p. 283 ff.

I do not feel myself debarred from calling attention to anything which has occurred in the course of my audit during the year which indicates loss or waste, or anything of that kind, which I think it is well that Parliament should know . . . if I find the result 'of administrative action has been a loss or wastefulness of public money, then I think it is not going beyond my duty of reporting, as an officer of the House of Commons, if I call specific attention to matters of that kind, even though the account itself would not disclose the facts . . .[8]

In other words, within the executive system itself, Parliament has placed a permanent executive officer with the task of controlling the executive elements engaged in spending: It has provided for an officer as continuous and as professionally interested in legality and economy as they are in spending. His legal status is of the essence of his utility. He is appointed by the Crown, during good behavior, is removable only on a joint address of both Houses of Parliament. His salary is a charge, like that of judges, on the Consolidated Fund. He has a judicial status. He reports to Parliament. In short, he is, in reality though not formally, a servant of Parliament, to control the executive; and he has a position independent of the executive whom he is to control, even of the Treasury. His reports are of the highest importance, for they, by anticipation, prevent illegality and, retrospectively, discover illegality and criticize wastefulness. Nor is this all: the Comptroller is aided by, and in turn aids, a special organ of the House, the Committee on Public Accounts.

It is clear that parliamentary control is imperfect unless it receives the report of the audit of public accounts, and more, unless it proceeds to an examination thereof. Until 1861 such an examination was spasmodic and badly organized.[9] Since 1861 a Committee on Public Accounts has been set up every session "for the examination of the accounts showing the appropriation of the sums granted by Parlia-

ment to meet the public expenditure." When the Comptroller and Auditor-General were established, the circle of financial control was complete.

The Comptroller is advisor to the chairman of the committee.

I always attempt, as far as possible, to reserve final judgment. My reports are intended to enable the committee to scrutinize the matter with the assistance not only of the Accounts and my reports but by oral cross-examination as well.[10]

The composition of the Committee on Public Accounts is important. It consists of fifteen members. Its chairman is a member of the opposition, sometimes a former financial secretary to the Treasury, and the rest of the members are distributed according to the party composition of the House. It examines the reports of the Comptroller, who personally helps it, and Treasury officials are also present. It may, and does, call for department accounting officers and whatever information it finds appropriate. Thus it is enabled to penetrate the financial and administrative fastnesses which are closed to the amateur. Its investigations, as any one of its reports will show, are very thorough. Finally, it reports to Parliament, which sometimes discusses the reports. Far more important than parliamentary discussion, even on its rare occasions, are the Treasury minutes which embody the chief reformative findings of the committee and go, like barbed arrows, to the culpable departments.[11]

Now it is true that the Committee on Public Accounts acts not only retrospectively, but late: for the Comptroller's reports do not reach Parliament until one year after the expenditure has been incurred, and only about a year after this can the committee report. However, departments do not like the smart of public censure, or Treasury reprimands. When matters are indefensible, the pecuniary responsibility of one or other official may be

---

[8] Report, 1903, Question 756; and Report, 1946, Questions 4163, 4242, 4259 ff.
[9] Cf. Durell, *op. cit.*, Chap. III.

[10] Report, 1946, Question 4302.
[11] Cf. the interesting Treasury document called *Epitome of the Reports from the Public Accounts Committee, 1857-1925* (1927, No. 161).

involved, for in extreme cases the committee may recommend disallowance. The Treasury itself may be challenged for permissions or prohibitions for which it is responsible. One committee chairman said: [12]

There is a great deal of human nature in the world, and fear is one of the greatest helps in keeping men straight. The fear of the Public Account Committee, and the very searching examination that takes place there, does a great deal to help in the path of rectitude the members of the civil service.

On the whole, then, in England the cabinet is mistress of finance. It is indubitably responsible for it, while the Chancellor of the Exchequer is, above all, the controller of expense. The control exercised by the House of Commons lies between the almost impossible margin of overthrowing the government on policy, and tinkering with small economies, in the main retrospectively. Suggestions to reinforce the power of the House of Commons are dependent for their efficiency upon more time and expertness of its individual members. Should they go far, they would damage the independent expert economy of the Treasury (which is universally lauded as of the highest value), and the power of control and responsibility, the concentration of which in the cabinet is the best guarantee of the maximum economy.

The vast increase of public expenditure and the multiplication of the agencies of public administration have left the House of Commons perturbed about financial control. In 1946 it was proposed [13] that the Estimates Committee and the Committee on Public Accounts be amalgamated into a single Committee on Public Expenditure. The reasons advanced were that both these committees deal with the same subject matter, though the former deals only with the current estimates while the latter reviews the accounts of the past year after they had been audited. Both, again, were compelled to range backward or forward, wherever comparisons were necessary for effective judgments. It was possible in the existing system to have gaps not surveyed in useful time by either committee. The fact that the chairman of the Estimates Committee is a member of the Committee on Public Accounts was not regarded as an adequate provision for cooperation. The experience of the Committee on National Expenditure during the war led to the conclusion that a larger committee than either of those in operation would permit subcommittee operations, expert staffing, and specialization, and therefore effective services to the House of Commons whose weakness in grasp of financial detail had been demonstrated. It was intended that the Comptroller and Auditor's status should remain unaffected either in relation to the departments or to the committee.

The proposal was strongly resisted by, among others, spokesmen for the government, especially when it was suggested that one of its merits was that the committee would develop a staff of experts. The fear was expressed that they would inevitably move into the criticism of policy, which was the concern of the government and the House of Commons, and would be tempted to intervene in everyday administration and produce troubles for the executive and conflicts between the House and the government departments. The government spokesman said: [14]

A committee such as is suggested would place a very heavy burden on senior officers, and inevitably hamper the efficiency of executive action by importing delays and cramping initiative . . . The fear here was that the Public Expenditure Committee would be liable, as was the Select Committee on National Expenditure in the war, to drop on Departments about current activities . . . If that is so, and they are liable to send for officers of Departments at any time about something or another that they think they should take an interest in, then the officers are liable to be pulled up at any time, and possibly examined, about current administrative matters. That has two consequences. (1) It is liable to be a

---

[12] Debates, 5th series, Vol. XXXVII, p. 424.
[13] Third Report, Committee on Procedure, October, 1946, Nos. 189-91.

[14] Cf. *ibid.*, Herbert Morrison, evidence, *Questions*, 3245 ff.; and Government Memorandum.

drain on the time of the higher civil servants, and an interruption of their work. (2) It is a little bit liable to make them lose their nerve; because if they have a Minister chasing them around day by day and a committee of Parliament liable to drop on them any day about something that is happening at the time, they are a little nervous as to who their master is; and one of the things which is very important about the Civil Service is that you should not make it dictatorial on the one hand, and you do not want to make it too nervy on the other—because once it gets nervy it loses confidence and dithers . . .

Then we get into the argument as to who is responsible for executive current administration, the Government or Parliament. I say it is the Government that is responsible. It is responsible to Parliament, but if Parliament is going to set up another duplicating set of administrative experts to take an interest in current administration, there is going to be a clash between Parliament and Government which I think would be bad . . . Parliament's business is to check the Government, throw it out if it wants to, go for it, attack it, criticise it, by all means, but Parliament is not a body organised for current administration—not in this country. They have had a go at it in France, and the United States, and I do not think too much of it.

The government resisted the proposal successfully.

Other countries desire the main principles which underlie the English system: clarity of the budget, considered discussion, and responsibility of a single authority for proposals of expenditure, but for various reasons have hardly attained it.

Weimar Germany came closest to English practice. Weimar procedure was regulated by articles 85 to 87 of the constitution and the *Reich* Budget Order (*Reichshaushaltsordnung*) of December, 1922, a law passed with the majority required for constitutional amendment, and again amended in March, 1930.[15] These were the principal legal dispositions concerning the budget and the examination of accounts, but the rules of procedure of

the *Reichstag* and the *Reichsrat* were also of importance, since they established standing committees to deal with proposals for expenditure and taxation. The net effect was to secure the completeness, the unity, the clarity and good faith, the specialty of appropriation, of the annual budget, and its previous acceptance by Parliament. Upon certain things doctrine, rather than law, had its uncertain work, as in England; in particular, in the thesis that the money voted by Parliament was a maximum; that, according to the principles of sound public finance, this was not a command to the government to spend, but only permission; and that the government should spend only as economy required. Both academic and parliamentary controversy revolved around this. Further, the principle of economy, which in England is not legally stated but is in practice applied by the Treasury, was definitely stated in article 17 of the *Reich* Budget Order: "Only such expenditures may appear in the budget as are necessary for the maintenance of *Reich* administration or the fulfilment of the duties and legal obligations of the *Reich*," and further, article 26 declared, "appropriations (*Haushaltsmittel*) are to be administered efficiently and economically (*wirtschaftlich und sparsam*)." These clauses, in fact, were submitted as the written foundation for the doctrine that the government need not spend the appropriations. To secure economy, the law gave the Minister of Finance special rights and obligations which were hitherto vested in him by convention. A cabinet resolution of October, 1923, required that he be consulted by his colleagues whenever projected statutes or administrative measures had financial consequences and gave him the right to send inspectors into the departments and require reforms—all, of course, with the right of appeal to the cabinet. Article 21 of the *Reich* Budget Order and article 32 of the rules of procedure of the cabinet gave the Minister of Finance a legal priority over other ministers, and probably they formulated what in fact occurs in England.

---

15 Cf. R. Schulze and E. Wagner, *Die Reichshaushaltsordnung*, 2nd edition (Berlin, 1928). with Appendix on reforms of 1930; Kühnemann, *Haushaltsrecht and Reichsetat* (Berlin, 1930).

Expenditure and observations whose acceptance in the Budget the Minister of Finance has rejected, are subject to the vote of the Cabinet upon the motion of the competent Minister, only, however, if matters of principle or otherwise appreciable importance are concerned . . . If the Cabinet votes against the vote of the Minister of Finance to exclude an appropriation or observation, then the Minister of Finance has a right to protest. The appropriation or observation can then only be put into the Budget if this is resolved in a further vote by a majority, and when the Chancellor votes with the majority.

This, of course, was entirely subject to the combination of parties in the cabinet: and when the Minister of Finance belonged to a tactically weak group his formal supremacy was as nothing, and, in fact, the ministership of finance went to the Chancellor's party or to an expert from outside Parliament.

The parliamentary stage differed from English procedure. The government approaches the *Reichsrat* first, and this had full powers of amendment and rejection. In the *Reichstag* there were three readings, the first reading being the great demonstration like the English budget speech. Only the principles were discussed, however, and then the bill went at once to a standing committee (number 5) on the budget, called the Chief Committee. It consisted of thirty-five members, corresponding to the party strength in the *Reichstag*. This was the principal stage of money bills. The estimates were here discussed for months, with the appropriate ministers, officials, economy experts. All the necessary documentation, library facilities, and secretarial aid were available; and for specially difficult and involved questions, a permanent subcommittee was employed. The second reading was a discussion on the committee's series of reports. The third went over the ground again, beginning with a general discussion. There were no criticisms on the work of the committee: ministers were in command and were responsible, and certainly with a group system and an unrestricted right of financial initiative on the part of private members, chaos would have followed any freedom in the full *Reichstag*.

The great obstacle to parliamentary control of financial policy in England was absent in Weimar Germany: the convention that the government alone is responsible for it. There was theoretical controversy over the right of the parliament to initiate increased charges, but there was more about its right to increase or decrease expenditure. The second reading in the full *Reichstag* was considered a waste of time and prevented a speedier voting of the budget without any compensating benefit. The right to initiate or raise expenditure was also censured, and the English rules regarding this were praised in the *Reichstag*,[16] for as the rules of the *Reichstag* stood, amendments could be moved on the second and third reading without previous examination by the Committee of the Budget. But Germany, like France, suffered ultimately not from defective rules but from an anarchical party system. Though, in Germany, this anarchy was not so old as in France, its fruits were such obstruction to the annual financial legislation as to produce emergency decrees and a dissolution of the *Reichstag*, and public shame had to accomplish what public spirit was first too weak to do.

France. French financial procedure to 1946 has long been a byword among the connoisseurs of parliamentary pathology.[17] Although French theory is of remarkable excellence and clarity, here, again, the rules are better than the spirit in which politics are conducted. As we have seen, the two vital points around which any sound procedure revolves are the independence of the Minister of Finance and the self-control of the legislature: the former requires a strong cabinet, the latter strong parties. In both these things France is defective. The long strug-

16 Moldenhauer, Minister of Finances, *Reichstag*, May 26, 1930. Cf. also W. Dorn, *Bericht des deutschen Juristentags* (Salzburg, 1928).
17 Cf. G. Jèze, *Cours de finances publiques: Le Budget* (Paris, 1922), and *Cours de Finances Publiques* (Paris, 1935-36); E. Allix, *Traité Elémentaire de la Science des Finances* (6th edition, Paris, 1931); and for a popular exposition, G. Bonnet, *Les Finances de la France* (Paris, 1924).

gle between legislature and executive in the nineteenth century naturally impelled the deputies to demand complete parliamentary freedom in financial matters: freedom to raise and lower appropriations and taxation, to amend or reject the budget, to tack all sorts of general reforms to financial grants, to discuss projects without limitation or coherence, and to attach interpellations to the financial resolutions. This led to intolerable abuses: the humiliation of the government, the voting of uneconomical appropriations to impress the country and win the support of organized groups, the retardation of the annual votes, and the destruction of a single responsible authority.

In 1911 and 1920 important reform of the rules of procedure occurred. (Note that in both these years there was a strong majority on the side of reform and that in both years, also, national and international difficulties compelled reform.) In 1911 it was forbidden to attach interpellations to the discussion of the budget, and additions to expenditure could henceforth be debated only after report by the Commission of the Budget; and a time limit was set to speeches. This had little effect. The trouble was more deep seated. Hence the reforms of 1920.

In regard to the Finance Law no amendment or additional article tending to augment expenditure could be put after the three sittings which follow the distribution of the commission's report in which the relevant chapter appears. No augmentation or diminution of expenditure could be proposed simply to raise a debate on ministerial policy (*à titre d'indication*). This was a notorious vehicle for parliamentary exhibitionism as well as the occasion for bona fide but untimely debates on administration. When an amendment or additional article fell within the competence of one of the permanent commissions and was endorsed by at least fifty signatures, it was sent to this commission if the Commission of the Budget or the government required it. This was in order to secure at least some expert discussion on the matter before the Chamber debated the matter, and even to

get impertinent demands postponed or settled. No proposition tending either to augment salaries, indemnities, or pensions, or to create services, employments, or pensions, or their extension outside the limits of the law already in force, could be made in the form of an amendment or article additional to the Finance Law. The discussion of the budget could not be interrupted by certain resolutions.

Outside these restrictions, of course, the deputies could initiate increases of expenditure and taxation (while in the House of Commons the prohibition is, for private members, absolute). The abuses arising out of the right of deputies to propose additions of expenditure to the government's budget may be appreciated from M. Tardieu's statement that in little over a year he was bombarded with proposals amounting to the expenditure of 15,000,000,000 francs! Such proposals worry the government and strangulate parliamentary proceedings. Hence, in February, 1934, partly as the result of the fears inflamed by the riots early in that month against the legislature, a new rule was adopted (article 73, Finance Act). Every project requiring increased expenditure or decreased revenue must provide for "collateral revenue, apart from the proceeds of loans, which are not already authorized in the Budget Act"—a rule so difficult to fulfill and so unpopular as to promise if not to achieve parliamentary continence.

The constitution of 1946 stipulates that the government submit the budget to the Assembly, though the deputies have the constitutional right to "initiate expenditures." Yet (article 17) "no proposals which would tend to increase expenditures already decided upon or create new ones may be presented during the discussion of the budget and of prospective or supplementary appropriations."

The rules of procedure of the Assembly of 1947 leave no doubt about the passage of the financial initiative and almost monopoly to the executive. We may repeat the rule: if the consequence of a bill or an amendment is to increase public expenditure or decrease the revenues of the nation, the *départements*, or the *communes*, then no debate can occur earlier than eight days after the request is made to the president of the Assembly in order that the Commission of Finances may be consulted. Nor can the bill or the amendment be put on the agenda unless they provide the revenues to meet the expenses proposed or make up for the reduction of income. Furthermore, deputies cannot (article 68) introduce into the laws of the budget or provisional or supplementary credits anything but dispositions directly concerning the receipts and expenditures of the fiscal year; nor can they introduce any additional article unless it tends to suppress or reduce an appropriation or to create or increase a receipt or to assure the control of public expenditure. The debate in the Assembly on each chapter of the budget is summary only, unless the government, or the Commission of Finances, or a regularly deposed amendment requires an extended discussion.

Before 1939 there was no such allocation of time as in England—only simple closure—so that the government was browbeaten and delayed long past even a reasonable period after the beginning of the new financial year. Owing to the fragmentation and conceit of the groups and the synthetic and quaking majority which supported the cabinet, the Minister of Finances was in normal times not able to implement the rules which gave him authority over the estimates of his colleagues. For they could soon break away from his dictates and even from the vote of the cabinet, and actually do battle with him before the Chamber and its Commission of Finances. But a Commission of Finances as it operates in France may enhance the weakness of the Minister of Finances and encourage the deputies to tergiversate. Even in the desperate plight of 1948, the Commission of Finances was at odds with the Schuman government over the deflationary, foreign-devaluation, and gold-market measures deemed essential to save France's internal and external economy.

Let us consider the organization and functions of the Commission of Finances of the Chamber of Deputies of the inter-war years, and then continue the record to the present. Since 1920 all financial matters have been concentrated in one commission, that of finances. It consists of forty-four members (the Senate's, of thirty-six); it divides itself into subcommittees corresponding to each ministerial department, and these have special *rapporteurs* under the superintendence of the *rapporteur-général* of the commission. All the estimates come before it, and all the taxation proposals. It advises all the other commissions of the Chamber where their work touches finance. Its connection with the Ministry of Finance is continuous, giving advice and sometimes admonition, and receiving the information it wants. It has an adequate secretariat and general equipment, meets almost every day, and assumes the position of the authority responsible for the finance of the country. In these matters all depends upon the spirit which animates the body. In ordinary times the Commission of Finances is not so much the competitor of the Minister of Finance as it is his master: he can do nothing unless he convinces it.

Now it may happen, and frequently does, that while the party composition of the commission remains constant, that of the cabinet has altered. The commission is in a position to force upon the cabinet its proposals or be its friend. Moreover, the deputies have no reserve in wishing and securing the overturn of a ministry, even for rather personal ends. They are, then, the masters of finance, and the *rapporteur-général* is a very important person, who, if we follow actual experience, appears before the Chamber proud of his budget, determined to support the view of the commission, and dealing freely with policy, and who enters upon those calculations of national wealth and taxable capacity and needs for expenditure which in England are associated only with the Treasury and the cabinet. In 1925 the commission virtually dismissed M. Loucheur, not content with his taxation proposals, and so dealt with his successor, M. Doumer, that the cabinet staggered, only to fall a few months later.[18] In 1925 and 1926 the commission harbored twelve former ministers! In the experiments of Callaux and Poincaré in 1925 and 1926, the presidents of the commissions of both chambers played a critical and masterful part, even in the remaking of the cabinet. Again in 1932, 1933, and 1935, governments fell because the commission challenged their budgets, while others survived only by making large concessions to the commission's counterproposals. Only very solid cabinets could stand up against the commission. The president and the *rapporteur* of the commission usually find their way into the cabinet in the course of time. Although, then, the commission does most useful work, it encourages the anarchy of the Chamber and takes responsibility from the Minister of Finances without being able to assume it itself.[19] Yet at the root is the chronic evil of party divisions and personal ambition.

The status of the Commission of Finances in the Fourth Republic is almost identical with that in the Third Republic. The rules are much the same. It becomes ever more evident that its operation is the same. The reason is the same.

For purpose of audit, France has a court of accounts (*cour des comptes*) composed of independent officials to examine and report upon expenditure, as to both legality and wisdom.[20] The Fourth Republic's constitution (article 18) gives the authority to regulate the accounts to the National Assembly, assisted by the court of accounts. The Assembly charges the court with all the investigations necessary for the purpose. The president and *rapporteur général* of the Commission of Finances and, if necessary, the presidents of the various commissions, may correspond with the court in regard to any inquiries and studies with which it is charged.

For auditing purposes, Weimar Germany had a court of accounts which was

based on article 86 of the constitution and articles 87 to 126 of the Budget Order. It was independent of the government, and took orders from no other authority in the Reich: it was empowered and obliged by the law only; that is, it was in a judicial position. The power of appointment of its president, deputies, directors, and counsellors was vested in the *Reich* President, with countersignature of the Minister of Finance. They had to have the prescribed qualifications for judgeship or for higher administrative or technical service: at least one third of them had to have judicial qualifications. They had the guarantees of office accorded to judges of the Supreme Court. They reported not only on the legality of expenditure, but on the economy of financial transactions of all kinds and on whether institutions and places had been maintained, or expenses incurred, which could have been retrenched without jeopardy to the administrative object.[21]

The United States Budget System. We turn to a system vastly different from the foregoing, because based upon the principle of separation of the legislative and the executive powers—the American budget system.

Before 1921, the United States budgetary arrangements were chaotic:[22] the Treasury stitched together the uncoordi-

[18] Cf. *Revue Politique et Parlementaire*, 1926; *Revue du Droit Public*, 1926, p. 451 ff.
[19] A. Soulier, *L'Instabilité Ministerielle* (Paris, 1939).
[20] Cf. Allix, *op. cit.*

[21] Schulze and Wagner, *op. cit.*
[22] For the situation before 1921 see W. F. Willoughby, *The Problem of a National Budget* (Baltimore, 1918). For a separate account of the reform movement cf. G. F. Weber, *Organized Efforts for the Improvement of the Methods of Administration* (New York, 1919); and F. A. Cleveland and A. E. Buck, *The Budget and Responsible Government* (New York, 1920). On the system see W. F. Willoughby, *The National Budget System* (Baltimore, 1927), which contains a good bibliography; A. E. Buck, *The Budget in Governments Today* (New York, 1934); D. T. Selko, *The Federal Financial System* (Brookings, 1940); Report of the President's Committee on Administrative Management, 1936, Chap. III; G. B. Galloway, *Congress at the Crossroads* (New York, 1946); F. Morstein-Marx, "The Bureau of the Budget," *American Political Science Review*, August and October, 1945; and A. Macmahon, "Congressional Power of the Purse," *Political Science Quarterly*, June, 1943.

nated, unrevised estimates from the spending agencies, and when these arrived in Congress they were unstitched and divided among the parallel Congressional committees. No concerted balancing of revenue and expenditure occurred administratively or legislatively.

The Budget and Accounting Act of 1921 establishes the following system. It vests in the President the transmission to Congress of the "Budget," which sets forth in summary and detail the estimates of expenditure "necessary in his judgment" for the year, his estimates of receipts, statistical information and balances regarding the finance of past years and the ensuing year, and other informatory data. He recommends action to make good predicted deficiencies and surpluses. In short, there is concentrated in the President the centralized consideration and recommendation of public finance. More, all other executive intervention is excluded by the injunction that no officer or employee of any department shall submit to Congress or its committees estimates, requests, or recommendations regarding appropriations or revenues. This is sometimes overtly, but more often privately, evaded.

To assist the President and to do the preparatory work for him, a special service, the Bureau of the Budget, was created in the Treasury Department, but by the Reorganization Act of 1939 it was transferred to the executive office of the President. Its director and assistant director are appointed by the President, and the bureau operates under rules prescribed by him. This is the workshop of the budget system. However, it has no independent force over the departments but is an investigating and collating authority: in the first place, its authority over the departments resides in and emanates from the President. The President enforces by rules the access of the bureau to the departmental information it wants, and its authority to secure changes. Each department is obliged to appoint a special budget officer who prepares the departmental estimates. The bureau aids and informs Congress as it requests. All, then, on the executive side depends upon the energy and capacity of the bureau, and very much upon its director, and upon the character of the President. Both together they can approach the British or German system in efficiency: together or apart they can cause the whole system to fall into weakness and contempt. The cohesion does not derive, as it does in the British system, from united responsibility to the Commons and the people: it is much more indirect than that, and hence requires an adventitious, independent probity.

No doubt need now be entertained that this independent morale and determination have been created, especially since 1933. From a handful of staff, its corps had grown to 40 in 1935 and to 600 in 1944. Its director is a member of the Presidential cabinet. Though he is not under the Treasury or legally constrained to work as a subordinate division, the relationship between the two financial departments is extremely close, and the personality of the Director of the Bureau of the Budget may well outtop the Secretary of the Treasury. Since, also, it is very rare that the President decides policy in cabinet session, and since the Director has direct access to him, it is between these two men and sometimes the Secretary of the Treasury that the cardinal financial decisions are made.

The functions of the Bureau of the Budget concern not only the estimates, but also administrative efficiency. Its activities and significance in the latter category are dealt with in another part of this volume. But it can be seen that any responsibility of this kind must allow it to penetrate into the actual management of the other departments, at a stage where the operations which call for funds will be malleable by the bureau. Also, as has already been observed, all bills emanating from the government departments must be cleared with the bureau, so that here again, bills which may involve expenditure or affect revenue may be controlled. Finally, the bureau has direct powers to receive the estimates, and all attendant and supporting information, and to recommend to the President what shall be his answer to the demands.

For this purpose the bureau has a considerable, but still insufficient, number of examiners, some of whom go into the field offices of the various executive agencies and from time to time examine the estimates on the operational spot. The bureau hears the justification of the spending departments and debates with them their claims. It reports to the President, who is very free to change at his own personal discretion the total and the items presented to him. He will take advice from his director of the bureau: but he will also ignore it for a favorite project, or he will return the budget for more economies where the party situation and electoral prospects require it.

By now, the bureau has a firm grip on the administration of the various departments. It knows what is going on, and it is able to measure the demands made upon it, and so to balance the various demands against each other in relationship to each other and then as a whole against the revenue that will have to be raised. On the latter the Treasury naturally has a strong word, sometimes a decisive one, to say, for it is responsible for tax proposals. Furthermore, since the beginning of 1946 it has been necessary to have regard to the recommendations and contentions of the President's Economic Reports which outline the general economic situation and prospects of the nation. (In the British Treasury all these factors—estimates, proposals for taxation and debt management, the general economic situation and reports thereon—are dealt with in combination. A further unifying process occurs through the collective responsibility of the cabinet.) The result is the budget of the United States government for the fiscal year.

Yet all is far from well in spite of the improvements traced so far. It is clear that an inward, cogent articulation of estimates and request for expenditure, the true needs of the departments, their managerial competence in their several departmental domains no less than cooperation of all of them in a grand dynamic march of government, is far from having been achieved. The Hoover Commission reports leave no doubt that the system just limps along rather distraughtly. As might well have been foreseen, the problem is a far bigger one—no less than that of the problem of the United States chief executive itself; and therefore the matter is intimately related to the discussion in Chapter 26, on the United States Presidency.[23]

The essential difficulty of American financial procedure still remains, in spite of the highly beneficial results of the new system. Congress may do as it likes with the Presidential proposals, for to it, under the constitution, they are little more. The committees and the two Houses may at any stage play ducks-and-drakes with the nicely balanced budget. In fact, the Committee on Appropriations, set up in 1920 with a large number of subcommittees, has adopted the practice of not increasing, though they may decrease, appropriations—and in every year the committee has granted less than the President asked for. The House usually slightly increases the amount reported. The Senate usually increases this slightly, owing perhaps to the large power generally possessed by individual Senators and their log-rolling. The amount is decreased in conference. The net difference between the Presidential suggestions and Congressional grants amounts to about .5 per cent. Thus Congress has subjected itself to considerable self-restraint, the first commandment of parliamentary efficiency.

Grave deficiencies still dog Congressional control over finance. The appropriations subcommittees take hearings on the estimates within their purview. They hardly spend enough time to get a thorough grip of the subject. It should be noted that these hearings are in private, even excluding other members of the parent committee, so that a demand for funds or the line taken by the committee is immune from public challenge.

23 See Commission on Organization of the Executive Branch of the Government: "General Management of the Executive Branch," February 1949, and Appendix E; "Budgeting and Accounting," and Appendix F, especially this latter; and "Treasury Department."

The members of the subcommittees do not serve long enough to become masters of the departments for which funds are being asked. They report so late in the year to the parent committee that the latter cannot exercise a coordination of the diverse estimates, nor be really master of the suasions of its infants. It is possible for the officials of the departments who are heard by the committees to mystify the committeemen, who may spend an inordinate amount of time on small red herrings that are not even odoriferous. Whole blocks of estimates go through without question at all. And yet, and yet, the officials know that if they are ever caught in some even minor deception they will be very roughly treated by Congress and the public. It must be admitted (I base this on my own observation) that committeemen make many arbitrary cuts in the appropriations—and this must lead to departmental overestimating on the theory that some will be bargained away. Furthermore, the bargains made in conference committee are hidden from the public. It has been proposed that the two Houses shall form one appropriations committee, rather than have a dual and duplicated system as now exists. The crushing duality of the United States system exists nowhere else in democratic government.

Until 1921 the United States audit arrangements were defective. Then the Budget and Accounting Act created a General Accounting office to which were accorded the two things which the old comptrollership of the Treasury lacked: independence of the executive, and power to report not only upon the legality of financial operations but on Congressional mismanagement or inefficiency and to recommend improvements. This arrangement proved to be awkward and obstructive, because (a) Congress gave the Comptroller-General, by statutes, various uniform rules to apply to all departments equally, but (b) more serious, he took his powers to mean not postaudit but obstruction of current expenditures by current audit! This, it will have been

noticed, is vastly different from British postaudit practice.[24]

Under the Reorganization Act of 1945 (section 7) the Comptroller's office was made part of the legislative branch of the government, thus emphasizing the Congressional authority over finance, its expenditure and administrative activity in general. The Bureau of the Budget manages the monthly apportionments of the appropriations to the various spending agencies. The appropriations are normally for the fiscal year and normally unexpended balances lose force with the end of the fiscal period, although there are some—such as those for big construction projects, housing, roads, airplanes, and certain grants-in-aid—which may be carried over to succeeding years until the job is completed.

Above all, there has never been within either House a combined view and authorization of both revenue and expenditure. Each part of the public finances is treated by separate committees which never meet together: no single survey and policy balances revenue and outgo! [25]

The report on Congressional reorganization made drastic recommendations to remedy these extremely grave faults. Among them are: the early Congressional establishment, each session, of annual budget totals beyond which the appropriations may not go unless borrowing is provided to meet excess expenditures; better staffing of the committees; abolition of secret sessions; full consideration by the parent committee of subcommittee reports; and a three-day term during which the committee proposals shall be before the House before consideration.[26] The United States pays heavily for the separation of powers!

In section 138 of the Legislative Reorganization Act, the statute required a "legislative budget." It required the two revenue and appropriation committees of

24 For American practice see H. C. Mansfield, *The Comptroller General* (New Haven, 1939), and the relevant chapters in C. H. Pritchett, *The T.V.A.* Chapel Hill, 1943).
25 The Bureau of the Budget attempts to supply unity.
26 A poor device to secure attention.

each House to meet and report not later than February 15 in each regular session a budget report and consequent resolution containing a determination of anticipated appropriations and revenues for the fiscal years:

If the estimated receipts exceed the estimated expenditures, such report shall contain a recommendation for a reduction in the public debt . . . The report shall be accompanied by a concurrent resolution adopting such a budget, and fixing the maximum amount to be appropriated for expenditure in such year.

Of course, this section assumed that one month was sufficient time to do this properly or to do it at all; that the committee's decision would be able to govern the appropriation committees in their power over their bills; that the required annual debate on the national debt would compel the establishment of a responsible-minded budget. None of these assumptions has been borne out: ways and means—that is, revenue policy—is still almost entirely independent of the amount to be spent, and the quantities of expenditure in the various estimates which make up the total. Party feeling, intraparty disagreements, hostility to the chief executive, headstrong chairmen of the appropriations committees, sincere differences on the merits of administrative spending, genuine alternatives regarding taxation policy and debt reduction between Congress and executive and among the various groups within the parties, have almost entirely nullified the operation of the statute and denied the nation of the benefits it was intended to secure: [27] poise, balance, objective consideration of claims for expenditure, rational relationship between spending and taxing, and harmony between executive and legislature. Failure is admitted.

LAWMAKING BY THE EXECUTIVE DEPARTMENTS

ALL legislatures have been forced to devolve to the departments the making of rules and orders and regulations—in other words, a kind of subordinate legislation which has attracted a variety of names: "secondary," or "departmental," or "delegated," or "administrative," or "subordinate" legislation. The volume is immense measured by the number of such instruments,[28] and the political significance is grave judged by the extent of governmental authority so exercised over and on behalf of persons and property.

In Britain in 1890, 168 rules and orders were issued; in 1913, 444; since 1937 never less than nearly 1500 a year, and in 1945, 1706. In the United States, Theodore Roosevelt issued 1011 during his administration; Wilson, 1770; Coolidge, 1428; Hoover, 1424, and Roosevelt, 3711. (See United States Code of Federal Regulation.) The figures for the countries must not be crudely compared!

The Reasons for Delegation of Power to the Executive are various as well as inexorable. (1) In almost all countries it is due, first, to the excessive amount of business which falls on the legislature compared with the time available for conducting it. Since a choice has to be made, then one choice is to concentrate attention on the clear definition of the main principles of statutes, and to leave the derivative or incidental rules and orders for formulation by the departments. No legislature could find the time to fulfill this latter function even if it sat twenty-four hours a day, every day, and forever.

---

[27] Cf. Hearings on Legislative Reorganization Act, 1946, p. 159 ff. for testimony by the secretary and director of the Majority Policy Committee of the Senate.

[28] Until 1946, when the Statutory Instruments Act was passed, the Rules Publication Act of 1893 governed the general procedure for the form of orders and their publication and submission to Parliament. The 1946 statute superseded that of 1893. Among its reforms, which were mainly in the nature of simplification and standardization, it introduced the term "statutory instruments" to cover all orders, rules, and regulations made by ministers under statutory authority. It is a convenient and expressive term which ought to become of general usage. Cf. C. T. Carr, *Concerning Administrative Law* (New York, 1942); C. K. Allen, *Law and Orders* (London, 1947); Report, Committee on Ministers' Powers, 1932; Report, U. S. Attorney-General's Committee on Administrative Procedure (1944); and W. Gellhorn, *Administrative Law, Cases*, etc. (Brooklyn, 1947).

(2) Many of the problems dealt with by the law are of a complex, technical character; for example, the kind of machines or forms or drugs or animal diseases or safety devices which are to be regulated by law. Legislatures as at present organized are not in a position to master and decide these issues. They need scientific and technological experts to assist them by filling in the law.

(3) The rapidity with which new situations arise—for example, some new device in the coal mines, or some action by a foreign country regarding its economic policy, or some new unfair business practice—requires a certain administrative flexibility or discretion.

(4) (This applies more particularly to the United States), some fields of regulation are too unclear in their legislative demands for Congress to be itself sure of what to do in each case, and yet they are too important in Congress' estimation to be delivered over altogether to the executive. Hence a kind of experimental and developmental submission to commissions like the Federal Trade Commission, the Interstate Commerce Commission, and so on.

England. In England, since there is the closest correspondence between executive and legislature, administrative rules and orders are, in important cases, valid only after the legislature has signified its consent. As prescribed in the parent statute, some (about 3 or 4 per cent of those examined) are sent to Parliament for an affirmative resolution;[29] others are submitted and made subject to a nullifying prayer against them within a certain number of days; others are submissible but call for no proceedings by Parliament; others, again, do not have to be submitted. The regular time for lying before the House is forty sitting days. The requirement of submission to the legislature sharply distinguishes the control of subordinate legislation in England from that in the United States, France, and Weimar Germany. The power to make such orders

is wide in scope and can be fearful in compulsion, for though some of the orders are hardly more than mere forms for records, censuses, or statistical information, others govern the procedure for the enforcement of statutes which limit personal liberty or control property, or give benefits to some while withholding them from others (as in the demolition of slum property, the right to search, the denial of licenses to conduct business operations, and so on). The more comprehensive and pervasive the planning of human activities through government, the more massive this power must come to be. It has raised the weightiest criticism and stimulated ideas for controls.[30]

Hardly any member of Parliament is individually equipped to challenge such rules and orders; and the House, as a body, is even less equipped or ready to review them. Unless any special interest, economic or otherwise, is spectacularly affected, no challenge is voiced. But the opportunity is open—and sometimes good advantage is taken of it. The rules and orders are made by the departments, sometimes after compulsory consultation of advisory representative bodies; some may pass through parliamentary twilight, and be subjected to a real public scrutiny only when they cause expensive litigation, because they happen to be *ultra vires.* Even, then, their political reasonableness, as affecting public liberty and utility, may be judged by no tribunal. (The House of Lords in 1924 led the way when it established an improvement in the procedure respecting rules and orders: no motion for an affirmative resolution of the House in connection with orders may come before the House for discussion until it has been discussed and reported upon by the Special Orders Committee, appointed annually.) Public petitions are entertained when the order is of a private-

---

[29] Cf. Third Report, Select Committee on Procedure, 1946, Evidence of Sir Cecil Carr, p. 243 ff.

[30] Cf. Lord Hewart, *The New Despotism* (London, 1929), especially Chap. VI; C. R. Allen, *Bureaucracy Triumphant* (Oxford, 1931), especially pp. 1-106. For a more moderate discussion cf. F. J. Port, *Administrative Law* (London, 1929); C. T. Carr, *Delegated Legislation* (London, 1921).

bill nature; where it is of a public-bill nature, a special inquiry may be recommended on grounds of policy, principle, or precedent.

Rules and orders are bound to increase with the evolution of the social policies of our time. It is equally certain that the lawmaking body is ill-organized for their control, while the ordinary courts of law are irritated and often incapable of properly measuring administrative necessity and justification by the standards they properly use in general. As the Committee on Ministers' Powers observed:

The facilities afforded to Parliament to scrutinize and control the exercise of powers delegated to Ministers are inadequate; there is a danger that the servant may be transformed into the master.

The increase of subordinate or delegated legislation during World War II, and the clear probability that governmental activity would increase when it was over, caused the House of Commons and publicists to turn to the subject again and again. Then, following a debate on May 17, 1944, the House established a Select Committee on Statutory Rules and Orders

to consider every statutory rule or order upon which proceedings may be taken in either House (subject to affirmation or annulment) and draw the attention of the House to provisions which (i) impose a charge on the public revenues, (ii) are made under an enactment which excludes challenge in the law courts, (iii) appear to make some unusual or unexpected use of the powers conferred by the statute, (iv) have been withheld from publication by unjustifiable delay, (v) call for elucidation of their form or support.

It will be observed that the terms of reference do not include any power over the "merits" or "policy" of an order or rule. This is because the instrument is supposed to be only the closer effectuation of the "merits" or "policy" of the statute, already settled by vote of Parliament. Yet politicians are still uneasy about the process, because the instruments could add to or vary the will of Parliament as stated in the statute (and in some cases perhaps they have).

The committee has an immense task: in 1943-44, of 1483 rules and orders it scrutinized 291; in 1944-45, 168; in 1945-46, 469; in 1946-47 of nearly 1900 rules and orders it examined 795 and drew the attention of the House to 6. It has the regular official assistance of the counsel to the speaker of the House of Commons, whose expert knowledge is made available in the form of memoranda and oral advice, without which the task of sifting would probably be impossible. The committee calls civil servants to explain matters it does not understand. It reports to the House whether there is or is not reason for drawing the special attention of the House to the rules and orders, which it deals with in batches within the time limits for action. Members of the committee are not bound to follow the report of the committee: it is still open to them, as to any member, to challenge an order where the statute has so permitted.

There is no doubt, judging by the committee's reports and by the recent challenges of rules and orders, that some members of the House are much more zealous than ever before in watching the stream of rules and orders. Further, the committee makes special reports regarding the procedure on rules and orders: on their drafting, and again, on the need for a more rational determination of what kind should be the subject of an affirmative resolution of the House and what merely subject to nullifying prayer. As time goes on, the committee must assist the establishment of more rational procedures and create a corpus of knowledge enabling better control.

The House has not the time for an adequate consideration of the committee's reports, nor have members sufficient time available for their own challenges: for only a half-hour at the end of the day's business is provided. Not two days in a session have been spent on an affirmation or prayers against. Various proposals for improvement have been offered. The chief one is the addition to the committee's powers of considering the "efficiency" of the rules and orders as a means of carrying out the purposes named in the relevant statute.[31] This proposal has been rebutted by those who are afraid of the committee's powers thus to "invade Whitehall"—that is, to intervene in the day-by-day administration of the departments.[32] Others have claimed that the committee should have power to raise matters of "policy." This proposal has been even more robustly gainsaid as trenching on the authority of Parliament, as a waste of time by going back over the ground already trodden by Parliament, and as challenging the authority of the government.[33] Some have even proposed that "particular" interests who feel aggrieved by any instrument should have the power to apply to the committee for redress: [34] this has been denied on the ground that it would leave the committee and thus the government open to hundreds—perhaps thousands—of challenges, and make laws unworkable. An instance given was a law relating to traffic offenses: other statutes would be as fruitful of complaints.[35]

So important is the subject that a thorough inquiry is promised. The most thoughtful expert's opinion is likely to be the shape of policy to come: [36]

With regard to the present proposal to extend those heads (the objects of the committee's supervision) to include policy and merits, it raises such important administrative considerations that the Government might feel obliged to prepare itself to resist challenge on party lines and the present impartial [sic] scrutiny would change its character. It would be necessary to hear witnesses competent to explain and defend decisions at the policy-determining level. . . .

There are indications that delegation of legislative power may have to be developed still further rather than to be fettered by a new type of supervision.

---

31 Sir Gilbert Campion, Third Report, Select Committee on Procedure, 1946, p. xliv ff.
32 *Loc. cit.*, Morrison, *Questions*, 3676 ff.; C. T. Carr, *Memorandum and Questions*, 4622 ff.
33 *Loc. cit.*, the same.
34 *Loc. cit.*, Questions 2960 ff.
35 *Loc. cit.*, Recommendation, para. 30.
36 *Loc. cit.*, C. T. Carr, Memorandum, paras. 2 and 4.

The United States. If the problem of subordinate or delegated legislation is also serious in the American constitutional system, its solution is so far very different from the British solution, for control by the courts, not the legislature, is relied on. From the beginning of the Republic, Congress found it necessary, when it had set down the principle or standard in the statute, to delegate to the executive, by statute, the power to frame rules and regulations. It is necessary to distinguish two species of such rules: (1) executive orders made by the President, emanating from his general constitutional responsibility to see that the laws are faithfully executed, whether the power has been explicitly conferred upon him by a statute or not; and (2) all others, emanating from the powers—given by statute to him and to the heads of departments and agencies—to make rules and regulations.

To the foreign observer it is at first sight astonishing that none of these rules comes before Congress for review and for annulment or positive acceptance. With the exception of an article of the Reorganization Act of 1938—which permits the President to make orders for better departmentalization of the administrative branch that become valid if not vetoed after a period by Congress—all other orders, rules, and regulations are challengeable only in the courts. The grounds for such challenge may be that they are outside the statute; or that they are made without due regard to the procedure provided in their mother statute; or that they are unconstitutional because the statute is unconstitutional or because they themselves infringe the constitutional guarantees. This kind of control, as we have already seen, is extremely penetrating. But it is not a control of policy, even so much as British practice has tried and been able to secure.

It is a matter for surprise that the report of the Attorney General's Committee on Administrative Procedure recommends against any submission of administrative orders to Congress.[37] Its main reason is that the method has not been successful elsewhere. But this is hardly true and it would seem to be shortsighted: for the success of Commons' control does not lie only in the number of rules and orders challenged and reversed, but in the effect on the action of ministers and officials induced by the anticipation that they may be challenged. Perhaps, however, the reason for rejection of Congressional control is that Congress may easily be an opponent of the executive, even when both are of the same party, and that Congressional procedure is already hideously cluttered up and confused. In view of these circumstances and the power of the special interests in the lobby, and in view of the fact that sometimes the two branches of the government are of different political parties, legislation would *never* get administered if the rules had to be submitted for the approval of Congress. The litigious and partisan temper would frustrate the administrative fulfillment of laws. Nor can it be omitted that the making of rules and orders is "executive" or "administrative" power, and that by the constitution this is the preserve of the President. Submission to Congress would raise difficult constitutional questions, just as, in reverse, such difficulties arise when Congress delegates what the Supreme Court defines as "legislation." But it is possible constitutionally, surely, for Congress to give itself the power of review over statutory rules and orders?

The clearly distinctive answer given by United States government to the problem of administrative legislation is the institution of commissions like the Interstate Commerce Commission, the Federal Communications Commission, the Federal Power Commission, and the Securities and Exchange Commission. These have variously been called "quasi-legislative," or "quasi-administrative," or "quasi-judicial," to indicate the mixed character of their functions. For Congress has entrusted them with the administration of laws like those regulating the railroads, radio broadcast-

ing, unfair business practices, interstate power utilities, and stock-exchange transactions. Congress was unwilling to vest the enforcement of these laws in the ordinary administrative departments, which it could have done as in other countries. But it believed a special procedure ought to be established for such acts as making orders to cease and desist from certain business or corporation practices, for putting into force certain railway freight and passenger rates, for improving railroad service, for issuing licenses and certificates of public convenience and necessity to operators of radio stations, and so on. Moreover, Congress thought the commissions should be multimembered, and not have only a single top policy director like the secretary at the head of an ordinary administrative department, and that such commissions should not be the preserve of one political party.

Weimar Germany. The phenomenon of "skeleton" laws, carried out by "administrative" legislation is witnessed also in European government: indeed, it preceded development in England and the United States. A much wider power to make rules was always recognized there as inherent in the executive, a product of centuries of autocracy; but the power is becoming less and less recognized as existing apart from empowering statutes or constitutional clauses. In Weimar Germany the cabinet was obliged to pass so-called *Rahmengesetze* (framework laws), while obtaining the power therein to fill out the law by executory regulations. Most of the *Verordnung* or *Verfügung* (rules) had to be first placed before various officially appointed representative consultative bodies in each department before they were valid. In some cases the assent of a parliamentary commission was required for their validity; in others, submission to the *Reichstag* for approval or challenge. As in England and the United States, the rules were challengeable before the ordinary courts, and in addition before certain "administrative" courts, for inconsistency with the statute (they had to be *intra leges,* or as the phrase would run in English and American practice, not

---

[37] Report, U. S. Attorney General's Committee on Administrative Procedure (1944), p. 120 ff.

ultra vires), and for their obedience to the processes for their creation provided in the statute.[38]

France. In France two types of rules prevail: *réglements* (simple rules), and *réglements d'administration publique* (rules of public administration). Their number has grown for much the same reasons as in other modern states.[39] Both are subject to actions for annulment by direct action before the *Conseil d'État,* or indirectly before the ordinary courts, when their validity is incidental to some case in which they are involved. In the Third Republic the power to make simple rules was deemed to have been given to the President of the Republic in article 3 of the constitutional law of February 25, 1875: "The President assures and superintends the execution of the laws." The power is now, by article 47 of the constitution of 1946, attributed to the premier —the president of the Council of Ministers. It is a change with some significance. The rule-making power was, under the Third Republic, amply used when emergency laws, especially on financial matters, were passed to deal with the oft-recurring crises. They were unavoidable instruments of governments which were themselves unstable and faced with distracted and incoherent parliaments. Rules of public administration are made on the basis of specific statutes, by the cabinet. As already observed, the *Conseil d'État* must be consulted in their drafting.

LEGISLATIVE CONTROL
OVER THE EXECUTIVE

WE have observed that parliamentary bodies were not exclusively engaged in

legislation but that their functions were mixed. Historical evolution has deposited with them what we broadly call the "control of the executive." This control is often referred to in English political discussion as being quite as important as (and some assert more important than) legislation, and as making Parliament the "grand inquest of the nation." Broadly, this means that the legislature is to keep the executive and the civil service within lines of policy which it supports.

Considerable imagination must be exerted to realize how significant to the welfare of the nation the control of the executive is. All modern states have assumed an immense range of governmental control, regulation over the multifarious activities of their many millions of citizens. In some cases they have proceeded to the actual conduct of widespread, strategically placed, economic enterprise: as the government credit, financing, farm and housing activities in the United States; the same in England with the addition of nationalization of the coal, transport, electricity, gas industries, the medical profession, and the Bank of England; and the same in France, with the addition of nationalization of coal, transport, banking, and so on. In all these instances there must be added the conduct of the social services and the provision of social security. The governments have thus assumed the responsibility for vast monopolies. They have no competitors. Their operators are the civil servants, who now, at headquarters and in the field, number millions. These are the managers of over forty per cent of the nation's income in Britain and over twenty five per cent in the United States. They are organized in complex ways in complex departments to conduct complicated operations to secure lawful ends which are themselves necessarily complicated. Their activities are sometimes merely routine, as when a postal carrier collects his letters and delivers them on his appointed route. But they are also crucial, standing at points in the social process where a single order controls the rights and activities of millions of men and women.

[38] Cf. Schlegelberger, *Rationalisierung der Gesetzgebung* (Berlin, 1928); and K. Dessauer, *Recht, Richtertum und Ministerial burokratie* (Berlin, 1928), p. 93 ff. E. Jacobi, in *Handbuch des deutschen Staatsrechts* (Tübingen, 1930), Vol. II, p. 236 ff.; F. Fleiner, *Institutionen des deutschen Verwaltungsrechts* (Tübingen, 1928), p. 70 ff.
[39] Cf. H. Nézard, *Éléments du Droit Public* (Paris, 1931), p. 222; Gaston Jèze, *Principes Généraux de Droit Administratif* (Paris, 1930), Vol. I, p. 378 ff.; Léon Duguit, *Traité de Droit Public* (Paris, 1923), Vol. IV, p. 666 ff.

The problem of the control of the everyday activity of government is the cardinal problem of contemporary government.

Now, before we enter into a discussion of the extent to which legislatures do now control the executive, the meaning of the word "control" needs definition. We do not mean that legislatures have, or pretend to have, or ought to have, the power of continuous intervention in administration and positive participation in the execution of the law. They do not, in fact, do more than act as the judge and the corrector of the cabinet and its administrative assistants. We could show, further, that it is almost impossible to do more than this (take, as an example, their financial powers!), and that where they confine themselves to this alone, the result of joint work of legislature and the executive is better than where the legislature attempts to interfere more positively.[40] We must, therefore, observe in what countries legislatures attempt to do more than control, and consider the lessons of that experience. One other point. It is not always necessary for legislatures or any controlling body to intervene. Their mere presence is sufficient to establish a standard of behavior for ministers and all public career servants. Marx declared that a specter was haunting Europe: in administrative control it must be contrived that a specter, the legislature, shall incessantly haunt executive officials! We must give due credit to the influence of the simple presence of the legislature, to the "silent rhetoric of a look." However, this is not all; nor it it enough.

Debates and Inquiries. Control of the executive has the longest history in England and very great importance is attached to it, some holding that Parliament's chief duty is still what it was before the enthusiasm for statute making began after 1832. Upon examination of the opportunities and machinery for control, we find that the House of Commons is reasonably but not fully effective. Let us consider the occasions when the House may inquire into the conduct of administration.

The first occasion is the debate on the king's speech to Parliament (the equivalent of the Continental "ministerial declaration"), which occupies something like 5 or 6 days. Then a little over 32 days altogether are devoted to the discussion of the estimates and other financial matters. Here, as we have pointed out, the discussion is not so much on the economy of the estimates but is rather a general examination of the administration of the department demanding supplies. And finally, we may count about 14 days a session (at the utmost) when the motion to adjourn the House upon a matter of public importance is accepted by the speaker [41] and a subject of administration debated, or when the government itself gives time for the discussion of substantive motions on important matters disturbing the public mind, sometimes called "votes of censure." Next, we may count 6 days debate on the Christmas, Easter, and Whitsun adjournments. Altogether, then, there are available nearly 60 days in each year when the House concentrates upon the subject of administration: this is 40 per cent of the time of the House.

It is impossible to state quantitatively how much time is devoted in such debates to general policy and how much to administrative detail. The two elements are blended, and the proportion of each varies from case to case. It can be fairly asserted that no item of administrative mismanagement can be regarded as immune from pursuit by the House of Commons. It is recognized that what may seem to be a detail—e.g., a veteran's pension not paid on time, or a late announcement of a rise in the price of cocoa—may involve a profound issue of public policy, general administrative weakness, or personal incompetence. No government can possibly resist the House of Commons' sense that something is rotten in the state, or fail, then, to offer the time for debate re-

---

[40] Cf. J. S. Mill, *Representative Government*, Chap. V.

[41] Cf. Sir Gilbert Campion, Memorandum and Evidence in Third Report, Select Committee on Procedure, 1946.

quested by the opposition (the leader of which is paid to conduct the opposition more efficiently). A special investigation may follow by a select committee of the House—as in the case of the disclosure of budget secrets, or the leakage of information from a government department—or a special tribunal of inquiry may be set up to make the attendant investigation. The power of the House of Commons may be regarded as peremptory over the administration: ministers bow to it, the opposition insists on it, the minority in the ranks of the government maneuver with it, and officials both dread and respond to its formidable strokes.

These controls over the administration occur in the full session of the House of Commons, not in the twilight of committees. All the members of the House participate in a chamber which is the single focus of the inquest. (The House of Lords has a parallel power of inquest.)

In addition to the regular order of inquest as embodied in the debate on the king's speech and on the financial legislation, and in addition to the special occasions of motions put by the opposition on more particular and critical occasions, there is another regular form of parliamentary control of the executive—continuous, everyday, always threatening and always occurring. This is Question Time.

Questions: Rules and Numbers.[42] All members of the House of Commons have the right to ask questions of ministers every day of the week except Friday. As the House sits Monday through Friday, this means that questions are in order on four days of the week. This is regular procedure all the year round when the House is in session. There are about one hundred and twenty days on which questions are asked each year. This is the field of operations.

It should be noticed that questions happen on consecutive days, and regularly,

with the week-end interval. The executive is under continual surveillance; the House is under continual obligation to think and interrogate. It is good for both. Question time lasts from shortly before 3 P.M. each day to 3:45 P.M. with a small margin—this is slightly less than an hour.

Each member has the right to ask as many as three questions for oral answer; he may ask as many questions as he wishes for written answer. The limitation on the oral questions is in the interests of fairness to all members, to thwart monopolists. Oral questions are "starred," written ones "unstarred"—an indication to the clerk of the House, which sort is intended. The answers to be "written" are published, like the oral ones, in the Parliamentary *Debates*.

A clear twenty-four hour notice must be given to the clerks of the House of oral or written questions to be asked. Since this means its appearance on the notice paper, questions may be answered from between twenty-four to forty-eight hours after handing in. The speaker or the minister may also be approached privately, by "private notice" by the member. This gives the opportunity of raising very important questions and skipping the time limit of notice. It is employed usually by a member of His Majesty's Opposition, or otherwise especially influential members of the House, with due sense of responsibility. It is an important safety valve for matters of urgency.

An average of seventy to a hundred oral questions are asked every day; as many more are written. The asking member, and any members of the House, may at once ask supplementary questions on matters arising out of the answer just given. It is a free-for-all, though the original questioner is considered by the House to have priority. It is clear that the more "supplementaries" are asked, the less time will be available for the original questions remaining on the list. Therefore the sense of the House keeps in check the supplementaries—readers of the Parliamentary *Debates* will notice that about three supplementaries are allowed. They are kept in a pretty terse form—for if they

---

[42] This account reproduces part of my paper for the Joint Committee on Reorganization of Congress, *Suggestions for Strengthening Congress* (June, 1946), p. 49 ff. Cf. also T. Erskine May, *Parliamentary Practices* (London, 1946), p. 381 ff.

were longer, they would be ignored, and the questioner would become very unpopular.

The purpose of the supplementaries is simple. For the original question, the minister is prepared with an answer, which has been formulated for him in the first place by his department but in which he has probably taken some part. But it is the purpose of the supplementary either to get additional information which has not been given, or, what is usually more likely, to pierce underneath the minister's guard and get him to divulge any state of affairs which he would otherwise not confess.

It is an excellent short probe. An intense passage-at-arms may occur. Official shortcomings may be revealed, and inferred from matching the supplementaries with the original answer. Smart official advisers attempt to anticipate the supplementaries. They sometimes succeed. More often they cannot. The strain on the ministers' readiness of mind, and parliamentary improvisation, and the stimulus to the hunting instincts of the members of the House, tones them all up. The supplementary may be very revealing. In civil life the maxim "Least said, soonest mended" is advised; in supplementary questions the maxim is, "Most said, Minister ended!"

No formal debate follows the questions, but a short, sharp debate, lasting from seconds to one minute, may burst out on any matter of importance. It may lead later in the session to a debate if members smell a rat.

The pressure on oral questions is very great, and in fact it is difficult to get more than about seventy answered per day. Those which are not answered orally are answered in writing. It has been recently suggested that an additional quarter-hour be allowed for questions; there seems to be a sentiment favorable toward the proposal, but it has not yet come under formal consideration.

Supplementaries are informally curtailed by the sense of the House, the tactics of the answering minister, the desire to get on to the next question—and formally, when the speaker decides that the business of the House is being retarded.

Though questions may be asked by anybody, in fact some fifty or sixty leading members of the House manage to get most in. This is natural selection, and nothing sinister. Also, the opposition puts more than half the questions, most of them by the leaders of the opposition, which may one day itself be in office and under questioning. But the rank and file of the government benches, that is, of the majority, are also busy questioners of the government, that is, of their own leaders.

The practice of the House, as interpreted by the speaker, requires that the questions be genuinely designed to elicit information. They always do; but that may not be their intention, and this is discussed in a moment.

There is another rule of greater importance. Questions can be addressed to ministers only where the subject matter is definitely a minister's responsibility. Thus, matters altogether outside the cognizance of government cannot arise. Also, the questioner must be very careful that he addresses the question to the right minister, otherwise the wrong one will address it finally to the right one, but the opportunity of oral answer may be lost owing to the delay. The officers of the House attempt to avert such misunderstandings. Where questions are on the more general responsibilities of the government—that is, on general past or future policy—the prime minister will answer.

Questions are sometimes "planted"—that is, are asked by a member in arrangement with the minister in order to give the latter the opportunity of making a statement on a subject which he deems ought to be imparted to the House. Again, there is nothing sinister about this. It is a part of useful relations between executive and House.

In order to avoid overpowering strain on ministers, who have their administrative and cabinet business to attend to, and in order to give members of the House the chance of directly interrogating ministers and not their understudies, the House has accepted a rota of days: for example, questions on agriculture and fisheries and commerce will come principally on one day, and those on foreign affairs, health, education, and so forth, on another day. But the questions are not all specialized to these days. Each day has a mixed bag.

Force of Questions. Every conceivable aspect of British government, from a minute problem in social services administration to the whole policy of the government—from little Pedlington to the course of foreign and imperial policy—may be the subject of questions. Starting no bigger than a man's hand, any question may develop into a crackling, intense storm, with thunder and lightning, and may even lead beyond the question hour into a full debate on government policy on a later day. There is a contingent, tense relationship, a kind of menace underneath the purring, which is exciting for the lions, for the gladiators, and for the public. There is real mental strife.

Questions are asked in full assembly of the House, not in the recesses of committee rooms. The House, often not fully attended, is most fully attended every day at question hour. Here is something dramatic and something that gives communion. Here is a focus for the grand inquest of the nation.

The first ostensible purpose of question time is to obtain information. If it is oral or written, it is fresh and addressed to a specific point. Other government publicity in printed form is very full but may not answer the daily questions in a man's mind. But the peculiar function of getting information by questions is not to reveal the mere facts about government activity, but to throw light on the condition of government in daily action and in daily preparation for tomorrow's action. It therefore has a contemporary and anticipatory quality. Members are trying to see what is over on the other side of the hill—and to do so early enough to influence the government before its commitment is absolute.

The ulterior purpose of the questions is far more important. Question hour is part of the apparatus of the House for controlling the executive, and for participating in the executive's course of action. It is the disciplinary quality of questions which is their characteristic and most significant mark. Members are trying to probe into the activities of the minister and the cabinet as a whole, and, behind these, the vast rabbit-warren of nearly a million administrators engaged in multifarious activities.

The minister is responsible for the administration of his department—the department is kept up to the mark by pressure brought to bear upon him by the House of Commons, and the pressure is continuously exerted through questions. Questions are formulated in a way as to suggest blame—that all is not well in this branch of public affairs, that there are weaknesses to answer for, not merely facts to give.

The minister is not simply giving information; he is answering an insinuated charge. He can answer this charge satisfactorily only by having his administrative department as perfect as man can make it. It is for him to vent his feelings on his departmental advisers if he is tripped up in the course of questions. His ministerial reputation with his party, with his cabinet colleagues, with his constituency, will depend on the showing he makes at question time. He is on incessant trial for the future of his own career—he is under cross-examination by any of six hundred members who believe that they could do the job better than he can. It is a serious ordeal. Moreover, it is a continuous one. He might get by with an evasion on Monday, but he is in the ring again on Tuesday. He may be witty and escape in a gust of laughter on Wednesday, but the questioner may trip him on Thursday. He cannot escape all his questions all the time. Often members will "gang up" on him with integrated questions, so that he cannot escape a barrage.

Effect of Questions. The effect on ministers, as all have admitted, is compelling. The effect is equally dynamic on the public employees who work behind the ministers, especially as the close official advisers attend the House of Commons in an official "box" behind the speaker's chair outside the bar, but close enough to advise a flummoxed minister at his whispered entreaty. There is an almost instantaneous transmission of the galvanic feeling of the House, through the minister, through his on-the-spot advisers to the thousands of civil servants who execute his policy. Woe to those who have failed him!

Questions put day by day for daily answering prevent administrative trouble or inefficiency from piling up to a point where it assumes scandalous proportions. The many minor operations make major surgery unnecessary. The minister knows the mind of the Commons, and can sense what the Commons will or will not tolerate. If he does not, he will be a parliamentary failure. The fact that he knows how far he can go is a great assistance to him in the assurance with which he can run his department. It seems to be a very worrying process, and it is; but it has the consoling effect that responsibility is then shared by the House of Commons. Hence, it is not necessary to put off criticisms of administration until they reach proportions where only a smashing sensational and disturbing investigation is necessary to set things right.

Questions have an important bearing upon the coordination of the administration's total activity. Any evidence that the departments overlap or that they stultify each other by want of cooperation or organizational inefficiency is immediately taken up, and the attention of ministers called thereto. (This benefit was not appraised in the section on administrative coordination of the report of the President's Committee on Administrative Management.[43])

Many questions are not even put in the form of asking for information, but in the form of "Is the Minister aware . . .?" followed by information given by the questioner. This is nothing but a deliberate drawing of the Minister's attention in public to some governmental matter which

should be put right. It may be an administrative grievance relating to a pension that has not been promptly enough settled at the member of parliament's direct request to the minister. Or perhaps it may be something which concerns civil rights, as in the Savidge case; or intervention in the Spanish war; or the badgering of Mr. Churchill about his policy in Greece; or the Secretary of War's threats to Mr. Duncan Sandys, M.P.; or unemployed-assistance regulations. Thus, in the first case, the use of strong-arm methods by Scotland Yard policy; in the second, a continual barrage of questions about Franco; in the third, questions which caused Mr. Churchill to change his policy; in the fourth, the allegation that the government was threatening prosecution of a member to prevent disclosures of their ineffectiveness in providing anti-aircraft guns; and in the fifth, discussion relating to riots because the unemployment-compensation regulations had taken no heed of the effect in various localities.

The temper of the House is made manifest to the government. The sentiment of the House becomes part and parcel of the government's policy.

Why then does the Government take notice? Why can it be jolted? That is the crucial issue, of supreme relevance to American circumstances. The answer is that there is a seamless web between government and the House of Commons. Members of the government are members of the House: elected in the same way, entitled to the same privileges, subject to the same obligations, living while it lives, losing office when it is dissolved. Without a fixed term like the President of the United States or of any cabinet member he likes to keep in office, the position of ministers is dependent on the credit they have with the Commons and the country, as demonstrated in office under cross-examination. They hold office because they are leading members of their party; they will lose it if they fall out of harmony with fellow party members to whom they have obligations. Their position is not fixed or absolute; it is contingent on their showing a daily level of quality. The opposition's

---

43 Cf. Chap. 26 below.

only chance of ever getting into office is to overthrow the government at a future election, discrediting them to the country. Questions may contribute to this.

No bar separates members from ministers. All are members of one body. The House has authority over everything, not merely legislation; it is master of the executive also. The cabinet are men who owe all their credit and strength to acceptance by the House of Commons after long apprenticeship as members who themselves used to ask questions and thereby show their quality. This is the supreme postulate: the impossibility of making a dividing line between legislature and executive in the British constitution

It will, therefore, be appreciated that questions derive especial value from the fact they are conducted in the full assembly of the House, in the full light of the national day. This is supplemented by the fact that many of the ministers, and often the prime minister, are in the House at question time, all together, one solid block, facing the House, infiltrated by the House.

Further, all acute questions get full reporting in the press (and not merely the major metropolitan press.) This opportunity to be noticed by the public is a stimulus to members to ask searching questions.

Ministers must answer questions, and in the end must answer them candidly. There are saving rules for the "public interest," and for the sake of not prejudicing pending negotiations, and for the internal administration of the nationalized industries and services. In wartime the Speaker is especially cautious to refuse questions which may help the enemy. The House allows latitude for withholding information, but the latitude is given in its judgment. A minister, or all ministers together, refusing to answer would find themselves voted out of office by a vote of no confidence. This is an essential factor in the situation—the House is master of the government; it cannot refuse frankly to answer proper questions, and what is proper is what the House says is proper.

A question's power over a minister in England is equally a power over the whole cabinet including the prime minister. Ministers take account of that collective responsibility in their answers; each commits all, and all, therefore, remember each. On the cardinal question of main direction, the prime minister himself will answer.

Proposals to limit the number of questions to two per member were rejected so as to leave freedom to members who had enough ideas to ask three. A suggestion to increase the time allowed for questions was not accepted, because it would trench on other business of the House, as well as impose further hardship on ministers and civil service. The time of notice has, on recommendation by officials of the Commons and the government, been extended from one to two days, on the ground that answers can often be soundly prepared only after extended fact-finding by cable, telegram, consultation, or research, and where policy is concerned, after much forethought. It was deemed better to lengthen the notice than to force the minister to give a superficial answer or ask for deferment. The disadvantage involved in the lengthening of notice, that often the question will not be answered in the same week, was regarded as less important than the advantage to the House of being able to get a well-founded answer, and then a fair deal from the administration. There is always the private-notice question to cope with matters of urgency.

What importance the Select Committee on Procedure attributed to questions may be gathered from its observation: "They regard the right to put Questions to Ministers as one of the most important possessed by Members. The exercise of this right is perhaps the readiest and most effective method of parliamentary control over the action of the executive." [44] So powerful is the influence of the questions on ministers and civil servants that ministers have sought to safeguard the daily

---

[44] Second Report, p. iii; the evidence in this report (January, 1946) constitutes a most valuable commentary on the practical operation of questions.

conduct of the nationalized services—the Bank of England, the coal industry, transport, electricity and gas, the public medical service, broadcasting, and so on—from close questioning in the House. It is feared that their employees would be so frightened of making mistakes that they would cease to be enterprising.[45] Here, is an issue with a history of controversy.[46] No government can commit the House to limit its questions, for the Speaker is master of the limits to questions, but there is no doubt that the Speaker would be guided by the sense of the House as led by the leaders of the majority.[47] It is my opinion that such important sectors of the national life will finally have to yield in very large measure to the questioning of the House.

Interpellations. The right of interpellation in France is not given by the 1946 constitution, but it is deemed to be an immediate and fundamental implication of the principle of ministerial responsibility. From the Revolution of 1789 the tradition and practice of a particularly strict accountability of ministers has developed and gives force to the principle. It is an important minority right, and a bludgeon wielded over the head of ministers. The interpellation is a kind of question, long and rather querulous, of the nature of an English vote of "no confidence," not like an English question. Its purpose is to put the government to the trouble of explaining its objects and methods in the particular branch of its policy and administration which is attacked. As the rules of procedure of March, 1947, now regulate it, the interpellation is thus handled by the Assembly:[48]

Any deputy may notify the president of the Assembly of his desire to make an interpellation, submitting a summary of it. It may be of the greatest width. The president next day informs the government and the Assembly. On the Tuesday afterwards the conference of presidents which settles the order of business fixes the time for the interpellation by agreement with the government and the interpellator. The Assembly can itself fix the day if fifty members endorse the interpellator's request; this is done without debate on the motion, and after hearing the government. Additional interpellations can be added to the original one, but not after the lapse of three sittings from the fixing of the timetable, and never (as used to be possible) during the interpellation itself. The government must be informed of these suggested additions and has the right to speak on them: the Assembly then decides whether they shall be admitted. This right of addition of interpellations was one of the most famous ways of embarrassing a government, for often, if it were seen that the government was in difficulties, additional troubles would be made for it in the mounting excitement of the chase. After the interpellator has started the discussion, it is open to any deputy to take part. On the *ordre du jour* of the day which winds up the discussion, one interpellator, the group presidents, the government, and the presidents of commissions may speak. Any deputy who wishes may have five minutes in which to explain his vote. In the heyday of its power it is the government which settles whether it will be interpellated and when; in the days of its weakening the government is obliged to accept interpellations which hasten its downfall.

Broadly, then, the ministers are subject to attack from many directions; in 1935 M. Laval was faced with some seventy interpellations of an exceedingly mixed character as the Chamber opened its autumn proceedings. It is to be expected, considering the nature of French deputies, that the government would be severely harassed by interpellations. The expectation was, indeed, overfulfilled in

---

[45] Cf. Debates, June 7, 1918, cols. 1649 ff.
[46] Cf. Lincoln Gordon, *The Public Service Corporation in Great Britain* (Oxford, 1938); Sir Arthur Street, *The Public Corporation in British Experience* (London, 1917); Sir Oliver Franks, *Central Planning in War and Peace* (London, 1947).
[47] Cf. Herman Finer, "The Central Planning Machinery in Great Britain," *Public Administration Review*, Spring, 1948.
[48] *Réglement*, Chap. XV.

the Third Republic.[49] The regular day for interpellations was in 1900 fixed on the Friday of each week and led to the presentation and adoption of the *ordre du jour;* [50] that is, there were some forty debates a year on interpellations alone. It will be noticed from the last few sentences that the deputies tried to find another way of making themselves heard— by debating the date of the interpellation. This practice was limited by new rules: only minister and interpellator might speak; the latter had only five minutes, and could raise the matter only at the end of the sitting.

The interpellation is terminable in one of three ways—without any vote at all, when the incident is simply closed; or by a vote upon the *ordre du jour pur et simple* or by the *ordre du jour motivé* (motived order of the day). The first-mentioned is hardly more than a question. The second is a resolution expressing no opinion on the merits or demerits of the government's case; it is a reservation of opinion, and the Assembly proceeds casually to the next business. But a ministry may have learned by the tone of debate, and from abstentions in the voting, that it is disliked, and many resigned because they were damned with praise too faint. The *ordre du jour motivé* is a definite vote of confidence in the government or a definite withdrawal of confidence. Thus: "The Chamber, considering the assurances of the Government, is of the opinion that the consequences to the mining industry have (or have not) been and will (or not) continue to be disastrous, passes to the Order of the Day." The negative is virtually an overthrow of the cabinet.

Now it was possible for interpellations to be joined, and frequently they were,

with the result that the diverse passions of the Chamber were joined and focused, culminating in a vote of censure on the government. This was a common way of defeating a government, and about three fifths of French ministries have thus fallen.

What, then, is the significance of the interpellation as a means of control of the executive? *First,* we must remember that it is not only the nature of the interpellation which destroys ministries, but the nature of the party system and the deputies' peculiar temperament and views of parliamentary rights. These are the root causes of the fall of ministries, and these have produced the most appropriate implement, namely, the interpellation.

Second, is the interpellation a good means of administrative control? It is certainly a frequent and sharp means, which causes ministers constant anxiety for the quality and direction of their policy and departments. Even where the interpellation is withdrawn and never debated, it is a threat, and we have seen that many are taken to an issue. But it cannot be good for ministers to be in hourly peril of fall, for this prevents them from attending with independent mind to the solid and long-period merits of policy, shakes their confidence, and puts a premium upon window dressing. There are some things which the deputy or the ordinary member of the parliament cannot appreciate until he himself is in command of the actual administration of a department. To question is often enough, with the ultimate reserve (not the immediate threat) of a right of destruction if the question is not properly answered. Interpellations, however, have been developed rather destructively. They too often unite factions into a temporary and sudden opposition only for the purposes of killing a ministry, and the main intention is not firmly to direct a government which is to continue in office, but to mend its ways. The system is too harassing when we consider the vast amount which a minister must do if he wishes to control his department with any firmness and completeness. Usually, however (and the figures given bear

---

[49] Summary (1924-28):

Interpellations	
No discussion	432
Discussion for fixing day of debate	231
Discussion, but not resulting in *ordre du jour*	27
Discussion leading to presentation and adoption of *ordre du jour*.	152
Total	842

[50] Cf. A. Soulier, *L'Instabilité Ministerielle* (Paris, 1939).

this out), the deputies are content with a really tumultuous oratorical jubilee; they do not mean anything by it, and the minister is able to get his Order of the Day voted after a general political address which concerns itself not very much with the details supposedly under cross-examination.

The Parliamentary Commissions. It has been made clear that the commissions have so developed as to exert a steady and not entirely wholesome pressure on legislative work. The truth is that the commissions discovered, by accident, an outlet for the repressed ambition of the ordinary member of the legislature, and have proceeded and will proceed to the point where something forcibly stops them. Their members can hardly be blamed for desiring not to be merely voting cattle. Their practices, however, while they have the effect of controlling administration, go too far, for they are neither so continuously interested nor so closely concerned nor so responsible as the minister, yet he is liable to constant interference and criticism of a dangerous nature.

French ministers complained all through the interwar years of being subject to "twenty legislatures," that is, the parliamentary commissions, and they were indeed excessively put on the rack of questioning and cross-examination. The public benefit was small as the proceedings were private. The commissions considered themselves to be as important as (if not more important than) ministers and officials, whose time they wasted both at sessions of the commission and visits to the departments. It may be that the bureaucratization of the French civil service was due largely to the bludgeoning tactics of the commissions. Ministers could bring their officials along to answer the questions and criticism of the commissions. On the whole, French control of the executive is too interfering at some points, and nonexistent at others. It is destructive rather than corrective. But a proper fusion of the methods of questions of the House of Commons and the committee hearings of the National Assembly offers a feasible way of improvement.

It is a question of proportion: how much to control or not to control? Therefore it is also a question of temper and good sense, as well as institutions. The French example of committees (commissions) of the Assembly endowed with a power to exercise administrative control has often been commended to English students.[51] It has hitherto been repudiated by leaders of Parliament, especially governments in office, on the ground of the excessive interference in day-by-day policy and the continuum of administration.[52] The objections are very weighty. But England, like the United States and France, may have reached a point where the size and importance of the administrative apparatus is so massive that such control by parliamentary committees, multiplying the scrutinizing power of the legislature and with expert staffs, may be unavoidable.

Weimar Germany followed the same general mode of parliamentary control of the executive as France. Questions, however, "small questions" as they were called, had to be endorsed by fifteen members and were answerable either in writing or orally during one hour of one sitting per week. Interpellations needed the endorsement of thirty members and had to be concisely and clearly drafted. Ministers set the date of discussion, and if they refused to answer altogether or for more than a fortnight then the *Reichstag* could put the interpellation on the Order of the Day. The interpellator was permitted an explanation of his question, and thereupon the minister replied. But only if fifty members requested a debate did one follow. Further, if a resolution was to follow upon the debate, at least thirty members were needed to support it, and as many members could demand that the resolution be examined by a committee before a vote was taken. If the interpellations were so many as to endanger the due completion of business, the *Reichstag* limited the interpellations to special days. It will be seen that the German system set

[51] Cf. Third Report, Select Committee on Procedure (1946).
[52] Cf. *ibid., passim.*

certain limitations upon the minorities which could hold up ministers. The limitations did not appear to be too severe. Virtually the rules said that only in matters which were important enough to find thirty who object could the *Reichstag* be troubled with their discussion, and this seems to me to have been more reasonable than the French practice, which though ideally splendid and democratic down to the meanest of individual members of the Chambers, makes democracy a farce by stopping publicly beneficial government for the benefit of the ambitions and vanity of deputies.

Committees for Recess and Foreign Affairs. The *Reichstag* committees were also continuously in touch with administration, but by no means so fussily as the French commissions. There were two committees mentioned in the constitution whose theoretical interest was very great, and the experience of which is worth a little attention.[53] We observed that however efficient parliamentary control is, there is still a portion of every year when there is no control at all. For this all ministers thank God; and both for the freshness of mind of the legislators, and their visits to their districts, the break in their sessions is beneficial. The makers of the Weimar constitution provided that a standing supervisory committee ("to safeguard the rights of Parliament") should function during recesses. Its number was fixed at fifteen, and later (1925) at twenty-one, and later still, twenty-eight. It was composed of members of the various parties. It did not sit continuously, but occasionally, in the recess. It confined itself to the discussion of the most serious events of the day: e.g., state of emergency in Bavaria, increases of salaries in the civil service, execution of the law relating to the defense of the Republic, financial guarantees to certain business undertakings, application of the budget surplus to the aid of agriculture injured by storms, and various statutory orders of importance. This seems to me to be an important institution, especially as it did not

worry the government continuously. It is enough if the government is aware that a representative of the legislature is existent to raise questions where deficiency or critical innovation is concerned. It is notable that the French constitution of 1946, article 12, provides for such an intersession supervisory committee "to exercise control over the actions of the Cabinet." It is the Assembly's secretariat, elected, as we have described, by the political parties according to their proportional group strength.

The second committee which found mention in the Weimar constitution was the permanent Foreign Affairs Committee. Its institution was the direct result of German democratic dissatisfaction with the secret conduct of foreign relations, and of a very common belief that if only the people were consulted, war would not lightly be undertaken or produced by unwise alliances and engagements. This view was extensively held, though it is very doubtful whether improvement is possible in the present stage of human greed and popular morality and wisdom. However, one thing is certain: that publicity of diplomatic negotiations is the first stage in preparing the mind to face the issues and so, perhaps, in the long run to change the present condition of international and domestic political morality. To this end the ratification of treaties by the legislature is a necessary step. America, as we have already shown, has both these institutions. France has both these institutions. In England, the making of treaties is still considered by the Conservative party to be a part of the royal prerogative, not needing ratification by Parliament, though this may be permitted, as of grace, to discuss treaties, while the Labour party submits treaties and presumably would abide by a vote of Parliament—yet no Foreign Affairs Committee exists although many people have demanded it.

In Weimar Germany there existed a standing Committee for Foreign Affairs, consisting of twenty-eight members. Its sessions were, like those in France and the United States, not open to anyone else except members of the committee. It

[53] Articles 34 and 35.

sat very often and heard ministers on current negotiations, or on events which affected or were likely to affect the *Reich*.[54] This meant that at least twenty-eight members and their substitutes and parliamentary friends were in touch with the march of events, and were able to raise an alarm when necessary. Further, ministers realized that there was a watchful committee, including members of the minority, which required a good reason for each stage in policy. The committee was often faced with an accomplished fact because the government negotiators had to make binding engagements. (Exactly this was complained of by the members of the French Assembly's Foreign Affairs Committee at various stages of the negotiations in May and June, 1947, of the six-power agreement regarding western Germany.) In spite of this, the mere presence of the committee and the need to answer its questions must have worked to influence the mind and activity of the ministers. The *Reich* Committee continued between parliaments, as well as between sessions.

American Methods of Controlling the Executive. In the United States the very basis of the constitution is that each branch of government shall go its separate way, and the executive finds no place on the floor of the House or the Senate. Attempts have been made to make the twain meet—in the committee stage of bills, and in the steady relationship between the Congressional leaders and the President and his cabinet. Yet these are not enough to satisfy Congressmen, or, indeed, the actual objective need for Congressional control. Congress has proceeded to control (1) by voting the estimates in very great detail, (2) by passing many acts regulating the departments and their functions in profound detail, (3) by discussing and voting detailed resolutions recommending certain lines of policy, and finally (4) by conducting investigations.

The methods here used have some merits and some deficiencies. They are overdetailed in matters of personnel, expenditures, and the structure of admin-

istration, and are not sufficiently broad and probing in the dynamic process of current activity. They are in annual stages: the controlling stipulations either occur before administration starts, if the statutes contain them—or else they come after the year for which the appropriations have been made has gone by. It is undoubtedly true (I have seen this from the inside) that the anticipation of being interrogated exercises a controlling and guiding effect on officials and their political chiefs. This could be improved in two ways. The first is by open, public sessions of the committees, for the temper of administrative criticism is in the long run more reasonable when conducted in public. Second, the narrowness of some of the committees in scope is to be corrected by the recent reductions in the number of the committees.

It will be observed that the United States Congress is still weak in something of the nature of the British system of public cross-examination of current policy. The need is met to a small extent by debate in the Senate, and if there is any justification at all for its want of curbs on debate, it lies in this, that the Senate can turn its attention at any time to some administrative scandal, and *a propos* of something else, relevant or irrelevant, make known its views. But the merits of the British question hour—incessant and in open forum—are certainly lacking. It has often been proposed that they should be supplied. A joint session of the two Houses at some convenient time—perhaps twice a week—would be of value, and should be experimented with. Yet there are drawbacks. The British system is not one that merely calls for information. Questions are a means of exerting discipline over the ministers and officials, because an answer is a commitment, and to discredit the minister is a stage in the game whereby the opposition appeals to the coming verdict, at the next election, of the people against the government. But in the United States the chief executive could not be interrogated. He would not submit to it; he has even on occasion ordered his own heads of departments not

54 Fr. Poetszch-Heffter, *Jahrbuch des öffentlichen Rechts*, (Berlin) XIII, 80.

to give Congress the information asked for, and here the law stands on his side.[55] None of his cabinet, when questioned, could commit the President, and if they did not commit the President, much of their value would be lost. Hence, the cardinal virtue of British questions—that they commit the executive—is not available in the United States system—the bogey again, the separation of powers.[56]

The characteristic inquisitorial method of supervising the executive in the United States is by Congressional investigations. Congressional investigations appear to have no constitutional basis excepting as an implication of the legislative power of Congress. Whatever the constitutional power of Congress, it has certainly cast its net of investigation very wide and deep, and in some cases (such as the Teapot Dome scandal, or the stock-exchange scandal, or the Garsson-May and Hughes-Myers war-contract scandals), has unmasked real villainy, or (as in TVA) has opened up the record and shown the baselessness of slander. Yet such a procedure is occasional, not continuous; it is cumbersome, and very slow. When it does come, the actual hearings develop almost into a prosecuting criminal inquiry, or, as Walter Lippmann has said, into a "wild and feverish man-hunt in which Congressmen do not stop at cannibalism." This is a grave infliction on officials. Yet investigations do, occasionally, force officials to make a valuable resurvey of their objectives and methods.

The basic governmental weakness of this way of attempting to control the executive is that after report, there is no guarantee of improvement at all. For legislature and executive, being separate, tend to become hostile, and refuse to take each other in good faith, and there is nothing to remedy this.

The report of the Joint Committee on Reorganization of Congress made the very

wise proposal (15) that the practice of creating special investigating committees be abandoned. Instead, it proposed that the regular standing committees be the continuing supervisors of the administration of the law, with the power of subpoena. The advantages of this proposal, carried into formal effect by the Act of 1946, are obvious and abundant. But the special investigating committees have not ceased to be appointed.

The different methods and spirit of parliamentary control of the executive prevalent in England are well expressed in some answers given by the Rt. Hon. Mr. Herbert Morrison, then Deputy Prime Minister, to questions asked by the Select Committee on Procedure in March, 1946. He said: [57]

. . . it is perfectly proper and, indeed, to the public advantage that Parliament should jump in; a short, sharp vigorous debate on the adjournment, even for only half-an-hour, in which the Government is thoroughly exposed and knocked about, would have a far more rapid, beneficial effect than a number of meetings of a select committee, the result of which may be that the Department may become demoralised waiting for the select committee's report, and it might, indeed, slow up the procedure of disposal . . .

But I do say, on the point of exposing a scandal, that a row on the floor in my judgment is quicker and the execution of the axe against the Minister is sharper than in the case of the necessarily more leisurely investigation of a select committee . . . sometimes party bias—a sharp vigorous attack—is in the public interest, and if a Minister is slipping up or something is badly going wrong, the quicker he is knocked about with all the bias, vigour and energy of which the critics are capable, the better. I want Ministers always in their lives to be apprehensive about these potential sharp and vigorous attacks. That is, indeed, under our Constitution the justification for the existence of the Opposition. It is a great blessing, and a great advantage always; and sometimes a great nuisance. But that is what it is for.

CONCLUSIONS

THIS chapter has thrown light on the immense amount of work society has thrust

---

[55] Cf. Mr. Truman's statement refusing data on loyalty, *New York Times*, March 16, 1948.
[56] See for further discussion of the applicability of British question hour to Congress: Herman Finer, *Suggestions for Strengthening Congress* (June, 1946), p. 49 ff.

[57] Third Report, Questions 3393, 3428, 3430.

upon modern legislatures. They desperately struggle with legislation and the control of the administrative departments. They are oppressed by the small amount of time at their disposal, especially if they are serious in a desire to mix with the people of their districts and to move about in the rest of the nation. The legislators need respite from the running of small administrative errands to which their constituents compel them, most pathologically in the government of the United States. However they may be chosen, or upon whatever qualifications, their duty indubitably requires them to specialize to a high degree in knowledge of the apparatus of government in order that they may master the methods of mastering it and may compel it to be the able instrument of a complex society with a passion for enduring freedom. It is an immense responsibility: so onerous, when one looks at the apparatus closely, that one wonders how even the small proportion of legislators who do rise to their obligations have been able to succeed. Above all, in an age of comprehensive government activity, involving the future as well as the present, the executive apparatus is stupendous in its extent and penetration. All the devices we have presented as constituting the machinery of control need repair and rational refinement. Their purpose, methods, and opportunities need also to be imparted to the people, whom they are to help and from which they in turn may get much decisive support.

Hence the vital importance of arranging for open public debate and for questioning the executive in a procedure which is accessible to people and press. Legislatures and executives, but the former more than the latter, have public teaching responsibilities. Their debates can be consciously made part of the regular education of the people. (They *are*, willy-nilly.) This does not call for broadcasting legislative proceedings—for the chance of an exciting debate on an important topic is hard to measure beforehand. It does call, however, for the decision on matters of principle in the full assembly,

or where relegated to committees (which should be as limited in use as possible), to open sessions there.

I am led to the conclusion that much larger parliaments are inevitable necessities of the modern state. They need more committees, or at any rate enough of them, and a representative, which means a larger, number of the legislators on the committees. If these, then, in the process of lawmaking and the control of administration, engage an excessive amount of the time of officials, the answer is that some small addition to the number of officials may be required in order that their number may be adequate to the task of answering for themselves and their colleagues to their controllers. This seems to me to be only rational.

DICTATORIAL LEGISLATURES

THERE is little point in talking about dictatorial legislatures. There is much more point in talking about dictatorial parties, and some attention has been given to this (p. 302 above). The *Reichstag* under the Nazi government was a pure facade, and the assembly, whose members had been carefully chosen by Hitler's hierarchy before submission to the electorate, were a mere claque to rise and applaud as directed. The *Reichstag* could be called only by the *Führer* and the president of the *Reichstag*, Goering. The laws, by force of the Enabling Act of March, 1933, were made by the cabinet, without discussion or ratification by the *Reichstag*.

The Soviet Union has a quadrennial election of the Soviet of the Union and the Soviet of Nationalities. They possess the supreme power in everything—law and administration. But the effectiveness of the Soviet is limited by two factors of dominating potency:

The *first* is the control of the elections by the Communist party, the only legal party and the only one that operates practically.[58] *Second,* the Soviet elects from its midst a body called the Presidium. This consists of thirty-seven members; its chair-

---

58 Cf. p. 255 above.

man is the President of the Soviet Union. The Presidium carries on the government of the Union in the time the Soviet is not in session. It is partly a legislative committee, and partly a cabinet which exercises decisive control over the Council of Ministers (formerly People's Commissars) in their everyday duties of administration. The Presidium is the continuous government of the Soviet Union in fact as well as law. And more so than in law, because (a) it has the right of making ordinances with the force of law (in fact, this is the regular process of lawmaking, leaving out such a law as the one that establishes the five-year plans); (b) it can dismiss and replace ministers, as they are incompetent or retire, in the intervals of Soviet sessions; (c) it can call an election if the two assemblies are in deadlock; and (d) while the assemblies are not yet elected, it exercises power.

The crucial point is: can the Supreme Soviet operate of its own will? The answer is "No." For it is convened by constitutional stipulation twice a year by the Presidium. But the constitution does not say when and for how long the Soviets are to be convened. In fact, the assemblies are called for sessions of something like seven to ten days, on two occasions in the year at a date that pleases the Presidium—on one of these occasions to accept the budget! [59] We know enough already about the difficulties of lawmaking in nations that are far from even approaching the U.S.S.R. in the range of their state activity to know that this is utterly inadequate as parliamentary government, or democratic control!

The mark of independence of a legislature is whether it can convene itself, regardless of the will of the executive. The question hardly arises in the British constitution because of the close correspondence of legislature and cabinet: the House is master. In the Weimar constitution it was stipulated that a petition of one third of the membership could get the *Reichstag* convened—a valuable provision. In the constitution of the Third Republic, the chambers met annually in January; remained in session at least five months; could be and were convened by the President (equals cabinet) at other times; and above all, could convene themselves if an absolute majority of the members of both houses required it. In the constitution of 1946, there is again provision for annual meeting; the total duration of interruptions of each session cannot exceed four months; it is thus in continuous session. Moreover, when it is not sitting, its *bureau* may convoke the Assembly, and it must do so when requested by one third of the deputies or by the premier. The United States Congress is practically independent, within the constitution, of the executive in the periodicity and length of its sessions. In democratic systems the legislature dominates the executive: in the U.S.S.R. in practice, and without constitutional denial, the Presidium dominates the Soviets. Or, in other words, the land is governed by the party and the administration, while the Soviets say "Aye," with no dissentients and no absentees.

---

[59] A good illustration for those who do not read Russian is in the verbatim report of the second session of the Supreme Soviet of the U.S.S.R., August, 1938 (Foreign Languages Publishing House, Moscow, 1938).

22

Proposals and Devices for Improving
Democratic Legislatures

THE actual electoral and parliamentary process already described presents a picture vastly different from that drawn in the pages of Rousseau and elaborated by democratic writers in the nineteenth century. The voter is becoming more than formally sovereign and equal: if he is free, he is not isolated; if unaided, he is not always rational.

In order to express the changing pressure of shifting interests, diverse and competing even within each man and woman, legislative assemblies are guided by all sorts of advisers and deliberative bodies. Advisory committees, commissions of inquiry, economic councils, and the "lobby" exert influence on cabinet and civil service. To judge the efficacy of this concourse of representative institutions, we must consider it as a single operating complex. It is not as yet well systematized, but certainly year by year the parts, old and new, are fitted together more rationally.

Yet there are defects, the chief of which are brought to light by (a) the theory of guild socialism; (b) discussion of the nature of the electoral system; (c) the problem of direct legislation; and (d) the problem of the compulsory vote.

GUILD SOCIALISM[1]

GUILD socialism is the product of two streams of thought: socialist and democratic. These together propose a state in which there shall be at once strict communal control of production and distribution and yet extensive self-determination. The theory of its political machinery revolves around the defects of representative government.

The Theory and its Defects. It is alleged that the central fallacy of representative government is the belief that the representation of one person's will by another is possible. The will is too comprehensive and too subtle in its multitude of components to permit of representation (Thus, originally Rousseau; thus, of recent years Cole and Webb.[2]) But if general representation is impossible, then a territorial system of representation of equal voters in their districts based upon it must be defective. How, in fact? The electoral issues submitted by the parties must be superficial, as empty as they are extensive. They must be dealt with centrally. They must be a confused multiplex, upon most elements of which the electors must necessarily be ignorant. Finally, the argument runs, the central legislature cannot help treating all citizens uniformly instead of diversely. Such a

---

[1] Cf. G. D. H. Cole, *Social Theory* (London, 1920) and *Guild Socialism Re-Stated* (London, 1920); G. C. Field, *Guild Socialism* (London, 1920); W. Y. Elliott, *The Pragmatic Revolt in Politics* (New York, 1923); and F. W. Coker, *Recent Political Thought* (New York, 1934).

[2] Sidney Webb, *A Constitution for the Socialist Commonwealth of Great Britain* (London, 1920), Introduction, p. xiii ff.

system is actually based on territorial con-stituencies in which, in fact, there is no real community of feeling or will since, though people live in the same neighbor-hood, they pursue very different interests. What, in fact, is there to bind the in-congruous, and often hostile, residents of any little area you like to take into a con-stituency? What unity is there which can be said to be representable? These critics answer, "Nothing."

Now this criticism of representation is true enough for actual developments in representative government since Rous-seau's time to make it, as a practical criti-cism, rather immaterial. To temper cen-tralization there is local self-government; to avoid legal uniformity there is the flexible application of statutes by rules and orders made by the administration, whether in the central or local bureauc-racy or through administrative tribunals, before which the interests concerned are represented. In most government depart-ments there are councils composed of ex-perts and representatives of relevant or-ganizations with consultations, or confer-ences, or hearings, or "adversary" hear-ings. Agents are elected to the legislature, appear before legislative committees, ne-gotiate with the cabinet and bill drafts-men. All these formal agencies of decision take no decision before previous discus-sion of their intentions with the pro-ducers, consumers, and cultural organ-izers. Political parties themselves are con-stituted by negotiation with certain groups.

If account of all this is omitted, the nature of modern representative institu-tions is gravely misrepresented. It may be rejoined that only exaggeration can pro-duce desirable reforms. But this is only partly true, for in the exaggeration itself there necessarily exist the germs of serious mistakes. The fascist régime in Italy was based, so far as theory is concerned, upon criticism of representative democracy anal-ogous to guild-socialist criticism, and nat-urally what was deemed to be its most powerful pillar was precisely its most faulty one, namely, the portrait of Rous-seauite "free" and "equal" abstractions

unqualified by all the actual devices of modern guild socialism.[3] In *Mussolini's Italy* I have shown how the fascist system, by instituting twenty-two corporations as the "representative" elements, really di-vided the land into twenty-two occupa-tional parties—or tended that way. Also I demonstrated that the corporations were not allowed to will the laws: the inte-grating will was Mussolini and any cronies he cared to consult. The corporative or guild socialist system is defective as an in-tegrating scheme of society, and would break the minimum foundation of perma-nent interests, the creation of centuries. The corporative state worked under the threat of coercion by the integrating ele-ment, the Fascist party. Without dictator and dictatorial party the corporations could not march together.

If the principle of government by con-sent of the governed is accepted, and if that consent is admitted to be shown in free elections, then the integrating will of the nation so emerges from election. If an integrated will is desired, it is most likely to be achieved on a territorial basis in which each electoral district assembles the voters, who are on principle regarded as equal. This is, at any rate, the principle which divides citizens from each other least; and indeed, it can be argued that its appeal to equality and its frown on per-sonal and social and economic differentiae of any kind encourage solidarity. Within the operation of this principle, it is then possible to make many subordinate con-cessions to the differences of corporate in-terests among men and women, and to allow for their representative influence. But once the territorial idea of represen-tation is denounced, and once corporate occupational representation is put in its place, there arises the insoluble problem of proportionately representing the cor-porate bodies. The problem is insoluble by voluntary agreement of the corporate bodies, because they will not accept repre-sentation according to their mere num-bers. Each industry or occupation or pro-

[3] Herman Finer, *Mussolini's Italy* (New York, 1936).

fession regards itself as socially and economically important beyond its simple numbers. It speaks of its production for the nation, its value as a component of national wealth, or (if they are doctors, let us say) of its basic importance as the foundation of all national well-being. They attempt to substitute a calculus of value for the simple arithmetic of men as men.

This so-called occupational or functional representation is socially and politically divisive if it is sovereign in the power to make law, because its animating spirit begins with the idea of differences, and not, as does the idea of territorial representation, with the idea of the equality of citizens. It confuses interests with will. Therefore occupational or functional representation can succeed only where it is subordinate; and it can be subordinate either to the democratically expressed will of a free electorate, guided by political parties, or to a dictator. In Mussolini's case it was to a dictator. His theorists asked me why England had not instituted the system of guild socialism (to them, the "corporate state") when England had been the originator of the theory. The answer was that Parliament was supreme, based on the freely expressed will of the people as equal citizens. Fascist Italy had abolished a free and equal electorate as the political will of the nation— hence the corporations could flourish, but still only as advisers, while the dictator alone willed their comparative ratios of representation.

Experience with economic councils (Weimar Germany and France) also demonstrates the truth of a corollary of this view, as we shall see presently. Serious difficulties had to be overcome in the apportionment of members for each group, and even when an arrangement was secured, hardly anyone was satisfied. Now, these fierce collisions occurred in bodies not with a power of final decision but simply with a power of consultation. Whether or not any of these bodies were in the majority in the economic council, their views were put before the public and ultimately modified by a *Reichstag*

or Chamber elected by territorial constituencies. Is it really conceivable that one could find even a temporary solution if the Guild Congress were a sovereign body?—if it handed down binding decisions and not mere expressions of opinion? The search for a numerical formula would surely end—as it threatened in actual experience—in a decision that since no ultimate test of the social value and conceit of each occupation could be objectively established, the only permanent peace-giving formula is: equal and universal suffrage to a common legislature: that is, the present system. Further, the assumption that men are so much more interested in the affairs of their occupation than in others is not borne out by analyses of voting in their occupational councils.[4] Recent studies have shown that a terrific amount of effort and attention to technique are required to get employers and employed to mind their own business.

The real difficulty, of course, is the management of a vast state which integrates thousands of different personal, local, and syndical interests. It is not soluble by disintegration and the consequent encouragement of guild conceit and selfishness (have we not all an interest in the prevention of corporate and personal abuse of possessions and cultural values as well as in a *post facto* correction of them?). But it is soluble by integration first, and then devolution—legislative and administrative—and always by consultation of the associations and localities. In the center of the integrative process are the communities we call political parties, and legislatures, and the conception of the numerical equality of citizens. Only those who are presumed to be equal will express themselves freely and accept the final decision; only those who are denied their claims to superiority will listen and obey. The present system, put into the

---

[4] Cole has handsomely thrown over the theory of representation he once held—cf. *The Next Ten Years* (London, 1929), p. 158 ff.—largely through a growing disbelief in his former theory that representation was the supreme good, and that representation must be ubiquitous.

form of the accompanying diagram, gives a good idea of the integration of, and mutual influence in and outside, the classical conception of representative government, and shows graphically how institutions have been created to overcome the chief defects announced by critics. (Yet, as we have amply seen, there is much room for improvement in the present system.)

riot decree of 1925, but raised to 173 in the law of March 19, 1936—also was based on delegates from the various occupational groups. Without entering into any great detail, this must be said of these bodies:

First, the *Reichwirtschaftsrat*: Though the government and the *Reichstag* were required to consult it before the introduction of laws of fundamental social and

THE VISCERA OF THE MODERN LEVIATHAN

Showing the Continuous Working Relationship between the Various Electoral, Vocational, Legislative, and Executive Organs of the Modern State

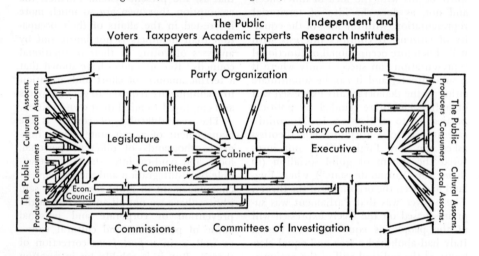

Economic Councils: Germany and France. Weimar Germany and Third Republic France attempted to steer a course beyond territorially based legislatures to include corporate assemblies: the former in the *Reich* Economic Council (*Reichwirtschaftsrat*) and the latter in the *Conseil Économique National*.

The former, based upon article 165 of the Weimar constitution, was an assembly of 300, later 200, formed by (1) delegations from employers and (2) employees of the occupational organizations, represented after a long process of cantankerous bargaining by numbers settled by the government, and (3) a group of government-named experts and consumers' representatives, to act as a balance. The latter—a body of 47 according to the Her-

economic importance, they very rarely did. Nor did the departments often ask for its advice. As soon as it came to speak as an assembly, it acquired parliamentary pretensions, and therefore was too much a rival of the *Reichstag*. Therefore it restricted itself to committee operations, in which its advice was technically good. But it split up into employers', workers', and consumers' groups for operation and voting, so that a blended policy was not obtainable from it. Hence it was cold-shouldered by everybody, particularly by the *Reichstag*, which was jealous, and therefore by the government, which was dependent on the *Reichstag*. It soon lost influence. A parliamentary assembly, elected by the people, believes it is unteachable as an expert on what the people want and need. It is. Hitler abolished the *Reich-wirtschaftsrat*.[5]

The scope of the *Conseil National Économique* was, according to article 1:

the study of problems affecting the national economy, giving opinions on government and private member bills when so requested, examining methods by which such bills may best be administered, and proposing measures for the control and organization of production and exchange.

The prime minister or his deputy was chairman.

In the thirteen years of its existence, the council was useful in making wide-ranging studies and in advising government departments. It, like the *Reichwirtschaftsrat*, worked through committees. The French government was obliged to submit to it bills of economic and social nature, and to report to it within a month what action had been taken on the council's recommendations. It prepared and adopted many reports on problems such as housing, the economic equipment of the nation, transport, foodstuffs, collective-bargaining contracts, and agricultural policy. It is possible to trace a causative influence of the council on the law on transport of 1934, on the collective-bargaining contracts and the forty-hour week of 1936, and, possibly, on the Monnet planning policy for capital equipment developed after World War II. Its recommendations to the government have, on request, included those on French port facilities, refrigerated storehouses, air routes to the East, public works, and the Commerce Exchange.

The Chamber of Deputies overcame an early jealousy of the council. It is noteworthy as a tribute to belief in its effectiveness as an adviser [6] that both drafts of constitutions after World War II included

an Economic Council, and this with little debate, as a matter of course.

The present Economic Council was established in the constitution [7] itself, because the Third Republic's Economic Council, though finally well-founded on the law of 1936, did not thereby acquire a status of clear and significant influence in relationship to the Chamber of Deputies and the Senate. Title III, article 25 of the present constitution prescribes:

An Economic Council, the statute of which is established by a law, examines, in an advisory capacity, projects and propositions of law falling within its competence. Such bills [*projects* and *propositions*] are submitted to it by the National Assembly before it takes them under consideration.

The Economic Council can, further, be consulted by the Council of Ministers. It must be consulted on the establishment of a national economic plan which has the object of full employment and the planned [*rationelle*] utilization of material resources.

The constitutional commission of the National Assembly itself formulated the law on the Economic Council, adopted October 27, 1946.[8] According to this law, the Economic Council is competent to examine bills of an economic and social character, excluding the budget and international treaties of an economic and financial kind, which require the approval of the National Assembly.

It will be observed that the status of the council is clearly consultative in this chief sphere of its competence. It cannot force a government to decide to consult it. There were some members of the Assembly who urged that the Council should have compulsory jurisdiction. But this idea was rejected on the ground that the Economic Council would then be "corporative" in character—that is to say, it would have a part in sovereign legislative power, or to put it in other words, would be a part of the will-organization of the nation rather than merely a thought- or

---

[5] Cf. Lindsay Rogers and W. Dittmar, "Die Reichwirtschaft, *De Mortuis . . ,*" *Political Science Quarterly,* December, 1935.

[6] Cf. G. Cahen-Salvador, "Le Conseil National Economique," in *Revue du Droit Social,* September-October, 1946; and Léon Jouhaux, "Le Rôle du Conseil Économique," *Revue Française du Travail,* August, 1947.

[7] Cf. *Séances de la Commission de la Constitution:* October 21, 1945, pp. 222 ff; 741 ff; June 2, 1946, pp. 58 ff, 463 ff, 680 ff, 770 ff.

[8] *Conseil Économique, Loi numéro 46-2384.*

interest-organization.[9] The *rapporteur,* a socialist, pointed out that to have accorded to the Economic Council an obligatory status would have meant the gravest submission of the agenda of the National Assembly to the Economic Council, since all laws have more or less an economic, social, and financial aspect.

The law goes on to say that the Economic Council *may* be asked for advice on drafts of simple decrees (rules and regulations) and of rules of public administration concerning the national economy. It *must* be consulted during the drafting of rules of public administration made in application of the laws which have been submitted for its advice. It *may* itself undertake the examination of economic, social and financial questions, and for this purpose conduct the necessary inquiries, and in conclusion put forward opinions and recommendations.

The Economic Council gives its counsel on the Plan,[10] and the bills and questions on which it is consulted by the government; on bills submitted to it by the National Assembly and its commissions; or on bills which it itself takes under advisement. It is limited in the time allowed it for such consideration to twenty days, or to the time set by the body requesting advice. Its opinion on rules of public administration arising out of law which it has considered must be given within thirty days.

We have already suggested that the procedure of the National Assembly has provided for the interweaving of the work of the Economic Council and the operations of the Assembly and its commissions, and the law on the council further provides that the opinions of its minority as well as its majority shall come to the ear of the Assembly. Its recommendations must be printed and disseminated among the deputies, and must be read out before the opening of a debate in the Assembly. Furthermore, if the competent minister or commission wish it, the *rapporteur* of the council can participate in the Assembly's debates in order to put forward the views of the council.

Finally, at the request of the parties and of the interested ministers, the Economic Council can be seized with any question relative to economic and social disputes and may eventually play the part of arbiter.

Over the composition of the Economic Council, there occurred hot disputes of the order already mentioned of the Weimar *Reichwirtschaftsrat:* that is to say, disputes about the nature of the constituents and the ratio of representation. It was desired not to set up a competitor to the National Assembly, which must be and remain the central sovereign body in the government. It was not desired to duplicate the many diverse consultative bodies which advise the departments, though whenever the Economic Council wished to bring them into its proceedings it would be able to do so. It was not desired to gather together a body of diverse notables who would be little more than honorific additions to it. Nor was it sensible to stuff the council with every possible representative of every possible interest in the country. In other words,

The commission preferred the conception of a council with inter-professional recruitment, less packed, but more synthetic in its structure, as well as strongly articulated, and above all not running the risk of appearing . . . . as an economic hold-all welcoming in its precincts representatives not infrequently honorific.[11]

The Economic Council contains 164 members who are appointed thereto for three-year terms. They are thus distributed:

(1) 45 nominated by organizations most representative of workers, employees, officials, technicians, engineers, and managers;

(2) 20 representatives of industrial enterprises thus distributed: (*a*) 6 from nationalized enterprises, (*b*) 14 representatives of private enterprises, among which a distinct and proportional representa-

[9] *Débats parlémentaires,* October 3, 1946, p. 4372 ff.
[10] Cf. below, Chap. 24.

[11] Pronteau, rapporteur, *Débats,* October 3, 1946, p. 4370.

tion is assured to big, small, and medium enterprises;

(3) 10 representatives of commercial enterprises, among which a distinct and proportional representation is assured to small commerce;

(4) 10 representatives of artisans.

(5) 35 representatives nominated by the most representative agricultural organizations;

(6) 9 representatives of cooperatives (2 for production, 2 for consumption, 5 for agricultural cooperatives);

(7) 15 representatives of overseas territories;

(8) 10 representatives qualified in French intellectual life (la pensée française), in particular, intellectual workers in the economic and scientific domain;

(9) 8 representatives of family associations;

(10) 2 delegates of federations of societies of wounded, during the period of reconstruction.

All the foregoing delegates are nominated, for each category, in part by professional organizations which are most representative, and in part by the territorial groupings of chambers of commerce and chambers of professions.

It should be observed that the only category which is not designated by a constituent group is that of the intellectual workers. It was proposed, but rejected, that these should be designated by associations, universities, or scientific academies. They are nominated by the government.

Ministers, undersecretaries of state, and commissioners named by the government have the entrée to the Economic Council and must be heard when they request it. Members of Parliament may attend the sessions of the Economic Council. The presidents and rapporteurs of the parliamentary commissions may attend the sessions of the council's commissions.

The Economic Council is mistress of its own procedure, and may conduct its discussions in open or closed session. The suggestion that it should regularly hold public sessions was combated by the rapporteur, who disclaimed any intention to reduce the public impact of the council but drew attention to the observations of M. Cahen-Salvador, the secretary-general of the Economic Council of 1936.[12] Since these are so similar to those expressed in relationship to the privacy of the sessions of the Reichswirtschaftsrat, not a priori but after experience, they deserve quotation: [13]

How is it possible not to be anxious about the consequences of debates carried on in public?

The atmosphere of the Assembly may be changed thereby. The cordiality of relations encouraged by closed sessions risks attenuation or disappearance. Attitudes of command would replace frank explanation. Instead of precise discussion, oratorical tirades would reign. Members would seek less to convince than to parade, less to dissipate misunderstandings than to entertain them in order to draw advantage from them, less to discover motives for reconciliation than to display the reasons for disagreement.

Public deliberations followed with passion by interested listeners, spied on with a malicious vigilance by opposition newspapers, would soon assume, especially in a nation fond of eloquence, a spectacular turn. Words would take precedence over action.

The suggestion that the commissions of the Economic Council might take the place of the consultative bodies within the departments was rejected as mixing different functions. These were more specialized in composition and had a different and narrower purpose than the commissions of the Economic Council.

The composition of the Economic Council does not duplicate that of 1936, but is very similar to it.

We may conclude with the rapporteur's characterization of the Economic Council's function: [14]

The increasing complexity of economic problems, the extreme importance of their solution for the rebirth of the nation, and the technical knowledge this requires, establish a duty for government and Parliament alike of surrounding themselves with all the qualified advice necessary for the sound utilization of all the material resources of the country.

12 From article cited, p. 307.
13 Débats, October 30, 1946, p. 4374.
14 Ibid., October 2, 1946, p. 4711.

Placed by the side of the National Assembly, the Economic Council is called to play a part of the first importance through its advice. It will enlighten it, orient it, and guide it in the discovery of the best solutions. And, concerning itself with very diverse problems, the Council will also express to the government the opinion of men who most usually taking a practical part in production, will bring along with the fruit of their special experience a desire to contribute to the co-ordination of the economic forces of the country.

One of the ideas leading to the creation of the *Conseil Économique* was, according to M. Cahen-Salvador, the desire—and certainly the need—to overcome the specialization of the government departments. His own words are very revealing, since he was not only the secretary-general of the prewar *Conseil,* but he was by profession president of a section of the *Conseil d'État,* that is, the supreme organ of administrative leadership. He said: [15]

Who does not see that each government department, having a defined sphere of power, is naturally inclined to make itself not only the interpreter but also the advocate of the demands of the professional groups which are within its province—and that the ministers, in their turn are—by inclination towards easy solutions, the fear of risks and conflicts, or the quest of popularity—very much readier to support the demands of their administrative clients than to discuss their rightfulness.

The potential value of such economic representative bodies is indubitable. Yet it is imperative that they should never be regarded as more than advisory, since no one would wish to confuse the line of the elected representative body's responsibility for policy. Nor must such an economic council trouble the pride of the popular assembly. It is necessary, though difficult, to arrange the timetable of legislation and debate in such a way as to take advantage of the timely advice of such councils. And, as the experience of the French Economic Council of 1936 suggested, much may be gained by deputing officials to sit with the councils and their committees.

Advisory Bodies in Britain and the United States. In British practice, consul-

tation with economic and social groups occurs by direct contact between them and the executive and the legislature, and by the use of devices like the royal commissions of inquiry. In view of the success of these methods, it has proved unnecessary to provide an additional advisory body. The channels of consultation are so much more closely connected with the executive than the legislature that they are further examined in Chapter 23 on the British cabinet.

In the United States, the nearest approach—and a valuable one at that—to an extraneous, unelected advisory body was the National Resources Planning Board. Its composition and appointment were markedly different from the counseling agencies already discussed: it had a board of several departmental political chiefs, an advisory committee of three "experts" from outside, and a professional staff of full- and part-time researchers. It was an adviser to the executive, and, through its reports, a mentor of Congress and the public. But except for its postwar reconstruction reports (especially that on *Work, Relief, and Social Security*), its counsels were of very long-range outlook and of basic, scientific-research character (e.g., *Technological Trends*), rather than concerned with more immediate policies.[16] Nevertheless Congress regarded it with hostility: it might have outpaced the members of Congress in intellectual ability and public-spirited forethought. Congress abolished it. In so far as its functions survive—and certainly the need for its functions is still pressing—they have been assumed by the Bureau of the Budget and the research units of other executive departments. So long as Congress hears all interests in honestly conducted committee procedure, and so long as it is expertly staffed, this will suffice. But the executive branch still needs its own omni-departmental and especially omni-interest consultant body or bodies; for the executive has a vital legislative as well as politico-

---

15 *Loc. cit.,* p. 302.

16 Cf. J. D. Millett, *The Process and Organization of Government Planning* (New York, 1947), especially pp. 137-52, for a thorough gifted analysis. Cf. also Chap. 26.

administrative contribution to make also. In part, the need is filled by the Council of Economic Advisers, a body of three appointed by the President, as required by the Employment Act of 1946. The act requires Congress to receive the council's regular sessional reports for study and to consider them in a special joint committee. This arrangement also is discussed further in Chapter 26 on the American presidency.

ELECTORAL SYSTEMS

Now we have given reasons for doubting whether there is ever likely to be a representative system which does not depend, in the principal, decisive resort, upon decision by a majority of members representing the citizens as equal. Indeed, we are certain that in the long run there is no other alternative. Then the question immediately arises how best can one attain exact representation.

Establishing the Constituency. The ideal system—that is to say, a system having exactness of representation as its only object—would be that in which the whole nation was taken as a single constituency, where lists of candidates for the whole number of members of the legislature could be presented and advocated by anybody. Such an arrangement, if it could be organized, would provide an exact reflection of majority and minority groups. But its defects are not only serious, they are actually destructive of the values most people want from representative government. Because it presupposes a national campaign, it centralizes authority in the party machine to organize the issues and conduct the campaign. It permits the least degree of local and personal adaptation of the candidates. It abolishes by-elections. It makes the contact between voter and program immediate, when what is needed is the mediation of a candidate between the two, so that he may explain the program to the voter and modify it after observation of the voter's reaction.

In default of this arrangement, what is to be adopted?—the division of the country into constituencies sized according to convenience and equity. Convenience implies that the constituency should be not too large for the maintenance of personal contact between candidate and voters, and, of perhaps more importance, between the local party associations and their clientele in the neighborhood. Equity implies that the constituencies shall be as nearly equal in population as possible. When this principle is applied, not once and for all, but continuously as the distribution of population changes in times of mobility—when it is applied simply and without "management"—then it can be taken by the law of averages, and in the long run, there will be no undue advantage to any party and no disadvantage to any, by reason of this cause alone.

Two practical questions then arise: (1) What is a reasonably sized area, and ought there to be only one or more seats per constituency? (2) In fact, are politicians so unfair as deliberately to produce or maintain inequitable election districts? A word or two on the second question first.

The United States more, perhaps, than any other country has familiarized us with the practice of "gerrymandering" (even as it has invented the word). To "gerrymander" is so to arrange the shape of constituencies that your own party's majorities, however small, are spread over the largest number of constituencies possible, and your opponent's majorities are made as large as they can be in each constituency certain to be won by him, but are restricted to as few constituencies as possible, especially where the contest is close. Now, men seek to cast out the devil from themselves by pledging themselves to a constitution. And in most state constitutions it is provided that electoral districts shall be compact in form, contiguous in territory, and contain the maximum possible equality of inhabitants. Yet even within those requirements the bosses and their henchmen act effectively. However, the system provokes retaliation and public contempt, and if the majorities are spread too well, a slight turnover in votes may cause a loss of the seat.

In England, redistribution has been decided on as an agreed all-party measure of both parties,[17] and has been carried out by an impartial body of commissioners.[18] On the whole, a laudable fairness rules the question. In Germany the principal unfairness until 1919 was in the obstinate refusal to redistribute seats which had been first distributed as far back as 1867; its particular system of proportional representation after 1919 was scrupulous in its equity. In France, what has been called *géographie de circonstance* was extensively practiced until the 1920's, more so before 1870 when the semi-autocratic executive had a vested interest in a pliable parliament. Under the rule of the parliamentary commission on universal suffrage and of the government, which introduced distribution bills, the amount of fraud was small. Like all the manipulators of redistribution, the government found the greatest difficulty in dividing well-knit neighborhoods, whether cities or urban districts, when their population was above the maximum number of inhabitants per constituency; and when the government had planned its redistribution, the parliamentary commission reviewed it in the light of evidence presented by the existing deputies. Yet until 1946 the constituencies varied all the degrees between 22,160 (Lozère) and 120,000 (Grenoble), though the aim was to put the regular minimum at 40,000 and the maximum at 100,000.[19]

Single-member Constituencies. The problems raised by single-member constituencies are different according as the majority required is absolute or relative. In the English and American systems, usually also in the British dominions, only a relative majority (known as a "plurality" in the United States) is required to win the available seat; in other words, whatever the number of candidates, the one at the top is elected. Now this may have results which may be considered to be highly inequitable, for it is

17 Cf. John Morley, *Life of Gladstone* (London, 1905), Vol. II.
18 Cf. report of Electoral Boundary Commissioners, 1918, and Speaker's Conference on Electoral Reform and Redistribution of Seats, May, 1944.
19 *Rapport Supplémentaire* No. 4625 (Baréty), *Chambre des Députés*, 1927.

TABLE 14—BRITISH GENERAL ELECTION RESULTS, 1929 TO 1945, FOR SEATS ACTUALLY CONTESTED

Year	Party	Votes (in millions)	Seats
1929[a]	Conservative	8.660	256
	Labour	8.385	288
	Liberal	5.309	59
	Others	2.94	5
	Total	23.647	608
1931[b]	Government parties	14.532	493
	Labour	6.648	46
	Independent Liberal	.106	4
	Others	.371	5
	Total	21.657	548
1935[c]	Government parties	11.790	405
	Labour	8.325	141
	Independent Labour Party	.140	4
	Independent Liberal	1.443	38
	Others	.300	8
	Total	21.998	596
1945[d]	Labour (and L.L.P. and Commonwealth)	12.150	397
	Conservatives	8.665	189
	Liberals	2.240	12
	Communists	.103	2
	Independents	.157	14
	Miscellaneous anti-Labour (including Liberal National)	1.450	26
	Total	24.765	640

a Seven seats were not contested. Cf. R. W. G. Mackay, *Coupon or Free* (London, 1943), p. 33.
b Sixty-seven seats were uncontested. *Ibid.*, p. 34.
c Forty seats were uncontested. *Ibid.*, p. 36.
d Fifteen seats were uncontested, but they are included in the totals of the seats. Cf. Macculum and Readman, *British General Election, 1945* (Oxford, 1947), pp. 248–52.

clear that as soon as more than two candidates compete, the topmost candidate may secure election by a minority of the votes cast in the constituency. This may produce injustices in some constituencies and general nation-wide misrepresentation.

In Great Britain, for some years after the rise of the Labour party with the continuance of the other two parties, many three-cornered contests were fought, with perturbing results. The results are shown in Table 14.[20]

Now it may be argued that the luck of the ballot will be evenly spread among the various parties, as a whole. This may be so, and at one election luck was almost exactly evenly distributed. Yet it is only hazard. The progress of constitutional development shows a continuous desire of mankind to ascend from hazard to controllable principle.

What is to be done? Neither the French nor the Germans before the introduction of proportional representation nor many parts of the British dominions leave the matter to chance. They use either the second-ballot or the alternative-vote system.

The Second Ballot and the Alternative Vote. Both repose on the principle that no one should be returned to Parliament who only has the support of less than 50 per cent of the voters.[21] They make an attempt to secure an absolute majority for the ultimately elected candidate, but they proceed by different methods. The second-ballot system involves a general election which, in each constituency, gives either one of the candidates or none an absolute majority: if the former, he is duly elected; if the latter, then a second election occurs, when all the candidates below the top two drop out, and the second contest is between these two. This second ballot occurred in France up to 1914, a fortnight after the first; by the Electoral Law of 1927 it occurred one week after the first.[22] In 1946, however, France established proportional representation, which is described presently. For the German *Reichstag* up to 1918, similarly.[23]

The merit of the second ballot is that it gives people the opportunity of reconsidering their vote when they know by the first result that certain candidates are out of the running and that their choice is now restricted. Many cannot have the man or woman they most prefer; they are given the opportunity of deciding which of the remaining candidates is nearer their first preference. There is one other merit: the successful candidates will make law and control administration. It is, in the long run, essential that the general body of citizens shall be satisfied with the equity of the system of government, and they are most likely to be satisfied if it can be shown that government rests on a majority of popular votes as well as of parliamentary seats. Now, the majority produced by the system of the second ballot or the alternative vote is a kind of second-best, not a wholehearted first choice, and it cannot be called as sound a majority as if it were composed altogether of first preferences. Yet the people may think so, or at least be satisfied that this majority, however compounded, is better than pure minorities. The statesman cannot reject such a factor.

Yet decades of actual electoral experience have demonstrated serious demerits in the second-ballot system. They are concisely and authoritatively represented in a report of the French Chamber of Deputies:[24]

(1) The respective situation of parties is falsified. It is impossible to gauge the importance of the various political groupings by reference to the results of the second ballot; the victories won on the second ballot are the product of a transaction most often obtained to the detriment of ideas and programs; (2) It often happens that these bargains are arranged under conditions which have nothing at all to do with political contests and which M. Dessoye, *rapporteur* of the Law of 12 July, 1919, called "obscure anxieties"; (3) The possibility of a second election even falsifies the results of the first. A large number of electors, in fact, use the first ballot for manifestations of sympathy or personal rancour and wait until the second round to ex-

---

[20] In the election of 1945, 117 minority members were elected.

[21] J. H. Humphreys, *Proportional Representation* (London, 1910).

[22] Rabany, *Guide General des Élections* (Paris, 1928).

[23] Julius Hatscheck, *Parlamentsrecht* (Berlin, 1915), p. 388 ff.

[24] *Rapport Supplémentaire*, No. 4625 (Baréty), *Chambre des Deputés*, 1927.

press their political sentiments. Others, finally, give their votes to such and such a candidate, solely to produce another election; (4) The second ballot engenders a recrudescence of violence which is not calculated to heighten the morality of the election. Further, it is an extra source of expenses, and the prospect of a second round may suffice to keep out of the struggle candidates who are poor.

Now, some of these criticisms apply more particularly to France; not that they will not apply elsewhere, for every institution has its consequences, good and bad —but the intensity and quality vary in different human and organizatory environments. Matters, for example, were particularly bad in France because of the weakness and multiplicity of parties and a tradition of electoral corruption—there is ample evidence of the unholy bargains produced, especially in the interval between the ballots. From France we have the phrase that the elected deputy is "the prisoner of the minority"; [25] from Germany before 1919 the term *Kuhhandel,* cattle dealing, among the parties. Nor were, nor are, the arrangements made between the parties, before and during the elections, for mutual support at the first or second ballot, always kept. Who knows what emergency will arise in the space of four years to make it nationally impolitic as well as undesirable for the party that engagements should be kept? Nor is the location of responsibility clarified. The second ballot was indeed disturbing, since, in French conditions, it decides the complexion of the new chamber. These were the numbers of second ballotings:

1889	211	
1896	178	
1902	174	
1906	157	in Assemblies
1910	227	of about 600
1914	252	members.[26]
1928	425	
1932	359	
1936	424	

[25] Cf. Bonnafous, *Le Scrutin d'Arrondissement et la Politique* (Paris, 1926).
[26] Cf. Georges La Chappelle, *Les Elections Legislatives* (Paris, 1924, 1928, 1932, and 1936).

To avoid the evils peculiar to a second ballot, the alternative vote was invented. In this system there is only one election, and the voter numbers his preferences at once, saying, in effect, "If my first-preference candidate does not succeed, then divide my second and third vote preferences among the top candidates." There are two ballots in one operation.[27] This, in fact, avoids the double expense and the double turmoil, but it does not get rid of interparty bargaining which occurs before the election. There is no doubt that the arrangement gives a peculiarly forceful position to the minorities, in the election as in the legislature: a direct product of the electoral method in combination with the existence of several independent parties determined to live in independence. Confusion in the executive begins with electoral confusion.

Proportional Representation: Theory. From the standpoint of exact representation alone, the systems already discussed may be improvements on the single-member constituency with relative majority, but they have still serious defects. (1) The actual majorities and minorities may still not be proportionately represented in the house; (2) certain small minorities may still not be represented at all. These criticisms have been urged by a long line of theorists and politicians without distinction of party, and their political import must not be underestimated. Nothing less than the authority of government is in question. At some junctures and in some legislatures a few votes may make all the difference, for years. It is of the greatest importance that no citizen should have sound reasons to believe that he is being commanded, perhaps coerced, it may be in most vital matters, by a minority. Hence the demand for mathematically exact representation of the electorate.

What does this involve? It involves always, whatever the diverse technicalities and whatever the size of the constituency, multiple-member constituencies. The number of seats available must be large enough to give to each coherent, well-

[27] Cf. Humphreys, *op. cit.*

knit group of voters with a faith sufficiently different from that of others the assurance of independent existence.[28] The number might be 5000 or 10,000 or 30,000, or smaller or larger—how much it shall be must depend upon the total number of representatives which are considered to be sufficient, and not too many, to compose a technically convenient legislature. Only if there are constituencies with several seats can there be the independent representation of minorities and majorities—for it is obvious that one man cannot be all things to all men.

Now it is rare that a judgment of a system is formed by reference to a single merit or demerit, and so with the various arrangements for proportional representation. If there were no adverse consequences to count then we should say, "Representation means mathematically exact representation; the single-member constituency stands in the way; it must be abolished." Omelets cannot be had without the sacrifice of eggs. Is the omelet worth it? That is the question. It is urged by many students that the procedure involved in producing mathematically exact representation involves the loss of other very important qualities in government, and that this must be taken into account in a judgment of the system. The issues involved become most clear if we review two of the many varieties of proportional representation possible. I take first the system which actually operated for the German *Reichstag* from 1919 to 1933, and then the system instituted in Fourth Republic France.

Proportional Representation in Weimar Germany. The principle of proportional representation was laid down by the Weimar constitution, and special laws determined the details of the system.[29]

The original arrangement was elaborated hurriedly in consequence of the sudden determination to hold elections for the Constituent Assembly of 1919. The impulse to proportional representation was immensely strong; it was compounded of devout worship of democracy by the revolutionary parties, belief that governmental justice was obtainable only by proportional representation, and the terrific reaction from the injustice of the old single-member, second-ballot system and the maldistribution of seats.

Broadly the characteristics were these:

The whole country with 65,000,000 inhabitants was divided into 35 constituencies (*Wahlbezirke*). (Great Britain, with 47,000,000 inhabitants, has about 610 constituencies.) The average size of a German constituency was 1,700,000 inhabitants, or about 1,150,000 registered voters. The largest was Württemburg, with a little over 2,500.000 inhabitants, and the smallest, East Hanover, with about 1,000,-000. These constituencies were then further grouped into 16 conjoint constituencies (*Wahlverbände*); in some cases the original constituencies were left, in others two or three were combined. The average number of seats per constituency was eleven.

The parties established a list of candidates for each constituency. The characteristics of the list are important: parties were named on the list; this was not so originally, but by 1924 politicians had discovered that the names of the candidates were insufficient indication to the voters. In addition, on the ballot paper, each party was designated by a number, and this was determined by the strength of the party in the last *Reichstag*, e.g., the Social Democrats, List I.

(1) It was not compulsory to name more than four candidates; that is, after the first four candidates were named on each list, the voters might be confronted with and might vote a blank support to a party organization which had the power to fill the places to which it became entitled.

(2) The list in any one constituency could be joined with that of any other within the conjoint constituency upon

<hr>

[28] For the case of proportional representation cf. Humphreys, *op. cit.* and *Practical Aspects of Electoral Reform* (London, 1922). Cf. also F. A. Hermens, *Democracy or Anarchy?* (Notre Dame, 1941); C. S. Hoag and S. H. Hallett, *Proportional Representation* (New York, 1937); and for theory and Irish practice, J. Hogan, *Election and Representation* (Dublin, 1945).
[29] Cf. article 22, and G. Kaisenberg, *Die Wahl zum Reichstag* (3rd edition), 1928.

declaration, and this gave small parties the opportunity to combine their strengths by arrangement in different parts of the country. Thus there were large constituencies with your list of candidates, and the possibility of combining your list with that in a contiguous constituency.

(3) Each party established a list of candidates for the whole of the Reich (*Reichslist*).

(4) The electors had one vote each. They had to accept the whole list and nothing but the list, by marking across in a circle at the top of the list in the ballot paper, and the votes went to the list, not to separate candidates.

(5) For each 60,000 votes a party was entitled to one member: e.g., for 260,000 votes, there were four seats plus 20,000 surplus votes.

(6) Now, in a perfect system of proportional representation, such surplus votes, which might be as many as 59,999 in any constituency, must not be lost. Therefore all surplus votes were collected and aggregated within each of the sixteen conjoint constituencies, and, again, for each 60,000 of these the party got one more seat. But if the surplus in any constituency was not more than 30,000 or over, the surpluses were not counted. Finally, surpluses in the conjoint constituencies (and in single constituencies where the parties have declared for a direct transfer to the *Reichslist*) were swept together and ascribed to their *Reichslist* of candidates. Here, again, each block of 60,000 votes secured a candidate for the whole *Reich*. If after this division there were still surplus votes, then the fraction of 30,000 and over obtained one seat. There was one qualification: in order to avoid the fostering of small parties, no party could receive more members from its *Reichslist* than it obtained in the constituencies. For example, if a party had four members in the constituencies it could not have more than four from the *Reich* surplus. The system was almost perfect in its equity from the standpoint of a "snapshot," but not quite. For we must not forget that, though the intention

was to be absolutely equitable, small and scattered parties were deliberately put at a disadvantage to avoid the fragmentation of the party system and the consequent difficulties in forming stable coalition governments.

(7) There were no provisions for by-elections; therefore, when the ordinary lists were being drawn up by the party organizations, substitutes were added to provide for possible vacancies.

Thus the general characteristics of the system were: the largeness of the constituencies; the length of the lists; the combination and reward of the surpluses, particularly on the *Reichslist* (this, together with the ascription of seats to each 60,000 votes obtained, earned the system the title of "automatic system"); and the absence of by-elections.

Weimar Germany had eight elections under this system, on which important hypotheses may be based. Whereas there was a fervent belief in the system at the outset, within a decade there were serious doubts, and plans for reform before the *Reichstag*.

In judging an electoral system three main questions always arise: is it mathematically equitable? does it produce a wholesome contact between constituents and representatives? does it favor or jeopardize governmental stability? To the first the German answer is, "Yes"; to the second a decided, "No"; to the third, that it jeopardizes governmental stability. Upon what facts and reasoning are these answers returned?

The system tends to split up big parties and to encourage the formation and independence of separate groups. Before 1918 there were seven big parties in Weimar Germany; in 1932 over a score were electorally alive. The tendency was toward a further disintegration. How far was proportional representation, in fact, responsible? German social conditions, even apart from the electoral system, favored the creation of electoral parties, partly owing to the national genius for association, but largely owing to the full and sudden onset of democratic government with its fissiparous temptations, in an age when the whole world was affected by a rather implacable division of economic and class interests. In England and in the United States, the party system preceded contemporary social and economic sectionalism, and still contains, though with enormous strain, the hostile elements.

Yet proportional representation itself positively contributes to the aggravation of successful sectionalism. In England a small party—for example, the United Empire party (1931)—would fail to secure a single seat and would either die out or make alliances. (So later with the Commonwealth party, a World War II mushroom.) With the German system, its surpluses over 30,000 in a constituency of, say 500,000 would be swept together, and the small party would receive seats. In Germany it was possible for the Christian and the atheistical peasantry to be separately organized; for the Catholic and the Protestant or atheistical artisan to be separately organized; for the large and small landowners to maintain separate groups; for the National Socialists to confront international socialists; for the Liberal party to lose, one by one, its constituent middle-class elements, which organized severally; for the Communist party to thrive under a rigid separation from democratic socialists.

The evil is grave, for two reasons: *First,* it makes more difficult the formation of governments, for by giving the groups independent strength in their own right, one more corporate conceit and resistance is fortified. *Second,* and perhaps of greater ultimate importance to society, is the driving of a number of nation-wide wedges deep into the body of the electorate, producing sections which it is important not to make hostile (as this does) but to integrate. A human tendency may be either promoted or counteracted by an institution. And the separatist mentality is promoted by the automatic-list system, and counteracted by the single-member majority system.

The list system causes vested interests to gain control of parties. Parties can calculate accurately, within a margin of

10 to 20 per cent, how many members will get in. In single-member constituencies they cannot: for that is a system of ever contingent electoral revulsion. Economic interests approach the party leaders and offer support of all kinds in return for the names on the list. This happens in all modern democracies, but it is easier to effectuate with the list system.

The central difficulty of the system is, of course, the large constituency and the long list, which inevitably throws into the hands of the parties, and more, the central council of the parties, the selection of candidates. It is even complained that the principle of direct election is infringed by the extent to which the parties intervene between the electors and the candidates. Further, if the party leaders settle the lists of names, they can demand unconditional allegiance from the successful candidates, and as a result the members' attention is turned always more to the party machine than to the constituency. Now, we have shown that in England also the parties are centralized and have a strong control over candidates, but there is always the chance that the candidate and the constituency may revolt. There is a rather subtle personal relationship between the member and the constituency which makes the dictatorship of party leaders effectively challengeable. A constituency may rather pride itself on the heterodoxy of a member above the average in ability; and at any rate the member has a definite circle of constituents to whom to appeal. In the German system, to whom could the heterodox appeal for support? He was one of a team, and was hand-picked.

Nor should we forget that whereas in England 640 local associations of each party participate in the choice of candidates, and in France 679 (1946), and in the United States 435 Congressional electoral districts, in Germany there were 35, or even less, centralized authorities for the choice and placing of candidates. Which system better promotes the real selection of a representative, or in other words, which is more representative? Further, a very large number of members were not elected in the constituencies at all, but from the *Reichslist*, which was established by the central party organization. Thus about one sixth to one ninth of the total membership of the *Reichstag* came from the *Reichslist* in various elections.[30] In other words, in regard to a large number of candidates, those elected on the surpluses, the electors did not know at all for whom they were voting, nor in the end, who were elected.

In the place of a large number of personal contests, there are conflicts of national party programs; not that in the first case there is no reference to personal character and deviations from the program. However, there is a difference and its effects are variously valued. Some say that stable, unyielding party machines and programs fostered by the system are desirable. But the main, I believe the overwhelming, body of opinion considers the concentration of power in the party leaders and party officialdom a dangerous source of misrepresentation of the dynamic and inventive impulses of the party. After all, if local and sectional differences are made impossible within existing parties, an extra reason is supplied for the formation of new ones.

Further, the campaign becomes less intensive, and more extensive: that is, it does not occupy itself with the cultivation of the individual voter by personal appeals, but in the institution of monster demonstrations, like processions, in which the mechanical apparatus for making a noise or creating a diversion is predominant. It is argued that the system makes it impossible for new leaders to grow and take command of the party forces. (This is a direct corollary of the previous argument.) But this is already going too far; it did not prevent Hitler and Brüning from coming to the fore. Yet there is a better chance for technicians in Germany to enter Parliament, since it is possible to calculate pretty certainly on the capture of seats, especially on the *Reichslist;* but is that desirable?

---

[30] From *Hauptergebnisse der Wahlen zum Reichstag,* published by the *Deutsches Statistisches Amt* after each election.

Between 1924 and 1933 projects of reform were plentiful, for on the whole, Germany was profoundly dissatisfied with the consequences of the system. The Germans wanted the equity of the system but not a number of small parties, which endangered the stability of government. They wished to rid themselves of the machine character of the party and to establish a more living connection between the deputy and the constituency. The common suggestion is single-member constituencies. These constituencies would be grouped into about fifteen associated constituencies. Each member would fight alone in the single-member constituencies and if he got the quota (e.g., 60,000 votes) he would be elected. If more than the quota were obtained, the surplus would go to his party colleagues in other constituencies who would benefit in the order of the votes they themselves had earned. At this point the reformers parted company, some wishing to abolish the *Reichslist,* others to maintain it.

Proportional Representation in Fourth Republic France. The Fourth Republic has instituted proportional representation, not without much agony. None of the parties wished a return to the single-member constituency and the second ballot. All spoke of abstract electoral justice, but it is notable that each was spurred on by the advantages to it of proportional representation. The strongest advocates of it were the Communist party—to the point of establishing one single national list! They regarded the single-member constituency as an agency of unholy compromises, where the Right would vote for Communists and Communist votes might be used for Right-wing deputies. They were the most resolute opponents of the voters' exercise of a preferential choice among candidates—whether on national or departmental or more local lists—and above all, they resisted the proposal of the M.R.P. allowing the voter to write in candidates not in the list or split his ticket —called *panachage.* The big parties were prepared to be brutal at the expense of the weaker, like the Radical-Socialists and the Right-wing groups, by keeping them off the slate unless they had lists in at least twenty departments, or by denying them the benefit of a share in the distribution of surplus votes above the quotas, when all gathered together, unless they had obtained over five per cent of the total votes cast at the election. These unjust proposals came to nothing.

The law of October 5, 1946, makes the departments the electoral constituencies, except that the six largest are each divided into a number of more conveniently-sized constituencies. Each party or other grouping puts up a list containing the number of candidates equaling the number of seats for the constituency. This number is settled in the law: the largest is ten candidates for Finistère with 483,000 registered voters, and the same for Gironde with 515,000 voters; the smallest the Basses Alpes, with two candidates and 56,000 voters—the others range between. No lists may be incomplete; no names may be written in by the electors; the candidates are put in the order of the party's preference and will be elected unless the voter states a preference, which he may do by writing in a preferential number on the ballot paper. The voter may vote only for one list. The seats are first distributed to each list of candidates according to the number of votes obtained by the list, divided by the average votes cast by the electorate per seat available. Then the seats in each list are divided in the order presented or according to the preference expressed. No provision is made for remainders to be nationally gathered and again divided, as was the case in the Weimar Republic.

It cannot be disputed that what led to this change in postwar France was a universal disgust with the single-member constituency, where electoral horse trading was promoted by the want of firm party organization and loyalty and was further aggravated by the second-ballot system in pursuit of an absolute majority for the winning candidate. However, a further extremely important motive was the feeling of each party that since it was not likely to win a majority by itself, which would have given it the single-handed control of the legislature and the executive (as is normally the case in England), it was just as well to compound for a system which would assure it of all the votes that it could muster as a minority. For the certainty that it could not be ground down by the operation of the fortunes of nonproportional representation—even if by giving this up it lost some chance of being overrepresented—gave it a continuing strength in negotiation with other similarly placed parties in the formulation of the laws and the formation of cabinets. Proportional representation would enable them to harden their hearts. A cause of proportional representation, therefore, was the multiplicity of parties: and conversely, an effect of it is the further encouragement of such a multiplicity. No party was more coolly calculating in this debate than the Communist. If it were a majority, so much the better, power would follow numbers. If it were a minority, then polling all its strength and obtaining a proportionate number of deputies, it could not be left out of account in the process of government. And when the time came to establish the constitution, it used the common acceptance of proportional representation in the electoral process as an argument for carrying it through with relentless logic in the procedure of the Assembly, wherever power was located: for example, in the Assembly's presiding *bureau*.[31]

The Communist party's logic was also combined with its determined, complete control over the parliamentary actions of the deputies, and arrogation of the right to compel these to resign from the Assembly or Council of the Republic when the party leadership thought desirable. Though there is not much complaint from the various deputies of the leadership's control in any party, independent publicists deplore the party oligarchical tendencies of proportional representation, reducing the independence of the deputies.

Of course, there is no such thing as

---

[31] Cf. p. 482 above.

P.R. in the Soviet electoral system: winner takes all!

DIRECT LEGISLATION

THE difficulties of representation have sometimes led to, among other things, the demand that parliamentary and party government shall be at least mitigated, if not displaced, by the direct action of the people.

Its Varieties. The maximum demand (as in the Bolshevist theory of government and that prevalent in some American states) [32] is for the right to elect and recall, at short intervals, all the elective officers of government, judicial and executive, except the legislative. In the French constitutional debates of 1946, the French Communist party expressed an inclination for recall of deputies, failing which the party claimed the right "on behalf of the people" to compel deputies in the party to resign from the Assembly. A more moderate demand is for direct legislation, that is, the initiative and the referendum. In both of these devices the people are formally called upon immediately, and not through the intervention of political parties, to record their votes on projects submitted to them. In the referendum, the legislature refers its work to the people for approval or disapproval. In other words, by the referendum, it is intended that the people shall have the opportunity of passing judgment upon a bill which has already been dealt with by the people they have elected; by the initiative, it is intended that they shall be able to introduce legislation which their elected representatives have not, for some reason, already handled.

Its Advocates. Now as soon as these institutions are examined, it will be seen that their merits are built upon real or presumed deficiencies in modern parliamentary systems.

(1) The arguments were most fully adumbrated, in relation to a practical constitution, in the German Constitutional Assembly of 1919. Direct legislation was recommended to correct the internal difficulties of Parliament resulting from the fragmentation and uncompromising attitude of political parties. These difficulties of Parliament either produced unholy partisan arrangements, giving a majority to an accidental coalition, when the result ought to be referred to the people, or else prevented legislation from getting beyond the initial stages. In other words, the party system may be so lacking in suppleness that it splits up the general will, and the only way to retrieve the general will is to take the proposals directly to the people. The fear that a temporary majority will unfairly rush into legislation is very strong.

(2) Next, as in the example of the Australian constitution, direct legislation was recommended as a device for breaking a deadlock between the two chambers. This is an old, tarnished claim of the British House of Lords. It was, in fact, apart from the use of direct legislation in constitutional amendments, proposed by Preusz as the only occasion for the use of the referendum in the German constitution.

(3) Direct legislation was proposed as a corrective of the petrifying effects of proportional representation (a mistake and its corrective both together!), it being argued that the system used in Germany would promote the permanent reign of a number of party officials and the hierarchy of leaders. These might be stupid and ossified, and the means to make a fresh wind blow was a direct appeal to the people!

(4) Finally, conservative parties usually believe that direct legislation is, on the whole, conservative rather than progressive. What this means, and whether and why it is true or untrue, we explore presently (p. 564 ff.). Its converse is the Leninist-Stalinist argument that the people are not bold social reformers, and therefore a vanguard must pioneer for them and even over them!

It is already clear, however, that the discussion of direct legislation cannot take

---

[32] Cf. J. Q. Dealey, *The Growth of American State Constitutions* (Boston 1915); and W. Brooke Graves, *American State Government* (New York, 1936).

place in a vacuum, but must be put into this context: whether, on the whole, the complex of representative institutions (the parties, the vocational and cultural groupings, etc.), which already produces a very close approximation of popular will and legislative result, can be improved by direct legislation.

Existing Legal Arrangements For Direct Legislation. Let us begin by observing the actual conditions prescribed for the exercise of direct legislation. Distinctions are made between constitutional, ordinary, and financial legislation. In most of the American states (but not in the federation),[33] in Switzerland,[34] and in Australia, a constitutional amendment must be compulsorily referred to the people for their direct vote. We have already explored the reasons for this: certain rights and obligations are considered to be so important that a change is made especially difficult. We also showed that the essential aimed at is care in the legislative process, and that this is produced by a compound of the actual electoral process, the quality of parties, the quality of the men and women in the parties, the nature of parliamentary procedure, and the general

---

[33] The account relating to the United States has been obtained from A. L. Lowell, *Public Opinion and Popular Government*, 2nd edition (New York, 1919); A. N. Holcombe, *State Government in the U.S.A.*, 3rd edition (New York, 1931); A. F. MacDonald, *American State Government* (New York, 1940); A. W. Bromage, *State Government and Administration* (New York, 1936). These books refer to the older treatises of Oberholtzer and others, which are, however, of small critical value. Cf. also V. O. Key and W. W. Crouch, *The Initiative and Referendum in California* (Berkeley, 1939); W. Schumacher, "Thirty Years of People's Rule in Oregon," *Political Science Quarterly*, June, 1932; J. K. Pollock, *The Initiative and Referendum in Michigan* (Ann Arbor, 1940); and particularly H. Gosnell and M. J. Schmidt, "Popular Law Making in the United States" (New York State Constitutional Convention Committee, 1938), Vol. 7.
[34] The account relating to Switzerland is from Lowell, *op. cit.*; Felix Bonjour, *Real Democracy in Operation* (London, 1922); L. C. Brooks, *Government and Politics in Switzerland* (New York 1918), p. 134; W. E. Rappard, *The Government of Switzerland* (New York, 1936), p. 55 ff, and *La Constitution Fédérale de la Suisse* (Neuchatel, 1948).

probity of the civilization in which these function. There is no escape from the conclusion that whether or not a formal and compulsory referendum on constitutional amendments is desirable depends upon the combination and relative quality of these elements in different countries. In England as we have shown, the House of Lords, and the circles of whose minds it is a specimen, certainly believe in the desirability of such a referendum. Its formal introduction involves the duty of writing the constitution, and reforming the body which can demand such a referendum, as in Switzerland, where 50,000 votes may initiate amendments; so in many American states, and in Germany under the Weimar constitution.

On ordinary laws there is curiously no initiative in the federal authority of Switzerland, for most of the arguments which apply to the other forms of direct legislation would seem to apply to this: but the cantons have this form. However, the constitutional initiative is wide enough to include ordinary legislation when proposed as a constitutional amendment, and this, which is found in some states of the United States also, is a defect rather than a merit—to put ordinary laws into the constitution. Several states in the United States have the ordinary initiative, the practice having been begun in 1898. In the German constitution of 1919 the initiative on ordinary laws also appears. In America more states permit the initiated law to go to the people directly, than allow it to go indirectly through the legislature first, for the amendment or counterproposal. In America also, all the states having a constitutional initiative permit the direct placing of the amendment before the people. In the Swiss federation (and formerly in Weimar Germany) the proposal goes first to the legislature. The American practice of permitting direct proposition to the people has the serious potentiality of reducing the credit of the legislature and permitting badly drafted and unsound legislation.

In Switzerland, many American states, and Weimar Germany, laws already passed may be referred to the people upon petition of a certain number of voters. This is called the *optional referendum*. In all these cases, no distinction is made between one proposal or another according to their natural subject matter or according to the complexity or technical difficulty of the legislation. The ordinary conditions having been met, the people are sovereign, except in the cases where the result infringes a superior constitution, as in the United States, Switzerland, and Weimar Germany.[35]

However, in some cases direct legislation is subject to certain statutory or administrative limits. Thus, in the Swiss federation the referendum can be applied only to laws "and resolutions of general application and which are not of an urgent character." This clause has been interpreted as excluding treaties, the budget, and grants-in-aid for local improvements. A similar "urgency" clause is found in the American state constitutions: [36] in the German federal constitution and in the German state constitutions there are also similar exemptions.

Now, what is the inward significance of these limitations: urgency, general application, and finance? The makers and interpreters of constitutions have feared the ignorance or the selfishness of the voters. Have they had good reason for this fear? Experience shows that they have. The people have been irrational in regard to sanitary measures, on the grounds that their individual liberty will be limited; niggardly, and even spiteful, in relation to the salaries of public officers; inclined to get special advantages for their own locality without any account of the public cost; and steadily against the assumption of tax burdens although prepared to receive public benefits. Evidently the people needed assistance and leadership.

---

[35] Equally in a state within the German *Reich*. Cf. F. Fleiner, *Schweizerisches Bundesstaatsrecht* edition (Tübingen, 1923), p. 274 ff; There is an edition of 1935.

[36] Cf. Lowell, *op. cit.*, p. 175: "Urgent for the public peace, health or safety." The power is freely used. Cf. also W. F. Dodd, *State Government* (New York, edition 1928), pp. 517-19.

Let us consider the results of experience somewhat more closely, first in Switzerland and the American states and then in Weimar Germany.

Direct Legislation in Switzerland and the American States. Numerically, the opportunities of direct legislation have been amply used in Switzerland and the American states—in some American states too often for the peace of the electorate, its interest in the subject, and its capacity to discriminate and judge. In Switzerland the referenda from 1874 to 1939 showed the Swiss people to be anxious for liberal political rights, severe to murderers, unfriendly to the process of centralization, in favor of tariff duties, occasionally anti-Semitic, a drag on state activity in the control or management of industries, supporters of domestic virtue (in the marriage and liquor laws), steadily austere (especially in the cantons) in relation to the payment of public officials, and unenlightened regarding public-health measures. On the whole one may say the effect has been gradualist; or, in other words, the assemblies were ahead of the people. Moreover, the people have certainly not acted spontaneously, but have, in fact, been strongly incited and whipped up and informed by the same processes of electoral campaigning by political parties and ancillary organizations as we find in democracies without direct legislation. In the American states, direct legislation has fairly effectively coped with the organized spoliation of the public by industrial, commercial, and financial bandits, and has effected constitutional reorganizations. The technical subjects like administrative reforms or election procedure have called forth less response than moral issues like education, cruel sports, liquor. Apart from this, a generally conservative and parsimonious attitude was adopted both to proposals emanating from the legislature, and more so, naturally, to the groups of reformers who initiated proposals. Conservative treatment has been given appropriations for education, and proposals involving taxation, and the principles and machinery of taxation. The initiative has given a heaven-sent opportunity to professional and manufacturing pressure groups to push proposals for their special advantage, while the citizens in general have not been impelled to initiate measures.

Now these very results might confirm the belief of some people in the virtue of the referendum at least. On what is this obvious conservatism based? It is due to the natural selfishness of the individual who can be made to bear a social burden only if he is thoroughly informed as to its meaning, its individual benefit to him as well as the social benefit—or, failing this, if he is either induced to trust certain leaders who can take a broader view than he (especially as the main burden will be not on the leader but on other people), or, again, if he is simply compelled by those who know better. Direct legislation places the weight upon the first of these factors.

But, as we have seen, the average elector is not highly educated or naturally apt to place confidence in education, so that unless there is a radical alteration of our present form of living and formal social education and culture, the making of law will be confided to people who cannot bear the burden. Forthwith they become the natural prey of political parties and pressure associations who, in most cases, think for them and force them into paths the character of which they cannot independently understand. We have already shown that some politicians succeed by window dressing and the offer of free pleasures and the pretense that there are no burdens to be borne. In most cases, that is, at the present stage of democratic development, unavoidable: otherwise the people would destroy themselves.

These considerations are borne out by observation of the actual voting in direct legislation both in Switzerland and the United States. Broadly these conclusions emerge: that the percentage of voters is small, the average being barely 50 per cent, this rising to as much as 70 per cent and 80 per cent in issues which stir the moral conventions or the property instinct, and falling, though rarely, to 20 per cent and lower where important but technical issues relating to administration are involved; that the votes in direct legislation are most usually between 10 per cent and 20 per cent lower than those for candidates for legislative and administrative office; that the votes are often exceedingly close, and this, combined with the smallness of the total vote, often results in a change of the law by a minority of voters. It seems quite clear from the accumulated results in both countries that an extensive and real opinion prevails and can be expressed on the primary and elemental issues, such as are embodied in the Ten Commandments, but that they are clearly at sea as soon as they are asked to make judgments involving a careful process of going back to first principles. Not that the first class of subjects does not merit or require thought, but the prejudices about them are so widely shared and so intensely believed to be true that many people will vote, and decide.

The lessons taught by experience of the referendum and the initiative are reinforced by studies of those who habitually return an answer of "No opinion," or "Don't know," in public opinion polls.[37] It has been found that when specific information is called for—thus, knowledge of tax rules or labor statutes or the names of officials and ministers or the effects of a tariff—some thirty per cent declare ignorance. Where a definite attitude is asked—for example, toward Presidential or senatorial policy, or toward barring strikes in wartime—then about fifteen per cent betray ignorance. If men and women are questioned on broad policy—for example, whether lend-lease should be extended to allies, or whether a policy of neutrality is advisable or whether the United States should pursue a path of neutrality or enter into war—the ignorance or apathy drops to between six and nine per cent. Confronted, again, with a speculative question—such as whether the Soviet Union will fight against Japan when the European war is over, or

---

[37] See E. T. Britton, *The "No Opinion" Factor in Public Opinion Research* (unpublished thesis, University of Chicago, December, 1947).

whether the Senate will endorse the entrance of the United States into the United Nations—there is a marked increase of expressions of "Don't know": rising to thirty per cent in some cases, and hardly falling below fourteen per cent. Finally, where answers are solicited to general questions of morals, religion, and social intercourse—such as a belief in God or immortality, the faithfulness of husbands and wives, the propriety of antemarital sex relations, the regulation of liquor traffic, honesty of views between husband and wife—almost everybody has an opinion and expresses it: only about five per cent are silent.

Those who habitually have no opinion are Negroes, the lower economic groups, people with small education, women, persons over forty, the rural element, those dwelling in the South. It will be inferred that some of these groups have common characteristics; and again, they are at the same time nonvoters in primary and general elections.

When we ask then, what good has direct legislation done in the countries where it has been actually used, the answer must surely be that these countries, save for the combating of the dishonest "bosses" in the American states, are no better off and are probably worse off. This is certainly the opinion in America. The Swiss idealize their system more than the Americans, but when one examines their opinions they are seen to be of small substance. Consider the utterances of Bonjour: [38] "It is the surest method of discovering the wishes of the people—an excellent barometer of the political atmosphere." But we have seen that the people's wishes can be destructive, when the people have not met together to discuss the consequences of their activity and are not enlightened by those who are informed and wise. He proceeds: "It compels the legislator to conform with the aspirations of the people, if he does not wish the fruit of his labors to perish." But the legislator's fruits may be so good that they ought not to perish, and the aspirations of the people many be uninformed, unintelligent and vindictive. "It puts an end to acute conflicts between people and governments, and provides one of the safest barriers there can be against revolutionary agitation." To this the answer is that the conflict is ended by brute force—that is a majority decision, which has in some cases been an exceedingly small majority, and sometimes a minority of the whole electorate. As for a barrier against revolutionary agitation, Bonjour himself says (though in regard to the initiative) that in the direct war-tax proposal "the Socialists made their appeal to the lowest instincts of human nature." Nowhere is there proof adduced that legislatures or parties are better or worse off since the introduction of direct legislation. It is highly probable when all is said and done that we will continue to emphasize the party system as a medium of government—especially for larger states with complex interests and greater difficulties for the propagandist. There may be an advantage in the initiative as a legal residuary instrument of correction against blocs and unrepresentative legislators—but how did they get there?

Let us now consider the special case of Weimar Germany.

Direct Legislation in Weimar Germany. Articles 72 to 76 [39] regulating the use of the initiative and the referendum, in some cases for ordinary laws and for constitutional amendments, were used several times, and were, in fact, a very mobile element in the constitution.

Let us first observe the German limitations on the initiative. (1) There were excluded certain subjects relating to finance. These limitations resulted from two motives: first, the conviction that the people could not know sufficient of law, administration, and public and private finance and economics to give a rational

---

[38] *Op. cit.*, p. 114.

[39] Cf. the commentaries on these articles in G. Anschütz, *Die Reichsuerfessung* (Berlin, 1930); F. Poetzsch-Heffter, *Gesetz über den Volksentscheid*, June 27, 1921, etc. The best description and commentary is G. Kaisenberg, *Volksentscheid und Volksbegehren*, 2nd edition (Berlin, 1926).

decision on the subject; and second, the fear that the organized groups, either favorable or hostile to central and local civil servants, would too often attempt to upset the existing situation. The financial limitations were quite broadly interpreted in practice, as we shall see, and the broad interpretation finds a majority of defenders among lawyers. [40] In this interpretation it is interesting to find adduced the experience of various countries, and of England in particular, where the initiative in finance is either located in the government entirely, or where Parliament is subjected to severe limitations, and the considerations which there hold good certainly hold good of direct legislation *a fortiori*.

(2) The second class of limitations on the initiative comprehended the special majorities required. Thus: where a referendum was in challenge to a resolution of the *Reichstag*, a majority of the registered voters must have participated in the referendum (article 75); that is, the referendum has no force at all unless at least half the voters polled valid votes. The reason for this provision was obvious, when we remember American and Swiss experience. It gives rise, however, to the tactics during a referendum of telling those who are against a project simply to stay at home and not register their votes. Further, where, according to article 76, a referendum with the force of a constitutional amendment occurs, its acceptance by the majority of the registered voters was required. Thus those in its favor need over one half of all the registered voters positively for them. Again the tactics of the opposition is to tell voters to stay at home, and to argue that the initiated project is a constitutional amendment. What is a constitutional amendment has also been rather widely interpreted.

Until the advent of Hitler, there were seven "popular" initiatives. Upon two only was the full procedure [41] carried out; the rest were abortive. The first, an abortive popular initiative, was that of the *Reich* Federation for Housing and Leaseholds "to amend the law on Housing." It was accepted by the government, but its promoters themselves dropped it.[42] The same association proceeded with a new proposal, and this was rejected by the government as a finance law. In April, 1926, the Association of Small Savers initiated an amendment of the Devaluation Laws. It was rejected by the government as a law affecting the budget. The government argued that "a law which materially amends the whole financial situation is inherently and without a doubt a law affecting the budget . . ." Schmitt [43] held that the term "law on the budget" properly refers to any law "the substance of which is by monetary measures to provide new income for the state's finances or to put new burdens upon it." In 1927 the *Reich* association of those injured by the devaluation of money [44] initiated a measure to return to the monetary valuations of debts, contracts, etc., before January, 1924. This was rejected by the government on the grounds that a finance law was involved.

The government's interpretation of the financial and constitutional nature of an initiative is final, the constitution having provided no other authority to decide this or to act as a court of appeal.

Two initiatives went through all prescribed stages: the referendum on the

---

[40] Cf. the discussion by Carl Schmitt, *Volksentscheid und Volksbegehren* (Berlin, 1927). Naturally, they are not convinced of the legislative capacity of the people. This attitude is of a piece with their vindication of the right of the judiciary to review the acts of Parliament and the executive for their constitutionality. Cf. Chap. 9, p. 153 ff.

[41] The procedure was provided in the Law Relating to the Referendum, for which see G. Kaisenberg, *op. cit.*, and the law relating to voting procedure at general elections; also, cf. F. Poetzsch-Heffter, *Jahrbuch des Öffentlichen Rechts* (Berlin, 1925).
[42] This led to the rule that after six months an abortive initiative lapses.
[43] *Op. cit.*
[44] Cf. F. Poetzsch-Heffter, *Jahrbuch des Öffentlichen Rechts*, 1929, p. 136. In the text I have omitted mention of the Communist party's initiative of October, 1928, demanding the cessation of work on the armored cruiser. It failed for lack of support in the preliminary stage.

expropriation of the princes, 1926,[45] and the referendum on the Young Plan of 1929, or, as it was cunningly termed by its promoters, the Freedom Law, or the Law to Prevent the Enslavement of the German People.

On the basis of Weimar German experience, we may answer several important questions:

(1) Is the vote on the referendum materially different from the distribution of votes as given to the political parties at the immediately preceding general election? It is not. In the election of December 1924, the Majority Socialists and Communists alone had together polled 10.5 million votes; these parties managed the referendum campaign, and the votes in its favor amounted to 14.5 million. In the second instance the general electoral vote and the referendum vote were even closer.

(2) Do the political parties keep out of the campaign? On the contrary. They enter with all their apparatus of propaganda, their appeals to party loyalty, and arguments which relate the proposition to the general policy of the party. In both cases where the referendum was carried through—the referendum on the expropriation of princes and the referendum on the Young Plan—two parties, the extremes on each wing, actually initiated the proposal. From the first moment each party declared its attitude and to the last advised and marshalled its rank and file. In the second instance the German National party was split by the action of the extremist Hugenberg: the Left wing of the party seceding on the ground that such extreme action tended to make impossible any governmental coalition between the party and other nonsocialist conservative groups.

(3) In what sense, then, is the initiative "popular"? In no sense different from the issues which are treated by the parties through the medium of the legislature and general elections.

(4) Was the issue "clear-cut" from all others? If so, the referendum is a useful remedy against the alleged defect of representative government that it is based upon elections where the multiplicity of issues confuses the electorate and destroys the sense of the mandate. The issues here were certainly not clear-cut. They were made part and parcel of a general system of constitutionalism, the theory of private property and Socialist reconstruction, of international affairs and public finance as a whole. They were related to the programs and policies of the parties. The most significant example of this was the questionnaire put in the *Reichstag* speech by Dr. Curtius in defence of his government's refusal to accept the referendum project: [46] "If the proposal is accepted, what will be the next step? If such an alternative is accepted, what is the answer to the derivative questions which will arise as a consequence? At such a stage, what steps will be taken by the proposers?" He thereby showed that any government can take the responsibility for the proposal of a referendum only when its *sequelae* have been envisaged and sound answers provided to meet all the unavoidable and closely integrated consequences.

(5) How does the referendum affect the position of a government based on parliamentary responsibility? The government is seriously embarrassed and confused. Its program of legislative work is suddenly interrupted by the necessity of aiding or opposing an enormous agitation toward which, by the constitution, it is bound to state its attitude. Further, in a system based on coalitions of more than two parties, often precariously balanced, the result is, at the least, to heighten the instability of the government, and to cause confusion and personal and group collisions, which cost energy to try to overcome, often without success. The referendum has no pacifying effect: on the contrary it inflames antagonisms by reminding men of their existence.

(6) Did the referenda threaten the prestige of Parliament? The answer is,

---

[45] F. Poetzsch-Heffter, *loc. cit.*

[46] Speech, *Reichstag, Stenographische Bericht*, November 26, 1929.

decidedly! For one of the most effective weapons of the parties and committees is denunciation of the parliamentary system and that particular *Reichstag*. It is a body of talkers; it can come to no decision because of the fragmentation of parties; it is congested with legislative and administrative duties; it is unjust; it has no courage. The weapon was used without mercy.

(7) Were the referenda educational? Insofar as they meant extra campaigns of public speaking and a special overflow of printed discussion in newspaper and pamphlets, the answer is affirmative. But can we be so sure when we take into account the character of the propaganda? You either appeal to prejudice or you teach: if the former then there is no education, and in the instances confronting us there was an almost absolutely unbridled appeal to certain simple but powerful prejudices: property or not, a violent assertion of patriotism or not. Here are some of the titles of pamphlets in the princes' expropriation referendum of 1926: "Property is Theft!" "Five Hundred Years of Robbery by Princes!" "Not a penny to the Princes!" "Rich Princes, Poor People!" "Law or Robbery in the Republic?" In the second instance, the very name of the proposal, the "Freedom Law," and the "Law against the Enslavement of the German People" were irrational incitements. The proposers have every inducement to be virulent and unmeasured and nothing to restrain them like subsequently continuing legislative or executive responsibility. Ministers were subjected to the cruelest abuse, and being in office, were handicapped in their replies.

It must be admitted that the people learn something from every additional dose of propaganda, but the dose is at least as bad as it is good. Who will dare to say that in time they help the good and eject the bad? If we contrasted what actually occurred with real education, we should contrast two or three months' inflammatory and irresponsible demagoguery with a process which should last years—a process in which the proposal would have been explained in all its parts to small groups of people of no more than twenty, and its connections with other parts of the existing body of laws and regulations carefully traced, its furthest ramifications and proximate and distant consequences weighed in terms of finance and subjective burdens placed upon various groups in the country and in foreign states, and the meaning of them all sedulously made clear. If education were the purpose, and a rational, considered, and sincere popular decision were required, these things would need to be fulfilled. In fact, they were not fulfilled. For the time was not available, and instead of the teachers who would have been needed, let us say about one in twenty of the voting population (that is, two million teachers), there were simply a few thousand party speakers, special associations like the "League for the Defence of the Seventh Commandment," and a handful of journalists. How many were made to realize that if they expropriated without compensation on this occasion rightly (let us say), they would have established a moral rule in the community not subject to careful discrimination when other groups were to be expropriated? How many were ever taught the results of attempting to force the hand of foreign governments by peremptory commands to one's own?

(8) Finally, the referendum gave to the discontented parties the chances of agitation, not only for something just, but out of malice, spite, and revenge for having suffered losses at the preceding elections and for their exclusion from the cabinet. If it is said that the referendum is proper in the third or fourth year of a legislature's life (and against that there is a great deal to be said), it must be observed that in Germany the referendum of 1926 was instituted by parties which failed at the elections of December, 1924 (in other words, the *Reichstag* had existed for only fourteen months when the referendum was proposed), while in the referendum of 1929 the *Reichstag* had sat for sixteen months and was again dis-

turbed by the extreme Right which had done badly in the election of 1928.[47]

The constitution of the U.S.S.R. empowers the Presidium on its own initiative or on demand of one of the Union Republics to conduct a referendum on proposed legislation (that is proposed by itself). The power has never been used; but Mr. Vyshinsky promises that *when* it is, it will not be in the corrupt bourgeois conditions of the lands beyond the pure pale (*op. cit.,* p. 335 ff.).

Such experience would, perhaps, warn us not to accept direct legislation as a remedy for the defects of parliamentary government. It improves nothing: neither the laws nor the people. It disturbs without providing solutions. It is an appeal from a court which has the makings and some of the equipment of a wise legislature, to all the crudities of a majority vote. Its operation leaves stark naked the physical power of numbers, surely not a desirable thing. The public cannot but be ignorant of the facts of the situation; the referendum campaign makes it no better, and it may make it worse, for many people are prepared to vote for what they immediately want without considering whether it is good for them or others in the long run. If, in spite of the teachings of experience, there are people who still say the will of the people ought to prevail, so it should. But let it not be pretended that this is the best medium through which it may do so. If what we have said about the process of govern-

ment in previous chapters is true, we should all be better served if our concern were fixed upon the reform of the party system; we should strive, then, to make the parties more responsible-minded, more sensitive, more masters of the social sciences. They would become conscious teachers, leaders, and trustees chosen for the qualities proper to such functions and for that of legislator. At any rate, the question of the referendum is the question of the quality of a country's political parties.

COMPULSORY VOTING

MANY people do not use their right to vote. Surveys show that in England the percentage of voters is about 75 per cent, sometimes a little more; in France recently about 80; in Germany about 75. In the United States about 70 per cent (in 1920 and 1924 there were low points of 60 per cent) vote in Presidential elections, while Congressional and state elections show, on the average, a worse record. (For the United States we must make allowance for Negro nonvoters in the South, who are excluded by fraud or force.)

Causes of Nonvoting. Why do not all the people vote? The reasons for nonvoting are inferable in two ways: first, one can examine into who are the nonvoters, and secondly, one can inquire of nonvoters why they do not vote. (It is also possible to interrogate them on their general character and interests, and make inferences.)

The first question has been answered in a variety of studies for the United States, and by the method of asking which groups of the population show the higher proportions of voting. Thus one study,[48] the results of which are corroborated closely

---

[47] On July 14, 1933, the Nazi government established its own referendum—without the popular initiative. It was used three times. The first was in November, 1933, to ratify the government's withdrawal from the League of Nations. The second was after the German-Austrian *Anschluss* in April, 1938 had been consummated. The third time was in August, 1934, when Hitler fused the posts of chancellor and president (on the death of Hindenburg) and the form of the question was "Do you German man or woman agree that. . . . ?" There were overwhelming votes of "Yes," to Europe's ultimate damnation. This form of referendum cannot hoodwink anyone: its intention was not to derive authority from the people, but to boast that benevolent dictatorial authority was being used for their own good.

[48] S. M. Connelly and H. H. Field, "The Non-Voter," *Public Opinion Quarterly,* Summer, 1944, pp. 175-87. See also A. Davidson and P D. Anderson, *Ballots and the Democratic Class Structure* (Stanford, 1943), *passim;* Charles E. Merriam and Harold Gosnell, *American Party System* (New York, 1949); and McGraw-Hill (publishers) *Recent Social Trends,* Vol. II, p. 1507.

enough by the rest, shows that the top quarter in the economic scale votes most, even when they have not had the highest education. Leaving economic welfare out of the question, the college people vote most, next the former high-school attendants, least of all those who do not attend beyond grade school. The older voters, those over 40, vote more than those between the ages of 21 and 39, in the ratio of 76 to 59. Among the workers, the voters in order of voting are white-collar workers, with farmers, manual laborers, and "service" occupations least of all. Recent arrivals in America vote more than do the persons of two and three generations settlement. Votes are highest in the great metropolitan areas and then trail down in the smaller ones, with the voting smallest in the rural areas. Of course, in general the Negro votes least of any group in the country: the reasons are obvious. Jews

and Catholics vote more than Protestant religious groups.

To the second type of question—asking the nonvoters why they do not vote—the best-formulated answer is that provided by Gosnell's study of nonvoting in Chicago.[49] The results are shown in Table 15. To make this study applicable to other countries would require considerable adjustment in the details and proportions, but its framework is representative of nonvoters everywhere.

There is no doubt that many of the answers Gosnell obtained were evasions designed to make the answerer less culpable than he or she was. For example, I should hazard the guess that 12.1 per cent is too high for illness. As Vauvenargues said: "Illness suspends all virtues and all

---

[49] Charles E. Merriam and Harold Gosnell, *Non-Voting* (Chicago, 1924).

TABLE 15—REASONS FOR NOT VOTING GIVEN BY
NONVOTERS INTERVIEWED: CHICAGO

Reasons For Not Voting	Percent Distribution
Physical Difficulties:	
Illness	12.1
Absence	11.1
Detained by helpless members of family	2.2
Legal and Administrative Obstacles:	
Insufficient legal residence	5.2
Fear of loss of business or wages	5.5
Congestion at polls	0.8
Poor location of polling booth	0.8
Fear of disclosure of age	0.3
Disbelief in Voting:	
Disbelief in woman's voting	7.8
Objections of husband to wife's voting	1.0
Disgust with politics	4.3
Disgust with own party	2.0
Belief that one vote counts for nothing	1.5
Belief that ballot-box is corrupted	0.7
Disbelief in all political action	0.4
Inertia:	
General indifference	25.4
Indifference to particular election	2.5
Neglect: intended to vote but failed	8.4
Ignorance or timidity regarding elections	7.1
Failure of party workers	0.9
Total	100.0

vices." Inertia provides for 44.3 per cent of the total, and perhaps this should be increased.

The Compulsory Vote. At any rate, is it worth while forcing all but the decrepit to vote? This is done in Belgium, Switzerland, and Australia.[50] In the first-named country the compulsory vote was introduced in 1893 when the suffrage was very widely extended. Until that time the results of voting under a limited franchise were on a par with those in England and France, but in the local government areas the results were disturbing. But it was argued that the comparatively heavier voting for the central legislature was obtained only at the cost of propaganda and discipline extremely expensive in energy and money.[51] The opposing theories were *(a)* that the vote was a civic "right" which the citizen might use or not, as he wished; and *(b)* that the vote was a "social right"—that is, a right to be exercised in the interests of society—and that therefore society might regulate its employment. The latter argument is analogous to the contention that the parliamentary privilege which protects a member of a legislature in the free expression of his opinions is not his alone but an attribute of the whole legislature, for its benefit and instrumental to its effectiveness. (We shall meet such arguments again: arguments which lead back to their proponents' ultimate metaphysics of society and which are not seldom at least a partial product of their material interests.) The strong practical reasons for the compulsory vote were the expense and difficulty suffered by the political parties in bringing the people to the poll. Moreover, the moderates were more afraid of electoral inertia than of the extremes: for the extreme voter would go to the poll voluntarily, not so the moderates. Thus, the Belgian voter is forced to vote, under penalty enforced by the justices of the peace. The fines are small, but they seem

to have been effective.[52] It is not surprising that the proportion of the electorate voting was always over 93 per cent (except in 1919, for which adequate extraneous reasons can be given). Excuses accepted are illness, absence abroad, absence for business; and not many are prosecuted compared with the total of nonvoters. In Switzerland some cantons have the compulsory vote, some not: in 1925 the cantons with it showed a poll of 86 per cent of the electorate, those without it only 72 per cent.[53]

In Australia, the Commonwealth Electoral Act of 1924[54] made it the duty of every elector to record his vote. Excuses may be made to the returning officers on a proper form which must be filled in by the nonvoter. The penalty for inexcusable nonvoting or nonjustification is between ten shillings and two pounds. The effect of the compulsion may be inferred from Table 16,[55] which shows very clearly the increase in voting after the passage of the Act of 1924.

And in every election for the House of Representatives and Senate, as well as

TABLE 16—AUSTRALIA: EFFECT ON NON-VOTING OF THE COMPULSORY VOTE ACT OF 1924

	Percentage of the Electorate Voting for	
Election	*Senate*	*Representatives*
1901	53.04	55.69
1917	77.69	78.3
1922	57.95	59.36
1925	91.31	91.39

[50] Also in Argentine, Hungary, Denmark, Luxemburg, Czechoslovakia, and Italy.

[51] J. Barthélemy, *L'Organisation du Suffrage* (Paris, 1920), p. 477 ff.

[52] Cf. Harold Gosnell, *Why Europe Votes,* (Chicago, 1930), p. 103: The first nonexcused abstention was punished by a reprimand or a fine of from one to three francs. The second offense within six years was punishable by a fine of from three to twenty-five francs; the third offense within ten years by the same fine and public posting; and the fourth offense within fifteen years by disfranchisement for ten years in addition to a fine and public posting."

[53] *Ibid.,* p. 129.

[54] Commonwealth Electoral Act (Compulsory Voting), No. 10, 1924. Codified with slight amendments, 1928, No. 17.

[55] From report of Royal Commission on Australian Constitution, 1929, p. 31, and *Official Year Book,* 1930.

every referendum, since that time, something like 95 per cent of the electorate has voted.[56]

What motivated enactment of compulsory voting in Australia? Members of Parliament were disgusted by the abstentions. "Ever since the federation was established, of all those who have been returned to the Senate during the last twenty-four years, on only four occasions has an individual senator been returned by more than 50 per cent of the votes enrolled." [57] How, under such circumstances, could members speak in the name of democracy and the majority? It was believed that if voters were compelled to vote they could the more easily be made to acquire an informed interest in politics. It was urged that the State already spent large sums of money to enroll electors. Further: "If the people exhibit no interest in the selection of their representatives, it must necessarily follow, that in the course of time there must be a serious deterioration in the nature of the laws governing the social and economic development of this country . . ." [58] It was pointed out that Queensland, which established compulsory voting in 1915, managed to poll over 82 per cent of the electorate, while the rest of Australia polled about 55 per cent.

What does all this show? That it is possible to make people come to the polling booths and write a figure or make a cross on a piece of paper if they are threatened with the fine of a few shillings unless they do so. It enables the politician to say with conviction and demonstration that he represents a majority of the people. It makes it easier to get people to the poll. In some a political consciousness will be awakened. Notice, however, the substantial dangers: to vote under duress is no proof of the will to vote, capacity to vote, or right judgment. The politician may say he represents a majority of the people: but in fact, 30 per cent or more have

voted who do not care enough about politics to vote, let alone to inform themselves, except under duress. It is easier to get people to the poll. Is that for the good in politics? Is that not bound to make the task and therefore the efforts of political parties easier rather than harder? And there is a great deal to be said for imposing the greatest rather than the least strain on political parties. Finally, is it worth while to force a few into political paths at the cost of forcing the congenitally apathetic into giving an unavoidably ignorant and perhaps contemptibly cynical vote?

Gosnell [59] shows quite clearly that a high percentage of voters is, apart from compulsion, brought out by momentous issues, keenly contested and closely contested individual constituencies, and well-organized and active parties: thence comes the fullness of the sovereignty which is' the prize of the victor.[60] He establishes some correlation between proportional representation and the size of the vote.[61] He shows also that there is more voting in urban than in rural communities; among skilled than unskilled workers.

Hence, when scholars like Barthélemy advocate the compulsory vote one is astounded at the argument:[62]

Abstentionism falsifies the sincerity of universal suffrage and prevents the normal operation of government by the majority; what becomes of representative government in a country where one third of the electors do not vote? The deputies—for we must take into account the votes obtained by the candidates who failed—do not represent the half of the electorate, and it is the half plus one of this

---

[56] Commonwealth of Australia yearbook for the various election years and referenda.
[57] Debates, Australian House of Representatives, July 24, 1924, p. 2446.
[58] Debates, Australian Senate, 2nd reading, July 17, 1924, p. 2180.

[59] *Why Europe Votes* (Chicago, 1930).
[60] Where there are constitutional limitations, as in the United States, interest and therefore voting tends to diminish. The same holds good, of course, of local government, which is severely limited government.
[61] Yet, says Gosnell (*op. cit.*, p. 183) regarding Germany: "It is true that the novelty of the system has now worn off and that its very stability has tended to lessen interest in voting, but the drop in the poll has been very slight."
[62] J. Barthélemy, *Rapport*, Chambre des Députés, *Le Vote Obligatoire* (1922), No. 4738, and *Droit Constitutionnel* (1926), p. 296 ff.

representation which governs the country. Forty million Frenchmen are subject to laws voted by the elected of two millions of citizens.[63] Under those conditions, the supposed national representation gravely risks being only a singularly unfaithful expression of the essential features of the nation. There is, further, a powerful interest in obtaining the votes of the mass of citizens who do not use the pointer of political passion. The obligatory vote brings to the polls the moderate voter, and favors the moderate parties which are often less well organized for the electoral struggle than the extreme parties.

Is this not a complete abdication of political science? The professor proceeds:

Once again, the obligation to vote is part and parcel of customs in Belgium; it produces no discontent there; it is an excellent means of civic education.

It is of outstanding interest in a theory of politics that the French Communist party was ferociously hostile to the proposal to institute the compulsory vote for elections in France. They wanted the votes to go to the most eager and zealous organizers.

There is no help for representative government in devices like direct legislation or the compulsory vote. They either ascribe to the elector capacities which he does not and cannot possess, or else seek to overcome the alleged defects of political parties by obliging the citizen to undertake functions for which he has no interest or no aptitude. They ignore the unuttered lesson of the polls of public opinion in the United States, Great Britain, and France, that on every subject there are some 10, 15, even 20 per cent of those interrogated who "Don't know," which not infrequently means "Don't want to know." They forget the advantages of division of labor, and undervalue the numerous agencies of public opinion other than elections. They suffer, moreover, from the grave disadvantage of not concentrating the voters' attention on the conditions of improving the personnel, methods, and purposes of political parties. Hope lies not on these devices, but in the more adequate selection and education of candidates for office, and in the marked improvement of schools and adult education.

---

[63] Does he mean that if 70 per cent vote, then one half of this—or 35 per cent—of four million of the electorate (before women voted)—may rule, and that of this, only two million may represent the majority in the constituencies?

Part Five

CABINETS AND CHIEFS OF STATE

The heart of a statesman should be in his head.—N A P O L E O N

Those who are in the Ministry of State must imitate the stars, which, though the dogs bark, do not refrain from giving light or pursuing their course: such abuse should not be allowed to shake the Minister's probity, nor make him swerve from the resolute march towards the ends which he has proposed for the good of the State.—R I C H E L I E U

Part Five

CABINETS AND CHIEFS OF STATE

CHAPTER 23
The British Cabinet and Its Authorities

CHAPTER 24
The French Cabinet

CHAPTER 25
The German Cabinet System: The Fall of the Irresponsible
Executive

CHAPTER 26
The United States Presidency

The heart of a statesman should be in his head. — NAPOLEON

Those who are in the Ministry of State must imitate the stars, which, though
the dogs bark, do not refrain from giving light or pursuing their courses; such
abuse should not be allowed to shake the Minister's probity, nor make him
swerve from the resolute march toward the ends which he has proposed for
the good of the State. — RICHELIEU

23

The British Cabinet and Its Auxiliaries

In pondering on the nature of executives, the student will do well to bear constantly in mind the characteristics of governmental leadership suggested earlier.[1] We have already indicated the principal parts of modern political machinery, namely: the electorate, the parties, Parliament, the cabinet, the chief of state, the civil service, and the judiciary. The middle terms—the cabinet and the chief of state together—comprise that which is usually called the executive. No deliberate philosophy on a single occasion distributed the work of government among its organs; these were made and endowed with power, each according to separate contingencies. Hence the executive comprises an assortment of functions which cannot be accurately inferred from the name, but can be known only by historic explanation and enumerative description. Indeed, all the executives have some legislative functions, even the American. And while in Continental parliamentary systems the executive is also the legislative leader, in the British system both the executive and the legislative functions are fully and inseparably blended in the cabinet.

The evolution of the executive need not occupy us long, for it has in many ways remained the residuary legatee in government after other claimants like Parliament and the law courts have taken their share, and we have indicated the history of the aggrandizement of these

authorities in other places. It is most useful to look upon the executive as the residuary legatee, for that explains the mixed nature of its functions and parts. In early times all power, of every kind, lay with the prince and his narrow circle of advisers or intimidators. It not only executed policy but planned it and sat in judgment.[2] The movement for responsible government caused portions of the power to be taken over by other institutions, the remainder itself being subjected to certain norms of constitutional morality and controlled by the new organs. The legislature, the courts, the people, the

[2] Cf. J. F. Baldwin, *The King's Council in England during the Middle Ages* (Oxford, 1913); A. V. Dicey, *The Privy Council* (Oxford, 1860), older than Baldwin's work and much exploded by it; E. R. Turner, *The Privy Council* (Johns Hopkins, 1928) and *Cabinet Councils in the Seventeenth and Eighteenth Centuries* (Oxford, 1932); A. B. Keith, *The British Cabinet System, 1830-1938* (London, 1939); Paul Viollet, *Histoire des Institutions Politiques et Administratives de la France* (Paris, 1912); Le Comte de Luçay, *Des Origines du Pouvoir Ministeriel en France: Les Secretaires d'État* (Paris, 1868); A. Chéruel, *Histoire de l'Administration Monarchique en France* (Paris, 1855); Dareste de Chavannes, *Histoire de l'Administration en France* (Paris, 1848); M. L. Hinsdale, *History of the President's Cabinet* (New York, 1911); W. H. Smith, *History of the Cabinet of the United States of America from President Washington to President Coolidge* (New York, 1925); Cf. L. D. White, *The Federalists* (New York, 1948) and L. K. Caldwell, *The Administrative Theories of Hamilton and Jefferson* (Chicago, 1944).

[1] Cf. p. 22 above.

parties grew to marvelous dimensions, yet they never denuded the executive (as the monarch and his ministers were called) clean of all but executive work. Even the fullest new modeling of government, that in the American states and federation at the end of the eighteenth century, established an executive which was more than a mere executive. And it is still anxiously debated whether the United States President is an executive compact only of the several definite powers assigned to him, or a more general executive with undefined residuary authority as well (like the European or British as Hamilton purposed). Even Montesquieu, as we saw, counseled no complete separation. Lawmaking was abstracted, but some lawmaking yet remained; justice was removed to a securer residence, yet large powers were reserved; control over the permanent officials was vested in the legislatures and courts too, yet not entirely; while the field of foreign relations has only in recent years shown signs of being relinquished by its ancient holder.

Now, the same tendencies which molded the executive in its modern form also caused the growth of a distinction between the chief of state (the King or the President or the Governor General) and the body of ministers or the cabinet, giving the former a principally decorative and symbolic position, which is combined with independence and permanence of tenure, while the cabinet has been made (and is) politically operative, reproachable, and removable, acting in fairly strict dependence on the elected legislature.[3] This is the council of ministers or the cabinet—sometimes also called the government or the administration, though these terms are a little wider than the former. Both these parts of the executive have important functions, and, though what holds good of one country does not exactly

hold good of others, of all save the United States this is clearly true: the most important political powers are exercised not by the chief of state but by the cabinet. Since this is so, and since it has a closer and more vital relationship to the electoral, deliberative, and controlling institutions which we have recently discussed, we treat of the cabinet first.

THE GENERAL CHARACTERISTICS OF THE CABINET SYSTEM

It need not be argued that the political characteristics we have described may be and are combined variously in different countries, even where the same terms are used to name a system which is believed to operate like the British model. In fact, as the course of the analysis will amply show, there are very significant differences of aspect and purpose. Broadly, however, there are certain common qualities and purposes which show themselves in the composition of cabinets and in their functions.

Cabinets are small bodies of men selected from among the leaders of the majority party or parties of the legislature, usually from members of that body, and holding office and exercising governmental power as long as, and in the measure which, the legislature permits. The people do not directly come into contact with the civil service nor does the legislature. The parties impel, but do not formally lead, the legislature. They employ a special agency, a trustee, a delegation from among themselves, to mediate for them. If we had not already in mind that etymologically a committee is an expressly selected and delegated body, we might call the British cabinet a committee of the legislature: it is that, except that the process of selection is not express choice by the legislature, and is indirect and complex, while the articles of delegation are rather vague and elastic.[4]

The members of such executive com-

---

[3] For the development of the system in the British Dominions see A. B. Keith, *Responsible Government in the Dominions* (Oxford, 1929), *The Government of the British Empire* (New York, 1935), and *The Constitutional Law of the Dominions* (London, 1933); and R. M. Dawson, *The Government of Canada* (Toronto, 1947).

[4] The French constitution of 1946 (article 45) is very strongly impregnated with the spirit of express legislative mastery over the Council of Ministers.

mittees man the departments of government each directing and controlling the
everyday administration of one great
branch of government activity. Collectively, they decide the execution of policy
and the making of laws, the order in time
of their items, how earnestly the tasks
shall be undertaken, how much money
shall be spent, and in what way the money
shall be raised. This includes both foreign
and domestic affairs. They explain to the
legislature their motives, intentions, and
reasons; they pilot their projects toward
legislative acceptance; and they answer
for the march of administration, which,
by their acceptance of office is deemed
theirs and only theirs. They are responsible; that is, it is acknowledged that
blame and praise will attach to them according as—in the opinion of the legislature and the interested members of the
electorate—they work woe or weal. The
whole apparatus of government, every
factor in the creation and execution of
political decisions, revolves around them,
concentrates upon them, radiates from
them, though often not with frictionless
celerity or to the universal satisfaction,
and, normally, with much grinding and
clanking. So powerful is this body, so busy,
so ubiquitous, that the charge of tyranny
is leveled at it, and gloomy prophecies
are made about the decline of legislatures. We have yet to see how much there
is in such charges and prophecies. But this
is true, that the energizing, responsible
center of government and ultimate decision is in the cabinet. Let us consider
these matters more closely in regard to
each country. When we do, we shall find
that for various reasons, very potent in
the past, but which may not persist always, the British cabinet system, the
mother of all, is by far the most efficient.

THE CABINET IN BRITAIN

THE British cabinet consists not of all but
only of the principal ministers of the
Crown.[5] All the ministers, together with

the undersecretaries and parliamentary
secretaries, form the "government" or the
"administration." Which ministers are included in the term "principal" depends
partly upon precedent and partly upon
the convenience of each government. Also,
the numbers vary within small limits, it
being necessary to comprehend all the
important branches, and to allow for committees of the cabinet to be formed without too much duplication of membership.
An excess of numbers, however, causes the
loss of the best psychological and physical
conditions of effective deliberation. The
number (about 20) is, of course, larger
now than it was in the beginning or middle of the nineteenth century (9 or 11),
because the state has a much wider sphere
of activities.[6] The ministers of the Crown
Act of 1937 defines "cabinet" ministers
as those notified as being such in the
London Gazette, the publicity daily of the
state. Further, it seems to me that the
variation regarding inclusion of the Post-
master General shows that importance is

by A. B. Keith), Vol. II ("The Crown," Part I),
Chap. III; S. Low, *The Governance of England,* revised edition (London, 1915), p. 167;
John Morley, *Notes on Politics and History*
(London, 1914); Ivor Jennings, *Cabinet Government* (Cambridge, 1936).
[6] Cf. Sir Robert Peel, *Mirror of Parliament*
(1835), p. 1797: cited in A. E. Todd, *Parliamentary Government* (Spencer Walpole edition, London), Vol. I, p. 283.

In 1948, following certain changes made
at the end of 1947, the Labour cabinet con-
sisted of only sixteen members. They were:
Prime Minister and First Lord of the Treas-
ury; the Lord President of the Council and
Leader of the House of Commons; Secretary
of State for Foreign Affairs; Chancellor of the
Exchequer; Minister of Defence; Lord Privy
Seal and Leader of the House of Lords; Lord
Chancellor; Secretary of State for the Home
Department; Secretary of State for the Colonies; Secretary of State for Commonwealth
Relations; Secretary of State for Scotland;
Minister of Labour and National Service;
Minister of Health; Minister of Agriculture
and Fisheries; Minister of Education; President of the Board of Trade. There were seventeen other ministers not in the cabinet. The
student will notice that India no longer appears in the cabinet; and that owing to the
establishment in 1947 of a Ministry of Defence, the Secretaries for War and Air and the
First Lord of the Admiralty ceased to be cabinet posts—not necessarily forever.

[5] Cf. W. R. Anson, *Law and Custom of the
Constitution,* 4th edition (Oxford, 1935, edited

partly defined with reference to the possible range and fluidity of policy. An office which like the Post Office has a rather limited range of controversial business and a vast scope of mere routine does not need the special attention of the cabinet. The same is now rather obvious of the Secretaries of War and Air, of Food, and Fuel and Power by contrast with the Minister of Defence, or the Ministers of Agriculture or Labour.

Ministers are ministers of the Crown, that is, they are formally appointed and dismissable by the Crown. But this action is hardly more than formal and symbolic, as we shall see more clearly later. The Crown appoints but does not choose; it dismisses but does not control; it acts on but does not determine the occasion of dismissal. For the power behind the throne is the authority of the people, to which government has been made responsible. The people almost exhaust their authority in the choice of Parliament and this body, to which a large sphere of sovereignty is ascribed by constitutional lawyers, applies the test of responsibility to ministers. But we have seen that people and Parliament are themselves organized and directed by political parties, and that it is difficult, indeed, to discover the distinct identity of these three bodies.[7] In the British system of government the trinity is an almost seamless unity.

This trinity cooperates by continuous interaction in the selection of the leaders of the party, and among them the prime leader. The Crown may, formally, choose anybody as chief minister, but government will cease if the choice made by the factors of popular control is flouted, because Parliament will not vote the laws or financial provision such a government requests and citizens might not obey or pay their taxes. Hence the Crown cannot avoid entrusting the formation of a government to their indubitable choice. I say indubitable, for if there is room for doubt, if there is an alternative, no rule exists,

either in statute or convention, to bind the Crown to choose one way rather than another, and a government must be formed by reference to the democratic practicability of the choice as viewed by the personal predilections of the king or queen.[8] Conditions have, since 1820, left little, though some occasional room for doubt as to who are the leaders of the parties, and therefore hardly any room for the personal choice of the sovereign. Before that time, there were hardly such agencies as political parties, but only fluctuating "connections" among leading families and the groups of interests attached to them. This situation, lending aid to special rivalries, together with the imperfectly acknowledged sovereignty of the people or even of Parliament, gave the Crown considerable latitude.[9] When factions and "connections" were transformed into parties, the division turned more upon the principles of government. Then, when government became actively lawmaking and socially ministrant, principles more and more settled party allegiance and singled out the man who best represented them.[10] When, finally, parties were consciously organized on a basis of dependence upon the people, they became the selective agents of leadership, and, providing they were not in doubt about who did and ought to lead them, the Crown could not be in doubt. In recent

---

[7] Cf. W. E. Gladstone, *Gleanings* (London, 1879), Vol. I, p. 224.

[8] Cf. W. F. Buckle and G. E. Moneypenny, *Life of Disraeli*, revised edition (London, 1929) 2 vols. (Note: Subsequent references to this work will be to the volume and chapter of the six-volume edition, page references will be from the new two-volume edition. All biographies frequently referred to will be indicated by their short title, omitting the author's name.)

[9] Cf. W. R. Anson, *op. cit.,* Vol. II, Part I.

[10] Yet the biographies of *Canning* (Stapleton), *Lyndhurst* (Martin), *Peel* (Parker) and *Disraeli* (Buckle and Moneypenny, to 1860), among others, now reveal quite clearly how unsettled principles were, and more, how slight was the connection between particular leaders and those principles. Could that be otherwise when England so suddenly took the plunge into a steam-driven civilization? Peel's perplexity and the drama of his career seem to show that the new world came far too abruptly for men to realize its meaning until they had grappled with its problems for years.

years the "machine" and the parliamentary members and their prominent men have determined these questions without the shadow of a doubt at special conferences.[11] Thus in 1922 the Conservative Carlton Club chose Stanley Baldwin to succeed Bonar Law; in 1937, Neville Chamberlain to succeed him; and in 1944, Winston Churchill became leader of the Conservatives at the invitation of Conservative party headquarters. In the Labour party, the body of Labour M.P.'s choose their leader; but his arrival among the few possibles is by election to high office in the party by the Annual Labour Conference. The development of the party caucus and conference has relieved the Crown of an onerous task of selection.

The Prime Minister Makes His Cabinet.
Until recent years also the appointment of a prime minister was not a difficult problem, since not only was each party definite about which of its leaders should be called upon, but there were only two parties, one of which was necessarily in a majority. However, since three parties have arisen, owing to the growth of the Labour party and nondecease of the Liberal, the former simplicity was lost between 1923 and 1945. We shall also see later that Continental systems do not operate so simply, and their experience, which is now used as a warning in Great Britain, may one day be scanned as a necessary lesson. The prime minister thus indicated, is entrusted with the formation of a government. Under contemporary circumstances he does not refuse, because he need not. He is well aware of his strength, whether it is in numbers, as in majority parties, or in tactical situation, as in the minority Labour government of 1929. Until 1931 it had not been necessary for a British prime minister, in contemplating the possibility of office, to make a formal pact of coalition with other parties by way of an agreement either on policy or sharing offices, both a notable consequence of Continental conditions.[12] This, however, happened in 1931,[13] in the following circumstances.

In 1929, the elections returned 287 Labour members, 256 Conservative, and 59 Liberals. The Labour government being in a plurality, the King called in Mr. MacDonald, the Labour leader, to form a government. In the absence of an official union between the Conservatives and the Liberals the most likely viable government was Labour, and it must govern until it should find it impossible—when it might be replaced by a coalition of some kind, or might appeal for a dissolution in the hope of a clear majority. It was harassed by the double opposition and harrowed by the unemployment brought on by the Great Depression. Finally, the cabinet itself split on the problem of balancing the budget—whether to overcome the deficit by reducing unemployment benefits, or by raising taxation, or by acquiring more revenue by establishing a general tariff system for the first time in history. Mr. MacDonald deserted his Labour colleagues, and joined with Con-

---

[11] Cf. *Disraeli*, Vol. III, pp. 951-57: William Beresford (Conservative whip) to Lord Stanley, January 22, 1849: "I have discovered that the plan that they at present intend to adopt is not to propose D. as Leader in a general meeting of the Party, but being themselves organized to go down to the House, and for him thus backed to virtually undertake to be Leader, not by election, but *de facto*. . ."
Disraeli's leadership was treated as an accomplished fact in an official letter of the prime minister to the Queen (*Queen Victoria's Letters*, March 16, 1849), and further confirmed by the recognition of the whip and members of the government. "Thus, without any regular nomination or election, but by a natural evolutionary process, the lead of the Opposition passed to the fittest."

[12] This situation, however, pertained during the Crimean War, when Aberdeen's coalition cabinet was in office—from December, 1852, to February, 1855. Upon the resignation of the Aberdeen ministry, Palmerston attempted to reconstruct the coalition cabinet, but the Peelites (Graham, Gladstone and Sidney Herbert) resigned within less than a fortnight. Nevertheless, the period of political compromise ended only with the death of Palmerston in 1865.

[13] Cf. Herman Finer, *Future of Government* (London, 1946), p. 84 ff.; and see MacNeill L. Weir, *The Tragedy of Ramsay MacDonald* (London, 1938); Sidney Webb, *What Happened in 1931* (Fabian Tract, London, 1932); Philip Snowden, *Autobiography* (London, 1934), Vol. II, pp. 929-61.

servative and Liberal leaders to form a coalition government.

Critics of the Crown allege that the King had personally appealed to Mr. Mac-Donald to take this course. The truth is not known. Such critics think the King should have accepted the resignation of the Prime Minister and with it that of his cabinet, and then called for a dissolution. But suppose the outgoing Prime Minister had, after a conversation with the King not asked for dissolution? Was it for the King to decide that for himself? Or should he have then gone to the leader of the next largest party, the Conservative, and then, if they found government impossible (as they would because the Labour party alone could have outvoted it), called for a dissolution? Should this be done during such a crisis?

At any rate, the coalition government was formed. The government then took some urgent remedial measures, abandoned the gold standard (which the leaders had promised they would not do) and then dissolved. They went to the polls as a coalition. But their principles differed. They made an "agreement to differ," defended in the House of Commons by Mr. Baldwin as proper in the circumstances, and supported by his argument that the British constitution was very flexible and even vague, and that the people were not averse to trying a cabinet so heterogeneous.[14] Within a few months the system broke down, precisely because it ran counter to the spirit of the constitution, which above all requires clarity of principle and indubitability of responsibility. The followers of the parties in partnership became restive, and when the tariff issue was raised acutely, some of the Liberals and some of the Labour members seceded. The others who remained may well be regarded as having joined the Conservatives, the dominant party in the coalition.

The prime minister's choice of colleagues is not controlled by the Crown, though on rare occasions the personal aversion of the monarch has been the means of keeping men out of office.[15] Fortunate is it, that the prime minister is unembarrassed by the personal wishes of the Crown, for his task is already formidable. The experience of a hundred and fifty years teaches us what an extraordinary combination of considerations dictates the composition of a cabinet. The prime minister seeks for ability in general counsel, for capacity to manage a department, for ideas and governmental initiative. These are not guaranteed by mere cleverness. For many other qualities distinguish men: industry, rapidity of intelligence, courage, a peaceful character which compels others to quiet consideration by its mere presence, sincerity—and the list is not exhausted. All these are required and the ideal cabinet is the one in which there happens to be the proper amalgamation of talent and character to serve the contemporary needs of the departments and the wants of the country.[16]

Today, the demands are far more exacting than at any previous time, for the amount and importance of governmental business is immense; the relationship of government to the economic and social pursuits of the country has become a blood relationship. The positive responsibility of the cabinet is passionately urged by almost every group and individual in the country, while criticism is continual and searching. Considerations of ability are important for the Chancellorship of the Exchequer only second to that of the prime minister. Is it not a remarkable illustration of the underlying impor-

---

[14] Cf. Debates, February 8, 1932.

[15] E. g., Queen Victoria "was a little shocked at Sir Charles Wood . . . designating the *future Government*, and selecting Lord George Bentinck, Mr. Disraeli (!) and Mr. Herries as the persons destined to hold *high offices* in the next Government" (The Queen to Russell, December 19, 1847). Cf. *Disraeli*, Vol. III, pp. 1165-66, and A. G. Gardiner, *Sir William Harcourt* (London, 1923), Vol. I, p. 464, on the Queen's dislike for Dilke; and S. Gwynn and G. M. Tuckwell, *Life of Sir Charles Dilke* (London, 1917), 2 vols., Vol. I, p. 303.

[16] Derby had to refuse because he could not rely on sufficient men of capacity. Cf. *Disraeli*, Vol. III, p. 1375 ff., and Queen Victoria's Letters (1st series), Vol. III, pp. 79, 80, Memorandum of January 31, 1855.

tance of economics and finance? (Perhaps another age may deem the Minister of Education or Religion, if there were one, second in importance only to the prime minister.) But the confidence of the City is necessary, even if, as since 1946, the cabinet's intentions are radically to reform the economic institutions of the country when City popularity, of course, could hardly be expected. But active hostility must be averted. Men with the quality of gifted organizers are needed, like Herbert Morrison, the "planner" in the cabinet of 1945.

Yet it is not upon capacity for the actual work of government alone that the prime minister may base his choice. Ministers must be good debaters in order to satisfy the House of Commons and the House of Lords that their admiration deserves the continuance of confidence. They must be able to deal with opposition criticism and, of quite as much importance, be good platform speakers and popular with the electorate. They must be on good terms with their own party. A party leader is entitled, in a democratic system, to believe that, be his cabinet never so bad, the curtailment of its life through lack of the arts of popularity will ultimately cause the country to suffer if the opposition is, as a sequel, called to form a government. There is the logic of the party system.

Then the question arises: shall all wings of the party be represented in the cabinet? Shall any attempt be made to include representatives of the various powerful industrial groups? This especially arises in Labour cabinets in England, since the trade-union groups are so large a part of the party; nor is it possible not to pay respect to those who have risen from social humbleness. In the Victorian age the problem was to include the castle and Vere de Vere,[17] later the great capitalistic interests; the problem now is to include and digest the factory and cottage as well as the politician by career, to the possible loss of aggregate efficiency. Another con-

sideration gives pause: how far shall heretical groups be included? Shall they be conciliated by inclusion or braved by exclusion for they have their following among the voters? [18] It depends upon the prime minister's temperament, the extent of the cleavage, the size of the dissentient minority, and the personalities of the prime minister's counselors and the leaders of the minority.[19]

The personal likes and dislikes of the prime minister have much weight. Former membership of a cabinet provides difficulties: an enemy will be made by exclusion; weakness may be the result of inclusion. But the prime minister is not a free agent. He has grown to leadership with others who are almost as good as he: in twenty or thirty years of common service in the same party and in the Commons, in opposition or in ministerial posts of varying rank. They have tested each other's strength and weakness, and all together have been tested by their opponents in years of debates, party conflict, and perhaps office.

Some of the men he is choosing are themselves possible substitutes, should something occur to prevent his own accession to office. He is no Caesar; he is not an unchallengeable oracle; his views are not dooms. He is always on sufferance and its terms are whether he can render indubitably useful service. At any time a rival may supplant him. The little group of leaders when in opposition are held together only loosely, and the conditions of their loyalty are not permanently fixed. Friendship, confidence, and policy suffer transformations. One or two or three who are needed by a potential prime minister

---

17 Cf. *Disraeli*, p. 1160, on the formation of the Derby-Disraeli cabinet, 1852.

18 "In 1846 the attempt to include the Peelites in Lord John Russell's Cabinet (formed 5 July) was frustrated by Peel himself" (Disraeli in a memorandum); the result was a purely Whig cabinet (*Disraeli*, Vol. III, Chap. I, p. 817). Cf. Spencer Walpole, *Lord John Russell* (London, 1889), Vol. I. So with the difficulties on the formation of the second Labour government in 1929—the Left-wingers were excluded by Mr. Ramsay MacDonald.
19 In October, 1946 the Labour cabinet of 18 was composed of 3 teachers, 6 trade-union officials, 3 lawyers, 1 physician, 4 professional politicians, and 1 cooperative-society expert.

may make terms about themselves and others, in regard to office and to policy. There may even be stipulations regarding the nature of leadership. The interactions and the negotiations settle the terms of colleagueship, the respective offices, and the nature, sometimes even the holder, of the prime ministership. But the indubitable prime minister—he who towers over his colleagues by reason of definite party selection, electoral popularity, character, and talent—has indeed a mighty power over the rest, for he has office to give. And only those who have seen the flushed faces, the anxious shuffling and nervous twitchings of the aspirants can know what a sovereign influence over men is thus exerted. When office is their life breath, we cannot be surprised that men pant for it: no spectacle of men in stress is pleasant. Thus, in the rather heated vagueness of an excited consciousness, do the prime minister and his colleagues associate in the formation of a cabinet, not without the frenetic advice and persuasion of unofficial tadpoles and tapers. The African jungle is not the only place where men do war dances and beat themselves into a frenzy in preparation for a kill. Salisbury was heard to say (from personal experience in forming a cabinet): "The Carlton Club resembles nothing so much at this moment as the Zoological Gardens at feeding time."

The Implications of Responsible Government. The principle of responsible government has certain institutional implications. The conventions of the cabinet system are: (1) that members of the cabinet are, as a rule, members of Parliament; (2) that they are necessarily members of the majority, whether of one party or of a coalition; (3) that they hold office only while Parliament and the country do not obviously withdraw their confidence from a minister or the entire cabinet; (4) that the cabinet acts as a unit in face of other governmental bodies, and this implies a certain predominance of the prime minister over his colleagues. We more closely investigate these implications *seriatim*.

Ministers are members of Parliament, that is, they are already elected or are found a seat upon taking office. There have been no exceptions to this, except the apparent exceptions of abnormal times. Such was the case of General Smuts, who was made a member of the Imperial Cabinet in 1917; but the exceptional position is obvious—the normal peacetime cabinet system had been suspended, and the special substitute body adapted to the supreme political direction of World War I was called "cabinet" from habit. But when Ernest Bevin became Minister of Labour and National Service in 1940, he was not a member of Parliament: a constituency was soon found to elect him.

It is clear that the principle is not unintentional, and that it has certain valuable consequences. It was deliberately maintained despite the numerous Place Bills which were designed to exclude from the House those holding place under the Crown. Although it seemed obviously dangerous to an eighteenth-century assembly to risk the sapping tactics of the king's friends by their formally proper appearance on the floor and in the precincts of the House, there was something to be said in favor of the efficiency of a government that is the product of legislative and executive cooperation. Moreover, it often happens that to exclude your enemies is simply to create a rival in an unassailable place. To command them into your continual presence is to have them under a surveillance, which does more than surprise their intrigues, for it irresistibly insinuates itself into their habits of thought, and attends, spectre-like, even in their private councils. This is simply the institutional application of the psychological truth: "Out of sight, out of mind." Hence the principle of ministerial membership of Parliament in England was deliberately excepted from the eighteenth-century acts to exclude from Parliament those holding a place of profit under the Crown.[20]

---

[20] The Act of Settlement (1701), the chief instrument, provided the basis for admitting ministers to the House—though in itself it was a statute which limited the number to be admitted, it did not exclude all. So insistent

Where the principle has not remained, as in the United States, specially devised arrangements have had to be established to secure its manifest benefits. For those benefits are that the mind of the legislature may be made known directly to ministers, not only in set terms and in explicit detail, but also by the activity of that compelling emanation, the "sense of the House," which men like Peel, Disraeli, and Gladstone treated with such respect; and, reciprocally, the minister may answer in direct debate for his administration. Much may validly be learned of the intrinsic worth of a man from the direct and continual observation of his personal demeanor, his features, form, and gestures, and the prodigal indiscretions of his facial expression. The fact that he has been a member of Parliament for some years (sometimes as many as twenty) has already acquainted him with its manners and modes, and taught him a parliamentary tact and a respect for his former colleagues which makes for the smooth and honest working of the system. The courtesies which he as a private member desired and obtained from ministers he now gives. This is not to pretend that office does not create a gulf between ministers and others: there is a saying in France that there is a greater difference between a minister and a deputy than between deputies of opposed parties—but it is a bridged gulf, with easy and frequent communication.

The mutual accessibility of ministers and members is the essence of the system. It is only a minor disadvantage that it excludes from consideration for office any but members (or potential members) of Parliament, talented outsiders, and ex-

perts. A final judgment of the system obviously depends upon how far the Houses are a reservoir of talent, and how far the civil service comes to the aid of the cabinet with its technical assistance. Nor is the cabinet, or any minister, precluded from seeking advice wherever it may be found: they have their week ends and their Beveridges! (The Parliamentary Debates of 1943 contain the very instructive episode of the government's forbidding its civil servants from advising Sir William Beveridge in the preparation of his work, *Full Employment in a Free Society*.) A kind of sporadic and unofficial cooptation is always going on. In the election campaign of 1945 Mr. Churchill sought to scare the electorate with the bogey that some Labour ministers and a potential prime minister might have to answer for or take advice on policy from the executive committee of their party. He ignored the fact that the Conservative ministers and prime ministers regularly took counsel with their party and their friends outside Parliament.

The Large Number of Ministerialists in Parliament. The number of ministerialists in Parliament is necessarily high, for altogether they number about 35, and their undersecretaries and whips add another 40, while one cannot leave out of account the parliamentary private secretaries, another 35. The number is about 16 per cent of Parliament's membership, and 35 per cent of a party of, say 300 (but somewhat less when the number in the Lords is subtracted). It is a direct product of the large scope of state activity and the need each department has for a distribution of departmental and parliamentary work. But it causes the immobilization of an appreciable proportion of the House for the task of criticism, and the creation of a fairly solid block which is as anxious to maintain itself in office as to make a good use of its power. This is one among other reasons why the special function of criticism is concentrated in the official opposition. There is always quite a large and interested weight favorable to the suppression of opposition in one's own

---

was Parliament on the responsibility of ministers that until 1919, when members became ministers their seat was automatically vacated, and they then had to seek re-election after new cabinets came into existence, except for the posts immune by old statutes. By the Re-election of Ministers Act, 1919, ministers appointed within nine months after a general election needed no re-election. In 1926 the provision regarding re-election was abolished.

On the general theme see Edmund Burke's *Thoughts on the Present Discontents*, 1770 (World's Classic edition, Oxford), Vol. II.

party, for office may be too easily exalted above conscience, though, to the office-holder, it appears that office actually serves conscience. The only way out of this situation is to double the number of members of Parliament, a reform which we have already shown (p. 541) to be desirable on other accounts. Some attempt is made by law to restrict the number of ministerialists sitting in the House of Commons, and the intention of the act was to reduce executive influence upon it. But its method is antiquated, for it does not allow for the expansion of state activity and the increase of departments. The proper method is to reduce the proportion by increasing the total membership of the House.

The Report from the Select Committee on Offices or Places of Profit under the Crown, 1941 (no. 120), recommended that to maintain the independence of mind of the House of Commons, a conscious attempt should be made to limit the numbers of ministerialists in the House: the number of ministers would be limited to sixty (including undersecretaries), and the number of parliamentary private secretaries by a "convention" announced in a governmental statement of intention. This report was the result of an inquiry stimulated by an action of Mr. Churchill's. In 1941, Mr. Churchill insisted that Mr. Malcolm MacDonald should not be deprived of his seat in the House on being appointed High Commissioner of Canada. He even introduced a special bill to grant him immunity. The House was anxious for its independence. Therefore it undertook an inquiry into the history and present situation of membership of the House as affected by the holding of office. It recommended limitation of ministerialists to some 10 per cent of the membership of the House.

The House of Lords as a Reservoir of Ministers. The peculiar bicameral system of the British constitution has always dictated that some of the ministry shall be members of the House of Lords. Until 1867, when the constitution was a real if not a formal oligarchy, the cabinet included peers as of social, if not legal, right.

The question was, rather, how many commoners should be included. Since 1867, rapid evolution toward universal franchise, the rise of the party system, and the development of democratic sentiment have reversed this policy. The larger number of ministers are commoners, a very small number, peers; and though we may say that Conservative governments contain more peers, owing to the party's social predilections and the nobility's predilection for that party, other parties have come to regard this element from the strictly utilitarian standpoint of their talent, their money, their influence, and to arrange regular representation in a House which still has constitutional powers. This is specially true of the Labour party's connection with the House of Lords.

The number of peers in the Labour cabinet in 1948 was two, both of whom had been commoners and were created peers by the Labour government for its own representative purposes in the House of Lords. One was the Lord Chancellor.

Political Unanimity of the Cabinet. The cabinet is, of course, composed of members of the party or parties commanding a majority in the House of Commons. The magnificent qualities of the British cabinet system are the clear and immediate corollaries of the special qualities of the British political parties. In so far as the parties are unique, so is the cabinet system. And if the characteristics of the parties lead back to the material and spiritual history of the nation, and the tight smallness of the island and its geographic setting, then the cabinet's distinctive qualities lead back to these also. Other lands work under other conditions, as we have already to a large extent appreciated.

We have generalized the usually proclaimed principle that ministers must belong to the same party, by saying that they must belong to the party or parties commanding a majority in the House of Commons. The principle was proclaimed in the halcyon days when two parties seemed to rule the country, and when everything seemed to suggest that there could never be more than two, even where strife and wild Irishmen abounded. Then, obviously, the principle of responsibility to the legislature meant the selection of the cabinet from the majority party. There was much less internal cohesion in nineteenth-century parties than later generations supposed, and often so much positive dissension that it was not seldom an impossibility to keep together as a government; and not infrequently some sort of coalition between wings and body supported a cabinet. But while the simple and happy external reign of two parties persisted—as it once again does, more clearly than ever—certain obvious governmental advantages resulted.[21]

These advantages were, for the electorate, a choice between two opponents and no more, and this, again, resulted in a fairly simple task of choice, and, for the cabinet, the possibility of unembarrassed leadership. A closer examination of each of these characteristics is important. We have already treated of parties in a democracy, and especially emphasized their organizing and educating functions: and a first judgment might be, the more parties the better. It is clear, however, that given the present quality of the average elector's education and native sagacity, the elector is hardly likely to be able to distinguish between more than two points of view on the same question, particularly

as this is sure to be exceedingly complicated and explained with evidence which, to a specialist, may seem crude and simple, but which to the common man seems exasperatingly subtle. Consider the criticisms of the jury system, where only one issue is before the court! Where there are many parties, they are obliged either to cease to explain in detail, because detail cannot be understood (and this is not good for the elector or for themselves) and rely upon exaggerations of principle uttered catchword-wise, or else to proceed with detail and confuse the voters' minds. Despite the doses of detail, it cannot be said that the electors have arrived closer to an independent and considered judgment than when only two alternatives faced them. Indeed, the reverse is truer. Issues may have been put in faulty generalization. But the competition between two parties brings out their implications. And finally, the House of Commons becomes the workshop of their application to the infinite varieties of the truth.

The party composition or the cabinet is even more important to sound governmental judgment and decision than it is to popular control. It is, indeed, an extraordinary proposition, at first sight, that ten or twelve or twenty men can sufficiently agree on every political problem to accept the principle of collective responsibility. Bagehot has said: "No two people agree in fifteen things; fifteen clever men never agreed in anything; yet they all defend them, argue for them, are responsible for them." The answer, however, is Gladstone's answer:

Rational cooperation in politics would be at an end, if no two men might act together, until they had satisfied themselves that in no possible circumstances could they be divided. [And again:] What are divisions in a cabinet? In my opinion, differences of views stated, and if need be argued, and then advisedly surrendered with a view to a common conclusion are not "divisions in a cabinet." There are, of course, many differences of view; but the question is, can the differences be accommodated? Obviously, the best condition of such accommodation is common allegiance to the same party.

21 Because the government so clearly emanates from election and from the party organization which has organized for and fought the election, there has always been a close and intimate relationship between, on the one hand, Parliament and the cabinet, and on the other hand, the party leaders and the machines outside them. The former participate in the formulation of policy with the latter, and sometimes the personnel of each are identical; this can be seen from Keith Feiling's *Life of Neville Chamberlain* (London, 1946). It is surprising (except for the never-failing queerness of electoral tactics) that Mr. Churchill should have tried to scare the electorate during the campaign of July, 1945, with the charge that the Labour leaders were responsible to an "unknown body"—the National Executive of the Labour party—to whom they could be required to divulge confidential information. Apart from errors of fact, this charge was an error of reasoning. Cf. *Report,* Annual Conference, Labour party, 1946, p. 5.

Though men and women often prefer the satisfaction of desires and ideas which directly benefit themselves more than others, there are loyalties and objectives which cause men to subordinate personal pride, acquisitiveness, jealousy, to the policy of a party. But only of their party, for it is by their voluntary choice that they are members, and, if it meant nothing to them, they would not follow it. Men and women flock to a party out of general instinctive bent towards it, together with strong social habit. It can be expected, therefore, that where a cabinet is simply the acknowledged group of leaders of a common party, the best psychological conditions for successful operation exist. The members are not without personal motives, but these are mitigated by deference to their fellowship in a party, and, if not to the merits of its immediate policy, at least to the danger of the conquest of power by the opposition. On the whole, the best interpretation—full faith and credit—not the worst—self-seeking—is placed upon the action of any member of the cabinet. Where, however, as on the Continent, several parties enter a coalition, the parties cannot avoid entertaining some suspicion of their colleagues. And since, further, their coalition is certain to come to an end one day, when, instead of being brothers-in-arms, they will be parliamentary and electoral opponents, they cannot avoid being continually on their guard against ruses, and ready with a challenge, nor ready to snatch some advantage for themselves, to the detriment of the national well-being as interpreted by the whole cabinet.

This brings us to the vital good in a cabinet system based upon a single party.[22] Somewhere in the state it is of sovereign necessity that there should be a forum where men may not only be absolutely frank with each other, but may be obliged to be frank with themselves. Its members may be as frank as they like in discussion, and they will be heard and met with like frankness, for there is a principle of unity between them reliable, in the last resort, to hold the cabinet together, and its followers satisfied, even if there are some resignations. At least the trial of strength, and the contest of minds, take place in a broad-minded and sympathetic forum. Everything encourages creativeness, for the creator knows that he will not be killed without good cause. If there is an advantage, the party reaps its credit. Where parties enter a coalition, such complete frankness is impossible, for frankness often involves ridicule, the break-up of the cabinet, or the surrender of hostages to electoral opponents. Hence timidity, equivocation, and crises, and, where strong men meet, continual friction and public recriminations. Even where two hostile wings of an English party have met in a cabinet, these results occurred, with the addition that the balance of forces was every day shifted, and there was considerable secret diplomacy between meetings of the cabinet. In the interest of creativeness the most desirable basis for a cabinet is one party, and this is to be weighed heavily against other considerations which would produce government by coalitions—such as, perhaps P.R. and such as extremism of personal and sectional views.

Nor is this all. It is obvious that in all ordinary circumstances the British cabinet, which is based upon a single party, is necessarily sure of a majority for its proposals in Parliament. Once an electoral majority is obtained and the leaders have been almost automatically installed, the rank and file follow them. The severest difficulties and anxieties of the leaders are pre-electoral, not postelectoral, and once in office they may proceed with all dispatch and vigor, with, on the whole, very little to fear from defection. For the nature of the party system, and of the electorate, may condone and even applaud those who murmur against the leaders, and, generally, this is wholesome; but it will hardly countenance revolt more than once. The terms of a pact in a

---

22 The "agreement to differ" of 1931, referred to above, p. 580, left a bad taste in everybody's mouth, and Mr. Snowden, on resignation from its restraints and subterfuges, publicly and venomously spewed it out! Cf. his *Autobiography* (London, 1934), Vol. II.

coalition government, however, can never be stated so precisely as to avoid quarrels about their meaning, nor can all men in each group be forever sworn to their leaders' bargain. Nor, finally, can a coalition government avoid surprises, and when they come there is immediate strain between the leaders and between these and their respective followers. The majority-party system encourages energy and decision, whether the policy is doing or not doing; the coalition system promotes timidity and vacillation, as we shall show in the section on France and Germany, and proved the death of democratic government in Italy, Spain, Poland, and Austria.

The experience of Great Britain in 1929–31 shows clearly the great advantage of the majority-party cabinet system by revealing the weakness of a cabinet founded upon a minority and dependent upon votes uncertain from day to day. The cabinet stumbled from one embarrassment and humiliation to another, and was unable to carry through legislation without mutilations and postponements. Recasting was disagreeable on account of the defeat of policy. To the electorate, the government appeared weak in intention, though, in fact, it was weak only in numbers and unable to control the time table of the House. With all the native energy and creativeness in the world, such a government is obliged to fall back on the defensive, and to eat the humble pie it had previously prepared for the opposition parties.[23] When a cabinet is split, or composed of a coalition, neither the electorate, nor even the skilled historian possessed of all the archives and memoirs, can discover who was really responsible for a

policy. Nor can the electorate ever know truly the proportion of responsibility for resultant policy borne by the government and a two-party opposition which marches into different lobbies at each division, not infrequently bifurcating.

The judgment of the body of electors on this situation is sound. It is adverse to the existence of more than two parties. We need not inquire how far this judgment is self-made, or how far it is uncritically tradition and the diffusion of the views of political leaders and publicists.

The Confidence of the House of Commons. The tenure of office by the cabinet depends upon its control over a majority of the House in matters which it holds to be vital. These must naturally be specific aspects of policy, legislative and administrative, and the cabinet's general repute and authority. When either of these is successfully challenged by an adverse majority, then it is obvious that ministers cannot go on—that is, if the adverse majority is really intent upon its course. For the machinery of government can be brought to a standstill by refusals to grant supplies and to renew annual legislation like the Army Act. But these sanctions are only the ultimate weapons of an outraged House, not the machinery and conventions which daily move the cabinet. The undue emphasis which Dicey has placed upon these sanctions ought to be modified, for the convention of dependence upon a majority is so well established and so permanent an ingredient of political mentality, that nothing else is likely to be needed save in revolutionary circumstances. To that point the convention has always operated quite successfully.

If cabinets were in office more for its sweets than for the fulfilment of policy, there might be a danger that they would flout the wishes of the Commons. But, in fact, policy has been a vital concern of governments, and any serious attack upon this or their general position has caused the resignation of one, or several, or all ministers. The methods of withdrawing confidence are by outvoting a governmental proposal or attacking a department, or accepting a vote of censure or no confi-

---

23 Some Labour politicians vowed, as the result of this experience, never to form a government again, as a minority. Circumstances, apart from appetite for power, can be easily imagined where they would have disavowed the vow. This is, of course, entirely different from their entering the coalition under Mr. Churchill in May, 1940, and remaining until the end of World War II. Even then, many members of the party were restive under the political truce, which nevertheless was maintained, very honorably, by all parties to the bargain.

dence. The latter is, for the whole cabinet, more deliberate and deadly than the former. For, on the attack upon a special policy, minister or cabinet may concede a point which is not vital, or may quibble about the small margin by which it was defeated, or else—where the opposition is composed of two wings (whether parties or groups of a party, whose cooperation in a majority is casual and not likely to form the basis of an alternative government)—there may be occasion for doubt about the sense of the House. But a vote of censure is inescapable.

Is there, on the whole, and truly, much reality in the power of the House of Commons over a ministry? The power of the House itself existed only before the organization of the electorate by modern political parties, when the House was not so completely dependent upon the electorate. When parties were evenly balanced or split, and loyalty to a program and a leader were not so strictly the qualifications for candidature and election to the House, there were surprises and upsets in the division lobby supported by the fairly free groupment of malcontents with the regular opposition.

Since the rise of strong party organizations, the uncertainty of confidence and power has been removed from the House to the inner councils of the party. Differences cannot be settled by open secession, for the electoral penalty is apt to be very severe, or the threat of it is. At the most, the dissentients among the followers of the cabinet can ventilate their grievances in the House in order to frighten the government off its original and challenged course, as in the revolt of forty members against the Labour government's foreign policy in November, 1946, carried as far as debate, but concluded by their abstaining from a vote! Only in abnormal times are the parties likely to be really troubled by parliamentary secessions, when a sharp crisis afflicts the country and new paths have to be sought. Such was the vote of some forty Conservative members against Mr. Chamberlain on May 10, 1940, in passionate protest against his totally blind war leadership.[24] He still had a majority, but his best followers had repudiated his conduct. He gave way to Mr. Churchill's war coalition.

For the rest, the settlement of such disputes (for example, within the Labour government in the fall of 1947 on whether the iron and steel industry should be nationalized and on whether the House of Lords should be reformed) is rather a domestic matter of the party, with the very remote possibility of an appeal to the House of Commons. This means that there is little or nothing to be feared by a cabinet which rests upon a single-party majority for its policy—that ministers individually, and the ministry as a unit, are safe. The cabinet may make concessions to their own party heretics, as of grace, but the House of Commons cannot compel the cabinet to an involuntary course. Further, votes of censure are no more than demonstrations to the public that some part, or the whole, of the opposition is carefully watching the government on behalf of the people. The term has the ring of doom in it, for "vote" sounds as though censure were already resolved and proven. It offers the opportunity on both sides for a full-dress debate: for the government certainly put all their goods into the window, and both sides attempt the highest number of votes that can be mustered. Every member of the House knows very well that the resolution is simply a feeling pretext for a debate and nothing more. Where a government is founded upon a minority of the House, the vote of censure necessarily takes on a more dangerous character. The niceties of a vote of censure mattered very much when the House of Commons was remote from the constituencies in publicity and there was no permanent organization linking it to its constituents, but since the almost definite settlement of policy and government at the polls, responsibility and confidence have become electoral, not parliamentary. Cabinet responsibility is plebiscitary, not representative, responsibility; the House

---

[24] Cf. Winston Churchill, *The Gathering Storm*, Vol. I, chapter 17 (New York, 1948).

has become the agent and mentor of the public, and rarely takes independent decisions. But it is a fierce watchdog that always glowers and growls, worries at the ministers' heels, and barks the alarm of "Strangers!" Once more we see how responsibility has been taken over by the political parties.

Lest any foreign observer mistake the nature of cabinet responsibility, and erroneously subscribe to the creed that the cabinet is not responsible, a few more words are necessary on this score.[25]

The cabinet cannot be turned out as a result of a Commons' vote of no confidence so long as it retains the support of its own rank and file. Does this mean that it has ceased to be "responsible" strictly to the House of Commons? Now, if responsibility means that the cabinet feels obliged to answer to the criticism and admonitions of the House, of the opposition, as well as its own party dissentients, then rigorous responsibility persists. For, as we have seen, the standing rules of the Commons, and certain strong conventions, guarantee to the critics the time and opportunity to challenge the cabinet's activity. Never a day goes by without this barrage flinging flame and lead at the cabinet. A vital factor in this process of discipline is that the nation is socially cohesive and territorially small enough for a fierce public light to beat continuously upon the central forum. The next election is always in the making; it is never out of sight, it is never out of mind. Both cabinet and opposition will have to appeal to the people for power; enough of the people and their mentors are on the doorstep watching the process inside the House. We have seen that the number of votes that separate the winner from the loser in the general election is small enough for future victory to be uncertain, for effort to reverse it to be encouraged,

and for struggles by the cabinet to avert a change in fortune to be compelling. Both sides therefore conduct constant maneuvers to raise themselves in the estimation of the public, and to discredit the other side. The voting figures in the House are secondary to the total cumulative effect of the record of both sides in action and argument. Even if present defeat is not turned into future victory and office, more votes and more seats have their influence upon the will of the government. A constant warning heard in the House is that the cabinet must not forget that nearly one half of the voters did not vote for it. This is an insistent menace. No government can ignore this fact; nor does it.

This process of argument, continued day by day and face to face, keeps the government responsible in policy and administration. Any mistake, any lack of feeling for legitimate and reasonable argument, may cost it public credit and seats.

Finally, the cabinet is not a thing apart from the rank and file of the House. Ministers are themselves rank and file. They are simply the leading members of Parliament of the party which is in the majority. They were nurtured in the House; their apprenticeship in that assembly was their testing and their selection ground. They think and speak and feel as members of the House. They are simply an extension—sometimes outside the House, with special responsibilities—of the membership of the House itself. Their responsibilities are not different in kind, whether legislative or executive, from those of their fellow members of the House. Both they and the rest of the membership of the House feel the same responsibilities, though in a different degree. Every member of the House feels that he is responsible for making statutes, and for executive policy, and for the good conduct of administration, in the same general character as does the member of the cabinet. No hiatus yawns black between them: they are members of one and the same body. Where the one ends and the other begins is not to be determined by any incision mark, still less by a cleft.

[25] I may say, in passing, that I have observed that a quite emotional nationalism still excites some political scientists, who seek to rebut criticisms of their own form of government by drawing wrong conclusions from their usually casual and surface observation of the operation of other systems.

Embracing them there is a seamless web. If these facts are ignored, then the British constitution cannot be understood, nor, *a fortiori,* can any system with which it is compared. The ignoring of these elementary phenomena has led to lamentable errors of emphasis in comparisons between American and British systems.[26]

If a decisive illustration were needed of the power of the House over the will of the cabinet, the reversal of the Labour government's current of emergency and planning policy in August of 1947, might be given.[27] The opposition had no chance at all by mere votes to deflect the cabinet from its path. But its continued, steady onslaught on the government's policies in finance, export, capital investment, labor, and wages, and its emphasis on the short-term rehabilitation problems as compared with Labour's long term planning policy, shook the government's own confidence and beliefs, and mobilized national opinion and focused its burning power on ministers. As a result, the cabinet was compelled to bring in a number of drastic immediate measures, to drop some ministers and appoint new ones, to reconstitute its own planning machinery, and to introduce a reign of enhanced austerity. The formidable impulse thus imparted by the opposition—not unwelcome by some members of the cabinet since it gave them a power by which to discipline the attitude of others in the cabinet—was of lasting effect. The promotion of Sir Stafford Cripps and the relative relegation of Hugh Dalton in November, 1947, flowed from the pressure of the Commons.

Apart from this, the student may very

[26] Thus in the controversy between Don K. Price and Professor H. J. Laski in *Public Administration Review,* Autumn, 1943, p. 317 ff., and Autumn, 1944, p. 347 ff. They have lunged past each other, fiercely stabbing what does not exist. See also the article on administrative responsibility by C. J. Friedrich in *Public Policy* (Harvard, 1941).
[27] See Herman Finer, "British Planning and Nationalisation," *International Labour Review,* March and April, 1948, and "British Central Planning Machinery," *Public Administration Review,* Autumn, 1948.

well be amazed—if he accepts the view of those who disparage the controlling power of the House of Commons over the cabinet—at the fact that on the Coal Nationalization Act, the Transport Act, the Electricity Act, the Town and Country Planning Act, and the Agricultural Act, (that is, the main nationalization acts of 1946 and 1947), scores and even hundreds of amendments moved by the opposition were accepted by the government, though its votes, if it had insisted upon them, could have voted down any proffered amendments.

The Prime Minister and His Colleagues. It is an accepted generalization that the prime minister is *primus inter pares,* that is, first among equals. This rests upon the observed facts in most of the cabinets since Walpole's time, that one man is called upon by the Crown to form a cabinet, that he makes the ministry and distributes offices, presides over cabinet meetings, and that if he decides to resign for any reason of policy, as distinct from personal incapacity, the cabinet breaks up. No statute settles the status of the prime minister; his salary is still drawn in part as First Lord of the Treasury, an office bound up with the premiership since 1721. Only in 1906 was a formal position in the table of state precedence accorded to the office. And only in 1937, in the Ministers of the Crown Act, does the office appear in a statute, for there (clause 4) it is laid down simply that "there shall be paid to the person who is Prime Minister and First Lord of the Treasury an annual salary of ten thousand pounds." Indeed, the notion of a prime minister was not to the taste of the eighteenth-century Venetian aristocracy, who preferred to divide power locally into counties and centrally into cabinets of impotent mediocrities. The story of the challenge to Walpole's position, the first to be called "prime minister," is well known. The protest was one founded on personal and factional jealousy, and not on any impartial consideration of the relationship between the prime minister and his colleagues as it concerned the efficiency of government.

It is obvious that one man may stand out in importance above his colleagues in open competition with them in the political arena. It is just as obvious that unless one is given a formally prior status there must be an incessant competition for it *de facto*. But this is not a condition of efficient government once there is a fairly well-marked difference between rival parties and once responsibility to the people is in any degree acknowledged. For such competition is bound to split a cabinet into real, if veiled, factions, and to put a premium upon the separative forces whenever a difference of opinion arises. A symbol of unity and a practical guarantee of unity are necessary. Some one person must be given a formal predominance which, in itself, will overcome the acerbity or intolerance of private opinions in the cabinet. To rely upon the personal popularity and talent of the man would make the office an object of ambition and a source of contention. No form of government has been able to avoid this conclusion. Not all politicians are willing to admit its necessity. But however it is hidden or counteracted or denied, it exists. A symbol and instrument of unity in the cabinet is necessary: something which shall prevent waste of effort and competitive friction, secure regularity in leadership, and avoid indecision. To achieve this in practice, one minister has been given the prime ministership. In Britain this has come about empirically, and the results are embodied in not very definite conventions. In other countries, British experience has furnished the basis for an attempt at written definition. In Britain the pre-eminence of the prime minister is shown and is secured by (1) the chairmanship of the cabinet, (2) the leadership of Parliament, (3) his position as chief channel of communication with the Crown on general policy, and (4) his acknowledged position in the country as leader of the party and the embodiment of the highest political power.

It is, of course, obvious that an incapable prime minister may ruin his conventional position. Sometimes (like Peel, Disraeli, Gladstone, Lloyd George, or Churchill) he so far towers above his colleagues that he could dispense with the artificial support of convention without disadvantage to government; sometimes (like Addington, Portland, Goderich, Melbourne, and perhaps Baldwin) he is so weak that without this authority he would be impotent. How can the latter contingency possibly arise? It may arise when death or a sudden political crisis results in the rather abrupt realignment of parties and colleagues, so that the prime minister from a previous dispensation is surrounded by ministers whose cooperation with him, and among themselves, is untried and incalculable. Nor is political judgment finite; it may always be modified by some new event revealing more clearly, and comparing, the character and strength of men. Sometimes, then, the prime minister is a weak plaything of the rest of the cabinet; sometimes he is a superior, cooperating, colleague; sometimes, when danger and character combine, he is close to being a dictator—on sufferance and with a limited term.

Even as the prime minister makes his cabinet, so he has the power to unmake it, by resignation or forcing individual resignations. He may even counsel dissolutions to achieve this. According to Lord Oxford and Asquith, the prime minister always submitted the question of dissolution to the cabinet for ultimate decision.[28] But this was not followed by Mr. Baldwin in 1923 or 1935, nor by Mr. Churchill in May of 1945. Ramsay MacDonald's use of this power in 1931 caused the Labour party executive to frame rules to control the action of the leader in regard to his cabinet. He would be required to consult a committee of three persons appointed by the parliamentary Labour party (the members in Parliament) in the formation of a cabinet; he would be subject to majority decisions in the cabinet; and he would recommend dissolution only after decision of the cabinet confirmed at a

---

[28] Lord Oxford and Asquith *Fifty Years of Parliament* (London, 1926), Vol. I, p. 194.

meeting of the parliamentary Labour party.[29]

Against the governmental advantages which issue from the existence of the prime ministership, certain disadvantages must be noticed. The prestige attaching to the office may on occasion result in an undue demand for deference to the opinion of the man, and too narrow a view of the extent of loyalty to be expected from ministers, so that independent views and ideas are forbidden. This has occasioned much distress to some cabinets, and it has occasionally deprived the country of the benefits of collective wisdom. The Baldwin cabinet of 1924 to 1929, the MacDonald cabinet of 1929 to 1931, the Chamberlain cabinet of 1937 to 1940 are cases in point. The ideal prime minister would put into the common stock his own real individual inventiveness and feeling, without forcing the situation by appeal to his formal superiority, and would use his position in the last resort, no more than to avert an actual split, so that the diverse views on the public good should be fully and maturely weighed against each other and the contingency which they are to meet.

Let us consider the significance of the facts about the prime minister's positions of power. (1) The prime minister is chairman of the cabinet, unless prevented by illness or by other engagements. There was a time when the king presided. But this appears to have stopped when ministers in the reign of George I made their resolutions privately before the cabinet meeting, no doubt because at certain points they were collectively hostile to the political pretensions of the Crown, and perhaps because a spiritual gulf developed between Englishmen and the alien king still connected with the state of Hanover. The king enjoyed his mistresses; his ministers enjoyed becoming masters. It is well known that in England and the Anglo-Saxon countries generally, the chairman of any committee attracts a special kind of loyalty, engendered by the

vague feeling that business is expedited and improved by order and that one must be prepared to suffer the chairman's ruling for the sake of the collective enterprise. A casting vote is usually inherent in the chairman; that in itself gives authority, though it should be noted that the cabinet does not take decisions by vote. The popular phrase, the "chair," indicates quite clearly, however, that loyalty is extended not to the incumbent but to an impersonal thing which embodies functional rules. It is clear that the prime minister is at an advantage.

(2) The prime minister is leader of Parliament, nowadays, invariably, leader of the House of Commons. This means that the principal announcements of policy and business are made by the prime minister, that questions on nondepartmental affairs, and upon critical issues, are addressed to the prime minister. (He may be closely assisted—as, in the Labour government of 1945, Mr. Attlee was assisted by Herbert Morrison as "Leader of the House of Commons.") The prime minister is recognized in the Commons to have an immediate authority to correct what he considers to be errors inferrable from any of his colleagues' statements, whether in or out of the House. No cabinet minister would consider he had such a right of correction or reprimand concerning any of his colleagues or the prime minister, but the prime minister exercises such a power, and no one says him nay; on the contrary, the power is considered a right. Generally, the House looks to the prime minister as the ultimate oracle in the matters of doubt where ministers do not give it satisfaction, and as the fountain of policy.

(3) The prime minister is the chief channel of communication with the Crown on matters of public concern; but he is not always only a channel, for we have seen too many examples of the Crown's connection with individual ministers behind the back of the prime minister. What is meant is that the reports of the cabinet councils are made by the prime minister, and that this account is not revised by his colleagues, and that, in emergencies,

---

[29] Cf. Annual Conference, *Report*, 1932 and 1933.

the Crown will first consult the prime minister.

(4) Most important of all, however, is the position of supremacy which the prime minister possesses from being chief of his party. Since William Pitt's time, the interval between a man's entry in Parliament and his accession to prime ministership has only on one occasion been less than thirteen years, and it has more often than not been over twenty-five. No colleague can dispute the significance of this, nor alter the terms of that leadership without either an appeal to the party or such conspicuous merit that the party itself initiates a reform movement in his favor. But this would take years of effort against all the latent sentiment of loyalty which has been created and stored to support the prime minister, a complex of feelings and ideas resulting in such inertia that a leader cannot be dislodged: he goes only when he removes himself by sickness or age (Baldwin, 1937), or flagrant incompetence (Chamberlain, 1940). The tendency is to support the leader against his colleagues, unless there is such scandalous ineptitude that it cannot be hidden even from the stupidest of voters, or unless, as in 1931, a contingency occurs upon which the minister remains in office while a large number of his cabinet secede owing to radical differences of policy. But this point is rarely reached in the modern state. No one knows, and no one cares, where other ministers dwell, but the innocent of innocents knows the meaning of 10 Downing Street. Consequently the prime minister has tremendous authority over his colleagues. They are, in detail, severally answerable to him, the embodiment of cabinet unity and supremacy. This it is which makes a cabinet to be the prime minister's cabinet, and gives him authority which may, if he wishes, undo a majority vote of the cabinet against him; for, finding himself in a minority, he may threaten resignation which will extinguish the adverse majority by extinguishing the cabinet. Moreover, the prime minister was *ex officio* chairman of the Committee of Imperial Defense and at Imperial Conferences. It is of interest to note that in the account of the cabinet given in Gladstone's *Gleanings,* published in September, 1878, the prime minister's position as head of the party is ignored; the gulf between that time and this is as wide as the great party organizations and the franchise which have grown so extensive since 1880. The cabinet, thus composed, is admirably appropriate to its functions, simply because its functional development has by gradual stages governed the nature of its composition.

Once again, it is here necessary to utter a warning, that the status of prime minister must not be thought of as involving his superiority to and independence of his cabinet. The desire on the part of some students to glorify the office of the President of the United States, to give its leadership justification, has caused them, unwarrantably, to point to the prime minister and urge that he stands high above and aloof from his colleagues, giving them orders and deciding "top policy" while they become subordinated into something like the political heads of departments in the United States government. The thought is ridiculous: it is wishful thinking: it is misleading for Britain and for the United States. The prime minister is solid with his colleagues; the party has cemented them together as a multiple but a corporate executive.

CABINET RESPONSIBILITY

IMPORTANT above all is the concentration of responsibility in the cabinet—responsibility for the continuous management of affairs. This responsibility was once toward the Crown; then it became divided between the Crown and Parliament; after 1832 it inclined much more toward Parliament than toward the Crown; since 1867, it is to Parliament tempered by daily regard to electoral and party opinion. Indeed, the electorate and the parties are organized to exact this regard, so that although the formal public arena of answerability is the House of Commons, the questions and the answers are always molded with conscious and necessary reference to the constituent bodies outside it.

Now, the existing treatises on the British constitution insist that the cabinet is responsible in two senses: that every minister is responsible individually for the work of his department, and that ministers are responsible as a body for each department and for general policy. This convention involves the need of explaining its practical daily operation, and what we are to understand by "responsibility." The convention means, in the first place, that certain work is definitely devolved to a known body of men and women, and that thereby each minister is made responsible for a single department of state, while being a member of a body which collectively acknowledges that it is answerable for all administration and policy. Each minister becomes the supreme ruler of a department. He may, if he wishes and if he can, do all the work of that department. But he finds that he cannot do more than generally direct the chief permanent officials in the few critically important matters of high administration, and elaborate, with their constant cooperation and counsel, policies for his branch of the national life. This is, in our own day, a tremendous task, and can be accomplished only by the aid of the civil service, which serves ministers of any party impartially. The minister's task is, on the departmental side, one of stimulus and direction; on the parliamentary and electoral side, advocacy and defense of what he and his colleagues are doing, and, as long as they are in office, they and they alone are assumed to be doing all that which is, in fact, being done. From the standpoint of Parliament and the people, the minister is the department; behind him stands an office, with an address, enclosing a vast reverberating vacuum, and this vacuum is created by the principle of civil service anonymity. The fiction is consciously preserved so that the keen searchlight of criticism shall travel swift and straight, and not be refracted by passage through the medium of the bureaucracy about which Parliament and the public cannot learn very much. The minister is liable for an almost instant answer regarding any of the millions of incidents which may occur in his relations with foreign states, or in all his own counties, towns, districts, parishes, regarding the claims and accidents of the most insignificant individuals, regarding even, let us say, the improper official execution of a diseased cow—he is answerable for all men, animals, things, and natural phenomena, within the purview of his office. He must satisfy the House: and should he not do so, he may be compelled to resign, if the matter is sufficiently grave, having regard to the whole political situation.

What does this last proviso mean? It means that a minister who is regarded as incompetent by the House may be forced to amend his ways by the fear that his colleagues will consider him individually culpable and too incompetent to warrant their intercession. Thus Mr. Shinwell in 1948 was demoted from the cabinet as Minister of Fuel and Power to Secretary of War, because he was too powerful an irritant to the opposition. This decision in any case depends upon the situation of the country and the cabinet's view of the gravity of the offense, and the importance of the man and the deed in the context of their general policy and reputation. On the whole, the Chancellor of the Exchequer and the Foreign Secretary may be said to be exempt from the fear of individual fall, though not of responsibility, because their offices are such important parts of the general policy of the government that its joint fall would almost certainly follow upon their defeat. And yet in December, 1935, the Foreign Secretary, then Sir Samuel Hoare, was dropped—made a scapegoat—in response to a storm in the Commons and the country. Also in 1935, the House made a minister recede on his unemployment regulations, and in 1940 on the wartime restriction of civil liberties. During World War II many individual ministers were dropped after Commons' criticism. And in November, 1947, for the simple and innocent indiscretion of informing a parliamentary journalist of the contents of his budget speech in the lobby of the House and immediately prior to the speech, which details were published in the newspaper before they were told to the House of Commons, one of the ablest Chancellors of this generation, Mr. Dalton, was compelled forthwith to resign from the government. As his prime minister said, "The Chancellor of the Exchequer must be above suspicion in the matter of his discretion."

The Consolidation of Cabinet Business. As a matter of fact, it is rather difficult to fasten any but the blame for quite small and routine departmental matters upon a single minister without involving the whole of the cabinet. Just as local government has become integrated with the work of the central authority, so that today there is hardly any real localization of an important subject of government. And just as there is an enormous and ever-growing integration between individual and governmental enterprise, so have all the individual departments of government become articulated. Fiscal policy unites them all: the economic and social planning activities of the state are impossible without a consciously and densely interwoven regard by each minister for the field of his colleagues. Begin with transport problems and you come to coal, to roads, to the iron and steel industries, to facilities for agricultural freight; begin with mass unemployment and there is no end to the domestic interests or foreign territories involved. The Minister of Labour sets the ball rolling, and involves the Foreign Office; but this involves the Colonial Office, which has jurisdiction over many Mohammedans. Or there is a question of cattle imports raised by the Ministry of Agriculture, whereupon the Board of Trade and the Treasury become unavoidably implicated for maintaining the balance of payments. And so on. Only in the minor matters are the departments entirely self-regarding; and these, as a matter of fact, can hardly ever occupy the personal attention of the minister.

The Location of Responsibility. Hence, even apart from the political value of the principle of collective responsibility, the actual condition of state activities compels solidarity. The history of English government since 1689, shows, however, a steady development of the principle of collective responsibility, not as a means to the efficient coordination of services, but as a means to locate and intensify the sense of responsibility. The purpose is not merely to secure one body because it is one and therefore unmistakable, although that is important in the highest degree. It is also to secure that each member of the cabinet shall be his brother's keeper, especially if he is a particularly weak or a particularly headstrong brother. Even if ministers do not actively play the proctor over their colleagues' policy, the theory is that they ought to. The knowledge that an individual's error may entail collective damnation is supposed to intensify each minister's interest in all branches of administration.

This principle is effective in British government, but like all principles it is as effective as circumstances will allow: the more the pressure of departmental routine, the less can ministers be interested in the activities and speeches of their colleagues; individual interests are so very various that it is only on the very highest and critical matters that the principle operates. The presumption, however, exists, and it is advantageous. Every minister has the duty and the right to discuss and in all ways to offer to improve his colleagues' policy and administration. The disadvantage of the system was pointed out by Morley: "The Chancellor of the Exchequer may be driven from office by a bad dispatch from the Foreign Office, and an excellent Home Secretary may suffer for the blunders of a stupid Minister of War." This cannot be avoided if the good in the cabinet system is to be retained: for to enact individual responsibility would be to encourage each minister to defend himself by pleading his colleagues' culpability, and to be always on his guard rather than open and frank when in council. Nor, as we have shown, is it possible to sever distinctly one branch of public business from another—and the defense would then be, "Had he not done that, and insisted on the other, I should never have been obliged to do this." That way lies the downfall of unity of the cabinet, of frankness in council, and indubitable location of responsibility. We shall see that other manners prevail in other nations.

Would it be possible for the government of the country to be conducted by a changing assortment of ministers regardless of party ties? Yes—if the foreign policy never involved the Exchequer in unwelcome expenditure; if it never raised issues affecting domestic industry, agriculture, and commerce; if it never caused a disturbance in imperial relationships; and similarly between the various other departments. Yes—if men were content to manage their own department only and to have no other interest either in policy or sympathy with groups of their fellow citizens. These conditions are normally quite impossible, though they are nearly realized in the United States presidential executive. Hence a certain pre-established harmony of policy is necessary; hence, an agency, party association, and collective responsibility is indispensable.

Collective Responsibility versus Collective Decisions. However, the principle of collective responsibility means only that ministers answer as one, and in the same sense, for any action in the lifetime of the government. It does not mean—at least, it has not meant—that there is always or often collective counsel or decisions upon everything, even of importance. So much was admitted by Gladstone. We know, for example, that three or four men of outstanding talents and public importance have ever formed, with the prime minister, an informal but definite association called the "inner" cabinet. This is not, and never has been, an institution with recognized public status; it is the spontaneous creation of resourceful kindred souls, as may be proved from anyone's experience of committee work. In English history we see this varying body of cognate leaders fashioning the most important policies, deciding on important offices, settling parliamentary or electoral tactics, with a very energetic day-by-day interchange of thought among them constantly proceeding. They shape their policy and get the cabinet to agree; or see ministers individually and persuade them to agree when the cabinet meets; or act without at all consulting the rest of the cabinet. Yet the whole cabinet is responsible. Collective responsibility has been interpreted to extend to ministers' speeches in the country, since these might seem to commit the whole cabinet.

Then the immense expansion of departmental work and the increase in the number of departments makes full discussion impossible. The minister is too overburdened by his own concerns to be so fully informed or interested in other matters that his judgment is in any sense considered and real. From weighing up the loss of revenue if rebates for local rates are given on playing fields, the Minister of Health must suddenly turn to constitutional reform in Kenya; from speculating upon Soviet propaganda in the British Empire, the Foreign Secretary may be asked to vote on the inclusion of the formula "genuinely seeking work" in an unemployment-insurance bill; while a Chancellor of the Exchequer, overwhelmed with preparations for the Budget, is worried into violently prompt considerations of trade policy with the Dominions or a sharp rise in world prices. He is apt to continue to think of his own work while his colleagues are discussing matters of joint concern. Further, the size of the cabinet has increased in proportion as the principal governmental departments have grown in number. Discussions are either conducted with a loss of concentration, or, if some take up more than their arithmetical share of time, the rest contribute nothing but a vote.

However, it is an exaggeration of serious proportions to hold with one former Conservative cabinet minister that: [30]

The one thing that is hardly ever discussed is general policy . . . The whole system is one

---

[30] Cf. L. S. Amery, *The Forward View* (Oxford, 1944), pp. 443-45, and *Thoughts on the Constitution* (Oxford, 1947), pp. 86-89. Both these works are seriously marred by an antiquated view of the constitution, in which the initiating governing power of the Crown (the cabinet) is over-stressed and the power of parties, Parliament, and the electorate undervalued and even disparaged.

of mutual friction and delay with, at best, some partial measure of mutual adjustment between unrelated policies. It is quite incompatible with any coherent planning of policy as a whole, or with the effective execution of such a policy. It breaks down hopelessly in a serious crisis where clear thinking over difficult and complex situations, definite decisions (not formulae of agreement) and swift and resolute action are required.

This judgment is wildly exaggerated and a little irrelevant. It omits altogether from the account the fact that "general policy" is made by the political parties, if the word "general" has a meaning. It isolates the cabinet from the other policy-forming institutions of the nation. It depreciates beyond what is real the interchange between the core of the cabinet ministers who form the "inner cabinet."

These facts, and the need to secure mature consideration of policy, have caused the development of the practice of submitting particular branches of policy to committees of the cabinet, of which a more detailed consideration is undertaken presently.[31] This practice is almost as old as the system itself, but in recent years it has become more urgent than before, owing to the enormous growth in the amount and complexity of business. As matters arise upon which preliminary study is essential—that is, where a policy has to be elaborated from the first careless inspiration, and where it must be measured by the standards of the scientifically possible —*ad hoc* committees of three or four members are appointed from the cabinet, members especially interested or capable being selected, or indeed, almost selecting themselves by their acknowledged interest or capacity. These prepare the subject, with the aid of departmental experts and friendly nonofficial advisers, and report to the cabinet, which may do whatever it wishes with the recommendation, but which is likely to accept with little amendment, owing to the casual nature of their knowledge of the subject and the burden of their preoccupations. This development is necessary and beneficial and is bound to go further. Collective council is

not absolutely necessary to collective responsibility where members of the cabinet are all of one party, and linked, as they are, to the electorate by the bonds of a party program. Furthermore, as we shall see presently, various ministers have come to be grouped in permanent cabinet committees for large interdepartmental planning, to save the cabinet's time and to free it for the highest policy of all.

It will be appreciated that a cabinet will resign as a body only if its over-all, essential policy is rejected by a frontal assault in the Commons, or by the firm repudiation of some branch of its policy on which it places exceptional significance (for example, housing or food-subsidy policy, in a Labour government) and which is usually closely bound up with its general character and policy; or if it is overtaken by internal differences and loss of self-confidence and needs the fresh breath of a popular re-election to redefine its policy and restore its authority and courage. If, in what may be the long interval before such pressures come upon it, there are individual examples of ministerial incompetence or sustained and irreconcilable opposition within the cabinet, what is to be done?

More and more, as the cabinet as a whole becomes impregnable because it possesses a party-prefabricated solid following in the Commons and the country, it is both a necessity and the practice for the prime minister (and the inner cabinet group) to obtain the resignation of the errant minister and periodically to reform the cabinet—and thus to satisfy the needs of efficiency, the self-respect and prestige of the cabinet and the party, and to cease to present a weak flank to the Commons and the press and the nation. The Labour government began in 1945 with a cabinet of elders of the party, and events and experience caused it to carry out successive reconstruction to substitute the younger men now tested in minor office and in Parliament. There is a noticeably increased tendency since World War I to maintain the integrity of the cabinet by discarding the incompetents and such incubuses as may be technically

31 Cf. p. 604.

capable but whose personality is so prickly as to draw upon the government, which must get its business done, uglier opposition than necessary. But some ministers may be dissatisfied with the cabinet, and they may not be able to persuade their colleagues to change their policy. They may then resign—like Mr. Eden, Mr. Duff Cooper, and Lord Salisbury, in 1938 and 1939 after Munich—to signal their disagreement, and may explain their position by letter and then in a special time available for them in the House of Commons, after which they will take their chance that their own persuasion and political events may vindicate them in the future and some day restore them to office.

Unanimity and Secrecy. This brings us back at once to that which we were concerned to labor in a previous page: namely, that the vital principle of collective responsibility is the homogeneity of the party upon which the cabinet is based. The spiritual condition of vigorous, frank, and independent creativeness, which is productive of so much good, is that there should be only a small risk of disruption and self-seeking; and this is provided by the political unanimity of the cabinet. Another condition, which is made really practicable only by the existence of political unanimity, is the secrecy of the cabinet proceedings.

Cabinet meetings are very private. This characteristic appears to me not to have commenced on any grounds of modern utility. I should think it was rather that, at first, royal councils were private because, in the days of conquest and challenge to the throne, the success of many royal policies depended upon surprise, and because strong government was secured by the authority which attaches to mystery rather than by open public consideration, and, later, because the Crown and Parliament were in conflict. Since 1832 the government of the day has had to secure its inner deliberations from the premature attention of an organized opposition in Parliament and the country, too well aided by the press whose eyes and ears are everywhere. Further, since

government is so pervasively occupied with the economic and social order, any policy may affect thousands of powerful and wealthy citizens, whether they be "economic royalists" or trade unions, so that if a secret is divulged before action is taken, it may happen—indeed, it has happened—that such citizens have evaded the government's intentions. Another thing must be remembered: to disclose what happens at the cabinet is inevitably to disclose differences among its members: to do that is to give the opposition the opportunity of playing upon those differences, and inevitably to cause a breakdown of united responsibility and to encourage mutual recrimination and individual reticence and distrust among ministers. Finally, publicity must reduce the independence of mind of ministers in relation to each other, and, by exposing them to the intervention of public opinion, reduce their mature, rational, and independent contribution to the process of policy making. A prime minister put his finger on the heart of the matter when he declared [32] that privacy of discussion "could only be made completely effective if the flow of suggestions which accompanied it attained the freedom and fulness which belonged to private conversations—members must feel themselves untrammelled by any consideration of consistency with the past or self-justification in the future." He wanted "irresponsible license in discussion." Inklings of these truths are to be found in the memoirs or speeches of cabinet ministers, though none expresses the whole philosophy.

The secrecy of cabinet proceedings is safeguarded by law and convention. The Official Secrets Act of 1920 forbids the communication to unauthorized persons of official documents and information, with heavy penalties. (The law was enforced in 1934 by a fine against Edgar Lansbury, son of a former cabinet minister, George Lansbury, in the biography he wrote of his father in which a memo-

---

[32] Lord Salisbury, in Gwendolen Cecil, *Life of Salisbury* (London, 1921), Vol. II, p. 223.

randum submitted to the cabinet was published.) The rest is convention. If a minister wishes to speak or write in his defense on leaving the cabinet, convention requires that he obtain permission of the Crown, whose servant he formally is, but this means getting permission from the prime minister—sometimes not impartial in the matter. Sooner or later, in biographies or defense in the Commons or Lords, the facts seep out—but rather later than sooner: that is to say, when publicity can do no harm to contemporary mutual trust and faithfulness of ministers. The guesses of the journalists may be inspired, but they are only guesses and can be brushed off as only guesses.

It is of special urgency in days of high nationalism and warlike friction between impassioned nations that the cabinet's state of mind not be made the subject of distracted and inflammatory debate until it has arrived at a considered policy. We may remark also that if secrecy helps to produce unanimity by preventing the obtrusion of public and disturbing elements into discussion, political unanimity is a very important condition of secrecy. Both help to concentrate responsibility upon a single unit, the cabinet, and since, also, responsibility is shared by all, and since no exact discrimination appears between the real and the supposed authors of a policy until long after the event, the more care has to be taken about the inclusion of people in the cabinet, for no one may be included who is so incapable as to cause its better members to fall.

Efficiency of the System. We have still to determine the real meaning of "responsible," but we postpone its consideration until we have indicated the significance of certain subsidiary facts. The cabinet, constituted and responsible as we have described, is the energetic, driving force in a government. In each department it sets the direction of administration, and a fairly harmonious tendency permeates them all. Economic and political circumstances (analyzed in the chapters on party) and a fortunate instinct for the basic necessities of government endowed England for a considerable part of the last century with the sufficient semblance, and sometimes with the reality, of a two-party system. This meant that there was assured to the majority party a stable period of government, which, from the Grey ministry which began in 1831, to 1940, amounted to an average of three and three-quarter years per ministry.

The effect was that not only did the whole ministry have time in which to consider, introduce, and pass its legislation, but it also had time to affect considerably the execution of the law, which, up till 1850, was perhaps more important than legislation as a part of modern statecraft. Nor is that all; for if we excluded the transition ministries when parties were in an abnormally fluid state (such as the first Peel ministry of 1834-35, the first and second Derby-Disraeli ministries of 1852-59, and one or two in the early home-rule period), we should find the average length of a cabinet substantially longer than three and three-quarter years. Each minister can never hope to learn everything about his department, but he can hope to learn much about his civil service advisers and sometimes impress his personality and politics upon them. This cannot be done in a short time, for the minister is usually an amateur and knows little about the office to which he is appointed. There is some good in this, for he is often prepared to overturn bad precedents as well as good. At the end of six months he is just beginning to know his own men and the rudiments of their craft. How can he be effective unless he has time to go further and become capable of independent decision? Though it may be argued that with the certain prospect of only a short term in office, the minister will be the more energetic, we may be sure that such energy will be no more than frantic. Only a long period in office gives men the knowledge, the composure, and the appetite to undertake large projects which will bear fruit in their time. Moreover, it is essential to give every holder of authority in the modern state ample time for second thoughts—for the issues are so complicated that only personal experience and touch can unravel the wrappings of their novelty and make real their quantitative and correlated weighing. The convention and the practice of the responsiveness of the civil service to ministers is partly the result of their length of time in office.

The cabinet gradually hammers out its program of legislation, bringing its general principles into closer relation to the concrete possibilities as disclosed by careful examination of the advice of the administrative experts and scientists, and by the arguments of Parliament. The crude clay of desire is fitted into the mold of natural possibility, and the result desired is attained with the minimum of violent collision and coercion. In this process the cabinet is not in relation with Parliament alone, but with its party and the deputations of citizens who treat with individual ministers. It learns just how much Parliament and the public want and can take: and so also receives constant psychological collaboration. There is a continuous exertion of influence upon the cabinet by the public through channels other than the formal representative body, and this influence, already large in our own day—so large as badly to frighten those who desire the exclusive location of publicity and regularity in representative bodies—is bound to become larger. After so short and special an experience of parliamentarism, we have not yet exhausted the possibilities of governmental invention. It has been found that action through the constituencies, the parties, and Parliament is too slow and technically too irresponsive to meet certain emergencies—while men, in each other's immediate presence, arrive, for good or ill, at understandings which are impossible amidst the exaggerations and distortions of "representation." In these cases it has happened that some members of the cabinet are deputed to intercede: usually in cases in which the need for the continuity of social services would sooner or later necessarily involve the government in what seemed, before the basic industries were nationalized, to be a dispute between two nonofficial groups over an apparently private matter (as in transport or coal mining or the textile industry or the price of food), since nationalization is clearly of universal concern.

The cabinet, as we have already shown, has a very effective control over the time of the House, and this enables it to decide the priority of business and the amount of discussion allowed to each item. This has been possible only when majority-party cabinets have existed. Ministers also guide the standing committees even where only details are supposed to be in question. We have also shown how the custom of the constitution and the procedure of Parliament throw upon the cabinet sole responsibility for the finance of government, with the attendant benefit that ways and means are correlated to expenditure by one mind, and that policy and finance are considered in a continuous and living relationship. Then the cabinet is the more securely attached to the House by its whips.

Before the country the cabinet is a unit: answerable, energetic, and more than a mere official governing body: it is an ornamental-philanthropic convivial institution, whose attendance at city banquets, motor shows, new hospitals, football, cricket, and boxing matches of national, international, and imperial importance, and the opening of sewage works and maternity homes brings it into brotherly touch and familiar *tutoyage* (in England indicated by the application "old" or followed by the diminutive form of the name) with rich and poor, giving to all the illusion that, after all, "there is no sovereignty except mine."

The Status of The Crown. Between the cabinet and the Crown there is a continuous and close contact. Here we have only to make some general observations. Ministers are formally "His Majesty's Ministers," but convention has made them the people's ministers, and responsibility, which was formerly to the Crown, is responsibility to Parliament and the people. This responsibility is assumed by the minister by his acceptance of the principle that all the public acts of the Crown need countersignature by a minister. The countersignature is the sign that responsibility to the sovereign, whatever the sovereign may really consist of, is accepted. The person of the Crown is thus almost entirely lifted out of the sphere of political decision. Yet there are certain conventions which still provide the Crown with the possibility of political activity. They are *first,* that the Crown has the right to information about cabinet decisions and parliamentary proceedings; and *second,* that the Crown has the right to communicate with (to warn or encourage) its ministers, either through the prime minister or directly—both of these on the basis that the Crown should have the right to explanation of that for which its consent is asked.

Once those rights are existent, the way is open for any amount of royal influence which the cabinet, Parliament, and the country are prepared to tolerate. They are not in our own day inclined to tolerate much, but though it is puny, it is more than what is recognized by those who imagine that the plenitude of governmental power has passed from the hereditary to the elective institutions. Broadly speaking, since the death of Queen Victoria, royal intervention has been used only to advocate the unity of the nation, at times when party and group warfare has threatened to cause violent dissension, and to promote "national" and imperial interests in international affairs. All depends upon personality and talent, but the hereditary, symbolic, and specially manufactured social status of the Crown enable it to exercise a unifying influence in cabinet counsel. It is not a power *behind* the cabinet, but *by* and *with* the cabinet, and, of course, never against its determined will. It has some field of personal authority in certain cases of dissolution of Parliament; and in the creation of peers to help a government to carry a policy through the Lords.

The Nature of Cabinet Responsibility. If responsibility is supposed to keep cabinets in the path they ought to go, what is the motivation and directing force in responsibility? Responsibility means that a position of trust is held; that is, that

power can be used only within certain defined limits. The question is, then, who draws those limits, who watches over them, and what is the punishment for their violation? Until 1689 the limits were drawn by the Crown, and the Crown itself was prompted by some reference to the state of opinion in the country and Parliament and among its friends. No organized and acknowledged institution expressed the limits of royal discretion, for Parliament spoke as a congeries of individuals or groups, neither unmistakably nor in unison; the people were subject, not sovereign; the state of representation was purposely vicious; while there was no question, until matters reached a revolutionary point, of really disciplining a king in the only effective way then known—by civil war.

Since 1689 the successful governmental contrivance was found of an irremovable but powerless Crown, and a powerful but removable ministry. Between the time when the early system was driven to its fall, and the rise of the modern system, the device of impeachment was tried— that is, a formal trial of the conduct of a minister before the House of Lords, which might end in exile, imprisonment, fine, or death. (The United States constitution contains this prescription regarding the President—article II, section 4.) This method of imposing political responsibility failed because in its time it was difficult to distinguish the part played by the Crown and that played by ministers in any specific act of government. Even had it not failed on this account, it would have deserved to fail on another: it was too serious a penalty to use for small errors, and too dreadful to carry out in any case. For to govern is to venture to create, and no creation is without risk of error; while even when a policy is successfully realized, the more successful it is, the less will political opponents like it, and the more jealous and ready to impute sin will they be. To prescribe a grave penalty for failure to satisfy avowed opponents is to paralyze government, while heavily to penalize error is to extinguish experiments the results of which must always be speculative. Supposing impeachment and execution were the consequences of an ill-timed return to the gold standard! Mr. Churchill would have been condemned to death in 1925 by followers of J. M. Keynes! A mode of settling responsibility was needed not so suspiciously partisan or criminal in aspect; and with it a means of punishment was required severe enough to discipline leadership yet not so severe as to kill it. These things were found in collective responsibility on a party basis, and the loss of office when this had been abused.

Now there have been times when the House of Commons itself has decided the terms of satisfactory cabinet leadership. There were years when parties were fairly evenly matched and liable to disintegration and would transfer their allegiance upon the issues presented to them. This state of affairs ceased to exist in 1896, and even before that, from 1867, did not exist save on matters relating to Ireland: that is, the cabinet had not to face a possible defection and loss of office as correctives. What then? Of what use, in such circumstances, to say that the cabinet is responsible to Parliament? The truth is that the responsibility of cabinets need not be forced, and yet responsibility may be none the less strict if the cabinet voluntarily accepts the burden: that is, the convention of *quod populo placuit leges habet vigorem* has grown up and constitutes part of the ever-effective controlling spiritual force of English politics.

This convention might continue and operate beneficially in its vigorous youth, and by virtue of the memory of the disaster which befalls politicians and people when it is disregarded, but men too soon forget the lessons of other people's experience. At the date when the House of Commons ceased to be the headmaster of cabinets and, reversing the parts, came instead under the cabinet's tutelage, the cabinet learned to obey a new mentor: the people. If it does not please the people, it loses votes for its party, and this means a loss of its own power and a gain for the opposition. At least, the cabinet

thinks so; and *this belief is the vital animating principle of the British constitution.* The House of Commons is the forum of debate, and the theater in which is conducted the comparatively rational dissection of conduct, but the investigation and the defense are not, in the ultimate resort, for the House: the ultimate spectators and judges are the party councils, the multitudinous groups, societies and associations, and the voters.

The Meaning of Office. Is that all? To lose office? No graft? None! Is there nothing stronger in the constitution to keep ministers continuously impelled by a sense of responsibility to the people? Can this possibly be effective? Strangely enough, it is. The prospect of losing office is a very strong corrective in British politics! For when office is lost, prestige evaporates, dignities are transferred, authority and dominion vanish! The man is smaller than the office, and friends turn away to new sources of favors *ubi bene ibi amicus!* The world treats the unlucky and the unsuccessful with ill-disguised contempt. The House no longer hangs upon their lips, and it is not altogether pleasant to lose official emoluments. Although most men sighingly protest that duty alone forces them to suffer the intolerable burdens of office, only those who are in office, or sure of it, make such complaint: the rest are strangely silent. Nor is any desperate energy or dispatch shown to leave office. For though all the motives we have insinuated do operate, there is still one of greater strength: and that is, that those who possess office in Britain control a vast range of political opportunity. All that they strive to amend in a faulty state, all that they desire to protect from savage aggression, becomes possible when they are in office and impossible when they are out. It is a question of who shall, for a stretch of time, be sovereign or subject—you, your class, your idea of your country, or other people and their ideas and interests? Gladstone speaks sound sense on this subject.

The desire for office is the desire of ardent minds for a larger space and scope within which to serve the country, and for access to the command of that powerful machinery for information and practice which the public departments supply. He must be a very bad minister indeed who when in office does not do ten times the good to the country that he would do when out of office, because he has helps and opportunities which multiply twenty-fold, as by a system of wheels and pulleys, his power for doing it.

The number of careerists, pure and simple, is rather smaller in British politics than elsewhere, and the number of men and women positively and passionately devoted to their own idea of social amelioration greater. Gladstone has been quoted, but a more recent prime minister avows the same passionate attachment to power. Neville Chamberlain confided in his private diary on the publication of his brother Austen's political letters: [33]

He has not the eagerness of temperament and the inexhaustible vitality of Father [Joseph Chamberlain], which kept him ever revolving some constructive idea . . . I believe I lie somewhere between the two . . . there are very few and brief moments when I feel I can't bear to talk or think of the politics that have become my main purpose in life. Indeed, my fear is always lest this prime interest should obliterate my other interests in art or music, or books, or flowers, or natural history.

The potent impulse of duty to society, the strong and irrepressible disposition to "give the lead" to other people, the avidity for power and prestige, the enjoyment of the tumult of business, the itch for fame coupled with the half-conscious memory of revered statesmen of the older school, and the sheer blind loyalty to a party—all play their part in driving men and women into politics and place. Take any or all of these factors, make one or all an intensely strong urge in an individual's life, then threaten to balk the free action of that passion, and is that not surely a compelling regulator of the statesman's action in politics? Hence office means much; and its loss also; and those pleasures and pains are the sanction of responsibility.

Moreover, as we have already shown,

[33] Cf. K. Feiling, *Life of Neville Chamberlain* (London, 1946) p. 287.

there are no formal limits to the sovereignty of cabinet-*cum*-Parliament. Cabinet responsibility and the whole electoral process are intimately bound together. This means that the cabinet has considerable latitude in the freedom to initiate and execute policy. After all, the cabinet consists of the leaders of the majority in Parliament and among the electors and the managers of the party machine. It will go beyond the possible margin when, like Peel, it emancipates the Catholics or repeals the Corn Laws, or, like Gladstone, springs Home Rule upon its party, or, as in 1935, pursues obstinately a foreign policy of appeasing potential aggressors. But with time and care, persuasion and coaxing, it can exploit to advantage the prestige and status and leadership and the accumulated loyalty of a decade or two, into an initiative independent, at least, of previous pledges to the electorate. Thus Disraeli and parliamentary reform, thus, the Labour government and the abundant fullness of its nationalization program of 1945-49 and particularly its reform of the House of Lords; so, especially in foreign affairs, and in many minor matters. Nor is there any doubt that this is good democracy. So long as government is for the people, and by their frequently elected and recallable representatives, it is proper that they should lead the people as well as follow them.

The cabinet system could not work at high efficiency were it not for a number of accessory factors in designed combination. These are: (1) the organized arrangement of the cabinet's work through committees, interdepartmental coordinative arrangements at the official and ministerial level, served by the cabinet secretariat and the economic, statistical, and planning staffs, and linked with official consultative bodies representing economic interests; and (2) the neutrality and anonymity of the civil service, not less than its superb ability. These may be called *technical factors*. There are others which may be called *party factors*: (3) party control through the caucus and representative devices, and (4) the continuous existence of a "shadow" or "ex"-cabinet composed of the leaders of the opposition. Each will be discussed in turn.

CABINET COMMITTEES, SECRETARIAT, AND ADVISORY BODIES

THE discussion of this accessory factor is rather more extensive than the rest, owing to its peculiar role in a democratic socialist state.

Before 1916, the cabinet met without any carefully planned agenda. Of these meetings no minutes were officially taken, though the prime minister sent a note of the result to the Crown, and other ministers scribbled private notes of what occurred.[34] There was serious need for such a plan of business and a formal record of transactions, as the many complaints by ministers and their fretting secretaries about the haziness of cabinet decisions show, and as the number of important disputes about the distribution of responsibilities historically demonstrates. From time to time some records were drawn up, but a continuous recording secretariat was late in coming—*first,* I think, because of the convention of secrecy, and *second,* because of the atmosphere of suspicion and factious hatred in politics of 1689-1832, partly due to the lasting consequences of the change of dynasty, when the minutes of the previous body of ministers (one can hardly say cabinet in a modern sense) might have been used as the basis of parliamentary recrimination and even impeachment. Then, *thirdly,* when the growth of business might have already pressed for new developments, individual ministers were probably too busy with their own work to think and demand a better system, leaving it to the prime minister and the "inner" cabinet to decide the order of business. But today the appeal is openly

to the people; no minutes can involve a cabinet more than their policy has already done; and the way was clear, from 1900 at least, for these formal records. The spirit of "it-is-not-done" was not, however, overthrown until World War I showed that it was humbug; and since the advent of Lloyd George's war cabinet in 1916, the cabinet has had a secretariat, agenda, and minutes. The secretariat was also in close personal relation with the Committee of Imperial Defense of which the prime minister is chairman;[35] in 1938 when the great first secretary, Sir Maurice Hankey, retired, his successor, Sir Edward Bridges, became secretary to the C.I.D. also. But in World War II the Committee of Imperial Defense was merged in the War Cabinet organization, and after it, as will be shown presently, its successor became an integral part of the committee organization of the cabinet.

It must be borne in mind that the Cabinet meets normally once a week, and yet the control by government of the social and economic life of the nation is remarkably extensive and penetrating. To acquit its obligations so that the nation may thrive, a mere meeting of the cabinet is palpably far from enough even with emergency meetings when necessary. The cabinet needs help. Gradually since 1919, more swiftly during World War II,[36] and even more resolutely and consciously since 1945 an advisory and revolutionary system has been constructed to serve the cabinet. Its features are: (1) cabinet committees, and then the official auxiliaries: (2) the cabinet secretariat or offices, (3) an Official Steering Committee, (4) the Economic Section of the Cabinet Secretariat, (5) the Central Statistical Office, (6) the Central Planning Staff, and (7) the Industrial Productivity Committee. Working with it very closely also are (8) the Treasury, the Departments, and the Corporations, and (9) consultative auxiliaries and working parties in industry.

Cabinet Committees. The cabinet does a considerable part of its work through

---

[34] For an account of this body, concerned with the military problems of the Commonwealth and Empire, and linking the British cabinets to the governments of the Dominions, see H. Finer, "Cabinet and Commons under the Impact of War," *Political Science Quarterly,* September, 1941; and M. Hankey, *Diplomacy by Conference* (London, 1947), Chap. 4.

[35] Cf. Hankey, *op. cit.,* Chaps. 2 and 3.
[36] Cf. Finer, *op. cit.,* pp. 321-60.

committees of itself. Their number, their exact terms of reference, when they shall report, who shall compose them, are entirely in the hands of the cabinet, especially of the prime minister. They are parts of the cabinet—its agents—and have no being apart from it; their status is not and cannot be independent of it. It is only by accident that the existence of the committees may become known: their composition is not officially disclosed in order to preserve the principle of collective responsibility. As Herbert Morrison, Lord President of the Council, explained to the House of Commons: [37]

I cannot take my honorable friend far into the secrets of Cabinet organization . . . The Cabinet is responsible for the acts of Government, just as Ministers are directly responsible to the House. How the Cabinet does its business, and to what extent it delegates certain things to Cabinet Committees is, if I may say so, the Cabinet's business because it accepts the responsibility. I can only assure my hon. Friend that decisions on policy, according to the nature of the decisions and their importance, the degree of their significance, and also the degree to which they may cause trouble and controversy in the House or the country, are settled at the appropriate level. That is, of course, the responsibility of the Government. These things are settled by one committee wherever possible, but the number of committees to discharge a series of functions is, of course, a matter of convenience and administration. . . It is not, of course, the practice for Governments to reveal the membership or chairmanship of Cabinet Committees if they can possibly help it. Indeed, we do not often reveal that they exist. . .

Of course, a name disclosed is an aperture for public criticism: and the criticism would seek to differentiate between the contributions of the named and unnamed participants in cabinet policy making.

A cabinet committee is composed of several ministers chiefly concerned with the subject matter to be decided. The chairman is usually the minister principally concerned. They often have at their sessions law officers and such civil servants as may be useful. They report to the cabinet, usually an agreed policy,

and thus save the cabinet's time. If agreement is impossible, then the unsettled issues are decided by the cabinet. Thus, they serve the prime minister by coordinating departments at a subcabinet level, and make feasible his "span of control" responsibilities.

The committees are of two kinds, temporary and standing, the former sometimes called *ad hoc*. Every now and again an *ad hoc* committee is set up to handle a special difficulty—thus, the development of atomic energy or the establishment of the national medical service as a going concern, given the refusal of most doctors to enter the service. Of this committee the Minister of Health was chairman. A housing committee functioned in 1945 and 1946, and perhaps later still, to prepare and facilitate the developing stages of the government's housing plans. At any one time there may be more than a score of these cabinet committees, most in operation more or less *ad hoc,* more or less permanently. Of recent importance were the Manpower Committee and the Fuel Committee. Their purposes may be inferred from the necessity of converting the economy of World War II to peacetime needs, the long economic emergency in the aftermath of the war, the nationalization of fuel and power, and the relationship thereof to exportable manufactures upon which the British standard of living precariously depends.

Among the standing committees of the cabinet are (1) the Legislation Committee; (2) the Defense Committee; (3) the Lord President's Committee; (4) the Policy Committee [38] (formerly Committee on Overseas Economic Policy); and (5) the Production Committee [39] (formerly the Minister of Economic Affairs Committee).

(1) The Legislation Committee is the

[37] Debates, February 28, 1947, cols. 2129-32.

[38] Includes the Prime Minister as chairman, the Minister of Economics, the Chancellor of the Exchequer, the Lord President of the Council, the Foreign Secretary, and the Minister of Labour.
[39] Includes the Minister of Economic Affairs as chairman, Trade, Labour, the Treasury. Town and Country Planning, Fuel and Power. and Supply.

former Home Affairs Committee, presided over by the Lord President of the Council, who in the Labour government of 1945 is deputy to the prime minister and leader of the House of Commons. It scrutinizes all legislation coming from individual ministers for technical and substantive characteristics, and deliberates on the priority and tactics of passage of the bills and other procedure in Parliament.

(2) The Defense Committee is of peculiar importance. At the end of World War II the Cabinet did not revert to the prewar Committee of Imperial Defense system, but instead adopted for defense purposes the arrangement which had served so exceedingly well during the war. In the war, the Prime Minister, Mr. Churchill, had assumed also the office of Minister of Defense and became thereby a superior unifier of the three armed services, War, Air, and Navy.[40] He was chairman of a Defense Committee of the Cabinet which included the ministers principally concerned with military operations and the Ministers of Production, of Supply, and of Labour and National Service. It was served by the Chiefs of Staff, themselves properly grouped in a committee, and by joint staffs for planning, supply, and the rest. Thus, planning for defense and action for defense were combined.

This arrangement has been adapted to peacetime purposes and, above all, linked organically with the economic and social planning activities of the government.[41] The Minister of Defense is now a permanent part of the machinery of government and a member of the cabinet. The Defense Committee is under the chairmanship of the prime minister, but since his load of business is heavy, the Minister of Defense regularly deputizes for him. The supremacy of the prime minister's authority must be noted. The membership of the committee is kept flexible, but, unprecedentedly, the government indicated its permanent nucleus: the prime minister, the Minister of Defense,

the Service Ministers, the Lord President, the Foreign Secretary, the Chancellor of the Exchequer, the Minister of Labor, and the Minister of Supply—ten ministers, of whom six are in the cabinet. The prime minister's formal chairmanship was explained to the House of Commons as follows: [42]

. . . the Prime Minister presides over the Defence Committee precisely because the wider aspects of defence with which I am now dealing must be dealt with by the authority of the Prime Minister who has to take full account not only of the claims of defence, but also of the claims of all the other activities of the nation, and obviously that could not be handed over completely to the Minister of Defence.

The Defense Committee, normally under the Minister of Defense, deals, under the cabinet, with:

The organization for national defence in its broader aspect, including both current questions of high policy in the sphere of defence, and also the preparation of plans over the whole field of government activity, both civil and military, for mobilising the entire resources of the nation in a major war. . . It will be responsible for the review of current strategy and also for the preparation of plans for the country's transition from peace to war. . . .[43]

Besides his duties of presiding, the Minister of Defense is responsible for (a) the broad apportionment of available resources between the three services in accordance with strategic policy, the framing of a policy of research and development, and the correlation of production programs; (b) the settlement of questions of general administration on which a common policy for the three services is desirable; and (c) the administration of interservice organizations, such as Combined Operations Headquarters and the Joint Intelligence Bureau.

(3) Most important for civil economic and social planning until September, 1947, was the Lord President's Committee. At that time its scope became less

---

[40] Finer, op. cit.
[41] Cf. Central Organisation for Defence, Cmd. 6923 (H. M. Stationery Office, 1946).

[42] Debates, October 30, 1946, col. 625.
[43] Cf. Central Organisation for Defence, p. 7.

clear and certainly was narrowed. Its title indicates its chairmanship. It is composed of ministers primarily concerned with home affairs and (to September, 1947) economic affairs—that is, all departments except Foreign, Colonial, Dominions, and Defense. This cabinet committee came into existence in 1940 (undergoing various transformations) with the cardinal purpose of bringing into regular and unifying contact the many departments involved with home and economic problems so that they might unitedly prosecute the main lines of policy required of them by the War Cabinet. The War Cabinet uttered its directives after it had heard the strategy prepared by the Defense Committee. The Lord President's Committee would declare how far its segments of the nation were able to meet the requirements of a strategy; would ask, if necessary, for modification of strategy; and in the end, would make commitments. Many disagreements were solved in this committee, relieving the cabinet and securing a concerted, reliable basis for military and production efforts.[44] The Lord President was one of the very few —usually eight—members of the War Cabinet. Other ministers besides those names above attended committee meetings when it was desirable.

(4) In the postwar period this committee was retained and it is still in active operation, but in respect of economic affairs it was supplanted in September, 1947, by the Policy Committee. This Policy Committee (or Committee on Overseas Economic Policy) has authority over the whole range of the nation's economic affairs.

(5) Until September, 1947, the Lord President's Committee coordinated all the domestic departments. It was the link between other committees of the cabinet, especially the "Home Economic Committee," also presided over by the Lord President of the Council, and the "Overseas Committee," presided over by the prime minister. It brought together the

research auxiliaries of the cabinet and serviced the committees with the latter's abilities. It supplied the cabinet itself with fully made or partly manufactured policies, as the result of deliberation and the settlement of differences at the ministerial level. Where agreement proved impossible to obtain, it appealed the raw material to the cabinet itself. (Any minister, of course, retains the right to appeal to the cabinet, and if the latter wishes, may attend the cabinet for a hearing.)

The Lord President's Committee surveyed the whole field of government (excluding the foreign): social services, social security, physical planning, housing, health, education, police, civil defense, pensions, and local government. Coupled with the fact that Mr. Morrison was at the same time deputy leader of the House of Commons and chairman of the Legislation Committee, a valuable unity of foresight and departmental concert was in the making. Mr. Morrison had the robustness of mind and body to carry it along, until a serious attack of phlebitis in the late winter of 1947, when, in any case, the disastrous urgencies of the Great Blizzard necessitated reorganization of the system.

When the reforms of September, 1947, were made, that is, when Sir Stafford Cripps was made Minister of Economic Affairs, he became heir to the "Home Economic Committee," Mr. Morrison's hard-driving ministerial committee. It became known as the "Minister of Economic Affairs Committee"—and more recently as the "Production Committee." The Minister of Economic Affairs presides over it (it will not be forgotten that Sir Stafford later became Chancellor of the Exchequer, while still holding the title and powers of the Minister of Economic Affairs), and it is concerned with the day-to-day coordination and promotion of the economic program. The Production Committee has command of the entire program of production for domestic and export purposes, including coal and power, building, shipbuilding, agriculture, the allocation of raw materials, and capital investment.

44 Cf. especially Sir John Anderson, "The Machinery of Government," *Public Administration*, Autumn, 1946, especially p. 153.

The various cabinet committees are served by subcommittees; and ancillary to each are committees of officials, to furnish the expert information. All the committees are thus personally linked to each other to a very considerable extent and simultaneously to the cabinet. The system is highly integrated and coherent, but the work that burdens ministers of cabinet rank who are at the same time members of cabinet committees is backbreaking.

The Cabinet Secretariat. The cabinet secretariat performs strictly secretarial functions. It circulates the memoranda and other documents necessary for the work of the cabinet and its various committees; marshals the agenda for each cabinet meeting under the direction of the Prime Minister; performs the same service for the cabinet committees under directions of the respective chairmen; circulates the notices of meetings; records and distributes to those who are concerned the cabinet's conclusions and draws up the reports of cabinet committees; and keeps the papers and conclusions of the cabinet subject to the cabinet's directions.

This means that the work of the cabinet and its committees is carefully prepared for before the meetings; that the general arguments, but not the record of the opinions of identified individuals, are set down together with a conclusion. The secretary sometimes insists on getting a formula for record where otherwise none is offered or where the discussion is inconclusive. It has been suggested that he sometimes needs to show "no little ingenuity and even inventiveness" in drafting it.[45] When the conclusions are reached, the secretariat sees that each minister involved in the conclusions gets his appropriate part, when it is for him to convert the decision into administrative action.

Only the secretary is present at cabinet meetings. He sits on the right-hand side of the prime minister and personally takes the record of the meeting. Naturally, the preservation of neutrality and anonymity, the two stoical characteristics of the British civil service, find their apotheosis in him—beyond the suggestion of even a discreet smile, it is said.

It should be emphasized that the secretariat is not advisory to the cabinet or its committees: it is secretarial. For advisory functions there has been established another part of the apparatus, to which we now turn.

The Official Steering Committee. Under Mr. Morrison, the Official Steering Committee was the central piece of machinery to assist the cabinet in planning. It functioned until November 20, 1947, when it disappeared in this form to reappear in another, under the aegis of and auxiliary to the Minister of Economic Affairs.

The Official Steering Committee consisted of the permanent heads of departments or their deputies representing the key economic departments, together with members of the Economic Section of the Cabinet Offices, the Central Statistical Office, and the Lord President's own office of planning advisers, administrative experts, "idea men," and scientific consultants. This, according to Mr. Morrison, formed "the central economic team responsible for gathering and assessing economic intelligence, preparing forecasts, framing economic plans, advising Ministers on the advantages and disadvantages of these plans, and keeping under review the execution of plans when authorized and put into operation."[46] There can be little doubt that it owed its conception to the interwar speculation on planning problems undertaken by men like Sir William (now Lord) Beveridge, by the research organization called *Political and Economic Planning* (the secretary of which became Herbert Morrison's assistant in the Lord President's Office), and by the present author. It secured coordination at the official as well as at the ministerial level. It spawned a number of

---

[45] Cf. L. S. Amery, *Thoughts on the Constitution* (Oxford, 1947).

[46] Cf. "Economic Planning," *Public Administration*, Spring, 1947, p. 6.

"working parties" (by which is meant "subcommittees," not the working parties that inquire into the reconstruction of the various British industries). Thus, one would be estimating the total manpower available and its forward distribution on various assumptions; another would be assessing the trend of investment and the problem of its guidance to meet immediate needs and prevent the onset of a depression; and still another would be watching the import-export relationship. They would thus produce the raw material for future estimates for planning purposes.

The "working parties" and the committee as a whole were simply advisory. The departmental representatives brought with them the not inconsiderable research and planning resources of their own individual departments and took back from the committee the view of the common good it had discussed and provisionally agreed to. From the Official Steering Committee there ascended to the Lord President's ministerial committee the predigested plans and estimates, forming the material on which the "political" mind could operate and eventually finding its way to the cabinet, so far as that was necessary. From the cabinet, through the Lord President, there descended to it indication of the general roads the cabinet was prepared to tread, having regard to its commitments to the country and Parliament.

The Economic Section of the Cabinet Secretariat. The Economic Section of the Cabinet Secretariat, a corps of professional economists, was established in 1941. It filled a yawning gap in the coordination of wartime effort, since to that time no extradepartmental body had worked parallel with the government on the intellectual plane. It receives all economic information marshaled by the various government agencies (central, local, and corporate) and repairs any gaps by its own research. It comments on the cabinet and cabinet committee information that comes in to it and prepares a picture of the general economic landscape to which the facts are tending, with warnings and fore-

casts of the probable outcome of actions or omissions to act. It serves the cabinet as a regular duty; but it also serves the various departments, and especially the Central Planning Staff when called in. It prepared the White Paper on *Employment Policy* of May, 1944, the *Economic Surveys* for 1947, 1948, and 1949—the so-called annual "economic budgets" which were an important advance in the statecraft of a planning age—and the White Paper on *Capital Investment* of March, 1948.

The Central Statistical Office. The Central Statistical Office was established as part of the cabinet secretariat in 1941, to produce a developing statistical series, general and comprehensive in nature, as an index to economic and social trends. It does not replace the statistical services of the various departments, which are highly developed and specialized, but looks at the figures from a different point of view, making correlations the department would not make and answering planning questions they would not seek to answer. The various excellent departmental statistical analyses assist and integrate with the analyses of the Central Statistical Office. Its systematic picture of trends is published in the *Monthly Digest of Statistics,* indispensable to forecasting and therefore to planning. It is of the highest political importance that this *Digest,* commenced during World War II for private circulation in governmental circles only, is now available to all. This means that the opposition may challenge the cabinet's plans with the very figures upon which they are based.

It is noteworthy that the planning activities of the government have necessitated the gathering of facts about business and industry more frequently and specifically than has hitherto been practiced in the censuses of production, taken at five-year or longer intervals, or gathered when royal commissions of inquiry investigated particular segments of the economy. The Statistics of Trade Act, 1947, empowers the government to require estimates and returns of any person carrying on an undertaking, for the purpose of obtaining information necessary for the interpretation of economic trends and the provision of a statistical service for industry and for the discharge by the government departments of their functions. The gathering of this information is limited to the nature, size, location, and acquisition of the undertaking, its employees, remuneration, rent, taxes, capital assets, and other matters strictly connected with the general purpose.

Before moving forward to an account of the Central or Interdepartmental Planning Staff, which was established in March, 1947, it is relevant to draw attention to the government's conception of planning machinery to be instituted as auxiliary to government. The ideas are to be found in the White Paper of *Employment Policy* of May, 1944, and in the *Economic Survey* of 1947. The essence of the matter is coherence of minds, exactness of information, the earliest apprehension of the movements in economic and social life that must be mastered in order that the plans may come true, and help from industry in gathering information.[47]

The *Economic Survey* of 1947, in particular, sketched the organization and method of preparing "economic budgets," each relating the needs of its sector of the economy—thus, the defense forces, transport, agriculture, manufacture for export, housing, factories, plant, and so on—to the resources of manpower and material needed and available to satisfy its demands. These would be coordinated and shaped with attention to the total manpower and other resources available and the special problems of foreign exchange, capital equipment and maintenance, fuel, and power.

Central Planning Staff. Up to the time of the *Economic Survey* of 1947 (say March, 1947), the government experimented with the machinery already described. The government and its official advisers were too wise to believe that administrative machinery is prior to the functions it is to serve. They recognized that there was as yet no final compre-

hensive plan of objectives, and that there could not be, given the peculiarly contingent nature of the British economy, so dependent on foreign markets and international relations. But it was found that the machinery was not integrated enough to cope with the urgent short-term problems of a "siege economy" under threats of failure, often through the actions of foreign countries (such as the decontrol of prices in the United States) of which little previous notice could be had. Hence, a new piece of machinery, the Central or Interdepartmental Planning Staff, was established to provide a more comprehensive planning staff than the Official Steering Committee and a more organized contact with industry.[48]

In establishing the Central Planning Staff it was recognized that the foundation of the economic planning work would continue to be done in the departments. No outside organization can know enough the detail, the living inwardness and complexity, to be mastered—and mastered only because scores of men have been specializing in the departments it may be for thirty or forty years! But it had been found that the ordinary members of the top levels of the departments, willing and able as they were, could not give the appropriate time and attention to the Steering Committee. The Government therefore required the appointment in each department of a "whole-time planning staff, under a senior officer, charged with special responsibilities in that field." These officers would be the members of a joint planning staff something like that so successfully developed in the war for military production purposes. The main strength is the departmental planning officers, but to secure effective direction from the center, the government appointed a full-time executive head of the staff. It was recognized that this Chief Planning Officer must be a man of the most special attainments, and the Government appointed Sir E. N. Plowden, a distinguished wartime official who had come in from and returned to private industry.

---

[47] Paras. 81 and 82.

[48] Cripps, Debates, March 10, 1947.

The departmental planning officers are administrative-class officials high up in the hierarchy. Each has at least one associate whose duties are so arranged that he can concern himself mainly with interdepartmental staff work. The assistants work together in groups as needed for specific pieces of planning. The Chief Planning Officer himself needs and has only a small staff for programing and for secretarial duties.

The Central Planning Staff (in the cabinet offices at the outset) is concerned with the whole field of forward planning. It works in closest relationship with the Economic Section of the Cabinet Secretariat and with the Central Statistical Office. Indeed, since November, 1947, when it was switched to the Treasury, under Sir Stafford Cripps, there are observers who declare that the Central Planning Staff and the Economic Section resemble each other so very closely in function that they must either duplicate or share the work of forethought. By rational agreement between the chiefs of each organ, it is shared.

Appraisal. The planning system so far described, especially before the advent of the Central Planning Staff, suffered from three weaknesses.

(1) Full departmental autonomy still existed, despite the ministerial committees, specially the Lord President's. (These committees, of course, in many instances secured full cohesion below the cabinet level.)

(2) The permanent heads of the departments were far too busy to become planning statesmen as it were; they might be planning statesmen if they had the planning staffs, as set up by the Central Planning Staff arrangement.

(3) Within the Cabinet, the principal economic ministries were not organized hierarchically: they battled for pre-eminence; none was on top.

For the moment we have done with the first two weaknesses. Let us consider the third a little more closely. In a planned economy, who takes precedence —prime minister, Chancellor of the Exchequer, the president of the Board of Trade, or the Lord President of the

Council? Or, to omit the appellations and revert to the essential functions, the chief of the whole executive; the master of expenditures, taxation, and fiscal policy (including the expansion and contraction of credit); the controller and regulator of imports of all kinds, of rationing, and the targets for exports; or an organizer of planning? In fact, the Chancellor, the President of the Board of Trade, and the Lord President worked closely together, but what direction they should take was determined by argument among them, and the prepotency which won the day was not founded on superior status or necessarily on the merits of the case. The House of Commons sometimes asked, "Who goes in to bat first?" The answer depended on rational agreement, but there are plenty of rational alternatives from which the less rational may be picked—and the picking is sometimes determined by force of personality.

Two basic problems were met and answered under this system of interministerial bargaining. The first problem was the compromise between the short-term emergency situation of the country just emerged from five years of desperate sacrifice and privation and anxious for a little ease (an emergency especially connected with the "dollar gap"), and the long-term attempt to mend the worn-out and devastated permanent productive equipment of the nation and to improve on it. The second problem was the fiscal problem of cheap or dear credit. Both these problems were aggravated by the losses caused by the stoppage or slowdown of production due to the Blizzard of the winter of 1947, followed by the loss of American dollars due to the international convertibility of sterling permitted in July and August, 1947.

Again, drastic changes were necessary in objectives, and therefore in machinery. His austerity and drive caused the Prime Minister to appoint Sir Stafford Cripps as Minister of Economic Affairs on September 27, 1948, with an authority over all the economic departments. In November, on the resignation of the then Chancellor of the Exchequer, Mr. Dalton, the Minister of Economic Affairs became the Chancellor of the Exchequer also. With the appointment of Sir Stafford as Minister of Economic Affairs, the Official Steering Committee lost most of its functions to the Minister's own committee and staff. The Minister was to coordinate the policy and activities of the production and economic departments. This would now be in the nature of an expediter superior to the departments. By the November change, the hiatus between fiscal policy and economic planning was abolished.

Some changes (already noticed) in the ministerial committees and the auxiliary agencies naturally followed. The Lord President's Committee still remains for noninternational, noneconomic coordination and planning.

The ascendancy of Sir Stafford Cripps since his double promotion is evident. Most of the younger men in the government are Cripps's friends and protegées. This personal arrangement provides for a slant which is of the essence of every plan. It is one which has been supported not only by the cabinet as a whole, and by the party, but also by the opposition, which through its arguments in the Commons mobilized opinion and helped drive the government toward more attention to the short-term economic problem, to some extent for public and non-party reasons.

The Industrial Productivity Committee. The progress of scientific research is also linked to the deliberations of the cabinet. Before World War II, the state promoted and benefited from scientific research through the Department of Scientific and Industrial Research, other specialized research bodies belonging to the various departments of the government, and grants to the universities. During World War II Mr. Churchill established a unit of scientific advisers to the cabinet, of remarkable value to the prosecution of the war. When the Lord president's office became the center of planning under Mr. Morrison, a group of scientific advisers was set up therein, and the advisers participated at appropriate points in the research and planning

program. As time passed, this was not considered enough, and in December, 1947, the government created the Industrial Productivity Committee: [49]

To advise the Lord President of the Council and the Chancellor of the Exchequer on the form and scale of the research effort in the natural and social sciences which will best assist an early increase in industrial productivity and further to advise on the manner in which the results of such research can best be applied.

The chairman of the committee is Sir Henry Tizard (formerly president of Magdalen College, Oxford, and now also chairman of the Government's Defense Research Policy Committee), and the other members are government scientists, university scientists, scientists from industry, a member of the Central Planning Staff, the director of the Economic Section of the Cabinet Offices, and the Lord President's personal secretary.

The Treasury, the Departments, and the Corporations. The major department of government is the Treasury, headed by the Chancellor of the Exchequer. Its outstanding status is symbolized by the fact that the Prime Minister holds the office of First Lord of the Treasury. The Treasury controls the estimates of all other departments and is the master of the civil service in the sense that it decides the numbers, pay, and qualifications of the entire service. Its Establishments Branch, its Organization and Methods Branch, and its Training Division gave it a part in the managerial planning of all the other government departments. The Treasury's responsibility for approving the budget and its obligation to devise the ways and means of raising revenue make it the engine of fiscal policy which harnesses and is harnessed to the total economic productive and distributive operations of the nation.

In the high state of nationalization which Britain attained in the years following 1945, the Treasury became the master of the Bank of England. Furthermore, the nationalization statutes made

---

[49] Debates, December 18, 1947.

the Treasury the financial and account-ant superior of the national transport, coal, electricity, gas, and communications corporations—the controller of their de-velopment policy, in most cases the guar-antor of their loans and in a sense (as agent for the cabinet) the weaver of the widespread planning activities of the na-tional corporations. The Treasury com-bines the major functions of a number of United States agencies—the Treasury Department, the Bureau of the Budget, the credit-granting agencies, the Federal Reserve System, the Securities and the Exchange Commission, and the more im-portant functions of the Civil Service Commission. In a planning nation it has sovereign functions concurrently with whatever department or minister is spe-cifically vested with the direct economic operations that planning requires.

When the changes of November, 1947, occurred, some planning and administra-tive changes became necessary. The Chan-cellor was given a third undersecretary, by the side of the Financial and the Patronage secretaries, namely, the Eco-nomic Secretary to the Treasury.[50] The Central Planning Staff with its director was transferred to become part of the Treasury organization, though retaining its identity. It remains in close touch with the Economic Section of the Cabinet Sec-retariat and provides interdepartmental services under the direction of the Chan-cellor of the Exchequer. In this, the staff which served the Minister for Economic Affairs cooperates.

Consultative Auxiliaries and Working Parties in Industry. In order to benefit from the industrial and financial experi-ence of private enterprise and the advice and good will of labor at the earliest mo-ment in the inception of plans, and also to gain friendship from those who will be affected by the plans, an Economic Planning Board was appointed on July 7, 1947. The chairman is occasionally the Lord President of the Council and more usually the Chief Planning Officer. The

membership consists of three nominees of the Federation of British Industries and the British Economic Council (a pri-vate body representing private industry); three nominees of the Trade Union Con-gress; the permanent secretaries to the Board of Trade, the Ministry of Labor, and the Ministry of Supply; three persons from the Central Planning Staff; and the director of the Economic Section of the cabinet secretariat.

There are several other consultative groups. In close touch with the Chancel-lor, and either directly or indirectly with the cabinet, is the National Joint Advis-ory Board, made up of employer and em-ployee representatives, which is consulted in the early stages of high economic policy —for example, wages and prices policy. The planning requirements of the nation are disseminated through the National Production Advisory Council on Industry and its regional boards in order to get the maximum agreement and obedience without the coercion of executive com-mandments to industry. Finally, the Trade Union Congress is consulted at almost every step of major economic and social policy development, for it repre-sents almost all of the organized workers.

Early in 1946 the president of the Board of Trade set up working parties in a number of industries, each consisting of twelve representatives of management, labor, and the public, with an independ-ent chairman. These groups had the task of examining the various schemes and suggestions put forward for improving the organization, production, and distribu-tion methods of their respective indus-tries, and of reporting on the steps which should be adopted in the national inter-est to strengthen the industry and render it more stable and more capable of meet-ing competition in home and foreign mar-kets. Their reports have constituted nothing less than plans for the renewal of the industries, and very far-reaching recommendations have been adopted from them. (The report of the Cotton Industry Working Party, for example, is remark-able evidence of what can be achieved by rational consideration of the state of an

---

[50] Douglas Jay, former University teacher, au-thor of *The Socialist Case* (London, 1936).

industry. It is of first-class importance to students of planning as an exhibition of method in studying its subject—it is a high and conscious exercise in foresight.)

The Industrial Organization Act of 1947 implements the activities of the working parties. It applies to industries which are not to be nationalized because it is deemed that private enterprise is better able to conduct them. It enables the minister, after consultation with the workers and employers organizations, to establish a development council for the industry with the object of increasing its efficiency and productivity. The order establishing such a council requires parliamentary endorsement. Where no council is established, the minister may make a levy on the industry for the promotion of scientific research. These councils are designed to carry into effect the recommendations of the industrial working parties.

Survey of Auxiliary Bodies. Thus, the British cabinet is surrounded by expert help channeled directly to it, or to its committees, or to individual ministers who can thereupon better contribute their own and their department's part to the knowledge and sagacity required by the cabinet. Continuously, an ascending stream of figures, facts, interpretations, forecasts, will-creating and will-created probabilities, sifted and reflected upon, reaches the cabinet, where decisions are made or the raw material of decision is converted into recommendation and command. Continuously descending from the cabinet, through its departmental assignments and through its committees, flows a general commitment of will and policy, initiative and determination on the course to be followed, but asking guidance, advice, and the facts which settle the bounds and pace of the possible.

It will be observed that the planning system is different from politics like the French and the Weimar German which set up economic and social councils. Also discarded were proposals like that of Sir William Beveridge for an economic general staff, a body of planners outside the departmental scheme and outside the cabinet to develop and hand on a plan to the government as the executant. Statesmen were rightly skeptical of an arrangement which would vest a planning function in a group of men who are not inside the administrative organs, not saturated with detailed knowledge of operating possibilities, not responsible for final decision and responsible execution.

The various bodies that have been described as offshoots of the cabinet or as created by it to offer assistance from outside are in continuous, busy, and intermeshed operation—the drive coming from the cabinet, the ministers, and the House of Commons urging on by exhortation, alternative proposals, questions, debate, and storms.

Thus, the cabinet arrangements in the center of the system may be visualized as a pyramid.[51] At the summit is the prime minister, acting through the whole cabinet and his chairmanship of the Economic Policy and Defense Committees. For his assistance, he is flanked by three ministers —the Chancellor of the Exchequer, the Lord President of the Council, and the Foreign Secretary. These, again, marshal the activities of other cabinet and noncabinet ministers through committees, ministerial and administrative. There is both devolution of work and responsibility and integration of mind and objective. The system is to a considerable extent the result of Mr. Attlee's own personal interest in efficient government—a not unwelcome testimony to the value of early years as a political scientist.

Yet it is urgent that the fact that the prime minister is "at the summit" be not construed as above and superior to his cabinet colleagues: he is one with them.

The Neutrality and Anonymity of the Civil Service. If the civil service were to change with every government, dire confusion would follow upon every assertion of the principle of responsibility. Even in the same party some members are elderly and tired; and some are trustworthy, but not undeniably bright. One

---

[51] Cf. discussion in Francis Williams, *Socialist Britain* (New York, 1948).

thing or the other: either responsibility and neutrality—or a political civil service and an inefficient, indeed, chaotic administration.

Cabinet ministers are not usually experts in the field of work of the department to which they are assigned. They may be accidentally; but they are not chosen purposely for expertness. Rather are they chosen because they have for long shown a special interest in and aptitude for that field. Yet their career has been parliamentary, not professional. They must rely on the advice and managerial assistance of the civil service officials: that is, career men who have mastered the details of their departmental business by many years of exclusive application. On the one hand, ministers are supposed to be aware of all the activity that is going on in the department, its operations affecting millions upon millions of people all over Britain, and, so far as some departments are concerned, beyond the seas. The officials must be given direction and impetus, in accordance with the statutes giving them their scope, and thus fulfilling the will of Parliament. On the other hand, the minister needs a body of experts to advise him on the proper, the most efficient, and least expensive way of defining new policies and embodying them in statutes. To render these services, the indispensable instrument is the civil service.

At the top of each department, then, stands the minister and one and sometimes (but rarely) two undersecretaries from his party. This constitutes the entirety of the political direction and office-holders. Immediately below these stands the permanent secretary of the department, the head of the pyramid of public servants. The crucial relationship is that between the political chief and the permanent chief. It is founded on two conventions: neutrality and anonymity.[52] By *neutrality* is meant impartial service with equal loyalty rendered to any chief of whatever incoming political party. Such loyalty has, almost without exception, been accorded to the political parties by the British civil service. It requires of the civil servant that he exercise all his talent and intellectual gifts and that he use appeal (not force) of character to advise his minister on the value to the nation of the minister's declared objectives and yet to yield to him when that objective has been decisively fixed by the former. Beyond this, it requires that the permanent officials advise the minister on alternative ways and means, and further, propose to him objectives and methods he has not thought of. Behind the permanent secretary looms a vast staff which is master of the human and natural and social sciences the minister needs for the fulfillment of the trust committed to him.

On pain of sure disaster, the minister must listen to and heed his secretary's advice. He will not readily do so unless either (*a*) he is convinced of the loyalty and impartiality of the permanent staffs, or (*b*) he can bring in with him his own trusted experts. If the system allowed the latter alternative, the magnificent benefits of career non-party experts would be lost. It is essential to be sure of the former. Their training at the universities, their life-long nurture and immersion in the British political tradition, their existence as citizens among other citizens have combined to support such official impartiality. Some men may sometime have been under strain of conscience and temper on this account: but with almost negligible exceptions, all have rendered the nation the inestimable service of completely faithful assistance to the ministers. The direct evidence of this is overwhelming. But if a recent expression of it were necessary, no one is in a better position to express it and to be believed than Lord (formerly Sir Maurice) Hankey, first secretary to the Committee of Imperial Defense and the cabinet secretariat, posts held with consummate distinction for over twenty years. He said:[53]

---

[52] See for fuller analysis, H. Finer, *The British Civil Service* (London, 1937).

[53] Cf. *Diplomacy by Conference* (London, 1946), p. 16.

The permanent head of a great department of state is on almost the same footing of intimacy with his political chiefs as they are with one another. Ministers talk before them with the same freedom as they do with their colleagues. These men would sell their souls before they would sell their chiefs.

Yet, some critics who have been worsted by Karl Marx's suspicion that men cannot be impartial, but must fatalistically follow only the line of their personal economic interests, have set forth theses tending to throw mistrust on the general observance of the convention of neutrality. They have pointed to the fact that many of the top civil servants in Britain are from the upper-middle and the upper classes and from the older universities. This still, despite an increasing tempo of change, is true. But the conclusions drawn from this outward-seeming truth (a stereotype, as Chapter 14 on public opinion has explained) are crassly false. The cry of "representative" bureaucracy has been set up; it implies that if the officialdom of a nation is not to a large degree representative of the class strata within it, it cannot be loyal to the interests of the less privileged groups, and, specifically, would not properly serve a Labour government.[54]

These ideas demonstrate the misfortune of judging the plain observable facts through the abstractions of a transcendent theory of history. The civil servants of Britain at the top of the administrative summit could not be disloyal to ministers for several plain reasons. First, if some tendered wrong advice, others would find a way of reaching the minister. *Sieve number one.* Second, the unfaithful would fear being detected in the course of time as the source of erroneous policies: their general professional reputation would suffer among their own colleagues. *Sieve number two.* Third, the minister is watched, as we have narrated, by his cabinet colleagues: if the civil servant deceived the minister, he could hardly deceive the cabinet: that is a fully delibera-

---

[54] Cf. J. D. Kingsley, *Representative Bureaucracy* (Antioch, 1943).

tive body, with something of a counter-check in its own cabinet secretariat. *Sieve number three.* Fourth, if the cabinet let a mistake through, the sieve of House of Commons questions stands peremptorily to sift out nonsense. Let it be remembered that the close assistants of the permanent chiefs are present outside the bar of the House in attendance on the minister during question time—they suffer palpitations of the heart as well as he. *Sieve number four.* Finally, the press has its representatives on the spot, and the parties have their own research institutions—*sieves number five and six*. The whole house of gaudy Marxian cards blows down!—for it is not political science! Moreover, if a Labour government's policy is being pondered, one other consideration is of the most significant weight. A Labour government gives the administrators something to administer. Is it to be supposed that men who have devoted all their lives to housing, or town planning, or road construction, or economic planning, or currency and credit affairs, are prepared to sabotage their own opportunity of creative work at the apex and approaching end of their own careers, when here at last is something splendid to build? something to do? a memorial to be won?

British civil servants are *anonymous*: that is, their names are not brought into debate as the inventors or executors of policy. This insures that their voices will not be lifted in advocacy or denigration of policies. If they came into the public light, they would be favored by some politicians and hated by others. They would lose a reputation for impartiality: and their advice—and soon they themselves—would necessarily be discarded. It is rare indeed that a civil servant's name comes before the public. This means that all responsibility, all praise and blame, are concentrated on the minister and the cabinet. The line of responsibility is not obscured or confused. It is the minister who will be shot. To avoid this fate he sees to it that his permanent staff do their job properly. They understand it, and he understands it: consequently each appreciates the qualities and compulsions of the other, with humorous and cynical lapses. They are not punitive to each other. They do indeed collaborate in a very honorable, pleasant, and fruitful fashion: someone once said as the Victorian wife devotedly served her husband—they never quarrelled in public—while the wife was never insulted in company by her husband, nor did she ever let her lord and master know that he was anything but perfect.

When a minister knows that he cannot put the blame on his civil servants, he is stimulated to judge their advice independently and carefully, and to insist that they shall do their best. That he is answerable to Parliament causes him to insist that others shall be answerable to him. Further, the efficiency of representative government depends upon the use of the expert knowledge of the officials; and only the belief that the advice they tender is scientifically impartial and not suspiciously biased will induce ministers to rely upon it and come fully under its influence. Thus, let it be noted, how upon the highest council of the nation—the cabinet—there is brought to bear the expertness and coordinating advice and assistance of the administrative class of the civil service. In 1939 they numbered roughly 1500: in the aftermath of World War II—a new world —nearly 4000. In this relationship of cabinet and administrative class resides the virtue of the British constitution. (In the United States, the *Report of the President's Committee on Administrative Management* declared in 1936 that the President needed help, and proposed six aides for him, and three units—fiscal, planning, and personnel—to tether all the government to him. It was hardly enough.)

PARTY ACCESSORIES TO THE CABINET

THE simultaneous spread of the democratic theory, with the emergence of the leaders of a party above the rank and file of the ordinary member of Parliament, has resulted in more or less systematic attempts of the rank and file to assert themselves against the cabinet. In the Conservative party this has shown itself, from time to time, by the formation of "diehard" or "ginger" groups, and these have attempted to drive the cabinet along the path of the "true" Conservative tradition, which seemed to get lost in the necessary compromise and concessions of parliamentary life, and in the ever-present consideration that, while a firm, bold policy is most desirable, it may cause such a loss of votes at the approaching election that the power to do anything at all will be taken away. The party leaders found no great difficulty in bringing members to heel, for loyalty to leaders is a strong element in the party of authority.

In the Labour party the matter has been more embarrassing. Upon the assumption of office in 1929, the usual practice of periodical meetings of the executive committee and the party became impossible, and its place was taken by a "rank-and-file" committee. But it is most interesting to observe that its intervention came practically to nothing, for as the cabinet is the only body in the state which can really appreciate the pressure of necessity in the business of government, and since urgency is always an overruling plea, the cabinet finds itself able to convince the rank and file that they must give way, and they do. Moreover, the country is normally on the side of the cabinet, which *does*, rather than of Parliament, which seems chiefly to *talk*. Yet it is good that the cabinet shall be conscious of a lively following, for that is one of the ways by which it is compelled to pay attention to the comparative rightness of its own, its followers', and its constituents' suggestions. When the Labour government of 1945 began to operate, the party set up a small liaison committee between rank and file, the leader of the House (Morrison), and the whips. But also no less than twenty party groups, one for each main branch of government, were established for the same liaison purposes.[55] They frequently meet to interrogate the minister. Their chairmen are experts, and men of demon-

---

[55] See Annual **Report, Labour Party Confer**ence, 1946.

strated independent character. One peer is included in each group.

THE "SHADOW" CABINET

THE opposition has gradually developed an organization to grapple with cabinet leadership, an organization not so good as the latter but good for its purposes and for the efficiency of the system. The former cabinet ministers form what has variously been termed the "ex-cabinet," or more recently the "shadow cabinet." From time to time it has been disputed whether the leader of the party, be he a former prime minister or a newly chosen person, shall consult only former cabinet ministers or shall take council with others. Practice naturally varies from leader to leader. In the Labour party the matter is decided by the periodical elections of the parliamentary executive, though others are not thereby excluded from nonofficial council. Elsewhere, though the "inner cabinet" and other strong members constitute the acknowledged group in the "shadow cabinet," the circle is not absolutely exclusive. Mr. Churchill's part voluntary, part obligatory exclusion from Mr. Baldwin's "shadow cabinet," following differences upon Indian policy, is an interesting example.

More important is the plain fact that the opposition feels the need for permanent organization and council. Nowhere has the necessity and value been so well recognized as in Bolingbroke's *Spirit of Patriotism*. The doctrine is perfect. There were times when the opposition was practically without a concerted lead, when it fell to the strongest and ablest to lead as he wished or to be sniped at by the rivals in his own party. Those days have departed forever, for the immense public benefit of an organized opposition has been fully recognized. The opposition of one day will be the government of the next, but the condition is that it shall maintain its identity and appear always with an alternative program, which will be regarded by the electorate as a pledge. The coming elections must be prepared

for as carefully as the government itself prepares for them, and sails trimmed to arrive at the desirable port. Then, the issues in government have become so obviously the apportionment of power, rights, and duties among contending social groups that a restraint upon the cabinet is plainly seen to be more necessary than before, and in order to restrain, it is obligatory to act according to plan, and systematically to match strategy to the opponent's attack.

These things impose a "shadow cabinet": something which shall continue the policy of its former and more powerful self, think and create in preparation for a fresh tenure of office, make commitments to the public for the future,[56] and meanwhile use the authority and strategy of a united body to obstruct, humiliate and bind the cabinet of the day. It cannot rely, as the cabinet can rely, upon the aid of the departments of state, except when this is embodied in published parliamentary papers and the information evoked by parliamentary questions and debate, but it has a substitute in its party-headquarters research department and the occasional help of paid experts. It is in constant touch with its chief campaign managers, the propaganda sections, the constituencies, here stalking cabinet ministers and replying to their speeches *seriatim*, and now and then meeting the party in conference. Moreover, the "shadow cabinet" arranges debate, entangles the cabinet, probes it here and there, discredits it, obtains electorally dangerous admissions, treats with the government whips for time and closure, and, when the cabinet is a minority government, forces concessions and imposes amendments. Finally, its rank and file are thus held together, given consistency and direction, and imbued with a united and vigorous spirit.

So far has the opposition become a regular institution that it has been dubbed "His Majesty's Loyal Opposition," and its leaders, of course, receive a correspond-

---

[56] As when in May, 1947, the Conservative party pamphlet *Industrial Charter* committed the party to the continuation of the nationalized services as at that date.

ing recognition—being asked to social functions by court and people and being consulted by the government when national and imperial isues require a united front, especially on questions of national defense. All this is governmentally good, but even better is the omnipresent, compelling, stimulating effect upon the cabinet: if it is true that this may in the last resort appeal to the people, it is equally true that the appeal cannot but be in part dictated by the opposition. In 1937 the importance to the state of organized and loyal opposition was recognized in the Ministers of the Crown Act, when, as in Canada [57] since 1905, a salary of £2000 a year was provided for the leader of the opposition. Mr. Baldwin argued that this financial endowment would protect and encourage the independence of the leader. Others were afraid it would lame him, make him acquiescent, almost a civil servant! Mr. Baldwin's view is right.

WEAKNESS AND DIFFICULTIES OF THE CABINET

The Burden of Work. We have already mentioned the unfortunate effects of the large size of the cabinet upon the ability of each minister to participate effectively in the formulation of policy. Yet the amount of work to be done by the cabinet and the tremendous burden upon each minister—departmentally, parliamentarily, electorally, and socially—have the further tendency to foreclose any thought beyond the immediate tasks. The period of office is a period of practical work, not of reconsideration and creative survey. One minister has impressed me with the burden borne by him and his cabinet colleagues now that, in addition to departmental, parliamentary, and cabinet duties, preparation for and attendance at cabinet committees is necessary. Hence the special importance of the secretarial and planning assistance to the cabinet and the continuous deliberations of political parties.

Necessary Trips Abroad. Other burdens now raise difficulties. Participation in world affairs imposes upon several ministers (the prime minister, the Foreign Secretary, the Colonial Secretary, and the Chancellor of the Exchequer) rather long occasional absences from the country or from current domestic business.

Personnel Difficulties due to the Party Process. Cabinet ministers must have won their way upwards in Parliament, and, as we have suggested, in that ascent the party rivals engage in a mutual scrutiny of each other's qualities which is altogether unceasing in its minuteness and intensity. For the public good it is salutary in the highest degree. Yet the path to Parliament and thence to the cabinet is that of popularity—if not with the whole electorate, at least with one or other of the various groups supporting the government, of which prime ministers are sensitively cognizant. Hence the amateur who obtains office is not always a gifted amateur. Compared with the abilities of some men who have never ventured into politics at all, and certainly of experts at large, he may be singularly mediocre and worse. Weak men, incompetents, are sometimes appointed to office or to inappropriate departments, out of such considerations of popularity, sometimes gained and faded a decade or more ago, or through the personal esteem or friendship of the prime minister.

Further, while it is true that the average age of cabinet ministers at entrance in the cabinet is about fifty-five,[58] some cabinet ministers, and certainly some prime ministers, are much older—in their sixties and seventies. Being the seniors of their party they are automatically called in to form cabinets. But as the biography of Neville Chamberlain has conspicuously shown, they are physically ailing far beyond the demands of office in our time. For the task is devastatingly heavy: attendance in Parliament, speeches in one's constituency and in the country generally, participation in party confabulations

---

[57] For the Canadian experience see R. M. Dawson, *Government of Canada* (Toronto, 1947), p. 396 and *passim*.

[58] Cf. Harold J. Laski, "Personnel of the British Cabinet," in *Studies in Law and Politics* (Yale, 1932) p. 195.

and conferences, and contribution to the work of cabinet committees—the last of an exacting kind. A man of fifty-five, in good health, has the experience ripe for affairs of state, without the weaknesses of age. As age mounts beyond that, by no means all cabinet ministers have the energy and stamina required for their duties, though they may have the wisdom and judgment. This can be a penalty which offsets the need and advantage of ministers' having served an apprenticeship in the House of Commons and having been responsible to it. In the second year of its office, the Labour government of 1945 found it essential to reconstruct, leaving out some of its aged incubuses, and bringing in several very young ministers.

The Power of the Threat of Dissolution. Some of the spontaneous and valid creativeness of the House of Commons is dissipated by the threat of the cabinet to dissolve if it is overcome upon a matter it deems vital. Now this point has been falsely overstressed. It has been phrased as though the cabinet were in the habit of letting the House know that it will definitely dissolve upon such and such provocation, as though members were coerced only by the thought of their election expenses. This is not so. The operation is much more subtle, and sometimes unintentional. It operates thus: when the cabinet lets it be known that a matter is vital, by sending out strong whips, not only its own recalcitrants are compelled to take thought, but the formal opposition must seriously consider whether the issue is really big enough for an electoral contest, and whether they are likely to be able to take over the government. If, on the whole, the political position is not quite in their favor they are likely to yield ground, wholly or in part. In short, each issue is determined not by the objective goodness or badness of the policy, but by whether the opposition can successfully carry the matter in the country, and this depends on (*a*) the nature of the issue itself, (*b*) the general state of political opinion in the country, and (*c*) the condition of the finances and organization of the party for the coming fray. But these matters hardly arise where the opposition is in a minority (which in the last two generations has been almost always) or unless the government party is likely to split (which is very rarely). Hence the opposition cannot do more than obtain that effect upon government policy which its debating talent, the reasonableness of its argument, and the calculation of favorable electoral chances, conspire to give.

Unwieldy Size. We have already observed (p. 577) that the British cabinet is a rather large body. It is half as large again as French and German cabinets. It is too large, it has often been said, for prompt and effective discussion and decision. This is true: one hand knows not the charity performed by the other. In default of devolution, the only feasible remedy seems to be a regroupment of the ministries into eight or ten, each with an adequate number of undersecretaries. To a ministry thus composed these could be added up to four ministers without departmental responsibilities. But good committee organization within the cabinet and its auxiliaries can overcome the unwieldiness of too large a cabinet. The use of ministers without departmental responsibilities—the Lord President of the Council and the Lord Privy Seal, almost sinecures—is in operation. As already shown, the cabinet in 1947 had been reduced to sixteen.

It is sometimes deplored that the system we have described divides the country into a set of men who strive their utmost to get things done and another set who do their utmost to obstruct them. Thus Shaw and Wells, men for whom I have a religious respect. I understand the urgency of their complaint—they wish the rotten foundations and the ugly and deceiving façades to be swept away at once. So do I. But the parliamentary and cabinet system springs from the loins of ordinary human beings, and their ultimate demand is the amplest liberty to do as they like and restrain others from doing as others like. This wish, when organized, is the democratic theory, and its organized practice is the party system, and cabinet government its natural flower. Are we so sure of ourselves, and the wisdom and goodness of the intentions of others, that we can surrender the right to obstruct?

On the whole, with the exceptions here and there noticed, the British cabinet system offers quick, vigorous, thoughtful, and responsible leadership; it is controlled, but not stultified; threatened, but not executed; questioned, but not mistrusted; politically partisan, but not personally malicious; restrained as much by the spirit of responsible power as by its institutions and sanctions; and Januslike, it looks at once out to the far-flung people and through the corridors to the gathered, exacting senate.

The cabinet controls (on terms and during its good behavior) the law-making assemblies, the making of law, the time table of the Commons and the Lords, the Parliamentary committees, the making of executive rules and orders, the estimates, the taxing power, the public corporations —all on the terms that it satisfies the legislature, which normally, it is sure to do because cabinet and legislature are one. What it plans it can do: what it legislates

it can find money for: what social benefits it decides should be bestowed on groups of the population come within its administrative gift: what coercion is necessary is lent to it by the legislature. It is master of the whole administrative apparatus. There are no hybrids like the independent regulatory commissions in the American system, and all the departments come under the vigorous swing of the cabinet. It is rock-like in its stability compared with the French cabinet under whose aegis the Monnet Plan is carried forward. It is umbillically tied to the people, as contrasted with the Soviet planners who tie their people noose-like to their own self-willed convictions. In plan-formulation and plan-execution it is the supreme engineer, compact of responsible will and dynamic initiative, epitomizing knowledge and the general good, and driving the plans home through the civil service.[59]

---

[59] For an inside view of the cabinet, the reader should compare David Lloyd George. *War Memoirs* (London, 1933); Winston S. Churchill, *The World Crisis* (London, 1923-28); and same author, *Their Finest Hour* (New York, 1949).

24

The French Cabinet

THIS chapter analyzes the French cabinet system as it operated during the Third Republic; indicates its weaknesses and ultimate collapse in the military defeat of 1940 and the attempts to cure those weaknesses in the interwar years; and examines the provisions of the 1946 constitution.

THE EXECUTIVE IN THE THIRD REPUBLIC

IN France, the effective executive of the Third Republic was, as in England and Germany, the direct issue of the parties as in Parliament assembled. The chief of state, the President of the Republic, was more than a figurehead, but not much more. The brunt of government was borne by the cabinet, or, as it is called in France, the *Conseil des Ministres*. As we have already seen in the case of England and shall in the United States, the efficiency of the executive is governed by the combined effect of its legal power, its conventional attributes, and its party and personal composition.

Cabinet government based fully upon parliamentary consent came only in 1875, with the simultaneous institution of ministerial responsibilty to the chambers and the establishment of a nonhereditary chief of state, elected by the chambers for a short term. The constitutional laws of the Third Republic provided (1) that every action of the President of the Republic must be countersigned by a minister; (2) that "ministers are collectively responsible before the chambers for the general policy of the government, and individually for their personal acts"; (3) that "the President of the Republic is not responsible for anything except in the case of high treason"; (4) that "the President of the Republic communicates with the Chambers by messages which are read at the tribune by a Minister"; (5) that "Ministers have the entry to both Chambers and may speak when they wish to," and they may make use of the assistance of commissioners designated, for the discussion of a specific project of law, by decree of the President of the Republic; and, finally (6) that a law declared urgent by both chambers must at once be promulgated, but that within the normal time before promulgation, that is, within the course of the month following the transmission of the law to him, he may require a parliamentary redeliberation of the law.

Responsibility. The constitutional laws of 1875 were the first since the Revolution to make clear that the responsibility of ministers meant principally political responsibility. Previous constitutional law and theory had not clearly distinguished between penal and political responsibility, nor had the former been decisively relegated as a minor and rare incident of office.[1] What, then, did political respon-

[1] Cf. Leon Duguit, *Traité de Droit Constitutionnel* (Paris, 1925), Vol. II, and E. Pierre, *Traité de Droit, Politique et Parlementaire* (Paris, 1922), Vol. I, para. 105.

E.g., the constitution of 1848 provided: "In all cases of ministerial responsibility, the Na-

sibility mean? As in England, it meant nothing more than that where the matter was sufficiently serious, a minister would be deprived of the power to pursue a political career, because the chambers would withdraw their confidence and the electorate might not return him. The attempt to find a more precise meaning failed, although the Chamber of Deputies once attempted to invest it with serious meaning.[2] The result has been a rather unsettled relationship between the government and the chambers. Pierre said it meant that the government must hide nothing from the chambers, that these had a continuous right to control and modify its policy and administrative activity. He did not, however, think that the cabinet should fall whenever one or some or all ministers displeased the chambers. "The question of confidence, which is distinct from that of responsibility, does not arise unless the Government considers that it would be dangerous not to attempt to make its own will prevail." This is only the French equivalent for the English insistence that the government need resign only on vital matters. Pierre said that the minister ought to stay in office unless he has been directly and gravely repudiated, but until that point has been reached, an adverse vote should be followed by bending, but not breaking. He was constrained (by events, I am sure) to admit that the principle of collective responsibility as it operated in France did not preclude a cabinet from permitting one of its members from speaking and voting in a sense different from that held officially by the cabinet. Thus in 1904, Combes, president of the Conseil, explained to the Chamber that there was nothing wrong in a difference between two ministers:

I do not think that it is to be imagined that x and y in consenting to join the same Cabinet

thereby repudiated their life-long doctrines. The Cabinet does not pretend to realize an absolute homogeneity. . . It pretends to reflect very exactly the republican majority of this assembly composed of four groups each of which professes divergent opinion on certain points.

That was almost the exact opposite of responsibility as it is known in the British system; for there it is pretended that unanimity exists, and the pretense is founded upon a reasonable expectation that men of one party, though of different shades of opinion, may by lifelong cooperation and mutual loyalty arrive at the unanimity and common will of a compromise.[3] We shall see that in France certain conditions made this presumption quite impossible and that, in fact, political practice virtually deleted the words "collectively responsible" from the Third Republic constitution. The question now is, what conditions governed the operation of these clauses? Four stand out in the highest relief: (1) the cabinet had no power to dissolve Parliament; (2) the chambers were composed of a multiplicity of groups; (3) the Senate demanded ministerial attention since it might have troubled, if not overthrown, a cabinet; and (4) the commissions were rivals of ministers. We must now examine what these conditions imply.

No Cabinet Power to Dissolve the Chambers. The constitution gave the President of the Republic the power to dissolve the chambers before the expiry of their legal term, provided he could obtain the assent of the Senate to such a policy. This article was dictated by the monarchists' desire to secure a strong, if not a monarchical, government and to make the President and the Senate forceful counteragents to universal suffrage and the Chamber of Deputies, while the republicans saw in the Senate a check upon the arbitrary use of the power of dissolution by the executive. But the first attempt to use this machinery, on May

tional Assembly can, according to circumstances, send the inculpated minister either before the high court of justice or before the ordinary courts for civil compensation." The constitution of 1852 abolished ministerial solidarity and provided for the minister's responsibility to the chief of state only.
[2] See Pierre, *op. cit.*, Vol. I, para. 107.

[3] Cf. Walter Bagehot, *The Character of Sir Robert Peel* (London, 1856), in *Works* (Longmans, 1915), Vol. II.

16, 1877, by the royalist President, Mac-Mahon, was so shockingly against the contemporary sentiment of the country that it was never repeated. Nor is that all. Parliamentarists were able to persuade the electorate, and, of course, themselves, that the power of dissolution ought not to be used. The motive of the deputies was obvious; they wished to retain their seats as long as possible and to act against any government, as they wished, with electoral impunity; and they were able to sustain this desire by the argument that the chambers represented the sovereignty of the nation. This again was sustainable by mere reference to the *Seize-Mai,* which produced the habit of regarding dissolution as a *coup d'état.*[4] The possibility of dissolution was never mentioned in normal times: it was no more than hinted at as a faint possibility—rather a fancy—when the dizzy turbulence of the chambers was plainly bringing government not only to a dangerous pass but into contempt. (It received, however, increasing favor from the parties of the extreme Right.)

Let it then be understood that no power of dissolution existed in France. The Chamber of Deputies always lasted its full legal term—four years. The government of the day had no weapon with which to ward off onslaughts, or to attack and disperse a parliamentary conspiracy, even the most factious. The political effects were dire. As factiousness could not be subjugated, sovereignty was thrown into the hands of any group, however small, which any time possessed the balance of power. Two or three men in a key group might decide the fate of a ministry, and even if they did not possess the power to overthrow the government, they might easily possess the power of throwing it into a state of fearful anxiety and of dictating vital changes in its program. Thus the government had the power of neither defense nor retribution. That was

a serious evil, for it meant that the value of its technically informed counsel was wasted for Parliament and the country. It might have been compelled to relinquish its considered policy for the unsifted inspiration of a small knot of willful men.

In 1934, after the February riots before the Chamber of Deputies—an undoubtedly serious attempt on the part of Right-wing groups and fascists to start a revolution—the prime minister, the long-bearded senescent Doumergue, called in to appease the country, proposed various reforms of the constitution. Chief among them was the restoration of the power of dissolution. His radio address to the people on September 24, 1934, stressed the need in view of the short-livedness of cabinets. "The governments may have among them men of ability but it is known in advance that there will be no time to give those men an opportunity to prove themselves, for the majority on which they depend may not be able to continue . . ." He proposed that the consent of the Senate should no longer be necessary for dissolution, except during the first year of the existence of the Chamber. The project was examined by the Chamber of Deputies' Commission on the Reform of the State[5] and, by a vote of twenty-one to three, was recommended with the exception that the President was not to be able to dissolve the Chamber earlier than three months after a general election or after a previous dissolution. Though some years before the Socialist party had favored dissolution, they now joined the Radical Socialists to oppose it in the Chamber. They did not propose to throw away their dominating position in the balance of governmental powers; nor did individual deputies intend to surrender their personal political power. (Tardieu had favored the reform, advocating it in his *L'Heure de la Décision* of January, 1934.) Doumergue was forced from office by dissentients from his proposals. Naturally, the Senate was hostile

[4] Cf. J. C. C. Bodley, *France,* revised edition (London, 1907), pp. 230-31; J. Barthélemy, *The Government of France* (New York, 1924); A. Siegfried, *Tableau des Partis Politiques* (Paris, 1930).

[5] *Bulletin des Commissions,* No. 47, May 1, 1934, p. 2919.

to the curtailment of its constitutional powers. There was some force in the argument of opponents that the cabinet in France could never be strengthened by the power to dissolve the Chamber, because it was inherently unstable, since no party ever came near to commanding a majority. (The provisions of the new constitution on this subject are discussed presently, p. 640.)

The Groups and the Cabinet. In France there are many groups, and, by the power to command ten or fifteen votes, a leader may become the dictator of government. In the Parliament of 1924-28, there were ten groups and thirty-one members belonging to no group; in that of 1932, sixteen groups and twenty-six non-affiliated members. No group ever secured a majority in the Chamber; hence, every government was a coalition.

The Terms of Coalition. The initiative in the formation of the cabinet had to be and was taken by the President of the Republic. He had obviously a number of choices—the chambers of 1928, 1932, and 1936, for example, contained three possible majorities—and even apart from considerations of policy, which have always moved Presidents in their approach to a ministry, personal preferences also had weight, as with Poincaré and Clemenceau. But the President was concerned to find a practicable government, and his principal anxiety was to discover the basis of a working majority, even if it should not be that which would best meet his own policy. With this intention he conferred first with the presidents of the Chamber and the Senate. This custom began with MacMahon, who actually offered the formation of a cabinet to the Presidents themselves, on the assumption that since they had been elected to their pre-eminent position by parliamentary majorities, they would naturally be able to form a ministry. They refused, but on several occasions the president of the Chamber of Deputies became prime minister. The suggestions of the Presidents were translated into offers made to various party leaders—and in some cases, to certain outstanding men who belonged to

no party at all—to form a government. These leaders, who were often without any organized party following,[6] consulted with friends to discover where the greatest strength compatible with the longest time in office was to be sought: was it entirely on the Left, or would it be among the moderate groups, or must an attempt be made to induce a Right group to cooperate with the moderate Left? The chairmen of the Foreign Affairs and Finance Commissions were consulted by the President of the Republic and the aspirant prime minister, to give light, and sometimes weight, to their quest. Then the groups were approached. These were not usually engaged by their leaders, but held a meeting to determine their attitude. They had various things to consider: whether they wished to serve with this particular person at their head; whether, accepting his person, they could accept the policy; whether, accepting these, they could cooperate with the other groups of the "combination"; and further, whether the number and importance of the ministries and under-secretaryships were satisfactory. One section—the Socialist party —never accepted office to 1936, but was asked for its engagement to vote with the government, or to abstain on certain occasions, in return for hostages of policy.[7] Nor was this all: the creator of the cabinet was careful to include as few small

---

[6] E.g., in 1914 Briand was not inscribed in any group; in 1919 Millerand was a *sauvage;* and even Poincaré and Laval might fairly be included.

[7] Cf. Maurice Privat, *Les Heures d'André Tardieu* (Paris, 1930), for an excellent analysis of the various changes of government in 1929-30. Cf. also for the relationship between Radical Socialists and Socialists, Edouard Herriot, *Pourquoi Je Suis Radical Socialist* (Paris, 1923) Cf. also Georges Suarez, *De Poincaré à Poincaré* (Paris, 1926), and L. Marcellin, *Politique et Politiciens* (Paris, 1928), 4 vols., and *Voyage autour de la Chambre* (Paris, 1925); J. Barthélemy and Paul Duez, *Traité de Droit Constitutionnel* (Paris, 1933); V. Haikal, *Le Président du Conseil* (Paris, 1938); A. Soulier, *L'Instabilité Ministerielle, 1871-1938* (Paris, 1939); E. Girard, *La Crise de la Démocratie et le Réinforcement du Pouvoir Exécutif* (Paris, 1938); E. Berl, *La Politique et les Partis* (Paris, 1932).

groups as possible, for the larger the number of included groups, the greater the compromise on principle, and the larger the number of joints, the greater the fear and prospect of fissure.

Now, if two conditions had been present, the "concentration" cabinet (or the *combinaison,* as it is called) would have sufficed and would have lived a long time compared with its actual length of life. The conditions were, *first,* that the groups should enter the combination as one man, and *second,* that they should remain faithful to the combination. Neither of these conditions existed, and neither could exist. The first did not and could not exist because every group contained dissentients, who would not follow their leader's person or policy, or who sought their own advancement by the overthrow of one ministry, hoping that the formation of a new one would find them more favorably placed to dominate or command office. The fact was that the conventions of party loyalty were not accepted in France, as they are in England, owing to the inability of the deputy to subject himself and his special convictions to public policy as interpreted by common consent. There was no way to force him into a state of discipline since dissolution was impossible: hence Jacques could always find an argument to prove that he was as good as his master. Nor did the vote of the group, whether it was unanimous or split, reveal the true state of mind of the groups: nor did it afford a guarantee that in other circumstances the conditions of today would be accepted by the same number. It was a fact well known, also, in all parliaments that men sometimes rise by intransigent opposition, while when they faithfully follow .the government they are expected to be silent and supine.

Nor could the coalescing part of the group be relied upon for long. The full difficulties of a program could not possibly be adumbrated in the few days of cabinet making, and as soon as they became patent in the course of the cabinet discussion, the signs of a rift appeared. Further, the coalition could not control the future; at any moment an anarchist might throw a bomb, a bank might fail, an army or civil service or Stavisky scandal might be unearthed, a cruiser might sink, a clash between army or naval forces might accidentally occur thousands of miles away, riots might occur—and a new question of principle would suddenly be thrust upon a cabinet of many jointed pieces, and a hungry, tumultuous, and theatrical assembly. No original loyalty held the French cabinet together: it was the adventure which did all, or failed; and it failed too soon.

The Opposition. The opposition was quite as badly organized as the cabinet. It had no such recognized authority as in England. It was composed of a fortuitous junction of heterogeneous, often bitterly hostile, groups. The cabinet suffered all the defects of being the result of concentration, but at least it concentrated groups more approximately likeminded than the opposition. There was, of course, no single opposition, but several opposition groups, and they became one opposition not by combining, but by converging. And then, having attained a kill, they diverged. The government was therefore faced by no consistent and regular machinery of criticism, but by irresponsible lethal attacks from all sides. For the attackers could not be sure that they themselves would form part of a government; and if they could be sure of this, they could not be confident of the policy in which they would be engaged. Hence their criticism was not tempered, as in England the opposition's criticism is tempered, by the thought that it might one day have to be justified by practice. A premium was placed upon exaggeration and incitement. It was never a responsible commitment. Nor was that all. The opposition, as a single body, was only a momentary phenomenon and disappeared at the precise time when the President of the Republic might desire to call it to office. It was often only a few votes (hardly a score) more powerful than the government it had overthrown; scarcely able, even if united, to govern. The groups, however, were back in their respective camps as self-righteous as could be, and some of them could not possibly hope to form a new government, while some of the old groups must remain in the next combination.

Short-lived Cabinets. The result was, of course, ministerial instability. Between 1873 and 1940, there were about one hundred cabinets.[8] Each cabinet lived on the average a span of a little over eight months. There were, counting cabinets of less than a week, about ninety-five ministerial and parliamentary disturbances, a condition which has powerfully contributed to bringing parliamentary government into contempt. The instability is better appreciated if we leave out of the average four ministries of great length for France. Thus Waldeck-Rousseau was in office practically three years, Combes over two and a half years, Clemenceau two and three-quarter years (1906–09), and again Clemenceau (1917–20) nearly three years; in all eleven and a quarter years. Table 17 is also revealing.

TABLE 17—FRANCE: DURATION OF
CABINETS, 1873–1940

Duration	Number of Cabinets, 1873–1940
6 months and under	50
6–12 months	31
12–18 months	9
18–24 months	1
24 months and over	8

From 1928 to M. Daladier's government of April, 1938, there were twenty-five cabinets, of which only Laval's first cabinet and Blum's Popular Front each lasted a year.

Now, each of these changes of ministry meant no complete renewal of all the offices, for one or more groups stayed in the new combination—sometimes little

more than the overthrow of a prime minister occurred. Ministerial changes were, in fact, *ministères de replâtrage,* replastered ministries, and the practice of re-plastering was sometimes called *dosage,* or "dosing" a dying patient. As a rule, between one half and three quarters of the previous ministry served in the new one. This is indeed a mitigation of all the administrative evils which might follow. Yet the consequences are sufficiently bad, as we shall see from a closer inspection of certain statistics. Further, the political facts practically extinguished the phrase of the constitution, that ministries were collectively responsible. There was hardly ever a complete clearance of a defeated ministry. There were frequent individual resignations.[9] It must have been felt that such frequent changes of the whole ministry were too disastrous. Yet these individual resignations weakened rather than strengthened the ministry, and they were often the immediate prelude to a downfall. Once the deputies tasted blood . . .

Intermittent Premiership. The value of a prime ministership is lost if the man has not a long and unbroken span of office. In France from 1873 to 1928, there were thirty-eight different presidents of the council;[10] their average length of office was thus almost exactly eighteen months. And there were fifteen more different ones between 1928 and the capitulation in 1940: that is an average service

TABLE 18—FRANCE: TOTAL LENGTH OF
SERVICE OF PRIME MINISTERS, 1873–1940

Duration of Ministry	Number of Cabinets 1873–1928	1928–1940
Under 6 months	10	7
6–12 months	13	5
12–18 months	3	2
18–24 months	5	1
24–30 months	1	0
30–36 months	2	0
36–42 months	1	0
42–48 months	0	0
48 months and over	4	0

[8] These calculations begin in May, 1873, in order to rule out the formative period after the war of 1870; and exclude several cabinets which lasted less than a week, as these were little more than attempts to form a government. The student must overlook some very slight discrepencies: the figures on the same basis are hard to obtain in a single series.

[9] Consider especially the succession of Ministers of Finance from 1924 to 1928.
[10] Omitting cabinets lasting less than one week.

of ten months. But some held office for fairly long spells, and recurrently. Table 17 is valid for continuous prime ministership: Table 18 for total service as prime minister.

Further, the prime minister came not as of right, with previous acquiescence of followers and the deference of his colleagues. Much of his time was inevitably spent in attempting to secure a practical supremacy, indeed, merely to keep the cabinet alive!

The Cabinet's Loss of Administrative Control. Few men held their departments long enough to make an informed impression about the quality of their activity. Nor were they in office long enough to learn from the results of their own legislation, or to initiate far-sighted policies. We must remember also that French ministries were peculiarly liable to loss of time from practices which are more fastidiously regulated in England—deputations, visits from members of Parliament and members of commissions, etc.—for they had not learned that to be the tribunes of the people is to have in mind the whole people and not to give way to the solicitations of the persistent few. A duty is owed to the inarticulate but it is not paid. And the added seriousness of such a situation is this: that the people and the administrators, finding that the responsible minister can do so little, are tempted to deny the value of democracy altogether, and to suggest the establishment of administrative syndicalism, in which the technical head of the service appears before Parliament and does the creative work which a minister should do —a regular French heresy! [11]

In spite of the palliating argument that upon the fall of a ministry some ministers remain in the next cabinet, there was a serious discontinuancy in the headship of departments. Thus for the period 1873 to 1940, some sixty-seven years, Table 19

shows the number of incumbents in the principal departments.

TABLE 19—FRANCE: NUMBER OF MINISTERS, 1873–1940

Foreign Affairs	27	War	41
Interior	37	Navy	42
Finance	38	Justice	55
Agriculture	42	Commerce	52
Instruction	41	Works	55
Colonies	42	Labor (since 1906)	40

Thus the average amount of change varied between once in two and a half years, and once in one and a half years. Moreover, even where there was continuity of office it was with different colleagues, with a different prime minister, and based on a different parliamentary coalition.[12]

The Senate and the Cabinet. The Senate was an extra source of difficulty to the government. Governments were overturned by the action of the Senate five times in the history of the Republic, and the government could not get its legislation through the Senate without taking special time and trouble to do so. Further, it suffered interpellations upon its policy in that chamber also. Now, the Chamber of Deputies had secured a primacy over the Senate as a representative of the people, and ministries defeated in the Chamber but sustained by the Senate had no chance of life at all. Though min-

---

[11] Cf. Henri Chardon, *Annales, Académie des Sciences Morales et Politiques, Sciences et Travaux* (Paris, 1928), p. 361 ff., and Robert de Jouvenel, *La République des Camarades* (Paris, edition 1924), Part II.

[12] This table does not, however, include an account of the ministries held by prime ministers. J. L. Heinberg (in an article in the *American Political Science Quarterly*, May, 1931, on "The Personnel of French Cabinets, 1871-1930") and counting on the basis of eighty-two premierships, says: "During thirty of the eighty-two terms, the premier has held the portfolio of foreign affairs; during twenty, that of minister of the interior; ten, that of justice; five, that of finance; and he has been without portfolio during four terms."
On the constitutional law of the matter (and this is one more proof of the vagueness of constitutions), Duguit takes the view that the government is as responsible to the Senate as to the Chamber; Esmein that the English practice was intended to be followed and ought to be considered as implied by the French constitution. Cf. L. Duguit, *op. cit.*, Vol. IV, p. 853 ff.; A. Esmein, *op. cit.* (7th ed.). Vol. II, p. 234 ff.

istries harassed or defeated in the Senate but sustained in the House might, and did, go on living, there was always the possibility that the obstruction of the Senate (as in 1890, 1896, 1913, 1925, 1930, 1935, 1937, and 1938) might so discredit or disgust a government as to cause its fall. Hence the government in normal circumstances had to walk warily; the question of confidence was put in the Senate ten times between 1896 and 1924, and several times after that in debate.

The government assured itself of support by taking some of its ministers from the Senate; and in this way, too, it secured the help of many capable statesmen. From 1873 to 1940 the Senate contributed twenty-two prime ministers out of a total of fifty-four, and rather more than one out of three ministers. Thus ministries always contained at least two members of the Senate, and often more.

The Commissions and the Cabinet. We have already seen (p. 493) that the commissions played a large part in the legislative, financial, and administrative work of government. They contained old and experienced members of cabinets and were the nurseries of future ministers. They weakened the ministers because they were powerful rivals and the chambers looked to them for guidance, whereas in England the sources of inspiration were purely ministerial. Moreover, they were the deputies and senators organized as continuous guilds, and they always acted as prosecuting attorneys and professional defensive societies, towards ministers. They could not see why ministers should arrogate to themselves full control and sole leadership. Ministers were able, therefore, to suggest that the blame for faulty projects, inappropriate administration, waste of time, and tardiness was upon the commissions, and no one could discover the exact truth of the matter. The commissions again, by their power of departmental penetration, were able to prepare the parliamentary defeat of the ministers.

The truth was that France was governed by a parliament in which the basis of action was almost one of unanimous consent, or *liberum veto,* and government either lived weakly on sufferance or snatched not infrequently at short-term dictatorial power (*pleins pouvoirs*) to carry out the most urgent defenses against financial or administrative collapse. A quasi-advocacy of the commissions—advanced on the grounds that they enabled former ministers to continue work in the field of government they had formerly tended, to control the new ministers, and to keep themselves in training for a return to office—is plausible, but omits the incoherence and vacillation produced by divided authority.

The President of the Republic. It is clear that in such a system the President of the Republic may claim and obtain more power than the Crown in England. For he represents continuity against change, and his experience is not lightly to be discarded by the cabinet. There were two types of cabinet meeting: the *conseil des ministres* and the *conseil de cabinet.* The former was a meeting of ministers with the President of the Republic as presiding officer, and it deliberated on policy: the latter met under the presidency of the prime minister and deliberated on tactics: the one was national, the second, parliamentary. In five years the President saw on the average eight or nine governments, as shown by Table 20. The dullest could not have lived without learning, nor could the lessons be without effect upon the ministers. More, if he was a creative statesman like Grévy or Poincaré or Millerand, he could not be without an added influence upon the council. And history shows that the Presidents who desired it were part of the efficient executive of France.

As for the President of the Republic, whose legal term was seven years, he was elected by absolute majority of the two assemblies meeting together. Though eligible for re-election, only two Presidents were ever re-elected for a second term: Grévy in 1885 and Lebrun in 1939. The office was not intended to be strong, and it was Clemenceau who declared that he always voted for the most stupid. Indeed, Clemenceau and Herriot failed of election. The Presidential powers embraced the whole of the executive powers, but they were exercisable by the Council of Ministers, with parliamentary responsibility. It was an office of dignity rather than power. But it could be influential, for Presidents like Poincaré could occasionally keep out of cabinet office statesmen like Clemenceau. All had influence in the Council of Ministers, but none against the will of the chambers, and none, even if they tried like Millerand (1920–24), could put up a ministry of their preference against the will of the chambers: Millerand was broken and forced to resign in trying this. But it was

tween two branches: a cabinet and a President. The French tried to overcome this cleft by electing weak submissive men to the Presidency: but the weak can destroy a nation as well as the strong.

Commissioners as Technical Assistants. The constitution gave ministers the right to assistance by commissioners during parliamentary debate. This right does not exist in England and cannot exist in the United States in open session, but it is of long lineage on the Continent. It is a very valuable gift to ministers who may have on their benches experts to prompt them, and even to speak in their place

TABLE 20—FRANCE: PRESIDENTS AND CABINETS, 1879–1940

Name	Years	Number of Cabinets	President's Term in Years
Grévy, first term	1879–86	9	7
Grévy, second term	1887	3	2
Carnot	1887–94	10	6 and 6 months
Casimir-Perier	1894–95	1	0 and 6 months
Fauré	1895–99	5	4
Loubet	1899–1906	4	7
Fallières	1906–13	9	7
Poincaré	1913–20	12	7
Deschanel	1920	1	0 and 7 months
Millerand	1920–24	5	3 and 9 months
Doumergue	1924–31	15	7
Doumer	1931–32	3	0 and 11 months
Lebrun, first term	1932–39	15	7
Lebrun, second term	1939–40	3	1

a power available to the President that at cabinet crises he could turn to one rather than the other wings of the Chamber where either was equally able to get support in office. That Herriot tried in 1939 to become President, and that Clemenceau had also tried vainly in 1919, is a sign that according to the character and ability of the man the Presidential office was one of considerable power. This was further demonstrated when the weak, amiable, mustachioed Lebrun had not the backbone to resist Pétain and his colleagues when they capitulated in 1940: he could have resisted, he could have reappointed Reynaud, he could have appointed a noncapitulationist—he tamely resigned. It is better that executive responsibility should not be divided be-

where the technical answer or information is beyond them. In Britain the officials, by simple custom, stand by the speaker's chair and whisper their lifesaving help to the ministers. In France, the commissioner might mount the tribune. The practice of the constitution permitted the help of the commissioner in the case of bills, resolutions, and interpellations. The commissioner was expected not to make saucy retorts in the manner of ministers or deputies; and a respectful demeanor was expected of him. Nor was he permitted to seem to take the responsibility for any action which was the minister's, and the minister, too, was held strictly responsible for all the actions of his department. Further, it was determined that questions must be answered by ministers.

There is an obvious benefit in this practice. It is clear that the expert can deal better with difficulties than the minister, especially ministers so short-lived. The technical nature of many bills has proved a serious strain on ministers in modern legislatures, who have to be coached and are unable to draw on the deep sources of professional knowledge. But there are disadvantages. *First,* it takes away from the dignity of ministers who are often demonstrated to be mere figureheads. *Second,* ministers are the less compelled to master all the details relevant to a policy or a statute. *Third,* sometimes officials whose actions are in question are brought forward as commissioners to answer for themselves, and though it is true that they know the facts, the minister rather should be at once their cross-examiner and their advocate. Yet with careful limitation the practice should be useful in all legislatures [13]—the limitation being that which in France is aimed at and on the whole, attained (the Fourth Republic continues the practice): [14] that the commissioner is nothing more than the technical assistant of the minister, and never his substitute. In the United States the appearance of officials before the committees of Congress at hearings fulfills the same function—even more effectively.

An Unorganized Cabinet, and Remedies Applied. Until 1914 the French cabinet had no rules of procedure, no agenda, no minutes, no secretary. There was even less preparation for its work than in England till then. Subjects were introduced by the ministers or the president of the Council, at haphazard, and were treated by a desultory and usually a tediously long and indecisive conversation. In 1916 Ribot created a secretariat of the cabinet on the model of the secretariat of the war cabinet created by Lloyd George. This was transformed by Painlevé and Clemenceau into an undersecretaryship of state attached to the presidency of the council. This organization brought together infor-

mation for the prime minister and co-ordinated and energized the work of the individual departments.[15] The organization ceased to be continuous after World War I, depending upon the varying personalities of the prime ministers.

Complaints were many that the cabinet was not equipped appropriately for its tasks. It was suggested that there should be more careful and considered attention to the projects prepared by the ministries and their consultative councils.[16] It was urged that the presidency of the council should be aided by a permanent council which would promote both continuity of policy from cabinet to cabinet and the ascendency of the prime minister.[17] It was also proposed that the number of independent ministries should be diminished[18]

---

[13] Cf. Pierre, *op. cit.,* paras. 641, 642.
[14] Constitution, article 53; *Réglement,* article 44.

[15] Cf. *Revue du Droit Public,* 1919.
[16] Cf. M. Lepine, in *Annales, Académie des Sciences Morales et Politiques, op. cit.,* p. 339.
[17] Cf. Maxime Leroy, *Vers une République Heureuse* (Paris, 1922), p. 86; Henri Chardon, *Le Pouvoir Administratif* (Paris 1912), p. 407; A. Schatz, *L'Entreprise Gouvernementale* (Paris, 1922), p. 230. See especially P. Dubois-Richard, *Revue du Droit Publique* (Paris, 1919), and *L'Organisation Technique de l'État* (Paris, 1930). The author was head of the administrative secretariat of Prime Minister Alexandre Ribot in 1917. In the article referred to, his opinion is as follows: "Even if the Chief of State has wide powers it is still necessary to organize the Prime Ministership and give it a bureau of research and coordination. . . In the first place, the following question must be answered: what are the tasks to be performed by services under the Prime Ministership? Now on this point, both experience and reason indicate that the first thing is to give the head of the government every means of forming his opinion with a knowledge of all the logically significant points; that the next thing is to secure the execution of the decisions arrived at, with a minimum effort and in a minimum time; obviously, the services which correspond to these two separate aims are of a very different character: on one hand documentation and research services are needed, on the other coordination services." Cf. also, M. Dendias, *Le Chef de l'État et le Rajutement de l'Exécutif* (Paris, 1937); P. Lions, *La Présidence du Conseil* (Paris, 1935); and V. Haikal, *op. cit.*
[18] The number of ministries in 1873 was nine; in 1890 eleven; in 1900 twelve; in 1928 (November) fifteen, in the government of Henri Queville, September 14, 1948, fifteen.

to improve collective counsel and provide the opportunity for a more rational, and less minute, division of functions.[19] Some recommended that there should be two cabinets, one composed of the ministers concerned with more "technical" duties and the other composed of "political" ministers,[20] and even that the form of ministerial responsibility should give way to government by a council of permanent officials, organized strictly according to the technical necessities of modern social services and acting with much more independence and publicity than hitherto.[21]

In 1925, a decree sought the creation of a systematic and permanent secretariat to the prime minister. Its work was to fall into four categories, each administered by a special section: (*a*) preparation for cabinet meetings; (*b*) centralization and dissemination of economic facts; (*c*) advice on administrative and judicial reforms; and (*d*) publicity. Further, other bodies, like the Economic Council, the Council of Housing, and the Council of National Defense, were to be brought into contact with the cabinet. This secretariat was composed of civil and military officials detached from various departments to assure a liaison, and to form the personnel of the undersecretaryship of state of the presidency of the cabinet. But within a few months the whole apparatus disappeared, under Poincaré's prime ministership, for reasons of economy.

If the arrangement disappeared, the need remained. In the wake of the antiparliamentary storm of February, 1934, Doumergue's reform proposals included the establishment of services of coordination for the prime minister. He said: [22]

You realize that I expect of a well-organized cabinet, with a president recognized by the constitution at its head, possibilities of governmental action which do not exist today. In my proposal, the prime minister ought to be provided with the assistance of a permanent, selected personnel above all, of small number, brought in from the great government departments. Helped by these services, the prime minister could follow attentively the activity of every ministerial department and could see to it that the one did not burden the other, and that suggestions initiated, activities, and efforts, should be coordinated for the common good. To the prime minister's office, besides the services of central statistics and the general secretariat of the superior council of national defense, there will be attached the reorganized *conseil national économique*.

Doumergue's general idea was carried out by an article of the French budget law for 1935,[23] followed by a decree carrying it out.[24] The article merely prescribed: "The minister in charge of the prime ministership shall have under his direction the administrative services of the prime ministership." The term used constantly is actually "presidency of the Council" and not "premier" or "prime ministership"—a term not unusual in French practice and designed to emphasize the organizing, chairmanship, function of the prime minister. The secretariat or the offices of the prime minister, according to this decree, consisted of a small permanent staff of clerical and administrative officers, and in addition, a floating personnel not exceeding fifteen (later twenty-five) released from their own regular departments for the purpose for each prime minister in turn. From this floating personnel one was appointed secretary-general of the administrative services of the prime minister. It was open to the prime minister to choose persons from outside the government public services to be members of the floating personnel; M. Blum, for example, appointing a university teacher, two former deputies, and three journalists.

The permanent nucleus of the prime minister's administrative services supplied him with material relative to the legis-

---

[19] Cf. Documents, *Journal Officiel*, 1921, p. 339, *Rapport*, report of Minister of Foreign Affairs; Th. Barnier, *Au Service de la Chose Publique* (Paris, 1926).
[20] Henri Leyret, *Le Président de la République etc.* (Paris, 1912), p. 148.
[21] Cf. Henri Chardon, *op. cit.*, in *Annales*, p. 381 ff., and "Probus," *L'Organisation de la Démocratie* (Paris, 1918).
[22] *Le Temps*, October 5, 1934: radio speech.

[23] Article 23, *Loi des Finances*, December 24, 1934.
[24] *Journal Officiel*, February 2, 1936.

lative activity of the Chambers, and took care of his correspondence and of the secretariat's files and library. The floating personnel—organized deliberately on a nonpermanent basis for each prime minister, so that he might be able to choose those whose individual capacity, character, and personality he found agreeable—acted as his general staff or administrative "brains trust," to whom he could devolve administrative missions, while they could relieve him of the burden of onerous high management duties and keep him linked with the various departments, as eyes and ears, and also as arms carrying out his directions. They received, sifted, settled, or passed on, as the case required, the importunities or the mere questions put by deputies and senators and members of the important public, coming direct to the prime minister or sent on by individual ministers to whom they were in the first place directed. Furthermore, the prime ministers used the floating secretariat as reports on specific problems.

In addition to the secretariat as instituted in 1935, the prime minister office had one or two parliamentary undersecretaries. They relieved the prime minister of many of the political duties—such as reception of public delegations, and the fulfillment of errands and commissions concerned in the maintenance of a parliamentary majority—which could be sloughed off safely by the prime minister. Inevitably, he organized the agenda of the cabinet meetings. But neither he nor the secretariat kept or transmitted minutes, or performed the general supporting services to the cabinet as a whole, as the British cabinet secretariat has done since 1916. Perhaps, in the nature of the shaky, short-lived, ill-matched, patchwork, coalition cabinets, that was and is impossible.

The decree of 1936, organizing the administrative services of the prime minister's office, also subordinated certain special agencies of government under the direction of the prime minister, combining their budgets in that of the prime minister's office. These agencies were: the central services for Alsace-Lorraine, the general secretariat of the superior council of national defense, the national labor council, the national economic council, and the central statistical office.

In spite of this organization, which in itself was wise and sound, though not perfect; in spite of the fact that some ministers held the same office for many years, though intermittently; in spite of the fact that former ministers often continued their activities in the parliamentary commissions—the French cabinet was mortally sick. It gained no strength from the newly established administrative services of the cabinet—a sick cabinet made them sick also.[25] For the prime minister enjoyed no strength of his own: he could not be a good master while he remained the timorous slave of several parties. In addition, it was a steady custom for the prime minister to hold a departmental office, and by no means as a formal chief: over thirty prime ministers held the office of Foreign Secretary; over thirty that of Minister of the Interior; a dozen that of Minister of Justice. It has been exceedingly rare for a British prime minister to hold a departmental office: it is an exception, like that of Ramsay MacDonald, whose vanity and messianic conviction that he could institute world peace impelled him for a time to hold the office of Foreign Secretary. As though the French prime minister had not occupation enough—or, had he, as prime minister alone, sufficient occupation? At any rate, he seems not to have been able to trust any other person to conduct foreign relations, or to govern the electoral and patronage-controlling offices, and the local-government supervising functions, of the Ministries of Justice and the Interior.

Thus, the French cabinet system possessed neither the party stability of the British government, nor the fixed term, if incomplete governing authority, of the American Presidency.

The Third Republic made so brief and inglorious a resistance to the nazi on-

---

[25] For a fairly up-to-date account by a French life-long observer, see Joseph Barthélemy, "La Présidence du Conseil," *Revue d'Histoire Politique et Constitutionelle,* January-March, 1937.

slaught of the late spring of 1940 because its political parties had shredded the nation, while the nation, considered as a multitude of individuals, had disintegrated the parties. So much was this so, that firm and stable government was not feasible. The permanent officials could not be controlled and directed, nor their actions appraised and corrected. No energetic masterful lead could be given them, because ministers were not in office long enough to get a grip on the departments, still less to discover and eradicate those who were disloyal to the democratic republic. No one was in office long enough to care to conceive the orders that ought to be given to the civil and military arms of the state, to raise its welfare, and to defend it against the secular and brutal enemy across the Rhine.[26]

THE EXECUTIVE IN THE FOURTH REPUBLIC [27]

THE advent of the Fourth Republic seems to have made no radical—perhaps no considerable—difference in the situation, es-

---

[26] Cf. *before* the débacle: R. Poincaré, *Au Service de la France* (Paris, 1926-33); A. Werth, *Destiny of France* (London, 1937), and *France and Munich* (London, 1938); M. Belgion, *News of the French* (London, 1938); D. W. Brogan, *France under the Republic, 1870-1939* (New York, 1939). For both general criticism and suggestions, more or less technical, for reforms, see: L. Blum, *La Réforme Gouvernementale* (Paris, 1936); G. Suarez, *Briand* (Paris, 1938); *Annales du Droit et des Sciences Politiques*, 1934, Nos. 2 and 3, symposium, "La Réforme de l'État"; R. Aron and A. Dandieu, *La Révolution Nécessaire* (Paris, 1935); Joseph Caillaux *et al.*, *La Réforme de l'État* (Paris, 1936); M. Ordinaire, *Le Revision de la Constitution* (Paris, 1934); J. Barthélemy, *Valeur de la Liberté et l'Adaptation de la République* (Paris, 1935); R. Capitant, *La Réforme du Parlementarisme* (Paris, 1934).
[27] Cf. *after* 1940: L. Levy, *The Truth About France* (London, 1941); E. J. Bois, *Truth on the Tragedy of France* (London, 1942); "Pertinax," *The Gravediggers* (New York, 1944); Pierre Cot, *Triumph of Treason* (New York, 1944); P. Reynaud, *La France a Sauvé L'Europe* (Paris, 1947), 2 vols.; M. Ribet, *Le Procés de Riom* (Paris, 1945); A. Michel (pub.), *Pierre Laval, Le Procés* (Paris, 1947); Gordon Wright, *The Reshaping of French Democracy* (New York, 1948).

pecially concerning the executive. It is true that all the resistance parties desired firm, swift government with the clear objective of social and political renewal. It is also true that the Pétainist reaction had placed the heaviest emphasis on deficient leadership as the decisive cause of the national disaster, and had substituted for the reign of the chambers the supremacy of a reactionary, irresponsible chief of state. But the French are a democratic people: and so France once again insists that the government shall be conducted by the properly elected representatives of the people. In other words, France is again in the régime of political parties. General de Gaulle, President of the provisional government in Paris from November 21, 1945, to the date of his disgusted resignation on January 20, 1946, was (and is) an enemy of this system, and in several uncompromising speeches before and after his resignation, proclaimed the need for government *above* the rule of parties. Thus (Bayeux, June 16, 1946):

It seems necessary to us that the Head of the State should be elected so as really to represent France and the French Union, that it should be his function to ensure the proper functioning of institutions above the parties and to make the permanent interests of the nation prevail in the midst of political contingencies. It seems to us necessary that Parliament should be one, that is to say, that it shall make laws and control the government, but should not itself govern either directly or through intermediaries. This is an essential point, and implies that the executive power must not proceed from the legislative power, even indirectly. . . At a time when it is clear to all how the State is undermined by the impotence and division of the parties, is it good to ordain that these parties dispose at their will and without counter-weight of all the powers of the Republic? When everybody observes the deplorable results of Ministers being dependent on their parties, is it good to arrange for this system to become definitive?

De Gaulle was repudiated, and resigned. Did the people accept or reject his constitutional notions? They then seemed to be relieved. The *Service de Sondages et Statistiques* conducted a poll on this question on October 15, 1945. In favor of a strong presidential régime were 46 per cent; 39 per cent were against; and 15 per cent expressed no opinion. But of the extreme Left only 21 per cent were in favor; of the Left, 35 per cent; of the Center, 61 per cent; of the Right, 81 per cent. Yet the numbers in the Left parties were so much greater than those on the Right and Right-Center. In September, 1946, 11 per cent polled favorably for de Gaulle's becoming prime minister; 30 per cent for his becoming President of the Republic; 39 per cent that he should have no political function at all; 20 per cent "did not know." The Communists voted 80 per cent against his being in politics; the Socialists, 54 per cent; the Left groups, 41 per cent; the M.R.P., 11 per cent; and the Right, 5 per cent.

It was in this period of torment and stress that the draft and the final constitutions were drawn up. The course of the discussion must be, in the interests of clarity, quotation of the articles of the constitution of the Fourth Republic which concern the President of the Republic and the president of the Council of Ministers (or cabinet) and the cabinet, with a commentary on their significance, particularly in the light of the debates in the two separate commissions on the constitution of the national constituent assembly and the debates in the assembly itself.[28] It is convenient to begin with the Presidency of the Republic, though any severance of this does violence to the integration of the plan of the executive.

President of the Republic. The President of the Republic is dealt with chiefly in title V of the constitution. Article 29 prescribes:

The President of the Republic shall be elected by the Parliament. He shall be elected for seven years. He shall be eligible for re-election once only.

The article means that the President is elected in a joint session of the two chambers. The M.R.P. and Right parties were insistent on election by both chambers.

The Communist party contended to the last for election by the National Assembly only, their purpose being to have a simple and clear government by the unobscured will of the popular assembly. Some groups even suggested the addition of other bodies, regional, municipal, and colonial, to the chambers as an electoral college. Their purpose was similar to the purpose of the M.R.P.—to secure a Presidency of the Republic who would stand above parties, be strong in his own right, and be "the incarnation of the permanence of the state and the arbiter among parties." [29] This idea, which, with the M.R.P., led to the attempt to build up a strong President with ample independent powers, commended the provision that the President's term should be longer than that of the chambers. Though one suggestion was that it should be six years, it was finally left at the term in the former constitution. There were stated three alternative ways of choosing the President: by popular election, or by election by the Assembly, or by a special college. No one spoke in favor of the first—the dictatorial danger was too menacing, and the French were worried by the nefarious results of the duality of the executive, as between president and chancellor, in Weimar Germany.[30] The third alternative was too fantastic. The constitution makers reverted to the practice of the Third Republic.

However, two differences may be noticed. The Third Republic required an absolute majority of votes for election. The new constitution says nothing about this. But it is understood that the old stipulation applies. However, the M.R.P. had attempted to raise the voting figure, and the rejected draft constitution actually required a two-thirds majority—but this was when only the National Assembly, not a bicameral session, was the electoral body. Furthermore, on the insistence of the Left, re-eligibility was allowed "once only." One other point is worth mention. The draft constitution re-

---

28 *Séances de la Commission de la Constitution:* April 25, 1946, and October 2, 1946, referred to respectively as I and II.

29 Commission, *Séances,* p. 119.
30 Cf. Chap. 25 below.

quired that voting for the President should be by open not secret ballot. The Third Republic had no stipulation regarding this, but it practiced secret ballot. The Communist and the Socialist parties were content to leave any such prescription out of the constitution altogether and leave it to the assemblies to decide on their own procedure. But the M.R.P. and the Radical-Socialists were eager for the express provision of secrecy. The former, especially, re-espoused the secret ballot, on the ground that since they wanted a strong and independent Presidency, who would need qualities of tact and diplomacy and even of "international clairvoyance" (surely a veiled reference to de Gaulle), he must not be a political appointee and partisanship must not be stressed, which it would inevitably be if his electors voted openly. The general body of the constitutional committee preferred open voting in order to emphasize the direct responsibility of members of the chamber. By a very narrow margin, the provision whether for open or secret ballot was left out of the constitution.

There is little point in reciting the various powers attributed to the President of the Republic, for the simple reason that article 38 requires that:

Every act of the President of the Republic must be countersigned by the President of the Council of Ministers and by a Minister.

This double countersignature signifies that the political responsibility for the acts are taken by those who so countersign. Since no countersignature is likely to be appended unless the countersigner is satisfied that the act is politically sound and defensible before the chambers, the real political will is not the President's but the prime minister's and the cabinet's. In other words, the President of the Republic is put into much the same status as his predecessors of the Third Republic and much in the political position of the Crown in England.

The Left parties were determined to avoid a split or dual executive which might cause a conflict of authority and obscure the true source of responsibility.

This was by no means to the taste of the M.R.P. and the groups of the Right, who fought hard for an independent, forceful President and against a President who should be only "King-log." They fought, but lost, a battle against the Left parties, in favor of retaining the right of pardon in the Presidency—a sign of majesty. The Left parties preferred to put the right of pardon into the hands of a committee of the National Assembly—especially the Communists, who saw the potential political implications of some acts of pardon —and it was finally assigned to the Superior Council of the Judiciary and to the President. Against the strong opposition of the Communist and Socialist parties, the M.R.P., threatening disruption of the triparty coalition of that time, won for the President of the Republic a potential "suspensive veto" on laws coming from the chambers which was almost identical with that of the Third Republic. For article 36, which requires the President to promulgate the laws within ten days of their receipt (or five in an emergency), permits him to "ask that it be reconsidered by both chambers; this reconsideration may not be refused." In vain did the other parties observe that if this required, like all other acts, the countersignature of the prime minister, it was stupid to establish the power; in vain, also, their reminder that the power had never been used throughout the Third Republic!

What is noteworthy is that the former powers of appointment to high offices and ambassadorships and so on (article 30) are now exerciseable "in the Council of Ministers," and that the President has no longer the obligation of the execution of the laws, which obligation has been placed squarely on the shoulders of the prime minister. It is also noteworthy that he no longer, as before, has the "disposition" of the armed forces, but, here, instead, simply presides over and orders the minutes kept of the superior council and the Committee of National Defense; he bears the title of commander-in-chief of the armed forces, but certainly without the implications which the title has for the power of the United States President. He was refused the power to require the president of the Assembly to read messages addressed to it (much desired by the M.R.P.) but was permitted only to address messages to it. No longer has he the right to negotiate and ratify treaties: but only the right to be kept informed of the progress of international negotiation, and then to sign and ratify all treaties.

On the other hand, the M.R.P. and the Right parties were able to put into the constitution an article (32) not to be found in that of the Third Republic, namely:

The President of the Republic shall preside over the Council of Ministers. He shall order the minutes of their meetings to be recorded and shall preserve them.

On this subject, protracted and heated debates occurred.[31] We have already observed that it became the practice of the Third Republic to hold two kinds of ministerial meetings, the *conseil des ministres* and a *conseil de cabinet*. At the former the President of the Republic presided, and here were transacted the most high acts of statesmanship, which certainly concerned and affected the political plans and prospects of the cabinet, but which rose above mere day-by-day political considerations. Such meetings gave the President of the Republic the opportunity to throw in the influence which came from long tenure of office compared with the normal cabinet, and such brains and character besides as the President possessed. But the cabinet meetings considered and took decisions on these questions also, and in addition were concerned with the problems of leadership of the chambers, and the balance among the political parties. The M.R.P. were adamant on writing the President's conventional status into the constitution. The party argued that the President of the Republic must preside over the cabinet if he was to keep in touch with the national affairs, and if he was to be, as they wished him to be, "charged with the permanent interests of the

French community." [32] If he were of no political weight, they argued, then let him be elected in an entirely different way. The Communists were particularly hostile to this provision: they wanted the President excluded from the cabinet altogether, not even present. But the M.R.P. argued that if he were so excluded, it would be impossible for him to be the guardian of the constitution and of the bill of rights. And, indeed, as we have pointed out,[33] the President of the Republic is president of the constitutional committee (article 91) which determines whether the laws passed by the National Assembly involve amendment of the constitution, and this includes the Preamble of Rights. Though this argument did not satisfy the constitutional committee (it was rejected by 24 to 18 votes), nevertheless the M.R.P. succeeded in making it a successful part of its case in the campaign of compromises.

As for the establishment of minutes of these meetings—that is, of the Council of Ministers, not the Cabinet Council—we have already drawn attention to the fact that such minutes were never hitherto kept. On this subject, an honest and patriotic conservative leader, M. Louis Marin, said: [34]

To the great scandal and shame of our country, we are the only nation which has never had minutes of this kind. It was even forbidden, out of a concern for respecting the cooperation of ministers—that is to say, to stifle their responsibility—to take notes during cabinet meetings, on pain of being admonished. This method was still in application in 1939 and 1940.

Who will ever understand—when all assemblies of any kind (I am not speaking of political bodies alone) are provided with councils of administrators and a council of directors and arrange for the taking of such accounts of the meetings as are necessary to fix responsibilities and to stimulate the directors and are necessary also from a practical point of view—how it could happen that in spite of so many projects of law and so many protestations, that

---

[31] *Séances*, I, p. 121 ff.

[32] *Séances* II, p. 121.
[33] See p. 154 above.
[34] *Journal Officiel*, September 5, 1946, *Débats*, p. 3523.

there were never instituted minutes of the councils of ministers, that is to say, of a meeting of men bearing the heaviest responsibilities and having in their hands the destiny of the nation?

Thus, the Fourth Republic has instituted a President of the Republic hardly differing in total political character from that of the Third Republic.

We turn now to the Council of Ministers or cabinet, dealt with principally in title VI of the constitution.

Prime Minister and Cabinet. The makers of this part of the constitution faced three problems. (1) They had to secure a prime minister with a status and authority above that of the unstable contract between the coalition parties that form the cabinet. (2) They needed to make of the cabinet itself more of a team than it had ever been under the Third Republic. (3) They sought to secure the dependence of the cabinet on the National Assembly, collectively and individually, and yet to avoid the ministerial instability which had cursed the previous régime.

Article 45 set out with due form the procedure for the appointment of prime minister and cabinet. Whether at the beginning of a parliament or after a crisis, the president of the council is "designated" by the President of the Republic. It was formally decided not to call the "prime minister" by that name or merely by the name of "president of the council," but to use the name of "president of the council of ministers." [35] (Yet henceforward, "president of the council" is here used alternately with "prime minister" or "premier.") After the designation of the prime minister, he submits his program and the policy of the cabinet he intends yet to constitute. If the Assembly signifies its acceptance, he then proceeds to collect his ministers and submits himself and them to the Assembly. When all together have received a vote of confidence by a roll-call vote and an absolute majority of the deputies, the President of the Republic signifies their formal appointment. The constitution actually puts this in a negative form, saying that prime minister and cabinet may not be formally appointed until this vote of confidence is obtained.

This arrangement [36] came to be known during the debates as "the double investiture," and the word "investiture" was even desired by the M.R.P. as a symbol of the appointing authority of—the President of the Republic!

The "double investiture" resulted from a compromise between those—especially the Radical-Socialists led by M. Herriot, the veteran cabinet-builder—who wanted a return to the procedure of the Third Republic, and those who wanted something else. The latter was an amalgam of the M.R.P. and the Left, who wanted a clearly discernible well-endowed leader of a team. They wanted the first discussion and vote by the Assembly when the prime minister-designate individually came before it, to be on his policy. That is to say, the leader and the policy were to be prior to the formation of the cabinet; unity would precede coalition; the Assembly would have created unity first. This idea went along with the M.R.P.'s hope (which proved vain) that the President of the Republic would have a strong hand in the choice of prime minister. The two together would have made a strong executive. It must be remembered that at this time the M.R.P. was largely a party of de Gaulle and was attempting to make a constitution to his liking, but it also manifested and still does manifest a sense of the unity of the nation and therefore advocates the strength of its central institutions as transcending the diversity of social groups within the nation.

It would have been possible to elect the prime minister and cabinet in the National Assembly. The Right-wing groups were horrified that this would make the prime minister the "assembly's messenger-boy." The Communist party showed a

---

[35] *Séances,* I, p. 98.

[36] It operates unless *"force majeure* prevents the national assembly from meeting," a proviso designed originally to meet the case of an enemy's occupation of the country, but later extended to any forceful obstruction.

strong inclination for this. The Socialist party harked back rather to the procedure of the Third Republic, though it did not side with the M.R.P. by any means. Indeed, in pursuit of the Communists' policy of weakening the executive (which the Communists knew they could not capture for themselves, but which, if ever they obtained a majority in the Assembly, they could always elect or dominate), the first and rejected draft of the constitution actually prescribed in article 73 that, "The national assembly elects the president of the council of ministers at the beginning of each legislative term by open ballot and an absolute majority of the deputies." And so also for the filling of vacancies by death, resignation, or otherwise. This method would have weakened the President of the Republic by permitting him only the presentation of candidates to the Assembly. It might also, as was pointed out, have caused protracted delays in the election of the executive—an eventuality which was emphasized by those with a knowledge of the working of the Prussian government in the Weimar period.

The opposition of M. Herriot and his friends to the double investiture was based on a common-sense judgment of what was most likely to happen in the future. They argued that it was more practical to vote on the whole cabinet than on the prime minister alone, since he would never be able to keep the promises he made to the Assembly without the co-operation of the ministers he had yet to seek and appoint, and they could hardly be expected to accept office entirely on his unqualified personal terms. He would later be put in the position of being judged on what he had promised: but less notice might be taken of his predicament in considering what he was able to do with his colleagues. The two steps seemed also to open the way to delays. The Communist party spurned any return to a situation in which the president of the republic would actually appoint prime ministers while knowing that their cabinets would fail or that they would not even be able to gather a cabinet to-

gether, in order by his astuteness to bring in the man he himself wanted when the others had been proved failures. The Communists quibbled long over the right word to use, whether "appoints" or "designates," in order to reduce the president of the republic's role to its weakest terms, and so strengthen the dominion of the assembly, or, in their own language, the "people's will." The Socialist party—remembering, without doubt, the designation of Pétain and Laval to the highest positions in the state at the capitulation, indeed Pétain's signature of capitulation before he appeared in the Chamber—insisted above all that the prime minister-designate obtained no political authority from the president of the republic, that he remained designate only until the national assembly had spoken its will.

The suggestion of the commission of the constitution carried the day: to sever the general policy of the prime minister from that of the cabinet, and to set the prime minister above the "contract between parties," in order to give him the extra authority which comes of his own individual and prior acceptance by the assembly. The commission made every effort to build up the distinct authority and responsibility of the prime minister, or, as the Socialists put it, "to organize the function of prime minister." Manifestly, the strength and mentality of the parties must decide whether this will be of any practical value. For, as the commission itself recognized, no man would accept designation as prime minister without having previously taken soundings on whether he would thereafter be able to find a viable cabinet. And, of course, what he later was able to achieve would depend on bargains already struck. Events since the beginning of the operation of the new constitution have shown a reversion to Third Republic type. Yet it was worth trying. The student will observe the attempt to arrive at the practical predominance enjoyed by the prime minister in the British cabinet system—*primus inter pares* (much quoted, and the Latin tags descriptive of his standing disparaged)—and the predominance of the *Reichs-*

kanzler in the Weimar German constitution. The unity, the strength, the stability, and the leadership of the executive as social, economic, and moral pivot was craved by all parties, except the Communist, which preferred the centrality of the legislature—the supreme soviet, and spurned anything in the nature of a separation of powers.

It is not of subsidiary importance that the authorization of the prime minister's and cabinet's appointment is founded on an absolute majority of all the deputies, on a roll-call vote. This is far removed from the excited pluralities, with furtive abstentions which left everybody guessing, of the Third Republic. The article has placed more open responsibility on the deputies and the parties: it may work valuably.

The ministers so chosen, after formal appointment by a decree of the President of the Republic, are (according to article 48) responsible "collectively to the National Assembly for the general policy of the cabinet and individually for their personal actions." They are not responsible to the Council of the Republic.

The constitution makers were anxious that incompetent ministers should be relieved of office, but it was difficult to put this in a form which did not involve the downfall of a cabinet. The difficulty was the greater as all parties were anxious to institute arrangements to strengthen the position of the cabinet as a whole against the will of the excited and tempestuous Assembly. Some suggestion was made that it might be possible to draft the constitution in such a way as to leave it open to the Assembly to censure a minister without destroying the cabinet. The difficulties are plain: the minister is presumably carrying out the policy of the prime minister. He may carry out a whole party with him in his troubles. And what would occur if a prime minister insisted on retaining a minister who had been censured? The common sense of the problem was to leave it to the prime minister to handle his ministers as the political situation required in his own discretion, based on judgment of the Assembly's

wishes and the balance of power among the parties.

We now turn to the problem of bringing responsibility home to the cabinet as a whole. The problem was to assure the cabinet of a reasonable tenure of office, and yet to assure responsiveness to the will of the Assembly. The solution revolved around votes of confidence and censure in the Assembly, and, on the other hand, the power of dissolution vested, under conditions, in the cabinet.

Article 49 declares:

A question of confidence may not be put except after discussion by the council of ministers; it can be put only by the president of the council.

The vote on a question of confidence may not be taken until one full day after it has been put before the assembly. It shall be taken by roll call.

The cabinet may not be refused a vote of confidence except by an absolute majority of the deputies in the assembly.

Refusal to give such a vote shall automatically result in the collective resignation of the cabinet.

It will be noticed that the prime minister is given some predominance, in that no other minister can raise the question of confidence before cabinet or Assembly, which, according to the debates in the constitutional committees, they might well do in a state of excitement. The purpose was to introduce more deliberateness in critical situations, and to make the cabinet a team under the prime minister.[37] The one day's delay before the debate is, as it was recalled in the constitutional committee, to avoid the upset of a cabinet in "the fever of an all-night sitting."

The deputies are put into reins by being confronted with responsibility. For they cannot wreak their will on a cabinet so easily as in the Third Republic, where to overturn a cabinet a plurality of votes

[37] Cf. André Philip, *Débats*, September 6, 1946, p. 3556: "The government ought only to put the question of confidence rarely; after cabinet deliberation, when everyone has maturely reflected and the prime minister has assumed the responsibility."

in the Assembly was enough, and when, therefore, as happened not infrequently, deputies undermined a government by abstention from voting. There may still be abstentions, but the government is secure unless more than fifty per cent of the deputies declare themselves openly and positively against the government.[38]

Much debate occurred over the well-used practice of the governments of the Third Republic which frequently put the question of confidence in their efforts to rally the members of the parties forming the government's coalition. It was asked whether the newly instituted procedure could be effective. For it was pointed out that the whisper could be sent circulating round the corridors that the cabinet was about to resign if obstructed. What the M.R.P. wanted was that the government should be stable: but the Communist party, and in a rather lesser measure the Socialist, was hostile to a cabinet which would be able to threaten the Assembly with a crisis, especially as the cabinet was to receive a power of dissolution.

We now turn to the Assembly's initiative in the overturn of a government. Article 50 says:

---

[38] An illustration of the operation of the constitution may be offered. On September 5, 1947, the Ramadier cabinet received a vote of confidence of 292 for and 254 against, with 54 abstentions. It was reported that the Prime Minister offered his resignation to President Vincent Auriol, and that the latter refused it, contending that it would be contrary to the constitution unless the Assembly had shown by a clear vote that it wished the government to resign. Then, on November 9, 1947, after being prime minister since January 21, 1947, M. Ramadier resigned, as his majority was not large enough, in his opinion, to support the considerable economic reform measures needed, and to face the steady succession of strikes. M. Blum appeared before the Assembly the next day, but he did not get the absolute majority of votes—he obtained 300 votes whereas he needed 309: 277 votes were cast against him. M. Robert Schuman appeared two days later, and obtained a vote of confidence of 412 votes against 184; the Assembly rallied to him, with the exception of the Communists.
See, for a survey of recent practice, C. A. Colliar, "La Pratique de la Question de Confiance sous la IV République," *Revue du Droit Publique*, April-June, 1948, p. 220 ff.

Passage of a motion of censure by the national assembly shall automatically result in the collective resignation of the cabinet.

The vote on such a motion cannot be taken until one full day after it has been made. It must be taken by roll call.

A motion of censure may be adopted only by an absolute majority of the deputies in the assembly.

This is article 49—on the cabinet's right to seek a vote of confidence, and so browbeat the Assembly—in reverse. It also institutes more responsibility in the Assembly's procedure than formerly existed.

The full import of the procedure regarding votes of confidence and of censure emerges from the constitutional provision of the power of dissolution—for this gives a sanction to the government's threats to resign. The constitution says:

If in the course of an eighteen-month period two ministerial crises occur under the conditions set forth in Article 49 and 50, the council of ministers, with the concurrence of the president of the Assembly, may decide to dissolve the national assembly. Dissolution shall be proclaimed by a decree of the president of the republic in accordance with such decision.

The provisions of the preceding paragraph may not be applied before the expiration of the first eighteen months of the legislature.

The cabinet has thus a recourse against the caprice of the Assembly: more, the right of dissolution was supported by Socialists and Radical-Socialists and the M.R.P. and parties of the Right—three quarters of the Assembly—because it was recognized that dissonance might well arise between the will of the Assembly and that of the government and that of the nation. The nation would be arbiter. This was not pleasing to the Communists, who wanted nothing of dissolution, contending that its threat would reduce the deputies to servility. They were afraid of executive strength. They even preferred silence in the constitution on the procedure of votes of confidence. Whereas the Socialists recommended dissolutions as a remedy for the insensitivity produced by proportional representation, the Communists expressed the traditional fear of plebiscites.

The question then was how to implement and yet limit the cabinet's right of
dissolution. The M.R.P. was prepared to
institute no limitation at all: to leave it
to the cabinet to challenge the Assembly
whenever it thought proper, and if necessary to take the quarrel to the country.
This was strongly opposed by M. Pierre
Cot (at one time *rapporteur* of the committee on the constitution, and a Left-
winger) with the sensible contention that
if this happened, France would supplant
a system of ministerial crises with crises
of government, that successive dissolutions would overthrow, perhaps, the constitution itself. He and others pointed
out the inconclusiveness of the frequent
dissolutions under the Weimar constitution, and the exacerbation and public instability they caused. If in Britain the
right of dissolution was not limited by
any constitutional provision, the stability
of British politics must be borne in mind
compared with the volatile French temperament.[39] Then the M.R.P. was persuaded at least to allow a closed season on
dissolutions—say, the first six months
after election, during which the Assembly
might find its center of gravity, its equilibrium. The Socialists proposed this
closed season. The Communists proposed
a limitation of dissolution by allowing it
only after three crises (rejections of votes
of confidence or passage of votes of censure) in two years. The M.R.P. countered
with "two crises in two years." From the
chairman of the constitutional committee
the idea of an eighteen-month season emanated. Pierre Cot pleaded for a longish
tenure of parliaments: there was already
a moral crisis, there would be an economic and a monetary crisis—France must
beware of adding a political one: "If
short governments are bad, short parliaments are worse!"

Article 51 represented another compro-

mise. The Communists did not like it:
the M.R.P. was adamant for the right of
dissolution. The Socialists were worried,
as were the Radical-Socialists, about the
freedom of the Assembly to conduct its
deliberations without being intimidated
by the government's threat of resignation.
The Communists persistently pointed to
the fact that a cabinet can, at times propitious to it, maneuver a first and a second crisis—they seemed acutely to fear being sent to the country for an election
campaign. The Socialists saw value in dissolution and an appeal to the country,
since dissolution would come at irregular
intervals and would submit a crucial
question of policy to the nation. The
Radical-Socialists had even proposed that
the second chamber be compulsorily consulted as a condition of dissolution!

Thus, the process of menacing the Assembly to obtain a crisis is regulated; the
process of throwing a government out is
regulated. Therefore the rude freedom of
a government to dissolve is restrained.
Nothing can stop a government from resigning if it wants to do so; but a resignation, on considered policy or out of
personal ambitions or caprice, does not
count as one of the crimes which provide
a qualification for dissolution. On the
other hand, the Assembly has something
to risk whenever it provokes the government to a point where it asks for a vote
of confidence. For if the vote is given, it
strengthens the government and humili-
ates the opposition groups; while if it is
denied, a dissolution may occur, and the
opposition may be punished by the electorate. The power of dissolution certainly compels the Assembly to look outward to the people, and be sure that their
opposition is not factitious and popularly unjustifiable.

Thus the Assembly and the government
have a free hand in the first eighteen
months of a legislature. After the lapse
of this time, when two ministerial crises
have been suffered in any eighteen-month
period, a dissolution may occur. The Assembly can be irresponsible, if it wants
to be, for a year and a half; after that, if
it sins, its sins may be its downfall. The

---

[39] *Séances*, II, p. 71: "English procedure,
which consists in dissolving the Commons in
case of ministerial crisis, cannot be applied
in France, where temperaments and mores are
different, and where the same traditions of
political stability or party organization do not
exist."

government, on the other hand, is at the Assembly's mercy for a year and a half: after that, if it is clever, it might enjoy as much as a year and a half of power. For if it suffered one ministerial crisis, its enemies must ask themselves who is likely to be in power after them to enjoy the power of dissolution which will come after the next, the second, crisis—and this must surely give them pause about the first. Some argued that as the government that dissolves ceases to hold office (as shown below), dissolution would be used cautiously, if at all.

No government has fallen as a result of the use of the "vote of confidence" articles; none has been in a position to threaten dissolution, possibly because no group, except the de Gaullistes, have expected to gain by dissolution. But, if we omit de Gaulle's two premierships covering September 11, 1944, to January 20, 1946, there have been seven premiers since that date, including the latest, the Radical-Socialist Henri Queville, cabinet. All resigned in the old-fashioned way.

This leaves open the question: Who governs during the elections after a dissolution? Some made the egregious suggestion that the presidents of the parliamentary commissions should do so. Most denied the right of the dissolving government to be the interim government, for there is tremendous fear in France that those who control the government (and especially the Ministry of the Interior) control the elections—especially, they argued, in a time when radio propaganda has become of such influence. The Socialist spokesman on this subject declared: [40]

In my opinion, the exercise of power between the dissolution and the elections must simultaneously offer the guarantees of impartiality and of being automatic.

From the first point of view, it seems to me a delicate matter to keep in office a government which dissolved, because by this very fact, it has taken sides against the assembly. It ought to be replaced by a neutral government, not liable in any way to suspicion of partiality.

From the second point of view, it seems im-

possible to proceed to the designation of a new government, because it might happen that the assembly would not facilitate this, which would obstruct the mechanism of dissolution.

It is perforce necessary to resort to an interim government.

In the British system, the dissolving government remains in power until the results of the elections are known; or it may happen that a government which has resigned gives way to one which takes over from it, and this in turn conducts the government during the election period. But this implies that all parties trust the government not to manipulate the elections in its favor.

The M.R.P. and the parties of the Right opposed interim government by the Assembly itself. But the M.R.P. accepted the idea of all parties in the Assembly having a right to participate in the interim (or, using the Anglo-Saxon phrase, the "caretaker") government. But, as a price for this concession, it wanted the President of the Republic to be at its head! This was firmly rejected by all other parties. Then the question was: Who should head the caretaker government? It was agreed that it could not be the dissolving prime minister. This left only one other "national" possibility: the president of the National Assembly. This solution was accepted by the Socialist and the Communist parties and the Radical-Socialists, but resisted by the M.R.P. and the Right groups. The former gained a victory. The consequence was article 52 of the constitution, which runs:

In case of dissolution, the cabinet, with the exception of the prime minister and the minister of the interior, shall remain in office to transact current business.

The president of the republic shall appoint the president of the national assembly to be the president of the council of ministers. The president of the council of ministers shall appoint the new minister of the interior with the approval of the secretariat of the national assembly. He shall appoint as ministers of state, members of party groups not represented in the government.

General elections shall take place not less than twenty and not more than thirty days after the dissolution.

[40] Séances, II, p. 77.

The national assembly shall convene by right on the third Thursday after its election.

The discerning reader will notice the importance, therefore, of the composition of the secretariat of the Assembly.[41] He will also notice that article 52 on the exercise of the right of dissolution requires the government to obtain the concurrence of the president of the Assembly! This is to give extraordinary power to the presiding officer of the legislature—and must lead to all sorts of politically tricky problems. It certainly stimulates the fight for the presidency of the legislature: it is bound to check the use of dissolution.

It only remains to add several other stipulations of the constitution to complete the picture of the executive under the Fourth Republic.

As we have already mentioned, the prime minister is vested with the power to ensure the execution of the laws; with the power of appointment to all civil and military offices (with certain exceptions); with the direction of the armed forces and the coordination of measures necessary for national defense. These acts require the countersignature of the appropriate ministers. Ministers have access to both chambers and their committees, and have the right to be heard whenever they request it. The prime minister may delegate his powers to a minister. In the event of the vacation of his office by death or otherwise, the cabinet appoints one of its membership to act as prime minister temporarily.

On the whole, the constitutional assembly acted wisely in all these provisions. It did the best that thought could propound, and that the equilibrium of parties could allow, to repair the mischiefs of the executive under the Third Republic.

Procedure and Secretariat of the Cabinet under the Fourth Republic. The procedure and organization of the cabinet are founded on rules adopted by the Council of Ministers itself in April, 1947,[42] but this is based on the re-adoption of the secretariat arrangements instituted in 1936 and operating to 1940. The prime minister has his own Secretary of State; the Council of Ministers has its secretariat much as before.

The "secretariat-general to the government," the body of permanent officials, prepares the agenda of meetings, whether of Council of Ministers or Council of the Cabinet, conferring with the President of the Republic and the prime minister. The receipt of communications from the public and from the various ministers is regulated as to the interval preceding submission to the meetings. The convention of secrecy of the British cabinet appears in the French rules in writing:

Secrecy of the deliberations constitutes a state obligation which engages the honor of all present at meetings of the council of ministers.

The secretariat keeps minutes of the meetings which are submitted for approval to the prime minister and then signed by the President of the Republic and preserved in his archives. In order to maintain coherence among the various departments, various laws and regulations provide for interdepartmental committees, conferences, and commissions, rather like the system of cabinet committees in Brittain but in France more formalized in legal and regulatory texts. But these need integration with the work of the cabinet. When any of these is unable to secure agreement on the matters within its competence—whether a report for the cabinet, or the draft of a decree to be made under its authority—the prime minister presides over a meeting of the ministers and, where necessary, of their departmental chiefs. The secretariat of the cabinet organizes and serves these special conferences also. The secretariat receives from the various ministers copies of all the various rules and regulations, circulars, and instructions of a general order which they establish for the application of the government's decisions.

---

[41] See p. 481 above.
[42] *Réglement intérieur des trauvaux du gouvernement, avril 22, 1947, notes documentaires et études*, No. 605, *Série francaise CXXXI*; following *Décrets*, July 25, 1945, and September 1 and 29, 1946.

The secretariat is in charge of the procedure for the preparation of laws. It receives all the documents and information and correspondence concerning a project proposed by one or more ministers and elaborated by conferences or other communications between them. This goes to the prime minister and to the *Conseil d'État* for its advice, and then is circulated together with the *Conseil d'État's* report to all cabinet ministers and to the President of the Republic. There follows a further stage of consultations among all concerned, assisted by the secretariat.

At this point the integration with the Economic Council or the Assembly of the French Union occurs. It is now decided at what point of time and in what form the advice of these bodies shall be sought. When this arrives, in a period fixed by the cabinet, the secretariat circulates it to those concerned. On discussion of projects by the National Assembly, whether introduced by the government or by the deputies, the secretariat watches the stages and keeps the ministers concerned informed and alert; and when the law is passed and to be promulgated, the secretariat is in charge of the routine for securing the countersignatures of the President of the Republic and the ministers concerned. A rather similar process of vigilance, notice, stages of discussion, and registration, occurs for decrees of various kinds, and the secretariat also takes care of transmission for publication in the *Journal Officiel.*

A weakness still exists in administrative coordination in that there is no counterpart to the British permanent undersecretaries, but rather the several bureau chiefs at the head of parts of the department. The British system was rejected by the constituent assembly.[43]

Thus, the prime minister, or in official parlance, the president of the Council of Ministers, conducts the government of the French nation, set in the midst of a fairly well organized series of agencies, auxiliary to him and his cabinet. He is responsible for the main lines of governmental policy. He has his own immediate personal political assistants in his office as prime minister. His ministers share responsibility with him, but not with the measured and assured solidarity of the ministers in the British cabinet. They have the assistance, over and above their departmental officials, of that special characteristic of French administration, consultative councils, often several connected with each department. Drawing them all together, as a unit, is the prime minister, and helping him in this process to attain some view of what is to be done, why it is to be done, and what means are to be depended on once the decisions have been taken, is the secretariat of the government. This links the cabinet and the individual ministers with the four assemblies which constitute the representative bodies in the Fourth Republic's constitution: namely (1) the National Assembly, which is will-determining, (2) the Council of the Republic, which plays a minor part in the formation of the sovereign law-making will, (3) the Economic Council, which is consultative and based on the functional groupings of the nation, and (4) the assembly of the French Union, designed to give a consul-

---

[43] M. Jacques Bardoux: cf. his *La France de Demain* (Paris, 1936), papers edited for the *Comité Technique pour la Réforme de l'État.* Representing the Republican peasant and social group, and himself a professor of law, he proposed to limit the number of cabinet ministers to ten, in the constitution. He also recommended the institution of departmental permanent undersecretaries, saying: "The minister assures contact with opinion and liaison with parliament. The secretary-general assures contact with traditions and liaison with the departmental sections. The ministers represents evolution; the secretary-general, continuity. The minister talks, the secretary-general writes. The minister passes; the secretary-general remains. One, that is, the minister, commands; the other, that is, the secretary-general, executes." The M.R.P. reporter of the draft constitution did not meet the argument, but explained that he was profoundly convinced that "departments must not be administered by technicians, but on the contrary, by men of profound general culture, not having suffered professional deformation and, yet capable of discerning and solving the problems of our own time." Cf. *Journal Officiel, Débats,* September 5, 1946, pp. 3526-7.

tative voice to the overseas possessions on matters concerning the whole empire.

Again, the prime minister and the cabinet are linked to the specific economic planning machinery provided to implement the Monnet Plan broadly as follows. The decree of January 3, 1946, created a "council of a plan of modernization and equipment." It prescribed the powers to be exercised by a commissioner-general for the Plan. The council was established as a subordinate of the presidency of the Council of Ministers. The objects of the Plan were to increase production, foster investment in the basic utilities and equipment of the nation, develop the standard of living, make good the devastation caused to the nation's production capacity, and promote full employment. The council of the Plan is composed of the prime minister and ten ministers at the head of the principal departments concerned with the economy and reconstruction, including the Minister of Foreign Affairs, and, in addition, the Commissioner-General for German and Austrian affairs and the Commissioner-General of the Plan. The prime minister and the Minister of National Economy appoint twelve or fourteen other members, chosen for their special competence. Under the prime minister, the Commissioner-General has his own staff. He acts as the permanent delegate of the prime minister in all departments for the purpose of establishing the Plan. He is a member of the economic committee, of the interministerial committees on German and Austrian affairs, of the National Economic Council, and of the National Council of Credit. He may pursue whatever inquiries he finds necessary in any departments of the government and may secure their cooperation. All agencies of the public administration are ordered to give him the information he requires for the establishment of a comprehensive budget of the national economic situation, while the departments concerned with the national economy must communicate to him their various plans and proceedings. Thus assisted, he is further helped by many consultative committees of employers and workers, of experts and high departmental officials and professional bodies, which he sets up but the decreeing of which is reserved for the prime minister on the proposal of the commissioner-general. At his disposal the Minister for National Economy puts various of the institutes of research which are located in or under the supervision of that department—for example, the Institute for Research into Prices and Fluctuations, the Division of Capital Development, and the National Center of Economic Information.

Thus, truly valiant efforts have been made by the founders of the Fourth Republic to achieve a steady leadership which sees things whole. The machinery and procedures are provided; what is lacking still is the unity and harmony of the electorate, which alone, by providing a stable majority party or a congenial coalition, could secure the movement and oneness of which leadership consists. For the French have lacked and still lack the spirit of Whig politics, as expressed by that Edmund Burke who foresaw the lethal effect on French polity of the Revolution:

They believed that no man could act with effect, who did not act in concert; that no man could act in concert, who did not act with confidence; that no men could act with confidence, who were not bound together by common opinions, common affections, and common interests.

25

The German Cabinet System

In this chapter it is proposed to describe the executive under the Weimar constitution,[1] and then to sketch briefly the nazi executive. This is followed by some short general observations and a word or two on the executive in the U.S.S.R.

THE FALL OF THE IRRESPONSIBLE EXECUTIVE

FROM the abortive provisions of the Frankfurt constitution of 1849, down through the struggle in the 1860's between the *Reichstag* and Bismarck, through the discussion of the chancellorship in 1871 and 1878, through the autocratic career of Bismarck, clear down to the allegations of President Wilson in 1918, no "responsible" government existed in Germany. In the center of the German *Reich* under the

Weimar constitution was, however, a responsible ministry. The experience of Germany with cabinet government is certainly of high scientific interest, though it embraces little more than a decade.[2]

The Nemesis of Irresponsibility. World War I revealed two weaknesses of the old irresponsible ministerial system of Germany and Prussia. That system assumed broadly that there was no necessity for an agreement between government and people before action was taken. This operated not badly in fair weather, for it takes a fool of astronomic dimensions to do immediate and obvious damage to a great modern state. But much more was demanded from government in war than in peace. In England and France the people knew their leaders—or believed they did; they believed that ministers were men of their choice, and had been accustomed for generations to the view that a responsibility rested upon themselves for that choice. It was natural to expect them to support even the mistakes of their leaders, and to repair any damage by extra effort. The state was in danger, and they were the state: they must defend themselves, and for this, no effort, naturally, ought to be refused. Indeed, World War I was fought by liberals and radicals, just as many men of the Left as of the Right! In Germany this was not so. While the victory and the stories of victory warmed the

[1] On the Weimar Republic and its fall, see, among others: S. W. Halperin, *Germany Tried Democracy* (New York, 1946), which has an excellent bibliography; Hitler, *Mein Kampf* (New York, 1940); R. T. Clark, *Fall of the German Republic* (London, 1935); A. Rosenberg, *History of the German Republic* (London, 1936); E. A. Mowrer, *Germany Puts the Clock Back* (London, 1933 and 1939); K. Heiden, *History of National Socialism* (London, 1934) and *Der Führer* (New York, 1944); Arnold Brecht, *Prelude to Silence* (New York, 1944); H. J. Heneman, *Growth of Executive Power in Germany* (Ann Arbor, 1934); F. M. Watkins, *The Failure of Constitutional Emergency Powers* (Cambridge, 1939); H. E. Fried, *Guilt of the German Army* (New York, 1942); Otto Braun, *Von Weimar Zu Hitler* (New York, 1940); A. C. Grzesinski, *Inside Germany* (New York, 1939); Ruth Fischer, *Stalin and German Communism* (Harvard, 1948).

[2] Cf. C. J. Friedrich, "Development of the Executive in Germany," *American Political Science Review,* April, 1933.

hearts of citizens, all was well—they were at one with their government. But after two years of indecisive war, industrial conscription, and food difficulties, a questioning began which could not be stilled. Nor could even the presence of the Kaiser, the hereditary king of Prussia, with the dominant constitutional sovereignty, the All-Highest himself, overcome the sullen apathy of the munitions makers. For they saw that they were not the state—that they and their political parties, however big and well-organized, had no real control whatever over leadership and therefore over the destiny they were asked to accept. Moreover, the real state of the country and the military situation was known only to a very few. It was not necessary for the government to consult the parties; there was no compulsion to do so. It was, however, more necessary than anywhere else in the world to maintain the illusion of absolute, if not of speedy, victory, for the prestige of success, not the sense of shared responsibility, was the title of the ruling class to its office. In other countries the public mind was always stimulated by the news that danger loomed; in Germany it was necessarily drugged. Suddenly, then, out of the blue, after inordinate exertions, and unparalleled privations suffered on the continuous and immaculate assurance of victory —suddenly, Army headquarters itself was heard to be in despair! The system collapsed. It has been said that it fell through a class war, "literally over a piece of bread."

Large masses of the middle classes and the peasantry seceded from the Conservative party and the National Liberals. The Catholic Center, reminded of its Christianity by Erzberger and of its Christian trade-union following, moved to the Left. The direction of the war, which meant the direction of all Germany, had since the end of 1916 fallen into the hands of Ludendorff and the general staff, and the Kaiser had been effaced. The opposition hardened. Already in March, 1917, the Social Democrats, the Independent Socialists, and the National Liberals demanded a constitutional committee to revise the

constitution. The demands became clamorous. At Easter, constitutional reforms were promised for after the war, the main promise being the institution of direct and equal suffrage in Prussia, the agitation for which had begun before the war and had continued with increasing, and then critical, emphasis. The famous Peace Resolution, won against the government and Ludendorff, was carried in the Reichstag. Bethmann-Hollweg fell, Michaelis fell, Hertling fell. The government was in a permanent minority. The Russian Revolution eliminated a foreign foe, but the sealed carriage from Switzerland to Russia which contained Lenin, with whom Ludendorff successfully infected Russia, proved to contain a powerful toxin to which Germany succumbed. The Spartacists formed on the socialist Left. Strikes broke out. Could the country be rallied?

The Transition to a Parliamentary Executive. Attempts were made. At the end of 1917, Von Payer, of the Progressive party, was made vice-chancellor, and the deputy prime ministership of Prussia was given to Von Friedberg, a National Liberal member of the Reichstag. A law passed in August, 1918, on the composition of the Reichstag and proportional representation in large constituencies, added forty-four seats in the hitherto underrepresented industrial constituencies. This would never have been done by the government and conservatives save under the most terrible duress. Woodrow Wilson, the former American professor of political science, pressed Germany toward democracy by his notes refusing peace negotiations with the autocracy. On September 30, 1918, when an armistice was already being sought by the supreme war council, the Kaiser, in a decree directed to Chancellor Hertling, promised a parliamentary system.

I wish that the German people should cooperate more effectively than before in the determination of their destiny. It is therefore my will that men who have the people's confidence shall participate in a large measure in the rights and duties of government. I bid you to bring your work to a close by continuing the work of government and to put into operation the measures I want, until I have found a successor to you. For this I await your proposals.

Prince Max of Baden, a ruler with a reputation for political liberalism, was appointed chancellor, with a cabinet of secretaries of state chosen from the *Reichstag* and made "Commissioners [not members] before the *Bundesrat*" in order not to forfeit their membership of the *Reichstag*. Prince Max introduced his government to the *Reichstag* on October 5 with a declaration reminiscent of those made by newly formed French cabinets.

On October 22, a bill amending the constitution was introduced by the government "to free the new government from its constitutional limitations which still stand in the way." The amendments were as follows:

(1) Declarations of war required the confirmation of *Bundesrat* and *Reichstag;* treaties of peace and other treaties within the scope of federal legislative competence needed the consent of both houses.

(2) The imperial chancellor required the confidence of the *Reichstag* for the conduct of his office. [It is because this had never yet existed in Germany or Prussia that I have so often said that the German political parties were not sovereign.] The chancellor was to bear responsibility for all acts of political significance undertaken by the emperor in the execution of his powers under the constitution. The imperial chancellor and his substitutes were to be responsible for the conduct of their office to both houses.

(3) The nomination, seconding, promotion, and retirement of naval officers and men had to be countersigned by the chancellor. (These had hitherto been within the uncontrolled competence of the Kaiser.)

(4) The chancellor's countersignature was required for the highest appointments in the state contingents of the army, and for the appointment, seconding, promotion, and retirement of military officers in the state contingent.

(5) For the good government of their contingents, the war ministers of the states were responsible to the *Bundesrat* and *Reichstag*.

Thus the irresponsible executive had been overthrown. The reforms, too, were suspended by the revolution and by the abdication of the Kaiser and princes. The impetus of change thereby grew stronger and produced the constitution of August 11, 1919, and especially the clauses on the executive. For two months the floods of constitutional desire let loose a storm which seemed to threaten the chances of parliamentary democracy—for the soviet system across the Russian border was strong meat for feverish spirits. The threat was, however, without substance, and in the elections of January, 1919, for the constitutional assembly, majorities were returned for whom the parliamentary way and the cabinet system were the very breath of their political lungs. The smoothness of the transition, and the revulsion from Leninism, proved later to indicate so full an acceptance of the democratic spirit as to let the Nazis in.

THE CABINET SYSTEM OF 1919

LET us consider the cabinet system as instituted by the constitution and molded by political behavior. These things will be observed: the incomparably more detailed regulation of the system in the constitution and other documents, the intentions leading to the adoption of the system, and the effects of the party system upon it.

Above all, an error of classic dimensions was made: the executive was divided into two agents—cabinet and President—with confused responsibility, all the more serious in a nation with a multiple-party system. The tradition of and passion for a strong executive proved the German undoing.

The Constitutional Articles. The Weimar cabinet system was formally based upon (1) certain articles in the constitution,[3] (2) certain articles in the law of the budget,[4] and (3) the rules of procedure relating to the imperial government.

---

[3] Articles 52-59.
[4] Article 21 chiefly.

A President, elected by the people, had a number of powers:[5]

all orders and decrees of the President . . . require for their validity the countersignature of the Federal Chancellor or the competent Federal Minister. The countersignature implies the undertaking of responsibility.[6]

This went not far beyond the terms of the old constitution, and the virtue of responsibility lies, as we have seen, in the body to whom responsibility is owed. This article said no more than that the President was not responsible—that some one else was—but said not whom.

Responsibility was broadly defined further on in the constitution.[7]

The Chancellor of the Federation, and the Federal Ministers require for the administration of their office, the confidence of the *Reichstag*. Any one of them must resign, should the confidence of the House be withdrawn by an express resolution. . . . The Chancellor of the Federation determines the main lines of policy, for which he is responsible to the *Reichstag*. Within these main lines each Federal Minister directs independently the department entrusted to him, for which he is personally responsible to the *Reichstag*.

It will be observed that "for the administration of their office" would include the countersignature of Presidential actions; and for such administration, responsibility was to the *Reichstag*.

The rest of the clauses deserve further comment. Unlike the French Third Republic constitution, provision was that responsibility should be to the *Reichstag*, the popular assembly, alone. This arrangement marked the tremendous gulf between the Weimar constitution and the imperial constitution from the standpoint of federalism, for it is a recognition and a guarantee that the body representing popular unity is paramount over the *Reichsrat* which represents states—while in the old constitution, the *Bundesrat* was the source and guardian of federal leadership.

What then prompted this arrangement and the consequent problems? These

clauses originated with the creator of the constitution, Preusz, and were accepted, in their original form, by the States Committee which examined the constitution before its introduction into the constituent assembly.

Let us examine Preusz's view up to this point. He rejected both the nonparliamentary executive of the United States, and the conciliar system of Switzerland, in which the government is a directly elected committee of parliament. Instead he provided for a titular executive (the president) popularly elected, and a responsible cabinet. Of the cabinet he said (and notice in italics some of the weakness):

The President of the *Reich* is not limited in the selection of Ministers and most importantly, of the Chancellor, to members of Parliament; because *it is by no means an essential requisite of the parliamentary system that the leading statesmen shall be members of Parliament;* but it is quite essential that they shall conduct the government in agreement with the parliamentary majority, and that they must resign should the majority deny them its confidence. For the general policy of the government the Chancellor is responsible; and ministers are appointed by the President upon his nomination. These are, however, not, as hitherto, nonindependent and subordinate helpers of the Chancellor, but stand toward Parliament as independent statesmen responsible for their Departmental administration.

Observe, then, the emphasis on the departmental character of the ministers! Preusz continued:

For the formal responsibility of the Chancellor for every individual Department would, as in the past, so in the future, be a fiction weakening the true political principle of responsibility.

That is, let us have done with a mere fiction, and concentrate upon those who do the work, those to whom the chancellor is obliged by the pressure of business to devolve the work, and let us hold them directly responsible.

And the agreement of the parliamentary majority with the general direction of the government's policy does not necessarily include the acceptance of the administration of each individual Department. Much more will the desirable influence of Parliament over the practical conduct of administration be strengthened, *where Parliament can produce changes in the conduct of individual Departments without a change of the whole Government.*

Preusz thus put his finger on one of the small practical weaknesses of collective responsibility for all and everything in the British system, and attempted to obtain the advantages of ministerial stability with true parliamentary strength in criticizing and eliminating unsatisfactory ministers. He saw the British constitution in books; and perhaps the passage out of Morley's *Walpole* struck him—as a German desiring efficient government—with more force than it really possesses. For we have already shown that collective responsibility makes ministers preternaturally aware of the infirmities of candidates for office, and causes them to restrain the foolish. Even then, a colleague who has really committed an error in an unimportant matter may be dropped, while if there has been an important error the minister may save his colleagues by resigning. While ministers command a sound majority for all except a particular departmental policy, it is the minister, not the cabinet, who will go.

Preusz was not convincing in showing that his differentiation could be made to work. His concluding remarks on these clauses serve to show that he was unsure of his ground, for he said:

Out of this arrangement of the relationship between the Chancellor and Departmental Ministers, practice will cause a more collective co-operation of the government, without the "collegiate" system being formally prescribed for it by the Constitution, a thing which is not to be recommended in the interests of *clear* political responsibility.

Thus he envisaged collective action, and could therefore have safely prophesied collective general policy, and a collective feeling of responsibility and collective resignations in most cases. Further, had he reflected that, in the future, cabinets would be composed of members of a large

number of different parties, he would not have imagined that any arrangement could possibly produce any clarity of political responsibility. In introducing the project into the assembly, Preusz added little to his explanation: the chancellor was now "President of the Imperial Ministry," and the "collective" system was not prescribed but was left to the molding force of practical needs. This sounds as though already the chancellor's superior status was reduced to nothing more than the position of the British prime ministership, and as though practical experience already showed the inevitability of collective counsel and responsibility.

In the Constitutional Committee. We now follow the project into the constitutional committee. There two tendencies prevailed: (1) to strengthen the chancellor, and (2) to set out more clearly the nature of the relationship between ministers and the "Government" as a collective body. (1) The chancellor, in Preusz's draft, was appointable by the President, but the ministers were to be nominated by the chancellor and only then appointed by the President. Then, apparently, the Presidency was strengthened at the expense of the chancellorship, by an amendment that both chancellor and ministers should be directly appointed and dismissed by the President. The reporter of the constitutional committee on this part of the constitution was Clemens von Delbrück, himself a former Secretary of State in the Empire, and son of Bismarck's colleague and vice-chancellor. He showed that several parts of the machinery were lacking. Insufficient, for instance, was said regarding the power of the chancellor and his relation to ministers. Was a "bureaucratic"—that is, a "chancellor" system envisaged, or was it to be a "collective" organization? Von Delbrück so expressed the problem:

To create an institution in which power and unity are combined, that is to say, a responsible institution—*one* responsible institution let it be noticed—must arise in which all the threads come together, an institution which is in the position to supervise all the items of business in broad features; and we must, on the other hand, decentralize not only in depth but in extent.

Von Delbrück's suggestions were adapted to this end, and were supported by reference to federal and Prussian history. He suggested (1) that ministers should be appointed only on the nomination of the chancellor; form ought to add authority to what would, at any rate, be the practice; (2) that the chancellor should preside over the government; (3) that the government as a body should create rules of procedure to be ratified by the President. All these things would strengthen the chancellor, and this must be done lest "on one fine day government get entirely out of hand." Then (4) there should be an express provision (till then not suggested) that "the chancellor decides the general lines of policy." This gives the chancellor the power to intervene in the administration of each individual department with some such observation as: "I warn you that the policy of the department is no longer in accord with the lines I have laid down. On the other hand, it must be said that the ministers, within these lines, are independent in the conduct of the branches of business entrusted to them." (5) Now, since Prussian and federal experience had shown quite clearly that certain things affect all departments, arrangements must be made for their collective treatment: all bills, including the Budget, all differences of opinion about the treatment of affairs touching several departments, and other matters already allowed for by the constitution—e.g. the dissolution of the *Reichstag*. (6) Finally, let the resolutions of the government be taken by majority vote, and give the chancellor a casting vote. This would enhance the importance of the chancellorship.

The general opinion of the constitutional committee seems to have been that neither a purely collective nor a purely chancellor system was appropriate, and von Delbrück's conclusion was that a chancellor system was not wanted, while collectivity was necessary to abolish contradictions—hence his suggestion for decision by vote. In short, something—not exactly defined—between the Bismarck system and the cabinet system with collective counsel and responsibility was sought, but it was not positively and comprehensively stated what this should be. There are points beyond which inventive political thought cannot reach, since the number and magnitude of the interrelated and present-future changing imponderables cannot be precisely and fully seized in words. Then, we cannot help quieting our doubts with simple inklings, and prescribing only the very little which seems certain.

Final Adoption. Von Delbrück's additions were accepted almost verbatim by the committee and the *Reichstag*, hardly a word being said in discussion or explanation of the cabinet system in the second and third readings of the assembly. What, then, had been created? A government: "The Federal Government consists of the Chancellor of the Federation and the Federal Ministers"; that is to say, apparently, a governing body, a council. Were all subordinated to the council on equal terms? The intention was to give the chancellor a distinct and effective primacy, and this was believed to have been accomplished (1) by naming him as a separate party in the government; (2) by his power to choose his ministers; (3) by his presidential authority over the government: "The Chancellor presides over the Federal Government and directs its business, according to standing orders drawn up by the Federal Government and approved by the President of the Federation;" (4) by his right and power to determine the main lines of policy; and (5) by his power to give a casting vote. Were people thinking of a collectivity when they thought of "government"? Perhaps; indeed, most likely; but we do not really know. Preusz seems to have expected this to come about.

The only express arrangement for subordination to the government as a collectivity was in article 57:

The Federal Ministers must submit to the Federal Government for advice and decision the draft of all Bills, also all matters for which such a course is prescribed by the Constitution, or by law, as well as differences of opinion upon questions affecting the sphere of action of several Federal Ministers.

The Rules of Procedure and the Budget Act. Even the rules of procedure and the special position given the chancellor by the Budget Order did not preserve the legal dogmas from unceremonious repudiation by the political parties. But before we examine this and its causes, let us consider the contributions made to German government by the Rules of Procedure and the Budget Order.

The Rules of Procedure were made in 1924, that is after five years' operation of the new system. Until that time the ministers had cooperated either without formal regulations or on the basis of casual rules. By 1924, then, there was experience of ministerial business and of the dependence of the ministry upon the *Reichstag* to go upon. The Rules of Procedure are also interesting examples of the German passion for committing their social arrangements to systematic statements of law. No other country, save Weimar Prussia, had or has such rules in such deliberately and carefully planned arrangement. Let us briefly consider their contents.

The Rules fell into four sections: the chancellor, the chancellor's deputy, the Ministers, the government.

The Chancellor. The chancellor, informed of all important measures, laid down the main lines of policy for the ministers. Contemplated changes or new policies of the ministers had to be brought to the chancellor for his decision.

The Chancellor's Deputy. At the chancellor's suggestion, the President of the *Reich* could appoint one of the ministers to deputize for the chancellor, in which case the chancellor determined the scope of the deputization.

Ministers. The minister's field was largely determined by the chancellor except where a policy touched more than one department when other ministers were called in, and ministers likely to demur had to be conferred with.

Deputations were, as a rule, receivable only by the appropriate ministry; a common reception might be given when the subject required it. The chancellor received deputations only exceptionally and as a rule only at the instance of a minister.

Foreign negotiations were to be conducted only through the Foreign Office; its assent and cooperation were required should other ministries desire to negotiate. Interviews touching foreign affairs were not permissible without previous arrangement with the Foreign Office.

The Government. The following subjects were to be brought before the government for discussion and decision:

(1) All projects of laws, all matters prescribed by the laws or the constitution, and the differences of opinion on questions which touched the business of several ministers.

(2) Drafts of all orders of general political significance; public announcements and citations from public archives where these should occur simultaneously by the *Reich* government and the states; suggestions for the appointment of high and unclassified officials and assistant secretaries, and for the variation of the established conditions of certain civil service posts. Further, matters of general or foreign importance of broad economic or financial effects had to be brought to the attention of the government. Attempts were of course made to reconcile differences that arose among the ministers.

Rule 24 was designed to secure the full concentration of leadership in the government and to avert disunity in relation to the branches of the legislature. When the Federal Council suggested important changes in a government bill, the government had to be consulted on the next step; similarly, if a minister concerned took exception to a proposed amendment. Important amendments offered by the *Reichstag* had the same effect. Where the case was urgent and a decision had to be taken at once, then agreement with available ministers was required.

All bills resolved upon by the Government are to be represented in the *Reichstag*, the Federal Council, and the Economic Council concordantly, even if individual ministers hold a different opinion. All officials, directly or indirectly concerned, are prohibited from acting against the views of the Government.

At cabinet meetings there were regularly present the chancellor, the ministers or their deputies, the secretary to the Chancellor's Department, the chief of the President's Office, the chief of the Government Press Service, and a clerk. The deputies had full rights of discussion and voting. Ministers might, where this seemed desirable, and with the agreement of the chairman, introduce a permanent official, who might be present only for the time and the specific purpose for which he was called in. This arrangement seems to me of extraordinary value in the modern state and, of course, it has from time to time been followed in England, when officials are called in to help ministers in matters where policy and technical knowledge cannot be separated, and do especially important service in cabinet committees. Minutes are taken, and the relevant extracts distributed to the various departments.

The Minister of Finance. It is well understood in the British system that the Chancellor of the Exchequer has a position of exceptional importance, and often of extraordinary power. The reason is simple: the Chancellor of the Exchequer must find the money which his colleagues have planned to spend. He must not be driven to impossible demands upon the public, and, therefore, he has been provided with a power of defense. Besides this, however, there is his own positive sense of responsibility for the industry and commerce of the country, and for the private purse of the citizen. A Gladstone or a Harcourt or a Snowden is strong, and in single combat with any minister, is usually sure of victory. Disputes of any magnitude become cabinet questions, and there the battle is between the Chancellor of the Exchequer and the majority against him, for the support of the prime minister. The Chancellor of the Exchequer and the prime minister together are, in all ordinary circumstances, irresistible.

German law followed the essentials of English practice. In the *Reich* Budget Order of December 30, 1922, the Minister of Finance was provided with a veto over the inclusion of expenditure or a rider in the budget. This veto could only be overcome by a majority of the cabinet and if the *Reich* chancellor was in this majority. In other words, Minister of Finance and chancellor could together settle the budget. This arrangement was forced into law by the financial difficulties of the postwar period. Yet the rule, which also appeared in article 32 of the Rules of Procedure, did not square with the constitutional clause that decisions were taken by a majority vote. Indeed, both von Delbrück and one other member of the constitutional committee emphasized that ministers ought not to become dependents of the Minister of Finance. The order was therefore passed with the majorities required for constitutional amendments. It is obvious that, legally, the position of the chancellor and the Minister of Finance was by this order raised above that of other ministers and above the position given by the constitution, while the other ministers had been made legally subordinate for financial purposes. It is a well-known fact, however, that where men enjoy a legal predominance they will very probably acquire an actual predominance, owing to the compelling effects of legal concepts on the mind of those who come into relation with them. Nor does the effect threaten to stop at this point: for a power in one direction is a power to intimidate and bargain in every other. It may be overcome by the political resources of the other ministers: but it is still a power to overcome, which requires a countervailing force.

THE ACTUAL OPERATION OF THE WEIMAR SYSTEM

CAN the predominance of the *Reich* chancellor be inviolate? Is the Minister of Finance assured of the power given him by the constitutional amendment? Do majority votes decide matters? All these things may be subjects of formal prescription, and again, formally, they may follow the course provided by the constitution and the Rules of Procedure, and yet the balance of political forces may govern the actual substance and nature of the formalities. Thus a chancellor's main lines of policy may be written down by him and be formally called his: yet what was established may have been the result of the compulsion of a party whose cooperation was essential to his ever having been able to accept the chancellorship. A Minister of Finance may threaten to use his veto power over an estimate, but what if he is told that its use will cause him to be outvoted on an ordinary measure which his party considers vital? A majority and a minority in the cabinet are in the process of formation: the minority asks for concessions and, unless they are granted, it is prepared to withdraw from the government. No better governmental arrangement can be made in the existing state of parties in the *Reichstag* and the country. The majority must to that extent give way. In short, the majority vote is based not upon the equality of ministers but upon the political strength of each in the special circumstances. There is no doubt, when we consult the experience of Great Britain and France over a long period, that various ministers assume different significance at different times. Sometimes there is a kind of instinctive subordination to the Foreign Minister, sometimes all defer to the departments concerned with unemployment, and almost always the Treasury is rather overpowering.

The experience of Germany shows that the party system so filled up the formal bottles of the constitution that these burst. *Formation of Cabinets*. We have shown in the cases of England, France, and the United States that the composition of the executive determines its power. So with Germany; here as in England and France, all went back to the character and number of political parties. Had Germany had a two-party system or something near it, then the constitutional articles might have been made to work in admirable and accurate accord with their intention: but it had not. The President of the Federa-

tion appointed and dismissed the chancellor, and, on the latter's recommendation, the federal ministers. This article appeared to give the President a free hand with the chancellor, and the chancellor a free choice of ministers, including the Minister of Finance. In fact, the President was very narrowly limited in his choice; and the chancellor, before he could accept the chancellorship, needed to get a group of colleagues. But these could normally afford to be extremely exigent before they entered his government. For the German Parliament, like the French Chamber of Deputies, was divided into a number of parties, none of which, after 1919, was able to approach a majority of the assembly. The situation therefore dictated coalition ministries. Thus the President was obliged to find a chancellor who, to discover a coalition, could fulfill two conditions: obtain a *Reichstag* majority, and maintain it for an appreciable time so as to avoid political vicissitudes. This second condition had been borne in upon the Germans by their own long experience of stable if autocratic government, by their desire for regularity and order in all things, and by the warnings which obtained from their intellectuals who ever paraded French ministerial instability as something which Germany must at all costs avoid. On at least one occasion, von Hindenburg, when President, threatened to dissolve the *Reichstag* unless his own nominee speedily found a coalition.

The principle that the largest party was to be called in to lead the government, provide a chancellor, and form a ministry was rejected for the principle that the prime consideration was the speediest formation of a practicable cabinet. After the elections of May, 1924, the German National party press urged that the President would violate the principles of parliamentary government if he did not choose the chancellor from that party, as the largest; yet Chancellor Marx of the Center party was asked to form a ministry, and the Nationals were left in the opposition. Again, when the Stresemann ministry fell, in November, 1923, the German Nationals insisted, in a letter from the leader of the party to the President, that "as parliamentary usage demanded," one of the opposition parties should be entrusted with the formation of a new government. They themselves were prepared to accept office, dissolve the *Reichstag*, and consult the people anew to see whether, indeed, the country was not turning to the Right for a government. To this the President answered (1) that the constitution left him full discretion in the matter; (2) that the use of this discretion had on his part been directed to securing "a personage whose political position seemed to promise most hope of the speedy composition of a workable Cabinet;" (3) that confidential discussion with *Reichstag* group leaders had convinced him that the opposition parties offered no hope of this, and (4) that even the German Nationals had admitted their readiness to follow a chancellor of the Popular party and the Center. It is to be remarked that, in this letter, Ebert admits his partiality for a coalition of the Left rather than the Center, and says he accepted the Center only because his first attempts had failed. In later and more crucial stages of the Weimar *Reich*, President von Hindenburg bargained with von Brüning and with Hitler, and his personal wishes (and therefore those of his private nationalist and conservative entourage) emerged as public policy, to the final accession of the Nazis.

Short-lived Cabinets. From February, 1919 to January, 1933, there were twenty cabinets; that is, each cabinet lived for eight months. There were various reasons for this weakness. Of very great importance was the disturbing and uncontrollable effect of foreign pressure upon Germany. Every time a crisis occurred in German foreign relationships, the balance of political strength and loyalty was rudely disturbed, since passions were so roused that often one could best govern by resignation from the government. Thus I count at least four cabinet downfalls as due to unavoidable foreign events. Another three defeats were due to the *malaise* of a new constitution: the Kapp *putsch,* stringency of measures against Saxony

and Bavaria, a conflict over the national flag. Four cabinets resigned when general elections went against them. Von Brüning's Center party had less than one half the strength of the Social Democratic party in the years 1928-32, but it was von Brüning who was chancellor. Other cabinet downfalls can be so explained. The first, a government of the Weimar coalition—Social Democrats, the Center, and the Democrats—fell after over a year of office (October, 1921, to November, 1922) owing to general weakness and the inability to attach to itself the party just on its Right—the German People's party. The chancellor, Wirth, of the Center party, was too uncomfortably placed to be able to pursue a steady policy without more support. In the second of these cabinets, Stresemann's Great Coalition, which included the previously named parties and his own, the German People's party, it was impossible to keep the parties together for more than seven weeks (August 4 to October 4, 1923), as the Social Democrats refused to give the government a free hand in matters of social legislation. The third cabinet to fall through parliamentary weakness was the Luther coalition of Center parties and German Nationals. This lasted ten months (January 16, 1925, to October 29, 1925) but did not prove strong enough, and a minority government in which the Democrats replaced the German Nationals took its place after six weeks of negotiation, only to fall four months later. The fourth cabinet of this series was similar in composition to Luther's minority government of the Center parties and the Democrats, but with Marx of the Center as chancellor, lived from May, 1926, to February, 1927—that is, for seven months—dying as the result of a vote of no confidence passed by the parties of the Right and the Left—the German Nationals and the Social Democrats. The circumstances of the last two years of the Weimar *Reich* have been explained already (p. 395 above).

Continuity in Office and Membership of the Reichstag. There was rather a large rotation of office due to the rapid changes of ministry. But some members appeared in cabinets again and again, and acquired a large amount of official experience, but it was usually varied, and German practice was far nearer the French than the English in this respect. Though there were twenty cabinets there were only eleven chancellors (von Brüning was chancellor from March, 1930, to May, 1932).

Now, the constitution nowhere provided that the ministers must be members of Parliament. Article 33 gave the *Reichstag* and its committee the right "to require the presence of the Chancellor and any Federal Minister;" while "the Federal Chancellor, the Federal Ministers, and Commissioners appointed by them have access to the sittings of the *Reichstag* and its Committees . . . At their request, the Government must be heard during debate." Here was ample power to secure a due attendance of ministers in the *Reichstag*. The arrangement made it possible for ministers to be chosen outside the circle of members of Parliament. There were undoubted advantages in this, providing the cabinet was, for the large majority, from the body of Parliament itself. It was not wise to attempt to dispense too largely with the process of electoral and parliamentary training and selection. Even if this were not so, we can be sure that members of Parliament would not be prepared to relinquish claims to office. Now, German political experience was the experience of a nation governed by experts. That experience was not forgotten, and it is not yet widely held to have been improper. On the contrary, it was generally agreed that expertness ought to find a place in the cabinet. The result was that though the overwhelming number of cabinet posts went to politicians, some very important ones went to nonparliamentary experts—in all some 24 ministers out of about 150 (in the first 15 cabinets). Luther, for example, was twice chancellor, Minister of Finance, Minister of Justice, and Minister of Food, and even declared himself nonparty. Cuno, another chancellor, was not a member of the *Reichstag*. Finance, Food, Economic Affairs, Transport, the Post Office, and the

War Office, have been held by ministers who were not members of Parliament. This device is used not only to include men who have masterly administrative ability, but also to withdraw bones of contention from the negotiations for a coalition, for, at least, exception will not be taken to these men on the ground that some particular party is receiving an advantage. The holding of the War Office by nonparliamentarians like von Schleicher, an intriguer and for a few days chancellor, was dangerous to the Republic.

Votes of Confidence. If we had not been taught that the living constitution may be and is always very different from its written clauses, we might imagine that the Weimar constitution was wise in distinguishing the responsibility of the chancellor and the whole government from that of any one minister, by providing that the chancellor was responsible for main lines of policy and the ministers for departmental policy, and that they must resign should the House withdraw its confidence by express resolution. We saw that Preusz desired the benefit of collective counsel without the disadvantage of a fall of the government when any one minister was to blame. Now, it could have been prophesied that such system could not possibly work, because, having regard to English and French experience, no easy line can be drawn between main lines of policy and the departmental application thereof. We foresaw that it would be impossible, having regard to the close-woven texture of modern governmental business and to the conditions of cabinet making, for a minister to be sacrificed without the cabinet itself falling. These prognostications were realized. Many votes of no confidence have been proposed and three did their fell work—but none was directed against a single minister: all were leveled at the cabinet. Some, but very few, ministers left cabinets because their pet policies did not receive furtherance, or because foreign events occurred with which they did not wish to be officially associated. But individual ministers were not attacked by express resolution; cabinets stood or fell together.

What, then, was the nature of the votes of confidence? It was agreed among constitutional lawyers of repute that the constitution meant that a government possessed the confidence of the *Reichstag* until this was "withdrawn." The government might, it did, but it needed not, ask for any express vote of confidence upon entering office or thereafter. This latitude was extremely important, because it meant that a cabinet led by a minority party might be tolerated and not overthrown, though no one was really happy about its composition or policy. Meanwhile that cabinet (the von Brüning régime is an example) could make law by the emergency decrees under article 48 (see below, p. 660) and still be tolerated for fear of either dissolution of the *Reichstag* or national disaster.

Now it is clear that there are degrees of confidence and no confidence. The constitution said that ministers must go if there is an "express resolution withdrawing confidence." We who are tactful know that mistrust may be conveyed without the use of explicit terms; we also know that we may avoid the expression of no confidence, and yet safeguard ourselves by not voting in positive favor of a resolution of no confidence—for from such a vote it does not follow that we positively have confidence. Parties in the *Reichstag,* therefore, who did not wish to overturn a government, but who were strong enough to do so (e.g., the Social Democrats *versus* von Brüning from October, 1931, to May, 1932) might and did vote against a resolution of no confidence, without considering that they supported the government, and with involved explanations to their constituents that they did or did not partly or wholly trust the government. Another method of parliamentary trimming was to give a "limited" vote of confidence; that is, assent to one or more activities or to a policy for a specific time. This form of vote of confidence became very frequent owing to the changing relationship of groups and governments. It enabled the parties to in-

jure and weaken the government by substituting "limited" for "full" confidence, and then dishonestly to explain away their position to electors who cannot follow whether their action was right or wrong in the circumstances. The President of the *Reichstag,* Löbe, suggested that the term *"billigen,"* which means no more than "to accept," ought not to be used alone to indicate acceptance of a government declaration without the addition of a definite statement of confidence. He believed it would be better to have the French practice, where the government declares that it stands or falls by the voting of a majority for a resolution which it designates. In this way there would be a positive and explicit expression of opinion within the terms set by the government. To me, this seems a very reasonable suggestion.

Had the government to resign if the majority did not vote expressly for a positive resolution of confidence in the government? To abstain from voting, or to vote against, is not an explicit withdrawal of confidence. Only once (Stresemann in November, 1923) did a government resign on the rejection of an affirmative vote of confidence, but that was the only occasion upon which such a vote was rejected; and on that occasion the chancellor had directly challenged a clear vote. Many votes of no confidence have been put by the opposition groups, but only three were accepted, and these led, of course, to the fall of the cabinets involved.

Beyond what we have already said, governments resigned, of course, when their *Reichstag* difficulties made progress with their policy impossible. Their fall was promoted also by differences between ministers. Thus von Schleicher in the last convulsions of the Republic tried a very eclectic coalition on December 2, 1932. He could not have stood, even if the President had not abruptly dismissed him.

On the day when President von Hindenburg appointed Adolf Hitler to be chancellor, the Weimar cabinet system, as well as the whole constitution, may be said to have ceased to exist, for though Hitler did not fully install his own dictatorial system for some months, nevertheless the die had been cast, and the era of terror had begun.

The advent of Hitler had many deep-seated social, psychic, and spiritual causes, but one of the causes was constitutional: the constitutional clauses let him in, above all the two-forked split executive. It can be argued that if there had been no von Hindenburg as President, then another President, using the powers that von Hindenburg used, could thereby have kept Hitler out. This is true: but still the constitutional clauses placed authority in the hands of an executive who was only remotely responsible to the people, as against a cabinet with heavy immediate tasks, based on an immediate responsibility to a fluid party and parliamentary foundation.

The President held office for seven years, and was eligible for re-election (article 41). This was in face of a *Reichstag* with a legal duration of four years, and liable to dissolution. More serious in the tests of strength and the conflict of authority was the fact that the president was elected by direct election of the people. This, as in the case of the United States President, gives very substantial moral support to a President: he can always think of himself as at least equal or even superior in authority to a chancellor issuing from no better a popular ocean of will than his own. Indeed, he owed a *duty* to the constitution. This constituted a serious cleft in the will-making authority at the head of the state. The French system is better, precisely because it allows the will of Parliament to dominate the presidency, and because it attempts to bring about a harmony between the cabinets which emanate from it and the Presidency by electing Presidents of no will or of good will. In the complex modern state, with its heavy duties of harmonizing social groups, a constitutionally arranged bifurcation is crass stupidity.

To the President were given, as we have seen, very ample powers of exerting his will in the formation of cabinets, and the dissolution of the *Reichstag*. He could give or withhold from a chancellor the weapon of dissolution. It was denied to von Brüning, and he was dismissed. It was given to von Papen, because von Hindenburg liked him. It was denied to von Schleicher because von Papen personally persuaded von Hindenburg in December, 1932, to try Hitler rather than to support von Schleicher in his attempts to make and keep a government going. He was given these powers in the articles we have already related; and they became strongly effective because the parties were so disintegrated that he had ample choices for the kind of coalition which should lean on the parties the president liked rather than disliked. Hindenburg leaned to the Center and to the Right—"national," as the term went.

President von Hindenburg had acquired massive strength from three sources: election, reputation, friends. As for election, he succeeded Ebert, the first President, who had served from 1919 to his death in 1925. In the first ballot, in 1925, von Hindenburg was not a candidate. The Social Democrats obtained 7,-800,000 votes; the Center party candidate, 4,000,000; a Liberal, 1,600,000; a Bavarian Catholic, 1,000,000; the Right parties' candidate, 10,800,000; Ludendorff, for the fascists and anti-Semites, 200,000; a Communist, 1,900,000. Let it be noticed that in 1925, there were nearly 11,000,000 Right votes; and practically no Hitler votes. If the Left and middle parties had got together, they could have had their own candidate. In the second ballot, the Right parties, smart enough, put forward von Hindenburg. In this election von Hindenburg's war leadership, and his age, and his nonparty position put him at the head of the poll—a "nonpolitical" man to exercise the most political of offices! Here is an index of the civic ignorance and negligence of the German electorate. He polled 14,656,000 votes; the Catholic Center candidate 13,-752,000 votes (concentrating the votes of Left, liberals, and middle groups, but losing Protestants to von Hindenburg because the Center candidate, Dr. Marx, was a Catholic); and the Communist Thälmann, 1,931,000. If the Communists had not been led by Moscow into their steady antiparliamentary attitude, their votes could easily have turned the tide, and Thälmann would later never have died in Hitler's concentration camp, or Russia been devastated by Hitler's legions. (Perhaps.)

The years 1925 to 1929 had been good ones for the *Reich*. By 1932, however, the full force of the depression had brought the blackest despair, and with it, had stimulated the advance of Nazi votes. Hitler was drawing to himself all the discontented groups, discontented about anything whatsoever—but especially those discontented about the nationalist humiliations in the Treaty of Versailles and about Germany's military weakness and inferiority, and the desperate unemployed and anti-Communist strata. The streets were already full of Nazi-Communist murderous clashes; parliamentary proceedings had become a farce as the extreme wings interrupted the sessions with disorder and actual pitched battles. Von Brüning had had to rely on the President's confidence to keep him in office, and to govern by the issuance of decrees, under the toleration of enough votes (heavily Social Democratic) to avert a vote of no confidence. Hitler was put up as Presidential candidate. The Social Democratic votes went to von Hindenburg: the results were von Hindenburg, 19,400,000; Hitler, 13,400,000; and Thälmann, the Communist, 3,700,000. Brüning—who had been sustained by von Hindenburg, as chancellor—and his Catholic Center party were fighters for von Hindenburg—now 80 years old and hardly able to attend to business for any stretch of time in the day.

The power of the President was amply supported by these votes. He possessed three powers of outstanding constitutional importance: the power to select the leader of the cabinet; the power to sustain him with his decree-making power under article 48; and the power to dismiss the chancellor. It is necessary to examine the nature and use of the latter two powers.

Article 48 and Emergency Decrees. Article 48 concerned two things: one, the power of the *Reich* to enforce *Reich* law on the states if these did not duly execute them. That is not important in this context. The clauses that are significant read thus:

When security and order in the *Reich* are seriously disturbed or endangered, the *Reich* President can take measures necessary for their restoration; if it is necessary, he may intervene with the use of armed forces. For the purpose of restoring safety and order, he may temporarily suspend, wholly or partly, the fundamental rights in the Constitution in Articles 114, 115, 117, 118, 123, 124, and 153.

The *Reich* President shall without delay inform the *Reichstag* of any measures taken by virtue of the first and second paragraphs of this article. At the request of the *Reichstag* such measures must be rescinded.

Particulars are determined by a *Reich* law.

The details never were so determined, so that there was lacking a second official opportunity for the consideration of the scope and gravity of the article, when, if necessary, it could have been better defined. The first opportunity had been available before the constituent assembly: but there was surprisingly little discussion of so vital an article, perhaps because the times were turbulent and a birch-rod in the cupboard implicitly desired, and because the deputies may have thought that the *Reichstag* was master and some day would make precise all that was still vague. One deputy, an Independent Socialist, foresaw that the safeguards of submission of the decrees to the *Reichstag* would be insufficient as a safeguard, and warned desperately against the coming of a President who might be antidemocratic.

This article looks as though it were concerned only with riotous or military situations, like those permitting martial law in Britain or a state of siege in France, or permitting the United States President to use his powers as commander-in-chief of the forces. But it was sufficiently nebulous in terminology, and new in its establishment in a young democracy, in a land used to authoritarian executives, that it could be and was used, *first,* to restore physical order. But when the economic situation became difficult, and above all, when there was no chance of getting a parliamentary majority for necessary policies, economic and social, it was used, *second,* to make laws on taxation, unemployment pay, rents, assistance to agriculture, harvesting of crops, banking, price regulation, tariff schedules, corporation laws, and many other matters of the highest controversial and political nature. Chancellor von Brüning did not commence this practice, but he powerfully used it. In this he was supported by von Hindenburg, who had come to like him, and the *Reichstag* did not reject the decrees by a vote of no confidence. During the adjournments of the *Reichstag,* the chancellor was virtually without responsibility to anyone except the President for such decrees.

Thus arose the practice of so-called "presidial cabinets"; that is, cabinets having no positive support by a majority in the *Reichstag,* legislating by the use of the Presidential decrees, tolerated by the *Reichstag.* By 1932, the President was fully imbued with the idea that in the uproar and depression and parliamentary disintegration, it was right and proper and constitutional to use the power in this wise.

Add one other factor. The President named the chancellor; the *Reichstag* was supposed to support the cabinet; the cabinet must leave office if the *Reichstag* withdrew its support positively; but the President could dismiss the chancellor. The relevant article (53) reads:

The *Reich* Chancellor and on his proposal the *Reich* ministers are appointed and dismissed by the President.

Hence, when the arch intriguer von Papen, a World War I spy, a member of the Catholic Center, and a Junker, wormed his way into the confidence of the senile von Hindenburg, he induced him suddenly, in May, 1932, to dismiss von Brüning. Then followed a von Papen cabinet, uncongenial to the *Reichstag.* Von Hindenburg gave von Papen the dissolution he had refused to von Brüning. Von Hindenburg and von Papen were prepared to offer Hitler seats in the cabinet. Hitler corresponded with von Hindenburg, who refused to give him the chancellorship for which he held out, with the backing of the president for another "presidential cabinet" backed by article 48, for the Nazis could get no parliamentary majority either.

The elections in November again returned an impossible chamber, with the Nazis in the lead. Von Hindenburg refused Hitler once again, but at the same time von Papen and the President himself were kindly toward the Nazis, repealing for their advantage the decree against private uniforms and the Nazi Storm Troops. Violence rose in a murderous crescendo. The pair at the top ousted the Prussian Socialist cabinet on the excuse that it could not keep order, all under article 48. When the *Reichstag* met in August, 1932, von Papen was overthrown by the largest majority in Weimar's history, 510 against 42. A dissolution followed. The Nazis were still the largest block of voters and holders of *Reichstag* seats, but they lost heavily in the November elections, in part because the Prussian *coup* had been contested before the Supreme Court and the proceedings had clearly shown the corrupt and brutal nature of von Papen and Hitler. Even von Hindenburg was affected by these events, and von Schleicher was given von Papen's place as chancellor. At this von Papen joined Hitler. Out of personal hatred he persuaded von Hindenburg to dismiss von Schleicher. Von Schleicher could not get a *Reichstag* majority, and so the Catholic von Papen argued that Hitler in combination with the German Nationals might make a viable government. Von Schleicher was dismissed: Hitler was appointed chancellor.

HITLER'S EXECUTIVE

OF course, under section 3 of the *Reich-ministers* Law (March 27, 1930), Hitler took the oath of office to "abide by the Constitution and Laws of the German People."

Ostensibly as an answer to the *Reichs-*

tag fire, von Hindenburg issued a decree under article 48, suspending the constitutional guarantees—freedom from arrest; free expression of opinion; freedom of the press, association, and meetings; the secrecy of letters, posts, telegraph, and telephone; judicial control of search warrants; and protection of property.

The Enabling Act of March 24, 1933, followed. Henceforward, all laws, including financial, might be enacted by the government, whether they were of a constitutional nature or not. The *Reichstag* thus became a facade. All laws thereafter were decrees of the cabinet. The *Reichsrat* was abolished. The *Reichwirtschaft* was outlawed. When von Hindenburg died on August 2, 1934, a decree of Hitler's cabinet merged the chancellorship and the Presidency: the dual role was ratified by a plebiscite a couple of weeks after von Hindenburg's death. In July, 1935, the title of *Führer* replaced the dual title. It would be an act of pedantry to enter into the detail of the organization of this dictatorship in which the constitution of the dictator and of his Nazi party became the constitution of Germany and was within an ace of becoming the constitution of the whole western world. The eight volumes of *Nazi Conspiracy and Aggression,* the documents produced in the Nuremberg war-guilt trial, contain the elaborate picture; Volume IV is especially concerned with the organization of the cabinet and the party,[8] while Supplements A and B contain the succinct closing addresses of prosecuting counsel and the defence, each, in his own way, describing the foulest behavior in human annals.

The general outline may be given. The principle of the system was "All responsibility upwards and all authority downwards," the summit being the leader of the state and the leader of the party.

The constitutional power to make laws outside the *Reichstag*—added to the chancellor's powers to make decrees and to govern, combined with the powers of the President as prescribed by the Weimar constitution—concentrated in Hitler's hands all power of every kind: executive, legislative, and judicial, and command of the armed forces (Law to Remove Distress of People and State, March 24, 1933; Law on Sovereign Head of the German *Reich,* August 1, 1934). The separation of powers was rejected and indeed scoffed at. The Minister of Justice, Dr. Frank, declared:[9]

This measure means a turning away from the liberal principle, of the separation of powers in reuniting the legislative with the executive power, and on the other hand a turning away from parliamentarism, since the self-responsibility of the leading personalities has taken the place of anonymous resolutions in the legislature.

The laws, with a few exceptions when the *Reichstag* was permitted to assent to the projects introduced by the *Führer,* were made by simple ordinance and promulgation. The more fundamental ones were drafted by the Minister of the Interior, and submitted to the cabinet. Others were drafted by the minister in charge of the particular department, were then sent to all members of the cabinet, and after a lapse of time for objections were considered to have been passed by all. Cabinet meetings were rare: there were meetings between the *Führer* and the men he wanted to see. A decree of his own set up a private cabinet for high policy, defense, and foreign policy. The laws were signed by the *Führer,* and were usually countersigned by the appropriate minister or ministers. The function of this countersignature was in reality nugatory—it was but a relic. Yet it was theorized about, as everything had to be theorized about that the dictator suffered to

[8] See W. Ebenstein, *The Nazi State* (New York, 1945); F. Neumann, *Behemoth,* 2nd edition (New York, 1944), E. Fraenkel, *The Dual State* (Oxford, 1942); E. R. Huber, *Verfassungsrecht des grossdeutschen Reiches* (Hamburg, 1937); U. S. Government Printing Office, *Nazi Conspiracy and Aggression,* Vols. IV, V, and VI; Pechel, *Deutsche Widerstand* (Zurich, 1947); L. Lochner (ed.), *The Goebbels Diaries* (New York, 1948); U. Von Hassel, *Diaries* (New York, 1947); Hans Rothfels, *The German Opposition to Hitler* (University of Illinois, 1947).

[9] In *Zeitschrift der Akademie für Deutsches Recht* (February, 1937).

exist by accident. Countersignature was supposed to maintain the responsibility of the ministers to Hitler: to vivify them by the idea that they also were *"Führers"* not merely clerks; and to produce a team spirit, where there was no team. For the theory supplied by the obsequious professors was that this was no "chancellor system" as had existed, nor a "prime minister system," but something especially heaven-dispensed.

This system of irresponsible political direction was supported by a number of pillars, chief of which were (1) the unity of party and state; (2) the control of the civil service; (3) the control of the judiciary; and (4) the fighting toughs and secret police.

(1) The Nazi party was given a monopoly of political life. The Law Prohibiting the Formation of New Political Parties, of July 14, 1935, prescribed:

The National Socialist German Workers' party is the only political party in Germany. Whoever undertakes to maintain the organization of another political party, or to form a new party, is punishable by hard labor up to three years or imprisonment from six months to three years, unless the action is punishable by a higher penalty under other provisions.

To get out of a jail was impossible once in it: and the "higher penalty" referred to was the interpretation of sedition and criminal activities established by the Nazis and rendered by the ordinary courts, or, more, the People's Court, which sat in secret and was manned by party members, especially the SS men. Further, the law of December 1, 1933, declared the party to be "the bearer of German political sovereignty, inseparably intertwined with the state." Its status (by this law) of "corporation of public law" gave it certain immunities in its property and activities because actions against it were triable in the administrative courts with a favorable jurisprudence to its purposes. The chancellor was leader of the party, and its supreme lawgiver and disciplinarian. He normally operated through a deputy: the vile Martin Bormann.

The deputy leader of the party was an *ex officio* member of the *Reich* cabinet. He participated in making the laws. He reviewed all nominations for high administrative and political offices. His local subordinates at all levels of government downward territorially had the same power of control, nomination, and rejection. (Cf. p. 210 above, on the position of the states and municipalities.)

Fitted into the party were various pillars and auxiliaries: the *Sturmabteilungen;* the *Schutzstaffeln;* the Students', Women's, and Physicians' associations. They were fighting militias. They had access to the best jobs. They were spies and denouncers of their fellow-citizens and professionals: for spying and denunciation were cardinal party duties. (Law, March 29, 1935, and Law of the Deputy of the *Führer*). The party members benefited from the rules of *lèse majesté*. They were bound to report contemptuous remarks about the party, and especially to resist open attacks upon it. To the SA and the SS certain rights of immediate self-defense were given. Within the party, strong discipline prevailed, all from above, administered in courts within the party. Action on the state by the party was confined by the decrees of the *Führer's* deputy to the channels ordained by him.

(2) The controls over the civil service have already been noted (p. 302 above). The exaction of loyalty to the *Führer* was personal and total. For example, article 3 (1) and (2) of the Civil Service Law of January 27, 1937:

A position in the public service is proof of confidence on the part of the state leadership, which the official must justify by being constantly aware of the added duties which his position imposes upon him. *Führer* and *Reich* demand of him true patriotism, a spirit of self-sacrifice, and complete dedication of his efforts, obedience to his superiors, and comradeship towards his colleagues. He must be a model of loyal fulfilment of duty to all his fellow citizens. He must be faithful unto death to the *Führer* who assures him his special protection.

The official must at all times support without reservation the National Socialist state and in all his behavior must be guided by the fact that the Nazi party, in indissoluble union with the people, is the basis of the German idea of the State. He must report to his superiors occurrences which might endanger the existence of the *Reich* or of the Nazi party, even when he has not learned of them in the course of his official duties.

(3) In the German system of government, the judges were civil servants, but the Weimar constitution required that they should be independent, obeying only their judicial conscience. But the theory of the Nazi state, presented to the courts from time to time and not infrequently by the Minister of Justice to the Nazi organization of lawyers, was that the Nazi movement superseded the Weimar constitution, in so far as laws and decrees canceled or altered its terms, and above all in so far as the will of the movement was expressed in the *Führer's* speeches. Hence, the judges were now subordinate to the *Führer's* will, and the "healthy popular feeling" about law was to prevail over judicial scruples based on the written statutory or case law. Dr. Frank, Minister of Justice, declared: [10]

The Judge is not placed as a sovereign authority in the State above the citizen, but is a member of the living community of the German people. It is not his duty in enforcing law, to impose on the community of the Volk or to resuscitate ideas of universally recognized values [that is, natural law concepts—*author*] but to safeguard the very definite order of the national community, to eliminate dangerous elements, to prosecute all acts which harm the community, and to reconcile all differences between the members of the community. . . . The Judge has not the right of judicial review of decisions made by the Führer and issued in the form of law or decree.

(4) Finally, the SS was a special corps of Hitler's toughs, the militia of the régime, chosen for purity of blood, with weight, height and girth prescribed—the equivalent in the twentieth century of Frederick William's tall grenadiers of the seventeenth, but more murderous and assigned for special duties. They were closely interwoven with the Gestapo, or secret police, headed by Himmler: the torturers, murderers, concentration-camp maintainers, spies, informers, and the rest. Of these the Law of February 12, 1936, said: [11]

The duty of the Secret State Police is to expose and oppose all social forces which are dangerous to the State, to collect and evaluate the results of these discoveries, to inform the government and keep the authorities of all kinds informed. . . The orders and business of the secret state police are not subject to review in the administrative courts.

This barbaric despotism wrought its wickedness in the midst of Europe unmolested from January, 1933, until September, 1939, when, much against their will, Britain and France were forced to preserve themselves against it. Nor did the United States challenge it by force, and hardly by words, until some time in 1941. The Soviet Union had even become allied with it in August, 1939. Those who connive are themselves besmirched.

The arms and the lives sacrificed to liberate the nations of Europe and the U.S.S.R. from the black, murderous tyranny of the nazis and all who connived at their wickedness or supinely condoned it also liberated the German people from themselves and the compulsions and cruelties within them. The grand question is whether, when the occupying powers leave, they can govern themselves in liberty and cease to hanker after the destruction of the liberties of other peoples. It is in doubt.

GENERAL SURVEY OF EXECUTIVES

THE analysis of the executive brings to light certain truths. It is obvious that a nonresponsible government is impossible and dangerous, save for very exceptional moments in the life of the modern state. Responsibility to some body representative of the people is needed as much for the well-being and capacity of the leader as for the enforcement of a sense of responsibility. Loss of office is, in the western world, at least a sufficient sanction of responsibility, while impeachment and

---

[10] *Nazi Conspiracy and Aggression*, Vol. V. Much of this is execrably translated.

[11] *Ibid.*, Vol. V, pp. 346 and 456; and Vol. IV, pp. 193 and 732.

civil and criminal liability are either unnecessary or too grave to be used. Responsibility of this kind admitted, the problem becomes one of finding the best conditions of centrality in leadership. The two chief methods are the parliamentary cabinet and the nonparliamentary President. There is every reason to believe that the parliamentary cabinet is far superior to the Presidential system; indeed, the latter has nothing which can be urged in its favor except the very devices which are desperately invoked to overcome its inherent defects. It is possible to concentrate to such a fine point that all the benefits of collective counsel backed up by the weight of a political following are lost. On the other hand, in the French and German cabinet systems, parliamentary committees dispute executive leadership, and contribute to the obscurity of responsibility, and this, if possible, is to be avoided, as it is in the British system. Modern cabinets are overburdened, and to meet their obligations they use expert commissioners to help them in debate and explanation and expert technicians either in the form of a council or as individual attendants upon the cabinet, and their rules of business are more and more being adapted to the complexity and intricacy of their work. Not all of them are as rationally organized as is necessary. Collective responsibility rather than individual responsibility is an almost inevitable consequence of the inseparable weft of all government business—and the vital importance of each part of a government's policy to the rest—and besides this, indubitable indication of responsibility is only possible where a unit confronts the legislature and the people.

The sources of healthiness or unhealthiness in cabinet government are to be traced to the party system, for this connects the government and the parliament, and the government and the people, and the government and the opposition. Of all the systems we have analyzed, the English by good fortune and the predominance of political ability over other spiritual dispositions, have produced the best. In other countries representative government in general (and the parliamentary executive in particular) has fallen into contempt. In some it ran the serious risk of replacement by a dictatorship. In a few, it has already been replaced by dictatorship, because the fragmentation and number of parties, and their mutual intolerance based on grounds of policy or personal egotism, result in a most disturbing instability of the executive. This experience provides a fresh criterion of the nonparliamentary executive of the United States—for at least, whatever the shortcomings of that system, the executive is fixed for four years, and stability is a tremendous advantage in the modern world of highly sensitive industrial, commercial, and financial human relationships based upon continuity of operation, credit, and meticulous calculation of the future. A moment's consideration of the effect on industry of taxation, tariff, and employment policy will teach that.

Yet the executive, as we have treated it, lacks the final touch: that is, an understanding of the part which the chief of state plays in the process of government. We have already indicated that the members of the cabinet, especially the prime minister, attract loyalty by reason of their high status as well as by their utility. They are credited with being more than they are because they are where they are. Men and women defer to Presidents and Kings, even when these are in fact able to do far less than that with which they are credited.[12]

THE EXECUTIVE IN THE U.S.S.R.

The student will notice in Table 21 that there is a kind of duality in the system of the U.S.S.R., with "executive" functions divided between Presidium and the Council of Ministers, until recently called the Council of People's Commissars.

The mechanism is thus constituted. The Soviet fresh from the elections elects forty-two members from its midst: one of them thereby becoming President of the Soviet

---

[12] Chap. XXVI in Vol. II of the original two-volume edition of the present work (Melhuen and Co., London, 1932).

TABLE 21—COMPARATIVE CHART OF EXECUTIVE ACTION*

Executive Action	British Cabinet	United States President	Fourth Republic France: Cabinet	Weimar Constitution: Cabinet	U.S.S.R.: Presidium	U.S.S.R.: Council of Ministers
Calls Parliament	Yes	(Self-called)	(Self-called)	(Self-called	Yes	
Dissolves Parliament	Yes	No	Yes	Yes	Yes, if dead-locked	
Makes laws	No	No	No	No	Yes	
Introduces laws	Yes	Quasi	Yes	Yes	Yes	
Produces budget	Yes	Quasi	Yes	Yes	Yes	Yes
Exercises veto	(Abeyance)	Yes	No	No	(Not arising)	
Appoints ministers	(King)	Yes	(President)	(President)	Yes—Soviet	
Dismisses ministers	Yes	Yes	No	Yes	Yes	
Appoints arms chiefs	Yes	Quasi	Yes	Yes	Yes	
Declares war	Yes	(Congress)	(Assembly)	(Assembly)	Yes	
Makes treaties	Yes	Quasi	(President)	(Assembly)	Yes	
Commands forces	Yes	Yes	(President)	(President)	Yes	Minor—yes
Ambassadors						
Appoints	Yes	Quasi	(President)	(President)	Yes	
Receives	Yes	Yes	(President)	(President)	Yes	Yes
Makes rules and orders	Yes	Yes	Yes	Yes	Important—yes	Secondary—yes
Directs foreign affairs	Yes	Yes	Yes	(President)	Yes	Minor yes
Maintains public order	Yes	Yes	Yes	(President—art. 48)	No	Yes
Appoints civil service	Yes	Makes higher appointments with Senate	Yes	Yes	Yes	Yes
Appoints judges	Yes		(President in council)	Yes	(Elected by Soviet)	
Is administrative chief	Yes	Quasi	Yes	Yes	Yes	Subordinate planning
Is responsible to legislature	Yes	No	Yes	Yes	(Must answer questions)	
Grants pardons	Yes	Yes	(Assembly)	Yes	Yes	

*This is avowedly a rough sketch for what it is worth: no one may use it without all the textual qualifications in mind.

Union; among the others are ample vice-presidents to represent the various republics. Its authority extends to the issuance of edicts between meetings of the Soviet, so that, as the latter are few and far be-tween, it is the continuing lawmaking body of the land. "New law" is to be made by the Soviet—but what that is nobody has defined, except that comprehensive planning legislation is submitted to the

Soviet for approval, and the budget goes to it also, for debate. The virtual power of lawmaking is thus in the hands of the Presidium. Furthermore, it interprets the laws. It convenes the Soviet twice a year, for as long as it wishes. It is never enough for the real work of legislation. It has the power of removing and appointing officials, including the Council of Ministers between sessions of the Soviet. Thus, save for some formal ratification of the action of the Presidium in the selection and dropping of ministers, the shaping of the cabinet and its entire control therefore lies with the Presidium. The other powers will have been noticed in Table 21. The Council of Ministers is a cabinet, with collective purposes, and with individual responsibility of ministers for their special departments. The departmentalization is highly developed, since the state is in command of most of the activities and thoughts of the people of Russia: at the moment there are the chairman, Stalin; eight vice-chairmen; and forty-five ministers. Both Presidium and ministers

are answerable to the Soviet. As these two bodies, in their Communist party roles, have chosen the members of the Soviet, by means of their control over the party, and as the Soviet meets for so brief a time with so heavy an agenda of applauding speeches before discussion and vote, answerability is a fiction.

Rather more important to notice are the tight organizational bonds which link Presidium, Council, and Politbureau of the Communist party, fully facilitating the dynamism and control of the last over and through the other two.[13] The Politbureau is all-Communist, and quintessence of Communist; and the other two bodies are fully Communist also. But, even more important, some leaders hold office simultaneously in Presidium, Council, and Politbureau—one head that thinks for three and assures Communist party sovereignty.

[13] Cf. Julian Towster, *Political Control in the U.S.S.R.* (New York, 1948), Chap. XI; and Andrei Vyshinsky, *The Law of the Soviet State* (New York, 1948), passim.

26

The United States Presidency

THE UNITED STATES PRESIDENCY

THE power, spiritual and physical, lodged in the people and government of the United States prodigiously outweighs that of any other nation in the world, far beyond that of any other democracy. The domestic use of this power for America's own internal economic well-being also increases or destroys the daily bread of hundreds of millions of foreign men, women, and children beyond her borders. The exercise of her might in the international congregation of seventy independent states, through friendly acts or pressure on the will of some of them, governs their independence and their security, and helps to settle whether their institutions shall be more or less democratic in spirit. Since the United States is transcendentally mighty, her constitution is by so much more a ruling force in the constitutional life and fate of all other peoples no less than of her own.

It can never fail to be a matter of profound anxiety on the part of the rest of the world, or of the 150 million Americans, that the American system of government disintegrates the leadership of Congress, and then largely stakes the fate of itself and the world of nations with which it is merged by physical oneness, upon the character and ability of one solitary man in the White House: that is, upon an accident. It is not a little terrifying to think that though the stakes are so high, ruin as well as bliss is risked on a single throw.

It is not intended here to make an elaborate analysis of the chief executive, as the history and concrete circumstances are readily available.[1] It is, however, urgent to assess the functional strengths and weaknesses of the institution, especially in comparison with foreign executives.[2] The

---

[1] The chapter is founded (1) on the well-known standard biographies, autobiographies, and diaries of the Presidents—e.g., Grover Cleveland, *Presidential Problems* (New York, 1904)—and some of the cabinet officers, e.g., Gideon Welles; (2) on the historians of particular Presidents or cabinets, like J. G. Randall, *Constitutional Problems under Lincoln* (New York, 1926), or Burton J. Hendrick, *Lincoln's War Cabinet* (Boston, 1947), or J. P. Tumulty, *Woodrow Wilson as I Knew Him* (New York, 1921), or A. S. Link, *Wilson on the Way to the White House* (Princeton, 1947), or Arthur Schlesinger, Jr., *The Age of Jackson* (New York, 1945); (3) on the documents on origins like Max Farrand's *Records of the Federal Convention* (New Haven, 1911), fully exploited in Volume II, chapter XXIII, of the two-volume edition of this work; (4) on studies like C. C. Thach, *The Creation of the Presidency* (Johns Hopkins, 1922), and N. J. Small, *Presidential Interpretations on the Presidency* (Baltimore, 1932), H. B. Learned, *The President's Cabinet* (New Haven, 1912), and M. L. Hinsdale, *History of the President's Cabinet* (Ann Arbor, 1911), and J. Hart, *The American Presidency in Action, 1789* (New York, 1948).
[2] Our understanding has been enriched by the studies of the Presidency as an office, such as E. S. Corwin, *The Presidency*, 2nd edition (New York, 1948); W. E. Binkley, *The President and Congress* (New York, 1947); E. P. Herring, *Presidential Leadership* (New York, 1940); and the reminiscences of Frances Perkins, *The Roosevelt I Knew* (New York, 1947); Henry L. Stimson and M. Bundy, *On Active Service in Peace and War* (New York, 1948);

illustrations chosen, are, for impressiveness, contemporary, but the generalizations are rooted in the development of a century and a half.[3]

The American Presidency has six outstanding characteristics:[4]

It is a "made" executive, but it has grown;

It is a "solitary" not a "collective" executive;

It is popularly elected, in practice directly;

It is more than an executive;

It is separated from Congress;

It may be tinkered with, but cannot be reformed.

A "MADE" EXECUTIVE

THE authority of the Presidency has verbal bounds, since the executive was created and defined in writing by the constitutional convention. Most of the authorizations are specific. It was the general

James Farley, *Jim Farley's Story* (New York, 1948); Robert Sherwood, *Roosevelt and Hopkins* (New York, 1948); Harold Ickes, *Twelve Years with Roosevelt* (New York, 1949); Cordell Hull, *Memoirs* (New York, 1948).
[3] Cf. chapter on the Presidency in Vol. II of the original edition of the present work.
[4] For the more immediate problems of fitting the Presidency to his contemporary responsibilities it is necessary to consult: Symposium, "The Executive Office of the President," *Public Administration Review*, Winter, 1941; Harold D. Smith, "The Budget as an Instrument of Executive Management," *ibid*, Summer, 1941; and N. M. Pearson, "A General Administrative Staff to Aid the President," *ibid.*, Spring, 1944; Paul Appleby, "Organizing around the Head of a Large Federal Department, *ibid.*, Summer, 1946; Louis Brownlow, "Reconversion of the Federal Administration Machinery," *ibid.*, Autumn, 1946; "Symposium on Federal Executive Reorganization," by Wayne Coy, J. P. Harris, and Don K. Price, *American Political Science Review*, December, 1946; Charles E. Merriam, "The National Resources Planning Board," *ibid.*, December, 1944; F. Morstein-Marx, "The Bureau of the Budget," *ibid.*, 1945, pp. 653 and 869 ff.; F. Morstein-Marx, *The President and his Staff Services* (Chicago, 1947); Lindsay Rogers, "The American Presidential System," *Political Quarterly*, Oxford, October, 1937, and, most recently, the Reports of the (Hoover) Commission on Organization of the Executive Branch of the Government, February-March, 1949.

—though by no means unqualified—intention of that body to establish an executive of assigned powers, not a general residual executive with "inherent" powers and a "prerogative,"[5] as had emerged over the centuries of constitutional battle in Britain and the Continental states. The states, under colonial rule as when they asserted their independence, were resolved on a subdued executive and a dominant legislature.

The "executive power" is vested in the President. He is commander-in-chief of the armed forces of the United States, and of the militia of the several states, when called into the actual service of the United States. He has the power to require the opinion in writing of the principal officer in each of the executive departments. He has the power of reprieve and pardon. He has the power to make treaties, with the advice and consent of two thirds of the Senate. To him is granted the power to nominate—with the advice and consent of the Senate—ambassadors, other public ministers and consuls, judges of the Supreme Court, and all other officers of the United States whose appointments are not otherwise provided for, which shall be established by law (but Congress may vest the appointment of these latter officers in the President alone, in the courts of law, or in the heads of departments). He is vested with the power to fill vacancies during recess of the Senate by commissions expiring at the end of their next session. Then, too, he is assigned the duty of giving Congress information on the state of the Union and recommending to their consideration such measures as he shall judge necessary and expedient. He may convene extraordinary sessions of the Congress. He has the obligation of receiving ambassadors and other public ministers. "He shall take care that the laws be faithfully executed." He shall commission all the officers of the United States.

This is a "made" executive: that is to say, one which was deliberately designed

[5] Cf. W. R. Anson, *Law and Custom of the Constitution* (Oxford, 1935 edition), Vol. II, Part I, "The Crown," Chapter I.

to take a certain place, a limited place, in a constitution along with other powers also defined. But, quite apart from the intentions of the constitutional convention, the terms of his authority are elastic, for they are in words, general words. Thus, "commander in chief"—on what occasion, when, and for what purposes? Thus, "the executive power"—is the model the European or the British king? Does executive power reach beyond the confines of the list of specific grants? What of the recommendation of measures to Congress?—in person, or by transmitted written message?—advocated with what force, authority, and instrumentalities (for "recommendation" could be rhetorical or perfunctory)? The reception of ambassadors, their appointment, the making of treaties—these can combine in a weighty power. And, finally, the obligation to see that the laws are "faithfully executed"—how vast a discretion to energy or laziness, to zeal or apathy, to courage or timidity, to coordinative power or administrative fecklessness, to width and force of managerial drive and political marshaling of forces for success, or to negligence and ineptitude! Nor is this by any means the end of uncertainty—of closure or opportunity of effective initiative. For one great party grouping, anti-Federalist, Whig, Republican, in 1789 and thereafter, resolutely affirmed and fought for the supremacy of Congress and the subserviency of the Presidency. Thus, Thaddeus Stevens's claim in 1862 [6] was but the intenser echo of doctrines first uttered in 1788:

We [Congress] possess all the powers now claimed under the Constitution [that is, Lincoln's claims!] even the tremendous power of dictatorship.

The Presidency is very largely what the incumbent is willing and able to make it, taking account of the problems and conditions of the time. Jefferson, Jackson, Lincoln, Hayes, Cleveland, McKinley, Theodore Roosevelt, Woodrow Wilson, and Franklin Delano Roosevelt made it

a center of the most active and effective governmental leadership. In theory and practice, or simply in practice, they proceeded on the view that they could do all that a political situation demanded, in the public interest, that was not forbidden by the constitution or that did not conflict with some other institution like the courts or Congress to whom the constitution had assigned definite powers. "The situation demanded"—it demands and offers what the founding fathers never dreamed of.

Theodore Roosevelt's claim is the most assertive and Franklin D. Roosevelt's the most elevated. The former founded his administration on

my insistence upon the theory that the executive power was limited only by specific restrictions and prohibitions appearing in the Constitution or imposed by Congress under its constitutional powers. My view was that every executive officer, and above all every executive officer in high position, was a steward of the people bound actively and affirmatively to do all he could for the people. . . I decline to adopt the view that what was imperatively necessary for the Nation could not be done by the President unless he could find some specific authorization for it.[7]

Franklin Roosevelt, taught by the unprecedented experience of connection with the White House from youth, experienced in the governorship of New York, and inspired by the plight of the "forgotten man," declared within a few days after his election in November, 1932:

The Presidency is not merely an administrative office. That is the least part of it. It is more than an engineering job, efficient or inefficient. It is preeminently a place of moral leadership. All our great Presidents were leaders of thought at times when certain historic ideas in the life of the nation had to be clarified....Isn't that what the office is—a superb opportunity for reapplying, applying in new conditions, the simple rules of human conduct to which we always go back? . . . . Without leadership, alert and sensitive to change, we are all bogged up or lose our way.

In a poll conducted and appraised by

[6] *Congressional Globe*, Vol. XXXVII, Part 2, p. 440.

[7] Theodore Roosevelt, *An Autobiography* (New York, 1913), p. 389.

Professor A. M. Schlesinger,[8] six Presidents were judged as "great": Lincoln, Washington, F. D. Roosevelt, Wilson, Jefferson, and Jackson, in that order. The common quality of their greatness, admitting many imperfections in the minor arts of administration and political tactics, was their soaring moral élan endowed with the native might to sweep masses into their swift flight towards answers to crises that supplied durable unity, freedom, justice and welfare to the whole nation.

A "SOLITARY" EXECUTIVE

THE constitutional convention desired to secure an unmistakable focus of responsibility and avoid confusion; and to encourage vigor and despatch in judgment and decision. The weak colonial governors were in disfavor. Hence no plural or collective executive, like a cabinet or council of ministers, was established, though it must never be forgotten that a multiple executive was proposed only to be dropped for reasons not fully reported in the records of the convention.

All constitutional responsibility is focused on one man and one man alone. The constitution even provides for his impeachment. The consequences are interesting and dangerous.

No collective responsibility in a group of men equal in status, with perhaps some ascendency in a prime minister, was sought. None has developed. Something called the President's cabinet, always including the ten departmental heads and usually others, was evolved. Yet, in reality, no cabinet exists, in the sense of a constitutionally responsible multiheaded council for the exercise of the chief executive's power. The cabinet is a mere collection of Presidential minions, "clerks" as they have been called. The President's will is supreme, whatever they may advise, because his responsibility is sole and plenary. Indeed, it is rare that the cabinet is called together; rarer still that it discusses major issues; and prac-

tically never that it makes a corporate decision. The President makes up his own mind, whatever the votes—when, indeed, votes are taken.

The talk of a cabinet, then, is specious: it is a cabinet at a meeting to hold conversations, perhaps at times to deliberate, but hardly ever to create a collective will that shall govern all including the President. The President floats above it, and aloof. He is not merged in a team; he is detached.

Though business may be distributed, partly by the Presidential wish and his general executive power, and partly by statutes of Congress which vest various administrative powers in the several heads of departments, no real sharing of authority occurs. That this weighs on the Presidential mind can be inferred from many utterances and action taken by all the Presidents. Franklin D. Roosevelt offers a particularly significant illustration among hundreds. At a press conference on December 20, 1940, he said: [9]

There were two or three cardinal principles; and one of them is the fact that you cannot, under the Constitution, set up a second President of the United States. In other words, the Constitution states one man is responsible. Now that man can delegate, surely, but in the delegation he does not delegate away any part of the responsibility from the ultimate responsibility that rests on him.

We have called this a particularly significant example because precisely this statement was seized upon by Roosevelt's political opponents on the Joint Committee of Investigation of the Pearl Harbor Attack, in order to fix on him the prime responsibility for that lamentable event, and they quote his words in evidence against him.[10] Every President is personally liable to be smitten in conscience, self-respect, and political reputation, by the boomerang of his own delegation of authority; responsibility—that is, punishability—is inescapable. He distributes

---

[8] *Paths to the Present* (New York, 1949), p. 96.

[9] Cf. *Public Papers*, 1940, p. 623.
[10] Cf. Report, *Investigation of the Pearl Harbor Attack*, Doc. No. 244, U.S. Senate, Washington, July 5, 1946, pp. 541-42.

business, or Congress does, but, whoever acts, he alone takes political responsibility. He therefore is careful not to devolve authority, which still attaches to him. It is always only a distribution of business. For whatever may be the actual demonstrable errors of his cabinet heads, political blame will come back to him. The President takes the greatest political risk in surrendering some of his authority into the keeping of others. If he is a conscientious man, this is a painful strain on him. He is torn between the impulse not to share power with others, though he has so crushing a burden himself, and the impulse to give it and then feel that unless he watches its use closely, Congress and public opinion will make him smart with blame. Congress may have given power and responsibility to a departmental chief, provided him with funds, instructed and encouraged him at its hearings yet since the President bears responsibility for executive competence, he cannot find relief from departmental concern, for he cannot cut the knot the constitution has tied.

It is an impossible burden. And, in fact, it cannot be borne in a governmental system so widely and deeply active as the American of the twentieth century is obliged to be. Too much responsibility paralyzes the will, for the imagined consequences are too fearful. An excessively concentrated accountability causes incomplete devolution of work to subordinate agencies, and a process of frantic intrusions and exits, by the chief executive, in the alternations between relief and accumulating anxiety. When the President is a weak man—which by the bargaining, contractual, almost casual, nature of the forces producing a nomination, he is liable at any moment to be—the pitiable man is reduced to a frightened whistling for courage, and policy to collapse.

The constitution and its conventional apparatus have provided him with no one he can fully trust; no one to lend him acceptable and dependable counsel; no one to encourage him with the sincerity that comes when a colleague's political fate is bound up with the results of the encour-

agement he gives. How much easier is the British cabinet minister's task, and how much lighter the prime minister's, even though the latter's power is not reduced and limited by any federal division of power, or checks and balances, or the exclusion of some matters from governmental jurisdiction altogether, as under the United States constitution.

It is not to be wondered that Presidents have been obliged to set up "kitchen cabinets" and "brain trusts" and "Assistant Presidents." In their constitutional loneliness they must confide in some one. In more fortunate circumstances they might have had a group of political party colleagues on whom they could rely, on whom they might have been compelled to rely. But the political parties are loose and divided; they have not been tightened up by a constitutional provision which would have been astringent to them by calling for a responsible *collectivity,* the top leadership of the party, as in the British government. Therefore Presidents have given and taken their confidences through personal friendships. By their nature these may be constant, or inconstant; competent or incompetent; lasting for days or months, not so often for years. The President does not look merely for ability, but for the signs of congeniality and trust—the small man in his way, with old-time small-town cronies, the great man, like Franklin D. Roosevelt, among the élite of intellect and character. Instead of decision by cabinet, we have decision by tête-a-tête. Notice how, on the death of one President, and the succession of the Vice-President of that same party, the former's departmental chiefs flee Washington, while the new chief executive brings in his own "gang." Frances Perkins's description of the Roosevelt cabinets [11] fits the stories of previous Presidencies and corroborates that given verbally to the present author by other members of Roosevelt administrations.

But as the years went on, Roosevelt's cabinet administration came to be like most previous

11 *The Roosevelt I Knew,* p. 377.

ones—a direct relationship between a particular cabinet officer and the President in regard to his special field, with little or no participation or even information from other cabinet members. Certainly almost no "cabinet agreements" were reached. Something about our governmental form and the tensions between the legislative and executive functions seems to make fully responsible cabinet action unlikely.

This account is corroborated by circumstantial stories. The effect of the last man in to see the President is most often decisive. The disputant who appears at the White House, as contrasted with the other man who stayed away, wins a superior influence.[12] Cabinet members take deliberate care to safeguard their departmental concerns from cabinet discussion, with mutual understandings for suppression. One of those especially trusted by the President lunches with him weekly. Here is a fortuitous assemblage of regional, local, sectional, vocational, and "party" chieftans, each with his own fief; some, but few, with broad views of policy; some, but not all, loyal to the President's person and comprehending the import of his policy. They have come into politics for a time; they do not expect to stay; they will retire soon because they are sick or disagree with the President or are merely unwilling to shoulder an unprofitable burden or wish to repair their fortunes in their private business. Or they will cling to office, despite disagreement with the President, useful or not to the public welfare, and the President will not eject them as early as the public good demands because he may offend the chieftain's followers or clients, and so lose support in Congress or popular votes if he contemplates a second term.

Yet there is still a drawback: the President cannot wholly trust them. For they may involve him in trouble, and they are behind-the-scenes operators. In that case, what becomes of the Philadelphia Convention's desire to secure an indubi-

table locus of responsibility? The President is still "responsible," but it is a nominal responsibility. His backstairs mentors have not been tracked down and punished, or pilloried before an electorate which may make him or them or his party suffer for misgovernment at the next election. A cabinet on the British and even on the Continental model constitutes the principal part of the executive: there is little in the kitchen (I do not say "nothing"): there are enough advisers to render a "kitchen" unnecessary: the overt cabinet is the group, as a group, to be held to responsibility.

This element of solitary, and not plural, responsibility is the plague spot of the American constitution in the twentieth century. All remedial gadgets must break against its insidious obstinacy. For above all, it destroys from the beginning to the end the possibility of coordinating the work of policy making and administration that has been distributed, and the various work of the agencies and departments and commissions set up by statute. No one man can coordinate so much with so little. Nor can one man, with this unique responsibility, take advantage of the technical and personal devices which from time to time have been proposed and even established to assist him to coordinate the vast proliferation of executive bodies. For we revert always to *his* responsibility, his pride, and his conscience.

Some further observations on this theme are essential, especially in the light of the recommendations made by the Report of the President's (F.D.R.'s) Committee on Administrative Management of 1936, and partly embodied in the Reorganization Act of 1939. As laws have followed laws, the agencies of administration have increased in number. These were not, as they are in normal British and European practice, fitted into as few chief directing departments as possible. By the time the committee reported, over one hundred separate organized departments existed, with the obligation of reporting to the President, and headed by chiefs many of whom drew their authority

---

12 It may be known that the present author was for nearly a year at T.V.A. headquarters in Knoxville, Tennessee, during its most critical year 1937-38.

not from him but from the Congress. Among them were the ten great departments of "the cabinet"; and many commissions, agencies, administrations, and authorities under the President but not within these departments. Some twelve agencies were altogether independent of the President's surveillance. Indeed, the President's Committee on Administrative Management went so far as to say that "a headless fourth branch of the government, responsible to no one," had "planlessly grown." It proposed twelve major executive departments fitted together in one all-comprehensive scheme.

The committee's resounding slogan was, "The President needs help," and it rang true. Accordingly, at the very center of the administrative structure, to assist the President and form a better organized White House staff, the committee proposed six executive assistants to the President in addition to existing secretaries who dealt with the public, with Congress, the press, and the radio. Their only function and status was so defined:

When any matter is presented to the President for action, affecting any part of the administrative work of government, to assist him in obtaining quickly and without delay all pertinent information possessed by any of the Executive Departments, *so as to guide him in making responsible decisions;* and then, when decisions have been made, to assist him in seeing to it that every administrative department is promptly informed. . . . They should be possessed of high competence, great physical vigor, and a passion for anonymity.[13]

One of the principal architects of the Committee as well as of its work (Louis Brownlow, the gifted director of the Public Administration Clearing House of Chicago) explained in its simplest form the purpose of this arrangement:[14]

The President's Committee decided to propose that the Executive Office of the President should perform only those functions, the responsibility for which could not be delegated

by the President. The "non-delegable" functions are those by which an executive may control the policies of his departments, while leaving to the head of each department decisions which are peculiar to its activity and the work incidental thereto. . . . According to our distinction between "delegable" and "non-delegable" functions, a staff function such as purchasing may be centralized or decentralized as expediency may require, but in either case can be well delegated; whereas managerial functions by which an executive can control his organization, especially budgeting, planning and personnel, must be performed in the Executive Office.

They looked to special assistance to the President by the Bureau of the Budget, a planning agency (perhaps the National Resources Planning Board), and a personnel unit.

The Reorganization Act of 1939 implemented much of this central-office reform. Yet still the Presidency did not work; because it *could* not work, even with this assistance. The very minor effectiveness of the reforms could have been and was prophesied. Not that the committee was at fault: without bricks and straw no one can make an administrative heaven. It was hamstrung by the logical defects of the whole system of responsibility within which the President worked. In 1942, I made this judgment on the reforms:[15]

The White House staff was increased as recommended, though time must show whether the physical and psychological attributes proposed for the assistants have been recruited. Experience hitherto, perhaps distorted by World War II, has shown the utility of the staff, but of a kind rather different from that which was planned and expected. A strong president, impatient of administrative apparatus in time of war, and even in time of peace, will hardly wait for his orders to sift down to the departments, or for information to be sifted up to him. He is likely to pass beyond his administrative assistants who are go-betweens, and make direct contact with his cabinet officers (the heads of the great departments) and the mightiest agencies. To him, his assistants would seem to clutter up his path; and to the impatient heads of departments they must appear as obstacles to be circumvented. This is

---

13 Report, p. 5.
14 Louis Brownlow, "A General View," *Public Administration Review,* Vol. I, No. 2, pp. 104-5.

15 *Future of Government* (then in mss.), p. 120.

in the order of what has happened; and the president in wartime has dealt with most agencies directly and through political confidential men and old friends.

The committee had its mind consciously focused for the time being on administration. But the President is not merely an administrative manager. He is, in addition—and blended to a point where even theoretical severance is impossible—a legislative leader, and something of the leader of a nation-wide political party. And the severance of administration and policy is only rarely possible. This the committee even affirmed, but it acted as though its affirmation conveyed no command to it.

These predictions have been borne out. They have been attested by many observers. One of the former White House staff has, in a brilliant article, admitted the insufficiency of mere administrative arrangements, and (in my opinion) without intending to do so, has demonstrated the collapse of the single, solitary chief executive for our time. Here is the crux of his constructive criticism: [16]

There remains the need for special facilities designed to capture in each particular matter before the President the best thinking available. Indeed, this fusion of thought by which all the resources at his command are brought to bear upon his business is a foremost function of the Executive Office ... another unit is required in the Executive Office vested with responsibility for so coordinating the various lines of staff work that every action paper reaching the President becomes a dependable end-product of joint analysis from different angles. . . Matters placed on the President's desk should adequately reflect not only a government-wide point of view, but also the contribution of different kinds of staff analysis, especially managerial thinking and policy thinking.

All of this has to pile up on the desk of one man! The new device suggested has the purpose of "continuing analysis of the flow of policy recommendations presented for the President's decision." But one man cannot do it! That one man

[16] Wayne Coy, *American Political Science Review*, December, 1946, p. 1124.

must always escape to other advice, either outside the apparatus designed or through its network, or himself escape from giving any answer at all. At least some of the answers must be perfunctory and therefore both incompetent as well as irresponsible, while others will not be made by the President at all. When a President is swamped with responsibility he is, paradoxically, tempted to "off-the-cuff" decisions, for how can he genuinely let his duty invade him? The amount of business is beyond one man's capacity or conscience. One solitary man must, surely, look for short cuts. The President needs help, as the Committee on Administrative Management declared; but he needs the help of a dozen or fifteen men, good and true, who bear a direct responsibility *with* him (not *to* him) to the public and the party and the Congress.

Ten years after the reforms mentioned had been put into partial effect, the Hoover Commission, in its Report on General Management of the Executive Branch (February, 1949), returned to the charge as though the committee of 1937 had never had the slightest effect. Indeed, the charges of inefficiency are more serious: "Authority is diffused, lines of authority are confused, staff services are insufficient. Consequently, responsibility and accountability are impaired." (p. 1). And, again, "The line of command and supervision from the President down through his department heads to every employee, and the line of responsibility from each employee of the executive branch up to the President, has been weakened, or actually broken, in many places and in many ways" (p. 4 ff).

The main reforms suggested are three: better integration and dovetailing of the departmental structure, leading to a smaller number of departments; increased Presidential staff services; and more offices of a supervising kind over the functions of government to be lodged in the Executive Office of the President— the latter would be (in addition to the White House Office), the Bureau of the Budget, the Council of Economic Advisers (to be one man, only), the National

Security Council, the National Security Resources Board, and an Office of Personnel.

What is of supreme interest to the present discussion is the newly suggested Staff Secretary. It is essential to give the proposal in the Commission's own words (pp. 22-23):

At present there is no one place in the President's Office to which the President can look for a current summary of the principal issues with which he may have to deal in the near future; nor is a current summary of the staff work available on problems that have been assigned to his advisers, his staff agencies, or the heads of departments and agencies.

To meet this deficiency, the Commission proposes the addition of the staff secretary. He would not himself be an adviser to the President on any issue of policy, nor would he review (in a supervisory capacity) the substance of any recommendation made to the President by any part of his staff.

The Commission believes that this recommendation will facilitate teamwork among the President's staff, the agencies of the President's Office; and any Cabinet or interdepartmental committees which are studying problems for the President.

If possible the staff secretary, like the executive clerk, should be a career public servant.

The staff secretary should keep the President currently informed of work which has been undertaken by various parts of the President's Office, by the Cabinet committees, or by interdepartmental committees or special advisory committees. He should inform the President of any difficulties which have arisen because of the overlapping of assignments or conflicts of policy. He should make the inventory of interdepartmental committees referred to in [an earlier recommendation] . . .

We need not dwell long on the uselessness of this proposal as a measure of any importance in helping the Presidents to make competent and responsible decisions, whether administrative, or on a higher plane of policy. It wants only the slightest amount of imagination to be spent on the words (in the quoted passage) "current summary", and then the disclaimer that the summarizer would not "himself be an adviser . . . on any issue of policy." Even if he were not, who that was being summarized would believe it, and not take steps to avert an unfavorable summary? Moreover, how could a single staff secretary even with assistants be big enough to do the job? How could he possibly *not* inject his values into the account given to the President? How could the President not suspect him of such personal interpretations especially if there were complaint made by a department chief?

How could he tell the story of "overlapping" and "conflicts of policy" without really doing the Chief Executive's own work?

The President cannot be helped through a single funnel upwards.

The Presidency needs to be put into commission. It needs distribution among fifteen equals, each of whom is fully the master and the servant of his own portion of responsibility and of all common policy which comes to them as a collective unity. You can coordinate if you have divided; you can divide if you can trust; you can trust if you alone are not saddled with all responsible decision. To apply a famous dictum of de Tocqueville's, used by him to describe the centralization of the *ancien régime* in France: when you centralize in a solitary President, you risk apoplexy at the center and anæmia at the extremities, or a red face and palsied hands. Nor is that all: if no full authority can be granted a departmental chief, how is one to induce men of stature to seek office and stay there?

All these proposed administrative gadgets may well help a little on lesser matters, and even that is to be much applauded. But every gadget calls for another gadget to stop up the still-existing leak, *ad infinitum*. Still, the reservoir of responsibility is so high and heavy that it will flood the channels made for it: what is needed is one collective reservoir and its sharing among a dozen or more interconnected basins, with free circulation among them all. The proposed reforms still leave the President high and dry, for they still leave him responsible for too much.

Nor is this all. The heads of departments are granted authority and are saddled with responsibility for their department by laws made in Congress. It has been found impossible to stop them from appealing to Congress for the funds and the legislation to implement their departmental policy, whether or not that conflicts with the President's.[17] Close observers admit in desperation that independent staff work for the President (for example, especially through the Bureau of the Budget) may do much to enforce regulations and controls and prepare long-range plans, but *cannot* build up a unified program of policy and legislation.

---

[17] Hardly a week passes without some such episode as the following. In April, 1948, Secretary of Defense Forrestal proposed a program which among other things provided for fifty-five Air Force groups. This, it must be remembered, involves proportionate magnitudes in the other parts of the armed forces; and all together have financial consequences which must be harmonized with the total budget, and therefore with taxation policy, and to some extent, therefore, with general economic policy. The original proposal was presumably made with the agreement of the President, and based on a theory of American commitments in foreign policy. At the hearings before the House Armed Forces Committee, however, Air Secretary W. Stuart Symington pleaded for seventy groups. Congress supported him against the President (presumably) and the Secretary for Defense. At his press conference of April 15, 1948, the President made some non-committal remarks when asked if he would discipline the Air Secretary. The foregoing confusion occurred in spite of the establishment by statute (July 25, 1947) of a Unified National Military Establishment, and of the National Security Council—composed of the President, the Secretary of Defense, the three armed services' secretaries, and the chairman of the National Security Resources Board—to advise the President on national defense. It nicely illustrates the weakness of the Presidency, and the administrative intervention of Congress.

Such cases are repeated as fast as it is possible to print a book. On April 28, 1949, the Secretary of the Navy resigned because the newly appointed Secretary for Defense had forbidden the construction of an aircraft carrier, which had been approved twice by the President, by the Bureau of the Budget, had been included in the budget message of the President on January 3, 1949, and passed by the House on April 18, 1949. The exchange of letters suggests but does not disclose the President's part in all this. See *New York Times*, April 27, 1949, for texts.

It is now newly suggested that a unit in the Executive Office of the President shall convene the appropriate department heads to formulate a common approach. Disagreement would lead to an appeal to the President, with the department heads in session with him. This proposal is an attempt to reproduce a cabinet. But the department heads are men who own no exclusive allegiance to the President: they owe some of it at least to Congress. They are men of the President's party, but the party is not a loyal phalanx. To say they are men of his "party" implies a common policy and loyalty that are far from existing.

Indeed, as one contemplates the collection of incongruous personalities in American cabinets from the beginning, but more especially since the end of the nineteenth century, it is ridiculous to mention the word "party." They are usually appointed because they have or are supposed to have some special interest or expertness in the field of that department —Henry Wallace in Agriculture, and then in Commerce; Jesse Jones in the Reconstruction Finance Corporation; Clinton Anderson in Agriculture; Henry Morgenthau, Jr., in the Treasury (because Mr. Roosevelt had a personal faith in him); Chester Bowles in price administration; Frances Perkins in labor welfare; or Wilson Wyatt as housing administrator, and so on. They are opinionated men; their natural pride is not moderated by party loyalty and solidarity with their chief executive. Their loyalties are divided between the President and their own department; they may sway between the President and Congress; they are torn between their own personal ideas and those of the President. In Mr. Roosevelt's administration of 1933 he had appointed a Director of the Bureau of the Budget, Lew Douglas, who had avowed the policy of a balanced budget and had been attracted by Roosevelt's declarations in favor of this in the campaign of 1932, and at the same time men like Tugwell, Ickes, and such-like, who were enthusiasts for public works which would require deficit financing. In 1935 the Frances Perkins social security proposals were refuted in Congressional committee by her own colleague, Secretary of the Treasury Morgenthau, who objected, successfully, to the proposed universal coverage. These examples are representative of the many which constitute the history of Presidential administrations.

In November, 1945, President Truman, after a ragged process of consultation with some of his advisers, and after these themselves had never met as one body, set forth his wage-price policy, crucial to all postwar reconstruction—foreign and domestic. Within a few days, a different version was published by his Secretary of Commerce, Henry Wallace. Again, Mr. Truman refused the advice of his Secretary of the Interior, Harold Ickes, on the appointment of an administrator of navy oil lands, and the account given of their relations by the latter shows clearly the nonexistence of cabinet discussion and the flight of Presidents to the men they find personally congenial. When the Senate refused to have anything to do with Mr. Pauley, the President's nominee and one of California's Democratic machine leaders, this same man was later appointed by the President to another office—and was very soon obliged to resign office on allegations that he had speculated in grain with inside information. Mr. Ickes' statement on his own resignation (*New York Times,* February 13 and 14, 1946), gives a grim picture of the Presidency.

Crasser examples abound in the foreign policy of the nation. Especially in relation to Russia in September, 1946, the President and Mr. Wallace were able to make matters difficult for Mr. Byrnes, the Secretary of State, while all the staff work in the world did not prevent Mr. Truman from making a *gaffe* on a truly cosmic scale. The story of American policy on Palestine since 1946 is equally calamitous.[18] At times no one knew whether there was a policy at all, or if so, whose it was—the President's, the State Department's, of which rival parties in the State

Department, or of the Senate Foreign Relations Committee. In the end, in November, 1947, the United States stood for partition of Palestine at the United Nations, but did not provide for the armed force necessary to support its view of international justice. After four muddled months in March, 1948, it withdrew its own recommendation—for so incoherent had the process of policy making been that the administration had never counted and accepted the cost. It thereby condemned Palestine to bloodshed. A similar executive-legislative tangle became apparent when the executive, having played a trump card in March, 1948, against the Italian Communists by proposing the return of Trieste to Italy, was set back by Congress' proposal to include Franco Spain in the European Recovery Program!

Another tragic and sickening (Senator Vandenberg called it "cynical") example occurred when Representative Taber, chairman of the House of Representatives Appropriation Committee, on June 8, 1948, led his committee—and with it the House itself—to cut more than one and a half billion dollars from the European Recovery funds, though the policy requiring the amount had been duly embodied in a statute passed by both Houses and signed, with special ceremony, by the President, over a month before. The statute in question, the European Recovery Act, had its origin in a speech made by Secretary of State Marshall in June of 1947. It was followed by negotiations among sixteen European nations for a joint scheme of economic reconstruction, requiring effort and bringing its rewards only after cooperation over a period to the end of 1951. The scheme was fought with the greatest malevolence by the Soviet Union and its satellites. It was a part of a world-wide economic recovery policy, but also a policy of containment of the expanding Russian power. Its promise stabilized France to set herself firmly and successfully against Communist-party aggression and subversion; its imminence fortified the Italian non-Communist government to resist, successfully, the bitter attacks of the Communists and

18 Cf. Bartley Crum, *Behind the Silken Curtain* (New York, 1947).

affiliated Left Socialists. Congress did not make up its mind until after the Secretary of the Interior and the Secretary of Commerce had produced voluminous and cogent reports to show the effects of America's assistance on America's own welfare, and to demonstrate its capacity to produce and deliver what it had promised. The statute was not passed until after the most careful and lengthy hearings had been undertaken in Senate and House, with testimony submitted to the most searching cross-examination from the State Department, the Department of Commerce, the Department of the Interior, other departments, and after a nation-wide debate of unrelenting intensity.

Finally, after many anxieties and despair that short-sightedness would ruin the hopes of Europe and the world, the program was voted, even then with less of an appropriation than was thought really adequate to the general policy. But the statute *was* voted. On its basis, an American administrator was nominated by the President and consented to by the Senate; his organization, the Economic Cooperation Administration, began to formulate the firm but intricate lines of its policy of supervision and administration of the plan, and the staff was being built up. The European peoples expressed their gratitude, and for their part set up a continuing organization of the fifteen nations, with a secretariat; and their own budgetary, trade, and currency policy became intermeshed with the promised and voted advances.

Mr. Taber and his friends decided, then, that they would not supply the money for a policy which had been voted for overwhelmingly by their own party, under no duress, and commended, after inquiries on personal visits abroad, by their own Congressional colleagues and leaders. Senator Vandenberg pleaded (June 10, 1948) that the House "not make indirect use of the appropriating function to veto these declared policies of Congress, and thus to brand these policies before the world as capricious, unreliable and impotent. We cannot build leadership for peace

upon any such shifting sands." He quarreled, he said, "with the final, overall, meat-axe technique . . . equivalent to a horizontal 20 per cent cut, which in my opinion guts the enterprise. In one fell swoop this takes away something like a billion dollars without a scintilla of regard for all of the carefully screened figures upon which all ECA estimates were made . . ." He observed that the action of the House "keeps the word of promise to the ear but breaks it to the hope."

The incident is full of instruction to the student of American government. The executive's foreign policy meant nothing to Mr. Taber. The Senate's foreign policy of his own party meant nothing to him. The statute containing a policy predicted on a quantity of funds meant nothing. His authority was divorced from the authority to make the policy and offer promised abroad. His authority almost alone could shake the credit of the United States and make infirm the tranquillity of several democracies. He seemed to owe no duty to the Republican leadership. Seniority had won him his place, and egotism moved him to use its power. Senate and House were at odds; their policy committees so laboriously set up by the Legislative Reorganization Act of 1946 (which at the same time raised the salaries and provided expert staffs for Congressmen) were not of timely avail to produce a harmony of policy and expenditure. And all the gadgets manufactured to secure a unity of action of ways and means and appropriations committees, and of executive policy and Congressional will, did not prevent this erratic, capricious behavior, and a profound shock to the whole world (with the exception of the Soviet Union, whose friends began at once to say, "I told you so!"). Was Mr. Taber moved by vanity? Was he affected with a desire to draw attention to himself in an election year? Was he a sincere isolationist? Was he confused? Was he merely spiteful? Is he misanthropic?

The memoirs of Sumner Welles, Raymond Moley, and Cordell Hull combined throw an authentic and tragic light on incoherence and mismanagement of foreign policy from 1933 to Pearl Harbor. The Pearl Harbor Report reveals a want of alert coherence between White House, the Secretaries of State, War, and Navy, and the Chiefs of Staff, with some proper blame on the first, or, more reasonably, on the system.[19] Other studies throw light on the lack of solidarity at the center—fumbling in the formation of policy, and stumbling and staggering in its fulfillment.[20]

Even with so potent and clever a President as Franklin Delano Roosevelt as compared with the busy cipher, Harry S. Truman, the President needs twelve or fifteen men of his own stature, of equal responsibility with him, equal in accepting party leadership and loyalty. And he and they need the ever-operative assistance of some sixty career men, heading the departments permanently, under the political secretaries—the cream of the crop of an "administrative group" of perhaps 10,000 or 12,000 at all ages on the scale from cadets to mature men and women, to be their advisers, their staff, their arms of administration. All need a Congress organized for, and alert regarding, its function of making collective and unified the policy of the scattered elements of the administration, by everyday, regular, organized, public criticism. Pearl

Harbors, domestic as well as foreign, may be avoided where a collective fifteen are responsible, and where the Congressional five hundred badger them with relentless questions.

On this latter point, an extract from Representative Frank B. Keefe's report on Pearl Harbor is apposite. He says: [21]

Those who find American public opinion responsible for Pearl Harbor accept an entirely false theory. Enlightened public opinion is based on accurate information. The American people, if kept well informed of their real diplomatic position, do not need an incident to unite them. If foreign policy and diplomatic representations are treated as the exclusive, secret information of the President and his advisers, public opinion will not be enlightened. The very nature of the consequent public alarm places the armed forces of the Nation in effective readiness and may even deter an enemy from executing its planned attack.

Without fully accepting the Representative's conclusions—especially regarding the kind of facts that the President can at any stage divulge to the public—or without condoning his motives, it may be ventured that public opinion would have been riper if Congress had had the right to ask questions of the executive. Some one of the five hundred would have been the permanent gadfly of the executive, a gadfly he could never forget, and that would have given alertness and tone to the Secretaries and have compelled a unified not a diversified judgment on their part.

According to Mr. Stimson's *Diary*, President Roosevelt was much exercised, and even baffled, by the problem of awakening the public and yet not alarming it in the two weeks before Pearl Harbor.[22] He considered but postponed a message to Congress. But the problem would have been solved where the executive was under an obligation to appear before Congress regularly.

The lack of a central *thinking*, focusing body of advisers at the top is acknowl-

---

[19] I cannot subscribe to the narrow-minded fault-finding of the minority report by Homer Ferguson and Owen Brewster, in *Report, Investigation of the Pearl Harbor Attack, op. cit.,* pp. 495-573; but they are not without reason in declaring (p. 567):
"The most powerful men next to the President in authority—men bound to obey his orders and serve without stint, were not far from the President's side; and any one of them, if so instructed, could have found and alerted the others. Secretary Hull, Secretary Stimson, Secretary Knox, General Marshall, and Admiral Stark were nearby. They could be reached quickly by means of communication at the President's command." But—the President and the Secretaries, though fully informed and in frequent contact, were not continuously in collective contact, and their apprehensions were sufficiently diverse in point and intensity to fail to have an inescapable defensive impact on the military and naval arms."
[20] A. W. Macmahon, J. D. Millett, and G. Ogden, *Federal Work Relief Administration* (Chicago, 1941).

[21] *Report*, Vol. V, p. 266.
[22] Cf. the hearing on the Pearl Harbor Attack, Part II, p. 5427.

edged by observer after observer of the Washington apparatus of government, however reluctant in the beginning they may be to admit any deficiencies in the American constitution.

The evidence of a former assistant Director of the Bureau of the Budget,[23] particularly gifted, confirms the truth demonstrated in every cabinet: how much more competitive than cooperative are the cabinet members among themselves and even in relation to the President. He emphasizes that the departmental heads cannot help the President nor administer their departments adequately through the bureau chiefs. Yet he repudiates the idea of "a rigid, special corps." And he wishes the staff leader at the head of department (apparently picked out of the civil service and put on a special register managed by the Executive Office of the President) to exercise the highest managerial supervision of whole department. Yet he expects this man to be responsible only for "staff cross-reference and synthesis," without a "monopoly on the function of staff representation to the secretary." "Without explicit *authority* to do so, it [the staff-leader arrangement] does it within the limits fixed by an absence of authority." This same observer-participant and political scientist has himself declared that in Washington, *political* sense is lacking, and has endorsed a foreign observer's suggestion that what is lacking is "to *think* . . . in terms encompassing all of the elements of the scene." This is indeed Washington's cardinal deficiency. But it is a deficiency that *cannot* be repaired by the "chairman" idea, nor by multiple approaches to the departmental head. Not, at any rate, as the first principle of organization. That first principle must be a pyramidal line of authority, from mere clerical secretaries to *one* top, all-surveying, permanent administrator. Authority must first be lodged with him: without that, integration cannot be expected. Then, authority being focussed, indubitable, and plenary, he may exercise it by cross-reference among his

[23] Cf. Paul Appleby, "Organizing Around the Head of a Large Federal Department," *Public Administration Review*, Summer, 1946.

aides, and by chairmanship, and by other tricks of the trade, as do his British counterparts, the permanent undersecretaries. But Appleby has certainly carried the analysis further and more courageously than previous writers—out of the bitterness of experience. Improvement cannot be achieved without a career administrative group, serving for life, if good enough so to serve. This subject is closely linked with the discussion of the top permanent personnel (below, Chap. 33).

THE CONSEQUENCES OF POPULAR ELECTION

THE President is popularly elected, and owing to the development of the parties and the nominating conventions, he is virtually directly elected. Consequences follow.

In an age where ideologies consciously challenge the very value of law and government, it is a serious weakness that the system of election may lead to a minority President. Wilson won the 1912 election by a minority of votes, and there are other, earlier instances. Such an event might occur at a time of grave distress and excitement. The parliamentary system of producing an executive body will be seen, on reflection, to avoid the grim crudity of unproportional representation to this extreme; or, as in practically all Presidential elections, even the entire repulse from executive influence of a very large minority.

The weight of a whole country behind the President gives him tremendous authority, and makes of him a focus of what millions expect. His popular authority is certainly needed in his relationship with a heterogeneous Congress: his veto and his message-making power would be worth nothing without it. But that popular support can be altogether dissipated by a mind. and character not attuned to the opportunities it gives and the qualities it demands. "I felt as though the heavens had fallen down on me!" was Mr. Truman's exclamation on learning that the responsibilities of the Presidency were his. And he certainly acted like a crushed man.

The Presidential campaign comes nearest to a unified nationwide consultation on policy. From this standpoint, Congressional and Senatorial elections are marred by excessive localism. The approach to Congress is obstructed by local and sectional barriers; a sum must be added up of diverse and rival elements before a policy can be pieced together. The President is a unit: each time he speaks, at any rate, the policy is one, though, of course, it need not remain so for more than a few days. With popular support, he is expected to unify, and, unifying, is expected to lead. That leadership he is pressed to undertake because a party has selected and made him the one man that best represents them, however badly that may be. He takes charge of the fulfillment of the laws that his party friends in Congress make—that is, one half the business of government. From that half emerges a knowledge of possibilities and necessities which hitherto Congress has not been equipped itself to provide so well as he. Hence, he is in a splendid position for legislative leadership. But more than this: with the development of mass communications (the press always, but in our time especially the radio), the reciprocal influence of Presidency and people has become immense. Perhaps no executive in the world—past times included, and dictatorships not excluded—possessed a status and vehicles of communication so powerful to educate a people in facts and responsibilities, and into mutual support of each other, as the President of the United States. If he fails, it is a personal failure, not one of position or opportunity. By awakening the people, even by his power to do so, he has a steady potential influence over Congress.

Yet is not this customary contrast of the beneficial unity of the executive with the injurious disunity of Congress at least a little exaggerated? The assertion of unity has often been made. For example, Polk's message to Congress at the end of his fruitful and forceful tenure:[24]

The people by the Constitution have commanded the President as much as they have commanded the legislative branch of the Government to execute their will. . . . If it be said that the Representatives in the popular branch of Congress are chosen directly by the people, it is answered, the people elect the President. . . The President represents in the Executive department the whole people of the United States as each representative of the legislative department represents portions of them.

But is there a real, practical, effective unity of will and policy?[25]

Popular vote for the President has involved the constitution in the weakness of the succession to the President. It is difficult to think of a more unfortunate arrangement than the simultaneous election of a Vice-President. If he is strong, the office is politically dubious, because he is less representative: if he is weak, he has not only not been wanted, but he has deserved not to be wanted. It seems to me that the best solution would be the abolition of the Vice-Presidency, and the return of the succession back to the people. Within a short time after the demise (or the resignation) of a President, say, two

---

24 J. D. Richardson, *Messages and Papers of the Presidents* (Washington, 1897), Vol. IV, p. 664-65.

25 Cf. the more modern, extended, and reasoned statement of a noted student: "That it [the steady aggrandizement of the influence of the executive in determining legislative action] has much to commend it cannot be questioned. Among the things in its favor, first mention should be made of the fact that the chief executive has a representative character in relation to the electorate that is not possessed by the aggregate of members constituting the legislative branch. These members are elected to office by relatively small subdivisions of the country. . . . Rightly or wrongly, it is impossible for them not to give consideration to the manner in which proposed legislative action will affect self-interests and those of their direct constituencies. . . . No such difficulty confronts the chief executive. He is elected by and represents the entire electorate. He, moreover, is, with rare exception, the acknowledged leader of the dominant political party and has been entrusted by it with the responsibility of using its best efforts to secure the translation into an action of the pledges made by his party. Strategically, he thus occupies a strong position. He represents the entire country in a way that the individual members of the legislature do not, and cannot. . . ." W. F. Willoughby, *Principles of Legislative Organization and Administration* (Washington, 1934).

or three months, there ought to be an election for President, to hold office for the full term. In the interim, several "caretaker" devices are possible: the speaker of the lower house; or the ranking member there of the President's party; or the Secretary of State. For a people to choose almost by accident, certainly by an involved compromise, and practically in ignorance, a Vice-President who may well become President, has been clearly shown to be an extremely costly business for the nation, and (it cannot be ignored) for other nations also. It has happened seven times. The story of Mr. Truman's nomination, and the unworthiness of the motives producing it, are awful warnings, deserving notice.[26]

Like the British prime minister, a President gives hostages as he moves along toward the supreme position. But the prime minister gives his hostages to his party colleagues: the concessions he makes to them in policy and in promises of place, are confined by the fact that party allegiance is strong. He cannot be capricious. There is method in the madness. The American President has not usually risen alongside the party chiefs: he has often risen in open hostility to them. The party is assisted by all sorts of "outsiders" among the henchmen of the local bosses, and powerful men not thoroughly saturated with party loyalty. Hence the extraordinary caravan of miscellaneous entrants into the administration at home and abroad. They may never have met before in their lives. At most they may have the merest passing acquaintance. They may hate each other as the result of incitement in casual press rumors. They drift to-

gether from the most incongruous careers with the most inharmonious outlooks. Thus, Daugherty appointed by Harding; Ray Lyman Wilbur by Hoover; Mr. Woodin by Franklin D. Roosevelt; Messrs. McAdoo and Mellon by Wilson; (Mr. Hoover himself as Secretary of Commerce); Mr. Pauley and Mr. Snyder and Mr. George Allen by President Truman; several in the Franklin D. Roosevelt "Brain Trust" soon to be dispersed and discarded; Jesse Jones as head of the RFC. by Franklin D. Roosevelt; Colonel House and Robert Lansing by Woodrow Wilson; the egregious George Harvey and later Joseph P. Kennedy in the London Embassy; the too-clever "Boss" Flynn in Canberra—almost. Hence, also, the incoherence of Presidential policy, and the frequent public brawls between two or more of the President's departmental chiefs, and sometimes between himself and one or more of the participants. Thus Milo Perkins and Henry Wallace; Henry Wallace and Jesse Jones; Leon Henderson and William Knutson; Donald Nelson and William Knutson; Sidney Hillman and William Knutson; President Roosevelt and General Johnson, and also Raymond Moley; Cordell Hull and Sumner Welles; Harold Ickes and (the proposed) Edwin Pauley and the President, in which Mr. Ickes ventured to doubt the word of President Truman in public, and even to suggest that a President may be at least terminologically inaccurate.

No limit seems to be irrefragably placed on the number of terms the Presidency may be held by one man. Until Franklin D. Roosevelt's time, it seemed to be taken for granted that two terms was a not improper rule. None had even tried for a third. Whatever the motivation of Roosevelt in flying in the face of tradition, a strong case could be made for his action on the ground that the European war required that his eight years' experience be continued. He himself urged this. It is interesting to observe that a forceful argument against this was the burden of the office on the health not only of Roosevelt but of any man at the age when he is likely to become President. A fourth term fol-

26 Cf. E. J. Flynn, *You're the Boss* (New York, 1947), p. 180 ff. For a review of the problem of the Presidential succession, and legislative proposals regarding it, see R. S. Rankin, "Presidential Succession in the United States," *Journal of Politics*, February, 1946, and E. S. Brown and R. C. Silva, "Presidential Succession and Inability," *Journal of Politics*, February, 1949; and for the election figures and situations, A. M. C. Ewing, *Presidential Elections: Lincoln to F. D. Roosevelt* (Oklahoma, 1940), and C. A. Berdahl, "Presidential Selection and Democratic Government," *Journal of Politics*, February, 1949.

lowed, victorious against the Republican argument that a Democratic President had better not be elected, because if a Republican Congress were, that President would be stultified! After this experience, there is more psychological freedom for at any rate three terms. The constitution itself leaves the door wide open to the needs of the nation, intentionally, according to the Records of the Convention.

The Republican Congress voted [27] a proposed constitutional amendment in 1947 to the effect that

No person shall be elected to the office of the President more than twice, and no person who has held the office of President, or acted as President for more than two years of a term to which some other person was elected President shall be elected to the office of President more than once. . . .

All the more reason for redoubled efforts to improve the quality of the political parties, and seriously to reconsider the central stipulations and conventions of Presidential government.

MORE THAN AN EXECUTIVE

THE constitution intended that the executive should be more than a mere executive: it very considerably modified the pure idea of the separation of powers. He has become a very active legislative leader [28] as well as an executive.

On the executive side, attention need be drawn only briefly to his remarkable powers of appointment and dismissal of officials, high and low, and his power to conduct foreign affairs.

Appointment and Dismissal of Officials. To safeguard its interest in the execution

of some administrative functions, Congress has attached restrictive rules to some dismissals: thus for members of the tariff commission, where Congress has deemed the agency to be quasi-legislative. The *Humphrey* case (1935) decided that. But where the office is administrative (and that is a matter of judgment by the Supreme Court, if an issue is taken to it), then the President, particularly because he is responsible for the faithful execution of the laws, cannot be restricted in his power to discipline by removal. Even the Tenure of Office Act of 1867, deliberately passed to thwart President Johnson, and designed to secure the administrative supremacy of the Senate, fell before the necessities of unified and directed administration. The Myers case (1926) reaffirmed the Presidential power. This does not invalidate rules designed to secure fairness to the official, or the efficiency of the service. A more interesting test came in 1938, after Roosevelt had removed Morgan, chairman of the TVA and the latter sued for salary. The Courts took the view that the TVA was an "administrative" agency subject to the necessary disciplinary power of the chief executive. This, although the statute and the debates leading to its passage had fostered the principle that the TVA was to have some independence and be clothed with the flexibility of private enterprise.[29] Yet it was a proper decision. It is a tremendous responsibility therefore that inheres in the President.

Conduct of Foreign Affairs. As for the conduct of foreign affairs, the President is limited by the knowledge that he had better conform to some general estimate of the mind of two thirds of the Senate, lest he suffer repudiation, as Wilson was repudiated by that body over the Treaty of Versailles and membership in the League of Nations. But within that very wide limit, the President is most potent in his diplomatic powers. He may make important agreements not by treaty but by "executive agreement!" Their range has been extremely wide: the limitation of

---

27 February 6, 1947, House of Representatives, 285 to 121; amended by the Senate, March 12, 1947, 57 ayes, 23 noes. On March 21, 1947, there were 81 ayes, 29 noes! in the House of Representatives. By January, 1949, 22 state legislatures had ratified, two had rejected, it.

See Everett S. Brown, "The Term of Office of the President," in *American Political Science Review*, June, 1947. See for the problem of the Presidential succession, Joseph E. Kallenbach, "The New Presidential Succession Act," *ibid.*, October, 1947.

28 Cf. p. 686 below.

29 Cf. Herman Pritchett, *TVA* (Chapel Hill, 1943), Chap. 7.

naval forces on the Great Lakes (1817); the agreements with various nations on the "Open Door" in China (1899 and 1900); the ending of the Boxer Rebellion (1901); the limitation of Japanese immigration into the United States (1907); the recognition of special Japanese rights in China (1917); the exchange of destroyers for bases with Britain in 1940. And so on. The courts uphold such agreements.[30]

In addition to this, the President has the power, as commander-in-chief, to order the movement of United States troops and navy, a power used scores of times [31] where his ideas of the interests of the United States in various parts of the world have required a show or the use of force. Consider the effect of Mr. Roosevelt's sending of troops to Iceland before America entered World War II, and the order to the Navy to shoot at German craft molesting American vessels.

At least as important is the everyday power to take the initiative and make declarations to the nation and the world. For example, the protracted relations with Japan, culminating in Pearl Harbor—negotiations designed to reduce Japanese power and pretensions, and to "baby them along" until American opinion and arms were strong enough to resist injustice more forcefully. Or the Rooseveltian negotiations with Hitler in 1937 and 1938, and the withdrawal of the American ambassador from Berlin in 1938. Once again, the abrupt thoughtless action (not taken in cabinet, but in colloquy with one adviser!) of Mr. Truman in cutting off Lend-Lease from Britain in 1945; and his personal difficulties in understanding the importance of not allowing a public statement on Russia on one basis by his Secretary of Commerce while his Secretary of State was negotiating with the Russians on a different basis, and the effect of this on the stability of other nations.

The importance of the Presidential dip-

lomatic power lies in its enormous scope and its value for the interests of the United States and the rest of the world. It happens that the United States is the most powerful nation in the world, by reason of her population, her level of education and culture, and her economic and military power. What a commanding instrument to wield in world affairs! The whole world's balance depends upon American clarity and firmness. Unfortunately, the constitution is not such as to assure peace to other nations, ally or enemy. For the source of diplomacy is so broken, confused, and obscured that other nations are unable to obtain an assurance of constancy and definition. The President may say one thing; his Secretary may say another; other members of his administration may speak altogether differently in public; and even if they say the same thing, which is a matter of guesswork to diplomats abroad, Senatorial sentiment must be considered. For a vigorous dissent by the Senate will arouse opposition in the nation, sufficient perhaps to wreck the policy, certainly to make the rest of the world uncertain how *effective* Presidential declarations are. Clarity more than charity is the duty owed by the United States to the rest of the world, whatever the policy. Mr. Stimson supported the League in its dealings (sometimes) with Japan over Manchuria with approval and assurances in 1931: but all foreign diplomats knew that this was a futile form of support.[32] They ignored it in practice because it was not a commitment. Perhaps the advent of the Security Council and the General Assembly of the United Nations will compel clarity, by compelling a bipartisan policy, and above all, after the Palestinian fiasco and reversal, by teaching that policy must be calculated many moves ahead. If that occurs, the Presidential initiative will still exist, as well as all the other instrumentalities of his constitutional authority, but it will be exercised in commission rather than individually. Significantly, it will be-

---

[30] Cf. E. M. Borchard, "Executive Agreements," *American Political Science Review,* October, 1946.
[31] Cf. Grafton Rogers, *World Policing* (published by World Peace Foundation, New York, 1945).

[32] Cf. B. W. Wallace "How the U.S.A. Led the League in 1931," *American Political Science Review,* February, 1945.

gin with party discussion and interparty agreements.

The considerable part of the executive in initiating the making of law has already been described.[33] It is very significant but ill-organized, chiefly because Congress does not recognize it, except grudgingly, and as an encroachment on its own powers. The President occupies a curious position as legislative leader. He is not quite the leader of his party, which can mean only the score of chieftains who are in and out of Washington from their local fastnesses of bossdom, or from the citadels of big business or big labor.[34] In the one serious attempt by the President (small as that attempt was) to secure for himself a party following by intervention in the primaries, his failure reinforces the validity of the advice offered him by his national chairman, Jim Farley, and reinforces the knowledge we have that the party is a more or less fortuitous gathering of local chiefs. Farley advised Franklin Roosevelt: [35]

... the job of the Democratic National Committee is to work for and assist in every way possible in the election of the party candidates. It denies to no man the right to aspire to office and it has absolutely no concern with, or in, the primary or convention struggles for these nominations. As individuals, the members of the National Committee may have their favorites, but as a body, the organization's hands are off and will continue to be off. These nominations are entirely the affair of the States or Congressional districts, and however these early battles may result, the National Committee will be behind the candidate that the people themselves choose. This goes for every state and every Congressional district.

The President deleted the last two sentences, Mr. Farley reports.

The platform is not drafted with his assistance and for his engagement, unless he happens to be in office at the time of preparation for the coming campaign. He is under no obligation to take notice of its promises; and conveniently, they are not usually so hard and fast that deviation from them is either technically difficult, verbally discernible, or stirring to the conscience. And yet—he can hurt his Congressional friends by slack execution; he can help them by the loan of his experts; he can destroy their efforts by the use of the veto; and he feels some responsibility to the fortunes of that vague entity called "the Party."

In times of emergency, like a bad depression or after a war, he could be a creative leader. He has resources of *expertise,* and freedom from the tyranny of localism—a high and central view that can contribute potently to helping men and women all over the nation to understand and accept a policy that is different from the policies of the several sections, the states, and the parties in conflict! He may take longer views than any of these; and provide against the consequences to all that will be the result of complete and uncompromising bargainers' insistence on their own full claims, or successful logrolling by the groups at the moment most strategic for enforcement of their predatory will.

Such a contribution was made, in a degree unprecedented since Lincoln, by Franklin D. Roosevelt. His immediate successor seems not to have had his inspiration of objectives, his flair of method, his talent to seek, find, and keep counsel, his genius of maneuver, and his fortitude to withstand immediate rebuffs for long-term and nation-wide values. Let the legislation of Theodore Roosevelt, and of Woodrow Wilson, and of the New Deal era, be recalled, that is, the most important in economic and social significance: the initiator was the President and a few personal and Congressional friends. Consider the vetoes, also, of Theodore Roosevelt regarding water power; Hoover on the TVA; and F.D.R. on tax legislation, on the soldier's vote, on bills establishing price-ceilings, on the CCC (and the food-subsidy program), among many others.

---

[33] Cf. p. 442 above.
[34] James A. Farley, *Jim Farley's Story: The Roosevelt Years* (New York, 1948), pp. 120-21.
[35] For example, Mr. Truman at the Jackson Day address, March 23, 1946: "My friends in Congress have got to make up their minds whether they are for the veterans' rights or whether they are going to bow to the real estate lobby."

Then it can be appreciated how powerful a President possessing mind and moral strength plus one third support in Congress may be to influence policy, directly by quashing a law, or indirectly, by letting his views be known beforehand, so warning Congress off certain behavior unless it is sure of a majority originally and later of a two-thirds vote to override him. By his veto power, a lashing last word in a public argument, the President is a permanent participant in Congressional calculations. For all this legislative leadership the President certainly needs help, abundant help, but a different kind of help from the gadgets so far used or proposed. For they do not deal drastically enough with the obstructions of the power to provide for the nation's needs, as evidenced by pains and stresses that can be removed from society at the cost to only a few people of some trivial and unjustified privileges.

Though these criticisms must not be ignored, it can be happily acknowledged that advisers around the Presidents have rendered them and the United States signal service in inventing and operating a number of auxiliary staff organizations without which the Presidents would be lost indeed. This development may be said to have properly begun with President Taft's Commission on Economy and Efficiency. A very brief indication of the character of these services must be given.

The Executive Office. They consist, first, of the Executive Office of the President: that is, of the Bureau of the Budget, the Liaison Office for Personnel Management, an Office of Emergency Management, the White House Office already discussed,[36] and the Council of Economic Advisers. The Executive Office was established by the Reorganization Act of 1939, and the scope of authority of the various units is defined in various statutes and executive and administrative orders. The Bureau of the Budget was first instituted by the Budget and Accounting Act of 1921, and has since undergone valuable transformations. The Liaison Office for Personnel Management is all that remains of the recommendation of the President's Committee on Administrative Management that the three-man Civil Service Commission should be transfigured into a single Civil Service Administrator to be the President's adviser and manager of all personnel affairs throughout the civil service. The recommendation was rejected by Congress from fear of excessive power in the executive, and by suspicion that the service might be opened to spoils. Instead, the Liaison Office is a rather attenuated, untethered link between the President and the Civil Service Commission. The Office of Emergency Management exists only on paper in the form of two administrative orders of 1940 and 1941. For its purpose—to provide an organization to cope with national emergencies, such as domestic disasters of flood, earthquake, drought, and so on—was overwhelmed by the emergencies of World War II. It operated, therefore, only in wartime, when it devised the governmental procedures and machinery for the preparation and conduct of the war. When the Office of War Mobilization was established in May, 1943, the liaison activities of the Office of Emergency Management came to an end—but not the office.

Two units of the Executive Office remain for discussion, the Bureau of the Budget and the Council of Economic Advisers.

The Bureau of the Budget. The role of the Bureau of the Budget in the preparation of the fiscal legislation of the government has already been described.[37] Emphasis was placed upon the influence of the bureau in producing something like a rational harmony among the competing claims for expenditure, and therefore of the policies of which expenditure is a monetary index. The budget-making power is a mighty arm for the integration of administration and policy, and its establishment by the Act of 1921 added much strength to the Presidential office. It was, however, observed that the Bureau, whose director is appointed solely by the

---

President, can exert its authority on behalf of the President, only if the President disciplines the departmental chiefs —and this he is not in a position to do, comparably with the British prime minister, though vastly more able than the French prime minister. In the Bureau of the Budget, a lively, elevated, and constructive President has a splendid instrument for progress, welfare, and good sense, in national policy and administrative cohesion and tempo. Yet this is not proof altogether against the disruptions of Congress when the Budget passes through its deciding hands, nor against the surreptitious appeals of department chiefs to Congressional friends for support against the chief executive's "decisions."

Down to 1933, the Bureau of the Budget restricted its activities almost exclusively to those mentioned. From that time, and later under the impulse of recommendations from the authors of the Report of the President's Committee on Administrative Management, it became a more comprehensive engine of Presidential control, especially under the direction of Harold Smith.[38] It increased its staff greatly, and recruited the specific talents appropriate to its various functions. As prescribed in Executive Order, September 8, 1939, it undertook

To supervise and control the administration of the budget.

To conduct research in the development of improved plans of administrative management, and to advise the executive departments and agencies of the Government with respect to improved administrative organization and practice.

To aid the President to bring about more efficient and economical conduct of Government service.

To assist the President by clearing and coordinating departmental advice on proposed legislation and by making recommendations as to Presidential action on legislative enactments, in accordance with past practice.

To assist in the consideration and clearance

and, where necessary, in the preparation of proposed Executive orders and proclamations, in accordance with the provisions of Executive Order No. 7298 of February 18, 1936.

To plan and promote the improvement, development, and coordination of Federal and other statistical services.

To keep the President informed of the progress of activities by agencies of the Government with respect to work proposed, work actually initiated, and work completed, together with the relative timing of work between the several agencies of the Government; all to the end that the work programs of the several agencies of the Executive Branch of the Government may be coordinated and that the monies appropriated by the Congress may be expended in the most economical manner possible with the least possible overlapping and duplication of effort.

It was not quite foreseen that the Bureau of the Budget would emerge as the outstanding weapon of the President in the armory of several advised between 1933 and 1937. Some as we saw, fell by the wayside. Another, the Office of Government Reports, was stillborn. But the Bureau of the Budget has thrived and has given valuable hints to other governments how to establish efficiency—at the second level.

The National Resources Planning Board. The Council of Economic Advisers is, in some sense, the successor to the National Resources Planning Board, and some attention must first be given to the latter. The Board was conceived by the Report of the President's Committee on Administrative Management as one of the three instruments by which a single-man Presidency could secure some control over the gigantic apparatus of government: the fiscal element was to be taken care of by the Bureau of the Budget, the personnel element by the Civil Service Administrator, and governmental planning by the National Resources Planning Board. The Board succeeded the National Resources Planning Committee established in 1935 by an executive order of the President. Its work was directed by gifted political scientists, economists, and administrative experts, and its researches and day-by-day functions were conducted by a well-quali-

---

[38] Cf. especially F. Morstein-Marx, "The Bureau of the Budget," *American Political Science Review,* 1945, pp. 653 and 869 ff.; and Harold Smith, *The Management of Your Government* (New York, 1946).

fied staff, partly part-time. It produced a series of remarkable reports, looking into the future of American natural and human resources, the variety of governmental units and their aptness to the social reforms of the future, and, most urgent of all, the remedies for economic depressions. Also, by preparing reports and lending experts, it fostered regional and local planning conferences. Some of its directors also gave direct personal advice to the President at his request. It was another form of "brains trust," more institutionalized, more academic, more remote from the invention of immediate policy, and especially concerned with foresight beyond the range of instant necessities, with themes fundamental to the problems of the day but still below the political surface.

The Executive Order of September, 1939 gave it an even ampler scope, not unnaturally, since one of the authors of the Report was the leading spirit in the National Resources Committee. That Report proposed: [39]

This Board should serve rather as a general staff gathering and analyzing relevant facts, observing the interrelation and administration of broad policies, proposing from time to time lines of national procedure in the husbanding of our national resources, based upon thorough inquiry and mature consideration; constantly preparing and presenting to the Executive its findings, interpretations, conclusions, and recommendations for such final disposition as those entrusted with governmental responsibility may deem appropriate.

It was to be only, and never was more than, a plan-making, not a plan-ordaining or plan-executing, body. It recommended, but made no decisions. For it was recognized that decision lay with the executive and finally with Congress. It was, that is to say, a "thought-organization," not a "will-organization." It would be useful, declared its framers, only "in proportion as it is detached from immediate power and responsibility."

[39] President's Committee on Administrative Management, *Report with Special Studies*, (U.S. Government Printing Office, 1937), p. 29.

Accordingly, the Executive Order established the Board. Its functions were defined as follows:

(a) To survey, collect data on, and analyze problems pertaining to national resources, both natural and human, and to recommend to the President and the Congress long-time plans and programs for the wise use and fullest development of such resources.

(b) To consult with Federal, regional, State, local, and private agencies in developing orderly programs of public works and to list for the President and the Congress all proposed public works in the order of their relative importance with respect to (1) the greatest good to the greatest number of people, (2) the emergency necessities of the Nation, and (3) the social, economic, and cultural advancement of the people of the United States.

(c) To inform the President of the general trend of economic conditions and to recommend measures leading to their improvement or stabilization.

(d) To act as a clearing house and means of coordination for planning activities, linking together various levels and fields of planning.

The Board functioned to the middle of 1943, when Congress abolished it. Congress felt so hostile to it that it provided that its functions should not be transferred to any other agency, nor performed after the date of termination. For the Board had produced some remarkable reports on the state of the national economy. Even apart from their remedial recommendations, the mere record of the facts disturbed the conscience of the legislators. It acted as a reproach to the hard of heart; it indirectly accused them of not doing their duty. President Roosevelt made some parts of the reports into the ingredients of his messages and recommendations to Congress—especially so regarding antidepression measures, and the combating of want, disease, unemployment, and lack of education. The new "bill of rights" proclaimed in the message of January, 1943, comes from the Board's reports, and especially from its leading spirit, Professor Charles E. Merriam.

The Council of Economic Advisers. It is easier to abolish a governmental agency than to abolish the obstinate need for the functions it serves. In 1946 Congress was compelled by the sentiments of economic improvement nurtured by experience of a war and the economic and social ideas clarified by argument during it, to set up the Council of Economic Advisers to the President. (Indeed, some politicians had proposed a committee of cabinet members to work with an advisory council.) The general political purpose was to use government to provide "full employment" and to attain higher standards of living. Congressional opposition, however, succeeded in qualifying this clear objective to read: [40]

creating and maintaining, in a manner calculated to foster and promote free competitive enterprise and the general welfare, conditions under which there will be afforded useful employment opportunities, including self-employment, for those able, willing, and seeking to work, and to promote maximum employment, production and purchasing power.

All the agencies of government would be utilized and coordinated for this purpose, as a continuing policy and responsibility. To enable the President to play his part, a Council of (three) Economic Advisers was established by the statute, in the Executive Office of the President.[41] To enable Congress to play its coordinate part, Congress established its own Joint Committee on the Economic Report of the President. At the beginning of each regular session of Congress, the President transmits to Congress an economic report setting forth an account of current conditions of employment, production, purchasing power, and the trends of these factors, together with a review of the federal government's economic program, and the relationship of all these matters to the responsibilities for economic prosperity imposed on the government by the statute. It is the Joint Committee's business to report to the Congress its "findings and recommendations with respect

to each of the main recommendations made by the President in the Economic Report."

Actually, the Council of Economic Advisers have thought it wise to make a midyear report also. The economic report is the President's. It is not the exclusive production of the Council of Economic Advisers—headed by the economist Professor E. G. Nourse—but is the product of their findings, and of the assistance and advice of his cabinet and of the various departments. The Council consults with a number of advisory committees in which business, labor, agriculture, consumers, state and local governments, and educational and research institutions participate.

Perusal of the Reports show indubitably that they are the Council's work. It is difficult to divine what the Council can possibly mean when they say, "The ultimate judgments entering into the Economic Reports to the Congress rest with the President." [42] The solitary man does not know a thing about the subject! All they can mean is that he has accepted the advice of others, and assumes responsibility for the analysis, and above all, for recommendations for action.

The Council of Economic Advisers differs from the National Resources Planning Board in keeping strictly to an advisory-analytical role, and not attempting to plan public works or conservation developments, and so on. It is most careful to keep itself from proposals of policy; and though this is difficult to do given its object and scope, it is possible, and the Reports show that it is done.[43] So far has its first chairman accepted the need to remain apolitical, that he has expressed very emphatically the view that the councillors should not appear before Congressional committees to express views on legislation which is pending. For this might entail them in a tangle before the Con-

[40] Full Employment Act, February 20, 1946, section 2.
[41] See a very interesting article by E. G. Nourse and B. M. Gross, "The President's Council of Economic Advisors," in *American Political Science Review*, April, 1948.

[42] *Economic Reports of the President* (New York, Reynal and Hitchcock, 1948) p. ix.
[43] *Ibid.*, p. 14. Cf. also E. G. Nourse, "Economics in the Public Service," *Proceedings American Economic Association*, in *American Economic Review*, Vol. 37, 1947.

gress in advocating or disagreeing with the policy the President has decided to follow. Yet the other two members feel that they ought to extend assistance to the Congressional Joint Committee when it is considering the material contained in the Economic Reports.

Although the Council is advisory, through its close cooperation with the Bureau of the Budget—which is the repository of so much knowledge about every department of the government, and which values the economic analysis provided by the Council for its own budgetary purposes—it becomes of some influence in drawing the departments together.

The President even has the Council appear at a cabinet meeting each quarter to present for discussion a survey of economic developments and problems! Yet the student must still remain a little skeptical when he reads, after less than two years of operation, that "The result of the Council's participation in cabinet meetings has been to help bring the thinking of department heads to a more unified consideration of the central economic problems faced by the President." [44] The Hoover Commission rightly proposed that the Council give way to a single economic adviser.

With this apparatus available, no excuse can be offered for failure by the President or Congress to take the best measures that economic science can suggest for assuring economic prosperity so far as government can assist this. Whether the advice is taken, however, depends once again on the political considerations which induce men to act or neglect to act—that is, on the balance of group wills in the community—and the judging of these is the President's business. And here, precisely, the President is still without the real assistance he needs as a creator of policy—equal colleagues equally sharing responsibility for a common end of which all are conscious and to which all are loyal.

Interdepartmental Coordination. Vari-ous interdepartmental arrangements have existed or exist for administration to achieve certain comprehensive goals. For example, the Office of Economic Stabilization during World War II acted to govern the national economy from the standpoint of prices; and, in order to do so, the Director, appointed by the President, had the widest conceivable authority, with the approval of the President, to issue directives of policy to all the Federal departments and agencies concerned. Similarly, the Office and Director of War Mobilization, from the standpoint of maximum production. Similarly, again, with immense powers, laid down as in the previous instances by Congress, the Office and Director of War Mobilization and Conversion, for the orderly return to a peace economy.

In the bill of July 26, 1947, organizing the three armed forces under a Secretary of Defense and setting up a combined National Military Establishment, a National Security Council was established. It is composed of the President, the Secretary of State, the Secretary of Defense, the Secretaries of the three armed service departments, and the chairman of the National Security Resources Board. Its function is to advise the President on national defense. It is highly reminiscent of the Defense Committee of the British cabinet. (The reasoning behind it may be read in Senate Committee print, Committee on Naval Affairs, 79th Congress, 1st Session, 1945, "Unification of War and Navy Departments and the Postwar Organization for National Security.")

Finally, the President is assisted from time to time by the reports of special commissions of inquiry, appointed by himself. Examples are the President's Commission on Higher Education (July, 1946); another (under his authority as commander-in-chief) the Scientific Research Board (October, 1946); or, again, the President's Advisory Commission on Universal Military Training (December, 1946).

When all this is said, what does this far-reaching Presidential auxiliary apparatus amount to? Almost certainly, many

---

[44] Nourse and Gross, *op. cit.*, p. 290.

minor matters of interdepartmental administration are solved on interdepartmental lines, but these mainly rank below the really important political sphere. They are not by any means decided by a steady, rational supradepartmental common mind. And, above all, the President knows practically nothing about them and decides even less.

I can properly assert, on the basis of full first-hand evidence of perhaps two score top participants at or around the assistant-secretary level in Washington, that their attempts at policy coordination condemns them, whether or not it finally succeeds or triumphs at the very top level, to nerve-wracking, tormenting negotiations, started, carried on, broken off, restarted, achieved with compromise. When the process is finally abortive, there is sickness at heart, discouragement and despondency, cynicism, and nervous breakdowns. For these officials will admit, they do not work, as their British official counterparts work, within the broad, fairly firm framework of a policy made by a political party ruling the whole process of government, or, where the party has not yet made up its mind, the prior existence of a party ethos always pregnant with a policy. There, the officials are effective within a circle forescribed, but it is not an absolute circle—they may help to create it. When they have done their share of the work, the pail will not be kicked over and the milk spilled. As one tortured Washington official declared: "Our British colleagues live in the paradise of the bureaucrat!"; and he meant only that their work, when done, is not destroyed. For there is imposed on the top administrative officials in Washington, a task of weaving together policies that are the proper responsiblity of the political party and the responsible executive. This should not be asked of them, and the system needs refashioning in order that what belongs to party and President should be done by party and President. To ask it of the administrative chiefs is to ask for complete or partial failure and the wreckage of health.

The brains, the character, the energy, the impetus—all are there, but they are not geared to central inspiration. There is no concert. One man has not the capacity, though he bears the responsibility, to produce a concert. In spite of all the apparatus of advice and coordination, the President swings about untethered to the whole administrative machine—he is a stranger to it.

If the gravamen of the Hoover Reports on "The National Security Organization" and "Foreign Affairs" be identified, it consists in this feeling that the President is removed from immediate immersion in the stream of affairs and that his advisers are separated from him by the responsibilities and authority with which Congress has invested them, while the President has his own kind of responsibility. The National Security Board and the National Security Resources Board (responsible for advising on the total mobilization of all the resources and manpower of America in the event of war) are not truly his instruments, though they are necessary aids to the fulfilment of his own responsibilities. Similarly with the conduct of foreign affairs: numerous agencies own a segment of relations with foreign powers, and these often are intermeshed with their duties to domestic American life. Foreign affairs, defense measures, the economy, ought all to come under a coherent regular responsible survey by a body which has a collective responsibility. But, now, interposed between the President and some of the department chiefs, stand the interdepartmental committees mentioned and various others, while at the center stands a solitary man, hardly other than a stranger to the various chieftains who come "to brief" him, irrelevant and bewildered.

The idea of the Hoover Commission that the Executive Office would have several advisers and coordinators of large segments of government business—the economy, the budget, defense, resources planning—would seem to offer to the President a kind of new super-cabinet: this could be so, and work well, *if* these men saw eye to eye politically, and *if*, with the President, they personally felt a corporate responsibility, and *if*, moreover, their relationship of authority to the heads of departments were satisfactorily settled. The Hoover Commission's idea that rather than these statutory interdepartmental committees, the cabinet should spawn cabinet committees as and when it thought proper is sound: they should stem from the center of responsibility, that is to say, from the President and his cabinet, and not invade the center by advancing from the outside fortified with Congressional authority, fixed in its terms of responsibility, and divided in loyalty, inflamed with conceit. The assumption is, however, that a real "cabinet" exists—but it does not. The two reports mentioned above are permeated with the embarrassment of recognizing sole Presidential responsibility in the last, that is, the controlling resort, and the difficulty of devising a way whereby the aid given by their chosen instruments could be really made to impinge on the President's mind. I incline to the belief that "ne'er the twain shall meet," or, if so, then only by the accidents of personality.

THE EXECUTIVE SEPARATED FROM CONGRESS

WE always return to the root of the trouble. Legislature and executive have been severed, though not completely. The executive has even been banished from the floor of Congress in open responsible appearance, though its presence is required, perhaps excessively, in committee hearings and investigations.

Congress makes the laws and Congress furnishes the funds. This at once nourishes its corporate pride and its alienation from the executive. Each is invested with its own responsibilities: it is obliged to think of those first, always possibly above considerations of good government. For it was originally believed that government could be good only when these psychological occlusions were established.

It has already been borne in on the reader how enormously wasteful a system it is that severs executive knowledge from Congressional lawmaking, and executive administration of the laws from the direct everyday impact of those who have made them; and that separates the making of policy from its fulfillment. This is the normal predicament, even where a President and his party are well in the saddle in both Houses. But even then tremors occur—and general faults of time table, priority, and emphasis—because some men in the party, who themselves might have been high in the leadership, dislike the President. They become uncooperative: sour, conceited, obstructive; responsibility is obscured, and what should be done is neglected. How much more so does this mutual stultification, but chiefly that of the President, weigh upon the nation, when, as too often happens, the party cannot simultaneously dominate legislature and executive! Each then steers a course towards a full victory over the other at the approaching elections: neither is willing to assist the other wholeheartedly, though each may make pretense of this as an election tactic.

At the best of times, the executive arrangements for the due order of business are spoiled by the private and more or less surreptitious appeals of department heads and subordinates to Congress for laws and money and administrative permissions. This contravenes the rules of the Budget and Accounting Act of 1921, and flies in the face of the repeated orders of the presidents. Congress, not President Roosevelt, settled the dispute between his Secretary of Commerce Wallace and Jesse Jones, his Federal Loan Administrator, whatever the President's wishes in the matter.

The President's persuasion of Congress is undertaken through most tenuous processes and ramshackle contrivances which continually face breakdown. Leadership is always at long distance, even if an Alben Barkley is in the Senate as Mr. Roosevelt's devoted agent. See, for example, their clash over the tax veto in 1944.[45] The student might well compare that clash and the language used during

---

[45] *Congressional Record, 78th Congress*, Col. 1981 ff.

its settlement with those of Clarendon as he describes the relations between Charles II and the House of Commons in 1661. Clarendon writes: [46]

These ministers had every day conference with some select persons of the House of Commons, who had always served the king, and upon that account had great interest in that assembly, and in regard of the experience they had and their good parts were harkened to with reverence. And with those they consulted in what method to proceed in disposing the house, sometimes to propose, sometimes to consent to what should be most necessary to the public; and by them to assign parts to other men, whom they found disposed and willing to concur in what was to be desired: and this without any noise, or bringing many together to design, which ever was and will be ingrateful to parliaments, and, however it may succeed for a little time, will in the end be attended with prejudice.

This is not far from a verbatim description of the United States constitution in the twentieth century in one of its most vital parts.

A Suggested Remedy. To remedy the weakness, the Report of the Joint Committee on the Reorganization of Congress [47] made the following proposal:

That the majority policy committees of the Senate and the House serve as a formal council to meet regularly with the Executive, to facilitate the formulation and carrying out of a national policy, and to improve relationships between the executive and legislative branches of the Government.

This, argues the Committee (which did not lack sifted information), is "in order to narrow the widening gap between the executive and the legislative branches." On this body such members of the President's cabinet as may be desirable would serve. Manifestly, when the two branches of the government are in the hands of different parties, such a hyphen would be neither desirable nor possible. Naturally, the act "to provide for increased efficiency in the legislative branch of the

government" did not provide for the above-mentioned arrangement among its clauses. If it had, one more law would have been condemned to almost certain desuetude. For the efficiency of such a joint committee depends on the willingness of the two branches to undertake and work it smoothly. But this depends on (a) the power of the President to rely upon the following of Congress when he has made commitments to the leaders, and they have made reciprocal commitments to him; and (b) the power of the President to prevent his own cabinet ministers from betraying him by a deal with Congressmen behind his back. Neither of these foundations is as yet built. The Report of the Joint Committee even admits elsewhere that party members are free to disregard the resolutions of their own caucus! The arrangement would be built on sand. And yet, every such structure *may* be a slight contribution to putting more responsibility on men to consider the views of a collectivity. Not much is to be expected of the device, but it must not be altogether discredited: it should be tried.

Congress Intrudes in Administration. What disintegrates the executive, both when he seeks to form overall policy and again when he is bent on driving all the departments and agencies as a single team (this need not be done by any means too tautly), is the undoubted right of Congress to intrude in the executive and administrative field. The constitution limits only the number of subjects on which Congress may make laws, not the matter over which in each case it has authority. Congress passes and always has passed laws and resolutions and financial provisions which prescribe administrative functions, define the contours of policy in each agency, ordain specific administrative organization therein, and lay down principles of administration, procedures, and personnel.[48] (The Tennessee Valley

---

[46] Edward Hyde Clarendon, *Life of Clarendon* (Oxford, 1843 edition), p. 1093.

[47] Report, Joint Committee on Organization, March 4, 1946, U.S. Senate, No. 1011, p. 13.

[48] Cf. Justice Brandeis in *Myers* v. *United States:* "Obviously the President cannot secure full execution of the laws, if Congress denies to him the adequate means of doing so. Full execution may be defeated because Congress

Authority statute is representative and very graphic.) Congress can tie the hands of the administrators of any agency very tightly, and it does. It gives them an extra wring, or loosens them, year by year when the budget estimates for each agency come before it. In doing this, Congress is making a quite rigid pattern within which the President is left very little discretion to guide, inspire and coordinate.

Already within eight years of the commencement of the federal government, Fisher Ames wrote to Hamilton the results of his own observation: [49]

What we call *the government* is a phantom... The heads of departments are head clerks. Instead of being the ministry, the organs of the executive power, and imparting a kind of momentum to the operation of laws, they are precluded of late even from communicating with the House, by reports. In other countries, they may speak as well as act. We allow them to do neither. We forbid even the use of a speaking-trumpet; or more properly, as the Constitution has ordained that they shall be dumb, we forbid them to explain themselves by signs. Two evils, obvious to you, result from all this. The efficiency of the government is reduced to its minimum, the proneness of the popular body to usurpation is already advancing to its maximum. *Committees are already the ministers;* [50] and while the House indulges a jealousy of encroachments in its functions, which are properly deliberative, it does not perceive they are impaired and nullified by the monopoly as well as the perversion of information by committees. We think the executive power is a mere pageant of the representative body—a custos rotulorum, or master of ceremonies. We ourselves are but passive instruments, whenever the sovereign people choose to speak for themselves, instead of our speaking for them.

It is no wonder, then, that the committees have, in the course of time, found it

declines to create offices indispensable for that purpose; or because Congress, having created the office, declines to make the indispensable appropriation; or because Congress, having created the office and made the appropriation, prevents, by restrictions which it imposes, the appointment of officials who in quality and character are indispensable to the efficient execution of law."
[49] Cf. Alexander Hamilton, *Works*, 1851, Vol. VI, p. 201-3, Jan. 26, 1797.
[50] Author's italics.

necessary to equip themselves with the same sort of expert staffs that the executive has, and that to these have been attributed functions and character very like those recruited in the British civil service for the assistance of ministers—a matter already noticed.[51] It is no wonder that the Congress has established the curious hybrids in administration: the regulatory independent commissions, like the Interstate Commerce Commission, the Federal Power Commission, the Federal Communications Commission, the Tariff Commission, and so many others, which, in the words of the President's Committee on Administrative Management, constitute a "headless fourth branch" of the government.[52] They were so established because Congress would not trust the executive with the administration of the main principles of policy which Congress might have confined itself to laying down in the act. Being thus established, they are not within the President's administrative power of control or inspiration. Nor is it to be marveled at that the powers given by Congress to the great interdepartmental offices previously referred to (price stabilization, of mobilization, of reconversion), actually grant their directors a power of control and direction far surpassing that exercised by the President himself under the direct grant of the constitution.

Thus, the Congress skirmishes in and out of the administrative agencies with its permissions and prohibitions, and thrusts deep into their organization and working.[53] Thus, also, Congressmen claim

[51] See p. 456 above.
[52] Cf. R. Cushman, *The Independent Regulatory Agencies* (New York, 1941).
[53] A particularly instructive example of Congressional interference with the administrative process comes to mind. In an executive order of June 24, 1938, the President authorized the Federal Civil Service Commission, among other things, "to establish practical training courses for employees in the departmental and field services of the classified civil service . . ." The Commission took its task seriously, and, working with the Council of Personnel Administration, the Office of Education, the heads of the employee unions, various officials throughout the government, and

and exercise rights of visit and interrogation, in their individual capacity, to the
individual departments, and even to the
individual bureau chiefs and other officials. And, naturally, some of the administrators become their friends, and so also
the friends of the economic groups they
and their visiting Congressmen serve.
This lacerates administration, and pulls
and plucks at it, until it slumps askew.
The commonly harmonious values are
subservient to the war of all against all,
and the President cannot but be at the
mercy of the engines he is supposed to
utilize. What can he do alone?

Deliberately, Congress commandeered
for itself the power to lead on the day it
banished the executive chiefs from the
floor of Congress. It thereby shattered the
cohesion of the executive for the executive's own business. And, simultaneously
it threw away the cohesion of its own proceedings by destroying an integrating executive nucleus that might have come
into its midst replete with knowledge and
stimulated by responsibility for enforcing
policy at the point where the clauses of
the law are being quickened into life.

The logic of the system has impelled
and still impels Congress to fly in the face
of John Stuart Mill's logic of representative government—that a popular numerous body is eminently fit to control administration, but not itself to conduct it.

THE PRESIDENCY CAN BE TINKERED WITH, NOT REFORMED

THE United States is more fortunate in
its government than the lands of Europe
which rule themselves through a cabinet
system founded on parties too numerous
to provide a stable and decided executive,
for it has avoided confusion and excessive fluidity. At any rate, it stands for four
full years, and if necessity should desperately press, it may serve as magnificently
as in World War II. Yet it approaches
the European governments in lack of
effective vigor: Presidents may make
many strong declarations, few are the
means for fulfilling them. Nevertheless,
the United States has been more fortunate
than France, partly due to the fact that
at any rate only two parties have occupied the main scene of legislation and
executive control. When the need for
action has become burningly urgent, what
was needed was carried by a bipartisan if
not a partisan grouping. Yet it is not
enough.

*Comparison with British Prime Min-
ister.* The British prime minister is happier than the chief executive of the
United States, for his choice of partners
is to a large extent made for him: it is
made in the least troublesome way in
politics, through the gradual selective
process of a free parliament and a party
in which a high degree of mutual trust
prevails because men are bound together
in a common enterprise in the service of
common principles. The harmony (always relatively speaking), is a pre-established harmony. He is more fortunate
than the President of the United States
because he may normally rely on the continual and current assistance of almost
all of his cabinet. It is their duty, indeed,
to bring him aid and comfort, not least
when it is in the form of frank criticism
and even resistance based on party principle. All of them are political in the best
sense of the word. He knows how far he

other persons, it produced a report leading to
a new unit of training administration, and
appointed, March 16, 1939, a Coordinator and
Director of Training. Then a revised report
was prepared called "The United States Civil
Service Commission's Part in Federal Training," projecting many activities. It must be remembered that in-service training has now
come to be recognized by every modern state
in the world as essential to the proper performance of the tasks of the public service.
But when Congress was asked for appropriations to implement this recommendation
which had taken many months of hard work
to devise, the funds were refused. (See *Annual
Report*, Civil Service Commission, June 30,
1939, pp. 46-47). In 1946, the British civil
service established an elaborate system of in-
service training, substantially inspired by
American thought and this latest experience.
But once its advisory bodies had made recommendations which the Treasury could accept,
and the cabinet had decided to support the
policy of the Treasury, the House of Commons found the money—there was no hiatus
between executive and legislature.

can go because his stablemates are with him continually, and all together face the common ordeal of the Forum, where some six hundred men, ready to take their places, are endowed by the people with the right to take them to task about detail even as about the most lofty principle.

The prime minister is mightier than the American President if he can carry his cabinet with him and then convince Parliament (and party affiliation has already made the latter an almost foregone though far from certain conclusion). For he is master not only of the executive but also of all legislative leadership and particulars. A seamless network holds together the prime minister and the cabinet and the Parliament. They are flesh of each others' flesh, in full sovereignty, for neither constitutional limitations nor courts declare them out of bounds: and they are still flesh of each others' flesh even when they are thorns in each others' flesh. The cabinet ministers cannot, as they succeed in doing in the United States, contrive to keep their departmental affairs out of cabinet discussions. The cabinet is precisely the place where all the cards are on the table, and where no one can keep the hand dealt to him covered up. Every man has the right to require his colleagues' hand to be placed face up. Nor can a British cabinet minister be maneuvered according to the rules of the game, as in the United States, not to challenge his colleagues' policy: the rule is that he is a minister precisely to do so. Most ministers will have been so apprenticed and selected that they can (as not more than one or two in an American cabinet are ever able to) offer valid contributions to the policy of all the other members of the cabinet. Each British cabinet minister is responsibly more fortunate than the departmental chiefs in the United States, because while he may be irked by the intervention of a colleague, it assists him, and enables him the better to bear his responsibility because it is thereby shared. And all of them together are better placed to take the initiative in administration and proposals for lawmaking, because they have learned to appraise and follow the "sense of the House." When that is accomplished they have shared their responsibility (which always sits heavy on the head that wears a crown) with Parliament. They can always answer: "You were accessories before and during the fact!"

No such comforts or permissions and easements exist in the American system: it is powerful and powerless, harsh, laborious, and stultified. It has not even the advantage of a steady, united, and responsible opposition, for the factors that disintegrate Presidential leadership do the same damage to the party in the minority. Opposition there is—strenuous and strident. But it consists of the uneven sum of individual acts of opposition by Representatives and Senators. It is scattered, sporadic, unsteady, not too well informed, and lacks the moderation that issues from admitting that criticism invokes a principle of public welfare and that criticism constitutes a self-commitment for a future spent in office. For the separation of powers precludes any reasonable assurance of future office, or the power to implement one's policy if one ever attained it.

Suggested Remedies. Can it be remedied? No substantial remedy exists outside a surgical one which will introduce an equivalent of the British system. All gadgets may be tried: they will effect small improvements:

(1) Most radically, on this lesser plane, all branches of the government—House, Senate and President—should be elected for the same term—four years—and at the same time. That would produce a collective, national searching of heart, vigorous and vast.

(2) Two or three question periods a week before a joint meeting of both houses might be instituted. Yet what is the use of questions unless they are of disciplinary force and can exact commitments of the executive as the British are and do? Nevertheless, let them be tried. But what would happen if the President and his departmental officers were confronted with questions by a Congress held

by a hostile party? Congress would lampoon them: a bear garden would result.

(3) The British government has found urgent and inescapable the need for an administrative class of career officials composed of some forty permanent undersecretaries and nearly four thousand assistants to them leading upwards to the political apex in a pyramid of age and experience. The French have accepted the need also. How much more desirable is this governmental device in a system where not only may different political parties follow each other from term to term in legislative and executive power, but where the President, because his party or his friends in his party have lost power in Congress, may suddenly find himself riding astride little more than a few cronies playing beggar-my-political-neighbor. One great permanent sturdy administrative bridge is needed—always open and open to all—over which both Congress and President of the same or different parties may safely travel—not the anonymous half dozen plus a précis-making staff secretary!

(4) Is it necessary to go beyond this? Undoubtedly. The Presidency should be truly collective: and that body should have the right of dissolution of Congress on vital issues in the estimation of the President and his group. Then the President would be elected at the same time as the new Congress was being elected. Elections might then be fought on emergent issues, whereas at present, issues are fabricated for elections at fixed times, putting a strain on everybody's honesty.

Nothing short of a radical reform can raise the government of the United States to the capacity needed to solve its domestic problems and to play its rightful part in preserving itself and furthering justice in the developing world order. If not, one day, a disaster will surely overtake the nation and its world neighbors. What do I mean by a disaster? Such things as not having coped reasonably and bravely with the prices problem after V-J day. Or, not having a unified mind to tell the public the truth about industrial production difficulties. Or not having

the unified will (of course, a steady opposition is always assumed) to take measures early enough to cope with depressions. Or not having a settled enough state of mind, owing to executive-legislative disintegration, to deal justly with capitalist and labor monopolies, oppressions, and cessations of work. Or not achieving adequate clarity and constancy to fulfill international obligations. Or suffering surprises like Pearl Harbor and its train of deadly consequences.

Many American political scientists recognize this picture. Indeed, their own research has principally contributed to its painting. Perhaps nothing can be done, since tradition, law, geographical extent and diversity may doom the land to incoherence of outlook and belief, and an invertebrate party system. Indeed, the government of the United States exhibits some of the incoherence which would undoubtedly characterize a world government, if it were democratic, and for the same cardinal reason—geographical extent and diversity.

It may be contended, when the student looks at European affairs, that after all, America has not done so badly in providing liberty, order, justice, and wealth. Do not democracy, freedom and justice, prevail, and at the same time is not the standard of living the highest of all anywhere? The point is rather that much more freedom for many more people could prevail, that justice could be more nobly conceived and more effectively administered, and that the standard of living could be higher for a far larger proportion of the masses, if the government were better built and conducted. The cavalier reply cannot be impeccably made that the land is so well off. One third of the nation is still ill-housed, ill-clothed, ill-fed, and sick for lack of adequate medical attention. A not inconsiderable contribution to American welfare happens to have been made by climate, land, and natural resources. So propitious are these that they have even encouraged governmental waste.

If the Cabinet System were Introduced. It is possibly a useful exercise to speculate broadly on the possible consequences of introducing the cabinet system in the United States, and then upon the factors probably inimical to its success.

. A true collective cabinet, with a solidarity of responsibility, would be of assured value only for the coordination of the administrative departments, and the production of a concerted legislative policy. It could be quite successful and valuable in the former function, assuming an inward genuine solidarity of political outlook, but it would still be marred by the power of Congress to make laws which virtually dictate how administration shall be conducted. If Congress were at sixes and sevens in making these laws, so would the administration be in spite of the solid cabinet. As for the policy-creating power, the cabinet might be solid, but the cabinet could not be sure that its propositions, any more than today, would ever become law. A cabinet would depend as much on the good graces of Congress as the President does now.

Consolidation of Powers. It is therefore obvious that something more is required than merely to institute a solid collective cabinet. That something in addition must, I think, mean that either the cabinet is given all of the legislative power, or that to the Congress is added the executive power. It does not matter which of the expedients is adopted: the overriding principle is that either shall have the plenitude of power, that power shall be undivided, that responsibility shall be unseparated. If the entire power of government went to the Congress, then Congress would in time create its own coherent leadership, even if the constitutional reformers had not already done so. Whatever the details, the main feature would be that the executive would emerge from the leaders of Congress, like the British cabinet or the French council of ministers. All the advantages of a unison of legislative policy and executive fulfillment and leadership would then be available. If, on the other hand, the executive were endowed with both legislative and executive power in their entirety, then the executive, being elected, and

founded on the principle of democratic representation and responsibility, would endow himself and be compelled to work with a council of leaders from the majority party. It might be a smaller council known as the cabinet, or a larger one which is the Congress and its committees. It might even be that this cabinet would be composed of the leaders of the Congressional committees, though in a vastly superior position of power and influence than the chairmen of committees today.

Hence, we see that to ordain a plural cabinet with collective responsibility is not in itself effectual to reform the system. We may also infer that the separation of powers, the existence of checks and balances, frustrates reform. It may be useful, but it is trifling, to propose question-time in Congress for the executive, solitary or collective, and to propose the regular presence of the executive and departmental chiefs on the floor of Congress. While the powers of proposal and of disposal are in different hands, the government remains weak. If the separation were overcome, then, in spite of the fact that the states retain a very large field of power, enough has already been granted specifically to the national government, and even more conceded by the Supreme Court, that a good, strong, active government would have been instituted. If, then, the present trend to the increase of federal powers continued, political parties might more seriously found themselves on public and national principle. They might better fit their organization to carry out the various functions to which we have given so much attention. The greater the amount of power, the wider the scope of government sovereignty to work weal or woe to men and women, to cities, states, interest groups, regions. The keener the interest in the quest for power and for votes, the keener also its accompaniment, the quest for as many votes as possible to challenge and oppose the majority. This would invigorate party principle, animate party organization, evoke and intensify the loyalty of leaders and followers in the electorate, the Congress, and the cabinet.

Power exercised in its entirety—that is, legislative and executive by one party—would solidify the opposition. The existence of an opposition, coupled with responsibility entire in its scope, and collective and therefore simple and single in its appearance, would stimulate the solidarity of the cabinet and its feeling of obligation for the public welfare. In other words, if somehow the reform were accomplished, it would go far to cure some of the evils which are often rightly stated to be the reason why the reform is not being undertaken: that is to say, the inchoate, the inarticulated, nation-wide parties. Local bossism might succumb to central leadership, if it were potent and brilliant, just as in the Presidential leadership of 1936 and 1940 Franklin Roosevelt was able to triumph even though the Democratic machine bosses detested the New Deal, for their own local tenures depended on the triumph of the candidate.

Obstacles to Reform. What factors are inimical to such reform? True, it would, if instituted, invigorate and reform the party system. But could it do so enough to become a viable system of government? It must be acknowledged that several powerful factors stand against the possibility. The first is the geographic range of the country, with its nature-determined regions, and the economic interests and therefore political loyalties based upon them. The most obvious is North and South. Another is East and Middle West. Another is the corn belt and the manufacturing and commercial regions. There are many others. Can a policy be found which can unite regional interests in a party, not merely for an election, but for decades and decades, so that a recognizable entity—party—survives the years, even if changes occur in its outlook? This is exceedingly doubtful. It is doubtful also whether the peculiar complex class composition and outlook of the British political parties can possibly have its counterpart in the American political environment, since the history and present composition of American economic groupings and opportunities have their own peculiar characteristics. Nor can the various interests of states and cities be ignored. It would seem as though the very range and variety of American geography and economic interests doom the nation to inarticulated parties. If this be granted, the government is bound to be at once disarticulated, and only in the spasms and agony of disaster to make unified forward surges in policy. If party unification and loyalty were missing, so would the Congressional be, and so also, the cabinet's unity.

Other obstacles exist to a full cabinet system, furnished with the conventions that guide it in Britain. The Senate was deliberately set up to perpetuate regional obstructions on national government; consciously to disrupt unified political parties if they should ever arise. A constitutional amendment could abolish the Senate, but if the Senate were abolished, it would not reduce the natural factors in the American polity which produced the Senate in the first place: that is, once again, regional diversity. A cabinet system requires that we assume a legislature based on the homogeneity and the solidarity of the free and equal representatives who represent free and equal citizens without distinction of territorial blocs, or regional vested interests.

Though it may seem a little recondite, it is not altogether without point to observe that in Britain the existence of an hereditary chief of state—the Crown—helps considerably in maintaining the smooth operation of the cabinet government. The chief of state symbolizes the unity and continuity of the state, the political order: is a point of reference for dissolutions and the appointment and resignation of ministers. He is a fixed point in fluctuation. It has already been appreciated how difficult a problem it was to provide against a dangerous and inefficient dualism of the executive in Weimar Germany, and in the France of the Fourth as well as the Third Republic. One of the awkward problems of statecraft is the election of the chief of state: if by the people, he may seek power and he will certainly have been defamed by some of the parties at the election. If by the legislature, then he will suffer the same fate of defamation and will most likely be weak. What would be the equivalent problem, what the chief of state, in an American system of cabinet government? The national government could hardly dispense with a chief of state separate from the prime minister and cabinet, and this chief of state could hardly avoid interfering with the cabinet.

Further reflection suggests that if the single executive gave way to the multiple executive in the United States government, the cabinet might be disintegrated by the demand of the various sections of the country for their own members of the cabinet in it. And, again, if the two-party arrangement did not continue at least as well as it now operates and if the government were no longer one of separated but of combined powers, the United States, having committed so important a stake to the political fight, might see the institution of multifarious parties, as in France or Germany or Italy, though inspired by different factors and seeking other objects. Then a cabinet system would be no gain, but a loss; for it would have cost the nation the executive stability provided by the fixed term, and transferred frustration from the separated powers to the segmented political parties.

Thus, it may be of the utmost importance to make a radical change in the central governing institutions of the United States; yet history, geography, and traditions may be insurmountable obstructions to anything but minor reforms.

Presidential Responsibility. Some observations on the nature of the President's responsibility need to be added. They are necessary because some men who see little hope of improvement in Congress believe that the "responsibility" for good government has been transferred to the presidency, since he is the only central political institution voted for by the whole people as a single national community, whereas the House of Representatives and the Senate are only the uncertain sum of hundreds of local elections in which local issues and local outlooks predominate.

Now, the President is "responsible" in the sense that he is vested with certain obligations by the constitution. So much is certain. But, in the first place, nearly all of those obligations and rights, whether executive or legislative, are expressed in highly general terms. That generality of expression throws back "responsibility" to the man in office. It is not outwardly to a document or the popular legislature that he must look to discover the clear lines within which he ought and is able to work. The contrast between Harding and Coolidge and Franklin D. Roosevelt demonstrates that. Therefore, the "responsibility" is mainly moral, that is to say, it stems from his own conscience and character. No Congress can harm a do-nothing President like a Calvin Coolidge, nor chastise a deserve-nothing like Harding; no Congress can altogether check the daring, like Jackson, or quell the bold and courageous, like Lincoln. His office is his, and he retains it for his four years. Congress can punish a President who desires to get things done, when he asks for money and laws for his purposes; but it cannot punish a President who is not interested in policy and action, for then it has no sanction over him. Accountability as responsibility is significant only in the case of active, aspiring, presidents. It may be urged that the President has a responsibility which issues from the fact that the people have elected him, and that he therefore owes them a duty. A duty may indeed be implied when a man has either asked for or not denied the candidacy. But the important question is, How is this implied duty to be made concrete and fulfilled? Presidential candidates are not usually given to being specific over the whole range of policy. In some branches they have no competence, for it belongs to Congress. They conduct a campaign in company with some party friends—they give one knows not what hostages to them. Many situations are obscure at the time of election. Where is the responsibility for dealing with them later? It may be argued that the candidate ought to be conscious himself of his policy and specific in his commitments. This desideratum may be not only conceded but even urged. But though a Presidential candidate may be the author of promises, he is not the master of their fulfillment.

Assuming that a responsibility is acknowledged to the people, it cannot be comprehensive, it cannot be specific, it is incapable of full and specific performance: though the performance may, in fact, be partial and specific, and even clever and appropriate to the problems at the moment when they are actually reached. Assuming, once again, that the President is responsible to the people as the nation as distinct from the people in Congress assembled, how can the responsibility be brought home to him in the years between his election and the end of office? It may only be by deputations, correspondence, and the press, the consultation of public opinion polls, of which the greatest as well as the first master was Franklin Roosevelt. Can this be said to be an exact responsibility? The continual stream of public comment, appeals, reproaches, and scorn may induce or lash him into promise and action. The polls of popularity are watched and followed with considerable sensitiveness by the dweller in the White House. It still leaves the President to formulate his will on the matters brought to his attention in this way. He can transmit the impressions and impulses he receives to Congress, he can stimulate the stream of communication to him and to Congressmen by the use of publicity devices: the radio and the press conference, and the White House chats to visitors, and speeches on special occasions in various parts of the country. He can bring together and exert appeasing influence upon conflicting groups in industrial warfare. He enjoys unrivaled opportunities and prestige for the mobilization of public opinion. But his responsibility to use them—and, having used them, to transform the aroused emotions and wills into law and administration—is still once again to be determined only by his own conscience and character. His term of office is not subject to the will of a controlling Congress, nor, unless he desires a second term or more, to the people's will. Hardly even where a President is anxious to secure re-election is it possible to think of "responsibility" in the sense of accountability, as it operates to rule a cabinet in Britain or France.

All the rest—with the exception of that rusty but still constitutionally available method of impeachment for crime and misdemeanor—all the rest is moral responsibility, the affair of a President's conscience, the pangs he feels. It can either be insufficient, as in the case of the weak Presidents, or it may, as in the Presidential attempt to reform the Supreme Court, be excessive accountability as responsibility stimulates, moderates, and guides; it is the preceptor and corrector of government; and this office is best managed where the government (in this case, the President of the United States) must account to an intermediate body between it and the people, so amorphous and widely scattered. And it becomes the more sensitive and helpful an instrument where both the agencies of government, the controller and the controlled, are not assured of fixed terms of office.

Responsibility and the Facts. Hardly a day goes by without a threat by congressmen that they will not find the funds for the President's policies, especially for foreign policy and military expenditures, unless the President "tells us all the facts —all." Now neither the House of Commons nor the French National Assembly is ever told all the facts. Nor can any assembly of hundreds of people, nor the people as a whole, ever be told all the facts, at the time they themselves demand. For one thing, the facts in their entirety that may be requisite to a right policy may not be available even to the executive. For another thing, some of the facts (in foreign policy especially) cannot be immediately told, lest they should make peaceful continuation of negotiations impossible. To tell may actually undermine the nation's ability to defend itself by the disclosure of information, by revealing that the nation is able to get information through its secret service or through the cracking of a foreign power's codes.

Far more important is the truth that a point is frequently reached where a transition from the facts to a decision must be undertaken though all the facts desirable are not yet obtainable. Policy is very frequently the offspring of inference, and no other basis than this is at hand. Yet the policy must be formulated and applied without waiting, lest events bring irrevocable disaster to the statesman and his people. But it is precisely at the frontier of inference and guesswork, in the twilight zone between facts about the past and firm resolutions about the future, that Presidents and Congresses may most seriously differ and dispute. The point has been admirably put by Justice Jackson speaking in 1948 for the Supreme Court in *Chicago and Southern Air Lines v. Waterman S.S. Corp.* (68 S.Ct. 431): "They [executive decisions as to foreign policy] are delicate, complex, and involve large elements of prophecy."

In the British system of government, and even perhaps in the French, though it is weaker, the unintermittent merging of executive and legislature, the ever-continuing life in each other's physical presence, is some assurance of the unison of mind which leads to a unison of guesswork, and therefore to a sharing of responsibility for policy. It enables a measured trust in the executive that purges a peevish demand for "all the facts." The United States President is, on the other hand, compelled to face the task of correct inference from uncertain premises alone—this is a burden of all governments, everywhere, and at all times in human history. It is a dreadful burden for a solitary man, even if assisted by a few faithful friends, to bear alone. Accompanying it is a twin burden: that the knowledge of the facts and the consequent guesses must be carried forward in a state of tentativeness and uncertainty, in a condition merely of temporary probability and yet of possible final certainty, in face of a clamant people

anxious to learn what sacrifices, what burdens, what happiness or unhappiness the future holds in store for them, and a people also, to whom the President owes an accounting. Particularly when the horror of war or the misery of depression is being faced is it difficult, as electorates now are, to release the secrets of fact and conjecture, when this may mean undeliberate, emotional behavior by popular groups, which would not occur later when time and events have ripened and made concrete the surmises which the statesman is obliged to nurse. The President is in a position where he can see much further than most people in the nation, even than the most enlightened publicists, but he is in a position where he must not talk as much as undutiful ones. He must bide his time, suffer the criticism until the day of reckoning, and hope that his prophetic thinking is sound enough to redeem his repute because it served his people. A true political party system tends to guarantee that the executive and the legislature share in common the values involved in inference and prophecy. Without it, the President bears an awful burden indeed.[54]

Planning and the Presidency. If it is ever found necessary—under stress of war or the emergency of a more disastrous depression than that of 1929 to 1936, or, more likely still, under a democratically developed conviction that social control of economic activity is conducive to liberty and welfare—to institute planning on something like the scale of contemporary Britain, then no doubt can possibly prevail that the Presidential system must undergo the most drastic reform. With it Congressional-Presidential relations would be transformed. A new coherence among the institutions of leadership and control would need to be established, and a real sharing of responsibility would have to replace the crude checks and bal-

[54] Professor Charles A. Beard's utter failure to acknowledge these truths about guesswork utterly vitiates his study of Rooseveltian foreign policy between 1933 and Pearl Harbor. Cf. *Roosevelt and the Coming of War* (New York, 1948).

ances of the horse-and-buggy age. The struggle against George III in the eighteenth century was different in kind from the twentieth century's encounter with giant masterful economies and relations with spirited and powerful independent sovereign nations, and the instruments of man's contemporary well-being should be appropriately contemporary.

A recent study has made a most cogent and comprehensively stated case for planning auxiliaries for the President.[55] But what stands out starkly in the argument, and what the sincere author finds to be an obsession to which he must continually return, is the constitutional power of the President by himself to thwart or advance the policies which emerge from his advisers. He says:

It is obvious that the administrative effectiveness of a central planning agency must depend on its relation to the President. The Office of the President is more than a government institution; it is even more than the reflection of the peculiarities of an individual personality. No organizational device can strengthen the backbone of a timorous President. No administrative arrangement can alter a fundamental conviction of a chief executive. The experience under the Employment Stabilization Act of 1931 clearly revealed that a mere legislative declaration of policy and the establishment of some administrative machinery did not automatically produce administrative action. President Hoover was not disposed to move even under the conditions which were overwhelming him. The answer was not different administrative machinery, but the election of 1932. Planning leadership, then, in the last analysis must always depend upon the personality of the chief executive.

The same single-handed power of the President to make or mar the government of the nation appears from reflection on one of the most interesting proposals ever made to surmount the combined effect of the separation of powers and the solitary executive. It is that made

by Professor W. Y. Elliott, before the Joint Committee on the Organization of Congress.[56] He proposed the institution of some half-dozen councils or committees, each covering a broad field of policy and administration: thus, foreign affairs, defense, fiscal policy, social security and social services, physical resources, commercial policy, and legal and organizational matters (civil service, etc.). Each of these councils or committees would be manned by a number of departmental chiefs, and it may be some of their immediate advisers, and some Congressmen of both minority and majority parties. Presumably, the chairman would be the departmental chief whose department was the principal focus of the field of policy covered—thus, for foreign affairs, the Secretary of State, or today for defense, the Secretary of Defense, and so on. The proposal was in part stimulated by President Roosevelt's action at that time of taking the Republican leaders as well as his own party friends into consultation on foreign relations, and by the operation of the Committee of Imperial Defense in England. But the proposal was not wedded to the chairmanship belonging to the principal department chief, since its author talks of the President placing direction in the hands "of a trusted staff adviser, who could act as the focal point for the formulation of policies." And, furthermore, the author had proposed to the President's Committee on Administrative Management that the six aides to the President should conduct coordinating work in this very sense.[57] It would be left entirely to the President to decide whether the opposition would be members of the committees, and to him also what individuals should be called, whether of his own party or not.

Then, the six committees, already coordinating large provinces of cognate subjects, would themselves be marshalled by a single chief of staff to the President.

[55] Cf. J. D. Millett, *The Process and Organization of Government Planning* (New York, 1947) p. 163. In both a civil and military capacity the writer has been close to the centers of federal governmental planning.

[56] *Hearings*, Joint Committee on Organization of Congress, June 26, 1945, Part 4, p. 951 *et seq.*
[57] *Ibid.*, p. 964.

It is essential that the President should have . . . someone who would perform the kind of "Chief of Staff" functions that have been put upon, first, Justice Byrnes, and now upon Judge Vinson in the Office of War Mobilization and Reconstruction. Such a Chief of Staff, either especially named, or made Director of the Bureau of the Budget, might readily organize these staff functions of the six groups . . . for bringing together in a manageable way the reporting of information, the research, and the policy clearinghouse upon which both President and Congress must depend. I would make bold to say that during the five years that I have spent in Washington, the major difficulties which we have encountered have arisen from the lack of adequate staff planning and coordination of policies, quite as much as from the inevitable difficulties of an improvised administration faced with the gigantic problem of modern war. We need to look ahead as to the effects of policies, of conflicting jurisdiction, and not to have all our time taken up in trouble-shooting avoidable messes.

These staff assistants to the President, at the head of each committee, were not designed as super-cabinet officers, but chairmen of advisory staff committees, whose responsibility would be to the President through a chief of staff. "Short of the President, and in the last analysis, of Congress itself, there can be no ultimate policy resolution" under the existing arrangement.

The prime problem still remains with us: Could such coordination be effective, even on a lower plane than the highest policy, while all policies, and especially crucial and unresolved ones, must go to the President, and when all those that are resolved virtually take the authority out of the hands of the President though still leaving him with responsibility? Could he possibly yield the supreme coordinating authority to his top chief of staff without emptying himself of power? The answer to that lies in President Roosevelt's admission, reported earlier in the discussion.[58]

The President needs more than help: he needs to be put into commission—but a true collective commission, virtually elected by the people, and merged with the legislature. It is no longer possible to repeat, with what seems to have been an air of satisfaction, Justice Brandeis's dictum that the doctrine of the separation of powers was adopted by the convention of 1787 "not to promote efficiency but to preclude the exercise of arbitrary power. The purpose was not to avoid friction, but, by means of the inevitable friction incident to the distribution of the governmental powers among three departments, to save the people from autocracy." [59] It may be true, but is it relevant?

If, then, radical reform is not possible, let us not believe that an incantation about "responsibility" and the wealth of the United States is enough. We owe ourselves clarity.

I have put the difficulties in the way of reform with full force, so that it may not be argued either that I do not know them or that I ignore them. Yet such difficulties may be overcome by a change of mind among those who can lead public opinion. It is a change of mind and intention that is needful. What an era of continued impotence, floundering, and corruption would British government still have suffered, if Jeremy Bentham and his one handful of friends had not dared to invent what was necessary and right, and proceeded to agitate for its acceptance! No vested interest in small-time pottering ought to be allowed to obstruct the upsurge of young men devoted to a new and more effectual vision.

What is of the most urgent importance is that no American student, and still less any American teacher, should permit himself to be seduced into not seeing faults and remedies just because they may have been rehearsed by foreign observers. The most public-spirited attitude surely is that which may be suggested by Rembrandt's picture, "The School of Anatomy." The teacher stands at the table with the scalpel; the body is laid open; the students observe. Is the man with the scalpel concerned with the nationality

---

[58] P. 671 above.

[59] *Myers* v. *United States*, 272 U.S. 52 (1926).

of the dissected body, or is medicine his first loyalty? Can you identify the nationality of the man on the dissecting table? Will the gazing students shut their eyes, simply because the teacher may have come from abroad, from Padua, or Bologna, or Oxford, to the things revealed to their minds by his neutral steel of insight? And, if the heart laid open should prove not to have done its duty to the now no longer living arteries, will they because they are Dutch, and the teacher is French or Italian or perhaps a Spanish friend of Cristofero Columbo, say, despite the final cold facts, "The heart, nevertheless, is sound"?

Part Six

THE CIVIL SERVICE

If there were always at the head of the administration a man whose comprehensive genius embraced all the circumstances, whose responsive and flexible mind knew how to conform its plans and wishes thereto; who, endowed with an ardent spirit and a tranquil reason, were passionate in the pursuit of the good, and calm in the choice of means; who, a judge upright and sensible of the rights of different classes of the community, knew how to hold the balance between their pretensions with a steady hand: who, conceiving a just idea of the public weal, promoted it without precipitation, and, considering the passions of men as a fruit of the earth, proportioned their development to that of eternal Nature, and set up no picture of perfection except to excite his own courage and not to irritate himself with the obstacles. . . .—N E C K E R

Nothing goes by itself: that is one of the errors of administration.—N A P O L E O N

27

The Civil Service in the Modern State

THE function of the civil service in the modern state is not merely the improvement of government; without it, indeed, government itself would be impossible. The civil service is a professional body of officials, permanent, paid, and skilled. Its numbers are a measure of the activities of the state and an indication of its nature. Already the totals of public employees—taking central and local government together, and including the industrial staffs—range from some one in ten of the gainfully occupied in the United States to something like one in five in Britain, France and Germany. The increase during the last hundred and twenty years is shown in Table 22, and it can be forecast that the numbers will increase.

THE GENERAL ASPECT

FEW doctrines are more productive of error than that which avoids the solution of the difficulties of state activity by abstractly relying upon the term "institution." It is certainly a valuable gain made in the written and oral teaching of the last fifty years that the too familiar abstractions of "sovereignty," "state," "government" have been at once reduced in their traditional authority over our minds and enlarged in body and perspective to mean concrete institutions.

Yet institutions are nothing more or less than men. No institution rises above the quality of its inventors and personnel. The ultimate possibilities of solving problems of government lie in the nature of the men and women who compose the institution. Plato did not err when he concentrated upon the training of his Guardians, and much political thought since his day has been a rediscovery of his supreme insight.

Modern governments assign the rights and duties of government to almost all "uncertified" people over 21 years of age. Our inquiry into the practice of government has already included the voters and their representatives. It must now proceed to consider these among the population who have adopted the service of the state as a professional career. We have, indeed, already made it plain that the efficacy of state action is far from being dependent upon the professional servants of the state alone, for it receives its animation and direction from the psyche and resources of the general population among whom the civil servants work. It is equally true, however, that be the population and their resources never so favorable, the quality of state action can be reduced to a base level by the unsuitability of the professionals and their organization.

Indeed, this problem tends more and more to outweigh any other in the modern state and even to assume a critical importance. For the actual and immediate application of political power to cases varying from one person to the whole population is carried on by the

TABLE 22—THE GROWTH OF CIVIL SERVICES[a] (CENTRAL AND LOCAL[b]): 1821–1946

Year	Great Britain[c]		France[e]		Prussia[f]		Germany[g]		U.S.A.[h]		Year
	Civil[d] service (thousands)	Population (millions)	Civil service (thousands)	Population (millions)	Civil service (thousands)	Population (millions)	Civil service (thousands)	Population (millions)	Civil service (thousands)	Population (millions)	
1821	27	14.1	—	30.4	[1800 23 [1850	11.6	—	—	8	9.6	1821
1841	17	18.5	90	34.2	25	15.0	—	—	23	17.1	1841
1861	59	23.1	248	37.4	—	18.5	—	—	49	31.4	1861
1881	81	29.7	379	37.6	152	27.5	452	45.4	107	50.2	1881
1901	153	37.0	451	39.0	250	35.0	907	56.9	256	76.0	1901
1911	644	40.8	699	39.6	342	41.0	1,159	65.4	370	92.0	1911
1921	958	42.8	1,212	39.2	390	38.1	1,753	63.2	597	105.7	1921
1928[i]	1,024	44.7	1,008	40.7	443	39.1	1,187	64.4	609	122.7	1928
1946	2,336	47.8	1,429[j]	40.5	—	—	—	—	2,128	146.0[k]	1946
Labor force (approximate)	—	21.0 (1946)	—	21.0 (1946)	—	14.0 (1939)	—	34.0 (1939)	—	60.0 (1946)	

[a] *Caution.* In spite of the greatest care and use of the best sources, these figures are only approximate: it is highly dangerous to compare those for each country in different years (since census methods and scope have varied), and even more dangerous to compare the figures for different countries since here even the definition of civil service varies. We have attempted to include all paid, professional, full- and part-time civil servants of the central and local authorities, *excluding* military and naval services, judges and magistrates, police and teachers. We have *included* all other civil servants whether "established" or "unestablished," whether administrative, clerical, manipulative, or "industrial" (i.e., postal and railway workers, for example), whether drawing salaries or fees or wages. The task has been exceedingly difficult, and there are errors and uncertainties. A fascinating history could, of course, be written, recounting *why* the growth we record took place. Cf. F. Morstein-Marx on this subject relating to Germany, *American Political Science Review*, 1935, p. 451 ff.

[b] We attempted originally to include only the servants of the central authority, but France and Germany lump *all* officials together; their method was followed in order to get the major amount of comparison possible.

[c] Census returns, occupational analysis, for 1861–1921; for 1928, *Treasury Memoranda to Royal Commission on Civil Service, 1929*, with 1921 figures of local government servants.

[d] No local government officials included until 1861. In earlier years there were none; later, not available until 1861. The apparently astonishing leap after 1901 is due to the inclusion of large classes of "additional" workers, i.e., mainly industrial and manipulative. The census, before 1911, was unsatisfactory on this score.

[e] Computed from *Bulletin de la Statistique Générale de la France*, October, 1913, article by Lucien March, "Contribution à la Statistique des Fonctionnaires." Figures for 1841 are those for 1839, and are *central* officials only; figures for 1861 are really for 1866. Figures for 1921 are from Census (*Statistique Générale*), Vol. I, Part IV; for 1928, from information supplied by Lucien March, of the *Institut de Statistique de l' Université de Paris*.

[f] Figures for 1800 and 1850 represent central officials only, and include police. They were supplied by ministerial director, Dr. Arnold Brecht, of the Prussian Ministry of Finance, with

civil service, and not by the people, legislature or executive. How far does a close
view of the apparatus of public administration warrant such a judgment of the
importance of the part played by the civil
service? The answer to this question
hangs upon two considerations: the nature and the extent of state activity, and
the comparative contributions therein of
the politician and the administrator.

It must already be quite clear that the
salient feature of modern government is
its positive and wholesale activity. That
does not mean that in earlier ages the
state either theoretically or actually abandoned a positive part. We have seen, on
the contrary, that this was not so, and
that, in fact, the state from its inception
onwards claimed and exercised the power
to regulate and control social activities
over large territories and wide fields of
human enterprise. Except for a short
period, from about 1800 to 1832, state action did not slacken though it may have
been incompetent. It is highly probable,
also, that the regulatory power of the
state will go on increasing, perhaps for
centuries. That which is novel about
modern state activity, and that which,
also, causes us to believe vaguely that it
is an entirely fresh phenomenon, is its
extent and method. Nothing like such
regulation of human activity has been
attempted outside ancient theocracies.

Further, this activity differs from the
old in its scope, its minuteness and its
instruments. In scope, it hardly fails to
envisage any branch of the moral or material sides of human endeavor. The
record is written on the roads, the gutters,
and the buildings, and spells what the
state has done in order that society may
have a modicum of wisdom, protection
of person against criminals and mechanically propelled vehicles, environmental
and personal defense against deadly bac-
teria as well as against economic misery.
The annual thousands of rules and orders, the detailed and present plan of
activity of all modern states, reveal how
the state concentrates upon each individual and weaves his every impulse into
the myriad-threaded warp of its existence.
No second in the day is unprovided for;
and for the many simultaneous events of
each second there is the exact and predetermined form or officer. Though some
may not admire, few can fail to wonder
at, this vast, involved scheme, which no
single mind has ever completely analyzed
in even a thousandth part of its extent.
The state is everywhere; it leaves hardly
a gap. But it is different today than, say,
in the eighteenth century, when it could
do little more than make a claim to power
by issues of statutes, orders, proclamations, and rules, while now its own professional servants calculate, control, and

reserve. Thenceforward to 1911 they were obtained by computation from the *Statistisches
Jahrbuch für den Preussischen Staat*, which began in 1903. Figure for 1921 from *Beamten-Archiv*
(1921) with allowance for local government; for 1928 from *Finanzstatitichen Teil der Statistitichen
Korrespondenz*, Berlin, October 3, 1930. Naturally, the Prussian figures are from 1871 onwards
a constituent part of the *Reich*'s. They must not be added together.

g Occupational census in *Statistik des deutschen Reichs, Neue Folge*, 1882, 1895, 1907, 1925. For
1928 the analysis in *Wirtschaft und Statistik*, 1930, p. 650. When the Prussian figures are subtracted from those of Germany (which includes all the states, all the local authorities, and the
federal government), the figure remaining is one for all the other states and local authorities
and the federal authority.

h *Statistical Abstract of the United States*, 1930, Table 177. *This is for the federal authority only.* To
find the full number of American central and local services would involve discovering undiscoverable figures of the forty-eight States and all the local authorities.

i Of which about 1.4 million are local, including teachers. Nationalized corporations
excluded of *Monthly Bulletin of Statistics*.

j Of which about 360,000 are local, including teachers. State industries excluded. Figures
supplied by French Information Service (New York) from computations of the Civil Service
Commissioner in attendance on the President of the Council of Ministers.

k Add some 3,000,000 for states, cities, counties, etc. Figure in table is for June, 1947. U. S.
Bureau of the Census.

apply those commands. Where formerly the state was wont to issue a proclamation, it nowadays deputes an officer. Few states have ever imagined that to command was enough, but no states until the eighteenth century began to employ public administrators on a scale sufficient to make the commands effective. Where the state used to rule by punishing offenders after the law was broken, it now anticipates errors of personal and corporate behavior and seeks to prevent them by the action of its officials. Even in the eighteenth century only one state, Prussia, had arrived at anything like our modern perception of public administration managed by a force of people, especially and systematically trained, recruited, and paid, to the exclusion of any other occupation, to execute the commands of the state.

The civil service is as much the product of the spiritual and mechanical factors of western civilization as are all other political institutions. The nineteenth century turned away from the impotent survival of unsalaried, untrained officers, who, as the records of the seventeenth and eighteenth century show, were illiterate and unwilling whether they were of the common people, the lesser gentry, or the nobility. Gradually the "honorary" officer ceased to play a part in translating the commands of the estate into social and individual behavior.

For two things were realized, though not uniformly in the countries under discussion. The first is that a rational order in industrial effort and organization demands the inclusion of all the best-skilled elements to do the required work, regardless of their social position, religious beliefs, political party, and (more recently) their sex; and the exclusion from the administrative apparatus of all those with such adventitious qualities, but lacking the specific skill. The tendency toward economic rationalism which triumphed to such a degree in the field, the factory, the office, and the stock exchange triumphed also in the creation of the civil service.

Second was the realization of the social advantage of division of labor. More conspicuously in the nineteenth than in any other century, did people group themselves into trade and professional categories moved by the vague sense that only in this way was the maximum amount of skill and productivity attainable. Society could now obtain the high standard of living which had become its god, by the knowledge and use of scientific technique functioning in a highly complicated organization. This technique could only be acquired in its minutest exactness, and practiced with the highest efficiency, if people undertook only as much as could be mastered. One branch of such science and art was administration or management, and such a profession of administration could be exercised under either private employers or the state. Indeed, recent discussion goes far towards assimilating private to public officialdom for purposes of scientific analysis. The activities of the state grew enormously for reasons we have described elsewhere, and with them, naturally, the managerial class [1] necessary to carry them out. It is clear, then, I think, that the growth of some of the cardinal and least-questioned principles of modern civilization brought about the establishment and growth of a professional civil service, and that the realization of those principles would have been impossible without such a service. Nor must we forget the part played by the democratic urge of "the career open to the talents," produced by the belief in the equality of men, the desire for freedom of opportunity, and hatred of the official privileges of the aristocracy.

Modern states, then, directly employ very large numbers of people who make the service of the state a life-long professional matter. It would be possible, or it is at least conceivable, that the legislatures, jealous of the public officials, might themselves attempt to formulate the rules and regulations to implement the statutes. If they did so, we have amply

[1] I used this term ten years before James Burnham's *The Managerial Revolution* (New York, 1941), and use it still without his extreme conclusions.

shown that they would need to increase their own numbers enormously, reorganize their timetable, and revolutionize their working habits and procedures. They would in fact have to supply themselves with whole-time experts. And if they tried to emulate the ancient city-states and to accomplish the actual enforcement of law by officials who were elected for short terms and unpaid, the laws would in fact not be enforced. The task to be done is immense (departments of government employ anything from two or three thousand to over a hundred thousand). The intricacy of the task, the need for continuity and regular and punctual attention, with a sense of enduring and unslackening responsibility, and above all, the scientific and technical knowledge required, make impossible any substantial reliance for the actual operation of the services on the people, the legislature, the political parties. A reading of the list of the hundreds of different jobs under the broad classifications of any civil service will indicate the concrete activities for which alone a lifetime must be spent to secure mastery and efficiency in practice.

The part played in government by the civil service is, then, of tremendous importance. In what respect are they governors? What is their part relative to that played by those other and elected elements who stand in the closest connection with them?

The earlier discussion in the chapter on the separation of powers has explained the politico-administrative connection. The business of the electorate, of legislatures and chief executives, is a double one: it is compounded of conflict and propulsion. They undertake to overcome popular opposition to their schemes for using the national resources, and by a multitude of devices, from academic discussion to the ruthless use of violence, they make their scheme effective. Those who triumph, and thereby come into possession of the legitimate power of the state, could, it is conceivable, employ their own party followers to help them to carry out their policy, and for centuries, in fact, this was considered good poli-

tics and adequate administration. But this practice was made impossible *first,* by the growth in the scope and detail of social policy, the division of labor, which, claiming the continuous energy of men in a set and special field, reduced the number of potential party rank-and-file; and *second,* by the need for technical skill. Thus the political power acquired by electoral victory, or through the influence of the privileged, had necessarily to be distributed among the few who acquired authority to command, and the many who were permanently employed to serve by the best technical means. Because the authority of scientific technique has so won its way among all sections of the population, it is now an almost universally accepted idea that those who professionally serve in a technical capacity can do so without affecting policy, or if they affect policy, that they do this impartially, without political tendencies and intentions and as a result of the sheer scientific value and significance of their advice and their assistance. They are the human transmitters of general forces and laws and nothing more. It is because a dozen or a score of men cannot today manage millions of people without a large body of servants and much machinery, and because a vast range of science, which the politician does not possess, is required to accomplish this, that we say that though the legislature, the cabinet, and the presidents may rule, the civil service administers.

It is a mistake in observation to lay the main weight on the public services as the "core of the modern state." "The core" is a misleading metaphor: it obscures the practical as well as the theoretical supremacy of public opinion and the elected legislatures and executive. Being a mistake of observation, it is accordingly wrong doctrine. It is, moreover, likely to be productive of a faulty public ideal. (Max Weber was first responsible for this bias.[2]) But an enormous and indispensa-

---

[2] *Parlement und Regierung* (München, 1918), p. 14: "In the modern state the real government effectuates itself neither in parliamentary debates nor in royal proclamations but in

ble service is rendered by the great corps of professional and scientific and administrative and clerical experts, together with their manipulative assistants. They contribute special expertness: they know the facts. They work as continuously and as long as a rational plan for the job to be done dictates, not under the artificial limitation of electoral periods. Whereas the politician who directs them is the instrument of popular desire and will, the public official supplies the natural or social-scientific veracities which determine how desire may be fulfilled or whether it must be modified or abandoned. He indicates ways to satisfy desire or will with the minimum sacrificial obligations which citizens must bear if laws are to be carried out. I need go no further in praise of the expert, though in view of some essays on the limitations of the expert—by whom our civilization lives—it would be in order.[3]

THE NATURE OF CIVIL SERVICE ACTIVITY

WE must now attempt to answer the question: what general qualities distinguish the activity and organization of state servants? and we may do this by describing them with comparative reference to the qualities of private industry. In this way we shall discover the features upon which to fix our attention.

The Urgency of State Services. Not all the services rendered by men to each other come equally under control of the state. Some, indeed, are entirely uncontrolled by the laws. There are very few such services. It is easier to see the varying extent of control, which ranges from the official registration of contracts to the actual stipulation of prices and the management of industries; from the cleansing of a street to the compulsory isolation of a fever-stricken citizen; from the application of general principles of "public-

policy" to the compulsory supply of certain services.

What impelled men to force the state to take upon itself these functions? These functions were undertaken because they were so essential to the maintenance and continuation of the state desired that their conduct could not be left to the privately established institutions of individual persons. This was shown by experience. Fear, pride, pity, charity—and a hundred other human elements—operated along devious and amazing ways to cause men to demand the large-scale, socialized, and permanent organization of certain services. Such were the relief of the destitute and the organization of the labor market, the provision of public health services, free education, the building of highways, the running of postal services, and many others.

All these services have certain common qualities. All have a quality of urgency, an urgency which takes its tone from the publicly accepted philosophy of the time. They are urgent because a high standard of living is desired, or because illness or death may result from their absence, or because—we do not quite know why—it is morally right, and here our reasons border on the mysticism of religion and are supported by vague conceptions of God, Progress, Evolution, Reason, World History, the Future, and many other things to which we have as yet given no name. When the urgency of these desires seems unlikely to obtain satisfaction from the independently created agencies of individual men, the state is asked to shoulder the burden. And so the state, as we have already said, becomes many things: a telephone, telegraph, and postal company, one enormous hospital, an army, a navy, an electricity-supply company, an association for the organization of trade relationships with other countries and within its own territory, an informative research service, a giant school with many grades, an insurance company, a bank, a coal mining corporation: the list of the state's incarnations is inexhaustible. But the state is incarnate because a special urgency affects each of these services.

---

the exercise of administration in daily life, necessarily and unavoidably in the hands of the civil service."
[3] Harold J. Laski, *Limitations of the Expert* (Fabian Society, London, 1935); Ernest Barker, *Reflections on Government* (Oxford, 1942).

It is a risk—nay, a peril—which the majority of inhabitants cannot contemplate undertaking (so experience has shown), to leave private, uncoordinated activity in charge of such services. Hence the special emphasis upon continuity in the public services; the tendency to keep governmental activities immune from judicial control and punishment; the great prestige attaching to official appointments, with the frequent corollary that men serve with their highest energies regardless of monetary reward, while with some the power flies to the head, and their conceit issues in disobliging "bureaucratic" behavior.

Large-Scale Organization. An activity of the state has usually been commended for control or management by the state because it is desirable that roughly the same main principles should be operative all over a large area (e.g., public education), or because safety of health or person demands it (e.g., motor-truck certification), or because it is economical to plan and operate over a large area (e.g., transport), or because some peculiar efficiency is to be obtained by central initiative (e.g., management of coal mines). For economy it is necessary to avoid duplication of lesser staffs and to concentrate control and operation in fewest hands. This is not a doom of the state's activities. Decentralization is possible and is one of the rationally conducted acts of modern administration.[4] But usually the organization under one control is large. Hence, much administration is accomplished not by immediate personal confrontations of the situation to be solved—and all situations are local and personal —but from afar, by writing, and report, and recording, and paper analysis. This is mitigated by the fact that modern communications make possible more than ever before action or investigation on

the spot by central officials. The defects of centralization are also mitigated by the remarkable development of standards and units, costs, and results, so that local observers can transmit to the center reports and figures which have the same vivid meaning at the center as they have at the extremities. Yet the personal impact of the complainant consumer is desirable. Too much public service activity is still impersonal.

Monopoly and No Price. The state's services are completely, or almost completely, monopolies; and the state renounces almost entirely charging the consumer a price, or a direct *quid pro quo* for value received. It treats all its clients alike, and does not charge what the markets will bear or make a profit on one citizen to recoup itself for the loss on another. The public services operate, fundamentally, to make universal provision of a necessary service to all who need it. The principle of price in a competitive market full of competitive consumers is discarded.

Since the state has a monopoly, its service cannot be judged by the results attained in like industries operating outside state control. Nor can the citizen threaten to find a competitive service of supply. Since the state charges an equal price to all, or no price whatever, a quantitative estimate of value is lacking, and the consumer is deprived of the ordinary means of expressing his judgment. As a rule, the consumer measures the difficulty of earning—or the unwillingness of parting with—his money, against the satisfaction he anticipates from a commodity or service he desires. He can pretty flexibly register his judgment of the comparative value of different quantities of goods at different prices by means of a price paid or withheld. Anticipation of his demand causes the production of goods in the special quantity and quality and time called for. The supplier who meets the conditions profits in proportion as he meets them: he who does not tends to become insolvent. There is a fairly direct relationship between efficiency and profit, value and payment, in the free

---

[4] Cf. D. H. Truman, *Administrative Decentralization* (Chicago, 1941); Herman Finer, *English Local Government*, 4th edition (London, 1949); G. D. H. Cole, *Regional and Local Government* (London, 1947); William Anderson and others, *State and Local Relationships* (Chicago, 1947); David Lilienthal, *T.V.A.* (New York, 1944).

equal before the law . . . Public privileges or disadvantages of birth or rank are to be abolished." In France the jurisprudence of the *Conseil d'État* is thus summed up in Jezè [9]: "All individuals fulfilling certain conditions, fixed in a general and impersonal manner by the organic law of the service (law, rules, general instructions) have the legal power of demanding the service which is the object of the public service: this is the principle of the equality of individuals in relation to public administration." The Bank of England charter under nationalization requires the governors to be "equal and indifferent to all manner of persons."

These principles exclude partiality: do they exclude adaptability? They do not in theory, but they tend to in practice. As state activity increases, this principle of fundamental equality with appropriate difference becomes of more and more importance in the relationships of public and service. It excludes differences of treatment which are liable to creep in, such as political antagonism, sex preferences, and religious and class differences, but the very serviceability of official action requires that there shall be differences of treatment according to the nature of the time, place, and person.

Limited Enterprise. Public officials are officials; they are not politicians or statesmen; they are not legislators. They may be and should be advisers, and must be executives. But their enterprise is not their own to decide upon. They cannot take the liberties or property of the citizen at their free discretion, offering him in return certain services or goods as a businessman does. They operate within the minimum and maximum permissions stated in the statutes. Admittedly and necessarily the statutes give them some discretion, always under the safeguard, however, of political executive direction and control, and of legislative and judicial remedies. The faults of officials are therefore frequently the faults of the laws,

not of themselves. Sometimes they suffer from the frustrations of eager men limited by what they regard as irrational blinkers on useful activities and ideas. But just as the private entrepreneur will not be rewarded for the services he is not asked to produce, and may think how silly his customer is, so the civil servant is obliged to administer the laws which do not permit him to supply what he personally likes. If he did otherwise, the cry of "despotism" [10] would rightly arise. The effect on the mentality of the service is discouraging: that in private industry continuously encouraging.

Public Accountability. Democratic systems of government have established devices to keep the public servant accountable, or responsible, to the representatives of the people. How necessary these devices are can be appreciated from some of the observations already made regarding the monopoly and largescale nature of the services. They live, as one observer has remarked, in a goldfish bowl: [11] their every activity is liable to Peeping Toms, and the Peeping Toms can punish them. This cannot but inject in them an appreciable caution, a determination not to make mistakes. They will insist on records and files, will carefully consider the law before a decision is reached, and even then will hedge. Accountability makes for hierarchy and subordination, as the top men try to avoid involvement in responsibility by subordinates. It tends to dampen the independence of mind and contribution which the younger men in the department may make to policy building, for the chief will accept only what he can defend. Resolute attempts therefore must be made to institute deliberately counterhabits to the tremors and rigors induced by the peering eye and the prodding finger. A story is told of the United States Department of Agriculture in the New Deal days. A public-spirited new arrival in the department thought how useful it would be if he

---

[9] *Les Principes Généraux de Droit Administratif*, 3rd edition (Paris, 1925-30), Vol. III, p. 20.

[10] Cf. Lord Hewart, *The New Despotism* (London, 1928); and James Beck, *Our Wonderland of Bureaucracy* (New York, 1932).

[11] J. Juran, *Bureaucracy* (New York, 1944).

could transfer the income from one activity to expenditure on a fresh activity. When the department's legal adviser was asked what possible objection there could be to this good idea (and note that he was asked), his answer over his oldfashioned pince-nez was, "They cut off King Charles' head for that!" But in dictatorial states, also, the head looks upward to the dictator or falls off. Hence a congenital tendency to "red tape," *paperasserie,* and *Vielschreiberei,* and a special fear of rashness.

"Establishment" or Hierarchy. The rather inflexible determination of the scope and nature of state activity by the executive and legislature, and the impossibility of prompt and frequent resilience, result in the conception and practice of an "establishment," that is, a carefully graded hierarchy and number of posts with duties and salaries to match. This is not normally alterable or escapable, so that civil servants affected by the public atmosphere of free and developing industry which surrounds them, and faced with an almost certain prospect of no exceptional changes in their favor, become very sensitive about promotions, and their morale can become pathologically affected unless special attention is paid to the equity of the promotion system.

Grading of Its Members. Both the impossibility of accurate money measurement of the civil servant's output, and the ultimate impossibility of legislative control of finance unless based upon a few simple, unchanging standards, impel to the creation of grades or classes of servants. Legislative control would be quite impossible if every head of a department had the right to bargain with each servant on an independent basis; this may cause great unfairness as between one kind of duty and another.

Directness of Government. Since the civil service is concerned with the direct execution of government in relation to the citizens, and since it is immediately compelling, it is naturally disliked. All groups feel that their burdens in the state are more significant than their gratifications from membership of it. That

is a universal tendency of human nature. The bearer of ill tidings, moreover, is not seldom personally blamed for the disaster. There must always seem to be too many civil servants: they must always appear to be officious and hard of heart: and the benefits which they have to bestow must always seem to be slowly and grudgingly given. There are few citizens, indeed, who can see into and beyond the action of an official, and detect the ultimate groups and interests upon whose behalf he is, in the last resort, acting in any particular instance. Public officials are too often blamed for the law and the policy made by the legislative or executive, when the latter are really at fault.

Lack of Ruthlessness. The services do not act primarily to make a profit. They are largely philanthropic. Many services were assumed by the state on philanthropic grounds, and, in recent years, to improve the condition of the worker pained by the insecurity of his economic lot. Ruthlessness is banished, because it is believed that the state ought to be a "model" employer, and further, the "established" nature of the service tends to exclude personal competition. Hence, "once in the service, always in the service." Neither colleagues nor superiors care to speak with harsh judgment of each other or subordinates, personal reports are frankly discriminatory, disciplinary power is seldom employed, and dismissal as a penalty is exceedingly rare. It becomes a special concern, then, to discover the conditions of restful, inventive work, *within* these limits.

Anonymity and Impartiality. The modern system of ministerial responsibility and of changing political executives unequivocally demands that civil servants shall do their work without personal public blame or praise for policy, and that they shall act with impartial, but enterprising and unrelaxing, helpfulness to governments of any party complexion. This demand involves certain rules and standards of conduct to be obeyed by both ministers and civil servants, and especially affects the methods of recruitment, the political and economic rights

misdirected zeal. Authority causes some men to grow, but others only to swell. Bureaucracy is not public officialdom; it is the infirmities of a profession, for which well-known practicable prophylactics and remedies exist.

The problem of bureaucracy is not a problem of the public offices alone. It involves the three elements in the state: the bureaus, the legislature, and the public. Each has its indispensable contribution to make, and the fulfillment of it by any two can be frustrated by the default of the third. The legislature owes, above all, careful drafting of the laws so that responsibility may be clear and tasks defined. It owes a twentieth-century rationalization of its machinery and methods, so that it may survey—amply, patiently, and thoughtfully—the work of millions of public producers. And, supremely, it owes to the nation the deep sincere obligation of treating public servants as average business men and women working for their living in the business of the public. This implies that partisan injustice and spiteful sneers be restrained, and that the legislature conduct its necessary and desirable investigations not as operations of torment or as self-righteous exhibitions of hatred and contempt or as invitations to the public to spit upon alleged sensational scandals. It is easy in a democracy to get the public to laugh away its political assets, and someone is always ready to cheer the iconoclast. If the members of the legislature make a goat of public officials, they cut off democracy's right hand. An awful responsibility is incumbent on parliamentary institutions in this, the twentieth century.

Finally, the public has its duties. It must recognize that the consumer is sometimes wrong. It need not condone inefficiency; it ought to make complaints. But it owes a self-control over spite and derision and it ought to hear both sides. It should not permit its legislators to cry out, "Good hunting!" whenever they see a civil servant. To hate government is infantile, for government is necessary. And what is necessary should be suffi-

ciently respected to encourage the invention and application of improvements. It should never be forgotten that a vast part of modern private enterprise has—either by deliberate collusion or by the manifest benefits of large-scale organization—come under single managements, which, because they lack competition and are of great size, have succumbed to the diseases we know as "bureaucracy." [16]

Finally, the supreme importance of recruiting and retaining persons stands out like a beacon in the efficiency of the public service. If the right people are obtained, they are able to know and do all the things that otherwise cumbrous procedures must be invoked to do. Such are decentralization; correct division of the work among departments and divisions and subdivisions; [17] proper marshaling and leadership of the technical forces; useful application of advisory and research committees; and then, as level upon level rises to the final political governors in the executive and the legislature, coordination of the persons and authorities necessary to advance stage by stage in reasonable progress. These divisions of function come about because a single human being is unable to do everything all the time: as the technical jargon goes, his "span of control" is limited.[18] The distribution of responsibilities occurs in order not to overload any single official with more than science teaches us he can bear. But then, again, for wise policy and effective action the parts must again be brought together, once more because of the limitations of the individual: he sees his own job intensively and his eyes get glued properly, thereto. Yet something must transcend the pieces that compose the jigsaw puzzle of state. Or-

---

[16] This much is well demonstrated in Professor Marshall Dimock's monograph on *Bureaucracy and Trusteeship in Large Corporations* (Temporary National Economic Committee Monograph, U.S. Government Printing Office, 1938).

[17] Cf. Schuyler Wallace, *Federal Departmentalization* (New York, 1941).

[18] Cf. *ibid.*, and L. Urwick and Luther Gulick, *op. cit.*

ganization does this but again, organization is worked by human minds. The personnel problem then is sovereign. Inferior men and women can defeat the finest departmentalization, whether at the center, whether between the center and the localities, whether in the form of release of powers to quasi-subordinate functional bodies. Personnel is sovereign. If men and women are competent enough, they can give life even to inexact, confused, and rough-hewn demarcations. Personnel is the sovereign factor in public administration. Will and mind are first; they engender policy; and mechanism is subsidiary to function.

In the coming chapters, accordingly, attention is confined to personnel problems; and within that focus is another, namely, concern for the top manage-

ment, or administrative, groups. Apart from considerations of scope, the reason for this is the supreme importance of the advisory and directing function at the summit. But also, the broad masses of the service offer fewer tough "public" problems, seeing that they perform either the average jobs of the service or the highly specialist ones. The tempo and morale and creativeness of these is either unamenable to any very considerable improvement by managerial tactics, while the specialism carries with it qualities of morale and professional standards which are at once definable, examinable, and controllable, whether top management is good, bad, or indifferent. The problem here is chiefly how to release upwards by promotion those of exceptional talent into the administrative class at the apex.

28

Origins and General Character: Germany

WE now seek to deepen our understanding of administrative problems by reviewing in broad outline the administrative experience of a number of countries. Each country has its own history, each its own direction and pace in the course of the last three centuries, and therefore each regards modern questions from a different point of view and asks them out of a different experience.

The country with the longest serious study and experience of a civil service and its problems is Germany. What I have to say here is the common heritage of Germany, but in the main it refers more exactly to the history of Prussia. The character of that influence in known to all the world as "bureaucracy." This was more the outcome of historical accidents than inborn temper, and now that it is challenged by the sovereign popular assemblies, it is likely to change its nature within a generation or two. No biological feature stamps Prussia as inevitably bureaucratic, but merely an accident of organization in the past, remediable perhaps in the future. Ancient purposes compelled her to forge bureaucratic instruments. The political error was not that such instruments were ever used, but that they were retained after their primary purposes had been accomplished.

If, from an early date, the German civil services were bureaucratic, they were also regarded as professions conferring great honor upon those who followed them. Indeed, in every state the civil service was the most honored profession, though in some, like Prussia, the higher military services were considered slightly superior. It was not snobbery that set this standard, but service and the expectation of service to prince and people. At a time (1723) when England and America in this respect were barbarian, and France profligate, rules of training and recruitment were formulated in Prussia which successfully provided efficient staffs. Indeed, it is plain that energies as mighty as those which England devoted to the creation of parliamentary institutions were in Prussia turned to the establishment of administrative institutions. While England was founding the constitutional state by the bloody struggles between the Stuarts and Parliamentarians, Frederick William, the Great Elector of Brandenburg, in struggles as bloody, consolidated his state, uprooted the remnants of feudal administration, and created the administrative organization indispensable to an efficient absolute monarchy. In 1688 when the Great Elector died, his legacy was an army and a civil service; in 1688 when William of Orange ascended the English throne, the English reward of a half-century's efforts was a sovereign Parliament. Thenceforward the cleverest young men in England passed (or did not pass) from the universities to the political parties and the House of Commons, while the clever young German, whether a Bavarian, Prussian, Hanoverian or Saxon, passed through grade after grade of actual and diverse administrative service, to become a statesman. Each system has its advantages and disadvantages, and each its philosophies. Political science in England maintained the turn it had taken prior to and during the Parliamentary struggle: it concerned itself principally with the question of political liberty and obligation. In Germany, cameralism, or the art and science of government by administrative departments (*Kammer*), attracted the best minds of the seventeenth and eighteenth centuries.

EARLY HISTORY

Recruitment. In Germany attention was early turned towards the problem of recruitment. This is, of course, the vital problem of the civil service. All depends upon the quality of the servants, and this is, to a large extent, governed by the terms of recruitment. Necessity and chance, as in all growth, had a large share in directing earnest attention to recruitment. The earliest formally qualified civil servants were the so-called "hired Doctors" (*gemietete Doktoren*) of the late fifteenth century. They were councilors forming part of the permanent or occasional entourage of the prince, and learned in the law.[1] There was, of course, no systematic organization of recruitment; the doctors of the law were engaged as they were needed, for the business of the rudimentary state did not require continuous services: in that it differs vitally from the modern state. The majority of the court officials who constituted the civil service of the time were men of high ecclesiastical status and of the nobility. These learned councilors were usually in the employ of more than one court. It is interesting to notice that with the institution of "hired doctors" there was introduced in Germany that connection between the civil service and legal training which is characteristic

of that country, and which has fallen in the course of time from being its highest glory to being, perhaps, its gravest defect.

In the next century, the full social and political force of the New Learning began to be felt and the reign of great states was beginning. The universities began to exert a vivifying effect upon intellectual life, and the state to develop from the private "estate" of the prince—the *seigneur*—into a more public thing. One set of officials acting in the localities in the service of the prince were concerned with military, police, and miscellaneous duties, including supervision of the municipalities; a second set were specially occupied with financial affairs; and a third conducted the administration of police, though, in the primitive division of powers, this included many things which we should today call administration. These central officials who, in Bavaria and other states, acted locally, were a powerful instrument of centralization owing to their education, which made them the frequent arbiters in disputes between powerful men, town, guild, and estate councils. Most of these officials were nobles, but in proportion as learning was required for the execution of their duties and as legally trained *bourgeois* became available and tended to be preferred by the antifeudal centralizing princes, the nobles were gradually forced to acquire a modicum of skill, either by formal instruction at the universities or by making the Grand Tour (*Kavaliertour*). The nobles lost ground rapidly in the two official categories where reading, writing, arithmetic, and legal skill were required: that is, in the financial and the judicial offices. For the office of defense and maintenance of the peace the non-learned, warlike noble was sufficient unto the time. At this date two troubles afflicted Germany which required more than a subsequent century of effort to eradicate. The large estate owners were made the royal officers and they were paid, as most officials then were, not in money, but in kind, the produce of the royal domains. The economic interest of these estate-owning officials tended to overcome their principles of

---

[1] Cf. S. Isaacsohn, *Geschichte des Preussischen Beamtentums* (Berlin, 1874), Vol. I; A. Lotz, *Geschichte des Deutschen Beamtentums* (Berlin, 1909), pp. 33 *et seq.*; C. Bornhak, *Geschichte des Preussischen Verwaltungsrechts* (Berlin, 1885), 3 vols.

good administration, and it became necessary to separate the economic management thereof. At the same time, the actual property of the noble was by no means completely under the direct government of the royal authority. A second danger threatened: one, indeed, which we shall show later (p. 750), entirely demoralized French public administration for two critically important centuries: the sale of offices and the alienation of jurisdiction. Under this system the office became, in the rudimentary condition of financial administration of the time, an easy means of producing revenue. A great deal of the State's field of administration was delivered over to private proprietors and towns. But Germany was energetic enough to purge herself (not entirely) of hereditary jurisdiction and sinecurists by 1700, while France succumbed.

The Reception of Roman Law. From the beginning of the sixteenth century, Roman law exerted a powerful influence upon the civilization of the Continent.[2] It taught the absolute authority of the *princeps.* The authority and the justice of the latter were pitted against those of the estates and localities, and caused the growth of a large popular literature of legal handbooks. The reception of Roman law, which took place over a period of two and a half centuries, can be said to have reached its completeness about 1550. The uncodified, largely unwritten and uncertain law of the Germanic states, varying from place to place and from court to court, and hardly deserving the name of application, since the subjective feeling of justice of the judges was paramount and unconnected with general principles, gave way gradually to a unified, crystallized, codified set of legal principles, the logic of which decided the fate of any particular case. The courts of law and administrative positions were opened only

to schooled lawyers.[3] There began that close and continuous and fruitful connection between the universities and the civil service which has not yet ceased and which other countries began to organize only about three centuries after this time.

At the same time, officialdom was influenced by the new conditions of commerce and law in other important directions. The councils of the prince received a more permanent and systematic organization than before, and both sessions and the division of work became more regular. The learned officials began to be paid in money and their contracts with the prince provided for their tenure and superannuation. To their character of mere servants of the prince's person they added that of servants of the public, for in the fiscal and other arrangements they made with the estates, the prince's opponents, they had to render justice not only as between prince and estates, but as between the various branches of the estates. The official councils became the resort of those who sought prompter justice than the occasional circuits of the courts could give, and by the end of the sixteenth century such official councils to advise the prince were accepted,[4] and were by the estates demanded, as indispensable to good princely government. Their cosmopolitan learning, their wide experience, and their conceptions of sovereignty made their temper anti-estate and anti-local. Since they were schooled, they could be turned to a variety of jobs, and in the consequent notation they learned the art of administration. Their centralizing spirit earned them the hatred of the estates, for, following the deliberate policy of the princes, they were frequently not natives of the state, but foreign-born, since these were more likely to side with their master than with the estates. Officials of the kind we nowadays call subordinate, or in Germany *subaltern,* were drawn from the middle class, obtained experience in town administration, and had a grammar-school education. They sometimes reached

---

2 See Stintzing, *Geschichte der Deutschen Rechtswissenschaft, Erste Abteilung,* pp. 21 *et seq.;* W. A. Holdsworth, *History of English Law,* 2nd edition (London 1922-38), Vol. IV; Stolzel, *Brandenburg-Preuszens Rechtsverwaltung und Rechtsverfassung* (Berlin, 1888), Vol. I, "Erster Teil."

3 Stintzing, *op. cit.,* p. 52 *et seq.*
4 Cf. Lotz, *op. cit.,* p. 58.

the highest offices. The usages of the time included the receipt of presents as well as fees.

The Seventeenth Century. It is in the seventeenth century that we can better see the growth of the modern state exerting its inevitable influence upon the civil service. The civil service was the royal answer to feudal pretensions and local patriotism. As loyalties and services were withdrawn from their feudal and local possessors, they were transferred to the centralized civil service. Broadly, they combined almost complete centralization with careful, deliberate, and clever organization of the various central councils. A central financial and budgetary system, a privy council for high politics, and a central and supreme judicial court were set up. The administrative center of gravity was the Exchequer (*Hofkammer*). The Exchequers then laid down financial policy and drew up financial legislation; they were the controlling authority for the royal domains, an appreciable source of wealth and power in a day when states were small. They collected the state revenue and administered its debts. They fostered handicrafts and trades and markets, planned tariffs, and were the personnel authority. The Exchequer became the central point of the economic system, for state activity was then not characterized as "interference": it seemed to be the expected and natural process. The Reformation threw further duties upon the state: *viz.*, education and poor-relief.

THE RISE OF THE PRUSSIAN CIVIL SERVICE

PRUSSIA now commenced to develop rapidly until it became the foremost state in Germany, and an example to the rest. Its exemplary and brilliant progress was largely due to the same kind of accident which in France led to deplorable results —the accident of birth. Between 1640 and late in the eighteenth century—let us say until the French Revolution—Prussia had the fortune to be ruled by four kings of whom three had administrative genius of a high order: these three, the Great Elector, Frederick William of Brandenburg

(1640–88), Frederick William I (1713–40), and Frederick the Great (1740–86), reigned in all for about 110 years.

The General Course of Development. It is almost impossible to appraise sufficiently the importance of these years of intensely energetic administrative drive. This directing force came at just that epoch in the life of the state when it was most urgently needed: that is, when all the spiritual and economic interests of men demanded a medium for their realization which the towns, counties, duchies, and other small and separatist areas of government no longer adequately afforded.[5] It came at a time, too, when its results in terms of administrative organization were bound to have an influence stretching as far as the institutions and mind of the nineteenth century. The Thirty Years' War caused tremendous material, spiritual, and institutional damage, and it threw upon the survivors the burden of reorganization of at least the revenue and military system. The state was extended in territory and population, and thus the number of civil servants within a single organization increased. It increased, too, because there was ascribed a field of activity to the state not again equaled till recent years. The sovereignty and *jus eminens* of the princes, which now obtained an absolute form and suffered decreasingly from challenge, was linked with the positive character of the state. A new technique was demanded, for the contemporary economic processes and morality required promptitude in judgment, honesty and energy in administration, intellectual equipment of the civil servants, and a reform of the old councils and chancelleries. The economic-*cum*-administrative science of cameralism began, and it taught the importance of a trained civil service.

Prussia was given a great impetus "to strengthen the civil service as the concrete means of unity, as the chief organ of state

---

[5] This is, perhaps, most brilliantly described in G. von Schmoller's famous essay, "Das Merkantilsystem," in *Umrisse und Unterscichungen* (Leipzig, 1898).

unity." [6] The Great Elector considered the Privy Council and himself as the unifying and supreme authority over all affairs of state. The character of the Privy Council had changed from that of an advisory to an executive organ. Some of the chiefs of the various departments were appointed members of the Privy Council so that they brought special knowledge to bear upon the discussions and, further, knew exactly how far their department was called upon to execute the decisions. There was a continual process of accumulation of business in the hands of the state and a continual creation of special organs to deal with it.

The whole country was the better brought under the control of the central authority by the institution of the *Statthalter,* a local regent appointed by the prince. They were non-natives of their particular province, and, being appointed members of the Privy Council at Berlin, they constituted a bond of union between the center and the localities, making of the resolutions of the Council a local reality. The *Statthalter* was important till the end of the seventeenth century, when the opposition of the estates and the provinces to central domination having ceased, they became unnecessary in their crude early form. Few were natives of the district in which they served, for in accordance with the nature of the state of the time, not the least important quality of a civil servant was his impeccable loyalty to the central authority. The civil servant was first the outpost of royal power: other qualities were essential, but only after this.

This twofold aim of centralization and militarization accompanied another which we nowadays describe as paternalism. In the actual experience of the Prussian state, however, it was found easier to realize the aims of the first two, but not so easy to create a civil service which should produce good fruits from the third. For centralization and militarization are inimical to paternalism: the former is only rarely

its appropriate tool, while the latter is its competitor and consumes its substance. Until the end of the eighteenth century, paternalism continued to be a faithful expression of the state, along with centralization and militarization. But the tendency was for it to lose its value compared with the others, and centralization and militarization became the predominant characteristics of the Prussian civil service. Forms predominated over purpose; command over the substance of commands; hierarchy over colleagueship; discipline over free creation; routine over local and personal invention; and at the end of Frederick the Great's reign, the charge of "bureaucracy" begins, not to end even in our own day.

The War Commissariat and the Chambers. We have anticipated the results of development. Let us retrace our steps. In the middle of the seventeenth century, the armies were nationalized. Prussia created a standing army directly administered by the state; and the formerly mercenary officers, captains, men, equipment, and so on, became socialized. Naturally, the war commissars became permanent state administrative officials: they had their local areas and central department. The government became a recruiter, and since money economy was yet in a backward condition, it had to become a barracks and feeding agent. The localities were directly called upon not merely to pay taxes in money, but to supply billets, food for men and horses, stabling, arms, and clothes. This led to penetrating interference with the life of the citizens, caused interference with civic administration, with guild and market conditions, and not least, with the bane of the seventeenth century, inns and tippling houses.[7] When natural economy gave way to money economy, the war commissars were brought into direct contact with the taxation system of the country. From 1680 onwards, the war commissars stood in the very front and center of public administration. They were obliged to take into consideration everything that could increase the ca-

---

[6] G. von Schmoller, "Der Deutsche Beamtenstaat in 17 and 18 Jahrhundert," in *ibid.*

[7] Cf. *idem.,* p. 299.

pacity of the citizen to pay his contribution toward the maintenance of the army; taxation systems and reforms, the excise which would be increased by greater production, the general police measures which would free the people of material and moral defects, and social welfare institutions like the promotion of good agriculture and manufactures. They became tax officials and local police authorities and overcame the independent tax officials of the states, so that thenceforward the state predominated in this field through its own officials. The central directory of war was created, the *Generalkriegskommissariat*, to exercise control and direction over the local commissariats —the best-hated branch of administration in the state, best hated, that is, by the estates and the cities, and Frederick William's testament acknowledged the difficulties of the situation. It was the soul of the new state. As one of the ablest of German administrative historians has said, "Prussia was then not a land with an army, but an army with a land." [8] In 1712 the *Generalkriegskommissariat*, which had split off from the Privy Council, was reorganized to cope with its accretion of duties: one of its divisions was devoted to taxes and excise, another to military affairs, and the third to administration and administrative jurisdiction. State power and civil equality were its pillars.

Meanwhile, from 1651 onward, the financial and economic divisions of the former local agents of the central authority, the *Amtkammern*, were given an independent status, and connected with a central division of the Privy Council. These local *Kammer*, and the central authority supervising them, had a field of activity comprising the contemporary equivalents of what is now the work of the British Treasury, Board of Trade, Inland Revenue Office, Ministry of Agriculture and Fisheries, and other economic administration scattered through the British government departments.

Both the war commissariats and the chambers took away from the power of the old claimants—the governing bodies which represented the local and feudal authorities. These authorities had till recently possessed the power to judge the competence of the chambers wherever they were disputed, but gradually this power of judgment was withdrawn, and all matters relating to the *statum politicum et oeconomicum* [9] were transferred to the chambers and the commissariats themselves. Administrative departments had arrogated to themselves an extensive field of justice. It was secured that the state departments should decide the limits of sovereignty and private law. By a series of instructions between 1713 and 1725, chamber or administrative justice [10] was set in the ascendant until the reforms of 1808; but the extent to which it is maintained is still a point of distinction between Continental and Anglo-Saxon institutions. Its later development and significance is discussed in another chapter (Chap. 36).

Centralization and the Civil Service. The centralization of the country proceeded apace. As in contemporary England, there was no local government system in organic connection with the central authority: none which, made by the central authority or evolved from its own necessities, had formed an efficient association with the central government. The towns and other great estates ruled themselves. Voluntary administrators, called *Kreisdirektoren*, performed the tasks of local government in unions of estates, and they and their districts became the basis of the Elector's local government arrangements. The establishment of a standing army had led to the appointment of state commands for these districts, and, naturally, continuous negotiations between these and the *Kreis* authorities took place. It was not long before the work of the Commissars was transferred to *Kreisdirektors*. But instead of being self-elected, they now came to be appointed by the Crown, and as the office grew in importance and

---

[8] Ernst von Meier, *Hannoversche Verfassungs und Verwaltungsgeschichte, 1680-1866* (München 1898, 1899), Vol. II, p. 409.

[9] Lotz, *op. cit.*, p. 115.
[10] Cf. *Acta Borussica* (edited by G. von Schmoller, O. Hintze, *et al.*), Vol. III, p. 682 ff.

required technical knowledge, they gradually became central professional officers under the direction and pay of the central authority. Thus a local authority was created which represented at the same time both the central authority and the local interests; that authority had come into being out of military necessities and for more than another century the military spirit pervaded its administrative activity; that activity naturally became extended over a very large number of economic and social activities; and it was a rural not an urban institution.

The towns were brought under the supervision of the central authority by the institution, in 1680 and following years, of tax commissioners to whom the municipal excise officials were obliged to account. At first they were traveling commissioners, making their circuits twice a year.[11] Soon their tasks were increased, for, as tax officials, the central authority required them to undertake various detective activities, for example, into the rate of payment for entry into citizenship, or the fees asked for admission into guilds. With the assistance of municipal magistrates, they became courts of justice in cases of tax frauds and insults to tax officials. They were made the inspectors of weights and measures; new taxes upon bakers and slaughterers were put under their management; and little by little they came to supervise the whole field of municipal administration, and to control the trades—guilds, building, and brewing. "By 1722 the Tax Commissioner had practically become the guardian of the town, which lost all independence."[12] He had under his control a host of medical men, and lesser officials like police and bailiffs, statisticians, and clerks. Tax collection ceased to be his primary business: his vocation became the control and supervision of the life of the municipality in the name and the interests and under the direction of the central authority. He was the clearest symbol, as he was the most

active agent, of the police state, the bureaucratic state on its paternalistic side. He combated local simony and nepotism. He was not, however, a wheel which turned independently of the other cogs set in movement by the energetic Hohenzollerns—he was a member of the war commissariats, where he exercised weighty authority. He had no judicial authority, but the commissariats had, and they judged the cases he brought before them. The tax commissioner's profession was the training ground for the best Prussian officials of the eighteenth century,[13] and they brought to their central departmental duties a fund of experience which explains why the Prussian state, incapable constitutionally of being reformed from outside or "below", could at decisive times be reformed from within or "above."

There was by now, in the first quarter of the eighteenth century, a civil service large for its time. Posts (nationalized in 1650), taxes, customs, forests, salts and mines administration, the schools and the church, in country and town—all demanded a large number of officials, capable officials, most of whom were recruited from subaltern army officers who had finished their service. The wakeful vigilance and grim earnestness which enabled the Hohenzollerns effectively to demand the efficiency and accountability of their presidents, ministers, and councilors was continued in the relations between these and their subordinates in the early days, at least, of these institutions, and with variations from chief to chief.

Energy and System. So far only the pioneer work had been done, great as that was. Men had been chosen for the state services of great capacity, occasionally of extraordinary talent, the field activity had been plotted out on an extensive scale, the enemies of the state suppressed, and a measure of competence and honesty introduced into the civil service. The organization, though so far approaching systematic form, was still loose and tentative, the authorities confused and

---

[11] Cf. G. von Schmoller, *Preuszische Verfassungs-Verwaltungs und Finanzgeschichte* (Berlin, 1921), pp. 151-52.
[12] Lotz, *op. cit.*, p. 121.

[13] G. von Schmoller, *Deutscher Beamtenstaat*, p. 300.

overlapping. The new ruler added system, formulated the rules of recruitment for higher officials, purged (by no means entirely) the service of the dishonest, and infused it with a fresh energy.

The quality of this energy is more important than the institutions which were created, but we cannot omit the institutions, because they work upon mind and energy, now improving, now spoiling, what springs from inward source. Schmoller best describes Frederick William's character, and it was this which, to the extent of the possible, recreated the character of his officials. He entered upon his work with "modest, fatherly economy, with Protestant conscientious morality, with sober rationalistic consideration, but also with the shrewd intensity and force of an unbendable will." [14]

The institutions energized by this intense spirit were ingeniously planned. In all the central departments the "collegiate" principle was thoroughly carried through, in order to avoid the predominance of any one man and to secure the benefits of collective wisdom and continuity of policy. Collective responsibility was enjoined. The councils were responsible, especially for accounts and for the probity and competence of their subaltern officials. The councilors were expected to create the means of narrowly watching all those at work in their department, and they were to make use of "spies" to inform themselves. Yet they were to examine with care the reports made by the spies lest the reports did an injustice to their subjects. Even the king himself had spies all over the country to report upon the conduct of ministers and officials.

Various instructions settled exactly the hours of work, procedure, and official secrecy. Employment outside the official service was prohibited, the acceptance of presents was prohibited, excise officials were forbidden to buy confiscated goods, and from those who handled money a guarantee was required. The officials who came into direct contact with the public were ordered to be polite, and the insulting of merchants was punished with a fine for the first offence and with imprisonment for the second. The tax commissioners were ordered to keep personal records of the local officials. Residence in the neighborhood of the work was exacted, and the conditions of leave were rigidly regulated. For breaches of the regulations there was a series of heavy fines, which were imposed. A Spartan quality was introduced into the service. Perfect accounts were expected, and expenditure beyond the budget was charged against the official. The king now undertook the examination of estimates, and each was obliged to receive an assent. Along with these sources of information about the nature of his state, the ruler had regular reports at various times of the year from the various central and provincial authorities. The royal example operated downwards through all grades of the service, and the spirit of strict subordination, the forcible exaction of the last ounce of duty from those who were obliged to render it, became part and parcel of every member of the administration. Direct explosions of the royal wrath were feared, and there yawned always the gulf of delation by colleague-spies. The king's example compelled imitation even to the farthest corner of the kingdom.

Provisions for Civil-Service Recruitment. In this reign the first formal rules of recruitment were established; and, fundamentally, they have ruled the German state ever since.[15] Already in 1700 written and oral examinations had been prescribed for military judges and judicial councilors. By the judicial order of June, 1713, it was laid down that no subordinate judge was to be appointed and no advocate was to practice without passing the examination prescribed by the state. If there were several competitors for posts, the best candidates were to be accepted in order of merit. Soon after this the *Protonotarien*, the highest clerical officers and the secretaries of the law courts, were required to pass a written examination before appointment. All this, of

14 *Deutscher Beamtenstaat*, p. 287.

15 Cf. *Acta Borussica*, Vol. I, *passim.*

course, presupposed a thorough legal training at a university, and in 1723, such a training was expressly required, and at a native university, the University of Halle, about which we shall have something further to say a little later (p. 733). Aspirants to the service could be allowed to participate in the procedure of the courts, but without a vote, before taking their state examination. Thus began the system still adhered to in Germany of the *Gerichtsreferendar*: the aspirant to the judicial service, who takes his university examination, and is known as a *Referendar* while he undergoes a period of preparatory service, after which he takes the final state examination to become an *Assessor,* the first rung of the judicial service. In 1737, a minimum of legal knowledge was prescribed for all other officials, in whatever departments or institutions, who participated in the administration of justice. This affected the relationship between noble and citizen, to the general advantage of the latter, since even those who took part in the administration of justice in virtue of feudal survivals were now obliged to acquire their university diplomas.

The rules of recruitment for the higher administrative service were not prescribed until later. And it should be specially noticed that these differed materially from those applicable to the judicial service. Experience was at first considered a better preparation than any formal training that could be invented, for general administrative work. Apparently, this, which occupied itself directly with promoting the economic welfare of the country, was the king's favorite branch, for upon being asked by the general directory in 1723 whether a place could not be found for the son of a deceased chancellor, he answered: "Examine him to see whether he has sense and a good head; if he has, let him be employed in the Kurmark War-and-Domain Chamber; if, however, he is a fat-headed devil, make him a member of the Supreme Court of Cleves, he's good enough for that." [16] Yet considerations of efficiency soon found their expression in a genuine though rough-and-ready procedure. The Instruction (of December 20, 1727) establishing the *Generaldirektorium* contained the general statement of qualifications: the presidents of the commissariats and chambers should have the same qualities as members of the general directory:

clever men as could be found anywhere, Evangelical, Reformist or Lutheran by religion, faithful and honest, with intelligent vision, possessing sound information about commerce, manufactures, and other cognate subjects, but also able with the pen: above all, they must be native subjects, but a foreigner of extraordinary ability can be suggested; they must be persons who are capable of anything for which one wishes to use them.

It was expected that the candidates should have taken courses at Halle, Frankfurt, or Konigsberg in cameralism—that is, in administrative science—and in agriculture and forestry. The university diploma was a prerequisite, ordinarily, to office. Young men were brought into the service after such a preparation and were then employed, without pay, in the departments, so that they might acquire practical experience of administration before they were given a permanent situation.

Here, in these university candidates, we see the lineal ancestors of the modern *Regierungsreferendar*: the government or administrative aspirant, then called *Auskultator*. In 1748 the qualities and studies of the candidates for government service as *Auskultator* were laid down in an instruction:

They must have occupied for at least one year such a position as would have given them the opportunity to obtain a knowledge of agriculture, cattle breeding, brewing and brandy manufacture, as well as trading accounts and extracts, as well as the surveys and valuations; during the winter they should learn something of administrative policy in the neighboring towns, and finally, they should make a record of what they thus learnt.

---

[16] Ernst von Meier, *Franzosische Einflusse auf die Staats- und Rechtsentwickelung Preus-* *sens im XIX Jahrhundert* (Leipzic, 1908), Vol. II, p. 65.

The state did not leave to chance the creation of the requisite faculties in the universities, but in 1727, Frederick William established a professorship of cameralism at Halle and Frankfurt to teach "the principles of agriculture and police, also the institution of surveys of offices and estates, and also the efficient administration and government of towns."

It is convenient not to break off here, but to pursue this history of recruitment to the final point it reached before the storm of the French Revolution and the period of the great reformer at the turn of the eighteenth century. Theory marched with practice, and the specifically German contribution to economic and political science of the eighteenth century occupied itself continually with the problems of the formation of a satisfactory civil service.[17] For example, Gasser, first professor of economics at Halle, shows clearly how insistent were the royal desires to change the basis of admission into the service from legal training to a more general education. The lawyer is too involved in pedantry and tricks.[18] Zincke [19] pointed out the need for a broad education in all the sciences appropriate to the state's task: namely, "to improve and perfect all that constitutes the temporal weal of its members." Justi,[20] himself in the Prussian service of mines for some time, emphasizes the importance of cameralia or *Staatswirtschaft*: that is, the whole complex of administrative-*cum*-economic-*cum*-planning-science taught at Halle University. The state may be compared to a machine; hence all its parts—that is, the offi-

cials—must be appropriately recruited and managed to its purpose.[21]

The examination system was rounded off principally by rules laid down in 1748 and 1770. A candidate for the higher government service must have had a good academic record. Upon application to the government, he was first given a written examination by a particular department, and then followed an oral examination before the Chamber Examination Commission. The one year's experience in a local department in accordance with the rules we previously described was required, in addition to the academic preparation upon which the examination was based. The commission reported to the department, the latter to the general directory. The second and final examination was taken with permission of the department, no period between the first and second being prescribed. It consisted of a written part, in which there were papers in jurisprudence and in administrative science (*polizei*) and in the survey and valuation of an estate, and an oral part, which could ramify over all branches of finance, natural law, and other subjects contiguous to the science of public finance. Some of the records relating to these oral examinations are extant and show with what comprehension and thoroughness the examiners executed their work, if not their victims.[22]

The Civil Service a Profession. What now, we may ask, was the essence of this development? The administration of the state had been professionalized: that is to say, it now depended upon a body of men permanently employed upon special work, their activities being uniquely at the service of the state and being purposively regulated and disciplined to accomplish its specific ends. A system of educational preparation had been established the like of which no other state demanded until the lapse of more than another

[17] G. Marchet, *Studien über die Entwickelung der Verwaltungslehre in Deutschland von der Zweiten Hälfte des 17 bis Zum Ende des 18 Jahrhunderts* (Munich, 1885), and A. Small, *The Cameralists*, (Chicago, 1909).
[18] Small, *op. cit.*, p. 210. Gasser said: "His Majesty the King of Prussia resolved to establish *Professores Oeconomicae* at the universities of Halle and Frankfurt, who should teach the students the principles of agriculture, *policy,* and also the establishment of budgets of offices and estates, and, further, the proper administration and government of towns."
[19] *Ibid.*, p. 228.
[20] *Ibid.*, p. 294 ff.

[21] J. H. G. Justi, *Gesammelte Politische und Finanzschriften,* etc. (Copenhagen and Leipzic, 1761), Vol. I, p. 8.
[22] Cf. Ernst von Meier, *Die Reform der Verwaltungsorganisation* (Leipzic, 1881), pp. 30-34.

century, and in its composition there was secreted the most appropriate training imaginable for the eighteenth-century state, by no means without lessons for our own day: for it required a knowledge of real as well as of written things, and both kinds of knowledge appertained to the actual institutions by which men earn their living and pursue their social destiny. A resolute, impartial, energetic, and honest spirit had been breathed into the service, and it became, side by side with the military career, the vocation *par excellence* of the most ambitious young men. Henceforward, the civil service became a career to which many families, generation after generation, contributed their talent, and it was a deliberate purpose of Frederick the Great's to draw into the civil service successive generations of the same family to create the proper mentality of servants of the state. The noble received a certain preference, but less under Frederick William than under Frederick the Great, and even then only if the minimum regulations had been met.[23]

The state had been almost altogether centralized; it performed an enormous range of duties. Any central survey of policy was left to the cabinet, the king's immediate entourage of trusted advisers. The political testaments of Frederick the Great, as well as his actual manner of government, show clearly how the reins were all brought into the cabinet and thence to the Crown.[24]

A well-conducted Government must have system as well-knit as any system of philosophy; all measures taken must be well-considered, and finances, policy and the army must move together towards the same purpose which is the strengthening of the State and of its power. Now, a system cannot emanate except from one mind; therefore it must issue from that of the King. . . More vividly affected by what he thinks, than by the thoughts of others, he will follow his plans with the fire necessary to make them succeed; and his pride which attracts his interest to the work will become useful to the country . . . Sovereigns of the first kind (who themselves rule) are like the souls of their State. . . They have, like God (who uses a mind superior to that of men in order to operate upon their wills), penetrating and industrious minds, to execute their plans and to fulfil in detail that which they have projected in the large; their ministers are properly instruments in the hands of a wise and clever master.[25]

For nothing had Frederick the Great more contempt than the French practice of a weak king and mutually independent and hostile central departments.[26]

DECLINE AFTER FREDERICK THE GREAT

THIS might have proved for a century or more to be an efficient system of government. But already there were two features that might easily become defects: the service was militarized, and one personality, the king's, overshadowed all the rest.

Militarization. The service was militarized by Draconian discipline and by the rigidity of its classes. The subaltern ranks of the service were intentionally filled with those who held subordinate posts in the army. From these officials the king required "enthusiasm, regularity and punctuality, and unconditional obedience to directions and official regulations." [27] The frequency of war caused occasional surpluses of men in the intervals of peace, and the jobs in the local services of the central authority were almost entirely made over to the miltary candidates. This service was on the whole subordinate to the first purpose of the state—the extension of its dominions. Infused with military spirit and dedicated to military ends, it was quite natural that under Frederick William and Frederick the Great, its paramount purpose should spoil the instrument for any other objects perhaps more desired by the population, the true interests of which were welfare rather than international glory.

---

[23] Ernst von Meier, *Französische Einflüsse* etc., Vol. II, p. 58.
[24] *Die politischen Testamente Friedrich's des Grossen,* edition of Professor Gustav Berthold Volz (Berlin, 1920), pp. 37, 77, etc.

[25] *The Anti-Machiavel,* published by Jean van Diven (Hague edition, 1741), p. 276.
[26] *Ibid.,* p. 37.
[27] Lotz, *op. cit.,* p. 159.

One personality overshadowed and drove all the rest! The Prussian state before 1740 had been compared to a great school and the king to a headmaster.[28] What should happen when the task grew too big, or when external pressure took the mind of the genius away from domestic affairs? It was inevitable, if that should happen and civilization produced these conditions, that the wheels would continue to turn for a limited time, and then require adjustment, not to another great man and many "average" subordinates, but to "average" men only.

The Polizei-Staat. What was radically at fault with the apparatus as a form was its dependence upon an impulse from above and within, and upon its own strength and knowledge. It would have been extraordinary for kings who called themselves the "first servant of the State" to serve on any other terms but their own, or to admit the superiority of anybody else's wisdom. They could not admit either the wisdom or the right of the people to determine the main lines of policy. Political theory as yet opposed such a field of liberty, and the administrative science of cameralism did not provide for the participation of the administered. All roads led to what is now called the *Polizei-Staat.* We have already explained that *Polizei* in seventeenth- and eighteenth-century administrative and political science did not mean the mere maintenance of the peace. Its connection with constabulary was inappreciable. It comprised almost all that we know today as the administration of economic and social institutions. Mayer, the German constitutional lawyer, defines it shortly: "Police: that which gives the whole its distinctive mark, and becomes a comprehensive and systematic working-up of the human material available in order to lead it towards a great goal." Its outlines were: strict obedience of the subjects to the king, who was the first servant of the state; the legal omnipotence of the royal will; a civil service which was the expression of this will; and in practice, the enormous range of the state's power.

Toward the time of the French Revolution, the system no longer operated with the effectiveness of a generation earlier. Cameralism and mercantilism—it is possible even to talk of state socialism—had led it into a range of activities which could be successful only by decentralization and popular cooperation; the military spirit had overcome that of social service, and strictly disciplined hierarchies ramifying through a large country were mentally too inflexible to invent the necessary devices to vanquish routine. The service was obedient but lacked that personal interest in the result which is the salt of industry. The single-headed genius had departed and multiple-headed Demos was not yet called upon to propel the machine or renew its defective parts. While Frederick William had been the personal president of the general directory, Frederick the Great and his cabinet now directed activities by memoranda, and the central departments increased in number. When Frederick the Great died, the directory had lost its cohesion and the cabinet its driving force. But, says one of the greatest authorities:

this police-power operated grimly and unmercifully; with an impulse of eudamonistic and social welfare it threatened to annihilate the definite private sphere of individual freedom. It threatened, as Tocqueville said, to change society into a prison or a barracks. In an Administrative Order of Baden in 1766 the following appeared: "Our Royal Administrative Council is the natural guardian of our subjects. It is its duty to lead our subjects from error and show them the right path; to teach them even against their will how to manage their own domestic affairs." Were this standpoint accepted, then ultimately one would be obliged to place a State official by the side of each citizen for life.

The Revolutionary Age. There now took concrete and institutional form those conceptions of social relationships and government which were proclaimed by the pioneers of the French Revolution. The Physiocrats and Adam Smith powerfully challenged the economic assumptions of

---

[28] Schmoller, in *Preussische Jahrbücher* (Berlin), Vol. 26, p. 552.

Colbertism and cameralism, and they could be no less explosive of the political institutions which embodied them. In Kant and his colleague Kraus,[29] at the University of Königsberg, a stimulus was given to political and economic individualism and to the reign of law in which each individual should be regarded as an end and not as a means. The enlightened despotism of Frederick the Great and Christian Wolff were discredited by these new prophets, and those who sat at their feet in 1780 and the following decade were the foremost officials toward 1800. If the startling ideas and events of these years made immediately no great inroads upon the institutions, they did upon the mind, of Germany, and yet only as a "revolution from above." The influences of laissez faire and democratic theory were effective in Germany only upon a portion of the bureaucracy, and, further, upon the philosophers. It is fair to say that philosophy was affected more than the men with practical power. The fact was that monarchical ideas were strong because the monarchy had not been inefficient, and it had deadened the people with military discipline and conserved the economic and social privileges of a landed nobility.[30]

The centralized military and police state held together until Napoleon smashed it. Only its desperate need caused King Frederick William III to invest supreme authority in Stein, the only man who was able to conceive, if not realize, the essential reforms. It was not Stein alone who conceived the reforms, settled their principles, or worked out their details. He was encouraged and helped by colleagues and subordinates of equal genius in their own spheres: von Schon, Hardenberg, Scharn-

horst, Gneisenau, Vincke, and the two brothers Schrotter and others. But he was possessed by the passionate desire for his end, the capacity for sustained endeavor, and the flaming but controllable impatience, in the degree of intensity which convinces the doubtful and overcomes the obdurate. This spirit, aflame and invincible, was conducted by a mind and character formed and tempered by affairs. Experience as a Prussian official for nearly a quarter of a century had taught him the nature of the Prussian bureaucracy; and to him, that nature was synonymous with ossified weakness.

Stein's criticisms were directed against both the form and the spirit of the administration. He looked to reforms in the direction of decentralization and the popular consultation, and a rearrangement of central machinery. As regards the latter he suggested, in order to overcome the growing gulf between the special departments and the lack of unified direction, that in place of the cabinet (which though atrophied allowed of illicit influence upon the Crown) there should be a council of heads of departments who would be relieved of concern for details, and would direct and supervise the execution of the general policy of the country only. In this system the king was to receive advice only from these ministers, and to command through them only. This would limit personal government and, at least, weaken the influence of territorial differences which had hitherto been emphasized owing to the division of departments upon a provincial basis. A single treasury was to take the place of the numerous treasures. Over and above the suggested ministry there should be a Council of State (*Staatsrat*) to exercise an even more general and common directive influence upon the various departments of government: to give advice on new legislation, to discuss questions affecting all or many departments. It was to be composed of the princes, ministers, high officials, and others appointed by the king. This Council, whose uses seem to the critic to be an unnecessary addition to the ministry, never came into existence. We have already used the term "Min-

---

[29] See Ch. J. Kraus, *Staatswirtschaft*, 5 vols. (Königsberg, 1808-11).

[30] G. P. Gooch's *Germany and the French Revolution* (London, 1920) amply shows this. Those who have worked on the first-hand materials of Gooch's book cannot fail to bear tribute to its conscientious and able scholarship.

Cf. for another survey of the eighteenth-century Prussian bureaucracy, W. L. Dorn, "The Prussian Bureaucracy in the Eighteenth Century," *Political Science Quarterly*, 1931, 1932, pp. 75 ff., 403 ff., 259 ff.

ister." It was Stein's project to abolish the "board" or "collegiate" system, and to have a single head for each department. These heads in council, under the permanent presidency of the king, would have had many points of resemblance to the early cabinet system in England, but since Frederick William III preferred one minister to act as intermediary between him and the others, a cabinet system could hardly be said to have come into existence: instead, one minister became predominant and this gave rise to the modern German chancellorship and Prussian minister-presidency which still strongly retain and reveal their embryological features.[31]

The provincial authorities were to be reorganized so that each branch thereof corresponded in extent of administration with a special central department; and it was suggested that all affairs which could be left to the independent local execution by these provincial authorities ought to be. A large reorganization of the local agencies of the central authority should then follow.

It is at this point that Stein utters those opinions about Prussian administration which most concern us.[32] His criticism of the bureaucracy was sharp:

We are governed by *paid, book-learned, disinterested, propertyless* bureaucrats; that will suffice so long as it suffices. These four words contain the character of our and similar *spiritless* governmental machines: *paid,* therefore they strive after maintenance and increase of their numbers and salaries; *book-learned,* that is, they live in the printed, not the real world; *without interests,* since they are related to no class of the citizens of any consequence in the State, they are a class for themselves—the clerical-caste; *propertyless,* that is, unaffected by any changes in property. It may rain, or the sun may shine, taxes may rise or fall, ancient rights may be violated or left intact, the officials do not care. They receive their salary from the State Treasury and write, write in quiet corners, in their departments, within specially-built locked doors, continually, unnoticed, unpraised. And then again they educate their children for equally useful Statemachines.—One machine (the military) fell on October 14th, 1806. Perhaps the writing-

machine will have its 14th October! There is the ruin of our dear Fatherland: bureaucratic power and the *nullity of our citizens!*

The civil service lacked life, inventive power, ability to serve the needs of the population, enterprise: impotence had overcome it and it was out of touch with the life which surrounded it.

The Bureaucracy in the Nineteenth Century. Judgments of that kind continued to be passed upon the civil service throughout the course of the nineteenth century. What is extraordinary, however, is that the rest of the world somehow formed the belief that this civil service was the ablest in the world; and in fact, it did some first-class work. Even while Stein was writing in retirement, it carried out, under Hardenberg's chancellorship, many far-reaching reforms, and it continued to do so until after the middle of the nineteenth cenutry, without the co-operation of a representative assembly.

By 1800, a reform should have been made of the educational preparation for the civil service to correspond with the tasks set by an age new to Germany. It is material, therefore, to review the type of criticism passed upon the ethos and the mentality of the service. (We later—Chapter 31—proceed to a study of recruitment in the nineteenth and twentieth centuries.)

In 1844 there appeared at Hamburg a small book entitled *Bureaucracy and Officialdom in Germany.*[33] The author attempts to show how enormous is the size of the service, an exercise which earlier and later generations have all enjoyed. He arrives at a total of 700,000,[34] and says: "These 700,000 promote the welfare of the subjects, secure their life and property, administer education and in-

---

[31] Cf. Chap. 25 on the German cabinet system.
[32] From the Nassau Memorandum.

[33] *Bureaukratie und Beamtentum in Deutschland, I. Preuszen* (Hamburg, Hoffmann and Canute, 1844), p. 72. The author's name does not appear, and the book purports to be a translation from the English of a Lord's steward who was in Germany for nearly ten years. But the book is written with so much animus, such a bitter hatred of the bureaucracy that it is doubtful whether an Englishman would have been so interested in German affairs.
[34] They include the judicial authorities, the teachers, and the clergy.

struction, judge evildoers, and edit, inspect, super-edit, control, decree, foster, journalize, chew over, insinuate, execute, remit everything, and so on."

The service had become a caste, sundered from the rest of society, in particular owing to the stringency of official secrecy, which unduly prevented civil servants from discussing affairs with the public whether orally or through the press. Our anonymous writer remarks that "it is a curious contrast that the first Protestant State of the Continent uses, as the basis of its administration, a principle which is the strongest pillar of Ultramonism." (Not so curious or surprising, as we shall see when we arrive at the end of our discussion of modern administration, Chap. 34).

Like the Catholic Church, the civil service tolerates no deviation from the faith, not the slightest, lest one change produce a greater. Fearful of losing its power, it does not accommodate itself to progress.

The spirit of Prussian administration is in many respects in direct contradiction to the spirit of the Prussian State, that is, the Prussian Government, and should the Government desire to be never so liberal, the Administration will maintain the opposite tendency as long as it can. The contradictory elements are, on the one side, the spirit of the Reformation State, on the other, organization according to the military State. The former is the ally of popular activity, the latter the resort of reactionary administrative activity. Bureaucracy can as well be compared with the military system as with a hierarchy, and is often compared with it. The three are parallels: military, hierarchy, bureaucracy: all rest upon the divine right of despotism, which wills no exception, no leniency, no progress, but only blind devotion and the eternally unchangeable acknowledgment of its infallibility. The three maintain themselves by unconditional obedience; the means by which obedience is maintained is fear; and this is maintained by dependence. The dependence of Prussian Civil Servants is rigidly secured by two devices: secret reports and the strict maintenance of official secrecy. The former reminds officials every moment of their superiors; the latter of the office.[35]

The result is a machine directed against the people, at least, when the people's will is something other than the will of the civil service. Within itself the organization receives its direction and energy from suspicious severity, and the control of detail by superiors, not from trust of the freely exercised discretion of subordinates. The moral strength of the officials is not evoked; and with all its mechanical accuracy the administration lacks a spirit of honor.

There are many other opinions of interest in this brochure, but the chief substance has been given and it shows, we think, where the fault of the Prussian civil service was considered to lie in the decade 1834 to 1844. A year afterwards this criticism was supported by a book called *The Prussian Bureaucracy*.[36] Its temper is similar to that which we have just described, but it surveys the field with a more level and composed demeanor. It is antipathetic to the civil service because that service is not directed and controlled by the people, and the author deems that from this fact flow a number of evils, chief of which, summarily described, are bureaucracy in the service and the political nonentity of the citizens. Since 1815, in fact, the civil service had been the instrument of oppression of liberalism, and it is not surprising to find here as elsewhere judgment centered not upon any examination of the technical efficiency of the civil service in its admitted purposes, but upon the political complexion of the critic. Were the writer convinced of the value of an absolute, antiliberal state, then the civil service seemed to him a splendid instrument; but were he in the ranks of those who (like Börne and Heine) fought for a liberal constitution, then the civil service was at once dubbed a "bureaucracy" and reproached with showing all the worst features inherent in such a governmental system. The author whose work we are now discussing confesses this power of the point of view over the judgment, for he says: [37]

---

[35] *Ibid.*, pp. 34-35.

[36] Karl Heinzen, *Die preuszische Bureaukratie* (Darmstadt, 1845).
[37] *Ibid.*, p. 71.

It is one of the chief purposes of this book to show, by an appeal to facts, that the Administration in Prussia is in no way qualified to be a substitute for the Constitution, that much more, it is the Administration which makes a Constitution most urgently necessary, together with the freedom of the Press and every kind of publicity belonging thereto.

It is from this level that the author surveys and describes his field. Another critic says that it is not the organization that makes a civil service bureaucratic, but the spirit that moves the organization.

By bureaucracy we here naturally mean not the form, but the spirit, not the body, but the soul. We mean what has generally come to be denoted as bureaucracy: the surplusage of officials and their activity, the abuses and evils of officials and departmental authority. The word bureaucracy is invective, which we cannot properly translate into our mother-tongue any more than we translate such words as despotism, canaille, etc.

This bureaucracy directly issues from Prussian absolutism. For absolutism is to be maintained only by centralization and a military and civil army. Although such absolutism came to pass under previous rulers, bureaucracy originated only when the head of the state lacked energy and benevolence.

In such a system it was bound to happen that the civil service felt its significance and status to be bound up with opposition to the people. It was forced by the situation in which it was placed— as defender of absolutism against the demand for representative government—to make its primary purpose consist of its own continued being and activity. It could not criticize its own composition and seek to remedy its defects or invigorate its spirit, nor could it tolerate criticism from without. Benevolent in intention, in manner it could not but be oppressive. "In England orders were given by the ministers who acted on behalf of the people; in Prussia orders were given by the civil service not only to themselves but to the people." The relationship between civil servant and the public may be epitomized in the words of the author as: "The limited vision, the

pedantry, the dark ignorance, inhumanity and arrogance" of the official, and the lack of remedy of the public.

This continued until the recent past to be a characteristic of the German civil services, not merely the Prussian, and history quite clearly shows that the reason of it is the lack of parliamentary institutions, or, perhaps it would be truer to say, the parliamentary state of mind. While that state of mind lacked force, absolutism prevailed, and every civil servant was bound to be actuated by the intentions—benevolent, offensive, and defensive—of the master spirit.

The relationship between superior and subordinate is analyzed with much acuteness of mind and is evidently founded on experience. On the one side there is the lust for power and dominion, with their cognate qualities and behavior, and on the other side, cringing servility, sycophancy, and those habits which men develop to propitiate the objects of their fears, and, further, the necessary degeneration of all qualities of initiative and independent creativeness in the official.

The secret reports constitute a vital element of the German civil service: an indispensable incentive to produce the character approximate to the times before the advent of democratic control. The system threw the civil servant entirely under the domination of his superior. Until the constitution of 1919, these reports could not be inspected by the person reported upon, and though, between 1845, when this account was written, and 1919, a disciplinary procedure was established which went far to abolish the arbitrary, the civil servant could never know what sort of a storm was brewing which might one day unexpectedly burst upon him. The moral atmosphere of the departments was charged with mistrust, espionage, fawning humility, and minor treachery. The compelling proof of political importance is inclusion in the constitution: and the right to inspect these reports was included in the constitution of 1919.

Survey. Before we can pass to a consideration of the German civil service during the period from 1850 or thereabouts to the present (which we shall do in Chapter 31), let us survey the position so far reached. Prussia (and with some variation the other Germanic states) was governed in the middle of the nineteenth century by an official hierarchy which was intensely bureaucratic in temper, uncontrolled by any popular representative institution and contemptuous of such, enjoying a jurisdiction of exceedingly wide extent and managed through centralized institutions, excellently efficient in formal and routine functions, and adept at the drafting and interpretation of rules and laws. This efficiency was assured by the rules of recruitment, and the ascription of a special social prestige to the civil service. These did not any longer produce inventiveness and plasticity of mind. Of this we have Bismarck's assurance, based upon his own experience as *Referendar* just before 1840. We shall see that as soon as Germany was called upon to serve positively and construct in the field of modern social and economic problems, instead of merely to keep order, the civil service was deemed either to be insufficient by itself and to need the aid of other institutions, or to require a radical reform of its education.

The books and the men I have consulted lead me to believe that between 1815 and 1871 the technical efficiency of the Prussian civil service was of a very high grade, and on the whole quite sufficient to the tasks imposed by the political, social, and economic conditions of the time. Not, indeed, until the third quarter of the nineteenth century did that country begin to be shaken by the mighty travail of a new order of state and society, and until the issue of that travail required official care, the old dispensation worked not unsatisfactorily.

Social Composition of the Service. The Prussian civil service was in its upper ranks the product and the monopoly of two classes—the nobility and the upper middle class, or the "bourgeois patriciate" as it is commonly called. The avenue to power was not open to the classes lower than these, for the necessary educational preparation presupposed means

which could maintain a young man in easy and respectable circumstances until the age of about twenty-seven or twenty-eight.[38] Even were these means available, yet further obstacles were placed in the way of general recruitment: the candidate was required to be "friendly to the state"—that is to say, conservative, of "good" family, a member of students' *corps* or a reserve officer, and as a rule a Protestant Evangelical. Hanover was especially subject to the class monopolization of the civil service. There were certain advantages about this method of recruitment: the family tradition of state service was a valuable guarantee of loyalty and devoted industry; the young men had a habit of government; and a sameness of origin gave rise to *esprit de corps*.[39] But what was praised as *esprit de corps* [40] by one set of people was blamed by ever greater masses of the population as the "caste spirit," not something which impelled to the *élan* of concerted activity but that which fostered a forbidding exclusiveness. The habit of government learned on Junker estates was apt to take on a sinister aspect to those who experienced its exercise—class rule and class government were bitterly resented, and the bureaucracy (especially those who were drawn from the army) was the anathema of the growing working-class movement. Loyalty and devoted service are not synonymous with administrative and political creativeness, nor with service to the whole of society regardless of class privileges. But here the discussion of German bureaucracy must merge with that of other countries. We shall compare their ultimate solutions in the same chapter, Chapter 34.

---

[38] Perthes, *Staatsdienst in Preuszen* (Berlin, 1835).
[39] Cf. H. Oncken, *Rudolf von Bennigsen* (Stuttgart, 1910), Vol. I, p. 33 ff.
[40] Cf. Hegel, *Philosophy of Right*, para, 297: "The members of the executive and the State officials constitute the main part of the middle class, in which are found the educated intelligence and sense of right of the mass of the people . . . The sense of state and the most conspicuous education are found in the middle class, to which the State officials belong."

29

Origins and General Character: France

WE must make acquaintance with the chief characteristics of the administrative institutions and manners to which the France of the nineteenth and twentieth centuries was heir. For the history of these later years has consisted very largely of the attempt to escape from the deficiencies of the administrative organization and spirit developed in the centuries we call collectively the *ancien régime*. The attempt to escape has been less forceful than the avowal, so that the *ancien régime* is still more than a reminiscence.

The features of French administration which leap to the eye from the study of its development are centralization, *Étatisme,* the venality of offices, the passion for place, the caste differentiation of officials, the popular detestation and suspicion of public administration, the establishment of administration, and the establishment of administrative law. All of these, excepting the venality of offices, are still present in modern France, but with differences of importance due to the influence of respect for private and local liberties and the abolition of arbitrary government. The venality of offices was killed by the revolutionary principle of "the career open to the talents," though it has taken over a century to destroy its successors, favoritism and patronage, and to replace it completely by recruitment by merit. These qualities are products of the *ancien régime*. The widely-current popular notion that centralization and the

power of the state are Napoleonic creations is erroneous: Napoleon was given as many opportunities as he made.

THE RISING TIDE OF CENTRALIZATION

Its History. France is the classic home of centralization, as it is of the doctrine of royal sovereignty, and for the same reason. These are not emanations of the French racial character, but the direct results of French feudal arrangements, which created hundreds of independently privileged lords and localities. The first result was a polyarchy indistinguishable from anarchy, though it was then the natural order of society, and the second, rivalry between the equally privileged for personal predominance. This competition among ducal houses filled the twelfth to the sixteenth centuries with war, rapine, daily violence, assassinations, murderous treachery, cynical ruses, misery among the common people, and periodical despoliation of the *bourgeoisie,* while kings and would-be kings died early and sudden deaths by poison or the dagger. Yet fitfully a single power added to its dominions. The usual phenomenon of centralizing power was witnessed; the Crown called to its aid not nobles, but clever and insignificant persons, and it showed mildness toward the *bourgeoisie.* By the end of the fifteenth century, monarchy had established itself, and from that time it sought to make good its hard-won authority by the imposition of its governing will all over its diverse conquered lands. The days of the centripetal forces were numbered.

From the accession of Louis XIV, the monarch was unchallenged by feudal pretenders, and it turned its attention away from the first task of all governments, the reduction of opposition, to the second, the regular provision of daily utilities. Long reflection upon the struggles of the monarchy with its noble competitors has convinced me that the grimness of French centralization was a direct and natural answer to the ungovernable refusal to be governed. Its exaggeration exaggerated centralization, which persisted throughout the reign of Louis XIV and Louis XV: in both it was the source of bitter complaint by the parliaments and local authorities. Under Louis XVI it continued to function, but towards the time of the great Revolution its character softened, its despotism became, in the language of the late eighteenth century, "enlightened" and "humanitarian." Nevertheless, a formidable despotism it was; the people had no effective part in either central or local decisions; and it required even more than the Revolution of 1789 to secure it.

Let us see through what institutions this centralization operated. The monarchical power was extended by the institution of intendants: that is, by representative managers or administrators. Their history appears like successive waves from a central source. A weak and transitory movement first begins. The next is more definite as the purpose of Richelieu and Colbert behind it is more conscious and deliberately planned, and it overwhelms the ground before it by its purposeful force. The tide is full in the last years of Louis XIV and the reign of Louis XV, and it masters all obstacles and it recedes only when the monarchy under Louis XVI is affected, though not completely convinced, by the strange but compelling philosophies of the democrats and the Encyclopaedists.

The Intendants. Much has, however, been said about the intendants. Some writers relate them, though remotely, to

the *missi dominici* of Charlemagne and the *enquesteurs royaux* of Saint Louis. A careful and discerning historian, M. Hanotaux,[1] shows that the intendants began as itinerant justices, of inspectorial and appellant rather than original jurisdiction—began, that is, in the institution known by the graphic name of *les chevanchées des maîtres des requêtes de l'hôtel.* The *maîtres des requêtes* were judicial officers who originally received complaints and requests addressed to the king, and reported these to him; they sat in judgment, with the king, upon these requests. In the interests of royal justice, which not infrequently was in competition with that of the parliaments and the relics of feudal courts, they went on circuit through the provinces.[2] These were their status and functions in the middle of the sixteenth century with which we are now concerned; their later history is interesting but belongs to another part of this study.

The intendants first appeared in the provinces in the company of the commanders of the royal armies when civil or foreign war was rampant. Tentatively established earlier in the century, they were withdrawn during the Wars of the League. They exercised powers which varied with the necessity for the exercise of power. They were called "intendants of justice, police, finance, victuals and of the military authority," and "commissioners sent into the provinces to execute the orders of the King." Their functions with the armies soon became insensibly attenuated, especially as the armies left; and the term "commissioner," which savored of unsettled, warlike, abnormal times, ill-accorded with the character of the intendants after the *Fronde,* and was, in fact, mainly used as a term of disapprobation by opponents of centralization before and after the great Revolution.[3] It took nearly a century, from about the

---

[1] G. Hanotaux, *Origines de l'Institution des Intendants des Provinces* (Paris, 1884).
[2] Cf. Albert Babeau, *La Province sous l'Ancien Régime* (Paris, 1880), Vol. II, Chap. I.
[3] A. de Tocqueville uses the term in *De l'Ancien Régime* (Paris, 1850).

last quarter of the sixteenth until the middle of the seventeenth century, for the intendant to shed his military character and become part of the normal apparatus of government.[4] At first *gens de lutte,* they now had become *gens de bon ton.*

From the beginning, the intendants roused the hostility of the quondam rulers of the provinces and towns. These early intendants did not stay long—a year or two was usual—and gaps of years often elapsed between the withdrawal of one and the commissioning of a successor. Further, their powers varied. They intervened in matters which were peculiarly liable to cause local disaffection: justice, finance, and municipal politics. In the first, they came into conflict with the nobility and the clergy, whose claims they often had to deny, and against whom they had to give judgment. In regard to finance, they had the power to examine the accounts and procedure of the collectors of taxes and deal with malversations, and to see that recalcitrant evaders were pursued. Their judgment was above appeal save to the royal council. And they could participate in the work of all courts of justice, preside even, give judgments, while the judges and royal officials were commanded by the Crown to obey and implement their decision. They settled differences between the officials themselves. In municipal politics they received powers which enabled them to call a truce to disputes of local factions which in some places resulted in chronic disturbance of the peace, and these powers became in the long run so great that local self-government became disastrously limited, the forms remaining with the municipalities while the authority was transferred to the intendant.

The intendants were chosen among the most intelligent and dependable members of the king's council and they correspond with the secretaries of state, sometimes with the king.[5] In the province they ap-

plied the *raison d'état* as learned directly in the council of state, and they did not stay in the province long enough to suffer this to be modified; often, indeed, they attained high power in the Council of State. Just before the reign of Louis XIII and the advent of Richelieu, their powers were already great, and an increased assurance is observable in the tone of the royal commissions—the words *power, authority, commission, special command, will* and *ordain, enjoin, authorize, approve* and *validate* are scattered with generous profusion.

With the advent of Richelieu the final state in the development of the intendants commenced. There was a change of such striking quality in spirit that many historians have ascribed to Richelieu the inception of the system. But Richelieu's genius consisted in the infusion of the existing institution with the full creative force of his own personality. It was the beginning of creative centralization, and Richelieu's innovating genius and fierce energy electrified the provinces, and in time reduced them to submission, but not to complete acquiescence. Intendants were sent to every *généralité* (divisions of a province) except the two or three nearest to Paris. The mere reception of an intendant by a province was, however, in those days a victory for the monarchy, for the *Parlements*: i.e., all the lawyers, in particular, were desperately hostile and the centers of local resistance. The numerous edicts and statutes gave them unlimited opportunity to challenge royal power, and they used the fine arts of interpretation to invalidate the intendant's jurisdiction. Their ultimate resort was the refusal to accept any royal commission which they had not registered, that is, discussed and accepted as due law.

The celebrated *Code Michaud,* an *ordonnance* to reform the kingdom, was drawn up in 1629. Article 58 of that code prescribed the powers of the *maîtres des requêtes,* and in such wise that its negotiation by the *Parlements* was certain. At

---

[4] Boyer de Sainte-Suzanne, *Intendants de la Généralité d'Amiens* (Paris, 1865), p. 87.
[5] Cf. Le Comte De Luçay, *Les Secrétaires*

d'État depuis Leur Institution jusqu'à la Mort de Louis XV (Paris, 1881), Chap. III.

a distance of twenty-three articles from this, that is, in article 81, was insinuated the rule that "No one can be employed in the office of intendant of justice or finance, deputed by us in our armies or provinces, who is . . ." and then follow a few prohibitions. The institution was thus established in the law, for discussion ceased at article 13, and article 81 was passed without discussion.[6] The *Fronde*, in fact, was the last attempt of the vested interests of feudalism to put off the triumph of the absolute state; the nobles united with the richer *bourgeoisie* to smash the power which threatened to make away with their privileges and to collect the taxes it demanded. The absolute state won, in terms too easy as the Revolution afterwards showed—and the trustees of this victory were, for the next century and a half, the monarch, his ministers, and the intendants.

Colbert. Under the rule of Colbert, supported by Louis XIV, whose application to administrative detail earned him the name of *roi administrateur*, the powers of the intendants increased in effectiveness.[7] Wherever any of the older authorities showed a weakness—as, for example, in the affairs of the clergy and the universities—the intendants stepped in to advise, control, or directly administer. Wherever there was no authority adequate to new tasks projected by the ministers—the making of roads, canals, bridges, fortifications, and the regulation of industry—the intendants were saddled with new functions. They were expected by the king to control the *Parlements*, and they did, though in the face of shrill remonstrances.[8] We shall see later how perfect centralization was rendered impossible by the sale and hereditary nature of offices: how, since the revenue derived from these was essential to monarchical policy, this very necessity meant the creation and maintenance of independent magistrates who could oppose the royal power.

Colbert was an utterly callous administrator. Once convinced that his purpose was good by *raison d'état* (or, as we might say, with perfect truth to political psychology, *raison de l'état Colbert*), he searched for the means best adapted to fulfil it, and this discovered, he had none of our conventional scruples: he dismissed, appointed, rotated officials, gave and denied favors, served with his tongue in his cheek, and detracted his equals and superiors. The incarnation of order and industry, he gave neither rest nor indulgence to his colleagues, his subordinates, or, indeed, the king.[9] The passion of the reformer which he ceaselessly endeavored to conduct to the intendants is amply shown by his enormous correspondence.[10]

When we reflect upon the immense number of public activities which Colbert either established or extended, and remember that the efficacy of it all depended upon the initiative of the central authority, since this was unwilling to share power with the old local authorities, or quasirepresentative assemblies, we can understand what an enormous amount of driving power was needed at the center, and what minutely obedient instruments were needed at the extremities. Industries like lace, silk, and Venetian glass were established or developed; native

---

[6] Cf. Georges Picot, *Histoire des États Généraux*, 2nd edition (Paris, 1888), Vol. IV, 118 ff., for the code.

[7] A. Babeau, *op. cit.*; A. Chéruel, *Histoire de l'Administration Monarchique en France* (Paris, 1855), and *Histoire de l'Administration de Louis XIV* (Paris, 1865).

[8] Paul Viollet, *Le Roi et ses Ministres* (Paris, 1912), p. 536. This contains excellent bibliographies, and renders unnecessary more references than actually are here given on the intendants.

[9] The latter, who boasted that he *was* the state itself (or so a legend has it), was made the servant of Colbert's will by Colbert's flattery. Phrases like "Your majesty had told us in two words what the deepest meditation of the cleverest men in the world could invent only in several years" put the scepter into the hands of the servant.

[10] This appears in full in the *Correspondence Administrative sous le Règne de Louis XIV*, edited by G. P. Depping (Paris, 1850), 4 vols., especially Vols. III and IV; it also appears in excellent selection in Pierre Clément, *Histoire de Colbert et de son Administration*, 3rd edition (Paris, 1892). I give the references to Clément as this is most accessible.

workmen were prohibited from leaving France and foreign craftsmen were encouraged to enter; the guilds were entrusted with powers to regulate trade and industry and themselves needed regulation; commerce in the most important native agricultural products was carefully regulated; fleets, arsenals, bridges, roads, and canals were built; mining was encouraged; forestry was regulated and horse breeding developed; criminals and vagabonds were unmercifully pursued.

The Qualities of the Intendants. Locally, the intendants were the local points of all this activity. Now it is quite obvious that any such extent of state activity is unrealizable without a large and competent body of officials. This is exactly what France lacked. The intendants were judicially trained officers. They were men who had gone through the legal training of the day. This was exceedingly formalistic and could not be said to prepare young men for an administrative career.[11] At the most, it enabled them to know their legal place in a territory closely contested by other lawyers. But it did not follow that legal training had even that effect, for the consummation of this was a judicial office, and as these were purchasable and hereditable, the power to purchase was the real key to entrance upon a legal career, and the politics and administration of the day were reserved mainly to the lawyers.[12] Of these, those with influential relatives or friends at court or in the Church, or those favorites of favorites, male or female, obtained office and promotion by intrigues. As soon as one member of a family acquired office, he began to pull every available string for the benefit of his relatives. Even Colbert's

brilliant genius was several times shadowed and almost extinguished by men aspiring to the same career; and a man of the ability and noble nature of Olivier D'Ormesson was lost to the service of the state for the very quality—judicial integrity—that should have won him the highest office but did not because it was exercised against Colbert for his ruthless and lethal attack upon his predecessor Fouquet.

This does not mean that patronage always had or has bad results, for the king and the ministers had their own credit to guard. And this is precisely the defect of patronage: when the patrons care little or not at all for their own credit, the offices go to the worst, and the most competent keep out of the system or, through discouragement, cease to work. What was commended as a policy to increase the material welfare of the people tended to petrify and become a deadening tyranny.[13]

It is clear that the intendants could achieve nothing without the aid of subordinates, and all the minor officers in the employ of the various departments of the council of state were at their beck and call. Further, the officials, paid and unpaid, of the local authorities, were their servants also. Both classes of officials, as far as we can see, showed neither ability nor willingness. They were recruited in one of three ways: (1) they were elected (e.g., parochial collectors of the revenue) and like the English overseers of the poor of the same time were only too anxious to shuffle off their onerous and unpaid duties; or (2) they purchased their office, as in the case of most of the central authority's officials, and saw in it only the means of oppression and the extraction of the maximum fees, bribes, and the other profits, while they gave the minimum of service, all the while maintaining an irritating independence of the intendant; or (3) they were appointed by the Crown or the intendant at discretion,

---

[11] The examinations conducted by the legal corporations were farcical. See e.g., Ch. Normand, *La Bourgeoisie Française au XVII Siècle* (Paris, 1908), p. 652 ff.

[12] *Le Journal d'Olivier Lefèvre d'Ormesson,* edited by A. Cheruel (Paris, 1860), 2 vols., tells this story, and is an invaluable record of politics and administration under Louis XIV. Cf. also the careers of the Ormesson and Molé families in Normand, *op. cit.,* Chap. IV. The career of Colbert and his relatives is equally instructive.

[13] Ch. Godard, *Les Intendants sous Louis XIV* (Paris, 1901) sums up the jurisdiction of the intendants at the end of Louis XIV's reign (p. 440).

which meant, in fact, by the favoritism of families or mistresses. There was constant war between the intendants and the local administrative apparatus, yet without the use of the latter the intendant could not carry out his policy. The maintenance of harmonious relations with the local powers—the governors, the courts, the president of the estates (where there were estates) and the municipal leaders—therefore became of first importance, and it is not therefore surprising that not only the character of the intendant was important in this regard but that of his wife also!

Subdelegates. The intendants were quite early in their history (about 1640) obliged to appoint subdelegates [14]—at first for special occasions, later as permanent subordinates for all tasks—for primitive means of communication compelled the delegation of work to local agents. Colbert wrote to the intendants, individually and collectively, to employ subdelegates as little as possible.[15] It is clear that he was afraid that the full force of the will of the central government would be weakened by the employment of officials drawn largely from the locality. He complains that they will have private interests, affections, or hatreds which do not march well with the course of justice.[16] But the Crown was obliged to bend to the administrative necessities which it had itself created. The central authority began to treat with the subdelegates directly when this was expedient, and their expenses were paid by the king. What administrative necessity had initiated, financial necessity completed. In 1704, a subdelegacy—called an *élection*—was created by the Crown in every chief town of each administrative district, and the office was purchasable. Until that time the appointments were made at the free discretion of the intendants. As few buyers appeared for the office, they were suppressed in 1715. The duties were very vague and were as elastic as the intendant allowed them to be. These subdelegates

were paid by the intendant and by whatever fees and bribes they could extract.

There was thus established in the seventeenth century a system firmly under the direction of the central authority and extending practically over the whole territory of France. Its personnel was of very unequal quality, but some of its members were exceedingly capable administrators, and even more than that, men of fine character and genius. The later intendants, as we shall show, wore less and less the aspect of tyrants, and became benevolent administrators who were not seldom in conflict with the central authority for their local sympathies and sending a stream of reformative suggestions to it. Between the end of the reign of Louis XIV and the Revolution, there stretches more than half a century of administrative history which De Tocqueville has described in *L'Ancien Régime.* De Tocqueville does not spare the system; the full energy of his passionate belief in liberty and decentralization is directed to paint in its darkest shadows.

The centralized system had consolidated itself, and the intendants were its instruments. In several famous and eloquent chapters De Tocqueville draws up the catalogue of France's grievances. "The Intendant was in possession of the whole reality of government." He quotes the often-quoted remark of the notorious Law to D'Argenson:

"Sir, I could never believe what I saw while I was administering the finances. You ought to know that this kingdom of France is governed by thirty intendants. You have neither parliaments, nor countries, nor Estates, nor governors, I am almost inclined to add, neither King, nor ministers. It is upon thirty Masters of Requests, sent to the provinces, that their happiness or misfortune, their fertility or sterility depend."

The volume of work for which they were responsible is enormous and has ludicrous results. They administered the unpopular taxes, principally the *taille,* the capitation tax, and the *vingtièmes;* they administered conscription for the militia, undertook the execution of public works, directed the engineers in the

---

[14] Cf. Babeau, *op. cit.,* Vol. II, p. 68 ff.
[15] Viollet, *op. cit.,* pp. 552, 553.
[16] Clément, *Histoire de Colbert,* ol. II, pp. 11 and 12.

construction of roads, maintained public order with the help of the mounted police, administered poor relief and the work houses, promoted agriculture, and supervised all the regulations governing industry. Government had assumed the place of Providence. The results were in part ludicrous and in part tragic. Foolish regulations caused officials to undertake foolish tasks: they entered into the most minute detail, for example, to ensure that cloth was made of the right dimensions and quality while producer and consumer had other wishes entirely. But other effects were more serious; people and officials became accustomed to formalities, delay, overregulation, and a surplus of reports and statistics. No one could possibly understand or keep all the rules, and therefore both officials and population ceased to take them seriously. The localities had experienced the substantial extinction of all rights to self-government, and the center of power was in Paris; to Paris, therefore, the best talents flocked, further denuding the provinces of spiritual life. The country was in the grip of a rigid and deadening centralization, one, indeed, which so worked upon the habits of men that the Revolution could not finish with it, but had to let it return because there was no other mentality ready to fill the possible vacuum. When the enormous weight of a whole system reposed upon the king or one or two favorites, capable or not, it was inevitable that from time to time the power to make decisions should fall into the hands of the subordinate officials at the center. Hence the development of what is called "bureaucracy."

THE TIDE TURNS

As we have seen, the system had grown up in the course of some two hundred years, by a process of struggle followed by continuous and gradual consolidation. But on the eve of the Revolution—indeed, for a quarter of a century before it—changes were in progress which find too little consideration in De Tocqueville's accounts. In a brilliant study, a Russian historian has revealed their nature.[17] For various reasons, the center now exerted less influence upon its local servants; the chief reasons were the increasing complexity of affairs and the growing independence of the intendants.

The Intendants Change in Character. The intendants became domiciled in the provinces for long periods: twenty years was by no means uncommon; many served for longer, some for upwards of thirty years. Out of sixty-eight intendants who administered France during the reign of Louis XVI, twenty-four served in one place for more than twenty years, thirty-nine for at least ten years, and only eight for less than five years. Men entered their posts in early manhood and remained often till death. What a contrast this was to the short terms of office of the ministers in Paris, and to the early history of the system!

The result was twofold: the growth of independence *vis-a-vis* the ministers, and the development of local patriotism. People talked now of the intendant as "the man of the province."[18] The intendant became paternally interested in the province, made his peace with the competing powers, represented the special interest of his locality, and, besides carrying out the policy of the central authority with every benevolent regard for the well-being of his area, contrived social and economic experiments on his own initiative. Office of this kind had become a family career, and there are many instances of the succession of office in the same family and the ramification of collateral branches of the family among other offices either in the same or neighboring provinces or in Paris. There was frequent consultation among intendants directly and

17 Paul Ardascheff, *Les Intendants de Province sous Louis XVI* (Paris, 1909). If there is any bias in this study, it is only in the desire to point out that de Tocqueville was insufficiently discriminating about the period at which he placed the full force of despotic centralization. This was before 1760. Cf. footnote 8, and see Paul Viollet's *Histoire des Institutions Politiques et Administratives de la France* (Paris, 1903), 3 vols.
18 Ardascheff, *op. cit.*, p. 81.

not through the intermediary of the central authority: they pooled their experience and lent each other their experts. Their work was made the easier by their accumulation of offices: they remained members of the legal corporations, were members of the *parlements,* and in some cases were even the presiding officer of these bodies, and what could not be obtained with facility through one of these professional channels they obtained through another.

The intendants were drawn from a class susceptible to the winds of doctrine which blew so strongly in their time. They were of the class which Ardascheff has very ingeniously named the *noblesse d'État*—that is, the very rich *bourgeoisie* which had acquired high office by its talents and money, and in acquiring office had acquired nobility—the *noblesse de la robe.* Under Louis XIV the officials had been chosen from a poorer and humbler class, they had been the spear-heads of the attack upon the pretensions of the feudal aristocracy; as Saint-Simon called it, *"le règne de la vile bourgeoisie."* They were precursors and sometimes the ancestors of this new aristocracy to whom the chief offices of state, the financial and the municipal; offices, and the magistracy, were the natural heritage. They were the precursors of the absolute state; the Revolution proclaimed the overthrow of their power but did not accomplish it, and even the era of Parliaments and the career open to the talents is still largely dominated by their social and economic power. From this class came the thousand or so lawyers practicing in the *parlements* and the other high courts. They could not enter the *conseil d'état* as *maîtres de requêtes* until after at least six years' service, and this requirement reduced the source of recruitment to between two and three hundred. Other offices, retirements, and deaths reduced the office of *maîtres des requêtes.* Then not all who were qualified to be members of the *conseil* desired to be. So that the number of *maîtres,* eighty-four, was the source of the thirty administrators of the provinces.

These men were precisely of that class who formed the staple of the *salons* of the time. Reason, Benevolence, and Progress mastered their minds and phrases and began to affect their administrative behavior; they talked the Rights of Humanity long before the crowd began to enact them. Their administrative habits became milder; their projects savored less of the study and their own uncontrolled personal will; improvement became their passion; and "love of the people" softened the rigor of their aristocratic position.

Whether or not the despotism was enlightened, it was a despotism—which operated through the intendant and his subordinates. Though the intendant mitigated the full weight of centralization, yet it was still very oppressive. Though the relations of the intendant and the province became more harmonious and mild, the province desired representative institutions, for whether or not the intendant was actuated by "humanity," he was the scion of a caste whose interests and mentality could not but exclude most that was vital to the Third Estate.

Nor was this all. You cannot pretend to govern for the good of the people without finally causing the people to want to govern themselves. Any despotic government which includes the people's good is ultimately excluded by it. It is amusing—though the upshot was tragic—to see the intendants attempting to maintain unsevered in their one bosom two warring souls, each of which they loved with a great passion: the Humanity and Benevolence of their century, which impelled them to interfere, and the laissez faire of the economists, which hissed "Leave them alone."

The public documents of the last few years before the Revolution show the intendants perfectly willing to promote the well-being of their provinces, and becoming more and more able to do so. Learned societies of all kinds—agricultural and other—they sponsored; inventions they encouraged; public works of utility and embellishment they planned and executed. The history of Turgot in the Limousin [19] is by no means an isolated history, although the character of the man has made it extraordinary. Neither the character nor the ability of the intendants was to blame for the defects of the *ancien régime;* at least, by no means primarily. But the intendants were the whipping blocks, as are, always and everywhere, the officials of a machine whose purpose and propelling force are disliked.

The intendants, willy-nilly, were the instruments of extortion. They were the tools of the powerful modern state, which had taken over the government and social obligations of the feudal lords without taking away from these their privileges, or without sharing its power with the people, who, by taxation and personal labor, maintained that power. On this disparity of financial burden and privileges pivoted all the theories and acts leading to the Revolution.[20]

The people, charged with taxes, duties, services and obligations, of all sorts, complains of the situation and desires a better. . . It attributes, as is usual in the human mind, all the evils it suffers to the administrators it sees.[21]

When they attempted to even out the financial burdens by making their administrative practice violate the letter of the law, the whole of the privileged classes cursed them for meddling fools.

Provincial Assemblies. From long before the middle of the eighteenth century, there had been a strong undercurrent of criticism against the intendants. Aristocratic and democratic thinkers agreed in this, that the intendants should be abolished.[22] By the middle of the eighteenth century even the court was affected by anti-absolutist views, especially the entourage of the future Louis XVI. In 1778, provincial assemblies were actually set up by Necker in two provinces to moderate the centralization of governmental power.[23] In 1787 the system with some differences, was widely extended. The assemblies failed not in their life but in their conception. For they were conceived as part of the old social order, not as the instruments of a new. As parts of the old social order, they were compelled to maintain the privileges on the one side and the burdens on the other. Therefore they could not be given any powers which affected the financial system or the sovereignty of the established authorities.[24] The *Tiers État* was never allowed its full voting power, and even if it had been increased to any equality with the combined *noblesse* and clergy, the functions were strictly limited. The elective element of the assemblies was therefore impotent.

The Revolutionary Age. When legal equality replaced privilege, the way was open for representative assemblies and decentralization; the central authority did not need to be as tyrannous as before, and the two-century-old institution of the intendants died. If it was not difficult, once social forces had shifted, to decree the abolition of the intendants, it was not so easy to escape from the tradition which had been created. For a tradition is a motive power in men; what has been sanctioned is a persuasive force, and an expedient ready-made; it saves exertion and thought and secures obedience. The tools had been abolished, but not the spirit which used the tools: centralization

[19] A good account is in S. d'Hugues, *Essai sur l'Administration de Turgot dans la Généralité de Limoges* (Paris, 1859).
[20] This is not the place to describe the structure of society. It can be found in H. Taine, *Les Origines de la France Contemporaine* (Paris, edition of 1906), Vol. I of which is entirely devoted to this; in Alexis De Tocqueville's *De l'Ancien Régime* (Paris, 1850); and, on the administration of finances, Marcel Marion, *Les Impôts Directs sous L'Ancien Régime* (Paris 1910); and, perhaps, best of all in Necker's works.
[21] P. Renouvin, *Les Assemblées Provinciales de 1787* (Paris, 1921), p. 89.

[22] Thus the Marquis D'Argenson, *Considerations sur le Gouvernement de la France,* composed about 1747, and first published in 1764 (edition 1787, *Avertissement*).
[23] Cf. Jacques Necker, *Memoire sur l'Établissement des Administrations Provinciales* (Paris, 1778, Stael edition), ol. III, p. 333 ff.; and his *De l'Administration des Finances* (Paris, 1784), Vol. II, p. 189 ff.
[24] Cf. also Leónce de Lavergne, *Les Assemblées Provinciales* (Paris, 1863).

itself had not been abolished. Only the undemocratic quality of centralization had succumbed. There was no alternative that could be set against it as a thing efficacious and proved by experience. Theory and aspirations might have provided a substitute, but the Revolution and Napoleon both needed the old method; the Revolution to cause a complete and universal break with the social and political conditions of the past, Napoleon the better to usurp and make all provinces obedient to his will. The notion of laissez faire was ever foreign to the Continental mind, and the French did no more than salute and march past it; yet that notion is essential to the readiness to give and take local self-government. Revolution followed revolution, reaction followed reaction; and the impulse of each sudden change was to impress itself over the whole country. No régime had the time and security to grow mellow or experienced enough to share its power—none but the Third Republic. And then by the middle of the nineteenth century, when decentralization had to some extent been practiced, and when its value was beginning to be understood, the evolution of science, industry, and commerce turned all in favor of centralization, and the second half of the century was occupied in the struggle against the old and the new forces that maintained centralization. Of these more recent developments we must speak later (Chap. 32). One blazing truth stands out: centralization can be a democratic as well as an undemocratic device, for the people who make the laws in a democratic state may demand services of government which can only be produced by centralization.

The Caesar Complex. The memory of power of the central executive and its former pretensions has caused French Parliaments to be highly jealous of the modern executive. It has been impressed upon them that the central power was once an entirely unrestrained authority, that its acts were arbitrary, that it is still a restive entity animated by the old spirit, and that the old spirit functioned in such wise that only a bloody but glorious Revo-

lution could expel it. The means is thus identified with the end; and though the end was the real vice, it has the vicarious force of causing hostility to the means. And thus at every point these two, Parliamentarian and Official, find themselves in contrast. It is a sheer reaction from an historical situation, one of those undue reactions of which the history of government is almost entirely composed: an unfortunate quality of human behavior but one which human beings, who live by exaggeration, will take centuries to grow out of; on a large scale it is what the uncontrolled reflex is in simpler behavior.

CORRUPT METHODS OF RECRUITMENT

THE centralized methods of the *ancien régime* might have been supportable by the country if the officials had been competent, if the career at least had been open to the talents. But the career was not open to the talents, and very little heed was given to the problem of competence. This is a very striking difference from Prussia, and the advent of Revolution in France and the slow progression from autocracy to constitutionalism in Germany are in part direct effects of the difference in the quality of their respective bureaucracies.

The Venality of Offices. In France until the Revolution, almost every office, central and local, excepting the dozen or so highest offices in the kingdom, were attainable only by private purchase, gift, or inheritance. All public offices, that is, were a species of private property, and a voluminous jurisprudence governed their transmission. This jurisprudence is at pains to explain that the offices which were vendible and hereditable were of a two-fold nature: they were at once a property and a public function. Anybody, then, who desired to acquire an office had to purchase the property from the owner and be installed in the function. The latter gave the Crown the opportunity of demanding guarantees of competence, but in fact the Crown and its officers through whose registers the transaction and the installation passed did not demand such guarantees: they were gallantly content with fees, bribes, and other favors, personal or procured. Not every one with the price of an office was legally entitled to it, but in practice, every one obtained it at some price. Ability, however, unsupported by money or family, was almost certain of exclusion from public office. The system, in short, was venality tempered by favoritism.[25]

Venality began in judicial offices, was extended to financial and other officials, and in 1680 was extended to municipal officials. By the time of the Revolution there were 300,000 offices of this kind, equivalent, at a guess, to the number of all officials, central and local: that is, the judiciary, central and local (all the members of the bench and bar of the *Parlements*); the intendants; the financial, road, forestry, postal, and customs officials; the queerly-named officials to whom the protection and regulation of industry and commerce had given rise (like the gaugers of wine, the computers of hay, the salt salesmen, the coal controllers, the sealing-wax warmers, the measurers of cloth, the judges of leather, etc., many, indeed, being quite private employments); and the mayors, lieutenants of mayors, and police.[26]

What was the history of this singular institution? It was little more than a fiscal expedient adopted by impecunious kings and ministers, and so easy a means of raising money that once it was begun its evils were never for long obstacles to its extension. Just as some modern countries when hard pressed have inflated the currency as an indirect method of taxation, so the number of offices of finance was inflated and sold, the revenue and the commission from their sale being afterwards paid for by the people at large who were taxed to pay the salaries. The practice had begun as an occasional and unwelcome expedient in the fourteenth century, but in Louis XII's wars with

Italy, financial pressure compelled a large-scale operation of this kind: the exception now became the rule.

Prices rose, but there was a frantic buying. Ministers made the most of their financial discovery. As it soon became too difficult to invent new offices, the old ones were doubled or trebled—that is, divided up among several holders, who exercise their functions in rotation, or who did what the seventeenth and eighteenth centuries were too fond of doing, employed a humble subordinate to carry them out. Loyseau explains this eagerness to buy offices as arising from ambition which had engendered an *archomania* (or mania for office) which caused people to hurry to obtain them. In Loyseau's day a common proverb was that "there are always more fools than situations!"

Offices were sought, then, with a frenzied energy, and they were created with cynicism. Desmarets, one of Louis XIV's Comptroller-Generals, had proposed to the King the establishment of some quite futile offices, and the latter asked who would ever consent to buy such situation? "Your Majesty," replied Desmarets, "is forgetting one of the most splendid of the prerogatives of the Kings of France—that when the King creates a job, God immediately creates an idiot to buy it."[27]

The effects upon the administration of France were mixed, but the bad easily outweighed the good. No regard was had to competence in the vast majority of the cases. The law provided for an inquisition into the capacity of the candidate which was supposed to have reference to his character, his age, and "sufficiency": that is, in the case of officers needing a legal training, their legal knowledge, and in the case of the financial officials, their ability to cover any loss. All these things were neglected. The legal companies examined the legal officers: it was a farcical procedure. Only one rule of exclusion was practiced: orthodoxy to the Catholic, Apostolic, and Roman faith. In the offices nearest to the king, capacity as he or his mistress judged it was important, and it

[25] This is described and analyzed in Louis-Lucas, *Étude sur la Venalité des Charges et Fonctions Publiques depuis l'Antiquité Romaine jusqu'à Nos Jours* (Paris, 1883), 2 vols.
[26] Louis-Lucas, *op. cit.*, II, 30, footnote.
[27] *Idem.*

sometimes occurred that the king would find the means for the purchase of an office. A vast mass of talent was thus excluded, while there was no regulation of entry other than ability to purchase. The numbers of officials bore no scientific relationship to the amount and kind of work to be done; there were too many as a rule, and they often held office for only a short time. It was impossible for the Crown to exert any effective pressure upon them through a hierarchy, since each, having purchased his office, stood in a kind of independence to those above him. None of the devices which the nineteenth and twentieth centuries have found absolutely indispensable to the maintenance of an efficient administrative service could possibly come into being in such a system. There was an untrained, unregulated, and uncontrolled mass of people, to whom, above all, the function was a private property to be used as a means of personal power and profit by fees and bribes. The *Pot-de-Vin* is written large all over the history of France.

This system suffered from the same fault which private industry and commerce of the nineteenth century and of our own day exhibit: services were rendered for profit unequally—the best to those who could afford to pay for them, not to those who most needed them. Montaigne, whose father bought him a councillorship at the age of twenty-three, said: [28]

There is nothing more barbarous than to see a nation where, by legitimate custom, the function of judging was sold, where judgment was bought for cash down, and where justice was refused to those who could not pay . . .

The venality of offices gave rise to yet another evil. It encouraged the formation of an official caste. On the face of it, this appears unexpected, since money could always penetrate into the phalanx of official positions, but, in fact, fortune goes very largely by bequest within families, and one generation which possesses privi-

leges is always in a good position to come upon opportunities for its children. The office holders thus became a caste ringed round by money and privileges. The whole body of office holders was divisible into four classes according to the quality of ennoblement and privileges attaching to the office: (1) The highest and hereditary nobility, with its exemptions from taxation, was conferred upon the most important officers—the immediate advisers of the Crown and its governors and lieutenants in the provinces. (2) A second category (councilors of the *Parlements* and other courts of justice, and the high accounting officers) obtained simple ennoblement which did not pass to descendants unless the officer died while in possession of his office or had not resigned it until after twenty years of possession and service. (3) A lower category of offices conferred personal nobility; these gave noble pre-eminence but not nobility, and were not transmissible. (4) Lastly, there were offices which did not confer nobility of any kind, but only some of the immunities and exemptions enjoyed by the nobles—supplements, virtually, to their salary, such as exemptions from the *taille,* of the *tutelle,* from collectorship of the *taille,* etc.

All this nobility and seminobility felt themselves part of a class with interests and aspirations other than the rest of the people. The result was administratively bad. A corporative spirit grew up which made this class resist reforms and caused the higher officials to protect the lower from punishment, for "short, medium or long, the robe covered and set apart a *gens togata,* which much more nearly constituted an 'order' than the nobility." Two other effects were disastrous: the people could not but feel that this caste had nothing to do with them except to exploit them, and was therefore to be obeyed only in so far as coercion was inescapable; and a continuous temptation existed to those with the means to step into the official class and there seek distinction.

There are those, however, who can find something good in the worst institution,

[28] Pierre Clement, *Études Financières* (Paris, 1859) p. 13—"Montaigne Citoyen."

and the stream of comments on venality has left a certain deposit. (1) It enabled the Third Estate to acquire office,[29] whereas, presumably, without such a mode of recruitment the public services would have been exclusively occupied by the old nobility and their nominees. The parents of the Third Estate gave their children a good literary education in the hope that they might one day occupy high office. (2) The offices were taken out of the sphere of politics which, until 1789, were rotten with religious and factional intrigue. Purchase and heredity contributed to the establishment of families in whom professional traditions of science and honor were engendered and maintained, and this was far preferable to appointment by court favoritism. (3) Finally, it was argued that venality produced the nonremovability and official independence of legal officers—an extremely important gain at a time when the monarchy was molding everything, provinces, municipalities, to its purposes—it was a refuge from the rule of the arbitrary. It was apparently on this ground that Montesquieu, in his *Esprit des Lois,* finally favored venality.[30]

There were occasionally serious suggestions to abolish the system—mainly under Colbert—but financial pressure and the question of compensation defeated all projects. The Revolution made a complete and indiscriminate suppression of the institution, and it required four hundred decrees to accomplish this.

Favoritism. Government abhors a vacuum, and when the laws deliberately create such a vacuum by a revolutionary break, a new principle must be set up. The Declaration of Rights of 1791 established a new principle. Article 4 says:

All citizens, being equal before it [the Law], are equally admissible to all public dignities, situations, and offices, according to their capacity, and without any other distinction than that of their virtues and their talents.

The vacuum is, however, not properly filled until a method of measuring and choosing "virtues and talents" has been devised and put into operation. Such a method ought to be determined by a calm and mature consideration of the nature of the state, considered not as a static entity whose life history has ended but as a dynamic condition. But the practical conditions of a revolutionary period do not allow of such foresighted and wholesale plans: there are urgent and immediate contingencies upon whose solution hangs life or death. The vacuum is, therefore, filled by a rush of that very spirit which made a revolution.[31] It is natural that the revolutionist shall judge virtue and talent roughly and readily as whether you are for or against him: indeed, in a revolution people choose themselves. Also in a counterrevolution. And as revolution and counterrevolution succeeded each other at intervals until 1870, it is not surprising that no careful attention was paid to the problem of recruitment, and that republics and empires and consulates and kingdoms relapsed not into systematic venality but into systematic favoritism. The factions and the parties in French political life after 1789 were unrestrained by any fine tradition to the contrary. Favoritism chased venality out of France and reigned in its stead until recent years. And as nomination was abandoned to the will of the prince, so was promotion and dismissal.

Survey. The French have, therefore, an experience of administration which has made them unfriendly toward it. When their kings were administratively active, they suffered from his assistants; when those kings were libertines and occupied themselves in war or court intrigues, the people paid the price of a machine which they detested. At a time when Prussia was rising to European im-

---

[29] A. Thierry, *Essai sur l'Histoire de la Formation et des Progrès du Tiers État* (Paris, 1853), Chaps. IV and VII.
[30] Book V, Chap. 19.

[31] Taine's metaphor is different: *Régime Moderne* (Paris, 1906), Vol. I, p. 194: "By an amputation which is radical, complete, and extraordinary and to which history does not measure an equal case—with the temerity of the theorist and the brutality of the *carabin*—the legislator has extirpated the old institution as far as he was able . . ."

portance by the forceful and able administration of a succession of particularly brilliant monarchs, the administration of France was systematically ruined and its name and actions delivered over to scandal and mockery by kings of weak will, debauched lives, and a juvenile taste for the glories of war. Thus did the accident of birth and the nature-given geographical situation which produced costly wars conspire with human nature to erect a polity at once centralized and venal.

The shapes which the central administrative departments successively took are not of much importance; as everywhere else they began as an amalgam, then were sorted out first by area and later by cognate services and swayed between control by single secretaries of state and boards.[32] Higher, perhaps, than in other countries was the importance of the Comptroller-General of Finances, and this was because the finances were in a

chronically pathological state and everything was subordinated to the requisition of a large revenue.[33] Ministers came and went in remarkably quick succession.[34] In the story of Necker's administration and downfall, and in that of Turgot, the whole natural history of the *ancien régime* is written. There seemed neither energy nor stability at the center.

The organization of the nineteenth century was not, then, written on an entirely clean sheet. The gullies could still be seen in spite of attempts at erasure, and the pencil was apt to slip into the ancient grooves; or their appearance would so terrify the legislators that they would write what a calmer mood could not commend.

---

[32] Cf. Viollet, *Le Roi et ses Ministres,* and de Lucay, *op. cit.*

[33] Cf. Necker, *De l'Administration des Finances;* and de Marée, *Le Contrôle des Finances* (Paris, 1928), Vol. 2, Chap. XII.
[34] In the reign of Louis XIV the controllers served an average of eleven years each; in Louis XV's regency five years; in his own reign three years; and in Louis XVI's reign of eighteen years, they served an average of one and three-quarters years.

30

England: Origins, Reform, and Recruitment
of the Civil Service

ORIGINS

IN what respects does English differ from Continental administrative history? The ordinary English view of today is that England was saved from bureaucracy and centralization, with which the Continent is afflicted, by the innate individualism of its people, their stout resistance to the interfering propensities of all government, and their ability to adventure and attain their own well-being by independent enterprise. But these words hide more than they reveal. Perhaps the real cause of freedom from bureaucracy is religious and social indifferentism and material acquisitiveness. Let us turn from the hypothetical to that which is historically well founded.

The first striking feature in English administrative evolution is the small amount of conscious—or at least formal —thought bestowed upon the subject until the end of the eighteenth century. It is impossible after the reign of Henry III and his immediate successors to find a person of the mental caliber and strength of character of Richelieu, Colbert, or Louis XIV in France, or the Hohenzollerns of the late seventeenth and the eighteenth century in Prussia, devoting themselves with such ardor to the creation of a complete social scheme and an administrative system to support it,[1] for Thomas Crom-

well, Francis Walsingham, and William and Robert Cecil were restrained by imperious masters and a restive Commons. Whatever of administrative inventiveness there was went mainly into the organization of the Treasury, and the Chancery, the development of the Royal Council, and only lastly the Secretaryship of State.[2]

---

[1] The early history of administration is, of course, hardly distinguishable from constitutional history, since the administration revolves immediately around the king, himself anactive administrator at the center. For this history see W. Stubbs' *Constitutional History*, 5th edition (Oxford, 1891-96), and C. Petit-Dutaillis, *Studies and Notes Supplementary to Stubbs* (Manchester, 1930).

[2] Cf. H. Hall, *The Red Book of the Exchequer* (Oxford, 1896); R. L. Poole, *The Exchequer in the Twelfth Century* (Oxford, 1912); T. F. Tout, *Chapters in Mediaeval Administrative History* (Manchester 1920-33), 6 vols.; J. F. Baldwin, *The King's Council in England during the Middle Ages* (Oxford, 1913). And see further: E. R. Turner, *The Privy Council* (Baltimore 1927-28), 2 vols.; A. C. Andrews, *British Committees, Commissions, and Councils of Trade and Plantations, 1622-75* (Baltimore, 1908); and F. S. Thomas, *Notes for the History of Public Departments* (London, 1846). Also see the historical introduction to the volumes in the *Whitehall Series*, all published in London: T. L. Heath, *The Treasury* (1927); E. Murray, *The Post Office* (1927); H. Gordon, *The War Office* (1935); J. Tilley and S. Gaselee, *The Foreign Office* (1933); G. V. Fiddes, *The Dominions and Colonial Offices* (1926); M. C. C. Seton, *The India Office* (1926); E. Troup, *The Home Office* (1925); H. L. Smith, *The Board of Trade* (1928); F. Floud, *The Ministry of Agriculture and Fisheries* (1937); A. Newsholme, *The Ministry of Health*

English needs were not those which required for their satisfaction the extreme centralization and hierarchies of the Continent. Before the sixteenth century the modern state had hardly yet arisen out of feudal organization, and this provided for so much of the official work in its own peculiar fashion, in the manor, the corporations, and guilds, and by the clerks, the Church-learned dignitaries, and minor writers. The Chancellor and the Treasurer and the royal clerks who surrounded the king were his private servants. They did not come under external criticism until much later, since their work was at first so slight and their power so unpolitical that it did not cause public anxiety. When, in the sixteenth century, the nation became conscious of its identity, international and domestic, and the Tudors had raised the power of the Crown to a great height, the monarchy and by consequence its ministers were faced by a restive Parliament at the center of administration and by about two thousand justices of the peace and thousands of parishes at the extremities.[3] That is, at the center its pretensions and plans were subject to a valid external check, and the privy councilors in Parliament were harassed and checked when they attempted the high hand. Nothing like such a powerful and authoritative control over the administration existed elsewhere in the Germanic states or in France. In this respect England was a century and a half in front of them. This was a very important factor for the extent to which it limited the size, pretensions, and quality of the administration. In the localities there was a ready-made administrative apparatus which cost little or

nothing.[4] When men like Burghley—no longer royal servants and clerks, and since about 1601 given the significant title of Secretary of State—began to pursue a positive state policy in relation to industry and commerce, they relied upon this local machinery. But what costs nothing usually gives nothing after the waning of the first excited patriotic impulse, and parliamentary Colbertism as it has been called, or mercantilism, petered out and ultimately did more harm than good because the administrative instruments indispensable to state activity had not been consciously devised to fit the law to be applied. This lazy hand-to-mouth method is apparent in every branch of national administration. The ends were desired, but not the means which alone could have attained them. An attempt was made at the end of the sixteenth and the beginning of the seventeenth century consciously to invigorate the administration of the Poor Law (which was the core of a local administration), and when it failed, the sun set on such efforts at administrative efficiency, not to rise again for two centuries. Continental thinkers have expressed their admiration of England's freedom from bureaucracy, and this admiration has been focused by the works of one great worker—Gneist—upon English local administration, the nature of which in the seventeenth and eighteenth centuries preserved the country from centralization.

The administrative apparatus of England from the middle of the sixteenth to the end of the eighteenth century worked so badly as to call forth law after law from the central authority, each complaining that the preceding one had not been properly executed. The preambles to these laws were little essays in administration, compounded of complaints, scolding, and exhortation. It is impossible to estimate in quantities the financial loss and the physical and spiritual misery suffered by the people of the parishes and the towns of England because there was

---

(1925); L. A. Selby-Bigge, *The Board of Education* (1927).

See too, Dibbens, "The King's Secretaries in the Thirteenth and Fourteenth Centuries," *English Historical Review*, Vol. XXV, p. 430; most importantly F. S. Evans's excellent study of *The Secretaryship of State, 1558-1680* (London, 1924); K. Pickthorn, *Early Tudor Government* (Cambridge, 1936), 2 vols.; and M. A. Thompson, *The Secretaries of State, 1681-1782* (Oxford, 1934).

[3] Cf. Charles A. Beard, *Early History of the Justice of the Peace* (New York, 1904).

[4] Cf. the studies of local administration by Sidney and Beatrice Webb.

no central officer to watch and control the behavior of the local authorities. It was enormous and terrible. However, the hierarchical, centralized, overdisciplined system of Prussia was avoided, and the detailed *étatism* and organized venality of France found no place. Instead much made for the development of administrative self-reliance.

The many ambitious laws made by Parliament were carried out not by the professional agents of the central authority, but by the local gentry of the upper and middling class. These were unpaid and nonprofessional. No qualifications of literacy or study were required of them. The conscientious among them could acquire the modicum of law necessary for their decisions from the justice's manuals and the customs of others. Their reasoning and judgments were not directed by authority; no excessive numbers of regulations or minutes hampered them; and no representative of the central authority supervised their activities. The authority they exercised appeared unstrained and natural to the mass of men, for the justices of the peace occupied their positions in virtue of their local economic fortune and social status. They were the landowners and therefore, in an agricultural society, the hereditary rulers. Their acres prevailed. As neighbors their rule was accepted with the minimum amount of questioning we accord to one of our own group. It is the "outsider" whose presence raises questions and whose pretensions conduce to discussions of their justification; the "outsider" it is who provokes the democratic *quo warranto*? The justice of the peace was not one of these, interfering in the name of the king or the queen or the state, but simply settled the everyday difficulties of two or three villages—and in partnership with his fellows, at quarter sessions, settled more important questions of order, roads and bridges, the well-being of the poor, prices and wages, and such-like affairs for the benefit of the country. Quarter sessions had a few officers—but for the rest, the everyday work of administration was done by even more immediate neighbors of the governed, the parish officers.

All these officers were directly of the people, serving for their term compulsorily and often unwillingly. They knew vividly, and in detail, the nature of the life of their community, and when they desired, did not find it difficult to distinguish the circumstances of one person from the other. Moreover, the people knew them just as well. Accommodation of governors and governed is of the first importance in successful and liberal administration: and this local mutual knowledge rendered easy of attainment. The opinion of the governed promptly and continuously influenced the governors—sometimes too easily as in the removal of nuisances, the relief of the poor, or the reduction of assessments for rates.

This was clearly a system in which the habit of self-government was fostered, at least for the aristocracy and squirearchy; here the legend of immemorial right of local government could develop vigor and stamina. The sense of freedom from external direction and control was not disturbed by the actual machinery which brought the central government and the local officials in town, county, and parish into the semblance of loose coherence. It was nonbureaucratic—that is, it was not exercised by officials trained for work in a particular department of state with habits of mind formed by professional activity in those departments.

The method of administration was largely judicial, that is, it was exercised at the level of the county and its districts by justices of the peace, who supervised and corrected *post facto*, rather than anticipated and intervened before and during the event. This is an important distinction between the administration of the nineteenth and twentieth centuries and the methods of the eighteenth. The judicial is after the fact, corrects and applies remedies; the administrative implies the appointment of an official to anticipate the future, to watch whether appropriate or erroneous administration will occur, with the responsibility for setting rules designed to guide action and avoid error, and with personnel having continuous responsibility to intervene to secure that the rule work as previously designed.

Yet the justices were on the local spot, and their wide acquaintance with men, interests, and policies enabled them to give good common-sense directions even if they were only remedial and of benefit in the future, and as persons, they influenced day-by-day administration. The method of keeping the local parochial officials up to a tolerable standard of duty was to "present" them or the parish as a whole before the judicial sessions of the county, that is, to charge them there with nonfeasance or malfeasance or negligence, and the rest. They would be fined if remiss in their tasks of, for example, apprenticing a pauper child, assessing rates, neglecting to remove nuisances (health hazards), not keeping up the roads and bridges, or not fixing the scales of wages and prices and conditions of apprenticeship. When the parties appealed, as they might, the central authority's judges on circuit gave judgment: and this settled the lines along which the matters in dispute were to be administered in the future: in reality a rule of administration was established. This soon found its way into the justices' manuals. The central judges took back the information they had locally obtained and in the Privy Council their views were shaped into a new, amending law. A kind of local, part-time inspectorial system was established in the institution of the common informer. In many cases, any person informing of a violation of the law received a share of the fine if the violation were established in court. This rudimentary detective arrangement no doubt kept officials rather more alert than they would otherwise have been, and brought more cases of maladministration to the courts than would otherwise have been corrected. Since all concerned—official, informer, and justice—were local residents in a land of villages, movement away from which was very rare, the system had its administrative merits. But it would have been surprising if the local situation

was continuously encouraging to informers.

An attempt was made between 1587 to about 1640 to institute stronger, directive, administrative control from the center.[5] It failed mainly because the onset of the civil war broke the continuity of central authority. And the outcome of the civil war was to vest local government in the hands of the substantial families of the localities until far into the nineteenth century.

The country was, in fact, more concerned in the seventeenth and eighteenth centuries to control the executive as a policy-making body than as an administrative organization. It was not anxious to seek to tap the sources of efficient government so much as to limit the power to govern without parliamentary consent. The Crown was not interested especially in highly efficient administration: all it sought was the right to appoint or give to its ministerial friends the right to appoint and employ in freedom from parliamentary control. Its interest was patronage.

Thus, while the Continent in these centuries elaborated an administrative system centralized and militarized or venal, and in Prussia professionally schooled, England devoted her energy to the perfection of constitutional restraints on the Crown. Prussia and France sought to flourish by "inner colonization," and so widened the scope of domestic government and bore heavily on the people through officials. England's eyes were directed across the seas to foreign colonization. The former exploited the people at home: the latter, far-away peoples. So England was spared the full rigor of domestic tyranny by officials.

This noncentralized, nonbureaucratic, local-gentry system of government was in part made possible by certain accidents of geographical position and historical fate. The comparatively unchallenged supremacy of a single political authority was accomplished by the Norman con-

---

[5] Cf. S. and B. Webb, *English Poor Law History* (London, 1932), Part I, Chap. II.

quest—five centuries before such a boon was gained by either Prussia or France, even if two or three hundred years were still needed to consolidate what in 1066 had been a first surge of centralizing authority. In geographical situation England was favored also: insular and isolated, invasion became difficult once a navy had been built for defense. It did not need to insist, as Prussia and France were obliged to, that the country, with strong neighbors not many miles distant, must be one and indivisible. It was not necessary as the price of survival to knit the country together with a thread of steel whose ends were in the hands of the central authority. Conscription of neither persons nor localities was necessary. The sea saved England for long from the administrative and despotic centralization imposed by the Continental state's addiction to the *raison d'état*. Then, also, England, through distance, was not pervaded, like the Continent, by the authoritarian influence of Rome either in her legal structure and spirit or in her religion.

Thus, free and liberal in her local administration (if anarchic and not altogether efficient, just, or charitable), and early in her rejection of excessive state activity at the center, England slid into the industrial era, when revolutionary changes had to be made to refit the administrative structure and methods to new compulsions and new opportunities. She did this, having lost the American colonies through patronage appointment of incompetents at home and to colonial offices.[6]

REFORM: FROM PATRONAGE TO OPEN COMPETITION

THE government departments are largely the creation of the last hundred years or so, and they have increased in numbers and personnel particularly since about

1870.[7] This is easily understood. The Industrial Revolution compelled society to equip itself to meet new material obligations on a vast scale. Health, poverty, education, communications, trade, agriculture, colonies, manufactures—all now disclosed elements which demanded large-scale regulation and compulsion. The political philosophy of the utilitarian school and the Tory humanitarians resulted in inquiry into these elements and in adoption of the necessary measures. At first only the dead environment—drains, buildings, factories, roads—was to be altered, but it soon began to be seen, most vividly in the sphere of public health, that men were no less important parts of each other's environment. Consequently state activity spread wide and deep. Expenditure grew and the numbers and efficiency of civil servants increased. From 1832 onward the numbers grew rapidly, and there is never a retrogression worth remark. But the expansion is not at a regular rate; it occurs by sudden spurts which may be correlated with the state's legislative and administrative assumption of new duties, or with the expansion of already established services. The figures in Table 23 were obtained from Parliamentary returns up to 1832, and since then from the censuses for England and Wales. The numbers include all administrative and clerical staffs, messengers, and postal officials; they exclude industrial staffs for which there are no facts. The different bases of the censuses and the paucity of explanatory comment on the civil establishments make it impossible

---

6 Cf. L. B. Namier, *The Structure of Politics at the Accession of George III* (London, 1929), 2 vols.; and G. M. Trevelyan, *Early History of Charles James Fox* (London, 1880), Chap. III.

7 Thus the Ministry of Agriculture was established in 1889; the Development Commission, 1909; Board of Education, 1899; the Local Government Board (now the Ministry of Health), 1871; the General Register Office, 1836 and 1874; the Ministry of Labour, 1911; the Department of Overseas Trade, 1917; the Department of Scientific and Industrial Research, 1919; and the Ministry of Transport, 1919. Every department has been extended by tasks unimagined by the generation which died around 1900. In and after World War II came such departments as the Ministry of Fuel and Power, the Ministry of Town and Country Planning, the Ministry of Civil Aviation, the Ministry of Supply, Ministry of Food.

to offer more than the crude figures given, but they show the striking increase, especially since 1881.

We are served today by an administrative machine which only in the last years has been converted from a planless improvisation into a well-ordered engine [8] both powerful enough and sensitive enough to satisfy modern needs. The the years 1689-1855; the second commenced in 1855. In the first period, attention was not directed toward improving the quality of the officials: the quest was not for aptitude, but mainly for the political purity of the House of Commons and the electorate.

1689 to the Nineteenth Century. The revolution of 1689 had given Parliament

TABLE 23—GREAT BRITAIN: GROWTH OF THE CIVIL SERVICE, 1797–1947

Year	Numbers	Remarks
1797[a]	16,267	
1815[b]	24,598	Here began parliamentary demands for "economy."
1821[c]	27,000	
1832[d]	21,305	"Exclusive of many persons who have returned themselves simply as Clerks, Messengers, etc., and many
1841[e]	16,750	who are engaged also in trade."
1851[f]	39,147	
1861	31,943	
1871	53,874	Some workmen included, but how many not stated.
1881	50,859	Telegraph and telephone service not included.
1891	79,241	
1901	116,413	Great expansion in post office since 1891.
1911[g]	172,352	Telegraph and telephone service now included.
1914	280,900	Includes Scottish and Irish services.
1922[h]	317,721	On the decline from the peak of war expansion. Excludes about 20,000 transferred to Ireland; includes Scottish services.
1938[i]	347,700	Last pre-World War II year.
1947[j]	717,000	Receding from wartime peak; some growth due to postwar controls and planning.

[a] and [b] R. H. Gretton, *The King's Government* (London, 1913), p. 111.

[c] and [d] House of Commons Paper, July 12, 1833, on Reduction of Offices. This title is significant of Parliament's attitude; but the House of Commons was not then anxious about "bureaucracy"; it was troubled by the increase of expenditure.

[e] From *Occupation Abstract*, in *Accounts and Papers*, Parliamentary session of 1844.

[f] From analysis of Census figures, in appendix to Report on the Re-organization of the Permanent Civil Service, 1854; papers, p. 439; Vol. 13, p. 36.

[g] and [h] Cmd. 2718; 1926, Memorandum on Present and Pre-war Expenditure.

[i] and [j] Cf. H. M. Government's *Abstract of Statistics*, May, 1948.

modern history of the British civil service begins in 1855. Up to that time, the offices of state fell into the hands of the ruling political party and were used to bribe and reward their followers. There were two periods of occupation with reform of the civil service. The first covered

the supremacy over the Crown, and to safeguard this sovereignty Parliament determined to exclude from the right to its membership any official holding a place of profit under the Crown. The civil offices were thus a pawn in the struggle between Parliament and the king. In this way the mass of officials were and still are excluded from Parliament. Exception was made, of course, and still continues, of

[8] Cf. Sir Warren Fisher, *Evidence, Royal Commission on the Civil Service*, 1929, p. 1267, paras. 3-6, Memorandum.

the ministers of state. They are the link between Parliament and the administration. Acts of Parliament went even further in the attempts to exclude officeholders from politics. In 1712 postal officials of higher rank were forbidden to take any part in elections, but the majority of lower officials were still allowed to vote. In 1782, the very apogee of the corrupt sale and gift of offices, the campaign of Edmund Burke for economical reform obtained a partial success in a statute of that year. The Act of 1782 disfranchised customs, excise, and postal officials, and this prohibition was maintained until the year 1868, but entry to these offices was still used as a political favor.

It is worth pausing here a moment to consider Burke's views. He was, perhaps, the first statesman to see the problem of the civil service as one of the efficiency of the administrative branch of government. His great speech of February 11, 1780, was entitled, "On Presenting to the House of Commons a Plan for the Better Security of the Independence of Parliament and the Economical Reformation of the Civil and other Establishments." [9] He said that uppermost with him

was the reduction of that corrupt influence, which is itself the perennial spring of all prodigality, and of all disorder; which loads us more than millions of debt, which takes away vigour from our arms, wisdom from our counsels, and every shadow of authority and credit from the most venerable parts of our constitution.

But he spent most of his speech on proving to the House how all the departments suffered from "the grand radical fault: the apparatus is not fitted to the object nor the workmen to the work."

Nineteenth-Century Criticism: to 1855. As in the history of local government and of most other English institutions of this period, there was a silent massing of the opposed forces of Utility and Patronage. We must not forget in this period the pioneer work of Jeremy Bentham. In his

[9] Edmund Burke, *Works*, World's Classics edition, Vol. II, p. 303 ff.

Official Aptitude Maximized, Expense Minimized (first published in 1830, being a series of papers composed between 1810 and the later year), he lays down the general basis for a reform of the corrupt officialdom and rank patronage of his time. In his *Constitutional Code* (Book II, Chapter IX, section 5 *et seq.*), he constructs in detail a code of official appointment and pay which shows his inventive mind at its best. Readers may well turn their eyes to this fine piece of reasoning, which anticipated more than all of our modern methods of civil service recruitment and other conditions, and they cannot fail to admire Bentham's marvelous power of mind, though they may smile at some of the grotesque practical suggestions which follow from his philosophy of human nature.

In 1849 the Permanent Secretary of the Treasury, Sir Charles Trevelyan, pointed out the defect of the civil service of his day: it was overstaffed, inactive, and incompetent, and people commonly considered the civil service as the last chance of a livelihood for young men who were too stupid to be successful in the open competition of the professions outside and for the old who had already failed. A rule had been made by the Treasury in 1840, for all departments, that "clerks appointed to the principal offices should possess a competent knowledge of book-keeping by double entry"— but it was obeyed by nobody. Those people who made the service a profession were habitually cheated out of promotion to the highest offices by the nominees of the powerful. But England was spared the great defect of the American "spoils" system—the rotation of offices—the product of a democracy oversuspicious of its executive, possible in a system where the executive has a fixed term of four years but not in a system of cabinet government where Parliament can be dissolved and ministers dismissed at any moment.

Reform was undoubtedly caused by the pressure of business on the civil service and by the mental energy of the utilitarian philosophy. The latter was already having its effect not only upon every aspect of government, but even upon the old universities which were in the 1830's and 1840's awakened from slothfulness, their endowments for scholarship now being competed for by examination. Indeed, Macaulay, the future reformer of the civil service, was a Fellow of Trinity by competitive examination. It was the age of the machine and engineering triumphs, and the civil service was perhaps now in men's minds taking on the aspect of one machine among many, to be renovated according to new needs. From the old system England was delivered by the invention of the method known as "open competitive examination" as a test of fitness to enter the service.

The germ of this idea was generated in the reform of the English administration in India, and was carried out in the Charter Act of 1833. A special school, Haileybury, where Malthus had been a master, had been established in 1813 for training those nominated to be Indian civil servants, and entrants to this had to undergo a difficult examination. The training was educationally of a high grade, and the discipline strict. But patronage still played a large part in appointments and entry to the school. The act of 1833 prescribed that, in future, four candidates were to be nominated for each vacancy and that the nominees were then to compete in "an examination in such branches of knowledge and by such examiners as the Board [of Control] of the Company shall direct" (section 105).

Yet this Indian reform issued from more general causes and together with other like reforms. A new class, the upper commercial and manufacturing men, now entered politics, especially with the Reform Act of 1832. They were accustomed to business efficiency, to the rational fitting of management and methods to purpose, and to strict account-keeping. Furthermore, local police and health and poor-law assistance administration had been reformed in 1829 and 1835 under powerful utilitarian influences. Colonies had been lost through incompetence. Judicial relics of authoritarian and barbarous penal ages were under attack by the new men who argued that men were good, if not free altogether from sin, but that institutions as they were corrupted them.[10]

In 1853 the charter of the India Company came before Parliament for revision, and Macaulay, brother-in-law of Trevelyan,[11] well-versed in Indian affairs and English university conditions, secured the complete abolition of patronage and the acceptance of the principle of open competition of all comers. It is important to appreciate the character of Macaulay's suggestion, for it has dominated the English theory and practice of recruitment and promotion until today, in the Home Office as well as the Foreign and Colonial Services. The essence of his argument is to be found in this part of his speech to the House of Commons (June 23, 1853):

It seems to me that there never was a fact proved by a larger mass of evidence, or a more unvaried experience than this: that men who distinguish themselves in their youth above their contemporaries almost always keep to the end of their lives the start which they have gained.

In July, 1854, Macaulay was called upon by Sir Charles Wood, Chancellor of the Exchequer, to head a committee of distinguished men (including the principal of Haileybury College, Benjamin Jowett, then tutor and later master of Balliol, Oxford, and Sir George Shaw Lefevre, who had had long administrative experience) to report upon the recruitment of the Indian civil service. His scheme of open competition and his list of subjects and marks were accepted in their integrity. Open competition was thus invented and put into practice for India, and it became the pattern for reform of the civil service,[12] and later

10 Cf. S. E. Finer, Jr., *Sir Edwin Chadwick* (London, 1949), Vol. I; and K. B. Smellie, *A Hundred Years of English Government* (London, 1934).
11 Permanent Secretary of the Treasury.
12 Later in his speech Macaulay cleverly analyzed the operation of competitive examinations: "Under a system of competition every man struggles to do his best; and the consequence is that, without any effort on the part of the examiner, the standard keeps itself

still a model for the United States and the envy of France.

Meanwhile an extensive and careful inquiry had been set into operation by a Treasury minute of November, 1848. It ran as follows:

The First Lord and the Chancellor of the Exchequer state to the Board [of the Treasury], that they consider it desirable that an inquiry should be instituted into the present state of the establishment of the Treasury, and into the arrangements and regulations for the distribution and conduct of the business, in order that such changes may be made as may be required to secure the highest practicable degree of efficiency, combined with a careful attention to economy, etc., etc. . .

Lord John Russell was then prime minister, and Sir Charles Wood the Chancellor of the Exchequer. The inquiry into the various departments was directed and in part conducted by Sir Charles Trevelyan, who was later joined by Sir Stafford Northcote. They were assisted by one or more members of each department examined. The reports cover about 450 pages, including the general report by Northcote and Trevelyan on "The Organization of the Permanent Civil Service." It is interesting to notice that the term "civil service" in reference to the home establishments was now used for the first time. The report was issued in November, 1853, together with an opinion upon it by Benjamin Jowett, the

up. But the moment that you say to the examiner, not 'Shall A or B go to India?' but 'Here is A. Is he fit to go to India?' The question becomes altogether a different one. The examiner's compassion, his good nature, his unwillingness to blast the prospects of a young man, lead him to strain a point in order to let the candidate in if we suppose the dispensers of patronage left merely to the operation of their own minds; but you would have them subjected to solicitations of a sort it would be impossible to resist. The father comes with tears in his eyes; the mother writes the most pathetic and heart-breaking letters. Very firm minds have often been shaken by the appeals of that sort. But the system of competition allows nothing of the kind. The parent cannot come to the examiner and say: 'I know very well that the other boy beat my son; but please be good enough to say that my son beat the other boy' " (*Hansard*, Series 3, Vol. CXXVIII, pp. 754, 755).

Master of Balliol, Oxford, and collaborator with Macaulay in the Indian reforms. About forty other distinguished people in public life and education were also asked for their comments, which were sent in between January and June of 1854, and the whole was placed before Parliament as the "Report and Papers relating to the Re-organization of the Civil Service." The plan was greeted by John Stuart Mill as "one of the greatest improvements in public affairs ever proposed by a government." This improvement consisted of that which Macaulay's Committee on the Selection and Training of Candidates for the Indian Civil Service was at about the same time recommending for India. It was the abolition of patronage and the admission of people into the service at prescribed ages and by means of competitive examination. Two other principles were laid down. The commissioners recognized that a clear distinction could be drawn between the intellectual and routine work of the service, and demanded an appropriate division of labor and a separate type of examination for each. This involved classing civil servants—a problem which has never ceased to give trouble, and which has never given complete satisfaction.

A further point in these recommendations calls for remark. Thinking mainly of the higher administrative posts, the commissioners laid down another principle, which still, but with some modifications, holds good in Britain, and distinguishes the British type of recruitment for that class from recruitment in other countries, notably France and Germany. The report was antagonistic to any technical preparation for the examination for such posts, for the commissioners had their eye upon the classical and mathematical education at Oxford and Cambridge of their day. They were impressed by Macaulay's argument that

men who have been engaged, up to one and two and twenty, in studies which have no immediate connexion with the business of any profession, and the effect of which is merely to open, to invigorate, and to enrich the mind, will generally be found, in the business of every profession, superior to men who have, at eighteen or nineteen, devoted themselves to the special studies of their calling. Indeed, early superiority in literature and science generally indicates the existence of some qualities which are securities against vice—industry, self-denial, a taste for pleasures not sensual, a laudable desire of honourable distinction, a still more laudable desire to obtain the approbation of friends and relations. We, therefore, think that the intellectual test about to be established will be found in practice to be also the best moral test that can be devised.

Macaulay was so sure of his prescription of seeking for evidence of superior mind rather than specific information that he even ventured that the competitors could as well be examined in Cherokee or Iroquois as the European classics and that the test would be as valid for the administrative object of his search; not information, but mind: *non multa sed multum,* not many things but much.

The principles here set out still stand as the foundation of the English civil service. There have been modifications in the course of the ninety years since that time owing to the growth of technical studies at the universities, but to a large degree the general foundation of liberal studies remains. The "mere smatterer" is not wanted. Even today the study of the humanities and history, in their classic and modern shapes, is strongly believed to produce the best type of administrative officer.[13] This belief has much to commend it, for it is not the knowledge of school subjects that is wanted in the

administrator, but a way of thought, a mental and moral discipline. The aim is not to secure an expert but an administrative officer who is capable of becoming skilled by contact with his actual work and able to say at what exact point an expert shall be called in. The examinations demand an education which will produce candidates with the highest power of enlightened common sense.[14]

The outlook, power and quickness in comprehension, the gift of dealing with people, the readiness to take the initiative and to assume responsibility, are all in the main highly developed when the business to be transacted is seen by the Civil Servant against a background of other knowledge of the type through which the mind has become developed.

The highest class of administrative officers thus provided has gone under different names (e.g., the upper grade, the first division, the administrative class), but it has so far consisted of the pick of the Honors men in the classics, history, and science (including mathematics) courses at the older universities, with the bias on the two former. From the upper and higher middle classes of the country—the only ones until quite recently who could afford such an education—came generations of young men into the service who had precisely the liberal, literary turn of mind, without professional prejudices or bureaucratic pedantry, fitted to work hand in glove with the parliamentarian, to act unoppressively toward the public and smoothly direct the departmental energies. The composition of that class has since World War I been undergoing a process of change and so also the demands upon it of a new era in national life. To this I revert later.

The commissioners laid down certain other rules for efficient and convenient recruitment of officials. (1) All examinations should be conducted by a single authority standing entirely outside the separate departments. This would secure

---

[13] This statement is rather more true of the Committee on the Civil Service Class I Examination of 1917, than of the present policy of the civil service commissioners, which is to draw recruits from a large variety of schools. The bias of the Committee is shown in this representative extract from its report (Cd. 8657, 1917): "To teach the classical learning and develop classical scholarship there was at work in 1914 a great band of scholars equipped by the tradition, the organized learning, and the experience of four hundred years. . . A large proportion of the most able students have gone in the past to classics, and we cannot alter the natural habits, the prepossessions, and the system, that have caused the most gifted among literary students to follow the ancient studies."

[14] Lord R. B. Haldane, "The British Civil Service," in *Journal of Public Administration,* Vol. I, p. 29.

effectiveness and consistency; and in this England, Germany, and the United States have followed much the same path, while France differs, having an examining authority in each department. (2) Examinations should be held at regular intervals and not for special appointments, which would conduce to making it known as an annual event to all potential candidates. (3) Successful candidates would be allowed to enter the departments of their choice in order of their place on the pass list (except since 1919 into the Treasury); not so in France or the United States. (4) There should be a period of probation before candidates were finally placed on the established staff.

Only part of the recommendations were carried into execution, and this, in the teeth of strong protest from the clubs, political and social, from politicians, and from everybody who had something to lose by the reform.[15] Macaulay, wandering into Brook's in March, 1854, found everybody astounded by Trevelyan's plans for the abolition of patronage at home. The storm from clubland almost swept Trevelyan, the Sir Gregory Hardlines of Trollope's *Three Clerks,* out of office. A remark made by the latter in 1875 (before the Playfair Commission on the Civil Service) is too interesting to put into a footnote; the italics are mine.[16]

I wish briefly to explain the circumstances which led up to the Report of Sir Stafford Northcote and myself on the organization of the Civil Service. *The revolutionary period of 1848 gave us a shake,* and one of the consequences was a remarkable series of investigations into public offices, which lasted for five years, culminating in the Organization Report.

1855 and After. By an Order in Council of May 21, 1855, the Civil Service Commission—the Central Board of Examiners—was established, with three members, with tenure during the pleasure of the Crown, "to conduct the examinations of young men proposed to be appointed to any of the junior situations in the Civil Establishments." The Commission would decide upon the age, health, character, and requisite knowledge and ability for the discharge of their official duties, and would give a certificate to this effect precedent to the appointment. The extent of the actual reform was this: (1) competition, not compulsory but permissive, was made the basis of appointments, but only throughout the ranks of the junior offices; (2) the power of appointment, following the issue of the commissioners' certificate, was still in the hands of the political heads of departments; and (3) a six-months' probation period was established. Abuses were thus limited, not entirely swept away. People of mature age who had special qualifications for a special post were not required to have the Commission's certificate.

It was twenty years before party attacks upon the work of the Commission ceased and it was left to work in peace.[17] The

---

[15] It is interesting to remember that Gladstone, who urged on this reform, did so on the ground that the higher classes would get administrative power. He believed, in 1854, that the aristocracy of this country were superior in natural gifts, on the average, to the mass, and that with their acquired advantages, their "insensible education," irrespective of book-learning, they were immensely superior. See the letter to Lord John Russell, January 20, 1854, in appendix to John Morley's *Life of Gladstone* (London, 1905). Queen Victoria was much perturbed by the suggested reforms and consented to them most grudgingly (*Letters,* February 7 and 17, 1854).

[16] *Parliamentary Papers,* 1875, Vol. XXIII, p. 100. It is remarkable that Trevelyan's services to the English government, at home and in India, have not yet received a mark of gratitude in the shape of a full memoir. The *Dictionary of National Biography* gives scant information about him. Born in 1807, at Taunton, he was educated at the Grammar School,

and at Charterhouse, and thence proceeded to Haileybury. He entered the East India Company's Bengal Civil Service as a writer in 1826 and rapidly rose to high administrative office, his interest and endeavors being directed especially to public education and finance. In 1838 he returned to England, and from 1840 until 1859 he was assistant, and later permanent, Secretary to the Treasury. It was in this period that he helped so materially to bring about the reorganization of the Home Civil Service. In 1859 he returned to India as Governor of Madras.

[17] Cf. Anthony Trollope in an article in the *Fortnightly Review,* October 15, 1865: "We,

Superannuation Act of 1859 supplied a sanction to the rules of the Order in Council of 1855 by providing that with certain special exceptions (professional officers of mature age being the most important), no person should thenceforward be deemed to have served in the civil service and to be entitled to a pension unless he should have been admitted with a certificate from the civil service commissioners.

In 1870 the Order in Council of June 4 completed the edifice thus created—its essentials were these. (1) The test of open competition was made obligatory practically throughout the service. (2) In the case of professional officers, the civil service commissioners might dispense with the examination test if they thought fit. (3) Certain officers appointed directly by the Crown (in 1914 these still numbered about three hundred, now considerably reduced) needed no certification whatever by the commissioners. (4) For certain situations, where the head of the department wished to dispense with an examination, the civil service commissioners could consent at the request of the head of the department and of the Treasury. This allows for the appointment of distinguished men from outside the service: a rare but valuable occurrence. (5) Lastly, but very importantly, the Treasury, which necessarily had powers of coordination and control permeating all departments because of its financial responsibilities and powers, was given special authority in the field of departmental organization. It was to approve the rules for testing candidates made by the Civil Service Commission and the departments, and the periods at which examinations should be held, the number of vacancies, and the grouping of situations to be competed for.

Your Majesty's Civil Service Commissioners, humbly offer your Majesty this our Tenth Annual Report.' Thus the dread document now under notice is commenced, reminding us with terrible earnestness of the quiet progress of the years. Here is their tenth report, and it was but the other day that we were discussing whether these Commissioners would ever have real existence!"

Since 1870 the development of the civil service has been marked by a series of thorough inquiries, always searching for improved efficiency. There were the Playfair Commission of 1875, the Ridley Commission of 1884-90, the Macdonnell Commission of 1910-14, and the Gladstone Committee of 1918, and all of these had before them the questions of classification, recruitment, and promotion, all interdependent parts of a single problem. It should be noted that there is no one general statute for officials as there is in the United States and Germany, and since 1946 in France. The foundations of the civil service are established, for the most part, by Orders in Council and Treasury Regulations and not by acts of Parliament. They were drawn up under successive cabinets in accordance with the recommendations of royal commissions; Parliament was not asked in any effective sense to ratify them, although it occasionally discussed their general character, and the Treasury and the Civil Service Commission were made the custodians of their execution.[18]

HOW THE SERVICE IS CONSTITUTED

THE civil service numbers 946,000, of which some 250,000 are industrial staffs. The remainder, nearly 700,000 nonindustrial civil servants, fall into the classes shown in the accompanying table. This number falls broadly into four great groups.

For all these classes save one, the principles of recruitment need little discussion here because their work is rather specific and this carries with it a concrete definition of the qualities required. So with executive work, though this is a little more difficult of definition than the other classes (and difficulties also are naturally experienced with some of the units in the inspectorate). So with the clerical, the typists, and the professional

18 They are brought together—at least the gist and references thereto—in Royal Commission on the Civil Service (1929), Appendix to Part I of Minutes of Evidence. *Introductory Memoranda Relating to Civil Service* (63-149), 1930.

scientific and technical staffs, where a well-known course of training is provided by certain responsible bodies. Little attention will be paid to these or the industrial and manipulative staffs in the following discussion of recruitment; some attention is given to them in the sections on promotion and political and civic rights (in Chapter 34).

The class with which we wish mainly to concern ourselves here is the administrative class. In 1938 it numbered about 1500; at the peak in World War II it numbered about 4800; it will become normal at about 4000. This is the pivotal

amendments, and various kinds of public explanations. They are responsible for the control of staff, and for the execution of the work of the department.

Let us be very clear, before another step is taken, about what this administrative class truly signifies. It is a body of advisers, a "brains trust" to use an American colloquialism, the immediate aid of the minister at the head of the department. Each member of it, in his own way, at his particular level in the hierarchy, will contribute not merely information to the minister, but the ingredients of supreme policy. At the top the two or three

TABLE 24—Numbers of the British Civil Service: October 1, 1947: Nonindustrial Staffs Only [19]

	Whole time		Part time		Total*
	Men	Women	Men	Women	
Administrative	3,864	517	27	9	4,399
Executive	40,528	9,839	237	69	50,520
Clerical and subclerical	130,436	121,023	195	7,087	255,100
Typing	222	28,628	4	1,507	29,605
Professional, technical and scientific	38,693	3,425	471	57	42,382
Minor and manipulative	127,664	56,178	25,075	25,541	206,650
Technical ancillary	44,419	7,787	156	143	52,356
Inspectorate	4,505	708	89	5	5,260
Messengerial, etc.	28,378	12,015	818	7,043	44,324
Total	418,709	240,120	27,072	36,461	690,596

* Includes part-time staff counted as half units.

and directing class of the whole civil service. From the permanent secretaries down to the assistant principals they are responsible for transmitting the impulse from their political chief, from the statutes and declarations of policy, through the rest of the service and out to the public. They translate the wishes of the political side of government into workable and legally valid rules; and to that end they use scientists and lawyers as they are required. It is their business to gather together and weave the strands of science and law necessary to the determination of policy by the minister, and this may issue in the drafting of projects of law, amendments thereto, answers to parliamentary

men at the head of the department will be almost the minister's permanent other self.[20] This has already been emphasized in the chapter on the British cabinet. It cannot be re-emphasized enough. Their functions include making the department work in order that the laws may be carried out. But the average of about a hundred members of the administrative class at the head of each department are there to amass, develop, sift, improve, continue, and carry to minister after minister the knowledge of the function and policy of the department in relation to those of all other departments. They are the department's permanent wise men.

[20] This is described with masterly illumination by a distinguished former member of the class, Sir Henry E. Dale, in his *The Higher Civil Service of Britain* (London, 1941).

[19] House of Commons, Debates, December 17, 1947.

The Educational System and the Civil Service. It will already have been appreciated from the discussion of the relationship between the higher civil service and the universities that the two are consciously integrated. The same principle in general holds good for the various lower grades of the services: it is attempted to organize the various classes in such a way as to tap the nearest related level of the schools. This is a valuable procedure: for by arranging the age limits and the nature of the recruiting examination for the service, the pupils can, at their respective ages, look toward entrance into the service and use their ordinary curriculum so to do. Two things result: a regular expectation, for those who wish it, to enter the service at the completion of their curriculum, and therefore any special preparation in view of the examination; yet the pupils are not obliged, as in most other systems of civil service, to be especially coached in subjects the civil service wishes, yet extraneous to the ordinary curriculum. Hence, the schools need not, for vocational reasons, be compelled to go outside the subjects and the methods of teaching commended by reasonable pedagogy for students of the age group in question.

The Local-government System and the Service. Though British public administration is highly decentralized (though less so than in the middle or at the end of the nineteenth century) and though local government has large discretion over the bulk of municipal and social services, there is, through various devices, strong and effective central control, supported by grants-in-aid from the central authority equaling over fifty per cent of the local government expenditures, excluding the public utilities.[21] The organizing, regulating, admonitory, advising, scheme-sanctioning, auditing, and inspecting controls are administered by the central civil servants, and, in the higher range of policy and action, by the administrative class.

It must be remembered also that the nationalized occupations, though not under civil service, are yet directed and supervised at the top level by the minister at the head of the government department related to the nationalized industry,[22] and this means the administrative group at the head of the civil service.

HOW THE ADMINISTRATIVE CLASS IS CHOSEN

THE administrative class is open by competitive examination to men and women between the ages of 21 to 24. In 1925, the class was opened to women on the same terms as to men. As the age indicates, it recruits mainly from the Honors-degree men of the universities. This class is recruited also by promotion from the lower classes of the service, and those who are so promoted, as well as those who enter by examination, enter first the administrative cadet corps, called the junior grade, which serves as a training ground for their new duties. The numbers of such promotions are small enough to give a reasonably certain prospect of more responsible office later. From 1923 to 1935 the class was recruited to the extent of 278 by competition and 82 by promotion. The annual relationship of promotees to entrants is erratic. There is a probation period of two years, at the end of which there is either discharge or reversion to a lower grade if the probationer is unsatisfactory.

This class is the hub of the administrative wheel; on one side it is attached to the parliamentary machine, on the other to the executive arms of the administration. To it is imparted a direction and velocity by the minister; from it there emanates advice which has been drawn from the specialists, the inspectors, the experts, and vocational and social representative bodies. Its advice penetrates beyond the minister to Parliament and the public; into it, through Parliament and the minister, passes the force of public, which is tranmuted by it into com-

---

21 Cf. Herman Finer, *English Local Government* (fourth edition, 1949), Part IV.

22 Cf. Herman Finer, "Planning and Reconstruction in Britain" *International Labour Review,* April 1948, p. 283 ff.

mands to the specialists, the inspectors, and all the classes of the service, in each department, in the local authorities, in the dominions and colonies and foreign countries, down to the final manipulative officer, to the end that the things politically willed shall actually be done. It is obviously the crux of the administrative side of government. As such it has naturally received and deserved much attention.

We are concerned with its duties and its preparation to fulfill them. The administrative class itself formulated its duties in evidence for the Tomlin Commission,[23] and it is reproduced in full, since incidentally it is itself a good example of the quality of the class.

The volume of official work which calls for decisions affecting the public is nowadays such that it is physically impossible for the Minister himself to give the decision except in the most important cases. And further, even when the issue is one which can and must be submitted for the Minister's personal decision, it has to be fairly and fully presented to him so that the material facts and considerations are before him. The need for services of this kind is present in every department which has a political head.

There is another common feature of all work which is strictly administrative in character. It is usually described—for instance, by the Reorganization Committee of 1920—by the somewhat general expression "the formation of policy." What is meant is, we think, this. The business of government, if it is to be well done, calls for the steady application of long and wide views to complex problems: for the pursuit, as regards each and every subject-matter, of definite lines of action, mutually consistent, conformed to public opinion and capable of being followed continuously while conditions so permit, and of being readily adjusted when they do not. Almost any administrative decision may be expected to have consequences which will endure or emerge long after the period of office of the Government by which or under whose authority it is taken. It is the peculiar function of the Civil Service, and the special duty of the Administrative Class of that Service, in their day-to-day work to set these

wider and more enduring considerations against the exigencies of the moment, in order that the Parliamentary convenience of to-day may not become the Parliamentary embarrassment of to-morrow. This is the primary justification of a permanent administrative service. Vacillation, uncertainty and inconsistency are conspicuous symptoms of bad administration. The formation of policy in this limited sense—subject always to the control of the Minister and to the supreme authority of Parliament—is typical of administrative work in all departments and in relation to all subject-matters whether of greater or of lesser importance.

All administrative work is carried out under statutory authority or, in certain fields, under the prerogative powers of the Crown. To a large extent it consists in the application to particular circumstances of general principles laid down in the statutes, or the administration of financial provision made by Parliament, in pursuance of the powers vested in the Department in that behalf. It involves necessarily the preparation or study of proposals for the alteration of the existing law in the light of changed circumstances, new policies or experience. It is indeed true that proposals for amending legislation within the administrative sphere do, to a large extent, and perhaps mainly, emanate from Departments. The statement that these processes form an important part of the work of administration affords, however, no ground for any suggestion that the Civil Service seeks to usurp the functions of Parliament itself. The functions are essentially different.

These, we conceive, are the common characteristics of all administrative work, whatever the subject-matter. In each particular branch of that work other characteristics will also be found, but they are special to those branches. For example, in the Board of Education and Ministry of Health, the important function of maintaining good relations with the autonomous Local Authorities, while securing in general the application of those standards of local administration which Parliament desires, is a type of work which is not found in a Department like the Customs and Excise or the Admiralty. Similarly, in some branches but not in others, one of the functions of administration is the determination or policy in the light of technical advice, which has to be weighed and balanced against other non-technical considerations, such as financial conditions or the state of public opinion.

Thus the efficient performance of the ad-

---

[23] Appendix VIII to Minutes of Evidence: *Statement* submitted by the Association of First Division Civil Servants, 1930.

ministrative work of the various Departments calls in all cases for *a trained mental equip-ment of a high order, while in the particular case powers developed in some particular direction are needed. In some spheres, what is most wanted is judgment, savior-faire, in-sight, and fairmindedness; in others, an in-tellectual equipment capable of the ready mastery of complex and abtruse problems in, for instance, taxation or other economic sub-jects, imagination and constructive ability.*

It is important to distinguish between the substance of administrative work and its form. The latter may be a memorandum, a draft regulation, an inquiry, a conference or inter-view, a verbal decision or instruction to a sub-ordinate, or a minute on official papers or an official letter. The substance of it is the exer-cise of a sound and informed judgment upon the subject-matter in hand; and this is equally true whether that judgment be final or to be submitted to higher authority.

The sentences which describe the qualities have been italicized in order to bring home their full import. And yet even the whole passage does not quite reveal all the gravity of the problem. For the men who enter this class are not merely secretarial; *they are the young shoots who may twenty years hence be permanent heads of the departments or very closely associated with them.* Their position in the governmental process will be not merely instrumental to, but creative of state policy. The significance of this must at once be appreciated.

The Permanent Secretaries have usually had perhaps more than twenty years of very varied official experience before they attain their position; and it is extremely rare for any to have served in only one department; indeed, just before World War II in the thirty principal depart-ments, twenty-three had served in one or more other departments. At that stage there is considerable transfer from de-partment to department. Those entrants, who, tested by time, experience, and comparison with their colleagues, have ascended to one of the first fifty positions in the service, are, indeed, men of high quality. Ministers soon learn, by taking cautious stock for a time, the respective

zones of usefulness of themselves and their permanent subordinates. If they are too ignorant or lazy to learn—and it is proper to say that some have been—they are helped by their cabinet colleagues, or they sink into pompous quiescence. In that case, the day-by-day administration runs routine-wise, while general policy is unchanged or is made by the initiative of Parliament or the cabinet. The perma-nent staffs can be excused a little impa-tience with that minister who cannot immediately understand their account of what two decades has taught them, as well as he who too rashly assumes that it may be learned and confuted in as many hours.

Sir Warren Fisher has stated the prin-ciples of cooperation soundly:

Determination of policy is the function of Ministers, and once a policy is determined it is the unquestioned and unquestionable busi-ness of the civil servant to strive to carry out that policy with precisely the same energy and precisely the same good will whether he agrees with it or not. That is axiomatic and will never be in dispute. At the same time it is the tradi-tional duty of civil servants, while decisions are being formulated, to make available to their political chiefs all the information and experience at their disposal, and to do this without fear or favour, irrespective of whether the advice thus tendered may accord or not with the Minister's initial view. The presenta-tion to the Minister of relevant facts, the ascer-tainment and marshalling of which may often call into play the whole organization of a De-partment, demands of the civil servant the greatest care. *The presentation of inferences from the facts equally demands from him all the wisdom and all the detachment he can command.*[24] The preservation of integrity, fearlessness and independence of thought and utterance in their private communion with Ministers of the experienced officials selected to fill the top posts in the Service is an essential principle in enlightened government as—whether or no Ministers can accept advice thus frankly placed at their disposal, and accept-ance or rejection of such advice is exclusively a matter for their judgment—it enables him to be assured that their decisions are reached only after the relevant facts and the various considerations have, so far as the machinery of

24 Present author's italics.

government can secure, been definitely brought before their minds.[25]

If, then, such a status and service are to be the culmination of a regular career, the preparation and the continued training of the entrants are of great moment. If all that were required were any single one among the qualities in the italicized passage for each individual job, then, perhaps, the specific tests might be invented, though this is improbable since each quality is itself rather nebulous and composite. But the difficulty is immensely increased when we reflect that to each job several of the qualities are essential, and that as the administrator proceeds in his career, now one and now the other, and all in various combinations, will be called upon, and this not with precise predictability. It is doubtful whether the nature of the problem has ever been considered as rationally as it deserves, but three generations of muddled development have brought us within sight of a solution.

The Method of Study. It is clear that the subjects of study matter less than the method of study, and that the demonstration of mind is more important than the display of information. The aim is not to recruit a departmental expert, but to discover a mind which for capaciousness and vigor will continually be able to master the technicalities of the job, indeed, a succession of jobs, through promotion and transfer. At a comparatively early stage, for example, the young administrator will be cooperating with colleagues and subordinates in sifting the information from persons and documents: that is, in deciding what is and is not important enough to go forward to the administrator and political heads of the department as relevant ingredients in the making of policy. Macaulay, then, was perfectly right to look to unspecialized university studies. It is clear that the excellence of this test and to some extent of the nature of those studies must depend on the tutorial method employed, and on the spirit and outlook of the uni-

25 Tomlin Commission, *Minutes of Evidence,* p. 1268.

versities. On the whole, the universities, old and young, look rather to the building of a liberal character than to the production of erudite, unpractical pedants or very practical technicians. The finished product is to hold his learning like a gentleman; he is to be a man of the world with a well-trained mind; he is to be a superb thinker. If there is a choice between the liberal, tolerant mind, and efficiency, then efficiency in the harsh and aggressive sense is well lost. This has accorded well with the general character of the people—indeed, it is its produce —and of Parliament. It has tempered the inevitable intrusions into private lives, of liberty, and property, which state activity implies.

As to the tutorial method, this is sufficiently different from that of other countries with similar civil service problems to give a special character to the British system. In the United States there are too many lectures and textbooks and too little severe individual wrestling with problems; they know more than all about it, but do not know what it is all about. In Germany a similar situation existed, except that students, not being forced to attend lectures, studied very hard privately because the examinations were stern, far sterner than in American universities. So also in France, but the clarity of the language and the civilized tradition are a salvation.

In these two Continental countries the tendency is to produce a highly doctrinaire type of recruit for the civil service. In England, especially at the older universities, with numbers small in comparison with other countries and with these numbers the result of a very heavy competition for admission during the secondary-school age, there is less lecture and textbook teaching—which is merely passive study—and much more personal contact between student and tutor. The subjects studied are not many, but they are studied deeply enough to make possible and awaken critical effort. The method is almost Socratic. In small seminars, or individually, the undergraduate brings his paper containing his own individual answer to some problem in political science, history, ethics, lingual or mathematical principle, produced by himself from books or documents recommended by his tutor. For an hour or more the effort is submitted to a ferreting, worrying, persistent examination, accompanied by suggestions to the student, recommendations of further or alternative reading, the indication of alternative solutions and points of view, and a further spontaneous cross-examination of the student's defensive explanations. The student learns to parry—a very important technical accomplishment in administrative life. His whole effectiveness depends not on what he knows but on how he can handle his knowledge to solve a problem. The tilling of his mind is exceedingly intensive. Through a subject, but only through it, he is learning a method and *savoir faire*. Quite unconsciously the student is preparing himself for work in administration, for it is rather like the process of holding the politician's (or his superior's) proposals for action or inaction to the touchstone of penetrating reason, so that the elements are ranged before one, to be recognized and evaluated, chosen or discarded, as the politician then desires. It is a critical mind that is being trained. As an Oxford don once said: [26]

[Oxford philosophy] . . . affords to the future civil servant or lawyer an unrivaled training in precision of phrase and elucidation of phraseology. Anyone who has really mastered this book [Professor Joseph's *Essays in Ancient and Modern Philosophy*] will have a mind ready to expose loose thinking and short cuts in arguments: he will in fact be a champion debunker of wordy nothings—but he will not be equipped with any understanding of the social problems of his own or Plato's world, nor will he have gained much insight into the real movement of scientific thought. He will have learnt not to understand problems, but to expose fallacies. Not one of his deep-seated prejudices or presuppositions will have been touched, though certain rationalisations of them will have been shown to contain contradictions. But he will have been armed with

a *dialectical* still sufficient to destroy the arguments of everyone he may chance to meet.

This is high praise mixed with criticism, and the criticism I take to be too severe.[27] Supposing, however, this tutorial method should be applied to world history, political science, economics, sociology, to "Modern Greats" at Oxford, the Economics and History Tripos at Cambridge, or a degree in economics and political science elsewhere? Then, I hold, the critical minds thus produced are of the greatest benefit to democratic government, for the politicians and the social philosophers and missionaries are only too eager and fruitful in their proposals for reform or inaction, and the civil service is urgently needed as their critical assessor, even, as Graham Wallas once pointed out, as "the Second Chamber."

Subjects of Examination. This brings us to the subjects of the examinations, after a discussion of which we may be able to sum up the value of the preparation for this, the highest grade of the service. It was natural that in the middle of last century and for decades after that, classics, mathematics, moral philosophy, history, and law, which were the chief subjects of university study, should be the only subjects of the examination. But classics, because of the foundations and scholarships and the eight-century old tradition, continued to bulk very large in the administrative examination, even when many new faculties had been established. For the men who made the recommendations to the civil service commissioners had been students a generation or two ago. As educationists they were less concerned with administration, which is serviceability, than with scholarship, which is the production of mind as mind. "We consider that the best qualification for a civil servant is a good natural capacity trained by a rational and consistent education from childhood to university . . . We do not wish candi-

---

[26] R. H. Crossman, *New Statesman and Nation*, November 30, 1935, book review.

[27] For another relevant extract from the report of the Committee on the Civil Service Class I Examination (Cmd. 8657 of 1917), see footnote 13.

dates to adapt their education to the examination; on the contrary the examination should be adapted to the chief forms of general education." [28] It must, of course, not be thought that the study of ancient philosophy or classical history and literature is inappropriate to the preparation of administrator's activities. Properly taught, they teach all sorts of social and political lessons.

Yet the civil service commissioners have yielded and included in their syllabus no less than eighty-four subjects.[29] Of recent years, criticism of the curriculum has centered upon the advantage in marks given to the classical and history schools compared with political science and economics. The figures show that for the eleven years 1925 to 1935, classics supplied thirty-five out of every hundred entrants, history twenty-five, modern languages eight, economics and politics seven, mathematics six, and mixed history, languages and literature seven. The last five years show no appreciable change in the proportions—classics and history still supply well over fifty per cent of the administrative class. (History, be it remembered, is often "government.") The balance of marks has recently been more fairly redressed, and we may expect more entrants from the older and the younger universities offering these subjects. *It is important to insist that it is the method of studying and learning and not the subject of information which is of moment in selection for administration.* Yet there is an advantage in studying the social sciences—for there the mind is being trained and the judgment formed through reflection upon causal relationships in phenomena which are the immediate setting of the services to be administered. Much more could be urged in their favor—but the more conservative claim is claim enough.

The Value of the Preparation. We are now in a position to assess the value of the preparation and selection for the administrative grade. The competition is very severe, for the situations attract the most capable among the undergraduates of any year. Only a combination of extraordinarily high intelligence, intellect, and character can be successful. The civil service commissioners have devised a method of marking to secure "that no credit be allowed for merely superficial knowledge."

We may hope that these qualities will in the future be drawn from a far wider group in the nation than is at present the case, for examination (1925 to 1936) shows that nine Oxford and Cambridge men are successful to every one from all other universities, despite the fact that they have only less than one third of all the male university students. Of the Permanent Secretaries appointed between the wars to be the head of the government departments, forty came from "public" schools, eleven from grant-aided schools, five from Scottish schools, and five from other sources, and then all via Oxford, Cambridge and Edinburgh. Now it may be argued that some of those who enter from the older universities will have arrived by scholarships from the public elementary schools and from municipal secondary schools. This is true: but examination of the lists shows that even in the twelve years before 1937, nearly 62 per cent of the recruits come from the public schools (especially from the few famous ones), although such schools have a total of only 15 per cent of all the secondary school attendance in the country.[30] Almost all come from the comfortable middle and upper classes. These have great virtues, as anyone who knows them will gladly acknowledge: charm, and tact, and literary facility. They are usually incorruptible and have a high sense of public duty. They are "constitutional." They may have impenetrable social prejudices, but these are not usually rampant, and above the basic prejudice,

---

[28] See E. L. Woodward, *Short Journey* (Oxford, 1946), for the luminous autobiography of an Oxford don and of teaching at Oxford.
[29] See appendix to my *British Civil Service* (London, 1937).

[30] In the 1936 competition, thirty-nine out of fifty-two entrants to the administrative grade came from "minor" public schools and municipal secondary schools.

is a mind which has been taught to ask questions. They are capable of a considerable degree of *esprit de corps*. But it is questionable whether they can ever easily escape from the sense of superiority unconsciously assimilated in their country or suburban homes and public schools and colleges. They are too alien to their subordinates, perhaps insensitive to impressions from clever "outsiders," and not markedly ruthless in the exposure of incompetence in their own ranks. If their composition included the memory of misery, hunger, squalor, bureaucratic oppression, and economic insecurity, perhaps a quality would be added to their work in the highest situations which could not fail to impress the minister at a loss for a policy or an argument. How essential it is for the state to be served by all kinds of talents and experience! Everyone must acknowledge that failing inborn sympathy or personal experience, the significance of many social situations is ignored or underestimated.

Also, it is urgent to remember that the education so far obtained is not the end, but only the beginning, of men's spiritual development. They have learned only the rudiments, and that in books and from hearsay: they enter the service between the ages of twenty-one and twenty-four. They emerge from the gray cloisters and the twilit halls, and in a few months enter the massive stone buildings forevermore. They lift their eyes from the second-hand books, and open them again on the dog-eared second-hand files. It is clear that something more than the present system is necessary for successful administration. There is direct evidence that the present system is not quite perfect. There is, first, the evidence of Sir George Murray (a very great administrator even among Victorian stars) before the Macdonnell Commission of 1914. He said:

What I was thinking of was this: That while the men who are drawn from the Class I Examination are, I think, very good for the purposes for which they are required for the first ten, or twelve, or fifteen years of their official life, I have at times been rather disappointed at finding how few of them emerge satisfac-

torily from the ruck and come out as really capable heads of departments.
[Chairman:] Will you just explain a little further? Is there, do you think, anything defective in the original way of selecting the first-division men, which explains the fact you mentioned of their turning out badly when they get to fifteen or twenty years' service?
[Sir George Murray:] I did not wish to say that I thought they turned out badly as a body, but merely that I should have expected that more of them would have been better qualified for the best places that were open to them. But I do not think that anything you could do in prescribing the subjects for examination or in making any change in the methods of appointment, could possibly affect that.

The comment made upon this by the Committee on the Class I Examination was: [31]

If among those selected by open competition there are not always to be found a sufficient number who, after many years of service, are, by virtue of their initiative, force of character, freshness of mind, and constructive ability, fit for the highest posts, the fault may lie in the system of training after entry, and in the conditions of subordinate service; it need not lie with the competitive system.

Before the Tomlin Commission of 1929 most heads of departments argued that the entrants might do in their raw state for other departments, but that for *theirs* some previous administrative experience was desirable. Sir Warren Fisher said that some of the heads of departments came to him about their recruits, "some censorious and some purring like cats."
Remedies for Defects. The remedy lies in three measures. The first is to make the two-years period of probation a real testing time, so that official and department may sever connections if they are not suited, and at the same time, a training period. This was, in part, the intention of the Reorganization Committee of 1920. It said:

Men and women so recruited should be regarded as a Cadet Corps from which selection should be made to higher administrative posts. . . .

[31] Paragraph 13, pp. 10 and 11.

In 1935 an able American investigator asserted [32] that the weaknesses of this class were:

(1) the lack of knowledge and appreciation on the part of administrators of the affairs of the outside world except in so far as they pertain to their work, (2) the lack of knowledge of the activities and policies of the departments of government, other than those in which they serve, and (3) the failure to consider public administration as a science with a body of fundamental principles, and the insistence on treating it as an art or mystery revealed only to those who have followed the initiatory rite through which they have passed, or alternatively as a faculty inborn, which is denied to all who are not blessed with it at birth. There are notable exceptions, but this indictment may safely be brought against the great mass of the members of the class. It is submitted that the principal reason for it is lack of proper training, although facilities for it are readily available.

Now, since 1919, the Treasury has demanded a period of service in other departments before it chooses its own recruits. The Ministry of Health has initiated its recruits into the organization of the department for some weeks. The Ministry of Labour has sent its recruits for a six-months tour of duty to provincial offices, after two years' service. The Colonial Office sends its officers for a two-year tour of duty to a colony or dominion, after some years of service. The Foreign Office and Diplomatic Service were amalgamated in 1919 partly in order to secure a circulation of men from London abroad and back to London, so that first-hand knowledge might flow in. It is more than ever important, as the omnipotent hands of the state stretch out toward all of us, that civil servants shall early be fitted for their specific tasks, and that they shall get to know the public, as living individuals, even if only for a short time. It is an effective way of helping a civil service from degenerating into a bureaucracy. The administrative class itself is emphatic on this question.

We consider it important that the probationary period (normally two years) should be rigidly enforced and that the officers should be discharged before or at the end of that period unless it is reasonably certain that they will become efficient administrators. In the absence of this certainty their retention is not only opposed to the interests of the public service, but it is a mistaken kindness to retain in the service a man who is unlikely to be fitted for promotion and may subsequently have to be discharged on the ground of inefficiency at an age when it is much harder for him to obtain other employment. [33]

Hitherto, after such a period of training (but usually only after undirected perambulations about the building), the civil servant has entered into the long spell of forty years' hard labor in the office. How shall he be kept alive and inventive? There is a serious chance of slavery to routine, the loss of inspiration and inventiveness, the falling into a deep, long groove. Sir S. H. Wilson, permanent undersecretary of state for the colonies, expressed his doubts to the Royal Commission of 1929 (Question 20,981) in these words:

I picture to myself a man going into the civil service at the age of twenty-two or twenty-three, or whatever the age is, coming from the university, passing the examination, and sentenced for the rest of his life to live in Whitehall, and to come up by train every morning from Woking and go home at the same time every evening, always seeing the same people, always dealing with the same work. I think it requires very little imagination to realize what that man must become after about twenty or twenty-five years, if he does not see more of the world. I think it is wonderful that they are as good as they are.

Of course, natural emulation among colleagues and the motive force of promotion—along with love of the job itself —stimulate administrative virility. A glance at the pyramid of the administrative class will show that the men in the lower ranks must bestir themselves if they are to reach the top at a desirable age. Table 25 shows the age distribution on April, 1946, of a representative sample

[32] Harvey Walker, *Training Public Employees in Great Britain* (New York 1935) p. 13.

[33] From statement cited p. 769 above.

comprising two thirds of the administrative class, excluding assistant principals (the lowest stratum of this class) and temporary civil servants, but including wartime temporary civil servants since fully employed.

Then, too, there is an incentive in the refreshing effect of attachment as private secretary to ministers and even prime ministers, and as secretary to departmental committees and royal commissions —a post which involves the planning and management of the enquiry, the scrutiny, analysis, and marshaling of evidence, presence at the examination of witnesses and at discussions between the members, and the drafting of the report. Nor, nowadays, as distinct from years ago, can the

must be substituted. The Report of 1853 clearly recognizes what was being lost when the sheltered occupation with security of tenure was to be consequent on successfully passing an examination:

[Outside professions] supply a corrective which is wanting in the Civil Service, for as a man's success in them depends upon his obtaining and retaining the confidence of the public, and as he is exposed to a sharp competition on the part of his contemporaries, those only can maintain a fair position who possess the requisite amount of ability and industry for the proper discharge of their duties. The able and energetic rise to the top; the dull and inefficient remain at the bottom ... their course is one of quiet, and generally secluded, performance of routine duties, and they consequently have but limited opportuni-

TABLE 25 [34]—AGE DISTRIBUTION OF THE ADMINISTRATIVE CLASS OF THE CIVIL SERVICE (REPRESENTATIVE SAMPLE): ENGLAND, 1946

Civil-service Position	Age of Direct Entrants			Age of Promotees from Other Grades		
	Over 41	Under 41	Total	Over 41	Under 41	Total
Permanent secretary	16	1	17	6	—	6
Deputy secretary and equivalent	25	1	26	17	—	17
Undersecretary and equivalent	55	9	64	46	2	48
Principal assistant secretary	32	7	39	27	2	29
Assistant secretary	96	105	201	195	44	239
Principal	53	175	228	446	113	559

educative effect of many personal contacts with local authorities, foreign representatives, deputations from social and industrial groups, business and labor representatives, and clamorous or helpless individuals be dismissed as potent factors in bringing the fresh breezes of real life along the interminable corridors of Whitehall and through the baize doors. It has been shown, within the service, that a severe apprenticeship does inform and train the cadet very considerably.[35] Yet there is a curiously muted and aloof air about the official life. Some artificially organized stimuli are essential: if the boisterous, dangerous storms of the independent businessman's existence are excluded, then deliberate "air conditioning"

ties of acquiring that varied experience of life which is so important to the development of character.

That is, *competition* ceases; the ruthless, pitiless competition of private business, which drives men out of business and a livelihood unless they can master themselves, their environment, sufficient science, and their colleagues and clients, and sell their services or goods to those who demand them or can be persuaded that they need them.

One such stimulus would be to give them a year of work (out of the two years' probation) divided between six months with the local authorities, and six months in a foreign country or countries.[36] But

---

[34] From *The Reform of the Higher Civil Service* (Fabian Society, London, 1947), p. 29.
[35] H. E. Dale, *The Higher Civil Service of Great Britain* (London, 1941).

[36] Something like this has now been recommended (and instituted by the Treasury) by the Report of the Committee on the Training of Civil Servants (Cmd. 6525; 1944). The operation of the Treasury training scheme is re-

if they learn that life goes on outside their departments, and not by their grace; that people can be different without being cranks; that there are alternative principles entirely to those upon which life in their class and nation are organized, it may be that the true inward value (or valuelessness) of their own civilization and function will become the more evident after comparison and reflection. They might be asked to report upon the foreign treatment of some subject falling within their own department. Once in the department, the administrators should receive six months' leave with full pay, for study abroad, every seven years or so.[37] Then, from the age of thirty-five onward, they should take part in the training arrangements of the subordinate grades, in the hope that they might, in teaching them, learn something about themselves.

Finally, as the Tomlin Commission remarked, great care must be taken not to appoint too many cadets in comparison with the number of higher situations, for to do that, as the First Division Association testified, was to condemn energetic, capable men to the perdition of repeating themselves *ad nauseam!* Up to 1934, only one third at the age of thirty-four could rise to principal; one third to assistant secretary at forty-five; one fifth to principal assistant secretary; one seventh to deputy secretary, and one seventh to secretary, about the age of forty-eight if at all.[38]

The Viva Voce Test. In pursuing the subject of the fitness of the administrative group's selection and promotion for the work to which it becomes assigned in the passage of time, it was convenient not to stop and examine one of the factors which weighs heavily in the entrance examination: the interview. The interview is designed to give the civil service commissioners some evidence of personality, even character. It may be that the written tests are some evidence already; and Macaulay clearly declared that young men who in competition with their fellows of the same age had shown superiority in studies might be regarded as having shown character also since they could not have prepared themselves for the success they had attained without having applied themselves to their studies and having eschewed sensual pleasures, or wine, women, and song. The problem of selection for character is still the *pons asinorum* of recruitment to the public services everywhere.[39] The British civil service experiments with the interview.

The interview, or *viva*, was established in 1917 on the recommendation of the Committee on Class I Examination, which said:

A Royal Commission expressed a cautious inclination toward a *viva voce* examination, but made no definite recommendation. The Consultative Committee appointed by the Board of Education on Scholarships for Higher Education in their report, 1917 (Cd. 8291) say that there should be a *viva voce* examination.[40] On this point as on almost every point of our report, we are unanimous. We believe that qualities may be shown in a *viva voce* examination which cannot be tested by a written examination, and that those qualities should be useful to public servants. It is sometimes urged that a candidate, otherwise well qualified, may be prevented by nervousness from doing himself justice *viva voce*. We are not sure that such lack of nervous control is not in itself a serious defect, nor that the presence of mind and nervous equipoise which enables a candidate to marshal

---

ferred to in the Fifth Report from the Select Committee on Estimates (with Minutes of Evidence), "Organisation and Methods," No. 143 of August, 1947. Cf. below, Chap. 34.

[37] Something like this also has been proposed by the Committee on the Training of Civil Servants. Cf. below, p. 783.

[38] The Fabian Society's *The Reform of the Higher Civil Service* (London, 1947), written by civil servants, recommends that promotion should be so organized as to bring the best people to high posts at a comparatively early age. It recommends these promotion zones: assistant secretary, 32-40; undersecretary, 35-49; deputy head or head of department or equivalent, 40-52.

[39] Cf. Oscar K. Buros, *Educational, Psychological and Personality Tests of 1935-36* (New York, 1937).

[40] Actually they were concerned with the selection of candidates for scholarships, and not with the choice of administrators.

all of his resources in such conditions is not a valuable quality. Further, there are undoubtedly some candidates who can never do themselves justice in written examinations, just as there are others who under the excitement of written competition do better than on ordinary occasions. . . We consider that the *viva voce* can be made a test of the candidate's alertness, intelligence and intellectual outlook, and as such is better than any other. . . We consider that the *viva voce* examination should not be in matters of academic study, but in matters of general interest, in which every young man should have something to say.

The civil service commissioners not only supported this reasoning, but vindicated the actual proportion of the marks assigned to the interview. As subjects to the value of 1000 marks must be offered from the numerous options, and as all candidates must in addition thereto take an essay paper carrying 100 marks, English 100, present-day knowledge 100, everyday science 100, and an auxiliary language 100, while the interview carries 300 marks, the latter was no less than one sixth of the total marks for the whole examination. It is an important proportion, and it has had the effect of greatly altering the position of many candidates on the list as settled by the written examination.[41] This excessive proportion of marks to the total obtained until the 1937 examination, when the commissioners' regulations even increased it from 300 out of 1800 to 300 out of 1300! We deal first with the experience of the *viva* down to 1936, and this will show how serious is the commissioners' new step.

The board of interview consists of certain distinguished figures in university education, and some retired civil servants. Its business is not to place people by their excellence in discussion of a "subject," but to place them for "alertness, intelligence and general outlook," clearly a subtle and laborious task, if it is taken seriously. In fact, the interview until World War II lasted about a quarter of an hour; it occurred usually before the

examination, since there are many candidates; it was therefore not based on the subject matter of the examination. In form, it was a desultory conversation, indefinite and almost void [42] regarding the scholastic career and the social interests and activities of the candidate. Nothing much was tested by it, and hardly the qualities mentioned in the regulations. In fact, the college tutors' testimonials played a considerable part in the result.[43] Further, the method did not make sure of retaining the good, or of getting rid of the bad.

Now a test of this kind lends itself too readily to the suspicion that qualities other than those appropriate to the service have undue weight. At any rate, two tests of the figures and methods make clear the intrinsic untrustworthiness of the test. An analysis of results from 1924 to 1929 shows that [44]

on the average when a candidate submits himself for the *viva voce* test, there are forty marks which may be added to or subtracted from the true measure of his personal equation, and these forty marks will be added or subtracted in a haphazard manner. But the *viva voce* test on which is awarded 300 marks maximum, lasting perhaps fifteen minutes, and carrying with it the random plus or minus forty marks, may be altogether decisive. That this is the case may be seen from a consideration of results in recent years. . . This element of chance may actually operate in the same way as if a candidate's fate were being decided by the tossing of a coin or the throw of a dice.

A more serious reflection on the system emerges from the investigation undertaken by the International Institute Examinations Enquiry. This body established a replica of the civil service *viva voce* examination and discovered that for the same candidates, but by the different boards, differences of as many as 92 and 70 marks were shown in extreme cases, with the average difference of 37 marks. The board of enquiry commented:

---

41 Tomlin Commission, *Evidence*, p. 60, para. 19.

42 *Ibid.*, Question 1419.
43 *Ibid.*, Question 1375.
44 *Public Administration*, April, 1930, pp. 231-36.

These extreme differences . . . amounting to 20 to 30 marks out of 100, and the average difference of about 12 marks out of 100, point to the unreliability of the interview test, and indicate the great influence that this test might have in the final placing of a candidate in a Civil Service examination . . . we must conclude that the different influences of the Boards have been sufficient in this case to mask the common influence of the same set of candidates.

This was further borne out by comparison of the marks awarded by individual examiners, which varied very much, but less so than the common results obtained by the boards as such.[45] One candidate put first by a board was put thirteenth by the other, another put seventh by the first board was put eleventh by the second, and so on.

These results show definitely that the evidence on which the examiners could judge the candidate was different in the two cases, that is, that the two interviews were so differently conducted that we might almost suppose different candidates to have been examined.

This nebulousness of result is not difficult to explain. Between the private business interview and the civil service *viva voce* test a profound difference exists. In the former, the employer knows in great detail, and from reality, the nature of the actual job to be filled, and capacity to fill it is preferred to adventitious qualities which may be engaging but unprofitable. The civil service board of interview do not know the exact nature of the situation, although that they should is shown by the requirements for the Colonial Service, that interviewers who have been to the colonies be included in the board. If anything at all is in their consciousness, it is a very vague picture indeed, and it can hardly be a kinetic one—that is, include the possibility of development to meet greater responsibilities in the years to come. They will never see, and certainly will not lose money by, a mistake, and so they are more likely to be influenced by superficial characteristics. A "nice" boy, with engaging manners and a pleasant accent, has a much better chance of having his relevant qualities assessed excessively than the rough diamond has of securing arithmetical justice.

If we really care about the efficiency of the civil service as an instrument of government, rather than as a heaven-sent opportunity to find careers for our brilliant students, these principles should be adopted. The interview should last at least half an hour on each of two separate occasions. It should be almost entirely devoted to a discussion ranging over the academic interests of the candidate as shown in his examination syllabus, and a short verbal report could be required on such a subject, the scope of which would be announced at the interview. As now, the interview should be a supplementary test and not a decisive selective test. The interviewing board should include a business administrator and a university administrator. The interview should come after and not before the written examination, and if this means some inconvenience to candidates and examiners, then they must remember that they are helping to select the government of a great state, and a little inconvenience is not to be weighed against such a public duty. The university tutors' reports should not be consulted until the interview stage has been concluded and marked. More weight might be justifiably accorded such reports if the reporting tutors from various colleges and universities met to determine a common policy of self-restraint in hymning their students' virtues. Finally, since the arbitrary will still prevails, it ought to be limited by the reduction of the interview marks maximum from 300 to 150.

It is deplorable, and utterly amazing, to find that on the recent revision of marks [46] of the various subjects of the written examination, the civil service commissioners not only missed the opportunity to make this reduction in the weight of the interview, but for some un-

---

45 *Examination of Examinations* (New York, 1936).

46 Cf. The regulations for admission issued by the Civil Service Commission (currently, London).

announced reason actually increased it! The *viva* used to be 300 out of 1800: it is now 300 out of 1300. The results of three or four years' work, culminating in and tested by the written examination, are to be more than ever the sport of an interview conducted as we have explained! This reflection is not brightened by the changed formula for the *viva*.

The object of the interview is to enable the Board to assess his suitability for each of the Services for which he is entered, and in framing their assessment the Board will attach particular importance to his intelligence and alertness, his vigour and strength of character, and his potential qualities of leadership.

The important terms in the definition do show an advance, in that it is now recognized that the Board is searching for administrators, that is to say, for men and women who can not only think, argue, and write, but also devise, act, and lead.

It is gratifying that since the end of World War II, exceptional attention has been paid to interviewing for the administrative class. The period of interview has been lengthened to something like three quarters of an hour, candidates are sometimes interviewed twice, the questioning is more thorough, and the discussion by members of the board afterwards is more deliberate. This is an improvement in itself, not to mention the extended "personality" tests for older postwar entrants, discussed later.[47]

ADMINISTRATORS, SCIENTISTS, PROFESSIONAL AND TECHNOLOGICAL SERVANTS

An exceedingly important aspect of administration is the relationship between the administrative class and the scientists, technicians, and professional men. These latter include barristers, solicitors, doctors, architects, engineers, and scientific and technical research staff. Below them are draughtsmen, technical assistants, supervisory staffs in industrial establishments, clerks of works, and foremen of works. Their importance for public administration needs no extensive descrip-

tion. It is enough to say that there is hardly any step the state wishes to take, in devising the law or executing the details of policy in all these services, without vital dependence at some stage on the advice of a scientific expert. Two examples may be given: a policy of national physical fitness and the advice of biologists and nutrition experts; the execution of a housing and slum clearance policy and the advice of architects, engineers, and surveyors.

Two questions arise (1) the recruitment of these officials; and (2) the relationship of their special expertness to the administrators and the minister, that is, the political chief of the department.

Recruitment. As to their recruitment, there are no really serious problems. As specialists, they have the publicly recognized qualifications. When individual vacancies arise they are advertised, and a selection is made by the method of competitive interview. There are, in fact, some five hundred distinct grades. Inquiry has shown the difficulty of pooling all posts in order to have common recruitment, which might allow of a choice of candidates on intellectual grounds wider than the narrow specialism. Some improvement is, however, possible, especially in the case of the research staff, and had recently been instituted.[48]

Role in Policy Making. What of their cooperation in the making of policy? The specialists maintain that the parliamentary head, in weighing the recommendations of his administrative subordinates, should be "fully seized of the nature of the technical advice upon the matter under consideration."[49] They urge

---

[47] Cf. p. 784.

[48] Cf. Report, Barlow Committee on Scientific Manpower, Cmd. 6824 of 1946. Cf. also *Science and the Nation*, issued by the Association of Scientific Workers (Pelican Books, 1947). The development is not unrelated to the stimulus of war, followed by the exceptional needs of stricken postwar economy, and the conscious planning of national prosperity through nationalization of basic industries and other policies culminating in the planning institutions auxiliary to the cabinet system described on pp. 608 above.

[49] Cf. para. 48, App. XI, *Minutes of Evidence, R.C.C.S.*, 1929-1931.

arrangements to effect this, even proposing a system of advising the minister by boards composed of administrators and specialists. If this was not feasible, then there should be a right of access to the minister on technical questions, and denied, at the same time, to the mere administrators. Their motives for these demands are not difficult to define. They wish mistakes to be avoided. They alone can tell where, when, and how the technical mistake will occur. The administrator may not appreciate the need for consulting them, and even if he consults them, the full force of their advice may not penetrate his misinformed obstinacy or abate the impetus of his ignorant enthusiasm. It may be also that some specialists believe that they know not merely what will be the scientifically appropriate course, but that their ideas on the good and evil of policy are as good as, if not better than, the administrator's. If their advice is not taken on the scientific order they may be discouraged in their efforts; if their advice is not courted on policy, good teamwork may be jeopardized.

The solution, it seems to me, is properly this. On policy there can be only one hierarchy of responsibility—it is that which passes down from the political chief through the permanent secretary and his administrative assistants. For theirs is precisely the education, training, and status designed to make policy: that is, to weigh up *all* the technical considerations in relation to each other, and to compose a harmonious pattern of values by reference to the expediency implied in the ruling political party's notion of Justice and the Good. As to the urging of scientific considerations directly on the minister, this is equally to be rejected. The minister's mind may be a fresh mind, but it is a raw mind. He is in no position, normally, to appreciate the full civic value of a specialist's advice, by reference to all the invisible and inaudible technicians who would also need to be heard before the balance of advantage and disadvantage could be struck. And what of the administrative feasibility of a plan? Shall he be personally confronted by all the specialists? If he were, the poor man would wallow in a chaos.

The minister needs a focused white light; the experts offer a (to him) rather vague, blurred, if fascinating spectrum. Such a spectrum is also all that is obtainable by a board composed of political chief, administrators, and specialists, and it is a spectrum which would only be produced at a loss of time. We can imagine the minister waiting outside the door and asking the Permanent Secretary, "Well, after all that, what do you think we ought to do?" The Permanent Secretary and his assistants provide the sharply focused white light for the minister. It is the only system under which the chaos of technical advice can be reduced to the order which action, that is to say, administration, vitally demands—the relevant being utilized, the rest discarded, with the maximum speed possible in view of the intrinsic toughness of the problem to be solved. Someone must do the picking and choosing, someone must be responsible for the broth, and, as in the nature of the democratic political process, it can rarely be the minister, it must be the minister's other self, the permanent administrator. The specialist ought not to feel aggrieved about this, for the administrator himself risks being discouraged by the minister's refusal of his advice. We are all instruments in a higher social purpose. Yet, if it is the specialist's nature to know more and more about less and less, it is the administrator's responsibility, on pain of being untrue to his function, to seek out perseveringly, and to weigh seriously and long, the science which research discovers and the expert secretes. Nevertheless, the specialist ought not to be denied the opportunity of promotion to the highest administrative posts, if he can show, by experience, the qualifications for them, and deliberate search must be made for the scientists of administrative attainment or promise.

The persistence of the government scientific workers, aided by their colleagues in their professional associations, and furthermore assisted by the tremendous rise in the prestige of science during World

War II, won the concession proposed in the last sentence, as the result of a recommendation made by an expert committee which advised the Treasury.[50]

THE WEAKNESSES AND IMPROVEMENT OF THE ADMINISTRATIVE CLASS

THE relative weaknesses of the British administrative class of civil servants have flown from (1) their comparatively narrow recruiting ground, and (2) the lack of deliberate and systematic training on entry into the service.

Recruitment. The first weakness is rapidly being overcome by the extension of the educational freedoms to a point where no really eligible mind fails to receive an open opportunity of competing in the entrance examinations. Figures given in the House of Commons [51]—see Table 26—show a progressive change in opportunity to enter the administrative class by open competition.

Of course, practically every one of these then went on to Oxford or Cambridge before taking the civil-service entrance examination. A grant-aided school means a school maintained or assisted by public funds, managed wholly or partly by the public authorities, and requiring a considerable proportion of free places. It must be remembered that the "public schools" are themselves considerably various in their social composition and economic status. The boarding public schools as distinct from the day schools supplied only 33.8 per cent of the entrants in 1925–37. (Note too the proportion of the higher ranks of the administrative class recruited by promotion,

which is almost tantamount to saying recruited from the middle and lower-middle and working class; this proportion is measurable by Table 25, based on a two-thirds sample of the service, given on an earlier page.[52])

Although this widening of the recruiting ground of the civil service was true of the twenty years before World War II, there were still obstacles. The Education Acts of the postwar reconstruction period, and the increased grants by the government to the provision of scholarships by the municipal and other educational bodies leading to the universities, as well as a trebling of the university accommodation, will set the seal on this beginning and promise. Moreover, the development of social studies, already highly success-

ful, will provide many students with that educational channel to the public service. It is important that ignorant sneers at history and classics as an approach to the public service be deferred until the meaning of those studies is considered.[53] History is the history of man and his struggles to control his environment and get along with other men; the classical studies provide this insight also. Surely they are incomparable qualifications for a public administrator—if they are pursued deeply enough to teach a man how to think, or, at any rate, the importance to mankind of thinking before acting?

Training. As for the second weakness,

TABLE 26—ENGLAND: SCHOOL BACKGROUND OF CIVIL SERVICE ENTRANTS, 1905–37

Period	Total	Percentage from Public Schools	Grant-Aided Schools	Scottish Day	Miscellaneous
1905–14	283	74	27	18	28
1919–25	197	63.5	43	18	11
1925–37	263	61.8	21	41	15

[50] Cf. *The Scientific Civil Service,* Cmd. 6679, 1945, p. 12, paragraph 13.
[51] Cf. Debates, May 8, 1946.

[52] Cf. p. 776, above.
[53] It will be noticed that the more recent reforms in university education in the United States—as exemplified in the Harvard Report on General Education, and the college courses on "civilization" and "the humanities" in the colleges of Columbia University and the University of Chicago—return to the older conceptions, with benefit to the students and the nation.

various remedies have been suggested and are being applied. Discussion about training has resolved itself into two stages of thought. At first, during World War II (when the "phony" period of the war had evoked the erroneous impression that the civil servants were at fault), it was suggested that a staff college should be established to train would-be civil servants and further train those already in the service.[54] But on reflection, this was rejected, on the general ground that it appeared castelike and that it was not desirable to unify the mentality of civil servants. A powerful truth resides in the latter observation. In the social sciences, we are not so sure of the truth as to subject civil servants to one set of administrative, economic, or social propositions. It is far better to leave the students free, even to force them, to scatter widely among the different colleges and meet the different minds which have been reflecting on the problems involved. That, also, will enable the service as a whole, or each department when it arrays all its resources of talent, to see a more comprehensive truth and more multifarious alternatives, for the benefit of the minister and the public. This system, then, was rejected. (It should be observed that as soon as the policy of "waging war" began, and civil servants were decisively led by ministers, the service performed miracles, winning the enthusiastic praise of ministers, Parliament, and public.)

Still the problem of postentry training remained. The Treasury Committee on the Training of Civil Servants, especially appointed in February, 1943, to examine the general problem of training at all levels of the service and to consider whether a staff college should be established, published a masterly report in May, 1944. It rejected the idea that entrants should go to a staff college, especially if it were to be one in which tuition was given to private business also. And, in fact, the recently established adminis-trative-staff college is a private-business-management college. But the committee recommended that a few civil servants might attend as an experiment. "It is extremely difficult to find a firm foundation on which could be based a method," says the Report,[55] "common to both business and Civil Service." The Report appears to base this on the rather specialized business practices which would have to be taught. The members of the committee could not have failed to reflect on the different sense of equities prevailing in business and the public service.

They recommended alternatively (and their plan is in effect) an entrance course of some two or three months, conducted by the director of training and education of the civil service itself, with assistance only from university circles. This would be on a two-day-per-week basis. The purpose is to shorten the process by which the entrant forms his own administrative standards and "professional approach." Lectures, reading, and discussion would give him: explanation of the functions of the departments, and their financial and parliamentary background; departmental, managerial, and procedural techniques; knowledge of the implementing of large-scale administrative schemes of the past; an introduction to cooperation with the public; indoctrination with high civil-service standards—urgency, accuracy, decision, avoidance of incomprehensible instructions and uncertainty of purpose; and an approach to statistics and their logic and purpose.

This training is *pari passu* with responsible work in the departments. The school would become a clearinghouse of ideas, and would be used also for refresher courses, and could be assisted by visits from men of commerce and industry.

The entrant is also to be given work in branch offices where the liveliest business is going on, with a senior officer to serve him as tutorial friend. Departmental talks, and visits to various departments and offices, at all levels, are designed to give him a bird's-eye view of the service.

---

[54] Cf. Sixteenth Report from the Select Committee on National Expenditure, October 1942, "Organization and Control of the Civil Service," No. 120, p. 37.

[55] *Ibid.*, p. 17.

Where a department has local offices, real work in the field for a substantial time is arranged.

To refresh those who have been in the service for some years, a period of secondment is proposed for those over the age of thirty. There may be periods of observation in commerce and industry or in local authorities (in Britain these are closely connected with the central government and are in a sense its local arms). Above all, those of special ability obtain sabbatical leave for study at home or abroad: this is applicable to those "selected for the promise they show of being worthy of eventual promotion to high administrative work." [56]

This, then, is the provision for the administrative class, and the maintenance and improvement of its traditional preparation and status. Vacancies arising after the end of World War II will be filled in the traditional way.

For the five hundred administrative-class posts to be filled in reconstruction examinations for the service after the war, considerable preference is given to veterans and those who served in civil employment of a warlike character. The prerequisites are university standard degrees of at least a second-class-honors level: the examination is simplified. In addition to the interview as described, a leaf is taken out of the Army method of selecting officers—groups of twenty to thirty candidates spend two or three days at a center, at state expense. A skilled staff mixes with them, and applies individual and collective intelligence and personality tests, interviews, discussions. This test enters heavily into their rating.[57]

This test, it should be noticed, is applicable so far only to those who are entering under the postwar reconstruction scheme, and they are several years older than the normal entrants. It may be that the experiment of the two- and three-day

protracted personality test will be so successful as to warrant introduction into the usual process of selection for ordinary entrants. If the method succeeds, it may be the best answer yet given to the hitherto unanswered problem of selection for character as well as for intellect. Some observers, admittedly on the basis of a short period of trial, believe it is possible that the intellectual qualities will be sacrificed to the animated, kinetic qualities in the recruits. If so, it would be a parlous adventure, since the posts to which these entrants may eventually be promoted require, as we have abundantly shown, the highest of intellectual attainment and power. The writer has heard sufficient about the selection method at the closest quarters to be willing to hope that it is a most valuable new technique of recruitment.

BRITISH AND AMERICAN CONTRASTS: SOME VITAL PROBLEMS YET TO BE FULLY SOLVED

In the writings and discussions of administrative personnel during the past few years, the contact of American and British students has been singularly fertile. A confrontation of some current ideas will serve to clarify problems on both sides of the Atlantic. I shall confine myself here to: (1) the idea that the British civil service is a "class" and not a "representative" civil service; (2) the problem of age at entry; (3) the problem of whether the administrative grade should be a career; (4) the problem of recruitment qualifications.

The "Representativeness" of the Civil Service. It has been abundantly admitted by British students that the social basis of recruitment of the civil service in the past has been too narrow. (It has been so admitted in this work.) This teaching was passed to American scholars. British students of the civil service have insisted on the need for a body of officials drawn from all classes in a state which has many social problems because it has classes. They have hoped thereby to secure the assets of wide and dynamic sympathies. But their concern was for something more,

[56] See *Whitley Bulletin,* May, 1949, for details.
[57] Cf. for a full and critical account, Ninth Report, Select Committee on Estimates, "The Civil Service Commission," July 28, 1948, Nos. 203, 205; and House of Lords, *Debates,* May 26, 1948.

and perhaps it was a concern at least as acute as that for social representativeness, and perhaps even its search was for a quality beyond that: they desired that all the most distinguished talent in the nation should get its outlet for the sake of the nation's welfare. They desired also that no talent which had a capacity for development and happiness in the public service should be allowed to wither.

As soon as these things are admitted, it seems an almost inevitable act of Nature that the admission should be transformed into an exaggerated, distorted historical thesis and prophesy. The nefarious influence of Karl Marx must be brought in to show that Britain is about to succumb to the weight of a civil service which is "unrepresentative," and in which, therefore, civil servants appointed as they have hitherto been would not impartially and honorably serve a Labour government. Nothing is said of the effect of the massive changes in the public sentiments regarding the objectives of the state which have occurred since World War I. Nothing is allowed for the changes in the tendency of teaching at the older and certainly the younger universities. No account is taken of the change in the appointment of teachers at universities and the effects of their teachings upon the entrants to the service. No weight is given to the substantially changed attitudes to state activity in economic and social matters. And the sovereign position of the House of Commons as the acknowledged democratic master of the service is left high and dry, as though it were irrelevant to the problem.

Instead of repairing these omissions, a puking version of Marx is taken from the exaggerations of men who have sucked at Marx until they have become bloated. This is the doctrine taught by one treatise, and, of course, it is so simple that it is lapped up eagerly by those who have no direct knowledge and by some who enjoy what the Germans call *Schadenfreude.* Thus: [58]

---

[58] J. D. Kingsley, *Representative Bureaucracy* (Antioch, 1945), pp. 278-80.

There are, obviously, points beyond which a man cannot go in carrying out the will of another; and the fact that those limits have seldom been approached in the conduct of the civil service since 1870 bears witness to the unity of the middle-class state. [Why the "middle class" should serve the aristocracy at the helm till toward the end of the nineteenth century is not explained.] The convention of impartiality can be maintained only when the members of the directing grades of the service are thoroughly committed to the larger purposes the state is attempting to serve; when, in other words, their views are identical with those of the dominant class as a whole. . . What can be said with little fear of contradiction, is that the civil service as now constituted would be much less representative of a state in which labor wielded power than it has been of a state in which that prerogative belonged to the upper middle classes. . . Would this be a source of difficulty? I am inclined to think that it would, for I am arguing that bureaucracies are responsible only to the extent that they are broadly representative. . . Nor is there much in the social background and experience of members of the administrative class to lead one to believe that as a group they would be able to participate creatively in the development of a Labour program.

This passage is a tragedy of historical misconceptions; is founded upon false history; and is the fruit of a misbegotten determination to see history as it is not, in the name of Marx Almighty, through one of his more erratic prophets.

Look at the leaks in this thesis! "The larger purposes the state is attempting to serve." "Thoroughly committed." "Their views are *identical.*" But the British civil service is now serving a Labour government more enthusiastically than it served interwar governments. The prophecy is wrong: then the history must be wrong. It is, crassly.

Finally, in this respect, the reader may be begged to compare the discussion of parliamentary control on page 530 ff. above, with this supporting statement by the author of the views quoted above on this page (in the same article):

I have said very little in this chapter concerning the formal devices of parliamentary and judicial control. . . I regard them, in any event, as of distinctly secondary importance. Responsibility is not to be secured through governmental forms or systems of checks and balances,—though these may sometimes help.

There could hardly be more political error compressed into so few words. And the following words of that author directly after this passage, which is about the Weimar constitution, betray a want of understanding of that system and its breakdown, and a determination to stick to a point even though it is nonsense.

Age at Entry. The British civil service restricts entry to certain age limits; the American accepts entrants to quite advanced years—to the junior professional assistants up to thirty-five. What is the British purpose? It is quite deliberate. The service of government is regarded as having a character of its own. It is different from business, from art, from teaching, from other professions. Its objectives are individual, its spirit and methods are special. A government servant must observe certain equities towards all clients which the businessman grows rich by ignoring. He must hold himself responsible and accept the procedures and public obligations, as an artist, loyal only to his own artistic conscience, does not. He must cooperate with others in his own division, in a situation of subordination to some and of command over others, and must work as a partner with other departments, while a physician or an architect has only immediate duties to a client. And unlike the teacher, his business is not only to think, argue, and research for absolute truth, but to employ a combination of unequally valuable truths to fulfill an urgent specific task. As Paul Appleby has reminded many American students,[59]

Government is different: the dissimilarity between government and all other forms of social action is greater than any dissimilarity among those other forms themselves.

The British civil service has drawn the conclusion that young people should come into the service at an age when their

[59] *Big Democracy* (New York, 1945), p. 1.

minds are open to influence by the individual character of government activity. This is a profession with its own proper characteristics. One illustration alone is permitted here. Some day a civil servant will have reached a point in his career where he is called upon to take a judicial decision in a dispute between men of lower rank and the state, or between private business claims and the state, or between two local authorities, in something like adversary proceedings. In that situation, everyone will claim that he ought to be judicial-minded. How are we to be sure of his impartiality unless he has received his training in the work of the department almost all his life, so that he not only knows the subtle factors involved and the laws and the practice, but also has attained control over his passions in the interests of impartiality? Much of the controversy over justice in the ordinary courts as against administrative justice revolves around this. Not that early entrance and life-long service are infallible conditions of judicial-mindedness: but is it better to be without any guarantee?

The American civil service is more impressed with the idea that the service should be open to anyone: that it should receive talent for a specific job wherever the candidate has mastered the written qualifications for that job. This idea ministers to employment opportunities. It also seems to promise freshness of mind, and specific work contributions. Yet it lets in men who soon get out; without a comprehension of their relationship to the whole administrative apparatus and to the President and to Congress; without a permanent interest in the service. All observers fear that it is not so much refreshing as disturbing. It has its values; it has its decided disadvantages. It is one of the chief factors making it impossible in the United States for federal service to be a "profession" of civil service.

The Administrative Grade as a Career. This leads directly to the problem of making the administrative grade a career. The British definitely establish a life career. This is a promise to the best minds of each generation that if they are content to give up the chances of fame and fortune in the professions, in the arts, and in business, and if they devote their minds and consciences to the service of the state, they may look forward to hard work, intense mental exertion, creative endeavor, the building up of their country, a comfortable salary but not a fortune,[60] and a comfortable pension and social honor at sixty. This, in Britain, does attract extremely able entrants. By far the largest proportion remain and grow and are worthy of the high authority to which they finally are promoted. In the end they are the advisers of ministers: career statesmen, as it were. They are immersed in high policy and participate in the nation's most moving events.

Some American observers affect to believe that the seeming assurance of a career must result in mental rot. But this is simply a hypothesis or suspicion. The facts count: there is no mental rot. Instead, a very intense emulation prevails among the younger men in the depart-

---

60 The salaries were to 1949:

Head of a major department £3,500
Deputy head of major department £2,500
Undersecretary £2,000
Assistant secretary ....£1,200 to £1,700
Principal ....£ 800 to £1,100
Assistant principal ......£ 275 to £ 625

The last three categories have a bonus of £60 a year for cost of living, to be amalgamated with the basic salary. The pound in normal times buys at least fifty per cent more than the American dollar equivalent. It may be remembered that it is designed that the "assistant secretary" and above categories should be reached at ages 32-40, 35-39, and "deputy head" and "head" at 40-52.

In February, 1949, changes were made as follows:

Secretary to the Treasury £5000
Head of a major department £4500
Deputy head of major department .£3250
Undersecretary £2500

The change was made on recommendation of the Committee on Higher Civil Service Remuneration (Cmd. 7635), because (a) the burden of work and responsibility had increased, (b) the cost of living had risen, and (c) the new boards of nationalized industries and the specialists in the national health service are paid quite high salaries.

ment; the opinion of colleagues in the service is a tremendous spur—a continual one—to enterprise and above all to mental exertion. Promotion is by no means certain; the approval of one's colleagues is contingent and very exacting; the rise to the permanent secretaryship is a considerable hazard of more than one in a hundred; ministerial rebuke or praise and indirectly by the House of Commons is always possible. The belief that men who enter a professional career will rot is an offshoot of social values which imply that men will not do fine work except under the lash of competition and dismissal, and the spur of material rewards. These values are not British values. Societies are different.

How can you recruit and keep four thousand advisers and assistants to the executive, and indirectly to the legislature, without offering men a career which will ask from them permanent and exclusive devotion, and require that they shall equip themselves in every way for their particular task?

Some men can be brought in as social need dictates at a later age, and so displace the chances of promotion of others already there. The British Treasury rules provide for this. The hazard is known. But if the proportion of those so entering becomes large, then the inducement to unqualified life devotion to the impartial and anonymous service of the supreme political authorities in the democracy has fled. You cannot have the cake of due mature, loyal advisership to the sovereign authorities, which they need as a life-and-death function of social democratic societies, yet eat up the cake by denying an assured career to the kind of people who will more surely give such service.

It is noteworthy that one of the experts, of long experience in political science and in the service of the Civil Service Commission, Sir Ernest Barker, threw out the suggestion that older men and women should be appointed to the top grade of the civil service, so as to make room for minds and characters nurtured in social experience.[61] But when it came to the actual establishment of such a project, he became more tentative. A more recent proposal by writers who have themselves held fairly high civil-service posts recommends a regular recruitment of applicants from the public for positions fitting the age zone of thirty to forty. In addition, it is recommended that the Treasury experimental arrangement to recruit some twenty per cent of the entrance places into the administrative class from elsewhere in the service be made a permanent feature. Furthermore, it is the Treasury's postwar long-term normal rule to recruit some twenty-five per cent of the regular examination entrants rather more on the basis of personality than of supreme intellectual attainment. These arrangements go far toward remedying any stiffness which may have entered into the collective mentality of the administrative class. Yet there is still an undoubted and a justified anxiety whether if the arrival at high positions after years of service is narrowed and subject to more hazards by promotions from outside the class, and by new entrants in response to public advertisement, the attraction to the university generation will still remain as strong as hitherto. Time must test this.

Recruitment Qualifications. Of course, the foregoing observations lead directly to the problem of entrance qualifications. The American system virtually says to anyone, whatever his preparation, in whatever school, or business, or scientific or professional training: "If you can pass our examinations for this specific job, you can have a job; and you can get promoted to any other job if you do your present one well, as retirements and deaths provide vacancies." Thus technicians of all kinds can and do enter into positions where administrative qualities are needed: that is, where perception of intradepartmental problems arise for solution; where interdepartmental cooperation is needed; where fruitful compre-

hensive ideas for the progressive march of the whole function and public service department and the government are required; where advice of a part-managerial, part-political nature must ascend to the top; where the making of laws, and the high strategy of law enforcement, are all involved. It is a thousand-to-one chance whether the man taken in because he can do a specific job today will be the administrator who is needed in the new situation of several or many years hence. American students admit repeatedly that it is not a good chance. Yet they are overwhelmed by the feeling that the career ought to be open to anyone who now can fill the bill, and by a kind of tempestuous faith in the fresh-minded entrant, who will wake up everybody else in the service.

It is very reminiscent of the Jacksonian view, stated in his first annual message to Congress, that, "The duties of all public officers are, or at least admit of being made, so plain and simple that men of intelligence may readily qualify themselves for their performance . . ." When Jackson spoke, no brain was needed to guide the work of two million officials, or to devise the ways and means of securing a job for all, or giving parity to the farmers, or conserving natural resources subject to rapacious use by entrepreneurs, or equipping the might of America for the continuous task of making justice and peace prevail in the international order.

British ideas are different. They plan to recruit a great body of administrative statesmen, culminating in some forty permanent undersecretaries. That is their supreme concern: to provide the changing party cabinets with permanent expert advisers, and to enable ministers to rest assured that all matters of managerial detail will be handled by the secretaries once ministers have given their main propulsion to them. In the administration a kind of permanent counterpart to the political ministers is essential: to do all the thinking that ministers must do, and be aware of all the facts of which a minister ought to be aware and yet cannot be because he is not a career man in administration; to be the focus and bearer of

[61] Cf. W. A. Robson, editor, *The British Civil Servant* (London, 1937).

the science and technology and social considerations contained in the entire personnel of the department, and to garner the aid that can be brought to it from all other departments as need requires. This is the principal object of the British system, and it does it very well. We have already seen the mechanism by which these men, sometimes called planning officers themselves, or the men in charge of such planning and intelligence officers, are brought together in a central planning staff or as the official counterpart of committees of ministers acting under the immediate direction of the cabinet. Their integration is not merely the result of a specially established machinery of coordination, but their minds are already woven together by an approach to a common education. They begin with many common assumptions about human nature, as history and philosophical and literary study have taught them it, and this, in the province of high policy. Of course they have different outlooks; of course they have competitive ambitions; but of course they also have many ideas in common. Policy and coordination begin there. Administrative integration begins at college; it is seated in the mind.

To these great advantages, the British civil service must sacrifice the possibly remarkable administrative talent of some technician or professional worker, for normally (it sometimes happens) he cannot get to the administrative summit (though he may receive equal pay) which is reserved to those who have been educationally prepared and have thereafter followed the practical apprenticeship laid down for them on the ladder that leads to proficiency in the special office of supreme advisership to minister and Parliament. That that course is hard, well-designed, and effective is shown by the success of the arrangement, and the testimony of those with most intimate knowledge.[62] That it requires some improvement in detail, and occasional departures,

is no reflection on the main service rendered.[63] That a good technician will not be a splendid administrator is not thereby proved in general: he may be, but can you uproot a wholesale success on an individual chance?

Admonition regarding Education for Civil Service. It is a truth applicable to all civil services that the part that education can play in the preparation of an official is relatively small, especially if by education is meant only the years at college and university; and if all the years before that and the education in the family and all social activities and influences are omitted or underrated. To administer is to act, to make up one's mind, to influence other people to carry out desired policies, to combine and compound the ingredients in a situation so as to find the particular key that unlocks the obstinate door. It is the educational process as an opportunity of selecting from among the many who present themselves, rather than education as a direct making of an administrator that, perhaps, should be stressed. It is not the cognitive but the affective elements in personality that urge on to action. The truth of this is obvious from a glance at the list of qualities set down in the British and American civil service rating forms for the determination of efficiency for promotions or advancements in salary. (p. 858 ff.) It will be noticed that perhaps seven out of ten of the qualities are not educable, that is to say, while it is possible to describe them and perhaps to devise exercises in them, they are almost uncontrollable inborn psychological and even physical qualities. This means that the process of selection is even more important than has hitherto been admitted.

THE CIVIL SERVICE AND THE VALUES IT SERVES

THE discussion of the recruitment of the higher civil service of Britain could not have failed to awaken the sense that we

---

[62] Cf. H. E. Dale, *The Higher Civil Service of Great Britain* (London, 1941).

[63] Cf. Report of the Committee on Training of Civil Servants (1944).

have not been concerned with a merely utilitarian instrument of a materialistic society. Values have been suggested which go beyond so limited and ungenerous a function. The civil service obeys a government but it serves a society, an ancient corporate personality with life today of a myriad facets, and a future of spiritual as well as the grosser needs. The British conception of its civil service is the British conception of government and civilization as a whole; for good or ill it is not a hand-to-mouth affair, nor a helter-skelter improvisation of a handful of administrative mechanics armed with a few brash generalizations about intelligence tests, efficiency records, rating scales, and the husks of a knowledge of human nature gathered from a hurried study of organization charts. It is not a temporary camp of prefabricated dwellings to which anyone may easily repair and may shortly leave. It is rather like a stately home designed with many wings, housing standards and conscience, and built to last many generations. It incarnates a pattern, a design, a concatenation of values, for living in its entirety, embodying values and graces beyond the materialistic only. Burke best expressed its inward parts in his *Reflections on the French Revolution:*

... the state ought not to be considered nothing better than a partnership agreement in a trade of pepper and coffee, calico and tobacco, or some other such low concern, to be taken up for a little temporary interest, and to be dissolved at the fancy of the parties. It is to be looked on with other reverence; because it is not a partnership in things subservient only to the gross animal existence of a temporary and perishable nature. It is a partnership in all science; a partnership in all art; a partnership in every virtue and in all perfection. . .

Clearly the manning of such a dynamic partnership cannot be left to chance or to narrow views of "efficiency." The higher civil service of Britain seeks permanent statesmen—that is its problem. That they are in part managers as well as statesmen is true and certainly makes the problem more complicated; but it is even more certain that the quality of statesmen will

always be the paramount quest, since that is the deepest need.

Roger Ascham's *The Scholemaster,* published in 1570, not so long after Columbus discovered America, wrote this tribute to Nicholas Metcalfe, the Master of St. John's College, Cambridge, who died in 1539:

This his goodnes stood not still in one or two, but flowed aboundantlie over all that Colledge, and brake out also to norishe good wittes in every part of that universitie: whereby, at his departing thence, he left soch a companie of fellowes and scholers in St Johnes Colledge, as can scarse be found now in some whole universitie: which either for divinitie, on the one side or other, or for Civill service to their Prince and contrie, have bene, and are yet to this day, notable ornaments to this whole Realme.

Hitherto, a considerable proportion of the entrants to the administrative class have been the sons of the high professional classes and, some, the members of the aristocratic families; quite a number have come from clerical families. In all of these has reigned a high sense of moral purpose; and this is cultivated at the universities, which have been residential. Graham Wallas, my teacher, himself the son of a religious minister, used to refer to men of this sort as "secular saints." It would be fulsome to apply this term indiscriminately. But the names of Trevelyan, Mowat, Eyre Crowe, Sir John Anderson, Lord Beveridge, Harold Nicolson, Oliver Franks have attained wide public fame. Hundreds of their counterparts, less well-known, attest the enduring public spirit of the administrative class, their devotion, and the conversion of their parents' religious into a secular ministry.[64] There is no indication that the new

[64] I refer for illustration to Bernard M. Allen, *Sir Robert Morant* (London, 1938); Lord Beveridge, *The Beveridges in India* (London, 1938); Cyril Connolly, *Enemies of Promise* (London, 1935); Dean W. R. Inge, *Vale* (London, 1934); *Sir Oswald Murray*, by Lady Murray (London, 1936); Beatrice Webb, *My Apprenticeship* (London, 1926) and *Our Partnership* (London, 1948); Harold Nicolson, *Lord Carnock* (London, 1930); and much may be learned from Sir Ernest Barker's *Father of the Man* (London, 1948), for he has been a

classes that are now entering the service have not inherited this devotion to the public service, which implies a large subordination of self to the present and future welfare of the great community, a fulfillment of self by assisting the establishment in the community's focus, the state, of more justice, more charity, more abundance, less pain, a fuller consciousness of truth.

THE CIVIL SERVICE IN THE CONTEMPORARY STATE

Do the expansion of state activities, the nationalization of the basic industries, the planned regulation of all others, the management of all-comprehensive social security, the objectives of full employment and deliberate progress toward a rising standard of living, impose an important change in methods of recruitment of the civil service?

The answer can depend only on the difference, if any, in the nature of the task of the government. Four changes may be discerned, and it will be observed that they are of degree rather than kind.

(1) The functions of government have changed in scope: a much more comprehensive intervention in social life has occurred. This change dictates the need for imagination of relationships among the branches of the government, the departments, and the agencies. Is this new? Between 1832 and 1948, is an enormous contrast: but is there much contrast between 1928 and 1948? Some contrast there is, and it is of importance. But civil servants have been coordinating for decades. The awareness exists, and if it did not at the official level, it would be speedily brought home at the cabinet and cabinet-committee level. It might be rejoined that it is from the civil servants that cabinet ministers must obtain their understanding of the need for coordination: this is true, up to a point; each helps the other, or averts mutual hindrance. Some clearer consciousness of the width and the compli-

cated problems in coordination, an extra alertness about this, a rising emotion about it, are required. This can be given in one or two courses at college, or in the in-training period now established by the Treasury. It calls for no important change in the general education and recruitment methods of the service. The need is partly met by the establishment of the Central Planning Staff, which, being rooted in the officials of the various departments, must agitate an everyday awareness of the responses each departmental group of officials must make.

(2) Contemporary state services place more emphasis on the future. Nearly all of them require the government to forecast what the great public groups will do. The officials must take the statistics of the past, carry them forward for a recognition of trends, and then ask themselves what probabilities of future behavior will vary the trend. This is a cardinal task of planning. Indeed, guesses must be made about the variables cleverly enough to judge what statistics must be gathered in the first place: for these will be gathered in order to assist in finding answers: the problem properly defined is half the answer. Sir Oliver Franks has stated the matter, from personal experience, in these words: [65]

The second [danger in planning activities] is to forget the real nature of the economic activities to which the planning refers. Since central planning concerns the future and what can be done with it, it is necessarily occupied with extrapolation from the present. Trends and tendencies must be isolated and analysed so that forecasts may be built up and estimates made. This cannot be done by purely intellectual processes: or if it is, the results are certain to be unreal and bad guides for practice. An awareness of how things happen is required, of the interrelations of commercial and industrial processes, of the factors which enter into the business decisions of business men. That is why good forecasting and estimating is an art though using all the scientific techniques that the study of statistics has made available. It is not the art of what wartime nomenclature called the back-

teacher of aspirants for the civil service and an examiner for the Civil Service Commission for some forty years.

[65] *Central Planning and Control in War and Peace* (London, 1947).

room boy. It requires knowledge of the world as well as highly specialized training. It is no criticism of the Civil Service to say that it has not enough experts of this kind. There are not enough in existence. But it must be the first concern of the Civil Service to increase their number if there is to be central planning and control in peace.

How can the "awareness of how things happen" be taught in a university to undergraduates of the normal youth of undergraduates? It cannot be, by hypothesis. And as we look at postgraduate students, several years after their undergraduate education, can we believe that they have acquired an "awareness of how things happen"? We cannot. They are both raw material. Is the answer then to bring in men from the outside as a regular wholesale procedure for recruiting the civil service? They cannot surely have mastered more than one trade, or two? Can we be sure that they could be employed exactly where their awareness would fit? There is a case for bringing in some from outside—a proportion of the total recruited annually, and the procedure of choice must be exceedingly careful so that in the search for those who know how the business mind works, there may not be lost to the service some kind of mind at all. The solution lies in the proposals already advanced, that a proportion of the higher civil service be recruited from the outside in the age zone of thirty to forty; that a fair proportion rise from the other grades of the service; and that all, once in the service, be given training, with opportunities every few years of travel and first-hand observer-participant experience in business. If this does not help toward discovery of the personnel needed, no other road exists. It is clear, however, that promotion policy must be directed toward keeping out of the positions requiring the specific awareness we are discussing those who have not the kind of talent which fits the situation or can be trained for it.

(3) If these requirements were met, they would take care of the third characteristic of administration in the planned state,

especially the British, whose prosperity is precariously poised on its imports-exports balance: speed of reaction to the first signs that the future is in movement. It seems unavoidable also that even if it is not desired to change the traditional principle of recruitment—namely, that candidates shall be examined in the subjects they themselves have freely chosen to study—and even if emphasis is still placed on the humanities (which I hope it will be), a strong case exists for requiring the subjects of government and economics. If this is not feasible before, then rigorous study of these subjects must be required after, entry into the service.

We now turn to the final quality which has become especially important in the planned state: practical initiative. Nothing was more significant during the debates on the nationalization of the Bank of England and the coal industry than the unanimity of House of Commons opinion that these industries must not be recruited "like the civil service." It is not fatally sure that a unanimous House of Commons is always right. It was, at any rate, not clear and specific in its anxieties. Civil servants hitherto have in many situations been obliged to take the initiative. It is difficult to think of any who are not required to, and that with continual promptitude. In any case, the nationalized industries have their own free recruitment methods, almost as free as any private corporation. (Whether they will be able to maintain it so over a long period is another question.) Is there a difference in the kind of initiative between the action of a Ministry of Health official in conducting an inquiry into a slum-clearance scheme, and an official of the Ministry of Fuel making sure that the complaints of the consumers' councils in the coal industry have stated their case and have been properly heard by the ministry? It would seem not. Is there a difference in kind between a land-purchase agent of the government buying land for a government storage-house in 1928 and in 1958, just because at the new date the goods to be stored are cotton bought and sold by the government? I do not think so. Is a new kind of treatment required where a regional export council (a representative body) must be urged and persuaded and invigorated by an official of the Board of Trade? Yes, undoubtedly. Is there a new kind of initiative required in deciding that more money should be invested in coal or transport? Hardly; for the proposition would come from the boards concerned, and high Treasury considerations would be involved. But perhaps a suggestion might come from the Treasury, when someone would have to initiate it. It would seem then that the answer is complicated and mixed. It is mainly to be answered by the methods of promotion, transfer, and training, and the training itself must insist on the need for a mood of alert prediction in the civil service. There will be much occasion—in a state which follows the general policy of full employment and a rising standard of living and equalized distribution—for the higher civil servants to cogitate and to digest and prepare suggestions of policy to implement the major decisions made by ministers and the House of Commons, and to make pioneer suggestions which emerge from the close scrutiny of practical and spiritual trends.

Yet all these things do not seem to me to add up to a case for departure from the main traditional principles of recruitment, though they do for their intelligent and rational qualification. For part of the difficulty is the wholesale nature of state activity. It is impossible to find a separate appointing process for each individual civil servant, fitting him to the particular job which is vacant. Even if this could be done, one would be dogged by the next attendant problem of following that same civil servant, individually, through the promotion stages up the ladder of responsibility; and if one were so followed, all would need to be. The permutations and combinations would elude the most elaborate form of control over appointments and promotion. No legislature could exercise its right of control over the appropriations for its civil servants if such individualization were carried out: how could they compare men and jobs and salaries? And, therefore, a radical change is not only unnecessary but infeasible.

Finally, to put all the emphasis on the civil servant is to commit a grave error in proportion. The stimulus to initiative in the planned state comes from the political parties; from the organized producers and consumers, the workers who want more money and less hours and better conditions on the job, and the various groups of consumers who in some cases (like coal, credit, houses, transport, electricity and gas) pay a price for the service or commodity; from the minister who wants to make a good showing in the eyes of Parliament and the public; and from the House of Commons that has the right of asking questions and making its will prevail. If all these institutions, and many more, remain alive and virile, they will continually provide stimuli to efficiency and initiative which cannot be ignored by officials of even average conscience.

31

Recruitment in Germany in the Nineteenth and Twentieth Centuries

INEXORABLY the spiritual and material conditions of nineteenth-century civilization began to affect the recruitment of the public services. Inexorably, but only gradually, and with much opposition from obsolescent ideals and vested social interests. An extraordinary break came round about 1875: the countries in which modern industry and the modern spirit had come to their most vigorous and self-conscious efflorescence then made sudden haste to renew their civil services, for the logic of industrial and commercial efficiency was irresistible. In the chapters which follow we continue to sketch the general development of the administrative services with special attention to the methods of recruitment. We are primarily interested in the branch of the civil service which shares in governing—that is, the higher administrative class. It is in this respect that modern states show differences, and characteristic differences; and that the evolution of the modern state is best observable. While, therefore, tracing the general assault upon patronage and the state's adjustment of its machinery to its purposes, we shall (1) deal with the higher services first, then (2) compare them and try to estimate the significance of their development and ultimate results, and (3) indicate, but very briefly, the solutions adopted for the subordinate classes.

THE RISE OF LEGAL TRAINING: TO THE 1870's

AFTER the reforms of the French Revolutionary period, there followed a time of conservatism and consolidation. In old Prussia the civil service was a nationwide and continuously operative economic institution. Its training had been adapted to its functions. But between 1815 and the last quarter of the nineteenth century a number of new conditions caused a very vital variation of the mode of recruitment. A vast mass of legislation, as distinct from administration, was required to meet social and economic needs. The state was renewing itself, and the duties and rights it was creating to accomplish this were often in the direction of freeing industry and commerce from its regulation. While, therefore, it was not adding to its administrative work it was making law, and it felt the strong need for civil servants with a good legal training, and, moreover, a training in private law. Again, since administrative law and its procedure were being sedulously developed, great importance was once more attached to legal training. Further, the constitutional struggles had for their object the legal restraint of arbitrary officialdom, and Parliament saw in a legal training of officials a good means of teaching them a practical respect for law. This, the legal restraint of officials, was the German idea of the "rule of law," a substitute for the "rule of law" in the Anglo-Saxon political tradition, namely, that no official could act otherwise than under the authority of a popularly responsible legislature. The Germans called it the *Reichstaat*. Nor were the individualists in this very temperate heyday of German laissez faire unready to secure limitations upon the activity of the administrative official similar to those of the judge.

Until 1879, therefore, the old practical and cameralistic preparation suffered continual modification which favored legal studies. The authentic note of the eighteenth century is still heard fully in the Prussian instruction of 1808. Candidates are expected to have studied thoroughly political science (*Polizeiwissenschaft*), technology, statistics, experimental physics and chemistry, botany and agricultural economy, and to have had the opportunity of acquiring practical knowledge of the most important trades, especially of the agricultural. They were no longer required to have worked in one of the domain administrations. Their examination was written and oral and they were accepted only if "they combined thorough theory in the required sciences with a sound, well-exercised judgment." [1]

In 1817 a change is already observable. Besides the preparation in the usual branches of knowledge, in languages ancient and modern, in history and mathematics, there is required thorough knowledge of the law, at least some practical knowledge of agriculture or some other chief industry, and as far as possible practical work as auscultator in the courts. The effect was not to put law into the foreground, but it was certainly to introduce a competing element and a relative depreciation of the position of the social sciences. However, the decisive change in emphasis did not come until 1846 when practice in the law courts became the rule and in agriculture or industry the exception. The chief requirement now became practice in the law courts and

the passage of the second examination in law for entrance to the superior courts. All that was now required of the cameralistic and agricultural sciences was "at least general acquaintance" therewith. Finally, there came the decisive "second examination" for the attainment of a permanent position, as *Regierungsassessor*. This examination was written and oral; the former consisted of three theses, one dealing with a subject of political science, another of administration, and the third of finance, the latter two being of a more practical nature.

By 1846, the predominance of legal studies was firmly established, and the final break had been made with the eighteenth century.[2] Most interesting is the downfall of the importance of agriculture. As interesting, too, is the cessation of practical work in agriculture and industry as a preparation for public service. It betokened the conscious withdrawal of the state from positive economic and social activity. The social sciences ceased to have their old importance as the foundation of a civil servant's training, but worse still, their cleavage from actual practice caused them to become excursions in the literary history of theories. They became less a scientific preparation than an exercise of memory, and the universal weed which forms upon the soil of circumscribed and theoretic studies, the "coach" or "crammer" appears, without resort whereto it was now almost impossible to pass the examination. In 1866 it became necessary to reconsider the Regulation, partly owing to public and parliamentary criticism but more particularly owing to the extension of Prussian rule.

The law of 1869 regulated entry into the higher judicial service, by abolishing the intermediate law examination at the universities, and setting up only two examinations, the first, the university law examination taken after at least three years' study, and the second, the great state examination, taken after at least four years of preparatory service. Until 1879, administrative officials were re-

---

[1] Clemens von Delbrück, *Die Ausbildung für den höheren Verwaltungsdienst in Preuszen* (Jena, 1917), p. 6.

[2] *Ibid.*, p. 8 ff.

cruited from the judicial assessors trained in this way. These judicial officials might have received a one-year's training in an administrative department as part of their four years' preparatory service: this was the intention of the government, but the Prussian Parliament rejected the proposal as it feared the undue influence of the executive.[3]

We now come to a period in which the position of legal studies is consolidated, but no sooner is it consolidated than parliamentary and public critics are compelled to criticize the efficacy of legal studies as a preparation for the administrative work of the modern state. Moreover, university teachers of law became thoroughly dissatisfied with the nature of the curriculum since they realized that it may have serious effects upon the efficiency of the service. A very lively controversy therefore begins, as to the scope and method of legal studies.

LEGAL TRAINING SUPPLEMENTED: THE PERIOD TO 1920

GERMANY was now full in the strong current of industrial civilization and the sense of state activity which had weakened a little between 1815 and 1870, but had never fundamentally suffered, now not only recovered its old strength but went beyond it in scope and energetic persistence. The higher officials' experience had taught them that the best administrative officials were to be obtained by a special training in which the study of economics and finance at the universities and the acquisition of exact knowledge of the conditions of public life and administrative law and practice during preparatory service were of equal and high importance. A government measure before the Prussian Parliament in 1874 acknowledged the necessity of a special preparation for higher administrative officials. It admitted that the entrant to the service could not obtain a knowledge of administrative institutions and adminis-

trative law at first hand: the more, in fact, that he devoted himself to law, the less would he be able harmoniously to relate written law and the practical necessities of life. A thorough knowledge of the indispensable sciences of economics and finance could only be obtained by their early, long, and serious study, and, as an adjunct of legal studies, would be entirely insufficient. Further, the Diet suggested the application of these proposals to the chief presiding officials of the local government areas [4] as well as their immediate subordinates, who alone were affected by the government proposals, and recommended that in the Ministries of the Interior and Finance only persons who had acquired the qualifications for the higher judicial service should be appointed.

Law Education versus *The Social Sciences.* After prolonged debate, open and occult, the Prussian Diet, the House of Peers, and the government arrived at a compromise.[5] The regulations applied to divisional directors and members of a government district, and the higher administrative officials adjoined to the overpresidents and government-district presidents, with the exception of justiciars and the technical officials. It may seem strange to the English reader that the regulations concerned what appear to be primarily local officials, but, indeed, such a mixture of central and local government powers were exercised by the authorities we have named that, in the present context, and in almost every other, they are to be regarded as departments of the central authority operating outside Berlin for a limited part of the territory. In any case they were until 1879 (and to Hitler's time they still were) the first office held by aspirants to the higher administrative departments; thence, after a preparatory period, they might be promoted to the central departments. The regulations were not made to apply to presidents of

---

[3] Cf. Friedrich von Schwerin, *Die Befähigung zum höheren Verwaltungsdienst* (Berlin, 1908), p. 5.

[4] That is, to presidents and divisional chiefs of the *Regierungen; Landräte, Kreis und Amtshauptmänner,* and *Oberamtmänner.*

[5] Law of March 11, 1879, and regulations of May 29, 1879.

the government districts or to the over-presidents of the provinces or to ministers.

The rules relating to training persisted until 1906, and were until then the object of controversy, and after certain reforms in 1906 continued to dominate conditions until the Revolution of 1918. The main provisions of the law were as follows: the qualification for entry into the higher administrative service was at least a three-year university course in law and political science; and the passing of two examinations. The first examination was the legal examination as prescribed in the law of 1869. The second, the state examination, was to take place before the "Examination Commission for Higher Administrative Officials." The second examination was preceded by a preparatory period of two years in the courts and at least two years in the administrative departments. Preparatory service took place in local government, urban and rural. The subject matter of the second examination was Prussian public and private law, and economics and public finance. The examination was written and oral—the written part consisted of two theses—six weeks, or a little longer, being allowed for the completion of each.

Very little had been accomplished by this law to meet the nature of the claims which society was beginning to make upon the higher branches of the civil service. Had it not been for the Prussian Parliament's fears, a separate examination might have been created based upon the social sciences. But in the existing state of politics the Parliament could only credit the government with the intention of using such an examination to reject "undesirable elements." [6] The result was that, in practice, law still retained a favored position. At the examinations very little emphasis was laid upon knowledge other than that which was directly legal, and in the best of cases the social sciences were introduced only as subordinate to law. As there was no special examination for these subjects, there was no certainty at all as to the attendance of the candidate at lectures. The natural result of the regulations and their busy apprenticeship made it impossible for them to do justice to the social sciences without the generous help of a "crammer." Two things had, however, been gained: it had been admitted that the legal and the administrative careers were separate and ought to be prepared for differently, and provision had been made for an apprenticeship period with the local authorities. Criticism came from two sources: from the universities which were teaching law and economics, and from practical statesmen, in office or in Parliament. It is instructive to review briefly the nature of their argument.

The Universities. It is quite obvious that if civil servants are selected by tests based upon a certain prescribed university training, the value of that test is to be sought in the actual nature of the training. Between 1879 and 1906, and even after this date, the universities showed many signs of serious dissatisfaction with the manner in which students applied themselves to their work, and with the intrinsic value of the law studies. Among the critics were Schmoller, Gneist, Gierke, and Jhering, and there were many others whose reputation, though not as world-wide as these, yet counted for much in Germany.[7]

The Defects of Legal Training. The gravamen of their charges was this. The teaching of law had fallen into a state of sterile dogmatism.[8] Where the theory of law was taught at all, it was not kept in a wise relationship to the actual law as it appeared in everyday practice, but was not seldom composed of a fabric of doctrines based upon a tissue of major premises untested by reference to the nature

---

[6] Cf. Von Delbrück, *op. cit.*, p. 15.

[7] The whole subject is treated, and the views of the principal contributors reviewed, in *Rechtsstudium und Prüfungsordnung; Ein Beitrag zur preuszischen und deutschen Rechtsgeschichte* (Berlin, 1877), by L. Goldschmidt, judge and professor of jurisprudence.
[8] Cf. Adolph Wermuth, *Ein Beamtenleben* (Berlin, 1922), p. 31 ff. This goes back to 1880. Wermuth became Secretary of the Imperial Treasury, and *Oberbürgermeister* of Berlin.

of social life. Analytical work, in which history and economics were used to explain the growth and operation of the law, was very rare, and this lack exercised an unfortunate influence upon seminars and lecturers. The main cause of this dry abstract and detailed dogmatism was the nature of the Prussian legal codes: they were isolated from the surrounding life of the other Germanic European states, they were neither the perfect continuation of the old German customary law nor corollaries of Roman legal principles, but curious mixtures tinctured with the theories of the men—great men, of course—who had written them. Their very minuteness of detail inhibited mental elasticity in their treatment. Only the great teachers could rise above the compulsions of these codes. The student was then apt to be trained to repeat a number of formulas, obtained no grasp of legal principles and, therefore, since he had an examination to pass, learned to pass it by a short period of concentrated memorizing. This was quite natural, since the most successful conditions for memorizing are definite dogmas and the stimulus of an approaching event.

If the law were to be taught with due attention to its sociological nature, a period longer than the prescribed minimum of three years was essential. Neither law by itself nor law together with an adequate preparation in economics and political science could be mastered in less than three and a half years, some said in four. And even the three years then prescribed could, at that time, be reduced to two, as the one year's service in the army was counted in.

It is common knowledge, of course, that exceedingly great care has to be taken in the teaching of any nonexperimental faculty. The student is obliged to occupy a merely passive and receptive position toward the teacher, and a large variety of devices must be consciously used to stimulate attention and awaken cooperation. Of all such nonexperimental studies law has, perhaps, the hardest task in getting itself accepted by the average student. Most humane of all in its social effects, it

is least human in its form. It ties the mind and tires it. The most successful law school in the world, Harvard, has succeeded in solving the difficulty of vividly interesting the student only by converting the student into a judge and the seminar into a court for particular cases, by the case method.[9] Only a very few gifted teachers in Prussia had made an approach to such a system, and, for the rest, the students, finding that their lectures were merely expositions of what was already exposed in textbooks and commentaries, spent their time in riotous living and passed their examinations by memorizing laws, but not learning law. For this we cannot entirely call the teaching to account: the traditions of studentship have a great deal to answer for. This was followed by a "cramming" establishment.

The students, in the fashion still permissible in Germany, divided their three years among various universities. There was no means of controlling their work or attendance at lectures, and when the first examination threatened they gravitated to the university in which conditions were easiest.

Those whose social antecedents proved satisfactory to the high local and judicial authorities to whom they applied for admission into the preparatory service then spent their time in a minutely regulated order of duties—regulated, the law of 1869 declared, to give the novice experience of all branches of judicial practice—the bar, the notary's office, judgeship, and office work. All this in four years! The result, says Goldschmidt, was only to reduce real talent to pettifogging routine. (It did, in fact, drive both Bennigsen and Bismarck out of the service.)

We have already said that economics and political science became the hand-

---

[9] And even this entails the penalty that the student loses, or rather never acquires, a sense of the whole system of law and its total significance in the social order. Cf. Josef Redlich, *The Common Law and the Case Method* (Carnegie Foundation, Bulletin No. 8, 1914); also cf. R. Valeur and E. Lambert, *L'Enseignement du Droit en France et aux États-Unis* (Paris, 1929).

maiden of the law. Students learned that few, if any, questions involving real study were likely to be put to them. These studies, then, were given only perfunctory attention, although the law required satisfactory knowledge of "the principles of political science." The universities, conscious of their importance as preparatory and selective institutions for the judicial and civil service, frequently expressed the wish to make more of these studies. But the examination is the only effective sanction of such a policy, and the examination did not demand this knowledge. Law had become divorced from its origin and its purpose, and a narrow and pedantic formalism had invaded a field in which pre-eminently the truth of real life is essential. This evil was unfortunate for the judicial service, but since the preparation for the judicial service in its first four years or so was also the preparation for the administrative service, it threatened to become disastrous for the latter also.

The truth was that economic life had taken such a direction that the state was bound to interfere with its processes, and this interference could only be properly carried out by appropriately trained officials.

Yet the predominance of law did blight the student who aspired to the administrative service. He did not appear before a Judicial Court of Examiners, but before the "Examination Commission for Higher Administrative Officials." The examination was to determine whether the candidates could be considered "capable and thoroughly prepared successfully to occupy an independent position in the higher administrative service." But they had, excepting for their two years, followed the same course as their judicial colleagues, and their choice of ultimate career was not always decided upon until the latest possible time, that is, after two years of preparatory judicial service. Further, the final examination was taken before practicing jurists, at the most a teacher of law was included, but never a teacher of political science.

Political Critics. Bismarck found the

civil servants of so little use that he set up an Economic Council.

In the 1890's the desire for reform became widespread. From now on the discussion of faults and remedies become of radical importance since the problems disclosed are elemental and affect all countries. Public discussion was first initiated by the Finance Minister, von Miquel, in 1895. He suggested a reduction of the time spent by administrative officials in the judicial service from two years to one, so that they might have a longer time in which to learn administrative law, social policy, economics, and other branches of science. The long time spent in the courts merely took away from the time which should be devoted to that which was ultimately to be the life career.

A lively discussion in the press followed, and in 1902 the government introduced a project into Parliament. The main object was to lengthen the university course to three and one-half years and to reduce the preparatory course to the same period. After much delay the government conceded a reduction of the work before the courts to nine months for civil servants. The overwhelming opinion was that it was very desirable that at least a part of the time should be served in nonstate institutions: like the Chambers of Agriculture and Commerce which on the Continent have an official representative status.

Away from Mere Book-Knowledge. This is the problem which has arisen wherever sincere thought has been bestowed upon the question of properly training officials: How to overcome the natural effects of book knowledge? Can it be left to the student's own devices? Ought there to be a preparatory period in the service—or outside the service? Will travel be of value? The necessities of the modern civil service go further: it is not enough that officials see the levers they have to pull, but that they should be vividly acquainted with the nature of the enormous tangle of objects and men attached to the other, the invisible, end of the lever. Plato long ago warned us not to teach with our backs to reality and our eyes only upon moving shadows.

Public discussion revealed clearly the most important fact which had caused perturbation before and which has since been the subject of anxiety. "In Germany," the minister said, "officials attain to responsibility and independence at too late an age." In other countries the young man of thirty was already in the center of independent activity, and even in Germany, in other professions, the man of thirty could look back upon a number of years in which freshness, resolution, and energy had already accomplished a great deal. This raises a question of great significance.

From 1906 to 1920. The result of the discussions was the Act of 1906, in which the main lines of criticism were given effect. This act functioned until 1920. Let us imagine that we desire to enter the administrative service after 1906.[10] We would be obliged to take at least a three years' course of law and political science at a university and then take the first law examination at school. Our university teachers are hardly satisfied with our stay at the university for only three years, but the government holds that as we spend more time in this way, we shall ultimately enter upon our duties at an age when all our freshness of mind is gone, and when, therefore, they can do very little with us. Now while we are at the university, it may be true that we shall be wasting some time—perhaps a good deal—if we join one of the students' corps,[11] but it will more than repay us in the long run, since relatives and friends, even people who

are not related to us who once belonged to the same corps, will give us a helping hand and will prefer us to other candidates, other things being equal or even more than a little unequal.

The final examination comes. The subjects are public and private law, legal history, and principles of political science and economics. The examiners are by statute instructed to explore our knowledge and insight into the nature and historical development of law, and to see whether we have a general legal and political science education necessary to our future profession. We now approach our four years of practical work, and it is fortunate that we are not of the generation before 1906, for they were obliged to serve two years in the law courts before proceeding to their real work; we have only to serve one year in the courts, and this may be reduced to nine months by the Ministries of Finance and the Interior. We stand no chance of entrance to the next stage unless we are Protestant, anti-Socialist, of "good" family: that is, if we are Catholic, or Jew, or Socialist or otherwise of Left-wing politics, or are of working-class family.[12]

The year or the nine months pass. They were not wasted. For the courts to which we were attached—the *Amtsgericht* or the *Landesgericht*—gave us a very good insight into procedure and administrative law in actual practice. We have now to be accepted into the preparatory service by the president of one of the fifteen prescribed government districts—an official of high status and important powers. Our English colleagues have no such arrangement as this whereby an authority other than the central departments chooses us. And, in fact, the practice in Prussia has not been quite unchallenged. It is the ancient Prussian practice, but suggestions for modifying it were made in 1875 and later. The government as a rule wanted to leave the matter as it is today in order to avoid burdening itself with duties which can be quite well performed else-

[10] This description is based upon the best two commentaries: upon von Schwerin, *op. cit.*, then member of the Examining Commission for Higher Administrative Officials; and Wandersleb, *Die Befähigung Zum höheren Verwaltungsdienst* (Berlin, 1927), then, assistant secretary in the Prussian Ministry of Commerce and Industry; and upon private information.

[11] Cf. for a good description of student life in the Corps, Hermann Sudermann's novel, *Der Tolle Professor;* also Presber's *Mein Bruder Benjamin;* see also G. Michaelis, *Fur Staat und Volk* (Berlin, 1922), and Bismarck's *Reflections and Reminiscences,* the first few pages.

[12] Cf. another angle, L. W. Muncy, *The Junker in Prussian Administration* (Brown University, 1944).

where, and its parliamentary supporters argued appointment by the government as futile. For the ministers could not possibly know enough to exercise a proper choice, whereas the local authorities who were responsible for the practical preparation of the candidate could more justly take the responsibility of choosing. It was further feared that central appointment would result in political higgling, since the central authority was subject to a great deal of parliamentary pressure. On the other side it was emphasized that central choice would mean uniformity of principles and a cessation of misunderstandings and suspicion about the motives of the president of the government district.

The three and a quarter years of preparatory service are so regulated as to give a conscientious servant a splendid opportunity of acquiring wide experience. The sanctions available to the president are such that any servant who ultimately stays in the civil service is certain to have made good use of his time; for the president may put off the final examination and, in cases of gross misbehavior or waste of time, even dismiss the referendar. The three and a quarter years are divided up as follows: twelve months with a *Landrat* (the executive officer of a local government area known as the *Kreis*), three months with a small popularly elected or municipal body, at least fifteen months with the government district Authority, and the district committee (*Bezirksausschuss*). As referendars, we will be placed in those local authorities, urban and rural, where we shall get an opportunity to survey a wide field of administration, to see the whole process of government in a particular area. It is probable that we shall be sent to a municipality of the first and second size and there we shall be overwhelmed with the enormous scope of its work and finish by being confined to some special branch only. If the opportunity occurs, we shall be made deputy of the head executive official —like the *Bürgermeister*—for a time, and every attempt will be made to awaken the feeling of self-sufficiency and responsibility. Care will be taken, according to the Rules, to give us work and explanations which will systematically promote our understanding of the social sciences, though attempts will be made to avoid weighing us down with details. When we are in the government district authority, our work will be so organized that we shall see the whole field of its activity, including the educational and financial division, but wherever a particular situation is not calculated to add to our comprehension of principles we shall be spared. Our apprenticeship will stretch from thorough occupation in the registration and accountants' office to the making of verbal reports in departmental meetings, and traveling commissions to state and non-state institutions. In the subdistrict of the government district—the *Bezirk*—we are employed for many months, since here it is possible to take a continuously active and rather significant part in the work (the authority is, of course, not nearly as important as the *Regierung*). Every authority under which we serve makes a report upon us, and the *Landrat* pays special attention in his to our relationship with the public in the district. A final and comprehensive report is made by the *Regierungs-Präsident,* and all the reports are put before the examination commission.

The *Regierungs-Präsident* decides when we are fit to take the final examination. This is done by requiring the apprentice to make a considerable report upon some subject arising in the course of his work. There is no legally stated field of investigation; it is left entirely to the president and the referendar to determine. It may be on the practical or the theoretical side. It may be financial or institutional. But it is desirable that its preparation should require a thorough acquaintance with constitutional and administrative law.

The Final Examination. The final examination is written and oral, and extends over the public and private law valid for Prussia, and, further, constitutional and administrative law as well as economic and political science. The question of all questions is: Is the referendar likely to be able to act independently and successfully in the higher civil service? Has he a sound enough grasp of the duties and purposes of the state in economic and financial matters? On each of two days we write a dissertation on a topic (till then undisclosed) with the aid of certain reference books which are provided in the examination rooms. A third day is occupied in the preparation of a verbal report. Then follows an oral examination. A candidate who fails may reappear once more; a second failure is followed by exclusion from the higher civil service.

The striking feature of the topics set for examination is their extreme practicality and technicality, and their wide range. Not that all are technical: some are upon the history of economic and social theory. The vast majority ask for judgments upon a narrow set of circumstances; the answering of these clearly demands a fund of exact knowledge, a firm grasp of legal and economic principles, comprehension of the conditions of the effectiveness of institutions, and the ability to focus correctly the general light of science on particular cases. Little or no room is left for metaphysical adventuring, and the confines within which doubt and curiosity might arise are rather narrow.

On the whole, the German procedure compared with the British shows a wide and important variation: the German being based much more upon the correct use of authorities, the British more upon personal judgments. If this diagnosis is correct, the situation it reveals is important, for it may be that much of the formalism with which German bureaucracy has been charged by native critcis was due to the spirit and training which have their expressions in this type of examination—nay! to the ultimate view of private and public life which engender these. The examiners believed that these were the proper questions to ask, they held this belief because they had a mental picture of the kind of civil servant they wanted to secure: men learned to the point of pedantry, and logical. This produced civil servants more useful in a static than a dynamic state; excellent interpreters of the past but not inventors of the ways and means of the future; apter to explain than to evaluate; and inflexible in the power to make exceptions—which is nine tenths of administration. Where the Germans are lacking the British are rich, but the British have their own faults which we have analyzed.

REFORMS OF 1920 AND THEIR CAUSES

THIS system of recruitment operated until 1920, when minor changes were made. Those changes were the first results of a rather widespread feeling that thorough reforms were necessary if the civil service were to acquire the qualities essential in the modern state. Since the creation of the Empire in 1871, Prussia's influence went far beyond its own boundaries; its indigenous effect was over two thirds of the territory, and when we add that the choice of officials for the imperial departments was from the various states in some rough proportion to their importance, the significance of the Prussian method was great enough to rouse widespread interest and even anxiety. Then came World War I. The unfortunate are morbidly curious about the causes of their downfall. A flood of self-criticism was the result. The liberal Germans were determined as never before conscientiously to master the parts of their gigantic political machine.

The classic sign of this spirit in the context of administration was a short tract by the statesman and administrator, Clemens von Delbrück.[13] It was written a year before the end of the war.

Law versus *the Social Sciences.* Delbrück starts with the already familiar analysis of the political economic activity of the modern state. The nature of this activity imposes upon the administrator a task vastly different from the judicial function. The judge works within rigid norms and does not judge by the conse-

---

[13] *Die Ausbildung für den höheren Verwaltungsdienst in Preuszen* (Jena, 1917).

quences of his judgment but by those norms. The administrator, on the other hand, has a wide field of discretion, and the consequences of his actions are of the essence of his decisions.[14]

He must, therefore, know what economic and political consequences his decisions will have for the individual and the community. He must arrange his measures that they benefit the public welfare and do not injure the individual without necessity. He must also be zealous to serve the individual, as far as he can, without injury to the community. In economic measures the administration is preeminently free in its resolutions and is bound to the law only in respect to their formal conditions and execution . . . Allegory was wont to show us Justice with bound eyes, and if we desired to pursue this figure, we should picture administration with eyes very wide open.[15]

The task is a particularly delicate one in a constitutional state, for the civil service must maintain an impartial attitude in a policy founded upon and directed by party conflict. It must serve the people and not antagonize Parliament, take political decisions but avoid political enmities. The impartial position of the civil service is emphasized in a study by another writer, who points especially to the need for keeping the great economic and social groups, technique and capital, in social order. Such qualities as this implies cannot be bred by the study of law: only the social sciences can serve.[16] But this does not mean that the administrator is to be trained in the social sciences only; for law must have its place, though a subordinate place, in the total scheme.

For How Many Years Shall Training Last? Delbrück then turns to the question of the length of training. This question had troubled German opinion for years. Delbrück remarks that the German higher civil servant does not get the opportunity of independent work until he is about thirty. Not until he is about thirty-five does he, perhaps, become a *Landrat*: that is, an official with an appreciable scope of power and responsibility. This training is too long. Delbrück is, in this opinion, only one of many voices. The noted economist, Professor Schumacher of Berlin, speaks from his own experience (as Delbrück does) when he says: [17]

I am not sorry that I was once a referendar—I learnt an extraordinary amount during that time; but I must assert that I suffered very much under the oppressive feeling that I was entirely chained up just in the years when I most strongly felt the impulse to act. Since then, I consider it to be one of the worst faults of our general organization that we let a great part of the most valuable talent in its most important years of growth wear itself away with waiting in nonresponsible and, to some extent, insufficient work. [Here the Assembly cried: "You are right."] . . . It is fundamentally unsounded to take away from a young man until nearly thirty both economic responsibility for himself and material responsibility for his work.

This view is represented in other places also.[18]

---

14 *Ibid.*, pp. 26-27.
15 The antithesis has also been put thus: "The administration of justice and administration are inherently different. This is demonstrated already by the fact that the judge has a list to work through, that is, the cases laid before him, and he can only deal with these. Beyond this he has no initiative. The administrative official, who merely settles cases which are brought to him by the public, is a very bad official. His office demands more of him. He must take action independently, draw matters to himself, and often himself provide the most important part of his work. He must pursue the needs and the development of life and economic activity; he must preconceive the uniqueness of separate things by the aid of creative fantasy, and make decisions. For this purpose the law is not an end in itself but a means to an end. Law only affords him the possibilities and limits of his activity. With the judge it is otherwise, although I am strongly of the opinion that the creation of law is the business of a judge, yet as a rule, he will do no more than subsume cases under their respective paragraphs." Nostitz, *Verein für Sozialpolitik* (Kiel, 1920), pp. 140 ff.

16 W. Brück, *Das Ausbildungsproblem des Beamten in Verwaltung und Wirtschaft* (Leipzig, 1926), pp. 14-15.
17 Schumacher also humorously remarked that the thwarted desire for activity caused the production of a substitute: "that pretentious bearing toward others that has so often given offense." Cf. *Verhandlungen des Vereins für Sozialpolitik* (Kiel, 1920), p. 77.
18 Brück, *op. cit.*, p. 34.

It is a valid and vital criticism of German recruiting methods. The British method has been strongly opposed to putting off the age of responsibility by a long period of preparation. The men who thus expressed their opinions about responsibility did not define it. They only felt its definition. But expressly to define it is to assert unequivocally why it cannot be put off to a late age, as well as why, too, an early age may equally be disastrous. Responsibility in office means freedom of judgment and action combined with unlimited liability to suffer the natural consequences of a mistake or enjoy the natural consequences of success. This implies in a person thrown into such a position some kind of spiritual balance between his own various faculties caused by his contact with the possibilities of pleasure or pain and with the objects or persons who form the material upon which his official judgment and activities are to be exercised. They will have an effect upon him, as he upon them. The result of the experience is to produce in the responsible person a knowledge of himself (it may be deep or superficial), of other people, and of inorganic environment. He will learn, in the uninfluenced measure of his capacity to learn, how much and how little man can do to secure a control over nature, and what personal contribution he is able to add. He will measure his own strength and weakness, and learn the worth of his own personality. And measuring this, he can measure that of others, and again, knowing others, he can again recoil upon himself and estimate his own place and value. No study yet invented offers so subtle and extensive a variation of happenings upon which to exercise judgment as human affairs themselves. For every object of study has its own nature, the way in which it is manageable, and the impression it produces upon the mind. The full effect of this is to be felt only by unhindered and unaided access to the objects themselves and the joys and sufferings emergent directly from them.

It is clear that the sheltered and cloistered life of book knowledge, with parents paying your way, and a long preparatory service when you are neither civilian nor civil servant and when not a pittance is paid you and not a day passes without tutelage—that all this places a screen between the spirit of the novice and his own personality. There is no connection between what you eat and what you produce. You answer not to those who may suffer by your activity, but to some one who stands between, who cannot take you completely au sérieux. The tenets of the schools are not graven into the character by the power of immediate abrasive reality. That is, you are devoted to an academic prescription which is not really appropriate to your profession. And the longer this goes on, the more powerful do the inhibitions or the incitements uniquely created for and by this prescription isolate you from neighboring aspects of life, sometimes from life itself.

It is a moot point exactly where to draw the line. Freshness of mind is at times strangely akin to dangerous ignorance. Some academic and tutelary guidance is essential. It can obviously, however, be overdone. And this as much as the study of law made the German civil service pedantic, authoritarian, and unadaptable.

Von Delbrück was accordingly opposed to any lengthening of the university course. He suggested the abolition of the nine months of judicial service for the administrative officials. Nine months would be won for administrative preparatory service, and whatever of private and criminal law these officials needed they could learn at the university where, however, administrative law should be their chief legal study. The proper subordination of law to the other studies, but the combination of the two, would be useful not only for administrative officials, but also for all those who desired to serve in local government, journalism, or Parliament. Von Delbrück looked forward to a single faculty uniting political science with jurisprudence. The studies should be followed by the first university examination, a preliminary to the preparatory service.

Theory and Practice. The next topic is, like the question of age, a widely discussed one: what can be done to secure that, when the student enters the service, his judgment shall be less theoretical than it is after the ordinary university training? We have already adverted to this problem. One solution discussed but rejected by Delbrück, is the introduction of a practical year into the middle of the university course. (Delbrück states an alternative: one year's employment in a local authority before the student enters the university.) It is urged that the practical work would enliven the students: their elementary lectures would prepare them for this year, and their practical year would prepare them for their final and advanced lectures. (Delbrück rejects the intermediate year on the ground that it would increase the academic years to four: and the alternative suggestion on the ground of its impracticability.)

German teachers likened the student with an economic and law degree to a medical student who begins practice without clinical experience.[19] There is an extraordinary unanimity of opinion about the "world strangeness" (*Weltfremdheit*) of the German official. There is not the same unanimity of view about its remedy. A director of a private business insists [20] upon the necessity of practical study before an occupation can be undertaken, and says that no system whereby the student goes for short periods (weeks or months) into one business after another can give him the required intensity of experience, since an unbroken stretch of time is necessary for him to become really acquainted with the conditions of labor, and the working class, and social legislation, and taxation relating to industry. And a professor of law and economics [21] analyzes that which the student may expect to derive from a practical year: he would learn

the sheer difficulties of daily life, the realities with which he is not familiar without experience, especially if his family are professional people. He must participate in menial tasks, and somewhere be, for a period, a cog in the great machine, whether it is a handicraft, or industry, or agriculture—where, does not matter, it is enough that he participates somewhere—so long as he somewhere learns the nature of the frictional difficulties of real daily life and obtains a really deeper insight into the world of labor and for a time works shoulder to shoulder with the mass of workingmen.

An administrative official of wide experience in the training of referendars in the preparatory service warmly recommended that the university course of study should be divided into two parts; one of elementary law and economics lasting two years; then two years of varied practice; followed by a final two years of study. For the administrative official was essentially a man of decision, yet the referendars who come under his charge were the least ready to take a decision.[22]

They believe that when they have once weighed up all sides of the subject, their work is at an end. I have been able to embarrass the referendars in theoretical and practical training by asking them, after they had most beautifully reported upon the legal and material circumstances of a case: "Now, what will you do? How will you solve the problem? To whom will you write? In what manner will you write? Is there anything more to be done? How will you begin operations?" They were nonplussed, and realized that the difficulty begins precisely at the point where they thought the subject was exhausted.

The only agreement indeed so far reached upon this vexed question was that something ought to be done to mitigate the ossifying effect of book knowledge and lectures. The most general solution offered was much greater use of seminar work, discussions, and practical exercises (papers, reports, and so on) by the students.

The discussion leads one back inevitably to purpose of training. Is it learning that is required, or a quality of mind, difficult to define, but which roughly is

---

[19] Professor Jastrow, *Verein für Sozialpolitik*, p. 21 ff.
[20] *Verein*, p. 82 ff.
[21] Professor Fuchs in *Verein*, p. 93.

[22] Dr. Saenger of Berlin, *ibid.*, p. 173 ff.

ability to learn, judge, and act? It is not knowledge, but manipulative, managing power, the recognition of the nature of the task, and the ability to devise and use the appropriate implement. This is the capital contradiction which must be fought out not to the victory of either side, but to that compromise which will produce the best civil servant. Of this, I believe Professor Schumacher had the clearest understanding and his words have the obvious stamp of the real.

The need of actual researchers is always extraordinarily limited; the need of men, on the other hand, who, without being learned, have acquired real scientific self-training, is in a civilized nation constant and growing if it is not to be stunted.[23]

In the schools the training must proceed upon the basis that everything supplies a problem to be solved. Science is an incessant struggle with problems. Schumacher continued:

Only in such a struggle which is always renewing perception, can clarity, the preliminary condition of everything else—*and first of all clarity toward oneself—be won; that feeling for actual limitation which distinguishes expertness from dilettantism* and is always and everywhere the proof and sign of true education . . . and self-understanding gives us the possibility justly to match together our own powers and our self-constructed aim, and upon this basis only does clear intelligence of the outer world develop; and there develops also the strength to overcome successfully the mightiness of error and delusion; the instinctive certainty of feeling, to which true competence which remains conscious of its limits, may finally unfold.

It is the mode of thought, the art and process of reasoning, that is to be sought; of course, as applied to the whole economic and social system. And this will give a judgment how to remove the unfavorable and enhance the favorable. It is impossible for even the most informed economist to know all that there is to be known about economic life—it is too vast.

Changes between 1919 and 1933. The

constitutional revolution of 1919 gave an opening for the introduction of changes in the recruitment of the higher civil service, and these changes were based upon the development of opinion since the coming into operation of the Act of 1906. The main changes were indeed accepted in the Prussian Diet with hardly a dissentient voice.[24] The Act of 1920 [25] amended that of 1906; it left the basic lines of that act fundamentally undisturbed, but modified them in respects calculated to energize the service in the future. The preparatory service was reduced from four to three years. The preparatory service began with judicial service of only six months. An alteration as significant as these was produced by the reform of the law examination which all law and administrative students had to take as a preliminary to the judicial and administrative services.[26] The immediate result was the regulation of the first legal examination. In the written examination about one quarter of the time was definitely assigned to constitutional and administrative law, and in the oral, which lasted two days, one day almost entirely to economics and political science.

The judicial term was served as before in a small court of first instance (the *Amtsgericht*). The preparatory service of two and a half years was spent in much the same way as before, with shorter stages. Finally, the appointment of certain officials to be the mentors of the referendars (which began in 1906 and proved itself a successful arrangement) followed by an extension of their activities. They were given special leave to attend the lectures of the Institute for Further Education in Political Science, and they met together at this Institute for discussion of their problems.

---

23 *Ibid.*, pp. 77-78.

24 Cf. Wandersleb, *op. cit.*, p. 13.
25 July 8, 1920, *Gesetzes Sammlung*, p. 388.
26 Cf. especially *Die Juristische Ausbildung in Preuszen* (Berlin, 1928), composed in the Prussian Ministry of Justice; and David, *Rechtstudium und Preuszische Referendarprüfung* (Berlin, 1928). Cf. also Weinmann, *Die preuszische Ausbildungsordnung für Juristen* (Berlin, 1927).

SURVEY OF GERMAN EXPERIENCE TO HITLER

(1) At the beginning of the nineteenth century there was a change in the training of civil servants: from the group of economic sciences collectively called Cameralism the weight was put on the study of law. This gave satisfaction for a time, because the state modified its previous positive activity and served by policing and emancipating.

(2) Environment and ideas changed under the influence of the industrial and commercial revolution, and the study of law as a training ground for administration was found wanting.

(3) In place of law what may be called neocameralist studies—that is, the social sciences—assumed the predominance in opinion, and the legislation of the twentieth century has accorded them an important place in practice. It is agreed, too, that the social sciences should include some law, mainly public law, but there should also be attention to the elements of private law.

(4) A period of preparatory service was always a part of the training: its value is definitely established by experience. It is applauded by everybody concerned. When differences arise they are upon the question of whether any time, and how much, should be spent in private industry. Practice with the local authorities and the local self-governing authorities is of capital importance in the modern state, which cannot dispense with local government, and where proper cooperation between the center and the locality may make all the difference between good and bad government—in terms of the satisfaction of the people and the economy of means.

(5) It was found that university training may easily result in administrative sterility. The safeguards against this are vital teachers and methods which impress the students with the practical importance of their work and inspire them to cooperate with their teachers in the mastery of a task and the solving of a problem. This first: then come adjuncts to book study, like occasional visits and practice.

(6) It is desirable in the highest degree to set administrators to work, on their own responsibility, at the earliest possible age. For the best training for life is life itself. The German method was criticized as devoting too long a time to preparation.

(7) The discussion of the place of law in the training of civil servants has produced a secondary discussion: the place of economics and political science in the training of lawyers and judges. The result, in theory and practice, was important, since no one qualified as a lawyer for the first rungs of the ladder to the bench without some university training in these subjects.

(8) Germany has had an extremely long and continuous history of interest in administrative efficiency. The interest is an illustration of her political character, and her psychology in politics could be written by deduction from this as a major premise.

(9) The actual selection of those who had qualified themselves in the prescribed way resulted in "closed" competition, keeping out republicans, socialists, atheists, those from poor families, the liberal-minded, and unorthodox in a monarchical and authoritarian state.

(10) German officials, carefully selected from restricted social classes and political outlooks, served a peculiar state in a peculiar way. They took orders from a monarchy that was not responsible to the people, and day after day administered in opposition to a *Reichstag* which could nag but not command them, because it was not the sovereign representative of the people, whose political parties, having the hypercritical temerity of the impotent, carped at and alienated them. They were instruments of a highly centralized state whose tradition of authoritarian government, benevolent or not, had shown no break in selfconfidence and paternalism for three centuries. They were devotees of a polity which had risen, flourished by military success, and exulted in kneeling on men and women abjectly obedient, even servile. They always looked upwards for orders: and

what they received in sternness they passed on in undemocratic rigor. They were friends of the people on their own terms only.

THE NAZI RÉGIME AND THE CIVIL SERVICE

THE creation of a civil service imbued with duty and a "sense of state" was a valuable legacy to the Weimar Republic had it known how to purge its inimical elements. It was a heaven-sent boon to Hitler's government, because the nazi movement had an uncanny and ruthless ability to subdue and exploit other people's noblest loyalties.

The higher civil service inherited by the Weimar coalition governments was on the whole monarchical and author-itarian-minded, and saturated with a stronger or fainter contempt for the democratic or party-state, though there were exceptions.

As the civil service had its "well-ac-quired" rights to place and pension, which it received in return for its life of selfless devotion to the service of the state, and especially the right not to be demoted even if transferred, and as there were not many places of equal rank to which a man might be transferred, the Republican governments did little to rid themselves of cryptoenemies. Nor were they impelled to by their political beliefs, for these included tolerance and fairness to individuals. Furthermore, within a very few years, the Weimar parties were no longer in a majority, and could not do as they liked, without raising a great parliamentary storm. When a "Rightist" attempt at a *coup d'état* was made in 1920, the high civil servants, indeed, sided with the Republican government, and lent all aid to defeat that attack. When von Papen in 1932 attacked the govern-ment of Prussia, once again many officials, but now not so many as before, defended the Prussian government. Yet the dom-inant tendency was nationalistic, author-itarian (though not arbitrary), and legal-istic.

For Hitler this was an ideal founda-tion. In the first place, most of the high officials (and the middle and lower ranks for that matter) were ready to serve him because he had been appointed by the President of the *Reich* in accordance with the letter of the constitution. Secondly, they obeyed commands because the ex-ecution of Hitler's laws and decrees was constitutionally based on the Enabling Act of March 24, 1933. Thirdly, the nazi movement was expert in taking measures to bend to their will the personnel of government. It did this in the following way.

A series of laws on the civil service be-ginning with the Law for the Restoration of the Professional Civil Service, April 7, 1933, swept away the "well-acquired" rights mentioned above. It gave to the government the right to purge the service of persons of non-Aryan descent, and others "who because of their previous political activity do not offer the assur-ance that they will exert themselves for the national state without reservations." More laws and decrees filled out this statute.

Some civil servants fled for their con-sciences and their lives. Others stayed because they felt conscientiously that they might temper a terrible régime by their counsel, their fairness, and their moderation. Other officials had had no connections at all with politics, and still continued in their nonpolitical work of economic, or social, or statistical, or tax administration, and so forth, in which, as it were, the Nazis were "neutral." Furthermore, the important posts, or new posts, in police administration, especially the secret police, and in the organization of suppression, went entirely into the hands of Nazi fanatics.

For the rest, the Nazis contented them-selves with a moderate purge. Those who were allowed to remain, or wanted to re-main, were subordinated to the Nazi political chief, or party supervisors, or Nazi appointees. Thus, Professor Brecht observes that of 1663 Prussian members of the higher civil service in field positions, 28 per cent were either dismissed as "un-reliable," Jewish, or the like (12.5 per cent), or dismissed or demoted to lower positions for "administrative reasons" (15.5 per cent). In the middle brackets of the civil service, including especially the clerical class, only 3.46 per cent were so affected.

The top personnel close to the political chiefs in charge of policy, propaganda, foreign affairs, and the control of the local administration were drastically purged and replaced.

Next, to make sure of the new appointees, and the survivors, new Nazi law subordinated all civil servants to the *Führer* and the party. Whereas they had hitherto taken an oath to protect the constitution, they now took this oath: "I swear that I shall be faithful and obedient to Adolf Hitler, the leader of the German *Reich* and the people, that I shall obey the laws and fulfill my official duties conscientiously, so help me God" (Law Regarding Public Officials, January 26, 1937). This law imposed a number of detailed duties on public servants. It was a code of discipline, and subjected them to the power residing in the *Führer*-ship and cabinet. For nearly one hundred years the German civil service had been governed in its official duties and demeanor, as well as in its behavior outside the office, by a comprehensive and exacting code of duties. This was turned to Nazi use. And now the service reverted to the three-centuries-old practice of secret reports on subordinates, which had struck such terror in them, and aroused so much hatred, and had been abolished by the constitution of 1919. In the law of October 20, 1936, preferential treatment was prescribed for entrants who were party members, and those who deserved especially well of the party. In these cases apprenticeship could be waived altogether or reduced in term. Promotions in office were made dependent on unconditional support of the Nazi movement. The Law of July 10, 1937, drew into the *Führer's* hands personally the appointment and even the retirement of all important officials. The Civil Service Code of 1937 required the deputy party leader and the local *Gauleiter* to certify the political reliability of entrants.

A campaign to secure their membership in the party was conducted, and the Foreign Office officials joined as a body. (They thus avoided victimization of those in the office who were not Nazis.) The campaign was not fully successful, and perhaps also the Nazi movement was not anxious to have a mass following, for by 1939 only a little over 28 per cent of the 1,500,000 members of the Civil Service were members of the Nazi party. Yet, 28 per cent is an ample figure. Not until somewhat later was party membership decreed obligatory for entrants to the public service.

Under the Weimar government, the civil-service trade unions, or associations, were guaranteed their free right to exist, though later denied the right to strike. But they were free to flourish and carry on the work of improving the professional situation of their members and their friendly services. They were, indeed, a model of professional propriety and helpfulness. The Nazi government brusquely changed this. All civil service associations were put under the wing of the Nazi party as one of its ancillary and supporting organizations. Its chiefs were Nazis and its objectives perverted into instruments of Nazi policy and philosophy.

In spite of these internal and external measures, penalization, and blandishments, the German civil service remained an extraordinary blend of loyalties, by no means nazified, though serving the Nazi state.

The Review of the Foreign Press published by the British government during World War II contains numerous instances of the fulminations of the Nazi hierarchy against the permanent civil service, especially the old-line officials, for their unbending will.[27] The shortage of manpower made it necessary to restore to their offices some of those who had

27 Cf. also the joint statement of United States Ambassador George Messersmith and R. H. Geist, Counsellor of Embassy, in *Nazi Conspiracy and Aggression*, Vol. V, p. 39 ff., for a discriminating account of official responsibility.

been retired, and there was much anxiety whether a proper balance was being maintained between good Nazis sent into the field and others who remained in the civil service. Hitler finally burst out in the *Reichstag* on April 26, 1942, against the civil service, and that body unanimously sanctioned the rights he claimed as *"Führer* of the Nation, Supreme Commander of the Armed Forces, Chief of the Government and Supreme Executive Power, as Supreme Justice and the Führer

of the Party" . . . without being subject to existing legal provisions of obliging every German national to do his duty by whatever means he deemed appropriate without instituting any procedure otherwise prescribed!

It is clear that the denazifying of the German civil service needs the most discriminating care, and that a new spirit and new procedure of selection is required for the German government of the future.

32

Recruitment of the Higher Officials in France: Nineteenth and Twentieth Centuries

It was not until late in the nineteenth century that France was able to overcome the twofold inheritance of the *ancien régime* and the Revolution: favoritism and centralization. Favoritism, though not necessarily incompetence, was stamped on the French administrative system by the Revolution and Napoleon. The first had swept away venality, but in its place no public standards of competence had been created.[1] The factions had their own special tests of efficiency, the first of which was—in the center—loyalty to their principles, and—in the localities—elections carried on under conditions in which the elected officers could not act for fear of the displeasure of the local cliques and for lack of a properly ordered system and public force to support them.

NAPOLEON: THE MIRACLE OF THE REAL PRESENCE

Under Napoleon, a more settled and rational scheme of appointment was applied, because his rule was longer than that of the different revolutionary sects and his social schemes were more fully elaborated and applied. Nor, except as a joke and a means to personal power,

would he accept the ingenious paper schemes of the quaint Siéyès in which one of the consuls, the consul de la Paix, would nominate to all offices in the ministries of Justice, Interior, Police, Finances, and the Treasury, while the other nominated all those in the Ministries of Marine, War, and Foreign Affairs. Siéyès, said Napoleon, had put only shadows everywhere, the shadow of judicial power, the shadow of government. Substance was somewhere necessary, and he put it in the executive power.[2]

But since the whole social scheme was politically dependent upon Napoleon's personality, he could not abdicate the choice of the principal officials, nor, since his nature obliged him to make of France a vast barracks, could he avoid naming the civil generals of his host. And the hierarchal quality of his system must be more extreme than the extreme anarchy of the preceding decade. His very genius postponed the time when a system of impartial choice could be established to operate continuously and automatically according to the principles of its foundation. All revolved around the genius and personal destiny of this man. The spirit which moved him to conquer in battle, and to undertake battles at all, moved him to be grimly exigent of success in the civil field. What did it profit

---

[1] Cf. H. A. Taine, *Les Origines de la France Contemporaine, Régime Moderne* (Paris, 1882-91), Vol. II, p. 146; and cf. sections on "L'Anarchie, La Conquête Jacobine" and "Le Gouvernement Révolutionnaire" for details.

[2] *Ibid.*, p. 170.

to win a campaign and lose the rulership of his adopted country? He could not boast legitimacy as a title, but only performance. Therefore he recognized no airs and graces, no artificial distinctions or honorific titles, as a claim to office; he did not even exclude the capable *emigrés* who had returned, many at his bidding, but, side by side, he indiscriminately employed the able, whether they had formerly lived by royalty or risen by killing it. The talents were required. The success of his state depended upon a variety of factors which were all present. He knew exactly what end he wished to achieve—perhaps not in the very large, but at each successive stage of his evolution. This knowledge automatically prescribed the type of men he required; for his comprehension of the science and technique of civilization was encyclopedic, and his administrative talents so unprecedentedly marvelous, that to conceive the end was at the same time accurately to conceive the means. But to have stopped at the recognition of what type of men was needed would have been insufficient. Napoleon required and possessed the faculty of judging men, of knowing with little effort how much was actually promised by external indications, and then he was ruthless in stripping the establishment of incompetents. He, therefore, with few exceptions, personally appointed, promoted, relegated or dismissed the higher administrative officials, especially the *Conseil d'État:* [3]

A minister would not have dismissed a single official without the counsel of the Emperor, and all the ministers could change without two secondary changes in the whole Empire resulting. A Minister did not appoint even a clerk of the second order, without presenting to the Emperor a number of candidates and with them the names of the people who had recommended them.

We must not, of course, drive too far the notion which supposes that the Emperor had the time or knowledge for effective selection of all the thousands of

officials who now spread not over France only but far beyond its borders. But we may take it that all the officials from the highest down to what we should nowadays in England call the executive class were directly selected by Napoleon. It is said that he formed a group of some five or six hundred young men, whom he successively called to the highest functions, in order to keep out those old enough to have been influenced by the old règime. Chaptal says (but exaggerates): [4]

He needed valets, and not councilors, so that he arrived at completely isolating himself. The Ministers were nought but chiefs of the bureaus . . . He administered down to the smallest details. All who surrounded him were timid and passive. One studied the will of the oracle and executed it without reflection.

There were not lacking the incentives to good work. There was ever the knowledge that the marshal's baton lay in the drummer boy's knapsack. And all knew the violence of the Emperor's anger with incompetents, which extended to contemptuous dismissal accompanied literally by a kick! As in the army, the worship of talent was conducted of set purpose—loudly, publicly, ceremonially—and to pay and power was added social distinction. The Legion of Honor was now established. "The French," said Napoleon, "have only one sentiment, *honor;* we must nourish that sentiment, they need distinctions." Titles of nobility were restored just when the American constitution banished them. Political privileges were established, like the right to be elected in the *département* and the *arrondissement*. The children of those thus distinguished received scholarships to enter *lycées* and the great military schools. [5]

Then there was the fury of his own fierce energy. He watched by day and night, and in his prime he worked at an electric pitch of intensity, for eighteen hours a day. In six hours the year's

---

[3] Cited *ibid.*, p. 168.

[4] Cf. Comte de Chaptal, *Mes Souvenirs sur Napoleon* (Paris, 1893), p. 228. Chaptal was Minister of the Interior under Napoleon.
[5] This is occurring in the Soviet Union, it commenced at the beginning of World War II!

records of a prefect were examined, analyzed, the balance of efficiency struck, a scolding or reward administered, and reforms elaborated. One official said: [6]

I worked from morning until night with a singular ardor; I astonished the natives thereby, who did not know that the Emperor exercised upon his servants, however far away they were from him, the miracle of the real presence; I believed I saw him in front of me, when I was at work shut in my study.

That, indeed, was the culmination of the Napoleonic system, and the sole condition of success of this mode of appointment and promotion—the miracle of the real presence.[7]

In a previous chapter we referred to a treatise upon public administration dating from this time. Bonnin's analysis of the qualities of an administrator are the qualities sought by the Emperor, and essential to the Emperor's system.[8]

---

[6] Cf. J. C. Beugnot, *Mémoires* (Paris, 1896), Vol. II, p. 372. Cf. also for many interesting passages on Napoleon's qualities as administrator, *Memoirs of M. de Bourienne*, edited by D. Lacroix (Paris, 1829); Bourienne was Napoleon's private secretary for some years.
[7] Comparison may be made with Frederick the Great: Macaulay's essay is very intelligent in this regard.
[8] Cf. C. J. Bonnin, *Principes d'Administration Publique*, 3rd edition (Paris, 1812), Vol. I, Introduction. (I am glad to think that my researches in France enabled me to bring this work to the attention of the English-speaking world.) E.g., p. 152 ff.: "All officials in the administrative system are and ought to be nominated by the prince, because they are his direct agents for the execution of the laws and the management of public affairs, and because, being the guarantor of such management, selection ought to be abandoned by him. Otherwise, it would be to will the effects without willing the necessary causes, because the causes would not produce the effects. Further, these officials participate, by the nature of their functions, in the Government of the State, since without them the prince could not act. To act it is necessary for him to have in his power the means of action, and these means depend upon his choice, without which his moral responsibility would be null, his action paralyzed, because he would no longer have at his disposition the knowledge of men, place and time." So also in regard to promotion, dismissal, etc.

FROM NAPOLEON TO THE THIRD REPUBLIC

THE fall of Napoleon took the pith out of his system, and his definitely conscious and energizing will gave way to a tawdry mock constitutionalism in which a king, Church, and the Chambers strove for mastery, and within these bodies there were violent intestine quarrels. Recruitment, let us say, in 1812 had been based upon a principle of Napoleonic efficiency, and this principle had been far in advance of anything at that time pertaining in England. In an incredibly short time the spirit faded and it was replaced by almost precisely those administrative manners which had their apogee in England under George III. But in France the consequences were worse, for their patronage extended to the prefects, subprefects, and mayors of all the localities. The evil penetrated all the members of the state. For each entity which strove for power—the cliques around the throne, the husbands of beautiful women, returned *emigrés* conscious of their family's services to the ancient royalty, clerical and anticlerical, ministers and deputies, republicans, Napoleonists, the Center, the Right, and all the other varieties of parliamentary groups, old noblesse and new noblesse, upper-middle class of former creation or recent acquisition of wealth—each was covetous of jobs for itself, for its friends, for its supporters, as present rewards or promises for the future.

The genius of Balzac [9] has left for us a picture of those times; and he shows us in the matter of a single career that capacity, industry, and public spirit succumbed to incapacity, inertia and selfishness. Occult influence decided appointments and promotions among the thirty thousand officials, and this influence had nothing at all to do with ability to carry out administrative tasks. The results were lack of subordination, since the power and status of the superior were never upon a steadfast foundation; lack of incentive, since dismissal and promotion could result from adventitious causes; and

---

[9] In *Les Employés*, dated July, 1836.

the swelling of the numbers because jobs were a currency which all sought. Gixion, Balzac's hero, says:

Serving the state today is not like serving the prince, who knows when to punish and when to reward. Today, the state is every one. Now, everybody is not concerned in anybody. To serve every one is to serve no one. No one is interested in any one. A clerk lives between two negations. The world has no pity, has no respect, has no heart, no brains: it is an egotist, it forgets tomorrow the services rendered to it yesterday. In vain can you search within yourselves to find . . . that from the tenderest infancy you had a talent for administration, that you are a Chateaubriand as regards reports, a Bossuet as regards circulars, a Canalis as regards memorials, or the genius of dispatches. There is a law of fatality against administrative genius; the law of promotion which results from it. This fatal method is based upon the statistics of promotion and the statistics of mortality combined.

Attempts at Reform. From the time of Napoleon to the Third Republic, France lived, with occasional but reprehensible lapses, under a bureaucracy thus composed. And in that time, although there were reformers pertinacious enough to cause discussion of reform legislation, there was never a majority in favor of reform. Even when there were majorities in favor of the major premises—"All offices should be filled only by the capable"—and successive majorities for secondary premises and the detailed conclusions which followed, by the time the Chambers arrived at voting upon the entire syllogism and its legislative embodiment, the majority had mysteriously disappeared. It is a brave class or clique that will disown itself, and the evils which Balzac portrayed are described again and again in the periodical *rapports* made by parliamentary commissions well down into the Third Republic. There were many legislative attempts at reform,[10] but though they were made by the best parliamentary leaders, perhaps because

they were made by those who stood above the common level they failed, with the result that the French civil service was by the 1930's regulated by a number of uncoordinated statutory clauses, a vast number of decrees made by successive governments, and the jurisprudence of the *Conseil d'État*.

All attempts at making a general *statut* were defeated. Why? It is clear from the parliamentary proceedings and maneuvers concerned with each attempt that only in recent years has the administrative efficiency of the service come to rank even as important as other factors in government and society. In the decades between the return of the Bourbons and the Third Republic the desire to limit the arbitrariness of government was uppermost in the minds of the opposition, while those in authority insisted upon the need for free discretion. Until recent years, indeed, the whole régime was in peril: hence the power to control the service was fought for on both sides as the power to appoint only the friends of the régime. This caused undue emphasis upon the sovereign power of the government, whether royal or republican, to make appointments as it wished. Hence, even Parliament accepted the view that the terms of recruitment should be settled by royal *ordonnance* or *règles d'administration publique.* This placed the burden of care for efficient administration upon the ministers: they could not bear the burden, and they abused their power. Further there was never a coincidence of the attitudes of the government, the Chambers, and the civil service. Each took a different course according to its own particular exigencies, and these never coincided: hence, although many projects were introduced and pressed they always failed. Moreover, in the Third Republic, even when it was well established, no government was sufficiently agreed upon a project, nor was there a cabinet majority to support it in the Chambers for a time sufficient to secure the passage of a law: there were government projects and the counterprojects of the Chamber and its commissions, and though the

---

[10] They are best reviewed in A. Lefas, *L'État et les Fonctionnaires* (Paris, 1913); this includes the Briand-Maginot project of 1911. I have verified Lefas' account by examining the various *rapports* he quotes.

differences between them were sometimes small, they were large enough to cause the downfall of the measures because the government was too preoccupied, too unstable, and too short-lived to carry anything through.

The civil service statute is the will-o'-the-wisp of French politics. The ultimate question is why there was not such agreement upon their matter that a measure was possible. The ultimate answer is that French politicians were interested in other things than efficient administration: and the existence of jobs was exceedingly demoralizing. The result was to cause pressure for arrangements more extreme than elsewhere: for syndicalism, and councils of administration instead of a minister in each department, to act as the employing and disciplinary authority. However, the claims of efficiency had to be met, foreign experience, the example of private industry, and the manifest need of administration were the impulses, and the French pursued a path peculiarly their own.

The First School of Administration. Even as far back as 1843 Laboulaye had suggested the idea of a special school of administration, from which the high officials of the departments would be supplied. And prior to that, Salvandy, Minister of Education from 1837 to 1839 and later from 1845 to 1848, had seen that a large part of the problem was to reform the faculties of law at the universities, for the men who entered the higher administration came overwhelmingly from the study of law. He wished either to organize a section of political science in these faculties, or to create a special school for the public services. The faculties of law and even the whole university defeated the propositions out of monopolistic jealousy and want of imagination and public spirit, and remained, indeed, obstacles in the path of reform down to the resurgence of France in 1945. And their law teaching was the driest and least human and intelligent that can be imagined: it verged on the caricatures of legal education.

In 1848, under the impulse of another Minister of Education, Hippolyte Carnot, a school of administration was established, by decree. It attempted to imitate in the administrative province what the Polytechnique did for the engineers, and what the military administrators and technicians did for the armed forces. It was to be a school "destined for the recruitment of various branches of the administration hitherto lacking in schools of preparation." But attempts to give the school a solid foundation by statute and parliamentary consent failed. The school lasted only eighteen months, admitting candidates between the ages of eighteen and twenty-two. They were to have three years of study, followed by a leaving examination. According to their position on the list, they would have passed into the various departments, including the prefectoral and overseas administration, with two years of probation. The school came to an end because funds were not forthcoming; because famous statesmen started courses but had no time to finish them; because no steady policy for continuous work had been provided for. It seems also that hostility was incurred by the faulty policy of wishing to make all higher administrative posts at one stroke the preserve of the school. Finally, the faculties of law were bitterly opposed to this rival; and the various departments were anxious to retain their full power over the recruitment of their special, departmental personnel.

THE CIVIL SERVICE IN THE THIRD REPUBLIC

NOTHING is more constant in French parliamentary reports than the view that it is impossible to regulate all departments of the government on the same principles, as in early years and substantially today in England. This was, in part, an attempt at obstructing reform, for if uniform rules could not be found they could not be applied, while different rules for each set of officials made the business so complex that either it was left to the individual minister's discretion or was left unregulated, and, indeed, there were the usual obstructive arguments about the impossibility of testing aspirant officials by examinations. In part, however, it was the almost unconscious acceptance of the principle that previous training, competition, and recruitment should be special to each kind of situation. The English general examination was not accepted: the organized German systematic law training was rejected and the German preparatory stages not thought of. Even as the technical schools produced engineers for the road service, so could various special schools produce the administrators for the various other services of government.

Principles of Recruitment and Training. French law and practice to World War II were therefore based upon two main principles: (1) the service open to the talents [11] and (2) the talents trained by a special education and selected by special tests for each department, the nature of the training and tests being decided by a rule of public administration [12] for each department.

The Principles in Practice. (1) The law excluded the refusal of an office to a citizen on grounds other than his "capacity, virtues, and talents," but there was a certain means of escape for the appointing authority in the jurisprudence of the *Conseil d'État,* which said that public manifestations of certain political, philosophic, or religious opinions might be grounds for exclusion, for such opinions might show that the person was incapable of fulfilling the particular office he sought.[13]

---

[11] Constitution, 1791, article 6; 1793, article 5. The latest form is in November, 1848, article 10: "All citizens are equally admissible to all public offices, without any other motive of preference than their merit and following the conditions which shall be fixed by the laws . . ."

[12] The rule of public administration cannot be made without previous consultation of the *Conseil d'État,* which cannot veto the rule but may comment upon it. The simple executive rules are made without submission to the *Conseil.*

[13] Cf. G. Jèze, *Revue du Droit Public* (Paris, 1912), p. 453 *et seq.,* on the *Bouteyre* case and its implications; and cf. Léon Duguit, *Traité,* Vol. III, p. 199 ff., who denies this limiting power.

(2) The power to determine the rules of recruitment lay with the Chambers, with the President (where Parliament had not made a law on the subject), and with ministers to whom the President delegated the appointing power and who had the power to regulate in detail the power given them by law or Presidential decree.[14] Most of the rules relating to recruitment, promotion, and organization of the departments are made on the basis of the laws of December 30, 1882 (Article 16) and April 30, 1900 (Article 35), which provide that the central offices of each ministry will be regulated by a decree in the form of rules of public administration inserted in the *Journal Officiel,* and no amendment can be made except in the same form and with the same publicity.

The conditions of recruitment of the officials corresponding to the British administrative class and the German higher civil service were settled by a number of rules of public administration: e.g., diplomatic and consular service, Ministry of the Interior, Ministry for the Colonies, Ministry of Labour, and others.

The chief characteristic of these decrees were: *(a)* the fact that almost all central officials were regulated by them; *(b)* the universal prevalence of competitive examination, in the main entirely open; *(c)* for the administrative grade *(rédacteur),* competition by examination and oral examination; *(d)* the technical character of the examinations; *(e)* the demand for previous proof of successful education: that is, advanced high-school diplomas; *(f)* the wide age limits for entry into the service; *(g)* the departmentalization of the test.

Let us illustrate this practice—for *Rédacteur* (Ministry of the Interior). For this position, the equivalent of a subordinate in the administrative grade of the British civil service, the following were authorized to take part in the competitive examination: members of the executive grade who had had at least two years in the service, past students of the

---

[14] For the legal details cf. Jèze, *op. cit.,* Vol. II, p. 450 ff.

École Normale Supérieure, or men with a *licence en droit, lettres;* or *sciences,* doctorate of medicine, or diploma of the *École libre des Sciences Politiques,* a diploma of the *École des Chartes* of the High School of Commerce, etc., etc. This requirement is to guarantee a certain level of education. The candidate must be under thirty (other departments: between twenty-one and twenty-eight, up to twenty-six, etc.). In this case, candidates had to receive the minister's permission to enter the examination; in other cases, entry for the examination was automatic after only conditions of nationality, army service, and medical examination had been fulfilled. The examination consisted of two written tests, and oral tests. The written tests comprised the making of a report, description, or comment on any of the general topics of a short list, and on any of a number of special topics. These all fell within the field of interest of the Ministry of the Interior or were cognate to it. There was no test in general knowledge, no general essay, no test of the mother tongue as in the English system, though this last was hardly needed at so late a stage considering the excellence of French secondary education and the national pride in literary grace.

The oral test did not consist as in England of a quarter hour of desultory conversation ending with the belief that the board of interview knows the man's character, but in oral tests upon the subjects contained in the list of examination subjects. Further, the candidate was given a set of minutes to study for a quarter of an hour and was asked then to dictate a letter on the subject for five minutes to a typist. For each part of the examination marks were awarded from 0 to 20. Then they were weighted thus: general question multiplied by 5; special question by 5; oral question by 3; dictation by 1. The examining commission consisted of the secretary-general of the department, or the personnel director (president); a director of the department; three principals; and one assistant (as secretary).

This body set the examination and rated the candidates.

We need not enter into the question of admission to the examinations—whether by previous interview as in the Ministry for Foreign Affairs, or by the various types of diplomas as in other departments. But let us notice that in the former, the written examinations (for the diplomatic and consular service) were on diplomatic history, economic geography, and public international law. For the *Conseil d'État* were required constitutional, political, and judicial organization, law in its many branches, and economics. For the *Inspection Générale de Finance,* the emphasis was upon mathematics, public finance (law and administration), and economics; similarly in the Ministry of Finances. In all of the services the oral examination was based upon the subject matter of the written examination. In the examinations for the Ministry of Agriculture, emphasis was placed upon rural economy and the law relating to agricultural credit, cooperative societies, public instruction regarding agriculture, etc.[15]

Once accepted into the service by this means, the *rédacteur* moved by regular stages to the top of this class, and might by promotion reach the supreme positions of *souschefs* and *chefs de bureau.* It will be noticed that nothing like the Permanent Secretary at the top of the pyramid of a whole department has been mentioned as the acme of the career: this was a grave shortcoming of French administration.

Very little more can be said about the upper branches of French administration since statistics are not available; indeed, only since World War II has an organization been set up which may collect them. There was favoritism, but more in promotions than in recruitment.

Appraisal of the Civil Service Under The Third Republic. The contrast with

15 Cf. for details the various decrees; some were given as a supplement to the calendar of the *École Libre des Sciences Politiques,* Rue Saint-Guillaume, Paris; cf. also Jean Bourdeaux, *Les Carrières Administratives* (Paris, no date, before 1930).

England and Prussia is remarkable: for these countries have a unified examination system, nontechnical in nature, and conducted by a body outside and independent of the departments. There were some good potentialities in the French method: for (1) it drew the candidate *ab initio* to the department in which he wanted to serve; (2) it required always a study of the economic and social background of modern state activities; (3) it brought the members of the department (as examiners) face to face with the candidates into their hierarchy, with the possibility of a better choice from the standpoint of public efficiency and smooth cooperation in the service. There were also disadvantageous potentialities: (1) the personal contact of heads of departments with candidates might very well result in favoritism; (2) the special knowledge might be narrow and superficially acquired.

Criticism of the examination methods hardly existed before World War II: the French were happy enough to have escaped from pure "spoils." But one great scholar, at least, preferred the English system because he believed it produced men who could think as distinct from those who merely mastered a special field of knowledge: [16] "a varnish which cracks and scales off at the first contact." Jèze believed that a general education would be enough, since most servants would never attain to really high rank until very late in life, if at all: why then require technical knowledge at entrance? [17] He believed that there should be a general culture examination at entrance, then, for promotion, technical examinations at successive stages. But this raises the more serious question of whether examinations at a later age are a just method of finding capacity. With all respect to Jèze, I am afraid that he was misled by

Lowell (whom he followed), for he dealt only with the examination and the subjects of the examination as determinative of culture. But the vital question really is the nature of university teaching, and I venture to say that this may, according to its character, give a general culture with very technical subjects and certainly with constitutional and administrative law and economics and political science, or an ossified pedantry to the most liberal subjects of education. Jèze and others also criticized the too great range of the syllabus.[18]

As regards the examining bodies, Jèze believed their composition to be conducive to co-optation and favoritism, and suggested the addition of independent experts from outside the departments.[19]

Lefas deprecated an attitude of hypercriticism regarding favoritism in official appointments,[20] and on the whole our own investigations bear this out. There were rules, rules of considerable merit, and the law and the administrative courts provided amply against gross abuses.[21] Even the old loophole (not unparalleled at one time in England) of entry through private secretaryship to the minister, was largely blocked: up till 1911 members of

---

[16] Jèze, *op. cit.*, p. 466 ff.

[17] *Loc. cit.*: "Given the age of the candidates at time of entrance, the extent of the syllabus for the competition does not often imply even a good culture. The candidates have very superficial knowledge, a varnish which cracks and scales off at the first contact. We ought to renounce encyclopaedic programmes."

[18] Cf. P. Dubois-Richard, *L'Organisation Technique de l'État* (Paris, 1930), p. 264 ff.: "A young man who wishes to succeed at the *Polytechnique,* after having passed the *baccalauréat,* is obliged to pass every day in his infancy and youth so many hours at his desk that he cannot find time to form his person and personality. Culture loses in depth, and even more in harmony, what it usefully gains in extent."

[19] H. Chardon (*Le Pouvoir Administratif* (Paris, 1912) believed that examinations wider than a single department and not intermittent (which separate departmental examinations can hardly avoid being) would raise the level of candidates, and render easier the assimilation of departmental grades.

[20] Cf. L. D. White, editor, *Civil Service in the Modern State* (Chicago, 1930), article by Lefas, p. 266 ff. Cf. also T. L. Barnier, *Au Service de la Chose Publique* (Paris, 1926). "In most of the public services, competition is today the basis of recruitment and free selection by the minister, by the prefects and even the majors, has been singularly reduced." Cf. also W. R. Sharp, *The French Civil Service* (New York, 1931).

[21] Cf. Jèze, *op. cit.*, Vol. II, p. 473 ff.

the cabinet of the minister were legally unregulated except by certain contradictory decisions of the courts: in 1911 a law provided that any appointments to public office from the ministerial cabinet or undersecretaries must be notified in the *Journal Officiel* before the resignation of the countersigning minister or undersecretary. Nor were ordinary civil servants who were appointed to a ministerial cabinet treated other than as the normal rules provide in regard to promotion. Yet this only requires publicity for an appointment made, it does not rule out or limit such appointments. Now, the decrees to which we have so far referred concerned only entrance into the administrative grade; they say nothing about the higher stages—*chefs de bureaux* and *directeurs,* the nearest equivalents of the English assistant secretaries to the Permanent Secretary. These are usually filled by promotion from those in the department and after many years of conspicuous service. But some were appointed from the ministerial cabinets. However, too much weight ought not to be attached to the explanation of the humorist: "Examinations are often made for fools who cannot get placed otherwise!"

In conclusion, we may say that the higher civil service of the Third Republic suffered from some serious shortcomings generally recognized and deplored, and yet not remedied owing to the instability of cabinets and passionate internecine social conflicts.[22]

(1) The various departmental services were highly specialized not only by function, which is natural, but by their educational preparation. Apart from the general education at the *lycée* or schools of that level, any general common state of mind was disrupted by specialized professional preparation of the kind already described. This flew directly in the face of the common sense of the French liberal critics, and compared unfavorably with the theory and practice of the higher civil service that efficiently prevailed in Brit-

ain. We have said that integration begins in the schools: France destroyed it, and the various government departments deliberately did so on wrong theories and for unworthy motives. What the departments put asunder, the unstable cabinets could not join: a united mind.

(2) Probation and apprenticeship were not real. No attempt was made to give postentry training, none to put the entrant through stages of practical work, and hardly anyone that entered was ever dismissed for unsuitability.

(3) The intellectual education received in the various schools that particularly provided for entrants to the public service was of a high grade, the highest in the world in point of the severity with which the student was compelled to attend to his studies. But it was heavily theoretical and synoptic. It was, in a sense, highly technical, even if the subject were law or economics. One has only to examine the textbooks to be convinced of this. The formulas were all cut and dried. They were answers but not thought-provoking problems. They did not whirr as reality whirrs. The studies had a remote, antiquated, uncontemporary, thin flavor about them. The truth was that France had dangerously slipped from any proper level of excellence in economic and political science studies: the books did not exist because Frenchmen did not write them. The reader will look in vain for a Hawtrey, a Keynes, a Robbins, a Hansen, a Wesley Mitchell in economics in the Third Republic. He will, in political science, miss a Corwin, a G.D.H. Cole, a Sidney or Beatrice Webb, a Graham Wallas, a Walter Lippmann, a Walton Hamilton, a Lawrence Lowell, a Laski, a Jennings, and so many others, and he will find nothing like the great series of commission and committee hearings and reports on administrative reform that adorn the Anglo-Saxon countries in the last four decades.

(4) All these things together resulted in a resistant autonomy on the part of the various departments and bureaus, an unintelligent *amour propre* that was culti-

[22] Nearly all the criticisms were aired vigorously in the Assembly, *Débats, Journal Officiel,* February and June, 1945.

vated and affected to the point of non-cooperation and even obstruction.

(5) Between the grade of *rédacteurs,* the administrative type, and the executive-clerical class, the arrangement of functions came to be confused, because no care was taken to establish and maintain the clear distinction between the higher duties and the routine. In departments recruiting from time to time for themselves, as vacancies arose, with their own division of functions, it often became convenient out of sheer slovenly expediency to give the lower ranks the work of the upper and the upper the work of the lower. The only way to check this is by the establishment of a class which runs through all departments, given integrity by a common education, a common examination, and a common status.

(6) Since no common class existed with its own career prospects, some departments attracted brilliant and ambitious men, while others could not even be filled. A single department, when it is of mediocre significance in the state and yet needs to be manned as much as do the others, is not an attraction when it is a trap into which one enters without the later chance of transfer. To be a member of a single class available for all employments, and with a right to request transfer and change in relation to all other promotees, spreads talent, and saves some of it from permanent frustration.

(7) The promotion system, from grade to grade, required that the promotee should go into the next higher position— by law. To make room for those who deserved promotion, more jobs than were necessary for the work were created. No notice was taken of comparative ability: promotions were given out of good nature. If men of special merit were required, some grades ahead, then they were often brought in by the minister by special decree, or some were brought in on an unestablished basis. Yet this produced more frustration for those who expected promotion, but who were defeated by the lack of rational system in the composition of the service.

(8) The service was on the whole manned by the upper bourgeoisie, which was not energetically democratic and in some of its branches was actually and even fiercely antidemocratic. Now, on the whole there were some opportunities for working-class and middle-class brains to get to the universities in France, because secondary-school education was freer than in England thirty years ago, where the number of free places in the secondary schools was strictly limited. Yet the cost of tuition and maintenance in the post-*lycée* period, at college or university, was a class restriction on entrance into the public service.

Now, much has been made of the social and political conservatism and antidemocratic flavor of the recruits entering from the *École Libre des Sciences Politiques.* Some observations on this subject are necessary. The school was established as a private foundation, with funds supplied by rich donors, in 1871, by a notable student of political science, Émile Boutmy. The purpose was to restore French government and administration after the defeat by Prussia, and especially to bring into political science and administrative studies some of the pungent air of reality these had always had in the nation across the channel. Several generations of publicists, politicians, and administrators were taught there to serve the Republic. It was a splendid idea!—but the school had its deficiencies. The first was that it could not of itself repair the specialization of teaching forced upon it by the structure of the administrative services themselves, and the nonexistence of a single administrative service which had a common education and was selected annually by a single assembled examination. Its teachers were inclined to laissez faire in economics and the legalistic approach in constitutional and public law. And it was, in the main, a school for the wealthy. During World War II it fell into irretrievable disrepute,[23] since the defeat was blamed on its teaching and products—

---

[23] Cf. *Débats, Journal Officiel,* June 21, 1945, especially observations of André Philip, *rapporteur-général* of the *Commission des Finances.*

and though this was far from being wholly just, there was enough in the charge that could be justified.

This judgment so far as it was well-founded took its grave importance from the kind of view expressed by Daniel Halévy: "Republican France has, in reality, two constitutions: one, that of 1875, is official, visible and fills the Press—this is parliamentary: the other is secret and silent, it is that of the Year VIII—it is the Napoleonic constitution which vests the direction of the country in the administrative corps." [24] One credible and gallant witness, by profession a member of the *Conseil d'État*, declares [25] that the upper ranks of the administration were taught by anti-Republican and even reactionary professors, leading to enmity to the Republic. He asserts that it was well-nigh impossible to get into the *Conseil d'État* or the Inspectorate of Finances and other departments without studying at the *École Libre des Sciences Politiques*. André Géraud, writing as *Pertinax* about "the Gravediggers of France," passes from blaming the Treasury officials to blaming the school which nurtured them: [26]

As I looked over the programs listing the various subjects taught in this institution, I was often amazed at the number of degree-spangled pedants who now replaced the founders. The majority of Treasury officials were recruited from this school. Vanity of examinations and competitions! These fellows were not chosen because of their intrinsic merit, the strength of their personality, or their fine character, but merely because of the supposed orthodoxy of their views, their powers of mimicry, their connections, and their position in Parisian society among the two or three thousand people who held the big jobs, set the fashion, handed out favors, and made the law. . . Inspectors of Finance [Treasury officials] were one huge family, and that connection could not be called healthy.

These men had loyalties, but they were not to the Chamber of Deputies; they had abilities but not those of a larger republican statesmanship. It was quite a habit of the Treasury officials to go into the employment of high finance after a few years in office. The double fault of the higher administration was that the officials were authoritarian and that the disjointed structure of the departments ruined the usefulness of such professional competence—in some, very high—and loyalty to the nation—in some, to *their* conception of the nation, very deep—as they had.

(9) The high officials, overdoctrinaire and disunited as they were, could not be and were not coordinated, harmonized, and driven toward objectives of national policy seen as a whole and steadily pursued. For the cabinets, their masters, were never in office long enough to make an impression, but always in office just long enough to cause an annoying disturbance and the comfortable sniggering reflection among officials that they were on the way out.

(10) Finally, the central departments, particularly the Ministry of the Interior, the Treasury, the Ministry of Justice, the Ministry of Education, and the *Conseil d'État*, were the strict unifying masters of all the French local-government units—*départements, arrondissements, cantons,* and *communes*. Though some decentralization had lightened the weight of financial and administrative controls emanating from Paris during the lifetime of the Third Republic, *la tutelle,* the central tutelage over policies, appointments, activities, and the regular budgets, was still one of the most rigorous and exacting in the world.[27] It operated in the main through the *préfet* in the *départements,* though the central offices' inspectors were also its instruments; and the *préfets* and his adjutants were the nominees of the Ministry of the Interior. Whatever was "bureaucratic," officious, and narrow-

[24] Cf. his *Décadence de la Liberté* (London, 1931).
[25] Pierre Tissier, *I Worked with Laval* (London, 1942), p. 7 ff.
[26] "Pertinax," *The Gravediggers of France* (New York, 1944), p. 364 ff.

[27] Cf. R. Maspétiol and P. Laroque, *La Tutelle Administrative* (Paris, 1930). Cf. also R. K. Gooch, *Regionalism in France* (New York, 1931).

minded in the capital, got itself reflected at any rate to some extent through France, with the exception of the big cities like Lyons or Marseilles. French local services were very backward compared with those in Britain and Germany.

The French Third Republic fell not only through the drying up of the sap of mind and devotion of all its high officials, but this had failed so badly as to make the radical reconstruction of the higher administrative service one of the principal anxieties of the Fourth Republic.

THE HIGHER CIVIL SERVICE IN THE FOURTH REPUBLIC

An attempt was made in 1937 to reform the recruitment of the higher civil service. It failed in the Chamber of Deputies chiefly because the problem had become so complicated that a democratic assembly in the conditions of the Third Republic could not see and force its way through all the jungle of vested interests, official and academic.

It is noteworthy that such a reform could only come in the wake of resurgence after defeat, and in a régime which was still of a zealous, warrior temper, and not yet delivered back to the habits of the Third Republic's politicians.

General de Gaulle, then head of the provisional government, commissioned a member of the *Conseil d'État* to undertake the mission of preparing a radical change.[28] It comprised a simultaneous reform of the higher administrative service and of the educational system: for a reform of one without the other was now acknowledged to be useless. After deliberations in the *Conseil d'État*, the Council of Ministers, and the Consultative Assembly, the combined ordinances, decrees, and regulations were published on October 10, 1945.

The Administrative Reform. Instead of the single *rédacteur* grade, which had here and there become confused with the executive and clerical officers, two high grades were now established: (1) civil administrators and (2) secretaries of administration.

The civil administrators are the group for which the recruitment reforms chiefly provide. They are almost identical with the British administrative class, and were consciously modeled upon it. All, wherever they serve, are subject to the same broad disciplinary rules, and they constitute one single group and career, whichever department they happen to serve at any time. Their hierarchy going upwards is: administrators-adjoint, administrative class *3*, then class *2*, then class *1*, and then class *"exceptional."* All of these are recruited through a newly instituted *École Nationale d'Administration*, from now referred to as the School. Their function has been described as: [29]

to fit the conduct of administrative affairs to the general policy of the Government, to prepare drafts of laws and rules and ministerial decisions, to formulate the directives to their execution, and to coordinate the march of the public services.

On the other hand, the secretaries of administration were rather like the "executive class" of the British civil service. The same authority describes them as "the technicians of the administrative services." He says of them: [30]

Their task is to assure the works of execution, current operations, and certain specialized functions which require sound administrative knowledge and experience.

They could be called top office managers. They fall into a managerial group, and two special categories, accountants and translators. These are recruited by an examination which is open to officials aged 35 and over and having five years of public service, and to young persons between

---

28 This was Marcel Debré (*Maître des Requêtes*) and then commissioner for the region of Augers, with France still under a war régime.

29 Cf. Marcel Debré, "La Réforme de la Fonction Publique" in *Revue d l'École d'Administration*, May, 1946, p. 34. Cf. also the annual calendars of the School, *L'École Nationale d' Administration* (Imprimerie Nationale, 1947), and the series continuing the *Revue*, entitled *Promotions*.
30 Debré, *op. cit.*, p. 34.

the ages of 18 and 25, holding a diploma of higher (secondary) education or the equivalent.

The Civil Administrators. The position of the administrative class, as it may be called henceforth, is clearly distinguished by its recruitment, its functions, its career.

The first task of the state is to assure itself of a flow of properly talented recruits for the administrative service. The School is concerned with the task of their further formation once it has found them. Essential to the discovery is the general prescription of what is being sought. This is described by the principal architect of the reform in these words: [31]

The "administration" is diverse in its composition. In this generic term are wrapped up services of very different nature. There are civil services of a purely administrative character and technical services, metropolitan and colonial services, home services, and services abroad. The magistracy, the university, and the armed forces are equally part of the administration.

It is diverse in its structure and its members. Certain services have a simple character of execution and those who carry them out have no part in the direction of the affairs of the State. Others, on the contrary, are at the very heart of the life of the nation, and their officers may be considered as influential collaborators of the political authorities.

When we talk of a School of Administration and when one envisages the administrative reform bound up with its establishment, the word "administration" has a special sense. It means that combination of services of a civil character which constitute the superior structure of the State and whose members have as their principal task to prepare or study the decisions of Parliament and the Government and then to direct their execution. It is among these officials that the Government would naturally choose a great number of its high officers, notably those who will occupy the situations which wield authority or of administration linked with policy.

Of the relevant services these principal ones come rapidly to mind: the central administrations of the ministries, the prefectoral and diplomatic services, the services of inspection, the administrative bodies concerned with law-making and control (the *Conseil*

d'État and the Court of Accounts). There are others like these.

This general description is vividly reminiscent of Macaulay's formula for the British civil service.

The French government rejected two ideas formerly suggested for the education of such a higher administrative career. One was modeled on the idea of the *Polytéchnique.* Here quite young men at once entered their career and were educated to it in this school, whence after three years of study they went off to their actual jobs. But this meant that the candidates were far too young and immature, coming direct from secondary schools. The tendency would be to impress upon them a single identical outlook. General culture would have been sacrificed to narrowness of the specialized administrative outlook—in a field where breadth was of the utmost importance. It was felt to be a little undemocratic, since it might be that those who had so young felt or been persuaded of the appeal of public service might be of an authoritarian temper, and only a small social class could afford such an education. Another idea was to bring from the universities to a special school of administration each year entrants chosen by competition. Here they would be prepared for their administrative service examinations. The students accepted would have their board, lodging, and tuition fees paid by the state. This idea was discarded, as it stood, because it did not thoroughly enough grapple with the kind of education given at the universities.

Two new ingredients were necessary: better university preparation of recruits for the public service, and a new institution for the intelligent development of those who had shown prowess in the new university stage.

The Reform of University Education. In the universities, and within the authority of the universities, there are established Institutes of Political Studies, or, in other words, faculties of political and social sciences. Their object is to co-ordinate and develop the work hitherto

[31] *Ibid.*, pp. 10-11.

undertaken by the other faculties in the teaching of economics, administration, and social studies, and to educate students in the work-methods and concrete problems of administration and social life. The true scope is the whole of the social sciences: the new object, animation and creativeness after so long a period of intellectual and spiritual infertility.

For some years the institutes will be established only in Paris, Strasbourg, Toulouse, and Lyons, for it is recognized that the reform will stand or fall by its products, and it is not deemed possible that enough of the right kind of teachers can yet be found for more institutes. No institute may come into existence unless its faculty, curriculum, and methods can first pass the very strict scrutiny of the *Conseil d'État*. Students can enter the institutes if they have a diploma of higher education (advanced secondary) on the list approved by the School. All candidates for entrance who deserve it and are needy are granted scholarships by the state. The state enters through its grant of scholarships, and also through the membership of certain officials and the director of the School on the "councils of improvement" which supervise the development of each institute, and through the president of the Council of Ministers' approval of their curricula and administration. The other connections between the state and preparation for the higher administrative service will become apparent later.

In their first year the students take an almost identical common course; in their second and third, many optional courses are permitted to accommodate some natural appetites and vocational interests. But specialization is banished. The purpose of the studies at the institute is a broad, liberal education, through the medium of the faculties of law and the humanities, with the additional focus of the social sciences. The education is by lectures, discussions, practical tasks, and seminar work. The teachers are the university professors and various authorities from the services and outside affairs, the latter to give a guarantee of "animation."

A severe examination at the end of the first year expels students not up to standard. After three years' work, a final examination leads to a diploma. The diploma is crucial—it is the first qualification for entrance into the School for those who do not come in by way of membership of the public service: it is the principal key to the public service at the top administrative level.

The School: L'École Nationale d'Administration. The School serves several purposes, incident to the formation of cultured and practical-minded civil servants. It replaces the separate, departmental, specialized entrance examinations, by a single annual competition. It provides for the people with talent but without means, because those who are admitted receive adequate payment as officials for the three years for which their studies now proceed. Receiving annually about ninety entrants who have already given proof of exceptional ability, the School has designed a combination of instruction by books and classes with a very clever succession of practical work-stages, in order to focus, make more concrete, living, and actively responsive to administrative tasks, their mind and habits.

Once again the students cover many subjects in the whole field of the social sciences: for illustration, the list includes administrative law and organization, legislation, administrative justice, fiscal and budgetary law, public accounts, public credit, economic legislation, labor relations, colonial organizations and legislation, international law, foreign policy and international problems, statistics, population theory, town planning, currency and banking, commercial policy, international transport, hygiene and preventive medicine, and social security.

Above all, the School sets its face sternly against the production of officials by mere book-knowledge, and against the merely formal principle of probation, which (as in almost every public service) had become a dead letter in practice. Most of the time at the School is spent in practice in the various administrative agencies.

What is of equally outstanding interest is that the School deliberately addresses itself to the problem of the moral cultivation of its officials. It will be remembered that it was to this that the mind of the English reformers of the middle nineteenth century was addressed, and we have already observed that the problem of character is one that still baffles those who recruit for the public service. The observations of the principal author of the French reform on the problem of moral education are particularly significant and well-styled, for they offer an insight into the nature of the civil service in the modern state. He says: [32]

It is not part of the mission of the School to play politics or to impose a doctrine. But the School must teach its future officials the sense of the State; it must make them understand the responsibilities of the administration, cause them to taste the greatness and accept the servitudes of their profession. It must do more. By a continuous effort made by its best professors, by recalling great examples and the great men in history, it must give to its pupils the taste for certain cardinal qualities: the sense of the humane that infuses life in every kind of work, the sense of decision which permits the taking of decision after the risks have been weighed, and the sense of imagination which is not afraid of any daring, any great deed. And even more than that. The founders of the first school of administration placed high hopes in the spirit which would animate their students. They were right, and it is proper today, on the eve of the years when the obligations of the service of the State will be heavier than ever, to relive the faith of the republicans of 1848 in the value of moral virtue taught and understood. When such is invoked, certain persons prick up their ears: they fear the reverse of the medal: a spirit of caste which would pervert the administration. But their judgment is superficial. The variety of the sources of recruitment for the School, the maturity already attained by most of its students, the determination to make them participate by numerous practical activities in the difficulties of life, are some of the elements which will prevent the School from becoming a closed chapel.

This ideal is so clear, that all that is now needed to make the services of the School plain, is a brief and bare description of its procedure and organization.

There are two separate examinations for entrance into the School, one for the students, the other for officials already in the public service. The former is taken by persons less than 26 years of age and holding the diploma of the institutes of politics, the latter by officials between the ages of 26 and 30 provided they have been in the public service for five years or more. (Some of the secretaries of administration will thus get their opportunities to rise.) The examinations are in the fields of political science and economics, but general themes, not specialized, are set the students. The generality of the examination extends to the setting of subjects covering a much wider field of university studies than those in the institutes, in order that those who have not yet thought of becoming civil servants should not be excluded from deciding to do so at this stage. The entrants from the civil service, who have not had time to acquire a general education, are given a specialized examination without a foreign language. All take a physical examination of some severity, and it may be added that all candidates must have accomplished their military service. The final proportion between the two classes of entrants will be decided by experience.

The School is organized in four sections: general administration, economic and financial administration, social administration, and foreign affairs. The candidates declare into which of these they would like an admission. The theory is that candidates should be given the opportunity of entering the vocation of their spontaneous choice, and that as specialization is inevitable, it should be neither ignored nor pushed to an extreme. In the entrance examinations, questions are provided enabling candidates to offer answers within their specialty; but care has been taken to avoid anything like four separate examinations. The examiners look for general culture, personality, and character, and the latter are appraised by

32 *Ibid.*, p. 22.

a very broadly constituted board of interview. Students are listed in the order of merit on one single list according to marks obtained, and they choose what section they wish to enter according to their place. If they cannot get into the section they want, they must go into some other—or try again next year.

Now that they have been admitted into the School, students come under the disciplinary code of the civil service, receive a salary, and commit themselves to serve the state for a period of twelve years, and, failing this obligation, to pay back to the state the three years' salary received at the School.

The three years are divided into a first year of practical work, and mixed arrangement of schooling and practical work in the second and third years. At the end of the three years the student-officials are classified by aptitude and competence: the incompetent and unworthy are expelled (they may be dropped for cause at any time during the three years). Their grades at the final classing are composed to the extent of one half for practical work and schooling, and one half on their final examination—and they are classed in their sections. But a general classing is also drawn up so that certain administrations like the *Conseil d'État* may take their recruits from diverse sources.

The governmental agencies which have so far been designated to be served by the graduates of the School are the *Conseil d'État,* the Court of Accounts, the highest level of the central administration of the ministries, the diplomatic and cognate services, the general inspectorate of finances and the general inspectorate of the administrative services, the inspectorates of labor, the administration of Algeria and the civil control of Morocco and Tunisia, and the prefectoral career. The relative centralization of French government makes all these posts of more than usual importance. As regards the prefectoral career, the present innovation is of especial importance since it brings to completion the development of the last three decades tending to take the career of prefect out of politics, and, furthermore, it is

the intention to create one service of the central controlling authority, the Ministry of the Interior, and its field services in the *départements.*

When the recruits enter the actual service of the state, they enter—like their counterparts in Britain, the assistant principals or administrative cadets—into a *début* stage. Some places, however, are kept for outsiders and promotees. Some places, also, are not available, since the ministers in their own discretion may make the appointments to positions of "direction and authority."

The Practical Training. Social value is placed by the School on the stages of practical training. It is, above all, desired to remedy the defect of all previous methods of recruitment, namely, to overcome the entirely theoretical knowledge by practice before the candidates enter on their own executive responsibilities. The critics of prewar French administration emphasize that its officials were more content to write a clever letter or a very complete report, or well-turned memorandum, rather than act anew. Moreover, it is desired to overcome whatever may still remain of the big-city outlook of the entrants by sending them to participate for some time in the provinces and the overseas territories, and also, to bring about the earliest possible contact between officials and labor unions, since so many come from the middle class. In addition, there are practical arts to learn from those already exercising executive responsibilities.

The various stages of practical training have been most carefully and precisely devised after comprehensive consultations with civil servants, with school groups concerned with scientific personnel management, and with private experts. The stages include spells of time in provincial and local administration in France and the overseas territories, in the central departments, and in the *Conseil d'État* and the various controls and inspectorates. There are stages of service in the different parliamentary bodies. The next series of experiences take place in the nationalized industries, and in private business of large and middle size which are soundly organized. The demands of a planned state, as well as the previous poverty of economic studies in France, have conduced to this stage, and there must be added the desire to impress the student with the idea that planning is not easy and that there is value and life in sound private enterprise. Finally, some if not all students, will spend some months abroad in the French services or in foreign public services or private enterprise.

What will be gained by this very well ·devised system of practice, or in-training besides a vivid, synoptic view? This: [33]

By such contacts, the future civil administrators will drink in progressively the sense of what is real and efficacious, the taste for action and personal initiative, a large comprehension of the most diverse social places, a comprehension made up of the knowledge of men and things, and also, let us hope, that sympathy for men which is the condition of all great work. . . By the end of these administrative training stages, the students will have acquired the sense of the State, not of a state abandoned to instable passions or disdainful of personal and local liberties, but of a state charged with pursuing in time, with continuity, its work of social progress imbued with respect for these liberties.

Further Education. France, like Britain during World War II, discussed the proposal that an administrative-staff college should be set up to cater for higher officials, as well as the younger generation, where all might be improved in general knowledge and administrative technique. This was inopportune. But something like it, to fulfill the task of refreshing those long in the service, was adopted, in the *Centre des Hautes Études,* the Center of High (Advanced) Studies. Its purpose is to re-educate and refresh officials who have been at work for some years in the technical and specialized and local services, those who have become blinkered through service in the same department for a long time. Its object is to bring them up to date, to enable them to widen their knowledge by the study of new problems, and to regain some breadth by mingling

with officials from other services and with men from outside the service. The courses and classes fall into three categories: general administration of the services managed by government for metropolitan France; imperial problems, like the political, economic, social, intellectual, religious problems arising out of the relationship between metropolitan France and the overseas territories; and the theory and practice of industrial enterprise and control by the State. Yet many important problems are studied in common by all those who attend the Center.

The Center achieves its object by means of lectures, discussions, research work, and practical in-training in the administration and in private industry. A carefully formulated scheme of "secondment" and rotation, bringing persons from the localities and overseas to the capital and sending some off abroad, is designed to lighten the monotony of their current careers.

The condition for entrance is to be between the ages of 30 and 45 and to have spent at least six years of service; or, to make room for entrants from outside, to have spent an equal time in private enterprise. A diploma certifies proficiency in the Center. It does not entitle its holder to office or promotion; but entrants from outside public administration, having gained a diploma, can use it as a qualification for entrance into the service.

The Personnel Agency, the School and Center. Thus it is hoped that the institution of the School will provide the regular entrants to the higher service from among the ninety or one hundred students accepted annually, and that the Center will help to revive the enthusiasm of the older generation. It must be borne in mind that these reforms are part of a renewal of the French state by men who took the leading part in the Liberation and in very many cases the resistance against the German occupation. The whole is infused with a spirit of high endeavor and action. Extra marks are given to students for athletic prowess, especially for ability to pilot an airplane or glider, or to parachute-jump. The designations taken by some of the classes already entering the School give

[33] *Ibid.,* pp. 59 60.

the pungent flavor of action: "Fighting France," "The French Union," the "Cross of Lorraine," the "United Nations."

The School is housed in the former premises of the *École Libre des Sciences Politiques.* It is maintained at the expense of the State. Its first director is a noted resistance combatant and one of General de Gaulle's former administrators in Brittany during the Liberation.

The connection of the School (and of the Center, since for the time being, the Center is administered by the director and council of the school) with the government is exceedingly interesting. It is directly within the authority and under the aegis of the president of the Council of Ministers. Under the president a direction of Public Service has been instituted to prepare the lines of a general policy for the public services and to build up documents and statistics. It formulates the coordination of status, principles of salary, pension schemes, and the organization of the services. It is assisted by one commission composed of the personnel directors from the various departments, and another representing the professional organizations of the officials. Side by side with the Direction is a Permanent Council of Administration. It is charged with studying and elaborating a policy for the public services, and, under the authority of the government, with imposing it on the whole administrative system, and thereafter with supervising the fulfillment of the statute of the public services. It is the sole council of discipline for the officials of the services recruited by the School. It is composed of a chairman, who is a president of a section of the *Conseil d'État,* six officials (three nominated by the civil service unions), and two persons from outside the civil service. The members are appointed in the Council of Ministers each for six years.

The School itself is administered by a director and a council of administration. The former is appointed by decree made in the Council of Ministers, and he cannot be dismissed without the reasoned decision of the School's council of administration. The council of administration has as its chairman, *ex officio,* the vice-president of the *Conseil d'État.* It contains members from the universities, the officials, and persons from outside the service, all nominated by the government. One of the officials is the Director of the Public Service, that is, the director of the bureau serving under the president of the Council of Ministers. Two of the officials are nominated by the civil service unions. The director of the School is assisted by an adjutant who is charged with organizing the practical training of the students and supervising their progress. The teachers at the School are drawn from the professors and administrators, and from outside these groups.

The discussion may well conclude with the remarks from a speech by the first director of the School on the occasion of the first commencement: [34]

The School must be a great School, *the* great School, into which one will be proud to enter, and from which one will be glad to graduate, which will form the best, the most poised, the most humane, the most sound of men. For such, tomorrow, must be the splendid officials of which the nation has need.

It will have been observed that here, in France, as in Germany and Britain, the problem of the higher civil service is approached in an atmosphere of dedication of service to the "State" which is the immediate incarnation of the national society. It is interesting to compare this with the manner in which the problem of the upper administrative levels is envisaged in the United States.

---

[34] *Revue de l'École Nationale d'Administration* (Paris, May, 1946), p. 55.

33

The United States Civil Service

AMERICAN experience of administration has been vastly different from anything we have so far described, for the offices of state and their services have been used—to an extent and for a span of time (until 1883) unparalleled in any other country—as the "spoils" of the victorious political parties. The reasons for this have already

they now stand. On June 30, 1947, the civilian employees in the executive branch in the continental United States numbered 1,849,781. Of these, 1,698,568 were subject to the competitive examination requirements of the Civil Service Act, amounting to 92 per cent of the total. This left 151,213 employees excepted from

TABLE 27—UNITED STATES: PERCENTAGE OF EXAMINABLE POSITIONS IN THE CIVIL SERVICE, 1883-1939

Year	No. of Positions Subject to Examination	No. of Positions In the Civil Service	Percentage of Positions Examinable
1883	13,780	131,208	10.5
1888	29,650	159,356	18.6
1893	45,821	180,000	25.45
1899	94,893	208,000	45.62
1903	154,093	301,000	51.19
1909	222,278	370,000	60.08
1913	292,460	435,000	67.23
1918	592,961	917,760	64.6
1924	415,593	554,986	74.8
1928	431,763	568,715	74.9
1930	587,665	608,915	67.7
1939	622,832	920,310	67.67

been given in part, and will be treated again presently. The remarkable and laudable progress since 1883 is shown in Table 27.[1]

Before entering upon the discussion, it is convenient to present the significant statistics of the United States civil service as

competitive requirements—a grave exception, yet in proportion to the total smaller by far than at any time in the history of the Republic.

As can be seen from the figures, the mighty days of spoils have passed away, and Europeans who still have "spoils" in their minds when they speak of the United States must modify their images very seriously. The largest amount of "spoils" are in the state and municipal

[1] Figures from 1883-1924 from *Annual Report*, U. S. Civil Service Commission, 1925, Vol. VIII. Figures for 1928, 1930, and 1939 from the Annual Reports of these years.

services: the federal government has cleaned itself.

THE PERENNIAL PSYCHOLOGY OF SPOILS

How did the federal government become sullied and what were the stages in its purification? Those in power in the state, whatever its form (monarchy, oligarchy, dictatorship, or democracy), are always likely to abuse their power to make appointments to public office. They are, at any rate, normally more likely to do this than to subject themselves to the prohibitions and difficulties required by attention to the public well-being. The public well-being is impersonal and intangible, it is comprehensive and remote, while the satisfactions to be obtained by following personal caprice in appointments are immediate and vivid. When one's own good is the first consideration—as, for example, in business—the conditions for the appointment of those best qualified to produce what is required are present, and in the long run, if bankruptcy is to be avoided, they prevail. But the results of public service are often impalpable, distant from the vicinity of the maker of appointments, and it still takes a great deal to ruin a whole nation by wasteful organization and extravagant payments to inefficient servants. Hence it is not a matter for surprise that a "spoils" system should have grown up in the United States: the amazing thing is that a democracy spreading over an area thirty-two times the size of England should ever have limited that system and controlled its own worst impulses in order to establish a system of appointment by merit! As Montesquieu has said, a democracy has peculiar need of virtue, for when, in other régimes, inefficiency is observed, there is the refuge of democracy, but if the people themselves lack virtue, where shall one turn? Yet a democracy is peculiarly liable to demoralize its administration; for its basic tenet is the equal worth of all men, while its fundamental machinery is a party system. The former causes all to demand a place, the latter must be stoked into continuous service by the provision of concrete satisfactions, money payments, honors, or public office.

We do not wish to describe in detail the progress by which the federal service of the United States proceeded from "spoils" to proficiency. Suffice it to say that the system of spoils began on a minor scale and apologetically with Washington, Jefferson, and Adams, became a torrent in 1829 when Jackson came into office, and from that time until 1883 swept through all the offices of government without legal let or hindrance, and most usually without moral inhibitions. From the Pendleton Act of 1883, when the Civil Service Commission was established, civil service positions were successively "classified" and subjected to objective rules of appointment, and the "spoils" system was steadily contracted. The questions which interest us are: (1) what were the discernible motives of the "spoils" system; (2) what were its effects, its machinery, and the obstacles and impulses to reform.

Motives of the Spoils System. (1) Spontaneous friendliness, conviviality, and generosity produced and produce spoils. We have to steel ourselves against such impulses to confer benefits upon our elective affinities, those who please by their manner, but especially upon our relatives. The lust of prestige, the feeling of power and virtue which nepotism produces, are very seductive, and compared with these things, the chances of being applauded for services to the Republic, especially in a party system of government, are faint. Moreover, it is easier to give away what belongs to the unseen public than what belongs to yourself. Vicarious generosity is one of the plagues of the world.[2]

(2) A more powerful motive in a democracy is the maintenance of one's own view of the constitution, the laws, and

---

[2] C. R. Fish, *The Civil Service and Patronage* (Harvard, 1904) p. 59: "In 1821 John Quincy Adams said that one-half of the members of Congress were seeking office, and that the other half wanted something for their relatives." Cf. L. D. White, *The Federalists* (New York, 1948) for this period.

their proper application.[3] It is argued that none will know this so well as one's own political nominees, and none will be so zealous as they. Hence an impulse to proscribe all opponents or neutrals and to appoint only indubitable friends. It is not relevant that opponents are technically efficient: that is an argument in favor of their proscription.[4] Better an incompetent supporter than a competent enemy. As a Massachusetts Republican clergyman preached in 1811, "But if ye will not drive out the inhabitants of the land from before you, then it shall come to pass that those that ye let remain of them shall be pricks in your eyes and thorns in your sides, and shall tear you in the land where ye shall dwell." [5]

(3) In a democracy, based as it is on party organization, the need for some commodity with which to induce and repay electoral services is great, and the greater it is, the larger the number of elective offices. In the United States this motive to create and use "spoils" was exceedingly strong, especially from the 1820's onward through the joint effects of the rising tide of democracy and the in-

creasing area of settled government.[6] This was the main cause of "spoils."

(4) The theory of "the rotation of office"—that office should not be held for long periods by the same incumbents and that everyone should have a chance of office—was put forward and practiced from a variety of motives. It was a means of stopping government from becoming a caste alien to the people,[7] a means of maintaining the responsibilty of officials to the people,[8] and in a democracy, based on the idea of the freedom and equality of citizens, it was claimed that all should have an opportunity.[9]

(5) As soon as one party began to proscribe enemies, the other party was obliged to do so; and the question then became, who would stop first? When that received no answer, the question became, could enough members of both parties stop at the same time, and how could they be induced to do so?

Not until 1883 was this question really answered, although the reform movement had begun over a decade before; and it was answered by a few politicians of abnormal decency with the help of the National League for Civil Service Reform. But first, of the effects of the "spoils system."

Effects of the System. An enormous number of offices—most, in fact—fell into the hands of the politicians. Every four years a large clearance was effected, and during each Presidential term other violent changes occurred. Sheer inefficiency was the first result; an increase in public costs the second; the creation of a class of officeseekers the third; political corruption the fourth; [10] a standing battle be-

---

[3] Cf. Jefferson (cited in Fish, *op. cit.*, p. 35): "If the will of the nation, manifested by these various elections, calls for an administration of Government according with the opinions of those elected . . . [T]his [removal of and replacement of officials] is a painful office; but it is made my duty and I must meet it as such. I proceed in the operation with deliberation and inquiry, that it may injure the best men least, and effect the purposes of justice and public utility with the least private distress; that it may be thrown, as much as possible, on delinquency, on oppression, on intolerance, on ante-revolutionary adherence to our enemies. . . It would have been to me a circumstance of great relief, had I found a moderate participation of office in the hands of the majority. I would gladly have left to time and accident to raise them to their just share. But their total exclusion calls for prompter corrections. I shall consult the procedure; but that done, return with joy to that state of things, when the only questions concerning a candidate shall be, Is he honest? Is he capable? Is he faithful to the Constitution?"
[4] Lincoln used the "spoils" system to build up the Republican party. Cf. Fish, *op. cit.*, p. 170 ff.
[5] Cf. Fish, *op. cit.*, p. 97.

[6] Marcy's speech and cf. Fish, *op. cit.*, p. 156; for the contemporary prevalence of the idea see *Better Government Personnel* (New York, 1936).
[7] Ellbridge Gerry: Rotation "keeps the mind of man *in equilibrio*, and teaches him the feelings of the governed, and better qualifies him to govern in turn." (Fish, *op. cit.*, p. 81.)
[8] *Ibid.*: "a check to the overbearing insolence of office."
[9] Jackson's message.
[10] Cf. Henry Clay (1829): "Incumbents, feeling the instability of their situation, and knowing their liability to periodic removals, at

tween the President and the Senate for the control of appointments and removals a fifth; and a terrific waste of time and labor on the part of the President and heads of departments, coupled with the real pain of refusal of applications for office, the sixth. Never had a state been so debauched. Officials were chosen through the loosely jointed machinery of Congressmen and the local party "bosses." Moreover, the parties preyed upon the officeholders' salaries, by "assessing" them at so much per cent for contributions to campaign funds, and this again caused a counterpressure for higher salaries, so that indirectly the parties were paid by the state. Finally, the political appointees were obliged to be politicians all the time to secure their future reinstatement. Worse still, politics and administration fell into public contempt.

Machinery of the Spoils System. How could the state continue to exist without governmental downfall? Even in a "spoils" system some good officers are chosen; and even in a "spoils" system there is not a clean sweep at every party change, since the newly elected executive has regard to his public prestige and has a modicum of regard for the public good, and once elected is independent for four years. There were Presidents who stood out against the removal of capable officials. Further, a long spell of office by the same party mitigated the revolutions in the service. Then it takes a great force to damage public administration very badly and very obviously. Finally, not until the 1870's and 1880's did the pressure of a complex, technical, and expectant civilization cause the federal authority to become active on a large scale requiring urgently a body of permanent and specially skilled officials.

Through what instrumentalities had the "spoils system" worked?—of course,

through the powers of appointment and removal. The constitution says that [11]

[the President] shall nominate, and by and with the advice and consent of the Senate, shall appoint ambassadors, other public Ministers and consuls, judges of the Supreme Court, and all other officers of the United States, whose appointments are not herein otherwise provided for, and which shall be established by law: but the Congress may by law vest the appointment of such inferior officers, as they think proper, in the President alone, in the courts of law, or in the heads of departments.

As to the power of removal, as we have shown, it is disputed whether it is an unlimited and illimitable power of the executive, or whether the Senate must be consulted, and whether Congress, having established an office and settled its tenure, thereby limits the Presidential power of removal.

What of the evolution of these powers? (1) "Ambassadors, other public ministers and consuls, judges of the Supreme Court" and all other officers—not "inferior" officers that is, at least heads of departments—were left to the tender mercies of the politicians, that is, the President and the Senate. The history of these officers is the history of political appointments—some justifiable, others not. (2) Over the rest of the "officers" Congress may exercise power, and it may operate by giving authority to the President, with the advice and consent of the Senate, the President alone, the heads of departments, and the courts of law. On this basis Congress had committed the bulk of the high administrative and technical offices to the mercies of the President and the Senate.[12] It committed to the same system the postmasters, the collectors of customs and internal revenues, registrars and receivers at land offices, district attorneys and marshals, officers of the Army and the Navy, and officials of the public health service and coast and geodetic survey—this is the bulk of contemporary

short terms, without any regard to the manner in which they have executed their trust, will be disposed to make the most of their uncertain offices while they have them, and hence we may expect immediate cases of fraud, predation and corruption."

[11] Article II, Sect. 2, para. 2.
[12] Cf. Lewis Mayers, *The Federal Service* (New York, 1922), p. 33.

spoils. It vested some power in heads of departments, and these, too, are liable to patronage, where Congress has not stated the mode of the appointment—which it has the perfect right to do.[13] Finally, after long years of administrative demoralization and with intense reluctance, Congress established an agency, the Civil Service Commission, with power to recruit, by merit, the officials which the President had the discretion to classify by executive order. This has given rise to the "merit" system for over 90 per cent of the whole of the federal service.

Obstacles to Reform. An intense struggle was needed to create the merit system, and the issue was complicated by these causes. First, the Congress was anxious to keep power out of the hands of the President and the heads of departments. To leave appointments solely to them was to give the executive the power to overcome the separation of powers (which was a dogma) by the use of patronage. Hence the chief preoccupation of Congress was rather to limit the removal power of the President than to increase his appointing power.

Next, by an unfortunate faith in the short tenure of offices, laws were passed establishing four-year terms of office for many official posts. This, the instrument of the theory of "rotation of office," was an application to administrative office, of measures properly taken, to secure the dependence of responsible assemblies upon the people. By a series of laws of 1820, 1851, 1872, and 1894, tens of thousands of officials in the customs, land, postal, and immigration services were made appointable for four-year terms. All these officers had to seek reappointment, and face the possibility of not being reappointed, every four years. In these circumstances, even where the Civil Service Commission examined the officers (as in the case of the postmasters), the examination could rarely provide good officials owing to the insecurity of the situation. The four-year term was an encouragement to political favoritism. All classified

[13] Cf. *U. S. v. Perkins* (1886), 116, U. S. 483.

offices and many others established by statute are permanent.

TOWARD A SPOILS-FREE CIVIL SERVICE

COMPARED with 1880 and the previous hundred years, a remarkable purification has taken place. Why and how?

Impulses to Reform. It seems that the exceptional irregularities in the Civil War period, due to the extension of government activity, had awakened attention to the problem. But the example of England in the preceding decade began to have its full force upon travelers and upon certain parliamentarians, like Thomas Allen Jenckes, Carl Schurz, George William Curtis, who were much above the average of their colleagues.

By 1872 civil service reform had forced its way into the party platforms, and in 1876, Hayes, the Republican candidate for President, and the favorite of the reformers, was elected President. His election was followed by the appointment of Carl Schurz as Secretary of the Interior, and the commissioning of Norman B. Eaton (afterward first Civil Service Commissioner) to write a history of the civil-service reform movement in Great Britain. The "political assessment" system came to be detested by officeholders and people and was the source of constant recrimination between the political parties, thus spreading the knowledge of abuses among the electorate. In 1876 Congress passed an act prohibiting the making or the payment of assessments among all servants or employees not appointed by the President and Senate. This and the executive order implementing it were little heeded. A Senate investigation committee of 1879 [14] showed (*a*) that the assessments were raised on a regular system, "follow-up" letters being sent to defaulters, and (*b*) that the President had approved the circular asking for contributions. The practice of assessments continued in the election of 1882.[15] In 1881

[14] Report, 46th Congress, 1st and 2nd session, No. 427, p. 2.
[15] E.g., Thomas, *Return of the Democratic Party to Power in 1884*, p. 85.
He says: "Great political battles cannot be

the National League for Civil Service Reform had been established; and in several states small associations were already at work. A case was fought in the courts, which held that the law against "assessment" was constitutional, and that the offender, the New York State Republican committee chairman, was guilty. At about the same time fraudulent arrangements were made by the second Assistant Postmaster-General and various subordinates to increase the number of certain special postal services and increase the pay for existent ones—profits to be shared. The propaganda of the reformer frightened the parties into inclusion of reform on their platforms. The evils had been fully exposed in the House Committee's report of 1868.[16]

An attempt at improvement had already been made in 1871. A Congressional statute had authorized the President to prescribe such regulations for admission in the service "as may best promote the efficiency thereof," and ascertain the fitness of each candidate in respect to age, health, character, knowledge, and ability "for the branch of the service into which he seeks to enter," and for this purpose to "employ suitable persons to conduct such inquiries." The President also obtained power thereby to regulate the conduct of persons appointed to the civil service. However, Congress, having given the President this power, failed to provide money for its execution. The result was the concentration of the reformers upon a new and more comprehensive statute. Neither party wished to spoil its chances for the Presidential election of 1884: the Democrats were in sight of power, the Republicans were within an ace of losing

it. For the few all-important votes an important, if unpleasant, concession had to be made. The reforming Congressmen, "exceedingly holy and wise," as an opponent called them, pressed. In 1883 the Senate, led by Pendleton of Ohio, and acting upon a bill drafted by Eaton (the historian of British civil service reform and the New York civil service), after a long and mainly scoffing debate [17] passed the bill by 38 to 5, with 33 members absent, while in the House 155 were in favor, 47 against, and 87 abstained. In the Senate, the majority was composed of 25 Republicans and 13 Democrats; in the House, of 102 Republicans and 49 Democrats. In the Senate the opposition were Democratic votes, the absentees mixed; in the House opposition and abstainers were well mixed among the parties.

The Civil Service Act. The Civil Service Act of 1883 is the legal foundation of the system of recruiting the officials to the non-Presidential-Senatorial positions, and of their various rights and duties, especially political. What are its main features? [18]

(1) It gave the President the power to appoint by and with the advice and consent of the Senate, three persons, not more than two of them adherents of the same party, as civil service commissioners, to constitute the United States Civil Service Commission. They are removable by the President alone.

(2) Their duty is to aid the President, as he may request, to prepare suitable rules to carry the Act into effect. These rules once promulgated, it is the duty of

---

won in this way. This committee cannot hope to succeed in the pending struggle, if those most directly benefited by success are unwilling or neglect to aid in a substantial manner. We are on the skirmish line of 1884 . . . unless you think that our grand old party ought not to succeed help it now. . . It is hoped that by return mail you will send a voluntary contribution equal to 2 per cent. of your annual compensation, as a substantial proof of your earnest desire for the success of the Republican party this fall . . ."
[16] Cf. 40th Congress, 2nd session, ii, No. 47.

[17] Cf. Senate Report, 47th Congress 1st session, No. 576; *Congressional Record*, 47th Congress 2nd session, 200-67.
[18] Cf. an act to improve and regulate the civil service of the United States (January 16, 1883, 22 Stat. 403). For the law and regulations and executive orders relating to the service, see any annual report of the U. S. Civil Service Commission (U. S. Government Printing Office), Appendix; and especially *Civil Service Acts and Rules, Statutes, Executive Orders and Regulations, with Notes and Legal Decisions*, as amended from time to time (Superintendent of Documents).

all officers of the United States wherever the rules pertain to help them into effect.

(3) These rules shall provide for the following, "as nearly as the conditions of good administration will warrant." (*a*) Open competitive examinations must be held to test the fitness of applicants for the public service now classified or to be classified. (*b*) The examinations are to be practical in character and to relate to fitness to discharge the duties of the service into which the applicants seek to be appointed. (*c*) The offices of each class are to be filled by those graded highest at the examinations. (*d*) The offices in Washington are to be apportioned among the various states and territories on the basis of their population. (*e*) A period of probation precedes absolute appointment. (*f*) Necessary exceptions from the rules are to be stated in the rules, and reasons to be given in the annual reports of the Commission. (*g*) The Commission is to conduct the examinations, make an annual report to the President for transmission to Congress, giving, among other things, suggestions for the more effectual accomplishment of the Act.

(4) Excluded from the effect of the Act are laborers and workmen and persons nominated for confirmation by the Senate.

To whom, now, did appointment by merit apply? It applied to the clerical positions already "classified" by an Act of 1853,[19] and a list of positions similar to these. Then, the act provided for the progressive classification of other servants by the initiative of the President and the help of the heads of departments.

The dynamic power was thus given to the President, and the history of "classification," or additions to the service recruited by the Civil Service Commission, is since then a history of the courage and vacillations of the Presidents,[20] the exigencies of party warfare and the craven fears of Congressmen, and the uninterrupted toil of the various Civil Service Reform Leagues.

This is enormous progress. Let us recapitulate the main features of the American system:

(1) Many important administrative and technical posts are still subject to political patronage.

(2) There are many minor positions in Washington and the "field" subject to political patronage.

(3) Some of the first category are appointed and maintained on principles of efficiency; some in the second category (e.g., Presidentially-appointed postmasters, and laborers) are examined by the Commission, but in these cases three candidates are presented for each nomination by the President, confirmable by the Senate.

(4) The great bulk of the service, professional, scientific, and clerical, is appointed after open competitive examination by the Civil Service Commission. However, by the rules made by the President under the Act, the Civil Service, "where the conditions of good administration warrant," excepts certain positions from competitive examinations and gives instead noncompetitive examinations. There are exceptions possible (by Rule II, Section 3) from examination altogether, amounting to several hundred in the central departments alone—without reasonable ground, having regard to their usual nature. There are certain exceptions from civil service appointment by statute. There are certain exceptions possible by Rule II, Section 10, where people may be appointed without examination when certain specific vacancies occur. This has made possible the appointments of special experts. Further, executive orders make special exceptions of experts, but mainly of widows of former civil servants, "for charity," about twenty to thirty a year.

The United States is not yet adequately strong in its higher administrative service, but it has other strengths: its attention to the theory and practice of classification; its experiments in tests for manipulative and simple executive officers; its contribution to the theory of "efficiency ratings"; its concern for postentry training;

---

[19] Cf. Mayer, *op. cit.*, pp. 41 and 47.
[20] W. D. Foulke, *Fighting the Spoilsman* (New York, 1919).

and its recently announced intention to utilize the various departments as recruiting agencies.

Spoils Nearly Ended. In the fiscal year ending June, 1930, the federal authority employed in the executive civil service [21] about 609,000 officials. Of these, 462,000 were subject to competitive examination on all the rules of the Civil Service Commission.[22] The rest, some 140,000, or nearly 25 per cent of the total, were appointed by other persons, it may be upon technically good rules of efficiency, it may be entirely out of political considerations. They were the offices in the gift of the politicians from the President downward, by the President with confirmation of the Senate, or by heads of departments, but some were subjected by Presidential decree to objective tests of merit.

How were the 140,000 constituted? The largest quota, comprising perhaps 98 per cent, consisted of post office employees [23] and artisans and unskilled laborers, and subordinate and temporary custodial and manipulative officials. The others, or some 3000 offices, consisted of the high directive and technical headships of the departments and ancillary bureaus in Washington and in the "field service." Many of the 98 per cent were subject to no objective tests of merit by any agency; and only a small proportion of the 3000 offices represented by the 2 per cent were anything but political "spoils," and it was this 2 per cent which coincided with the English administrative grade in its highest reaches, going down in some cases to what English students would define as the higher reaches of the executive class. Then, out of the 98 per cent, the postmasters of the first, second, and third class, numbering about 15,000, were examined by the Civil Service Commission, which then presented three candidates for

each post from whom the President and the Senate appointed one. In the 98 per cent, there were also some 2000 customs and revenue officers who were subject to no rules of appointment but were Presidential-Senatorial nominees.

In the years since 1930, widespread and beneficial reforms have been carried out. In June, 1936, the numbers of federal civil servants had risen to some 824,259 under the impulse of new functions to repair past shortcomings in social and economic reform and to palliate the miseries of depression. In that year some 60 per cent only were subject to merit examination. The President's Committee on Administrative Management recommended the extension of full civil service conditions "upward, outward, and downward." The President responded with the ordering of full civil service status for all postmasters in June, 1938. Then, the Ramspeck Act of November 20, 1940, gave to the President the authority to include all offices: but it directed the exclusion from civil service only of TVA, WPA, federally owned corporations, and as the President should decide, the positions in the appointing power of President and Senate, and the assistant United States district attorneys. The Executive Orders applying the President's power in this regard (Nos. 8743, 9004, and others) brought into civil service practically all positions not then covered by it. There are some exceptions [24]—they number perhaps 40,000 or 50,000; the estimate is difficult to make—for offices of a religious, or confidential, or safety or police and detective kind, and some temporary kinds of expert assistance, all United States attorneys and marshals, collectors of revenues and customs. But broadly speaking, the federal service was practically a system removed from spoils and was applying objective tests of merit everywhere, ex-

---

[21] This includes, of course, servants of the legislature and the courts.

[22] Therefore called the "classified" civil service.

[23] About 100,000 employees and postmasters of the *1, 2,* and *3* class and "star routes." Fourth-class postmasters were put into the classified service many years ago.

[24] There are 330,325 excepted positions. Of these, 200,000 are outside the Continental United States in occupied areas. Of the rest, large groups like the TVA., the FBI., and the Foreign Service have their own merit system. Those who are still patronage may be judged from the lists on pp. 43-55 of the U. S. Civil Service Commission, *Annual Report* (1947).

cept in the highest "policy-determining" or political secretaryships and assistant secretaryships. The federal service rose to a size of 3,000,000 during the war, when, of course, the posts were special war appointments and did not confer civil service status. The tide recedes: and it is expected that the federal service will regularly employ some 1,500,000 to 2,000,000 employees. All of these with the exception of top political positions have come under civil service tests, though the Senate still has a hand in the appointment of first-, second-, and third-class postmasters, numbering some 15,000, because the Senators help to nominate for the examination.

The attainment of almost full civil service, sixty years after the passage of the Pendleton Act, may not seem a remarkable feat in the complete span of a man's life. However, the achievement must be measured against all the grim and insidious opposition to it by politicians of all parties. The nastiest type of public men have set their hands again and again to prevent or mitigate or ruin the civil service system. The reform has been accomplished in the midst of a great industrial revolution, and convulsions of the public conscience. It cannot even be said that the battle is won forever since attacks continue, and one or the other party may one day debauch the service again for the sake of its electoral benefit.

THE CONTEMPORARY SITUATION IN THE
HIGHER CIVIL SERVICE

In the United States, then, at the present time, most technical posts, but not all, are filled by those who have been selected by the Civil Service Commission. Many of the civil servants' posts equivalent to the British or European officials at the very top, and between the minister downwards to the executive class in the nontechnical and merely administrative posts are political appointments. But this does not connote the entire absence of civil servants equivalent to the English, French, and German administrative grades appointed by merit. Only, the Americans have classified their servants in more technical terms and prescribe technical examinations for them. Below the rank of bureau chief, which is headship of a principal branch of a department, come the clerks of various ranks, and these are appointed by merit down as far as the unskilled laborer positions, an occupation exempted from the normal civil service tests but not from special tests which have in fact been established.

Absence of Satisfactory Top Management. Yet almost all offices down to and including some of the bureau chiefs are political appointments. (The Hoover Commission Report on "Departmental Management," page 9, shows that 32 out of 73 bureau chiefs are still not under civil service.) What is this political stratum? It includes the heads of departments or secretaries who are cabinet ministers, and properly, as in Europe, political appointments. Then, according to European practice, there would be a political undersecretary. In the United States instead there are occasional political undersecretaries, but always one or more political assistant secretaries for each department.

Next, downwards after the politicians, we should expect to find, as in British or German practice, the Permanent Secretary, a professional appointment by promotion after long service, at the head of a large staff of professional civil servants going down through all ranks in the capital and the provinces to the industrial staffs. But not so in the United States. In the first place, there is no counterpart to the Permanent Secretary and his immediate deputy with authority over a whole department. The next officers below the little group of political appointees are chiefs of various bureaus either independent of the departments (as the Government Printing Office) or subdivisions, rather independent, of the department. These are directed not by a Permanent Secretary, with a staff of assistant secretaries and principals as in England, but by the political assistant secretaries above, and then by the bureau chiefs. In other words, there is no career officer who links together and directs all the bureau chiefs in a whole department. Where the British have a well-forged career link between the civil service levels from the highest point downwards and the politicians at the pinnacle of authority, the United States administration has only a political hiatus or a meddler and some assistant meddlers.

Five factors obstruct America's way to the provision of satisfactory top management in her administration. (1) The first is an undue attachment to "technical" tests—a product still of a society and economy in the making and on the make. The Civil Service Act of 1883 is still the authority for "technical" tests. It must be remembered, also, that recruitment is not truly competitive: it is qualifying, and those that get the qualifying marks are held on the register for a length of time until a job turns up. Also, the "rule of three" prevailed: that is, the Civil Service Commission certifies three successful candidates for each post to the head of the department, from which he chooses one. The severity is lacking. (2) Politicians do not trust any top administrators but their own party friends—at least, as yet, not enough for long enough. (3) There prevails a partly genuine, partly propaganda idea that an administrative class is a social "class"—which is nonsense. (4) It is said that Congressmen like to make contact directly with bureau chiefs in immediate charge of operations, and not go downwards through one top administrative chief. (5) The creed still conspicuously ferments that anyone from anywhere can do anything, or should be allowed to try.

Political Chiefs and the Administrative Chasm. Accordingly, in the American administrative departments, the political secretaries and assistant secretaries occupy the place but hardly perform the functions of the Permanent (that is, the career) Secretary and his immediate career assistants in the British system. The American system is maintained by a number of arguments: some sound, others specious. It is sound to have political chiefs appointable and removable by the victorious party in the election: that is proper democracy. It is sound, though rather expensive, to have many assistant secretaries. It is not sound to give to those assistant secretaries the responsibilities that are administrative at the same time as they hold those that are policy-determining and politically punishable. For the road to the latter positions is not the road to administrative competence. If the assistant secretaries must be appointed, it is unsound not to appoint additional men to act as permanent career departmental chiefs in whom all the operative authority and work of the department shall focus. From these permanent departmental chiefs, upward, and suitably advised by the bureau chiefs, there should ascend departmental advice on policy and day-by-day law-fulfillment reports to the political chiefs above. The unfortunate crux of American administrative difficulties lies in the unfilled chasm between the political chiefs and the bureau chiefs, and with it the fact that the President "needs help" which the system still does not provide, and never can until the day of drastic remedies.

I compute that at the top of the United States civil service there are some 9000 professional and scientific and 7000 clerical, administrative, and fiscal posts above the salary of $7000. This is 16,000—perhaps a few more should be added to the top administrative group, organized as such; it is disintegrated. (The Hoover Commission, in "Departmental Management," page 60, making a *different* computation of "top management staff," totals 16,000 also!) A magistral pioneer study by Professors Arthur Macmahon and John D. Millett has revealed to us the true state of the national administration at its top levels.[25]

Vigor and freshness of mind have been extolled by many as the contribution which the political group of assistant secretaries may be expected to bring to the conduct of administration. What, in fact,

---

[25] A. W. Macmahon and J. D. Millett, *Federal Administrators* (New York, 1939).

do they bring? They are appointed on practically pure political (that is, campaign) considerations, nominated by the President, to be confirmed by the Senate. They are sometimes appointed before the secretary, the head of the department, is himself appointed, so that he comes into office, not quite knowing what his policy is yet to be, to find a *damnosa hereditas,* infantile in novelty, already on his doorstep. No party principle or platform unites all the assistants; none the secretaries: none the secretaries and their assistants. Loyalty is to a particle of the platform. Hence they are all specialists as to loyalties and their ability. Departmentally, secretaries and assistants have often been at terrible odds with each other as regards policy, ability, and personality. Their typical periods of office are two, or three, or four years: scant time, indeed, to master their departmental responsibilities or to understand their authority or to acquaint themselves with talent or to design instruments of cooperation. Instead, there is a fitful feverishness of activity, or impassivity and fecklessness. Such a means of appointing the highest directors of departmental administration gives little encouragement to interdepartmental cooperation. A majority of them are lawyers; some are businessmen and journalists, others teachers and owner-farmers; most of them have been to college: but what, administratively speaking, what merits do these unspecific qualifications provide? These haphazardly selected men, put like cuckoos into the position which could be occupied by a group of civil service career administrative statesmen, rarely include career men —rarely include experts in a given field of administration. Civil servants refuse to be promoted to such positions because they would be exchanging security for insecurity of tenure.

Owing to the operation of political parties in the United States and the influence of sectional and special pressures, the political chiefs are at best second-rate. While some are appointed at the age of forty to fifty, when administrative vigor and eagerness is likely to have given way to steady wisdom (if the wisdom was already in reserve), most of them are actually appointed at the age of fifty to sixty. Where then is the freshness of mind?

Thus, they cannot give administrative direction and counsel as their permanent (and younger) British counterparts can. They are faded second-raters (in a composite picture of course). They cannot freshen the tone of the enormous agencies over which they confusedly preside, or assure a more virile responsibility on the part of the mass of their subordinates. As the study by Macmahon and Millett concludes: assistant secretaries are "idling cogs in the national machinery." [26]

Bureau Chiefs as Administrative Bridges. This situation puts a tremendous burden for the good of the state on the bureau chiefs. They are hardly able to bear it; but they are the best that American practice now affords as coordinators of other peoples' work, leaders of large sections of administration, links between their own branches and those of other similarly placed chiefs, and advisers upward on the development of the laws, regulations, and policy.

Who are they? Macmahon studied only 62; Hoover, 73. But there are, at a guess, as no one can tell exactly, perhaps 1200 officials at bureau-chief level, whatever the title. Macmahon says they are "the key figures in national administration." Of the 62, 27 were full civil service officials, and 3 appointed by special terms equivalent to putting them into that career-tenure category. Another 14 had been promoted from inside the civil service, while 4 had virtually been promoted from civil service, state, or local administration. Thus, altogether 48 might be regarded as fully or practically career men. Of the 14 remaining, 8 had been recruited from outside, from work of a related nature, and 6 were purely political appointees.

They are nevertheless not men of assured and very long service. Some of the posts which are unprotected are lost at a change in the Presidency. Most others

---

[26] *Ibid.,* p. 302.

arrive at their status at about the age of forty-eight when retirement is not so very far off; while others resign to take jobs which may better provide for their later years. The jobs are held for something like eight to sixteen years and over; these stretches of time are substantial, and are remarkably so compared with the transient assistant secretaries. Men in comparable positions in the British civil service get there by about the age of forty; so that they have almost always twenty years of the highest responsibility before them, though not always in the same department. (My comparison is with a rank somewhere between that of principal and assistant secretary in the British system—admittedly a difficult comparison.)

These bureau chiefs are technicians or specialists. They are not an "administrative class" or "civil administrators" as in France since 1946. They have entered a department by an examination which required technical proficiency in the specific services of a grade of a branch of a special department. Most of them had a higher education: and more than half of them took postgraduate studies, many of which were specialist. It is understood that the way to promotion is to a large degree paved with postgraduate studies. But usually, American undergraduate education is not yet of the intellectual standard of British or European—there are fine exceptions, of course.

Thus, as the study demonstrates: "Bureau chiefs are critical links in the managerial chain. Their essential permanence is a prerequisite of command through the hierarchy as a whole." [27]

Proposed Reforms. What is the conclusion? The United States lacks administrative advisership or statesmanship at the highest level. Some bureau chiefs have fine gifts of general counsel, comprehension, and managerial ability. But the bureaus are chopped pieces of what should be some system (I do not say "a" system). The pieces are too finely chopped. How can they be put together to give the President and the secretaries

and the Congress the panoramic counsel they need? In the British system an administrative class has been the chosen instrument. It has some disadvantages: it requires that the exceptions, those who cannot rise to the height of responsibility and service, shall be left unpromoted; and it may suffer from the loss of the valuable assets that a technician with administrative gifts could contribute. But the only present remedy in the United States administration boils down to looking for the exceptions among the specialists and technicians, and culling them untutored, or giving them tuition, in administrative responsibilities and then seeing that they are transferred into the right places. If the reader will study the ingenious devices proposed by the authors of the Macmahon and Millett study for overcoming the infirmities in the system which they were at the most honorable pains to reveal, it will be seen that the exertions are so much more considerable than the promise of success that more serious changes are necessary. Something like the British system is necessary: I do not say identical. Its basic tenets, I think, are unavoidable; especially so where state activity involves the management and marshaling of the abilities of one and a half million civil servants, in a framework of political leadership in which the executive has an enforced separation—settlement with the Congress, and where the two may be estranged, even bitterly hostile, in cunning ways, because a different party is the incumbent of each. Man and wife being estranged, perhaps the children might benefit if trusty housekeepers managed the home—under direction, of course.

Apart from the internal meliorative suggestions of the Macmahon and Millett study, two ways have been proposed: (1) the appointment of administrative secretaries, and (2) the gradual building up of a class of administrative technicians.

(1) In some departments, though very few, there has been established—as a simple result of intradepartmental experience and initiative, and the empirical discovery of someone who merited the posi-

tion—the job of administrative assistant or administrative secretary. This position is close to the secretary, and provides for the services of general managerial and advisory duties. It could be universally installed. If it were, with a group of cadets to aid and follow their chief—and if there were a suitable avenue of entry into the group, with careful selection of the candidates whether from inside or outside the service, recruited in the hope of a regular career—it would provide the administrative body we think is indispensable to the government.

The Hoover Commission proposed that, under the department chief, the under secretary, and one or more assistant secretaries, all political appointments, there should be generally in addition, "an administrative assistant secretary who might be appointed solely for administrative duties of a housekeeping and management nature and who would give continuity in top management. They and certain other officials, as in the Treasury Department, where length of tenure makes appointment from the career service preferable, should be appointed from that service." [28] This is a truly ominous abdication! They have left policy to the bureau chiefs; they have assigned major policy where it has always been, to the politically appointed chief and his assistants; but all they want the "administrative assistant secretary" for is "housekeeping and management" duties, and continuity in top management! This is a lamentable misunderstanding of what is needed: beneath the political chiefs, a permanent, career, brains trust, to be responsible for advising on long-term policy, for expert policy assistance to the political chiefs, to be their friendly and subservient critics, as well as to see that the whole department is a smoothly running concern in its personnel, salary, disciplinary, cooperative, research, and fulfilment and enforcement responsibilities. What is needed is not merely a broom but a brain.

(2) Something of the nature of an alternative has been tried since 1934. Some American students of administration, above all Professor Leonard D. White of the University of Chicago, had for long been impressed with the value of an administrative stratum which would comprise not merely technicians and special experts, but men of general education, comprehension, and high intellectual ability.[29] He was influential as adviser and later as member of the Civil Service Commission. The Commission set up a Junior Civil Service Examiners' Group. The intention was to provide an entry into administrative situations. The minimum educational qualification was a bachelor's degree from an institution of recognized standing. Some 15,000 applicants between 1934 and 1941 took the examination (itself testimony to an enhanced interest in public service as a career); of these 7000 passed, while over 2000 in due course found positions in various types of work in the federal service. Nearly 2500 more entered this group from other examinations.

The examination was subsequently consolidated with one for junior professional assistant, still preserving the great width of its general appeal in the range of examination options. The scope was narrowed, however, by the requirement of special work in economics, political science, and public administration, so that some potential candidates were deterred from entry. Ten years' experience attests some moderate success of this mode of recruitment, as a few of the ablest of the rising civil servants come from this source. After World War II, the experiment continues; junior administrative technician, is, characteristically in the American scene, the title of the posts.

Yet how far from answering the real problem this innovation is may be seen from a consideration of (a) the posts that fall within the title of junior professional assistant, and (b) the qualifications. (a) The examination recruits administrative

---

[28] "General Management of the Executive Branch," pp. 38-39.

[29] Cf. his *Government Career Service* (Chicago, 1936).

technicians, archeologists, astronomers, bacteriologists, chemists, economists, engineers, geographers, legal assistants, librarians, mathematicians, metallurgists, patent examiners, physicists, psychologists, social science analysts, and statisticians. Already, then, the importance of the reform must be reduced to the administrative technicians, economists, social science analysts and statisticians—for these are the only groups in the list who are more especially fitted by education and purpose than the rest, who are chiefly the products of education in the natural sciences. The economists and the statisticians must be regarded also with some doubt, because their education is normally extremely narrow and specialized, even if it goes deep. It must be remembered that we exclude from the discussion natural ability to administer: for that is a factor common to all civil services and methods of recruitment, while we are here trying to isolate the effect of recruitment and educational requirements.

(b) When, again, we turn to the qualifications for entrance, we note two factors markedly different from those of Britain and France and from the classic system of Germany to 1933. First, entrance is possible between the ages of 18 to 35: much younger and very much older than in the other services. The problem of recruiting at too advanced an age has already been ventilated.[30] Second, the prerequisite for entrance to the position of junior administrative technician is *either* a full four-year course at a college or university leading to a bachelor's degree with at least 24 semester hours in public administration, business administration, political science, or industrial management or industrial engineering, with credit also for statistics, accounting, economics, psychology, and sociology to a certain limit— *or* at least three years of progressively responsible experience in general office work, one year of which must have been in administrative duties of the kind of work described for these recruits—*or* a combination of experience and education

at the rate of one academic year of education for nine months of experience. What then is the description of the work? This: [31]

Administrative Technicians will perform or assist in performing responsible work in one or more specialized fields of administration. The duties include assisting in organizational and procedural studies; preparing and reviewing budget estimates; doing recruitment, placement, position classification, and related personnel work; and performing other administrative duties.

When this is compared with the descriptions of the work of the higher civil service classes in Britain, France and pre-1933 Germany, the paltry, inadequate nature of American administrative reform along this particular road becomes all too plain.

The Problem Not Answered. The problem of inadequacy in the higher civil service is not solved, for two reasons.

(1) In the first place, no recognition has yet been given to the principle of an administrative class or administrative "brains trust." As yet it is not accepted that a career of administrator should be set up, devoted to administration, in the sense given to that word in the higher civil services of Britain and France.[32] The classification of the federal service provides no place for such a career, leading up to administrative assistant or secretary—as suggested by reformers but not yet installed. Most of those recruited by the examination just described have not undertaken the general work of administration—which means, in our context, the highest tasks of advice of ends and means in policy—but specialist services in personnel work, financial controls emanating from the Bureau of the Budget, and technical supervision and assistance in administrative organization and methods. The function of *thought,* comprehensive and synoptic, supplied by a widespread career group—*thought* covering grand sections of the whole administrative apparatus,

---

30 Cf. pp. 786 and 803 above.

31 Cf. Announcement No. 75, October, 1947, U. S. Civil Service Commission.
32 See especially pp. 786 and 822 above.

and sweeping its gaze over the whole of the Government from a lofty plane, unencumbered by administrative and clerical triviality—is lacking.

(2) The examinations show triviality also—no width, no philosophic wrestling —they are back into the routine of their subjects.[33] As a very enlightened examinee in this same entrance examination has said: [34]

It must be recorded, however, that the examination does not reflect the outlook of those who hold with Felix Frankfurter that our institutions of higher learning must be training schools for public service, not through utilitarian courses, but by the whole sweep of their culture and discipline.

One of the merits of British and French civil service recruitment is the very close correspondence between the educational system and the public service. This is made possible, fruitfully, by the coherence of the educational system, the consequence partly of a long history of culture and partly of the relative smallness of the territory served. But a deeper cause emerges as we reflect on these truths: both public services and educational systems are suffused with a like sense of standards of social conscience and mind. The United States is too young and otherwise busy as yet to have developed these. The time is fast approaching when America will have become a society, which is an aggregation of human beings living in each other's company on the basis of spiritual principle. As it is, the civil service tends to be merely one other kind of job.

In spite of much thought and many inquiries and reports every other year, and in spite of many audible claims that the daylight was about to break, in spite of millions of dollars spent in research on the subject by the learned foundations, the Hoover Commission could not but reveal great disappointment with the state of the public services. "Personnel Management," its chief contribution to the problems says,[35] "Not enough time and effort are being spent on recruiting our best young men and women for junior professional, scientific, technical, and administrative posts." It observes [36] that, of some two million persons in the federal service, no less than a half a million persons a year must be recruited "to fill vacancies caused by turn-over," admittedly "an indication of the existence of low morale." Yet most of the Commission's report is concerned with salaries and minor personnel practices and gadgets. Only Professor J. K. Pollock, who entered his own report [37] exhibits the glimmer of an insight into the problem of getting and properly placing in important policy positions "superior native talent."

In the light of this mole's-eye view of what service the Republic needs, it makes one almost grudge to acknowledge the possibility of the wisdom of the Commission's recommendation, that, under the authority of the Civil Service Commission, each department should assume responsibility for developing its own recruitment program, in order to meet its own special requirements. But, even that seems to re-enthrone the special expert, and to threaten the recruitment of departmental hierarchies, who, at the brains-trust level, will find cooperation difficult, since they will have remained in their own departments for many years after having come in with special talents for and special loyalties to it rather than to the federal service as a whole. It is another step away from coordination and a single career service with all the possibilities of cross-fertilization by transfers, within a single service framework and devotion. Patriots must be sick at heart to realize that almost all that has come out of the Commission, at much cost, and with so many years of administrative

---

[33] Cf. Princeton bicentennial volume, J. McLean (ed.), *Universities and the Public Service* (1949); cf. sample papers, obtainable from the British and United States Civil Service Commission. Cf. also V. B. Zimmerman and Dwight Waldo, "A Worm's Eye-View," *Public Administration Review*, Winter, 1942.
[34] *Ibid.*

[35] Page 3.
[36] Page 5.
[37] Page 47 ff.

studies behind it, is in Professor Pollock's words, "a report inclined to envisage the problem of building a career system entirely in terms of higher pay, promotions, and transfers." [38]

Postentry Training. The theory that training after entry into the public service was necessary to ensure the full development of the latent talents of each entrant, and to supplement a program of promotions based on the discovery of a gift for administration, is an especially American idea: more contributions have been made to this subject in the United States than in any other country. Indeed, the British innovations of the postwar era are very much the direct adoption of American ideas.

Several American departments at the federal level have for a long time instituted public administration courses of wide scope for their officials and for others that like to attend. The school in the Department of Agriculture is especially well known. On June 24, 1938, an executive order required the Civil Service Commission to establish practical training courses for the civil service, this in cooperation with the departments and the Office of Education. The Commission was empowered to give credit in promotions and transfer tests for attendance at such courses. The Commission produced an interesting policy entitled "The United States Civil Service Commission's Part in Federal Training" (May 12, 1939). The Congress did not, however, supply the necessary funds. Nevertheless, the position of coordinator and director of training was filled; since then the departmental efforts have been encouraged, and the Commission has set up a school for the training of those who in their departmental or field work have shown aptitude for ascension to top management. The personnel officers of the various departments are the talent scouts as well as the immediate supervisors.

Each year the personnel officers of the various departments nominate several promising officials for further training.

The Civil Service Commission chooses some thirty from among these and then, on its own premises, gives them three months' training in administration. It is, of course, not a general education, but highly specialized. Nevertheless, it is important as one of the apertures through which a talent for government on a high level may be given its opportunity of service. It may be that some of the talent which is available will be thus discovered. But, necessarily, it is bound to depend on departmental altruism: and being departmental, there is no all-seeing eye to spot the men wherever they may be. An alternative method is to spot all or very many of the best brains of the school generations together at one open competitive test, as in the British and French systems of entrance to the administrative class.

In the study by Macmahon and Millett to which reference has been made, emphasis is laid upon the fact that the bureau chiefs came from and received their graduate education at colleges of wide geographical dispersion. This was praised by the writers. Their general view coincides with that of the present author's that the diversity of training, especially in the social sciences, is a good to be retained and not restricted.

TENTATIVE SUMMARY

THE condition of the United States civil service is not a desirable one, and it has both political and administrative disadvantages. We have already dealt with the political defects of the system. The administrative disadvantages are plain: many incapable of the function they ought to fulfill are appointed. The "tone" and direction of departments and bureaus are subject to frequent change. The casual incumbent is not really interested in the fate of the subordinates, while some subordinates not only suffer from insuperable political obstruction to promotion, but suspect the political forces even more than they deserve. Incentive to technical excellence is reduced. The turnover rate is

[38] Page 55.

about 2.9 per cent each month. "Of acute concern to federal officials generally, "says the Hoover Commission,[39] "is the continuous exodus of executives and key personnel from upper bracket positions." One half of nearly seven hundred of such former officials left owing to low salaries and lack of opportunity for advancement, compared with private employment. Where, indeed, are the top "brains trust" positions in the administrative ranks? They have never been created.

If professional administration is lacking at the top, who conducts the work year in year out? Probably more falls upon the chiefs of divisions, chief clerks, and officers in charge than in other governments: that is, upon the top men in the professional and scientific and clerical-administrative-fiscal posts, let us say, the 8000 of the former and 4000 of the latter earning

[39] Appendix A, page 8.

salaries of over $7000 a year. Now it is a truth borne out by the general experience that in the grades below those which we have consistently called the administrative, the nature of the entry test, and therefore of the education implied, becomes technical in the sense that it requires either special knowledge of office routine, computation, etc., or knowledge of the law and practice of the particular services of the department. Thus the American system, by keeping the highest offices in politics, leaves only the routine ones in the service (of course, excluding "technical," "scientific," "professional" occupations), and has divided administrative leadership generally speaking between (a) politicians who are amateurs and soon pass from the field, (b) technicians, and (c) subordinate clerks. It is far from adequate to the needs of contemporary America.

34

Problems Which Arise After Recruitment

HUNDREDS of thousands of persons have entered the public service. Their function gives rise to a number of difficult problems springing from the nature of that peculiar employer, the public, and that rarity which is growing so much more common, the public employees. The public demands efficiency, at the least possible cost. The employees desire conditions of employment which they define as "fair." The problems are not dissimilar to those raised in modern private industry; and, of course, there are gradations of private and public enterprise, from the pure types of each, to those which approach the identity of the other. But, we are already aware, and shall become increasingly so, that the public services have special characteristics. This will be emphatically noticed as we traverse the contest of the demand for low-cost efficiency with the demand for fairness of treatment through the medium of the special problems of promotion, efficiency rating, classification, training and discipline, morale, loyalty, and civil and industrial rights.

PROMOTION

IT is the lower grades which are most interested in the arrangements for promotion. The upper grade has no obstacle external to itself to prevent its members from rising to the highest positions according to their capacity. But a social problem of serious proportions arises for those who have not been able to afford the education necessary to enter the higher grade, but who develop capacities and the ambition and desire which often accompany them. For the civil service as a whole, the impossibility of a proper outlet for this capacity means the loss of efficiency by resignation of the best officials, and a dreadful deterioration of morale, which occurs not only among the members directly affected but among colleagues, and the sheer waste of talent which does not find its appropriate expression.

Now, all countries give a rise in pay within the grade occupied—a stipulated annual increment from a minimum to a maximum. The regulations require that these shall not be automatic, but shall be given or withheld as a reward for maintained efficiency or as a punishment for unsatisfactory work.[1] In the United States civil service, the "efficiency-rating" system is designed to secure that promotion, demotion, and retention in the service shall depend upon tested efficiency.[2] That is to say, the regulations especially direct that the increments shall not operate automatically; and certainly the tendency of thought in recent years—born of public concern about the growth of the civil services—has been to demand the punctilious execution of these regulations. But this is a rare procedure, rarer, at least,

[1] Order in Council, clauses 20 and 36. Cf. Macdonnell Commission, Fourth Report, Chap. VIII, p. 3 ff.
[2] 37 Stat. 413, Act of August 23, 1912, Sect. 4.

than the fluidity of rewards and punishments in private industry. We are at present more concerned with real promotion, that is, a rise to a higher grade.

Arrangements for Promotion. Opportunities for promotion are in all countries rare. In England before the reform of 1919 there were no formal processes for promotion, no written and comparable records of achievement, and the opportunities for promotion to a higher class, though existent, were few in proportion to the numbers in the lower grades. When the service was reclassified after the Reorganization Report of 1920, the opportunities were increased,[3] but the new clerical class (a compound of part of the intermediate, the second division, and part of the assistant clerks) still complained and complains of want of opportunity—though we have shown that substantial opportunity to rise existed for very able executive and clerical officials.[4]

What, in essence, is the source of the continual complaints of the lower classes regarding promotion? It has a threefold origin. First, the service classes and their complements are fixed at strictly the number necessary for the work to be done, and this excludes a flexibility of promotional chances according to the contemporary availability of talent. Then too, the civil servant with some years' experience is embittered to think that others will come into a class above him upon recruitment by examination for which he, perhaps, had not the economic means, and that he will have to be subordinate to such entrants and perhaps, for a time, help them to learn their departmental jobs. And finally, the tests often bring into the service people too good for their jobs—they are too young to know this, and later fret at the standstill imposed upon them by rigid classification.

This is a terrible problem and, if a time should come when most modern utilities are socialized, the system might one day be violently disrupted by the

restless spirits who seek advancement. Two things are clear: on the whole, the best economy lies in an increase of the posts open to promotion beyond the number dictated merely by the work to be done—simply to give the lower grades a continual feeling of opportunity; also, early promotion is necessary.[5]

In Germany there was no possibility at all of an intermediate-grade official's being promoted to the higher administrative class. At the most, an official of long standing and experience might be entrusted with work of the higher grade as a substitute for a short time, but he did not become one of that body either legally or socially. (Somewhat similarly, staff clerkships in the British civil service are one outlet for the clerical service.) The relationship between the higher and the subordinate grades was indeed one of the current jokes. Arrangements have been made for promotion within the lower grades. Very similar arrangements existed in France as in Germany to 1946, but the reforms we have discussed allow for substantial promotions to the higher positions. In the United States, political nominees and technically highly trained officials keep the top levels closed, but the generous age limits of entrance enable capable subordinates who continue their studies to advance by re-entry into higher positions.

Two questions are opened by these arrangements for promotion. The first is, how far do these opportunities respond to the available talent and the demand for promotion? The second is, what are the tests applied to select for promotion?

Response to Desert and Need. The first question is practically unanswerable, for there is no accurate gauge of the available talent or the extent to which mem-

---

[3] *Ibid.,* Chap. VIII.
[4] Royal Commission on the Civil Service, 1929, *Statement of Case*, Civil Service Clerical Association, and evidence of W. J. Brown, p. 70 ff.

[5] Cf. Macdonnell Commission, Fourth Report, p. 61: "It is, we think, indisputable that there is no worse training for the real duties of administration, which requires freshness of mind, individuality and judgment, than a long period of routine work, however faithfully performed; if, therefore, a man has sufficient superiority to fit him for administrative work, this fitness should be ascertained as early as possible in his career."

bers of the upper grade ought to make room for those promoted. In this lack of accurate standard lies all the force and heartache of the lower grades; for they, like all of us, are apt to assess their personal capacity much more highly than the outsider will; and none of us will admit that he is not above the average. It is probably true that the clerical grades are too highly educated for the work they have to do, and that much of their training and ability is wasted. For their tests are pitched at a height needed for their most difficult work, and as soon as they have learned their routine, their everyday tasks make no increasing demands upon them. In private industry their talents would, in a number of cases—we must admit we cannot say exactly how many—respond to the stimulus of opportunities, self-made, self-sought opportunities. But in the civil service the opportunities cannot be made, and it is no use seeking them—for the opportunities depend upon the establishment, and the establishment depends upon legislative supplies, and these in turn depend upon policy and public opinion—all matters which no individual civil servant's enterprise can influence. The spirit of resentment in the lower grades is heightened by the fact that many are excluded from the full opportunities of the public service because they have not had the economic means to go through the training and pass the examinations set for the administrative class or the equivalents thereof. Perhaps these considerations account for the enormous turnover in the United States civil service, noticed in the previous chapter, especially as private employment opportunity is so much more abundant as compared with other countries.

The Rating of Efficiency. The second question offers an interesting insight into the nature of the state. The efficiency of the promotion system turns upon the means adopted to decide the relative merits of various public servants doing very much the same work. How close is the scrutiny, and how does it compare with the method of private industry? In private industry, in the businesses of small and middle size, but definitely less and less as the firm grows bigger, there operates an intensity of selective process, unknown in public services. The prevailing dictum is that "nobody is in business for his health." The motive is gain, and the understanding is that all should try to "get on." There is a certain fatalism in the "get on" convention in that to have "got on" is accepted as a sign of desert; rather than a standard of desert being set up to determine whether a man ought to get on or not. A certain ruthlessness is exercised by both employers and employed. The employer wants the best person at the top and the worst at the bottom, and the immediate index of the rightness of choice is the profit-and-loss account. Further, the relationship between employer and managers, and often even with individual workers, is close enough for the employer to sum up personal qualities. Nor is there any sense of colleagueship to prevent the expression of such a judgment. The tradition and spirit of private industry is all against it. The employer is accountable to no one: his own conscience, with its price registry of economic loss and gain, pity, sympathy, delight in power and efficiency, is the ultimate test. Or, rather, the private employer is accountable—to the consumers; but they have so far shown inordinately little interest in anything save cheapness, plenty, and quality.

Could not this system be introduced into the public services? To ask the question is to express its absurdity, impossibility, and to reveal the differences between public and private enterprise. To give an unlimited discretion into the hands of the higher officials, and to let loose ambition in the services, must ultimately cause the aggregate of salaries to rise or fall. The legislature would be presented with fluctuating estimates, and ought to examine the causes of fluctuation and attempt to relate the efficiency of the services to the increases or decreases. But that is impossible where the staff is so large and the services are not rendered to the public upon a price system. If the legislature did not control, but permitted taxation to be raised to meet the increases without discrimination, I think we may take it that the salary bill would steadily rise. Or, suppose that it were forced down, there would be dissension among the staffs insupportable where the services to be rendered are as basic as they are said to be. The only egress from this difficulty, and, of course, it is the one taken by public services everywhere, is to lay down from time to time a set of conditions of employment which will operate fairly automatically: i.e., to limit the discretion of the superior officers and the opportunities and ambitions of the subordinates.

In private industry the variations of price, quantity, and quality cover all good and evil: in the public services the elements of good and evil in the conditions of employment largely predetermine quality and quantity. Accountability to the legislature and the public limits the number of permissible alternatives in employment policy. Further, in a "closed" service—that is, closed off from the chances of independent development by the individual of useful and money- or prestige-earning services—the sense of interpersonal equity tends to become very strong, so that considerations of justice and fairness assume an important place. Hence a special emphasis upon impartial tests of the right to promotion. If we are dependent upon our superiors and not upon our own capacity in relation to the outside world, then our superiors' judgment must be subjected to equitable rules.

Seniority and Merit. The satisfaction of the claims to advancement in the public service is therefore obliged to take place under certain forms and conditions. The tendency is always to fall back upon sheer seniority, for this method has much to commend it. It is automatic, and avoids the need for making invidious distinctions between one person and another, of placing the young over the old, of measuring the responsibility for the result of promotion.[6] (Its main difficulties

are those of legal definitions of seniority.) It is safe for the official who is charged with making promotions to say, "The man has been in the office n years!" It satisfies a sense of equality. To the older people, seniority is a defense against the newcomer; to the bulk of men and women who are not ready to run the risks of their avowed belief in themselves, it is equitable and undisturbing. Indeed, for very many situations seniority, up to a certain point, is advantageous—those situations are the simple routine clerical duties where long familiarity with office conditions and steady loyalty are the best indicia for those who are to direct several subordinates.

However, both the controlling authority of the civil service on behalf of the public[7] and the representative associations of the employees have agreed on the necessity for a more rational system—the former to secure efficient work, the latter to institute tests of merit which shall not depend upon the personal favor of a superior officer. Such tests are, in respect to merit, difficult to devise owing to the lack of an openly competitive spirit in the employees, the absence of free enterprise, and the inability exactly to relate the monetary value of each servant's work in the total produced by the service. And personal favor can only be minimized, not entirely abolished.

Examinations for Promotion. The most prevalent test of merit for promotion is now competitive records of past efficiency. However, in some of the United States

---

[6] G. Jèze, *Revue du Droit Public* (Paris, 1912), p. 505: "Promotion by grade or class by senior-ity is very much open to criticism; it suppresses emulation, renders useless zeal and intelligence in the exercise of the function. Its only advantage is negative, it stops favoritism inherent in a discretionary power. The violent reaction against favoritism and the intervention of the politicians in the career of the officials explains, without justifying, the place which is more and more given to promotion by seniority."

[7] Cf. *Begründung* to Law on Salaries, *Reichstagsdrucksache*, 3656 (1927): "Naturally one must have the right to promote capable officials beyond the limits of their normal career. This is an incentive especially valuable for all and by its use extraordinarily unique powers are awakened and made useful for all of us."

federal departments examinations are given.[8] England, for the most part,[9] certainly considers these an interference with the ordinary official work of the candidate, and where the original test has been severe, the need for a supplementary test is an unnecessary imposition. In France it has been said that examinations for promotion are inappropriate, as officials must "less prove extensive knowledge than initiative, judgment, and tact," [10] and the theory of the inexaminability of elderly candidates has been propounded.[11] In Germany examinations were required for the promotions in the lower grade, but from two thirds the way up the service this ceased, and informal reports were used. The superior official simply keeps a fairly detailed record in a portfolio: the record is called *personalakt*.

France: Favoritism Abolished For Merit. A similar system was in existence, but less efficient, in Third Republic France, and more than a suspicion of favoritism clung to the system of seniority which strongly prevailed. In that country attempts were made for many years to bring about a change—to establish a legal proportion between the number of places to be attained by seniority and the number by merit—but none of them went beyond the stage of being referred to a Parliamentary commission. The projects also included arrangements whereby the promotions should be determined by a departmental council upon which the rank and file of the staff of the grade in question should have minority representation. To the present, promotions have been made according to the decrees regulating the departments, in so far as these decrees concern promotion, but some omitted to

regulate it. When the French use the term *avancement* they are concerned with movement upward in the same class, and also movement to higher grades. The former was more subject to seniority than the latter, and mainly gave the servant a higher salary. True promotion—that is, promotion to a higher grade—was mainly at the discretion of the head of the department, which meant in practice at the instigation of the superior officers. The law of 1912 attempted to secure a limitation of favoritism by providing for promotion lists, which were, in fact, generally drawn up each year, by the head of the department in council with some subordinates. Report forms covered education, character, conduct, accuracy, relations with superiors, and public and special aptitudes, and these were rated "bad" or "excellent" or given an arithmetical grade. But this only limited political favoritism; it did little more. This kind of limitation had a long history in France; and, indeed, the possibility of recourse to the *Conseil d'État* to maintain the principles of loyalty and sincerity to the spirit of the arrangement was (and still is) a firm safeguard against dishonest promotions.

In the Fourth Republic, civil servants have at last attained a thoroughly systematic status by the *Statut Général des Fonctionnaires*,[12] and this regulates promotion though the details must be supplied by a number of subsequent decrees. There are four great categories of civil servants: *A, B, C,* and *D,* separately recruited. For *C,* and *D,* which are lower in the hierarchy, competitive examination may open the way upwards into *A* and *B,* in which a small number of places are open for promotees, certainly not more than ten per cent. Various regulations provide for in-service training and access upwards. The promotion may occur by favorable placement on the regularly es-

---

[8] L. D. White, *Government Career Service* (Chicago, 1935); Lewis Mayers, *The Federal Service* (New York, 1922).
[9] Exception in the customs service.
[10] Caillard, *Rapport, Journal Officiel*, February 3, 1907, p. 982.
[11] Cf. Project of June 1, 1920, which provided for promotion by (a) examination, (b) inscription on a table of promotion, (c) special decisions. It was arranged that in the promotions within the same class, one third at least were to be by seniority.

[12] *Loi*, No. 46-2294, October 19, 1946; and see *Journal Officiel*, April 3, 1947, for Instruction No. 1 on the application of the law; Decrees No. 47-1236, July 8, and Decree of July 24, 1947, on joint committees in *Journal Officiel* of those dates.

tablished lists of promotables, where the record of past service and currently exhibited ability and attainments decides the order of merit.

The promotion procedure within the categories (or *cadres,* as they are called) is based on annual reports of the officials.[13] These are now very much like the British civil service report forms, and have something of the character of the numerical statement of efficiency as established in the United States civil service efficiency record system, both described presently. It is highly significant that the French civil service has adopted these ideas, and they owe much to the fact that some officials of the *Conseil d'État* and others were, during the German occupation, with the French forces in America or Britain. This is shown also by the establishment of joint committees of higher officials and representatives of the lower ranks for each department, very much like the British civil service Whitley Councils to be described shortly. These review the promotion lists, and they may at the request of a civil servant consider the revision of the list in the interest of the complainant. The list, which grades officials in order of merit, is founded on "a careful examination of the professional value" of the officials. It must be shown to all officials three days after it is made up, so that a challenge may be made by interested parties. No lower-grade officials can pass on the promotions of higher grade.

Within the categories there are two kinds of promotion: by *échelon* and by grade. The first is within the grade: it occurs by seniority and efficiency record, and brings to the promotee an advance in salary. The average time an official of average ability may be expected to spend in each *échelon* is the basis of efficiency: in proportion as his efficiency record marks show he is above the average, the years he is to spend in the *échelon* are reduced, and he gets quicker promotion; in proportion as he does not come up to the average, he stays where he is or may be retired. When he is at the top of his

échelon he may get promotion to a higher grade, but here seniority will not be taken into account: it is at the pure discretion of the higher service to select by merit.

Britain: Report Forms and Promotion Boards. The most ambitious schemes are the British and American. In the British civil service the system revolves around the annual report form and the departmental promotion boards introduced in 1921. Posts with a salary of less than £700 a year are involved.

The report form repays consideration. It prescribes a number of human qualities: knowledge *(a)* of branch, and *(b)* of department, personality and force of character, judgment, power of taking responsibility, initiative, accuracy, address and tact, power of supervising staff, zeal, and official conduct. (It is an extraordinary thing that exactly ten qualities are enumerated—is it due to addiction to ten questions in examination papers or the Ten Commandments?) But the relative importance of these qualities varies with different posts, and the fitness of an officer for promotion depends upon his personal combination of those qualities requisite to the work in the vacant post. The further down the scale of routine work, for example, the more would knowledge of branch and accuracy count; where the official comes into contact with the public, address and tact would be "weighted"; in the management of other people, personality and force of character and power of supervising staff would stand out. These qualities are then judged by the certifying officer as above, below, or on the average of the grade. Exceptional qualities, good or bad, are included in the report. Until 1938, a judgment was then made whether the officer was *(a)* eminently fitted for special and early promotion, *(b)* fitted for promotion but not for exceptional promotion, or *(c)* not fitted for promotion at present. If an official fell under the third judgment or was below the average of the grade through faults entirely his own, it was part of the equity of the scheme that he should be informed of this.

In 1938, as the result of a Whitley

---

[13] *Loi,* No. 46-2294, October 19, 1946, Title **IV.**

Council inquiry, the gradings were made rather more varied, thus: exceptionally well qualified; highly qualified; qualified; and not yet qualified. The gradings for the various qualities were increased from "above" or "below" average and average, to outstanding, very good, satisfactory, indifferent, and poor. Special reasons have to go with the reports of "exceptionally well qualified" and "not yet qualified," since they are regarded as being well above and below the average assessment. These more distinctive gradings were introduced as the result of twenty years of experience; and American practice, which began with an excessive number of grading distinctions but retreated to some extent to British simplicity, influenced British ideas. The extremes moved to each other as each learned about its own practical difficulties and the merits of the other.

Vacancies for promotion are made known through the promotion boards that exist in almost every department of English service. Evidence is gained from the supervising officer and also from the staff side of the Whitley Council of the department or of the district or office concerned. Appropriate forms are designed in order to indicate those qualifications that are not otherwise specified. The movement toward further education of the civil servant in both Britain and Germany is partly cultural, partly vocational. The result has been in Great Britain the establishment of the Institute of Public Administration and various schemes conducted by other civil service bodies connected with the civil service staff associations, and in Germany a much more ambitious scheme—the establishment in several great centers of administrative academies (*Verwaltungsakademien*). What is gained by this attention to promotion? No complete exclusion of favoritism is possible, as anywhere in life. For, if reports and personal records are drawn up, some one has to do this, and the personal factor still persists. But certain things are gained. The first is regularity of report. This means that there must be

recurrent attention to the relative merits of subordinates. The deliberateness at stated intervals conduces to conscious attempts at distinction and though there is in all countries a tendency for the certifying officer to tar all with the same brush, so that the total marks tend to prove that all are equally meritorious—distinctions are made.[14] The qualities mentioned in the British report forms break up the vagueness of judgment into a number of more specific questions, answers to which can only be given by close attention to their purport. The second gain which underlines and makes effective the first is the heightening of responsibility brought about by the possibility of a representation against a flagrantly unjust promotion.[15] And third, the staff feels that this dispensation reduces the possibility of jobbery, that they are having a "square deal," and that causes for suspicion and the furtive backbiting which is as bitter as gall in any "closed" occupation have been much diminished. The Royal Commission of 1929 (in its report of 1931) met the claims of civil servants even further—the precise terms of an adverse report are to be divulged, and sympathetic consideration is to be given to the institution of a departmental board of review which will include a staff nominee. These are important gains and well worth the time and energy expended upon the operation of the system.

Two variations of the system are worth mention. In some of the American states (Wisconsin most notably), an authority outside the department is introduced as a check upon the judgment of the departmental promoting officer; and in Australia, appeal machinery has been provided more completely than elsewhere to reduce the sense of grievance of officers who believe they are entitled to promo-

---

14 In one of the states of the United States, the regulations compel the certifying officer to place the servants in defined grades of merit in such and such a proportion—i.e., he is compelled to make a distinction.

15 The evidence before the Royal Commission, 1929, shows that such representations are made in individual cases.

tion but to whom others are preferred.[16] The Wisconsin system is based upon a report form very similar to that used in the British civil service. The information given in the report by the departmental superior is supplemented by the independent reports of the Civil Service Commission's examiners. They visit institutions and departments, and according to a privately circulated report of the Civil Service Commission, "In this work the examiner tries to get the officer to give a sort of word picture of each employee, noting especially those characteristics that are outstanding." The kind of information obtained is, of course, a great contrast to the percentage marks or comments on the report cards.[17]

The advantages claimed by the Commission for this method of personal inspection are (1) the information is more significant and vital, (2) "an appointing officer will gladly give an hour to talk over the work of his employer where he would consider the filling out of report cards as a bore, unnecessary red tape, put it off until the last thing, do it in a perfunctory way, and wonder if the reports would ever be looked at by the Civil Service Commission"; (3) close touch between the Commission and the departments fosters a spirit of cooperation; (4) the Commission is able to observe the need for reclassification and learn how best to formulate the examination.

It is quite obvious that this system can only work where the civil service is as small as it is in Wisconsin. There one approaches the manageable size of a not-too-large firm, and these personal contacts are not too costly and can be conveniently arranged. Further, the smaller the number of things to be compared, the easier the comparison; and one mind carrying a single standard minimizes the possible aberrations of judgment. Such a system could only work correspondingly

well in a large civil service if the number of the inspecting staff were large. The British civil service is some three hundred times as large as Wisconsin's, and the Prussian and Imperial and French civil services even larger. The difficulties are commensurately increased — more than commensurately, indeed, for the larger the number of human beings engaged in a task, the more difficult the agreement upon a single standard upon which to judge the officials they inspect. The solution is then one of two: either the establishment of basic principles and forms of comparison, or/and the decentralizing of selection for promotion. These are the inevitable effects of the largeness of the modern state and the vast number of civil servants it is bound to keep under a more or less centralized rule. At a certain point the economy of largescale organization seduces the ordinary man and woman from their longing for self-government.

This leads to the promotion method of the United States federal civil service: this is bound up with its efficiency-rating system and this with classification.

EFFICIENCY AND THE RATING OF CAPACITY

THE common notion is that civil servants have life tenure of their positions. This is nowhere true in law—for the law arranges for their dismissal or pensioning on grounds of redundancy or inefficiency. Yet in normal times, that is, when no great changes must occur (as after a war), the civil servant has come by practice to enjoy almost a life tenure, with superannuation to follow, though there is a remarkable turnover in American public services compared with others anywhere! [18]

What are the grounds of this lack of mobility? Some are the result of accidental, some of essential, causes. In the former class are the origins in royal tenure when the master would maintain favorites in office regardless of efficiency; the

[16] Cf. F. A. Bland, *The Government of Australia* (Australian Government Printing Office, 1943).
[17] Cf. W. E. Mosher and J. D. Kingsley, *Public Personnel Administration* (New York, 1941).

[18] Cf. *Ibid.*, p. 342 ff. In each year between 1925 and 1938 inclusive, not less than 13.0 per cent of voluntary quitting occurred. Cf. also figures on p. 843 above.

exceedingly confidential-authoritarian nature of the Crown servant of earlier days; the undue reaction against "spoils." Among the more recent and essential causes are the desire of the chiefs to save the trouble of change and the pain of dismissing others; the pressure of civil servants and their organizations (which is now paralleled in private industry); the fact that the civil servant is induced to educate himself to a certain standard for the service and to take the prescribed examinations; the desire to get good work by the promise of permanent employment (and special conditions regarding discipline, civic rights, etc.). These motives have been reinforced in their effect by the difficulty of measuring the efficiency of civil servants. What cannot be measured must be endured, lest one is mistaken or accused of injustice and favoritism. It is notable that with the increased consciousness about the importance of the civil service, and the improvements in the technique of rational employment methods, every civil service bestirs itself to challenge the notion of necessary permanence in office and the rigidity of its conditions. It declares a war on "dead wood." Can that war be won?

The quest of efficiency, then, had led to attempts to expel the atmosphere of security and automatic advancement that persists in the public services, and this obviously first depends upon whether efficiency can be "rated." No country has gone further in this than the United States, at least in theory. Its work may, when we have described it, seem pedantic and pretentious, but not a little of the world's progress has been won by such work.

Two things have combined to cause the United States to push the mechanism of "rating" efficiency further than development elsewhere. The first is the fact that the federal civil service (and the state civil services, for that matter) operate in a social environment intensely individualistic and acquisitive; the lack of other traditions, the freshness of the social adventure, the spectacle of fortunes extorted from nature and fellow men—all conspire

to add a keen edge to the mental weapons of these gainful and self-realizing human beings. The civil service cannot avoid measurement in terms of this environment. Its collective and its individual services cannot be rated in a fashion very different from those of General Motors or the Chicago stockyards or Western Union Telegraphs. Individual service, efficiency, advancement, and reward are inseparable terms: so are inefficiency and demotion (the opposite of promotion) and dismissal. Secondly, there is a tremendous interest in "personnel problems," Taylorism, scientific management, and "human engineering." These two influences — the individualistic acquisitive temper, and the enthusiasm for scientific management, the worship of salvation by technology—were strengthened in power by the general inefficiency of the personnel methods which long before World War I generated a strong and persistent reform movement.

From 1913 practical attention was turned toward the problem of heightened efficiency. A small new division was created in the Civil Service Commission called the Division of Efficiency with power "to investigate the needs of the several executive departments and independent establishments with respect to personnel and for the investigation of duplication of statistical and other work . . . etc., etc." In 1916 a Bureau of Efficiency independent of the Civil Service Commission was created to give effect, among other things, to the law of 1912 prescribing the establishment and use of "efficiency ratings" in the public service.[19] This law provided (sect. 4) that

The Civil Service Commission shall, subject to the approval of the President, establish a system of efficiency ratings for the classified service in the several executive departments in the District of Columbia based upon records kept in each department and independent establishment with such frequency as to make

[19] Cf. G. A. Weber, *Organized Efforts for the Improvement of Methods of Administration in the United States* (Baltimore, 1919); and cf. L. M. Short, *National Administrative Organization of the U. S. A.* (Baltimore, 1923).

them as nearly as possible records of fact. Such system shall provide a minimum rating of efficiency which must be attained by an employee before he may be promoted; it shall also provide a rating below which no employee may fall without being demoted; it shall further provide for a rating below which no employee may fall without being dismissed for inefficiency.

But no real investigation or progress took place until the appointment of the Reclassification Commission in 1920. This conducted one of the finest pieces of investigation ever accomplished in the history of public administration. Its terms of reference were the investigation of rates of compensation in the civil service and the reporting on what reclassification and readjustment of compensation should be made so as to provide uniform and equitable pay for the same character of employment. . . ." [20]

The Commission interpreted its terms of reference very broadly and found itself concerned with three main problems: (a) promotion, (b) the relationship between efficiency and movement upward in only one class and from class to class, and (c) classification of the service.

As regards (a) and (b) the findings of the Commission were:

that no uniform practice exists in the advancement of efficient employees at either salary or rank, both of which are commonly referred to as "promotion"; that salary advancements proper are controlled by administrative officers, while true promotions are usually made as the result of noncompetitive examinations; and that lack of assurance that efficient work will receive suitable reward injures the morale and reduces the efficiency of the entire service . . ." [21] "Because of the absence of any centralized control over promotions and advancements, it is impossible to generalize about the methods in selecting persons for advancement when a vacancy occurs. Some offices maintain fairly elaborate systems of efficiency ratings, and have a carefully developed plan for using them, including advisory committees, and some use an exam-

ination system for certain classes. In other offices the selection is made by the administrative officer with only such advice and assistance as he may choose to seek in the particular instance. In such offices the whole question turns on the administrator's knowledge of his force, his fairness, and his judgment." [22]

Equity as between the various kinds of work done in the service, and efficiency and good morale within each department, depend in the first instance upon a proper classification of all the services, and the problem of equitable promotion is dependent on the problem of proper classification. This is the lesson also of the civil services of Great Britain and France.

Now, the Civil Service Act of the United States and its applicatory rules [23] provided jointly that the higher positions in any grade should be filled by promotion unless no one was capable of filling the position vacant, and that promotions would legally occur only by examination or exemption therefrom by the Civil Service Commission. But, as the Reclassification Commission observed, promotion was, in fact, badly organized, and the United States had suffered the brunt of the two results of this: for more people than was necessary "blind alley" occupations existed, and second, there was a tremendous "turnover" of employment, to which the petrification of opportunity was undoubtedly a contributory cause. Although the Reclassification Commission advocated competitive examinations for promotion, its recommendations of the use of "efficiency ratings" to be regularly made in the departments and checked by a central supervisory bureau were later given effect, and this system has been made the principal basis of the promotion and demotion system. Now, before "efficiency rating" can operate there must be some way of comparing like with like, and this brings us back to the problem of classification, an indispensable foundation of equity and efficiency in

[20] Act, March 1, 1919, Sect. 9.
[21] Report of Congressional Joint Commission on Reclassification of Salaries, March 12, 1920 Part I, p. 20; 66th Congress, 2nd session, Document No. 686.

[22] Ibid., p. 54. Cf. also L. Mayers, op. cit., p. 310 ff.
[23] Sect. 7 of the Act of 1843, and Rule X, 1.

any great organization employing large numbers of officials.

CLASSIFICATION

THE problem of classification may be thus defined: to set all servants to work which is not too difficult nor too easy for them to do; and then to treat all who do equal work, equally, and where there is a difference in the amount and quality of work done, to proportion reward to service. Upon proper classification depends the efficacy of recruitment, the possibility of creating a rational promotion system, and the equitable treatment of people working in different departments. The experience of all countries shows how necessary is such a classification, though indeed it is very difficult to establish and to maintain a developing service, and practically impossible to satisfy the individual civil servant that he has been rightly placed in any particular category. Without categories there is no calculation, no comparison, no relative assessments and evaluation; and in a popularly governed state, particularly where publicity and government by political amateurs necessitates easily grasped facts and figures, control ceases where categories end. Yet it is the placing in categories which is bitterly resented by the restive, the ambitious, and the growing; and only the paramount necessities of a control which has ceased to be personal, because the thing controlled is of too great magnitude, can justify its deadening effects. Even the crab, said William James, would very likely be filled with a sense of personal outrage at having itself classed as a crustacean and would say, "I am no such thing. I am Myself, Myself alone." But the state is too large an employer to be able to make individual bargains with each of its servants; such bargains would make legislative control quite impossible; nor is there any accurate standard available to the public service, within itself, which could be used as a basis for the exact calculation of such individual contracts. The least amount of evil in state service is produced by the best classification.

The Reform of 1920. This is what the American inquiry of 1920, conducted by the Reclassification Commission, fully realized. Indeed, no one contemplating the situation of the American federal civil service at the time of the inquiry could have failed to realize the significance of proper classification. The Reclassification Commission found

that the Government has no standard to guide it in fixing the pay of its employees and no working-plan for relating the salaries appropriated to the character and importance of the work for which such salaries are to be paid, and that the designations of positions now appearing in the book of estimates are inaccurate and misleading.

The inequalities made tranfer from one department to the other—very desirable, within reason, as it prevents stagnation—a difficult process, since the salary differences operated as obstacles to free movement. Rational criticism and reform of promotion methods were impossible since these varied from office to office and meant something different in each department. The consequence was the degeneration of the morale of the service which could be expressed statistically by the turnover of jobs which in 1916 was 11 per cent. The way out of this administrative morass lay in instituting conditions of employment the keynotes of which should be *equity* and *uniformity*.

The basis of the system was classification; a special authority constantly to renew the classification; the relationship of salary scales to the grades then set up; and a promotion system based upon efficiency ratings, i.e., more or less exact statistical expressions of efficiency. The theory of classification involved the detailed analysis and description of every job in the government service—this was actually done at that time for over 100,-000 situations, and has been carried almost to completion. This recorded and defined a position—a specific job or office. To the description of duties is added a summary of qualifications required for their execution, and the lines of advancement.

All similar positions wherever they are in the service constitute a class. The next category inclusive of cognate "classes" is a series of classes or services (or "grades" as the statute of 1923 designated them). These are grouped into the great groups. The whole civil service fell, according to the Reclassification Commission, into three of these. Thus: There is a class of indexers in various departments; some grouped into the Departmental Publications and Information Service; this and other Services are grouped into (1) services involving clerical, office, or commercial work; (2) skilled trades, manual labor, public safety or related work; (3) scientific, professional, or subsidiary work.[24]

The essential importance of this method which differentiates it from evolution in other countries, is its conscious and minute attention to the nature of the job. Other considerations have been of some influence, even if not paramount, in Great Britain. English thought has centered rather upon the educational system of the country and the natural stages, secondary and university, at which its products were completed and sent out into the world of industry and the professions. Of course, a rough classification by the nature of the jobs was made mentally: their characteristics were enumerated in a broad unanalytical fashion, and then the classes so formed were related to recruits from the various grades of schools.

There is much to be said for the English system—taken as an extreme type—but inefficiency must be the inevitable result if it is carried to extremes. Its great advantage is that it does not influence the educational system to adapt itself to its detriment by deviation from the lines recommended by the nature of the educational process: also, it reduces the scope of the "crammer" for particular examinations. The American system classifies the jobs, and then expects the schools to provide the education to suit them. Its particular merit is to relate the nature of the specific job to the mind training required for it, and to produce a closer relation of capacity service and reward than other systems. Yet it also is anxious to secure some contact with the schools, the lack of it is serious, as it reduces the contribution of morale and general education which the schools can be made to give and which the service supremely needs.

The Act of 1923. The United States Classification Act of 1923 set up the Personnel Classification Board to (1) classify and (2) review and revise the uniform system of efficiency ratings setting forth the degree of efficiency for *(a)* an increase in pay where the maximum is not yet attained, *(b)* the continuance at the existing rate without increase or decrease, *(c)* decrease, *(d)* dismissal. Each employee was to be rated by the head of his department in accordance with this scheme of rating. "The current ratings for each grade or class thereof shall be open to inspection by the representatives of the board and by the employees of the department under conditions to be determined by the board after consultation with the department heads."

Later the administration and improvement of classification and efficiency records was vested in the Civil Service Commission.[25] Let us examine the scheme.

The first experience of it lasted until 1935. Its very meticulousness made a blunter method thereafter necessary. But the original model still exists in its outline and purpose. It is highly ingenious and very well illustrates the intense longing for a mathematical gauge of official capacity and the extent to which such an object can be produced. Discussion will revolve round the original system and be used as the basis for theoretical analysis, and then the later amendments will be noted.

---

[24] The classification that came to prevail, though applied only to a fraction of the service, is as follows: professional and scientific; subprofessional and subscientific; clerical, administrative, and general business; and custodial, labor, and mechanical.

[25] Cf. J. McDiarmid, "The Changing Role of the U. S. Civil Service Commission," in *American Political Science Review*, December, 1946.

A report upon each official was made every six months (since 1935, annually) on a special form called the graphic rating scale. A number of service elements are selected and appear upon this scale —they ordinarily numbered fifteen, but a sixteenth was kept for physical ability needed in certain positions in the custodial service. For the clerical and administrative staffs the number of elements— that is, qualities—used in rating an employee varied from four to ten, being usually five or six, the exact number depending in all cases upon the nature of the duties performed. It is clear that every class in the service needs for the exercise of its functions a different combination of these elements. Not only this, but among these elements some are more important than others. Therefore, not only is a selection of the elements necessary, but also a "weighting" of them, according to their importance, and this is expressed in percentages. Only experience can say what elements are necessary and determine their weights.

It may be asked, why stop at fifteen elements? The diversity of human occupation and services is more minutely divisible than these. The answer is that division has somewhere to stop, for without simplicity there may be confusion, and control is defeated. Once more the need for comparison and control of a multitude of officials by a single mind (the Civil Service Commission and Congress) dictates the situation. Further, the greater the subdivision, the more room for departmental choice of the elements, and again the difficulty of judging the relative merit in the aggregate of one official and another. Yet this analysis of human qualities is necessary in the public service because the principle of free price-making and free profit-making has been discarded as the consumers' check upon the producers' aptitude, and any control is therefore bound to be on the ingredients which may compose efficiency.

The service elements on the graphic rating scale were: (1) accuracy; (2) dependability; (3) neatness and orderliness of work; (4) speed with which work is accomplished; (5) industry, diligence, energy, and application to duties; (6) knowledge of work; (7) judgment, common sense, wish to profit by experience; (8) success in winning confidence and respect through personality; courtesy and tact, control of emotions, poise; (9) cooperativeness; readiness to give new ideas and methods a fair trial; obedience to the management; (10) initiative, resourcefulness, inventiveness; (11) execution of work; (12) ability to organize, ability to delegate authority, to plan work; (13) leadership; ability to get cooperation of subordinates, decisiveness, self-control, tact, courage, fairness in dealing with others; (14) success in improving and developing employees by informing them, developing talent, arousing ambition; (15) quantity of work (to be used only when accurate and competent output records are kept). Thus the United States succeeded, by five points, in putting the English report form in the shade. It is an interesting analysis of psychological working qualities.[26]

Departmental rating offices marked the scale in those elements already combined by the (then) Personnel Classification Board. In pitching their mental mercury at a standard, they were instructed to have in mind "reasonable performance standards for the compensation grade in which that class is found." When the rating was done, reviewing officers in the departments compared the rating of different rating officers and smoothed out the results of abnormal variations of standard. These were then submitted to a board of review (a number of higher departmental officers). The board discovered the percentage per element, multiplied it by the weight assigned to that particular element, and found the weighted average by totaling the weighted element ratings, and pointing off two decimals. The board of review were informed in a series of "suggestions" how to control the ratings. They were expected to prorate the ratings up or down in order that the final ratings should

---

[26] Cf. the more recent one, Appendix A.

come to an average of from 80 per cent to 84 per cent for acceptable workers. The result was the final efficiency rating. A report was drawn up in order of the efficiency ratings.

The eligibility of employees to receive specific salaries within the grade ranges, on the basis of their efficiency ratings, was indicated in a special table.

Survey of American Classification Scheme. I have entered into some detail in discussing this scheme because it is a fine illustration of the devices which the modern state is forced to adopt if it wishes to secure as strict a control over the efficiency of its employees as any private employer does. It is a tremendous apparatus, and a very delicate one, to have to operate, but short of a high degree of native public spirit, enterprise, and freshness of mind in the civil servant, there is no logical escape from such a system of control, if efficiency is really desired. If every penny is counted, and if for each penny the maximum of return is to be obtained, some such scheme is indispensable. For, as we know, the general defect of a civil service is its sheltered position. It is sheltered from the risks of trade fluctuations, from the thousand and one environmental and human vagaries which make all the difference between business success and failure. Its pay and other conditions of employment are not subject directly to what it can make by its service to a consumer who has alternative sources of supply. Its contract is founded upon one of the surest and most unchangeable bases; the authority of the state, the need people have of the state, of order, if not of specific services. And this foundation gives a sound title to taxation—the source of salaries.

Without, however, the possibility of movement, of fresh currents of desire, a standard of attainment and accountability without risks and threats, fluctuations in reward and punishment, the average human being tends to fall into a state of unenterprising complacency, fitting his habits and mode of life to his predetermined pay and position. The most universal popular complaint about the civil service is the somatic condition at which even fresh entrants ultimately arrive, and the disease is caused by lack of incentive. The mind and body, it is alleged, are simply not kept on the stretch, and they cease to be creative. It is a condition which is comfortable for the civil servants, and for the order and regularity of the service; in the slick performance of routine it is providential—not a single unexpected thing happens; but society is apt to be the loser. Security of service and regularity of advancement are indispensable for some occupations in life, though the argument may be driven too far: but for the mass of men they cause enterprise to run down to the minimum point at which slackness, though existent, is undetectable. The English, the French, and the American schemes are designed to restore movement, hope, despair, acquisitiveness, and so stimulate effort. Of course, the main allegation may be exaggerated.

This problem has become more serious in proportion as the state has further socialized various services; it is well-known in the great private enterprise monopolies of today.[27] In proportion as the circle of private enterprise decreases, the opportunities of comparison of conditions inside with conditions outside the service will decrease, and in proportion as laws are made, the activity of civil servants is at once dictated and confined. Further, the greater the number of services rendered by the state without a price, a direct *quid pro quo,* the fewer will be the bases for accurate rating of the produce of officials. The system we have just described is a perfect illustration of the extent to which judgments of the civil service are linguistic rather than numerical. Efficiency-rating schemes will become more and more universal, and, even as at the present time, legislatures have come to demand that estimates and accounts be presented to them in a form enabling comparison to be made between units of

[27] Cf. Marshall Dimock, *Bureaucracy and Trusteeship in Large-Scale Business* (Temporary National Economic Committee Monograph, 1941).

expenditure in one department and another, so must they, if they desire, in whatsoever form, to retain the control of the executive, obtain an insight if not an actual control, over the efficiency-rating machinery—the boards of review and the rest.

The efficiency-rating scheme that operated to 1935 was found to suffer from certain operational rather than conceptual defects. The numerical rating, which was taken to the second decimal point, was excessively refined. The moderation of the rating made by the immediate supervisor, by reviewers who softened the hard-boiled and fortified the soft-, aroused the wrath and unwillingness of the supervisors to take responsibility for a judgment not their own. The legislative requirement that as many ratings be above a stated average as below it, whether men were like that or not, caused all sorts of artificial contortions. To suit this system to the related increments, demotions and promotions dependent on minute differentiations became really impossible: a breakdown of the integrity of the rating system occurred. Who would rate so minutely with such dire consequences, and with the knowledge that perhaps the next-door supervisor was easier in his ratings?

In 1935 a simpler form was introduced,[28] with about the same number of service qualities, but without numerical calibration. Close to the British method, the ratings were: excellent; very good; good; fair; and unsatisfactory. To these corresponded respectively the consequences: promotable within grade if below top salary; the same; no salary change if receiving middle salary or above; if below middle, promotable not beyond it; reduce one step if above middle salary; dismiss from present position. The ratings are required to be considered when the force is reduced.

It should not be forgotten that, if necessary, the servant has a well-organized course of appeal to the Civil Service

---

[28] Cf. Standard Form 51, December 1943, p. 19, *Efficiency Rating Manual*, Civil Service Commission and Appendix A, below.

Commission against the rating to which he has been doomed, and that the supervisor who makes the rating is therefore challengeable, and may be called upon to state the grounds of his judgment. The rating form of each employee must be available to him for his inspection.

Finally, it is interesting to observe that the modern ideas of classification give to the agency which conducts it, a participation in general administration responsibilities, in that their task of periodical job-reviews is to be instrumental to reorganizations of operation and personnel.

Whatever the actual outcome of the American experiment, it is at least a valiant and capable attempt at finding a solution. We may, according to the amount of cynicism in our character, smile a little grimly at their belief that human nature is so to be analyzed, calibrated, and recorded, and that this is a practicable way of controlling it. But stranger things than that already exist in human institutions—e.g., you cannot become a civil servant without an examination. And with a change of social forms and state activity, stranger things yet will be generated.

The most recent reconsideration of the federal efficiency-record system (Hoover Commission) ends with a scathing denunciation of its inefficiency.

In its "Personnel Management" (p. 29), the Commission states that:

The present efficiency-rating procedures in the Federal Government have the effect of undermining supervisor-employee relationships.

It bases its conclusions on the fact that the system, under certain circumstances, makes mandatory either a public reward or a public penalty; that the supervisor's determination is subject to challenge and revision at three higher levels; that the efficiency rating process is based upon contradictory and unvalidated assumptions; and that the system is not used to the extent that it should be as an aid in the development of the employee and for the purposes of measuring the employee's potential usefulness to the organization.

All of this was predicted, based on common sense knowledge of human nature in administration over the centuries. It is an interesting question why such common sense came to be ignored? At any rate, bitter experience has confirmed it.

TRAINING OF CIVIL SERVANTS

WHEN officials have been recruited, especially at a young age, they are to the services merely raw recruits. It is true that many of them have by their education, even when not prescribed by the rules of recruitment, acquired a fairly accurate knowledge of the rudiments of their coming position and the role it plays in the whole picture of the profession. Yet this cannot be sharply clear and ever-impressive. Others, in the services which permit recruitment at an advanced age, may have acquired principles of business behavior perfectly appropriate elsewhere but not sufficiently judicious or equitable for the public services. Both these elements need specific induction into their work. It can, of course, be obtained by immediate immersion in the job, with the hope that the entrants will pick up what is required in the process of doing it. The result is not certain, may never be achieved, and wrong ideas may mar an official's work for years until accident puts him right, if it ever does. These are the cogent arguments for deliberately established procedures for postentry training.

There are others of at least equal importance. It will have been observed that much importance has in the previous pages been attached to the fact that the public services are "sheltered," that is, not subject to the continual competition that still prevails in many branches of private enterprise. We have stressed the relative lack of movement and animation by promotion or transfer or the invention of new jobs or demotion or dismissal. Now this is a relative, not an absolute, factor: in some grades and classes of the services there is substantial movement; in some big businesses there is little movement. It is essential that the public services should deliberately provide something which will stimulate thought and

aspiration. Educational courses are helpful in this, especially when they are linked with credits required for promotion.

Furthermore, as officials stay in the service beyond their first youth, some of the freshness of hope and courage fade in some. Some men and women become tired as they do in almost every walk of life. In politics the process is sometimes correctly called conservatism. In life generally it is sometimes seen as cynicism: a disbelief in the value of the function one is performing—not to the point of causing retirement, not a disbelief in one's own professional work any more than a disbelief in much else besides, but still, no energetic urge any longer dictates administrative enterprises: they no longer have, in Shakespeare's words "pith and moment."

This advent of the *blasé* years is expressed in a mild defensive tone by a British civil servant of long and successful career, in answer to the present author's charge of "cynicism." Sir Henry Dale says: [29]

This steady lengthening and widening of experience confirm in high officials a certain way of looking at things, a habit of mind issuing in a certain creed consciously or subconsciously held by most of them. . .

The substance of that creed may be compressed into five propositions, none of which is at all novel. First, pure reason is not at present the most important factor in human affairs. Second, even in the realm of pure reason there is much to be said for both sides on any complicated question which is fiercely disputed, and in the modern world all serious questions are complicated. Third, in a vast and highly organized society, great social, economic, and political changes (call them reforms if you like) cannot be made quickly without causing some unmerited suffering. Fourth, a minority which feels strongly and shouts loudly will often prevail against both the majority and the merits, unless the majority itself feels strongly. Fifth, in this complex and rapidly changing world, any great measure, whether legislative or executive, is sure to have results, often very grave results, which no one foresaw; in other words, the strongest intellect and the keenest in-

[29] Cf. his *The Higher Civil Service of Great Britain* (London, 1941), pp. 92 and 93.

sight cannot predict anything like the full consequences of important decisions.

. . . . It is possible to be enthusiastic for moderation and prudence. That is the attitude of mind which may, I think, be properly attributed to the chiefs of the Civil Service; will any sensible man call it cynicism?

Now, it is perfectly possible that this is not cynicism but wisdom. In order to make sure that this "stoical realism," as the author calls it, is the latter and not the former, and that it is truly the result of garnered experience and not the mere passage of the years, there is everything to be said in favor of measures which may offer to counteract the latter.

The general scheme of training set up in France in 1945 has already been noted, and it will be remembered the *Statut des Fontionnaires* requires training of civil servants of all ranks as part of the arrangements for promotion. We have also briefly traced the arrangements of the United States civil service for postentry or in-training, as yet not as complete in practice as is desirable.

Attention has been drawn to the interest of the British civil service in the matter, and a few further observations are desirable.

The *Report of the Committee on the Training of Civil Servants* [30] provides a general theory of training, and recommends the practical arrangements for giving effect to it. We are rather more concerned with the former than with the latter.

The recommendations of the Committee derive from two things: an appreciation of the faults of the civil service, and a view of the function of the civil service in the modern state. As to the faults, the committee reported: [31]

The faults most frequently enumerated are over-devotion to precedent; remoteness from the rest of the community, inaccessibility, and faulty handling of the general public; lack of initiative and imagination; ineffective organisation and misuse of manpower; procrastination and unwillingness to take responsibility or give decisions. We recognize

that these defects exist in some measure—though not so generally or in such degree as is often alleged—and whether they derive from the individual or the system, post-entry training must be directed to eliminating them.

As for the objects and general principles of training the committee said: [32]

At the outset we asked ourselves the question: "What is the object of training?" If the answer is that it is to attain the greatest possible degree of efficiency, then the word efficiency seems to need some closer definition. In any large-scale organisation efficiency depends on two elements: the technical efficiency of the individual to do the particular work allotted to him, and the less tangible efficiency of the organisation as a corporate body derived from the collective spirit and outlook of the individuals of which the body is composed. Training must have regard to both elements.

Five main aims present themselves.

First, training should endeavour to produce a civil servant whose precision and clarity in the transaction of business can be taken for granted.

In the second place, the civil servant must be attuned to the tasks which he will be called upon to perform in a changing world. The Civil Service must continuously and boldly adjust its outlook and its methods to the new needs of new times.

Thirdly, there is a need to develop resistance to the danger of the civil servant becoming mechanised by the machine; whilst we must aim at the highest possible standard of efficiency, our purpose is not to produce a robot-like, mechanically-perfect Civil Service. The recruit from the first should be made aware of the relation of his work to the service rendered by his Department in the community. The capacity to see what he is doing in a wider setting will make the work not only more valuable to his Department but more stimulating to himself. In addition, therefore, to purely vocational training directed to the proper performance of his day-to-day work, he should receive instruction on a broader basis as well as encouragement to persevere with his own educational development.

Fourthly, even as regards vocational training, it is not sufficient to train solely for the job which lies immediately at hand. Training must be directed not only to enabling an individual to perform his current work more

---

[30] Cmd. 6525, 1944.
[31] Para. 13.

[32] Paras. 15 and 16.

efficiently, but also to fitting him for other duties, and where appropriate, developing his capacity for higher work and greater responsibilities.

Fifthly, even these ends are not in themselves enough. Large numbers of people have inevitably to spend most of their working lives upon tasks of a routine character, and with this human problem ever in the background, training plans, to be successful, must pay substantial regard to staff morale.

The arrangements, put into force in 1945, after full conference with the representative organizations of the various classes of civil servants, are administered by a newly established Director of Education and Training in the Treasury.

Training schemes are devised in each department by departmental training officers under the authority of the establishment officers and the head of the whole department. They are devised and carried out with the cooperation of the joint committees, the Whitley Councils, to be discussed presently (Chap. 35). Training arrangements include reception of the new entrants by a specially appointed official in each department, who impresses upon them the prestige they must uphold, the functions they render to the community, and the history and functions of the department. Then attention is paid to the general system of working in a government office, the duties, organization, confidential nature of the work, discipline, and so on. Training follows in the actual duties. After this, mobility in the department is organized to relieve monotony and widen the official's outlook and comprehension. Those who show the qualities which make for effective supervisory duties are picked out and given tuition in personnel work.

The training so far mentioned does not include all that the training plans provide for. The departments encourage their staffs to acquire outside vocational qualifications, in some cases allowing time off and paying the fees. Lest this should be of a narrowing effect, the encouragement to further education extends to nonvocational education, in the form of university extension lectures,

evening classes, and such like. For this purpose the civil servants cooperate with the local schools and colleges.

It should be remembered that any qualification or distinction won at such courses, nonvocational as well as vocational, is recorded on the annual report form which may lead to promotion.

Within the departments, frequent conferences are held, to explain work procedures, the problems of implementing the statutes, the reason for new regulations, the problems raised by public complaints, the realization of policies old and new.

We have already referred to the special attention paid since the end of World War II to the initiation of the administrative class entrants into their work, and to the institution of the system of sabbatical leave for those who after a few years of service have shown exceptional promise. As to the former, a systematic course of lectures and seminars for two days a week over a period of two or three months teaches the nature and art of administration, the techniques the service uses, the standards of conduct it requires. This is combined with "live work" from the outset, and a well-thought-out rotation within the divisions of the department and spells of work in the field services of the department. This now replaces the old method of putting the man to work at once, and reliance merely upon learning from observation of others.

It will be surmised that the provision of additional opportunities of promotion, the appointment of officials especially concerned with personnel work, with listening to appeals, reviewing the personnel administration of subordinate supervisory officials, and the thorough fulfillment of a well-devised policy of in-training, means that more officials must be appointed and more expense incurred. Only the myopic or ill-willed would attack such expenditures and activities as uneconomic or wasteful. A small amount of expenditure on the appropriate arrangements in the respects we have noted can bring truly enormous benefits in return.

DISCIPLINE, MORALE, LOYALTY

GRATIFICATION of ambition, the acquisition of power, and increases of salary, are not the only incentives to good and better work. Often, indeed, these incentives cannot operate. Where a settled state of establishment has been reached, where all the prizes and the risks are foreknown, these tend to lose their virtue owing to their certainty, and States have found themselves compelled to introduce codes of discipline, more or less detailed, more or less severely enforced. The means to the enforcement of the conditions of work in private industry are well known and may be violent: the employer in person, or his representatives (the foreman, the subdirectors, the managers) are watchful for threats to the profit-making capacity of the firm, and the lame, the crippled, the incapable, the recalcitrant, may suffer many penalties up to the point of dismissal or enforced resignation. The non-competitive, sheltered nature of the public services blunts the edge of industrial discipline, for one cannot calculate quite so well how many pounds will be lost by certain special behavior. Further, the public services have a special dignity of a like kind to, but different in degree from, the great professions of medicine and law. The public services are, in its concrete forms, the state, and they may not behave like lesser associations in their everyday contact with their customers and their colleagues.

Disciplinary Regulations. We are now concerned principally with the regulations of the activity of civil servants designed to secure efficient work. In this matter Germany has the longest experience and is, indeed, the pioneer. Her rules are publicly known and constitute a large and definite chapter in constitutional jurisprudence. It is most convenient for exposition, therefore, to rehearse the German provisions, adding comments to the parallels or divergencies of the civil services of the United States, Britain, and France.[33]

(1) The civil servant is required conscientiously to discharge his office and all the duties directly appertaining thereto, in accordance with the constitution and the laws, to obey the official orders of his superiors, in so far as they do not contradict the law, and to behave worthily of the respect accorded to his office.

The obligation of obedience to a superior does not extend to action and judgment while member of a board. On the contrary, the official is there expected to observe only the laws and the statutory orders, and to make his decision and give his vote quite independently, according to his free judgment and the dictates of his conscience. He must never allow himself to be moved from this free decision by the fact that his superior is a colleague on the board and differs from him in opinion.

It is not the business of an inferior to question the material value, the policy, of his superior's order. He is sheltered from responsibility if the command passes four tests: it must be *(a)* within the local and material competence of the superior, *(b)* and of the subordinate, *(c)* not contrary to the laws and the constitution, and *(d)* regular in form. When the official does not obey, it is at his own risk. He becomes liable to disciplinary penalties if his disobedience is declared unjustified by the higher official or the disciplinary judge. Only an immaculate judgment on the part of the inferior will avoid a penalty. When the official is in doubt, therefore, he is counseled to obey, and then make a complaint afterwards.

This injunction of obedience is paramount: yet it will be noticed that it is qualified when officials are members of policy-creating bodies. Indeed, on such bodies, and even elsewhere in the hierarchy of action, it is important to protect and encourage independence of mind.

[33] I follow principally A. Brand, *Das Beamtenrecht,* 2nd edition (Berlin, 1926); A. Schulze and W. Simons, *Die Rechtsprechung des Reichsdiszplinarhofs* (Berlin, 1926), Sect. 8; Julius Hatschek, *Deutsches und Preussiches Staatsrecht* (Berlin, 1921 and 1923); and H. Assman, *Die Dienstvergehen der deutschen Beamten* (Berlin, 1926).

Frankness of opinion needs protection because it is the safeguard of the most precious element in administration: originality, inventiveness, new ideas, stimulation of emotion and emulation. In the British and the American civil service, the same rule derives in the former from the ancient service of the Crown and in the latter from the civil service statutes and executive orders. Yet in these services the spirit was favorable to independence of mind more than in the German civil service, whether before or during Hitler's régime. The political system and the society have much to do with the relative easiness of relations in the hierarchy in the democratic countries compared with Germany even during the Weimar period.

It will be convenient later [34] to quote the British doctrine of the duty of independence of mind in actual practice. At this point it is meet to draw attention to the defense made by the American State Department of two of its officials who had sent to the department from China reports which did not please Ambassador Hurley in Chungking, and against which he vehemently protested. The doctrine is exquisite.[35]

What it amounts to is that within proper channels they expressed to those under whom they served certain views which differed to a greater or less extent from the policies of the government as then defined. Of course, it is the duty of every officer of the United States to abide by and to administer the declared policy of his Government. But conditions change, and often change quickly in the affairs of governments. Whenever an official honestly believes that changed conditions require it, he should not hestitate to express his views to his superior. . . . I should be profoundly unhappy to learn that any officer of the Department of State, within or without the foreign service, might feel bound to refrain from submitting through proper channels an honest report or recommendation for fear of offending me or anyone else in the department. If that day should arrive, I will have lost the very essence of the assistance and guidance I require for the successful discharge of the heavy responsibilities of my office.

There is hardly a single administrative post, however humble in the hierarchy, whether strictly executive or policy-making, which does not contain some particle of doubt and change and growth. None should therefore be deterred by an even unspoken menace from opening his mind, none should be discouraged from expressing doubts by the tacit offer of rewards. It is the vital task of official superiors to nurture and defend the original-minded.

Something of this idea of independence of mind [36] is lodged in the theory of the public corporation as a form of administration,[37] best expressed perhaps in President Roosevelt's message to Congress recommending establishment of the TVA: "a corporation clothed with the power of Government but possessed of the flexibility and initiative of a private enterprise." And the student, while remembering the strength of the decision in *Myers* versus *the United States,* and *Morgan* versus *the TVA*, will not forget the essence of the rule favoring independence of mind in *Rathbun* versus *the United States* where the Tariff Commission was characterized as "free to exercise its judgment."

Of course, it is a matter of tact, sometimes of genius, for both superior and subordinate to appreciate exactly where the line must be drawn between immediate obedience and independence. Both are necessary: in executive posts, and the more urgent the service rendered the more so, is obedience peremptory, to act first and talk afterwards.

The development of planned economies, with the state in management of industries, has deepened the concern for independence of mind on the part of the actual day-by-day administrators of the

---

[34] Page 884.
[35] Secretary Byrnes' statement to the Senate Foreign Affairs Committee, December 7, 1945.

[36] Cf. R. M. Dawson, *The Principle of Official Independence* (London, 1921).
[37] Cf. L. Gordon, *The Public Corporation in Great Britain* (London, 1937).

[865]

banks, mines, power utilities, transport, steel plants, medical services.[38]

(2) Civil servants must carry out the duties of their office with the greatest sincerity and probity, without regard to private advantage; with the greatest impartiality, with all industriousness, and care. The official must be especially on his guard against partiality. Various decisions have made clear the meaning of this rule. For example, an official whose personal interest is likely to be materially affected in the exercise of his functions must withdraw from such an affair. No money may be accepted for benefits conferred by official activities. As to capacity to fulfill his duties, sheer ignorance, physical inability, or mental aberration would lead not to disciplinary action but to dismissal from the service. But the law acts with a disciplinary intention where such incapacity is or may be brought on by the official's voluntary behavior, for example, by dissipation, drunkenness, or waste of time such as that of him "who without permission from his superiors seeks out a colleague during service hours and talks over a private matter for an undue length of time." [39]

Beyond this there are many special rules, especially appropriate to different classes of work. For example, extraordinary weight is laid upon the impartiality and incorruptibility of the officials, and upon the absolute inviolability of secrecy of posts, telegraphs, and cables. We find similar special rules in the civil services of other countries also.[40]

(3) Civil servants must keep punctually to the hours of arrival at and leaving their work.

(4) Without the official's having a legal claim to extra pay, an extension or alteration of existing functions may take place, so long as the new work corresponds to the training and capacity of the official, and is not of an entirely different nature, and is derogatory neither to the normal activity of the official nor to the honor of his rank. When special help is demanded during a strike to make up what the strikers would normally have done, all officials are obliged to obey—even higher officials are obliged, where necessary, to do purely physical labor. These duties are nowhere stated so absolutely outside the German civil service.

(5) Civil servants are obliged to be truthful in official dealings, even when they are under a charge, and they must not pass over in silence important facts the disclosure of which is of concern to the department. This obligation of candor and truthfulness extends to information which is demanded about extra-official behavior.

(6) Respect for superiors is demanded, outside as well as inside the office, even when the superior is objectionable in character and demeanor. The forms of this respect have in Germany alone been construed in terms of superlative subtlety. For example, you may not omit the usual daily greeting, but women cannot be expected to greet their superiors first; [41] when your superior enters the room you must rise; and then, towards all officials, inside and outside the office, a respectful attitude must be observed, especially to any of a higher grade! The president of a Staff Council must preserve this respectful attitude even during the course of his presidential duties!

In their intercourse with the public, officials must always be courteous. They must avoid roughness and apathy; they must be friendly

---

[38] Cf. Herman Finer, "British Reconstruction and Planning," *International Labour Review*, March and April, 1948.

[39] Brand, *op. cit.*, p. 424 and footnote.

[40] Cf. British Revenue Officials (volume on administration, the instruction books): "Having regard to the technical and frequently contentious nature of the work, it is not always easy to satisfy taxpayers as to their obligations and rights under the Income Tax Acts, and it frequently happens that a taxpayer feels a sense of grievance for which there may be no grounds apparent to a member of the staff. In such cases, patient attention and a courteous explanation of the point at issue will do much to remove any sense of grievance and expedite the settlement of a case," etc., etc.

[41] A civil servant has answered this difficult question thus: "A woman civil servant nods first to a man when he is a superior officer, very old, or has otherwise a generally higher social standing."

and obliging; must try to further the affairs of all who appeal to them, and readily give advice and information to persons who are ignorant of the law and official routine, providing that official duties or the legitimate interests of others are not opposed thereto. Quiet and circumspection must be observed, since procedure may easily awaken an impression of violence and prejudice and make difficult the execution of business. The mode of dealing with the public also depends in a certain measure upon the educational level and the breeding of the individual, and the right way here will be indicated by the natural tactfulness of the official. Officials must be helpful to each other.[42]

(8) Officials must not allow insults to pass unnoticed, lest the service should suffer degradation.[43] By the Criminal Code (clause 196) an action lies against persons who insult an official (Beamtenbeleidigung). In cases where the official is in doubt about the significance of the insult, he may consult his superior, who may take an action for insult if this occurred during the exercise, or otherwise in respect of, the official's duties. Indeed, to maintain the dignity of the state (as authority), the superior may not consider whether the official was personally hurt or not and whether or not he desires an action to be taken. It is the office, Authority, which is of paramount importance. That this is so is proved by the opinion (which is, however, a subject of dispute) that the department has a right to forbid an official from taking action if the publicity of court proceedings would prejudice the interests of the service. In such cases, it is held by jurists of good repute, the personal claim of an official to satisfaction must give way to the interest of the department. The French Statut des Fonctionnaires reiterates the right of officials to protection against threats, assaults, insults, and defamation: the administration is obliged to protect them (article 15). Neither in British nor United States law and practice does this remnant of lèse majesté appear in a special form.

(9) Such behavior is enjoined in non-

official life that the dignity, confidence, and respect bound up with the office shall not be disadvantageously affected.[44] The Frederickian Code, the Allgemeines Landrecht, already forbade irregular life, gambling and the contracting of debts, and condemned officials who made themselves despicable by base behavior. Officials connected with any financial departments are forbidden to speculate, and this as well as drunkenness and frivolous contracting of debts may result in dismissal. Nor may an official deliberately endanger his health or protract his convalescence by foolish behavior. In short,

every official must in his extra-official life have regard to the special obligations which his official position imposes upon him. The official must therefore so order his general way of life to conform to prevalent opinions on virtue, manners, and morals. This duty he owes, not only to his master, the State, to which he stands in a special relationship of loyalty, but to the whole of officialdom, which ought to suffer in its ranks only worthy professional colleagues.[45]

The jurisprudence on this subject—the general moral behavior of officials in their private lives—is voluminous. For example, careful distinctions, which we need not investigate too closely here, are made in the matter of sexual relations, in order to separate self-regarding from service-regarding behavior. As soon as such behavior becomes publicly known and can redound to the discredit of the service, a breach of discipline has been committed. This discipline is especially strict (quite naturally) in relation to school teachers, and marriages must be notified as soon as they take place, including the name and profession of the father-in-law.[46] Again, drunkenness, occasional and chronic, is classed according to its effect upon the

---

42 Translated almost verbatim from Brand, op. cit., pp. 427-28.

43 Schulze-Simons, op. cit., p. 231; 22.12.13.

44 Cf. for France the doctrine (Jèze, op. cit., Vol. II, p. 91) of dignité de la vie privée. Its derogation is a service fault subject to official discipline.

45 Brand, op. cit., p. 429.

46 The severity of the rules was originally most marked in the financial departments—at one time, previous permission to marry had to be asked for and granted.

official, his cooperativeness, his dignity, and the degree of responsibility and sobriety strictly required for his work. Police officials have especially severe obligations of sobriety. In the matter of contracting debts, not only is the official himself watched, reprimanded, and fined when the matter becomes serious and damaging enough, but he is expected to stop his wife from frivolous domestic economy! Games of chance may be played, in good company, so long as one's economic independence is not thereby jeopardized!

Nothing like the detail and severity of this is reproduced in the British, French, and American civil services, though it is an understood rule that the service is not to be brought into disrepute and that officials must be capable of fulfilling their tasks physically and intellectually and morally, and that any shortcoming in these respects would, when punished, act as corrective examples on extra-official behavior leading up to inefficiency. But the method is not direct, it is roundabout. The British civil service is also hostile to gambling and moneylenders, yet it merely points out in a Treasury circular that there are no such things as good moneylenders, but only bad and worse.

The purpose of such principles, whether direct or indirect, is to prevent officials from falling under the influence of men outside the department to the extent that they may be afraid to exercise their duty energetically and impartially. If matters were left to themselves, it could happen that moneylending and gambling transactions and indulgence in strong drink and other sensual pleasures could ruin all the calculated relationships of authority among civil servants themselves. In private enterprise these matters are left much to themselves, though there are businesses and professions which tacitly or by stated rules exact good social behavior of their officials. For the most part, however, punishment is expected to come from business losses, and fine behavior is expected to be rewarded by success, that is, profits and prestige. As we have so often repeated, the rewards and punishments of official life are not usually as direct and

impressive: hence the establishment of rules anticipating possible aberrations.

(10) No official may take on any additional offices or employments, other than those for which he has asked and obtained permission of the appropriate departmental authority.[47] It is an axiom of the service that *all* the official's time and energy must be devoted to the proper fulfillment of official duties. (The right to take part in political activity is a special case to which we later devote special attention.) Paid membership of boards of directors or management of a limited liability company, cooperative society, or any other profit-making corporation is entirely forbidden to whole-time officials, but mutual provident societies do not fall under this ban.[48] Other types of subsidiary employment, like agencies for insurance companies, trusteeships, accountancy, editorship of periodicals, coaching, the carrying on of a craft or trade, require no permission. No such permission is given for the management of a tavern or an open stall. The wife, children, and servants of an official are given permission to carry on only those trades which are not likely to result in the degradation of official dignity. Nor is the official now given permission for continuous and regularly paid professional orchestral and concert performances.

(11) The civil servants must observe official secrecy.

These duties form a comprehensive code of behavior which the civil servant is obliged to respect.[49] Penalties of various grades up to the point of dismissal are attached to them, and their intention is to maintain the efficiency of the service. No state is without them, although there are differences of content and form. The tre-

---

[47] Cf. Brand, *op. cit.*, Part VIII, Sects. 147-52. Cf. also France, *Statut des Fonctionnaires*, articles 8-10, (a very rigorous set of principles): "interests of a nature to compromise his [the official's] independence."

[48] So almost identically in France since 1946.

[49] The rules were maintained throughout the Hitler period, and, indeed, were reinforced by additional duties designed to make the service even more subservient to political and top administrative direction.

mendous difference between Germany and other countries is this: that while she has a code stated quite publicly in a convenient form, Great Britain had only an incomplete set of Treasury circulars and minutes and departmental rules, without coherence and uninformed by a deliberately applied mind,[50] the United States has only departmental rules and a few clauses in certain statutes,[51] and France until the statute of 1946 had only a number of principles flowing from the general axiom that the service must serve the state, and these principles were enunciated occasionally by the *Conseil d'État*.[52] Secondly, whereas the Continent has a regular set of law courts (administrative tribunals for the most part) which are specifically competent in this matter, England relies upon the ordinary sense of justice of the departmental chiefs (which may or may not be a valuable safeguard), and in the final resort upon the minister and the Treasury, in serious cases, and extraordinary tribunals when a particularly striking scandal occurs, as in the Gregory and Bullock cases, and the United States upon the head of the department and review by the Civil Service Commission.

Discipline and Morale. These rules are ubiquitous and ever-present threats, and the essence of their purpose is subordination and devotion. They are, in a sense, of the nature of a state religion. They are those commandments which issue from the nature of the state, and are based upon the desire to maintain the state. An analysis of the nature of any one of these obligations ultimately ends in revealing some aspect of the general nature of the state—whether it be authority, or order, or service, or impartiality among the various social contestants for power. Given the nature of the state one can, on the contrary, work back to these rules: they are the inevitable expression thereof; and

who wills the one wills the other. Some may be practiced a little too roughly, some too mildly; some may be antiquated and deserve abolition, and again there are others which ought to be included but are not. But in their substance they are calculated to create a mentality and supply incentives so that the public services may operate effectively in spite of the fact that the rather violent discipline—the economic fears and aspirations—of the competitive and profit-making world is absent. They are in part a substitute for the rough justice of the manager, the foreman, and the customer's dissatisfaction with services and commodities produced by the private employee. But, of course, the great monopolistic businesses of the modern world, especially where their market is inelastic, are obliged to adopt similar methods to secure steady creativeness, and, in fact, they do so.

In the Gregory case, the Board of Inquiry set down the doctrine for the British civil service [53] and reaffirmed it in the Bullock case.[54]

. . . the Civil Service, like every other profession, has its unwritten code of ethics and conduct for which the most effective sanction lies in the public opinion of the service itself, and it is upon the maintenance of a sound and healthy public opinion within the service that its value and efficiency chiefly depend.

The first duty of a civil servant is to give all his undivided allegiance to the state at all times and on all occasions when the state has a claim upon his services. With his private

---

[50] Cf. Royal Commission on the Civil Service (1929), Introductory Memoranda (63-49), p. iv ff.
[51] Cf. U. S. Civil Service Commission: Annual Reports, Directory and Prohibitory Statutes, and Rules.
[52] Cf. Jèze, *op. cit.*, Vol. II, Chap. 2.

[53] Report of the board of inquiry . . . to investigate certain statements affecting civil servants, Cmd. 3037, 1928, p. 21.
[54] Report of the board of inquiry . . . to investigate certain discussions engaged in by the Permanent Secretary to the Air Ministry, Cmd. 5254, 1936. Sir Christopher Bullock had interlaced public negotiations regarding the charter of the Imperial Airways with the advancement of his personal interests. The Board said: "We do not say that he consciously used his official position to further his interests; yet we cannot but think that it was the official position he held that provided the vantage ground. . ." The report refers to the "lack of that instinct and perception from which is derived the sure guide by which the conduct of a civil servant should be regulated."

activities the state is in general not concerned, so long as his conduct therein is not such as to bring discredit upon the service of which he is a member. But to say that he is not to subordinate his duty to his private interests, nor to make use of his official position to further those interests, is to say no more than that he must behave with common honesty. The service exacts from itself a higher standard, because it recognises that the state is entitled to demand that its servants shall not only be honest in fact, but beyond the reach of suspicion of dishonesty. It was laid down by one of His Majesty's Judges in a case some few years ago that it was not merely of some importance but of fundamental importance that in a Court of Law justice should not only be done, but should manifestly and undoubtedly be seen to be done; which we take to mean that public confidence in the administration of justice would be shaken if the least suspicion, however ill-founded, were allowed to arise that the course of legal proceedings could in any way be influenced by improper motives. We apply without hesitation an analogous rule to other branches of the public service. A civil servant is not to subordinate his duty to his private interests; but neither is he to put himself in a position where his duty and his interests conflict. He is not to make use of his official position to further those interests; but neither is he so to order his private affairs as to allow the suspicion to arise that a trust has been abused or a confidence betrayed. These obligations are, we do not doubt, universally recognised throughout the whole of the service; if it were otherwise, its public credit would be diminished and its usefulness to the state impaired.

It follows that there are spheres of activity legitimately open to the ordinary citizens in which the civil servant can play no part or only a limited part. He is not to indulge in political or party controversy lest by so doing he should appear no longer the disinterested adviser of Ministers or able impartially to execute their policy. He is bound to maintain a proper reticence in discussing public affairs and more particularly those with which his own Department is concerned. And lastly his position clearly imposes upon him restrictions in matters of commerce and business from which the ordinary citizen is free.

We content ourselves with laying down these general principles, which we do not seek to elaborate into any detailed code, if only for the reason that their application must necessarily vary according to the position, the Department and the work of the civil servant concerned. Practical rules for the guidance of social conduct depend also as much upon the instinct and perception of the individual as upon cast-iron formulae; and the surest guide will, we hope, always be found in the nice and jealous honour of civil servants themselves. The public expects from them a standard of integrity and conduct not only inflexible but fastidious, and has not been disappointed in the past. We are confident that we are expressing the view of the Service when we say that the public have a right to expect that standard, and that it is the duty of the Service to see that the expectation is fulfilled.

The general rule necessarily holds good in every case where a special art or craft is pursued. Discipline is severe in proportion to the excellence of attainment sincerely desired. Bernard Shaw does not drink tea, coffee, or alcoholic liquors, mainly because he is loyal to his craft: has he not said that without them he kills nine out of ten thoughts, but having consumed them he loses the power of self-criticism? The most splendid code of systematic self-discipline is the Book of Spiritual Exercises made by Ignatius Loyola for the Jesuit Order. The novice passes twenty-eight days in devotional retirement. In this seclusion he is humiliated by the memory of his past life and troubled with a vision of future labors and sacrifices. He then learns the life and works of Christ, and chooses the specific path upon which he thinks to tread toward the divinely appointed goal. He is helped to enter into the spirit of the way of salvation made known by the Saviour; and before the resplendent light of this revelation, the novice annihilates his average nature and surrenders for ever to the commands and prohibitions adequate to the duties which he has now come to expect of himself. Each day starts with prayer, and then a *prelude,* that is, a strenuous imaginative evocation of men and places, or his personal vices, which he will be called upon to master during the day. He must obey the dictates of his preconception. Then (and on each day there is a different routine) he traverses a number of spiritual stations; surveys his sins and meditates upon their despicable baseness; reflects upon the distance of his fall from the possible maximum of human saintliness; and from the high morality of God, meditates upon, and even cries aloud, his worthlessness compared with the Lord's unbounded loving-kindness; vows that he will embrace the means of amendment, and repeats the Lord's Prayer. A ritual of penitence, all military in its qualities of discipline and subordination to the command of the former cavalry officer, Loyola, was prescribed, and it recalled in terms calculated to rouse the martial spirit, the eternal battle between Wrong and Right.

More modern and ordinary instances abound. An Olympic runner is made by careful diet, proper spells of rest, and disciplined exercise. A boxer suffers terribly during training; similarly with dancers, painters, and writers. They discipline their talents.

The ordinary, average worker is kept to this intensity of training, this carefulness of life, is kept "in form" by the prospects of advancement or of losing his job and by many other things which operate equally in the civil service as, for example, the opinion of his friends and the sneers of his enemies, a pure sense of self-respect, and so on.[55] The security of tenure, the colleagueship, the monopoly of unpriced services, reduce the strain and tautness and severity of the service of the state, and a deliberately invented and consciously inspired code of discipline is the necessary basis of progress. The desire for excellence of attainment must, if it is not spontaneous, be synthetically fabricated. Whereas in private employment the price of service in large part evokes obligations and restraints, in public employment the obligations and restraints which serve the public are not in strict proportion to the price paid to civil servants.

In some countries a note of religious solemnity is introduced into the whole arrangement by the institution of an oath

which civil servants take when entering the service. In bygone days such oaths were personal, that is, they were made to the Prince, King, or Emperor,[56] and it was to the personal service of these that the olden-day Chancellor, Marshal, and other officers swore devotion. The transformation of the royal State into the impersonal state has resulted in the oath being taken to the laws and the constitution. For these continue, or lawyers are prepared to demonstrate that they continue, though Presidents, Prime Ministers, and party leaders come and go. Weimar German officials had to "swear loyalty to the *Reich* constitution, obedience to the laws, and conscientious fulfillment of my official duties." [57]

The Obligations of Public Service. Supposing now that the present tendency toward maintaining state activity continues, that the state socializes: that is, manages a large part of the total economic activities to the exclusion of the present price- and profit-making machinery. Suppose it discards for the great basic neces-

---

[55] Cf. Carl F. Taeusch, *Professional and Business Ethics* (New York, 1926).

[56] E.g., the oath in the fifteenth century (in Prussia) was to the immediate master: to him was sworn faithful service, the care of his interests and those of the country, the prompt and careful execution of all official duties as well as the special orders of the master, and finally, the strict keeping of official secrets and other confidential information made by the master. (S. Isaacsohn, *Geschichte des preussischen Beamtentums*, Vol. I, p. 7.)

[57] Cf. constitution, 1919, article 176.

France: Under Napoleon as Emperor, civil servants swore obedience to the constitution and to the Emperor; this form remained until September, 1870, when the oath of service was suppressed. But Jèze says that the professional oath still exists. He condemns it, saying it is puerile, because a magistrate or a teacher will serve loyally in any case. "In fact, it is a practical and theatrical means of fulfilling the official ceremony of installing a public officer. It has no legal significance. The oath adds absolutely nothing to the service duties of the official." (Jèze, *op. cit.*, Vol. II, p. 94).

Great Britain: No oath. *United States:* No oath, but the TVA statute requires [Sec. 2(h)] that all members of the board shall be persons who profess a belief in the feasibiliy and wisdom of this act. The Authority requires this profession of all its employees. The requirement had its origin in the anxiety that enemies of public enterprise would thwart the TVA from within.

saries the principle of price for the principle of the best quality and greatest quantity to him who needs most, or even the principle of equal distribution? If the ordinary economic motives as they now operate are devitalized by the state provision of secure economic conditions, what principle of behavior must be put in their place to serve such a philanthropic state? If nationalized services are to operate with the maximum of beneficial effect and the minimum waste of energy and resources, it is not enough that they are manned by millions of civil servants who know how to go about their business, acting in an ingeniously-planned organization. A faith must animate and sustain them in the use of that knowledge, a faith akin in its steadfastness and compelling attraction to' that which moves great scientific, intellectual, and artistic natures. They must believe that their work and their surrender of easy satisfactions and daily indulgences are worth while.

A dynamic ethic is above all necessary, an insistent commandment, an unfailing "Thou Shalt" and "Thou Shalt Not." This ethic can have an enduring effect only if it is based on a deliberately inculcated scheme of beliefs about the debt owed by individual men and women to the society whose service is their purpose, and these beliefs must be held religiously. We have glanced at the present state of those beliefs as included in the codes of discipline of some great modern states. But they merely correspond to a degree of socialization which if it is not small is at least not yet as large as the programs of progressive political parties. Even conservative parties are socializers in the many things they would like to *force* everybody else to do: for conservatism is far from individualistic. It merely asks of the state different activity from that demanded by others; but, emphatically, it asks the state's intervention. If society, then, comes to rely upon the socialized operation of essential industries, its success will depend chiefly upon the quality of mind the civil servant brings to their conduct. And it seems to me that the qual-

ity of mind must fulfil the following conditions.

The civil servant must believe that the public welfare is his sole end, and that he is not entitled to spiritual and material adventures which conflict with this end. He must subdue desires for alternative satisfactions which are incompatible with the public welfare. When all constitutional channels, in the creation of which he will naturally have had a fair say, have been used in regard to his claims for pay, conditions of work, amount of leisure, etc., he must accept the result without that malice, sense of injustice, or revolt which would spoil his work. Since only what best serves the state is best, it is a breach of official faith to show favoritism or jealousy in the course of his official duties on grounds of race, creed, class, sex, family ties, etc. If he receives orders which are unsound, or is reprimanded, as he thinks, unjustly, his sense of obedience must not be weakened, and (without animus) he must honestly state what seems to him unfair and inefficient. The use of his leisure would need to be such as not to unfit him for the best performance of his duties. His inventive faculties must be continually kept at their fullest natural stretch. His imagination must, as far as it can, see through the forms and the oral and written reports to the human realities they represent. The representative assembly and its organs will lay down the limits within which he may act officially, and he owes obedience. Tolerant and kindly to those below him in rank and to the public he serves, he must use his official authority no more than the interests of the service require, and suppress the impulse of personal dominion since his command is held only as a trust for society.

These are austere conditions, and the task of cultivating them in several million administrators drawn from the average men and women we know is fraught with immense difficulty. Indeed, it may be asked, is the task even possible? We shall not attempt to answer that question here but we may indicate some of the elements into which the inquiry must be resolved. How far is the incentive to make private profit actually operative in modern industry? How strong are other motives, if present, compared with it? Was private profit the predominant motive when the young men or women first entered employment, or were they attracted by other prospects in their vocation? Would a freer choice of profession modify the desire for harsh competitive economic advantage, and fortify the strength of other mental and spiritual factors, such as delight in speculation, research, organization, handicraft, and so forth, essential to sound progressive industry? How far, in fact, has acquisitiveness been checked in professions and business? If it has been limited by an accepted body of ethics, what general effect has this had upon the behavior of those accepting it? Has there been, for example, much private rebellion against the code—did men "grunt and sweat under a weary life," and feel that they bore fardels?

For it is urgent to beware that we do not simply remove the human stress and pain from where they are resident in society to another place. Good statecraft is to move and redistribute them so as to reduce their incidence to the minimum possible. And it is all too easy to make mistakes: to create sheer ugliness and moral inhibitions without creating as much or more freedom, beauty, and moral development. Of this, the statesman must beware, and the cost must be anticipated. And, finally, we must ask whether we can possibly devise a system of education for children and adults which will enable us to inculcate the code of discipline—how far can we go along this road of changing the schools, the universities, and the environment, and thereby of subjecting impulses and restraints to our rationally conceived social plans? For the ethics of every profession will be found, on close analysis, to be not much higher and not much lower than the general decency of the nation as a whole. Their nature, at the least, is powerfully molded by the level of the surrounding and pervading civilization.

These are not easy questions to answer. They require an exact and critical research into human nature and the world in which it lives. But whether they are answered before we move into a more socialized or a less state-controlled life than we have now, the good we decide upon will be purchased by a price paid in the currency of such restraints as we observed in the official discipline of today.

These questions are not put with the idea of suggesting that the conditions are impossible of fulfillment. Nor are they expressed in an absolute sense, that is to say, the world is not faced with deciding to have all or nothing of socialization or a planned economy. There may be some branches of enterprise where the conditions can be fulfilled better than in others. There may be partial state control, short of full ownership and management, in which the controllers alone must satisfy the disciplinary conditions, while the rest are free. The full force of the principles regulating duty and incentive in a planned economy may not need to be applied to the general body of the workers under the higher ranks of the executive group, the intermediate foremen level.

What is to be learned, however, is that where the economy, as well as other phases of man's social behavior, is subject to social rule, it must be in the name of certain principles. Those principles can be fulfilled by a persuaded people and convinced officials. In proportion as persuasion and conviction are lacking and it is still ordained to proceed with the policies, then coercion must intervene.[58]

It is, therefore, emphatically evident that the democratic process, whereby no additional activity is assumed by the state and no extra piece of governmental ma-

[58] Here the reader should have in mind the Soviet planned economy, carried through and maintained without popular consent. Cf. A. Baykov, *The Development of the Soviet Economic System* (Cambridge, 1946). Cf. Stalin's speeches in *Leninism* (New York, 1942) regarding the uprooting of the kulaks and the inefficiency of the administration of the planned economy, especially the quality of the products. Cf. also S. and B. Webb, *Soviet Communism* (London, 1935), Part II, Chap. IX, "In Place of Profits," where they ask anxious questions regarding fear as an instrument of managerial control.

chinery is set up until it has been thoroughly warranted by open discussion and acceptance, is an essential element in good administration.

THE democratic principle has had at least as much influence upon the modern state as the principle of efficiency, and the public services have been powerfully affected by it. But the notion of authority still lies strongly embedded in the organization of the modern civil service, and though the democratic principle has had its influence, its effect is still only in the early stages of evolution. All kinds of motives combine to support the harshness and firmness of the state's authority over its servants, and these motives are grounded in the state's prestige and in its social importance. Decades have been required to bring some mildness into the state's relations with its servants, and the concessions have never been made but with great misgivings by their donors. Legislatures are in fact dreadfully frightened by civil services: they and society seem to be lost without them and lost with them, and they feel compelled to treat them in a way which has, in the last generation at least, not been tolerated by private employees. We have already in our discussions of discipline traversed some of the reasons for this.

Political freedom falls broadly into two parts—that which concerns the exercise of the vote and general political activity, and that which concerns candidature for legislative assemblies.

The Vote and Political Activity. No countries now forbid civil servants from voting, nor, as a special class, were they so limited in the nineteenth century. The tendency has been rather for civil servants to be especially welcomed as voters, not by the law, but in political practice, because the government in power (in France until 1871 and in Germany until 1918, the Crown's ministers in a mock-constitutional state) and the parties struggling for power have always hoped to influence civil servants to vote for them. Governments have always had a fairly easy task, especially in France, Germany, and the United States, in intimidating civil servants, and spying on civil servants has served to reveal any recalcitrancy. The importance of these votes in the aggregate can be gauged when we remember that the officials constitute a very substantial proportion of the electorate. We may take it, too, that there are fewer abstentions among civil servants than among other branches of the population. Further, they have, in bureaucratic countries, made very good canvasses. These qualities persisted in Third Republic France; in Germany they were cynically employed until 1918, when a great break was made with the electoral and bureaucratic past. In England the progressive disappearance of patronage and the growth of bribery and corrupt-practices legislation reduced the significance of this use of the civil service vote to a negligible proportion after 1870. In the United States the remnants of the spoils system leave Congressman and the Senator an ample field for ugly election practices in spite of very great progress in the last four decades.

At first, and to some extent even now, the civil service vote was encouraged by the politicians for their own purposes. But as the numbers of the civil service grew, and as its members became ever more aware of their collective economic interests, they became strong enough to threaten to make at least some members of the legislature the servants of their special interests. The threat from some bodies of civil servants, like dockyard workers and postal officials, was strong enough to constitute a problem. The way out of this difficulty was variously proposed as disfranchisement or as the creation of special constituencies.

No great harm has come from leaving matters to take their own course. It is too grave a penalty to debar a civil servant from voting when the result of that voting has, on the whole, so little effect. If civil servants were much more numerous than they are, and if their activities and power were not offset by other voters and associations, then some other arrangements would need to be made. We shall speculate on this theme later. But the vote has obviously come to stay.

Political Activity in France. The extreme of liberty allowed in political activity is to be found in France. But this is not based upon any consciously elaborated political activity at all; it comes about administratively, and is derived from the authority of the minister and the heads of the department to see that the officials do their work properly. Where, therefore, participation at meetings, the employment of time in writing, and canvassing, acting as treasurer, and so on, affect departmental activity, the means of its restriction is part of the ordinary disciplinary arrangements. But the tendency in France has not been generally to forbid or even narrowly to restrict political activity. It has been simply to turn it into "proper" channels: that is to say, to make it support the government of the day, and rid it of antipatriotic, antimilitaristic, syndicalistic elements, and religious suspects.[59] It has been said [60] that:

The same men who to purify the law of all Catholicism, asserted the indifference of the State to all doctrines, to-day recognize the State's right to have a doctrine; those who negated the soul say that it has the "charge of souls;" those who forbade it to challenge the ndependence of the mind by any philosophical preference, assign to it the duty of creating "the unity of minds."

The time is past when the personal records were the unfailing registers of political behavior. The jurisprudence of the *Conseil d'État* does not permit use of the disciplinary or promotional power on political grounds, but it denies to the official the right to act outside his work in such a way as to threaten to render inefficient his capacity for serving the common good as assigned to him in his official duties. He is safeguarded against surreptitious pressure by the *statut,* which declares (article 16) that his *dossier* must not include any mention of his political, philosophic or religious opinions.

Political Activity in Britain. British manners and institutions are much different. A comparatively high standard of public honor is combined with more subordination to the public welfare. Long years of electoral experience and efficient party organization have made civil servant canvassers unnecessary, while the tradition of the impartiality of the civil service is a strongly respected convention. Rational consideration has therefore been given to the subject, and a series of rules worked out by the various departments and the Treasury. Generally these allow political activity so long as it is not of a sort to bring the civil servant as an official into such conflict with other citizens that the public service would suffer damage in its dignity, authority, and reputation as an impartial servant of the community. The rules, therefore, affect the combativeness of the civil servant, and his occupation with politics while in official uniform or during his official hours. The Order in Council of 1910 embodied the traditional custom of the service that "employees of the civil service should take no overt part in public political affairs." Examples of departmental rules are the *Clerk's Instructions* of the Board of Inland Revenue which forbid any officer to become secretary of a political association or club, and the Post Office rule forbidding canvassing or other political demonstation while in postal uniform or serving upon a party committee concerned with furthering or preventing the return of a particular candidate.

In 1925 a Treasury Committee considered regulations governing candidature for Parliament and for municipal bodies of persons in the service of the Crown, and its report [61] dealt with political activity and the right of candidature, but

---

59 Cf. P. Harmignie, *L'État et ses Agents* (Brussels, 1911), p. 29 ff.; and P. Leroy-Beaulieu, *L'État Moderne et ses Fonctions* (Paris, 1890), p. 81.
60 Étienne Lamy, *Catholiques et Socialistes,* p. 38, cited in Harmignie, *op. cit.,* p. 30, footnote.

61 Cmd. 2408, 1925.

with special and almost exclusive attention to the latter. The committee required the maintenance of restrictions wherever the reputation for impartiality of the civil servant might be jeopardized. The main ground for such restrictions upon candidatures and political activity was this:

The constantly extending disposition of Parliament to entrust the exercise of quasi-judicial duties to executive departments without providing any of the established safeguards operative against judicial excess—such as publicity, right of audience to persons affected, statement of reasons for judgment, right of appeal, and the like—as well as the sharper alignment of political parties in these days, unite to make the high reputation for political impartiality hitherto enjoyed by the public service a more valuable national possession than ever before. We can feel no doubt that the confidence universally held in the existence of such impartiality is a most valuable guarantee for its continuance, and we can have no assurance that the existing ethic of the service would long survive that confidence if it were once lost.

The committee rejected the possibility that an alternative career, that of politics, should be opened up to civil servants. It would take experienced civil servants from the service, and would distract others by aspirations which might fail of realization. They were afraid that a public servant would use his office to help his political career and his political career to improve his official position. They accordingly recommended that participation in municipal government should be still permitted by departmental discretion, where it involved no moral or material interference with official duties. As for parliamentary candidatures, the existing civil service rule—that is, resignation on candidature—was to continue in effect. But the industrial staffs (munitions workers, shipbuilders, etc.) of the fighting services should be exempt. Some members of the committee thought that all industrial staffs and the manipulative and other subordinate grades should be free to pursue candidatures. But even here it was recommended that political activity in official uniform or in the area of service should be forbidden. The agreed recommendations were made effective by Order in Council, July 25, 1927. The departments which have local offices and connections with the local authorities prohibit their officials from standing for local councilorship.

Many civil servants, keenly interested citizens, remained restive under these restrictions, and after World War II raised the issue of political freedom anew, at a time when also great changes occurred in political and administrative organization. The most recent ideas are surveyed presently.

Political Activity in Germany. Before the advent of democratic government in 1918, the German government mastered the political activity of its servants and saw to it that none save "friends of the Government" or "Fatherland-faithful" citizens became and remained civil servants. The large military element which had the monopoly of the lower clerical and custodial grades was well enough disciplined not to need encouragement to occupy itself with political activity excepting as it pleased the government, that is, the Conservatives; and the upper civil service was in the main by birth and social position the supporter of the government, and those who were heads of the local authorities were the political agents of the government.[62] A long and bitter controversy raged round the position of the heads of the local hierarchy under the name of "the problem of the political officials."

The advent of democracy aggravated the problem. It was especially among the civil servants of executive and clerical rank—always the storm-center of agitation in the civil service—that resentment was felt about political limitations.

The change from monarchy to democracy threw Germany without any preparation into the very midst of all the bristling difficulties of the problem. The first impulse, as soon as parties became all-powerful, was for each party to use

---

[62] See H. von Gerlach, *Meine Erlebnisse in der Preussischen Verwalting* (Berlin, 1919); and A. Wermuth, *Ein Beamtenleben* (Berlin).

the civil service for all it was worth as "spoils" and as votes, canvassers, and election agents. Some things—some necessary—were done in the early months of the Revolution.[63] Then the constitutional assemblies of the *Reich* and the states set to work and produced the elements of a code. The main features in the *Reich* and in Prussia emerged from a consideration of article 130 of the constitution of August 11, 1919, and a series of decisions of the Supreme Administrative Court of Prussia. The constitutional clause said:

Officials are servants of the community, not of a party.

All officials are guaranteed freedom of their political opinion and the right of association. Officials are accorded special representative committees which will be constituted in detail by a law of the *Reich*.

We are here principally concerned with the second clause of this article—on the freedom of political opinion. This, when taken together with article 118, which gave all citizens the right to express their opinions freely but within the limits of the general law,[64] meant that the official was without any constitutional limits upon his political activity. But these constitutional rights were abrogated to the extent made necessary by the nature of their office.[65] This is a very good illustration of the argument sustained in the previous section on disciplinary codes and the need for an

official ethic. The constitutional rights of civil servants are limited by more than the general criminal law; they are not like ordinary people. These limits did not go so far as to exclude officials from the franchise, or to require that they should change their political party because it happened to have a point of view different from the government of the day. But officials must be held in check by remembering that their behavior might affect the belief in the impartiality of their official function. No admixture of official and political activity was permissible. Nor might any official superior use his authority to influence the political opinion and activity of those under his control. Officials were forbidden to use their official or social power to influence votes, and all political agitation in official precincts was strictly forbidden. The Supreme Administrative Court of Prussia decided that "freedom of political opinion" meant that any official might openly proclaim himself member of a political party, and that against this simple declaration no disciplinary action could be taken. Cases, however, arose where officials wore party symbols, like swastikas and Soviet stars, buttons, and badges, and since experience showed that these resulted in undesirable altercations and a disturbance of the peaceful continuity of official work, the exhibition of symbols during service was completely forbidden.

The penal code [66] forbade all officials, without exception, to promote or support, by positive activity, the efforts of political parties who wished to abolish the bases of the existing republican forms of the state by violence—as, for example, the Communist party or the Separatists. An official, for example, who participated in the formation of a "red army" had to be dismissed.[67] Behavior of this kind naturally was against the oath of office. The law on the Defense of the Republic [68] of July, 1922, which has been inserted into the *Reich* law relating to

---

[63] Von Gerlach, *op. cit.*
[64] I.e., the criminal law relating to libel and slander, etc.
[65] Cf. Brand, *op. cit.*, p. 486. The Prussian *Oberverwaltungsgericht* (1927) laid down very strong doctrine: "The right to freedom of opinion is no unlimited one, but finds its limits for every citizen in the general laws, and for the official further in the duties imposed on him by his duties, principally in the duty of obedience and loyalty, which forbids him from making a use of this right as unlimited as other citizens who are not under the compulsion of the unrelaxable official discipline in the general public interest. The office includes the whole of the official's personality. He is never a mere private citizen: in all his actions, even outside his office in the narrowest sense of the word, he must know and remember that his office binds him."

[66] *Reichsarbeitsministerium*, 23.2.23.
[67] Articles 82-84.
[68] Prussian Disciplinary Court, see *Deutsche Juristen Zeitung*, Vol. 24, p. 832.

federal officials, also imposes special duties upon them. They could not in public and during their functions promote movements for the restoration of the monarchy or against the existence of the Republic, by the misuse of their official status or by incitement or spiteful behavior, nor support such movements by calumniating, defaming, or bringing into contempt the Republic, the President of the *Reich,* or members of the present or a previous republican-parliamentary government of the *Reich* or any state.[69]

The administrative courts worked out the effect of the official duties upon constitutional rights in considerable detail. Where officials in the course of their political activity criticized the government, they were expected to endeavor to exercise the rights in a peaceful and a technically impersonal fashion. They could not fight the government either publicly or privately in a manner designed to stir up hatred, or agitate, or incite. What happens inside the service was not to be made known to outsiders not directly interested. Complaints about superiors might not even be published in a service journal. Officials were obliged to be very careful not to defame their superiors, or to engender dissatisfaction among officials and jeopardize the discipline and order of the civil service.

Thus the political activity of civil servants in Weimar Germany was limited. Civil servants could act and speak politically, but all in a muted key. It should be noticed that in Germany some of the officials were definitely political officials:[70] that is, their position was such that they had wide discretion in the execution of the plans of the central government; they shared, indeed, in the work of government in a very real sense, being in close and intimate contact with

ministers and sharing their confidence. These could not, under any circumstances, work against the government of the day, and were not allowed to attempt to criticize ministerial plans or projects in public.

On the whole, the Weimar Germans worked out a rational system, not too hard upon the civil servants and not dangerous or derogatory to the authority of the state. The interests of any state are in the maintenance of its authority, and this is based upon its spiritual awfulness and its temporal dignity and efficiency. The limitations upon the civil servants are designed to safeguard these qualities, in all their possible entirety, from the effects of unrestrained democracy. These limitations ought not to be drawn too narrowly since too sharp a differentiation between officials and public is bad for both. Everything which can make for community of life and understanding of governors and governed is important. The mistake to be guarded against is that of being unjustly restrictive to the official.

Political Activity in the United States. This, owing to an unfortunate administrative history, the United States has not been able to avoid, and her present law and regulations are rather of the nature of an undue reaction from the blatant evils of the "spoils" system than a rational settlement of the problem of political activity.[71] The Civil Service Act of 1883 gives the Civil Service Commission power to aid the President in preparing suitable rules for the civil service, and the rule which appears first in the body promulgated by the President runs:

No person in the executive civil service shall use his official authority or influence for the purpose of interfering with an election or affecting the results thereof. Persons who by the provisions of these rules are in the competitive classified service, while retaining the right to vote as they please and to express

---

[69] Cf. also G. Anschütz, *Beamten und die Revolutionären Parteien* (Berlin, 1931).

[70] These were classified in an order made by the *Reich* Ministry of Justice, 16.2.23, *Reichsjustizministerium;* cf. *Beamten-Archiv,* Vol. III, p. 322. The best general treatise upon the subject since 1919 is A. Köttgen, *Das deutsche Berufsbeamtentum und die parlamentarische Demokratie* (Berlin, 1928).

[71] The same may be said of Australia, Canada, and South Africa, and the regulations of these countries are almost identical with those of the United States. For the United States, see W. Chen, *Doctrine of Civil Service Neutrality in the United States and Great Britain* (University of Chicago Ph.D. thesis, mss., 1937).

privately their opinions on all political subjects, shall take no active part in political management or in political campaigns.

This provision is supplemented by the rule prohibiting political assessments, that is, the raising of funds for political purposes by more or less enforced contributions from civil servants.[72] It is extended in various ways by the Hatch Act.[73]

Candidatures for political conventions in the capacity of delegate, or service as an officer or employee thereof, are prohibited. Attendance is permitted, but not participation in the proceedings in any shape, nor public display of partisanship or obtrusive demonstration or interference. It is permissible to cast a vote at primaries, mass conventions, or caucuses, but not to go beyond this point, whether as an officer of the meeting, as a speechmaker, or even to take a prominent part in the proceedings. Preparing for, addressing, or organizing or conducting a political meeting or rally is not permitted. Nor is service on any political committee allowed. Even attendance at committees which are distinctly related to government policy at a time when campaigns are in progress may fall within the ban. It is permissible for civil servants to be members of political clubs, but not to be active in organizing them, or in making addresses to them, or to be officers within their framework. It is even dangerous to hold office in organizations established to secure social reforms, as they may take on a character of partisan political activity. There might even be a question asked where the more technical aspects of governmental reform were the object of some civic organization's program. It is permissible to make gifts of money or kind to political organizations, but they may not solicit, collect, receive, disburse, or otherwise handle contributions for political purposes. No such contributions

may be made directly or indirectly to secure the election of members of Congress.

Although employees may express their opinions on all political subjects and candidates, such expression may not occur in such a way as to constitute an active part in political management of campaigns. While an employee may wear a political badge or display a poster in his window or car, it is a violation of the law to make this into a partisan display while on duty.

The management of newspapers or editorial service thereon, where they are known as partisan, is prohibited; any kind of publication for or against parties, candidates, or factions is prohibited. Practically every kind of activity at the polls is prohibited, excepting the right to vote. Though the right of petition is safeguarded, if petitions are identified with political management or campaigns, the civil servant may not initiate them or canvass for their signature.

All these rules are interpreted in detail and quite strictly—at any rate, in theory. There are additional rules prohibiting the interference with the political freedom of any civil servant by other civil servants or by outsiders through the offer or refusal of jobs or promotions or dismissals, and so on, for political purposes.

These restrictions are exceedingly heavy: certainly in their overt completeness far more so than those in Britain and France. There are others concerning the holding of office in legislative assemblies, and even more important, being members of organizations whose political activities and general philosophy are disliked—such as fascist and communist groups. To this subject we return presently. It may be added that one of the bans on membership of political organizations related to affiliation with those that advocate strikes, and this also needs separate discussion later.

The action taken by the Civil Service Commission against offenders is displayed annually in its report.

Political Candidatures. Neither Great Britain nor the United States allows political candidatures of civil servants. The

---

[72] Criminal Code, Section 118 ff.
[73] Public Law, No. 252, August 2, 1939; amended July 19, 1940, and March 27, 1942. Cf. Civil Service Commission Form 3726, June, 1942, *Political Actions of Public Officers and Employees.*

early practice of the former was dictated by the fear that the executive would dominate Parliament at a time when the Crown and ministers showed every sign of desiring such domination. That fear has departed, but before it lost its efficacy it resulted in the theory of the separation of powers and its inscription in the constitution of the United States and most of the American states.[74] The present situation, which is very much the same for Australia and Canada, is dictated by the fear that the civil service would lose its reputation for impartiality if civil servants were allowed freely to become candidates and participate in the work of political assemblies. We have already (p. 869) quoted a passage from the report of the British Treasury Committee which reported upon this subject —impartiality is its theme. But there are other difficulties. The civil servant who becomes a member of a legislature might find it necessary to criticize his former chiefs, political and administrative, and to say things about his department which would breed a very ugly spirit in his office. How could he, then, at the expiration of his term, be reinstated without disturbance and personal friction? An alternative career would be created for some, and this would take their minds from their work; while the possibility of their translation to another sphere would cause all kinds of emotional disturbance among their colleagues and those seeking promotion. There is the further difficulty of their status in the department when they return from their parliamentary activities. All these and many more possibilities are not of such a nature that their importance can be gauged with any exactitude; we have no data upon which to judge how many people would be affected

with the desire to be candidates, and how many adjustments would have to be made through their alarums and excursions. But a fear remains. The general practice of English-speaking countries is, then, to exclude candidatures for the legislature.

The higher officials in Great Britain who are, by the nature of their duties, continually dabbling in politics, have not insisted on their claims. The subordinate officials have pointed out that officers of the armed forces had the right to enter Parliament. Dockyard workers, too, were in a condition of freedom in this respect.[75] Postal and customs officials, however, and the clerical and administrative staffs were obliged to follow the rule (by clause 16 of the Orders in Council of 1910) that "any officer seeking a seat in the House of Commons shall resign his office as soon as he issues his address to the electors, or in any other manner publicly announces himself as a candidate." The Treasury declaration first supporting this rule was made in 1884, and said that there would be public injury caused

by any departure from the conditions which, under Parliamentary Government, render a Permanent Civil Service possible, and . . . among those conditions the essential one is that the members of such a service should remain free to serve the Government of the day, without necessarily exposing themselves to public charges of inconsistency or insincerity.

The reply of civil servants [76] is that they ought to take as keen an interest and as controversial a part in politics as any other citizen. This does not impair their loyalty in administering a contrary policy, "and in place of the existing restrictions on the expression of those views all that was required was a code of professional discretion such as that expected of barristers and solicitors." They rely upon a "professional ethic." The committee sustained the Treasury's opinion. Resignation on candidature is the civil service

---

[74] Constitution, article I, sect. 7: "No senator or representative shall, during the time for which he was elected, be appointed to any civil office under the authority of the United States, which shall have been created, or the emoluments whereof shall have been increased during such time; and no person holding any office under the United States shall be a member of either House during his continuance in office."

[75] See Report of Committee on the Parliamentary, etc., Candidature of Crown Servants, Cmd. 2408, 1925.
[76] Report, p. 14.

rule in regard to Parliamentary candidatures.

France and Germany have a different history in this matter of political candidature of civil servants. In France up to 1852 there was a general tradition and practice of membership of the Chamber and the Senate by officials, until great abuses, both administrative and political, arose.[77] From 1852 dates the constitutional principle that every paid public office is incompatible with the mandate of deputy to the legislative body. In 1875 this general rule was adopted [78] and even a list of exceptions kept the ordinary civil servant from the Chambers. Since 1919 [79] if an official is elected to a legislative body he ceases for the time being to be an official, since office and membership are incompatible, but does not lose pension rights.

In Germany [80] before the Weimar régime, neither the *Reich* nor the states excluded officials from Parliamentary candidature and activity, and indeed, since the beginning of constitutional government in those states, special guarantees were created so that this activity might be unhindered. Later, under the kind of constitutional government pertaining before 1918, the difficulties of the double nature of the official, as official and private citizen, did not appear in all their severity. For the government excluded from its service all but those likely to be its friends, and political parties had no very effective part in constitutional life. It was even to the interest of the government to have its well-disciplined civil servants in the political assemblies as representatives of its point of view, as experts upon the subjects discussed, especially in committee, and as an addition to governmental voting power.

Prior to the advent of constitutional government, that is, under the despotism of the eighteenth century and its limited counterpart to 1848, the "people" found it rather to their interests to have officials included in the estates and other representative bodies, since they were able and since they were occasionally in the van of political liberalism, and as such a counterweight to the influence of court favorites. During the March days of 1848, liberal opinion, following the constitutional development of France, England and the United States, tended to demand the exclusion of officials from the assemblies. But other currents of opinion resisted, and the end was the maintenance of unlimited freedom of entry into Parliament, and of the rules which had previously been made to secure that officials should not find themselves dismissed for their ambitions or even experience undue hardship in obtaining leave *(Urlaub)* to which they had a statutory right.[81] Until the entry into force of the constitution of 1919, the situation in the *Reich* and Prussia, and almost all other states with small variations, was that all officials had unconditional freedom to participate in parliamentary and local government; [82] they obtained leave automatically upon election. This leave extended to the full session of the assembly and to short adjournments, but not to long prorogations. Officials were secured by special regulations against having to pay the cost of departmental deputies out of their salaries. In support of the existing situation were those considerations: the technical ability of officials, the loss to the dignity of the service if they were denied the free expression of opinion, and the value of their impartiality in assemblies

[77] Cf. E. Pierre, *Traité de Droit Politique et Parlémentaire*, 5th edition (Paris, 1924), para. 337.

[78] Law, November 30, 1875, article 8: "The exercise of public office paid out of State moneys is incompatible with the mandate of deputy."

[79] By the combined effect of the law of December 30, 1913, article 33, and the law of October 21, 1919.

[80] The history of the German law and practice is very ably described in Clausz, *Der Staatsbeamte als Abgeordneter* (Karlsruhe, 1906).

[81] The constitutional assembly of the North German Confederation, 1867, consisted of 40 per cent of active civil servants, and the same proportion appeared in the Prussian Diet. In 1867, thirty per cent of the German *Reichstag* were active officials; in 1898-99, fifteen per cent. It must be remembered that judges and teachers were included in these percentages.

[82] Cf. constitution, 1871, article 21.

which were more and more becoming a prey to violent economic and social conflicts. Against the right of candidature were the difficulties felt by the officials in combining office with party activity, the disorganization caused by sudden departures without leave and without proper arrangements previously made, and, from the point of view of the public and the parties of the Left, the increase of government influence by the activity and votes of parliamentary civil servants.[83]

The new constitution reiterated on the whole the freedom of political candidature. Article 128 gave "all citizens without distinction" the right to participate in public office, "in the measure allowed by the laws and in correspondence with their competence and services." Then article 39 [84] said: "Officials and members of the armed forces need no leave for the exercise of their office as members for the *Reichstag* or state Diet." This part of article 39 was word for word the same as article 21 of the constitution of 1871. But the second part introduced a novelty which was a significant extension of the right of free candidature. "If they attempt to acquire a seat in these bodies, then they must be granted the leave necessary for preparations for the election." The precise meaning of the word "necessary" *(erforderlich)* was left to the head of the department. No such leave preparatory to elections for the local authorities can be obtained, as it was thought that this would result in frivolous candidatures for the mere purpose of obtaining a holiday.

Germany had a very different problem to solve in the matter of political candidatures and activity, for her political system before World War I was radically different, both constitutionally and administratively, from the Weimar organization. The country assumed the democratic

method at a time when it was under serious and valid criticism, in spite of its many good features. Germany was badly scared by the rapid succession of short-lived governments and the instability of political life in the great states of today, and was especially anxious about the chronic defectiveness of French parliamentarism which had never been able to create an independent and efficient civil service. It was an act of great political bravery to dare the possible effects of democratic government upon the administrative system, but this was done. The result was that Weimar Germany was the most liberal country in the world in her interpretation of the rights of officials to participate in political life.

The Law of Officials under the Constitution of the Western Zones (1949) abolished the right of civil servants to run for legislative office.

SOME CONCLUSIONS ON POLITICAL RIGHTS AND DUTIES

ON the whole, then, civil servants are under strict prohibitions regarding the use of the civic rights available to all citizens. How far is this just? The answer is suggested by a consideration of three questions: the fundamental importance of impartiality and continuity of the public services, the situation as it is affected by the growth in the size and scope of state services, and finally, the rather wider issue of general loyalty to the entire political regime.

Impartiality and Continuity. Unwillingness to give officials any extensive political freedom is not due to mere caprice; it is due to the recognition, sometimes clear, sometimes vague, of the profound public importance of impartiality in the civil service—and it is a widespread and insistent recognition. We have seen this purpose immanent in the whole range of political activities—the state must not be injured, it must go on. Whatever the changes in the political constellation, however great the shocks in the world of political conflict and however violent its revolutions, the state, which is certainty,

---

[83] Clausz, *op. cit.*, p. 186 ff.
[84] Cf. also article 11 of the Prussian constitution: "State officials, employees and workers, and corporations of public law need no permission to exercise the activity of a member of Parliament. If they become candidates for the *Landtag*, the necessary time for preparation for their election is to be given. They continue to be paid their salaries and wages."

regularity, order, must continue. It must not cease: cessation is mortal. The instrument of continuity of services, which *ex hypothesi* are vital, is the civil service. Conceive the social and economic loss in modern Britain or France or Germany or the United States if the administrative services were the sport of political parties —the waste of organization, technique, expertness, professional zeal, and the adaptation which comes of years of regular and uninterrupted devotion to duties! All parties in the state must be sure of a highly efficient instrument, however diverse their policies, for no policy is worth the paper it is written on unless there is executive force behind it. Parties may differ on all things, but one thing is their common desire: power when they are in office, and such power is executive power. Our chief hope that political ministers and a helpless public will be prepared to learn from real science, resides in the flawless impartiality of their experts; and only the fact will create the confidence in it.

It is not surprising, therefore, that Weimar Germany inscribed official impartiality or neutrality into her constitution; that France has moved towards such a condition; that the Anglo-Saxon countries above all have created stringent prohibitions designed to serve political neutrality. The Anglo-Saxon countries are rightly afraid of their former selves. The question is whether in the present condition of acute political conflict in modern times this important constitutional rule can be maintained. For the more severe the struggle, the greater the temptation to use every means, legitimate or illegitimate, noble or base, to secure political advantage, that is, to win power over the adversary. In Great Britain, so far, the staff has been ready to serve any whom the elections and Parliament designated as the government. It is generally believed that this readiness will permanently prevail. This contention was well supported by the severe test of the Labour party's various tenures of office.

In the first edition of this work in 1932 I said:

It should, however, be said that at no time in English political history have these qualities of neutrality been subjected to a really crucial test. We have yet to see whether civil service neutrality can be maintained if burdened with any vital problem of conscience. We must not be too sanguine that our future is likely to be as free of social cleavage as our past. It should be remembered that during the General Strike of 1926, a large number of civil servants would not, on conscientious grounds, volunteer for duties outside those for which they were expressly engaged. Feelings were roused to a pitch where numbers of civil servants seceded from their association because they thought it had taken up a "disloyal" attitude. There are times, in fact, when the policy of a government directly affects the vital nature of the state. We should be foolish to imagine that old habits will continue to rule in such trying days. France is a chronic sufferer from official partiality—or at least, politicians pretend so. Excellent old civil servants in Germany attempted to sabotage the Revolution of 1918, and went a long way towards accomplishing their aim; [85] and even today the irreconcilability of parties produces a state of suspicion in which capable servants are obliged to leave. Yet the sense of service of the state made the civil service the saviors of Germany in the Revolution. It will be noticed that Germany in its "political" officials, France by political undersecretaries and occasional favoritism, and the United States by the number of offices of high administrative rank which may still be included in "spoils," have allowed themselves a safety-valve—official neutrality is not expected of them; indeed, the opposite is re-

---

[85] F. Giese, in *Das Beamtentum im deutschen Volksstaat* (Berlin, 1924) argued that civil servants ought to take the same attitude towards their service as Frederick the Great to the state—they held their powers, not for personal enjoyment, but as first servants of the state. Further, the service relationship is not to any personal superiors or masters, but to the state. "If this, the only right constitutional view, had been a common possession of the German civil service, then fewer officials would have fallen into so difficult a conflict of consciences on the fall of the monarchy and the entry of the Republican ministers; since they felt obliged to their imperial or royal masters, instead of, properly, to the Empire or their state, many believed that they might not recognize any other institution as official chiefs, although the new institutions embodied no other than the real and hitherto existent chief of the service, namely, the state." Cf. also E. Kleinstück, *Vom Wesen des deutschen Beamtentums* (Berlin, 1927), p. 30.

quired, and appointments take place to secure the subservience of these officials to those who appoint them. We shall not press this analysis any further, excepting to say that this impartiality will depend for its efficiency in the future more and more upon the deliberate training of officials to this end. We recall the opinons about official education expressed in Germany. It will be remembered that various writers insisted on the need for such a training in the social services that civil servants would be qualified to take a nonparty view, a view transcending parties: as one writer had it, they represent *the integrity of pure state mentality,"* another, "they serve the common good." [This is extravagant and impossible.]

The supreme importance of impartial service and counsel rendered by the civil servant to the political chief has already received some treatment.[86] It requires further consideration at this point, for it is bound up with the problem of political activity, since political activity which seems to attaint the administrative impartiality of the official renders him suspect to political leaders of the opposite side.

If the belief in political impartiality or neutrality of tendered advice and execution of commands should be shaken, we should be faced with the social tragedy that the political chiefs—who are unskilled and casual workers—would hesitate to accept the skilled aid of the permanent experts. They would be tempted to remove those they distrusted and put their own "experts" in their place. They would deny the value and possibility of the existence of objective science, natural, social, economic or administrative, and deprive the state, that is everyone, by depriving themselves, of all the benefits of knowledge from which the sepsis of partisanship has been removed. The case of Mr. Lilienthal and the Senate's hesitations to appoint him to the chairmanship of the United States Atomic Energy Commission, some Senator's attempt to have the FBI investigate that Commission for them,[87] and also the attacks on Dr. Condon of the United States Bureau of Stand-

ards, are indications of the serious possibilities. Political chiefs might use "Left" science or "Right" science, but not plain science; and the public welfare would be surrendered to wishful thinking.

If the public servant were a mere automaton, the problem would be easy of resolution. But it happens that he is human. Nor is that all. The relationship between official and political chief is a delicate and complicated one. More is required from the official than a dry memorandum, and a take-it-or-leave-it. His independence of mind as an official adviser is safeguarded by his loss of full political independence as a citizen. And his independence of mind is sorely needed. The view generally held in all civil services (as shown in Byrnes's statement, p. 865) is that the civil servant has a duty to press his views on his political chief: not to domineer, but to advise with force, and not too easily to desist. This principle was thus expressed in a British official document: [88]

Determination of policy is the function of ministers, and once a policy is determined it is the unquestioned and unquestionable business of the civil servant to strive to carry out that policy with precisely the same energy and precisely the same good will whether he agrees with it or not. That is axiomatic and will never be in dispute. At the same time it is the traditional duty of civil servants, while decisions are being formulated, to make available to their political chiefs all the information and experience at their disposal, and to do this without fear or favor, irrespective of whether the advice thus tendered may accord or not with the minister's initial view. The presentation to the minister of relevant facts, the ascertainment and marshalling of which may often call into play the whole organization of a department, demands of the civil servant the greatest care. The presentation of inferences from the facts equally demands from him all the wisdom and all the detachment he can command. The preservation of integrity, fearlessness and independence of thought and utterance in their private communion with ministers of the experienced officials selected to fill the top posts in the service is an essential principle in enlightened government, as—whether or not

---

86 See p. 614 ff. above.
87 Cf. for example, Truman's resistance in his veto message on Senate Bill 1004, *Congressional Record,* May 15, 1948.

88 Tomlin Commission, *Minutes of Evidence,* p. 1268.

ministers can accept advice thus frankly placed at their disposal, and acceptance or rejection of such advise is exclusively a matter for their judgment—it enables him to be assured that their decisions are reached only after the relevant facts and the various considerations have so far as the machinery of government can secure, been definitely brought before their minds.

Now men are very sensitive about high policy and the nature of the state, or in other words the interventions into their natural freedom made by others through the supreme force acquired in the name of the community. Their happiness is in issue, their years may be subjected to the domination of other people, their lives may be cut short. They are rightly sensitive about the ends and means of social authority. They will cast the conventions of official neutrality and anonymity to the winds if they find that these are being misused or cannot be relied on. It was never easy to establish these principles. It has taken over a century in each democracy, and there are unwitting and corrupt enemies ready to overthrow these achievements of civilization. It is, then, a nice problem at any given moment to weigh whether the principles have become firmly enough established in the public mind and part of the structure of the mind of officials, that the time-honored buttresses—the rules against political activity—can be dismantled. The answer must differ in each society, for not all are on exactly the same level of public spirit, political maturity, social equanimity.

The Effect of Growth of the Public Services. A point of time comes in the modern state when two facts exert a strong influence on the answer to the problem raised here. One is the growth in the number of civil servants in the direct employ of the state, and the other, a very probable accompaniment, is the assumption by the state of power over industries through the mechanism of public corporations. If the public services in the former began to reach the proportion of more, let us say, than one in five of all the families in the nation, would it still be tenable to deprive civil servants

of their political rights? It must be remembered that all civil services that forbid certain political practices to their officials also prescribe that they may not undertake such activities through their families either. If rights were limited, then a very important part of the dynamic, creative element in the nation is sterilized. This could not be afforded, as it would be a sheer loss of brains and character; and in all aspects of the democratic principle and its benefits it would not be right.

Now, it may happen—it has happened in Britain—that in order to avoid the rigidity of traditional administrative methods, including civil service recruiting by wholesale examinations, nationalized industries have been organized as public corporations. They have hundreds of thousands — perhaps millions — of employees. These serve the state; they are even under the supreme, ultimate direction of the government as to general policy. Why should they be free, as they are, of political restrictions and the regular civil servants not? Why are they free? Because it is recognized even without argument that so many citizens ought not to be limited in their political liberties: it is repugnant to good sense.

Indeed, the civil service staffs of Britain have requested that the whole matter be opened.[89] They have proposed [90] that no civil servant of any grade should be prevented in future from standing for Parliament, and that special leave should be granted, with pay, to prosecute his candidacy. They propose also that for local government office it shall not be required that the civil servant shall ask for previous approval: but that instead he shall merely notify his intention to the head of his department, who may then demur for cause. And, finally, they request the removal of the usual restrictions of serving on political committees, making speeches, canvassing, and so on, and that

[89] Cf. staff side representations, *Whitley Bulletin*, April, 1947, p. 52.
[90] The proposals are reminiscent of New Zealand's practice. Cf. L. Lipson, *Politics of Equality* (Chicago, 1948).

civil servants should not in future be under any disability to express political opinions publicly, except under the Official Secrets Act. They use the arguments used in the previous paragraph. They point out that it is difficult to justify a difference between the rights of civil servants and of employees of the public corporations. They argue that the time has come "to rely on the discretion and good sense of civil servants in these matters."

The General Issue of Loyalty. When states are threatened in their form of government, they try to make sure that at least they shall have no worry from their officials. These hold special positions of power and trust, and betrayal might mean downfall. We have noticed this in the evolution of the German civil service, and the rules on this in the French civil service. No special regulation of political principles is by law required in the British civil service: the days of the Test Acts and of Catholic disabilities are long over. Prior to 1947, the United States civil service had rules prohibiting membership of certain political associations. The Hatch Act (section 9A) said:

It shall be unlawful for any person employed in any capacity by any agency of the Federal Government, whose compensation, or any part thereof, is paid from funds authorized or appropriated by any act of Congress, to have membership in any political party or organization which advocates the overthrow of our constitutional form of government in the United States.

The Emergency Relief Appropriation Act of July 1, 1941, denied employment to any alien or Communist or member of the Nazi Bund Organization where the salary came from emergency relief funds. So also for posts in the National Youth Administration. In the shadow of World War II, the Civil Service Commission decided not to certify for employment any person when it has been established that he is a member of the Communist Party, the German Bund, or any other Communist, Nazi, or Fascist organization (June 20, 1940). And the act of June 28,

1940, prohibited employment where conviction has been obtained of a wide variety of "subversive" acts, mainly the suborning of members of the armed forces from their duty and the teaching and organizing of movements to overthrow the government of the United States by force.

Then on March 23, 1947 [91] President Truman issued an executive order requiring the purging of the government service of employees found to be "disloyal" or "subversive." This has required a general definition of loyalty, has involved the Attorney-General in listing all subversive organizations in the United States, and is aimed at not only members, but "fellow-travelers" of, any "totalitarian, Fascist, Communist, or subversive organization." It involves the checking of the loyalty of all existing officials—some 2,000,000—and of all entrants. To see that no one is done an injustice, each department has instituted a loyalty board, and above them all is a loyalty appeals board, appointed by the President, with a membership (at the time of writing) of highly trustworthy and competent citizens. The action was taken according to the order because

the presence within the Government service of any disloyal or subversive person constitutes a threat to our democratic processes . . . and maximum protection must be afforded the United States against the infiltration of disloyal persons in the ranks of its employees, and equal protection from unfounded accusations of disloyalty must be afforded loyal employees of the Government.

There can be no doubt that this move was dictated by revelations of spying by agents of the Soviet Union, first disclosed by the Report of the Royal Commission (Canada) [92] which investigated the communication to Soviet agents of secret and confidential information, especially relating to the atomic bomb. (Other disturbing facts had been learned about Soviet infiltration in European countries.)

[91] Cf. for documents with discussion, University of Chicago, *Round Table Pamphlet*, No. 511, "Loyalty and Liberty in 1948," January 4, 1948.
[92] June 27, 1948, Ottawa.

It cannot be avoided, in a time of international troubles, to safeguard the democratic state, with its generous and easy ways of life, against insidious subversion.[93] Neither Communists nor Fascists nor Nazis have the slightest respect for democratic principles or institutions. Each declared themselves the mortal enemy of the democratic state. Yet the self-restraint implied in definition and legal procedure and appeal is a tribute to the democratic constitutionality of the United States.

Shortly after the subversion of democratic government in Czechoslovakia by its Communist party in February, 1948, the British government established a policy of limiting the freedom of employment in the civil service of members of (or those actively associated with) the Communist or Fascist party or organizations. This consists of making sure that no one so associated as to raise doubts about his or her reliability is employed in connection with the work vital to the security of the state.

The prime minister stated that the measure was a security measure only. He declared: [94]

The State is not concerned with the political views, as such, of its servants, and as far as possible, alternative employment on the wide range of non-secret Government work will be found for those who are deemed for the reason stated to be unsuitable for secret work. It may, however, happen that it is impossible to find suitable employment elsewhere in the civil service with specialist qualifications, and in such cases there may be no alternative to refusal of employment or dismissal.

It will be noticed that the British policy is not as sweeping as the American: its criterion is security, not loyalty, although it must be admitted that the issue of loyalty is bound to arise in border-line cases where overt actions are not by themselves absolutely conclusive. Furthermore, the British scheme does not require the complete survey of all in the service, but will work through secret or public investigation of suspects. It admits of continued employment, though in posts not vital to security. As a safeguard the government appointed a committee of three former civil servants as a body to which appeal is possible. It conducts an inquiry into cases which the minister finds *prima facie* to require action; its report is in each case available for the minister—though his is the responsibility for any decision. An adequate procedure guarantees that a civil servant charged with disloyalty may easily clear himself of any unfounded charge.

So far, to May, 1949, the government exclude those about whom suspicions are justified from the headquarters staffs of the armed service departments and the Ministry of Supply.

The democracies have unfortunately been forced to learn lessons from the nefarious tactics of fascists, nazis, and communists since 1917. It is well for them that they have learned. It is as certain, even as it is necessary, for the sake of democracy itself, that they will apply the rule of law to make sure that justice is done and not abused.

It would, of course, arouse a deep feeling of injustice if taxpayers suspected that the servants they were paying—and nowadays the proportion of the individual's income which contributes to all forms of state expenditure is remarkably high, being about one fifth on the average in the United States and one third Britain—if the salaried servants were indeed unfaithful to the principle that the majority's opinion shall prevail while each minority is assured of the continuing right to try to turn itself by persuasion into a majority. For that is the principle violated when a civil servant cripples the civil service as an instrument of government, not to mention the damage partisanship does to technical efficiency. Resentment is bound to follow in a society where the civil servant and the public stand to each other in the relationship of paid servant and employer. In a well-ordered society where massive benefits and rights are interlaced and well-balanced with duties, licentious criticism

[93] Cf. Herman Finer, *America's Destiny* (New York, 1947), Chaps. VIII-XII.
[94] House of Commons, Debates, March 15 and March 25, 1948.

cannot be allowed. Opposition must flow through well-regulated channels and must not threaten certain fundamental tenets and hardly the constitution by unconstitutional means. The more benefits we wish to take for granted and enjoy securely in the state, the less may we attack its ultimate inward principle—in the case of the democracies, majority rule and the outlawry of violence.

One final point requires comment. One of the remaining objections of laissez-faire economists—who retreat from defense to defense—is that if civil servants have political rights they will associate and exact from the government, the budget, and the economy more than they are entitled to, and they will act as monopolistic producers and become slack and lazy. We will offer an answer to this question after consideration of the right of civil servants to associate and to strike.

THE RIGHT TO ASSOCIATE
AND THE RIGHT TO STRIKE

THE modern claim to associate in industrial and professional unions is, broadly, the claim to exert pressure upon employers for various ends, mainly economic. Association takes place for other reasons also: for mutual aid against the common risks of life and for the combined organization of pleasure and study. Mingled with these reasons is another which, from a general social standpoint, is of far more importance: the defense and pursuit of economic interests. For through the employer, pressure is directly exerted upon that portion of the community which consumes the product of those associated, and this, in turn, affects the economic position of other circles. Associations within the civil service may at any moment find it necessary to exert pressure upon their employer, that is, the Treasury, and through that, the legislature and the public.

The position of civil service associations is peculiar in that the services of their members are rendered to a peculiarly wide public, in some cases to almost every inhabitant of the country. Their services are as a rule monopolies: that is, there is no alternative source of supply. The services they render are of a particularly vital nature to society, indeed, that is why they have become socialized. Finally, the employer is the state, an institution of which undisputed authority is the essence, because that authority is so necessary and at the same time so liable to daily dispute. The state is a condition of subjection for us all, no matter what rights we obtain from this subjection and so many are ready to throw off this subjection when the opportunity offers that the state is forced to be especially stern. It is such a master that the civil service possesses. There are other, secondary, peculiarities, and these clearly emerge from the discussion of the right to associate among civil servants, and they determine, as we shall now see, the extent to which associations and the right to strike are permitted.

Associations and strikes have no inherent virtues and vices; these are no more than consequences of their purpose and actual use. Associations in the civil service have originated, like trade unions, to reform abuses and procure the amelioration of working conditions. They were a product of the nineteenth century, but of the late nineteenth century. They become most numerous and insistent in certain social conditions: the worse the conditions of employment in the civil service, the greater the number of associations and their bitterness of temper; the more developed certain theories of the state, the more factional and disruptive the associations.

France. France entered the last quarter of the nineteenth century with an administrative system full of mortal abuses. Uncertainty of tenure and rank, political favoritism in recruitment and promotion, classification which raised inequality of working conditions and salaries to the level of an organized system, spying and counterspying on the private, political, and religious activities of the civil servants, no guarantees that disciplinary measures would be justly conducted, contempt from Parliament and the public—

these were the main features of French administration. The Law of Associations of March 21, 1884, was the culminating point of a long struggle of workers and professions of all kinds to secure the right of association. This law gave workers exercising the same professions or allied vocations the right to unite without authorization in associations for the study and defense of their economic, industrial, commercial, and agricultural interests.[95] These associations could federate among themselves. The result of this law was the speedy formation of a host of syndicates, the originators of the modern French trade-union movement, centering in the *Confédération Générale du Travail*. No one during the course of the debates on the law of 1884 had dreamt of including the officials, but, at first slowly, and then with a rush, officials perceived the advantages of organization and began to establish associations. The administration stopped them. In 1887 the Minister of Education himself intervened with a letter addressed to the prefect forbidding such associations as "manifestly incompatible with the very notion of a public function." [96] Road sweepers, navvies, and similar workers in municipal employ made attempts of a like nature, were forbidden to proceed by the prefect and the Ministry of Public Works, but maintained a furtive existence. Other state employees in the tobacco and match factories were more successful—they were not counted among civil servants: in this way, the state railway employees were admitted to have a right to associate. These concessions were made upon the theory that such employees in similar public utilities, privately owned and managed, had the right to strike.

The government could not permanently repress the movements, and therefore the Radical ministry of 1894 decided

to still the tempest by allowing the associations to come into being under their good-natured sponsorship. Many associations came into being, the principal ones being those instituted by the postal, telegraph and telephone services. The teachers got their way. The mailed fist gave place to the approving smile: all in the vain hope that the associations would not defend themselves when attacked, and that they would be the friends of republican and anticlerical governments. For France was tempest-tossed domestically and internationally, and peace and unity at any price was desired, in order that monarchism, ultramontanism, and the foreign enemy might at need be vanquished. But official approval had not counted that the right of association might be construed, as for ordinary industry, into the right to the defense of professional interests. The manipulative employees, postal officials, warders, those in the public works departments and municipalities, and teachers, wanted more than the mere right of peaceful coalition. They wished full rights under the law of 1884. This was never accorded them by their masters, nor could they obtain it, legally, under the statute of 1884, for this was *limitative:* it limited the right to syndicate (i.e., to be an association with rights of aggression) to "economic, industrial, commercial and agricultural" interests. Yet outside it there was not even a legal right to form associations. In 1901 a new law on associations gave the government an opportunity to meet the demands of civil servants for associations without specifically according the right to strike as possessed by ordinary associations of private employees. All citizens could now form associations, with certain specific exceptions, but in these exceptions civil servants were not included. The result was an enormous expansion in the number of associations.

The ardent spirits among them were dissatisfied with this position. But to the ardor of the workers' leaders must be added the effect of syndicalist theory which for the French public services has been worked out by writers like Maxime

---

95 Cf. P. Pic, *Traité de Législation Industrielle* (Paris, edition 1937), p. 216 ff.; and A. Lefas, *L'État et les Fonctionnaires* (Paris, 1913), p. 140.
96 Pierre Harmignie, *L'État et ses Agents* (Brussels, 1911), p. 13.

Leroy [97] and Paul-Boncour.[98] These desired the break-up of the present centralized state, and the division of political and administrative power among vocational associations, of which the public services are only special aspects. The central coordinating body composed of delegates of the associations would issue general rules, and within their wide confine, the public services syndicates would arrange for their execution. There would be an end of the interference of Parliament in petty matters, and the syndicates would be able to regulate all their vocational interests, technical and economic, in a rational manner hitherto unknown in the politically demoralized condition of the French civil service.[99]

We need not proceed further with analysis of the syndicalist theory. But the resistance to the power of civil service associations contained arguments of great import in the modern state.

The first impulse of resistance is simply authoritarian. There is an instinctive feeling that the state will crumble, or, at least, will be severely shaken by the existence of associations. For however peaceful the intentions of the associations, any body which unites members with a definite and special interest becomes suspect. Adam Smith observed this when he said that whenever he saw two bakers speaking together he suspected a conspiracy against the public. And the history of associations, corporations and guilds, especially in France, has been one to deepen this suspicion.

The Minister of Commerce said in 1891:

If they could carry out for their own profit the law of professional unions, it would be against the nation itself, against the general interests of the country, against the national

sovereignty, that they would organize the struggle.

M. Barthou, in 1906, had the same suspicion (by this time with ampler justification): [100]

When the State manufactures tobacco and matches, it does not see any reason for refusing to its workers, any more than to private employees, the right to form trade unions. But when it exercises, in a general interest, the functions and the rights of the public authority, can it authorize civil servants to turn against it, equal to equal, in an imperative and menacing manner, the very authority with which it is invested? Now notice that after the postmen and the teachers, the customs officers and the tax officials, have demanded the right to form trade unions. There is only one word to characterize such a state of affairs: anarchy. . . The public service associations are violating the law; they are going counter to good sense, they are defying public order.

That is the context in which many people see this problem: it is defiance to the state, a threat to public order, a menace to sovereignty, indeed, mutiny. Defense to the state!—"Civil servants who share in public authority form a part of one corporation only, that which is the state —the nation itself!" [101] "To form a Trade Union . . . would be one part of civil servants open warfare against the nation!" [102] The gist of these arguments is pure fear of anarchy, and parliamentary conceit: deadening to liberty and provocative of violence, open or subterranean, and irrational repression.

A reasoned opinion regarding the exceptional position of the public servant is the second line of defense against the right to associate. This was best expressed by one of the earliest essays in resistance. M. Spuller, Minister of Education, quashed the attempt of the teachers in 1887 to form a trade union. His circular ran: [103]

A public situation is not a profession, in the same way as official pay (traitement) is not a

[97] Maxime Leroy, Les Transformations de la Puissance Publique (Paris, 1907).
[98] Cf. his article, "Les Syndicats des Fonctionnaires devant le Parlement," Revue Socialiste, January, 1906.
[99] This subject is treated in the last chapter of Harold J. Laski, Authority in the Modern State (New Haven, 1918). A more recent contribution is by G. Mer, Le Syndicalisme des Fonctionnaires (Paris, 1930).

[100] Harmignie, op. cit., p. 157.
[101] Rouvier, Chamber of Deputies, May 22, 1905.
[102] Jules Roche, Chamber of Deputies, November 17, 1891.
[103] Lefas, op. cit., pp. 143-44.

salary. The salary of the workman is higgled over penny by penny by him and the employer. . . Both of them ask but one thing of the state: liberty of struggle and competition. . . But official pay is, on the contrary, fixed by law and is not alterable except by the law. If we suppose that the pay seems small, is there any one of us who will pretend that officials have the right to form an association and if necessary go on strike to force the state to increase the scale? . . .

Is it not evident that once he has become a member of the national administration, the teacher cannot turn by turn present himself as an official, and in this quality receive fixed pay, demand guarantees of security, or to put it more clearly, irremovability, excepting for disciplinary penalty, and have the right to a pension; and then, all of a sudden, changing his character, put himself forward as a free worker, and demand, through the right of association, the means of defending his interests against the state, as a workman defends his at his own risk and peril against his employer?

Many a minister later made use of these same arguments: The civil servant has a secured status which imposes obligations upon other citizens. If he accepts that status he must, in return, relinquish the right to secure better terms by a show of force. We are obliged to guess at the fundamental ideas of state employment involved in this type of argument, for they are never stated. Probably people who argue in this way really mean that the state, through the legislature, has carefully considered in what exact measure the services it renders are socially important; and it has translated this estimate into terms of an amount of money in the budget. This expenditure was carefully related to the income of the country, its revenues, and the general currents of social and political thought. The state cannot do more than this, and, offering the salaries and other expenses of administration in the measure which it does, it is only able to continue to afford them if it obtains the calculated amount of service in a loyal, willing and uninterrupted fashion. If these conditions are not observed, if slack service, skulking, and interruptions occur, the national ability to pay is dissipated, and all state arrange-ments fall to the ground. It is a matter of state efficiency, directly inherent in the nonprofit basis of state services, and not only a matter of the dignity of the state. This seems to us the only rational foundation of this type of argument; for merely to say that once the terms are accepted one should not kick against the pricks is puerile; one must show good cause why the pricks exist. It is not enough to say, as M. Briand once said, that the state has not the same elasticity in its financial arrangements as a private firm.[104] Whether that really means anything is a doubtful point; and if it did mean what it appears to mean, and if that meaning were true (that the state cannot demand and obtain more revenue promptly), it would still have to be explained why this is so. And when M. Clemenceau sonorously recounts the advantages of state employment—peacefulness and certainty [105]—he is still obliged to say why not more of these can be given at the demand of the officials; but he does not.

Indeed, these arguments are but the unimportant outposts of the central and vital argument against the right of association. The right of association (with or without the right to strike) always offers a threat to the continuity of the services, unless the right is much limited. For once the right is granted, even with limitations, even upon sufferance, a psychological condition is established—one of group conceit, a consciousness of identity and power, separatist in feeling—liable to resist the aims of the state by the cessation of work. Now, in private employment (comparatively) such a feeling and such a liability do not matter very much: only a master is inconvenienced or ruined by such behavior; and as for the consumers, they have (or had before the rise of giant monopolies) alternative

104 Chamber of Deputies, *Débats*, May 13, 1907, p. 975. Briand's views regarding the strike underwent a mighty transformation between the time when he was seeking a seat in Parliament, and the time, say, when he became a minister.
105 Cf. Harmignie, *op. cit.*, p. 149 (April, 1907: letter to the teachers).

sources of supply.[106] But the services of the state are, *ex hypothesi*, vital in their nature, and as a rule monopolies—there is no alternative source of supply. They have been deliberately and especially selected from among many things made and services rendered spontaneously by developing society as being of a fundamental nature, which neither prudence nor compassion could leave to the free play of supply and demand. They have become essentials of modern existence: they are indispensable. Therefore those who undertake them may not jeopardize their existence by the strike or threat of a strike. People cannot even bear to think that they might cease: for if such a thought became widespread, uncertainty would have entered, and certainty is the essence of social efficiency.

The theory which we have just expounded has never been fully analyzed in France, though Hauriou,[107] Duguit,[108] and Jèze [109] go quite far. They do not pursue their analysis to its base, namely, that social life would be badly injured. The politicians have only realized its fundamental meaning when there has been a strike, as in the arsenals, the posts, and the railways. In those cases it seems to me that they have rather been incensed that something called National Sovereignty, or the Public, has been defied, than understood the exact meaning of the strike.[110]

The proper line of resistance to strikes in the public service was taken in a bill to regulate the right to strike, placed before the Senate in 1895. The minister who introduced the bill said: [111]

It is necessary to distinguish among the different enterprises those which constitute public services properly so-called, affecting the general order and even the security of the country, from those which involve nothing other than a question of finance. . . . It is only there that the very principle of nationhood is at stake, that the right of demanding exceptional protection for it appears to be incontestable.

They were services of such importance that they had been exempted, in the law on the army (1889), from immediate mobilization: for example, firemen, road workers, dockers, surgeons, chemists of the *hospices;* workers in the penitentiaries, forest officials, customs, posts, and telegraphs, and the technical administrative sections of the railway services; inland revenue officials, the administrative officials in the state tobacco factories, and the Bank of France.

This and other bills of a like nature never passed beyond their preliminary stages.

Instead, France was delivered over to parliamentary tergiversation of a most dishonorable and despicable kind, and

---

[106] The possibility of alternatives, of course, becomes less and less true as the process of amalgamation proceeds; and we have shown that as amalgamation occurs in vital commodities, the state forbids strikes and lockouts.

[107] Cf. M. Hauriou, Note in *Conseil d'État*, August 7, 1909, in Sirey, *Receuil*, Part III, p. 145 ff., re dismissal of officials on strike, without previous communication of *dossier* (Law, April, 1905). "In effect, by the acceptance of the employment conferred upon him, the official submits to all the obligations deriving from the very necessities of the public services, and renounces altogether all always faculties incompatible with a *continuity* essential to the national life . . . [These] fundamental conditions of the existence of a state demand, on the one side, that the public services indispensable to national life shall not be interrupted, and, on the other side, that officials shall live in peace with the government. Let us observe that we appeal not to the *raison d'État*, which is a dangerous notion, because the well-being of the state may often appear to be connected with momentary circumstances, but to the theory of the unconstitutionality of the laws, which cannot be invoked except in regard to the permanent condition of state life, which doctrine and jurisprudence shall have already determined, and which, in consequence, would not permit of surprises."

[108] *Traité*, Vol. III, Chap. IV.

[109] Jèze, *op. cit.*, Vol. II, p. 246: "The idea of the public service has other necessary consequences: public servants are forbidden all actions which might stop or go counter to the regular normal and continuous functioning of the public service."

[110] Also they were struck with fear, or said they were, regarding national defense. A strike left open the frontiers! This was a powerful argument on the Continent before 1914! After World War II it has certainly not lost cogency.

[111] Trarieux, *Sénat, Débats,* March 4, 1895, and Documents, 1895, No. 38. Cf. Lefas, *op. cit.*, pp. 180-82.

the futile logic-chopping of constitutional lawyers, who commenced with abstractions and ended with abstractions. Parliamentary futility ended in postal strikes in 1906 and twice in 1909. The first strike of 1909 lasted a little over a week, and what imagination could not teach, the facts did. Paris was isolated from the rest of France and the world; the Minister of Foreign Affairs could get no news about the Balkan crisis, several most urgent telegrams being delayed; business began to languish, as prompt and exact information was impossible to obtain; the food supply of Paris was momentarily endangered; the stock exchange was so badly stricken that the effects were felt in London, Brussels, and Berlin. Then, later in the year, a more nationalized cessation of work took place and lasted ten days; similar effects were felt, and to them was added the sabotage of material.

The results were vindictiveness against the officials' leaders, some reforms, the strengthening of governmental feeling against the associations, and the introduction of a number of bills before Parliament to establish *Le Statut des Fonctionnaires,* that is, a code of working conditions for officials, in place of the numerous unintegrated regulations adopted piecemeal and many of them liable to violation by the minister. These principles were maintained by French governments to World War II: no right to strike; a right of association and of federation among associations; the right of the associations to challenge all administrative decisions interesting them before the *Conseil d'État;* but no federation with other than civil servants' associations.

French legal theorists have differentiated between *agents* or *fonctionnaires de gestion* and *agents* or *fonctionnaires d'autorité.* In the former class are all officials who are merely executive, without discretion, involving public authority, that is, not essentially part of the state, and perfectly assimilable to ordinary private employees; while the latter class consists of those who are more intimately connected with the governing power. It does not matter so much whether the former class are subjected to the state, the lawyers argue, but certainly the officials "of authority" must be.

This distinction has given rise to a long discussion, every lawyer having a different system, pedantically created out of words challenged by every one else, and satisfactory to himself, but rejected with contempt by his "dear" colleagues. The process of argument has been as follows: Is this distinction between *agents de gestion* and *autorité* tenable? The lawyers answer, Yes! [112] Since this distinction is valid it can be at once translated into terms of the law of contract: the *agents de gestion* come within the category of private contracts, the others, in the category of public law. In the first case the State is simply an *employer,* in the second it is the *Sovereign-Power.* Syndicalists like Leroy [113] are especially devoted to this dichotomy, because all the employees falling in the first category are thus placed on a complete par as to their liberties with ordinary private workers.

Arrived at this point, the lawyers feel entitled to get over their difficulties by making havoc of the law of contract. (1) Does not the state contract just like a private company with the *agents de gestion?* Yes; for the state has often been compelled to pay damages like any ordinary citizen for a civil wrong. The *Conseil d'État* has admitted that in its judgments. (2) The object of the relationship between the state and the employee—is this not one that can be made by simple contract? To carry letters, count cards, add up figures, and sweep trains, are these not everyday objects of private contract? Yes; then why make a difference between the state and a private company? (3) What end is pursued by the contracting parties? Is not the state pursuing a simple end in treating with an individual; and is not the individual intent upon pursuing only his own interests and nothing more? This is so. Then the contract is identical with ordinary private contracts.

---

[112] Thus Hauriou, Duguit, Berthélemy. But Jèze says that the distinction has broken down (cf. *op. cit.,* Vol. II, p. 238).
[113] Cf. *op. cit.,* pp. 130-32.

It is extraordinary how this legal nonsense has blinded the eyes of otherwise clever people to the real facts of the situation. They discuss at length the nature of the contract made, the present condition of the contract, but this is not the problem. The problem is, what compels the state to demand submission of civil servants and to offer the conditions it does? It is in what lies behind the law, not in what is expressible in its inelastic formulas, that the political scientist is interested. All states prohibit strikes for all civil servants. Why? Not because they have not learned the law of contract in the university schools, but because of certain overpowering necessities. It is precisely these necessities which we desire to discover. Even the enlightened Duguit, by equating the state with a "public service corporation" (which was overstepping the mark), and by his attacks upon the theory of the moral personality of the state (an important service to law and political science), lent his authority to the school which divides the civil service into two classes. He says the *agents de gestion* are properly to be put on a par with private employees, although he himself cannot and does not make this distinction, but puts all public servants on a similar footing, demanding the right to associate for all of them.[114] For the erroneous notion that the state is a "public service corporation" and nothing more, by missing out the social conscience which the state imposes upon individual consciences when it undertakes a service, strips the state of its essential character. The conclusion is then easy, but full of error. And the attack on the moral personality of the state can go too far, for in destroying the notion of personality it may deny that its purpose is moral.[115]

The truth is that all public servants are employed in work which is of a specially important character in society. The reason which compels the public and the legislature to draw these services out of the hands of private industry is like the force which is applied at one end of a rod or a length of string: the science of mechanics proves that this force is present not merely at the end or at any separate spot in the length, but pertains all through the length and gives every particle in the length a character equally peculiar. Thus, in the public services, the essential quality of being public, the why and wherefore of their socialized nature, pervades the whole. Some part of the civil servant's activity, whether he is in the immediate confidence of the minister and gives orders to thousands of subordinates, or whether he is a post-office messenger boy, the temporary master of nothing more than a second-hand bicycle which is not his property,—some part of the civil servant's activity is state-determined, it lives and operates in virtue of that peculiar fellowship and conscience called the state, it derives its character from the state, and would be otherwise were it not of the state. To ignore this is to be unaware of the nature of the state or to have petrified the state in a legal formula which has no counterpart in life. Harmignie, who has collected and analyzed the French theories of *agents de gestion* and *agents d'autorité*, says quite rightly that if you take any particular act it is fairly easy to decide whether it is one or the other—an *acte de gestion* or *d'autorité*, but it is almost impossible to distinguish the *officials* into these classes, "because the same individual accomplishes now one, now the other kind of action."[116] Harmignie includes teachers, postal officials, and the clerical staff of the ministries in *agents d'autorité*: the first, because "they are the champions of the republic public authority, by their work of education itself, because this education should be civic"; the second, because one must think of "all that is confided to the postal service; for the probity, the devotion, the faithfulness which the service demands and the police-interest, on which the confidence of the public should be neither betrayed nor shaken"; and the third, because one must

---

114 Cf. his *Revue du Droit Public* (Paris, 1907), p. 410 ff.
115 *Moral*—not whether it is a good or bad morality.

116 *Op. cit.*, pp. 181-82.

remember "the occult but real administration exercised by them." [117]

We shall, in the conclusions which follow this discussion, analyze more clearly than has yet been convenient what it is in the public service which differentiates it from private or "free" services (though, in fact, *no* industry is free in the modern state), and what therefore distinguishes the civil servant from the private servant.

The constitution of the Fourth Republic introduced the right to strike. In its preamble the right to strike is generally guaranteed, but it is also stipulated that the right will be exercisable within the laws yet to be made to regulate it. So far as the civil service is concerned, the *Statut des Fonctionnaires* (article 6) does not take away a right to strike from them, but recognizes syndical rights to civil servants in their completeness. The organizations must deposit their constitution and list of directors with the head of the government department.

It must be remembered that this may well conflict with the rules of obedience to official superiors as stated in the very same law.

Germany. The Weimar *Reich* and state constitutions contained clauses giving freedom of association to all citizens (before that, the law was in a very anomalous state regarding trade unions), including the right of civil servants to associate. The *Reich* constitution contained two clauses relating to this question. Article 130 said: "All officials are guaranteed the freedom of their political opinion and freedom of association (*Vereinigungsfreiheit*)." Article 150 said: "Freedom of association for the protection and promotion of working and economic conditions is guaranteed to every one of all professions." The clauses do not contain any mention of the word "strike." This issue was indeed avoided deliberately by those who drew up these clauses, and for both civil servants and private workers, social control over the right to strike was left to particular laws and regulations. The consolidation of the Republic and the rebuilding of social order resulted in the denial of this right. We shall now retrace our steps, and return to the condition of affairs before the Revolution, describe the theories then adumbrated and on the whole generally accepted, and then analyze the effects of the revolutionary and post-revolutionary events, which led ultimately to the denial of the right to strike.

Before World War I, Germany was blithely unconscious of the problem of the right of association; at least there was no ground for anxiety. The social situation of the civil service at that time, and the legal condition reflecting it, is well summed up by a famous jurist.[118]

The obligation of public service differs from other relationships of obligation by the *oath of service* which must be taken by the servant and which is combined with the commencement of activities. This oath is variously formulated but contains substantially the same promise faithfully to carry out the duty with which the taker of the oath is obligated. The purpose of the oath is to strengthen the ethical element contained in the public obligation to serve, by invoking the conscience and the awe of God, since the ethical element is not completely tangible in law. The civil servant is, however, legally bound to take this oath. Thus we are again concerned with a legal characteristic of official obligation which arises out of that ethical element. And it is indifferent what kind of subject the official obligation may be. Military leaders can be provided with a specially hired following by a private law contract; they can be helped by a peasant whose horses have been commandeered for the public transport; they can also be provided with a military waggoner: the last alone fulfils a sworn duty which under circumstances demands from him for the same function quite a different willingness to sacrifice himself than is expected from the former two types; this measure he must himself discover from his loyalty to the service: and just for that reason he is sworn in.

This type of theory was general.[119] It postulated an all-powerful state, the immaculate nature of its authority, and,

---

[117] Cf. M. Hauriou, note in Sirey, *op. cit.,* 1907, Part III, p. 49; Cf. also his *Droit Administratif,* 3rd edition, p. 685, note.

[118] Otto Mayer, *Deutsches Verwaltungsrecht,* 2nd edition (Munich, 1917), Vol. II, p. 245.
[119] E.g., P. Laband, *Staatsrecht,* 5th edition (Berlin, 1913), Vol. I, pp. 4, 100, and 433.

therefore, the subjection of the people—in this particular respect the subjection of the civil servant who has a special ethical relationship with the state, servant of all. There was no question of the right to strike, and this in itself was not discussed. All that was discussed, and this with question-begging business, was the subjection of the official to a code of discipline given to the law of the state and the theory of its authority under an absolutist monarchical system. When the revolution came, the previous repression had engendered a tremendous amount of force against the old system, and the impetus of that force at first swept away more than mature consideration could, or afterwards did, justify.

Complete rights of association were promised to all, and these were held to include the right to strike.[120] A number of exceedingly well-organized associations arose, at present including practically every person in the *Reich,* state, and local government services. But little by little the *unlimited* nature of the right of association was suppressed. The opposition was based upon grounds with which we have by now become very familiar:

Taking into account the pension rights accorded to them, and the general interests of the whole economic system, which must be protected, the final conclusion of the right of association, the right to strike, cannot be accorded to officials as it can to private workers.

But the phrase *the general interests of the whole economic system which needs protection* is a more enlightened line of objection than was usual in France. Another point of view, the rational attitude of which is to be applauded, was:

The official must first exhaust all possible means of conciliation (*alle Instanzen*) and must then finally have applied to the legislature, which provides the means, before he makes use of this right. Both morality and reasons demand this.

In the constitutional assembly of the *Reich,* the debates [121] at once centered round the meaning of the word "association." The constitutional committee of the assembly, dealing with what afterwards became article 159, found itself called upon to choose either the original form of the clause written by Hugo Preusz, in which the word *Koalitionsfreiheit* was used, or some other word which would not give the impression that the right to strike was admitted. The reporter of the clause asked the committee to take it that the original form did not touch the question of the right to strike. Whereupon an official of the Prussian Ministry of Commerce said: [122]

According to the meaning which has been previously ascribed, to the word *Koalitionsfreiheit,* it is supposed to include the right to strike. Now it is suggested that the right of coalition ought not in any way to be limited. . . That is to say, at no time, in no condition of necessity, for no class of civil society, ought it to be limited: not for railwaymen, not for those who produce the most essential articles of consumption, not for people who control gas, fire, water . . . not for agricultural workers. I don't know whether the committee was really conscious of the full import of such a constitutional rule, and whether it really wishes to accept the responsibility for such a condition.

The word *Vereinigungsfreiheit* was chosen instead of the other: and an important member of the constitutional committee (Dr. Hugo Sinzheimer, a great authority on labor law) said, "we expressly declare that we do not wish to decide the question of the right to strike in the Constitution." [123] The only new ideas in full debate were the need for a right to strike as a counterweight to the organization of other industrial and professional groups in the state; and the difficulty of reconciling such a right with ministerial responsibility for the Budget.[124]

The issue, indeed, was positively settled, at this time at least by events, and

[120] Cf. L. Bendix, *Das Streikrecht der Beamten* (Berlin, 1922), pp. 5-11 (an intelligent book); proclamation of the Council of People's Commissaries, November 12, 1918; proclamation of Prussian government, November 13, 1918.

[121] Cf. *Bericht und Protokoll des 8. Ausschusses,* No. 391, p. 389 ff.
[122] *Ibid.,* p. 390.
[123] *Idem.*
[124] Heilfron, *op. cit.,* Vol. 7, p. 459 ff.

by the declarations of theory evoked by those events. A threatened railway strike in Prussia in the spring of 1919 drew from the government the following decree: [125]

The right of coalition does not justify a breach of contract. Every refusal of work without consent is therefore a breach of duty which involves legal consequences.

In 1920 the Prussian government made quite unequivocal declarations that the right to strike did not exist.[126]

The so-called right to strike has no inseparable connection with the conception of the right of coalition. The strike is only one of the means, and not the sole one, through which one can attempt to attain better economic conditions. Whether *this* means shall be used is to be decided by the mutually obliging rights and duties which were included in the condition of officialdom. If the concerted stoppage of work is not compatible therewith, then the so-called right to strike is not given with the right of coalition. In its application to civil service conditions, these principles lead to the conclusion that the civil servant must not strike. The civil service status is a status of loyalty. *As the state could not conduct an ordered life and could in no wise express its will, it must enter into a relationship with the civil servant which obliges the latter to a complete devotion to the state.* This condition of loyalty also appears from the fact that the official takes an oath of service. The special character of the official's status is expressed in important condition of civil service law. With due regard to the duties towards the community imposed upon him, the right is denied to the official capriciously to leave his work. For this reason also the majority are appointed for life and made dismissible only by means of statutorily regulated disciplinary procedure. Further, the rights of officials to specified salary, half-pay and pensions for dependents, are legally regulated and are specially guaranteed by the *Reich* constitution. In this specially formed relationship of rights and duties, the civil servant who strikes, at once breaks his oath and violates the official obligation he undertook. The strike is an unpardonable truancy from work and its consequence is that the servant, during the time of the strike, loses his pay and must expect formal disciplinary procedure against him

with the purpose of dismissal. By this none of the great interests of the civil servants is violated, because at their disposal are other means of making their views valid than the strike. Since the representative assemblies of the states have a far-reaching right of controlling their executives, as the representative councils have on local government, the official has a specially influential instrument to get his demands satisfied by their help. The opinion of the Prussian government in this matter is identical with that of the *Reich* government, etc.

This clear and well-founded statement became the basis and model of all future development. The disciplinary courts have maintained a similar attitude. The duties of the officials, which we discussed in a previous section, as stated in the *Reichsbeamtengesetz* of 1873, the various state civil service laws, and departmental regulations, limited the constitutional right to strike.[127]

Survey, and Comparison with Great Britain and the United States. The grounds for refusal of the right to strike, when we sum them up, were, broadly, three:

(1) If the state engages itself to give certain benefits to its civil servants, and by its institutions and traditions substantiates its engagement, it may as a matter of a fair bargain require a corresponding guarantee that it will not be subjected to the inconvenience, at the minimum, of a strike.

(2) The interests which the state has in the continuous operation of its services are of an urgent, life-and-death nature, and these must not be stopped lest a great calamity befall it.

(3) If the demands of civil servants are given ample constitutional channels in which to find their vent, and, if just, their satisfaction, then the strike must be relinquished as a means of forcing the state to surrender.

In our opinion the problem is substantially solved in these three propositions.

---

[125] Cited in Bendix, *op. cit.*, p. 38. I give only the essential parts.
[126] February 20, 1920, Prussian *Landtag*.

[127] Brand, *op. cit.*, Sections 159 and 159A; also G. Anschütz (Berlin, 1933), *Die Verfassung*, on article 159. Cf. also H. C. Nipperdey, editor, *Die Grundrechte* (Berlin, 1929-30), Vol. II, article 159.

We have already, in treating of France, expanded upon the first proposition. The rest of society is burdened with the provision of the officials' total remuneration; it cannot produce this without the security and steady continuation of all fundamental services, and therefore if it accepts the continuity of the burden, it not only *ought* to have (as a matter of everyday ethics) a *quid pro quo* in the matter of continuity of service, but it *must* have this, or else the source of its ability to pay the remuneration is gone. The moral claim is grounded in the economy of nature.

The second proposition, that the services performed by the state are so fundamental that they can on no account be allowed to cease, is of basic importance. It is indeed the root and center of the whole case against the right to strike; and this it is which frightens people even against the right of association. This fear is simply preconsciousness of danger to society of any interruption of the eternal round of industry. An analysis of the industrial and commercial life of any modern state shows that this fear is only too well justified, in the measure in which we grant that bread is better than liberty. The life of modern society is highly organized. Few activities are undertaken for the direct satisfaction of those who do them—the vast majority of commodities and services are produced for others than the producer. A delicate counterpoise of freedom and subordination of the myriad elements alive in society has been created as the necessary basis of social production and consumption. Most of the satisfactions of life have at least a particle of economic welfare allied with them, sometimes as the end and purpose of the satisfaction, sometimes as instrumental to a largely spiritual satisfaction. And the mass and quality of things done, thought and consumed which make up modern civilization are vitally dependent upon its high material welfare. Without this there would be neither means, nor leisure to enjoy the means, and all the conditions of work and worship would assume another aspect. Whether that aspect would be more pleasing to any

particular individual among us or not it is immaterial to discuss here. It is enough if we can admit that it would be otherwise. But we have everyday proof that the mass of mankind do not want it otherwise, and the plans of social regeneration made by the great leaders of thought are rarely based upon a reduction of the amount of wealth, but most frequently postulate consciously or unconsciously an increase in the riches of the world. Its true nature is disguised in the modern god, "The High Standard of Living."

This indispensable standard of living cannot be produced otherwise than by two main institutions: subdivision of labor, and credit. The first produces a number of independent, specialized and well-nigh nonversatile economic groups; the finished product of each is the raw material of the other, and the sectional services must be combined to attain any utility to a consumer. All economies—that is, the minimization of effort with the maximization of gain—are derived from the regular, steady, punctual and exact cooperation of otherwise unrelated multitudes, information about the market, transport, command of raw materials and labor long before the product can be consumed, and all the machinery of exchange is needed to help this method of indirect production at the highest pitch of efficiency. Everything, down to eighths, even thirty-seconds of cents must be calculated, anticipated, and weighed when supply and demand are being adjusted to one another. And the months and the years in which deliveries and payments are due are assumed—by operations in which people place confidence—to be here already. Time, which is mathematically-calculated interruption, has been abolished by the economic need for continuity; continuity would be abolished by interruption, if it returned unexpectedly. Not one of the innumerable factors in the calculation may be changed by an undue stoppage in its predicted orbit upon which so many other revolutions depend. A strike in one industry of importance may do grievous harm to the life of other parts of the community, who, so far from being immediate parties to the dispute, do not even know what it is about. The state is therefore compelled to demand the continuous fulfillment of social expectations. Who compels it? Society. We have reached a stage in the life of the state where even the dissidents and the well-nigh irreconcilables conduct their coercive (defensive or aggressive) campaign with order and regard for the basic necessities of life. The German railwaymen in 1920 were at pains to transport milk; the English coal miners would not let the mines get flooded; and in the General Strike of May, 1926, the British trade union organizations issued directions and made arrangements for the proper conduct of the nation's vital necessaries. In the French General Strike of November, 1947, similar restraints were observed.[128]

Now, in proportion as the services are vital to social existence, obedience to the state must be unconditional. Of such a character are the public services. Communications, revenue, health, the ordering of trade and industry and their various processes, which secure conditions of justice and physical health for the weaker members of society, and prevent, at least in part, waste and tyranny, the care of the poor, the widow and the orphan—our prudence and compassion have declared these things to be so urgent and vital that we will not have any but the state to administer them. In proportion as we do not admit that these can be given up we are driven to demand their continuity, that is, to forbid any right to strike; or to place this right under such restrictions that it loses its original meaning and force.

What is public, what is private, service? Now it may be said that all this proves nothing in particular about the *public* services. Does not the analysis we have made lead us to the conclusion that *all* great services—whether in private or in public hands—should be forbidden to strike, or allowed to strike only under

very limiting conditions? Such a conjecture was made already by Harmignie in the course of his discussion of French civil service associations.[129]

It is objected that the interdiction of the right to strike ought then to be extended to workers of the railway companies and of all services the monopoly of which is a concession and which are of public utility, as lighting, for example. We agree; it is necessary assuredly to take special legislative measures concerning the workers of these enterprises and to forbid them, under severe penalties, to suspend their work.

In most countries some limitations had already been established before the World War I. Apart from countries where a sheer authoritarian attitude was taken up by the government, as in Rumania and Bulgaria, limitations were strict, even stricter than in great modern democracies like Australia and New Zealand. The state had in Australia and New Zealand come to mean so much to the ordinary man, to give him so many rights, that these could not be maintained without corresponding obligations, for the obligations were part of the energy which produced the resources out of which rights were distributed. Therefore those countries placed all industry under a régime which put off the right to strike until the time when human reason had accomplished all it could. Courts of Conciliation and Arbitration were established, principles of a "living wage" were adopted, and strikes and lockouts, in private as well as the public services, were made illegal. It is quite clear that economic and other benefits are created by labor, capital, and organization: if these stop, the benefits cease; and the more carefully organized and planned the benefits are, the more indispensable is the continued work of its creators. The whole tendency of trade-union legislation in Great Britain since 1906 has been toward the limitation of the power to strike.

Naturally the state has first taken steps where it could most easily take them, namely, in relation to the officials in its own immediate service, but the doctrine

---

[128] Cf. The General Strike Order, Trade Union Congress Memorandum, given as Document No. 72 in Page Arnot's *The General Strike* (London, 1926), p. 160 ff.

[129] *Op. cit.*, p. 329.

which it has propounded is valid to many so-called "private" industries too. In Great Britain the subject attained little prominence until after the General Strike of 1926. Up to that time there had been an extensive growth of civil service associations which had met with no obstacle from the government. Very little, if any, discussion had taken place about the right to strike. No law forbade any civil service association to come into being, or, if it was established, to affiliate with outside bodies.[130] For the predominant purpose of British statesmen has been liberty rather than security and order.

The grades of the service below the administrative have for long felt a certain sympathy with the Liberal and Labour movements. The theory of the Treasury in regard to pay and conditions in the civil service is that they ought not to be more than that given by any employer outside the service. Therefore it was and is to the interest of the associations within the service to cooperate with the trade unions outside to raise the general rate of wages and improve the conditions of labor. Further, the service associations recognize the fraternal duty of uniting with other labor forces to increase their strength and give them aid in overcoming the hurtful qualities of the present organization of industry and commerce and society. Therefore the associations grew [131] and they affiliated to the Labour party and the Trade Union Congress. Not sympathetic to such affiliation, and self-excluded from it, were the top 20,000 of the administrative, upper clerical, technical and legal staffs. The division between these and the subordinate and manipulative grades is one between those who are in positions of command and those who take orders. Those who take orders are, in the mass,

allied with the Labour movement; the rest are, on the whole, satisfied with the state as it is, and are sufficiently well off not to feel the spur to join the party of criticism and reconstruction.

There was no prohibition of the right to strike: the rule then was and still is that the civil servant who does not obey this may be dismissed and even be denied his pension, without recourse in the courts!

Before 1926 affiliation had raised no great controversy,[132] though the affiliating associations were conscious of their peculiar situation—servants of the state yet allied with a party whose intention it is fundamentally to alter the nature of that state. The state, it was said in popular discussion, could not be sure of the uninterrupted service of those who belong to affiliated associations, since they are liable to be recommended to go on strike at any moment. The state had the right to expect members of the civil service to volunteer for any duties consequent upon the emergency. Civil servants enjoyed the special advantage of being a "sheltered" occupation, and the price of this was political neutrality. Against this view the attitude of the civil service associations was well stated in the ballot paper issued to members of the Civil Service Clerical Association, which, finding many dissentients in its ranks, took a referendum on the question. The association admitted affiliation, but denied that it was obliged to go on strike at the request of other labor organizations. As regards the position of civil servants as servants of the state, it argued there was no necessary inconsistency between civil servants doing their work faithfully and well, and yet at the same time being federated with other bodies of wage earners, through the Trade Union Congress, for the protection of their wage interest.

It was rejoined that if the demands of civil servants are given ample constitutional channels in which to find their vent, and satisfaction when found to be just,

---

[130] Cf. Bernard Léger, *Les Syndicats des Fonctionnaires en Angleterre* (Paris, 1929); cf. also H. G. Swift, *History of Postal Agitation* (London, 1900).

[131] For their present numbers and constitution, cf. statements submitted to the Royal Commission by the Civil Service Clerical Association, the Society of Civil Servants, the First Division, etc., and the Civil Service Clerical Association's Year Book.

[132] Macdonnell Commission, Fourth Report, pp. 99 and 100.

the strike must be relinquished as a means of forcing the state to surrender.

The issue was decided in a state of public temper rare in Great Britain. The trade unions were beaten until they were dazed, and Parliament, which had several times in the past few years been unable to find time to deal with a Trade Union Bill to limit the political and industrial powers of the unions, attacked the new and steaming dish with a really unwonted gusto.[133] The result was the Trade Union Act of 1927, clause 5 of which related to civil servants: [134]

... prohibiting established civil servants from being members, delegates, or representatives of any organization of which the primary object is to influence or affect the remuneration and conditions of employment of its members, unless the organization is an organization of which the membership is confined to persons employed by or under the Crown and is an organization ... in all respects independent of and not affiliated to, any such organization as aforesaid the membership of which is not confined to persons employed by or under the Crown or any federation comprising such organizations, that its objects do not include political objects, and that it is not associated directly or indirectly with any political party or organization. . . .

In May, 1946, the act was repealed, and the unions returned enthusiastically to affiliation with the Congress.

The United States civil service does not permit the right to strike, or even to affiliate with organizations imposing or proposing strikes against the United States. Thus the act of August 24, 1912 (37 Stat. 555) provides that postal employees will not be subject to reduction in rank or compensation or removal from the service for belonging to any form of organization of postal employees, so long as the organization is not affiliated with

any outside organization imposing an obligation or duty upon them to engage in any strike, or proposing to assist them in any strike, against the United States. . .

Then in a note on Executive Order No. 7916 of June, 1938,[135] the Civil Service Commission, commenting on the requirement that grievance procedures should be set up in each department (according to the order), gave its approval to the recognition in all departments of the right to join unions, free of the fear of victimization for such membership or nonmembership, and then generalized the strike prohibition for all civil servants.

How, then, does it come about that there are big unions of federal civil servants affiliated with the A.F. of L. and the CIO? It is managed by the repudiation of the right to strike contained in the constitutions of the civil service unions themselves, and by the refusal of the associations to accept unions which have not made such a repudiation.[136]

The Taft-Hartley Labor-Management Relations Act of June, 1947 (Section 305) made it unlawful for any person employed by the United States or any agency thereof (including any wholly-owned government corporation) to participate in any strike. The penalty is immediate discharge, the forfeit of civil service status, and a three-year ineligibility for re-employment.

We have already discussed the effects of a strike upon economic and social life. It could yet be argued by civil service associations that since the strike was a very remote contingency, no government ought to establish a restraint. But, indeed, the question is not merely one to be determined by the probability of the event, but of the omnipresence of a threat. The right to strike is no positive guarantee: it is the residue of the individual claim—and even legal right—to freedom of opinion and person. The right to strike is a

---

[133] Cf. Mr. Churchill's answer to a deputation of the Civil Service Civil Rights Defence Committee, representing all the affiliated Unions (March 1, 1927), reproduced in *The Post* (organ of the Union of Post Office Workers) for April 9, 1927. It is still of great interest.

[134] Sect. 5, Sub-Sect. 1 only is reproduced. The whole of the clause should be studied. Cf. also Statutory Rules and Orders, 1927, No. 800.

[135] Cf. Civil Service Act and Rules, etc., etc., November 30, 1941, p. 144. Cf. L. D. White, "Strikes in the Public Service," *Public Personnel Review*, January, 1949.

[136] Cf. D. Ziskind, *One Thousand Strikes of Government Employees* (New York, 1940).

result of the state's noninterference with the right to freedom of person. But when the state does not interdict, the result is that when men act in association, they feel that they possess an ultimate coercive power, a positive weapon. The possession of this weapon acts psychologically upon its possessors: it increases their will, as well as their power, to resist. It offers an alternative to negotiation with the good will of the other party. This brusqueness may jeopardize the public welfare; and it is the fear of this that is expressed by the opponents of the right to strike. Its legal acknowledgment may deliver over events to passion before all the devices of reason are exhausted. Yet its nonexistence may also set up against the guardians of public order so little resistance that they will act ignorantly, passionately, on private or class motives, and slur over the justice of civil servants' claims upon the public.

Constraint put upon civil servants, therefore, cannot permanently operate unless the state admits constraints upon itself, or to speak less abstractly, unless the people and legislature establish machinery which will control and at need coerce ministers, Treasuries, and heads of government departments to the end that they may act justly. For as has been said, the strike is not a right, it is a fact,[137] and "the right to strike is not one to be asked for, it must be taken!" [138] The whole of citizenship may be summed up in the phrase, *organized mutual self-restraint*. If this does not exist, strikes will come, right or no right. So that the strike being excluded, what are its indispensable substitutes? They are (1) institutions, in which civil servants can obtain a full and proper hearing, and in which their legitimate grievances can find redress and (2) public recognition that the authority of the people, of the legislature and ministers, has moral bounds, in that it must be willing to temper the doctrines of Treasury control and economy—both potential fetishes—with justice to officials. The second is the fundamental necessity. As the

civil service is expected to subject itself to the community, so is the community obliged to subject itself to the civil service. Enlightened nations have already made arrangements to guarantee this, while others still persist in the true belief that, for a time at least, exploitation is possible, and the untrue belief that discontent suppressed is discontent dissipated.

Collective Bargaining. Is collective bargaining in the sense that it exists in private enterprise conceivable in public enterprise? The subject has been raised chiefly in the Tennessee Valley Authority, which wished to establish a very enlightened personal policy, and it is inferrable as a problem from the discussions regarding the nature of the contractual relationship of civil servant and state. As regards the latter, it has been generally denied that civil servants fully established are in contractual relationship, whereas people engaged for a specific job may be put on a contractual basis. Normally, all civil servants are engaged according to the status prescribed by a law or an order laid down by the executive. It is denied that this is contractual, because it is desired to imply that though the official may resign he cannot strike. Therefore he cannot bargain collectively because, like the strike, this would imply an equal status with the state and imply the ability to shed engagements when it suited the civil servants in the event of a dispute.

The Tennessee Valley Authority was at first inclined to say that it had introduced collective bargaining, and it certainly established and worked processes whereby the point of view of both sides was as openly expressed as in any bilateral negotiations in private industry. Yet in the introductory statement to its Employee Relationship Policy, the Authority has clearly declared that its first duty is to the public.[139]

What of the argument that unless there were strong resistance against the unions of civil servants, they would exploit the

---

[137] Lefas, *op. cit.*, p. 199.
[138] Harmignie, *op. cit.*, p. 118.

[139] Cf. Civil Service Assembly (Chicago, 1943), *Employee Relationship in Public Service;* also S. Spero, *Government as Employer* (New York, 1948).

state for their own benefit? This was rather more plausible two or three decades ago before the problem became concrete: it was possible to speculate pessimistically in the abstract, and laissez-faire economists did so. They believed that bodies of civil servants would get their pay raised, or get their hours or intensity of labor reduced, or fall into well-paid inefficiency. They would do this, it was suggested, by pressure on members of the legislature, by lobbying, by threats to strike, and (in some electoral districts) by voting for pliable candidates. Time has shown the ridiculousness of these not-disinterested guesses. It might then have been realized that the number of officials was too small to have any decisive threat to the legislature; that it was practically impossible for the civil service vote to be so spread among all the districts that the civil servants' votes would decide the balance. On the other hand, if the civil service became very large, then the civil servant as citizen had interests in common with the rest of the nation superior to the civil servant as employee of the state. He also would have an interest in stability, or general political change or conservatism.

The Right to Strike under Socialism. If, again, the civil service comes to embrace several great occupations like power, fuel, conservation, transport, credit, housing, public medicine, steel, chemicals, and various others, then the workers in these occupations are more likely to be—indeed, experience now shows us that they are—in competition with each other for the division of the total national income in wages and taxation burdens and benefits, rather than in collusion with one another to exploit somebody else. The great battles of our time on the economic field are really battles between the occupations rather than between the workers and the employers or between the workers in public enterprise and the state as employer. But this latter tension does exist, for the state as employer is also the state as representative of the whole body of consumers. It is through the instrument called the "state" that the respective claims for wages,

hours, and conditions are made by the occupations upon each other; the state is the instrument of negotiation and adjustment, and, in the end, of enforcement. All this has become very manifest with the rapid and massive development of nationalization and intensive regulation of industries in Britain and Europe.

As for the right to strike, that itself is kept by labor unions in rationalized industries: where it is not recognized, as in TVA, strikes have nevertheless occurred. In the last final tension they may very well occur. If the ultimate right to rebel did not exist—though not acknowledged —then legislatures and governments and the personnel departments might become stonyhearted and authoritarian to public employees. But it is noteworthy that the leaders of the labor unions in the industries which have been nationalized recognize the need for new self-restraints by the workers themselves on their right to strike. It is asserted that the trade unions in a socialized or socializing state have gone beyond the field of combat with the capitalists, and that, as citizens and voters, they are themselves henceforth owners of the means of production. Upon them, therefore, now falls a responsibility, to get the best out of the capital invested, and the organization also, and to satisfy the consumers by good quality and the maximum production.

The old employer-employee relationship will continue to exist in nationalised industry, but in a fundamentally altered form. The employing authority no longer represents a limited private interest engaged in the pursuit of profits. It represents a public interest. The welfare of the whole community is its concern. It will conduct the industry as a social service, owing obligations equally to the workers it employs, the consumers it serves, and the people as a whole. New wage relationships, it seems to me, and a new technique in collective bargaining, must be evolved to meet this altered situation, as regards nationalised industry at any rate. . .

. . . I believe that we shall have to reexamine many trade union practices where they tend towards restriction; we shall have to do some fresh thinking about the historically conditioned principles of collective bargaining. . .

Reckless and irresponsible elements in our trade unions can work much mischief to-day. There have been unauthorized strikes and conflicts arising out of inter-union relations that are disquieting. . . Every responsible trade union official and every loyal member of the unions can see the dangers arising from unofficial strikes. . .[140]

---

[140] Speech by Charles Dukes, chairman, Trades Union Congress, Annual Report, 1946.

Thus, the new occupations and services in the public management, which yesterday were private enterprise, are hardly distinguishable in outlook from the civil service unions and the public as employer in the matter of responsibility for steady production. They were on the way to that assimilation even before they were nationalized, and they were nationalized because, in part, society now urgently required the assurance of their uninterrupted production.

35

Redress of Grievances and Guarantee of Rights in the Civil Service

THE machinery whereby civil servants can make their complaints heard and secure a redress of their grievances is broadly fourfold: the national and local representative assemblies and the Treasury (or Ministry of Finance); special representative councils like the Whitley Councils in England or the Officials' Representative Councils in Weimar Germany; courts of arbitration after the model of the industrial and wage courts for private industry; and formal arrangements with procedure of a judicial nature for the prosecution of established rights and the challenge of disciplinary sentences.

LEGISLATURES AND TREASURIES AS MEDIATORS

LEGISLATURES mediate between the civil service and the taxpayer. History shows that they are not liberal toward the civil service, but rather the reverse. It is to their interest in every country to act in such wise that they can triumphantly claim to be a champion of economy. No legislature has ever shown spontaneous generosity to civil servants. The atmosphere is one rather of meanness. Civil servants' salaries are easily accessible to economizing governments, and their professional ethics leave them defenseless against a barbarian public. In Great Britain there are many occasions when civil service conditions may be discussed before the House of Commons, but only a critical situation (like the Gregory case) or some rank injustice tactlessly committed can cause the House to turn its attention away from the more general matters of administration which are discussed during supply debates. But Parliament has no special machinery to focus and force its deliberate and detached attention upon grievances which may seem minor to it but which are important in the eyes of civil servants. Parliamentary machinery failing, the mediator between civil service and taxpayer is the Treasury.

The Treasury has been blamed for its tightfistedness.[1] But its general arrangements, financial and otherwise, for the civil service, have been quite liberal compared with other countries. Day-by-day grievances demanding adjustment of pay and conditions—adjustments which are fairly promptly made in private industry —may be met by the Treasury in a spirit of authority, churlishness, and unreasonable negation. However, the developments of the years since 1919 have on the whole encouraged much more reasonableness and understanding. Since the Establishments Division,[2] the Organizations and Methods branch, and special estab-

---

[1] Cf. Report, Machinery of Government Committee, 1918, Cmd. 9230, pp. 17-21.
[2] Cf. 16th Report, Select Committee on National Expenditure, No. 120 of 1942, "Organization and Control of the Civil Service."

lishment officers and divisions in the department have been instituted in the Treasury, its understanding of staff questions has been much enriched.[3] It cannot be denied that the Treasury still needs an impetus from the outside, and the civil servants a powerful means of advocacy, to secure a proper sensitiveness to staff questions. They cannot dispense with their associations.

The situation in Great Britain is, however, better than in Third Republic France. There the Ministry of Finance was overshadowed by the parliamentary commissions of the budget (and their sub-committees), and neither the Chambers nor the commissions showed any tenderness of regard for the civil service. Problems of staffing, bonus, and pay were met with feebleness, chicanery, illwill, ignorance, and self-seeking meanness and shuffling—everything, indeed, except wisdom and social spirit. Nor had civil servants the power to invoke the aid of Parliament by petitions exposing the policy of the executive in their regard. This privilege which the constitution of 1875 passed over in silence is a "natural right" for ordinary citizens and is available to British and American civil servants, but the French chambers never censured the government which suppressed it for officials. Though some civil servants sat in Parliament, the situation of the whole body was not thereby improved to any degree worth mention. The civil service was, indeed, compelled to conduct active practical campaigns, especially during elections, to secure attention to its demands. The great *Fédération des Syndicats de Fonctionnaires* (formerly adherent to the C.G.T.) had black lists of deputies who did not support civil servants' demands, and these names were communicated to the groups in the constituencies. The Federation in a resolution of its congress of 1924 said: [4]

It knows that it can count upon the absolute devotion of all its fighters to whom will fall the task of a giving to this organization the necessary vitality to cause to triumph at the elections not any particular party, but a current of opinion strong enough to combat the present influence of the great economic groups and to facilitate the evolution of syndicalism.

The Congress of the United States is not an open-minded court of appeal for civil servants. There is an exceptionally strong mistrust of the executive authority and an extraordinary (almost a vicious) spitefulness toward bureaucracy. It has been possible for civil servants to "get at" Congressmen and Congressional committees by backstairs organizations. But the virtue of this system from the standpoint of the civil service—accessibility—is offset by the great drawback of the sporadic, haphazard, unsettled, and partial nature of such solutions. There is no substantial or continuous guarantee in such machinery. The United States Treasury is not to be compared with the British Treasury either for the scope of its authority or for its energy and traditions in civil service matters. The division of authority over the civil service between Bureau of the Budget and Civil Service Commission is vastly different from that between British Treasury and Civil Service Commission, for the former is authoritative and dynamic almost entirely, the latter only trivially instrumental. Hence initiative is confused and disintegrated in the American arrangement.[5]

The Act of August, 1912, provided that: [6]

the right of persons employed in the Civil Service of the United States, either individually or collectively, to petition Congress or any member thereof or to furnish information to either House of Congress or to any committee thereof, shall not be denied or interfered with.

[3] Cf. description of this in evidence of Russell Scott, Royal Commission on the Civil Service, 1929, *Minutes*, Vol. I, and Warren Fisher, *ibid.*, pp. 1278 ff.
[4] Cf. G. Carrère and J. Bourgin, *Manuel des Parties Politiques* (Paris, 1924), p. 253.

[5] Cf. L. Mayers, *op. cit.*, p. 549.
[6] 37 Stat. 583. Cf. Report of the President's Committee on Administrative Management, p. 7 ff., and the special study by F. Reeves and P. David, *ibid.*, pp. 59-139. Cf. also J. McDiarmid, "Changing Role of the U.S. Civil Service Commissions," *American Political Science Review*, December, 1946.

This gave rein to the attempts at organization, and from 1916 the National Federation of Federal Employees has been able to exercise due influence upon Congress. The statutes creating the Reclassification Commission and the retirement system (1920 and 1922 respectively) were due in large measure to the activity of this organization, the latter statute being especially the result of the clever application of the strength of the employees' organizations. That strength is reinforced to a tremendous degree by the electoral power of the American Federation of Labor and the CIO, to which various employee unions are affiliated. The employees have been forced into a lobbying attitude by the inertia, ignorance, and incompetence of Congress. Before the organizations came, the employees suffered and had no convenient means of redress. Yet Congressmen like Ramspeck (himself once a political appointee) have induced a more rational atmosphere. The establishment (in 1946) of standing committees of the Senate and the House on Civil Service is an important improvement of procedure. Yet it is an extraordinary fact that the salaries of the top British civil servants are considerably higher (in a less wealthy society) than their American colleagues! Why?

In Germany one of the defenses against the right to strike was the alleged existence of ample other means for the redress of grievances. And, indeed, there is much solidity in this defense. Apart from the fact that civil servants had direct representation in the *Reichstag* and in the state parliaments, and in recognized organizations, the parliaments themselves were organized to give the civil service easy and prompt access to them. In the *Reichstag* the Fourteenth Committee (Affairs Relating to Civil Servants) discussed and settled the main lines and the details of civil service questions and laws before they went before the full House. The permanence of the committee, its smallness, its special field, all offered to both the public and the officials a rational consideration of their respective claims, although higher administrative officials,

members of the *Reichstag* and academic observers, argued that the civil servants exercised, perhaps, undue power.

REPRESENTATIVE COUNCILS

DURING the last generation the governing body in industry, private as well as public, has learned the value of creating councils in which representatives of the workers have a seat, and where the demands of both sides may be candidly presented and discussed.[7] The chief merit of this system is not that it necessarily gives the worker or civil servant any greater control over the conditions of his work than before, for that obviously depends upon the extent to which the employer is willing or compelled to waive the extreme use of his property rights, nor that it avoids conflict, but that it is possible for issues which rankle to secure a prompt outlet. Timely remedies may then be applied and injurious consequences reasoned over and appreciated before they come. He who hesitates is won.

The Whitley Councils in England. In Great Britain, until 1917, individuals and associations in the civil service, like the United States civil service till more recently, were obliged to act mainly by memorial which finally reached the head of the department and then the Treasury.[8] The chief disadvantage of this method was that negotiations were in writing, and personal discussion was almost entirely excluded. In 1917 a vast change was contemplated in private industry, and this had its effect upon the civil service. In private industry it became evident, especially during the war, that it was not only unsatisfactory conditions of remuneration that caused industrial unrest, but a desire to be consulted about these conditions, and to learn how far orders and policy were the arbitrary expression of the employer's personal

---

[7] Cf. literature on this subject published from time to time by the International Labour Office.
[8] Cf. Royal Commission on the Civil Service, 1929, Introductory Memoranda, pp. 70-71.

temper and how far a necessary condition of industry. In 1917 the Whitley Report on Relations between Employers and Employed was issued; it touched only the nonpublic industries.[9]

Civil servants pressed for the application of the Whitley proposals to the public service. By the end of July, 1911, a council of officials and representatives, after negotiations and the cabinet's approval, drew up a model constitution for the departmental Whitley councils. Generally, it was stated,[10]

The objects of the Council shall be to secure the greatest measure of cooperation between the administration, in its capacity as employer, and the general body of the staff in matters affecting the department, with a view to increased efficiency in the department combined with the well-being of those employed; to provide machinery for dealing with grievances, and generally to bring together the experience and different points of view of the administrative, clerical, and manipulative Civil Service.

There are many departmental councils on the model set out, with wide variations according to the peculiar circumstances of each department, and each has small numbers representing equally official and staff sides. The National Council, which considers the interests of the service as a whole, and to which the departmental councils are bound to refer general questions, is composed of fifty-four members divided equally between official and staff sides, whose representatives must be "persons of standing (who may or may not be civil servants)." It has consisted on the official side of the permanent secretaries of departments or other higher officials, and since 1922 of three members of Parliament. The Controller of the Establishment Branch of the Treasury is chairman. The staff side representatives must be appointed by civil service groups or associations [11] named in the constitution.

About one half the members of the staff side of the Council have been full-time officers of associations, the rest serving civil servants.

The Whitley Councils are concerned with the problems of nonindustrial staffs in posts carrying remuneration only up to £700 a year.[12] The industrial staffs have special industrial councils.[13]

The functions of the Whitley councils include (1) provision of the best means for utilizing the ideas and experience of the staff; (2) securing the staff a greater share of responsibility for the determination and observance of the conditions under which they work, and the determination of the general provisions governing recruitment, hours, tenure, and remuneration; (3) encouragement of further education of civil servants and their training in higher administration and organization; (4) the improvement of office machinery and organization, and the provision of opportunities for the full consideration of suggestions by the staff on this subject; and (5) proposed legislation so far as it has a bearing upon the position of civil servants in relation to their employment.

What is the authority of the councils? In 1919 negotiation between the perturbed staff representatives and official representatives resulted in a unanimous report which became, substantially, the constitution of the councils.[14] The constitution goes beyond making the councils merely advisory. It says that "the decisions of the Council shall be arrived at by agreement between the two sides, shall be signed by Chairman and Vice-Chairman,[15] shall be reported to the Cabinet and thereupon shall become operative." As for the Department Councils, their decisions "shall be reported to the Head

---

[9] Cmd. 8606 of 1917.
[10] Para. 21, constitution, National Council.
[11] On all constitutional questions cf. J. H. Macrae-Gibson, *The Whitley System in the Civil Service* (Fabian Society, London, 1922). See also L. D. White, *Whitley Councils in the British Civil Service* (Chicago, 1932), and E. N.

Gladden, *Civil Service Staff Relationships* (London, 1943).
[12] Including scales which commence below £700 but rise above it.
[13] Cf. Royal Commission on the Civil Service, 1929, *Introductory Memoranda*, p. 85. Cf. report on establishment and progress of joint industrial councils, 1917-22, published 1925.
[14] Cmd. 198 of 1919.
[15] A member of the staff side.

of Department and shall become operative." [16] Does this mean that the decisions made overrule the will of the cabinet and of individual ministers? At the tenth meeting of the National Council, a committee was appointed to clarify this question, and it agreed upon this definition:

The establishment of Whitley Councils cannot relieve the Government of any part of its responsibility to Parliament, and Ministers and Heads of Departments acting under the general or specific authority of Ministers, must take such action as may be required in any case in the public interest. This condition is inherent in the constitutional doctrines of Parliamentary Government and ministerial responsibility, and Ministers can neither waive nor escape it.

It follows from this constitutional principle that, while the acceptance by the Government of the Whitley system as regards the Civil Service implies an intention to make the fullest possible use of Whitley procedure, the Government has not surrendered, and cannot surrender its liberty of action in the exercise of its authority and the discharge of its responsibilities in the public interest.

This, if it means anything, means that a greater freedom is given to the official side, because if on consideration any agreed plan is discovered to have unexpected implications, it could be overridden on the grounds of cabinet responsibility. However, the term that agreements become "operative" does imply an obligation that in all normal cases they shall be operative. As in all negotiating assemblies based upon "instructions," discussions must sometimes be adjourned until fresh instructions are obtained. There is no voting—each side acts as a unit: and therefore each side must find agreement beforehand. In the background, with its hands on the ultimate strings, is the Treasury.

No Act of Parliament founded the Whitley system. It arose out of a promise made by the government of the day. And whatever strength it has is drawn entirely from the needs of the public service and the character of the men and women who compose the councils. Most of the coun-

cils have done much good work in the matter of promotions, discipline, and the organization and conduct of office work; especially is this true of the departments where small devices have great value because of the largeness of the staff and the industrial nature of the work—in the Admiralty, Post Office, and the Customs and Excise councils.

Naturally the National Council has been active on a wide scale. It has reported upon and received the reorganizations of the general principles and methods of promotion; a Superannuation Committee has codified the complex superannuation regulations; a Committee on Further Education has made its report on provision for the further education of younger civil servants, and lectures have been arranged by civil service bodies and an internal and external diploma of public administration has been created in the University of London. A bonus and a sliding-scale system to meet varying price levels have been secured, and, perhaps most important of all, the regrading and reorganization of the civil service has been effected. In preparation for the tasks of reconstruction after World War II, the Whitley council played a central and magnificent role: no single step was taken without its advice and report.

What has been gained by the institution of the Whitley councils? Something very important psychologically has been gained when there can be a semipublic review of a foolish, untactful, or despotic show of authority [17]—when resentment of arbitrary interference with habit is avoided. Then, too, officials below the top grade have now a feeling that in regard to promotion, leave, and other official benefits, any jobbery is likely to be detected and quashed. Too much must obviously not be expected from the system by the staff side. However, it is quite clear, from the evidence given by heads of departments and representatives of the

---

[16] Clause 19.

[17] In the departmental councils it is open to the staff side to discuss any promotion when the accepted principles have been violated; disciplinary cases may also be presented for discussion if the staff side wish it.

staff, that the departmental councils have actually produced an invaluable and indispensable atmosphere of good and easy relationship between superiors and subordinates—that is the universal testimony.

The power of the associations behind the councils is still required to maintain real official respect for the cases they advocate, and we can surmise, though we cannot exactly count the number of, small benefits silently won without overt conflict by the mere existence of organized and recognized *vigilantes.* The evidence before the Royal Commission of 1929 shows that matters are not always discussed in the formal meetings of the councils, but informal discussions occur between the leaders of the officials of the staff sides, and settlements reached at once.[18]

We may pass over developments in Third Republic France very rapidly, for there were so few, and the world has nothing of value to learn from them.[19] The French politician was interested in other things, while the civil service associations were driven into a position of syndicalist extremism.[20]

Fourth Republic France introduced a veritable revolution in the status of her officials, following the most enlightened practices of the world. A Superior Council of Public Service (*conseil supérieur de la fonction publique*)[21] is established by the *statut des fonctionnaires:* it is presided over by the prime minister or his deputy (it is almost certain always to be the latter) and it is composed of twenty-four members nominated by the cabinet, twelve on the proposal of the civil service unions. It is concerned with the high level

of civil service policy and with the establishment of a minimum living wage, and it coordinates the work and views of the departmental councils of the same kind. Its recommendations are forwarded to the prime minister. Each department or service has established administrative commissions on a joint and equal representative basis of high officials and rank and file. Their competence includes surveillance—and in some cases participation—in the process of recruitment, efficiency records, promotion, discipline, and more generally all questions affecting personnel. The rank-and-file representatives are elected by the whole body of officials in the various departments and agencies respectively. In addition, there are in each agency technical committees on a joint basis which handle problems of organization or administration, making recommendations when asked for them—here the rank-and-file members are chosen by the trade-union organizations that are most representative.

The Officials' Representatives Councils of Weimar Germany. Article 130 of the constitution provided that officials shall receive representative bodies by special law. Such a law was not passed, but individual departments established civil servants' committees (*Beamtenausschüsse*) temporarily to fill the gap, e.g., Ministry of Posts, Ministry of Justice, and Finance Ministry. The duty of the committee in the Ministry of Finance was to represent the interests of the officials before their superiors. The councilors were enjoined to act so that the sense of duty and joy of labor, the mutual confidence of subordinate and superior, were enhanced. Demands and suggestions of the staff relating to general personal affairs in the department were to be considered by the council and represented before the heads of the department. On the other hand, the superiors were to consult the opinion of the committee in the regulation of departmental routine and the hours of work, and in the laying down of principles for deputations, annual leave, sundry welfare institutions, and the reemployment of those dismissed from the

18 The report, 1931 (p. 137 ff.) suggests hardly any change, except the extension of facilities for staff representatives to carry out their functions.
19 Cf. Lefas, *L'État et les Fonctionnaires* (Paris, 1913). Cf. Ricard, *Droit et Jurisprudence en Matière de Postes, Telegraphes, Telephones* (Paris, 1931), Chap. VII.
20 Cf., for example, among the saner of those who desire the service turned over to the independent discretion of associations, Georges Mer, *Le Syndicalisme des Fonctionnaires* (Paris, 1929).
21 *Statut,* articles 19 to 22.

service. And when the person specially concerned wished it, the council was to give its opinion on miscellaneous welfare matters like refusal of leave, recommendations to physicians, distribution of dwelling places, and the problem of whether or not there was a right to an addition to pay on the ground of place of residence. The various ministries in the *Reich* and in Prussia established committees of this kind—they were purely advisory.

The ministries did not treat the committees as alternatives to the civil service associations,[22] but they several times expressed their desire that no individual cases should be represented by the associations, though they were always ready to deal with any exceptional case where misunderstandings and errors could be swept away.[23] Of the tendency to carry individual grievances to the associations, the *Reich* Ministry of Finance and the Prussian Ministry of Justice complained. The latter [24] pointed out with considerable justice that the associations were not in a position to sift out the truth or falsity of the complaints. Consequently, the department was unduly bothered with communications. The complainant is not well served by such a procedure since his complaints must ultimately revert to the place of their origin for investigation. But if the Officials' Committee were at once approached, it could quash groundless demands and recommend the substantial ones. Prompt and just decisions can be made in this wise. The special evil of approaching the association was, however, this: that the committees did not receive the amount and degree of work they were well fitted to carry out, and confidence in them was generally weakened.

Until now [1922] it seems as if the recognition that the Official's Committees when properly employed can be effective in an extraordinarily fortunate way has not yet found general extension. They can reinforce a strong bond of confidence between the individual official and the departmental authorities, as well as avoid superfluous written communications. Without prejudice to the pending statutory regulation of official representative bodies, let the departmental authorities already begin to act in a fashion calculated to maintain the status of the committees in all respects, so that they may be in a position to fulfill their duty for the welfare of the civil service.[25]

Here is a problem which has arisen in the relationship between the trade-union organizers and the works councils in private industry. It is very difficult, excepting in special cases, to lay down a rule as to where the competence of the one begins and the other ends. There is much good sense in the remarks we have quoted above; and we calculate that they will everywhere be necessary. For there are always individuals with grievances and idiosyncrasies who seek the stage as potential martyrs. There are those with a persecution complex, and other litigious to the extreme. It is a frequent thing to find a man or woman who prefers not to be tried by his or her peers, since chicanery and prevarication do not impose upon one's colleagues for long. And there are always ministers and heads of departments who do not like even the proper intervention of the association. Indeed, serious disciplinary problems are involved in the right to appeal from the head of the department.[26] The committees had not the executive force of the British Whitley councils, but they were nevertheless the moderators of minor distempers. The *Entwurf* (project) *eines Gesetzes über Beamtenvertretungen*, 1930, under discussion before the Nazi triumph is analyzed in the two-volume edition of this work (p. 1439).

Grievance Committees in the United States Civil Service. Thus, committees through which officials may represent their grievances are of exceedingly recent date. The United States civil service has

---

22 It was, perhaps, owing to the strength and the ability of these associations that the councils have not fully developed.

23 *Beamten-Archiv*, Vol. II, p. 31.

24 *Ministerialblatt für die preuszische innere Verwaltung*, October, 1922, p. 1082.

25 *Idem.*

26 The Royal Commission on Civil Service reported, 1929, against centralized appeal bodies for this reason. Cf. also F. A. Bland, *Government of Australia* (Sydney, 1943), Chap. 13.

some such grievance procedures in a few agencies—beginning with the supervisor of the aggrieved official, going up to supervisors, and here and there an agency or departmental appeals committee.[27] The system is still upon its trial, and even at its best is confined to the minor adjustments of staff matters which are in any case troublesome to superiors, and occasional consultation on matters like the general principles of superannuation, classification and promotion. The maintenance of rights cannot be as yet entirely left to such instruments. Officials must still rely upon their associations for a show of power. There is no authority without an awe-producing element, whether it be spiritual, like the force of personality, the impressiveness of talent or the appeal of justice, or simply physical, varying only in the manner and strength of its application. It is hardly possible for the civil service at present to forego either the one or the other; but in proportion as institutions of the kind we have just discussed are developed and full scope given to the former, the threat of physical injury (which of course carries with it spiritual disablement) will become more and more dispensable.

The arrangements so far indicated are not concerned with adjustments of pay, but only Britain provides a special court for clauses regarding the pay, in relation to the working conditions of the service, among the countries with which we deal, though Australia has a fairly long experience of a civil service arbitral court. We indicate the main elements only of the English system.

Early in 1917 a Civil Service Arbitration Board was set up as a result of agitation by civil service associations because the War had sent prices sky-high while wages lagged far behind.[28] Two motives can be seen at work: the realization that "There is no worse tribunal in the world for fixing a scale of wages than the House of Commons," and to free members of Parliament from intolerable pressure. The Board established by the executive authority of the government was to deal by conciliation or arbitration with questions arising with regard to claims for increased pay made by Government employees, except in the cases of industrial staffs, and where there was already recognized machinery applicable to the case. It referred only to posts under £500 a year. Suddenly as part of the general postwar attack upon government expenditure and the standard of living, the Board was abolished in February, 1922. The alleged grounds of abolition were that the Whitley Councils considered questions of remuneration. Now since the Whitley Councils can only declare and not enforce a recommendation this plea was fallacious, perhaps dishonest.

An intense campaign was conducted and ended with the reestablishment of the Board early in 1925. Its constitution is part of the industrial courts set up by the Act of 1919.[29] In the present case the court consists of a chairman who is either the president of the industrial court or the chairman of a division of the court, together with one member drawn from a panel of persons appointed to the industrial court by the minister of labor as representing the chancellor of the exchequer for the time being (this is the employers' representative), and one member drawn from a panel of persons appointed to the industrial court by the minister of labor after nomination by the staff side of the National Whitley Council. Civil servants and officials of civil service associations are ineligible for appointment as members of the court.

Only claims in regard to salaries of £850 and less can be referred to the court, unless by the consent of the parties concerned in the claim. When negotiation fails arbitration is open to the govern-

[27] The Executive Order of June, 1938, on the subject has not resulted in any substantial practical measures. See *Personnel Journal*, October, 1939, p. 151, *et seq.*

[28] Cf. Royal Commission on the Civil Service, 1929, *Memoranda*, p. 77 ff.

[29] Statutory Rules and Orders, 1924, No. 554/26; Treasury Circular, March 14, 1924; Rules of Procedure, November 28, 1927 (reproduced in Royal Commission on the Civil Service, 1929, Memoranda, Appendices).

ment departments on one hand, and the recognized civil service association within the scope of the National Whitley Council on the other hand, on application by either party. The matters which may be taken to the court are claims affecting emoluments, weekly hours of work, and leave. But claims can be made only for "classes," i.e., "any well-defined category of civil servants who for the purpose of a particular claim occupy the same position, or have a common interest in the claim." This provision limits the work of the court, and were it not so, individual cases, and cases of small groups, where inequalities in respective pay and work were concerned would cause a continuous rush of claims for related adjustment, and destroy any stability for the Treasury and Parliament. The whole problem of classification would be reopened and never closed. This, of course, unfortunately imposes hardship on some officials, and the hardship is a direct result of largescale organization, and the exigencies of parliamentary control. Civil servants are generally satisfied that they have secured a very valuable piece of machinery for removing grievances. It is acknowledged that the court is fair, patient, and thorough. But one criticism is heard. The Treasury is the sole interpreter of the terms of the judgments of the court, and may take action before submitting its intentions to the court.

The staff side have requested that the Treasury be limited in its power of interpretation, and that, say, the Ministry of Labour, should decide between its view and the Treasury view; and that there should be some limitation on the action of the government affecting remuneration and conditions of civil servants without first submitting such matters to the judgment of the industrial court. The government has rejected such requests on the grounds of their general political responsibility, which requires that they shall not be bound,[30] but the decision is practically always followed by the Treasury.

The Royal Commission [31] recommended no change in the constitution or jurisdiction of the court, except a wider definition of "class." From 1925 to 1939 over three hundred cases were submitted to the court, a few by the staff side of the National Whitley Council, rather more by the staff side of the departmental councils, and the bulk on behalf of associations or groups of associations.

THE GUARANTEE OF RIGHTS

How far does the state define the rights of civil servants—that is, the rewards and penalties of their work—and offer means of recourse against itself when the official feels these are violated? It is obviously unjust, and practically foolish, for the state to demand that civil servants shall deprive themselves of their defensive associations if it does not set up institutions which will offer them protection. All this raises many questions of formal law: the nature of the state as employer, the doctrine of autolimitation of the state's power, whether it is possible to sue the state. These questions have given lawyers, especially on the Continent, an enormous field of activity, and often caused them a tremendous waste of good time. For, in the end, these are not questions that can be decided by legal logic, and they would never have been raised did the state commence today without any legacy of its old absolute authoritarian self, a legacy which confuses the issue by setting up two fictions one against the other, state and subject. But we have learned that such problems are practically posed in terms of the interrelationship of social groups; and if we regard the present problem in this light, it is quite feasible—and not as may even be considered today, unnatural—to give the social group constituted by the civil service recourse against all the others who are served by it. It sounds different when we set the civil service and the state against each other. It has been otherwise in the past because

[30] Cf. declaration of Financial Secretary to the Treasury, March 9, 1926, and that of Prime Minister, February 2, 1927.

[31] Report of the Royal Commission on the Civil Service, 1929, p. 145 ff.

this opposition was construed into one of constant and necessary hostility. Though the last half century has witnessed a change of mind in this respect, there are still some who maintain the old tenets, and unfortunately the law has not yet caught up with even moderately enlightened opinion. Some countries still have sixteenth-century notions written and active in their statute books.

England. The British system still operates upon a legal basis as old as it is unjust. Arising out of the ancient doctrine that "the King can do no wrong," and that civil servants are servants of the Crown, it has been assumed that the Crown may dismiss its servants at pleasure.[32] No law or general administrative code lays down a scheme of disciplinary misdemeanors and accompanying penalties. A civil servant has no legal action against dismissal. His superannuation rights are ultimately determinable by the Treasury, for its interpretation of the acts is not challengeable in the courts. It may be pleaded that the head of a department would not hurt anybody unreasonably, and that the Treasury would rather be kind than cruel: unfortunately for human relationships, not all men are good or wise or well informed. Hence machinery is necessary to correct the deficiencies of men acting spontaneously.

The guarantee civil servants possess is the promise made by the Treasury in November, 1920,[33] as the result of a formula adopted by the National Whitley Council. This says that

except in cases which may give rise to criminal proceedings, full particulars of any charge against an officer's conduct shall be communicated to him in writing before any disciplinary action be decided upon.

The question of reports affecting promotion, that is, mainly the annual reports, was left to the consideration of the promotions committee: and this decided that in the case of adverse markings the

civil servant must be given a written intimation of his assessment, with particulars and reasons. Finally, when a report upon an officer in circumstances not covered by these arrangements reflects upon him adversely, he must be informed of the alleged defects in order to enable him to make explanations before the report is placed on record.

Nor does the Crown Proceedings Act, 1947, which permits private suits against the state, apply to the civil servants in his employment relationship to the state.[34] It does not imply a contract of service. The Royal Commission[35] recommended that in serious cases the civil servant shall have the right to oral proceedings before a senior officer of the Department. He may have associated with him a colleague, or a representative of his association. In all cases of misconduct the charge is to be written and supported by a statement of facts. This was fulfilled by a Treasury Letter of May, 1935, which deprecated any standardized practice.

United States. In the United States the principles and methods derived from the same source as the English common law on this subject prevail, and no improvements have been made upon it. The power of dismissal has been made strict and absolute by the judgment in *Myers* vs. *U.S.A.* and *Morgan* vs. *T.V.A.* though the right to answer adverse reports or to appeal against disciplinary action is in a vigorous state of action and development.

France. In France the evolution since 1905 resulted in the establishment of a series of legal guarantees for civil servants. This development is the direct issue of two legal institutions unknown to Anglo-Saxon law: the suability of the public authority and action for excess of power. These are explained further in Chapter 36 on *Legal Remedies against Public Administration and Administrative Law,* but a short indication of their import is necessary here. The suability

---

[32] C. S. Emden, *The Law and the Civil Servant* (London, 1927). Confirmed in *Rodwell* v. *Tithe Exemption Commission* K. B. D., April 5, 1944.
[33] Circular No. 57/20.

[34] *Treasury Letter,* January 30, 1948; *Whitley Bulletin,* March, 1948.
[35] Report of the Royal Commission on Civil Service, 1929, p. 173 ff.

of the public authority means that the state furnishes the opportunity for the challenge and the quashing of any of its actions which are inconsistent with the law, and redress for damage from the state. Such cases are ultimately heard by the *Conseil d'État*. Then, second, any person having a personal interest in such an *ultra vires* action may take proceedings in as easy and convenient manner as if he were conducting an ordinary civil action; in fact, the actions are easier to take.

For the safeguarding of his everyday working conditions, then, the French official has to look to two sources: first, his written or customary rights, and second, the *Conseil d'État* which will deny validity to any regulation or decision affecting him which violates the rights. As we have already seen, there is no single coherent statement of civil servants' rights: there are simply a number of decrees, rules of public administration, and departmental regulations affecting appointment, promotion, and discipline, and the financial and special laws of various dates affecting payment and pensions. All these establish interests for individual civil servants, and by the evolution of principles in case after case, the *Conseil d'État* has provided a sound guarantee of these interests. In regard to general disciplinary measures, the jurisprudence of the *Conseil d'État* is exceedingly extensive, since it was the first undertaken in point of time, before the middle of the nineteenth century.

The rules relating to appointments and promotion lists are maintained in this way. Dismissal, which is the greatest danger menacing an official, especially since it abolishes the title to a pension, is challengeable on the question of its regularity, its injustice, and its brusqueness.[36] Where Councils of discipline are established and have not been regularly invoked before a disciplinary penalty has been imposed, the penalty becomes invalid. Many cases have been raised on the basis of the law of 1905 which gives civil servants the right to inspect their personal records. The article says:[37]

All civil and military officials, all the employees and workers of all public departments have the right to the personal and confidential communication of all notes, memoranda (*feuilles signalétiques*), and of all documents composing their personal records, whether before being the object of disciplinary measures or a removal from office, or before being kept back in their promotion by seniority.

On all sides the *Conseil d'État* has hedged this right with defenses.[38]

What the French law has done, then, is to create the principle that a subordinate in the civil service is toward his superior in the position of an administered person. As the civil service may abuse its power *vis-à-vis* the ordinary citizen, so may the higher civil servants do to the lower.

Germany. The country in which rights and guarantees were most elaborately and firmly evolved was Imperial and Weimar Germany. If we reflect on what has been said about the jurisprudence of the *Conseil d'État* and then extend that to be perfectly comprehensive with every conceivable procedural guarantee, we shall acquire an idea of *Reich* and state guarantees to their officials. Every step, from admonition to retirement, was hedged with rules and procedural assurances. We have no space to recite the facts as contained in the various laws and regulations, or the machinery and procedure of decision.[39] We refer only to the general theory, known as that of acquired rights (*wohlerworbene Rechte*).[40] The Weimar constitution said (article 129): "The acquired rights of public servants are

[36] M. Hauriou, *Précis de Droit Constitutionel* (Paris, 1929), p. 587, and footnote.

[37] April 22, 1905, article 65. Characteristically of French legislative methods, this is in the Financial Act of the year. Cf. Librairie Dalloz, *Code Administratif* (Paris, 1930), p. 489.
[38] Cf. L. Duguit, *Traité de Droit Constitutionel* (Paris, 1923), Vol. II, p. 150 *et seq.*, and G. Jèze, *Revue du Droit Public* (Paris, 1912), Vol. III, p. 75 ff., re disciplinary cases.
[39] Cf. A. Brand, *Beamtenrecht* (Berlin, 1928) and A. Schulze and W. Simons, *Rechtssprechung des Disziplinarhofs* (Berlin, 1926).
[40] W. Schroder, *Die Wohlerworbene Rechte der Beamten* (Berlin, 1930).

inviolable." This gave rise to a vast literature of interpretation, and to several suits and judicial decisions. One representative of the officials went as far as to claim complete inviolability of rights in the future as well as the rights already acquired: [41]

The acquired rights are inviolable! The will and the clear phraseology have it that all rights belonging to officials ought not to be altered to their disadvantage. Thus this is not merely a program of the *Reich* Government, but, as previously said, a directly effective positive right. Article 129 of the Constitution by its form and purpose does not merely accrue to the officials employed at the entry into force of the Constitution, but it is effective for the future and guarantees also the acquired rights which were later established.

Some jurists were ready to claim that a constitutional amendment would be needed for any change in the status and salaries and working conditions of civil servants. Now, it is clear that changes of status cannot be for ever avoided; clearer still that civil servants cannot be granted complete immunity from the general fortunes of the society they serve, that their conditions of work and their salaries must to some extent be in fair relativity with the fortunes of all others in the nation. But the idea of acquired rights and of the constitutional guarantee was to produce carefulness, deliberation, and consultation, and to put a heavy drag on rough-shod legislative overriding of legitimate expectations. And among the things so guaranteed are classification, method of recruitment, rights to promotion, salary scales and increments, titles, rank, orders, symbols of honor, insignia and honors. There are elaborate rules concerning retirement, pensions, bonuses to the family, local cost-of-living bonuses, official dwellings, removal expenses, and travel; and the most minute prescriptions regarding disciplinary offences and the procedure (in order of gravity) of warning, reprimand, fines, suspension, and dismissal. The penalties are established with a split-hair exactness; and so also the detail of the intradepartmental stages of action by the superior against the inferior official or the latter against the former. And, then, outside the department, rises the structure of the administrative courts leading to the pinnacle, the *Disziplinarhof* in Berlin.

Whatever the shortcomings of German administrative justice, it provided a system of redress open to all workers in the employment of the state, even the humblest; it acknowledged that the state may do wrong, and obliged itself to admit its wrongdoing in just rules and independent courts. No other country approaches this yet.

The United States. In spite of many suggestions made from time to time by the Civil Service Commission and the associations of civil servants, the federal service has no such comprehensive arrangements, systematic and authorized by law or executive order, as Britain, France, and prewar Germany. But the Civil Service Commission's recommendations to the departments that such shall be promoted has resulted in a great variety of cooperation between employees and the directing personnel of the departments and agencies. The National Federation of Federal Employees (which is not affiliated with either of the two major labor organizations), the American Federation of Government Employees (A.F.of L.), the United Public Workers of America (CIO), various craft unions, and unions of postal workers furnish the pressure to secure representation of the employees' point of view, and to clear up injustices and grievances.

Their pressure regarding pay levels is one exerted on Congress, rather than through joint councils, though the TVA has a notable annual wage conference, which under the terms of the statute settles the rates for the ensuing year. As to hours, leave, pensions, tenure, discipline, and promotion policies, the civil service rarely takes a step without the participation of the employee organizations. This is achieved through the Labor-Management Advisory Committee of the Civil Service Commission, which is a standing

---

[41] Hans Assmann, *Wohlerworbene Beamtenrecht* (Berlin, 1924).

body, first established in November, 1942, consisting of two representatives from each of the three major unions, six representatives of management, and a member of the Commission as chairman. The committee has authority to initiate and recommend policies which will result in the effective utilization of personnel. This is reminiscent of the scope of the National Whitley Council in Britain; but it is not accompanied, as there, by departmental joint committees. In the departments, however, on occasion and from time to time, joint committees may be called, when they confer on working conditions, safety, in-service training, appeals, methods for adjusting grievances, leave, promotions, and so on. But, in the main, they are called only when particular grievance situations require attention.

It is a requirement in the departments that promotions, demotions, suspensions, dismissals, and other disciplinary action shall take place in accordance with the Commission's rules. Appeal procedures lead up to the Commission itself as the final instance.[42] Where an employee feels that he cannot of his own ability obtain just treatment, his organization will plead his case, and be admitted to do this. But this process does not include anything like the French departmental councils that keep watch and ward over the personnel record and promotions procedure.

On the whole, perhaps as a kind of compensation, American public employee unions are called before Congressional committees, during hearings on budget and other legislation, much more gener-

[42] Cf. Civil Service Law, Rules, etc., November, 1941, U. S. Civil Service Commission, and its annual reports.

ally and as a matter of course than is the case in any other country.

We have thus observed the majestic and sweeping march of the democratic countries from the rigors and meannesses of the absolute state to the reasonableness and decency of the present time as regards the conditions of work, discipline, and reward of the state's own servants. This has not produced a decline in efficiency, but on the contrary has been coincident with marked improvement on the quality of the service rendered, not only as a result of the responsiveness of a democratic government to a sovereign people, but as a result of better administrative activity in a strict sense of the word. Justice and kindness are not lost. If the mind is applied to the subject, it is possible to formulate an interrelationship of duties and subordinations which must be observed for efficiency—the grand object being settled by frequent elections, and rights and guarantees, freedoms and generosity, which being observed lead to peace of mind, happier cooperation, and therefore to efficiency. It is better, in administration to give much and get much, than to give little and be served grudgingly and sourly. Outstanding in interest is the dissolution of the ancient hereditary rights to public employment. Above all in significance is the steady assimilation of the vital economic occupations under private enterprise to the conditions of public enterprise or civil service; and simultaneously the reverse process of easier, more flexible, personnel management and relationships in the latter—learned in many cases from the practices of private enterprise and publicly advocated by the civil servants' trade unions.

36

Legal Remedies against Public Administration and Administrative Law

THUS the state is continuously managed by a vast body of professional expert servants who contribute by their technical assistance to the foundation of law and carry it out. There resides in the legislature, and ultimately in the electorate, the power to correct error and vice in either of these functions, but as we have seen, these bodies are far too cumbrous to deal with a succession of individual cases—various in character and extremely complicated in substance. They have neither the machinery, procedure, nor capacity adequate to such judgment. If abuse of power is to be corrected, the specifically appropriate court of judgment and procedure are necessary.

Let it be remembered that when the statutes have given power to the officials, they should be able in that measure to act. The welfare of specified beneficiaries and the public in general depends on action. The search for infinite controls of "administrative finality" may defeat the laws, paralyze the official, and protect evil-doers.

The remedies available to the public to compel civil servants to do their work in accordance with law—which is a slightly narrower field than that indicated above—are regulated variously in different countries. Their importance has come into startling prominence since one by one the consequences of the growth of state activity have become clear. The is-

sues raised, and still the subject of agitation, are: How can officials be restrained from illegally commanding, and forbidding, or executing acts?—how far ought an official to be suable in his own private fortune, and how far should the state be responsible for breach of contract and wrongful acts in the course of official duties?—and before what courts should such issues be judged?

These again arise from two considerations: the first from the financial inability (usually) of the average civil servant to pay compensation adequate to the damage done. The second consideration is more complex: the civil servant has duties of a peculiarly difficult nature, many of which involve (a) from technical considerations, immediacy of judgment, so that speed, for example, which may be the essence of success, may cause misjudgment; and (b) always the inevitable decision in favor of some individuals or social groups to the disadvantage of the property and amenities of others. Either of these may land a civil servant into trouble with some individual or group of citizens, and judgment of the legal rectitude of the action taken, which is the only point at present under consideration, should, if it were to be just, be undertaken only by those trained to an appreciation of the nature of the tasks, the functional responsibility, and the mentality of the official, judging by a procedure and with the statistical and documentary equipment appropriate to the issue.

The possibilities of official misbehavior are myriad. Power may not be used when it should be used. An official may go beyond the power granted by law. Power may be deliberately or unconsciously perverted to ends having nothing to do with the public service. Accidents may happen in the course of a proper use of power, to the detriment of citizens quite detached from the event. Or improper procedure may be adopted in the practice of official judgments. Or commands and prohibitions may be uttered without basis in law. Against these the citizen demands a defense and remedies. These should be specifically appropriate to the cases which occur, and regard must be had to the nature of official duties, while to rely, in cases of compensation, only upon the pocket of the official is to rely upon a vacuum.

The state of the law varies very much in different countries, owing to the peculiar constitutional history of each. England, which is so excellent in other things, was until very recently defective in this respect, the United States is little better, while France and Germany share the most honorable position.

ENGLAND

The Crown and the Citizen: to 1947.
(1) Until 1947, the central authority, as a public institution, was not suable for tortious acts at all, and for breach of contract only by a favorable answer given to a petition of right by the attorney-general. The legal grounds of this immunity resided in the feudal foundations of the doctrine that the king can do no wrong and hence cannot wrongly choose or instruct his officials.[1] Behind it was the de-

sire not to have the public authorities hampered in the exercise of their power either at the time of exercising it or in anticipation of punishment by the courts after the event. And there are some functions of government which do not brook being so hampered: the keeping of order, the suppression of foreign enemies, and so on. Therefore, in the matter of tort, liability was upon the individual officials, and suit was in the ordinary courts and by ordinary procedure since no others had been established expressly for this purpose. As regards contract, the proper entity to be sued had to be carefully searched out in a multitude of legal hiding-places, and even when discovered, the Crown might and did defend itself by a dozen or so unconquerable weapons of procedure.[2] Broadly, then, the state had created for itself a privileged position regarding contract, with no basis of modern utility, but, on the contrary, considerable public disutility in which claimant groups were unreasonably penalized.[3] Some government departments, for some matters, were subject to suit, as the statutes which established their functions, for example in the case of commerce-like operations of the Post Office or Office of Works put their contracts on an ordinary basis. Furthermore, all the public corporations before and since 1945 included the right to sue and be sued.

As regards tort, whatever remedy was available was only against the individual official directly responsible for the act, and could easily be entirely inadequate in

---

[1] The early history of the doctrine can be traced in Ehrlich, *Proceedings against the Crown, 1216-1377* (Oxford, 1921), Vol. VI; F. Pollock and F. W. Maitland's *History of English Law* (Cambridge, 1899), Vol. I, p. 516; and W. S. Holdsworth, *History of English Law*, 3rd edition (London, 1926), Vol. VIII, pp. 249-53 and 472-79.

[2] G. E. Robinson, *Public Authorities and Legal Liability* (London, 1925); and W. S. Holdsworth, "History of Remedies against the Crown," *Law Quarterly Review*, Vol. 38, p. 289.

[3] In 1822, C. J. Dallas (*Gidley* v. *Lord Palmerston*, 3 Brod. and B. 275) attempted to base the ministry of the servants of the Crown on this reasoning: "On principles of public policy, an action will not lie against persons acting in a public character and situation, which from their very nature would expose him to an infinite multiplicity of actions . . . The very liability to an unlimited multiplicity of suits would, in all probability, prevent any proper or prudent person from accepting a public situation at the hazard of such peril to himself."

terms of compensation to the grieved person, and was sometimes unfair to the official acting under administrative stress. The reason advanced for the maintenance of this situation was that it placed full responsibility on the official. This is true, though whether the psychological effect is always present, or always good, is a matter of considerable doubt; but the question arises, ought all the responsibility to be so placed? It is even questionable whether such responsibility is indeed, made continuously conscious, by the fear of punishment of this kind, in an official between the hammer of superior orders and the anvil of stubborn citizens or situations.

(2) A statute could make the Crown liable, but only by "express mention or necessary implication." Many statutes were invoked as "necessarily" implying the Crown's liability—without success, because the act was "a general enactment of the character of those enacted for the public safety," and the courts very strictly defined the term "necessary." This meant that the servant, in so far as he acted in an official capacity,[4] was immune from suit under such statutes. Yet this was an act of grace; there was no guarantee for the injured citizen.

(3) However, it was the almost invariable practice for the Crown to stand behind the official, to grant the petitions of right, and even to discover parties in cases of doubt, in order to make suits possible. Local authorities, being corporations, were assimilated to natural persons, and were, therefore, in relation to their own servants, in a condition of master and servant and were liable. However, the extension of central powers caused the local authorities to become, in certain matters, plainly an agency of the central authority, which so settled the terms of recruitment, dismissal, payment, and work that the service relationship was construed as one between the central authority and the servant. The result was that the central authority was immune from liability, the local authority was relieved of it, and the only recourse was against the official individually.[5]

(4) Officials enjoyed certain common law or statutory immunities from action: so police officers, executing a warrant regular on its face, and customs and excise officers in the conduct of a search; so, in the delimitation to six months of the period within which actions for tort in the exercise of a duty (not a power) against all individual officials (local or central) who were liable;[6] nor was there an action against a superior officer for the faults of an inferior officer unless the faults were clearly the act of the superior servant.[7]

(5) Local authorities and central authorities were amenable to action in the ordinary courts to compel them to undertake their specific duties, and to question the legality of actions undertaken.

Thus, in England until 1947 there was for a large sphere of public administration in the central authority and under its close control no redress in tort against the state, but only against individual officials. Their wrongful acts, further, were protected by certain limitations and permissions. Any suit, moreover, was and is heard and decided by the ordinary courts of law. In contract cases the citizen was badly hampered against the government.

The Crown Proceedings Bill of 1947. Although the government acted graciously in the matter of tort and contract, what was needed was a statutory guarantee of rights. The first Labour Lord Chancellor, Haldane, set in train studies to remove the ancient obstructions to justice: and in 1927 a committee of legal experts under the chairmanship of Lord Justice Hewart (a Conservative in politics) reported the need for amendment, together with a draft bill to secure it.[8] Not until the Labour government of 1945 was the subject resumed, and in 1947 the government carried the Crown Proceedings Bill.[9]

---

[4] Note the distinction between "performing public duty," and "his own personal act" (J. Wills in *Cooper* v. *Hawkins*).

[5] Cf. G. E. Robinson, *op. cit.,* p. 4 ff.
[6] Public Authorities Protection Act, 1893.
[7] C. S. Emden, *The Law and the Civil Servant* (London, 1923).
[8] Crown Proceedings Committee, Cmd. 1842, 1927.
[9] Public Statistics 10 and 11, Geo. 6, Chap. 44.

The phrases of the Attorney-General, recommending the bill to the House of Commons deserve quotation: [10]

It will very greatly fortify that principle of equality for all before the law which all of us are agreed is a fundamental part of the British way of life, and not the less so when we are progressing toward the Socialist State. . . . I do rejoice that it should have fallen to the present Socialist Government to resolve the doubts and anxieties which have obstructed action . . . and to give Parliament as a whole the opportunity of enacting what this bill, in fact, does, that the rights of the little man are just as mighty, and are entitled to just the same protection, as the rights of the mighty state."

He observed that one of the reasons pressing towards the reform was the rapid development of the contacts between the state and the life of the citizen.

The Crown Proceedings Bill permits the citizen to bring actions against the Crown, that is, the government or state, in exactly the same way and courts "as if the Crown were a fellow citizen." A person can enforce any claim as of right regarding contracts and torts. The state will admit liability for the wrongs committed by its servants or agents as any private citizen or public corporation does. It will answer for negligence, wrongful acts, default by its servants or agents, breaches of the common law or statutory duties—e.g. under the factory acts—to those it employs, and for breaches of duty arising from the occupation of premises or land.

There are some minor exceptions, to do with the Post Office's services, and accidents in the armed forces to personnel while on duty. The latter, of course, are taken care of in the armed forces' pensions schemes. But there are two major limitations. One is that the prerogative of the Crown (the government)—that is, its still unwritten power to defend the realm, administer the armed forces in time of peace as well as war, its power regarding aliens, harbors, patents, and the suppression of disorder and the maintenance of peace—relieves the state of liabilities to suit. A certificate to this effect put in by

10 Debates, July 4, 1947.

the Crown to the courts during pleadings will enable the courts to rule whether the limits of prerogative have been observed, or do not cover the action taken.

The second limitation of substance is that the state is not officially bound to produce documents which it believes to be in the interest of the public to keep secret. This leaves the government with power over definition of "public interest." The courts have, in the past, been unwilling to accept the responsibility of making such a decision. The government will take political responsibility for any attempt to hide what is material and what ought to be disclosed. In the course of discussion it was admitted by an Opposition speaker that some matters ought not be disclosed. For instance: [11]

If you are to make all confidential reports by civil servants disclosable, then the result will be that the state will not have the advantage of as clear, honest and forthright reports from its civil servants as it would have if they were protected.

The Rule of Law. Now, these present processes represent the contemporary result of what Dicey called the rule of law, by which he meant three things (of which only the first two are of importance here): [12]

(1) That no man is punishable or can be lawfully made to suffer in body or goods except for a distinct breach of law established in the ordinary courts of the land. In this sense the rule of law is contrasted with every system of government based on the exercise by persons in authority of wide, arbitrary, or discretionary powers of constraint.
(2) Not only with us is no man above the law, but [what is a different thing] here every man, whatever be his rank or condition, is subject to the ordinary law of the realm and amenable to the jurisdiction of the ordinary tribunals.
(3) The general principles of the Constitution are, with us, the result of judicial decisions determining the rights of private persons in particular cases brought before the courts.

11 Sir D. Maxwell Fyffe, Debates, col. 1692, July 11, 1947.
12 *Law of the Constitution*, 8th edition (London, 1930), p. 179 ff.

The Crown Proceedings Bill of 1947 has gone almost all the way to removing any obstruction to the rule of law in Dicey's sense, so far as the law and the rule cover the same ground.

Administrative Jurisdiction.[13] During the last forty years various government departments (which are not courts in Dicey's sense) have been made final courts of judgment in regard to many matters which fall within the scope of their work, which are not simply the narrow exercise of clear and indisputable powers, but are actually the construction of the law, an office usually fulfilled by the ordinary law courts. Thus the Minister of Health, the National Health Insurance Commissioner, the Board of Education, the Board of Trade, the Minister of Transport, the Railway Rates Tribunal, and other authorities, not being ordinary courts of the land or constituted as such, finally decide questions of fact so complicated and disputable as between parties—and thereby affect the person and property of the subject—that justice requires careful precautions. The appeal open to the citizen demands very careful procedure since the facts are technical and complicated, and the result affects property (let us say, a slum house) and the well-being of the public. Moreover, the fact that there is an appeal makes it look as though the department is a law court, owing to the appearance of a dispute between parties at law, or as the lawyers have it, a *lis inter partes.*

The essential issue is raised whether such procedure is or is not "judicial" in its nature. Was there something like "natural justice"? Lord Chancellor Haldane, in a very famous case, declared it was sufficient if the board acted judicially, saying that it must be "without bias, and must give to each of the parties the opportunity of adequately presenting the case made." The minister could not possibly be expected to do the work himself but must (and ought) to act vicariously through his officials. Oral hearings were

not necessary, nor was it correct to speak of the case as a *lis inter partes.* Beyond that the ultimate controlling authority was Parliament. The minister's judgment was unanimously sustained.

There is a considerable distribution of such administrative power,[14] and therefore Dicey's rule of law is, in practice, considerably modified. What is the significance of this power? This: that authorities which are not specially trained in adjudication, in aloofness, and which are as yet without procedure which leaves no doubts may take away liberty and property with redress,[15] though, it must be remembered the power to do so has been established not by them but by Parliament. On the other hand, the courts are nowadays faced with issues which they are not in a position properly to settle.[16] Yet neither the due safeguard of the individual called upon to surrender in the name of the community, nor the due safeguard of the social groups whom Parliament has decided ought to be benefited, should be unprovided for. The issue seems to invite in many cases a new type of administrative court in which the judicially trained and the administratively trained—served by their inquiry officers and acting under the well-known judicial forms of publicity, record, and evidence (with suitable modifications)—shall cooperate.

The report of the Committee on Minister's Powers (1932) put forward a number of principles which would offer safeguards to the citizen that the administrative departments were exercising their quasi-judicial functions judicially. There is no space to review them here. But they are designed to give the citizen due no-

---

13 W. A. Robson, *Justice and Administrative Law,* 2nd edition (London, 1947).

14 Cf. F. J. Port, *Administrative Law* (London, 1929).
15 Cf. Lord Hewart's indictment, *New Despotism* (London, 1929), pp. 43-44.
16 E.g., *Roberts v. Hopwood* (1925), 41 T. L. R. (444): "There are many matters which the Courts are indisposed to question; though they are the ultimate judges of what is lawful and what is unlawful to borough councils, they often accept the decisions of local authorities simply because they are themselves ill-equipped to weigh the merits of one solution of a practical question as against another. . . ."

tice, to make public inquiries necessary as a part of validity of judgment, to offer the citizen an opportunity of being heard, to place the act of judgment in the hands of judiciously tempered persons. This can be done, and not with great difficulty: it requires only the intention. What the committee was afraid of, and left to Parliament to watch, was that the intention would be weak. Their doctrine of ministerial interest is extremely interesting:

We think that in any case in which the minister's department would naturally approach the issue to be determined with a desire that the decision should go one way rather than another, the minister should be regarded as having an interest in the cause. . . It is unfair to impose on a practical administrator the duty of adjudication in any matter in which it could fairly be argued that his impartiality would be in inverse ratio to his strength and ability as a minister. An easy-going and cynical minister, rather bored with his office and sceptical of the value of his department, would find it rather easier to apply a judicial mind to purely judicial problems connected with the department's administration than a minister whose head and heart were in his work.

The Committee on Minister's Powers therefore wished Parliament to assign quasi-judicial powers to departments only exceptionally; and when they were so assigned thought they should rather be assigned to ministerial tribunals than to the minister. It must be admitted that in the majority of acts passed since that time, Parliament has not followed the advice given. It has felt that the danger of injustice was not so grave, and that somewhere a final decision must be made.

Administrative Law. Now we have touched upon a subject of the acutest controversy, but purposely without mentioning the name under which the controversy has been conducted—administrative law. For the introduction of the term Dicey is responsible. He borrowed the term *droit administratif* from France and gave it at once an erroneous and a sinister meaning. He takes his definition [17] from Aucoc's *Droit Administratif*, as follows:

Administrative Law determines (1) the constitution and the relations of those organs of society which are charged with the care of those social interests (*interêts collectifs*) which are the object of public administration, by which term is meant the different representatives of society, among which the State is the most important, and (2) the relation of the administrative authorities toward the citizens of the State.

This would seem as clear as any definition can be. But Dicey is determined to find a sinister meaning in it, and therefore says: "These definitions are wanting in precision, and their vagueness is not without significance." He then proceeds to discard any comparison of the two countries in 1905, when the edition was written, and instead goes back forty years: that is, to the time before France created its modern means of redress against the state and before England began to destroy hers. He soon loses his historical interest, and begins the process of whittling away the borrowed definition until *droit administratif* appears (p. 329) to be nothing more or less than a body of rules for the protection of officials who have committed abuses of power against the citizens:

the fourth and most despotic [as though all the others were despotic, though less so] characteristic . . . of *droit administratif* lies in its tendency to protect from the supervision or control of the ordinary law courts any servant of the State who is guilty of an act, however illegal, whilst acting in *bona fide* obedience to the orders of his superiors and, as far as intention goes, in the mere discharge of his official duties.

Finally *droit administratif* is made to appear as only, and no more than, the generalizations from the judgments rendered in the special courts, the *tribunaux administratifs*, for officials in their relations with the public.

Let us be clear, once for all, on the real meaning of administrative law, or *droit administratif*, or *Verwaltungsrecht*. By *droit administratif*, Berthélemy means this: [18]

All the services which combine to the execution of laws, excepting the services of justice,

---

[17] A. V. Dicey, *op. cit.*, p. 328.

[18] *Traité* (as in note 26 below), pp. 1 and 2.

are administrative services, and *droit administratif* is the sum total of the principles according to which their activity is exercised. . . Administrative Law analyzes the mechanism of the Governmental machine. How the machine is constructed is taught by constitutional law. How it works, how each of its parts functions, is the subject matter of administrative law.

There is surely nothing sinister in this. It is a little vague, like all definitions, but it is intelligible and not disquieting. In England there is such a body of law: and wherever there is administration and law, there is administrative law. It includes statutes, conventions, and case law from the ordinary and the special courts. Similarly with the German synonym: *Verwaltungsrecht.* "Administrative law is the legal ordering of the relationship between the administrating state and the subjects met in the process." [19]

If we take the lands of their origin as legitimately laying down the proper connotation of a term, then the most proper definition of administrative law in English is that by Port: [20]

Administrative Law is then made up of all those legal rules—either formally expressed by statutes or implied in the prerogative—which have as their ultimate object the fulfilment of public law. It touches first the legislature, in that the formally expressed rules are usually laid down by that body; it touches secondly the judiciary, in that (*a*) there are rules (both statutory and prerogative) which govern the judicial actions that may be brought by or against administrative persons, and (*b*) administrative bodies are sometimes permitted to exercise judicial powers; thirdly, it is, of course, essentially concerned with the practical application of the law.

In short, administrative law is no more mysterious or sinister than simply the law relating to public administration.[21]

We have dwelt upon this for two reasons. The first is to create a standard of criticism of the manner in which the term is used by some authors (Dicey, in the

past, and recent controversialists) who use it in the very narrow sense of such "judicial" action as is carried out by administrative boards and ministers, and the current popular notion that it means only law made by the departments in the form of rules and orders. These terms are dyslogistic; and therefore we come to the second purpose: to challenge the domination of an erroneous concept which inhibits reformative thought.

FRANCE

THE French monarchy of the *ancien régime* drew to itself all suits in which the authority of the crown was concerned, and it was able to do this because of its centralized strength, and the venal, if sometimes learned, composition of the *Parlements* which caused them to be despised by both people and monarchy.

In 1791 the ordinary courts were forbidden to handle administrative functions.[22] Beginning in the Year VIII, special bodies were created to judge administrative actions—the prefectoral councils and the *Conseil d'État* [23] above them and the ministers. And in addition, special bodies were established to decide such things as compensation to the state for the reclamation of marshes, and the institution of defenses against floods, and audit of accounts of public moneys. The administrative jurisdiction of the *Conseil* increased, and its *Comité du Contentieux,* under the chief justice, took charge of it. The jurisdiction was favored by reason of its cheapness and promptness.

In 1831 the procedure of the *Conseil d'État* was reformed to assimilate it to that of the ordinary law courts (similarly for the prefectoral councils, but not till 1862) and in 1848 the *Conseil* received the power to pronounce judgments instead of giving advice. The development of its jurisdiction was not unchallenged: liberals

---

[19] F. Fleiner, *Institutionen des deutschen Verwaltungsrechts* (Tubingen, 1922), p. 61.
[20] *Op. cit.,* p. 12.
[21] Finally admitted in Report on Ministers' Powers (London, Cmd. 4060, 1932).

[22] R. M. C. Dareste, *La Justice Administrative en France* (Paris, 1898).
[23] The *Conseil d'État* was primarily a legislative body, and a rule-drafting authority: it was also empowered to "settle difficulties arising in administrative matters."

like Dalloz and de Tocqueville tried unsuccessfully to get all matters founded on statutory law and concerning nondiscretionary matters before the ordinary courts, leaving to the *Conseil* those founded on prerogative and discretion.

Up to 1872 the *Conseil d'État* had only the right of adjudication in specific cases; in other words, it could not possibly grow beyond the small elasticity of a few granted powers. In 1872 it acquired a general and sovereign authority in administrative actions thus.[24] This is the supreme court. There are then subordinate bodies in the localities, like the prefectoral councils.[25] The *Tribunal des Conflits* decides in which courts disputed cases belong. This is a body not weighted to one side or the other, ordinary law-court judges or administrative judges, and so there can be no suspicion of undue influence on behalf of the government against the citizen.

The *Conseil d'État* itself consists of a large number of *conseillers, maîtres des requêtes,* and *auditeurs.* The first class give judgment while the two last classes prepare the judgments. The *auditeurs* are recruited by competitive examination from among those with the law degree of *licencié.* The *maîtres des requêtes* are recruited, to the extent of three fourths, by promotion from the *auditeurs,* the rest being appointed by the government at its discretion, while two thirds of the *conseillers* are recruited from the *maîtres des requêtes,* the rest being chosen at the government's discretion. The appointments at discretion offer a loophole for influence, but in fact, convention limits the government's choice to those high in the administrative service. This supplies direct experience of administration. Further, the *conseillers* are removable, but this does not occur, nor is the independence of this august body at all affected by the possibility.

The *Conseil,* the *Tribunal des Conflits,* and the prefectoral councils, administer between them a branch of law at once cheap and completely defensive of the citizen against injuries by public administration, whether by quashing of improper actions or by the grant of damages. The results of their judgments are not embodied in a code, though that may one day come, but the rules, taken together, give every individual citizen the right to require the *Conseil d'État* to judge the legality and equity of every administrative decision, and to repair momentarily the destructive results of illegal or inequitable action.

We do not intend to pursue in detail the jurisprudence of the courts, but we simply set out the main conclusions which its activity justifies.

Let one be guarded against considering administrative justice as "exceptional" justice. That would be to commit a grave mistake and a serious abuse of language. Administrative justice is not a dismemberment of the justice of the law courts. It is the judicial organ by which the executive power imposes upon the active administration the respect for law. The administrative courts have not taken their role from the judicial authority; they are one of the forms by which the administrative authority is exercised. To put the matter even more precisely, it may be said that the administrative tribunals are, towards the acts and the decisions of the administration, what the Courts of Appeal are to the decisions of inferior courts.[26]

Since there are some administrative actions which are necessary in terms of government, where a multiplicity of actions is likely, and where, too, the official is involved in the habits and urgencies of a vast apparatus, there must be a limitation upon the power to sue officials personally.[27] A distinction must be made between acts for which the servant is personally liable and suable in the ordinary courts, and those which are the result of administrative faults, for which the service as an entity is responsible. Such limitations and distinctions may be by statute or decree or judgment of a court. In

[24] M. Hauriou, *Précis du Droit Administratif et du Droit Public* (Paris, 1932), p. 505 ff.
[25] *Idem.*

[26] H. Berthélémy, *Traité Élémentaire de Droit Administratif* (Paris, edition of 1926), p. 1072.
[27] Cf. L. Trotobas, "Liability in Damages under French Administrative Law," *Journal of Comparative Legislation,* February, 1930, p. 44 ff.

France, the *Tribunal des Conflits* makes the distinction, and its doctrine is to be found in a series of cases commencing with the *Pelletier* case of 1873.[28] These settle the distinction (from case to case) between *faute personnelle* for which damages can be obtained in the ordinary courts, and *faute de service* or *faute de fonction* for which a suit lies in the administrative—that is, specially constituted —courts.

Faute personnelle is extremely difficult of definition, but it has been defined by the great French administrative jurist of the last generation as "that kind of fault which reveals the man with his weaknesses, passions, and imprudences."[29] Duguit gives this formula: "when the act, accomplished on the occasion of the service, is, however, an act foreign to the service, it is called, according to the consecrated terminology, the *personal* fault of the official." Some samples are: an official (properly) posts an electoral list, but (improperly) it publishes the fact that one man, an electoral adversary, had been excluded therefrom because of bankruptcy; a tax inspector points out irregularities at a tobacco depot (properly) and accuses a boy of theft (foreign to his administrative power); a teacher teaches his pupils to read (properly), and makes revolting remarks about God (that is a personal fault). The distinction is between personal impropriety from pursuit of a wrong purpose, and error due to incompetence and mistake when pursuing a right object. There is a tremendous controversy about the definitions of *faute personnelle* and *faute de service;* we cannot here discuss which of the disputants is nearest the truth; but in many cases the practical distinction is exceedingly difficult. Personal faults are judged and decided before the ordinary law courts; service faults before administrative courts, i.e., in the

localities, the prefectoral councils,[30] and the center, the *Conseil d'État.*

The state and the municipalities are responsible, can be sued in the administrative courts, and may be compelled to pay damages for any prejudice to property or life caused by defective action [31] —for a *faute de service,* that is, as Hauriou says, "the negligences, the omissions, the errors which are among the habits of the service, when those habits are bad." French jurisprudence speaks of a *grave (lourde)* fault; the idea being that it is beyond the average incompetence to be expected among the mass of men and officials.[32] Compensation by the state was admitted in the Revolutionary period in regard to property and public works, and is well established in the case of breach of contract; much of that is a development from the guarantee of individual property in the early constitution.[33] In this background the official may err by *excès de pouvoir,* that is, by going outside his legal powers; and one remedy is annulment of the act upon promulgation and before injury occurs (*recours pour excès de pouvoir*) or if the act causes injury, there is action for indemnification (*recours contentieux*). There are even signs that in the case of sheer unavoidable accidents, the public authority is responsible.[34] Such are cases where the fault complained of is not simply caused by *force majeure* (i.e., a purely external and totally incalculable and unavoidable factor) but by a fault of the service which cannot in the present state of science be assigned to specific cause.[35]

---

28 This case was not fought to saddle the government with fault and compensation, but to guarantee officials against the abuse of the right to sue them.

29 E. Laferrière, *Traité de la Jurisdiction Administrative,* 2nd edition (Paris, 1888), Vol. I, p. 648.

30 Cf. for their composition and activity, Bérthélemy, *op. cit.* (1930 edition), p. 1108 ff.

31 I.e., for lack of competence, violation of form, violation of a law, or misuse of power. M. Hauriou, *Precis,* p. 374, and Paul Duez, *La Responsibilité de la Puissance Publique* (l'aris, 1927), p. 16 ff. and p. 23 ff.

32 Léon Duguit, *Traité de Droit Constitutionnel* (Paris, 1926), Vol. III, p. 462.

33 *Idem.* in the case of *Pluchard,* 1909 (*Receuil-Sirey,* 1829), especially Duguit's general conclusion and notes on p. 470.

34 Duguit, *ibid.,* p. 469 ff.

35 *Couiétas,* November 30, 1923. Larnaude thus expresses the theory we have indicated above: "When this vast machine, called the State, a hundred times more powerful and a hundred

Now, not only is the state prepared to accept responsibility and pay damages for its own faults, but in some cases it pays damages for its officials convicted of a personal fault. This development is of late growth and owes some of its strength to the theoretical work of M. Jèze, who in connection with two famous cases [36] argued that a personal fault was always graver than a service fault and that the state should accept liability not on the basis of any fault, but as offering insurance against social risk of damage from the public services.[37]

Yet there are warnings against an extention of this practice, lest the official escape from personal responsibility altogether.[38]

We have already shown how the professional rights and duties of officials have been included within the jurisdiction of the administrative courts.

Finally, procedure is simpler than that of the ordinary courts and inexpensive.[39]

Thus we may say that in France, every illegal official act is challengeable either in the ordinary courts or in special courts where procedure, composition and doctrine give very generous guarantees that only that will be done which is legal, that only the legal which is done competently and with a proper motive will be permitted, and that a cheap and simple process will cause annulment and produce indemnification by the public authority responsible, and that even a personal fault may in many cases be indemnified by the public authority. One has only to analyze the judgments given by the *Conseil d'État* to realize what remarkable acumen has been applied to the problem of reconciling the process of government with the claims of individuals, and the close connection between the *Conseil* and the development of administrative science and law by academic masters.

GERMANY

THE legal redress of official infractions of the law or maladministration reached highly systematic and secure conditions in Germany (allowing for the hideous but transient reversion to barbarism between 1933 and 1945). This seems to be due to three things: the desire to secure a legal control of the administration, where for so long a political control was weak; a special love of law which was signalized by observers centuries ago; and the development of the theory of the *Rechtsstaat,* that is, the state which shall not act arbitrarily but only in accordance with law and morality. This latter was the contribution of liberal thinkers to German constitutional development. These, until the last quarter of the nineteenth century, sought a solution in the transfer of administrative jurisdiction to the ordinary courts, using the French differentiation of act of authority and simple acts of administration as a division between what should be left to the departments to correct and what should come before the ordinary courts. They pressed to its utmost what the German Conservatives had denied: the separation of powers. Indeed, the Frankfurt constitution of 1849 expressly prohibited administrative tribunals.

It is to Gneist, the constitutional and administrative historian, that modern German notions and institutions of administrative justice are due, for in his *Der Rechtsstaat* he demanded the creation of special administrative courts in the localities and at the court, formed of several members, and in the localities aided by unpaid laymen.[40] This offered

times more dangerous than the machinery of industry, has injured some one, those in whose interest it functioned when the injury was caused, must make restitution; the principles of solidarity and mutuality upon which our institutions are based, require it." Cited by R. D. Watkins, *The State as a Party Litigant* (Baltimore, 1927), p. 148.

[36] *Revue du Droit Public* (Paris, 1914); and Léon Duguit, *Transformations du Droit Public* (Paris, 1913), pp. 274-77.

[37] *Revue du Droit Public,* Vol. V, pp. 31, 586.

[38] Duguit, *op. cit.,* p. 489.

[39] See P. Duez, *op. cit.,* Part III, and Appleton, *Traité Elémentaire de Contentieux Administratif* (Paris, 1927).

[40] Published 1871, first as an allocation to the jurists who were members of the first German *Reichstag*.

the possibility of a reconciliation between the necessities of the administrative services and the need for judicial protection of individual rights. State after state began from 1875 onward to construct a system of administrative courts. The essence was to subject the public authorities to a regular control through special courts set in motion by actions by citizens, and to give this action a guaranteed basis, not a precarious one as the police state of the eighteenth century had, when it of grace permitted actions to be brought by citizens against it in the ordinary courts.[41] Gierke's formula is, "The *Rechtsstaat* is a state which sets itself not above the law but within it." [42] The result has been the growth of a system of jurisprudence in every respect honest and appropriate to administration and citizen. We shall consider its salient features presently.

The Fiskus. German jurisprudence recognizes the distinction between public and private law, and within the latter an old doctrine teaches the personality of the state as the bearer of rights and duties like any ordinary person, sole or corporate. Now this doctrine of the state's personality may (as Duguit has spent hundreds of pages in proving) have the evil effect of confounding the individuals with the state, and so of making the state almighty. But it has its very useful side in that the personification provides a suable entity: the *Fiskus.* This body, in all the government departments in which it is resident, has all the rights and duties in contract and tort of an ordinary individual or firm, and the suit lies in the ordinary courts. The courts proceeded further and created a doctrine of indemnification for damages to the recognized rights of the subject, and these covered both statutory rights and those of natural justice, or "subjective rights," as they are called in Germany.[43]

In the nineteenth century the liberal movements then went further along the line of the *Rechtsstaat,* to control the complex administrative relationships which were fast developing, while doctrine now identified the *Fiskus* with the state, but only on its property-law side, and practice confined this only, and not the new developments, to the civil courts. In the field of acts of authority by public administration, the new courts, administrative courts, became the givers of justice.

Article 131 of the Weimar constitution, especially by its extraordinary application by the *Reichsgericht,* ran:

If an official violates his official duty toward a third person in the exercise of public authority entrusted to him, the responsibility fundamentally rests with the state or corporation in whose service he is. Retrospective action against the official is reserved. The ordinary course of justice may not be excluded. The appropriate statutes shall make any more detailed regulation.

This unassuming article was so constructed by the *Reichsgericht* that it may be called the *ultima ratio* of the *Rechtsstaat.*

Thus the state took all liability for its officials (the immediately employing body, *Reich,* state, or local authority was liable). The person who had committed the error was no longer of concern,[44] and when an official was jointly provided for by a number of authorities, one or the other was judged liable. The decisions of the *Reichsgericht* and the state courts made the distinction, with which we are already familiar, between faults which are clearly of the service and those which are personal faults of the official. Here, as in France, the line was not easy to draw in marginal cases, and there were occasional anomalies. As in France, the wrong must have occurred in a duty toward a third person, not simply in a voluntary service which the law does not enjoin. Finally, the wrong must have occurred by intention or negligence.

The official was personally liable for

---

[41] Otto Mayer, *Deutsches Verwaltungsrecht,* 3rd edition (Munchen, 1924), Vol. I, p. 54 ff.
[42] *Zeitschrift für Staatswissenschaften,* Vol. XXX, p. 130; L. Mayer, *op. cit.,* p. 62 ("The *Rechtsstaat* means the maximum possible legality of administration").
[43] See George Jellinek, *System der Subjektiven Rechte* (Freiburg, 1892).

[44] *Reichsgerichtshof,* Vol. III, October 5, 1920.

criminal actions, as included in the Criminal Code, in the course of official duties: e.g., corporal injuries, violation of freedom, constraint, and torture. The jurisprudence of the *Reichsgericht* maintained that the "previous question" (*Vorfrage*, or *Vorentscheidung*), whether there was at all violation of official duty, must come before the ordinary Courts.[45] That is, there were practically no relics of administrative prejudice in tribunals of Conflict or their like.[46]

There was a class of case in which a wrong has been done, but where the fault could not be called culpable. This was similar to the French differentiation between an average or normal fault, which lies in the normal nature of men and the service, and a grave fault. It is for the grave fault that the servant or the state is liable in France; it was for the grave fault only that the servant or the state was liable in Germany. When the fault was normal, unavoidable in the normal state of human nature, no one was responsible (so according to the terms of the Civil Code, 839). But sundry statutes made exception from this state of affairs and positively asserted state liability in specific matters. So in various statutes regarding damage caused by riots when the public authorities were impotent to intervene effectively. Yet where such laws were not existent, the immunity of official and state ceased where the illegal action redounded to the advantage of the state. This was similar to the French tendency to compensate for risk, that is, where public works or activities caused special injury to a citizen.

The state or *Reich* could demand satisfaction from the official for the damages it had to pay, but his liability ceased to exist after three years. The officials of local authorities were in the same position.

Officials might claim that they were not responsible.

All this so far is concerned only with the amenability of the official and the official institution to the ordinary courts, though in the background there is the disciplinary relationship between official and state, a subject we have already analyzed in Chapter 34.

The intention of administrative jurisdiction was to secure that the orders of public authorities be legal by regard both to written law and to natural justice respecting life, liberty, and property.[47] It was their duty to state the law when that had been challenged, as it was the business of the English local government board to state what was right in the dispute between Arlidge and the Hampstead district council. Their work was recognized as of a contentious-judicial nature, and therefore they were established with the conditions of independence of mind. But since the subject which they had to judge is one—government—of a complicated technique, they were given the conditions, too, which would make this possible.[48] So far did opinion change since 1849 that whereas the administrative courts were constitutionally forbidden, the constitution of 1919 expressly required their creation: [49] "In the *Reich* and the states, administrative courts shall be created, according to statute, for the protection of the individual against orders and rules of the administrative departments."

Each state had its own system of courts, and although there was a movement for a *Reich* Appeal Court, such was not established.[50]

The Superior Administrative Courts in Prussia and the larger states were judicial authorities independent of the administrative apparatus, but in other states there were various kinds of connections with

---

[45] This is on the basis of article 131 and 11, Introductory Law to the Judicature Act (*Einfuhrungsgesetz Gerichtsverfassungsgesetz*). But the courts are permitted to exclude the procedure up to the decision of the question whether the challenged behavior of the official was legal.
[46] Walter Jellinek, *Verwaltungsrecht* (Berlin, 1928), pp. 316-17; F. Fleiner, *op. cit.*, p. 284 ff.

[47] Cf. Fleiner, *op. cit.*, p. 247.
[48] G. Anschütz (ed.), *Handbuch der Politik* (Berlin, 1920-26), p. 458.
[49] Article 107.
[50] *Vereinigung der deutschen Staatsrechtslehrer* (1929); *Wesen und Entwickelung der Staatsgerichtsberkeit: Überprüfing von Verwaltungsakten;* also *ibid.* (1925), *Der Schutz des öffentlichen Rechts.*

the administrative departments, or the ordinary courts. In Prussia the court was composed of a president, several Senate presidents, and councilors, all of whom had life tenure and were removable from office only by a decision of the full court. One half the members had qualifications for a judicial office, the rest for the higher administrative service.[51]

Procedure before the courts was in the form of a *lis inter partes*, i.e., a contest between parties, these being either individuals who opposed each other, or public authorities against each other, or the public authority against individuals,[52] and they were to each other as complainant and defendant in civil actions. Procedure was public and oral. Not only might the parties demand a review before the highest court, but other persons might require review on the grounds that the public interest was involved in the magnitude of the issue.

The main lines of the German system are clear. The citizen had good guarantees that the administration should not act outside the law, and damages were available from the public treasuries, while officials were well protected in their professional rights. Except in the lower instances there was no suspicion of *raison d'État*, since the courts were independent and properly trained, but some, though not serious, criticism was leveled against the admixture of administration and jurisdiction in the lower instances and the danger of political bias in the selection of the lay element, yet even there the lay element was recognized as a protection against bureaucratic perversion of power, and as a contributor of a special expertness, viz., that of the knowledgeable man in general social life. There was not a single Court, but a number of unrelated tribunals. They were the *Reich* Economic Court, the Insurance Court, Private Insurance Court, the Finance Court, the Settlement Court, the Patent Office, the Public Assistance Court.

Doubts have been expressed regarding the merits of administrative justice compared with the capable and impartial judgment in the ordinary courts; but on the whole they have succumbed to the consideration that the administrative courts were both independent and yet capable of judging propriety, legal and circumstantial, in government, a matter not so much within the capacity of the civil courts.

Limits to Remedy. One final point is worth mention. Everywhere there is a point which the courts and the law hold to be unreviewable and unchallengeable: this is what is called variously "discretion," *freies Ermessen*. What does the phrase mean? It means that the courts act with an eye to the reasonable conduct of reasonable men. Not to do this would be in every case to attempt to substitute their judgment of persons, facts, and expediency for that of the officials who are actually immersed in the thousand details and their conjuncture which call for their action or forbearance. Hence the courts make allowances for circumstances of time and place, especially situations of emergency, sanitation, civil disturbance, and military aggression. They refuse to prosecute the official's decision and effect beyond a certain point. If, in fact, they did not practice this forbearance, all administration would be paralyzed by fear of error. They allow, in American terms, "administrative finality."[53]

Somewhere, in short, the law courts must leave the officials' judgment free of challenge—not on law, not altogether on procedure, but on facts and expediency of action.

THE UNITED STATES

THE American federal authority has enjoyed an advantage over England, and suffered a great disadvantage: there has been no fiction of the infallibility of the government (Crown), but there has been

---

[51] Dieckmann, *Die Verwaltungsgerichtbarkeit in Preuszen* (Berlin, 1926), p. 41 ff., for the composition of the various courts.
[52] Cf. Dieckmann, *op. cit.*, p. 52.

[53] J. M. Landis, *The Administrative Process* (Yale, 1938), Chapter IV; Milton Katz, *Cases and Materials on Administrative Law* (St. Paul, 1947), Chapter VII.

the obstacle of the separation of powers. Yet while the latter has been steadily palliated by the partial vesting of judicial functions in administrative bodies, and the assumption of administrative powers by the judiciary, the state was not made liable for the torts of federal officials, and the doctrine of nonsuabilty of the state is well established.[54]

The state is not liable for torts committed in its service; executive officers are themselves civilly liable for illegal and unconstitutional acts done in their official capacity,[55] and cannot plead the orders of a superior officer. Where the officer has acted legally, but with unwise use of discretion, there is no liability.[56] Relief was obtained by petition to Congress for private bill, gravely encumbering its Claims Committee. But Public Law (601) of 1946 admits torts claims to a maximum of $1000 before any United States district court where the tort was committed while the official was acting within the scope of his office. Of course, no action is good where the act is exercised with due care or is discretionary.

There are the rights to obtain injunctions against illegal and unconstitutional activities, mandamus to compel the performance of nondiscretionary acts and to compel the exercise of discretion, but this does not extend to direction of the exercise of discretion.

During the last thirty years or more, the establishment of government corporations for commercial or industrial operations (for example, the TVA) has always been used to make the corporation suable as a private corporation or person would be. In fact, the courts are ready to accept the liability even where it is not expressly prescribed in the corporation statute.[57] Furthermore, the government may—and as in Britain before 1947, did—in special cases permit suit, and Justice Frankfurter indicated many of these in the *Keifer* case cited above. The most general of such permissions applied to contracts.

As regards contracts, the regime of petitions to Congress gave way in 1855 to the Court of Claims "to hear and determine all claims founded upon any law of Congress or upon any regulation of our executive department, or upon any contract, express or implied, with the government of the United States." [58] This and subsequent amplifying legislation and the judgments of the Supreme Court have carefully excluded the consideration of cases which "under the assumption of an implied contract, make the government responsible for the unauthorized acts of its officials, those acts being in themselves torts." [59] The Court of Claims is composed of judges holding the tenure *quam diu se bene gesserint,* and are appointed by the President, by and with the consent of the Senate. In evidence and procedure it is analogous to other courts.

[54] Cf. K. Singewald, *The Non-Suitability of the State in the United States* (Johns Hopkins University Studies, 1910), and R. D. Watkins, *The State as a Party Litigant* (Johns Hopkins University Studies, 1927). Watkins (p. 55) says: "We adopted it [the doctrine] without considering whether it was valid, essential or desirable . . . Historically there seems no other explanation than simply it was accepted by us as something belonging to the normal course of things." So until 1868 when a doctrine of utility was invented: *The Siren* v. *U.S.* (1868).
See especially J. D. Block, "Suits against Officials and the Sovereign Immunity Doctrine," *Harvard Law Review,* September, 1946, p. 1060 ff.
[55] Cf. Joseph Story, *Commentaries* (Washington, 1833), Sect. 1671, *U.S.A.* v. *Lee* (1882), 106 U.S. 196; *Cunningham* v. *Macon and B.R.R. Co.* (1883), 109 U.S. 446, 452; *Poindexter* v. *Greenhow* (1884), 114 U.S. 270.
[56] "Whenever from the necessity of the case, the law is obliged to trust to the sound judgment and discretion of an officer, public policy demands that he should be protected from any consequences of an erroneous judgement" —*Downer* v. *Lent* (1856), Col. 94. Yet malice, bad faith, and corruption, seem to leave an opening for recovery.

[57] Cf. also R. Cushman, *The Independent Regulatory Commissions* (New York, 1941); David Lilenthal and R. H. Marquis, "The Conduct of Business Enterprises by the Federal Government," *Harvard Law Review,* February, 1941. Cf. also *Keifer and Keifer* v. *Reconstruction Finance Corporation,* 306 U.S. 381 (1939); and J. McDiarmid, *Government-Owned Corporations* (New York, 1939).
[58] Act to establish a court for the investigation of claims against the United States: February 24, 1955, c. 122, 10, statutes, 612; and see *Williams* v. *United States,* 289 U.S. 553 (1933).
[59] *Gibbons* v. *U.S.A.,* 8 Wall, 269.

The most interesting and instructive developments in the sphere of administrative jurisdiction are those in the various great commissions like the Interstate Commerce Commission, the Commissioner of Patents, the Federal Trade Commission, and others, some of whose functions, the continuous and regular application of the law to very complex economic and technical phenomena, have been recognized by the Supreme Court of the United States to be judicial.[60] From these, however, after the advantages of administrative jurisdiction have been exploited, appeals are properly permitted.[61] We must leave to the reader the study of their technique, their safeguards for social as well as individual justice, and their relationships with the ordinary courts and with the institution of "due process" (previously described, p. 144).[62] Here only this need be said that various statutes require for the making of diverse rules and orders a procedure of notice to the public, of hearings, of consultations, conferences, even of "adversary" hearings. These have in many cases been independently developed by the administrative agencies, or

have been evolved under the impetus of judicial decision. Further systematization was attempted by the Walter-Logan Bill (vetoed, see p. 103 above). Finally, the lawyers had their way in the *Administrative Procedure Act* of 1946. This code of rules for rulemaking and quasi-judicial action of the departments is very elaborate and perhaps excessively clogs the administration at every stage of official initiative by offering opportunities to those aggrieved or about to be aggrieved to appeal to the courts for injunctions to refrain from action or to command action.

It must be remembered, of course, that the individual official who wrongs any party is himself liable to suit for damages, as in British law. Only in the cases we have mentioned does the government stand behind him to accept suit and pay damages if its functions carried out by its officials have injured others.

We have now surveyed the problems raised by the administrative features of the modern state in their evolution and contemporary form. We have seen the rise of the civil service, the forces which governed the formation of its character in different countries, and the influence of social forces, and democratic institutions upon its present qualities. Three features emerge, pronounced and striking: the search for impartial expertness; the attempt to control, legislatively or through the Courts, its potentially aberrant actions; and the attempt to reconcile police and ministrant functions with the freedom and security of the civil servant. These are still problems: they are unsettled; they are lashed by the flux of social forces. Yet what is the attitude of the public—the sovereign public—to these mighty machines of government and the conditions of their operation?

---

[60] F. J. Port, *op. cit.*, p. 276.

[61] This review is "limited substantially to two questions, first, whether there was evidence before the administrative body upon which reasonable men might fairly have arrived at the conclusions reached; and second, whether any rule or principle of law was disregarded in reading them." J. Dickinson, *Administrative Justice and the Supremacy of Law* (Yale 1927), p. 190.

[62] Cf. Report, *Administrative Procedure in Government Agencies,* committee appointed by Attorney-General, Document No. 8, 77th Congress, 1st session; *Administrative Procedure Act*, Legislative History, 79th Congress, Senate Document No. 248, 1944-46; Walter Gellhorn, *Administrative Law, Cases and Comments* (Brooklyn, 1947), and J. K. Hart, *An Introduction to Administrative Law and Cases* (New York, 1940).

37

The Public and the Services

THUS a multitude of laws and practices establish, direct, and control the public administrative services. What is the result? What do they produce? What does the public think of the product, and what ought it to think?

In every country there is a vast body of men and women drawn to the professional service of the state. Everywhere, and with few exceptions, they are highly educated, formally, in relation to their duties and to their counterparts in non-public industry, and this in spite of the "crammers" who live upon examinations. Yet this education and the related formal tests are nowhere entirely appropriate to the specific tasks to be performed, and the world is as yet merely stumbling toward a proper method of preparation and selection for the public service. For the truth is that under the common rubric of the "public service," and even within its broad general classes, the tasks are multifarious, each calling for a special aptitude—a different combination of "service elements" as the American administrative scientist would say.

In private industry there is supposed to occur a continuous process of selection by competition, and a minute adaptation to the local and personal diversities of the consumer. The profit incentive, the danger of bankruptcy, and the singleness (if narrowness) of mind of the businessman often produce this result. Hitherto, however, the public services, local as well as central, have concerned themselves rather with the production of wholesale quantities of uniform products at the margin of urgency, than with the creation of individual satisfactions in the vast field of individual desires. The developments of the last quarter of a century, however, in state and municipal ownership and management, leave no doubt that the field of their legitimate and useful operations is very large, and quite as large is the variety of forms in which they can become effective: there is a judicial control, judicial-*cum*-administrative control, administrative control, and complete state ownership and operation, and of these there are many subtly different varieties, from complete administration in a centralized department to high decentralization and quasi-public corporations.[1] The tests of capacity must be correspondingly diverse.

The clerk in the colonial office, the inspector of education, the director of the electricity department, the chief of a savings-bank division, the diplomatic service, the Treasury examiners of estimates—for each of these there is the optimum training. So far, capacity to learn, tested generally, and such attributes of character as honesty, vital to the public services, have been sought. They are not enough. The simple motives of security, respectability,

[1] Cf. Herman Finer: *The T.V.A.: Lessons for International Application* (International Labour Office, 1944); and Herman Finer, *Municipal Trading* (London, 1941); also Herman Pritchett, *T.V.A.: an Administrative Study* (Chapel Hill, 1943).

and social prestige, especially of the great classes of the disinherited in a modern society, may have been enough in a world where only one twentieth or thereabouts of the productive population were civil servants, and where initiative had not hitherto been of first importance; but they are insufficient in a dynamic state.

All the civil services show remarkable zeal, but the law and the nature of the service tend to confine this zeal to rigid and narrow channels. The exhilaration of adventure and conquest does not exist, while legal permissions and prohibitions which surround the task and the office produce a cautiousness, sometimes a veritable misanthropy. *Le règlement* is not only the excuse for sloth, but sometimes really causes it.

Moreover, the slowness of personal transfer and circulation, and the sense that there is an "establishment" which nothing can alter, engenders and nourishes the feeling that one is in a rut from which it is not worth while to attempt to emerge. Incentive is blunted, and discouragement sets in, and leisure comes to be enjoyed rather than applied. Yet there are conspicuous examples of men who have found themselves in the service of the state, and whose impersonal passion for their work survives the temptations of an acquisitive society and the comparative smallness of their salary, so that the state is often served at one half or one quarter or even less the rate of pay obtainable outside its ranks. Such men and women, put into key positions, are of inestimable value as the leaders of their staffs, especially the younger generation. Give men significant public work with decent, not extravagant, rewards, and the talent available is more than abundant.

Public responsibility produces a tendency difficult to resist. It is overroutinization and overconscientiousness. In the end, whatever the technical answers to technical complaints, the state services have to reply to the public in or out of the legislature, in terms of the cultural or civilization value of their actions. Too often the quantitative answer which settles, if it does not convince, the complainant or opponent is, by nature, not available. A linguistic answer must be given. That is, it must be persuasive, and as the office must answer for it, two things occur: the reports go from official to official up the hierarchy to the chief, and, when in doubt, risk is not taken so much as passed on, and records must be made, kept, and consulted as the warrant of justification. Time and audacity, the mother of invention, are apt to be lost, all around.

The power of the state is immense, and whether as policeman or tax collector, or licenser of automobiles, or controller of agricultural research—whether as gas works or passport office—it confronts the citizen with the aspect of inescapable doom. The civil servant is part of a machine of domination, and accession to office, according to reports from all countries, tends to produce in him an overbearing attitude which sometimes merges into tyranny. This, even when it falls short of legally challengeable misfeasance, can be extremely painful. Roughness and authoritarianism is infrequent in England, as the service has always been confronted by a strong Parliament and sense of self-government, but there is a growing dislike of the expert, founded partly upon his prevalence and partly upon public ignorance. France has more of it—partly owing to the tradition of *la puissance publique*—partly to the French petty bourgeois veneration of officialdom (when they or their relatives are, or are likely to become, officials)—and partly to the official's defensiveness against a critical and sarcastic public, out of self-compensation for the insults and reprimands showered downward in a strongly hierarchical system, and out of the spontaneous sullen malice of the miserably underpaid.

In Germany the services have still the authoritarian tradition, an intentional sternness. But all that a nation can do is being done to smooth the rough edges and convert officiousness into good offices. The civil service schools and associations work for this end. The constitution declares the rights of the public very clearly: "Every German has the right to make requests or complaints to the competent department or representative body in writing." In fact, even before this declaration of rights was made, the public was very ready to approach officials, especially the local *bürgermeister,* who in some cases is looked upon as a veritable Providence. Why not?

For the major civil services it would be possible to extract (as from the decisions of the *Conseil d'État* and the general code of duties of German officials) a set of strict injunctions to civil servants that their behavior to the public be always irreproachably considerate and well-measured. Such injunctions are very urgent, since an aggrieved citizen is faced with a dilemma: either to suffer rough treatment without the possibility of turning to an alternative source of supply of the service, or to make a formal complaint and be obliged to go through a wearisome course of correspondence long after the first smart has passed away.

In every country the public is hostile to the official because at some time or other, as an inspector or a tax collector or a medical officer or what not, he comes to take away, not to give—it is in the nature of his task to limit one's freedom and property. This is not done for himself, though he may feel some satisfaction in doing it—he may feel powerful, stern, a *deus ex machina,* yet in the end the deed redounds to the benefit of certain individuals and groups in the background. One experiences the deprivation, but the social benefit is not so easily discernible, just because it is social and diffused rather than immediately personified. The public fears the official and the extension of official activities, because it feels there is no chance of appeal, no alternative to official judgment. It cannot understand, without careful tuition, why officials receive pay and pensions—why, indeed, they are needed at all. All other businesses explain themselves. In Germany advertisement is less necessary than in England, because the activity of officials has for over a century been an honored part of the general civilization to which all are accustomed. Even so, the German civil service associations do not maintain a sulky

silence, but keep themselves well in the public eye, both inside and outside Parliament. A few among the public everywhere recognize the significance and difficulties of the official's function; ought not steps to be taken through every medium of publicity to overcome the hostility and distrust? (Yet there is a valid difference between information and touting for support.) [2]

Supposing one were asked for a civil servant's vindication in regard to the public, what would it be? This, I think:

I possess great power, and I may do you harm. I do not, however, act for myself, but for the public good as determined by the legislature or the local authorities and often by direct representations from the public. Nor do I act arbitrarily, but according to rules which are equally valid for everybody. Not my will prevails, but the will of other members of the public. If, therefore, you quarrel with my powers, you should not blame their immediate executor but their ultimate creator. Yet, of course, some discretion is necessarily left to me, and I know that I ought to exercise this with all politeness, understanding, and the infliction of the least amount of necessary pain. Like all men—like you, for example,—I am sustained in my work by my pay and other rights, my zeal is not consistently as its highest level, and I have alternations of mood (sometimes I am alert, sometimes slack), yet I will not deny my services because they are troublesome to me and because they are just a little beyond the minimum which will forestall and avoid complaint, but positively seize opportunities to be helpful, fitting the remedy carefully to the case. Your own roughness, accent, and social standing may affect me, but I will try to avoid letting them improperly bias my reasoned judgment. Business would proceed more speedily and appropriately if you would cooperate with me by recognizing my difficult position and treating me with sympathy rather than hostility, if you read all the rules which you are supposed to read and keep, before you fly into a temper because mistakes have occurred, and if you willingly cooperated on the various committees which are and should be established for collaboration.

Even with all the arrangements and personal control which conduce to smooth working of the service and satisfaction of the pub-

2 Cf. J. L. McCamy, *Governmental Publicity* (Chicago, 1939).

lic, I may still suffer from unsympathetic treatment because ultimately I am the representative of the state—that is, the whole of the public! You will of course enjoy my power and applaud it when it does you some immediate good: I must beg you to recall the significance of my work when I have to weigh the rest of the public good against you. I at least am a member of a body which is neutral in the state, or rather helpful to all. You cannot buy more of my services if you happen to be well off, you will not get less if you happen to be badly off; you will not be passed over

if you belong to one particular party or given special privileges if you belong to another. We represent the unity and collective control of the state. I give the whole of my time to the work, and am as entitled to my pay and pension and other rights as any other worker. If my services are intangible or misunderstood they are nevertheless productive and important. Without them, your state will be nothing but a desert full of the discordant noises of people giving contradictory orders: It will crumble and cease to be a state—for a state is coordinated action.

38

Concluding Observations

CAN one fail to acknowledge that the most amazing quality of the processes of democratic government described in the foregoing chapters is the amount of rational self-control exerted by human multitudes? (Or is it self-indulgence? Could they be worse if they tried?) In other contexts it may matter whether this self-control is itself a blind, impetuous instinct, or something open-eyed and superior to instinct. Here that question need offer no challenge. We stand astounded at the subtlety, complexity, the coordination, and the undefeatable persistence of the deliberating mind, which works to make its multitude of values prevail in a social medium incalculably more convoluted than man's brain—seeing opportunities, alert to apertures, quick to retreat from a noose, ingenious to invent the paths of advance and escape, *homo faber,* the smith hammering, tempering, shaping, and fitting! Self-government is a miracle wrought by reason that wrestles with the Dionysiac and other volcanic rages of human nature; and it is no wonder that it is as yet an imperfect miracle.

Some political scientists take keen pleasure in observing the degree to which men are nonrational and nonconscious as they create and work their governments. Some especially delight, as did Faust in Goethe's drama, in playing with the question, "Which came first—the Word, or the Mind, or the Force, or the Deed?". For some indulgent moments they enjoy a bout of cynical inebriation with the idea

that institutions arose without kindness aforethought and unblessed with any measured choice and thought regarding values, ends, and ways and means. Without denying the insurgency of the irrational and the unconscious, let us acknowledge the tremendous philanthropic inventiveness of men in the art of government, for, at the very least, that is a spur for future inventiveness and a promise of reward for the agony of courageous thought.

VINDICATION OF DEMOCRACY

THE principal, indeed, the desperate, task of democracy is to maintain itself; its next, to improve and refine itself. This question needs solution: what Marxism is to Soviet Communism, and what Racialism was to the Nazi State, X is to Democracy; hence: What is X? X is the value that is most hospitable and least hostile to all the other values which burn in man sometimes at such intense heat that were it untamed, the commonwealth would melt away.

It can hardly have escaped notice that the present work has devotedly avowed the tenet that democracy is the "right" form of government for mankind. Democracy's needs have been used as the standard of valuation of the efficiency of the institutions and procedures of government; and imperfections of conviction, obscurities in values, and mismanagement in action have not been ignored. The criterion itself needs justification: it is the X we seek: we have to find an answer to the question why democracy is "right."

Like Locke and Rousseau (with the qualifications set forth in Chapter 5 on *Democracy*), I believe that of all forms of government the world has so far experienced and of all those conceivable, democracy is "right," and that, as a major expediency within democracy's own values, the majority is "right." It remains to be asked what is the meaning of "right."

I quote the masters. Locke said: [1]

And thus that which begins and actually constitutes any political society is nothing but the consent of any number of freemen capable of a majority to unite and incorporate into such a society. And this is that, and that only, which did or could give beginning to any lawful government in the world.

Rousseau declared: [2]

It follows from what has gone before that the general will is always right and tends to the public advantage; but it does not follow that the deliberations of the people are always equally correct. Our will is always for our own good, but we do not always see what that is; the people is never corrupted, but it is often deceived, and on such occasions only does it seem to will what is bad.

All that Locke and Rousseau mean is that the principles on which autocracies, aristocracies, theocracies, monarchies had been founded in the past, and the values by which they had been defended, could not muster for themselves as much reasonable assent as democracy. If we look for the most lawful or righteous principle of government, that which will involve the least coercion and feeling of coercion, democracy is less open to discredit by rational argument than any other principle of collective living in the large areas in which multitudes now live.

Now, a deservedly famous liberal, Lord Acton, was ill at ease with these enthronements of democracy. He objected that "The Revolution taught the people to re-gard their wishes and wants as the supreme criterion of right." [3] This is hardly a fair description of the doctrines of Rousseau or Siéyès. What they taught was that the people had the right to wish and want and create policy, not that there was never stupidity or brutishness in what they wished or wanted. It is clear that the word "right" is being used in two different senses, refers to two different orders of value. In Rousseau's sense, in Locke's and in my own, the "right" is concerned with the problem of who ought to exercise authority? But Acton confuses this with the question, who is most likely to be *wise?* A world of difference lies in the distinction, and some further probing of it may help to answer, what is X?

Acton believed that no one, whether the one or the few or the many, should rule with unlimited power. What then should rule the rulers? At various points in his writings, the reign of principle is expressed as "Reason," or a "higher law," or "the law of Heaven," or a "code not made by man," or "a law of nature," or "the voice of universal reason, through which God enlightens the consciences of men."

The issue is, through what medium is moral rectitude to enter the body of society? Acton may argue that God alone is right, or only Reason is right. But assuredly God is vapid without a vicar, and right is ethereal without an agent. This, then, is the crux: through whom is Reason to speak, carried by what means of communication will it be found?—and the question is, also, for whose satisfaction ought we wait, who is the proper judge?

Surely the values held by the multitude will decide the rectitude of any social principle, custom, law, or agency as it touches the happiness and sense of what is right of each and all. It is, of course, well understood that in any political situation where an opinion is called for, something more than the individual's values is involved: there is the body of facts which the mind receives into itself, the facts of

---

[1] John Locke, *Essay on Civil Government*, Chap. VIII, Para. 99.
[2] J.-J. Rousseau, *The Social Contract* (1762), Book II, Chap. III; and on the "majority," Book IV, Chap. II.

[3] Lord Acton, *Essays on Freedom and Power* (Boston, 1948), p. 167.

history and of contemporary occurrence in the close and distant environment. Yet Francis Bacon's *Novum Organon* and his *Advancement of Learning* have amply warned us not to believe that those are our values that we first see without self-criticism, that we may be deceived by ourselves and the Idols of the Tribe, the Cave, the Market Place, and the Theater. What is tremendous in its significance for political science and political action is this, that even when the question on which judgment is required is analyzed into most minute parts and propositions, when they seem to have been taken back to questions of demonstrable historical, statistical, psychological fact alone, none except a very few physical facts are scraped entirely clean of value judgments or can be. The bone of social fact is never scraped clean of values; the bone itself, its shape, size, and matter, is itself compact of values. I say this, advisedly, after searching inquiries conducted in group work with the ablest of colleagues. And, it is important to say it, for it faces us with the challenge, how are the different, and potentially conflicting values, to be reconciled —assuming that one is interested in reconciliation? What is "right" will be the morally least challengeable method of reconciliation, the principle that divides us least—assuming that one is interested in minimizing the divisions among men.

Even supposing the political facts to be commonly accepted and demonstrable to the common satisfaction, men are still faced with the judgment: What do they mean for me? What rights against others do they confer on me? What duties, and to whom, do they imply? To whom ought I defer? To what services ought I devote my brief time, my only true capital, on earth? And when this last is said, it will be remembered that some men's values include immortality.

Even where the bare bones of fact are clearly presented—e.g., in United States housing policy—the fact that, as compared with other nations, the American steadily spends a much larger percentage of his income on his automobile, his picture theaters, and his cosmetics than on his hous-ing it is still but a minute particle of all that a person needs to know in making of policy. If all the relevant facts were clean and dry, and agreed, he would still be baffled by their number, which run into thousands for his whole integrated domestic and international policy, and the significance of each when fitted with the rest would be not what the facts could cry out for themselves but the value which the policy maker imputed to them as he made a plan to act and conducted himself in the course of action.

All of man's personality all through time, his internal balance of personality, unique as it is and mutable in its own unique way in every second of his life, is involved in his valuation of any single decision in social life. Jacques Maritain rightly observes: [4]

I am known to other men. They know me as an object, not as subject. They are unaware of my subjectivity as such; unaware not merely of its inexhaustible depth, but also of the presence of the whole in each of its operations, that existential complexity of inner circumstances, data of nature, free choice, attractions, weaknesses, virtues perhaps, loves and pains; that atmosphere of imminent vitality which alone lends meaning to each of my acts.

The crucial question then is this: is this personality to be asked for its *acceptance* of social policy or to be coerced into obedience and seeming acceptance? Is government to fall back on physical fear? If voluntary acceptance is chosen, it is happiness, or at least it minimizes unhappiness, which some have accounted to be the proper end of morality and politics. And, even if man's happiness be not regarded as of any importance, and is discarded with contempt, as it was by Hegel and Carlyle as unworthy of man (and God!), even if Virtue is regarded as the superior end or value, it would still be cogently tenable that this end requires the voluntary assent of one's own standard of value. For to have another man's idea of virtue forced on one or to achieve triumphant rule by cheating is hardly virtuous, and to be obsequious to his decrees

[4] *Existence and the Existent* (New York, 1948), p. 76.

for fear of punishment puts one's virtue out of action as much as if it were annihilated.

Yet, it ought to be asked, is there no value, no virtue, no reason, possessed by some one man or men so demonstrably, so convincingly, that all men ought to accept them, can receive them, and be happy? The answer is a reluctant but firm and dispassionate No! Neither revelation nor scientific proof nor the examination of man's mind and will in the course of history points unchallengeably to any man or a few who have possessed, possess, or may possess, the truth infallibly for all time, for all circumstances, and for the satisfaction of all of us. That declaration is the cold and pallid faith that defines by inference the "right" of democracy. For it defines our duty to live in and for a polity which secures and guarantees to others (who would therefore guarantee to us) the social and governmental arrangements which will constitute the maximum resistance to force and oppression, give the maximum latitude for spontaneity of ideal and action to all, that is, which will keep the way open for diverse values and loyalties and yield the least ground for the sacrifice of one person by another.

Many will hate such a faith—as I shall show that Nietzsche did—because it entails the acknowledgment that their own brand of perfection has no valid claim of itself to rule the rest of the world. Acton would have to yield and subordinate *his* idea of wisdom or reason (at least to some extent) to this overriding faith and its discipline. But this principle has its merits even for an Acton. For the chief social consequence of the tenet that a single unifying indisputable ideal cannot be discovered either in revelation or scientific test is the principle of supporting everybody everywhere in the maintenance of those institutions which provide men with the freedom and latitude to fit themselves, their qualities and desires, where they most happily can, with the maximum permissions and allowances of the right to dwell elsewhere in thought, opinion, occupation, and place, with abundant grounds of appeal, and the chance of

mercy and redemption over and above the assurance of justice. Such a polity is the frame of a universal freedom, defensible by each for all because the defense of freedom for all is the maintenance of freedom for each. Inside this philanthropic frame of freedom, and not transgressing or overthrowing it, all faiths and minds and values should find their initiative and momentum, and though there must be limits, their avenues of development, and a not too oppressive haven from rivals and enemies.

This is, perhaps, the principle which will find the maximum, though not universal, acceptance in the long run. It is therefore also justifiable for short-run situations when patience and tolerance may be on the point of collapse in face of some bitter complexities in social change. Forbearance can cogently be asked for in short-term troubles as a sacrifice to avoid threatening the long-term good.

This, then, is the answer to the desperate cosmic question mark. It needs to be briefly restated, and the consequences of its rejection suggested.

When it is said that democracy (and through its major expediency, the majority) is "right," it is asserted that all individual values deserve the right to be heard, and that when they have so been heard and manifested themselves to attract attention and commend themselves, it is right that the reconciliation shall be made by all voices equally heard. Values can be called "interests" or the "religions" of individuals or groups if it will make the matter clearer. The Nietzschean view would utterly discard this "right." Here is a characteristic passage: [5]

The essential thing, however, in a good and healthy aristocracy is that it should *not* regard itself as a function either of the kingship or the commonwealth, but as the *significance* and the highest justification thereof—that it should therefore accept with good conscience the sacrifice of a legion of individuals, who, *for its sake,* must be suppressed and reduced to imperfect men, to slaves and instruments. Its fundamental belief must be precisely that so-

---

[5] *Beyond Good and Evil* (New York, 1937), para. 258.

ciety is *not* allowed to exist for its own sake, but only as a foundation and scaffolding, by means of which a select class of beings may be able to elevate themselves to their higher duties, and in general to a higher *existence*. . .

The implications of the antidemocratic philosophy are plain: Nietzsche is saying that some men have the right to be so sure of their morals that they kill others for their victory. The implications are that there need be no attempts to persuade; that indeed, such attempts are undesirable, for they cannot possibly succeed since one man will not comprehend the merit of the other man's values; and that steady repression, with murder as the ultimate means if necessary, may be undertaken. It means that an antidemocratic society must undertake the permanent application of force. Such a society would have to face the continuous possibility of revolt following on conspiracies. It would contemplate with equanimity the unhappiness of the oppressed, and, of course, make their unhappiness certain. It denies to them from the beginning the possibility of virtue. It makes rancor and fear, of the rulers as well as of the ruled, the permanent psychological atmosphere of society. It denies peace, and therefore, time for reflection and experiment and, perhaps, reconciliation of values. It forfeits the possibility of evoking truth for it condemns diversity, the riches of individual uniqueness, and originality—it never allows the multitude sparks of originality to soar, to be added together, contemplated, and compared. It is as irresponsible as Hegel, when he said: [6]

Great men have formed purposes to satisfy themselves, not others. Whatever prudent designs and counsels they might have learned from others, would be the more limited and inconsistent features in their career; for it was they who best understood affairs; from whom others learned, and approved, or at least acquiesced in—their policy. For that Spirit which had taken this fresh step in history is the inmost soul of all individuals; but in a state of unconsciousness which the great men in question aroused. Their fellows, therefore,

[6] *Philosophy of History*, trans. by J. Sibree (New York, 1944), p. 30.

follow these soul-leaders; for they feel the irresistible power of their own inner Spirit thus embodied.

For Hegel did not leave it to the masses to decide whether they should follow or not; and he left the means to be judged not by them, but by history, which of course necessarily displaced the judgment to aeons away from the date of acts which he said constituted the "litany of lamentations" of whole peoples.

The "right" for democracy that we think we have established is, then, no denial of the right of all to initiative, to leadership; on the contrary, it vindicates it. In our inevitable divisions, the democratic is the polity that divides us least. In our inevitable fury, it moderates us most, compatibly with our continued creativeness. It is resilient and self-curative, not entirely without coercion, for that (alas!) is impossible, but deploying the minimum residue of coercion permitted after patient contention and reasoning enforced by the right of dissent and the right to have one's votes counted. It is the right to picture your view of the supreme good, as you see it, to all the public, even to operate that supreme good in a limited area and for a limited group of adherents (family, business, church, club)—and these, as it were, are inoculations for the whole of society. If a wound is made in the mind of the great community, the dissenters may rush to cure it; if a hole is torn in its body the believers in other values may gather together to fill it.

For many, like an Acton or a Nietzsche, the democratic "right" will not be the ideal best: for all, however, it may be the acceptable second-best: that is to say, that which permits their own best, their own Reason, their own *vox Dei*, a life and a chance of persuading others, which otherwise might be altogether denied to them. It is the arbitral principle which admits challenging argument, but it is the one which is open to the least damaging criticism when contrasted with those other principles of government which have for so long presided over the destinies of man. If there is a less vulnerable principle of "right," I should like to hear it. Provided —of course, provided—that one wishes to eschew force and fraud, and that one wants the reign of peace, while justice is being cogitated and instituted as conscience freely develops in the most extensive feasible area containing the greatest number of people.

The democratic "right" as we have been obliged to justify it, is the equivalent of the "civil religion" which Rousseau demonstrated [7] must be set up over all other religions if a state, that is to say, an order embracing millions of people with divers and ever changing religions, are to live peaceably together in the possession of their faith.

There is therefore a purely civil profession of faith of which the Sovereign should fix the articles, not exactly as religious dogmas, but as social sentiments without which a man cannot be a good citizen or a faithful subject.

THE RECONCILIATION OF VALUES?

IT would be a mistake to seek to brush away the real problem of the reconciliation of values by the belief that differences are differences in words, mere semantic confusions, and that if only the right formula in words can be found we need not be concerned for a principle of reconciliation or at least of peace. For this would be only to adopt Mephistopheles' mockery, expressed in Goethe's *Faust*, as our valid comfort.

Do not try tortured ideas to find,
Because when to concepts you are blind,
A word as substitute arrives.
With words fine arguments can be conducted,
With words whole systems may be constructed,
With words we can continue full believing,
From words not a jot is open to the thieving.

We do not seek to minimize the strength of clashing convictions. One of the most impressive lessons the political scientist learns is that the splendid minds to which nature has given birth do not often and never altogether agree with each other. Take any ten political philosophers in the two thousand years since Plato and Aristotle, and unique outlooks will be discovered among them all, and therefore unique interpretations and practical policies. Points of agreement there are: but the world-shaking fact is difference. It is possible to sweep away the differences due to diversity of interests, misunderstandings about words, dissimilar environments, the peculiarities of the age in which they lived. Yet when all this has been allowed for, and when mere factiousness and envy have been purged, a solid difference still remains. No amount of argument and experimental persuasion can budge them from their special vision. I do myself damage if I do not try to fathom to the end the ultimate assumption which is their integrity and incapable of being surrendered; I remain incomplete if I ignore the added consciousness it gives me; and being incomplete my duty will be less perfect and my services less valuable than they might be. A gulf must still be bridged. The principle that democracy is always "right" is the only one that can bridge it: though there have been and are forms of government which abridge not merely the gulf but the terrains of diverse personality which abut upon the gulf—which "make a wilderness, and call it peace!"

Edmund Burke has even warned us of the need to consult more than mere reason—or he might rather have said, reasoning—when we attempt to apply our knowledge of humanity to the conduct of government; that is to say, our differences are not only more than differences of words, but graver than differences of reasoning. He said: [8]

Politics ought to be adjusted, not to human reasonings, but to human nature; of which the reason is but a part, and by no means the greatest part.

This dictum did no more than revert to what Locke had called the "ocean of being" of man, but it did no less than foresee the mighty divers into black deeps of the human psyche, Schopenhauer, Nietzsche, Freud, and Freud's continuators and critics. This is not the place to

---

[7] *Contrat Social*, final Chapter.

[8] *On a Pamphlet Intituled The State of the Nation*, 1765.

accompany those explorers; but it is the place to say that an inkling of the fervencies which separate men was enough to persuade men like Burke to warn us not to look too deeply into the origins and cohesive bonds of society, and Burke is obsessed by their inscrutability. Yet it is not their inscrutability so much as the enmity that might be ignited by their clear-eyed scrutiny and a penetration to the passions beyond the thin confines of reasoning. This is not to say that men are not in much united—witness the area and the long periods of peaceful living, peaceful reform, and peaceful progress within each state. Much unites them; but much more might divide them if their polity was such as to involve a perpetual agitation of their differences. It is Nietzsche who prescribes free, forceful, unscrupulous adventures of the will, and it is equally Nietzsche who recoils with horror from the sight of the will at work: [9]

Alas for this mad melancholy beast man! What phantasies invade it, and what paroxysms of perversity, hysterical senselessness, and *mental bestiality* break out immediately, at the very slightest check on its being the beast of action! All this is excessively interesting, but at the same time tainted with a black, gloomy, enervating melancholy, so that a forcible veto must be invoked against looking too long into these abysses.

What is the political scientist to reply to the passionate, ferocious claims of the human nature which is deeper and fiercer than what may be too easily dismissed as but superficial Jeffersonian reasoning? If millions upon millions are to live in wide areas rocked in peace, with violence outlawed—*if* this value commends itself —then we are compelled, I think, to found our government upon a tactical ignoring of the furious claims of any one or few above any others, and to admit only a common right to expression and persuasion short of war and the immediate and present threat of force. But this is the democratic way. It demands some self-abnegation, even the self-control of press-

ing the democratic principle, especially the majority principle, to the point of absolute perfection. The older phrase for it is "ballots rather than bullets": a newer one may be supplied, but potential critics of morals and English are begged to forbear—"kid or kill"!

IN WHAT SENSE GOVERNMENT IS ONLY "SECOND BEST"

A BIOGRAPHER of Lord Morley, dilating upon that statesman's practical wisdom, used a phrase which not so long since was a cliché among political scientists, particularly those who in an exhibition of man-of-the-worldishness let us into the secret that the self-government of man is a difficult enterprise: "politics are one long second best." [10] Some consideration of the commonplace is relevant to an understanding of the justification of democracy.

Every one of us, escaping from the trance of habit, from time to time wins an idea of the "best" objects, methods, and procedures of government, or, perhaps more narrowly, some governmental device, a swift stratagem, for solving a troublesome problem, and with ingenuity we offer to square the political circle. This would be for the "best" of all concerned, "best" in objective and "best" in means.

Yet, on second thoughts, it is borne in upon us that someone must pay for the reform we have proposed. It may be that the cost makes its pursuance unprofitable. It may be also or alternately that success would require qualities human beings do not possess, and of these some may be of a kind that can never be possessed by any man, or are possessed by very few, or can be acquired but only at immense cost, or are attainable at the combined prices of effort and *time*. Sacrifice, resignation, abnegation, and time, are especially necessary ingredients where the "best" is founded upon the development, reconciliation, and the common acceptance of values.

Counting the cost, it is at this time that

---

[9] *Genealogy of Morals* (Modern Library, New York, 1937), p. 88.

[10] J. H. Morgan, *John, Viscount Morley* (London, 1924), p. 111; and see above, p. 7.

we recognize that we had better do the best, that is, now the "second-best," with the means and the time available to us. The intellect might do better, the heart might counsel braver new worlds, but the material is not yet to hand. Yet we may do better than we are doing by using the available material more aptly: our brains may advise us of a better situation than the one we accept—but not to the wished-for "best." *Quaere*: Is the unattainable "best" to be called "the best"? Or is the attainable best, given the material and the time at our disposal to be called the "best"? If it is the latter, it can no longer be apologized for as "the second best." Immanuel Kant somewhere names this so-called second best "the best compossible," that is, the best consistent with the circumstances. It is, of course, realized that from the standpoint of any idealist deeply attached to his ideals, and not prepared to concede the justification of democracy, which requires of him that he carry us by persuasion or not at all toward the fulfillment of his ideals, and which gives equal hearing and play to other and perhaps inimical ideals, what is achievable can only be the second best indeed. The temper of such a demand for the sectarian best may be appreciated from a letter of Lord Acton to Gladstone's daughter: [11]

But if party is sacred to me as a body of doctrine, it is not, as an association of man bound together, not by common convictions but by mutual obligations and engagements. In the life of every great man there is a point where fidelity to ideas, which are the justifying cause of party, diverges from fidelity to arrangements and understandings, which are its machinery. And one expects a great man to sacrifice his friends—at least his friendship—to the higher cause.

And it is no surprise, excepting in its candor, that earlier in the letter he confesses:

Politics come nearer religion with me, a party is more like a church, error more like heresy, prejudice more like sin, that I find it to be with better men.

The burden, as Lord Morley saw it, that made the second best tolerable *in lieu* of the best as Lord Acton wished it, is expressed in his understanding of the heavy operation of the machinery that we have quoted earlier.[12]

WHAT IS LOST AND GAINED BY WHOLESALE GOVERNMENT

IT is fortunate that we take for granted the unearned bequest that modern states are so large in area and population and the assumption that they should be so. But it is important to be deliberately aware of the consequences of size—of units of government which embrace as many as 150,000,000 in the United States, some 40,000,000 in France, nearly 70,-000,000 in Germany, nearly 200,000,000 in the Soviet Union, and approaching 50,-000,000 in Britain. Immense advantages to human existence, and not a few awkward ills, arise from what is a simple but stupendous fact, and we are not nearly conscious enough of this balance.

The primary advantage (and this does not exclude our understanding of the derivation and parallel advantages), is that over a large area, solicitous for the life of millions upon millions, peace reigns, violence and war are banned, and there rules the presumption of tranquil, uninvaded communication and exchange—that is, of Order. Connected with this, and in part its condition, is the highly probable assurance that if the present situation of interpersonal and intergroup value-adjustment is deemed unfair, a remedy may in the future be available by persuasion. Time and peace are needed for the appeasement of temper and the clarity of vision which *may* probably bring what is regarded by more as a higher justice. Time and peace may, in fact, not bring justice—but without time and peace, justice will far less certainly be won. Fears are relieved, hope is encouraged.

How priceless is this boon, for most people in the long run (not for all, for

---

[11] Lord Acton, *Letters to Mary Gladstone* (London, 1905), pp. 314-15.

[12] Cf. page 7.

some may hate the consequences), may be inferred from even a cursory recollection of the many centuries of war, and the struggles and hopes of mankind for peace, for world government, for a federation even, and in the last resort, merely for pacts of friendship and defense. What were the friends of the League of Nations and the United Nations not prepared (in theory, at any rate) to sacrifice in the subordinate inefficiencies of government in order to secure the benefits of peace?

Yet the wholesale nature of government gives birth to two evils which must never fail to be counted against its enormous profit. The first is the burden of centralization, which has a twofold nature: it involves the expense of officials and organization, and it cannot provide for direct, highly considerate individual treatment of the needs of all its individuals and groups. To these evils there are remedies and mitigations: but they require to be devised and applied. The second is the limitation on the liberty of subordinate groups within the larger community, when they are prohibited from exceeding persuasion and minor intimidations in pursuit of their ardent will and best beliefs. The cost to such subordinated groups (when they are subordinated, and they will not be subordinated for all time and in everything that concerns the commonwealth—they too will have their day), is best expressed by Hamlet:

For who would bear the whips and scorns of time,
The oppressor's wrong, the proud man's contumely,
The pangs of despised love, the law's delay,
The insolence of office, and the spurns
That patient merit of the unworthy takes . . ?

but it would not follow that the bare bodkin would be used to make the quietus of the oppressed: it might kill the commonwealth, by rebellion or revolution. Yet the democratic life urges them to be tolerant, patient, to bear misunderstanding, to suffer fools gladly, to risk futility. The French political philosopher, François Fourier, in his *Théorie des Quatre Mouvements* (1808), thought he might reduce the inevitable pressure of the great society on the individual by disintegrating France into many hundreds of self-governing societies, called phalansteries, each containing 1600 persons. In these small units it would be possible for the members to know and participate in the affairs of the whole without a cumbrous apparatus of government. But, clearly, he does not allow for either differences of values within the phalansteries, or differences among them. The idea is mentioned merely to underline how deeply some may resent the vexations of the wholesale community, and to suggest that smaller communities are not without their problems either. The organizational pressures of the wholesale area may be met by ingenious decentralization, and by such an education of the citizen as to teach him the access to office holders and the centers of authority. The wholesale state itself may be made more tolerable by obedience to the principle that no additional function is assumed by the state—or rather, is imposed upon it by the majority —unless it promises fulfillment of a social value intensely held by a substantial majority. It must be remembered that one of the advantages of collective action is the maintenance of union and peace over a large area of the earth: when we condone anew state activity, we win a general benefit over and above the specific one, so long as the place of freedom is guaranteed.

DEMOCRACY AND ECONOMIC WELFARE

Some critics of democracy and some of its good-hearted, but confused, friends express fears that democracy may be too weak a form of government to overcome the very awkward economic and social obstructions in the track of the nation— obstructions which, however, must be overcome because it is democracy's principal business to furnish high economic welfare for all.

Now, it is true that under democracy the raising of the standard of living will be forwarded exceptionally well. This is for two reasons. First, freedom of enterprise together with government regulation and activity will be developed in the measure in which the *whole* community —all its various interests and skills—demand it, with a considerable degree of willingness rather than coerced planning, and the poorer part of the community will be assisted to opportunity, education, and health in many ways by the social services and social-security arrangements. Secondly, it is also true that some political parties, perhaps all, will insistently preach the value of ever-higher standards of living.

Yet there are dangers to democracy in the insistence on inordinate economic welfare. It would be tragic to neglect the fact that democracy's keenest rival for man's devotion is economic welfare. The conflict between them is not absolute but is a matter of degree. Even in saying this, it is necessary to be alert to the dangers of the rivalry. For it would be wrong to promise rapid, almost immediate, increases of wealth in such quantity that the inventiveness, the resources, the skill of labor and management, could not possibly provide. Much popularity can be easily won by whipping up the expectations of the needy and encouraging indulgence in acquisitiveness. There is no more heart-warming experience on any political platform. Indeed, the appeal has its definite value: it makes people discontented with their lot when that lot is remediable, and it may even inspire men and women to rise out of their laziness and ignorance to engage in ingenious invention and aggressive enterprise. But unless those who speak in these terms be ruled by sincerity and sobriety, they play with fire, with arson for democracy. It is too easy to exploit poverty and misery, and arouse an acquisitiveness which, given lack of time and ability, is not satisfiable. Civilizations are full of proverbs and parables regarding the seductions of wealth: God and Mammon; the Golden Calf; "Man does not live by Bread alone;" betrayal for thirty pieces of silver; "for a handful of silver he left us"; and so on.

It is also true that for the easy, tolerant, and cheerful conduct of democracy without violence, a degree of economic abundance properly spread is necessary. It is not unfair thinking to relate the rise of civil liberties and democratic constitutions to the growth of wealth in Europe and the United States—though great care must be taken not to ignore other factors. It was Francis Bacon who advised the spread of wealth as a preventive of seditions. Yet to be sure of democracy, democrats must be temperate about acquisitiveness. Democracy is its own reward: it is not merely a means to an end: it is an end, and the most important end. To say otherwise is to fall into a materialism which could lead to a government of chains, even if self-imposed chains. Democracy in a reasonable time will lead to the maximum welfare; but the maximum welfare worshipped as a prior or competing standard might, if beyond any reasonable estimate of feasibility, kill democracy by incitement to unreasonable and violent discontent. What a democracy acquires it itself guarantees that its members may keep; what a revolution and a dictator, in the name of wealth first, donate may always be taken away by its givers, even if what is given is actually something more than an unfulfillable promise.

DEMOCRACY AND HAPPINESS

Democracy in modern gigantic states is a wholesale arrangement. As such it cannot possibly penetrate to the relief of some forms of unhappiness experienced by individuals and families. By hypothesis these would be different from the usual. Nor, given the kinds of happiness which alone may please people of special tastes and bents and family upbringing or fortune, is it easy to know what would make them happy, even if it were possible to transform the whole of society for the sake of the less numerous portion of the nation. A well-educated, well-administered democracy, with a long-nurtured, mature conscience, may render great services through the laws and its career servants in these ways. But in many areas the state cannot enter—we reach the non-political.

How small of all that human hearts endure,
That part which laws or kings can cause or
cure!
Still to ourselves in every place consigned,
Our own felicity we make or find.

These areas are the preserve of social action on a local scale, of fellowship, voluntary, personal, or in small groups: of free friendships, clubs, associations, societies, forums, the private practice of brotherhood. The state may assist with money or advice; by the loan of experts; by arbitration at request; by the setting of standards when abuses have made themselves evident—for example in the practice of psychiatry or the adoption of children. Above all, the government will assist by leaving the circle of freedom to private persons where it itself cannot positively help them and where they cannot injure others. Where democracy cannot creatively bring happiness, it is the aptest form of government to say that what would seem to make for unhappiness shall not be instituted.

OF THE INFLUENCE OF TIME ON GOVERNMENT

It is impossible to discuss the nature of government without repeated use of the words "patience," "tolerance," "waiting upon persuasion," "deliberation," "education," and others which are synonyms or nearly so. These words are all variations on the word Time, and the idea to be conveyed is that with Time every difficulty in interpersonal relations may perhaps be peacefully resolved, and to express the conviction that without the lapse of Time between the conception of an idea and its application in practice, errors and violence will be committed. Not enough attention has been given in political science to the effect of Time on the political process, though much, of course, is casually assumed. Economists habitually make a distinction between the short run and the long run, not that they follow out the consequences fully,

or that they can or should be required to distinguish quantitatively between the one and the other in general. Far too little concern altogether has been shown by political scientists, and so a few observations are necessary, for an important connection subsists between considerations of time and the theory of democracy.

The problem of Time in political science may be considered from four points of view: Time and Patience; Time and Knowledge; Time and Appeasement of Passions; and Time and—for want of a better word—Eternity.

Time and Patience. If a government craves short-run, swift results, for whatever reason—and time and temper are in this respect one and the same thing—certain consequences follow. It enters on its task with forceful drive, and presses men and means to secure obedience. By hypothesis it is condemned and condemns others to inaccuracy of diagnosis and formula. Its rough, driving energy and faulty prescriptions fail to give it complete satisfaction in time, and compel its subjects to undertake passive or active resistance or simply to be irresponsive to orders or persuasion because they are surprised and lack mental and spiritual preparation. Since time presses, the intractability of the citizen is met with the government's hatred, proceeding from frustration, and violence is thrown in to redeem what would otherwise be wasted effort and disappointment. A vicious crescendo of mutual torment gains momentum. Reciprocal understanding is diminished, and the wish to understand wanes with the increase of spite. The end being rabidly wanted, the means are degraded. This is to look at the subject from the point of view of the government.

From the point of view of impatient citizens and their groups—and it must be remembered that there is close correspondence between citizens and governments in democratic states—the prospect of the swift passage of time, the vanishing and wasted years, the duties undone, the hopes unfulfilled, must stir to frustration and ʿan the flames of a determination to revolt, to claim the rights of minority rule, to attest the right of violence, and to be unscrupulous about ways and means, that is, about government.

What misery would the world not have been spared if the Nazi and the Soviet régimes had not moved under the compulsion of short-term results? There is even a Soviet saying that its present generation is "the manure of the future." The consequences of not waiting on Time rippled out from these régimes over the whole world, partly as the result of the obstinacies of the domestic situation and the psychoses they produced, and partly as a campaign against the rest of the world to make sure that the neutral and the hostile should be converted or sterilized at the earliest moment. These men could not be sure of the future as they thought it ought to be: they looked on their lives as inevitably brief and wished to see results in their own time, sufficient at least to give them the guarantees of the future after their own death. Their purpose was to pin down, to hold down, the effect of future time on a generation or more while habit formed, the habit that would then be so iron-bound as not to yield to the inspiration of those yet to be born. Opponents must be murdered: dissenting minds must be obliterated. The rulers fretted against the ancient wisdom:

Some men with swords may reap the field
And plant fresh laurels where they kill;
But their strong nerves at last must yield;
They tame but one another still:
    Early or late
    They stoop to fate. . .

On a very dramatic level, the effect of the pressure of time on government may be seen in the ebb and flow of conflicting attitudes since the 1820's about the status and the civil rights of the Negro in the Southern states of the United States. To some the conflict of 1861 was "irrepressible," to others "repressible" and curative by time and peaceful change. Lord Acton showed no temporal zeal for emancipation: he saw the world *quod semper*

—everlasting. On a lesser scale, it is interesting to reflect that the robust methods used by the Tennessee Valley Authority in its struggles with the public utilities of the region sprung in part from the belief that the then directors could depend only on a single four-year term for President Roosevelt, and therefore the electricity corporations must be conquered in that brief period, or perhaps never.

Time and Knowledge. No one is born wise, though he may be born with the propensity to wisdom within him. Time alone teaches us the lessons of man's nature, in our own experience which carries conviction and validity far above what comes from reading and oral teaching. Not that the latter does not require time also. But experience itself affects all the senses, while the written word and the most vivid teaching rarely sets in motion all our nature. It takes time for any facts to be fitted into the world as it has come to be built in our minds. The truth is the coherence of all that we know and all that we can know. The full truth could not be known by any of us until all the experience of the whole of life has been counted, for failing this, our world of one day may be inconsistent with that which is attainable on a later day. Bernard Shaw somewhere remarks that we experience a sense of loss when we have learned a new fact. He does not explain this feeling that something has been lost. The explanation is that we have lost a world we labored to create; but now a new process of creation must be undertaken because, to allow for hospitality to the new fact, to provide it with a room, the whole of that world in all its parts must be remodeled. The facts must be *dwelt with* if their meaning is to flourish, and if they are to be valued for their relevance for the springs of action. Time is technical knowledge, knowledge of human nature, of the mind of man as revealed in a very long historic experience, the knowledge of the systems of ethics and their fate, the strengths and impossibilities of administration, understanding of the processes of valid thought, and, far from least, self-knowledge. Time enables us if not to conduct an experiment with life in our own time, at least to be present and observe.

The testimony to the truth of these observations has been given over the centuries by the wisest among mankind— it is in the poets as it is in the political philosophers, this "inseparable propriety of time," which as Francis Bacon showed in *The Advancement of Learning*, "is even more and more to disclose truth." Nothing wiser has been said on this theme than the passages in Burke: and it is a grave mistake for this reason, to charge him, as some have done, with being a "conservative" or a "pessimist." Only a shallow mind, irresponsible to the point of frivolity, can believe that a just and true policy may be prosecuted without an understanding of the vastest and most intricate thing the world has to show— human nature in its environment where it calls for a political act. The assumption, of course, is that we should act on knowledge and not merely on zeal, however merciful and noble that may be. It is better that Burke speak for himself, in only one of his appealing intimations: [14]

It is one of the excellencies of a method in which time is amongst the assistants, that its operation is slow, and in some cases almost imperceptible. If circumspection and caution are a part of wisdom, when we work only upon inanimate matter, surely they become a part of duty too, when the subject of our demolition and construction is not brick and timber, but sentient beings. . . Time is required to produce that union of minds which alone can produce all the good we aim at. Our patience will achieve more than our force. . . I have never yet seen any plan which has not been mended by the observations of those who were much inferior in understanding to the person who took the lead in the business. By a slow but well-sustained progress, the effect of each step is watched; the good or ill-success of the first gives light to us in the second; and so, from light to light, we are conducted with safety through the whole series. We see that the parts of the system do not clash. The evil latent in the most promising contrivances are provided for as they arise. One advantage is as little as possible sacrificed to another. We

compensate, we reconcile, we balance. We are enabled to unite into a consistent whole the various anomalies and contending principles that are found in the minds and the affairs of men. . . If justice requires this, the work itself requires the aid of more minds than one age can furnish.

It is suggested that if the good of all men and women should be sought by government, then the knowledge which fits the condition of all of them and their children's children is discoverable more faithfully in the form of the state which best provides continuity and duration and is avowedly founded on patience, and the principle of equality which best encourages men to speak out, and rebuffs the arrogant official's claim to know and act without consultation. If revelation requires encouragement and coaxing, and time to win all confidences, then democracy is an essential condition of the revelation of truth. The truth in political science is not submissible to the method of the natural sciences (who, indeed, would be happy if it were?): what the rigor of cause-and-effect demonstration is to the physical sciences, time is to the social and above all to political science. The penetrative, permeating effect of time on truth may best be seen perhaps in Marcel Proust's masterpiece, *Remembrance of Things Past*. The world will be happier with a Proust as its political scientist than a Karl Marx.

Time and Appeasement. It is possible that time is more than revealing—that it is appeasing. I cannot be dogmatic. Philosophers and poets believe so. Shakespeare, for example, says, in *Troilus and Cressida*, "Time's glory is to *calm* contending kings." What truth is there in this? Perhaps we could accept the view in the following process of argument. If we think of Time as being the property of the lives of the single citizens, then the young must grow older or, as we say, mature; while the already old will grow older still. It seems to be almost universally testified that the advancement to and beyond maturity is accompanied by an assuagement of passion, a moderation of temper, a cooling of emotion, a realiza-

---

[14] *Reflections on the French Revolution* (World's Classics) Vol. IV, p. 187.

tion of the extravagances of former hopes. A more modest sense of the importance and priority of wants is developed; the exacting demands on other people and on one's self are in later years acknowledged to be an excess of vanity. The progress is from Shakespeare's lover, "sighing like a furnace," to the soldier "jealous in honor, sudden and quick in quarrel, Seeking the bubble reputation, Even in the cannon's mouth," to the justice, "full of wise saws and modern instances." Where all may speak and act, as legitimate contributors to policy and government of the whole community, then the youthful dynamic is tempered with the reconciliations to existence of the middle-aged and the old, while the temperance of the latter is animated by the young of the living generation. I need not quote Burke again, for the famous passage in his *Reflections on the French Revolution,* extolling "the great, mysterious incorporation of the human race . . . never old, or middle aged, or young" is too well-known.

It is reasonably tenable that the polity that stipulates Time allows for appeasement: the democratic is a long-term régime. The democratic system and principle is liberated from the short-term frantic compulsions of one or a few persons obsessed, it may be, by the brevity of their own lives, and, by hypothesis, revolutionary as compared with the mass of other people, since their creed differs from that of the masses at the beginning and is obliged to remain eccentric for the sake of their credit and vanity.

Time and Eternity. To some, the Time of their own life is not the decisive, instigating factor of their actions within the span of their own life. They would hold that there is no value in seeking to alter the terrestrial future, and to attempt to do so involves a violence that debases the soul now. I cannot express this very well because either by nurture or by nature I have no clear comprehension or inward sympathy with this idea of reality. In default of my own evidence I adduce that of Aldous Huxley: [15]

---

15 *The Perennial Philosophy* (New York, 1945), p. 194.

For those whose philosophy does not compel them to take time with excessive seriousness, the ultimate good is to be sought neither in the revolutionary's progressive social apocalypse, nor in the reactionary's revived and perpetuated past, but in an eternal divine *now* which those who sufficiently desire this good can realize as a fact of immediate experience. . . The peace that passes all understanding is the fruit of liberation into eternity; but in its ordinary everyday form peace is also the root of liberation. For where there are violent passions and compelling distractions, this ultimate good can never be realized. . .

Whether such resignation does or does not involve the idea of personal immortality, it looks on mundane life (as Ecclesiastes does) as a brief instant, and its corollary is quietism. It is one strand in the Christian life, and as such has an important meaning for democracy, suggesting patience, toleration, and resignation and faith. Hence the Marxist regards it as "the opium of the people." Yet other parts of the Christian doctrine would spur to action. The political attitude appropriate to the sense of the insignificance of mundane future time for the political process would be long-suffering, charity, the abhorrence of violence, the counsel that affairs can wait, and if they do not, at any rate, in the end it will not matter even if an activist policy has created works, for they will crumble.

Even if this attitude is not held by even a small group of people in each nation in an absolute form, then it is still an ingredient in the values and habits of large numbers of people in a degree that varies from person to person—but all have traces of it, and the total is important for government.

The upshot of these considerations on Time is to commend the method of democracy in comparison with any other, except the *accidental* consonance of a necessarily short-lived dictator or small oligarchy with the values of the people they govern. Democracy is patient, reveals knowledge, appeases tempers and hatreds, and, proceeding on the principle that no legislature can bind its successor, makes no such fetish of Time as would prompt to major violence within the nation—that is to say, in comparison with other régimes.

THE DEMOCRATIC AND THE DICTATORIAL STATE

THE threads may now be drawn together. The dictatorial state promises and can deliver swift action of a radical nature. But experience shows that those we have learned to know in our own lifetime—the nazi, the fascist and the Soviet state, still fumble in the effort for full administrative success for lack of time, knowledge, and happy cooperation by the millions to whom they have promised to do good. The rights of freedom of speech, of the press, of association, of meeting, of dissent, of participation in the will-building of government, are destroyed, and where they are given any license at all it is to the accompaniment of chicanery and corrupt practices by which the substance is withdrawn. The fury of fanatical zeal, the frenzied disappointment with plans unfulfilled, the nagging fear of doubt and opposition in the unfathomable depths of the population, spurs them forward to an aggressor's descent upon the people, with a gigantic police force, an army of torturers calling for confessions and betrayals, with force to the utmost, imprisonment, transportation, slavery, and murder, as the instrument of peremptory success. And in this dispensation the citizen is severed from his fellows by the fear of betrayal; cannot pour out his heart even to the officials who are supposed to be his benefactors; is direly constrained to appear to share the values thrust upon him. Under duress the gifted must hide their talents; the average must obey in fear, in rancour, and in hatred. The way of life is closed tight against the literature, the science, the religion, and the philosophy of the rest of the world.

The miserable, fearful, subjects of a dictatorship are cast out from the highest moral choices, those which concern the way of life of all mankind; for their dignity is openly despised. Above all, for the sense of the sensitive that the years pass by under perennial frustration, no remedy is permitted which allows of peaceful change: they are entrapped in the bitter margin between fawning self-debasement and the hazards and blind extremity of revolution, revolution not even for the major purpose of changing the nature of the state but merely to change the personnel of an administration. Yes: perhaps for a time their material welfare is better than it was before; and perhaps there is a promise of better things for the future: but now and for any foreseeable and attainable time, there reigns the *angst* of a human mind and conscience writhing in the strait-jacket of alien values. The medicinal principle which a dictatorship like all other political systems contains is not the one which can be used as a daily diet, or, being used, can promise health: for it is either internal disruption of the dictatorial group or its overthrow in wholesale and protracted murder. Its medicine is brutality, even if heroic brutality, and brutality is a poison.

Democracy has its defects: the overcoming of hereditary privileges and the winning of equality takes time and strains the patience while the pain and stress of injustice continue to prevail. Collective action that promises vast benefits is retarded by special interests that hold strategic controls. Special ability and insights may be subordinated to the grosser claims of the mass of average men.

However, the political, social and economic gifts of democracy endow mankind with vast riches. We are so accustomed to the exercise of our civil rights that we have ceased to realize that they are as vital to our moral life as breathing is to our physical, and we take this miracle for granted! We can speak our minds, and so exercise our talents, relieve our protests, feel our dignity and community with our fellow men. We may soar on the wings of the evidence of all science, all art, all religion, all philosophy, from wherever and from whatever time they issue. We may in association with our like-minded fellow citizens freely join our efforts and fortunes to bring home to all the moral significance of our spiritual values and urge them to support our interests and defend with us the liberty that is threatened. We have the assurance that the sphere of our private life—our family, our diversions, our worship, our work —will not be invaded except by due process of law in which we have an equal say with any. We rest tranquil that officials and judges will not abuse us, and that they themselves will have to answer for discrimination and bias and unauthorized invasions of our private or public life to a public tribunal in which we, as of right, sit as judge and jury. These values, too often taken for granted, are so immense to humanity that it is advisedly impossible to express their magnitude: no terror, no cruelty, no stifling, no roughness, no cunning or chicanery, no strong-armed hypocrisy. It is all imperfect, of course: but compared with nondemocratic government of past times and the dictatorships of our own time it wears the halo of perfection. We know, too, that inequalities can be reduced as soon as a majority are convinced that they are really inequalities and have no contemporary usefulness as a social function. Since the law will be made and the administration be given momentum and controlled by us, the voters, and since our power can be successfully exerted by association and persuasion, the impulse of the system is to foster fellowship and a common conscience among all men. The medicine of democracy is secreted in its own beneficent nature: the retreat from a political mistake even as the way forward is an open one; it is majority persuasion taking its original impulse and life from any one, the humblest indeed, who may need to raise his voice; and it is a remedy that practically does not call for bloodshed. Its principle, broadly and steadily honored in the observance, is, Let live, and live! It accomplishes the dual feat, first, of fanning the enthusiasms of all who have values and yet keeping the flames down below the height where they might set the whole community in an all-consuming blaze; and, second, of bowing to the inevitability of gradualness while not succumbing to political sloth.

The contrast between modern nonresponsible or dictatorial government and responsible and democratic government is now more clearly seen. The former rests upon the pretension that a monopolistic and imposed party possesses the ultimate truth about the political destiny of humanity. That conviction is definite, sharp, and fanatical, and therefore brooks no opposition. But democracies admit the pragmatic nature of their search for perfection, and recognize that of perfection there is no single exclusive principle. Yet they surmise that if such there should be, it is one yet to be discovered in a process of evolution, and that if the unfolding is to arrive at soundness, it must be founded on the unfettered expression and interplay of all opinion.

Where then shall we look for the binding together of the world-wide network of mind and mind, to the end that the principles of democratic unity shall be applied and defended? The labors are, of course, divided among the exceptionally gifted and the universal body of men and women everywhere. The latter depend for the earliest intimations of vision and feeling upon the gifted, but must always have the last word, should they still want it, after having first heard and considered. And one of the unending tasks is to protect the open way for the gifted—for all the gifted of whatever persuasion—and equally to maintain the proper conditions by which the multitude's reflection upon them is promoted. Those with exceptional gifts are not divinely appointed; for all men are divinely appointed or none; they spring from the common body of the people. (I have seen Italian peasants who look the image of Fermi, the great physicist.) There are men and women of peculiar talent who can see across distances of social space inaccessible to the senses of ordinary men. Some have minds fitted by nature to comprehend the distant experience of humanity in time, that is, in history; others are geniuses of intellectual coordination, of immense span, who sense connections, correlations, and causality and can predict the shape of coming things—an Aristotle, a Montesquieu, a Hegel, a Marx, a Toynbee, and an H. G. Wells. Others are geniuses of psychological and spiritual insight: the un-uttered secrets of individual capacity and aspiration yield to them, and the hopes and fears of salvation dwelling in the labyrinth of each person emerges at their scrutiny: Socrates, Aquinas, Machiavelli, Spinoza, Rousseau, Burke, Bentham, Goethe, Shaw, Freud. There are geniuses of feeling and sensitivity, of justice and mercy: they feel more vividly and painfully than others with St. Thomas that "it is no part of Christian perfection to endure with equanimity the wrongs inflicted on other people." Often, therefore, they can express these feelings more vividly, and under their impulse sacrificially dedicate their lives to the establishment of remedies and opportunities for human society by preaching, teaching, or politically and socially building: Tom Paine, Thomas Jefferson, Elizabeth Fry, Lincoln, Robert Owen, Florence Nightingale, Jane Addams, Mrs. Sidney Webb. These stand on the summit, but close to them are many thousands, themselves able thinkers, critics, and intermediaries and popularizers, and some are practical political and social leaders. All such people think and feel earlier and differently from their fellow citizens in general, so much so that they may be repugnant to them. Yet these are the men and women who will—with the pains described by Hegel in his exhortations about "great" men—in the long run advance the freedom and happiness of all if they are tolerated for long enough to impress their message. For the sake of the general freedom their special freedom is above all necessary, and its defense is an obligation of the masses, returning incalculable benefits. The nation is blessed which cherishes its heretics.

The task of the plain man in a democracy is, then, not easy. The continuance and operation of this system of government requires that he tolerate and listen to innovation and adequately reflect so that he may distinguish between the sincere and the insincere, the well-wishers and the misguided, the genuine and the charlatans, the visions from the hallucinations, and so that he may decide how much of the contribution of each is not only for his own good now but for his own good in the long run, and not only for his own good in the long run, but for that of his neighbors all over the world.

In the dictatorial state, the pattern of man's perfect character is one man's vision; the teaching of "character" means the imposition of that mold, while good citizenship consists of submission to its confinement. In the democratic state, since perfection is yet to be discovered and is contingent on a continuing quest, the nature of the preferred character is the one that accepts plasticity and the principle of live and let live, of adventure and of self-expression leading to that end. While the dictatorial state thrusts the main emphasis upon obedience, the democratic places the accent upon the conditional terms of consent and the expression of disagreement. The dictatorial state removes responsibility from the conscience of the individual party member and tries to chloroform or hypnotize the mind; in the democratic, the conscience of the individual is fully responsible, refreshed by the beating waves of dynamic opinion, and troubled. Therefore, where dictators rule, the peculiar duty of a party member seems to be harder than that of the democratic citizen; but, in truth, the implied responsibilities of democracy are much more exacting. For self-government means, first, the government of one's self. That is why the democratic states vibrate, sometimes violently, and seem and are unstable. It explains why, therefore, the democratic states are not yet as fully democratic as the tasks implied in their own principle require; for the burden is heavy on citizens and party members who take their responsibilities seriously, and so too few of them do. A few well-organized, conscious, competitive, and honorable parties can make the tasks easier to fulfill. The dictatorships show that there is a clear alternative to the burdens of democratic citizenship; but is it nice?

We do not know to what the whole process is tending in its large and far-flung outlines. We cannot know. We do not even know the possibilities more than a little space of time away. It is a difficult and most sedative process to get to know. (Hence, Georges Sorel: "Away with blue-books: they reduce your revolutionary ardor!") We cannot be audacious about human potentialities, even though history is long. It is only a step from the sanguine to the sanguinary, and Hitler, Stalin, and Mussolini took it. Democrats have to grasp the nettle of their own hopes in the beneficence of freedom for the whole multitude, whatever the consequences of the freedom—that none, not the greatest, can prove the tenability of any one faith on which mankind can be united.[16] That nettle is (and it is wholesome, if prickly) that the true and the good are revealable, not at once, but as you go along, and as you keep the ways open for it from wherever it may come, by your modesty, your hesitations, your reflection, your listening, and encouragement of those who have something to say or, where less articulate, can signify by action. This is the philosophical moderator of the self-realization that is a basic tenet of democratic theory.

The criterion is the grant of all freedom to act and develop except to destroy or indubitably endanger that freedom. In the light of this, there are bounds to all forms of expression and action, for individuals, groups, classes, parties, and occupations; and a doctrine would elaborate and illuminate this. The nazis and the fascists produced such a doctrine in the form of history, philosophy, and civil studies, for their purposes. Its intent, not its content, is relevant. It was to serve to clarify the relationship between the kaleidoscope of hundreds of diverse events in the common man's environment and experience, the many everyday seemingly eccentric and arbitrary happenings and their civic relevance to him. It was to replace the chaos of the city streets by a world's meaning. It was on the way to achievement by the establishment of a doctrine of human destiny and duty, drawn from history interpreted by reason, to serve as the thread and signal of direction. It sought to bring nature, history, and

spirit into a conspiracy to subvert liberty. All things that the common man saw and heard and surmised, but could not correlate or draw meaning from, the nazis and the fascists suffused with coherence by relating to the focus of meaning which they had created. The Russian Communist party, concerned to secure continuous and dynamic loyalty, was forced to find an answer to the problem whether its members could be reliable unless they had absorbed the Marxian historical analysis and logic.

There is no doubt at all that the like can be achieved and made acceptable for and by democratic man, by relating the events of his society and the march of history to the essential democratic doctrine here proposed. Its requisite is Time, but Time may be economized by collective and persistent effort.

One hundred and fifty years ago, in the midst of the French Revolution, the Abbé Siéyès asked, what is the Third Estate?—and answered that it was nothing. And further, what did it want to be? —and replied, Something. And, finally, what ought it to be?—and declared, Everything! Today, the Third Estate is Everything, for the People hold the plenitude of power. A new era evokes new questions. What does the People demand? Equality. What does it chiefly want? Plenty. What does it need, and what ought it to give? Mercy. And of all the polities known to us, democratic government, with all its natural imperfections, is Mercy's most assured and durable instrument, and the best tempered.

Political science is confession: and to teach it is to confess. This does not mean that it is merely introspection, for the mind is not nourished only by what it contemplates within. Looking outward in time and in space, as well as deep down inwardly, the mind apprehends a world. And, in order that our good may not be wrested from us, it is imperative that along with its smiling certitudes, we confide the doubts and uncertainties, the weaknesses and ignorance of our world, to those who day by day can and must revive freedom and advance mercy.

16 Even when presented as Humanity, as in Auguste Comte, *System of Positive Polity* (London, 1875), on which see J. S. Mill's dissent in his *Autobiography*.

Appendix A

Standard Form No. 51
August 1946
U.S. CIVIL SERVICE COMMISSION

Form approved.
Budget Bureau No. 50–R012.3.

REPORT OF
EFFICIENCY RATING

ADMINISTRATIVE-UNOFFICIAL ( )
OFFICIAL:
REGULAR ( )   SPECIAL ( )
PROBATIONAL ( )

As of .... based on performance during period from .... to ....

....

(Name of employee)

....

(Title of position, service, and grade)

....

(Organization—Indicate bureau, division, section, unit, field station)

1. Study the instructions in the Rating Official's Guide, C. S. C. Form No. 3823A.
2. Underline the elements which are especially important in the position.
3. Rate only on elements pertinent to the position.
   a. Do not rate on elements in *italics* except for employees in administrative, supervisory, or planning positions.
   b. Rate administrative, supervisory, and planning functions on elements in *italics*.

CHECK ONE:

Administrative, supervisory, or planning................ ☐

All others................ ☐

ON LINES BELOW MARK EMPLOYEE

√ if adequate
− if weak
+ if outstanding

...... (1) Maintenance of equipment, tools, instruments.
...... (2) Mechanical skill.
...... (3) Skill in the application of techniques and procedures.
...... (4) Presentability of work (appropriateness of arrangement and appearance of work).
...... (5) Attention to broad phases of assignments.
...... (6) Attention to pertinent detail.
...... (7) Accuracy of operations.
...... (8) Accuracy of final results.
...... (9) Accuracy of judgments or decisions.

...... (21) *Effectiveness in planning broad programs.*
...... (22) *Effectiveness in adapting the work program to broader or related programs.*
...... (23) *Effectiveness in devising procedures.*
...... (24) *Effectiveness in laying out work and establishing standards of performance for subordinates.*
...... (25) *Effectiveness in directing, reviewing, and checking the work of subordinates.*
...... (26) *Effectiveness in instructing, training, and developing subordinates in the work.*

[956]

(10) Effectiveness in presenting ideas or facts.
(11) Industry.
(12) Rate of progress on or completion of assignments.
(13) Amount of acceptable work produced. (Is mark based on production records? _____ (Yes or no))
(14) Ability to organize his work.
(15) Effectiveness in meeting and dealing with others.
(16) Cooperativeness.
(17) Initiative.
(18) Resourcefulness.
(19) Dependability.
(20) Physical fitness for the work.

(27) *Effectiveness in promoting high working morale.*
(28) *Effectiveness in determining space, personnel, and equipment needs.*
(29) *Effectiveness in setting and obtaining adherence to time limits and deadlines.*
(30) Ability to make decisions.
(31) Effectiveness in delegating clearly defined authority to act.

STATE ANY OTHER ELEMENTS CONSIDERED

(A)
(B)
(C)

Adjective Rating

STANDARD

Deviations must be explained on reverse side of this form

Plus marks on all underlined elements, and check marks or better on all other elements rated.

Check marks or better on all elements rated, and plus marks on at least half of the underlined elements.

Check marks or better on a majority of underlined elements, and all weak performance overcompensated by outstanding performance.

Check marks or better on a majority of underlined elements, and all weak performance not overcompensated by outstanding performance.

Minus marks on at least half of the underlined elements.

Adjective Rating

Excellent

Very Good

Good

Fair

Unsatisfactory

Rating official ____

Reviewing official ____

Rated by _____ (Signature of rating official) _____ (Title)

Reviewed by _____ (Signature of reviewing official) _____ (Title)

Rating approved by efficiency rating committee _____ (Date)

Report to employee _____ (Adjective rating)

INTERPRETATION OF EFFICIENCY RATING

Your efficiency rating is an official record of the way you are doing the work of your job.

Excellent (E) means that performance in every important phase of the work was outstanding and there was no weakness in performance in any respect.

Very Good (VG) means that performance in at least half of the important phases of the work was outstanding and there was no weakness in performance in any respect.

Good (G) means that performance met requirements from an over-all point of view.

Fair (F) means that performance did not quite measure up to requirements from an over-all point of view.

Unsatisfactory (U) means that performance in a majority of important phases of the work did not meet job requirements.

INSPECTION

You are entitled to inspect the final ratings (not the rating forms) of all employees in your office or station.

SIGNIFICANCE OF EFFICIENCY RATINGS

An efficiency rating of "Good," "Very Good," or "Excellent" is necessary in order to receive a periodic within-grade salary advancement.

An efficiency rating of "Fair" requires a one-step salary reduction if an employee's pay rate is above the middle rate for his grade (the fourth step in six-rate grades).

An efficiency rating of "Unsatisfactory" requires that the employee be dismissed or reassigned to other work in which he could be reasonably expected to render satisfactory service.

Efficiency ratings are a factor in determining the order in which employees are affected by reduction in force.

APPEALS

If you believe your rating is wrong, you should first discuss it with your supervisor or personnel officer. You have the right, if your position is subject to the Classification Act, to appeal your rating within certain time limits to a board of review established for your agency. Appeals or requests for additional information concerning appeals should be addressed to the Chairman, Board of Review, care of Civil Service Commission, Washington 25, D. C.

Index